The Swahili People and Their Language

A Teaching Handbook

Published by

Adonis & Abbey Publishers Ltd
St James House
13 Kensington Square
London
W8 5HD
Website: http://www.adonis-abbey.com
E-mail Address: editor@adonis-abbey.com

Nigeria:
No. 3, Akanu Ibiam Str.
Asokoro,
P.O. Box 1056, Abuja.
Tel: +234 7066 9977 65/+234 8112 661 609

Year of Publication 2014

British Library Cataloguing-in-Publication Data
A catalogue record for this book is available from the British Library

ISBN: 978-1-909112-44-5

The Swahili People and Their Language

By

Dainess Mashiku Maganda & Lioba Mkaficha Moshi

Table of Contents

Dedication

To the African men and women whose history inspires new ways of knowing and learning while nagging our minds to search for other ways to remember, cherish, acknowledge and value identity exhibited through history. Without your lives, the world would never be the same and humanity would not look the same.

Acknowledgement

The thought for "The Swahili People and Their Language" was born out of our struggles to find suitable texts to teach our Swahili-Studies class. We thank the "Swahili Studies Students" whose thirst for learning inspired the birth of this book as they asked critical questions which compelled us to examine, revisit, and present the Swahili Coastal States and its people this way. We thank Dr. Fabian Maganda's scholarly advice and dedication and most of all the enormous time he devoted to create our maps. Dr. Josephine Dzahene-Quarshie was a great asset to this project mostly for her partnership and contribution of the section that brought in a vivid picture of Ghana's role in the promotion of Kiswahili. We salute our families for their enduring support in the work we do. We cannot forget our friends who cheered us throughout the process. We are especially indebted to the knowledge and wisdom of the Swahili people, whose presence has contributed greatly to the human history, allowing us to examine what it means to be rich, poor, adept, dominated, and successful and inhabit this world with other people while displaying a unique fabric of a multi-textured culture.

Salutation

I'm a Swahili, a living soul, a touch of humanity

I am from time past
I am still alive
I am a generation of peace
I am a revolving craft
I am a hidden history
Some say I never existed until my heart was felt
Some say I never knew much until history defended me
Some say I was never prosperous after they took what I had
Some say I don't know to live because they tell me how to live
Some say I don't advance because I never measure up to their
standards
Some say I will never succeed because I don't know business
I say look at me
I say look at the world
I say listen to your minds
I say search your hearts
I am who I am just because
I have what I have just because
I do what I do just because
I know what I know just because
I see the world just because
I speak but hardly anybody listens just because
I cry but hardly anyone hears my cry just because
I have riches but everybody wants it
I have made it this far just because
I am lagging behind just because
Please understand I am not to blame for my fate
Please understand you are not to blame for my fate
Please understand it is you and I to blame for my fate
But please rejoice for my life
Rejoice I am a Swahili

Rejoice I am special
Rejoice for what I bring in this world
You can't understand it all
You can't fix it all
You can't even deny it all
But you can accept
And you can honor my personhood
Understand and cherish that I am a human
I am a Swahili, a living soul, a touch of humanity

Preamble

To get students thinking and to prepare them to benefit from the contents of this book, it is critical to put forth critical information we know, should know or have heard about in a generalized manner about the Swahili people and their geographical locations. Some of what we know or may have heard may or may not be accurate about the Swahili people and their history of development or the lack thereof. To start the students off, we ask that they begin by trying to answer the following questions which, we hope, will help them to get stared in thinking about the critical issues and topics that will be explored in the book.

a. What is the Swahili Coast?
b. Do you think the people who lived in the Swahili coast didn't know anything until they were visited by other foreigners? This book will reveal the inherent knowledge of the Swahili people before the arrival of people from the Middle East, the Far East and the West.
c. Did the Swahili gain or lose anything by accepting visitors to their land? Mazrui (1999) note that the coastal people were not adventurous but what does that really mean? Does it suggest that people didn't go around or explore other parts of the world or does it simply mean they were contented with their way of life and how they operated on a daily basis? In the course of reading this book, we will discover that the coastal people had their own way of life, developed systems and principles that tailored their living and guided them through legislative processes that instilled different ways of self-governance.
d. This brings us to a series of questions: Did the Swahili people have their own civilization? What is civilization and how is it measured? It is our intention to point out specific information that has been put out by different scholars to show that there

existed a thriving civilization noteworthy of discussion in light of the overall definition of civilization.

e. What is the value of indigenous knowledge and what can we learn from the Swahili people's indigenous knowledge that served the development of their own brand of civilization?

f. What aspects of present day Swahili life that shows how the Swahili indigenous knowledge was altered or affected as the result of new adaptations?

It is true, as this book will show that colonialism is responsible for altering the effectiveness of the Swahili indigenous knowledge and other administrative structures. Needless to say, this may have opened the Swahili people's minds to new ways, while depleting their power of this indigenous knowledge in both governance and other ways of life.

Much of this book will also discuss language. Language is central because everything begins and ends with language. The Swahili people had their own language: Kiswahili, a Bantu language that has borrowed extensively from different languages both within its borders and other parts of the world. Such exposure to other languages has influenced the culture of the Swahili people including their value system that had a limited advantage to indigenous cultures of the Swahili people. Later in the book, we will revisit this point as when we discuss Mazrui and Mazrui (1999) on the politics of Kiswahili. The discussion shades light on the intricacies of both indigenous and acquired languages and underlines the struggle between the need to maintain a sense of linguistic identity while thriving to cope with the winds of globalization in the international market, a necessary demand for an international language competence.

CHAPTER 1

Introduction

Why this book

This book bridges the gap between information obtained from short summaries about the Swahili coast as found in a variety of sources and historical and political accounts that focus on the people of the Swahili coast and the roots of their language, namely Kiswahili. Most books on this topic tend to cover one specific area or issues such politics, history, identity, or cultural background of the Swahili people and the language. Scholars and teachers teaching African studies and Swahili studies in particular, find it hard to find one source that contains sufficient information. In this book, we try to merge the historical background of the Swahili people, their place then and now, while providing a more substantial background of their civilization, the rise and fall of their states as well as the spread of Kiswahili on the continent and beyond. We include works by different scholars whose archeological studies and oral histories help create a more satisfying account of the Swahili language and its speakers. We also add reflections intended to enhance classroom discussions.

To elicit students' cooperative learning, the book provides questions that guide them as well as encourage critical reading of different literature. The book is also an eye opener for those who would like to retrace their footsteps to the past in order to envision new pathways to the future. Students will also be exposed, through this book, views and perspectives about the African people. The reflections offered in this book will be an asset to those who might use it to teach about Africa, specifically the East African coast.

Overview

The book is divided into two major sections: history, language and society. The first part gives readers a background of the Swahili coast. Here we guide students to understand the location and explain how historians came to know about this part of the world. Hence we briefly highlight archeological discoveries and documents supporting the existence of the Swahili in different centuries. The second part is devoted to the Swahili language. We define the language, its speakers and its development. It is here that we also detail historical pathways taken by the three East African countries: namely, Tanzania, Kenya and Uganda in their use of Swahili during different centuries. The current status of Swahili nationally and internationally will also be discussed here. This last part is also devoted to the painting of a picture of the Swahili society. It is in this part we offer a discussion on the development and collapse of the Swahili States. We give readers a glimpse of the composition of the society at that time, the different social classes and what was seen as the characteristic of a member of the Swahili society. The conclusion of the book contains a summary of the key issues discussed and author reflections on topics discussed.

Framing the location

To better understand the area of interest; let us locate these Coastal states on the map of Africa, relative to other countries on the African continent and the countries known as Eastern Africa.

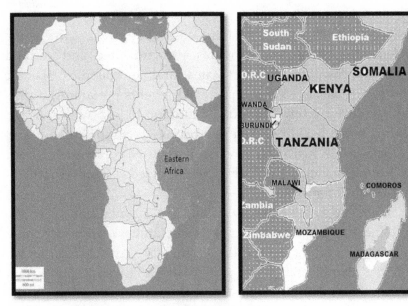

Map 1 & 2: *Map of Africa and the Eastern African Countries*

Note that the area of interest here is the east coast of Africa, specifically Somalia, Kenya and Tanzania (Tanganyika and Zanzibar), also the Comoros and Madagascar.

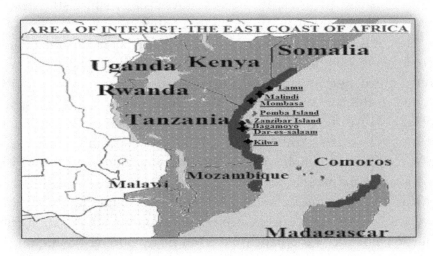

Map 3: *Area of Interest: The East Coast of Africa*

To understand the history of the Coastal States, we turn to the work of Kusimba (1999) that provides a documented and verified history of the Swahili Coastal States and its people. Specific information such as the location, particular events pertaining to this region will be drawn from this book in addition to few other sources. Images of historical buildings and key people illustrating issues and topics of the Swahili historical development are also compiled from different sources including personal knowledge and firsthand experiences of the area.

In his s investigation of the Swahili coast, Kusimba notes that the people, political order, and settlements in Zambezi were integrally involved with the commerce and developments of the Swahili Coast. In his study, Kusimba traced the varied roots of Swahili civilization from the hearths of African subsistence settlements to Sultan places. He refuted the claim by early explorers and researchers that the coastal cities and monumental architecture of the interior were carried to Africa as part of the conceptual baggage of foreign colonials of times past. As you will see, to better understand sub-Saharan African history, we must first divest ourselves of simplistic ideas of social and political development on the continent.

First, it is important to understand that, similar to Kusimba, many people were taught in school that African cultures had remained pretty much unchanged until European missionaries and colonists arrived in the late 19th century. They could not turn to their school books because those were replete with images of caravans led by ferocious bearded Arab and Swahili men, welding whips over emaciated slaves, chained together carrying ivory to the coast. However, grandparents may help to bridge this gap. As was the case for Kusimba, his grandfather helped him understand that the cultural diversity of African peoples preceded European colonization; that trade, friendship, and alliances between many different communities add to the exchange of ideas, information, and genes. Consequently, during his study on the Swahili coastal states, Kusimba was impressed by the main mosque at Gede, built more than 700 years ago. His guide attributed this and other significant sites to seafaring

18

Arabs and Arabized Persians who came to East Africa to trade and colonize the Coast.

Second, one must not undermine the power of the resources of the Swahili Coast which extended from Somalia through Kenya, Tanzania, Mozambique, the Comoros, and north-west Madagascar, to have attracted many people of diverse ethnic background and speaking many different languages. And for that reason, to understand the roots of the Swahili culture requires more than sorting through the history of these groups. It commands a deep and clear understanding of the 500 years of colonization needing to be unscrambled: conquest by the Portuguese who first rounded the Cape of Good Hope in the late 15th Century; and occupation by Britain and Germany after the Berlin Conference of 1884 partition of Africa. Third, it is critical to see how Colonization led to an influx of Europeans, Arabs, and Indians. Swahili towns were composed of numerous and diverse clans claiming different ethnic origins. For example, in the last two decades in Kenya, there was a tendency to regard the Swahili as an alien people. Unfavorable stereotypes of them as indolent urbanites were exploited to justify land appropriations and destruction of archeological sites, which represented a proud moment in East Africa's, indeed Africa's heritage.

The Swahili Coast

The Swahili Coastal States, also referred to as Swahili-City States, are old Swahili towns found along the eastern coast of Africa from Somalia to Mozambique. This is an expanded definition of the Swahili Coast because most people understand the Swahili Coast as the area covering Kenya and Tanzania and the associated islands. One can see the reason for that considering that Swahili speakers are mostly associated with this limited area. However, there is need to discuss Swahili States versus Swahili language which we will in later chapters.

The Swahili Coastal States are marked by visible features that include white washed houses of coral, a number of small mosques

19

where people of the Islamic faith from the immediate neighborhood gather for prayers. The mosques are also venues for after prayer gathering to discuss town affairs. To distinguish themselves, the Coastal Swahili people often stress the main difference between themselves and their neighbors to be dual heritage, which include immigrants from Shiraz Persia and Arabia who, for centuries ventured the African coast to trade.

History shows the Swahili coast was deeply involved with the outside world as early as the first millennium after Christ. They depended on the annual northeast and southeast monsoon to propel their dhows that sailed from the Arabian Peninsula and the Persian Gulf (see map below) As Kusimba (1999) shows, trading dhows sailed down this coast from the Arabian peninsula and the Persian Gulf to trade pottery, cloth, iron tools for African slaves, ivory, gold, timber, shells, dyes, and perfumes. It is through these contacts that the eastern coast of Africa changed so profoundly around the close of the first millennium AD.

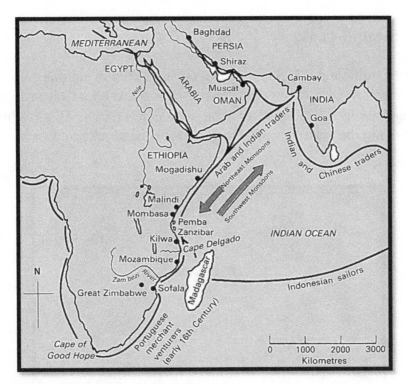

Map 4: Trading Routes

The Coastal States were also populated by Bantu-speaking people from the interior who migrated and settled along the coast stretching from Kenya to the tip of South Africa. It is of no surprise that merchants and traders from the Muslim world and India became interested in the region and subsequently settled here as they realized the strategic importance of the east coast of Africa for commercial traffic. An influx of Shiraz Arabs from the Persian Gulf and even small settlements of Indians started to settle in this area around 900 AD onwards. The Arabs who populated the Swahili coast called this region al-Zanj, which translated to: "The Blacks." It was the presence of these Arabs that created an opportunity for the control of Muslim merchants from Arabia and Persia. The major east African ports from Mombasa in the north to Sofala (Zimbabwe) became Islamic cities and cultural centers by the 1300's.

21

The Swahili Coast

The Swahili coast is believed to extend from 1º N in Southern Somalia to the mouth of the Limpopo River. It is a 20-200 kilometer wide strip of land over 300 kilometers long that extend from Mogadishu in Somalia to the north to Cape Delgado in Mozambique to the south.

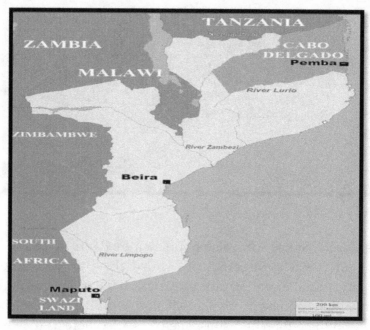

Map 5: Cape Delgado

The environments vary from coastal to the grasslands of elevated hillsides. Historically, the north of Somalia coast, offered entry ports to caravan routes to the Nile valley through such foreboding towns as the legendary city of Harar (see map 6 below), a prominent slaving center with business in cotton and coffee.

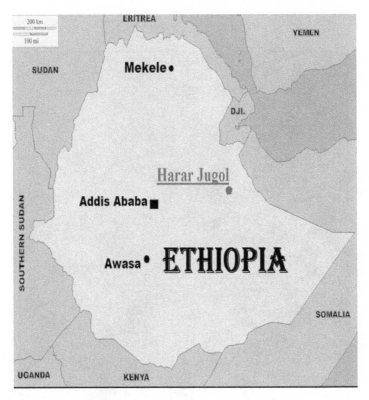

Map 6: *Harar Jugol*

The area also includes several archipelagos and islands in the Indian Ocean [the Comoros, Lamu archipelagos and the islands of Mombasa [Kenya], Pemba, Zanzibar, and Mafia [Tanzania] (also see map 3).

The major Swahili city-states included Barawa (Somalia), Mombasa, Gedi, Pate, Malindi, (Kenya), Zanzibar, Kilwa (Tanzania), and Sofala (Zimbabwe) in the far south (see map 3).

In 1506, Barawa (in Somalia) was reduced to ashes by a Portuguese fleet. It became a major Portuguese port, but in league with other coastal towns. In 1758, it liberated itself from Portuguese rule in and became part of the coastal alliances led by the Zanzibar Sultanate. Barawa was attacked again in 1840, by the Bardheere Jama'a (residents of the Bardera city) looking for an outlet to the sea (see map 7 below).

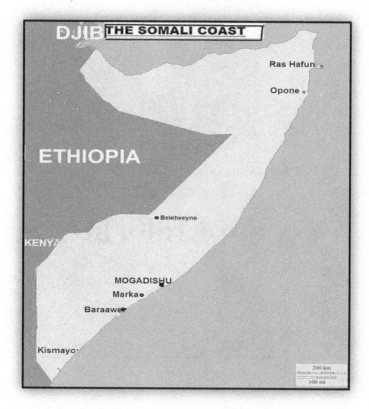

Map 7: *The Somali Coast*

The town of Barawa was burned and the people appealed to the sultan of Zanzibar for protection. But in 1889, Barawa fell into the hands of the Italians when the Sultan of Zanzibar was forced to agree to the annexation of coastal ports to the Italian colonial administration of the Horn.

This historical account is significant because it shows how the coastal cities were in constant attack as the different foreign interests grew over the available resources and passage to the Far East. African scholars who have researched this area have declared that these costal city-states were Muslim and cosmopolitan and they were all politically independent of one another. They were more like competitive companies or corporations each vying for the lion's share of the Indian Ocean trade. It is also fair to assert here that the savvy

24

trading skills of the Swahili coastal people constituted one of the major reasons for the coastal cities to become culturally cosmopolitan. Additionally the cultural mix of a Bantu, Islamic, and Indian influences enhanced this status. Needless to say, extensive commerce brought in additional influence from the Chinese through artifacts and culture. Note that, although the Arab, Persian, Chinese, and Indian influences were significant in the growth of Swahili civilization, the indigenous people should be credited with the skills found in the way the cities were run by nobility that was African in origin. Kusimba (1999) writes that the nobility was served by the commoners with some foreigners who made up a large part of the citizenry.

CHAPTER 2

The Coastal Towns

Overview

Kusimba (1999) gives an interesting account of the coastal towns. The old Swahili towns started to flourish as early as the 14th and 15th centuries. As other historians also have shown, these two centuries mark the coastal states' greatest time of stone building activity and architectural diversity. Such areas include Songa Mnara on the island of Kilwa, Gedi in Malindi, and Jumba la Mtwana in the north part of Mombasa. Others that were rebuilt were Shanga and Kilwa Kisiwani.

The question in many people's mind is how these places lost their vitality that has been replaced by under development and poverty. To some extent, one can consider the early disruption of trade to be attributed to the Portuguese intervention in the Indian Ocean from 1498. The Portuguese who raided these places and plundered them for their own good were interested in the gold resources in the area spreading from the Cape in South Africa to Zimbabwe and Mozambique.

New towns were established from the 18th – 19th centuries after the Portuguese had lost control of this coast and were heavily influenced by the new international demands for ivory and slavery. This interest contributed to what is known as the second Swahili boom period. This occurred alongside a heightening of power politics in the Indian Ocean and its closer incorporation into the world economy. The Arabs in Zanzibar were responsible for slavery, and in turn, strengthened their control of Zanzibar under the Oman rulers. The Oman rulers extended their control to cover the coastal towns. In the 19th century Mombasa was a key town. Newer ones included Bagamoyo and Kilwa Kivinje. Eventually, all of these towns became important slave markets. Later in 1860s, Dar es Salaam was founded by the sultan of Zanzibar, Sayyid Majid, as his own mainland town, his 'house of peace' to rival Bagamoyo. Shortly, we give a more detail account for some of these coastal towns with special emphasis on the major ones like Kilwa and Bagamoyo. Needless to say, the Swahili Coast towns are characterized with the remnants of their past florescence, the ruins of once prosperous towns. These remnants show that there were some elite mansions and mosques built in coral rag, and less elegant neighborhoods with the homes, markets, and workplace of the common citizens.

There is no question in the minds of historians and archeologists that these noteworthy relics were built by Swahili peoples about 500 to 800 years ago. Their culture was original and they interacted with and were influenced by centuries of economic contact with and colonization from southern Arabia, Western India, and Portugal. The world knew of the Eastern coast of Africa, its commerce, and its treasures. But the long history of the coast extends even further back in time, beyond the rumored voyages of Phoenician seamen, to even times when the coast was peopled by the first settlements of Bantu speaking, iron-using farmsteads that spread south along the coast to establish new settlements in eastern Africa.

Kilwa - Tanzania

Located on two islands close to each other just off the Tanzanian coast about 300km south of Dar es Salaam are the remains of two port cites, Kilwa Kisiwani and Songo Mnara. The larger, Kilwa Kisiwani, was occupied from the 9th to the 19th century and reached its peak of prosperity in the13th and 14th centuries. Kilwa is considered the most important city from the 12th – 14th Centuries. The main reason is that it controlled trade with the Mozambique Channel and Sofala, including high-quality ivory and the gold of Zimbabwe. Settlement and commercial activity started in the 9th century—same period as Shanga and Manda in the north (Kenya). However, Kilwa remained prosperous for about 3 centuries. A number of scholars documenting Kilwa's history tend to highlight ways in which Kilwa's positioning was advantageous to it-self. It lie's on an island, in a sunken sanctuary for security, hence, sheltered harbor for sailing craft of all sizes.

Map 8: *Location of Kilwa*

The town of Kilwa as such is divided into three different towns - Kilwa Kisiwani, Kilwa Kivinje and Kilwa Masoko. Kilwa Masoko is the most developed of the three and the regional hub whilst Kilwa Kivinje and Kilwa Kisiwani have spectacular historical attractions.

Kilwa Kisiwani: is an island reached by dhow and has an amazingly well preserved collection of ruins. On arrival as you sail from the mainland the most striking sight is the old Omani Fort, which is built on the foundations of an Old Port uguese fort.

The Big Mosque dates from the 12th Century and was once the

largest mosque in East Africa. The Sultan's palace is located directly south of the mosque and contains four graves. The small mosque dates from the 15th Century is still in use today. The large complex of walls in the west of the island is called "Makutani" and contains a palace from the 18th Century, another Sultanate's palace, and a mosque from the 15th Century. All the way to the east of the island there are the ground walls of the "Husuni Kubwa", once the largest building in tropical Africa.

Localguides give tours of the ruins and dhows can be arranged from the small jetty on the mainland. The site is quite spread out and you can easily spend a whole day walking around all the ruins. Tourists are advised to take  lots of water on tour because it can be very hot whilst touring the ruins which do not much shade around them.

Kilwa Kivinje: was an ancient Arabian slave and ivory trading town, where caravans departed for expeditions to the interior. When the Germans assumed control at the end of the 19th century, the colonial government built a fort and extended the town. Today you can still find a Market Hall, the Fort, and two pillars commemorating those who died during wars such as the Maji Maji War.

The History of Kilwa

The story of Kilwa begins around 960-1000 AD. It is believed that its encounter with foreign rule stared with the purchase made by Ali ibn al-Hassan Shirazi from Rersia, modern day Iran. He was one of seven sons of a ruler of Shiraz, Persia. His mother is believed to be a slave from Abyssinian. Trouble befell Ali ibn al-Hassan Shirazi whe his father died because his brothers drove him out of his inheritance from his father. He left Siraz and set sail out of Hormuz with his household and a small group of followers to Somalia. His destination was Mogadishu, the main commercial city of the East African coast. He did not stay long in Mogadishu because he did not get along with the elites of Mogadishu who drove him out of that city.

He continued to travel down the African coast and upon reaching Kilwa; it is believed he had the opportunity to purchase the island of Kilwa from the local Bantu inhabitants. According to one chronicle (Strong, 1895), Kilwa was originally owned by a mainland Bantu king 'Almuli' and connected by a small land bridge to the mainland that was often covered during high tide and appeared only during low tide. The price that was asked for by the king is believed to in kind, measured by colored cloth that could cover the circumference of the island. Later the king changed his mind and wanted to go back on his word but the Persians had started making changes to the island by cutting off the bridge and severing Kilwa from the mainland and making it an island and a colony of the Persians.

Kilwa started to become a busy trading post. Its fortuitous position made it a much better East African trade center than Mogadishu. It quickly began to attract many merchants and immigrants from the far north, Persia, and Arabia. In just a few years, the colony was big enough to acquire Mafia Island which became a satellite settlement. These commercial developments in Kilwa and Mafia challenged the East African Coast commercial dominance that was once held by the Somali ports particularly Mogadishu. Suleiman Hassan, the ninth successor of Ali ibn al-Hassan Shirazi (and 12th ruler of Kilwa, c.1178-1195), ventured further south and wrested control of the southerly city of Sofala. Wealthy Sofala was the principal entry port for the gold and ivory trade with Great Zimbabwe and Monomatapa in the interior. The control of Sofala increased the gold revenues to the Kilwa Sultans, allowing them to finance expansion and extended controls of the East African coastal states.

31

The wealth brought in by the gold trade meant that Kilwa had its own mint and was the only place in sub-Saharan Africa to issue coins It was this wealth and the prosperity of Kilwa that amazed the famous Moroccan trader Ibn Battuta who visited Kilwa in 1331 during the Mahdali dynasty and declared the city to be the most developed of all the cities he had so far visited. He commented favorably on the humility and religion of its ruler, Sultan al-Hasan ibn Sulaiman. He was particularly impressed by the planning of the city and believed that it was the reason for Kilwa's success along the coast. Ibn Battuta had stayed at the court of al-Hasan ibn Sulaiman Abu'l-Mawahib who ruled Kilwa from 1310-1333 AD. This period is noted as one that the major architectural constructions were made. These include elaborations of the complex palace of Husuni Kubwa and a significant extension to the Great Mosque of Kilwa, which was made of Coral Stone, and the largest mosque of its kind. Elaborations were also made to the market of Husuni Ndogo. All these are considered major relics that have remained an attraction to present day tourists to the area as well as much archeological work.

With a firm control of the rich island of Kilwa, the Sultanate ventured elsewhere in the 15th C. to claim control over the mainland cities of Malindi, Inhambane and Sofala and the island-states of Mombasa, Pemba, Zanzibar, Mafia, Comoro and Mozambique including smaller places now often referred to as the "Swahili Coast". The rulers of Kilwa also claimed lordship across the channel over a myriad of small trading posts on the coast of Madagascar (also known as *island of the Moon*). To the north, Kilwa's power was checked by the independent Somali city-states of Barawa (a self-ruling aristocratic republic) and Mogadishu which was the dominant city considered Kilwa's main rival. To the south, Kilwa's Sultanate control reached as far as Cape Correntes.

While the Sultan of Kilwa was the main ruling figure, he was considered a hierarchical head of the Kilwa Sultanate which was not a centralized state but rather a confederation of commercial cities ruled by internal elite's merchant communities with trade connections. The Sultan had the prerogatives of appointing a governor or overseer.

However, the authority given to these appointees was not consistent and could be reduced in some places to a mere representative than a governor with administrative powers (e.g. in outposts like Mozambique Island where the appointee was considered a true governor in the Sultan's name while in Sofala the appointee's powers were very much limited and equivalent to an ambassador.

It is useful here to highlight other factors that play into the unsung history of Kilwa and its resilience. The Sultanate built a Kilwa empire that was part of a large control largely built by the Iranian Bazrangids. Geographically and politically, the empire became an independent entity marked by the reigns of Emperor Ardashir the Ist of the Sassanid state who conquered the parent state of Bazrangi in southern Persia in 224. Emperor Ardashir's successor, Shapur I, annexed the southern shores of the Persian Gulf, as well as the region of Muscat on the Indian Ocean. This led to the removal of all final vestiges of Bazrangi independence on the Asian continent. Needless to say, Zoroastrian fire temples within the Kilwa Empire were preserved as a result of Bazrangi custodians. Sassanian sources, which include rock inscriptions and documents, discuss how the Bazrangids served important custodial functions at the Great Temple of the goddess Anahita in Istakhr (near Persepolis). The Kilwa Empire prospered even during the early Islamic era. However, the capital city of Kilwa was under siege by members of the native populations of East Africa. The city fell and nearly 2,000 of its inhabitants were devoured in a single week. In 980, the Zanj Empire was founded by Ali ibn Hasan and succeeded the Kilwa Empire. Recent archaeological searchings in the old Kilwa important sites such as Unguja, Tumbatu, Mtambwe, and Mkumbuu are giving hope on the history of the Bazrangid's founding of the Kilwa Empire and its status as a maritime power..

The Decline and fall of Kilwa

The prosperity of the port city remained intact until the last decades of the 14th century, when turmoil over the ravages of the Black Death took its toll on international trade. By the early decades of the 15th century, new stone houses and mosques were being built up in Kilwa. There were competitions with the royal dynasty from ambitious appointees, ministers and emirs, who played the roles of kingmakers, and *de facto* rulers against the Sultans of Kilwa, a phenomenon which resulted in the weakening of the empire. The most successful was probably Emir Muhammad Kiwabi, who ruled Kilwa for nearly two decades through several sultans, including him at one point. Throughout his long 'reign', Emir Muhammad constantly fought battle with his relatives including his nephew, Hassan ibn Suleiman (son of an earlier vizier) who he had previously tried to install as sultan but was resisted by the population of Kilwa. It was at this point when Emir Muhammad decided reserve sultanate to Kilwa sultans descending only from the royal dynasty keeping out families of viziers. By maintaining this stance Muhammad thwarted Hassan's ambitions to the throne. The last sultan installed by Emir Muhammad before his death was the royal prince al-Fudail ibn Suleiman in 1495. The man who succeeded Muhammad's post: Emir Ibrahim (known as *Mir Habrahemo* in Barros, *Abraemo* in Goes), helped al-Fudail crush the ambitious Hassan once and for all in a great battle outside Kilwa. But it was not long after this battle that Emir Ibrahim is said to have betrayed and murdered sultan al-Fudail. Rather than declare himself sultan, Ibrahim took power merely with the title of *emir*, and claimed to be exercising rule in the name of a son of an earlier sultan of the old royal dynasty. This was rather convenient for Emir Ibrahim since no one had seen or heard of this absent prince from which he claiming ancestry. Emir Ibrahim's usurpation was unexpected by not only Kilwa but also many quarters. Ibrahim met resistance to all those who revered Muhammad who had recognized the importance of constitutional propriety for peace in the Kilwa Sultanate. Most of the local governors of the Kilwa vassal cities, many who were either relatives or had owed their positions to Emir Muhammad and the royal dynasty, refused to acknowledge the usurpation of Emir Ibrahim, and began charting an independent course for their own city-states. Consequently, the writ of Emir Ibrahim only covered the city of Kilwa itself and possibly Mozambique Island. This was believed to be the condition of the Kilwa Sultanate when the Portuguese arrived. Portuguese scout Pêro da Covilhã, disguised as an Arab merchant, had travelled the length of the Kilwa Sultanate in 1489-90, and visited the ports of Malindi, Kilwa and Sofala, and delivered his scouting report back to Lisbon, describing the condition of the Kilwa Sultanate in quite some detail. The first Portuguese ships, under Vasco da Gama, on their way to India, reached the sultanate in 1497. Gama made contact with the Kilwa vassals of Mozambique, Mombasa and Malindi, seeking to secure their cooperation as staging posts for the Portuguese India Armadas.

In 1500, the 2nd Portuguese India Armada, under Pedro Álvares Cabral visited Kilwa, and reported seeing houses made of coral stone, including the ruler's 100-room palace, of Islamic Middle Eastern design. This visit changed the Swahili coast forever. The dominance of the Swahili coastal towns over maritime trade was affected by this arrival of the Portuguese. They end the Arabian and Asian connection by reoriented all international trade towards Western Europe and the Mediterranean. During the visit, Pedro Álvares Cabral attempted to negotiate a commercial and alliance treaty with Emir Ibrahim. But the Emir was not forthcoming with his answer and no agreement was reached. This resulted in another visit by a well-armed Armada in 1502, this time under Vasco da Gama. It was by far more mean-spirited and prepared to take no for an answer. Having secured separate treaties with Malindi, Mozambique and all-important Sofala, the Portuguese brought their menacing fleet to bear on Kilwa itself, and extorted a sizeable tribute from Emir Ibrahim.

Some have speculated that the Emir missed a golden opportunity to restore his fortunes by not being forthcoming in the first instance. If a treaty with Cabral had been reached back in 1500, the Emir might have secured the assistance of the Portuguese navy in bringing the half-independent vassals back under his sway. At least one Kilwan nobleman called Muhammad ibn Rukn ad Din (known to the Portuguese as Muhammad Arcone), did advise Emir Ibrahim to strike up an alliance with the Portuguese. The Emir turned around and gave Muhammad up as a hostage to the Portuguese and then refused to ransom him back. Consequently, Muhammad was subjected to Vasco Gama's wrath.) Notably, the vassals used the Portuguese to secure their permanent break from the Sultanate. The ruler of Malindi was the first to embrace the Portuguese, forging an alliance in 1497. After Emir Ibrahim was defeated through a coup, it was certainly not hard to persuade the ruling sheikh Isuf of Sofala (believed to be a nephew of the late elder Emir Muhammad) to break away. He signed a treaty with the Portuguese in 1502, and followed it up by allowing the construction of a Portuguese factory and fort in Sofala in 1505. As we know, Mozambique remained a colony of the Portuguese up to late 20th Century.

It was in 1505 that Francisco de Almeida brought his fleet into the harbor of Kilwa, and landed some 500 Portuguese soldiers to drive Emir Ibrahim out of the city. Almeida installed the aforementioned Muhammad Arcone on the throne, as a Portuguese vassal. Remembering constitutional proprieties, Arcone insisted that Micante, the son of the late sultan al-Fudail be his designated successor. The Portuguese erected a fortress (Fort Santiago) on Kilwa and left a garrison behind, under the command of Pedro Ferreira Fogaça to keep an eye on things.

© The Hebrew University of Jerusalem & The Jewish National & University Library

Portuguese rule was not very welcome particularly their imposition of Portuguese Mercantilist laws on the sultanate including the restriction on ships other than the Portuguese to carry trade to the principal coastal towns. This was seen as contentious because it essentially put many Kilwa merchants out of business.

The Portuguese did not stay very long. In 1506 after the assassination of Muhammad Arcone by the sheikh of Tirendicunde (a relative of Emir Ibrahim) and the succession rule of Micante who was later deposed because he would not be a Portuguese puppet. Sheikh of Tirendicunde then installed Hussein ibn Muhammad, a son of Arcone, as the new sultan. Chaos broke out in the city of Kilwa when partisans of Micante & Emir Ibrahim seized control of much of the city, driving sultan Hussein and the partisans of Arcone out of the city. They sought refuge in the Portuguese Fort Santiago while street fighting and fires broke out throughout the city. This forced Kiwa residents out of the city leaving it practically deserted except for a few roving partisan gangs and the terrified Portuguese garrison.

Hearing of the Kilwan chaos while in India, the Portuguese vice-roy Almeida dispatched a magistrate Nuno Vaz Pereira, to inquire into the matter. Upon arriving in late 1506, Pereira convened the competing sultans Micante and Hussein, and asked them present their dispute to him. Pereira ruled in favor of Hussein which allowed him to remain the sultan of Kilwa and then relieved the unpopular commander Fogaça of his duties to soften the blow and also lifted the mercantilist restrictions on Kilwa shipping allowing Kilwa to start trading with other Swahili coastal towns. These changes allowed the Kilwa refugees to return resulting in peace and tranquility to be resumed, but only for a very brief moment. The back breaker was the raise of the Hussein against Tirendicunde to avenge his father's murder. The town was brutally sacked, and numerous prisoners taken. Hussein then dispatched emissaries to all the vassal cities of the Kilwa Sultanate, ordering them to return to obedience if they wanted to remain safe. This forced vice-roy Almeida to reverse Pereira's decision of installing Hussein as the Sultanate of Kilwa by deposing him and reinstating Micante. He did this because he feared Hussein's tyranny and what it might do to the fragile Portuguese interests in East Africa. Thereafter, Kilwa grew to be a substantial city and the leading commercial entre port on the southern half of the Swahili coast trading extensively in gold, iron, ivory, and other animal products of the African interior for beads, textiles, jewelry, porcelain, and spices from Asia with states of the African hinterland and interior as far as Zimbabwe.

Studies at Kilwa

Interest in Kilwa, predominantly by archaeologists, was a consequent of two 16th century histories about the site, including the Kilwa Chronicle. Serious archaeological investigation began in the 1950s. In 1981 it was declared a World Heritage Site, and noted visitor sites are the Great Mosque, the Mkutini Palace and some remarkable ruins. Excavators in the 1950s included James Kirkman and Neville Chittick, from the British Institute in Eastern Africa. Archaeological investigations at the site began in earnest in 1955, and the site and its sister port Songo Mnara were named UNESCO World Heritage site in 1981 including an inscription on the List of World Heritage in Danger: 2004. There is a serious rapid deterioration of the archaeological and monumental heritage of the islands due to various agents like erosion and vegetation. The eastern section of the Palace of Husuni Kubwa (*Palace of the Queens*) is progressively disappearing. The damage to the soil caused by rainwater wash is accentuating the risks of collapse of the remaining structures on the edge of the cliff. The vegetation that proliferates on the cliff has limited the progression of the rain-wash effect, but causes the break-up of the masonry structures. The World Monuments Fund included Kilwa on its 2008 Watch List of 100 Most Endangered Sites, and since 2008 has been supporting conservation work on various buildings.

Songo Mnara was a Swahili stone town, dominated by the well-preserved remains of more than 40 large domestic room-blocks, five mosques, and numerous tombs. Room blocks wrap around and enclose an open, central area of the site where tombs, a walled cemetery and a small mosque are located. Compared to the 800-year occupation of nearby Kilwa, the relatively short, 200-year occupation of Songo Mnara makes it an ideal candidate to examine household and public spaces from a discrete period in time. Notable feature of the medieval architecture of Kilwa is the use of domes which is not paralleled anywhere else on the East African coast at this early period. With the exception of some domes in the palace of Husuni Kubwa all of the domes in the Kilwa area are supported on squinches. Elsewhere on Kilwa buildings are covered either with barrel vaults or flat roofs made out of wood and concrete. The Makutani Palace may be an exception to this as it seems to have had a wooden roof covered with palm thatch (makuti).

The name Kilwa today is used for three settlements: Kilwa Kiswani, Kilwa Kivinje and Kilwa Masoko. The ruins are confined almost exclusively to Kilwa Kiswani (on the island), whilst Kivinje and Masoko are both later settlements on the mainland.

Kilwa Kisiwani and Songo Mnara are two archaeological sites of prime importance to the understanding of the Swahili culture, the Islamization of the east coast of Africa and the extensive commerce of the medieval period and the modern era. These are islands, situated close to each other, off the Tanzanian coast. On each island a complex of ruins has been preserved, but those of Kilwa Kisiwani are by far the most important. As noted earlier, the site has been occupied from the 9th to 19th centuries and reached its peak in the 13th and 14th centuries. Among the many monuments these are some of the most important:

1. The vestiges of the Great Mosque, constructed in the 12th century of coral tiles imbedded in a core of puddled clay, but considerably enlarged in the 15th century in the reign of Sultan Soulaiman ibn Mohammed el Malik el Adil (1412-22).
2. The remains of the Husuni Kubwa Palace, built between around 1310 and 1333 by the sultan Al Hasan.
3. Numerous mosques.
4. The Geraza (Swahili for 'prison') constructed on the ruins of the Portuguese fortress.
5. An entire urban complex with houses, public squares, burial grounds, etc.

6.   The ruins of Songo Mnara, at the extreme north of the island of Songo, comprise five mosques and a number of domestic dwellings of puddled clay and wood within the enclosure walls. A poorly identified construction of larger dimensions is known as 'the palace'.

The ceramics and small objects gathered during the excavations bear exceptional testimony to the commercial, and consequently cultural, exchanges of which Kilwa, and to a lesser extent, Songo were the theatre. Cowry shells and beads of glass, carnelian or quartz were mixed with porcelain of the Sung dynasty as a medium of exchange from the 12th century. Chinese porcelain and Islamic monochrome faience continued to be the vectors of a bartering system well after the appearance of a monetary atelier at Kilwa.

The main buildings on Kilwa are the Great Mosque and the Great House, the Small Domed Mosque, the Jangwam Mosque, the palace of Husuni Kubwa and the nearby Husuni Ndogo, the Makutani palace and the Gereza fort. There are also important ruins on nearby islands including Songo Mnara, Sanje Majoma and Sanje ya Kate.

The Great Mosque which is a large complex structure dating from several periods consists of two main parts, a small northern part divided into sixteen bays and a larger southern extension divided into thirty bays. The earliest phase evident at the mosque is dated to the tenth century although little survives of this above foundation level. The earliest standing area of the mosque is the northern part which dates to the eleventh or tenth century and was modified at the beginning of the thirteenth. This area was probably covered with a flat roof supported on nine timber columns. The next phase included the addition of a large cloistered courtyard to the south supported on monolithic coral stone columns and a small chamber to the south-west covered by a large dome. This was probably the sultan's personal prayer room and the dome is the largest dome on the East African coast, with a diameter of nearly 5 m. Also belonging to this period is the southern ablutions courtyard which included a well, latrines and at least three water tanks. Sometime in the fifteenth century this arcaded southern courtyard was rebuilt and covered over with the present arrangement of domes and barrel vaults supported on composite octagonal columns, making this the largest pre-nineteenth-century mosque in East Africa.

Adjacent to the Great Mosque on the south side is the Great House which mostly dates to the same period as the latest phase of the mosque (i.e. eighteenth century). The Great House actually consists of three connected residential units each with a sunken central courtyard. Most of the complex would have been a single story although a second floor was added to some of the central area. The purpose of the Great House is not known, but it is likely that at some stage it served as the sultan's residence judging from a royal tombstone found during excavations.

To the south-west of the Great Mosque is the Small Domed Mosque which together with the Jangwani Mosques, they are the only two examples of a nine-domed mosque in this area. This building probably dates from the mid-fifteenth century (it is built on an earlier structure) and contains an arrangement of vaults and domes similar to the later phase of the Great Mosque. There are only two entrances, one on the south side opposite the mihrab and one in the centre of the east side. Domes cover most of the area of the mosque except for two bays covered with barrel vaults, one next to the entrance and one in front of the mihrab. The central bays are differentiated from the side bays by being wider and by the use of barrel vaults at either end, emphasizing the north-south axis. The dominant feature of the mosque is the central dome which is crowned with an octagonal pillar and internally contains three concentric circles of Islamic glazed bowls set within the dome. The two vaults to the north and south of the central dome are also decorated with inset bowls of glazed ceramics whilst the two domes either side of it are fluted internally; the other four domes are plain internally.

The other nine-domed mosque is of approximately the same date and is known as the Jangwani Mosque; it is located to the south of the Small Domed Mosque. Although more ruinous, excavation has

41

shown this mosque to be similar, with the same use of fluted and plain domes, and entrances only on the south and east sides.

To the east of the main group of buildings are the remains known as Husuni Kubwa (large Husuni) and Husuni Ndogo (small Husuni). The term Husuni derives from the Arabic term *husn* meaning *fortified enclosure or fortress*. Whilst this term may be appropriate for the the latter, its application to Husuni Kubwa seems unlikely for a palace complex. Husuni Kubwa is located on a coastal headland overlooking the Indian Ocean. It seems to date mostly from the late thirteenth or early fourteenth century and may well have never been completed. The complex consists of three main elements, the gateway or monumental entrance, the large south court and a complex of four courtyards which form the core of the palace. Also at the northern end of the complex there is a separate private mosque located on rocks next to the sea and reached by a staircase. The four courtyards at the northern end of the complex comprise an audience court, a domestic court, a bathing pool and a palace court. On the east side of the audience court are a flight of steps leading up to a flat-roofed pavilion which has been interpreted as the sultan's throne room. To the east of this is the domestic court which opens on to a complex of residential rooms, or beyts. The bathing pool consists of a sunken octagonal structure with steps and lobed recesses on each side. The palace court at the northern end of the palace is a sunken rectangular structure aligned north-south with steps at either end. The north set of steps leads to a further residential unit which overlooks the sea and the small mosque. It is possible that the sea mosque and the staircase represent the sultan's private entry to the palace. The royal nature of the palace is confirmed by a floriated Kufic inscription found during excavations which mentioned Sultan al-Hasn bin Sulayman.

By contrast Husuni Kubwa is a severe-looking building which fits the name Husuni (fort). It consists of a rectangular structure aligned north-south and measuring over 70 m long by more than 50 m wide. Thirteen evenly spaced, solid, semi-circular bastions protect the outside of the wall with one rectangular tower on the west side. The only entrance is in the middle of the south side and consists of a wide gateway leading into a gateway with the exit on the east side thus forming a bent entrance. Excavations have revealed the traces of a few structures inside but these may be later and do not give any indication of the function of the building which is unparalleled elsewhere in East Africa and suggests an outside influence. There is little evidence for dating this structure although it is thought to be contemporary with Husuni Kubwa.

The other two important buildings on Kilwa Island are also defensive structures although they seem to date mostly to the eighteenth century. The largest of these is the Makutani palace which was the residence of the sultan in the eighteenth century. This building is contained within a fortified enclosure known as the Makutani, which consists of two curtain walls fortified by square towers with embrasures. The wall was originally approximately 3 m high and crenellated. Although there is no trace of a parapet this could have been built of wood like many other features of the eighteenth-century remains at Kilwa. The palace occupies a position between the two enclosure walls and appears to be built around one of the earlier towers. It is the only building on the island still to have an upper floor which contained the main residential area of the palace.

The Gereza or fort is located between the Makutani palace and the Great Mosque. It consists of a roughly square enclosure with two towers at opposite corners. Although there is some evidence that the original structure was Portuguese, the present form of the building seems to be typical of Omani forts.

In addition to sites on Kilwa Island there are important sites on nearby islands. The earliest of these sites is Sanje ya Kate, an island to the south of Kilwa where there are ruins covering an area of 400 acres, including houses and a mosque. The mosque is of an early type with a mihrab niche contained in the thickness of the wall rather than projecting out of the north wall as is usual in later East African mosques. Excavations have shown that the settlement was abandoned before 1200 and most of the ruins date to the tenth century or even earlier.

To the east of Sanje ya Kate is the larger island of Songo Mnara which contains extensive ruins on its northern tip. The remains date to the fourteenth and fifteenth centuries and consist of thirty-three houses and a palace complex, as well as five mosques contained within a defensive enclosure wall. The remains at Songo Mnara are informative as they are one of the few places in East Africa where pre-eighteenth-century houses survive in any numbers. The houses have a standardized design with a monumental entrance approached by a flight of steps leading via an anteroom into a sunken courtyard, to the south of which are the main living quarters of the house.

Kilwa Society and Economy

Despite its origin as a Persian colony, extensive inter-marriage and conversion of local Bantu inhabitants and later Arab immigration turned the Kilwa Sultanate into a veritable melting pot, ethnically in differentiable from the mainland. The mixture of Perso-Arab and Bantu cultures is credited for creating a distinctive East African culture and language known today as Swahili (literally, 'coast-dwellers').[5] Nonetheless, the Muslims of Kilwa (whatever their ethnicity) would often refer to themselves generally as *Shirazi* or *Arabs,* and to the unconverted Bantu peoples of the mainland as *Zanj* or *Khaffirs* ('infidels', later adopted as a racial epithet by European settlers).

The Kilwa Sultanate was almost wholly dependent on external commerce. Effectively, it was a confederation of urban settlements, there was little or no agriculture carried on in within the boundaries of sultanate. Grains (principally millet and rice), meats (cattle, poultry) and other necessary supplies to feed the large city populations had to be purchased from the Bantu peoples of the interior. Kilwa traders from the coast encouraged the development of market towns in the Bantu-dominated highlands of what are now Kenya, Tanzania, Mozambique and Zimbabwe. The Kilwa mode of living was as middlemen traders, importing manufactured goods (cloth, etc.) from Arabia and India, which were then swapped in the highland market towns for Bantu-produced agricultural commodities (grain, meats) for their own subsistence and precious raw materials (gold, ivory, etc.) which they would export back to Asia.

The exception was the coconut palm tree. Grown all along the coast, the coconut palm was the mainstay of Kilwa life in every way - not only for the fruit, but also for timber, thatching and weaving. Kilwa merchant ships - from the large lateen-rigged *dhows* that ploughed the open oceans to the small *zambucs* used for local transit - were usually built from the split trunks of coconut palm wood, their sails made from coconut leaf matting and the ships held together by coconut coir.

The Kilwa Sultanate conducted extensive trade with Arabia, Persia, and across the Indian Ocean, to India itself. Kilwa ships made use of the seasonal monsoon winds to sail across to India in the summer, and back to Africa in the winter. Kilwa pilots had a reputation for extraordinary sailing accuracy. The Portuguese marveled at their navigational instruments, particularly their latitude staves, which they considered superior to their own. Nonetheless, the coir-sewn Kilwa ships were not seaworthy enough to brave the treacherous waters and unpredictable violent gusts around Cape Correntes, so the entire region south of that point was rarely sailed by Kilwa merchants. Inhambane was the most southerly settlement that can be considered part of the Kilwa trading empire.

Kilwa Kisiwani and Songo Mnara were Swahili trading cities and their prosperity was based on control of Indian Ocean trade with Arabia, India and China, particularly between the 13th and 16th centuries, when gold and ivory from the hinterland was traded for silver, carnelians, perfumes, Persian faience and Chinese porcelain. Kilwa Kisiwani minted its own currency in the 11th to 14th centuries. In the 16th century, the Portuguese established a fort on Kilwa Kisiwani and the decline of the two islands began.

The remains of Kilwa Kisiwani cover much of the island with many parts of the city still unexcavated. The substantial standing ruins, built of coral and lime mortar, include the Great Mosque constructed in the 11th century and considerably enlarged in the 13th century, and roofed entirely with domes and vaults, some decorated with embedded Chinese porcelain; the palace Husuni Kubwa built between c1310 and 1333 with its large octagonal bathing pool; Husuni Ndogo, numerous mosques, the Gereza (prison) constructed on the ruins of the Portuguese fort and an entire urban complex with houses, public squares, burial grounds, etc. The ruins of Songo Mnara, at the northern end of the island, consist of the remains of five mosques, a palace complex, and some thirty-three domestic dwellings constructed of coral stones and wood within enclosing walls.

The islands of Kilwa Kisiwani and Songo Mnara bear exceptional testimony to the expansion of Swahili coastal culture, the Islamisation of East Africa and the extraordinarily extensive and prosperous Indian Ocean trade from the medieval period up to the modern era. The key attributes conveying outstanding universal value are found on the islands of Kilwa Kisiwani and Songo Mnara. However, two associated groups of attributes at Kilwa Kivinje, a mainly 19th century trading town, and Sanje Ya Kati, an island to the south of Kilwa where there are ruins covering 400 acres, including houses and a mosque that date to the 10th century or even earlier, are not included within the boundaries of the property. The property is subject to invasion by vegetation and inundation by the sea, and vulnerable to encroachment by new buildings and agriculture activities that threaten the buried archaeological resources. The continued deterioration and decay of the property leading to collapse of the historical and archeological structures for which, as noted earlier, the property was inscribed, on the List of World Heritage in Danger in 2004

The ability of the islands to continue to express truthfully their values has been maintained in terms of design and materials due to limited consolidation of the structures using coral stone and other appropriate materials, but is vulnerable, particularly on Kilwa Kisiwani to urban encroachment and coastal damage as these threaten the ability to understand the overall layout of the mediaeval port city. The ability of the sites to retain their authenticity depends on implementation of an ongoing conservation program that

46

addresses all the corrective measures necessary to achieve removal of the property from the List of World Heritage in Danger.

The sites comprising the property are legally protected through the existing cultural resource policy (2008), Antiquities Law (the Antiquities Act of 1964 and its Amendment of 1979) and established Rules and Regulations. Both the Antiquities laws and regulations are currently being reviewed. The property is administered under the authority of the Antiquities Division. A site Manager and Assistant Conservators are responsible for the management of the sites. A Management Plan was established in 2004 and is currently under revision. Key management issues include climate change impact due to increased wave action and beach erosion; encroachment on the site by humans and animals (cattle and goats); an inadequate conservation program for all the monuments, and inadequate community participation and awareness of associated benefits.

Long term major threats to the site will be addressed and mechanisms for involvement of the community and other stakeholders will be employed to ensure the sustainable conservation and continuity of the site. There is a need for better zoning of the property for planning in order to ensure development and agricultural uses do not impact adversely on the structures and buried archaeology.

Bagamoyo - Tanzania

Bagamoyo is located at 6°26'S 38°54'E close to the island of Zanzibar and 75 km north of Dar-es-Salaam on the coast of the Indian Ocean.

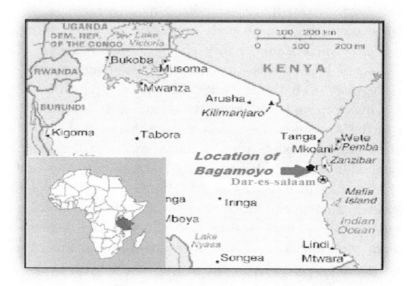

Map 9: *Bagamoyo in relation to other major towns*

In the late 19th century, Bagamoyo used to be the most important trading entre-port of the east central coast of Africa. The Indian and Arab traders influenced the history of this place greatly, and so did Christian missionaries and the German colonial government.

19th Century German garrison of Bagamoyo

This town is known for the historical ruins it hosts. These include the Kaole Ruins with remnants of two mosques and a couple of tombs

48

dating back to the 13th century. It shows the importance of Islam in those early Bagamoyo times.

Kaole Ruins in Bagamoyo, Tanzania

Bagamoyo was a small and unimportant trading center until the middle of the 18th century with most of its residents being fishermen and farmers. They traded fish, salt, and gum. In the late 18th century Muslim families relatives Shamvi la Magimba in Oman settled in Bagamoyo. By enforcing taxes on the native population, trading in salt from the Nunge coast north of Bagamoyo, they made their living. Consequently, Bagamoyo became a trading port for ivory and the slave trade in the first half of the 19th century with traders coming from places as far as Morogoro, Lake Tanganyika and Usambara travelling to Zanzibar.

The word Bagamoyo ("Bwaga-Moyo") means "Lay down your Heart" in Swahili. Scholars have proposed two theories behind this name. One is it refers to the slave trade which passed through the town (i.e. "give up all hope") or to the porters who rested in Bagamoyo after carrying 35 lb cargos on their shoulders from the Great Lakes region (i.e. "take the load off and rest"). Since Kilwa attained the status of being the major slave port, the name of the town most likely derives from the latter explanation.

In the year 1873, the slave trade in East Africa was officially prohibited though it continued secretly to the end of the 19th century. The Majumbe, Bagamoyo local rulers, presented the Catholic "Fathers of the Holy Ghost" with land for a mission north of the town in 1868. This became the first mission in East Africa. This caused the native Zaramo people, mediated by representatives of Sultan Majid and after 1870, by Sultan Barghash to resist. The mission originally intended to house children rescued from slavery, soon expanded to a church, a school, farming projects and some workshops.

 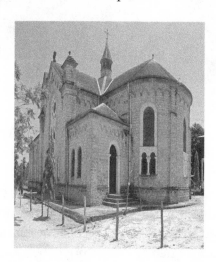

The old church in Bagamoyo,Second Catholic Church built by the missioners in Bagamoyo

In addition to being a trade centre for ivory and copra, Bagamoyo was also a starting point for renowned European explorers. They moved out from Bagamoyo to find the source of the River Nile and explored the African inner lakes. Richard Francis Burton, John Hanning Speke, Henry Morton Stanley and James Augustus Grant were some of them. In his lifetime, David Livingstone never went to Bagamoyo, but his body was laid in the Old Church's tower (nowadays named Livingston Tower) while waiting for the high tide to come so his body can be shipped to Zanzibar.

Bagamoyo was the first capital of Tanzania while serving as the German headquarters of German East Africa (first under the auspices of the German East African Company and then the German Imperial Government) between 1886 and 1891. Dar es Salaam became the new capital of the colony in 1891.

While Bagamoyo was the first capital of Tanzania under the auspices of the German East African Company, it was also the German headquarters of German East Africa and then the German Imperial Government between 1886 and 1891. In 1891, Dar es Salaam became the new capital of the colony. The town was apparently the birthplace of SS-Oberführer Julian Scherner-1895. When the German Empire decided to build a railway from Dar es Salaam into the interior in 1905, Bagamoyo's importance began to decline.

During World War I, on August 15th 1916, a British air attack and naval bombardment was launched on Bagamoyo. The Germans were overrun and the German garrison was taken.

Bagamoyo is today a centre for dhow sailboat building. There are efforts to maintain the ruins of the colonial era in and around Bagamoyo and to revitalize the town. Internationally, Bagamoyo is well known today by the Bagamoyo College of Arts ("Chuo cha Sanaa") which teaches traditional Tanzanian painting, sculpture, and drama, dancing and drumming. Bagamoyo is more diverse than some other areas of the country because of its various history and proximity to Dar es Salaam. There are also other centers of education, including a nursing school, a fisheries center, and an extension of the University of Dar es Salaam. The reconstruction of the road from Dar es Salaam to Bagamoyo has increased the number of visitors to Bagamoyo making it a new tourist destination with new and luxurious hotels springing up along the shoreline. Apart from the visitors, Bagamoyo is home to many ethnic groups, including the Wakwere, Wazaramo, Wazigua, Maasai, and Waswahili. Many different cultures coexist in Bagamoyo, including people of Arab descent although Swahili culture dominates.

Bagamoyo was recently designated as Tanzania's seventh world heritage site and is the oldest town in Tanzania. Bagamoyo's history has been influenced by Arab and Indian traders, the German colonial government and Christian missionaries. Although Bagamoyo is no longer the busy port city that it once was, Tanzania's Department of Antiquities is working to revitalize the town and maintain the dozens of ruins in and around Bagamoyo.

Bagamoyo was the major slave trading post in East Africa. Bagamoyo, which means 'lay down your heart' in Swahili, was probably given this name because Bagamoyo was the last place the slaves would stay in Tanzania before being shipped off to foreign lands. Although the slave trade officially ended in 1873, slaves continued to be sold and traded in Bagamoyo through the end of the nineteenth century.

During the slave trade, it was not uncommon to see hundreds of slaves walking through the streets of Bagamoyo chained together by the neck. Slaves were collected from the interior by capture, purchase or trade and then shipped to Zanzibar or Arab countries.

Dar es Salaam- Tanzania

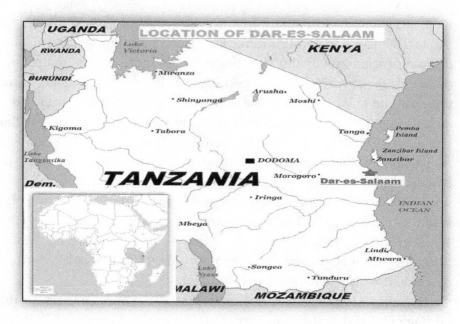

Map 10: Dar es salaam in relation to other major towns

Dar es Salaam means "heaven of peace" (in Arabic). It is located in a bay on the Indian Ocean. A United Nation' report (2008) on the State of African Cities as a framework for addressing urban challenges in Africa explains that the city of Dar es Salaam was first established in 1857 and was formerly known as Mzizima. Mzizima is a Swahili term that translates to "healthy town". In 1862, the Sultan of Zanzibar found it and gave it the name Dar es Salaam. It continued to be only a small port till the German forces; specifically the German East Africa Company, established a station there in 1887.

It is an important city currently and historically as it was the capital of German East Africa from 1891–1916. During World War II, it began to grow tremendously hosting multiple universities and technical colleges. The city is now the home to the national archives of Tanzania, as well as the National Museum of Tanzania.

German forces occupying Dar es Salaam in the 1980

From the 1960's to early 1990's, Tanzania was a strong supporter of the African liberation movements and many political exiles were hosted in Dar es Salaam. Hence, it was the capital city of Tanganyika from 1961 to 1964 and of Tanzania from 1964 to 1974 when Dodoma was declared the new capital. Although the Tanzania's National Assembly officially moved the capital to Dodoma in 1996 many government offices still reside in Dar es Salaam. The city is best known as the economic power house and the major port for Tanzania and other neighboring countries. In 1998 a bomb, planted by terrorist and believed to have been inspired by Al-Qaida, went off at the U.S. Embassy in the city of Dar es Salaam killing eleven people.

Aerial view of Dar es Salaam

The city's population has quadrupled since 1980. According to the 2012 census, the population of the Dar es Salaam region was 4,364,541. Dar es Salaam city accounts for 10% of the total Tanzanian mainland population. As the largest city it is the communication and economic center of Tanzania. The main industries of the city include, but are not limited to oil, textiles, clothing, shoes, cement, aluminum products, and pharmaceuticals. Although Dar es Salaam has limited access to the sea, it is Tanzania's main sea port exporting a number of goods mainly cotton, coffee, diamonds, and hides.

The business boom in this city is partly due to easy transportation access which began with the central railroad that was built during the colonial period. This railroad links Dar es Salaam on the east with Kigoma on the west. It passes through many small towns on its way to the west and branches off twice. The first branch leads to the northern regions of Kilimanjaro and Arusha with a small branch at

Korogwe that goes to the coastal town of Tanga which also serves as one of the key Tanzania trading ports. The second branch is at Tabora to link Mwanza, a port on Lake Victoria, to the central line. Kigoma is an important port on Lake Tanganyika. It serves both Rwanda/Burundi and the Democratic Republic of the Congo. The importance of Kigoma sored during the civil wars in the Lakes Region countries by serving as an entry port for refugees escaping the fighting in the respective countries of DRC, Rwanda, and Burundi. The second major railway from Dar es Salaam is popularly known and TAZARA (Tanzania-Zambia Railway). It was built by the Chinese and serves as Zambia's major access to the Indian Ocean through the port of Dar es Salaam. This was constructed at the height of the liberation movement for the Southern African countries of Angola, Mozambique, Zimbabwe, and South Africa when Zambia could not export or import its goods through the major sea ports of these countries. Dar es Salaam became the major port for the Zambian "Copper belt". The railroad also allows for quick travel as well as efficient commerce.

In 1891, the city of Dar es Salaam had about 4,000 inhabitants and extended only two kilometers from the Indian Ocean to the Hinterland. In 1980, the city expanded to 14 kilometers and recently, it boasts 30 kilometers. Dar es Salaam is a great port because of the way it is shaped but the low point is the traffic from all of the ships. There is increasing concern that the port might be in danger of losing business due to infrastructure issues, employee work ethics, and traffic to and from the port. The problem of corruption within the local police and Tanzanian revenue authority at the port is considered a major complication affecting the port's economic status. A journalist from one of the major newspapers in Tanzania, Mwananchi Communications Limited, noted on his blog the possibility of traders in Rwanda and Uganda withdrawing from shipping in cargoes through the Dar es Salam port effective September 1, this year, 2013. If the port at Dar es Salaam starts to lose some of its business, it will create a ripple effect that could cripple the rest of the city and the country as a whole.

The Dar es Salaam seaport

Another aspect that is of concern for the city of Dar es Salaam is that the central and local governments have not been able to control its growth partly due to the port access coupled with the rapid growth of its international airport that receives and dispatches planes daily across the globe. Thus, while the city is important historically, its significance in the global economy cannot be underestimated. It is the world's 9th fastest growing city with a population growth rate of 5.6. Many of its historic buildings are being demolished to make way to sky-scrapers to accommodate the influx of both foreign investors and new businesses. While the Ministry of Antiquities has jurisdictions over what happens to buildings of historic significance, it seems the quest to modernize and make Dar es Salaam a 21st Century city seems to win and silence the critics of historical preservation. The fast growth has also attracted Tanzanians from other parts of the country to make it the most densely populated city in Tanzania with a population density of 3,133 people per square kilometer.

Zanzibar - Tanzania

Located in the Indian Ocean, 25 miles from the Tanzanian coast, Zanzibar has a population of around 800,000. It is known for its rich history of early mankind habitation, the sad slave trade, the triangular trade network (between Arabia, India, and Africa) and the various ruling powers that controlled the island for long time. It is a city, a port and an island (usually known as Unguja). It has many archipelagos (small islands) and sits right next to the island of Pemba.

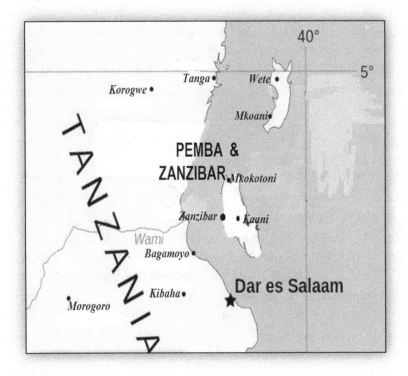

Map 11: Zanzibar

The Hadimu and Tumbatu ancestors who belonged to different ethnic groups in the mainland East Africa and who travelled to Zanzibar around 1000 AD were seemingly the first permanent residents of Zanzibar. It is believed that, since the Pal Eolithic, though not constantly, Zanzibar has been populated. At Kuumbi Cave, heavy duty stone tools were found in a 2005 excavation. Such findings suggested the site was inhabited at least 22, 000 years ago. Chami (2006) archeological discovery of a limestone cave report underlined the use of radiocarbon technique and proved Zanzibar was occupied around 2800 BC. Although some writers are not completely convinced, the glass beads possibly from around the Indian Ocean are traces of the communities in Zanzibar suggesting an early trans-oceanic trade networks. Juma (2004) identifies cave sites revealing that iron-working and farming communities during the mid-first millennium AD resided on the Mafia and Zanzibar islands, and indicating mud-timber structure settlements built at the onset of urbanism. On Zanzibar, these ancestors lived in small isolated villages making them easily conquered by outsiders because they could not unify and organize themselves into larger and strong political units.

Trade

Ayany (1970) shows trading routes with Zanzibar and the ancient Sumer and Assyria existed based on the ancient pottery findings. For example, near Eshnunna, an ancient pendant traded to copal, brought from Zanzibar, was discovered and dated ca. 2500-2400 BC. Traders from Arabia (mostly Yemen), the Persian Gulf region of Iran (especially Shiraz), and west India probably visited Zanzibar as early as the 1st century AD. They used the monsoon winds to sail across the Indian Ocean and landed at the sheltered harbor located on the site of present-day Zanzibar Town. Although the islands had few resources of interest to the traders, they offered a good location from which to make contact and trade with the towns of the East African coast. A phase of urban development associated with the introduction of stone material to the construction industry of the East African coast began from the 10th century AD. Historians write that Assyrians, Sumerians, Egyptians, Phoenicians, Indians, Chinese, Persians, Portuguese, Omani Arabs, Dutch and English have all been in Zanzibar at some point.

Traders began to settle in small numbers on Zanzibar in the late 11th or 12th century, intermarrying with the indigenous Africans. Eventually a hereditary ruler (known as the Mwenyi Mkuu or Jumbe), emerged among the Hadimu, and a similar ruler, called the Sheha, was set up among the Tumbatu. Neither had much power, but they helped solidify the ethnic identity of their respective peoples.

The Yemenis built the earliest mosque in the southern hemisphere in Kizimkazi, the southernmost village in Unguja. A kufic inscription on its mihrab bears the date AH 500, i.e. 1107 AD. The identification of villages presents the lineage groups that were common.

The Arabs were the majority of the landowners; they controlled 1,000 miles of mainland coast from present day Mozambique to Somalia. In 1698, Zanzibar became part of the overseas holdings of Oman. Later, the Oman ruler, Said bin Sultan, moved his court from Muscat to Stone Town on the island of Unguja. After his death his sons struggled with succession. As a result Zanzibar and Oman were divided into two separate realms. Majid became the first Sultan of Zanzibar. To this day, most of the wealth lay in the hands of the Arab community, who were the main land owners.

Colonial Rulers

Kaene (1907), Ingrams (1967) and Turki (2007) detail the history of Zanzibar tracing its colonial rulers to its dependence. The Portuguese were the first European explorers on this island. They were introduced by Vasco da Gama who visited Zanzibar in 1499. Around 1503 or 1504, Captain Ruy Lourenço Ravasco Marques landed in Zanzibar; he demanded the sultan give him tribute in exchange for peace. This was shortly after Vasco da Gama's visit, and from then on, Zanzibar became part of the Portuguese Rule that controlled Zanzibar for nearly 200 years.

The second rulers were Arabs led by the Sultanate of Oman who was a great trader for cash crops and spices; he gained control of Zanzibar in 1698 with a ruling Arab elite. He expelled the Portuguese as a result of a profitable slave trade and ivory together with a growing clove plantation economy. Slave trade was the third pillar of the economy in Zanzibar, giving it an important place in the Indian Ocean's Triangular Trade. The most notorious Sultan and slave trader was Tippu Tip. His accolades include: trader, plantation owner, governor, and most of all, a slave owner.

The Arabs built forts at Zanzibar, Pemba, and Kilwa. The Arab rule arose in 1840 when Sayyid Said bin Sultan al-Busaid (also known as Seyyid Said) moved his capital to Stone Town from Muscat in Oman. Using the slave labor, he developed clove plantations and assumed the governing of the Arab elite. Said encouraged other traders from the sub-continent of India to settle on the island and they increasingly took part in Zanzibar's commerce. In 1856, upon his death, his sons succeeded him. Zanzibar and Oman were divided into two separate principalities on April 6, 1861. From 1834/5–1870, his sixth son, Sayyid Majid bin Said Al-Busaid became the Sultan of Zanzibar, while his third son, Sayyid Thuwaini bin Said al-Said became the Sultan of Oman.

The Sultan of Zanzibar was in-charge of the Zanj region, an extensive portion of the east African coast controlling trading routes that extended further to the Congo River, around Kindu. This region was later changed by a German-British border commission in November 1886 to become a ten-nautical mile (19 km) wide strip along most of the coast of East Africa. The Zanj region included Mombasa, Dar es Salaam, all offshore islands, several towns in what is now Somalia and stretching from Cape Delgado in Mozambique to Kipini in Kenya.

The slave trade was a growing business that the British fiercely opposed. They gradually and then by force fought to gain control of the Zanzibar island. With the signing of the Heligoland-Zanzibar Treaty between the United Kingdom and the German Empire in 1890, Zanzibar became a British protectorate.

After the demise of Hamad bin Thuwaini on 25 August 1896, Khalid bin Bargash, eldest son of the second sultan, Barghash ibn Sa'id, declare himself the new ruler and took over the palace- against the wishes of the British government, which preferred Hamoud bin Mohammed. The British gave Khalid a one-hour ultimatum to leave but he declined, causing the British to open fire using their Royal Navy ships and destroy his Beit al Hukum Palace. This struggle ended in 45 minutes, hence the shortest war in history called the Anglo-Zanzibar War.

The destruction of Sultan Khalid's Beit al Hukum Palace

THE HAREM AFTER THE BOMBARDMENT.

The favored ruler, Hamoud took over and restored peace to the kingdom upon adhering to British request and ended the eastern slave trade in [[1987 please check this date to make sure it is correct]. He also compensated the slave owners. Ali, his son was educated in Britain.

In December 1963, both Zanzibar and Pemba became autonomous monarchs after gaining independence from Britain. A month later, many Arabs and Indians were killed, several more banished and thousands seized during the bloody Zanzibar Revolution war. The result was the birth of the Republic of Zanzibar and Pemba, and in April of 1964, mainland Tanganyika merged with Zanzibar to form what is now known as Tanzania. Needless to say, administratively, the island still remains a semi-autonomous region.

Today, many people visit Zanzibar to see many sites embodying its history (Michler, 2007). One of the sites is the Old Fort of Zanzibar which was built by the Omanis to protect the island from the

Portuguese in the late 17th century. For many decades, Zanzibar has been famous for its spices and slave trade. In the 19th century, historians attest that about 50,000 slaves passed through Zanzibar yearly (Gates & Appiah, 1999). As a result, the city became East Africa's central slave-trading port and many go to see the remains of the slave market place. Sadly, as many as 80, 000 Africans died on their way to the island every year (Owens, 2007). Others come to see the remains of the first steam locomotive in East Africa, which was found in Zanzibar during the reign of Sultan Bargash bin Said who ordered his noble carriage to be towed from town to his summer palace at Chukwani by a tiny 0-4-0 tank engine (Owens, 2007). Yet many people also visit Zanzibar to see the remains of the Sultan palaces, some of which are still well maintained and some even livable. They are especially attracted to the carved doors dating back to ancient times. Furthermore, there is a large seafood business with Zanzibar flourishing in the Indian Ocean. The beaches are very popular to all travelers, and most people who find themselves in Tanzania plan a day trip to Zanzibar itself. The island is accessible from Dar es Salaam both by sea and by air. It is fifteen minutes by air while a boat trip can take between seventy minutes and two hours depending on the speed of the boat.

Carved doors in Zanzibar

Lamu – Kenya

Lamu is located on Lamu Island on the Northern Coast of Kenya, and is part of the Lamu Archipelago. This island is part of the three largest islands in this coast namely: Lamu Island, Manda Island, and Pate Island. Lamu is one of the original Swahili settlements, and can only be reached by boat (dhow). It is a Muslim community with their lingua franca originating from Kiamu, but also they use Arabic and English. People here use Kenyan currency – Kenyan Shilling. They have 12 hour days with summer seasons that look and feel like winter. May through July, they have long rains.

Lamu Island[1] is a part of the Lamu Archipelago of Kenya. The Lamu Archipelago is located in the Indian Ocean close to the northern

---

[1]Source: Allen, James de Vere: *Lamu, with an appendix on Archaeological finds from the region of Lamu by H. Neville Chittick.* Nairobi: Kenya National Museums.

coast of Kenya, to which it belongs. The island lies between the towns of Lame and Kiunga, close to the border with Somalia, and is a part of Lamu District. The largest of the islands are Pate Island, Manda Island and Lamu Island. Smaller islands include Kiwayu, which lies in the Kiunga Marine National Reserve, and Manda Toto. Today the largest town in the archipelago is Lamu Town, on Lamu Island. The town is on the World Heritage List.

Lamu Old Town, the principal inhabited part of the island, is one of the oldest and best-preserved Swahili settlements in East Africa. Built in coral stone and mangrove timber, the town is characterized by the simplicity of structural forms enriched by such features as inner courtyards, verandas, and elaborately carved wooden doors. Lamu has hosted major Muslim religious festivals since the 19th century, and has become a significant center for the study of Islamic and Swahili cultures. The island is linked by boat to Mokowe on the Kenya mainland and to Manda Island, where there is an airport. There are no roads on the island, just alleyways and footpaths, and therefore, there are few motorized vehicles on the island. Residents move about on foot or by boat, and donkeys are used to transport goods and materials.

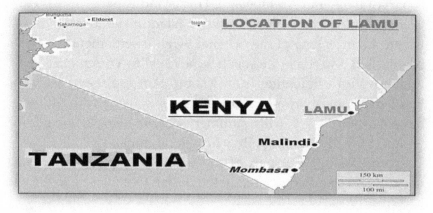

Map 12: Lamu Port

Lamu port was founded on the island by Arab traders at least as early as the fourteenth century, when the Pwani Mosque was built.

The island prospered on the slave trade. After defeating Pate Island in the nineteenth century, the island became a local power, but it declined after the British forced the closure of the slave markets in 1873. In 1890 the island became part of Zanzibar and remained obscure until Kenya was granted independence from Great Britain in 1963. Tourism developed from the 1970s, mainly around the eighteenth century Swahili architecture and traditional culture. The Old Town Lamu was designated a UNESCO World Heritage site[2] in 2001 based on (1) the architecture and urban structure of Lamu graphically demonstrate the cultural influences that have come together there over several hundred years from Europe, Arabia, and India, utilizing traditional Swahili techniques to produce a distinct culture; (2). the growth and decline of the seaports on the East African coast and interaction between the Bantu, Arabs, Persians, Indians, and Europeans represents a significant cultural and economic phase in the history of the region which finds its most outstanding expression in Lamu Old Town; and (3) its paramount trading role and its attraction for scholars and teachers gave Lamu an important religious function in the region, which it maintains to this day.

Pate Island is located in the Indian Ocean close to the northern coast of Kenya, to which it belongs. It is the largest island in the Lamu Archipelago, which lie between the towns of Lamu and Kiunga, close to the border with Somalia. From the 7th century, Paté Island was an early site of Arabic colonization. It long vied as a Swahili port with Lamu and with Takwa on Manda Island and came to prominence around the 14th century, but was subjugated by Lamu in the 19th century.

Public transportation is provided by a few mini buses (so called matatus). The main administrative centre on the island, with the police station, is Faza.

---

[2] Source: UNESCO documents

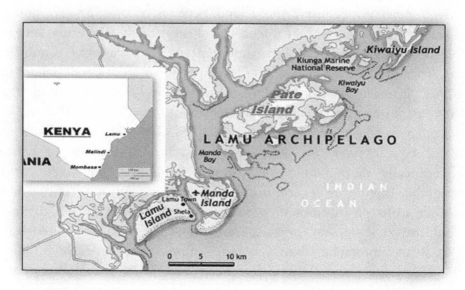

Map 13: *Pate Island*

Manda, also an island of the Lamu Archipelago of Kenya, is known for the prosperous 9th century ports of Takwa and Manda town. The island is now linked by ferry to Lamu and is home to Manda Airport, while Manda Toto Island lies to its west. The island is separated from the mainland by the narrow *Mkanda* channel.

Both Manda town and Takwa were probably abandoned due to lack of water in the first half of the 19th century. In the 1960s the Kenya Department of Agriculture recommended building several concrete catchments called *jabias* to capture rain water on the island. Two *jabias* were built and many families moved onto the island, farming maize, cassava, simsim and cotton.[1]

The Manda town ruins (by the coast on the NW side), were first explored by the archaeologist Neville Chittick in 1965. The town owed its origins in the 9th and 10th centuries to trade with the Persian Gulf. The chief trading commodity was probably elephant ivory; mangrove poles were probably also important. From the earliest period the inhabitants of Manda were building with burnt square brick and stone and set with a lime mortar. These building techniques are found only on the coast and on the islands of Kenya; they have not been used in the interior of the country,[2] whereas the bricks averaging about 18 cm (which "match perfectly ...in measure") are unique for East Africa for this period, and are likely to have been brought in from Sohar, inOman, initially as ballast in the sailing ships entering the port.[3] From the mid-9th century to the early 11th century buildings were also constructed from coral known as *coral rag* cut from dead coral reefs.

The large scale excavations which happened in 1966, 1970 and 1978 revealed an unrivalled prosperity for the period and include Chinese porcelain dating from the ninth century onward, Islamic pottery and glass, and local pottery datable by the associated imports. The most striking features of the town are the large sea walls built between the 9th century and the 13th century.[4] Running parallel with the sea with returns running inland, these walls built from large coral blocks are deduced to have been constructed partly to reclaim sections of the shore, and partly to consolidate the edges of the peninsula.

At the heights of its power the town covered some 40 acres (160,000 m^2) and its population is estimated to have been about 3,500. Manda prospered until the 13th century when it began to decline. The islands are reputed to be one of the westernmost ports of call of the great Chinese fleet of Zheng He, or even to be the resting place of a wreck of one of his ships. No direct evidence has yet been discovered of his visit, although it is known that he visited Mombasa, further down the Kenyan coast, in around 1415.

Lamu District is a district of Kenya's Coast Province. Its district headquarters is Lamu town. The district covers a strip of northeastern coastal mainland and the Lamu Archipelago. Lamu District has a population of 72,686 (1999 census) and its land area is 6,167 km. The district has only one local authority, Lamu county council and it has two constituencies: Lamu West and Lamu East There are extensive mangrove forests in the area. Kenya, South Sudan and Ethiopia have launched a controversial development project to build

a port, oil refinery and rail network near the island of Lamu. In addition to Lamu Town, there are three villages on Lamu Island
The economy of Lamu was mainly based on slave trade until 1907. Their exports include: Ivory, mangrove, turtle shells, and rhino horns.

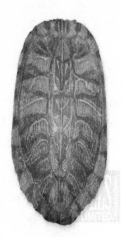

Turtle shells   *Rhino horns*

Exports were possible using the Uganda Railroad built in 1901. Tourism also boosted the economy of Lamu especially with people coming to visit the Headquarters of Lamu District.

Malindi- Kenya

Malindi is located on the Kenyan Coast. It lies off the coast of the Indian Ocean and northeast of Mombasa (Kenya's largest coastal town). Based on the 2009 census, Malindi is Kenya's fifteenth largest populated city with a population of 118, 265. Malindi is also the largest town in Kalifi County.

Malindi was established in the early thirteenth century by the Arabs. The Malindi officials established a relationship with the Portuguese and in 1498 they welcomed Vasco da Gamo, a great Portuguese explorer. Much to the dismay of the locals, the following year the Portuguese set up trading posts along the city. This established a colonial relationship with the Portuguese and the indigenous people of Malindi. The city remained wealthy, with most of the economic support streaming from agriculture and trade. The Portuguese presence remained prominent until the seventeenth century; with the construction of Fort Jesus in the neighboring town of Mombasa, interest in Malindi declined.

The sultan of Zanzibar assisted in restoring the city to its former wealth during 1861 to 1890. The abolishment of slave trade in 1873 and the growing tension between the African and Arab people of Malindi lead to the economic downturn of the city. This was followed by the establishment of British imperialism in the 1900's which lead to another economic boom from agricultural trading. Following decades of economic significance, Malindi stalled after World War II. Malindi was established by the Arabs in the 13th century. In the 1400s, it also established diplomatic relationships with both the Chinese and Portuguese forming a strong foundation for trade. In the mid-1990s, mass tourism began to "put Malindi on the map. Historically, Malindi was known to be a trade post for slave trade, rubber, fruit and ivory. Malindi is now mainly publicized as renowned tourist hub due to its spectacular beaches.

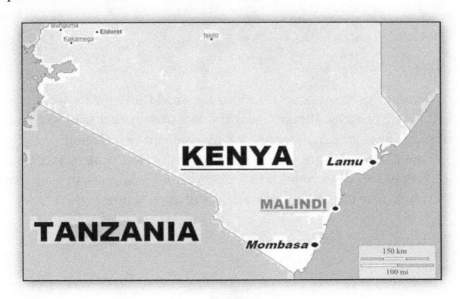

Map 14: Malindi The current economy in Malindi looks somewhat similar to how it was during the 14th century, just a bit developed. In

the past, the people of Malindi were dependant on fishing, hunting and agriculture. Their tourism-inclined economy focuses on many things-beaches, restaurants, hotels, coffeehouses, deep sea fishing, as well as a revived architectural industry and woodcarving. In those days, with not so many tourist towns, this proved to be of great economic gain.

Malindi brought people around the world to view its wonderful and exotic beaches. While that is the major attraction here, the Gedi ruins are another reason people visited and still visit Malindi.

The Gedi Ruins are remains of a Swahili town located near Gedi; the remains Gedi were declared a Kenyan national park in 1948, and they showcase examples of classic Swahili architecture.

The Gedi Ruins

With tourism at the epicenter of its economy, Malindi is known for its sandy beaches and luxurious resorts. It is a hotspot for Italian tourists in particular, but attracts thousands of visitors from the world each year. Malindi boasts 96 miles of breathtaking beaches and some of the most fascinating coral reefs on the coast of the Indian Ocean, which are preserved in Malindi Marine National Park. Tourists typically spend their time in Malindi indulging in water sports, such as scuba diving and snorkeling, enjoying various cuisines, and relaxing alongside the beach. The Vasco da Gama Pillar, a bell-shaped monument built in 1498 by Portuguese explorers, is a historic Malindi landmark and serves as another common tourist attraction. There, tourists explore historic grounds and shop for various souvenirs uniquely crafted by locals. In addition, wildlife enthusiasts are drawn to Malindi, because of its renowned safari adventures.

With tourism progressively increasing in Malindi, foreign investors in the resort town have begun to emerge as well. Billionaire and Italian socialite, Flavio Briatore, is pioneering the investments by building a 500 million dollar resort set to open in August, 2013. The exclusive resort will include a top of the line casino and private chauffeurs and boats to navigate its guests through the city of Malindi. It is said to be the first of its kind in all of Africa.

Mombasa-Kenya

Mombasa was founded in association with two rulers: Mwana Mkisi (female) and Shehe Mvita. According to oral history and medieval commentaries, Shehe Mvita superseded the dynasty of Mwana Mkisi and established his own town on Mombasa Island. Shehe Mvita is remembered as a Muslim of great learning and so is connected more directly with the present ideals of Swahili culture that people identify with Mombasa. The ancient history associated with Shehe Mvita and the founding of an urban settlement on Mombasa Island is still linked to present-day peoples living in Mombasa. The Thenashara Taifa (or Twelve Nations) Swahili lineages recount this ancient history today and are the keepers of local Swahili traditions. Even though today Mombasa is a very heterogeneous cultural mix, families associated with the Twelve Nations are still considered the original inhabitants of the city.

The exact founding date of the city is unknown, but it has a long history. Kenyan school history books place the founding of Mombasa as 900 A.D. It must have been already a prosperous trading town in the 12th century, as the Arab geographer Al Idrisi mentions it in 1151. Most of the early information on Mombasa comes from Portuguese chroniclers writing in the 16th century. The famous Moroccan scholar and traveller Ibn Battuta did visit Mombasa in 1331 on his travels on the eastern coast of Africa and made some mention of the city, although he only stayed one night. He noted that the people of Mombasa were Shāfi'i Muslims, "a religious people, trustworthy and righteous. Their mosques are made of wood, expertly built."

In 1498, Vasco De Gama, a Portugueses explorer, arrived on the shores of Mombasa. He was the first known European to visit Mombasa, receiving a chilly reception in 1498. This put a halt to the dominance of Arab influence for about 150 years. Vasco De Gama's arrival was mainly welcomed with hostility among the locals, but the tables turned when he made the King of Malindi his ally. Two years later, the town was sacked by the Portuguese. The Portuguese used their power to make the King of Malindi the Sultan of Mombasa. This insured that the locals had no choice but to obey the Sultan, who took orders from the Portuguese Government. Mombasa became Portugal's main trading hub along Africa's East Coast which led to the construction of Fort Jesus (which still stands today). The Fort served as the main hub for trading goods, a prison for slaves, and for the protection of the Portuguese from attacks by locals and foreign battalions. Local slaves were traded for goods coming from European countries

In 1502, the sultanate became independent from Kilwa Kisiwani and was renamed as Mvita (in Swahili) or Manbasa (Arabic). Portugal attacked the city again in 1528. In 1585 Turks led by Emir 'Ali Bey caused revolts from Mogadishu to Mombasa against the Portuguese landlords; only Malindi remained loyal to Portugal. Zimba cannibals overcame the towns of Sena and Tete on the Zambezi, and in 1587 they took Kilwa, killing 3,000 people. At Mombasa the Zimba slaughtered the Muslim inhabitants; but they were halted at Malindi by the Bantu-speaking Segeju and went home. This stimulated the Portuguese to take over Mombasa a third time in 1589, and four years later they built Fort Jesus to administer the region. Between Lake Malawi and the Zambezi mouth, Kalonga Mzura made an alliance with the Portuguese in 1608 and fielded 4,000 warriors to help defeat their rival Zimba, who were led by chief Lundi.

During the pre-modern period, Mombasa was an important centre for the trade in spices, gold, and ivory. Its trade links reached as far as India and China and oral historians today can still recall this period of local history. India history shows that there was trade links between Mombasa and Cholas of South India. Throughout the early modern period, Mombasa was a key node in the complex and far reaching Indian Ocean trading networks, its key exports then were ivory, millet, sesamum and coconuts.

In the late pre-colonial period (late 19th century), it was the metropolis of a plantation society, which became dependent on slave labour (sources contradict whether the city was ever an important place for exporting slaves) but ivory caravans remained a major source of economic prosperity. Mombasa became the major port city of pre-colonial Kenya in the Middle Ages and was used to trade with other African port cities, Persia, Arab traders, Yemen India and China.[7] 15th century Portuguese voyager Duarte Barbosa claimed, "[Mombasa] is a place of great traffic and has a good harbor in which there are always moored small craft of many kinds and also great ships, both of which are bound from Sofala and others which come from Cambay and Melinde and others which sail to the island of Zanzibar."[8]

In 1698, the town came under the influence of the Sultanate of Oman, subordinate to the Omani rulers on the island of Unguja, prompting regular local rebellions. Oman appointed three consecutive Governors (Wali in Arabic, Liwali in Swahili): Imam Sa'if ibn Sultan who ruled for less than a month in 1698; Nasr ibn Abdallah al-Mazru'i who ruled for 30 years (1698-1728); and Shaykh Rumba who succeeded him and ruled for three months in 1728. Thereafter, Mombasa returned to Portuguese rule under captain-major Álvaro Caetano de Melo Castro (12 March 1728–21 September 1729), then four new Omani Liwali until 1746. Thereafter, the information is disputable. Mombasa became a British protectorate from 1824 – 1826 under the administration of Governors when Omani rule was restored in 1826 and seven *liwalis* were appointed. Although Said bin Sultan of Muscat and Oman annexed Mombasa 1837, it was placed under British East Africa Association administration in 1887 which later became the Imperial British East Africa Company. Mombasa attained the status of the capital of the British East Africa Protectorate and the sea terminal of the Uganda Railway, which was started in 1896.

Mombasa was and still is inhabited by Cushitic-speaking people from modern day Sudan and Ethiopia who were the early settlers in Kenya beginning around 2000 B.C. Due to its strategic position, Mombasa was and continues to be a city sought for trade opportunities though under a huge Arab influence that heightened trade along the coast.

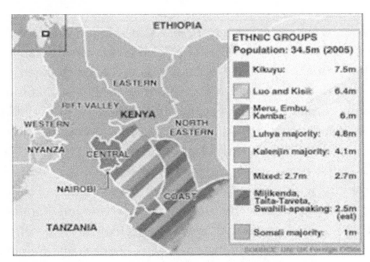

Map 15: *Ethnic groups in Mombasa*

75

Needless to say, many of the workers used to build the railroad were brought in from British India to build the railway, and the city's fortunes revived. The Sultan of Zanzibar formally presented the town to the British in 1898. In 1920 Mombasa became the capital of the Protectorate of Kenya, with its coastal strip under the sovereignty of the Sultans of Zanzibar. This changed after Kenya's independence in 1963 when it became part of the newly independent Republic of Kenya with Nairobi as its capital.

City of Nairobi

Nairobi began in the late 1890's as a railway camp as the British built a railway from Mombasa to Uganda. Originally named "Ewaso Nai Bari," meaning "place of cool waters," later changed to Nairobi because the British could not pronounce it. Due to Nairobi's cooler swampy climate, it soon became the capital of Kenya. Gaining its independence from Britain in 1983, it quickly became the center for agricultural economy. Now, Nairobi is considered "The Gateway to Africa" with populations from all walks of life. Nairobi is a cultural diverse city with populations from all major Kenyan Ethnic groups, including Kikuyu, Luo, Luhuia, Kalenjin, Kisii, and Kamba. At 20%, the Kikuyu tribe represents the largest amount of the ethnic group population. Nairobi is home to Asians, Europeans, Somalis, and a large amount of expatriates working for embassies and organizations planted in the city.

Mogadishu - Somalia

Mogadishu is capital of Somalia and port city to the world. According to Lionel Casson (1989), the word Mogadishu translated literally from Arabic; it means "The Seat of the Shah". The first references to Mogadishu date back to as early as1AD in the Periplus of the Erythaean Sea. The royalty of Mogadishu, called the Sultanate, developed with the influx of Emozeidi Arabs, beginning in the 9th or 10th centuries. Archaeological excavations have recovered coins from China, Sri Lanka, and Vietnam. Italy ceased Mogadishu from the Sultan of Zanzibar in 1892, making it a pseudo-colony of the Italian Government. Between 1949 and 1960, Italy ceased its control of Mogadishu and Somalia was made independent. On July 1, 1960, the State of Somali and Trust Territory of Somalia (formerly Italian Somaliland) United to form the Somali Republic, with Mogadishu as its Capital.

After a coup d'état on October 21, 1969 resulting from the assassination of the President of the Republic, the Somali Democratic Republic emerged. A civil war broke out in 1991, toppling the regime set forth by the previous coup. On December 3, 1992, the United Nations passed Security Council resolution 794 which approved a coalition of UN peacekeepers to enter Somalia. After many Islamic uprisings in the late 1990's and 2000's, Mogadishu is now in a time of relative Peace.

CHAPTER 3

The Livelihood Of The Swahili Coastal States People

Introduction

The word "economy" can be defined in many ways. The business dictionary describes economy as "an entire network of producers, distributors, and consumers of goods and services in a local, regional, or national community." To understand the economy of a people therefore, one must comprehend the different activities related to the production and distribution of goods and services in that particular geographic region, while recognizing ways in which they correctly and effectively use their available resources. In this chapter, we will briefly identify and highlight the circular flow of goods and services among the Waswahili from producers to consumers, and in more depth articulate the corresponding flow of labor and capital into the production process within the Swahili Coast. Later we will show how trading activities have been and can be enhanced through the use of Kiswahili in Africa and internationally.

A: The Making of the Swahili Coast Economy

As noted earlier, the Swahili Coast occupies an area that is about 10^0 N in Southern Somalia to 250^0 S. to the mouth of the Lompopo River (Sanseverino 1983:153). There is a considerable environmental variability along the Coast, as the region extends from the shores of the Indian Ocean to the grasslands of the elevated hillsides. The towns of the Swahili Coast created a unique culture in an important part of Africa, producing multi-textured ecological system, which suppressed the resources of any one portion of the Coast. One function of culture is the articulation of human populations into local environments. The Coastal Cities played a significant part in the transfers of goods from the African countryside to the dhows waiting to transport local commodities to markets and across the sea to Arabia. The coast was a crossroads, articulating its residents into a worldwide trading network. Goods produced in Africa went north to the Red Sea and the Persian Gulf, and beyond to the Malabar coast of India.

Much of the coastal town markets were influenced by manufacturers from the Far East who made their way into the area to trade and to collect goods much needed by the ready markets in Europe. Needless to say, East Africa's ports harbored sailors on the long sail from Europe to the Malabar Coast around the Southern Cape of Africa. The northeast monsoon winds that blew from October to April facilitated the passage of lateen-rigged dhows from the Red sea and Persian Gulf carrying the goods from the East to ports of eastern Africa. Because the area had stable settlements, investments in permanent residences, civic buildings, and religious edifices were easily established. Thus, the environment was welcoming and played a critical role in the development of the Swahili trading towns. They had rich and fertile soils plus a stable climate two vital factors that distinguished the farming populations from other residents who occupied the city and its vicinity. Merchants from the hinterlands of eastern Africa craved the imported goods also. Local trading nets – transfer of supplies to relatives and those offered at local markets, or carriage of tradable commodities by pastoralists to distance lands. Because the people of the Swahili Coast participated in the greater Indian Ocean trade network, their lives were completely changed over the years by assuming both the roles of farm goods producers and traders.

The Coastal Geography

Due to the dual roles discussed above, the Coastal people practiced agriculture capable of yields greater than those of subsistence farmers in order to sustain the hierarchy of individuals engaged in other occupations, trades, or politics. Their productivity was enhanced by the good climate and the rich soil. The coastal states stretch

Mogadishu in the north to Tanzania in the south. The Tanzanian coast consisted of mixed vegetation with large mangrove swamps along the lagoons and bays and scattered forested areas. The timber estates were very larger but were diminished as their worth increased in the Persian Gulf trade. In addition, the locals converted some of the forested area into much needed agricultural land. The most popular and vastly extensive trees were the Chlorophora Excelsia, (*mvule* in Swahili) which was exploited for its wood and for making furniture for local use and export to enhance the coastal economy.

The habitation of the coast and its hinterland was also endowed with many opportunities for a variety of economies. Foragers, pastoralists and farmers were drawn to the Coast by the resources of the forests, grasslands, and the Indian Ocean encouraging the growth of the coastal towns. These resources, some of local importance and others which were staples of the long distance trade, contributed to the development while forming the basis of the inhabitants' commercial traffic.

The Coastal Resources

The Swahili Coast's diverse ecological zones supported both agricultural and the abundance of fish. The Coastal plain and islands offered not only marine resources, but access to trade routes. The plateaus were suitable for hunting wild game, including elephant, rhino, leopard and lions, which provided ivory, rhinoceros horns, and cat skins respectively. These were considered items that were an important part of the long-distance trade from the first century onward. These include the rich mangrove and other forest furnished timber for construction there were export as well. It is believed that there are at least eight different kinds of mangrove species that provided lumber and the needed charcoal for forging iron, which was from ferruginous limonite sand found on many of the beaches. The animals provided leather and they needed the charcoal to tan hides. Some of the mangroves were used for firewood and for making red dye. Minerals were exported from the southernmost coast. These included cooper and gold. The cattle thrived because the scrub forest did not have the tsetse fly found in other areas. The importance of the Mombasa Island comes from its freshwater harbor that is effective in protecting the island from harsh weather. Gordon, Charles Alexander (1874) notes that the varieties of tree provided ample timber that was critical in boat and ship work as well as furniture and decorative doors.

The high tides on the Mrima coast extending to the southern Kenya border to the Rufuji (Tanzania) Delta made the soil fertile for good farming. Pemba and Zanzibar that are off the Mrima coast have some of the greatest population densities because of its agriculture and harbors. Flood plains of rivers leading to the Indian Ocean are key settlement locations. The fertile soil, a consequence of the annual floods, facilitated agricultural activities that included rice, maize, beans, peas, bananas, tobacco, pumpkins, and yams. Needless to say these activities did not produce a self-sufficient society because there was a very loose connection between these activities and the coastal trades. The farming was much more inland while the coast maintained its heavy reliance on fish and trading activities.

Because the economy in Africa depends on agriculture more than manufacturing, the success in agriculture on the coast depended not only on the astute farmers but also the soil. There are two kinds of soil in East Africa that are important here: the black cotton soils, and the sandy loams and red-dish clay. The black cotton soil is typically found in the seasonally flooded grasslands while the sandy loams and red-dish clay are more typical on other parts of the coast. The northern coast isn't as successful with agriculture due to distance away from the coast, low precipitation levels, and low soil moisture. Still, other regions like Zanzibar and Pemba are rich in resources, making them among the most densely packed settlements. One complements to the coastal civilizations is the ability to work together in complex networks. This made it possible for each group to be sufficient to thrive. The need for vital resources to be moved and traded created a momentum for small-scale trading networks making use of the rivers and sea to accomplish this. By having boats for fishing as well as to transport commodities efficiently from one place to another, the region melded together into and interdependent ecological zone.

The economy of the Swahili coast also depended on its indigenous population. Its rich resources made it an inevitably competitive area for human settlement and exploitation. The Lamu and Mombasa Islands commanded and to date continues to command excellent harbor facilities, with plenty of fresh water, and are surrounded by excellent fishing grounds. The islands and harbor have clean, fresh water and is easily defensible. As Nurse (1983) notes, the discovery of an eight-thousand-year boat-building tradition in Nigeria bolsters the claim made by historical linguists that the Proto-Sabaki Bantu speaking peoples arrived on the coast with a well-developed nautical technology that showed through their success and the general coastal settlement patterns.

The coastal people depended and still do on the coral reefs and sea shores for fishing. The Coastal swamps contain at least eight species of mangroves, each species thriving under slightly different levels of salinity. Mangrove poles have historically been used for building, firewood and charcoal for iron smelting and forging. Mangrove bark was, and still is, used for tanning leather. Mangrove poles and the red dye produced from the bark formed an important export to the Middle East. The Mrima coast extends from the southern Kenya borders to the Rufiji Delta in Tanzania. Southwards lie the eastern plains of Tanzania. The fertile, well-watered highlands are ideal for farming maize, beans, peas, bananas, tobacco, pumpkins, and yams. Explorers like Livingstone and Thompson [need year reference] reported this area to be densely populated with settlements along the Ruvuma, Lukuledi, and Rufiji Rivers.

The Significance of the Interstate and Intrastate Interaction

As noted earlier, the economy of the coastal states deeply depended on the interstate and intrastae interactions. The ecological system formed by these interactions of the various commercial interests around the Indian Ocean wove together the produce and peoples from a quarter of the earth. This was enhanced by the very reliable monsoon winds that moved from the northeast starting from October and lasting up to April. The rest of the year the monsoon reversed its course, moving from the southwest. This provided a reliable means to economically import and export goods from the far east to the coastal states. This interaction was,mentioned in the Periplus of the Erythraean Sea. Traces of Iranians, Chinese, as well as local coastal potters can be detected in many archeologically established Swahili settlements (Kusimba 1999)

Thus, the monsoons did not exist as a colorful part of the local environment, but as an important concomitant of economic life. In pastoral economies, there was little opportunity for permanent structures or need for a complexly stratified society. This was not the case for the Swahili Coast. Those who were able to capitalize on the trade routes earned wealth and high status in the society, because the stability of the settlements allowed investments in permanent residences, civic buildings and religious edifices. Needless to say, the wealth was not equally distributed because the Swahili coastal people were classified based on a number of factors. The inhabitants of the Coast were drawn from diverse ethnic religious, linguistic, and subsistence backgrounds. The social classes were often based on these divisions and may be considered as the primary factor for persistent designation, the haves and the have nots.

There were four main social classes:

1. The elite class: the *Waungwana*,which include the free, or nobly born. These are often associated with those who considered themselves the direct discendants of the Profet Mohamed, and by definition Muslim and very proficient in Arabic, the only acceptable language of the Kuran. The ability to read the Kuran was also associated with linguistic scholarship in Arabic.
2. The *wazaliwa*-defined as the descendants of freed slaves or has one of their parents (often the mother) a slave.

84

3. The *watumwa*-those who were slaves. Many of these worked for the elites an on the plantations owned by the elete group.
4. The *wageni*-these include anyone who was visitor to the coastal states or was a recent immigrant.

More has to be said about the *waungwana* because of the way this staus influenced the class system and the lingering effects to date. This group dominated urban life (to-date the implications can be realized in the fact that the affluent live in urban settings) and controlled the social, political, and economic structure of the community. Members of this group were defined by the designation (*i.e.* Ungwana: the ethic of "culturedness"-intellectual and artistic sensitivity) which gave ideological support to their control of wealth-creating activities, including land and labor. In addition to this prestigious designation, members of this group owned the fertile land, stretches of beach, and mangrove swamps. They had the ability to employ slaves to work these lands betokened. The status also gave members of this group the voice to make policy decisions in the affairs of the town. As such, membership in the *uungwana* was limited to those demonstrating blood ties to a well-respected ancestor who could supplement their kin-based claims to status with wealth, especially ownership of a stone house located in an elite section of the town. In addition, *Uungwana* privileges included the right to: religious scholarship; own property such as fertile farmland, stretches of beach land, mangrove forests, and fishing areas; own cattle; build and live in stone houses in one's own *mtaa* (neighborhood); receive, entertain, and trade with foreign merchants; elect town, and mosque officials; blow the great *siwa* (horn), at weddings; hold hereditary offices of *Mkuu wa Jela* (prison warden), *Mweka Hazina* (keeper of the town treasury), *Mkuu wa Pwani* (warden of the sea), and Khatib (Friday preacher); and the right to slaughter the expiatory ox after the cleansing ritual of *kuzinga mui* (rounding the town).

The accolades afforded to members with this status generated these regulations which prevented commoners from participating in lucrative international maritime trade with the Persian Gulf and Indian sub-continent, in order to concentrate authority and wealth in

85

the hands of land-holding elite. The elite monopoly of the harvesting of large trees prevented commoners from building their own boats and ship-building industry for the *wungwana* (elites). To maximize their profits from regional and interregional trade, the elite individuals invested in local crafts, including production of high-quality iron articles, copper ingots, wire and bracelets, shell beads, cowry shells, and textiles including raffia, kapok, and silk clothes for trade into the African interior. Because of their ability to wealth, they became sponsors of specialized crafts-men, such as boat builders, masons, gold and silver smiths, and coin casters. Without doubt, these privileges left little room (to-date) for those in the lover status to become economically at par with the *Waungwana* (the elites).

This explains why the agricultural sector was not profitable to small scale agriculture by the local farmers with limited resources in the Swahili Coast, as rains were sporadic and factored into crop production. Combined with the class system that had developed in the area, the productivity of local farming enterprises must be considered when positing the plunking down of a viable body of foreign trade and investiment on the African shore.

The vibrancy of the Swahili coastal people makes one wonder and the savy trading skills makes one aclaim some sofisticated cilivilzation in this part of the world that matches or surpases that which is considered to have arrived from outside the area. The question is what could have resulted from this if the indiginous civilization was allowed to grow and florish. Kusimba (1999) explains that the participation of the peoples of the Swahili Coast in the big Indian Ocean trade system started the process that transformed their lives. They attracted the attention of neighbors mainly due to their ability to use their local environments. As a result, many neighboring mercantiles in other powerful nations became highly interested in forming a prosperous elite but even more, they set the conditions for colonial exploitation.

Civilization like trade is not a monopoly of one place. Just as most areas master one resource, and are dependent on trade for the others, humans learn from each other in order to enhance what they already have. The Swahili Coastal people knew the importance of relying on each other to grow their economy by diversifying their resources. Lamu and Mombasa Islands are great ports for trade and fishing, but have little ability to grow food. Thus, they depended on other regions thar are agriculture based for their food security. This exemplifies the importance of the Swahili Coast showing that is not just its port cities that are important but it is an amalgamation of the different intertwined sub-civilizations which were dependent on each other. The port cities contributed, as did the plains and plateau regions, the mangrove swamps, and the agricultural groups. The map below shows how the colonial powers partitioned the agricultural land along the coast .

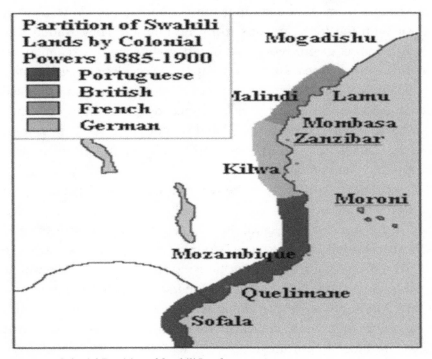

Map 16: Colonial Partition of Swahili Lands

Concluding Remarks

The significance of this chapter is the inter and intra trade interactions of the Swahili people, an important aspect of the economy of the region which was based on the Waswahili being the middlemen merchants of the long-distance trade between the northern Indian Ocean countries and those in the interior of Africa. As most traders do, these coastal stated traders settled in urban areas mostly along the coastline and some in large villages known as *mji* (city). The Swahili merchants, who also provided safe harbors for traders outside of the Swahili coast, had many complex skills which enabled them to provide facilities needed for mercantile exchange. They did this when the merchants from Asia used maritime seafaring vessels to meet at the coast with the foot caravans from the interior. They traded raw materials such as grain, ivory, gold, and mangrove in exchange for processed commodities such as weapons, porcelain, textiles, and beads. There was also Ferruginous limonite sands found on the beach and charcoal from the forest which they used to turn limonite sands into iron that was used locally and exported too. The vibrant commerce lasted for about two thousand years before it was interrupted by the Portuguese.

The vibrancy resulted from the fact that the Swahili people hand many skills, built very strong permanent houses using stones which birthed the "Stone-towns"-coral blocks set in narrow streets, and usually surrounded by walls. The "Country-towns," large village-like places which provided temporary housing, foodstuffs from gardens and fields, and slave labor were interspersed into the stone-towns. Rice and sorghums were the staple foods while tamarind, coconut, banana, and mango were other important crops and trees. Clove was perhaps the most important crop as it was mainly grown in large plantations formerly owned by Omani Arabs and traded highly. People living in stone towns had large plantations for growing exports through slave labor; those living in country-towns grew food for stone town dwellers but did not participate in the long-distance commerce. Together they formed a congeries of towns with one fundamental culture of economic interdependence.

For sustainable commerce, labor was a great commodity. It came from three main sources: the family and kin group, slaves, and hired laborers. Such labor categories are critical to understanding the Swahili economy as it defined social and political aspects of their economy. For instance, in the country-towns there was a sense of labor equality as men and women were considered equal, seeing their labor as complementary when men worked on clove plantations in the largest towns such as Zanzibar, Dar es Salaam and Mombasa, and women stayed home to handle domestic needs. Until the beginning of the twentieth century, slaves carried domestic works and agricultural ones in the Stone-towns. Since then, hired labor by non-Swahili immigrants and others from the country-towns did such jobs. Consequently, the Swahili settlements started having a shortage of seasonal labor, a persisting problem to this day.

Mazrui and Mazrui (1999) note the growth of the Swahili coast economy happened when an intensification of local agricultural and industrial production, as well as a growing interregional trade became rather necessary to the underwriting of the development of their complex society. The influx of wealth into the region certainly stimulated the growth of the different kinds of population centers. Settlements growth was the greatest in those areas that best attract trade, such as the mouths of major rivers or creeks. Settlements that had begun as modest fishing or farming hamlets gradually developed into towns and cities closely connected to the Indian Ocean. Egypt, Yemen, and the Indian sub-continent continued to be the main trading partners. A number of goods were imported but the Chinese Longquan, Tongan, and Ying Ch'ing were the most popular fifteenth-century imports. Others included the Islamic pottery which varied greatly in quality, but so too did the reintroduced ceramics from China, though it is also possible that some putatively Chinese pottery was actually made in Thai and Vietnamese kilns. The ability to trade these goods with various people outside the Swahili coast resulted in a social classification based on the wealth accumulated. Although each city made its own coins, many coins were used everywhere. Wealthier traders formed the elite group; there are indications that these individuals displayed their new-found wealth in personal architecture and the underwriting of civic and religious architecture. Both elite and non-elite women wore elaborate ornaments including gold, silver, and bronze bracelets and rings (a custom that continues to date).

The East Africa growing prosperity increased the market for exotica both from the African interior and from around the Indian Ocean as trade networks moved goods from small, rural communities to large ones, where those items were consumed or processed for further exchange or export overseas. The main players in East Africa at the time of the arrival of the Portuguese were Mwene Mutapa, from his mountain fastness at Mount Fura, in modern Zimbabwe, as well as the rulers of Kilwa, Mombasa, Malindi, Pate, and Mogadishu. Their trade networks also involved much of eastern Southern, central, and parts of West Africa. Mazrui and Mazrui also showed that the Portuguese noted, quiet early in their dealings with Africans that, "they are great barterers and deal in cloth, gold, ivory and diverse over wares with the Moors and other Heathen of the great kingdom of Cambaya". The many smaller settlements along the Coast played a similar role in the trade to rural villages of the interior.

The trade system played an important role in defining regional and interregional political hierarchies. At the time of the Portuguese intervention in East Africa, the local merchant class controlled their own day-to-day activities and commerce on the East Coast of Africa. Foreign merchants were present but were a minority. The principle language of the coast was Kiswahili. Trade with the interior was a long established practice. The most important "commodity" moving among interacting partners, however, was informational in Islam. There were several advantages associated with conversion to Islam. African Muslims freely traveled abroad for commerce, education, and pilgrimage. As the Swahili civilization grew in prosperity and power, large scale conversion to Islam in East Africa began in earnest, particularly during the years from the thirteen to the fifteen centuries.

The earliest known mosque on the Swahili Coast is at Shanga which was built in the mid-9th Century. The expansion in international maritime trade at this time increased competition between the commercial interests of the larger towns. The towns relied on merchant fleets that plied the Indian Ocean. Large polities, like Pate, Malindi, Mombasa, and Kilwa, invested in trade partnerships with interior societies and built watercraft used to ply the Coastal waters and interior rivers, collecting and selling trade items. Nevertheless, in many Coastal towns visited by the Portuguese were ships and boats from different Coastal and foreign ports. Sofala on the southern coast of Mozambique was the main artery for trade with the interior Kingdom of Mwene Mutapa, the source of considerable gold, copper, silver, iron, ivory, leather, and slaves. The Karimi merchants took control of trade on the Red Sea, established international trade with Cambaya and the wealthy and experienced Indian Vanya merchants from Gujarati.

It is without doubt that the greatest aspect of the Swahili Coast is the fact that it shared a common cultural, linguistic, and economic system. Islam and Islamic cultural ethos were the primary cultural pillars of the vast majority of the settlements and polities. Kiswahili dialects were mutually intelligible. The economic system was largely based on craft production and long-distance and international maritime trade. Wealth allowed the *waungwana* to create an elaborate internationalist culture on the edge of the African continent. The Elite families maintained strategic contact with one another and their trading partners, at home and abroad, through political and trade alliances, intermarriage and the exchange of the gifts, and only occasionally through military action. Furthermore, the military conquests (Arab and European) that came to the Swahili Coast came from other quarters, not from within and transformed the Costal States for ever. Left alone, these states could have developed to a world class economic center and perhaps Africa would never have been the same. Having this in mind and to better answer the question of who really built the sophisticated towns found in the Swahili coast, we turn, in the next chapter, to the work of archeology hoping to sketch an illustrative account of what the Indigenous Swahili people were capable of doing and how this information was obtained.

CHAPTER 4

Theories, Archeological Discoveries and Historical Accounts of Swahili Civilization

Introduction

Kusimba (1999) documents varied theories which arose from scholar's attempt to provide explanations of the existence and development of the Swahili civilization. This chapter is intended to review those theories and question further the assumption that the Swahili people did not have a civilization of their own prior to the arrival of the colonizers. One of the pressing questions is whether the Swahili civilization was imported? Historians suggest two major ways for studying historical accounts of a people. The first is oral history which explores a number of stories in order to determine the origins of specie that is specific to part of the world. What is known today about the Swahili people is derived from Portuguese chroniclers, Swahili informants, tribal/village folklore and the "literate elite" in the 16th Century. The second source is archeology. Combined, these two sources yielded explanations that we might consider as evidence for the growth of the Swahili Coast civilization. One theory from these sources indicates that the Swahili civilization may have been derived solely from outside sources (an immigrant culture). The second theory claims that there are enough probable courses to believe a local source (autochthonous culture). Some historical scholars believe that neither is sufficient and that the combination of the two theories brings us closer to an accurate account. In this chapter we present a chronological account of the key periods in the human history that marked the different stages of the rise of the Swahili Coastal States, covering the origination and growth of the Swahili civilization.

Theories on Swahili Civilization

The Diffusionism Theory was inspired by Friedrich Ratzel, founder of anthropogeography.

Friedrich Ratzel

Diffusionism is a theory which posits that large-scale ironworking, intensive agriculture, urban centers, monumental architecture, centralized kingdoms, and highly developed art all originated outside of Africa. The urban cities on the coast are a result of the migration of people from the Near East. It is however important to remember that the Europeans were the ones who wrote the article with such claims. In1948, the Royal National Park Service of Kenya Colony appointed James S. Kirkman the first warden of the national park- given him the right to excavate the land. Between 1948 and 1956, Kirkman excavated three mosques, a palace, 15 hours, the walls of Gede and several other sites. Over the next thirty years, Kirkman and his partner, Chittick, conducted an investigation of Coastal archaeology, with particular interest in architecture and the influence of Islam and trade.

James S. Kirkman

According to Kirkman, immigrants were drawn to the coast from less-prosperous relatives of foreign merchants, who remained abroad. Kirkman believed the newcomers were responsible for Coastal civilization because "without these classes the Coast would have remained a land of mud and grass huts like most of tropical Africa" (Kirkman, 1964). Swahili themselves traced their ancestry either to hinterland place called Shungwaya or to the Shirazi immigrants from Iran.

The External Origin Theory

According to Kusimba, the major theory about the Coastal people is the External Origin Theory which stipulates that the Coastal people did not exist prior to the arrival of outsiders, bringing with them the culture, civilization, and language). It explained settlement variations between Swahili towns as the result of different ethnic, cultural, and religious origins of the original colonizers. It satisfied a colonial world view, affirming the colonial role in Coastal history. It also attempted to assign present-day observations to the interpretation of life in pre-colonial cities.

Archeologists of the 20th Century are considered "new archeologists" because they created a different environment of debate that challenged some of the assumptions basic to early archeology.

Emphasis shifted towards elucidation of how cultures adapted through time necessitating other forms of investigating the study of cultural processes. The archaeological study on Shanga, (Horton 1996) revealed valuable information that shed new light about the Coastal States. The discoveries showed that the town was divided into 2 neighborhoods (mitaa) which varied in their quality and size, suggesting a degree of social and economic difference. It also disputed the theory of an external origin of civilization. Horton demonstrated that Shanga was founded as fishing, herding, and farming village. By the 19th Century, non-local artifacts found their way to the place, suggesting participation in local, hinterland, and Coastal trade as well as contact with the world across the Indian Ocean.

Though in contact with international commerce, the town demonstrates its roots in the African milieu. Indeed, the first houses built there were the round, sun-dried clay and timber huts that are commonly associated with the coastal Cushite and Bantu. In time, these houses were replaced by the rectangular coral rag and sun-dried clay and limestone houses still found in the area. Horton's interpretation of Shanga as an African settlement that gradually became more complex as its inhabitants expanded their trade networks directly contracted the External Origins Theory. Discussing the cultural identity of Swahili, Horton argued that the Swahili shared much of their culture with the other Coastal groups, that they shared a common heritage.

Through this theory, the large Arab population of the Coast in the 19th and early 20th Centuries and its strong cultural influence was pushed back in time several centuries. This necessitated new archeology. The 1960's were a time of innovation. It introduced new archaeologists, trained in anthropology and archaeology, versed in "culture process," who quested the research premises of an earlier generation of "descriptive" or "culture-historical" archaeologists. The new archeologists focused on how cultures adapted through time, the study of culture process- sought out the cultural development within a local situation.

In the 1970's, the External Origin Theory broke down. This theory was also challenged by many namely: Horton, on the basis of his decade long excavation at Shanga; J. de Vere; Allen's ethno-history; Wilding's analysis of local pottery; Nurse's and Spear's reinterpretation of the Swahili Chronicles, and Nurse's reinterpretation of the historical linguistic evidence.

Richard Wilding (1989:105) disputed the External Origin Theory, particularly its notion that Coastal and hinterland material culture had little in common. He found an increasing similarity in form and decorative motif of the ceramic wares of post- 14th century Swahili and rural groups (1980). He used this evidence to suggest that the first settlers at the Coastal sites were Cushitic-speaking pastoralists and foreigners, and that Bantu speakers played their part in the populating of the Coast at a later date. He argues that foragers, farmers, and traders combined forces to develop the cosmopolitan Coastal civilizations.

Nurse and Spear (1985)'s challenge concentrated on the locally produced traditional chronicles (14tth – 16th Centuries), they were written during the colonial occupation when the Coast's social, political, economic, and spiritual spheres were controlled by foreigners with roots in the Near East. He showed the Arab conquest of the Coastal produced a huge influx of foreign migration, a fact the chroniclers tacitly acknowledge in their attempts to legitimate the claims of the dominant classes, also pre-dominantly foreign in origin. Nurse and Spear found in the traditional histories of Mombasa, Kilwa, Pate, Lamu, and other towns a recurrent theme involving the arrival of settlers who through gift-giving to local inhabitants, were allowed to settle. The settlers eventually consolidated their claims on the land through magic, deception, warfare, and intermarriage with local princesses. The children from these unions became dominant and eventually wrested social and political power from the indigenous inhabitants.

In short, science began to re-access the local contribution to the beginnings and growth of these metropolises and the societies that supported them. Two notions now exist: The Swahili civilization derived from foreign sources, primarily migrants to the Coast, who brought their own cultural and social ideas with them. More autochthonous theory, suggesting the underlying themes of Swahili civilization were derived from cultural modes already inhering in the traditional folkways of the Coast.

Archeological work in Africa today

Lessons Learned from Archeological Studies

We join many historians in support of the fact that archeology can re-affirm a society's view of itself; create a new appreciation for one's past, and to establish adverse relationships with foreign cultures. Archeologists use a number of approaches which include new technologies such as Radiocarbon measurements, DNA determination, and perception of trace elements absorbed from ancient diets. They also use new techniques such as: systematic excavation, careful recording of provenience and identification and seriating artifact types.

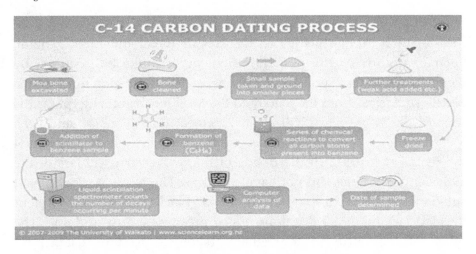

Before looking into how archeology presents the discovery of the Swahili civilization, it is important to highlight some critical aspects about archeological processes. One issue of concern is that the method depends on one's ability to transform field data into information. The concern here is the effects of one's own interpretation of the past vis-à-vis the data obtained. Often times the process is very subjective and biased. It is also true that one's interpretation can be formed based on the training received. Many of the archaeologists are foreign trained. They approach their field work with pre-conceived ideas, ideologies, and theories about what they may or may not find. As such, it is very difficult for a foreign or foreign trained researcher to do an interpretation that is completely unbiased and devoid of preconceived ideology and or theory. Much of the literature about the life in pre-colonial Africa shows an attitude that has been influenced by systematic marginalization of the continent.

Much of the perception of Africa in pre-colonial times was derived from a view of history that is a manifestation of an evolutionary course from 'a-historical' and primitive stage progressively moving upward toward civilized states. The model still persists in the mind of non-Africans and some elite African educated in the western ideology. One only needs to look at the way both print and social media treats any issue concerning Africa, be it a natural disaster or a human instigated disaster or development in general. Such an attitude produced the divisions made in the 19th Century by some historians to give us a continent divided into three parts: Northern Africa (from the Sahara to the Mediterranean), Egypt (as the center of a great civilization connected to Asia and the Mediterranean), and Sub-Saharan or Black Africa which was out of the realm of history. In the minds of many Western scholars of the 19th Century, Africa did not have a history. The term "Africa" meant sub-Sahara Africa (also referred to as 'black Africa): a continent deemed lacking either development or progress worth studying. The other Africa, north of the Sahara, belonged to the Asiatic and European worlds. Although Egypt signifies the passing of the cultural torch from the East to the West, it is not factored into the African equation.

The Africa of the imagination was an-historical, underdeveloped world, prisoner to its natural spirit, a place still at the threshold of universal history. Pre-historians, coping with explaining physical evolution, sought in Africa the evidence of early man and his culture, finding it convenient to adopt suggestions of social evolution to characterize and classify the remains they encountered. The Sahara was deemed a significant barrier preventing the movement of ideas from south to north, but which nevertheless allowed passage of them southward from Europe. The Colonialist world view denied the indigenous peoples a claim to their impressive monuments by asserting that they were the work of a variety of foreign migrants. As a result, irrigation terracing, earthworks, stone, monuments, and other evidence of advanced culture in eastern Africa were assigned to ancient settlers or the Hamites, driven down from the Horn by Islamic invaders in the 8th Century. Stigand (1913:116) noted that Swahili had a mixture of Arabic (vocabulary) but its grammar was Bantu. Stigand drew a conclusion that words which denoted civilized accomplishments derived from Arabic while those concerning day to day living came from Bantu vocabulary. It is evident that once you devalue a people's language, you also devalue their history.

Archeology and the Swahili Coast

As established earlier, archeologists are aware of the transformation of field data into information. Setting one's own interpretation of the past is a more subjective matter. One can easily quantify the contents of a pit but the significance of that pit and its role in some past culture is another matter. Often times the process is biased toward one kind of explanation or another, so much as to regard each individual investigator and the world view as a product of the expectations of his time and place prevailing conventional wisdom within the discipline. Where European trained researchers had difficulty was in interpreting the history of civilizations not ancestral to their own. The art and high achievement of the Greeks, Persians, and Egyptians, for example, were easily absorbed into the corpus of Western culture. Remains of past cultures, not immediately identifiable from the received history of literate peoples, were more difficult to fit into prevailing models for explaining the nature of the civilized condition.

Archaeology was first practiced by Europeans in the 19th Century to investigate questions concerning their historical worth. It diffused to Africa in a colonial setting. Archaeologists were originally interested in solving a set of problems revolving around: Stone Age cultures, early forms of humans and descriptions of monumental buildings. Archaeologists showed little interest in the history of the indigenous people, or the "primitives."

The Swahili civilization of the East African coast posed a problem of being interpreted from a political content interpretation rather than a cultural one because the culture was not considered 'high culture.' Thus the explanation of the Coastal civilization has several accounts: travelers, anthropologists, and others gathered over the past 500 years. These accounts often give rise to the investigator's description in support of some self-serving Western view of the nature of African society, or a story in support of the informant's world view. By controlling history, it is often possible to shape the present and influence future events.

The traditional accounts available for scrutiny are variously derived first from the anecdotes of the Coast and its rural countryside conveyed by Portuguese chroniclers and Swahili informants; and second by some gathered accounts among village or tribal folk, many of whom developed a sophisticated knowledge or understanding of the expectations of foreign observers and written accounts set down from the 16th Century onward by the "literate elite' of the Coastal states. There are two major explanations for the growth of civilization on the Swahili Coast: it was derived solely from outside sources, hence, it is an immigrant culture. The other claims it was derived from local sources, i.e. it was an autochthonous one. Kusimba (1999) argues the Swahili coast was a vital crossroads in the commerce of the ancient world.

When considering different explanations regarding the Swahili coast, we encourage you- our reader to seriously consider that the Swahili Coast was ethnically diverse and how it came to be so is critical to understanding the origin of its complex history and economic character. The making of the Swahili coast shows Europeans stopped in Mombasa and Zanzibar before launching their travel into the interior. Large numbers of Arab and Indian merchants, financiers, and crafts people came to East Africa to trade in slaves, ivory, rhinoceros horn, timber, copper, and gold, but also to fill the void left by the Portuguese expulsion from Mombasa in 1729. After the Portuguese expulsion, the Coast became an Oman colony, which lasted until 1964 when the Sultanate was overthrown by Zanzibaris, more than half of the new immigration occurred after 1840 when the Sultan Seyyid Said transferred his capital from Muscat to Zanzibar. Arab and Islam political and cultural dominance of the Coast was nearly complete. Europeans who encountered this formidable Arab presence on the Coast formed the opinion that the stone ruins they encountered were built by ancient Persian and Arab colonists. William Fitzgerald was told by the local informants that the ruins were built by their ancestors, described the ruins of Ras Kiamboni and Shakani as bearing witness to settlers from Arabia, Persia, and India. The presence of architectural mosques and tombs and the presence of datable imports from as far back as 650 years ago, suggested to Fitzgerald of a great antiquity and a forgotten race (Fitzgerald 1898:443).

The denial of African origins in the Coastal states had been repeatedly displayed to invalidate any civilization associated with the indigenous Coastal Swahili people. For example, wells and fragments of locally made ceramics and pottery imported from India, the Middle East, and China, point to the emergence of trade with the locals. Work on the ruins of Kilwa by the British Academy characterized the ruins as the remains of African civilization despite the noted influences from Arabia, Portugal, and India. Some archeologists like Kirkman and Chittick (British) argued that the Coastal towns were the work of immigrant Islamic traders who settled the Swahili Coast and adjacent islands in order to capitalize on commercial opportunities. Chittick credited the origins of Swahili civilizations to those lands around the Indian Ocean with which the local merchant class formed the closest trading partnerships.

The destruction by the Portuguese of the Costal economy was described by Vasco da Gama on his voyage to Calcut. The King of Kilwa is repeatedly described as an African and the King of African, although he claimed to be descended from the Old Shiraz Kings and his way of life was Arab rather than African. The Swahili themselves traced their ancestry to a hinterland place called Shungwaya or Shiraz immigrants from Iran. According to oral traditions, the Swahili left the hinterland sometime in the 16th century, fleeing Oromo pastoralists' aggression, shortly after they came to the Coast for the first time. This chronology would bring them to the Coast long after the founding of the Coastal cities. But, most major Swahili towns such as Pate, Kilwa, Mombasa, and Zanzibar, possess chronicles, which usually begin with the 10th century Shiraz colonization under Ali ibn Hasan ibn Ali of Kilwa and his sons. The traditional narratives, being political as well as historical accounts, were fraught with perils to those who took them too literally.

Facts on the Origin of Swahili Civilization

What Old Sketches and Documents Reveal

Among strong suggestions of a native Swahili culture can be found in what historians term old sketches. We mention one here to make a case in point. What we present here is not exhaustive but rather significant.

Bagamoyo Catholic Mission 1868-1893.

Father A Le Roy

Father Alexandre Le Roy Catholic, or Spiritan, missionary recorded the oldest documents of baptisms and marriages within the Catholic Church in East Africa. Bagamoyo, which as mentioned earlier is located at the Indian Ocean in Tanzania was recorded containing information about East Africa in the 19th Century. The documents showed that at the time of slaves, Christian missionaries were the first Europeans to arrive in East Africa in the 19th Century.

They arrived on Zanzibar in 1863 and established themselves on the East African mainland in 1868. The first mission-station was located in Bagamoyo and was named "St. Joseph's Mission Bagamoyo." The missionaries were appalled by the slave trade:

1,514,000 East Africans were captured and sold during the 19th Century.

Slave caravan 1

Efforts to fight slavery at the grass-root level began under the jurisdiction of Bishop Armand Maupoint of St. Denis on Reunion Island (Northeast of Madagascar). He witnessed thousands of slaves were imported there to work on the sugar cane farms and coffee plantations. The Bishop wanted to fight slavery in the "home land of slaves." He told the Spiritans "... to fight slavery at the grass roots level, to ransom as many slaves as possible, to settle them in villages and to teach them Christianity." (Henschel 1889:2)

Slave caravan 2

The liberating program was started from Zanzibar to Bagamoyo in 1863 by Father Anthony Homer and Etienne Baur who began mission work in Zanzibar. They bought slaves at the market and then set them free. He founded a "Freedom Village" in Bagamoyo in 1868. From Zanzibar to Bagamoyo Sultan Seyyid Majid granted Father Homer a large plot of land north of Bagamoyo for boarding houses for the boys, girls, and married couples. He conducted workshops and a church. The fathers trained the men to have certain skills and the sisters took care of the young females and taught them house-hold skills and nursing skills while the children received elementary education. From 1870-1893, the missionaries baptized 2,496 people who they ransomed from slavery.

Missionaries baptizing slaves

Bagamoyo missionaries wanted to take the gospel inland, but they faced many obstacles such as the cholera epidemic in Bagamoyo, German French War, hurricane Kimbungo. Consequently father Horner finally made his first exploratory trip in 1876. In 1887, Ft. Horner succeeded in opening the first mission station in the interior Mhonda. He was followed by one in Manderia in1881, Morogoro in 1882, Tununguo in1884, and Ilonga in 1885. "Record of Marriages" tell us who were married, when, and where they moved in order to advance the gospel. Historians can also use this data to see the average age of marriage during this time.

The Boshiri war: In 1888, members of the "German East African Society" took over administration of the East African coast, in Bagamoyo. The Germans ordered the Arab authorities to evacuate the administration building. Germans announced new public regulations, hoisted new fall, and brought in new policies. Because of the changes, war broke out and lasted up until the end of 1889.Twice the town of Bagamoyo was attacked, once by Boshiri and then by the German Admiral of the Navy, Deinhardt. Almost all the buildings in Bagamoyo were destroyed. 7,500 inhabitants took refuge in the mission.

In 1889 Hermann von Wissman was appointed Commandant-in-chief of "German East Africa" with the title, "Imperial Colonial Commissioner." On May 8, 1889, he attached the headquarters of

Bushiri, killing Bushiri and the supporters in Bagamoyo. This swiftly ended the war and the Germans took control of Tanganyika, called "German East Africa." In the 1890's all mission stations were running schools. Teachers became the new lay missionaries to East Africa. The new pastoral approach of "mission schools became very effective for the Church in East Africa. The former model of ransoming slaves continued. Altogether, 113 Spiritans worked in East Africa during the first 25 years. They had a strong commitment to the build the Catholic Church in East Africa by proclaiming the Good News of Jesus Christ.

Historical Chronology of the Rise of the Swahili

The following historical account is based on the works of Archeologists working on the East African Coast (cf. Kusimba – 1999 for a detailed account). They considered imported ceramics, coins, and historical records among the most accurate methods for determining Coastal site chronologies. By examining dates found in known ceramic kilns and securely dated places in the Middle East, the following periods [adopted from Kusimba 1999] were compiled as useful markers illustrating the existence of the Swahili Coast and the ultimate development that followed.

Period 1 (100 B.C. to 300 A.D.):

This is considered the earliest time when communities of Bantu and Cushitic-speaking communities were discovered. Very few sites can be associated with the time. These places were inhabited by iron-using farmers, whose descendants now inhabit much of eastern and southern Africa. They were characterized by a consolidation of a number of technologies-iron working, cereal production, pottery manufacture, and cultural patterns. Cultural patterns and social organizations of these Bantu speakers affected later cultural development on the coast. For example, he pastoralists, who adopted the practice of following their flock in the Nile valley, followed the rhythm of natural opening of pasture. The pastoralists and metal forgers played an important role in utilizing the varied environmental

108

zones of the coastal and its environs, establishing the conditions under which elaborating cultural arrangements developed. This era was marked by limited communication with the outside world.

Period II (300-1000 A.D):

The era is divided into two major phases. The first phase is called Azania. It took place between 300 and 600 AD. During this time, the Swahili increased their locally produced goods. They also had some artifacts from Far East trades, but not much compared to what they produced on their own. The second phase is called the Zanjian, and occurred between 600-1000 AD. There was a tremendous increase in communication with the Far East, which scholars suggest was motivated by maritime trade. This period was marked by the increased communication with the outside world.

Period III (1000-1500 A.D)

This is considered the classic age of the Swahili civilization. There was an emergence of autonomous Swahili city-states. The architecture was elaborate featuring stone buildings with coral walls. Scholars also indicate the coast at this time had a secure economic base. There was evidence of an increasingly complex social and political economy capable of supporting professional craftsmen. Trade with the interior increased-marked by glass beads and rock crystals from the interior of Kenya. As a result of the much intercommunication with the outside world, natives converted to Islam in large numbers causing expansion and extension of trade into the 14th Century. The use of coral stone in domestic architecture and tombs among the wealthy became prominent. 16th Century East Africans continued to maintain trade with people around the Persian Gulf, India, and Madagascar. At this time Chinese ceramics were popular. Much of the trade occurred at Kilwa mainly because of its strategic place. The location of Kilwa placed its elite in a tactical position to participate in, manage, and control much of the African trade between southern eastern Africa and other ports along the northern Swahili Coast, Madagascar, the Comoros, South India, Indonesia, and the Persian Gulf states. Gold, copper, ivory, slaves, and iron from southern Africa came to Kilwa via Sofala, the entry port to Zambezi. Cloth, glass, beads, cowry shells, shell beads found their way to the interior through the markets of Kilwa. This period was marked by a remarkable trading system and economic growth.

Period IV (1500-1950): Colonial Period

The growing trade attracted different foreigners as indicated. The Portuguese were among those who arrived in 1495 and found the Swahili Coast a thriving civilization intermeshed with a long standing complex regional and international trading system. The Swahili States fell into the hands of the conquerors because they were not united enough despite their savvy commercial skills. Hence, readers need to understand clearly the rise of Swahilidom in order to grapple with the dilemmas of scientific discoveries and historical explanations regarding the Swahili civilization. In some aspect, the explanation we offer may seem a repeat of the Swahili eras discussed above. However, looking closely at the account we present next, one can see the two are related but not similar.

The Rise of Swahilidom

Provided with the background above, one is able to see how the Swahili City States was shaped by a series of events and historical eras. Without doubt each historical period had a profound impact on the building of the Swahilidom. Kusimba reports that the first half of the 14th century was considered the 'golden age' of the Swahilidom due to maritime civilization and international commerce. Important sites include: Lamu archipelago-Manda, excavated by Neville Chittick, and Shanga by Mark Horton. Zanzibar was one of the main attractions then. There were several exports from the land of the Zanj (source of the name Zanzibar-Zenji Bar = land of the black people).The main import attractions in this area were ivory, iron, and slaves who were taken to work in the salt mines of Basra and to drain the marshes of lower Iraq. A question frequently asked concerning

110

the slave trade is: When did the slave trade decline and what effect did this have on the area? After the slave revolt in the 9th century – trade declined sharply although slave trade continued for another nine centuries.

In addition to trade in Zanzibar, the meadows of gold and copper from the south of the Swahilidom was another factor contributing to its development. The southern part of Africa brought copper and gold from Zimbabwe and the Limpopo bend. These were carried to the Mozambique coast, a land believed to be of Sofala. It produced gold and many other ornaments. The Gold Dinars created an economic stimulus that went beyond the Islamic empire, the Far East and Europe. History also shows the Swahili civilization carved out a small territory even further south around Sofala in Zimbabwe. While the northern cities of coastal Zimbabwe remained localized and showed little influence on the African culture further inland from the coast, the Sofalans actively went inland, deep into the African hinterland, and spread Islam and Islamic culture.

The Madagascar and Indonesian connection was another aspect of Africa, greatly intertwined and highly influential in trade. There was a critical connection between Madagascar and the Coastal states. Both of them were infiltrated by Arab sailors and Malayo-Indonesians who participated in raids occasioned by competition for the control of the commerce of this region. The involvement of the Swahili by providing alliances enhanced the Islamization of the harbor-towns.

The West and East also took part in the making of Swahili. Egypt, for example, played a key role in the development of the Coastal states by serving as a trade link between the Indian Ocean and the West. Doing this enhanced and opened up trade between the west and the Far East-India, China, other South East Asian lands, and Arab lands. Another significant historical account of the development of the Swahili has been told through what has become known as the story of the Great Mosque in Kilwa. Kusimba notes that what was unique about the Great Mosque was the focal point of the Swahili town, a place where people congregated on Friday to pray, the finest building in town. While it was the only ruin to survive the

Portuguese destruction, it also holds the history of the town to date. Scholars discern the 1300 boom of international activity in the town of the Great Mosque by looking at the massive and ornamental buildings activities, the monuments of the grand place of Husuni Kubwa, the elaborated arches, domed and barrel-vaulted extensions that still stand intact after the destruction to this day.

Placing the Swahili Coast in the World

When provided with the series of events, developmental eras and factors illuminating several features of the Swahili Coast, it is clear that this part of East Africa commanded and continues to commands attention.

First, the Swahili coast has played a prominent role in the world history. Solomon and his Tyrean allies were reputed to have dispatched trading fleets to the coast of E. Africa. Even the Romans trafficked there and the Egyptian goods penetrated its interior. In historic times, the north part of the Somalia coast offered entry ports to the caravan routes leading to the Nile valley through such foreboding towns as the legendary city of Harar, a prominent slaving center with thriving business in cotton and coffee. Its central reaches in Kenya and Tanzania connected the people of the flourishing kingdoms of the Great Lakes Region-Karagwe, Runyoro, and Buganda-on the Highlands to the Coastal towns, the markets on Zanzibar and the island archipelagos. In the south, ports along the Mozambique Strait trafficked inland to the plateaus of Zambezi and the mineral riches controlled by maShona kingdoms, ruled from marvelous places like Great Zimbabwe. Nowadays, the Swahili Coast is strewn with the remnants of its past florescence: the ruins of once prosperous towns, with the elite mansions and mosques built in coral rag, and their less elegant neighborhoods, with the homes, markets, and workplace of the common citizens. Such noteworthy relics were built by Swahili peoples about 500 to 800 years ago. Their culture was, on the surface, an Islamic one and they interacted with and were influenced by centuries of economic contact with and colonization

112

from southern Arabia, Western India, and Portugal. Despite this welter of external contacts, it was a culture that remained essentially African in its cultural roots and inspirations.

Second, the inhabitants of Swahili towns played a prominent role in the triangular mercantile trade making of India, the Persian Gulf, and East Africa. Even before the Portuguese, the Coast had been visited in times past by traders from the Orient. The world knew of the Eastern coast of Africa, its commerce, and its treasures. But the long history of the Coast extends even further back in time, beyond the land of Punt and rumored voyages of Phoenician seamen, to even times when the coast was peopled by transhumant foragers and herdsmen, and the first settlements by Bantu speaking, iron-using farmsteads before spreading on to the South along the coast to establish new settlements in eastern Africa. It can no longer be disputed that the first set of exchanges of the Swahili trade transferred iron and iron tools, as well as textiles, agricultural, animal, and marine products from place to place among otherwise independent communities of forages, fishers, farmers, and pastoralists, accepting products of the field and herd in return. Though receiving little to sometimes no credit, these exchanges laid the economic groundwork upon which the future prosperity of the Coastal cities would depend.

Third, the Swahili highlighted the ingenuity of the African genius to survive and prosper on their own. There was a tendency to believe that African cities were built by foreigners. It was tacitly assumed that the civilization which developed on the Swahili Coast was a by-product of the migration of people and ideas from the near and Far East. The origins of Swahili civilization were commonly believed to have been from an external trade between foreign immigrant merchants and the Near/Far East. The role of indigenous people was largely thought irrelevant to the question of understanding the origins of social complexity (Kirkman 1964:22). But Swahili culture is a vigorous multi-textured one, a result of a long and dynamic process of inter-action between indigenous Coastal peoples occupying a strategic place, the African cultures and non-African societies across the world's oceans.

As we showed earlier, as early as the first century A.D., Africa's trade relations with Eurasia became more institutionalized and centrally controlled by growing state societies and significantly contributed to bi-directional biological and technical transfers in the Old World. Boat building technology and camels enabled trade in gold, salt, animal products, and spices across the Indian Ocean and Sahara. Trade in Eastern and Southern Africa stimulated the growth of cities along the Swahili Coast and in the interior, centered at the Shona kingdoms of Zimbabwe. Research work on the Swahili Coast in the 20th Century focused on the following questions: Who built the complex urban towns of the Swahili Coast? What was their role in the Indian Ocean trade?

This distinctive cultural and ethnic character of the Swahili people – who are urban, literate, and Islamic, and seemingly unlike the other coastal peoples, who are rural, farmers, non-literate, and traditionally African in their beliefs, was regarded as evidence of their separate identities and cultural origins. This model nurtured the view that coastal towns were far too sophisticated to have been the work of indigenous Africans. Many academic quarters before 1980 held the Swahili coast as an extension of the Islamic world. It is assumed that Muslim people of the Swahili coast were colonials merely interested in exploiting the economic resources of the region. These works legitimated the tendency to look overseas to explain local coastal events, even though locally made material culture constituted nearly all of the archeological assemblages at all sites. In the next chapter, we explore in more depth the language of the Swahili people.

CHAPTER 5

The Kiswahili Language

In this chapter, we draw heavily from the works of Mazrui and Mazrui (1999). We also include works by other Kiswahili scholars who interrogate the different aspects of Kiswahili. For the most part, we show the spread of Kiswahili in Eastern and central Africa. While the spread of Kiswahili in these regions have taken place against a background of the interaction between church and state, it has also occurred in the interplay between economics and politics. In addition, three domains of social experiences surrounding Kiswahili exist: spiritual considerations, affairs of the state, and matters relating to the business of livelihood sustenance.

What do people say about the roots of Kiswahili?

The debate about the roots of Kiswahili has placed the language in the realms of Arabic as its origin while others suggest that the Swahili States are the custodians of the language and its various cultures. The Swahili Coast is the home for different ethnic groups with a large number of the Swahili speaking people. Thus Kiswahili and its culture dominated the Swahili coast with great political influence. With this background, Kiswahili is a Bantu language belonging to the Northeast Coast Bantu Sabaki sub-family (Middleton 1992, Hinnebusch 1976). Both Middleton and Hinnebusch demonstrate that Kiswahili is indeed a Bantu language and that it has borrowed heavily from Arabic. The borrowed words tend to mirror a set of specific cultural values, moral values, and literature which probably signifies the transfer of these ideas from Arabic sources. Arabic has been for some time and continues to be the language of learning for Islamic scholars in E. Africa. The Arabic aspects of the Kiswahili language remain important to elite Kiswahili speakers. The use of Arabic in the Swahili States can be compared to the situation in Europe where Latin was the preferred language of learning until the 19th Century. Arguments favoring Arabic over Kiswahili has often cited the fact that the Quran has never been translated to Kiswahili and that Kiswahili speakers who are Muslims recite the Quran in Arabic and not in translation. However this is somewhat similar to Latin which was embraced as a language of service to believers of Catholicism until Vatican II when other languages were included in religious services. The dominance and strength of Islam has managed to preserve the Holy Book in the Arabic language but it does not take away the fact that the Swahili people had a language of their own prior to Arab reign of the Coastal States.

The native Kiswahili speakers of the Coastal States easily adapted the Arabic and Islamic culture which allowed the language to be greatly influenced through borrowings. Swahili (or Kiswahili with ki = of) is derived from the Arabic word *sawahel* which means "coast").
Due to interstate and intrastate interactions, the language grew to become one of the most common and widespread of the lingua francas of the region (a lingua franca is a secondary language that is a combination of two or more languages).

Mazrui and Mazrui (1999) define Waswahili as those to whom Kiswahili is the mother-tongue and whose culture has been influenced significantly by Islam. Parallels can be drawn by comparing the understanding of who Jewish Moroccans are in relation to the Jewish faith and the relation that obtains between Christian Lebanese with their Christian faith.

Not all Kiswahili-speaking people are Waswahili. Native Waswahili speakers are outnumbered 30-1 by non-native speakers. Its rapid growth and spread is viewed as favorite to becoming the favored African language that might cause other languages, especially within the region, to die out. Currently there are more Kiswahili speakers than Swahili people. Because not every Kiswahili speaker is a Swahili person, those who consider themselves indigenous speakers must have a claim to the Coastal States ancestry. In addition to a wide spread on the African continent, Kiswahili speakers include those in the Diaspora, a phenomenon that has given rise to a variety of Kiswahili dialects which are distinct from the Coastal States standard Kiswahili. Speakers can be found in Somalia,

Kenya, and Tanzania, parts of Mozambique, South Africa, Zimbabwe, the Democratic Republic of the Congo, Rwanda, Burundi, Uganda, Malawi, Zambia, Ghana, the United States, Saudi Arabia, China, and other European countries.

Cross-Cultural influence on the Swahili Coast

Historically, Arabs are seen as those who "Arabized" the Swahili Coast, but there is also evidence of the Swahili Coast's influence on Arabs. Historians have tried to explain the by focusing on three possibilities. First there is the 1964 Zanzibar revolution. During this time, many refugees ran to the Arab world to look for a home and a job, taking with them the Swahili culture and language. The second possibility is the oil connection in the Arab countries that had an economic impact on rich Swahili people. There is a third component that we see. This is the role of the elite Swahili who sought intellectual connections with Arab countries and either intermarried or migrated to the Arab land. These elite are also credited with *Ulamaa* or learned ones, representing renowned poets and religious leaders.

Initially, the Kiswahili written form was influenced by the Arabic alphabet which is why for some time scholars insisted that the origins of Kiswahili was from Arabs and Persians (Mazrui & Mazrui, 1999). However, this has been refuted because of syntactic and other grammatical features found Kiswahili that are of Bantu origin and not found in Arabic. But, we cannot minimize the role of Arabic in growing the Swahili lexicon and the overall cultural influence to the Swahili speakers. The lack of scripts written in Kiswahili prior to the arrival of Arabs is not sufficient evidence that Kiswahili did not exist. Like many other Bantu languages, Kiswahili thrived in oral tradition and acquired written scripts much later in its evolvement as a prominent language. The earliest known document recounting the past situation on the East African coast was written in the 2nd century AD (in Greek language by anonymous author at Alexandria in Egypt and it is called the Periplus of Erythrean Sea. Scholars who suggest that Kiswahili is an old language point to the early expansion of

117

Swahili civilizations southwards of Somalia and Kenya to reach Zanzibar (from the Arabic word al-Zanj = *black)* and Kilwa.

Other influences on the Swahili coast and by implication the Kiswahili language are discussed in Mazrui and Mazrui (1999). They note that European colonization brought other linguistic and skill labor influences to the Swahili people. The Swahili people adapted to these cultures and skills to secure employment as the Europeans developed the industrial mode of production in their colonies. The need to adapt in order to increase one's opportunities and upward mobility has remained a tradition in Africa. For example, immigrants from Kenya, Uganda, Mozambique, Rwanda, and Burundi seek opportunities across the border in Tanzania to fill skill labor positions not utilized by Tanzanians. As a result, there is a cross adaptation process where immigrants learn Kiswahili to meet the Tanzanian requirements while Tanzanians learn English to meet the needs of the immigrants and investors. Consequently, there is a new linguistic phenomenon that is emerging that includes French and Portuguese (limited cases of Spanish mainly from tourism) in the development of new lexicon to meet the professional and social interactions.

To summarize, the nature of the Kiswahili language shows evidence of the influences noted above, the earliest ones associated with the interactions with various colonial powers: namely, Persians, Arabs, Portuguese, Germans and British. From the Persians came words like *chai* 'tea', *achari* 'pickle', *serikali* 'government', *diwani* 'councilor', *shehe* 'village councilor'. Such words bear testimony to the older connections with Persian merchants. The Arab and Persian influences on Swahili can be also found in the use of numbers. While the numbers *moja* 'one', *mbili* 'two', *tatu* 'three', *nne* 'four', *tano* 'five', *nane* 'eight', *kumi* "ten", are all of Bantu origin, the remaining numbers: *sita* 'six' *saba* 'seven' and *tisa* 'nine' are borrowed from Arabic. The Arabic word *tisa* actually replaced the Bantu word *kenda* for 'nine'. The Bantu word 'kenda'for can be found in many Bantu languages as the authors of this book can attest for its existence in both Kisukuma (Lake Victoria region) and Kichaga (Kilimanjaro region). Speakers of this languages have not adopted the Arabic term

118

tisa but rather inserts *kenda* into the mix when counting from one to ten. In addition, the enumeration by increment of tens beginning with number twenty is borrowed from Arabic: *ishirini* 'twenty', *thelathini* 'thirty', *arobaini* 'forty', *hamsini* 'fifty', *sitini* 'sixty', *sabini* 'seventy', *themanini* 'eighty', *tisini* 'ninety'.

Kiswahili has also absorbed words from the Portuguese who controlled the Swahili coastal towns from c. 1500-1700AD. The borrowings included: *leso* 'handkerchief', *meza* 'table' *gereza* 'prison', *pesa* (peso), 'money', etc. The Swahili peoples' love of bull-fighting, still popular on the Pemba Island, is a cultural borrowing from the Portuguese of that period. From German, Kiswahili borrowed words like *shule* 'school' and *hela* 'a German coin'. English is second to Arabic in loan words in Kiswahili. A few examples here include: *baiskeli* 'bicycle', *basi* 'bus', *penseli* 'pencil', *mashine* 'machine', *gauni* 'gown', *koti* 'coat' and many newer words from technology *kompyuta* 'computer' *twita* 'tweeter' etc....

The Spread of Kiswahili

There was an extensive spread of Kiswahili before way before colonization. For centuries, Kiswahili was the language of interaction between the people of the East African coast and its neighbors. These interactions were mainly associated with maritime trading as well as trading with the hinterland. As such, the interactions were instrumental in the early spread of the language to as far as the islands of the Comoros and Madagascar and to the south as far as the Mozambique and the Cape of South Africa. Trading with Arabs and other merchants from the Far East allowed the language to spread to Oman and the United Arab Emirates and to some parts in South East Asia. Also, trade and migration from the Swahili coast during the nineteenth-century helped spread the language to the interior of particularly Tanzania and beyond, reaching Uganda, Rwanda, Burundi, the (Congo Democratic Republic of the Congo and The Congo Republic) , and the Central African Republic. The coming of the missionaries facilitated the entry of Kiswahili into mainstream formal education in East Africa. Roy-Campbell (2001) shows that

Christian missionaries learned Swahili as the language of communication in order to spread the Gospel in Eastern Africa and credits the preparation of the first Swahili-English dictionary to a missionary.

The adoption of Kiswahili was not free of controversy. It spurred debate of merits of its uses vis-à-vis other possibilities. The two areas of concern are the use of Kiswahili versus other vernacular languages and Kiswahili versus English. Mazrui and Mazrui take us through the discussions in the following areas.

Vernacular and Proselytism

The debate was centered on the usefulness in the spread of the gospel. Vernacular languages such as Luganda (Uganda) or Luo (Kenya and some parts of Tanzania) were considered too drenched with associations and connotations drawn from native religious practice that were much further removed from Christianity than Islam. Making use of them risked conceptual distortion greater than what Islam presented with its association with Kiswahili. Kiswahili was also considered a transitional tool that could introduce European Christian vocabulary into the vernacular while it bridged the conceptual gap between European theological language and the indigenous spiritual universe in Africa. Thus, the popularity of Kiswahili as a language of choice for conversion led to Christianity being identified partly with knowledge of Kiswahili, both as written and as spoken language. The Livingstonian principle meant that Christianity could only be truly accepted in an African community by using conceptual tools of the indigenous culture and language. Therefore, Kiswahili as a lingua franca was unfit for reaching the "innermost thoughts of those undergoing conversion."

Missionaries versus Policy- Makers

The fact that missionaries used Kiswahili to spread the gospel specifically to teach people how to read the Bible, created controversy between church and state in the fundamental issues of educational

120

policy. Questions rose regarding the idea of training the mind (modernization) vs. converting soul (spiritualization). This debate pitted colonial policy-makers against missionaries. At the beginning, education was left to missionaries. Because of that, colonial administrators worried that mission schools were too narrowly focused on the spiritual at the expense of the intellectual and the cultural. The major concern of the policy makers was that the adoption of Kiswahili for the spread of Christianity creating unnecessary conflicts between religious goals and education goals.

The Colonial Period

During the colonial time, the role of Kiswahili was primarily a communication tool between the colonial administration and the local people. The colonial administrators pioneered the effort of standardizing Kiswahili for both educational and administrative purposes. Because Zanzibar was the epicenter of culture and commerce; the colonial administrators selected the Zanzibar dialect of Swahili (Kiunguja) as the standard. This dialect was then used as the formal way of communication in schools, in the media (newspapers and radio), in books and other publications.

Interestingly, the Germans had issues with both English and Swahili. To start with, they were worried about the Islamic ties with Swahili. A great controversy arose over how to handle the use of Swahili to run the government as an official language considering that the relationship between Islam and the uses of Kiswahili was very strong with many Arabic loanwords having infiltrated the language. And so, the Germans became hostile towards Kiswahili because they "took the official support for Kiswahili to be blatantly pro-Islamic." In addition, the Maji Maji rebellion which historians suggest happened because the indigenous people of Tanganyika wanted to drive out their German colonizers who charged too much tax, demanded intolerable child-labor, and relocated people from their villages to grow cotton as a cash crop. Turning to magic, Kinjikitile Ngwala, a spirit-medium leader promised to provide medicine able to turn German bullets to water ("*maji*" the translation

121

of the word *water* into Kiswahili). The belief and confidence that the medicine would work are what many historians propose empowered the people of Tanganyika to rebel. The Germans changed their minds after the Maji Maji uprising and the Meinhof's de-Islamization of Kiswahili. The problem with English in Deutschtum was that it posed a threat to the establishment of German cultural control over its colonies. English was used not only by missionaries but also by other foreigners to the community such as Indians. The Solution was to discourage English in East Africa and to establish German and Kiswahili.

Needless to say, Christian missionaries did not see a threat from Kiswahili associations with Islam in the early days of colonization and evangelism. It was widely believed that Islam and Christianity shared a common Middle-Eastern ancestry (monotheistic), and embraced many spiritual concepts and values. Kiswahili already contained vocabulary necessary to explain the spiritual concepts of Christianity. Also, the status of Swahili as a lingua franca with relevant religious concepts made it a good choice for conversion of indigenous Africans to Christianity.

Dr. J.L. Krapf

Kiswahili received a boost from the support of Dr J.L. Krapf who encouraged its use in the spread of Christianity in Eastern Africa. He saw Kiswahili as a perfect means for conversion (EXCEPT for Arabic script, which would leave the door open to proselytism from the Mohammedan among the local tribes). This was a threat because with that, the Waswahili could be Christianized and civilized. The Solution to this threat involved initiating the use of the Roman script in writing Kiswahili.

After independence, all three Eastern African countries (Tanzania, Kenya and Uganda) took different routes to ultimately make Kiswahili as an official language or one of the official languages in conjunction with English (to be discussed further in later chapters). The deliberate efforts by independent Tanganyika (modern Tanzania mainland) to promote the language, spearheaded by the late and first President of Tanganyika: later Tanzania, Julius K. Nyerere. Stites & Semali (1991) note that Tanzania's special relations with countries of southern Africa was the main force that propelled the spread of Kiswahili to the South, specifically to Zambia, Malawi, South Africa, Mozambique, Angola and Zimbabwe. This allowed Kiswahili to rise as the national and official language in Tanzania. Proficiency in Swahili is a requirement in all of government businesses. Although in Kenya, the official language is English the national language is Kiswahili. By comparison in Uganda, the national language is English with Swahili assuming a second position of importance, although widely use in the military.

The Faces of Kiswahili

The significance of Kiswahili in the past three decades has been both economic and political. Before independence, it was used as means of communication across ethnic boundaries. It was also a major tool as the three countries agitated for independence (to be discussed further in later chapters). Mazrui and Mazrui (1999) explain that the economic function includes horizontal national integration, which is defined as contacts across ethnic groups at the grassroots level. The political function of Kiswahili remains to be the promotion of vertical

123

integration, which implies creating links between the elites and the masses. It is here the history of Kiswahili, underscores Africa's dependency and decolonization. With the push for the use of Kiswahili in government settings, came a concern in the 1960's. For some countries, this meant those in political power needed to be proficient in both Kiswahili and English.

There is now a growing involvement in public affairs and policy. Mass involvement of the people varies from country to country depending on political systems and their emphasis on participation ideology. However, regardless of the varying ideologies, most political systems strive toward expanding popular participation (Mazrui and Mazrui 1998).

The spread of Kiswahili has taken place against a background of interaction between church and state and between economics and politics. Three main domains are of interest in this respect 1) Affairs of the State 2) Business of earning a living and 3) Spiritual considerations. These three domains caused Kiswahili to undergo changes in the political realm. The direction of change can be categorized into three social processes which indicate that the wider the arena of social interaction the closer the process is to opening up potentialities to a person. The first process describes an individual who feels comfortable only in his or her own clan while being held back from his or her fullest potential. The second process defines an individual whose allegiance is incapable of transcending ethnic affiliates and therefore has not experienced full potentiality. The third process describes an individual whose horizons are limited to the borders of their country leading him or her to not be sensitized to the international implications of social existence. These three processes are best understood through the concepts of detribalization, urbanization, and secularization.

Detribalization

Mazrui and Mazrui (1999) note that detribalization was among the changes embodied by the Swahili language. It was not a process by which people stopped thinking of themselves as a certain group (Example: Luo, Baganda, etc.) but rather a process that takes the form of changes in custom, ritual and rules, and a shift towards a more cosmopolitan lifestyle. In behavior, this meant people were no longer guided by the heritage of values and rules of their rural, ethnic community. In loyalty, however, they may identify with their native group more "ferociously" than ever after they leave: they become proud of their roots. Therefore, Kiswahili affected class formation. It played a critical role in diffusion of Christianity and Islam. This happened as those converting to Christianity and those to Islam used it in their worship, especially in inner cities where local native languages could not read everyone. Furthermore, Kiswahili led to politicizing of racial consciousness among blacks in eastern Africa. For one, if you didn't speak Kiswahili well, your native language became more apparent, leading you to be somewhat disconnected to the rest of the fluent and polished Swahili speaking group.

There is no doubt that Kiswahili creates new forms of national consciousness among the inhabitants of each of the East African countries. For example, the Kiswahili spoken in Tanzania differs from that of Kenya because of Tanzania's emphasis on standard Kiswahili[3]. On the other hand, Kenya and Uganda Kiswahili is considered more colloquial than standard because it tends to follow social and contextual discourse. The Kiswahili speakers from all three countries understand each other despite the minor differences in their usage. These differences are considered national and could be with the social interplay of the language within different political landscapes in East

---

[3] Tanzania pushed for the use of Kiswahili as a vehicle for nation building in the early 1960's and used it in other formal settings such as schools much earlier than Kenya did. Kiswahili in Kenya is a lingua franca but competes with not only English but also local "vernacular" languages such as Kikuyu in official settings including political forums and schools. See also Edgar C. Polome, "Tanzania: A Socio-Linguistic Perspective," in Edgar C. Polome and C. P. Hill, eds., *Language in Tanzania* (Oxford: Oxford University Press, 1980). Also David Laitin discusses language policy and nation building in Africa, and the existence of lingua franca like Kiswahili in East Africa (Cambridge: Cambridge University Press, 1992)

Africa; making it a cause of national consciousness once unnoticed. These differences could be considered a source of class formation where Swahili transforms peasants to proletarians, and independent rural cultivators to members of the urban workforce. Comparatively Mazrui (1999) notes, the diffusion of Christianity and Islam caused a formation of two religious cultures by building a comprehensive Muslim culture which had its own cuisine, ethics and aesthetics. Furthermore, the coming of the Christian missionaries in the 19th century accounts for the people's gradual adaptation of the missionary influences on their language and culture.

Urbanization

Urbanization accounts for the flux of people from rural areas to cities, a major cause for detribalization. While eroding rural ethnic custom and ritual, it expanded the scale of social interaction. It however, did not necessarily erode loyalty and identity. This process also led to the formation of a Lingua franca. As people had to co-habitat in a landscape where each spoke a different tongue, the need for a unifying language became natural. It was a necessity to their survival and existence. They had to make it work and indeed, this didn't occur as a formula they had to understand and apply, it was a coincidence of the human genius which allows people to form specific discourses according to the specific needs of the time, place and circumstance. Urbanization therefore also led to new politics of African nationalism after World War II. As Mazrui notes that some soldiers enlisted from Uganda served in Kenya and vice versa during World War II.

Ethnic intermingling in the barracks; new military routines and drills as well as soldiers far removed from their homeland heightened that sense of shared African identity. The concept of kinship was also magnified. Kinship is a literal consanguinity; a direct relationships of descent and lineage. It is associated with a dominant social myth, which takes it to imply a presumed descent from common ancestry. It also corresponds to a metaphor as a symbolism of the family responsible for enhancing cohesion without claiming literal

126

consanguinity or presuming it as a myth. Other association with this idea include: "Mother-country"; "Fatherland" and "Founding Fathers" as common ideas shared by Swahili speakers co-habituating and living in big cities from varied parts of East Africa.

Secularization

Secularization is defined as the activity of changing something (art, education, society, or morality) so it is no longer under the control or influence of religion. Of interest here are past and modern secularization. *Past secularization* of Kiswahili has been the declining significance of religion, both as an explanation of natural phenomena and as a basis of social behavior. Although religions like Christianity and Islam brought about change by broadening people's perspectives and introducing them to a larger world, but that change can also stymie progress, just as the ethnic religions can. It is, however, the case that the vast majority of Waswahili are Muslim.

The secularization of Kiswahili has been underway in the 20th century for a variety of reasons. Major promoters of the language have wanted it for social (secular) reasons, while gradual utilization of Kiswahili for spreading Christianity is underscored by religious experts. On the other hand, many believe western ideas, concepts and skills has been a major factor as the increase in usage of Kiswahili to communicate with Europeans helped to secularize it as well. One should not undermine the social change as also a factor. Social change on one side and linguistic change on the other constantly reinforced each other. As Kiswahili spread beyond the boundaries of the people who produced it, it has been called upon to serve the needs of other religious systems and other worldviews. Now, the contributions from Arabic to the Swahili culture are more likely to be political than religious. Meanwhile, European languages contribute more and more, leading to a new and complicated aspect of the language.

Modern secularization is a higher stage of the process of secularization, especially since the nineteenth century, is the stage of scientific method and of relatively advanced technological culture. How has this affected Kiswahili and its role in East African societies?

First, one needs to remember that Kiswahili is not a language globally used in advanced science. The main languages of science in Africa have been: English (Kenya, Tanzania and Uganda); German (Tanganyika and Ruanda-Burundi); and French (Old Belgian Congo, Rwanda, Burundi and Zaire). Kiswahili was used as an educational language, but only until the end of primary school. Thus, Kiswahili was not given a chance to evolve into a language of discourse and scientific analysis. Even though there have been efforts to import scientific words to Swahili in order to meet the challenges of doing science. There is no reason for Swahili not to develop to meet these challenges, considering languages like Japanese that have been able to develop both technologically and scientifically.

Mohamed H. Abdulaziz (1996) identified two features making English better suited for scientific vocabulary than Kiswahili. One is the process of lexical compounding which is achieved less easily in Kiswahili than in English. English is said to be a highly nominalizing language while Kiswahili tends towards a greater use of verbal constructions. In other words, a Swahili verb can be manipulated by adding different language aspects to it to bring a different meaning but English uses separate individual words to make sentences with different linguistic aspects. For example, the English sentence, "I love you" translates into a one Swahili word: *"ninakupenda"* by simply attaching the subject prefix, a tense marker, an object marker and the verb stem all together. This gives English an edge over Kiswahili because much of the scientific and technological vocabulary belongs to the nominal category. Nevertheless, Kiswahili has a remarkable capacity to adopt linguistic items from languages far different from itself, like German or Semitic. It is asserted that Kiswahili is flexible and robust enough to respond to the challenges of the scientific age. But what about "technicalizing" and "scientificating" the Waswahili? This also is possible as history shows room in the broad area of the technology of production. The goods produced elsewhere but consumed by Waswahili are assimilated into the language and people's lifestyle. The various activities ranging from nutrition to maternal and child healthcare: such as the use of reproduction

128

technology are aspects which have needed the Kiswahili to adopt. Different aspects of technology such as the cell phones, computer usage, and issues concerning war and peace, satellite, the mining and power industry, naturally compel the language to adopt terminologies from other languages. The Swahili speakers have already adopted for example, the different telephone terminologies such as, "phone card": literally translated as *simukadi* in Swahili, show how communication technology has made its way into Kiswahili and hence manifesting itself in people's daily conversations. Kiswahili has now become connected to different levels of businesses. Mining which facilitated a large labor force of Swahili speakers to mingle with other technologically advanced people who speak different languages needed a lingua franca to thrive. In the 1990's mining was especially popular and dominant in the Democratic Republic of the Congo and Shaba. Other areas we alluded to earlier include technology of reproduction: physical reproduction- nutritional values of foods, preventative care against dehydration, diarrhea, STD's and (AIDS). Sexual Reproduction brought such concepts and terminologies as planned parenting and birth control, which were strongly seen in clinics in Kenya and Tanzania but now these are prominent in Uganda as well. With military, language of the armed forces in Kenya, Tanzania, and Uganda updated military technology to require mechanical and technological skills: these were thought to be good for developing traits within each of the three countries. Today, the great interplay of military forces dealing with different issues of peace and governance warrant the use of Swahili. The recent political uproars in Kenya had President Jakaya Kikwete of Tanzania intervene and call the Kenyan elected officials to compromise and put away their differences, and Kiswahili played a major role.

CHAPTER 6

Functions of Kiswahili

Introduction

So far we have been trying to put across the idea that the Swahili coast of East Africa is a very important part of the region especially today within the new world order or disorder due to its rich history which, for the most part, is not very well known or for a good part misunderstood. Its uniqueness lies in the Swahili language and its function. It is the perceived functions of the language that provides the picture of what was before, what is current, and what will be in the new world order that is supposedly democratic and globally oriented.

We indicated earlier that the eastern coast of Africa changed profoundly around the close of the first millennium AD. Bantu-speaking people from the interior migrated and settled along the coast from Kenya to South Africa. Merchants and traders from the Muslim world and India realized the strategic importance of the east coast of Africa for commercial traffic and began to settle there. The cumulative effects on the language are clearly marked by its ability to borrow from the languages of the new inhabitants to enrich its lexicon. Recall from our earlier discussion that from 900 AD onwards, the east coast of Africa saw an influx of Shiraz Arabs from the Persian Gulf and even small settlements of Indians. By the 1300's, the major east African ports from Mombasa in the north to Sofala in the south became a trading magnet attracting traders from all corners of the world. Trading dhows sailed down this coast from the Arabian Peninsula and the Persian Gulf following annual northeast monsoon. Their main aim was to trade pottery, cloth, and iron tools for African slaves, ivory, gold, timber, shells, dyes, and perfumes. These items were named using the indigenous languages of the coastal people or new words that were coined to meet the description of the items to facilitate trade. Trade enhanced the development of a number of Swahili towns along the coast where the functions of Swahili were clearly pronounced during that period, a time when it was not in competition with any other language but rather embraced new lexical items to enrich its own. Needless to say, these opportunities allowed for the expansion of Swahili civilizations from Somalia and Kenya in the north to Zanzibar and Kilwa in the south. The expansion demonstrates the coastal resilience and the history also shows that the Swahili civilization carved out the territory for which we now claim to have exploited and continue to accord Swahili with important and critical functions. The areas served by Kiswahili are not just hinterlands of Tanzania, Kenya, Ugamda, Rwanda, Burundi, and the Democratic Republic of the Congo, parts of Malawi and Zambia, but includes several archipelagos and islands in the Indian Ocean, namely the Comoros and Lamu archipelagos, and the islands of Mombasa, Pemba, Zanzibar, Mafia, and Kerimba. Newer areas are closely associated with the politics of the region and these include Mozambique, Zimbabwe, Angola, and South Africa. These are countries that had to fight the colonial powers for their independence and sought refuge in the Swahili speaking states for over a decade. Consequently, there is a generation that was born in the Swahili states and assumed Swahili as their first language. Although the functions of Swahili are different in these areas, Swahili serves as a language of choice in specific environments.

The place of Kiswahili is viewed in relation to its central reaches in Kenya and Tanzania and connected to the people of the flourishing kingdoms of the Great Lakes and the Swahili coastal towns (Mombasa, Lamu, Malindi, Zanzibar, Kilwa (the island archipelagos, Mafia, Madagascar, Comoros, and the Seychelles). The functions of Kiswahili in these areas is what defines the Swahili culture as a vigorous multi-textured one, a development that has resulted from a long and dynamic process of interaction between indigenous coastal people occupying a strategic place, the African cultures of the interior and non-African societies across the world's oceans.

Before we look at the functions of Kiswahili in the various states, we need to define critical terminologies that will appear in this chapter. First, a *communal language* is defined as an indigenous language to only a section of a particular population in a country or countries and one that has not been adopted as on official language. An *official language* is one that has been designated to serve as a medium of communication in conducting the affairs of one or more departments of government. A *national language* is one that is confined primarily to one country and may or may not be regarded as the official language. A re*gional language*: is identified as one that is widely spoken by both natives and non-natives of a particular geographically contiguous region and has been adopted as national language by at least two of the countries of that region. A *world language* is one which has spread beyond its continent of birth, is widely understood in at least two continents, and is regarded an official language of several states in those countries.

These terminologies will be instrumental in understanding the place of Kiswahili at the national, regional, and global levels. We will attempt in the following sections to outline the functions in the key countries that have shown much progress in advancing the functions of Kiswahili.

The Place of Kiswahili in Tanzania

Located in the East coast of Africa, Tanzania has a population of 34.4 million people (URT Population and Housing Census, 2002). Socio-linguistically, this country has 127 living languages (Ethnologue 2012). Swahili is one of these languages and is spoken in diverse degrees of proficiency by over 90% of the population. Since Swahili serves the wider communicative needs of Tanzanians in daily socio-political and economic life, it is used as an official and national language, while other home languages provide for intra-ethnic communication needs

133

Map 17: *Major Languages of Tanzania*

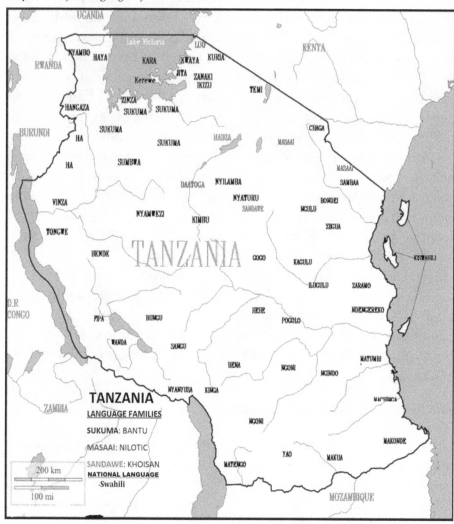

Ethnographically, people in the Islamic coast as well as some born in the urban areas, speak Swahili as their first language; these constitute only a small proportion (i.e., 10%) of Swahili speakers in Tanzania. The remaining speakers use one or two of the home languages and Swahili as a second language. Apart from Swahili and home languages, Tanzania recognizes English as an official second language, despite the fact that it is spoken by only 15% of the population (Rubagumya, 1990). English is used in school and also in information technologies, international relations, tourism, business, trade, and mass media. These services are concentrated in the urban areas.

The Historical Background of Languages in Tanzania.

Ever since colonization, Tanzanians have spoken and used their local languages to communicate within local areas (Mazrui 1990). However, Swahili was not an indigenous language in Tanzania, it finds origin from the Sabaki family of Mombasa Kenya. Swahili came to Tanzania as the Waswahili interacted with people from other parts of Africa for trade, business and education. Likewise languages of the colonizers (i.e., Arabic, French, Portuguese, German and English) contributed to the growth of Kiswahili with many borrowed words which became part of the language (Roy-Campbell 2001). In spite of such borrowings, one must remember that Swahili is a Bantu language with 80 percent of its syntax from Bantu languages though borrows some of its words from foreign languages (Hinnebusch & Mirza 1997). It is used in Eastern and Central Africa to communicate trans-tribally and, hence, it unites all Tanzanians.

Swahili helped facilitate the independence in 1961 and to make education available for the masses (Semali 1993). In the early 1970's, Tanzanians were proud of Swahili and even looked down on people who spoke English because it was regarded as aligning with the colonizers; speaking English was called "kasumba ya ukoloni," a colonized mindset (Roy-Cambell 2001). The emphasis on Swahili during the independence era caused English proficiency for most Tanzanians to suffer (Trappes-Lomax 1985). This pattern of inadequate English proficiency for many Tanzanians has continued to this day. Indeed, starting in the early 1970s, many Tanzanians favored knowing Swahili more than their local languages (Roy-Campbell 2001); they tend to see national identity as more important than their ethnic group identity (Wangwe 2005). This emphasis on Swahili led to it being the only language recognized as an African

135

language for African people while other languages in the continent failed (Semali 1993).

English and Kiswahili: The Germans who colonized Tanzania in the 1880s used Swahili as the language of communication to govern their colony, and used it as the medium of instruction in the first five years of primary education (Roy-Campbell 2001). After the World War in 1919, the British took over Tanzania from the Germans. When the British arrived in Tanzania in 1925, they created an official, standard Swahili and maintained Swahili as a medium of instruction (Rubagumya 1990; Blommaert 2004).

Under the British rule, Kiswahili was emphasized in the K-4 primary grades but English was the medium of instruction. After independence, Kiswahili was integrated into all schools either as a primary medium for learning or as a compulsory subject. In 1967, through the Education for Self-Reliance policy, Kiswahili was made the medium of instruction throughout the primary level of all government-sponsored schools. This policy was designed to provide education that fit the local conditions of Tanzanians.

Kiswahili was also introduced into teacher training colleges to ensure that teachers were fully prepared to teach in the language. In the 1970's, there was a movement in Tanzania to incorporate Kiswahili in post-primary education, and a concerted effort to provide teaching and learning materials in the language. However, by 1980 it was not evidence that the government had plans to shift mediums. In 1984, the Tanzanian government declared the use of both Kiswahili and English in post-primary education. This was heavily weighted by president Nyerere's own declaration to support the government's decision to have two languages in the school saying, "English is the Swahili of the world and for that reason must be taught and given the weight it deserves in our country."

The British' support of Swahili in schools, primarily as a subject, necessitated the emphasis on English as a medium of instruction in the last three years of primary school and six years of secondary (4 for ordinary high level and 2 for advanced) education (Roy-Campbell, 2001). As such, English took a new communicative role as an official language in the legislature, the judiciary, and administration outside the education system.

After independence in 1961, Swahili was the sole medium of instruction in Tanzanian primary schools and for adult education (Roy-Campbell 2001). According to Semali (1993), Swahili was one of the main vehicles in helping Tanzania reach near an 80% literacy rate soon after its independence; no other country in Sub Saharan Afroca was able to reach such a high literacy level in such a short period of time. Consequently, in 1962, the Tanganyika African National Union (TANU) party and government leaders made efforts to advance Swahili in the postcolonial period for the sake of freedom, patriotism, and cultural identity (Roy-Campbell, 2001). Realizing that Swahili was a fundamental instrument in securing Tanganyika's independence, these efforts were made because Swahili became a symbol for liberation and national unity (Semali 1993). Furthermore, since the 1980s, many scholars have attempted to promote the social status of African languages (Bamgbose 1986; Adam 1980; Semali 1996). Starting with the post-independence period, for example, the emphasis was on developing and promoting Swahili in order to cater to the wider communicative needs of the Tanzanian people. This effort concluded with the formation of Swahili Council of Tanzania, which was responsible for putting into practice the Swahili policy in the country (Roy-Campbell, 2001).

However, the Tanzanian people still view and recognize English as a "Highway to success" and "a gateway to social rewards," and most importantly, as an "Empowerment language" (Neke 2003, p.140). Such opinions towards English are not unfounded. In professional jobs for example, Neke indicates that the interviews for such jobs are usually (if not always) conducted in English, though Swahili is used in many work places in Tanzania. As a result, someone proficient in both English and Swahili language has an added advantage and stands a better chance of successfully moving upward socially than someone with Swahili only. In light of this, Tanzania still has great inequality in its social domains even though the country has been independent for over forty years.

Current status of Kiswahili in Tanzania

To show where Kiswahili is now in Tanzania, we highlight important issues worth considering. First, Kiswahili is the language still well understood and spoken by the majority of Tanzanians. This means most, if not all Tanzanians, can now communicate with each other through this medium. This indeed, is a powerful stance for Kiswahili. Second, students who learn in Kiswahili, in primary and secondary schools tend to perform better academically than when the use of English is employed (Birgit-Utne 2005). This shows the reality about Kiswahili as a language capable to propel its citizens to become educated in a basic level. This however is not a strong component to making it a language of power in Tanzania; it simply makes it a useful language as it has been. Third, though many Tanzanians understand and use Kiswahili not only in school, many do not support its continual use in school because they deem it detrimental for their economic success. Though the realty for many Tanzanians is that they end up in communities they grew and hence do the type of jobs not requiring English proficiency as I noted earlier, many still believe they have a shot in bettering their lives if indeed English becomes part of their skills.

Fourth, Kiswahili as a tool to unite Tanzanians from ethnically diverse background has been and continues to be highly acceptable. Provided Tanzania is no longer under colonial rule- at least physically, many Tanzanians don't struggle so much with their ethnic differences. They don't see this as an area of concern and therefore, Kiswahili remains in their mind as a national language but is not able to move them from a national level to international status economically. The question remains in their mind, why emphasize Kiswahili when English takes an upper hand in several major areas of communication, for example interaction with foreigners, some aspects of court proceedings, instruction in higher education, the internet and the drive by elite (elite defined as knowledgeable and economically wealthy) families to put their children in English medium schools.

The fact that many Tanzanians want to use English as the medium of instruction in school- from primary to secondary rather than using Kiswahili - is indicative of language ideology unaffected by the reality of the use of English within the country. In other words, many Tanzanians are not so much following logic in determining which language will help them survive and perhaps excel within their current contexts, they are thinking of what can be possible- the hope, the dream and the opportunity awaiting them but hindered by their lack of proficiency in English. Also, the perspective of language scholars encouraging the use of Kiswahili within the Tanzanian schools has not yet affected the negative ideology associated with Kiswahili in regards to employment.

Furthermore, leaders in Tanzania have not reached a consensus to the switch from using English in secondary schools to the use of Kiswahili. For example, a report in Tanzania's Guardian newspaper (2012) cited a former Member of Parliament calling for Tanzanian secondary schools to adopt Kiswahili as the language of instruction. The member made his declaration after a large number of Form IV (equivalent of high school senior) failed their 2012 national examinations. He said it was time for Tanzania to reassess the existing policy of English-language instruction. This is a testament of the ideological struggle regarding Kiswahili in Tanzania and how measuring its status is not a small matter.

In her article, Anna Rabin (2011) quoted another member of parliament who said, "We should not raise our kids to learn half English half Kiswahili." This remark was given during a debate on the Tanzanian budget allocation. I bring this to our attention here to show that Kiswahili has meant different things at different times for Tanzanians. Its status now is not only defined by the economic status of many Tanzanians, but rather the perspectives they hold based on varied factors. If we look at Kiswahili as a social language transcending ethnic barriers, this language has succeeded and stands on the highest possible rank in Tanzania. If we look at it as a language of commerce within the country, this language commands respect as many within the country and some without use it proficiently. If we look at it as the language of economic success, we find a divide; some Tanzanians are economically successful by entirely relying on Kiswahili and some indigenous language.

On the other hand, many believe their knowledge of Kiswahili is the reason they have not and will not go further in their social status. Though the Tanzanian government is often praised for its victorious support of a single indigenous language as the official national language, the battle for supremacy between English and Kiswahili continues to be a feature of Tanzanian political affairs and society. This struggle complicates the status of this language within the country. If on the other hand we look at Kiswahili as the medium of instruction and how those learning through it succeed or fail in academia, studies show it is doing well but now facing a new challenge. Having been undermined with the popularity and demand for English over the years, students' Kiswahili proficiency is not as high as it should, provided they use it in and outside of school. In fact, efforts to discourage its use in school have contributed greatly to students putting less effort in mastering it as a language in academia. They however have a high command of it non-academically. For example, the Uwezo Report (2011) primary school results show the

140

vast majority are not able to read a story in both English and Swahili. With this in mind, Tanzania has now at its table once again as the heated debate of what Kiswahili means for education but more importantly for society in general.

Though many scholars have shown the complexity of language of instruction, many focus on this issue rather on one direction. By this I mean, they write about this ongoing situation in Tanzania whereby Swahili is used in primary education while English use happens at the secondary and tertiary in English as both divisive and detrimental. Since only a small amount of students continue with post-primary education, very few students are therefore able to gain mastery of English. Researchers explore and continue to show the ability to speak English continue to be associated with class, consequently those unable to gain a post-primary education being further sentenced to lifetimes of unskilled labor.

What we find troubling and worth noting here is the tendency to have Tanzanians choose to use either Kiswahili or English in school based on whatever study or report done. I believe it is time we start thinking beyond the either or spectrum. Being versed in language instruction and indeed the teaching of a foreign language, we know one can learn both without sacrificing the other. If Tanzanians need to master English, they can do so while learning Kiswahili or in Kiswahili. If Tanzanian students are not excelling in English, is Swahili to blame or is it time someone looked at the way English is currently taught in Tanzania rather than thinking the abolishment of Kiswahili will automatically result in a new English proficiency in those students. The status of Kiswahili continues to be complicated because of this confusion between language proficiency and academic performance. Furthermore, we are yet to see researches done on Tanzanians who are making it big economically with little to no use of English whatsoever. As Tanzanians, we firmly believe in the access gained by knowing English but we are also convinced that Kiswahili is rising high internationally and soon, others will know Kiswahili more than Tanzanians themselves, which later on, will put many Tanzanians currently undermining this language in a state of being once again left behind when Kiswahili is gaining a commanding voice internationally.

Kiswahili in Uganda

In Uganda, the major beneficiaries of the spread of Kiswahili were the armed forces of both colonial and post-colonial East Africa. The Uganda experience is interesting because of the relationship between who ruled the country and who dominated the armed force. Both Milton Obote and Idi Amin come from the northern part of Uganda and were linked to the Nilotes. Consequently, the armed forces recruited mostly from the Nilotes who were very conscious of their separateness from the Bantu groups that were predominantly settled in the southern parts of Uganda. The Nilotes were especially alienated from the Baganda (Mazrui & Mazrui 1999). This relationship created ethnic rivalry among the groups (Acholi, Langi, Kakwa, Lugbara, Baganda, and Nilotes). It is also interesting to note that the rivalry necessitated the use of a common language for communication between them. Kiswahili became the language of choice across ethnic boundaries and even when Idi Amin came to power and eliminated many of the Acholi and Langi members of the armed force.

There is need to discuss briefly why Kiswahili experienced such a strong resistance in Uganda. One, the citizenry feared a process of "Swahilization" that they associated with a broader political "Kenyanization". The second reason was the perception of 'power' in Kenya which was closed linked to the white settlers. This fear of colonization necessitated a memorandum to the Colonial Secretary in London and the creation of Joint Committee on Closer Union in East Africa. The Buganda won inquisition allowing Luganda to be used in lieu of Kiswahili in administration and education. Having lost Kiswahili, both the missionaries and the administrators agreed to use English in post primary education where the vernacular languages were used. A colonial report from 1953 argued, "It [Kiswahili] comes in-between the study of the two languages [vernacular and English] as an element confusing the educational picture."

Administrators decreased their desire to have Kiswahili as a lingua franca more when there was a growing national consciousness and anti-colonialism movement in East Africa which was benefited by Kiswahili as the trans-ethnic language. Policy-makers began to move away from "over-promoting Swahili" because of the growing political consciousness of the people that was labeled as a "dangerous, post-war epidemic.

Outside the Ugandan army, Kiswahili gained political importance, especially during Idi Amin's reign despite the hostility and political decline associated with his brutal regime. This is because the Baganda saw wisdom in changing their resistance to Kiswahili and became the propagators of Kiswahili and its integrative functions in the army. The resistance was mainly from the perception that Kiswahili was an Arabic language and therefore foreign. Additionally, it's being adopted as an army language ge of authority and force. The society's response to the change of heart indicated a change in their perception of the social function of Kiswahili. The increasing functional role of Kiswahili in Kenya and Tanzania, its neighboring states, also encouraged and assured the Ugandans that it should not be just a military language.

To acknowledge the change, a Ugandan Scholar suggested that after the war, it was reasonable to assert that stopping Kiswahili was a means to reduce agreement within the African continent.
Two points worth highlighting here:

1. As Uganda pushed for independence, both Kiswahili and the vernacular languages were pushed out of the schools.
2. Since the National Resistance Movement lead by Yoweri Museveni, Kiswahili had once again another chance to be reintroduced into the schools.

As a result, a Ugandan mission was sent to Tanzania to study how they could reintroduce Kiswahili back into the schools. The Uganda Kiswahili Association began to train teachers who were to teach Kiswahili to adults. Kiswahili was once again made the medium of instruction for the first three years of primary education since 1952.

Consequently, Kiswahili has spread fairly widely in Uganda under the force of urbanization and migrant labor. A significant portion of the Uganda workforce comes from Kenya. For some time trade unionism was partially led and controlled by Kenyan immigrants, predominantly men. As such, the political economy of Kiswahili in Uganda was for a considerable length of time a language of men rather than of women. In 1972: 52% of Ugandan men were able to hold a conversation in Kiswahili compared to 18% women.

Working Class men in Uganda

Reasons why it become a language of the men:

- Rural-to-urban migration
- Employment in the urban workforce
- Recruitment into the armed forces

Kiswahili in Kenya

The City of Nairobi

The place of Kiswahili in Kenya is in relation to urbanization where its functions are highly pronounced in cities like Nairobi and Mombasa. This can be explained as a consequence of mobility with cities attracting ethnically diverse people who would require a common language to be able to conduct everyday business.

Like in the case of Tanzania (then Tanganyika) Kiswahili evolved into the primary language of politics in Kenya especially in the process through which the masses became increasingly involved in national agitation for African rights. The Kenya *mau mau* was an insurrection against the British, primarily led by the Kikuyu. It began in 1952 and ended in 1960. British rulers insulated the Kikuyu from the mainstream of the political process in order to depoliticize them. This insulation of the Kikuyus aided in their Swahilization. With leadership in both movements were in the hands of the same people, because of this, there was a rise in Class-Consciousness and Race-Consciousness. This manifested itself in different social and political arenas.

In regards to language policy in Kenya, the first decade of Kenya's independence witnessed very little change from the old British pattern. In 1957, the Ministry of Education created the Nairobi Special Centre whose objective was to promote English as the medium of instruction. The reason for this change was the undeniable students' academic failure sweeping the nation. The Nairobi Special Centre was created to look at ways to address the problem of high failure rates in both primary and secondary schools which was supposedly caused by poor command of English.

Right after Kenya gained its independence, English became the language taught in schools and Kiswahili never regained its status as an instructional language. Immediately after independence, the colonial linguistic legacy was challenged, but little change occurred. The Kenya National Committee on Educational Objectives and Policies was set up to identify more realistic goals for the country's education system and developed several options to reintroduce Kiswahili back into the school system.

The English language continued to be the primary official language, except in broadcasting. The Voice of Kenya led the way in popularizing the image that Kiswahili was the national language while English was the official language. There was also a Swahilization of the Kenyan government. As early as 1964, Kenyatta began demonstrating his desire to Swahilize the parliament. Later, in 1974, he ordered that debates in parliament from then on be conducted exclusively in Swahili. In 1970, during a meeting of the Kenya African National Union, they passed a resolution that set 1974 as the ear in which Kiswahili would be fully adopted as the official language of the country. Not everything went smoothly. In fact, there were some anomalies.

Due to varying views within parliament regarding the switch, in 1975, Kiswahili remained the language of debate in the legislature, but the legislation itself then came before parliament written in English (Mazrui & Mazrui 1999). During this same time, Kiswahili became the supreme language of political communication in the country. However, the official version of the constitution as fundamental law remained in the English language. The government didn't let those anomalies to continue for a long time; it instituted a number of amendments. In 1979, the constitution was amended to allow oral debate in the National Assembly to be conducted in either Kiswahili or English. A further amendment of the constitution required that parliamentary candidate will have to prove at the date of nomination that he or she has a high proficiency in both written and spoken Kiswahili and English.

The shift of the capital from Mombasa to Nairobi was an additional factor that enhanced the spread of Kiswahili as a lingua franca on a national level. Kiswahili in Nairobi had an easier time in the competition with the Kikuyu language than it had with Luganda in Kampala, Uganda. The Kikuyu in Kenya were not a privileged group. They performed the most menial tasks in town (sweeping streets, emptying latrine buckets). By the time of independence, very few Kikuyu politicians addressed meetings in Kikuyu.

Immediately after independence, the colonial linguistic legacy was challenged, but little change occurred. English became the language taught in schools and Kiswahili never regained its status as an instructional language. The Kenya National Committee on Educational Objectives and Policies was set up to identify more realistic goals for the country's education system and developed several options to reintroduce Kiswahili back into the school system.

Kiswahili in the former Belgian Congo

Kiswahili also penetrated into areas like the Francophone countries of the Democratic Republic of the Congo (DRC), Rwanda, and Burundi, where French was introduced through the Belgians. To understand the mitigating factors, one has to look at the linguistic implications of the Belgians and not the French introducing the French language to the people of these countries. Belgians have two languages, French and Flemish. At the on-set, it was not clear in Belgian Congo whether French or Flemish would be the language to be adopted. The Belgians revered and feared the French language because of its association with autocracy. The Flemish cultural affiliations with German afforded the Belgians the linguistic distance from the master. This attitude allowed the French language to thrive even though it was sandwiched, in some parts, between indigenous African languages and Flemish. It was important, therefore, to instill it in the schools that were largely controlled by the Flemish Belgians. The attitude that prevailed among the Flemish Belgians at the time, allowed Kiswahili to penetrate the Eastern and Southern parts of the Congo. Kiswahili provided the bond that the people needed. By the time the DRC achieved its independence, a substantial number of Congolese spoke Kiswahili with reputable proficiency. Kiswahili has since remained one of the important languages in the DRC in addition to the Lingala, and Kikongo. The Belgian Congo disagreement over language of instruction had to do with the use of French vs. lingua franca. The lingua francas included Lingala, Kiswahili, Kikongo, Tshiluba for primary education and French for higher levels. Advantages of using a lingua franca for state administration included the use of regulations in fewer languages. Besides, officers and commissioners could be moved without learning a whole new vernacular. There was a feeling that lingua francas also would be helpful and easier to use in administration facilitation. Thus, in 1928 Colonial Report included measures to introduce Kiswahili as dominant language for educational and administrative purposes.

The Spread of Kiswahili into the former Belgian Congo was also enhanced by economic changes and integration. First were the movement of Swahili and Arab traders in the earlier centuries, and then the emigration of colonial workers in the twentieth Century. Other factors include dated events. Specifically, in 1970 Katanga rebelled twice against the central government of Mobutu Sese Seko. Laurent Kabila (of Katanga) embarked on an effort to reunify the whole country in the 1990s after the murder of the Prime Minister Patrice Lumumba. In 1996 and 1997: Kabila mobilized Swahili language as the medium of command in a multi-ethnic army of rebellion. Many of the recruited fighters already had knowledge of Kiswahili. They formed secret participation of training officers and possibly troops from Rwanda and Uganda. Kiswahili became a kind of linguistic asylum for many Tutsi to reduce their ethnic vulnerability as speakers of Kinyarwanda. They could not entirely conceal their Tutsi identity, but Kiswahili allowed them to downplay it.

Other Aspects of the language

What does it mean to be "Swahilized"? The concept of being "Swahilized" takes on the fact that mechanical directions of words and concepts mostly come in English, and so get learned in English. Thus, "Swahilization" happens when an English vocabulary is somewhat modified to make it easier to understand when trying to teach/explain it. For example, the English word bank is written in Swahili as *benki*; oil as *oili*; carrot as *karoti*; and machine as *mashine*, just to name a few. When this happens, it increases English influence in growing Swahili vocabulary, but is growing the most within the military sects, making the armed forces the "intellectuals" of the future. Adding to this is the world of media such as the use of Television. In Kenya, Tanzania, Zanzibar, and Uganda, socialist politics slowed progress of the spread of Kiswahili. The story is rather different in each country but after regaining their independence, many countries adopted a more left-winged ideology. This means that original broadcasts on radio and television used, and consequentially spread, Kiswahili. The privatization of the media industry also facilitated the language to spread through such radio stations of Kenya Broadcasting Corporation (KBC) which used half English and half Kiswahili. The Kenya Television Network (KTN) however, broadcasted in English only.

In terms of radio, up until the end of 1990's, there were no purely Kiswahili stations which were large enough to compete. Hausa was used to broadcast in West Africa. Recently though, many local stations in especially in each east African country broadcast in Kiswahili: making it the dominating language in African radio. Even more, there is a growing presence of the language in international broadcasting. Swahili is broadcasted in the USA, Germany, and even Japan.

Adding to its expansion is the use of telephones in Kenya and Tanzania. For example, operators speak mainly Kiswahili and English but the actual conversations are mostly in Kiswahili. It is important to remember that before independence, phone conversations were mainly in English. In fact, not only telephone operators, in Kenyan airplanes such as the "Precision," which operates in East Africa, particularly from Tanzania to Kenya and vise versa, their operators use very little English. More recently, Kiswahili seems to have an upper hand compared to English. Ethnic languages of Africa and India are also important for families seeking to preserve their affinity to the ethnic languages. In the last decade these efforts were even more apparent than they seem to be at present. The role of India is critical just because of its business linkages with East Arica. Although international calls are mostly English-dominated, local calls within Africa or from Africa to India are mostly Kiswahili as a consequence of the strength of the business ties between East African and Indians with strong family and social ties in East African.

Changing Roles of Kiswahili

Naturally, language grows and therefore changes not only in its vocabulary but even more, it's historical, social, and political position transforms to integrate varied factors and players within and outside its connected speakers. Kiswahili started changing three decades ago and continues to evolve. Historically, Kiswahili served as an integration tool in three levels: 1) upper horizontal – which describes contact, communication, and interaction among elite groups, 2) lower horizontal – involving masses in contact with each other and able to establish linguistic basis for sustained interaction, and 3) vertical linguistic – defined as communication between rulers and the ruled. Kiswahili which is considered most important in East Africa was facilitated partly by labor migration. Since then, the role of Kiswahili has developed some variations based on formal political and social uses.

Mazrui and Mazrui (1999) note that from the time designated the colonial era, there have been four stages of integration (as experienced by Western European countries): 1) imposed hegemony (dominance of one group over others). This is when cultural perspectives become skewed to favor dominant group; 2) gultural integration: the intentional intermingling of varied ethnic groups and

150

unification through one language to allow trans-ethnic communication; 3) Economic integration: amalgamation of businesses and other trade networks to allow a flow of goods in and outside of East Africa through a unified linguistic medium; and 4) political integration- the efforts to foster a unified citizenry with a goal to help people live peacefully and unified under one nation state. These processes bring about two stages of national consciousness: 1) inner-orientation which is the desire to protect national interests, and 2) outer-orientation which is the national interests defined partly in international terms. The burning question is whether or not East Africa is approaching end of the first stage? Currently, the balance between English and Kiswahili is shifting as the number of Kiswahili speakers continues to grow prompting the question whether it is at the expense of English. But there is also evidence that the number of speakers of both languages is also growing but with Kiswahili having an upper hand in both use and preference.

In this decade, Kiswahili plays a great role in uniting different players in the social and political fields at the national level. For example, it is the language used by local politicians, economists, and a cross-section of elites to communicate. There is also evidence that now than a few decades ago, the preferred language in the textbook business is Kiswahili. Included in this trend is the publication of literary works such as novels, pamphlets, and other books intended to provide specific academic information. Kiswahili has also attained a prestigious role in journalism particularly in printed and broadcast news. It has successfully found its way into the technology used in mass communication. As such, the East African people are more willing to familiarize themselves with Kiswahili and minimize their orientation towards the use of English. To this extent, Kiswahili is becoming the language of the working class. Such a development can be explained by the process of detribalization that we discussed earlier. The process of detribalization moved people towards a nationalistic ideology. There was a transfer of loyalties, a movement from a kin-based loyalty to a class-based loyalty. People to people relationships and political participation have also played a role in the realized changes in the use of Kiswahili.

It was through the use of Kiswahili that a politician is able to reach a larger audience. This is important for the development of a democratic society. The need to use English for economic reasons is still preserved but in order for politicians to be elected and to serve their people effectively and efficiently, they have to use Kiswahili as required while the use of a politician's vernacular language is reserved for communication with the residence of the districts they serve politically. The emerging changes brought about by globalization trends are to be expected and there might be instances that would appear to undermine the gains made by Kiswahili to date. However, considering that changes were embraced during the colonial period followed by adjustments when independence was attained, it is not incomprehensible that changes brought by globalization and technological advancements will likewise be absorbed by the society.

We noted earlier that Kiswahili is gaining international attention but also exhibits a stiff competition with English. Needless to say its gains as demonstrated by its function as an official language initially in Tanzania and then in Kenya and Uganda subsequently is indicative of its resilience and its ability to exhibit international status compared to other indigenous languages of the African continent. To continue to excel, it will require advocacy and strategies for succumbing the challenges characteristic of emerging international languages. Such challenges include the adoption of technology, critical needs in print and electronic media, and the expanded use in the academia. In the next chapter, we expand this discussion to include the internationalization of Kiswahili.

CHAPTER 7

The Global Status of Kiswahili

Introduction

In the previous chapter, we introduced the conversation regarding the functions of Kiswahili in the coastal states and other hinterland states. These included Tanzania, Kenya, Uganda, and the Democratic Republic of the Congo. In this chapter, we explore the global status of Kiswahili taking into consideration that the coastal states can no longer claim a monopoly of the language. We will show that Kiswahili has gained ground both on the continent of Africa and beyond allowing it to claim a global scope. Like many other languages, Kiswahili does not only reflect its speakers and their lives, but also it is a conduit of social, political and economic success. It has the ability to contribute economically and to influence international play field on a plethora of issues involving communication.

Background

The dictionary meanings of the term globalize is 'make something become adopted on a global scale'. The term global has two interesting meanings: (1) "relating to or happening throughout the whole world, and (2) "taking all the different aspects of a situation into account" (Source: "Globalization" 1999:759). Most scholars who have written about globalization bear out some of these meanings in the definition of globalization. In his discussion on globalization and discontents, Joseph Stiglitz (2003) notes that globalization has been celebrated because of its assumed potentials. Not only is globalization a means to reduce the sense of isolation of those living in the developing world but also a conduit for the world's access to knowledge and innovations in technology. Globalization is seen as a means to forge closer integration of countries and peoples of the world by affording them unrestricted transportation and communication and by eliminating economic barriers that restrict a free flow of goods, services, capital, and knowledge. Jagdish Bhagwati (2004) notes that globalization has economic potentials that are evident in the way local economies have been integrated into international economies. Cumulatively, these considerations give us a foundation for the discussion on the role of language in globalizing the world and the potentials for the 99% of the world languages that have not been integrated in the global market.

The potentials for Kiswahili as a global language reside in the ability to attain and sustain prominence in the world as a global language. There is a difference between developing a language for global use and developing a language as an ideological tool. Global usage of a language enhances global understanding. However, when it is used for ideological purposes its function assumes an imposing and threatening value to the culture of other group of speakers. A shared language should be a bridge between cultures, a bridge that connects speakers and allows people to share cultural values, diverse views and knowledge, and promotes a global understanding and a polycentric society. If the ideology behind the spread of a language is to demonstrate power (military or economic), or to secure a competitive edge, or to manipulate a system at the expense of the less politically and economically powerful, then the global function of that language is defunct and the possibility to be globally acceptable is lessened.

Before we discuss the potentials for Kiswahili as a global language, we need to revisit some aspects that we have already touched on in earlier chapters on the influencing power of the English language, the language of choice during the colonial period in East Africa where Swahili now serves as either an official language or a national language and in some cases as both.

The Power of English

When speakers of English, particularly native speakers, refer to English as a global language, they often do so with a sense of pride and comfort. They do so because there is a lot of encouragement from political circles as well as the media that expresses the idea that English is the preferred communication tool across national boundaries. Those who do not agree with this sentiment, point out that designating English a global language provides an explicit excuse for L1 speaks of English to avoid learning another language (Crystal 2005). Needless to say, not everyone in the world speaks English. At the most it is the language of the elite and those who speak it do not always achieve communication because there is no clear common ground for all speakers whether native or non-native.

It is important to also point out that not all native speakers of English are thrilled with the idea of making English a universal (global) language. Their main concern is the loss of the cherished English cultural values and identities associated with the language. L-1 speakers clearly see significant differences between their culture and the cultures of non-L1 English speakers and fear that the culture and purity of their language will be replaced by a hybrid that is both alien and degenerate. This same racial exclusiveness of English was invoked in the early 19th Century when Britain was establishing its colonies around the world. Mazrui and Mazrui (1999) notes that English colonist learned the local languages of their subjects and insisted on speaking them even in those cases where the local subjects could speak English because they wanted to discourage the local people from considering themselves equals with their masters. In addition, the Englishman wanted to define the social distance that needed to be maintained with their subjects.

According to Mazrui and Mazrui (1999), Lord Lugard was not enthused by the native's acquisition of the Queen's language and contended that spreading the language to non-English people, was disrespectful to the English people and their cultural values. He could not fathom the possibility of non-native English speakers assuming a monopoly of the English language. Of course, Lord Lugard's concerns did not stop the spread of English in the colonies. The British produced the United States, which has, linguistically, been more successful in spreading English. The role of the United States in the world has also become more critical since Britain lost its power and prestige in its colonies and elsewhere in the world. The United States not only outspends Britain in teaching the language and broadcasting English news to the world but also contributes more than any other nation to science, technology, trade, sports, military power, literature, and theatre, all in English. Of course, the English native speakers are not very happy with that either. They do not consider the varieties of English in the United States and elsewhere to be legitimate and resent the way their language has and continues to be degenerated.

For non-native speakers of English, the spread of the language conjures mixed feelings. While the good is obvious, it is nevertheless a point of concern for those who consider globalization to be a dangerous path for the world to travel. There is concern that there is no regulatory body that would ensure that prejudice, exploitation, and unilateralism are not tagged onto the globalization ideology. It is without doubt that the language that we use selectively shapes our perceptions, the names we apply emphasize particular aspects of reality and neglect others, language names what exists, and the world is named by those who hold power. Because power is reflected in language and exists in the discourse it is not neutral. As such, language reflects the cultural values and perceptions of the user, the power in and behind language can be used to define who has control and determines when, how, and where a particular language should be used. Before we discuss these concerns further, let me turn my attention to the status and role of Kiswahili and try to answer the critical question, whether Kiswahili merits consideration for global use.

The Power of Kiswahili

There is no doubt that Kiswahili has gained ground as a language of choice by millions of people in East Africa and its neighbors. It has been transported to different parts of Africa and the West due to migration, both voluntary and as a consequence of ethnic wars, including the fight against colonialism and apartheid. Refugees from neighboring countries learn Kiswahili during their short stay in Kenya or Tanzania and keep the language when they finally immigrate to England, the United States, or other western countries. This is evident in the increase in demand for Kiswahili translators for agencies like the American based Language Line Incorporated and Pacific Interpreters Inc. that offer services to law enforcement, hospitals, legal services, immigration services, airline companies, and schools.

The number of people learning Kiswahili at institutions of higher education in the United States has also attained impressive numbers even though the enrolments are only high at the elementary and in special cases intermediate levels. We are also encouraged when we look at Europe and Asia where the enthusiasm is stronger and the objectives are better defined. At many of the European institutions of higher education, including private organizations, the study of Kiswahili is intense and purposeful. European institutions offer a more serious program of African languages, with Kiswahili topping the list. Many of their objectives are tied to development projects that are sponsored by the European Economic market, and specific agencies such as DANIDA and NORAD, to name only a few. Such examples offer us some perspective of the power and potential for a global use of Kiswahili.

There is also another motivation for learners and users of Kiswahili, namely the global performing arts. As we all know, hip-hop is no longer confined to the West where it has strong roots. Those who have had the opportunity to travel to East Africa recently would agree with me that Swahili hip-hop is gaining much popularity among the young people. That global dimension of hip-hop plays a role in attracting non-Swahili speakers to the lyrics and the associated performances even when the language used is not fully understood. Hip-hop offers a new avenue for learning the language through soft emersion and a way to share indigenous knowledge and cultural values that are not easily accessible through print media.

The attraction of Kiswahili hip-hop music to non-native speakers of Kiswahili is evident in the number of foreigners, particularly students and tourists, who buy hip-hop CDs and audio cassettes of this music and their keen interest in learning both the lyrics and the accompanying dance moves. The poetic nature of the lyrics makes it relatively easy for Kiswahili learners to learn the language and the dance moves. Interest in attaining fluency and high proficiency levels of the language also seems to be on the rise both at institutions in the West and at language centers in both Kenya and Tanzania. A good example are a number of institutions in bothe Kenya and Tanzania (e.g University of Dar es Salaam, State University of Zanzibar, the MS-Training Center for Development in Tanzania, Kenyata University, and Moi University) that, for many years, used to attract only a handful of learners of Kiswahili from Europe. Currently, they register more than two hundred students from Europe, the Americas, and non-Swahili speaking countries in Africa. The majority of these clients attend their summer programs while a minority group requests their services to coincide with the learner's academic term in their home countries.

Such examples demonstrate that Kiswahili is attaining a prominent status. Not only is this language powerful but also very symbolic. It has and continues to be used to shape the understandings of the world about Africa (even when we view this as being done at the expense of other African indigenous languages).

Undoubtedly, Kiswahili will achieve a recognized global power. The challenge is to establish a sustainable global need and importance among other global languages. The signs are there considering the growing use of Kiswahili in world media such as the Voice of America, and Radio Deutsche Welle, BBC radio and Television, and Asia radio and TV programs that come to many homes in East Africa.

Some of these programs are broadcasted to East Africa (especially Kenya, and Tanzania) on a regular basis (in some cases twice a day). In addition, Kiswahili has been identified by Microsoft for the development of scanner OCR that would identify Kiswahili text. Mr. Opiyo of the Nairobi Microsoft office (cf. Majira Newspaper, June 2004:2) noted that Kiswahili was selected because of its status, a strong African language that can stand a global test as a language of business and communication in East Africa. Other African languages that are being targeted include: Yoruba, Hausa, Somali, and Amharic.

The growing interest to expose Kiswahili to technology is also demonstrated in the move by Vodacom Airtel, Tigo, TTCL, and Zantel phone companies to regularly place advertisements in newspapers in both English and Kiswahili to advertise their services. Both companies have seen the wisdom of reaching all sectors of the public since the buying power or usage does not reside in the affluent only.

There is also growing Kiswahili literature including language textbooks and computer assisted programs for language and literature (cf. Moshi and Omar 2003). Several scholars including Ali & Mwakilo (2001) and Chuwa (2003) have developed manuals in Kiswahili that are intended to facilitate the understanding of how the computer works and how other writing programs such as Word Perfect could be utilized in Kiswahili. Microsoft (MS Word Journal 2002) listed a selected number of African languages (Amharic, Edo, Fulfunde, Hausa, Igbo, Kanuri, Swahili, Oromo, Somali, Sesotho, Berber, Tigrigna, Tsonga, Setswana, Venda, Xhosa, Yoruba, and Zulu) as prime targets for the development of user friendly operational manual in the local language. Needless to say, the expansion to cover these many languages is refreshing and demonstrates the growing global understanding of the need to be linguistically inclusive. Kiswahili leads the pack while it offers both the model and encouragement to other languages. Let me add that, currently, a spell-checker is in progress (spearheaded by Professor Arvi Hurskainen, University of Helsinki) to help editors who choose to write in Kiswahili. Without doubt, similar programs will be developed for

159

other African languages using the established template for Kiswahili (Legere 2005). As noted in Tafsiri Sanifu v. 6, published by the Institute of Kiswahili in Dar Es Salaam, a comprehensive terminology was developed and released by the Tanzania Swahili Council (BAKITA). Furthermore, Kiango (2004) attests that more than 20,000 lexical items were compiled by 1989.

These are, therefore, elements that are speeding up the process of globalizing the use of Kiswahili. The prediction is that once the need and value of learning and using Kiswahili is recognized like that of English, the quest for Kiswahili to attain a global status will be realized. The anticipation was demonstrated in a June 2004 surprising move by President Joachim Chisano of Mozambique at the African Union (AU) Assembly in Addis Ababa that offered a model for what is expected from African leaders, namely leading by example. President Chisano showed the hidden power of African languages by, unexpectedly, deciding to address the Assembly using Kiswahili. The Assembly was not prepared for this bold move and there was a brief moment of panic as the delegates scrambled to get translators to provide simultaneous translation. Needless to say, President Chisano was not swayed and continued with his remarks without worrying about the inability of the delegates to comprehend what he was saying. President Chisano's bold move, prompted President Obasanjo of Nigeria to follow suit by greeting the delegates in Kiswahili and thanking President Chisano for his bold move. Though symbolic, this move was both bold and commendable. President Chisano demonstrated the uniqueness of Kiswahili, reminding the delegates that they have been debating on the use of African languages at the assembly for over a decade and yet they had not moved to implement it. He wanted to show that this was the time to implement it, at the birth of a new organization, the African Union (that replaced the Organization of African Unity-OAU). President Chisano wanted to emphasize that the organization should change to reflect the world as it changes in the 21st Century. Africa and Africans should not continue to do business as usual. Rather, Africa and Africans have to assume their place in the global world and that language is one

160

avenue through which they can assert their authority and cultural power. President Chisano demonstrated the power of Kiswahili and its prospective global use. Needless to say, other delegates at the assembly who could have used Kiswahili did not follow suit. These included the AU Pan African Parliament President, the Presidents of Tanzania and Kenya, including their representative Ministers of Foreign Affairs, all of whom Kiswahili is either their first language, national language, and/or an official language in their countries. Other delegates who could also have seized this opportunity included Presidents and representative Ministers from Uganda, Rwanda, Burundi, and the Democratic Republic of the Congo whose Kiswahili is at least a second language, compared to President Chisano and Abasanjo who learned Kiswahili as their third or fourth language, undoubtedly for non-cultural reasons and motivations. President Chisano acquired the language when he lived in Tanzania as a refugee during the Mozambique liberation war from the Portuguese. The war lasted for more than fifteen years. It is not clear what President Obasanjo's Kiswahili skills are because his use of the language at the summit was limited to the salutation and the recognition accorded to of President Chisano for advocating for a wider use of African languages at the AU summit. Nevertheless, his gesture is well taken in the larger context namely demonstrating the global power and status of Kiswahili.

One other factor that we need to consider is the fact that Kiswahili affords us with examples that fit linguistic globalization. Compared to English, its use is not associated with the establishment of colonies. It is also not used for ideological reasons alone. Mazrui and Mazrui (1999) note that while Kiswahili was used to influence ethnic loyalties it was also an instrument for changing ethnic behavior, creating social classes and religious affiliations, and for providing racial identity and national consciousness. Its origins are believed to be along the coast of East Africa. It spread into rural areas around 1800 where it assumed the role of transforming East African peasants to proletarians, changing rural farmers to urban workers. Furthermore, although Kiswahili was deeply associated with the legacy of the mosque, it was later exploited by the church in its ministries for the purposes of Christianization. Among the Muslims, Kiswahili was a socialization tool among different ethnic groups and regions. This promoted a comprehensive culture of its own that transcended language as a mere communication tool.

Unlike English, Kiswahili averted a parochial form of ethnicity and a universalistic orientation. Mazrui and Mazrui (1999) correctly observes that the Swahili culture and Islamic religious background did not perpetuate a single heritage but multiple heritage that include a variety of cultures symbolized by food, ways of doing, and dress that brought Africans, Arabs, and Indians together. The language became a tool of communication for indigenous speakers to bond with others. The language thrived and spread despite initial resistance shown by missionaries who associated it with Islam and scholars whose description of the language tended to pit the coastal communities with the mainland communities. It was impossible to overlook its importance and the role it played in combining and synthesizing people from different ethnicity and backgrounds. The missionaries could not downplay the Middle-eastern monotheism exemplified by modified lexical items from the Old Testament found in the Quran.

Kiswahili shares some similarities with English in its effect of enhancing social interaction between different groups, breaking down ethnic loyalties and identities. People from different groups intermingle with ease creating a decline in ethnic customs. This, however, does not mean that these groups have abandoned their core cultures. Like in the case of today's English speakers, members of an ethnic group do organize themselves to meet their ethnic socialization needs, an aspect that explains the acceptability of different varieties that reflect the ethnic background of the speaker. In such interactions (includes wedding rituals, burial rituals, and other community festivities), ethnic languages are used interchangeably with Kiswahili, perpetuating code switching and code-mixing (Scotton 1979). Such endeavors afford the groups the pull of ethnic loyalty.

In East Africa, Kiswahili serves as a lingua franca among different ethnic communities and it is usually the language of the work place, market place, educational systems, and in Tanzania --more than the other East African countries, the language of government business. Evidence of Kiswahili's role as a lingual Franca is in the way it fostered the spread to other parts of sub-Sahara Africa. This extent of its spread provides us the confidence to speculate its potential as a global language in the 21st Century. Furthermore, the rapid nature of its spread and the ease at which it seems to be accepted by other communities explains its adopted role in the early 50s when it assumed a political function of fostering nationalism. It was the language the new breed of African political leaders used to impel for African nationalism and the African right to self-determination and independence.

In the preceding Chapter we showed how Kiswahili assumed a major role as a lingua franca when politics became a nationalistic movement in the 50s. It also assumed a bigger role in the armed forces of both colonial and post-colonial East Africa. We discussed the Uganda experience which we termed interesting because of the relationship between who ruled the country and who dominated the armed force. We discussed how both Milton Obote and Idi Amin treated the role of Kiswahili in Uganda just because of the ethnic diversities that seemed to influence the choice of a lingua franca for the time. We noted that this diversity forced Kiswahili to the army barracks to bridge the linguistic gap between members of the armed forces from the north (Nilotes) who were very conscious of their separateness from the Bantu groups that were predominantly settled in the southern parts of Uganda. To create a symbiotic relationship that was already maared by ethnic rivalry among the groups (Acholi, Langi, Kakwa, Lugbara, Baganda, and Nilotes), Kiswahili was adopted as a unifying language and remained the lingua franca of the arm forces. The spread of Kiswahili outside the barracks provided a political function for the language especially during Idi Amin's reign despite the hostility and political decline associated with his brutal regime. Because Kiswahili facilitated the expansion of the Ugandan's

163

social interaction circles, it was adopted later in 1986 as the official language of the army.

We also explained in the previous Chapter that the success for this development came from the Baganda's need to belong to the larger community of the Swahili speakers. Because the Baganda Royal family supported the introduction of Kiswahili the rest of the Uganda society warmed up to the use of Kiswahili. This was also a response to the increasing functional role of Kiswahili in Kenya and Tanzania, its neighboring states. It assured the Ugandans that it was not just a military language but a cross-boundary communicating tool. They did not want to continue to view the role of Kiswahili in the same way as apartheid South Africa viewed Afrikaans considering the image of brutality associated with the Ugandan armed forces under the various regimes especially that of Idi Amin. That era was disconcerting to many of the Ugandans. Kiswahili gained additional importance after Obote's return from exile to Uganda and the formation of the National Resistance Army (NRA) in the south under Yoweri Musoveni.

In Chapter 7 we also explored an interesting historical aspect of the languages that can be considered here as evidence of the power of Kiswahili outside of the coastal states. This is associated with its ability to penetrate areas like the Francophone countries of the Democratic Republic of the Congo (DRC), Rwanda, and Burundi, where French was introduced through the Belgians because of the linguist differences between the Belgians who spoke Flemish and the French whose colonial power advocated for the introduction of French to its colonies. The Belgians used their cultural affiliations with German to create a linguistic distance between the master and the subject as is often associated with the Germanic culture. This attitude that prevailed among the Flemish Belgians at the time, allowed Kiswahili to penetrate the Eastern and Southern parts of the Congo. Kiswahili provided the bond that the Congolese needed. Kiswahili has remained, beyond independence important language in the DRC in addition to Lingala, and Kikongo. Kiswahili, however, has been the most widespread of them especially in the economically rich parts, specifically the Shaba Province (formally Katanga).

A more recent evidence of the expansion of Kiswahili can be found in its integrative role in migrant labor communities in sub-Saharan Africa, states that achieved independence after a period of liberation struggle, and misplaced communities in refugee camps in Eastern Africa, and those who have been settled overseas after spending a number of years in refugee camps in Eastern Africa (these include Somalis, Rwandans, Burundians, and Congolese). These groups learned Kiswahili and now use it as a lingua franca in their new communities. Often, these groups select Kiswahili as the language of their identity when requesting an interpreter in England and America and also as a medium of communication with other displaced peoples from these four ethnic groups when they find themselves in the same communities abroad.

Further Considerations

As presently defined, globalization espouses a monolithic view of the world where the only surviving super power reserves the custodianship of the English language. To bring about a polycentric equation, advocates of a linguistic and cultural diversity need to be engaged in a much wider struggle for the creation of a polycentric world. If globalization is allowed to eliminate linguistic and cultural diversity, then there will not be a chance for the development of a polycentric world where diverse experiences and knowledge contribute equally to science and technology, the two driving forces of global understanding in the 21st century and beyond.

Walters and Brody (2005) correctly notes that when we advocate for a global language, we need to contend with the concerns of both sides of the debate. There are real concerns by both native and non-native English speakers about political, economic, and cultural consequences as they affect them should English become global and spread to all corners of the world. If Kiswahili should assume a recognized global role and in order to avert regional as well as continental fears, it should avoid the monolithic and possessive characteristics of English.

The fear of accepting English as the only global language is rooted in early histories of European languages that spread as a result of political, economic and military prowess. The Greek language, for example, existed in the Middle East for two hundred years due to the armies of Alexander the Great. Latin was spread by the legions of the Roman Empire, and Arabic spread in North Africa and the Middle East to foster Islam through the Moorish armies of the 8th Century. Included are Spanish, Portuguese, and French that resemble the English in the way they found their way to the Americas, Africa, and the Far East, mostly through expeditions and the quest to establish colonies through different means, including military force. Thus, we cannot blame those who fear that military power might come to play once again in the era of globalization.

We cannot overlook the fact that economic and military powers are the avenues of political influence around the world in the 21st century. While globalization aids economic competitiveness, it also creates a 'survival of the fittest' attitude amongst the competitors. The media is going to play a major role in aiding and abetting the economic competitions.

Consequently, the language or languages that occupy the central and subject positions stand a better chance of acquiring a global status due to the ability and opportunity to assume a multifaceted role of communication. The United States is currently the only standing super power and the custodian of English. The major currency of the world is the dollar (despite the fact that the Euro has gained the buying power slightly). The language of the dollar is English. The Europeans use English to communicate across their own borders and the rest of the world. As a result of colonization, Africa communicates with each other in English. As such, the center and subject positions of communication are currently occupied by those that have enhanced their economic and political power through the use of English.

The question that we need to address is, should the world accept the power of English as linguistically inevitable and therefore disregard any efforts to have a linguistically diverse world? Crystal (2005:508-514) enumerates the risks of accepting one language to serve the world. These include:

1. Elite monolingual linguistic: where one group assumes the monopoly of the language encouraging the development of complacent and dismissive attitudes towards other languages and cultures.
2. Manipulative tendencies: where the privileged group use their competitive edge to manipulate the system at the expense of those who have less power and lack the ability to use it. Consequently the gap between the poor and the rich would increase.
3. Marginalization: where some languages become marginalized and rendered not worth learning.
4. Language death: when a language is considered not worth learning, it becomes irrelevant and its ultimate death is hastened. This is a real danger for small languages and languages spoken in less powerful nations. This also perpetuates the mentality of "survival of the fittest".

Presently, Africa is confronted with these risks because of its dependency on foreign languages for communication, education, and trade. Thus, any of these risks are real. In his discussion of the Status of English in Africa, Schmied (1991) correctly observes that there are persistent inequities in practice and application of resources available to L-2 English speakers. Specifically African scholars face sociolinguistic or grammatical problems as they try to express their ideas in English in an English only academy. Furthermore, despite the claim for global English, many written works in English around the globe remain unpublished due to sociolinguistic stereo-typing of both the authors and the texts. Oftentimes, research by Africans that is enhanced by firsthand knowledge of linguistic phenomena that is particular to their first language is considered intuitive. This is an effort to distinguish between 'mainstream' researches from 'other' research practices. Unfortunately such categorizations reinforce Crystal's concern of manipulative tendencies by the custodians of the designated global language. The categorizations also explain why large amounts of works by non-L1 English speakers have limited access to English-based publications. Unfortunately, such limitations indicate missed opportunities for the exchange of ideas in written form between scholars of diverse cultures and linguistic backgrounds. It also defeats the meaning of globalization noted earlier that calls for the need to take all the different aspects of a situation into account. It is without doubt that information regarding interesting questions and phenomena are missed when we allow theoretical speculation from limited data source regardless of whether we are researching on language or anything else.

Because Kiswahili has emerged as the most developed African language, should the rest of Africa become apprehensive about its potential power in the future? Considering the role that Kiswahili assumed from the onset and the functions it continues to foster, it is unlikely that Kiswahili will be a threatening language if it were to become one of the global languages.

The origins of Kiswahili do not include political or economic power. The communities that have a rich culture associated with the language are not imposing to the extent of threatening the cultures of other communities where Kiswahili has spread or might spread in the future. Because those who currently hold the monopoly of the Kiswahili are non-threatening, the function that the language can successfully perform is that of building a bridge for global understanding. As noted earlier such a function is globally acceptable. By leading the pack, Kiswahili has an opportunity to advocate for the development of other African languages to fulfill both regional and continental communication needs. Kiswahili cannot be expected to fulfill that role alone. To avoid being compared to English, Kiswahili has to avoid being as racially or regionally exclusive of its indigenous speakers. In fact this would be out of character for Kiswahili since the speakers do not have the history of possessiveness of the language. As scholars, we should continue to encourage the practice of learning other languages and to persuade African political leaders to institute the learning of other African languages from as early as primary school and to reinforce it at secondary school level.

It is important to emphasize that a language does not become global or universal because of the size of the population it serves. Rather, it is determined by the function it serves and the recipients of these functions. We have historical evidence that provides us with this caution, the rise and fall of Latin which has largely remained a language of scholars of religion and classical studies. It became an international language throughout the Roman Empire and around the world as a consequence of the Roman's military power but not their numbers. As their power declined so did the language except where religious power remained (e.g. its association with the Roman Catholic Church). Adding to this example are Hebrew, Greek, Arabic, and French that were revered because of their supposed aesthetic values, clarity of expressions, literary power, or religious standing. Kiswahili has attractive attributes too, but scholars should refrain from using them as pre-conditions for their prominence and sustainability as a global language. Its resilience, success, and sustainability at the national, regional, continental, or international levels cannot be guaranteed by any one or multiple attributes it may exhibit. The attributes of Kiswahili should be viewed as motivating factors for students of language and their instructors as well as an example that could be used to encourage the development of other languages to promote global understanding.

There are those who would argue that promoting Kiswahili creates a grave yard for other indigenous languages (including associated cultures) in East Africa, particularly in Tanzania. I would argue that, contrary to such views, Tanzania has shown and has enhanced its cultural appreciation and diversity by the fact that its citizenry has accepted Kiswahili as a national identity and something that unites the people. Kiswahili is a national language that bears out some key cultural aspects that are shared across tribal boundaries. Needless to say the identity of East Africans around the world is associated with the unifying language of Kiswahili. Many individuals and communities have or are learning Kiswahili (these include many parts of Europe, Asia, America, and several African countries). In each of these places, one would tell you that there are a variety of reasons for teaching and learning Kiswahili. In the United States, there are over 100 institutions of higher education that have integrated Kiswahili in its mainstream curriculum, and it is often the popular choice for undergraduates who are required to study a foreign language for their graduation requirement. Some have higher goals and objective and may have found a career move that they think would put them ahead of their classmates after graduation. There are quite a number of students who have been studying Kiswahili over the years across the many institutions around the world who have made good use of that skill, perhaps working with key institutions of higher education, government and private agencies, and a variety of NGOs in Tanzania, Kenya, Uganda, Rwanda, Burundi, some work with the UN refugee settlement programs both in Africa and elsewhere. These individuals add to the numbers in Europe and Asia and constitute the growing power of Kiswahili and its potential for becoming a global language.

Concluding Remarks

As we consider the globalization of world languages, one would expect East Africans to find the national will to invest in Kiswahili. Though on a small scale, there is movement to incorporate Kiswahili in technological advancement. The recent investment by Bill Gates in the development of a Kiswahili version of the Microsoft (July 2004) and the utilization of new technologies like the cell-phones are encouraging aspect that create opportunities for Kiswahili as well as establishing an important role for Kiswahili in the 21st Century. It is also testimony to the current and future power of Kiswahili, dispelling the myth that technology and modern science can only be achieved through colonial or European languages, something that is a concern to many as the winds of globalization surge on.

It is obvious that scholars and leaders of the field of Kiswahili cannot afford to let these developments pass by and not seize the opportunity to place Kiswahili on the global languages map. By its ability to exploit innovations afforded by science and technology, Kiswahili has proved its new status among the world languages. The success attained by Kiswahili is, undoubtedly, an inspiration and encouragement for other African languages that have a large body of written literature that can be exploited by scholars of language, linguistics as well as other disciplines including science and technology. African scholars should realize that while it is important to continue to seek the important technological and scientific stimuli from other cultures, it is also important to be placed in the center of it all in order to encourage interdependence rather than dependency. Africa cannot continue to shy away from making critical contributions to the world cultures and the global world of the future. The globalization ideology will not do justice to Africa if Africans stay on the sideline and watch the winds of change go by. Africa has to view itself as an innovative constituency of the global world of the future. Africa must do justice to its own cultures, views, and use its scientific and technological culture as a potential to new global innovations.

The development of Kiswahili and its contribution to the development of the East African societies are part of Africa's preparations for a fuller involvement in world cultures, a global culture that is needed but must be compatible with the present stage of human understanding of the world and their realization of their potential as full contributors in the global village.

While Kiswahili strengthens its place among the world global languages, it is expected that other African languages will develop rapidly following the examples offered by Kiswahili. As a global language, Kiswahili stands the chance of becoming the mediator between the continent's constituencies, including the Diaspora. Kiswahili, therefore, is a piece of the African culture whose power to

171

penetrate the global world stands as a model for all other African languages. Its functions in society have clear consequences in the role as a world language in so far as knowledge expansion and dissemination is concerned, specifically in the political, scientific, technological, and social interaction spheres. At its early stages of expansion, Kiswahili passed the test of transforming class structures across communities in East Africa by promoting nationalism and social interaction between ethnic and religious communities. It can compete with English despite the fact that English will continue to aid various advancement processes (Mazrui & Mazrui 1999:188). Allowing English or other foreign languages to assume an exclusive role in Africa's technological advancement would, undoubtedly, encourage dependency while thwarting global innovations that could be influenced by the African cultures and experiences. It would also encourage the divisions that exist between rural and urban communities, pitting those who live in cities/towns against those who live in rural areas. Considering that African economies rely more on rural agricultural developments and productions and that the majority of the population is rural based, it would be a sad commentary if African leaders and scholars continue to allow foreign science and technology to be dispensed through the gates of foreign languages only.

Africans on the continent and the Diaspora have a responsibility to ensure that African languages assume a permanent place in the functional role of global languages. Africans should cultivate an optimistic view of the potentials for African languages in the global village of world languages. There is need to encourage the formation of a polycentric world that is defined and characterized by linguistic diversity. The role of the Diaspora is in ensuring that African languages assume a permanent place in the functional role of global languages. As noted earlier, the demand for African languages by the children of slaves and subsequent immigrants to the new world served as a catalyst for the need to teaching African languages of the languages in Europe and America. The demand allowed some African languages, such as Kiswahili, Yoruba, Hausa, Arabic, and

Zulu, to name only a few, to gain prominence as the commonly taught African languages in Europe and the West. Without doubt, the efforts of Africans are critically needed to continue to advocate and sustain the African languages at home and abroad. Compared to the teaching of African languages and linguistics in the 60s, 70s, and 80s, today's efforts appear weakened. The demand does not appear as intense, and the learner profile has changed dramatically. Consequently the teaching of African languages is, in some institutions, a service component of the curriculum instead of a critical academic component for a holistic curriculum that would contribute to the general knowledge and experience of the globalized learner. Kiswahili has paved the way for such endeavors.

It is also important to encourage leaders and the citizens of East Africa not to succumb to the pressure to de-emphasize Kiswahili by promoting English medium schools. It is sad to note that many of these schools have resorted to the colonial style of enforcing an English only environment in the English only schools. Students who are caught speaking their local languages or Kiswahili on school compounds are punished by hard labor or by withholding certain privileges like a trip to town for shopping or taking away their free time. There have been reports of students who were kept out of class to work in the school gardens as a form of punishment. The sad part is that these English medium schools have children in primary one who are hardly eight years old. The message these kids are getting from such punishments is that their local language or Kiswahili is inferior to English and that mastery of the English was the most important thing in their academic endeavors. Another message that these young people infer from the punishments they endure is that their language and cultures are unworthy of learning and would not make them successful in life. This was, unfortunately, the ideology that was perpetuated in education during colonial periods.

There is also need to encourage those in the Diaspora who advocate for a global use of Kiswahili to refrain from being contented with the minimal utilization of Kiswahili as is often demonstrated in the US in the adoption of Kiswahili names, words, and phrases in naming practices, the scattered use of Swahili words in children's books, children's theatre and films, and product labels (especially beauty products). Also, if Kiswahili is to be one of the global languages, we cannot be contented with the teaching of Kiswahili as an academic subject when its major accomplishment is to enable the learner to name objects. While we encourage those small steps, we should also cultivate the interest of those who want to learn the language because of their interest and hope to use it purposefully. Such learners are the likely global users of Kiswahili. As scholars we need to encourage lifelong learners, those that are willing to go beyond the object naming exercise. Accuracy in usage and the need to be functional in the language should be the key objectives both for the teacher and the learner.

Scholars should not take part in undermining the power of Kiswahili. When a language is trivialized, its power is also diminished. We should not allow a global language to be trivialized by inaccuracies that are correctable by scholars who maintain an activist role in promoting and perfecting a language. English, French, German, or other global language users do not trivialization their language. Kiswahili users should likewise take an active role in protecting and promoting it as accurately as possible. Using the word 'possible' here allows us to draw a distinction between standard and colloquial Kiswahili. A non-standard use of the language is acceptable while an inaccurate use of the language should be discouraged.

CHAPTER 8

Ghana's Role to the Promotion of Kiswahili

Introduction

In Chapter VII we discussed the place of Kiswahili in Tanzania, Kenya, Uganda, and the Democratic Republic of the Congo. All these countries form an East African cluster and their history of Kiswahili is comparable. For the most part they are an integral part of the Swahilidom. They are the framework for the discussion of the history, development and civilization of the Swahili Coastal States.

This Chapter, however, seeks to introduce a special case which looks at the promotion of Kiswahili within the African continent. Ghana, West Africa, is a special case because its role in the promotion of Kiswahili on the continent is both historical and highly commendable.

Ghana is one of the few non- eastern African countries that have played a significant role in the promotion of Kiswahili in the last fifty years. Ghana has contributed to the promotion of the teaching and learning of Kiswahili since the 1960s. Much of the credit goes to Dr. Kwame Nkrumah, the 1st President of Ghana (1957-1965) whose Pan-Africanist ideologies and advocacy for the adoption of Kiswahili as a continental lingua franca allowed Kiswahili to be institutionalized at the Ghana Broadcasting Corporation (GBC) and later extended to the Ghana Institute of Languages (GIL) and finally the University of Ghana, Legon (UG)

Kiswahili in Post-Independence Africa and Beyond

It is worthwhile at this juncture to revisit some aspects discussed in earlier chapters in order to frame Ghana's role in the promotion of Kiswahili. As noted earlier, Kiswahili has been and still is one of the most important languages in Africa and the world today (Moshi 2006,

Mulokozi 2002). It has seen significant development and expansion since the early to mid-nineteenth century due to the following factors:

1. the development of trade expeditions from the East African coastal area into the interior which emerged at the turn of the nineteenth century and led to the expansion of Kiswahili from east African coastal area into the interior on a large scale.
2. European missionaries to East Africa from the mid nineteenth century whose interest in the Swahili language for their missionary purposes led to the systematic study of the language and documentation of its grammar by them as well as the development of a Roman based writing system for the language.
3. And the late President Nyerere's (the first president of the Republic of Tanzania) promotion of the language as a National and official language and the medium of instruction for primary education in all public schools and a compulsory subject at secondary school level.

Europe, the Scandinavian countries, China, the USA and other states in their various capacities have contributed to the development of the Kiswahili language in the areas of international broadcast, academic research and publications, teaching and learning and ICT (Mulokozi 2002; Moshi 2006; Chebet-Choge 2012). The Organisation of African unity (OAU) now African Union (AU) has also recognised and promoted Kiswahili by establishing it as one of its six official working languages.

In East Africa, the East African Community (EAC) which is made up of five states; Tanzania, Uganda, Kenya, Burundi and Rwanda has also endeavoured to promote Kiswahili by adopting it as one of its three official languages (Kiswahili, French and English) as stated in the East African Community information Guide for Investors (Chebet-Choge 2012). Other than the EAC, Kiswahili has been adopted by the Democratic Republic of Congo (DRC) as one of its six national languages. It is a major lingua franca in countries such as,

Tanzania and Kenya, as well as major cities of Uganda, Burundi, Rwanda, the Comoros, and Somali. It is the medium of Instruction throughout primary education in Tanzania and parts of Kenya and a compulsory subject in primary and secondary education in Kenya. It is also taught in schools in Uganda. At the tertiary level it is taught in a lot of East African universities and in several non-East African universities. It is taught as a degree subject at the University of Dar es Salam, Tanzania, Makerere University in Uganda, Moi University, Kenyatta University and the University of Nairobi in Kenya,

Apart from Eastern African universities and educational institutions, there are universities in Northern, Southern, western and central Africa that have Kiswahili in their curricular. In Libya, Sebha University Kiswahili has been taught on a regular basis since 1984 and it is the most popular African language of the Department of Languages and African Studies with over one hundred students (*http://www.tripolipost.com/articledetail.asp?c=4&i=304125/06/2013*).

Other Libyan Universities that teach Kiswahili are Nasser University and Al-Feteh University (Chebet-Choge 2012). In Nigeria Kiswahili was taught at the University of Port Harcourt from 1979/1980 academic year until the early 1990s (Amidu 1996). Although there were commendable efforts to sustain the Kiswahili program it nevertheless collapsed due to lack of teaching staff. Also, in 1969, Nigeria initiated Kiswahili broadcasting through External Service of the Federal Radio Corporation of Nigeria (FRCN) also known as Voice of Nigeria. (http://www.voiceofnigeria.org/Kiswahili/ ourhistory.htm). Ghana is among the few African countries that seem to have been able to preserve some of the successful efforts to promote and develop Kiswahili in West Africa. Their contribution to Kiswahili dates as far back as 1961 when Tanzania attained its independence. Below is a historical appraisal of the Ghana institutions that have and continue to promote Kiswahili.

A historical Appraisal of Ghana's Contribution to the Promotion of Kiswahili

As noted earlier, Kiswahili in Ghana owes its existence to the late Dr. Kwame Nkrumah, first President of Ghana. In the early post-independence era, he was one of the African leaders who encouraged the adoption of Kiswahili as a continental language in order to promote Pan-Africanism (Chimera 2000; Chebet-Choge 2012). He showed his commitment to this call for Kiswahili as a continental lingua franca by championing directly or indirectly its adoption by some Ghanaian public institutions. These include Ghana Broadcasting Corporation (GBC), Ghana Institute of Languages (GIL), University of Ghana (UG) and SOS Herman Gmeiner College.

Kwame Nkrumah Mausoleum, Accra

Ghana Broadcasting Corporation

The Ghana Broadcasting Corporation (GBC) was established on July 31, 1935 by the British Government under the code name Station Zoy. An External Service unit of the Corporation was inaugurated on June 1, 1961, four years after independence. It was established to become "A true voice of Africa helping in the struggle for total emancipation and political union of African states" (Kugblenu 1975: 8-9). It was primarily initiated because Kwame Nkrumah, the then Prime-Minister saw broadcasting as an opportunity to propagate his Pan-Africanist message to his fellow Africans.

The External Service unit broadcasted in six languages: French, Hausa, Arabic, Kiswahili, Portuguese and Bambara (spoken in Mali, Burkina Faso and Senegal). These languages of broadcast at the external service were very strategic; each had a particular target area in Africa or beyond as their audience. The target audience for the Kiswahili broadcasting included Eastern and Central Africa. At some point there were over twenty hours of Kiswahili broadcasting weekly. The External Service put out current affairs programs that explained Ghana's viewpoint on burning issues affecting Africa and the world through informative, educative and entertaining programs. The programs also attempted to break cultural barriers and encouraged the promotion of African unity and highlighted the African liberation struggle (Kugblenu 1975). Frempong (2008: 5) saw the presence of the External Service as "an important tool of Nkrumah's Government Foreign Policy". Herd and Kugblenu (1978: 126) also state that the External Service Department became "one of Africa's ambitious international radio propaganda stations in keeping with Nkrumah's ambition to play a leadership role in the Pan-African Movement".

A survey of the program line-up of Kiswahili broadcasting during some months of the years 1965-1969 indicated that in 1964 and 1965, there was only one hour of broadcasting in Kiswahili from Tuesdays to Saturday. From 1966-1969 the number of hours went up to five hours daily from Monday to Saturday. The program line-up included news, music, current affairs as well as women and youth programs. The news included translations of opinions expressed in the major Ghanaian daily newspapers and weeklies. The Kiswahili programs were advertised in Kiswahili in a magazine that was published by the External Service unit: *Radio Ghana Calling*[4]. The contents of the Kiswahili programs as shown in the magazine included:

Habari za Leo na Mazungumzo ya Habari	'Today's News and Discussion on the news'[5]
Ghana Leo	'Ghana Today'
Muziki kutoka Kusini	'Music from the South'
Majibu ya Maswali kutoka Wasikilizaji	'Questions and Answers from Listeners'
Chaguo Lenu	'Your Choice'
Maendeleo Nchini Ghana	'Development in Ghana'
Muziki Wenu	'Our Music'
Wagombea Uhuru	'Freedom Fighters'
Maisha ya Wanawake Kiafrika	'lives of African Women'
Chaguo cha Mabibi	'Ladies' Choice'
Mambo mbali mbali ya Afrika	'African Issues'
Matokeo ya wiki	'Events of the Week'
Afrika Leo	'Africa Today'

To enhance the output of the External Service, a correspondent was stationed in Dar es Salaam to bring news from East Africa: Uganda, Tanzania, and Kenya. The broadcasting team included both Ghanaians and non-Ghanaians to meet the needs of the language areas. Some of the Ghanaian Kiswahili broadcasters were Sam Owu (*Radio Ghana Calling* June 1964: 15), E. Y. Kumi (*Radio Ghana Calling*, January 1967: 23), and Theresa Dogbe. Tanzanian broadcasters included Anna Msuya, Joe A. Mwetta (*Radio Ghana Calling* March, 1968:23), Rose Krescheiner (*Radio Ghana Calling* November, 1968:23) and Edith Tetteh (*Radio Ghana Calling* July, 1969:19)[6]. The *40 Years of Broadcasting* brochure of 1975, reports that there were some efforts at

---

[4] A copy of a page advertising the programme line up of the Kiswahili Service in a magazine Radio Ghana Calling has been attached as an appendix.

[5] Authors Translation.

[6] Edith Tetteh was married to a Ghanaian.

"Ghanaianization" of the External Service Unit. That is, there was an effort to recruit Ghanaians who were proficient in Kiswahili. This move, it seems, was motivated by the need to cut costs in order to save the External Service Unit. Needless to say, the Kiswahili Service was closed down[7] some time n in the late 1970s. The research for this contribution was unable to establish the actual year and date of the program's demise.

Ghana Institute of Languages

By an Executive Instrument (Bill) number 114 of 1963 the Ghana Institute of Languages (GIL) was established on September 3, 1963. The objectives for its establishment were to 'provide courses for instruction in non-Ghanaian African languages, foreign languages for Foreign Service personnel, and civil servants needed to advise the government and other public authorities in matters of national interest that were associated with the source countries of the selected languages. The institute was the first of its kind in Africa (Executive Instrument 114 1963:1).

This institution was close to President Nkrumah's heart for as mentioned earlier. It was directly under the auspices of the office of the President. Per the Executive Instrument, the Principal of the Institute was to be appointed by the President. After the overthrow of President Nkrumah in 1965, the Institute found a home under different units, first the Ministry of Education, then the Ministry of

---

[7] The study could not establish the exact date due to the unavailability of official documentation at the GBC as a result of a fire which gutted the Corporation burning its archives completely. It was also not possible to solicit information on this from any of the former staff of the Kiswahili Service because unavailability (either deceased or could not be located).

Foreign Affairs and back to the Ministry of Education where it has remained since.

The institute was made up of three Schools; School of Bilingual Secretary, School of Translation, and School of Languages. These three schools remain functional to-date.

According to Mr Christopher K. Angkosaala, head of Research Department and former Acting Director of the Institute, the Institute was established at a time when many citizens of neighbouring African States took refuge in Ghana as their home countries struggled for independence. The Ghana government provided education scholarships for some to study in Ghana and refugee status to political refugees.

Kiswahili was one of the founding languages of the Institute. In addition to learning the language, the Kiswahili students took classes in translation with focus on French - Kiswahili or Kiswahili - English. According to Mr Angkosaala, the Kiswahili Program thrived for over twenty years. Then the student numbers started to dwindle as more African states attained their independence. Many of the students and the political refugees began to return to their home countries. By mid 1980s, the shortage of instructors coupled with student attrition and logistical problems, the Kiswahili program was terminated. This was unfortunate considering that Kiswahili, as well as Hausa, were the only authentic African languages at the institute and they were the first to be terminated. Today the Institute offers courses in eight languages, including Chinese, German and Portuguese. Based on information on the Institute's Website, the current Director of the Institute is considering reintroducing both Kiswahili and Hausa in the near future.

University of Ghana, Legon

The University of Ghana was the third Ghanaian institution to be associated with Kiswahili in Ghana. It was during the 1963/1964 academic year that plans were advanced to expand the then Department of French Studies to include the teaching and learning of

Arabic, Russian, Spanish, German, Portuguese and Kiswahili. To support Kiswahili, contacts were made with the University of Dar es Salaam language department to establish alliances that would allow exchanges of information, teaching and research ideas, students and teachers (Annual Report 1963/1964: 17).

The Balme Library, University of Ghana, Legon

The University of Ghana appointed a committee to work on the expansion of the Department of French Studies to account for other modern languages, hence the Department of Modern Languages that was headed by Professor Rebecca Posner (ibid: 18).   Dr. W. O. Animfen, who served as one of the sources for the data used in this contribution, noted that the committee's decision to include Kiswahili as one of the languages to be taught in the new Department was likely to have been inspired by the desire to promote Nkrumah's Pan-Africanist ideologies. The establishment of the Kiswahili broadcasting at the GBC and the teaching of Kiswahili at GIL a few months earlier were also instrumental in the final decision to include Kiswahili in the overall University curriculum.   The Department was established in

October 1964. Between 964-1966 academic years, the Department offered Kiswahili at the general degree and subsidiary levels (similar to a Minor in the USA system). The teaching staff at the time was two part-time Kiswahili tutors, Dr G. S. P. Freeman-Grenville who was sponsored by the British Government through a bilateral agreement with Ghana and Mr Sam Owu, a Ghanaian who was also a Kiswahili newscaster at the GBC External Service, (Amidu 1996: 92). From the onset, staffing for the Kiswahili Section was a challenge because the Section did not have full-time teaching staff during the first few years of its establishment (i.e. 1964-1969). During the 1969/1970, the Section finally had two full time tutors, Mary Wagstaffe and Mr Sheik Kassim Hafidh, both from London. During this same year, there was one part-time tutor, B. A. Rashid from Dar es Salaam. The external examiner for that year was W. H. Whiteley from the School of Orienatal and African Studies, University of London (Annual Reporter1969/1970: 90). In 1972, the then Head of the Kiswahili Department at the University of Dar-es Salaam, Mr Maganga paid a two week visit to the Kiswahili Section (Annual Report 1972: 66). During the 1972/1973 academic year, T. B. M. Bugingo from the University of Dar-es Salaam was appointed under the UG's agreement with UDS to head the Section. Dr. Joan Maw of the School of Oriental and African Studies, University of London was the external examiner for that year.

In 1978, Mrs Hamida Harrison, a Tanzanian now retired and on part-time, joined the Section as a tutor. Over the years, scholars such as Professor Maganga and Professor Rubanza from the University of Dar es Salaam served as External Examiners for the Kiswahili Section. Until 1972, the UG relied mostly on the British government to provide the needed Kiswahili lecturers and external examiners most of whom came from the School of Oriental and African Studies, University of London.

In the 1980s and 1990s the Kiswahili Section saw an expansion in staff recruitment when four Ghanaians were hired as Lecturers. Currently the Section is composed of two-full time Ghanaians, a Senior Lecturer/Coordinator and an Assistant Lecturer and three part-time lecturers (one Ghanaian, one Tanzanian and one Kenyan) arrived shortly after. This trend clearly shows the resource based challenges that have besieged the Kiswahili Section in the Department of Modern Languages. These challenges did not dampen the enthusiasm of the parties concerned to see that Kiswahili was sustainable. In the current Undergraduate Handbook of the University, one can find at least 37 courses covering various areas of studies in Kiswahili language, literature, history and culture. The Department established a Combined Major program intended to expand the scope of the curriculum. To ensure a high level language proficiency for Kiswahili students, a selected group of students in their third year of studies are regularly sent to the University of Dar es Salaam for a one year study abroad program. The One Year Abroad Program was instituted in the mid-1960s and has been sustained to-date. Based on institutional agreements, students have been to Kenya, Zanzibar, and mainland Tanzania. Currently, students are sent to the University of Dar es Salaam only.

The Kiswahili Section of the Department of Modern Languages at UG has produced renowned Kiswahili scholars such as Professor Assibi A. Amidu of the University of Trondheim and the late Dr. Jonathan K. Mensah. For the 49 years that Kiswahili has been taught at the University of Ghana it was only during the 1967/1968 academic year that students were not admitted due to lack of teaching staff (Amidu 1996).

The SOS-Hermann Gmeiner International College, Ghana

In 1990, the charitable and non-profit SOS Kinderdorf International Organisation founded the SOS-Hermann Gmeiner International College in Ghana to offer academic programs that were designed to develop African students' sense of social responsibility and commitment to Africa's development. There was an opening for Kiswahili Studies and in 1995 a Kiswahili Program was initiated. The primary purpose for introducing the language was to give students from Eastern and Central Africa an opportunity to learn the language well enough to build their proficiency to native speaker level. This was intended to benefit the efforts already in the works, to create a strong lingua franca in Eastern and Central Africa. In addition the school wanted to highlight its Pan Africanism philosophy. The other languages offered by the school included French, Amharic and Spanish.

What the Department of Modern Languages at the UG, Legon is proud of is the fact that most of the Kiswahili teachers are UG graduates and are therefore a product of the Kiswahili Section. The Unit has also trained students from other parts of Africa including Kenyan, Zambia, Tanzania, Malawi, Lesotho, Zimbabwe and Uganda. In its prime years, the program had very few students, to start with only four. The numbers grew over the years to a total of forty five students in 2013 at various proficiency levels. According to Mr Shadrack Mensah who currently oversees the activities of the Kiswahili Program, there has been a very strong enthusiasm from the students enrolled or seeking out courses in Kiswahili. Their interest in the language comes from the fact that they can transfer knowledge gained to other courses in their program of study. The high enrolment numbers has encouraged the administration to keep Kiswahili in the College curriculum. This enthusiasm has also been met by a new initiative at the College that offers students a study abroad opportunity to spend about three weeks in Zanzibar.

Cumulatively, it is clear that Ghana has played a critical role in the promotion of Kiswahili over the years. It has shown dedication in both the teaching and learning of the language and in international broadcasting using the language. Although the External Service unit and the GiL were unable to sustain their commitment to promoting the language, the University of Ghana has held its end of the bargain steadfast. Furthermore the Kiswahili program at SOS Herman Gmeiner College continues to grow in strength and student interest.

Challenges Confronting the Consolidation of Kiswahili in Ghana and Beyond

As noted earlier, the University of Ghana has taken great interest in the Kiswahili program. This is important because it explains UG's long-term sustainability and commitment to the study of Kiswahili over the years. This was not the case for the Ghana Institute of Languages' (GIL) Kiswahili program that was available for over twenty years before it was forced to close down due to financial hardships. This happened despite their tremendous efforts to salvage the program. In part this had to happen because it did not start on good footing as it was faced with a series of problems since its inception. The problems were compounded as a result of the coup that deposed President Nkrumah. This caused the program to be moved from the President's office to the Ministry of Education, then the Ministry of Information and eventually back to the Ministry of Education. Obviously by de-coupling it from its original base it created an instability that was not healthy for growth and or development and eventually its demise. Furthermore, the institute was dogged by low student enrolments, scarcity of lecturers and other logistical problems that made it impossible to sustain the Kiswahili Program.

To explain the survival of the other languages of the GIL over the years, one has to look at the level of support the Institute receives from the home governments of these languages. Needless to say, the Kiswahili Programme at the UG has survived to-date despite the myriads of problems such as human resource and high attrition rates of students and a lack of equipment and tools for effective language teaching and learning. The Kiswahili Section has been branded the least endowed and therefore the endangered Section of the Department of Modern Languages in every sense of the word despite the fact that it usually has more students than the Arabic Section. One would have liked to see it endowed with more human resources. A recent attempt to get the Masters Programme approved by the University authorities failed because the proposal coincided with the resignation of one of the two Ph.D. scholars in the section. Interestingly, the other non-African languages sections receive substantial technical, human resource and financial support from the governments of their host countries (e.g. France, China, and Spain) through their various embassies in Ghana. The Kiswahili section does not enjoy any such support. Recently, though, the Kenya Airways initiated some financial support for the Kiswahili Students Club activities.

Over the years, the University of Dar es Salaam (UDS) has supported the Kiswahili section by hosting its Year Abroad Programme, but students have to bear the full cost. Consequently, the sustainability of the program is threatened by the high costs that the students have to incur to study at UDS. Other problems include the reduction in scholarship support from the Ghana Government and occasional delays in releasing funds for the program. A glimmer of hope that is associated with the posting of an Ambassador to Kenya from Ghana does not assure us either of the future ability by the government to sustain scholarships for the Year Abroad Program.

However, these challenges have not affected the enthusiasm found in students and the teachers associated with the program. This is attested by student enrolments over the years. Considering that in the first two decades of the program, student numbers at any given time were in the single digits, the gradual health of the Section is remarkable. Improvements are evident in the 1980s and 1990s with an average of 50 to 100 students and a present day sustained average of 190 students each year. The breakdown of the averages is as follows: first year (155); second year (24); third year (17); and final year (10).

As the break down shows, there is a very high rate of attrition right after the first year. This is a consequence of the luck of financial support for students in the program especially sponsorship for the year abroad language proficiency program. There is also a need for a language laboratory. Authorization for the construction of two large language laboratories for the Department of Modern languages has yet to be finalized. The expectation is that when the laboratories are completed, local immersion programs, which have already been approved by the University Council, would enhance the needs of the students who are unable to go for the proficiency strengthening year abroad program. Reduction or wavers of tuition by Year Abroad Program host institution would strengthen the sponsorship to allow more students to participate in the program each year.

Concerning the human resource challenges, the Kiswahili Section has resolved that the only way to ensure full capacity is to train its own faculty through staff development programs. To be able to achieve this there is need for external institutions to support the training of more Ph.D. And M.Phil. Students who would staff the Section upon completion of their training. This would be in addition to the requisite home unit to roll out its own graduate program for future staff development and sustainability of the Section. We are encouraged by the current initiative from the International Programmes office at UG which has offered to sponsor one teaching assistant to pursue graduate courses in Kiswahili through staff development. Furthermore, given the needed support for staff development, the University of Ghana could reposition itself to train prospective teachers to support the teaching and learning of Kiswahili in the West African sub region.

The Promotion of Kiswahili and its Prospects for African Unity

The quests for Pan-Africanism and African unity were punctuated by a call from famous African scholars and personalities for the adoption of a common language, Kiswahili for Africa. A common language was therefore deemed an important factor in the promotion of Pan Africanism. Chimera (2000) and Chebet-Choge (2012) report that Nkrumah and Wole Soyinka were prominent non East African scholars and patriots who advocated for the adoption of Kiswahili as a continental language for the whole of Africa. As the pro-term Secretary-General of the then newly formed Union of African writers, part of Soyinka's vision was to make Kiswahili a continental lingua franca. Furthermore Soyinka encouraged all African writers to work towards the translation of their works into this continental lingua franca (Jeyifo: 2004: xiii; Chebet-Choge: 2012). Soyinka spoke at the 1977 FESTAC about the need for African governments to adopt Kiswahili and made an appeal for a firm commitment to Kiswahili as the continental language (Gibbs 1980: 6).

The late President Julius Nyerere of Tanzania, Ayi Kwei Armah an African writer, and Professor Ali Mazrui, a renowned Pan-Africanist, are among the staunch supporters and advocates for the adoption of Kiswahili as a continental lingua Franca (Chimera 2000; Mulokozi 2002; Katembo 2008: 112). However, there has not been a strong movement from African countries in support of this proposal. The lack of interest is not only from African leaders but also from the African people. They were and continue to be mainly concerned about the cost of such an undertaking and the efforts needed to create a continental lingua franca.

Faced with these challenges the novel idea of a continental lingua franca seems to fizzle out of the struggle for African Unity. Various scholars and supporters of Pan-Africanism have in the past avoided the subject of an African linguistic unity as part of the quest for Pan-Africanism. What scholars have kept up through scholarly papers on Pan-Africanism and African Unity is interrogating the challenges that prevent Africa from achieving its goals of Pan-Africanism. Adogamhe (2008:17-26) for instance, discusses issues such as security, political and economic challenges that face the quest for African unity. However he fails to acknowledge the linguistic unity challenges. Scholars have failed to acknowledge what Nkrumah, the father of Pan-Africanism, saw in advocating for an African linguistic unity and that his vision had everything to do with finding the pertinent tools for the promotion of African Unity. President Nyerere of Tanzania used the unity factor as a foundation to enforce Kiswahili as common language for Tanzania. His success was instrumental in pulling in all the East African countries to consider linguistic unity as critical in the development of the African people.

There are various reasons why the African Union (AU) should work on getting the entire continent to work towards adopting a common language for the continent and to consider Kiswahili as the

190

likely lingua franca for this movement. There is no doubt that, a common language (linguistic unity) can be the means to an end in the quest for African unity in the areas of political, economic and geographical integration. The task is monumental but it is insurmountable. Cebet-Choge (2012) notes that the promotion of Kiswahili to cover the rest of Africa as a Regional Lingua Franca is achievable if all the leaders of African countries are willing enough to consider the proposal. It is disconcerting to think that while Europe, Asia, and America are showing tremendous interest in Kiswahili, African states do not seem to take any interest at all or are lukewarm in their vision for its success as a lingua franca of Africa. African leaders are contented with the use of the language of their former colonial masters (English, French, and Portuguese) rather than to develop linguistic unity across the continent using an African language. The lack of a Nyerere or an Nkrumah in the political scene in Africa has rendered the leaders of the Kiswahili speaking countries ineffective in advocating for Kiswahili as a continental language. These countries (primarily Tanzania, Kenya Uganda) have not set the example that would encourage other African countries to consider limited use of colonial languages (Moshi 2006). There is limited hope from the momentum seen in Ghana, Nigeria and Libya. These are African States that have shown some commitment to the promotion of Kiswahili. There has also been some movement in the south with the commencing of Kiswahili studies at the University of KwaZulu Natal in South Africa. The publicity that followed this inception is good for the purposes of encouraging other states to also take the lead.

An increased effort to support and encourage the expansion of the teaching and learning of Kiswahili in Ghana and indeed the rest of Africa can elevate Kiswahili to a position where all Africans can take pride in an African language assuming the unity forging role. It is, without doubt, the responsibility of the East African countries with the backing of the African Unity (AU), to take the lead and embark on a massive campaign to promote Kiswahili in the rest of Africa. Obvious, proponents of English did likewise to ensure English is a global language. We now see other languages looking for ways to secure a firm position on the global map too. China and France have stepped up their efforts in advocating for their languages globally. Granted, these are countries and not continents, the African continent is stronger as a larger body of advocates. . Because African countries have remained rather ambiguous with respect to an African lingua franca, even in their own states, a unifying language for the entire continent is by far more attractive when competing with the established languages like English, French, Arabic, and more recently, Chinese. The University of Ghana can be a useful platform in the promotion of Kiswahili in Ghana and the West African sub region. However, it cannot do it alone without, the needed support of all stakeholders. Funding will be critical to support the expansion of the existing Kiswahili Program at UG while efforts are made to revive and reintroduce Kiswahili in the institutions that pioneered it but were forced to close down because of financial hardships. With the available technological advancements, the promotion of Kiswahili through online instruction at different institutions of higher learning and even as early as primary and secondary schools across the continent is indeed insurmountable.

Conclusion

In conclusion, it is important to reiterate that although the promotion of Kiswahili in Ghana has been attributed to Nkrumah's quest for a united Africa, considerable efforts have been made by the country to sustain Kiswahili in Ghana long after the days of Nkrumah. The University of Ghana and the Government of Ghana have demonstrated commitment to the promotion of Kiswahili scholarship through the sustenance of the Kiswahili program and the offer of scholarships for Ghanaians who study Kiswahili. Both the late Presidents Kwame Nkrumah (Ghana) and Julius Nyerere (Tanzania) had a vision that translated to their advocacy for a united Africa. There is need to sustain these efforts already in place and to build on the successes shown by the East African countries, and the small steps made by Ghana, Nigeria, Libya, and South Africa. The University of Ghana and the Government of Ghana have demonstrated commitment to the promotion of Kiswahili scholarship by making the Kiswahili program at UG sustainable through teaching and scholarships for Ghanaians who study Kiswahili. Ghana's significant role in the promotion of Kiswahili over the past half century through its institutions (GBC, GIL, UG, and SOS College) is highly commendable.

Teaming up with Ghana, East Africa and indeed all who advocate for linguistic unity in Africa will enhance the potential for a successful promotion of Kiswahili on the continent of Africa and the Diaspora. This would also be in keeping with Nkrumah's quest for Pan-Africanism and African unity. This step if taken, in spite of obvious challenges, will go a long way to promote the economic and political unity that Africa seeks and deserves.

CHAPTER 9

Epiloque

Introduction

In the preceding Chapters we discussed the history, development, state, and status of the Kiswahili including the different roles its indigenous and non- native speakers have played in both developing and spreading it beyond the likely borders. We are cognizant of the fact that there are still a number of issues involving Kiswahili that still need exploration but for now we feel this suffices the objectives of this book as a reader for our students. In this chapter we want to focus on some issues that point to the need to continue redefining, strengthening, and expanding on the functions of the Kiswahili both locally and globally.

In discussing the origin and nature of Kiswahili, we define the Swahili States based on the definition of indigenous Swahili speakers. While this definition is true to its limitations, it is clear that we have reached a point where it could be extended to cover more ground. The growth of Kiswahili beyond the borders of the Coastal States provides a compelling case for extending the definition to cover other areas where Kiswahili functions are being realized in an extensive way. In other words, the definition should include States or places where Kiswahili speakers have enabled the functions of the language have reached a competitive status with those of English. These areas include where the language is spoken extensively, there are signs that it is taken seriously to the extent that it has been included in the curriculum at various schools and or institutions of higher learning, it has become one of the languages exploited in trade activities, cultural exchanges, and other aspects of globalization. This broad and rather generalized definition allows us to focus on a variety of issues concerning Kiswahili both at the continental and international levels.

We will focus on what is current in the efforts to develop and expand the use of Kiswahili language and culture, highlight progress made and the challenges facing these endeavors. We look at progress made through the eyes of different social and political players endowed with the power to make things happen as well as possessing the needed mechanisms which manifest themselves as organizations, institutions, commissions, councils or even committees for specific issues. We will also look at trends Kiswahili publications

Strengthening Kiswahili in Africa

In the last decade, a number of measures have been taken to facilitate the role of Kiswahili in the social, educational, political, and economic development in east Africa. As previously discussed, conversations regarding the importance of Kiswahili in Tanzania, Kenya and Uganda have been mostly for educational purposes. We now turn our attention to other aspects of Kiswahili.

To ensure that Kiswahili assumes a more prominent role in local politics, international affairs, economic activities, socio-cultural linkages, and educational, scientific and technological interactions that are necessary for development in East Africa, the three East African countries agreed to create a Kiswahili Council. According to the East African Community Education Portal (2013), this council was created in 1930 as a joint cooperation between The Republic of Kenya, The United Republic of Tanzania and the Republic of Uganda. An inter-territorial Language Committee whose members rotated seats (1930-1964) was formed to promote the standardization and development of Kiswahili. The rotation seats started with Dar es Salaam (1930-1942) followed by Nairobi (1942-1952) then Makerere (1952- 1961) and closed by returning to Dar es Salaam (1962-64). The expectations were very high and in time it became clear that the task for this council was too ambitious to manage. The decision that followed was to incorporate the council as a part of the University College of Dar es Salaam under the Institute of Kiswahili Research in 1964. This arrangement did not last long as it collapsed when East

African Community was dissolved in 1977. Needless to say, the designated language bodies continued to interact informally and then re-establish another avenue for formal alliances.

In 1999 the East African Community was reinstated and a treaty, Article 137 was signed. At the center of the agreement were the inclusion matters of cultural and linguistic fields, and the provision for Kiswahili to become the Community's lingua franca. In the same year, the corporate body, East African Kiswahili Council was born. The council had as its vision to promote and coordinate the use of Kiswahili for regional unity and to create sustainable socio-economic aggregates among the three partner states. Specifically, among other objectives, the council sought to: (1) promote Kiswahili by encouraging its use nationally, regionally and internationally; (2) spread Kiswahili through usage to convey African values such as gender parity; (3) support and encourage research in Kiswahili by developing advanced Kiswahili study centers; (4) offer aid to partner states to educate and produce Kiswahili communicators and teachers in all areas of society; (5) equip citizens with the Kiswahili literary and linguistic skills through curriculum reform; (6) stay abreast in international developments associated with Kiswahili; (7) encourage staff and student exchanges among Kiswahili institutions; (8) monitor the growth of Kiswahili in information technology; (9) examine where communication and technological use of Kiswahili is needed; (10) and to organize translations to and from Kiswahili. Though the goals and objectives of this council were established a while back, preparations to execute them were not put together until June 2008. This was necessary to allow applications to be made by partner states to host the commission. Despite the fact that such preparations were made, the process is still pending and there is cautious optimism that the 2008 objectives will soon be met. Activities within the East African countries seem to suggest that individually each country is taking some measures to support Kiswahili.

Despite the fact that much is being done to advance Kiswahili in Tanzania, there seems to be a disconnection between the way the academia supports Kiswahili and the public's view of how to socially utilize it in the public arena. To begin with, the *Baraza la Kiswahili la Taifa* (BAKITA) (formed 1967), indicated the desire for the country to promote Kiswahili as a critical and useful tool that unites and elevates African traditions, values and promotes national identity while at the same time making the Kiswahili speakers viable and willing participators in the task of building a national economy. These measures were taken very seriously by the Tanzanian Parliament as indicated in the *"Sheria ya Bunge Na. 27 ya mwaka 1967"*. It was record to facilitate all aspects of developing Kiswahili in the Tanzanian society. To ensure that this objective was met, BAKITA organized several activities within the country including educating the public on various aspects of Kiswahili through the media such as radio programs *"Lugha ya Taifa"* aired on Saturdays from 6:30 to 7 pm and *"Kumepambazuka"* from 1:30 to 3 early in the morning; television program-*"Ulimwengu wa Kiswahili"* aired on Tuesday from 1:30 to 2pm and Thursday: 11 to 11:30am. Continuing to-date, BAKITA gives advice to Kiswahili students and scholars writing about the language; nurtures emerging Kiswahili authors; facilitates the distribution of Kiswahili published materials; organizes services for Kiswahili translators; and examines the production of Kiswahili textbooks at all education levels within the country.

Furthermore, Tanzania started *"Siku ya Kiswahili,"* which is a Swahili day of celebration. This initiative has been in place since 1995 and its purpose is to unite Swahili scholars, learners and writers. Additionally, the event served as a reminder to the government of its critical role in developing Kiswahili. This event was also designed to be carried out across the nation but since its inauguration in1998, it has largely remained in Dar-es Salaam. This is evident on the BAKITA website which shows that the venue for the *Siku ya Kiswahili* 'Kiswahili day' between 1995 and 2007 has been Dar-es Salaam and no records are shown for any other venue on the Tanzania mainland except one time in Dodoma. Since 1998, Zanzibar (Tanzania Island) has held its own separate celebration, the latest being April 13th of

2013. In addition to BAKITA, several other Kiswahili promotion organizations have been formed in Tanzania (mainland). These include: *Taasisi ya Taaluma za Kiswahili* (TATAKI)- the university of Dar-es Salaam; *Chama cha Usanifu wa Kiswahili na Ushairi Tanzania* (UKUTA); and *Umoja wa Waandishi wa Vitabu Tanzania* (UWAVITA). Similar efforts have been launched in Zanzibar (Tanzania Island) through the *Baraza la Kiswahili la Zanzibar* (BAKIZA) and *Taasisi ya Kiswahili na Lugha za Kigeni ya Zanzibar* (TAKILUKI).

Kenya has also taken considerable steps to strengthen Kiswahili (Otieno, 2011). The Academy for African Languages (ACALAN) praised Kenya for elevating Kiswahili to an official language and for incorporating it in its Constitution and avail funds to support its development. According to the Star newspaper in Kenya, Grace Kerongo (2013) reported on a recent Kiswahili symposium, organized by Kiswahili Cross Border Language Commission of the Kenya chapter. It was held in Arusha, Tanzania from May 28 to June 1, 2013 to explore the way in which Kiswahili can be used for regional integration through the East Africa Community. Part of the symposium's aim was to re-energize the spirit of African unity in the region. The Research Institute of Kiswahili Studies of Eastern Africa, a research directorate within the National Museums of Kenya, established a Kiswahili International Conference since 2011 (The International Linguistics Community). Their second conference in 2012 was held in Mombasa where participants explored ways to develop Kiswahili in the same manner as other world languages. They examined possibilities for Kiswahili to play a role in phenomenological realities which include globalization, environmental concerns, interstate relations, ever changing education systems, and the need to facilitate African unity. Such events echo the earlier vision of the East African Kiswahili Commission whose establishment is still pending.

In addition, other East African countries such as Rwanda and Burundi are taking the lead in encouraging its citizens to use Kiswahili. For example, the News of Rwanda (March 2012) highlighted measures taken by the East African Community (EAC) to emphasize the use of Kiswahili in its community. Gahiji (2012) notes that one of the EAC members reported on a detailed plan of teaching Kiswahili to non-speakers within the region. The plan put the EAC department of culture in-charge of overseeing this initiative and Burundi is expected to host its center. Up until 2010, the language used as a medium of instruction in Rwanda was English and students pursuing a career in journalism in Rwanda were the only ones provided with modules for learning Kiswahili. For the most part, Rwandans who are able to speak or write in Kiswahili have been those in or have resided in Tanzania, Kenya or the Democratic Republic of Congo.

Among the measures to help facilitate the growth of Kiswahili speakers especially in East Africa, beyond Tanzania and Kenya, CHAWAKAMA (*Chama cha Wanafunzi wa Kiswahili Afrika Mashariki*-an organization of Swahili students in East Africa) was formed. CHAWAKAMA was founded in 2004 in Arusha by Swahili lecturers and students to facilitate communication and economic exchanges within East Africa. Their first conference took place in Kigali- Rwanda because, as the organization's secretary noted, "Rwanda, Uganda and Burundi, are countries where Kiswahili is not as much used as in Kenya and Tanzania" (The Rwanda Focus, November, 2008). In addition, measures taken by the Kigali Institute of Education to conceive methodologies of learning Kiswahili and apply them nationwide became part of the organizational structure of the CHAWAKIRWA (*Chama cha Wanafunzi wa Kiswahili Rwanda*- an organization of Swahili Students in Rwanda), Rwandan Chapter. More specifically, the Rwanda Chapter and the Burundi Chapter (CHAWAKIBU) decided to host a Kiswahili conferences starting with one in 2008 with the intention of drawing ideas from Kiswahili experts in Tanzania and Kenya. Other measures included buying and distributing Kiswahili textbooks, enriching the curriculum, and teacher training to offer Kiswahili as a language/subject in more than 200 schools in Rwanda (Mbonyinshuti, 2013).

Before we move to the international arena, it is prudent to briefly comment on Tanzania the designated champion of Kiswahili development and promotion. Observations show that efforts to strengthen Kiswahili around the country have also met with counter efforts whose intentions are to strengthen English in the public arena. Some Tanzanians believe these efforts undermine the use of Kiswahili. There is no question that there is a strong affinity to English across the country. This poses interesting questions considering Mwalimu Nyerere's (1st President of the Republic of Tanzania) efforts since independence to promote Kiswahili with the intention of minimizing Tanzanians' affinity to English. Die hard proponents of Kiswahili wonder what fifty years of independence (celebrated nationally in 2011) bought Tanzania if Kiswahili is still in second place to English which continues to win its visibility in the public arena. One need not go far to see the evidence as we observe new road-signs being put up to replace some that were changed to Kiswahili after independence. Most billboard advertisements for bus transportation and telephone companies on the highways are in English, names of shops, hotels, and restaurants are also in English. The interesting part is that this phenomenon is not just in big cities, it is in small towns and villages where most of the people do not speak English. A new barber shop, beauty salon, or beer parlor in the village is more likely to be named in English rather than in Kiswahili. In big cities such as Dar es Salaam, Dodoma, Mwanza, and Arusha, English-medium schools as well as English church services have become the new norm. Children hardly watch Swahili television shows but rather prefer the English shows and cartoons. Because most of Tanzania Swahili radio programs do not attract a big audience from the general public, broadcasters and producers include portions of English to be more attractive. There seems to be a slew of competing agendas between the public and the channels that know better and should be in the frontline in advocating for the development and appreciation of Kiswahili.

Strengthening Kiswahili in the Diaspora- Organizations and other Initiatives

The focus in this section is the efforts made outside the Coastal States to promote and develop Kiswahili. We are aware that Kiswahili is taught in some parts of Africa other than Eastern Africa such as Ghana as discussed in Chapter Eight. Outside of Africa, the big players include Europe, Asia, some Middle Eastern countries and the United States. We will, however, focus on the efforts made in the United States where other African languages have thrived too. For the most part we will concentrate on the motivation that led to the institutionalization of African language in the United States and how the interest has been sustained over the years. Kiswahili has been the major beneficiary of these efforts which explains why it is the most popular African language and a language of choice by both institutions and individual students who are interested in African languages.

Programs of African Languages (PAL) in the United States were formally established in the late 1950s as an integral and crucial component of the national Defense Act (NDEA) of 1958 that created African and other Area Studies centers (Dougherty 1993, Ruther 1994, Swenson 1999). At that time, the administration of African languages was placed under the leadership of Africanist scholars in linguistics, language pedagogists, and literature specialists. Although that has largely remained so, home departments have varied from institution to institution, ranging from Linguistics, African Studies, Literature, and African American Studies/Black Studies. For the most part, the languages have done relatively well in units like linguistics, African Literature, and Black Studies. Of the most popular African languages tough in the United States, Kiswahili tops he charts, featured in more than 100 institutions, both government and private. Kiswahili is also number one in the commonly taught African languages in the United States and without doubt around the world (Europe, West and South Africa, and Asia).

But who sponsors the teaching of African languages, and by default, Kiswahili? The main advocates are African Studies Centers and Institutes across the United States. However, the home units for the languages are usually Linguistics, Africa Literature and Black Studies Departments. It is in such units where one can find between 100 and 300 students learning Kiswahili in a given academic year. Most institutions offer Kiswahili up to four years, producing fairly proficient individuals who are ready to participate in research and other activities in a predominantly Kiswahili speaking area.

It will be remiss of us not to mention the force behind the sustainability of African languages in the United States with Kiswahili being the largest recipient of the sought out language by new learners of African languages. The 1987 edition of the directory of African and African-American Studies in the United States (Rana & Destefano 1987) 389 colleges and Universities in 44 States (including Puerto Rico) had flourishing African languages programs. At least 110 courses that comprised African Studies and African languages were taught at these institutions. An estimated 49 different languages were offered, the most frequently taught being Swahili (52) Arabic (24), Hausa (15), Yoruba (9), Amharic (6), Zulu (6), Bambara/Manding (5), Krio (5), Shona (5), and Afrikaans (3) and Igbo (3). When the directory was updated in 1993 an increase in the number of institutions teaching African languages had grown to 55 colleges and universities. However, the variety of languages had diminished. The most popular languages in the 55 institutions and colleges included: Swahili, Arabic, Yoruba, Hausa, Amharic, and Zulu. Swahili and Arabic have picked up more institutions (100), Arabic (55), while Yoruba (15) and Amharic (10) follow closely.

No one person or association can do it alone even though the task of persuading institutions on the need to institutionalize African languages is daunting. It was the status of African languages teaching and research in the United States that prompted scholars to organize and establish both the African Conference on African Linguistics (ACAL) and the African Languages Teachers Association (ALTA). In

203

the process of formulating the arguments for these associations, scholars were cognizant of the fact that the driving force that laid the general foundation for campus-based language and area studies programs of which African languages were beneficiaries (Lambert 1973, 1984, Thompson 11980, Clements 1989) was the need to provide graduate students expanded opportunities to study and conduct research in Africa after WWII. In the case of Africa, it led to the founding of the first programs of African Studies: Northwestern University (Evanston, Illinois 1948), Boston University (Boston, Massachusetts, 1953), Howard University (Washington DC 1954), Columbia University (New York City, NY 1958), and UCLS (LA, CA 1954). Early data show African Studies MA and PHD degrees as early as 1930s (Sims & Kagan 1976, Stutzman 1989, Clements 1989). Clements show that in 1933 and 1955 there were doctoral students who completed African language related theses at four different institutions: Chicago, Columbia, Pennsylvania, and Hartford. It is the wisdom of many of these scholars that benefited the field of African languages. The outcome of their efforts was the emergence of the African Language Teachers' Association (ALTA).

The birth of ALTA in 1988 (cf. Bokamba 2002) was necessary to highlight the realization that the teaching and learning of African language was being marginalized at the national level. The founding members were mainly from institutions with established African Studies Centers that were also funded by the US Department of Education through Title VI grants. Such Centers are to be credited for the arrival of many scholars from Africa with scholarships to study for their higher degrees at these situations while they spearheaded the teaching of the critical African languages (mainly Kiswahili, Yoruba, Housa, Zulu, Amharic, Xhosa, Bamana, Manding, to name a few). The ALTA founding members organized and facilitated the creation of a forum where pedagogists and linguists could discuss ways to sustain the teaching and learning of African languages in the United States. The strength was guaranteed considering that many of the African language teachers and experts, the African students and other scholars who were recruited by African Studies Centers and programs were behind the efforts and focused on promoting the teaching and learning of African languages.

The need to form ALTA as a body that brought African language teachers together was strengthened by ACAL which was already flourishing and had many of the language teachers as members who were contributing through their contributions to scholarship on African linguistics as a necessary conduit for the recruitment of future African linguistics scholars through the language classes they were teaching.

ACAL was born in 1970 at the U. of Wisconsin. The orientation was both theoretical and applied linguistics. ACAL legitimized the teaching, research, and learning of African languages in the United States. The study of African languages and subsequently research on African languages made the study of linguistics both theoretical and applied more exciting. African languages tested the pre-conceived theories of universal grammar. Field research data brought new questions to the field of linguistics, interrogating pre-conceived assumptions that all languages are basically the same in their underlying structures and that one theoretical framework could adequately handle their analysis. The data forced linguists to abandon the interpretation of world languages through the structure of western languages, particularly English. One of the authors for this book recalled being told by one of her professors that the linguistic knowledge of her first language was based on intuition and that her claims that her language could handle structures that were impossible in European languages and some selected other world languages was inconceivable. She was told that a noun which described a location could not function as a regular noun which must pass certain linguistic analysis tests to claim certain functions in world languages. Incidentally, these tests in question belong to a set of pre-ordained tests for legitimate functions that a noun can perform in an utterance that represents how human beings communicate with each other. Moshi (1993, 1994, 1995, 2000), through a series of publications

205

attempted to prove that languages are often unique to their speakers and may behave differently to the extent of disproving the notion held about universal grammar. ACAL gave many African languages and linguistics scholars the voice and the forum to challenge these pre-conceived notions and theories. To date, ACAL has continued the tradition of interrogating linguistic theories that are largely formed base on Indo-European languages. They have also produced results that have literally forced linguists to reconsider assumptions that influenced theoretical conclusions about world languages based on pre-conceived language universals.

Another event that propelled African languages in the United States was the birth of the National Council for Less Commonly Taught Languages (NCOLCTLs). NCOLCTL was enabled by the National Foreign Languages Council (NFLC) created in 1987 at John Hopkins University School of Advanced International Studies (SAIS) Washington DC. NFLC was a product of the President's commission on foreign languages and International Studies. The principal objective of NFLC was to improve foreign language capacity of the United States. Note that the President's Commission for the establishment of the NFLC postdates the movement for the establishment of African languages and Black Studies on college campuses. However, it was necessary for such a body to be the lever that hoisted the African languages to allow their needed visibility. As noted earlier, no other African language has benefited more than Kiswahili. Thus, its strength cannot be evaluated devoid of these events.

The NFLC organized conferences between 1987 and 1990 focusing on the need for the US to be ready to engage the world. These conferences allowed NFLC to influence the various foreign language fields. Richard D. Lambert, the then director of NFLC, provided leadership, strategic guidance, financial and material support to all LCTLs. The conferences promoted dialogue among scholars from different fields with expected outcomes of finding collective solutions to common problems. There was also a need to develop a coherent group of scholars with one voice advocating for foreign languages. NCOLCTLs used these goals to mobilize practitioners/linguists from different language fields. The role of linguists in the various meeting held by NCOLCTLs was critical especially that of the Africanist linguists. Their participation was seen by NCOLCTL as an added advantage that would raise its visibility. In the final analysis, it was the African languages members that shaped the direction of these conferences, the agendas that directly affected the language fields, and what eventually emerged as the federation of language associations under the NCOLCTL umbrella. Needless to say the Association Board members includes two scholars from the Swahili language field. The first President of the Association was Professor Eyamba Bokamba from ALTA and a member of the Swahili field and one who comes from one of the member Swahili States (by extension), the Democratic Republic of the Congo.

ALTA was one of the earliest associations to embrace NCOLCTL and to designate tasks and activities intended to further NCOLCTL's endeavors. ALTA's enthusiasm and developed under this umbrella helped to shape the direction of NCOLTLs as a new found vehicle for global understanding. ALTA was also the first one to initiate discussions on the language learning framework through organized conferences and workshops for its members. ALTA's leadership and representation on the NCOLCTL Board was a major advantage because it was able to work on two different fronts, the ALTA membership agenda and the ALTA's interest in the activities of NCOLCTL. The team style representation of ALTA on the NCOLCTLs Board enhanced its membership's understanding to appreciate the issues ALTA had to address within the language framework concept with special attention to the African languages' field specific perspectives. Consequently ALTA's field initiatives were used by NCOLCTL as guidelines to a generic development model from which other associations could draw examples. ALTA benefited most in the areas were material development, best practices national visibility (Bokamba 2002), the development of a pool of professional language teachers, and an attempt to change the culture of transient instructor pools at college campuses. As national tool and through its forums, NCOLCTL was instrumental in empowering many individuals teaching African languages at different institutions where they seemed powerless to initiate changes at institutional level.

ALTA was one of the major groups that enthusiastically embraced the NCOLCTL goals and objectives. Such an enthusiasm served NCOLCTL very well by helping NCOLCTL to raise its visibility during its formative years. ALTA saw an opportunity and exploited it despite its concern about its place in the new national body that was intended to advocate for all less commonly taught languages. ALTA was cognizant of the fact that there are less commonly taught languages and there are the less of the less commonly taught languages. 99% of the African languages fell in the latter category since only Swahili and Yoruba really fitted the less commonly taught languages description when compared to other less commonly taught languages like Chinese, Japanese, Korean, Russian, Hebrew, and the Turkic languages. Thus ALTA's fear of the marginalization of the African languages was real, that the definition of less commonly taught languages would only take a few of the African languages and ignore others. Accordingly, the relationship between NCOLCTL and ALTA had very strong under currents that the ALTA leadership was able to control to ensure its mission was served despite its fears of marginalization. ALTA made a very smart move by ensuring that Africa was well represented and that the continent was not viewed as a country. There were a number of ALTA members with leadership positions at the Executive Board in the early years of NCOLCT. I am proud to say that those leaders help shape the final NICOLTIC that is thriving now. Projects for NCOLCTL that were funded by the Ford Foundation found examples for other language associations from ALTA through the well thought out selection of projects that had respectable outcomes. NCOLCTL used the success shown by ALTA to convince FORD Foundation that their money was going to good cause and results were produced were beneficial and met the

Foundation's expectations. ALTA's success can be explained by its strong leadership at that time as well as members' willingness to transform the field of African languages. ALTA developed language task forces based on the language specific interests of its membership. The task forces were charged with the responsibility of recruiting new members to ensure that each specific language or group of languages represented the interests of the field. It was at this time also that ALTA realized an increase in its membership and program strength through workshops on materials development, teaching methodologies, mentoring, and outreach to K-12 and community organizations.

Within a year of operation the task forces created unprecedented enthusiasm in the field. Scholars and language pedagogists started to communicate with each other discussing best practices in teaching and learning. The latter resulted in a newsletter "Teaching ideas and resources for African languages" compiled and published by Indiana University under the editorship of Robert Botne, one of our finest linguists and pedagogist. The newsletter offered the field an opportunity to share classroom experiences. The Swahili field was very aggressive in exploiting the opportunities to develop. The achievements included the production of teaching and learning manual such as *Mwalimu wa Kiswahili* "The Swahili Teacher" and other innovative materials that included videos and online comprehensive teaching and learning materials. *Mwalimu wa Kiswahili* (Moshi, Hauner, Innis, and Nanji 1999) that was originally published by Binghamton, NY: Global Publications, IGCS is still in production though NALRIC publications, Indiana University and remains a popular reference manual for teachers of Kiswahili. To keep the enthusiasm of the task forces, the field leadership organized group meetings at different conferences, workshops, and meetings of interest. The most effective conference was ALTA's annual international conference which was inaugurated in 1997.

ALTA is therefore the best thing that happened to the field of African languages in the 90s. It provided scholarly support to teachers in Title VI institutions as well as non-Title VI institutions which were largely ignored before the inception of ALTA. The training that was offered in workshops in the early days of ALTA benefited the new breed of language teaches and coordinators who were at the time graduate students in different institutions and most of whom are now either in a tenured/tenure track or instructor positions. Kiswahili has always been the biggest beneficiary of the success from the different initiatives and organizations that had African languages in mind. Such success is obvious in the rapid field development, revitalization of Kiswahili language programs, and the establishment of a critical mass in each of the main institutions that teach Kiswahili as a critical subject in the institutional curriculum rather than just a language requirement for graduation.

In the last couple of years, the field has turned a corner and has realized that while it is important to be under the big umbrella of ALTA and NCOLCTLs, it has to show its maturity by spreading its wings. To make Kiswahili viable and to allow people interested in learning and teaching it to unite, exchange ideas, disseminate research on Kiswahili, and to educate the masses on the significance of valuing and cherishing Kiswahili, the field agreed to form an international association that focused exclusively on Kiswahili. The association was officially inaugurated in the USA 2012 and was named "CHAUKIDU"- Chama cha Ukuzaji wa Kiswahili Duniani. The central mission of the association is to celebrate the expansion, strength and place of Kiswahili in the world. It is still too early at this point to predict the future of the association but if history is on our side, the success of the association will, undoubtedly follow previous patterns considering that the main players in the association have remained loyal to and the strongest advocates of African languages, particularly Kiswahili. The prevailing enthusiasm is a strong indication that CHAUKIDU is destined to be a force to reckon with as an advocate for the place of Kiswahili in the world. CHAUKIDU has already formed alliances with other associations whose objectives include a focus on Kiswahili language and culture. Such associations include a media based arena, the VIJIMAMBO blog which celebrated its third anniversary this year (2013) in Washington DC. Of interest to us is its ability to organize a forum that invited Swahili language, culture, and Literature to make presentations at the event. To top it, VIJIMAMBO was able to secure the presence of the second President of the Republic of Tanzania, Honorable Ali Hasan Mwinyi to serve as the keynote speaker. This was indeed significant because it goes to add to the general feeling that the field of Kiswahili in the Diaspora is making an international impact. Currently, VIJIMAMBO and CHAUKIDU are planning other initiatives that would promote weekly or monthly exchanges among Kiswahili scholars.

A Look at Kiswahili at Institutes of Higher Education

Although Kiswahili is receiving a lot of attention beyond the traditional boundaries of the Coastal States and despite the fact that Kiswahili speakers who are spread across the globe play a big role in the development and expansion of Kiswahili, there are challenges that Diaspora proponents of Kiswahili face. We highlight the challenges by using two Institutions of Higher Education that are in the forefront of advocating for Kiswahili and which are microcosm example of other programs at various institutions (over a hundred in the United States) that engage in teaching and scholarship that involves Kiswahili. The selected institutions are the University of South Carolina and the University of Georgia. We plan to highlight the success and challenges for each of these institutions that are based on their program design models.

Kiswahili Program at the University of South Carolina

Kiswahili was introduced at the University of South for the first time in 1988 using graduate students as instructors. Because the instructors were students, the language was taught in the evening under the Continuing Education Department, as a strategy to promote the growth of a new language. The first instructor was a Kenyan who taught one class for four consecutive years. Upon his graduation on

211

his fourth year, his place was assumed by another teaching assistant, a Tanzanian. The teaching schedule remained the same utilizing evening hours but showing growth in student enrollment. To address this unprecedented growth, another class was introduced but was offered during regular day time class schedules. It is important to note here that since its inception, Kiswahili at USC has always been taught by graduate students except in the late 1990s when an instructor was retained to teach it because the school could not find a graduate student suitable to teach Kiswahili at the time.

The teaching model at USC follows from a "students' need design"- *mfumo wa uhitaji wa wanafunzi*. This model is not unique to USC but is common at more than fifty percent of the schools that offer Kiswahili to their students among other foreign languages. Students take Kiswahili as a foreign language but Kiswahili is not considered an integral part of their program of study. In other words, students have other languages they can decide on to fulfill foreign language requirement obligated by the institution. Comparatively, other foreign languages re attached to a larger program of study. For example, students studying Spanish would be majoring in Spanish Studies that may include Spanish Linguistics, Spanish Literature, Latin American studies, and so forth. Kiswahili does not fit in this pattern. Due to the low regard of the need for Kiswahili, a university such as USC would employ graduate students who are proficient in that language and going to school at USC to study for a Masters or Ph.D. degree. There is no requirement on the part of this student teacher to have any language teaching background and they are neither supervised by a senior faculty with expertise in the language through teaching or research. The advantages for the Kiswahili-speaking students in teaching the language is a small monetary compensation and a possible reduction of tuition or in some cases a fully paid tuition. The cost to the university in this arrangement is very low since the compensation is not counted as employment salary (very low) compared to what a professional or full time professor would be paid. The cost is, however, on the students because the

212

stability needed in the teaching of a language like Kiswahili tends to suffer due to the transiency nature of staffing - different teachers come and go after they complete their studies. In addition, the sustainability of the class heavily depends on enrollments. This is common at most institutions where specific course offerings are based on class enrollments. Low enrollments will cause a class to be cancelled at a moment's notice. Low enrollments in foreign languages, particularly African languages, tend to be affected the most and on a regular basis.

As we will see later, the program model adopted by institutions like the University of Georgia prevents such instability by safeguarding the needs of the students while preserving the integrity of the program. That mindset tends to grow and strengthen stability.

Another dilemma at USC is that Kiswahili is not part of its overall university curriculum. Thus, USC is not obligated to offer it even if the student demand to include it in their 'program of study' is high. Programs that are unstable like Kiswahili are the first to go when the budget requires adjustments. Enthusiastic program directors and or teachers like one of the authors of this book who used to teach at USC tends to safeguard the gains made in order to keep the language going year after year. Coupled with tenacity and ingenuity the said author helped to keep Kiswahili in the class schedules for a number of years while she was a graduate student. Her story is not unique, it can be told from many other institutions where Kiswahili is being taught or once upon a time it was taught on a regular basis.

These problems can also have roots in the way the teaching of Kiswahili is initially set up at a college campus. As noted earlier, was introduced at USC in 1988 with a graduate student instructor. The language started with one class offered through the evening classes program, namely, *continuing education*. The use of graduate students to teach the language continued and Kiswahili grew and courses for both evening and morning sessions were offered. It was in the late 1990's when the total number of Kiswahili students reached 40. At the beginning of 2000, new instructors joined the university and

213

propelled enrolments to reach 100 students by 2012. This growth convinced the administration to offer Kiswahili courses in the summer.

Despite such gains, Kiswahili lost its place at USC in 2012 at the departure of a long time graduate student instructor and an avid advocate of the teaching of Kiswahili at USC. The departure was a consequence of her completing her Ph.D. and subsequently being employed by a major university in the State of Georgia. USC's reluctance to secure a permanent instructor for its Swahili program has played a major part in the instability of that program costing students time invested in the program but unable to complete their studies to meet their desired career goals. Comparatively, the University of Georgia (UGA) caters for the students' needs and career goals, allowing them to pursue a certificate in African Studies or a minor in African Languages and Literatures. In the following section we will describe the model used by UGA.

Kiswahili Program at the University of Georgia

The Kiswahili program at UGA can best be described as a "departmental design"- *mfumo wa idara*, a phenomenon that is not common across the nation. At UGA, students can elect to have the Kiswahili courses as an integral part of their program of study in a specific department, in this case the Department of Comparative Literature. In other words, the student's degree or certificate objectives are strategically incorporated in the design to allow students to elect Kiswahili and be sure to have the courses available for their entire degree studies period. By selecting to study Kiswahili at UGA, a student has four goal oriented options, namely: (1) to fulfill a language requirement or to (2) obtain a Certificate in African Studies; (3) a minor in African Studies; (4) a minor in African Languages and Literatures. Swahili courses, like all other courses are enrollment driven but only at the elementary level. Once a student advances to the intermediate or advanced levels, they are guaranteed instruction in order to ensure that they fulfill their intended goals.

This assurance has been a major driving force for high enrollments. Every fall semester, there are at least three sections of twenty five students each and two sections of up to twenty students in the second year of language study. This structure was put in place when Kiswahili was initiated in 1988 and by being fully integrated in the overall university curriculum it has gained the needed status that is accorded the commonly taught languages like Spanish and French.

When Kiswahili was started at UGA in 1988, the university opened a permanent tenure track position which attracted a Ph.D. graduate from the University of California, UCLA and who was at the time a faculty member at Stanford University. Although the set up was that of an independent program with an appointed director, it was nevertheless nested in the Department of Anthropology which was also the home department for the Program in Linguistics. As such, Kiswahili was associated with the study of Linguistics and Anthropology from the onset. In 1992, the Kiswahili Program was moved to the Department of Comparative Literature, the home department for non-western languages. The move was necessitated by a restructuring of the Department of Anthropology forcing that Linguistics to be attached to the English Department. Consequently, the logical home for the Swahili program was the Department of Comparative Literature that already had the tradition of housing other non-western languages. No changes were made to the Kiswahili program; in fact its structure forced a change in all of the languages already in the Department elevating them to a program status with an appointed Director. Thus, the Swahili Program assumed permanent membership among a growing number of other language programs, namely Chinese, Japanese, Korean, Vietnamese, and Hindi. The move to Comparative Literature and its overall success motivated the university to initiate two more African languages, Yoruba and Zulu. Over the years, two more African languages were initiated: Amharic and Zulu (but did not do well and were place on hold for the time being). Needless to say, Kiswahili has thrived under this structure offering courses during the academic year, overseas study abroad,

215

and occasionally in the summer. The structure has not only been the most secure arrangement but also a design that makes logical sense and which allows growth and sustainability. The students who are likely to take Kiswahili as part of their degree program is not restricted to those interested in World Literature but rather include students from a variety of disciplines such as Engineering, Anthropology, International business, public health, international affairs, music, geography, psychology, only to name a few. Most students elect to study Kiswahili based on their future goals and objectives. Some have their eyes on international agencies (government or otherwise) that have interest in East Africa and other countries where Kiswahili is a possibility, non-profit organizations, agencies associated with the medical fields, and religious organizations.

The Kiswahili Program has advanced its curriculum by introducing other course on the study of Kiswahili focus on Swahili history, culture, civilization, linguistic ideology, political development, colonization and its effects on the language policy and planning, and religion. These students can learn the language for two or more years and can also take electives courses that focus on the areas listed above. The set up as described shows a wide spectrum that is both manageable and appealing to students. Consequently, the success gained over the years has not only strengthened the position of Kiswahili in the overall university curriculum but has also allowed it to become sustainable over twenty five years at UGA. The setup has also been enhanced by the willingness of the university administrators to staff the program with two permanent Ph.D. professors and additional lines for graduate assistants who are directly supervised by the permanent and full time faculty. Being housed in the Department of Comparative literature has also allowed the Program sustain its campus-wide status of a fully funded program instead of surviving through ad hoc budgetary plans that have a source of funding from soft money obtained through external or internal grants or even discretionary funds from the Dean's overall budget.

It is fair, therefore, to say that the teaching of Kiswahili at UGA offers a model that is reliable and one that the authors would like to advocate. Such a model guarantees growth, strength, and sustainability, especially in the Diaspora. It is also encouraging to those who are teaching in the program or the language because they can plan for a strategic development that is backed by commitment and job security. Job security is a major aggregate for job satisfaction, a big motivation for excellence in performance, and a guarantee for a healthy working environment.

Issue of Publication in Kiswahili

We bring the issue of publications in Kiswahili because knowledge of the nature of African publishing greatly helps us understand the context of African languages within their national states and transnational status. What we think is of great significance is the way this discussion lays a foundation to the understanding of the international dynamics and the role these dynamics play in structuring the status of linguistic trends in both local and other broader contexts. Publishing in African languages needs to be understood in light of history, politics, religion, social and even economy. The complex nature of language policies and realities in African countries, which are not only intricate but often contentious, affect patterns of publishing and also authorship. The challenges are also tied to the colonial legacies that affect the attitudes towards the varied number of languages spoken in the various countries. Needless to say, the challenges also reflect both national and international power relations that were established and continue to be pursued since independence. For the most part these inheritances shape both economic and educational policies in the former colonies.

Against this backdrop, when we look at where Kiswahili finds itself with regards to publication, we need to keep in mind that literary awards such as the Nobel, Commonwealth Literature, and even the

Africa-centric Nobel prizes seldom go to writers in African languages spoken by the majority of Africans. Thus, we cannot ignore the fact that the state of African publishing is intertwined with the state of African economies. Arboleda (1985:35) notes that, since the early 1980s,

Even more sharply pronounced is the comment from Magoba (2002) and Altbach (1999) a specialist on African publishing, who give a realistic picture of the state of publishers in African languages. They underline critical issues that are endemic to-date and are worth noting as important in our discussion. These include: the dominance of colonial or 'world' languages (particularly, English and French), that continue to be favored by governing elites; low literacy rates of readers; linguistic complications; limited markets; and reader purchasing power.

These issues are illustrative of the situation with Kiswahili publication in Tanzania and Kenya. M. M. (Mugyabuso) Mulokozi (2002), a Professor at the Institute of Kiswahili Studies, University of Dar es Salaam, declares that a lot needs to be done in Tanzania and Kenya. He shows laudable strides Tanzania and Kenya have made in Swahili publication but cautions that the endemic problems cannot be ignored. These include publishing policies that are rather too confining, poor writing skills, and most of the entire problem associated with distribution. He underscores the existence of many writers in East Africa, noting specifically those of the late 1990s, where there were five thousand Kiswahili active poets in Kenya and Tanzania. Sadly, much of their work was not published and those published were not distributed and remained only known within the national borders with very few known across the countries of Kenya and Tanzania. The problem of exploitation by cosmopolitan publishers was also endemic as is the case of the renowned writer and poet Shaaban Robert. Without downplaying the role of the global market on this topic, Mulokozi cites the problem of political and religious-motivated censorship by highlighting Ngugi wa Thiong'o, a prominent African writer whose publications in his native language met much opposition leading him to stop writing in his indigenous language. This is indeed a great setback in the quest to increase publications in African languages.

Jan Blommaert (1997) expresses the complication of publication in African languages using Kiswahili in a case study that shows that the issue of politics and Kiswahili publication is tied to matters of dependency, decolonization, and popular participation. For instance, in Tanzania, transnational publishers who ran the industry during colonization were joined with local publishers after independence. These individual, small publishing firms joined the nation-building project and began to choose, publish, distribute and promote literature in their own language. A good example is the the promotion of Ujamaa (familyhood/socialism). When this happened, writers had to change their writing to adapt to the new style whose goal was to promote the message desired by the country. Subsequently, many Tanzanian writers have tried to rid themselves this confining and filtering functions of the state-controlled mode of publication. However, the reality is that many Kiswahili writers had lost momentum and remain "generally marginalized, despised, and swindled' whilst publishing remains trapped in a socio-economic milieu that imposes 'financial, infrastructural, cultural, and political obstacles' in its path" (Albatch 1999: 37).

There have been efforts in the last decade that have brought both adequate organization and assistance to Tanzanian writers. Post-independence publishing saw the emergence of the University of Dar es Salaam's initiative under the leadership of the Institute of Kiswahili Research. This unit has been instrumental in key publications including new dictionaries, an annual journal of Kiswahili studies, literature books and books of poetry. In 2012, the Institute celebrated its 50th Anniversary, a commemoration that was organized by University of Dar es Salaam, the African Academy of Languages (ALCALAN), and UNESCO. The significance of this international conference and gathering is the marking of a milestone for Kiswahili, a commemoration of fifty years of the Kiswahili as a language of

African liberation, unification and renaissance. This joint effort in itself is a clear indication of the growth and expansion of Kiswahili, its role in Africa and the impact it has had across the globe.

Likewise, Kenya has made much progress in the use of Kiswahili. Nathan and Emily Ogechi (2002), both of Moi University Kenya, explain the scope of publishing in African languages, with special attention to Kiswahili in different academic levels in Kenya. They underscore that Publishing houses in Kenya, as many in East Africa fall under two broad categories: transnational/multinational and indigenous publishers. The former are mainly owned by western publishers and tend to be better established, owning numerous branches in several countries- an issue noted earlier. The latter categorize firms owned by private individuals and the government, which came after the multinationals. In this decade, Kenya has no shortage of publishers (Mulokozi 2002). Though mismanagement and lack of funds caused some indigenous publishers to fail (Chakava 1996), there is still a large number in existence. Specifically, there was a 60% increase in the number of publishing houses between 1977 and 1997 and 95% of those were indigenous. By the end of the 1990s, there were more than 130 registered publishers in Kenya. Unlike Tanzania, Mulokozi (2002:7) affirms that "Kenya's publishing and distribution network is intact." However, like Tanzania, it still faces serious problems namely: limited sophisticated Swahili reading market leading to publishers preferring to publish in English rather than Kiswahili. There is minimal Swahili readership outside the classroom. Most books in Swahili are either school textbooks or fiction (Okwanya 1990). Mulokozi (2002) correctly observes that not only books but there are even few magazines and newspapers in Kiswahili. As such, only Taifa Leo and Kenya Leo have national circulation implying that the Kenyan Swahili print media (newspapers) has not expanded.

The strides and problems still facing publication in Kiswahili do not end in East Africa. They simply expand and meet even bigger challenges internationally. We highlighted this issue first in the

African continent to set the stage for our readers to understand that while the issue is complicated in Africa it is even more complicated outside Africa. Using the United States of America as an example, publication in Kiswahili language has increased in some way but it is still lagging behind other foreign languages taught and/or used in the USA. However, Kiswahili is now part of the internet translation device; meaning, a person can indeed type a Kiswahili script and ask "google translator" to translate a text. There are also several online Kiswahili publications intended to help people learn Kiswahili. In order to provide a better picture that demonstrates where Kiswahili publication stands among other African languages taught in the USA we also looked at how it compares with non-African languages. One may find books in other foreign language-learning books and other materials. The main distributor of such materials around the world, especially in the USA is an entity known as *"World Languages"*. This source shows that there are 27 published Kiswahili teaching/learning books and some come with audio recordings and a total of 7 Swahili dictionaries. Furthermore, there are about 11 bilingual children's books for Kindergarten through 2nd grade listed on this website with an additional 12 suitable for grade 3 through 5. Thus, in this website alone, one can find a total of 23 books under the category of children's books which are basically original English books translated into Kiswahili. The site also shows popular books translated into many other world languages including English. Comparatively, the number of books in African languages is not insignificant but the margins are significant. For example, while Urdu has 20, Yoruba has11, Shona 10, Afrikaans 6; Amharic 3 while Akan and Zulu has none in the children's category (See table 1 below).

Table 1: *Books in African Languages represented on the "World Languages" Website*

Language	Children's books	Dictionary	Teaching/learning materials	Total
Kiswahili	23	7	27	57
Urdu	20	16	15	51
Yoruba	11	2	13	26
Shona	10	1	4	15
Afrikaans	6	1	9	16
Amharic	3	5	8	16
Akan	0	1	0	1
Zulu	0	1	4	5

In order to confirm whether the designation *"World Languages"* provided a really good representation of available children's books in the different world languages, we further explored the most popular websites used in libraries worldwide and one that the USA public libraries refer anyone searching for children's literature especially those not represented in hard copies- the *Children's International Digital Library*. Interestingly, here like the *World Language* source, Kiswahili had a total of 17 books, which is more than any other African language had.

From the table above, it is clear that the other publication categories that we explored shows interesting distributions in the availability of dictionaries and other teaching and learning materials for each of the listed languages. Note that while Urdu has 16 dictionaries, followed by Amharic (5), then Yoruba (2) while Akan has 1 and Zulu has 1. In Teaching/learning material, Urdu still leads with 15, followed by Yoruba (13), then Afrikaans (9), Amharic (8), and Zulu and Shona (4) each. Akan has none. Needless to say, this distribution should be taken with a grain of salt because with the publication and distribution problems still looming large, the representative data cannot be totally relied upon. This goes to illustrate the point we have been putting across concerning the status of Kiswahili publication. It is possible if one was to look elsewhere, such as the *Children's International Digital Library*, it is likely to see equal or less representation of language-specific materials published and distributed in the USA and around the world (See table 2 below).

Table 2: *Selected foreign language books represented on the "Children' International Digital Library (CIDL)" and "World Languages (WL)"*

Category	Language	CIDL	WL
African	Kiswahili	17	23
	Urdu	14	20
	Yoruba	0	11
	Shona	1	10
	Afrikaans	1	6
	Amharic	2	3
	Akan	0	0
	Zulu	0	0
	Total	**34**	**73**
European	Spanish	173	421
	German	79	77
	French	56	165
	Italian	44	59
	Russian	17	73
	Total	**369**	**795**
Middle Eastern	Arabic	30	119
	Total	**30**	**119**
Asian	Japanese	13	44
	Chinese	10	133
	Korean	6	78
	Total	**29**	**255**

Comparatively however, Kiswahili lags behind some of the languages in this table. For example, in the children's literature alone, Japanese has 44 books, Italian 59, German 77, Russian 77, Korean 78 books, Arabic 119, Chinese 133, French 165, while Spanish has 421 books. Kiswahili has a long way to go to catch up but its current status is commendable as a world language that has advanced beyond its African borders and is currently leading all the African languages in publication (see table 1 and 2 above).

What these numbers tell us is that languages taking an upper hand in publication are also leading in international business and demonstrate a strong international economic presence in the world. Kiswahili has not attained that prestigious place although it does represent a nation that is one of the rising economies in East at Africa and Africa in general.

Conclusion

What does this mean to advocates of the Kiswahili language, culture and its contribution to the civilization of the Swahili coast and the world at large? Literature teaches and moves humanity to look at the past in order to shape the future. It also discloses the genius of the mind played in the space of history while troubling the future even before it happens. Thus, no civilization is worth loosing, and literature is the best preserver of a people's history and a reliable documentation of a civilization. To ensure that this is in place, it is incumbent upon scholars to advocate and to look for ways to continue to grow the language that is the root of our symbolic place in the world. Language can be both a source of war and peace. Part of the goal of language sustainability should be to make the existing powerful achievements more salient as a step towards empowering those who are positioned in the non-powerful subject position in language conventions. In the case of Tanzania, Kiswahili has been the source of sustained peace and tranquility. That is the attained power. To sustain it, it is necessary to make it an economic power too in order to enable it to withstand the technological changes that might erode the confidence in the speakers as they strive to use resources available in Kiswahili to meet their economic potentials. Speakers should use the power that technology brings to bear to not only sustain what has been attained but also to grow every aspect of the language and its contribution to civilization.

By the same token, African leaders need to claim the power of their respective languages. It is only African leaders, especially those coming from Anglophone Africa, who do not exploit the power of their languages. Leaders from other nations do that all the time. When the citizenry see that their leaders are proud of their cultural heritage through language, they will respond positively and will grow the confidence to sustain the language through the development of its literary works.

APPENDIX

Suggested Activities and Revision Questions

Chapter I: Introduction

Student activity:

Using the internet, research the following cities/towns of East Africa based on the (a) to (f) outline.

City/town: Mogadishu, Kismayu, Lamu, Nairobi, Mombasa, Tanga, Dar es Salaam, Bagamoyo, Zanzibar, and Kilwa.

1. Historical background
2. Current political structure
3. Indigenous culture
4. Contemporary/popular culture
5. Special aspects about their cuisine (influence of new cultures)
6. Music (indigenous versus current trends)

Revision questions

1. What do we mean by 'the Swahili Coastal States', also known as 'the Swahili City-States'?
2. What are the main areas of interest in the study of the Swahili Coastal States?
3. Why is Kusimba a reference point of interest in the study of the Swahili Coastal States?
4. What other critical aspects of interest that one has to consider when framing the discussion about the rise of the Swahili Coastal States?
5. Geographically, how would you place the Swahili Coastal States/Swahili City-States?
6. What are the major cities associates with the discussion of these states?

7. What are the visible features that identify the Swahili Coastal State areas?
8. What groups of people can you find in these states?
9. Briefly outline the historical background of some of the key cities named in this chapter.

Chapter 2: The Coastal Towns

Student activity:

1. Revisit the activity requested of you in Chapter I.
2. Pick out the cities discussed in this chapter and compare notes.

Revision questions

1. Briefly describe the city of Kilwa highlighting its history and the different subdivisions.
2. Who were the key players responsible for Kilwa's development as a major trading post and then its demise?
3. Why do you think Kilwa was selected as the converging center for the coastal trade?
4. The second key Swahili Coastal city is Bagamoyo. What is the source of its name?
5. Why do you think the study of Bagamoyo gives you a "bird's eye view" of the history of the coastal states and cities?
6. Briefly outline the history and contribution of Bagamoyo to the development of the Coastal States.
7. Why is Bagamoyo often seen as the central point for the study of the Coastal States' maritime slavery?
8. Apart from the involvement of the Middle East and the larger Asian continent, how is the west associated with the development and history of Bagamoyo?
9. Outline the historical background of the city of Dar es Salaam.
10. Why is the city of Dar es Salaam important to Tanzania's economy?

11. What roles does the Dar es Salaam port and the railroads play in the economic vitality of the neighboring countries and how is this vitality currently being threatened?

12. Outline the historical background of Zanzibar showing its importance in the overall civilization of the coastal states.

13. What were the major trade attributes of the island and how is the island associated with slave trade?

14. What is the location of Lamu city and why is it an important Swahili Coastal-city?

15. Briefly describe its historical background that contributes to its importance.
    Why is Lamu referred to as an archipelago? What are the other places that are a part to this description and why are they important to the contribution and development of the Coastal States?

16. Another northern city that contributes to the discussion of the development of the Coastal states is Malindi? Outline its historical background and importance in this respect.

17. How did Mombasa come to be and how did it rise to become a key city of the Coastal States?

18. What has Mombasa got to do with slavery, Portuguese rule, and the control of the Coastal States' trade routes to the Far East?

19. What is the role of Mogadishu in the study of the Coastal States?

20. Nairobi is not a Coastal State but it is included in this Chapter's discussion. What is its importance in this discussion?

21. What do cities of East Africa have in common that support the theory of multiculturalism, a sense of shared history, and a global outlook?

Chapter 3: The Livelihood of the Coastal States People

Student activity:

1. Using your dictionary find out the meaning of: colonialism, inter-trade, and intra-trade.
2. Outline the ingredients that you think were not present in the Coastal States to allow outsiders to assume that they were not civilized and that they could be colonized and cut off from both inter and intra-trading opportunities.

Revision questions

1. Describe the ecological system of the Swahili coast and explain how it enhanced the economic well-being of the Coastal States.
2. How did the Swahili Coast advance their inter-trading and intra-trading practices? Explain the significance of the inter-trading and intra-trading opportunities that were afforded to the coastal people before being colonized.
3. Who were the major influences on the coastal economy and why was the interaction possible?
4. In a short paragraph, explain how the Coastal people found economic opportunities and how they organized themselves to manage the flow of goods inherent to the Indian Ocean trade.
5. What was the role of agriculture in the coastal economy?
6. How did the economic well-being of the coastal people affect the class system? Identify the classes and outline the privileges/benefits or the lack thereof.
7. The chapter discussions seem to suggest that the Swahili people were very prosperous and lived in a sense of inter-dependency with each other and had social skills that allowed trade to flourish. If that is the case, why do you think caused them to lack the unity they needed to fight off colonization which destroyed the perceived harmony?

Chapter 4: The Rise of the Swahili Coast

Student activity:

1. Look up the dictionary definition of 'Civilization'.
2. List all the aspects of life (socio-cultural socio-political, political economies, or otherwise) that you think fit into the given definition.
3. Design a step-by step plan on how you would integrate those aspects that seem to have been restricted from the dictionary definition into a definition that is more inclusive.
4. In your opinion and based on what you have read so far, did the coastal cities/towns of East Africa have a type of civilization not shared by the rest of the world. Do you think if such a civilization existed, it had any impact on Western Civilization?

Revision questions

1. Describe the historical periods that identify the rise of the Swahili Coastal States.
2. What evidence do you have that points to the fact that there existed a form of civilization on the Swahili Coast that was indigenous and particular to the Swahilidom and that benefited from interactions and influences from external sources?
3. How was trade organized by the Swahili people and what major commodities dominated this trade?
4. How was Madagascar and Indonesia connected to the trade and civilization of the Swahilidom?
5. Identify the northern and southern routes that became important in fostering the interstate trading and interactions.
6. How do you understand the triangular mercantile trade?
7. Why was the origin of the Swahili civilization not linked with internal factors but rather associated only with external trade?

8. How are the urban Swahili people distinguished from the other rural coastal people?

Chapter 5: Theories, Archeology and the Swahili Civilization

Revision questions:

1. What are the suggested ways of studying historical accounts about a people?
2. What are the assumptions put forth about the rise of the Swahili civilization and what are the sources of these ideas?
3. Who are Kulturkreissen and Kirkman? How are they associated with the concept of a Swahili civilization?
4. What is the External Theory and how does it reflect a dominant perspectives about Africa in general?
5. Archeology can untangle and shed light on people's history. Explain why this was still difficult in revealing the history of the Swahili Coastal States.
6. What are the accomplishments of the 20th Century archeologists and why did they consider themselves "new archeologists?
7. Who is Horton and what is his relationship with what we know today of Shanga town?
8. What was the main concern in archeological research and the interpretation of findings?
9. What is the general perception of Africa as a result of the way early archaeologists and historians portrayed the continent?
10. What do you know about Stigand and his view of the Africa he came into contact with?
11. Why was the interpretation of the Swahili civilization a problem to the 'new archeologists'?
12. List the important historical aspects of Bagamoyo that point to its place in the rise and fall of the Swahili civilization?

Chapter 6: The Kiswahili Language

Student activity:

1. What do you think are the main challenges for Kiswahili to establish itself in relation to other world languages like English?

Revision questions

1. Briefly describe the debate surrounding the origin of the Kiswahili language
2. What is the evidence for Kiswahili's relationship with Arabic? How does Kiswahili relate to other languages in the region?
3. Distinguish between a Swahili speaker and a Swahili person. Where would you find Kiswahili speakers?
4. What are the explanations for the Arab influence on the Swahili Coast?
5. Briefly describe the manner in which Kiswahili has been spread along the states and the hinterland (you may also list the features that describe the manner and extent of the spread.
6. Give examples of the influence from different colonial powers on the Kiswahili language
7. What were the linguistic impediments experienced by the missionaries whose main role was to spread Christianity in East Africa?
8. Why did the Germans have an issue with both English and Swahili?
9. Who was Dr. J.L. Krapf and why was he important to the debate about Kiswahili?
10. How was Kiswahili received after the East African countries of Kenya, Tanzania, Uganda attained independence?
11. The spread of Kiswahili has taken place against a background of interaction between church and state and between economics and politics. What are the three main domains of interest in this respect and what effects did these domains have on Kiswahili in

general?

12. What did Mazrui and Mazrui mean by 'detribalization' and what is its relationship to other aspects of the spread of Kiswahili namely "urbanization?

13. What is 'secularization' and why is it important in the discussion on the spread of Kiswahili? What do the authors mean by 'modern secularization'?

Chapter 7

Student activity:

1. If you were given a role of language policy advisor to the key Swahili States, what would you consider as necessary in trying to unify their systems in order to create a platform for Kiswahili to emerge as a regional language and perhaps a continental language?

Revision questions

1. When did most changes occur on the eastern coast of Africa and how?

2. The authors indicate that there are cumulative effects on the development of Kiswahili as a language. How are these effects marked?

3. What sort of opportunity allowed the expansion of Swahili towns along the coast?

4. How is the place of Kiswahili viewed?

5. Briefly describe the place of Tanzania in the study of Kiswahili and the Swahili people?

6. Briefly describe the historical background of languages in Tanzania vis-à-vis Kiswahili.

7. Outline the role of Tanzania before and after independence.

8. What is the relationship between Kiswahili and English in the Tanzania education system? Can the two languages co-exist and for what benefit.

9. Outline the four important issues that highlight the current status of Kiswahili in Tanzania.
10. What are the major differences and similarities of the status of Kiswahili in Uganda compared to Tanzania?
11. What is the status of Kiswahili in Kenya and what are the similarities and differences compared to Tanzania and Uganda?
12. What is the story behind the establishment of Kiswahili in the Democratic Republic of the Congo (DRC)? What other languages does Kiswahili have to compete with in the DRC?

Chapter 8:   The Globalized Status of Kiswahili

Student activity:

1. Based on the way globalization is used in everyday conversations, how do you understand it? Give examples of what you consider to be a global phenomenon.
2. If you were given an opportunity to design a class on world languages, cultures, and civilizations for a high school class, what would you   consider as important aspects to include from the civilization of the Coastal Swahili States

Revision questions

1. What do you think are the relationships between the status of a language, here Swahili, and the existence of a strong and globally recognized civilization?
2. Why do you think English is a powerful global phenomenon? How does Kiswahili power compare with that of English?
3. Who is Lord Lugard and why does he feature in the discussion on the power and role of English particularly in the British colonies?
4. List at least five elements that you think are being used to speed up the process of globalizing Kiswahili.

5. The authors of this chapter seem concerned with the role of African leaders in advocating for foreign languages instead of promoting African languages like Kiswahili. What examples did they discuss at length about this concern?

6. What do the authors mean when they say: "Kiswahili averted a parochial form of ethnicity and a universalistic orientation?

7. Give examples that show Kiswahili is serving as a lingua franca in East Africa.

8. What are the risks that Chrystal (2005) outlined to be considered when we accept English as the only world language? How do you understand these risks?

9. What advice do the authors give scholars of Kiswahili and political leaders of Kiswahili speaking States?

10. What do you think English should be doing more of to hold its position as "a global language" and what steps should Kiswahili take to catch up with English?

Chapter 9

Student activity:

1. Using the internet, identify countries and programs across the globe that use or provide instructions in Kiswahili.

2. Establish the year the program was initiated and if it is no longer in place which year it was dropped from the system and why.

Revision questions

1. Who is credited with the Kiswahili initiative in Ghana and what were the initial institutions that took up the challenge of promoting Kiswahili in Ghana.

2. What are the main factors associated with the development and expansion of Kiswahili in the 19th Century?

3. What constitutes the East African Community? What is the role of the organization in promoting Kiswahili?

4. What African countries teach Kiswahili as a subject?
5. What contributions to the Promotion of Kiswahili in Ghana are attributed to its first President, Dr. Kwame Nkrumah?
6. What institutions in Ghana were unable to sustain the promotion of Kiswahili and why?
7. When Kiswahili was initiated at the University of Ghana, who constituted the student body for the different courses offered?
8. What Kiswahili programs were popular at the Ghana Broadcasting Corporation?
9. What were the objectives of the Ghana Institute of Languages and what were its pressing challenges?
10. What aspects contributed to the establishment of Kiswahili at the University of Ghana?
11. What are the key challenges for the Kiswahili Section at UG and what does the author consider to be the long term remedies?
12. What does the author expect the continent of Africa to do to promote Kiswahili regionally and why?

Bibliography

Abdulaziz, Mohamed H. *Transitivity in Swahili: East African languages and dialects* vol.5.Rüdiger Köppe Verlag. 2006. Print.

Adogamhe, Paul G. "Pan Africanism Revisited: Vision and Reality of African and Development." *African Review of Integration*, 2.2 (2008): 1-34. Print.

Allen, J. de V. "Swahili History Revisited." *Seminar Paper #76, Institute of African Studies*, Nairobi: University of Nairobi, 1977. Print.

_____."The Swahili in Western Histography." *Seminar Paper #6, Institute of African Studies*, University of Nairobi, Nairobi, 1976. Print.

_____. "Swahili Culture and Identity." *Seminar Paper, Institute of African Studies*,University of Nairobi, Nairobi, 1976. Print.

Michler, Ian. *Zanzibar: The Insider's Guide* (2nd ed.), Cape Town: Struik Publishers, 2007. Print.

Middleton J. *The World of the Swahili: an African Mercantile Civilization.* New Haven: Yale University Press. 1992. Print.

Moshi, Lioba. The Globalized World Languages: The Case of Kiswahili. *Selected Proceedings of the 36th Annual Conference on African Linguistics,* Ed. Olaoba F. Arasanyin and Michael A. Pemberton, MA: Cascadilla Proceedings Project. 2006:166-175. Print.

Moshi, Lioba. *Locatives in KiVunjo-Chaga.* In Theoretical Approaches to African Linguistics Africa. Ed. Akinbiyi Akinlabi. Trenton, New Jersey: World Press, Inc. 1993: 129-145.   Print.

_____. *Time Reference Markers in Kivunjo-Chaga. Journal of African Languages and Linguistics,*15(1994):128-159. Print.

_____.*Time Stability, the case of Adjectives in Kivunjo-Chaga.* In Topics in African Linguistics. Ed. Salikoko Mufwene and Lioba Moshi. John Benjamin Publishing Co.   1995:141-159. Print.

Moshi, Lioba, Abdul Nanji, Magdalena Hauner, and John Mtembezi Inniss. *Mwalimu wa Kiswahili: A Language Teaching Manual.* Binghamton, NY: Global Publications, IGCS,   1999. Print.

Mulokozi, M. M. "Publishing in Kiswahili: A writer's perspective." *Publishing in African   Languages: Challenges and Prospects.* Ed. Philip G. Altbach and Damtew Teferra, Chestnut   Hill,   MA: Bellagio Publishing Network, 1999: 18–37. Print.

_____.*African Epic Controversy: Historical, Philosophical And Aesthetic Perspectives   On Epic Poetry And Performance.* Dar es Salaam: Mkuki Na Nyota Publishers, 2002. Print.

Mwita, A.M.A & D.N. Mwansoko *Kamusi ya Tiba.* Dar Es Salaam, GTZ. 1998. Print.

Neke, S. M. *English in Tanzania: An Anatomy of Hegemony.* Diss. Universeit Gent. 2003. Web. 23 September, 2013 http://cas1.elis.ug ent.be/avrug/pdf03/neke.pdf.

Nshubemuki, L. *Istilahi za elimumisitu: Kiingereza-Kiswahili.* Dar es Salaam: Forest Research Support in Tanzania, 1999. Print.

Gordon, Charles, Alexander *Life on the Gold Coast.* Memphis TN: General Books. 2009 [1874]. Print.

"Globalization." In *Encarta World English Dictionary.* New York, NY: Bloomsbury   Publishing, St. Martin's Press, 1999:759.

Hancock, Ian (ed.) *Readings in Creole Studies.* Gent: Story-Scientia. 1979. Print.

Head, S. W. and J. Kugblenu. "A Survival of Wired Radio in Tropical Africa." *Gazette,* 24.2 (1978). 121-129. Print.

Henschel, Johannes. *1868-1893 Bagamoyo Catholic Mission: What Old Sketches and Documents   Tell.* Dar es Salaam: Top Desk Production Limited, 1989. Print.

Hinnebusch, J. T. & Mirza, S. *Kiswahili: Msingi wa Kusema, Kusoma na Kuandika: Swahili: A foundation for Speaking, Reading, and Writing.* (2nd Edition) Lanham, New   York: University Press of America. 1997. Print.

Hinnebusch, T. Swahili: Genetic Affiliations and Evidence. *Studies in African Linguistics,* 6.(1976):95-108. Print.

Horton, Mark. *Shanga: The archaeology of a Muslim trading community on the coast of East Africa.* Memoirs of the British Institute in Eastern Africa 14. London: British Institute in Eastern Africa, 1996. Print.

Ingrams, William H. *Zanzibar: It's History and Its People,* Abingdon: Routledge, 1967. Print.

International Children's Digital Library. A Library for the World's Children,n.d. Web, 24 Sept. 2013. http://en.childrenslibrary.org/

In2EastAfrica: Academy lauds Kenya for uplifting Kiswahili Ed. Otieno, R. 24 August 2011. Web. 23 September 2013 http://in2eastafrica.net/a cademy-lauds-kenya-for-uplifting-kiswahili/

Jan Blommaert, "The impact of state ideology on language: Ujamaa & Swahili literature in Tanzania." In *Human contact through language & linguistics.* Ed. B. Smieja & M. Tasch   Frankfurt: Lang, 1997. Print.

Jeyifo, Biodun. *Wole Soyinka: Politics, Poetics and Postcolonialism.* Cambridge: Cambridge University Press. 2004. Print.

Chakava, H. *Publishing in Africa: One Man's Perspective*. Nairobi: East African Educational Publishers. 1996. Print.

Chami, Felix. "Excavations at Kuumbi Cave on Zanzibar 2005." *The African Archaeology Network: Research in Progress*. Ed. Paul Sinclair, Abdurahman Juma and Felix Chami Der es Salaam University Press, 2006, 95-106. Print.

Casson, Lionel. *The Periplus Maris Erythraei: Text With Introduction, Translation, and Commentary*. Princeton University Press. 1989. Print.

Chebet-Choge, Susan. "Fifty Years of Kiswahili in Regional and International Development." *Journal of Pan-African Studies*, 4.10 (2012): 172- 203. Print.

Chimera, Rocha. *Kiswahili Past, Present and Future Horizons*. Nairobi: Oxford University Press. 2000. Print.

Chuwa, Albina R. *Jifunze Kompyuta WP5. Hatua ya Kwanza*. Dar Es Salaam: IKR. 2003. Print.

Crystal, David Globalizing English. *What's Language Got to Do With It?* Ed. Keith Walters and   Michal Brody. New York, NY: W.W. Norton and Co. 2005, 504-514. Print.

Chittick Neville H. "The Coast of East Africa." *The African Iron Age*. (eds.) P.L. Shinnie. Oxford: Clarendon Press. 1971. 108-141. Print.

Education Science & Technology. *The East African Kiswahili Commission*, East African Community Education, 2013. Web.

Frempong Manso, Stephen Esq. "Evolution, Growth and Development of Media Pluralism: An Assessment of Policies Legislation and Regulatory Framework in Ghana." Web, 2008. http://www.wjecc.ru.ac.za

Fitzgerald, W.W.A. *Travels in British East Africa, Pemba and Zanzibar*. London: Chapman and   Hall. 1898. Print.

Gahiji, "Swahili Language to Be Given Emphasis in EAC." *News of Rwanda*, Web, 10 March,   2012.

Gibbs, James. *Critical Perspectives on Wole Soyinka*. Lynne Rienner Publishers. 1980. Print.

7. What are the visible features that identify the Swahili Coastal State areas?
8. What groups of people can you find in these states?
9. Briefly outline the historical background of some of the key cities named in this chapter.

Chapter 2: The Coastal Towns

Student activity:

1. Revisit the activity requested of you in Chapter I.
2. Pick out the cities discussed in this chapter and compare notes.

Revision questions

1. Briefly describe the city of Kilwa highlighting its history and the different subdivisions.
2. Who were the key players responsible for Kilwa's development as a major trading post and then its demise?
3. Why do you think Kilwa was selected as the converging center for the coastal trade?
4. The second key Swahili Coastal city is Bagamoyo. What is the source of its name?
5. Why do you think the study of Bagamoyo gives you a "bird's eye view" of the history of the coastal states and cities?
6. Briefly outline the history and contribution of Bagamoyo to the development of the Coastal States.
7. Why is Bagamoyo often seen as the central point for the study of the Coastal States' maritime slavery?
8. Apart from the involvement of the Middle East and the larger Asian continent, how is the west associated with the development and history of Bagamoyo?
9. Outline the historical background of the city of Dar es Salaam.
10. Why is the city of Dar es Salaam important to Tanzania's economy?

APPENDIX

Suggested Activities and Revision Questions

Chapter I: Introduction

Student activity:

Using the internet, research the following cities/towns of East Africa based on the (a) to (f) outline.

City/town: Mogadishu, Kismayu, Lamu, Nairobi, Mombasa, Tanga, Dar es Salaam, Bagamoyo, Zanzibar, and Kilwa.

1. Historical background
2. Current political structure
3. Indigenous culture
4. Contemporary/popular culture
5. Special aspects about their cuisine (influence of new cultures)
6. Music (indigenous versus current trends)

Revision questions

1. What do we mean by 'the Swahili Coastal States', also known as 'the Swahili City-States'?
2. What are the main areas of interest in the study of the Swahili Coastal States?
3. Why is Kusimba a reference point of interest in the study of the Swahili Coastal States?
4. What other critical aspects of interest that one has to consider when framing the discussion about the rise of the Swahili Coastal States?
5. Geographically, how would you place the Swahili Coastal States/Swahili City-States?
6. What are the major cities associates with the discussion of these states?

11. What roles does the Dar es Salaam port and the railroads play in the economic vitality of the neighboring countries and how is this vitality currently being threatened?

12. Outline the historical background of Zanzibar showing its importance in the overall civilization of the coastal states.

13. What were the major trade attributes of the island and how is the island associated with slave trade?

14. What is the location of Lamu city and why is it an important Swahili Coastal-city?

15. Briefly describe its historical background that contributes to its importance.
    Why is Lamu referred to as an archipelago? What are the other places that are a part to this description and why are they important to the contribution and development of the Coastal States?

16. Another northern city that contributes to the discussion of the development of the Coastal states is Malindi? Outline its historical background and importance in this respect.

17. How did Mombasa come to be and how did it rise to become a key city of the Coastal States?

18. What has Mombasa got to do with slavery, Portuguese rule, and the control of the Coastal States' trade routes to the Far East?

19. What is the role of Mogadishu in the study of the Coastal States?

20. Nairobi is not a Coastal State but it is included in this Chapter's discussion. What is its importance in this discussion?

21. What do cities of East Africa have in common that support the theory of multiculturalism, a sense of shared history, and a global outlook?

Nurse, D., and Spear T. *The Swahili. Reconstructing the History and Language of an African Society, 800-1500.* Philadelphia: University of Pensylvania Press. 1985. Print.

Ohly, Rajmund *A Primary Technical Dictionary English-Swahili.* Dar Es Salaam, Tanzania. 1987. Print.

Ogechi, O. N. & Ogechi, B. E. "Educational Publishing in African Languages, With a Focus on Swahili in Kenya." *Nordic Journal of African Studies* 11.2 (2002):167-184.

Owens, Geoffrey R. "Exploring the Articulation of Govern-mentality and Sovereignty: The Chwaka Road and the Bombardment of Zanzibar, 1895–1896", *Journal of Colonialism and Colonial History*, Johns Hopkins University Press 7.2 (2007): 1–55. Print.

Rabin, A. *Language of Instruction in Tanzanian Schools: Creating Class Divides andDecreasing Educational Standards.* Think Africa Press. 2011. Print.

Roy-Campbell, Z.M. *Empowerment through Language.* Trenton, Asmara African World Press. 2001. Print.

Rubagumya, C.M. A., Oksana, A. O. B., John Clegg, J. B., & Kiliku, P. A three tier citizenship: Can the state in Tanzania guarantee linguistic human rights? *International Journal of Educational Develop -ment*, 31(2011):78–85. Print.

Rubagumya, Casmir M. *Language in education in Africa: A Tanzanian Perspective.*Clevedon: Multilingual Matters. 1990. Print.

Rathgeber, E. "African book publishing: lessons from the 1980s." In *Publishing and development in the Third World*, Ed. Philip G. Altbach. Oxford: Hans Zell Publishers, 1992: 77-100. Print.

Social Sciences Online, 19 Feb 2004. Web, 23 Sept. 2013 http://h-net.msu.edu/cgi bin/logbrowse.pl?trx=vx&list=h-swahili&month=0402&msg=HZRThv6QiHOSSVEOAdUCTA

Sanseverino, H. V. "Archaeological remains on the South Somali Coast," *Azania*, 28 (1983):151– 164. Print.

Schleicher, Antonia. and Lioba Moshi The Pedagogy of African languages, an Emerging Field. Ohio State University, Columbus Ohio. Foreign Language Publication & Services, 2000. Print.

Schmied, Josef *English in Africa: An Introduction*. Longman, New York, NY. 1991. Print.

Scotton, Carol, M. The context is the message: morphological, syntactic, and semantic reduction   in Nairobi and Kampala varieties of Swahili. *Readings in Creole Studies*. Ed. Ian   Hancock, Gent: Story-Scientia. 1979: 111-128. Print.

Stites, R. & Semali, L. "Adult literacy for social equality or economic growth? Changing agendas for mass literacy in China and Tanzania." *Comparative Education Review*, 35.1(1991):44-75. Print.

Semali, L. The communication media in postliteracy education: New dimensions of literacy. *International   Review   of   Education*, 39.2(1993): 35-48. Print.

Semali, L. Indigenous education in Tanzania: A response to Arun Agrawal. *Indigenous   Knowledge and Development Monitor*, 4.1(1996, April):12-19. Print.

Stigand, C.H. *The Land of Zinj. Being as Accountant of the British East Africa, its AncientHistory and Present Inhabitants*. London: Constable. 1913. Print

Stiglitz, Joseph. *Globalization and its Discontents*. New York, NY: W.W. Notron & Company. 2003.

Strong, S. Arthur "The History of Kilwa, edited from an Arabic MS", *Journal of the Royal Asiatic Society*, 1895: 385–431.

Swilla, I. Languages of instruction in Tanzania: contradictions between ideology, policy and   implementation. *African Study Monographs*, 30.1 (2009):1-14.

The Rwanda Focus, "Swahili to help integration," 30 November, 2008, Web, September 24, 2011 http://focus.rw/wp/2008/11/swahili-to-help-integration/

Trappes-Lomax, H. English language teaching in Tanzania: a colloquium. *Utafiti: Journal of the Fac. of Arts and Social Sciences*, 7 (1985): 11-26.

Turki, Benyan Saud "The Sultan of the Arab State of Zanzibar and The Regent 1902–1905." *Journal of the Documentation and Humanities Research Center* 178(1997)

United States Department of State, *Countries of the World and Their Leaders* 2nd Ed., Detroit: Gale Research Company, 1975

University of Ghana (1964). University of Ghana Annual Report 1963/1964. Published by University of Ghana- Legon, Accra Ghana.

University of Ghana (1969). University of Ghana   Annual Report 1969/1970. Published by the University of Ghana-Legon, Accra Ghana.

University of Ghana (1972). University of Ghana Annual Report 1972. Published by the University of Ghana-Legon, Accra Ghana.

URT. *Population and Housing Census.* The National Bureau of Statistics, Dar es Salaam Tanzania. (2002). Web, 24September,2013 www.nbs.go.tz/population

Walters, Keith and Michal Brody *What's Language Got to Do With It?* W.W. Norton and Company. New York, NY. 2005. Print.

Wangwe, S.M & Van-Arkadie, B. *Overcoming constraints on Tanzanian growth: policy challenges facing the third phase government.* Dar es Salaam, Mkuki na Nyota. 2000.   Print.

Wilding, Richard. F. *The Shanga Panel: Proceedings of a Meeting to discuss the Findings of the Archeological Excavations at Shanga, Pate Island, Kenya.* Mombasa: Coast Museum Studies Occasional Paper no.1. 1987. Print.

Wilding, Richard. F. *The Ceramics of the North Kenya Coast.* Ph.D thesis. Nairobi: University of   Nairobi. 1980. Print.

Wilding, Richard. F. "Coastal Bantu. Waswahili." In Kenya *Pots and Potters.* Ed. By S. Wandibba and J. Babour, Nairobi: Oxford University Press. 1989: 100-15.Print.

*World Language Resources, Inc."*Worldlanguage.com the ultimate Language site, 1992 2013", Web. 24 Sept. 2013 http://www.worldla nguage.com/

Index

External Origins Theory, 96

F

Fitzgerald, William, 102, 103, 237
Flemish Belgians, 147, 164

G

German East African Company, 51
Ghana Broadcasting Corporation, 175, 178, 235, 239
Ghana Institute Of Languages, Vii, 175, 178, 181, 187, 235
Globalization, 153, 236, 238, 243
Great Mosque, 32, 38, 39, 40, 41, 43, 45, 111

H

Hausa, 149, 159, 172, 179, 182, 203
Homer, Father Anthony, 106
Horton, Mark, 96, 97, 110, 230, 238
Husuni Kubwa, 30, 32, 38, 39, 40, 42, 46, 112

I

Indian Ocean, 23, 24, 27, 33, 42, 45, 46, 47, 53, 55, 57, 58, 60, 62, 63, 65, 68, 71, 73, 79, 80, 81, 82, 83, 86, 88, 89, 90, 91, 96, 103, 104, 111, 114, 132, 228
Institute Of Kiswahili Research, 196, 219

J

John Hopkins University School Of Advanced International Studies, 206
Joint Committee On Closer Union In East Africa, 142

K

Kaole Ruins, 48, 49
Kenya, Iv, Vi, 16, 17, 19, 21, 23, 28, 44, 60, 63, 64, 65, 66, 67, 68, 72, 74, 75, 76, 82, 83, 94, 109, 112, 117, 118, 120, 123, 125, 126, 128, 129, 131, 132, 135, 142, 143, 144, 145, 146, 147, 149, 152, 153, 157, 158, 159, 161, 164, 170, 175, 176, 180, 185, 188, 191, 196, 199, 200, 217, 219, 231, 233, 238, 240, 242, 244
Kenya Television Network, 149
Kenyata University, 158
Kilimanjaro, 54, 118
Kilwa, Iv, 23, 27, 28, 29, 30, 31, 32, 33, 34, 35, 36, 37, 38, 39, 40, 43, 44, 45, 46, 49, 60, 73, 90, 91, 97, 103, 109, 111, 118, 132, 225, 226, 243
Kirkman, James S, 38, 94, 95, 103, 113, 230, 239
Kiswahili., Ix, Xiii, 15, 90, 115, 116, 119, 120, 122, 123, 128, 133, 136, 138, 139, 140, 141, 143, 148, 149, 151, 152, 157, 159, 160, 164, 170, 171, 174, 175, 177, 181, 182, 186, 191, 192, 196, 197, 198, 199, 201, 206, 209, 210, 211, 219, 220, 232, 233, 234, 240, 241
Kiwabi, Emir Muhammad, 34
Kusimba, 18, 20, 25, 27, 84, 86, 93, 95, 102, 108, 110, 111, 225, 239

L

Limpopo River, 22
Lingala,, 148, 164
Lompopo River, 79
Lumumba, Patrice, 148

M

Madagascar, 17, 19, 32, 105, 109, 111, 119, 132, 229

CPSIA information can be obtained
at www.ICGtesting.com
Printed in the USA
LVHW102134150722
723616LV00008B/413

9 781909 112445

ANESTHESIA SECRETS
Second Edition

ANESTHESIA SECRETS
Second Edition

JAMES DUKE, M.D.

Assistant Professor
Department of Anesthesiology
University of Colorado Health Sciences Center
Associated Director of Anesthesiology
Denver Health Medical Center
Denver, Colorado

HANLEY & BELFUS, INC.
An Affiliate of Elsevier

HANLEY & BELFUS, INC.
An Affiliate of Elsevier

The Curtis Center
Independence Square West
Philadelphia, Pennsylvania 19106

Note *to the reader*: Although the information in this book has been carefully reviewed for correctness of dosage and indications, neither the authors nor the editor nor the publisher can accept any legal responsibility for any errors or omissions that may be made. Neither the publisher nor the editor makes any warranty, expressed or implied, with respect to the material contained herein. Before prescribing any drug, the reader must review the manufacturer's current product information (package inserts) for accepted indications, absolute dosage recommendations, and other information pertinent to the safe and effective use of the product described. This is especially important when drugs are given in combination or as an adjunct to other forms of therapy.

Anesthesia secrets / edited by James Duke—2nd ed.
      p. ; cm.—(Secrets series)
      Includes bibliographical references and index.
      ISBN 1-56053-354-4 (alk. paper)
         I. Duke, James, 1957- . II. Series.
      [DNLM: 1. Anesthesia—Examination Questions. 2.
   Anesthesiology—methods—Examination Questions. 3. Anesthetics—Examination
   Questions. WO 218.2 A578 2000]

                                                99-048700

ANESTHESIA SECRETS, 2nd edition   ISBN 1-56053-354-4

Permissions may be sought directly from Elsevier's Health Sciences Rights Department in Philadelphia, USA: phone: (+1)215-238-7869, fax: (+1)215-238-2239, email: healthpermissions@elsevier.com. You may also complete your request on-line via the Elsevier Science homepage (http://www.elsevier.com), by selecting 'Customer Support' and then 'Obtaining Permissions'.

Printed in the United States of America

Last digit is the print number: 9 8 7 6 5

DEDICATION

To my best friends, my wife Renée and my brother Ron, with all my love.

CONTENTS

VI. ANESTHESIA AND SYSTEMIC DISEASE

CONTRIBUTORS

Richard D. Abbott, M.D.
Department of Anesthesiology, University of Colorado Health Sciences Center, Denver, Colorado

David T. Adamson, M.D.
Anesthesiologist in Private Practice, Salida, Colorado

Rita Agarwal, M.D.
Associate Professor, Department of Anesthesiology, University of Colorado Health Sciences Center; Co-Director, Acute Pain Service; Attending Anesthesiologist; The Children's Hospital, Denver, Colorado

Richard B. Allen, M.D.
Anesthesiologist in Private Practice, Rapid City, South Dakota

Jose M. Angel, M.D.
Anesthesiologist in Private Practice, Boulder, Colorado

Tanya Argo, M.D.
Anesthesiologist in Private Practice, Denver, Colorado

Robert F. Bossard, M.D.
Assistant Professor, Department of Anesthesiology and Pain Management, University of Texas Southwestern Medical Center, Dallas, Texas

Donald G. Crino, M.D.
Assistant Professor, Department of Anesthesiology, University of Colorado Health Sciences Center; Attending Anesthesiologist, Denver Health Medical Center, Denver, Colorado

Michael Duey, M.D.
Anesthesiologist in Private Practice, Denver, Colorado

James Duke, M.D.
Assistant Professor, Department of Anesthesiology, University of Colorado Health Sciences Center; Associate Director, Department of Anesthesiology, Denver Health Medical Center, Denver, Colorado

Stephan O. Fiedler, M.D.
Anesthesiologist in Private Practice, Denver, Colorado

Kevin Fitzpatrick, M.D.
Anesthesiologist in Private Practice, Brighton, Colorado

Matthew D. Flaherty, M.D.
Anesthesiologist in Private Practice, Greeley, Colorado

Robert H. Friesen, M.D.
Clinical Professor, Department of Anesthesiology, University of Colorado Health Sciences Center; Associate Director, Department of Anesthesiology, The Children's Hospital, Denver, Colorado

Timothy Fry, D.O.
Anesthesiologist in Private Practice, Denver, Colorado

Frederick M. Galloway, M.D.
Associate Professor, Department of Anesthesiology, University of Colorado Health Sciences Center, Denver, Colorado

Rose A. Gates, R.N., M.S.N., O.C.N.
Senior Instructor and Clinical Nurse Specialist, Department of Anesthesiology, University of Colorado Health Sciences Center, Denver, Colorado

David M. Glenn, M.D.
Anesthesiologist in Private Practice, Stanford, California

Julian M. Goldman, M.D.
Associate Professor, Department of Anesthesiology, University of Colorado Health Sciences Center, Denver, Colorado

Patricia A. Gottlob, M.D.
Staff Anesthesiologist, Colorado Permanente Medical Group, Denver, Colorado

Cindy Griffiths, M.D.
Anesthesiologist in Private Practice, Denver, Colorado

Cynthia K. Hampson, M.D., M.B.A.
Physician Anesthesia Group, P.S.; Sacred Heart Medical Center, Spokane, Washington

John Alden Hatheway, M.D.
Staff Anesthesiologist and Director of Pain Management, Naval Ambulatory Care Center, Newport, Rhode Island

Joy L. Hawkins, M.D.
Professor, Department of Anesthesiology; Director, Obstetric Anesthesia, University of Colorado Health Sciences Center, Denver, Colorado

Alma N. Juels, M.D.
Assistant Clinical Professor, Department of Anesthesiology, University of Colorado Health Sciences Center, Denver, Colorado

Jeremy J. Katz, M.D.
Assistant Professor, Department of Anesthesiology, University of Colorado Health Sciences Center; University Hospital, Denver, Colorado

Theresa L. Kinnard, M.D.
Associate Professor, Department of Anesthesiology, University of Colorado Health Sciences Center, Denver, Colorado

William V. Kinnard, M.D.
Pulmonologist, Boulder, Colorado

Lyle E. Kirson, D.D.S.
Associate Professor, Department of Anesthesiology, University of Colorado Health Sciences Center; Veterans Affairs Medical Center, Denver, Colorado

Paige Latham, M.D.
Assistant Professor, Department of Anesthesiology and Pain Management, University of Texas Southwestern Medical Center at Dallas; Director, Cardiothoracic and Vascular Anesthesia, Parkland Health and Hospital System, Zale-Lipsky University Hospital, Dallas, Texas

Lisa Leonard, CRNA, M.H.S.
Nurse Anesthetist in Private Practice, Denver, Colorado

Michael Leonard, M.D.
Chief, Department of Anesthesia, Colorado Permanente Medical Group, Denver, Colorado

Philip R. Levin, M.D.
Assistant Clinical Professor, Department of Anesthesiology, UCLA School of Medicine, Los Angeles, California

Ana M. Lobo, M.D., M.P.H.
Anesthesiologist in Private Practice, Denver, Colorado

John D. Lockrem, M.D.
Department of Anesthesiology, University of Colorado Health Sciences Center, Denver, Colorado

Steven J. Luke, M.D.
Anesthesiologist in Private Practice, Dallas, Texas

Laurel L. Mahonee, M.D.
Anesthesiologist in Private Practice, Denver, Colorado

M. Susan Mandell, M.D., Ph.D.
Anesthesiologist in Private Practice, Denver, Colorado

Lora L. Manning, B.S.N., MSNA, CRNA
Nurse Anesthetist, Denver, Colorado

Roger A. Mattison, M.D.
Department of Anesthesiology, University of Colorado Health Sciences Center, Denver, Colorado

Stephanie E. May, M.S.A., CRNA
Staff Anesthetist, Department of Anesthesiology, Denver Health Medical Center, Denver, Colorado

Gladstone C. McDowell II, M.D.
Anesthesiologist, Columbus, Ohio

Howard J. Miller, M.D.
Assistant Professor, Department of Anesthesiology, University of Colorado Health Sciences Center; Denver Health Medical Center, Denver, Colorado

Paul K. Miller, M.D.
Assistant Professor, Department of Anesthesiology and Critical Care Medicine, University of Colorado Health Sciences Center; Medical Director, Surgical Intensive Care Unit, University Hospital, Denver, Colorado

Jefferson P. Mostellar, M.D.
Anesthesiologist in Private Practice, Englewood, Colorado

Jeff S. Nabonsal, M.D.
Anesthesiologist in Private Practice, Brighton, Colorado

Kenneth Niejadlik, M.D.
Anesthesiologist in Private Practice, Denver, Colorado

J. Todd Nilson, M.D.
Department of Anesthesiology, University of Colorado Health Sciences Center, Denver, Colorado

Michael B. Ochs, D.O.
Anesthesiologist in Private Practice, Denver, Colorado

James A. Ottevaere II, M.D.
Anesthesiologist in Private Practice, Eau Claire, Wisconsin

Malcolm Packer, M.D.
Assistant Professor, Department of Anesthesiology, Denver Health Medical Center, Denver, Colorado

Robert W. Phelps, Ph.D., M.D.
Associate Professor, Department of Anesthesiology, University of Colorado Health Sciences Center; University Hospital; Veterans Affairs Medical Center, Denver, Colorado

Philip A. Role, M.D.
Anesthesiologist in Private Practice, Bonner General Hospital, Sandpoint, Idaho

Stuart G. Rosenberg, M.D.
Intensivist in Private Practice, Denver, Colorado

James W. Rosher, M.D.
Department of Anesthesiology, University of Colorado Health Sciences Center, Denver, Colorado

Peter Sakas, M.D.
Anesthesiologist in Private Practice, Boulder, Colorado

William D. Sefton, M.D.
Anesthesiologist in Private Practice, Andrews Air Force Base, Clinton, Maryland

Andrew A. Shultz, M.D.
Anesthesiologist in Private Practice, Denver, Colorado

Robert H. Slover, M.D.
Assistant Professor, Department of Pediatrics, University of Colorado Health Sciences Center, Denver, Colorado

Robin B. Slover, M.D.
Anesthesiologist in Private Practice, Salt Lake City, Utah

Steven J. Stein, M.D.
Anesthesiologist in Private Practice, San Antonio, Texas

David E. Strick, M.D.
Anesthesiologist in Private Practice, Atlanta, Georgia

Kenneth M. Swank, M.D.
Assistant Professor, Department of Anesthesiology, University of Colorado Health Sciences Center; Denver Health Medical Center, Denver, Colorado

William Turner, M.D.
Department of Surgery, Washington University School of Medicine, St. Louis, Missouri

Andrew M. Veit, M.D.
Assistant Professor, Department of Anesthesiology, University of Colorado Health Sciences Center; The Children's Hospital, Denver, Colorado

Elizabeth F. Ward, CRNA
Staff Nurse Anesthetist, Department of Anesthesiology, Denver Health Medical Center, Denver, Colorado

Douglas E. Warnecke, CRNA, M.S.
Department of Anesthesiology, Denver Health Medical Center, Denver, Colorado

Kelli Lambert Weiner, M.D.
Anesthesiologist in Private Practice, Fort Collins, Colorado

Lee Weiss, M.D.
Department of Anesthesiology, University of Colorado Health Sciences Center, Denver, Colorado

Charles W. Whitten, M.D.
Professor, Department of Anesthesiology and Pain Management, University of Texas Southwestern Medical Center at Dallas; Director, Anesthesia Surgical Services, Parkland Health and Hospital System, Dallas, Texas

Mark Wilson, R.R.T.
Respiratory Therapist, Denver, Colorado

Gene Winkelmann, M.D.
Anesthesiologist in Private Practice, Fargo, North Dakota

John H. Yang, M.D.
Department of Family Medicine, University of Colorado Health Sciences Center, Denver, Colorado

Teresa J. Youtz, M.D.
Anesthesiologist in Private Practice, Denver, Colorado

PREFACE TO THE FIRST EDITION

An anesthesiologist is a physician first. Ensuring an insensate state within the confines of the operative theater is much too narrow an interpretation of the specialty. The practice of anesthesiology is the practice of perioperative medicine, encompassing pre-, intra-, and postoperative care. The perioperative physician understands the application of physiologic and pharmacologic principles in the care of the patient undergoing the stress of a surgical procedure. He or she must appreciate the pathophysiology involved and the human as an adaptive organism. Though the specialty is rich in technical skills mastered through continued practice, the real skill is centered about sound judgment and a substantial knowledge base. It is these attributes to which we hope this book contributes in a somewhat unique way.

This text, like all books in *The Secrets Series*®, is designed in a question and answer format. *Anesthesia Secrets* is sufficiently broad that it should be of value to the medical student recently introduced to the specialty, to house officers at all levels of training, and to all practitioners preparing for board examinations. The application of this knowledge easily extends to clinical situations outside the operating room, encompassing preoperative and postoperative evaluation, and to problems encountered in emergency and critical care settings. We challenge the reader to examine the question and formulate a response before reviewing the answer in order to participate fully in the learning experience. We trust this method will prove both fun and stimulating. We hope you find this to be true and this text to be valuable.

James Duke, M.D.
Stuart G. Rosenberg, M.S.

PREFACE TO THE SECOND EDITION

My thanks go to all of the readers of the first edition. Favorable comments from residents and students have been their own rewards, and I was certainly gratified by the text's widespread popularity.

Since the first edition, no more hours have been added to the day or week to accomplish all of the tasks at hand. Recognizing that everyone's time is his most precious commodity, I have made earnest efforts to focus the discussions. Chapters on Congenital Heart Disease, Acute Respiratory Distress Syndrome, and Laparoscopy are new additions. As in the first edition, I hope you find this second effort valuable.

James Duke, M.D.

I. Basics of Patient Management

1. THE AUTONOMIC NERVOUS SYSTEM

William Turner, M.D., and James Duke, M.D.

1. Describe the autonomic nervous system.

The autonomic nervous system (ANS) is a network of nerves and ganglia that control involuntary physiologic parameters and maintain internal homeostasis and stress responses. The ANS innervates structures within the cardiovascular, pulmonary, endocrine, exocrine, gastrointestinal, genitourinary, and central nervous systems (CNS) and influences metabolism and thermal regulation. The ANS is divided into two parts: the sympathetic (SNS) and parasympathetic (PNS) nervous system. Activation of the SNS has been classically associated with the "flight or fight" response. The SNS and PNS generally have opposing effects on end-organs, with either the SNS or the PNS exhibiting a dominant resting tone.

2. Describe the functional anatomy and physiology of the sympathetic nervous system.

Preganglionic sympathetic neurons originate from the intermediolateral columns of the thoracic and lumbar region of the spinal cord (T1–L2, L3) and synapse at one of three different types of ganglia: the paired paravertebral sympathetic chain, the unpaired prevertebral ganglia, or a terminal ganglion. Preganglionic neurons may ascend or descend the sympathetic chain before synapsing. Preganglionic neurons stimulate nicotinic receptors on postganglionic sympathetic neurons by releasing acetylcholine. Postganglionic neurons synapse at targeted end-organs and release norepinephrine.

3. What peripheral receptors are involved in the SNS? What is the end-organ response to receptor activation?

Adrenergic receptors include the following: alpha-1 (A1), alpha-2 (A2), beta-1 (B1), and beta-2 (B2). Generally, A1, B1, and B2 receptors are postsynaptic, whereas A2 receptors are presynaptic. Alpha-1 receptor activation produces contraction of the vas deferens, trigone, ureter, splenic capsule, and prostatic capsule as well as arteriolar constriction, mydriasis, piloerection, salivation, and lacrimation. Alpha-2 receptor activation produces negative feedback inhibition for subsequent norepinephrine release. Beta-1 receptor activation produces positive inotropic and chronotropic effects on the heart while increasing renin secretion and lipolysis. Beta-2 receptor activation produces bronchodilation, liver glycogenolysis, and skeletal muscle vascular dilation.

Dopamine exerts adrenergic effects but also activates a physiologically distinct class of receptors known as dopaminergic receptors. The two clinically important dopaminergic receptors are DA1 and DA2. Activation of DA1 receptors produces dilation of blood vessels in renal, coronary, and splanchnic vascular beds, whereas activation of CNS DA2 receptors produces nausea, vomiting, and psychic disturbances. Exogenous dopamine cannot cross the blood-brain barrier.

4. Describe direct- and indirect-acting sympathomimetic agents.

Direct-acting drugs are agonists at the targeted receptor, whereas indirect-acting drugs produce the release of endogenous neurotransmitters into the synaptic junction. Sympathomimetics may be classified as direct-acting, indirect-acting, or mixed direct- and indirect-acting. Ephedrine

1

and dopamine are examples of mixed direct- and indirect-acting sympathomimetics, whereas phenylephrine is an example of a direct-acting agent. Mixed and indirect-acting agents lose efficacy with repeated administration or in catecholamine-depleted states.

Receptor Activity of Adrenergic Agents and Mechanism of Action

AGENT	RECEPTOR	DIRECT/INDIRECT/MIXED
Norepinephrine	A1, A2, B1	Direct
Epinephrine	A1, A2, B1, B2	Direct
Isoproterenol	B1, B2	Direct
Dopamine	A1, B1, DA	Mixed
Clonidine	A2	Direct
Phenylephrine	A1	Direct
Ephedrine	A1, A2, B1, B2	Mixed

5. What is dose-specific receptor affinity?

Dopamine and epinephrine demonstrate different receptor effects at different infusion rates. Dopamine has predominantly dopaminergic effects below an infusion rate of 3 µg/kg/min, beta-adrenergic effects from 3 to 10 µg/kg/min, and alpha-adrenergic effects at greater than 10 µg/kg/min. Therefore, dopamine may be infused at different rates to obtain a specific pharmacologic effect. Epinephrine has predominantly B2 effects below 2 µg/min, B1 and B2 effects from 2 to 10 µg/min, and A1 effects at greater than 10 µg/min.

6. Review the synthesis of norepinephrine and epinephrine.

Synthesis of norepinephrine begins with active transport of tyrosine into the adrenergic presynaptic nerve terminal cytoplasm. In the cytoplasm tyrosine is converted to dopamine by two enzymatic reactions: hydroxylation of tyrosine by tyrosine hydroxylase to dopa and decarboxylation of dopa by aromatic l-amino acid decarboxylase to dopamine. Dopamine is then transported into storage vesicles, where it is ß-hydroxylated by dopamine ß-hydroxylase to norepinephrine. Epinephrine is synthesized in the adrenal medulla through the same sequence of enzymatic reactions as norepinephrine, except that a majority of the norepinephrine produced is converted to epinephrine through n-methylation by phenylethanolamine n-methyltransferase.

7. Describe the metabolism of norepinephrine and epinephrine.

Norepinephrine is removed from the synaptic junction by two mechanisms: reuptake into the presynaptic nerve terminal and inactivation at non-neuronal tissues. Removal of norepinephrine by reuptake into the presynaptic nerve terminal produces neurotransmitters for reuse and is the most important mechanism of inactivation. Enzymatic metabolism of norepinephrine and epinephrine is by monoamine oxidase (MAO) and catecholamine O-methyl transferase (COMT); the important metabolites are 3-methoxy-4-hydroxy-mandelic acid (VMA), metanephrine, and normetanephrine.

8. Describe the pharmacology of common beta-adrenergic antagonists.

Beta-adrenergic antagonists, commonly called beta blockers, are reversible antagonists at ß1 and ß2 receptors. Beta blockers are used mainly in antihypertensive, antianginal, and antiarrhythmic therapy. Beta blockers may be cardioselective, with relatively selective B1 antagonist properties, or noncardioselective. Beta-1 blockade produces negative inotropic and chronotropic effects, decreases renin secretion, and inhibits lipolysis. Beta-2 blockade produces bronchoconstriction, peripheral vasoconstriction, and inhibition of glycogenolysis. In addition, some beta blockers have partial beta-agonist activity, and some have membrane-stabilizing or antiarrhythmic effects.

Properties of Selective Beta Blockers

BETA	CARDIOSELECTIVE	PARTIAL AGONIST	MEMBRANE-STABILIZING
Propranolol	0	0	+
Timolol	0	0	0
Pindolol	0	+	+
Metoprolol	+	0	0
Atenolol	+	0	0
Acebutolol	+	+	+
Esmolol	+	0	0
Labetalol	0*	0	0

* Also an alpha-1 antagonist.
0 = not a characteristic; + = has this characteristic.

9. Describe the pharmacology of common alpha-adrenergic antagonists.

Like beta blockers, alpha blockers may be selective or nonselective antagonists. Prazosin is the prototypical selective alpha-1 blocker, whereas phentolamine and phenoxybenzamine are examples of nonselective alpha blockers. Alpha blockers produce vasodilation and are used in the management of hypertension. When used as an antihypertensive, nonselective alpha blockers may be associated with reflex tachycardia. As a consequence, selective alpha-1 blockers are primarily used as antihypertensives. Labetalol is a nonselective beta blocker and a selective alpha-1 blocker used for treatment of angina, hypertension, glaucoma, and pheochromocytoma.

10. Describe the functional anatomy and physiology of the parasympathetic nervous system.

Preganglionic parasympathetic neurons originate from cranial nerves III, VII, IX, and X and sacral segments 2–4. Preganglionic parasympathetic neurons tend to synapse with postganglionic neurons close to the targeted end-organ, creating a more discrete physiologic effect. Both pre- and postganglionic parasympathetic neurons release acetylcholine as the neurotransmitter. The receptors are subclassified as nicotinic (ganglionic and neuromuscular cholinergic receptors) or muscarinic (postganglionic cholinergic receptors). The vagus nerve is the dominant nerve of the PNS. Vagal discharge affects the heart, respiratory tree, spleen, liver, kidney, bladder, and proximal intestinal tract. The PNS tends to maintain baseline function of visceral organs. Important effects of the PNS include bronchoconstriction, activation of the gastrointestinal system, miosis, increase in secretions, and bradycardia.

11. Describe the synthesis and degradation of acetylcholine.

Acetylcholine is synthesized within the presynaptic nerve terminal mitochondria by esterification of acetyl coenzyme A (CoA) and choline by the enzyme choline acetyltransferase; it is stored in synaptic vesicles until release. After release, acetylcholine is principally metabolized by acetylcholinesterase, a membrane-bound enzyme located in the synaptic junction. Acetylcholinesterase is also located in other nonneuronal tissues, such as erythrocytes.

12. Describe the pharmacology of common muscarinic antagonists.

Muscarinic antagonists, also known as anticholinergics, block all muscarinic receptors equally, with the exception of charged quaternary forms that do not cross the blood-brain barrier. Muscarinic antagonists produce bronchodilation, inhibition of secretions, and mydriasis, along with antispasmodic and positive chronotropic effects. Centrally acting muscarinic antagonists may produce delirium. There are four commonly used muscarinic antagonists: atropine, scopolamine, glycopyrrolate, and ipratropium bromide. Glycopyrrolate is a quaternary ammonium compound that cannot cross the blood-brain barrier and therefore lacks CNS activity. Ipratropium bromide is a poorly absorbed inhaled agent that is useful in the management of asthma by antagonizing the bronchoconstrictive effects of acetylcholine.

13. What features of the history and physical exam suggest autonomic dysfunction?
The signs and symptoms of autonomic dysfunction include orthostatic blood pressure changes as well as vasomotor, bladder, bowel, and sexual dysfunction. Patients should be asked about orthostatic symptoms, blurred vision, reduced or excessive sweating, dry or excessively moist eyes and mouth, cold or discolored extremities, incontinence or incomplete voiding, diarrhea or constipation, and impotence. Patients with autonomic dysfunction also demonstrate lack of heart rate variability with changes in posture (supine to erect). Evaluation of orthostatic blood pressure and heart rate changes is of key importance during the physical exam.

14. List some causes of autonomic dysfunction.

Diabetes mellitus	Rheumatoid arthritis
Hyperthyroidism	Systemic lupus erythematosus
Horner's syndrome	Paraneoplastic autonomic dysfunction
Pheochromocytoma	Shy-Drager syndrome
Human immunodeficiency virus	Fabry's disease
Amyloidosis	Heavy metal autonomic neuropathy
Uremia	Cis-platinum and vincristine chemotherapy
Alcohol use and withdrawal	Tetanus
Guillain-Barré syndrome	Botulism
Eaton-Lambert syndrome	

15. List some commonly used drugs that have autonomic effects.
Commonly used medications with anticholinergic effects include antipsychotics, antihistamines, tricyclic antidepressants, cyclobenzaprine (Flexeril), and amantadine. Sympathomimetic medications, especially indirect-acting agents such as ephedrine, should be avoided when a patient has recently consumed MAO inhibitors (a class of antidepressants) or illicit stimulants, such as amphetamines and cocaine. A combination of these drugs may produce a toxic, hypersympathetic response.

16. How can renal and splanchnic blood flow be preserved when sympathomimetics are used?
Dopamine is the agent of choice to increase renal blood flow when a sympathomimetic is needed because it dilates renal and splanchnic vasculature. However, at an infusion rate greater than 10 µg/kg/min, dopamine constricts renal and splanchnic vasculature by exhibiting alpha-agonist properties.

17. How is pheochromocytoma diagnosed and treated?
Pheochromocytoma is a catecholamine-secreting tumor of chromaffin tissue. Most tumors are located in the adrenal medulla. Signs and symptoms include paroxysms of hypertension, headache, palpitations, flushing, and sweating. Pheochromocytoma is confirmed by detecting elevated levels of plasma and urinary catecholamines and urinary VMA, normetanephrines, and metanephrines. The treatment for pheochromocytoma is surgical excision. Preoperatively, the patient should be given an alpha antagonist (to control hypertension) and hydrated. If the patient becomes tachycardic, a beta blocker is instituted. Intraoperatively, invasive monitoring is needed to detect fluctuations in blood pressure and to guide therapy. Intraoperative hypertension is controlled by intravenous infusion of an alpha antagonist or nitroprusside. Once the tumor is removed, the patient should be monitored for hypoglycemia and hypotension.

BIBLIOGRAPHY

1. Andreoli T, Bennett JC, Carpenter CCJ, Plum F (eds): Cecil's Essentials of Medicine, 4th ed. Philadelphia, W.B. Saunders, 1997, pp 815–817.
2. Drug Evaluations Annual, 1994. Chicago, American Medical Association, 1994, pp 210–211, 539–549, 680–683.

3. Lefkowitz RJ, Hoffman BB, Taylor P: The autonomic and somatic motor neuron systems. In Hardman JG, Limbird LE (eds): Goodman and Gilman's The Pharmacological Basis of Therapeutics, 9th ed. New York, McGraw-Hill, 1996, pp 105–140.
4. Low P: Clinical Autonomic Disorders: Evaluation and Management. Boston, Little, Brown, 1993, pp 157–197.
5. Moss J, Craigo P: The autonomic nervous system. In Miller R (ed): Anesthesia, 4th ed. New York, Churchill Livingstone, 1994, pp 523–577.

2. OXYGENATION AND VENTILATION

David T. Adamson, M.D.

Editor's note: Refer to Chapter 29, Hypoxemia and Pulmonary Physiology, and Chapter 83, Respiratory Therapy, to complement this discussion. Chapter 3, Blood Gas and Acid-Base Analysis, Chapter 23, Pulse Oximetry, and Chapter 24, Capnography, discuss monitoring oxygenation and ventilation.

1. What are the major causes of hypoxemia?

Low inspired oxygen (O_2) concentration: Common causes of decreased oxygen concentration (FiO_2) are low O_2 mixtures, depleted O_2 supply, or breathing circuit disconnection. In the normal situation, arterial oxygenation is a function of alveolar oxygen concentration. A hypoxic gas mixture delivered to the alveoli (low PAO_2) will result in a low arterial oxygen tension (PaO_2). This relationship is described by the alveolar gas equation where Pb is the barometric pressure, $P_{vapor\ H_2O}$ is the vapor pressure of water, and $PaCO_2$ is the alveolar pressure of carbon dioxide (CO_2):

$$PAO_2 = FiO_2 (Pb - P_{vapor\ H_2O}) - (PaCO_2/0.8)$$

This equation reveals a direct relationship between FiO_2 and PAO_2. The denominator in the equation is called the respiratory quotient (RQ). The RQ is a ratio of CO_2 production to O_2 consumption, and in a healthy patient the RQ averages about 0.8. The RQ is considered to be constant but can change with the patient's metabolic state and dietary consumption.

Hypoventilation: Most patients under the effects of general anesthesia are incapable of maintaining an adequate minute ventilation to deliver sufficient O_2 to the alveoli. This may be due to muscular paralysis or the ventilatory depressant effects of virtually any of the anesthetic agents used. This effect is usually overcome by using O_2-enriched inspiratory gases and by mechanically ventilating the lungs.

Shunt: In the normal healthy patient, arteriovenous shunting accounts for about 2% of the cardiac output (CO) mainly due to blood flow through the thebesian veins of the heart and the pulmonary bronchial veins. With adequate CO, this physiologic shunt is well tolerated. Disease states such as sepsis, liver failure, arteriovenous malformations, pulmonary emboli, and right-to-left cardiac shunts can create significant shunting that will result in hypoxemia. As shunted blood is not exposed to alveoli, hypoxemia caused by shunt cannot be overcome by increasing FiO_2.

Ventilation-perfusion (V/Q) inequality or mismatch: Ventilation and perfusion of the alveoli in the lung ideally have a 1 to 1 relationship that allows for efficient oxygen exchange between alveoli and blood. When alveolar ventilation and perfusion to the lungs are abnormal (V/Q mismatching), hypoxemia can result. Some causes of V/Q mismatching are atelectasis, patient positioning, bronchial intubation, purposeful one-lung ventilation, bronchospasm, pneumonia, mucus plugging, adult respiratory distress syndrome (ARDS), and airway obstruction. Hypoxemia due to V/Q mismatching can usually be overcome by increasing FiO_2.

Cardiac output (CO)/oxygen carrying capacity: Oxygenation of tissues depends on the carrying capacity of oxygen in the blood and delivery of blood to the tissues. This concept is described by the oxygen delivery (DO_2) equation:

$$DO_2 = (O_2 \text{ capacity})(CO)$$

where O_2 capacity is equal to $(1.39 \times Hb \times \%Sat) + (0.003 \times PaO_2)$. The 1.39 is the ml of O_2 that each gram of hemoglobin can carry, Hb is the hemoglobin concentration, and %Sat is the hemoglobin saturation. Multiplying the PaO_2 by 0.003 gives the amount of O_2 that can be carried in the blood as a dissolved gas (a very, very small amount). From this equation it is apparent that as cardiac output or O_2 capacity falls, so will the DO_2, which ultimately results in hypoxemia.

Diffusion: Efficient O_2 exchange depends on a healthy interface between the alveoli and the bloodstream. In severe pulmonary diseases, such as pulmonary fibrosis, pulmonary edema, and ARDS, oxygenation can be adversely affected, as O_2 cannot diffuse from the alveoli into the blood.

2. What is pCO_2 and how is it related to alveolar ventilation?

The amount of CO_2 in the blood, or pCO_2, is inversely related to the alveolar ventilation. This is described by the equation:

$$pCO_2 = (V_{CO_2}/V_{alveolar})$$

where V_{CO_2} is the CO_2 production of the body (for our purposes considered constant), and $V_{alveolar}$ is the alveolar ventilation (defined as minute volume less the dead space of ventilation). In general, minute ventilation and pCO_2 are inversely related.

3. What are the causes of hypercarbia?

Hypoventilation: As stated, decreasing the minute ventilation will ultimately decrease alveolar ventilation, increasing pCO_2. Some common causes of hypoventilation include muscle paralysis, inadequate mechanical ventilation, inhalational anesthetics, and opiates.

Increased CO_2 production: Although CO_2 production is assumed to be constant, there are certain situations in which metabolism and CO_2 production are increased. Malignant hyperthermia, fever, thyrotoxicosis, and other hypercatabolic states are some examples.

Iatrogenic: The anesthesiologist can administer certain drugs to increase CO_2. The most common is sodium bicarbonate, which is metabolized by the enzyme carbonic anhydrase to form CO_2. Rarely, CO_2-enriched gases can be administered. Exhaustion of the CO_2 absorbent in the anesthesia breathing circuit can result in rebreathing of exhaled gases and may also result in hypercarbia.

4. What physiologic effects occur in a hypoxic and hypercarbic anesthetized patient?

The most common effects of mild hypoxia and/or hypercarbia are hypertension and tachycardia due to reflex sympathetic stimulation. Effects of profound hypoxia and hypercarbia include myocardial irritability and depression, cyanosis, bradycardia, and circulatory collapse.

5. What effects do the inhalational anesthetics have on ventilation?

In the unanesthetized patient, ventilation is usually regulated to maintain pCO_2 and pO_2 at normal values (about 40 and 80 torr, respectively). While the drive to maintain ventilation is regulated by both CO_2 and O_2, the most important regulator is CO_2. This is made possible by chemoreceptors in the medulla and receptors in the carotid bifurcations and on the aortic arch. Chemoreceptors in the medulla are primarily sensitive to changes in CO_2 and subsequent changes in cerebrospinal fluid pH, whereas the carotid and aortic bodies are sensitive to changes in pO_2. The potent inhalational anesthetics such as halothane, isoflurane, desflurane, and sevoflurane greatly attenuate the ventilatory response to hypercarbia and hypoxemia (see Figure, next page).

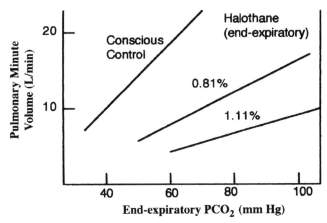

The CO_2 response curve shows the effects of inhalational anesthetics on the pulmonary minute volume with increasing pCO_2. As the inhalational agent is increased, the curve is shifted to the right, showing a decreased minute volume response to increasing hypercarbia. (Adapted from Foltz B, Benumof J: Mechanisms of hypoxemia and hypercapnia in the perioperative period. Crit Care Clin 3:279, 1987, with permission.)

6. What might be done to improve oxygenation?

Increase FiO_2

Increase minute ventilation

Increase cardiac output (oxygen delivery to tissues)

Increase oxygen carrying capacity (hemoglobin)

Optimize V/Q relationships (i.e., positive end-expiratory pressure [PEEP]/continuous positive airway pressure [CPAP])

Cardiopulmonary bypass

Decrease oxygen consumption from pain, shivering, or fever

Induce muscular paralysis

7. How does PEEP work?

PEEP increases oxygenation by maximizing the ventilation–perfusion relationship in the lung. By maintaining this positive pressure at the end of exhalation, alveoli that would tend to become collapsed are maintained in the open state, allowing for continued ventilation and O_2 exchange in lung units that would otherwise be perfused but not ventilated (V/Q mismatch). The lung volume at the end of exhalation is called the functional residual capacity (FRC). The FRC is the lung volume at the end of a normal expiration, which is about 2.5 L. The volume at which alveoli begin to collapse is called the closing capacity (CC). When the CC is greater than the FRC, airway collapse occurs. PEEP maximizes the FRC, keeping lung volumes greater than closing capacity, therefore maintaining open and functional airways. Some causes of an increased CC are obesity, increased abdominal pressure, supine position, ARDS, aspiration, pregnancy, and pulmonary edema.

8. What is the purpose of preoxygenation before the induction of anesthesia?

Preoxygenation is an important part of any general anesthetic. In an unanesthetized person, inspired room air contains approximately 21% O_2, with the remainder being mostly nitrogen (N_2). Not many people can go more than a few minutes without ventilation before desaturation occurs. If patients breathe 100% oxygen for several minutes, they may not desaturate for up to 3–5 minutes, because the FRC of the lung has been completely washed of N_2 and filled with O_2. The FRC is much less in patients who are obese, are pregnant, or have increased abdominal pressure. Neonates also have a disproportionately small FRC and will desaturate very quickly, even with adequate preoxygenation.

9. What is diffusion hypoxia?

Diffusion hypoxia is a decrease in pO_2 usually observed as the patient is emerging from an inhalational anesthetic where nitrous oxide (N_2O) is a component. The rapid outpouring of insoluble N_2O can displace alveolar oxygen, resulting in hypoxia. All patients should receive supplemental O_2 at the end of an anesthetic and during the immediate recovery period.

10. You are on call (your first), and, much to your dismay, your beeper goes off. You answer the page and are informed that Mr. Smith in the ICU has acute pulmonary edema and needs to be intubated. Your senior resident and attending are both unavailable. What will you need to intubate Mr. Smith?

When intubating a patient, whether inside or outside of the operating room, certain bare essentials must be present to ensure a safe intubation. They can be remembered by the mnemonic **SALT.**

Suction. This is extremely important. Often patients will have material in the pharynx, making visualization of the vocal cords difficult. Also, suction needs to be present to avoid the aspiration of vomitus or other material. Aspiration is **bad.**

Airway. The oral airway is a device that lifts the tongue off the posterior pharynx, often making it easier to mask-ventilate a patient. The inability to ventilate a patient is **bad**. Also, a source of O_2 with a delivery mechanism (ambu-bag and mask) must be available.

Laryngoscope. This lighted tool is vital to placing an endotracheal tube. Not having a laryngoscope present at an intubation is **very bad.**

Tube. Endotracheal tubes come in many sizes. In the average adult, a size 7.0 or 8.0 oral endotracheal tube will work just fine, but where prolonged intubation is expected, insert as large a tube as possible (e.g., 8.0 in women, 9.0 in men). The larger tube will prove beneficial should the patient require bronchoscopy and will simplify weaning from mechanical ventilation. Not having an endotracheal tube available at an intubation is **extremely bad.**

11. You have successfully intubated Mr. Smith, and now he requires a ventilator while his pulmonary edema is treated. The nurse turns to you and asks, "What settings would you like, Doctor?"

There are several easy rules to remember that will take the terror out of managing a patient who needs to be placed on a ventilator. They are **mode, tidal volume, rate,** and **FiO$_2$.** (First, you have listened for bilateral breath sounds.)

Mode. Whenever a patient has just been placed on a ventilator, the easiest mode to remember (which will work just fine initially) is intermittent mandatory ventilation (IMV). In this mode a patient is given all the breaths you set and can also receive breaths that he or she initiates.

Tidal volume. The average tidal volume for a normal patient is 10–12 ml/kg. For a 100-kg patient, a tidal volume between 1000 and 1200 ml would be adequate.

Rate. A good place to start the rate is 10–12 breaths per minute. With an adequate tidal volume, this will usually deliver a reasonable minute ventilation and maintain an acceptable pCO_2.

FiO$_2$. Always start with an FiO$_2$ of 1.0.

All of these settings will have to be adjusted to maintain acceptable pCO_2, pO_2, and airway pressures.

12. After returning to your call room, you receive yet another page from Mr. Smith's nurse. He informs you that he has received the blood gas analysis for Mr. Smith, which reveals: pH, 7.50; pCO$_2$, 30; pO$_2$, 50; Sat 84%. His ventilator settings are: tidal volume, 1000 ml; respiratory rate, 12 breaths/min; FiO$_2$, 1.0 (100% O$_2$); PEEP, 0. What can you do to improve Mr. Smith's oxygenation?

It would appear from the blood gas that Mr. Smith has a respiratory alkalosis, appropriate for the low pCO_2, indicating that he is receiving more than adequate minute ventilation (perhaps excessive). However, Mr. Smith is clearly hypoxic despite his inspired O_2 concentration of 100%.

Pulmonary edema prohibits lung alveoli from functioning properly, which has resulted in V/Q mismatch, causing the low PaO_2. The addition of PEEP can help to improve alveolar function and oxygenation and is usually administered between pressures of 5 and 15 cm H_2O. The most common initial level is 5 cm H_2O. One might also consider assessing for bronchial intubation.

13. What adverse effects could the addition of PEEP have on Mr. Smith?

1. Decreased cardiac output
2. Hypotension
3. Worsening hypoxia
4. Barotrauma (pneumothorax)
5. Increased intracranial pressure
6. Decreased urine output

PEEP can be a very useful tool to improve oxygenation; however, it is not without risks. Positive pressure is transmitted throughout the thorax when PEEP is applied. Any level of PEEP can decrease venous return to the heart and result in decreased CO, producing hypotension and hypoxemia. High levels of PEEP can result in trauma to lung tissue. Those most susceptible to barotrauma include patients with chronic obstructive pulmonary disease (COPD), bullous lung disease, necrotizing infections, tuberculosis, and lung transplants. Positive pressure transmitted to the venous system limits egress of blood from the cranium, elevating intracranial pressure. Sudden decreases in urine output with the institution of PEEP have been reported and are thought to be due to release of atrial natriuretic factor.

14. During a general anesthetic for which you are using nitrous oxide (N_2O) at a flow of 2 L/min and O_2 at 2 L/min, the wall supply disconnect alarm sounds. Upon turning on your E cylinder tanks of N_2O and O_2, you note that the pressure gauge for the N_2O tank reads 750 pounds per square inch (psi) and the O_2 tank's gauge reads 1000 psi. How long will you be able to deliver these gas flows before the tanks are empty?

All contemporary anesthesia machines have two sources of gases: the wall outlet and E cylinders attached to the machine itself. The cylinders are color coded and usually left shut off, being saved for use in an emergency.

A full green E cylinder of O_2 will have a pressure of 2000 psi and contain about 625 L of O_2. Since the O_2 is a compressed gas, the volume in the tank will correlate linearly with the pressure on the gauge. Therefore, a pressure of 1000 psi means the O_2 tank has about 312 L of gas left. At a flow of 2 L/min, there is enough O_2 in the tank to last 156 minutes, or about 2.5 hours.

A full blue E cylinder of N_2O will have a pressure of 750 psi and contain about 1590 L of N_2O. Nitrous oxide, being a compressed liquid, acts differently than the compressed gas in the O_2 tank. The pressure in the N_2O tank will stay at 750 psi until all of the liquid has been vaporized, and only then will the pressure in the tank begin to fall. At the point where N_2O pressure falls, there will be about 400 L of N_2O left. Since the N_2O tank in the question shows a pressure of 750 psi, we cannot tell how much N_2O remains by looking at the pressure gauge, and therefore cannot predict how long we can supply this gas (see Figure).

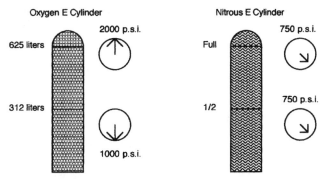

As oxygen is used, pressure in the tank decreases. In the nitrous oxide tank, the pressure remains constant until the tank is nearly empty.

15. What are the causes of a sudden decrease in end-tidal CO_2 in the anesthetized patient?

1. Low cardiac output
2. Pulmonary embolism
3. Venous-air embolism
4. Circuit leak or disconnection
5. Extubation
6. Obstruction of the airway or sampling tubing
7. Cardiac arrest

Anything that interrupts the perfusion of blood to the lungs or gas flow from the lungs will result in a decreased end-tidal CO_2. Beware of mechanical causes of decreased end–tidal CO_2, such as kinked tubing and disconnections.

BIBLIOGRAPHY

1. Barker SJ, Tremper KK: Physics applied to anesthesia. In Barash PG, Cullen BF, Stoelting RK (eds): Clinical Anesthesia, 2nd ed. Philadelphia, Lippincott Williams & Wilkins, 1992, pp 166–169.
2. Carlson K, Jahr J: A historical overview and update on pulse oximetry. Anesthesiol Rev 20:173–181, 1993.
3. Foltz B, Benumof J: Mechanisms of hypoxemia and hypercapnia in the perioperative period. Crit Care Clin 3:269–286, 1987.
4. Ganong WF: Review of Medical Physiology. Norwalk, CT, Appleton & Lange, 1987, pp 560–563.
5. Kharasch ED, Yeo KT, Kenny MA, et al: Atrial natriuretic factor may mediate the renal effects of PEEP ventilation. Anesthesiology 69:862–869, 1988.
6. Knill RL: Ventilatory responses to hypoxia and hypercarbia during halothane sedation and anesthesia in man. Anesthesiology 49:244–251, 1978.
7. Maarten JL: Does subanesthetic isoflurane affect the ventilatory response to acute isocapnic hypoxia in healthy volunteers? Anesthesiology 81:860–867, 1994.
8. Moyer GA, Rein P: Pre-oxygenation in the morbidly obese patient. Anesth Analg 65:S106, 1986.
9. Prough DS, Mathru M: Acid-base, fluids, and electrolytes. In Barash PG, Cullen BF, Stoelting RK (eds): Clinical Anesthesia, 3rd ed. Philadelphia, Lippincott Williams & Wilkins, 1997.
10. Weil MH, Bisera J, Trevino RP, et al: Cardiac output and end tidal carbon dioxide. Crit Care Med 13:907–909, 1985.
11. West JB: Respiratory Physiology: The Essentials, 5th ed. Philadelphia, Lippincott Williams & Wilkins, 1994.
12. Wyche MQ, Teichner RL, Kallos T, et al: Effects of continuous positive-pressure breathing on the functional residual capacity and arterial oxygenation during intra-abdominal operations. Anesthesiology 38:68–74,1973.

3. BLOOD GAS AND ACID-BASE ANALYSIS

Peter Sakas, M.D., and Matt Flaherty, M.D.

1. Why is arterial blood gas (ABG) analysis superior to noninvasive estimates of oxygenation and ventilation?

Pulse oximetry can readily and noninvasively estimate hemoglobin saturation (SpO_2), while blood gas analysis *measures* the partial pressure of oxygen (PO_2) within the blood, as well as measuring hemoglobin saturation. Saturation > 95% may correlate with a wide range of PO_2 values. The ABG analysis also calculates the arterial pH, bicarbonate (HCO_3^-), and base excess, which further define the patient's condition.

2. What are the normal ABG values at sea level?

Normal ABG Values

	SEA LEVEL (RANGE)	DENVER (ALT 5280 FT)
pH	7.40 (7.35–7.45 [± 2 SD])	NC
PaCO$_2$	40 mmHg (35–45 [± 2 SD])	34–38 mmHg
PaO$_2$	80–97 mmHg*	65–75 mmHg
HCO$_3^-$	24 mEq/L (22–26)	NC
SaO$_2$	> 98%	92–94%
Base excess	0 mEq/L (-3–+3)	NC

PaCO$_2$ = arterial partial pressure of carbon dioxide; PaO$_2$ = arterial partial pressure of oxygen; SaO$_2$ = arterial saturation with oxygen; NC = no change from sea-level value.
* PaO$_2$ varies with age and fractional concentration of oxygen in inspired gas (FiO$_2$).

3. Define the Henderson-Hasselbalch equation.

$$pH = 6.1 + \log (HCO_3^-/ 0.03 \times PCO_2)$$

The Henderson-Hasselbalch equation describes the relationship between the plasma pH and the ratio of plasma PCO$_2$ and HCO$_3^-$. The equation really tells us that the primary determinant of the plasma pH is the ratio of PCO$_2$ to HCO$_3^-$ and not the individual values alone. For example, a change in the PCO$_2$ may be accompanied by a change in the HCO$_3^-$ such that the ratio of the two remains the same and the pH does not change.

4. Describe the major acid-base disorders and the compensatory mechanisms seen when they are present.

Major Acid-Base Disorders and Compensatory Mechanisms

PRIMARY DISORDER	PRIMARY DISTURBANCE	PRIMARY COMPENSATION
Respiratory acidosis	↑ PCO$_2$	↑ HCO$_3^-$
Respiratory alkalosis	↓ PCO$_2$	↓ HCO$_3^-$
Metabolic acidosis	↓ HCO$_3^-$	Hyperventilation (↓ PCO$_2$)
Metabolic alkalosis	↑ HCO$_3^-$	Hypoventilation (↑ PCO$_2$)

The primary compensation (acute compensation) is generally achieved most rapidly through respiratory control of CO$_2$. Ultimately the renal system excretes acid or bicarbonate (chronic compensation) to reach the final response to the initial disturbance. Mixed disorders are common. Compensatory mechanisms never overcorrect for an acid-base disturbance; when ABG analysis reveals apparent overcorrection the presence of a mixed disorder should be suspected.

Rate of Compensatory Responses

PRIMARY DISORDER	PREDICTED RESPONSE
Respiratory acidosis	HCO$_3^-$ increases 0.1/mmHg increase in CO$_2$ (acute) HCO$_3^-$ increases 0.25–0.55/mmHg increase in CO$_2$ (chronic)
Respiratory alkalosis	HCO$_3^-$ decreases 0.2–0.55/mmHg decrease in CO$_2$ (acute) HCO$_3^-$ decreases 0.4–0.5/mmHg decrease in CO$_2$ (chronic)
Metabolic acidosis	PaCO$_2$ decreases 1–1.4/mEq HCO$_3^-$ decrease
Metabolic alkalosis	PaCO$_2$ increases 0.4–0.9/mEq HCO$_3^-$ increase

5. What are the major buffer systems of the body?

The bicarbonate-, phosphate-, and protein-buffering systems are the three major buffering systems. The **bicarbonate** system is primarily extracellular and the fastest to respond to pH imbalance, but it has less total capacity than intracelluar systems. Intracellular buffering occurs through the **phosphate** and **protein** systems. Intracellular buffering has a very large capacity, about 75% of the body's chemical buffering. Hydrogen ions are in dynamic equilibrium with all buffer systems of the body. CO_2 molecules also readily cross cell membranes and keep both intracellular and extracellular buffering systems in dynamic equilibrium. We commonly measure the status of the bicarbonate system because it exists in the plasma in large quantities and is readily measurable. Chemistry laboratories actually measure the total CO_2, a sum of all forms of CO_2 in the sample, such as bicarbonate, carbonic acid, and dissolved CO_2 gas. The bicarbonate value reported on ABG analysis is calculated from a nomogram using the Henderson-Hasselbalch equation and the measured values for pH and $PaCO_2$.

6. Does the liver have a role in acid-base balance?

Metabolism of protein usually results in net production of acid. The liver metabolizes organic acids, such as lactic acid, which conserves plasma HCO_3^-. Hepatic disease may lead to various acid-base disorders: respiratory alkalosis secondary to central nervous system stimulation; metabolic acidosis secondary to lactate accumulation or, commonly, coexisting renal disease; and mixed disorders due to combinations of these disorders.

7. How does the kidney influence acid-base balance?

The normal kidney maintains acid-base homeostasis by two mechanisms. Large amounts of bicarbonate (4500 mEq/day) are filtered at the glomerulus and then reclaimed prior to final urine formation. The kidney also excretes acid when hydrogen ions combine with phosphate and ammonia and are excreted in the urine. Renal failure results in decreased clearance of inorganic acids. **Renal tubular acidosis** (RTA) results when either proximal tubular reabsorption of bicarbonate (RTA type II) or distal tubular ammonium ion excretion (RTA type I) is impaired.

8. What is the anion gap?

A major tool used in evaluating acid-base disorders, the anion gap is the calculated difference between the serum sodium concentration and the sum of serum chloride and bicarbonate:

$$Na - (Cl + HCO_3^-)$$

The plasma is actually electrically neutral, and the "gap" is composed of anions we do not usually measure. The normal anion gap is approximately 10 and normally ranges from 8 to 12. When an acid load is present, bicarbonate ions titrate the acid, and consequently, the bicarbonate concentration falls. This drop in HCO_3^- increases the calculated anion gap. Increases in the anion gap usually indicate that the HCO_3^- concentration is being decreased by a titratable acid, creating a condition known as an **anion gap metabolic acidosis**. Anion gap elevation can occur with elevated serum HCO_3^- concentrations in mixed acid-base disorders as well.

9. Name several causes of anion gap metabolic acidosis.

Increased acid production from any of the following sources:
- Ketoacidosis (diabetic, alcoholic, or starvation)
- Lactic acidosis (hypovolemia, hypotension, hypoxia, toxins, or enzyme defects)
- Toxins (salicylates, paraldehyde, methanol, or ethylene glycol)
- Hyperosmolar hyperosmotic nonketotic coma
- Uremic acidosis (acute or chronic renal failure)

10. Name several causes of non–anion gap acidosis.

Non–anion gap acidoses are usually due to loss of bicarbonate rather than the presence of acid. Potential causes include:

Renal tubular acidosis	Interstitial nephritis
Diarrhea	Ureteral obstruction
Ureteral diversions	Drugs (e.g., spironolactone, acetazolamide)

11. Describe lactic acidosis and its causes.

Lactic acid is formed by glycolysis and arises from many metabolic pathways. Hypoxia, hypotension, hypovolemia, and sepsis all can result in states of **low tissue oxygen delivery**. Cellular metabolism of carbohydrate (oxidative phosphorylation) requires O_2; when O_2 delivery fails, the cells rely on anaerobic metabolism, producing lactate. Less common causes of lactic acidosis include diabetic ketoacidosis, liver disease, cyanide poisoning, widespread malignancy, and alcohol consumption. If a blood sample is stored for a prolonged period, the cells continually metabolize glucose to lactate and may falsely elevate the lactate content of the sample.

12. When is it appropriate to administer bicarbonate?

Metabolic acidosis is commonly treated with sodium bicarbonate, although this is controversial. Bicarbonate combines with hydrogen ions and, in the presence of the enzyme carbonic anhydrase, becomes CO_2 and H_2O. Patients with adequate ventilation can eliminate the CO_2. However patients with inadequate ventilation only accumulate more CO_2, which can readily cross cell membranes and contribute to intracelluar acidosis, a theoretical concern. Bicarbonate administration is best reserved for patients with adequate ventilation and pH < 7.20 (the pH that begins to cause generalized enzymatic and metabolic dysfunction).

Lactic acidosis may be due to tissue hypoperfusion, and therefore volume resuscitation and oxygenation should be addressed before attempting to correct the acidosis with bicarbonate infusion. There is no evidence that treatment of lactic acidosis with bicarbonate improves outcome.

Bicarbonate has been shown to be useful in renal failure, other bicarbonate-wasting states, treatment of certain toxic ingestions (such as tricyclic antidepressant overdose), and hyperkalemia. The bicarbonate dose is calculated as follows:

$$BE \times 0.3 \times \text{body wt} = \text{total base deficit}$$

Where BE is the base deficit in mEq/L, 0.3 is the extracelluar water percentage, and body weight is in kilograms. The total base deficit, in milliequivalents (mEq), is often corrected by approximately 50% and then reassessed with further ABG analysis.

13. What is a Clark electrode?

The Clark electrode, developed in 1956, measures the PO_2 in the blood sample. The oxygen electrode is based on the oxidation-reduction reaction of dissolved O_2 and water.

14. What is the Severinghaus electrode?

The Severinghaus electrode, developed in 1958, measures the PCO_2 in the blood sample.

15. What factors determine the value of $PaCO_2$?

CO_2, a major product of cellular metabolism, is primarily produced in the mitochondria and eliminated through the lungs. A simple relationship can be assumed:

$$PaCO_2 = VCO_2/VA$$

where VCO_2 is total body CO_2 production, and VA is alveolar ventilation. **Hypocapnia**, defined as $PaCO_2 < 35$ mmHg at sea level, can be caused by decreased production (e.g., hypothermia, neuromuscular blockade) and/or increased elimination (e.g., overzealous mechanical ventilation, hypoxia or metabolic acidosis with compensatory hyperventilation, or pulmonary parenchymal disease that stimulates J-receptors and increases VA). **Hypercapnia,** defined as $PaCO_2 > 45$ mmHg at sea level, can be caused by increased production (e.g., light anesthesia, hyperthermia, shivering) or decreased elimination of CO_2 (e.g., hypoventilation, increased dead space secondary to decreased cardiac output or pulmonary embolus, or rebreathing CO_2).

16. How does one determine if the PaO_2 value is "normal"?

First, determine the **alveolar PaO_2** using the alveolar gas equation:

$$PAO_2 = [(P_B–47)FiO_2] – PACO_2 \times 1.25$$

where P_B is barometric pressure, 47 is vapor pressure of water, and $PACO_2$ is the alveolar PCO_2, (substituted with $PaCO_2$ since they are in close approximation). The value of 1.25 is the respiratory quotient, which is an averaged value reflecting the amount of oxygen absorbed relative to the amount of CO_2 excreted. With a calculated PAO_2 and a known PaO_2 from the ABG the **alveolar-arterial oxygen gradient** (A-aD_{O_2} gradient) can be easily computed. For people age 50 years or younger (breathing room air), the difference should be < 20 mmHg. A larger value indicates a deviation from normal oxygenation status due to intrinsic pulmonary parenchymal disease. Hypoxemia with a normal A-aD_{O_2} is due to hypoventilation. Age can decrease the PaO_2, so an approximation of normal PaO_2 (breathing room air at sea level) is:

$$\text{Age-adjusted } PaO_2 = 102 - [\text{age in yrs}/3]$$

17. What are the more common acid-base disorders seen in the postoperative period?

    1. **Respiratory acidosis** is very common due to residual anesthetics and neuromuscular blocking agents, which blunt the response to rising $PaCO_2$.

    2. **Metabolic acidosis** may occur when surgical blood loss or third-space losses are underappreciated and volume resuscitation is inadequate.

    3. **Respiratory alkalosis** is also common due to pain or anxiety.

BIBLIOGRAPHY

1. Gal TJ: Monitoring the function of the respiratory system. In Lake CL (ed): Clinical Monitoring for Anesthesia and Critical Care, 2nd ed. Philadelphia, W.B. Saunders, 1994.
2. Mizock BA, Falk JL: Lactic acidosis in critical illness. Crit Care Med 20:80–91, 1992.
3. Schumaker PT, Cain SM: The concept of critical oxygen delivery. Intens Care Med 13:223–229, 1987.
4. Sorbini CA, Grassi V, Solinas E, Muiesan G: Arterial oxygen tension in relation to age in healthy subjects. Respiration 25:3–13, 1968.
5. Tremper KK, Barker SJ: Monitoring of oxygen. In Lake CL (ed): Clinical Monitoring for Anesthesia and Critical Care, 2nd ed. Philadelphia, W.B. Saunders, 1994.
6. Vender JS, Gilbert HC: Blood gas monitoring. In Blitt CD, Hines RL (eds): Monitoring in Anesthesia and Critical Care Medicine, 3rd ed. New York, Churchill Livingstone, 1994, pp 407–421.

4. FLUIDS AND ELECTROLYTES

Frederick M. Galloway, M.D.

1. Describe the functionally distinct compartments of body water, using a 70-kg patient for illustration.

    Various authorities quote different percentages for the different body compartments, perhaps because they base composition on total body weight. Because people vary greatly in adipose content (a tissue with relatively low water content), basing body fluid compartments on lean, or ideal body weight (IBW), is advised.

    The **total body water** (TBW) is 57% of the IBW (40 L).

    The **intracellular fluid** (ICF) compartment comprises 35% of IBW or 63% of TBW (about 25 L). It is the principal potassium-containing space.

    The **extracellular fluid** (ECF) compartment contains the remaining 15 L of TBW; it accounts for 22–24% of IBW and is subdivided into **interstitial fluid** (ISF) and **blood volume** (BV). The BV is 7% of an adult's IBW (about 5 L) and is composed primarily of plasma, plasma proteins, and formed blood elements, principally red blood cells. The plasma proteins generate a colloidal osmotic pressure, which is in part responsible for the distribution of water between the ISF and BV compartments.

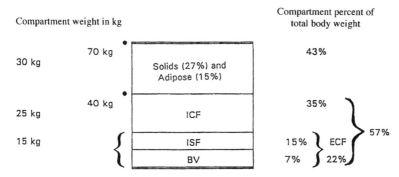

The compartments of body water based on 70-kg body weight.

2. Describe the dynamics of the distribution of fluids between the intravascular and interstitial fluid compartments.

The intravascular or blood volume and the interstitial fluid spaces (which make up the ECF) are in dynamic equilibrium, governed by hydrostatic and osmotic forces. Starling first described the microcirculation at the capillary level. The capillary hydrostatic pressure (Cp) at the arteriolar side causes an outward filtration of fluid, and the capillary osmotic pressure causes reabsorption on the venular side. A slight disequilibrium, as demonstrated below, produces a slight excess in the net filtration of fluid, which is subsequently returned to the circulation through lymphatics. Thus, intravenously administered crystalloid solutions distribute throughout the entire ECF compartment within minutes.

Forces determining outward filtration of ECF		Forces promoting reabsorption of ISF	
Mean capillary hydrostatic		Plasma colloid osmotic	
pressure (mmHg)	17.3	pressure (mmHg)	28.0
Negative ISF pressure	3.0		
ISF colloid osmotic pressure	8.0		
TOTALS (mmHg)	28.3		28.0

3. How are fluid requirements determined?

Fluid requirements are most closely related to metabolic rate. Both caloric requirements and oxygen consumption are measures of metabolic rate. Caloric expenditure per kilogram declines with increasing body weight. The following example determines the daily fluid requirement for a 40-kg person:

100 ml/kg/day for the first 10 kg	1000 ml
50 ml/kg/day for the second 10 kg	500 ml
20 ml/kg/day for the remaining 20 kg	400 ml
Daily fluid requirement for a 40-kg patient	1900 ml

The so-called 4-2-1 rule for calculating hourly requirements is a derivation of this calculation. The factor in each step of the calculation is simply divided by 24. Hence, 4 ml/kg is the hourly requirement for the first 10 kg, 2 ml/kg for the second 10 kg, and 1 ml/kg for the remainder of the patient's weight.

4. Describe a proper preoperative evaluation of volume status.

Proper evaluation includes an interview with the patient, consideration of the clinical context, physical assessment, evaluation of vital signs and other hemodynamic measurements, assessment of urine output, and evaluation of selected laboratory values. An organized approach is helpful.

1. **History and clinical context**
   • NPO (nothing by mouth) status—duration; volumes and composition of last ingested or administered fluids

- History of vomiting, diarrhea, excessive diaphoresis, diabetes (mellitus or insipidus), alcohol ingestion
- Review of medication, especially diuretic use
- Bowel preparations may result in 2–4 L of volume loss if not replaced.
- Have a high index of suspicion with certain conditions necessitating emergency operations and often accompanied by hypovolemia. Examples: ileus, peritonitis, bowel obstructions, gastrointestinal bleeding, burns, trauma, large bone and pelvic fractures, and febrile illnesses.

2. **Physical assessment**
   - Tailor the examination to the problem but always be thorough. Evaluate skin turgor, mucous membranes, capillary refill, edema (chronic—pitting edema; acute—periorbital and conjunctival edema), ascites, evidence of pleural effusions or pulmonary edema.

3. **Vital signs and hemodynamic measurements**
   - Pulse rate, pulse pressure, blood pressure, respiratory rate
   - Orthostatic changes in pulse and blood pressure
   - Central filling pressures—central venous pressure (CVP), pulmonary artery and capillary wedge pressures as well as derived hemodynamic indices, such as cardiac output and index, mixed venous oxygen saturation, and oxygen delivery and consumption

4. **Urine output**
   - Oliguria, defined as < 0.5 ml/kg/hr, is a useful sign of inadequate fluid replacement or inadequate hemodynamics. An adequate urine output in an adult is 0.5–1.0 ml/kg/hr. Urine output in adults of > 1 ml/kg/hr may reflect overhydration in the absence of loop or osmotic diuretics. Alcohol or anesthetics also may alter urine output. Children should have a slightly more vigorous output; neonates should have an output of 2.0 ml/kg/hr.

5. **Laboratory determinations**
   - Useful laboratory values in the assessment of volume status include hemoglobin, hematocrit, electrolytes, blood urea nitrogen (BUN), creatinine, proteins, urine osmolality, specific gravity, and sodium concentration.

5. Describe the progression of signs and symptoms with unreplaced acute blood loss and their correlation with volume loss.

BLOOD VOLUME LOST	SIGNS AND SYMPTOMS
10%	Thirst Vasoconstriction—veins
20%	Sweating Mild-to-moderate increase in heart rate Slight drop in blood pressure Decreased urine output
30%	Tachycardia (–120 bpm plus) Moderate hypotension High degree of vasoconstriction Cool, clammy, and pale Anuria
40%	Severe hypotension and tachycardia Mental confusion
50%	Coma—near death

Note that blood pressure is not significantly affected until approximately 30% of blood volume is lost despite a decreasing cardiac output. Early compensatory mechanisms, including peripheral vasoconstriction and tachycardia, may mask significant volume loss.

6. What are the goals in the resuscitation of hypovolemic patients? What is the preferred initial resuscitation fluid? How does it distribute?

The primary goal is the restoration of the microcirculation (tissue perfusion) and reversal of the hypovolemic state. These goals are accomplished only by restoring the extracellular fluid volume, both BV and ISF compartments. The initial resuscitation fluid of choice is a balanced salt solution that will distribute quickly into both the BV and the ISF compartment. The initial distribution of crystalloid is approximately one-third intravascular and two-thirds interstitial. Because of passage into the ISF, blood loss must be replaced 3:1 with crystalloid solutions to be effective. Dilution of intravascular colloid osmotic pressure favors further significant passage of crystalloid into the ISF. It has been estimated that if two thirds of a patient's blood volume were replaced with crystalloid solutions, the ratio of distribution between the ISF and BV would be approximately 10:1.

Initial resuscitation measures may result in a state of compensated shock, in which blood pressure appears normal, but diminished cardiac output persists, along with high systemic vascular resistance and tissue hypoperfusion. The patient remains somewhat tachycardic and anuric or oliguric and demonstrates a persistent metabolic acidosis with increased blood lactate levels. This situation cannot be ignored, for in patients with multiple injuries its persistence may predispose the patient to delayed sequelae of shock, such as multiple organ dysfunction and death.

Persisting indices of hypoperfusion, continued blood loss, and declining hematocrit (acceptable minimal levels depend on the age of the patient, coexisting disease, extent of injury, and expected future losses) suggest a need for blood transfusion. Transfusion therapy is covered in the chapters on hemotherapy and trauma.

7. What is meant by third-space losses? What are the effects of such losses?

The ECF compartment is composed of the blood volume and ISF volume. In certain clinical conditions, such as major intra-abdominal operations, hemorrhagic shock, burns, and sepsis, patients develop fluid requirements that are not explained by externally measurable losses. Losses are internal, a temporary sequestration of ECF into a functionless third space, which may not participate in the dynamic fluid exchanges at the microcirculatory level. The volume of this internal loss is proportional to the degree of injury, and its composition is similar to plasma or ISF. The creation of the third space necessitates further fluid infusions to maintain intravascular volume, adequate cardiac output, and perfusion.

8. What are the determinants of perioperative fluid requirements?

1. **Basal requirements.** In the absence of catabolic states (e.g., starvation, burns, sepsis, fever), anesthetized patients are close to their basal metabolic rate; the same is true for fluid requirements (see question 3).

2. **Preoperative deficits** should be estimated (see question 4).

3. **Blood loss.** Estimates of blood loss are derived from measuring losses accumulating in suction canisters, observing or weighing blood loss on surgical sponges ("laps"), looking at the drapes, and being vigilant for occult blood loss (hidden in the drapes or lost on the floor).

4. **Third-space losses.** Minor operations with minimal tissue injury do not exhibit much third spacing. The third space requirements for major abdominal operations may be significant. For moderate surgical trauma (e.g., open cholecystectomy), estimate about 3 ml/kg/hr; for more extensive procedures, such as enteral resections, estimate 6–8 ml/kg/hr; and for major vascular resections (e.g., abdominal aortic aneurysms), estimate 10–20 ml/kg/hr.

5. **Transcellular fluid losses.** Estimate losses from transcellular fluids, such as ascites, pleural effusions, enteral fluids (e.g., gastric succor), and fistulas.

6. **Effects of anesthetic agents and technique.** Through a combination of sympathetic suppression, vasodilation, and myocardial depression, general anesthetics quickly unmask hypovolemia. Many patients with previously adequate filling pressures experience a significant decrease in blood pressure with the induction of anesthesia. Although occasionally administration of vasoactive substances is needed, patients often improve with fluid infusion.

During major conduction anesthesia (subarachnoid or epidural), the vasculature experiences a local anesthetic-induced loss of sympathetic tone. Decreases in blood pressure usually respond to modest fluid infusions, but sometimes pressors are required to support systemic pressures.

Clearly estimating perioperative fluid needs requires skill and vigilance. Frequently the best assessment of adequate volume status is satisfactory urine output (see question 4). Patients with impaired cardiac and renal function and patients undergoing extensive procedures with significant volume shifts may require CVP or pulmonary artery (PA) catheter monitoring to assess adequately fluid and cardiovascular status.

9. What fluid and electrolyte disturbances are common in the perioperative period? Specify their cause.

1. **Hyponatremia** may be due to salt restriction in elderly patients, administration of hypotonic fluids, or absorption of sodium-poor irrigants, as during transurethral resection of the prostate (TURP) or when the uterus is distended to facilitate a surgical procedure. The inappropriate secretion of antidiuretic hormone (ADH) or excessive use of oxytocin (with ADH-like properties) also may produce hyponatremia; other causes include diuretics, adrenal insufficiency, nephrotic syndrome, and congestive heart failure.

2. **Hypernatremia** tends to be less common than hyponatremia. It may be caused by dehydration, gastrointestinal losses, diabetes insipidus, and renal failure.

3. **Hypokalemia** is most commonly caused by diuretics; look for hypokalemia in patients receiving β-adrenergic agonists.

4. **Hyperkalemia** may be drug-induced or iatrogenic; it also may be found in renal failure, diabetes mellitus, massive transfusion, and acidosis.

5. **Metabolic acidosis** is commonly seen in massive trauma or in extensive operations associated with massive fluid shifts.

6. **Hypocalcemia**—a decrease in ionized calcium—may be seen with rapid transfusion of citrated blood products.

10. When should hyponatremia be treated?

The rate at which hyponatremia develops and the presence of symptoms determine the aggressiveness of treatment. If hyponatremia has developed quickly, as during TURP, the patient may develop hypertension, bradycardia, confusion, apprehension, agitation, obtundation, or seizures; usually the sodium is found to be less than 125 mEq/L. The aggressiveness of treatment depends on the extent of symptoms. In the simplest cases, fluid restriction may be sufficient. More acutely ill patients may require diuresis or administration of hypertonic (3%) saline. Seizures require securing a protected airway, oxygenation, ventilation, and perhaps administration of anticonvulsants, although seizures are usually self-limited. Sodium bicarbonate provides 1 mEq of sodium/ml if a rapid sodium infusion is necessary.

11. How are body water and tonicity regulated?

The first mechanism involves release of ADH. ADH circulates unbound in plasma, has a half-life of roughly 20 minutes, and increases production of cyclic adenosine monophosphate (cAMP) in the distal collecting tubules of the kidney. The net effect increases tubular permeability to water and results in conservation of water and sodium and production of concentrated urine. Stimuli for the release of ADH include the following:

1. Osmoreceptors in the supraoptic nuclei of the hypothalamus have a mean osmotic threshold of 289 ± 2.3 mOsm/kg. Above this level, ADH release is stimulated.

2. A closely related mechanism for regulating body water and tonicity is the thirst reflex. Thirst center neurons are located in the lateral preoptic area of the hypothalamus, regulate conscious desire for water, and are activated by (1) an increase in plasma sodium of 2 mEq/L; (2) an increase in plasma osmolality of 4 mOsm/L; (3) an excessive loss of potassium from thirst center neurons; and (4) angiotensin II. Activation of the thirst center stimulates release of ADH.

3. Aortic baroreceptors and stretch receptors in the left atrium respond to intravascular volume and are sources of afferent innervation to the supraoptic neurons. Stretch receptors also give neural input to the sympathetic nervous system.

4. The effects of aldosterone on the renal tubules fine-tune serum sodium levels (see question 20).

12. What is the difference between osmolarity and osmolality? Is there a difference between osmolality and tonicity? How is the osmolality of blood determined?

In casual discussion, osmolarity and osmolality often are used interchangeably, but in fact they are different. Osmolarity is defined as the number of osmoles of solute per liter of solution; osmolality is the number of osmoles of solute per kilogram of solvent. Osmolality of blood may be higher than tonicity if the blood contains substances to which cells are permeable (such as urea or alcohol), which contribute to osmotic pressure but not to tonicity. Osmolality is measured by determining the freezing point depression of the aqueous solution; the freezing point is lowered by 1.86°C per osmol of solute. Osmolality can be estimated by the following equation:

$$\text{Osmolality} = 1.86 \, [\text{Na in mEq/L}] + [\text{glucose in mg/dl}] \div 18 + [\text{BUN in mg/dl}] \div 2.8$$

13. Discuss the synthesis of antidiuretic hormone.

ADH, or vasopressin, is an octapeptide synthesized in the supraoptic and paraventricular nuclei of the hypothalamus. It is transported attached to carrier proteins (known as neurophysines) down the pituitary stalk in secretory granules along the axons of the cells of origin into the posterior pituitary gland (neurohypophysis). There it is stored and released into the capillaries of the neurohypophysis in response to stimuli from the hypothalamus. ADH-producing neurons receive efferent innervation from osmoreceptors and baroreceptors.

14. List conditions that stimulate and inhibit release of ADH.

Conditions that Stimulate and Inhibit Release of ADH

	STIMULATES ADH	INHIBITS ADH
Normal physiologic state	Hyperosmolality Hypovolemia Upright position β-Adrenergic stimulation Pain Emotional stress Cholinergic stimulation	Hypo-osmolality Hypervolemia Supine position α-Adrenergic stimulation
Abnormal physiologic states	Hemorrhagic shock Hyperthermia Increased intracranial pressure Head injury Positive airway pressure	Excessive water intake Hypothermia
Medication	Morphine Nicotine Barbiturates Tricyclic antidepressants Vincristine Cyclophosphamide Chlorpropamide	Ethanol Atropine Phenytoin Reserpine Glucocorticoids Chlorpromazine
Result	Low urine output Concentrated urine	High urine output Dilute urine

15. What is diabetes insipidus?

Diabetes insipidus (DI) is caused by a deficiency of ADH synthesis, impaired release of ADH from the neurohypophysis (neurogenic DI), or renal resistance to ADH (nephrogenic DI). The result is excretion of large volumes of dilute urine, which, if untreated, leads to dehydration and hyperosmolality of body fluids. The usual test for DI is cautious fluid restriction. The inability to decrease and concentrate urine suggests the diagnosis, which may be confirmed by plasma ADH measurements. Administration of aqueous vasopressin tests the response of the renal tubule. Comparison of plasma and urine osmolality is useful; if the osmolality of plasma continues to exceed that of urine after mild fluid restriction, the diagnosis of DI is suggested.

16. Discuss the alternative treatments for DI.

Available preparations of ADH include pitressin tannate in oil, administered every 24–48 hours; aqueous pitressin, 5–10 U IV or IM every 4–6 hours; synthetic lysine vasopressin nasal spray, 2 U 4 times/day; and 1-deamino-8-D-arginine vasopressin (DDAVP), 10–20 U intranasally every 12–24 hours. Incomplete DI may respond to thiazide diuretics, chlorpropamide (which potentiates endogenous ADH), carbamazepine, or clofibrate.

Because the patient is losing water, administration of isotonic solutions may cause hypernatremia; in addition, excessive vasopressin causes water intoxication. Management during surgery may require a continuous infusion of aqueous vasopressin of 100–200 mU/hr after a bolus of 100–200 mU. Measurement of plasma osmolality (or estimation from serum levels of sodium, glucose, and BUN) as well as urine output and osmolality is indicated when vasopressin is infused.

17. List causes of diabetes insipidus.

Vasopressin deficiency (neurogenic DI)
    Familial (autosomal dominant)
    Acquired
        Idiopathic
        Trauma (craniofacial and basilar skull fractures)
        Tumor (craniopharyngioma, lymphoma, metastasis)
        Granuloma (sarcoidosis, histiocytosis)
        Infections (meningitis, encephalitis)
        Vascular (Sheehan's syndrome, cerebral aneurysm, cardiopulmonary bypass)
        Hypoxic brain damage
Vasopressin insensitivity (nephrogenic DI)
    Familial (X-linked recessive)
    Acquired
        Infections (pyelonephritis)
        Post-renal obstruction (prostatic, ureteral)
        Hematologic (sickle-cell disease and trait)
        Infiltrative (amyloidosis)
        Polycystic kidney disease
        Hypokalemia, hypercalcemia
        Sarcoidosis
        Medications (lithium, demeclocycline, methoxyflurane)

18. Define the syndrome of inappropriate antidiuretic hormone release (SIADH). What is the primary therapy?

Hypotonicity due to the nonosmotic release of ADH, which inhibits renal excretion of water, typifies SIADH. Three criteria must be met to establish the diagnosis of SIADH: (1) the patient must be euvolemic or hypervolemic; (2) the urine must be inappropriately concentrated (plasma osmolality < 280 mOsm/kg, urine osmolality >100 mOsm/kg); and (3) renal, cardiac, hepatic, adrenal, and thyroid function must be normal.

The primary therapy for SIADH is water restriction. Postoperative SIADH is usually a temporary phenomenon and resolves spontaneously. Chronic SIADH may require the addition of demeclocycline, which blocks the ADH-mediated water resorption in the collecting ducts of the kidney.

19. What disorders are associated with SIADH?

Central nervous system (CNS) events are frequent causes, including acute intracranial hypertension, trauma, tumors, meningitis, and subarachnoid hemorrhage. Pulmonary causes are also common, including tuberculosis, pneumonia, asthma, bronchiectasis, hypoxemia, hypercarbia, and positive pressure ventilation. Malignancies may produce ADH-like compounds. Adrenal insufficiency and hypothyroidism also have been associated with SIADH.

20. What is aldosterone? What stimulates its release? What are its actions?

Aldosterone, a mineralocorticoid, is the hormone responsible for the precise control of sodium excretion. A decrease in systemic or renal arterial blood pressure, as well as hypovolemia or hyponatremia, leads to release of renin from the juxtaglomerular cells of the kidney. Angiotensinogen, produced in the liver, is converted by renin to angiotensin I. In the blood stream angiotensin I is converted to angiotensin II, and the zona glomerulosa of the adrenal cortex is then stimulated to release aldosterone. An additional effect of angiotensin II is vasoconstriction. Aldosterone acts on the distal renal tubules and cortical collecting ducts, promoting sodium retention. Besides hyponatremia and hypovolemia, stimuli for aldosterone release include hyperkalemia, increased levels of adrenocorticotropic hormone (ACTH), and surgical procedures.

21. A 45-year-old patient scheduled for an elective cholecystectomy takes furosemide for hypertension. Preoperative laboratory tests are normal except for a potassium level of 3.0 mEq/L. What are the risks of proceeding? Why not give the patient enough potassium to restore the serum level to normal?

Hypokalemia favors the development of serious cardiac arrhythmias, especially in patients with ischemic heart disease or preexisting cardiac arrhythmias and in patients receiving digitalis. Acute hypokalemia is probably more serious than chronic hypokalemia. The total body deficit of potassium, primarily an intracellular cation, is not well reflected by serum concentrations. A patient with a serum potassium of 3.0 mEq/L may have a total body deficit in excess of 400 mEq.

Historically, standard anesthetic practice was to consider even modest hypokalemia as a contraindication to elective procedures. However, sufficient data have been gathered that suggest that patients without the above risk factors who are not undergoing major thoracic, vascular, or cardiac procedures can tolerate modest hypokalemia (possibly as low as 2.8 mEq/L) without sequelae.

As mentioned, serum potassium levels do not reflect true body deficits. Attempts at rapid correction of serum potassium levels poorly address the extent of the problem and are more dangerous than modest hypokalemia. In fact, rapid attempts to correct hypokalemia have resulted in cardiac arrest.

22. A 48-year-old hypertensive patient with chronic renal failure requires an arteriovenous fistula for hemodialysis and is scheduled for a general anesthetic. Potassium is measured as 7.0 mEq/L. What are the risks of proceeding? How can life-threatening hyperkalemia be treated?

Hyperkalemia may produce ventricular arrhythmias, beginning with premature ventricular contractions and progressing to ventricular tachycardia and fibrillation. Hypoventilation and acidosis worsen hyperkalemia, as does the administration of succinylcholine and potassium-containing fluids or medications. Many anesthesiologists believe that hyperkalemia > 5.9 mEq/L should be corrected before elective procedures. Patients with chronic renal failure are normally dialyzed.

Emergent treatment of hyperkalemia consists of three mechanisms. Immediate, direct reversal of cardiotoxicity is accomplished by administration of calcium chloride. Potassium can then be quickly shifted intracellularly as a temporizing maneuver to decrease the serum level by hyperventilation, β-adrenergic stimulation (e.g., beta-agonist nebulizer), sodium bicarbonate, and insulin and glucose. Removal of potassium from the body—the definitive (and time-consuming) treatment—can be accomplished by diuretics, Kayexalate, and dialysis. One should always consider hyperkalemia when a patient with renal failure suffers cardiac arrest.

BIBLIOGRAPHY

1. Goldmann DR, Brown FH, Guarniere DM (eds): Perioperative Medicine: The Medical Care of the Surgical Patient, 2nd ed. New York, McGraw-Hill, 1994.
2. Guyton AC, Hall JE (eds): Textbook of Medical Physiology, 9th ed. Philadelphia, W.B. Saunders, 1996.
3. Hirsch IA, Tomlinson DL, Slogoff S, Keats AS: The overstated risk of preoperative hypokalemia. Anesth Analg 67:131–136, 1988.
4. Kokko JP, Tannen RL (eds): Fluids and Electrolytes, 3rd ed. Philadelphia, W.B. Saunders, 1996.
5. Sterns RH, Cox M, Feig PU, Singer IS: Internal potassium balance and the control of the plasma potassium concentration. Medicine 60:339–354, 1981.
6. Vitez TS, Soper LE, Wong KC, Soper P: Chronic hypokalemia and intraoperative dysrhythmias. Anesthesiology 63:130–133, 1985.

5. HEMOTHERAPY

Jeremy J. Katz, M.D.

1. What is the average human blood volume?

In a 70-kg man, total body water comprises about 60% of body mass or about 42 L of fluid. This is divided between the intracellular compartment (40% of body mass or 28 L) and the extracellular compartment (20% of body mass or 14 L). The extracellular compartment is divided into the interstitial space (15.7% of body mass or 11 L) and plasma volume (4.3% of body mass or 3 L). The total intravascular blood volume comprises approximately 3 L of plasma plus 2 L of red cells for a total volume of about 5 L (see Figure). Total body water volumes vary with age, sex, weight, and body habitus. The estimated total blood volume (EBV) of an average adult male is about 75 ml/kg and that of the average female about 65 ml/kg. Females have a greater percentage of adipose tissue, which is less vascular compared to other tissues.

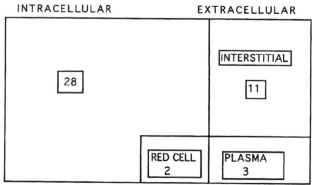

FLUID COMPARTMENT VOLUMES (L)

Volumes (L) of different body compartments (in a 70-kg male).

2. What are the physiologic adaptations to acute normovolemic anemia?

During surgery, acute blood loss is usually replaced with crystalline solutions, resulting in acute normovolemic hemodilution. Compensatory changes include increased cardiac output, re-distribution of blood to the tissues that are oxygen supply–dependent (such as the heart and brain), and increased oxygen extraction. The increase in cardiac output is due to factors such as reduced blood viscosity, increased venomotor tone and venous return, and increased sympathetic nervous system activity. Similar changes occur in response to hemorrhagic shock, but the compensatory changes may be overwhelmed in severe or prolonged shock.

3. What is an acceptable minimum preoperative hematocrit?

Rather than relying on a "starting" hematocrit as a "trigger" for transfusion, emphasis should be placed on the maintenance of an adequate hematocrit during the *entire perioperative period.*

Obviously the need for transfusion, the amount of blood required, and the decision to initiate transfusion will be influenced by a starting hematocrit. However, consideration should also be given to the patient's age, general health, the use of drugs that may interfere with the autonomic nervous system or hemostasis, the presence of disease that may increase oxygen demands, and a prediction of expected or ongoing blood loss.

While elective surgery has been successfully performed in patients with preoperative hemo-globin as low as 6g/dl (provided blood loss was minimized), patients with coexisting disease, particularly impaired cardiac function, are less tolerant of decreased hematocrit. Studies have shown a correlation between reduction in hematocrit and the incidence of myocardial ischemia, as evidenced by electrocardiogram (ECG).

In the absence of cardiovascular instability, perioperative transfusion should be considered at these hematocrit values:

	Hematocrit
Healthy patients	18%
Patients with well-compensated systemic disease	24%
Patients with symptomatic cardiac disease	30%

4. How is blood loss estimated?

There is no absolutely reliable way to estimate blood loss. Close attention should be di-rected to observing blood suctioned from the surgical field and that lost into surgical sponges and drapes. During cases with extensive third space fluid loss and major fluid resuscitation, es-timation of blood loss becomes even more difficult and serial hematocrits should be drawn. One way of estimating an "acceptable" blood loss prior to considering transfusion is as follows (illustrated with an example of a 60-kg man with a preoperative hematocrit of 42%):

- Estimate total blood volume (TBV):

    TBV (ml) = weight (kg) $\times$ EBV (ml/kg)

    [TBV = 60 kg $\times$ 75 ml/kg = 4500 ml]

- Estimate red blood cell volume (RBCV) at preoperative hematocrit ($RBCV_p$):

    $RBCV_p$ (ml) = TBV (ml) $\times \dfrac{\text{preoperative hematocrit}}{100}$

    [$RBCV_p$ (ml) = 4500 ml $\times$ 0.42 = 1890 ml]

- Estimate RBCV at hematocrit of 30% ($RBCV_{30}$):

    $RBCV_{30}$ (ml) = TBV $\times$ 0.3

    [$RBCV_{30}$ (ml) = 4500 $\times$ 0.3 = 1500 ml]

- Allowable RBCV (ml) loss to reduce hematocrit to 30% = $RBCV_p - RBCV_{30}$

    [RBCV loss (ml) = 1890 ml – 1500 ml = 390 ml]

- Then acceptable blood loss to reduce hematocrit to 30% (ml) = RBCV $\times \dfrac{100}{30}$

    Allowing for conversion of red cell volume to blood volume at hematocrit of 30%:

    [acceptable blood loss = 390 ml $\times$ 3 = 1070 ml]

5. For what is donor blood screened?

Donated blood is tested for blood group antigens and infectious disease markers. ABO and Rh antigen status are determined, and an antibody screen is performed to detect any unexpected red cell antibodies.

Infectious disease markers tested for include:
- **Syphilis**
- **Viral hepatitis:**

  Hepatitis B: hepatitis B surface antigen and antibody to hepatitis B core antigen assays

  Hepatitis C: antibody to hepatitis C virus assay

  Alanine aminotransferase: measured as a surrogate marker of nonspecific liver infection
- **Retroviruses:**

  Human immunodeficiency virus (HIV): anti–HIV-1, anti–HIV-2, and HIV-1p24 antigen assays

  Human T-cell lymphotropic virus-type I/II: antibody to HTLV-I/II assay

6. What types of red cell products are available?

- **Red blood cells:**

  A unit with citrate, phosphate, dextrose-adenine (CPDA-1) anticoagulant has a volume of 300–350 ml with a hematocrit of about 75–80%; addition of additive solutions reduces the hematocrit to approximately 60%.

  Indicated for increasing oxygen-carrying capacity and volume expansion for significant hemorrhage.
- **Red blood cells deglycerolized:**

  Stored in the frozen state

  Indicated for prolonged storage of rare red cells
- **Leukocyte-reduced red blood cells:**

  Indicated for patients with a history of previous febrile transfusion reactions
- **Washed red blood cells:**

  Useful in patients who have had previous severe allergic reactions
- **Whole blood:**

  Rarely used

  Obtained only with increasing difficulty; packed red cells are transfused in cases of less severe blood loss preserving plasma and other components for other patients

  Indicated only for symptomatic deficit in oxygen-carrying capacity together with hypovolemia of sufficient degree to be associated with shock

  The usual unit contains about 500 ml of anticoagulated blood with a hematocrit of 35–40%.

Federal regulation determines the duration of blood storage and requires that at least 70% of transfused red blood cells survive 24 hours after transfusion. Whole blood or red cells may be stored for 35 days with the anticoagulant preservative solution CPDA-1 and for 42 days when AS-1 (Adsol) or AS-3 (Nutrice) are added.

7. How should red blood cells be administered?

Suitable diluents include normal saline and isosmolar non–calcium-containing solutions, but the safest practice is to use only normal saline. Saline dilution will facilitate infusion and minimize hemolysis. Hypotonic solutions such as 5% dextrose should not be used to avoid hemolysis or cell clumping, and calcium-containing solutions should also be avoided to prevent clot formation.

A standard blood administration set with a pore size of 170 μm is recommended for infusion of red cell components. If only 1 or 2 units of blood are slowly administered to normothermic adult patients, warming of blood is not necessary. Warming is appropriate with rapid transfusion of large amounts of cold blood, in pediatric patients, and in those recipients with potent cold agglutinins.

8. What happens when a type and screen test is ordered?

The patient's blood is **typed** for ABO and Rh group and then **screened** for antibodies. The patient's red cells are tested against standardized commercially available anti-A and anti-B reagents for determination of the patient's ABO type. The patient's serum is also incubated with group A and B red blood cells to demonstrate the presence of the corresponding isoagglutinins.

The antibody screen has three phases, and the performance takes about 45 minutes. The patient's serum is tested against specially selected red cells containing all relevant blood group antigens for detection of clinically significant antibodies.

The donor's serum is also screened for unexpected antibodies to prevent their introduction into the recipient.

9. What is the difference between a type and screen and a crossmatch?

In 1984 the Food and Drug Administration modified standards and regulations to permit blood to be released for transfusion without a crossmatch, provided certain criteria are met.

If blood is needed for transfusion and the antibody screen is negative, only an "abbreviated" partial crossmatch is done. The patient's serum and red cells from selected donor units are mixed and spun for 15 seconds—testing only for ABO and Rh type. Units can be released within approximately 5 minutes. A full crossmatch is usually performed after the blood is released.

If blood is needed for transfusion and the antibody screen is positive, then a crossmatch is necessary, requiring about 45 minutes for completion. Instead of the patient's serum being tested against commercially available red cells containing known antigens, the serum is tested against red cells from selected donor units. In addition to verifying ABO and Rh compatibility, the crossmatch detects more unique antibodies.

DEGREE OF CROSSMATCH	CHANCE OF COMPATIBLE TRANSFUSION
ABO-Rh type only	99.8%
ABO-Rh type + antibody screen	99.94%
ABO-Rh type + antibody screen + crossmatch	99.95%

10. What type of blood should be used in an emergency situation?

Urgent need for blood may require incomplete compatibility testing. If time does not allow for complete crossmatching, the following may be transfused:

- type-specific, partially crossmatched
- type-specific, uncrossmatched
- type O, Rh negative, uncrossmatched

Type O blood lacks both A and B antigens and cannot be hemolyzed by anti-A or anti-B antibodies in the recipient's serum. The use of O red blood cells, which contain a small volume of plasma and are almost free of hemolytic antibodies, is preferred to that of whole blood.

The patient may be switched to type-specific blood even after transfusion of up to 10 units of type O red blood cells. However, when 2 or more units of type O, Rh-negative, noncrossmatched blood have been transfused, the patient should not be transfused with his or her type-specific blood until the blood bank has determined that the levels of transfused anti-A and anti-B antibodies have fallen to levels low enough to permit the transfusion.

Clerical or management system errors are the most frequent causes of ABO-incompatible transfusions. Each unit of blood should be checked prior to transfusion by two individuals to verify that the patient's name and identification number are the same as those on the blood unit. Expiration date, ABO, and Rh type should also be checked and the unit inspected for evidence of bacterial contamination such as discoloration, bubbles, and clots.

11. What are some of the complications of massive blood transfusion?

Massive transfusion is defined as the acute administration of more than one blood volume within several hours. Complications include:

- Coagulopathy due to:
  dilutional thrombocytopenia
  lack of coagulation factors V and VIII (labile factors)
  disseminated intravascular coagulation (DIC)—associated with hypoperfusion or he-
    molytic reaction
- Metabolic problems (related to blood storage):
  hyperkalemia
  citrate toxicity
  acidosis
  impaired oxygen-carrying capacity (due to reduced 2,3,DPG concentration)
  hypothermia

12. By how much will transfusion of a single unit of red cells increase the hematocrit?

One unit of red cells will increase the hematocrit by 3% and the hemoglobin by 1 g/dl in the average adult.

13. What are the risks of transfusion of infectious agents?

Human hepatitis viruses are the most frequently transmitted infectious agents. Before the introduction of testing for antibodies for hepatitis C virus, the frequency of transmission of hepatitis was believed to be 3% per transfusion episode. The risk of transmission of hepatitis C is currently estimated at 1:100 or less per unit and that of HIV between 1:250,000 and 1:500,000 per unit. Bacteria, spirochetes, and parasites may also be transmitted.

14. What type of transfusion reactions may occur?

- Hemolytic transfusion reactions
- Allergic reactions
- Febrile nonhemolytic transfusion reactions

15. How is a hemolytic transfusion reaction managed?

Most hemolytic transfusion reactions are caused by anti-A or anti-B antibodies during an ABO incompatible transfusion. They may occur immediately (during or shortly after a transfusion) or later (5–7 days after transfusion).

Clinical manifestations include fever; chills; chest, flank, and back pain; hypotension; nausea; flushing; diffuse bleeding; oliguria or anuria; and hemoglobinuria. General anesthesia may mask some of the clinical manifestations, and hypotension, hemoglobinuria, and diffuse bleeding may be the only visible signs.

When a reaction occurs, the following should be done:

- Stop the transfusion immediately and remove the blood tubing.
- Alert the blood bank and send a recipient and donor blood specimen for compatibility testing.
- Treat hypotension aggressively with IV fluids and pressor agents as needed.
- Maintain urine output: Treat initially with IV fluid and mannitol. Use diuretics and renal-
  dose dopamine if urine output is not maintained.
- Massive hemolysis can release potassium—monitor potassium levels.
- DIC may occur—the best treatment is identifying and treating the underlying cause.
- Check urine and plasma hemoglobin levels.
- Verify hemolysis with direct antiglobulin (Coombs) test, bilirubin, and plasma haptoglobin
  levels.
- Perform baseline coagulation studies: prothrombin time (PT), partial thromboplastin time
  (PTT), platelet count, fibrinogen level.

16. What alternatives are there to homologous blood transfusion?

- Autologous transfusion (the collection and reinfusion of the patient's own blood)
- Perioperative blood salvage (the collection and reinfusion of blood lost during and immediately after surgery)

• Intraoperative isovolemic hemodilution (the reduction of hematocrit or hemoglobin by withdrawal of blood and the simultaneous volume replacement with cell-free substitutes)
• Use of substitute products for replacement of plasma and blood volume

The primary goal is maintaining perfusion with adequate intravascular volume replacement. Provided therapy is appropriately monitored and fluids given at an appropriate rate, any solution will adequately restore volume status. Replacement solutions include various crystalloid and colloid products that do not provide additional oxygen-carrying capacity. Research is being carried out into the use of non–blood oxygen-carrying solutions, but none is yet available for widespread clinical use.

Comparison of Various Replacement Solutions

Physiologic crystalloid solutions (replacement volume is about three times that of blood loss because of distribution to the extracellular space; has only a transient effect)

Normal saline:	Iso-osmotic, mild hypernatremia and hyperchloremia with large volumes
Balanced salt (e.g., Ringer's lactate):	Hypotonic, causes fewer electrolyte disturbances

Colloids (replacement volume equal to that of blood lost)

Albumin (5%) or 25%):	Overhydration; pulmonary edema, particularly with use of 25% solution, due to absorption of interstitial fluid into the vascular compartment
Hetastarch (Hespan):	Affects coagulation—use moderate amounts < 20 ml/kg
Dextran (40 or 70):	Potential for analphylaxis, interference with platelet, red cell function, and blood crossmatching

BIBLIOGRAPHY

1. American Society of Anesthesiologists: Committee on Transfusion Medicine: Questions and Answers about Transfusion Practices. Park Ridge, IL, American Society of Anesthesiologists, 1992, pp 1–44.
2. Consensus Conference: Perioperative red blood cell transfusion. JAMA 260:2700–2703, 1988.
3. Cosby HT: Perioperative hemotherapy. I. Indications for blood component transfusion. Can J Anaesth 39:695–707, 1992.
4. Delima LGR, Wynands JE: Oxygen transport. Can J Anaesth 40:R81–R86, 1993.
5. Irving GA: Perioperative blood and blood component therapy. Can J Anaesth 39:1105–1115, 1992.
6. Leone BJ, Spahn DR: Anemia, hemodilution and oxygen delivery. Anesth Analg 75:651–653, 1992.
7. Mesmer KM: Hemodilution. Surg Clin North Am 55:659–678, 1975.
8. Miller RD: Transfusion therapy. In Miller RD (ed): Anesthesia, 4th ed. New York, Churchill Livingstone, 1994, pp 1619–1646.
9. Napier JAF: Red cell replacement in surgery. Transfus Med 7:265–268, 1997.
10. Nelson AH, Fleisher LA, Rosenbaum SH: Relationship between postoperative anemia and cardiac morbidity in high-risk patients in the intensive care unit. Crit Care Med 21:860–866, 1993.
11. Ramsay JG: Methods of reducing blood loss and non-blood substitutes. Can J Anaesth 38:595–612, 1991.
12. Rose D, Coutsoftides T: Intraoperative normovolemic hemodilution. J Surg Res 31:375–381, 1981.
13. Spence RK, Carson JA, Poses R, et al: Elective surgery without transfusion: Influence of preoperative hemoglobin level and blood loss on mortality. Am J Surg 159:320–324, 1990.
14. Stehling L, Zauder HL: How low can we go? Is there a way to know? Transfusion 30:1–3, 1990.
15. Transfusion Alert: Use of Autologous Blood. U.S. Department of Health and Human Services, 1989, pp 1–16, NIH Publication No. 89-3038.
16. Wedgewood JJ, Thomas JG: Peri-operative haemoglobin: An overview of current opinion regarding the acceptable level of haemoglobin in the peri-operative period. Eur J Anaesthesiol 13:316–324, 1996.
17. Welch HG, Meehan KR, Goodnough LT: Prudent strategies for elective red blood cell transfusion. Ann Intern Med 116:393–402, 1992.

6. COAGULATION

Jeremy J. Katz, M.D.

1. How does one identify the patient at risk for bleeding?

The most important factor is an accurate medical history. Questions about medications, including anticoagulants, nonsteroidal anti-inflammatory agents, and aspirin; excessive or abnormal bleeding; and medical conditions known to be associated with bleeding disorders identify most at-risk patients. Platelet disorders usually present with petechial hemorrhages of the mucous membranes and skin, whereas clotting factor disorders have a more pronounced clinical picture with spontaneous intramuscular, joint, gastrointestinal, and intracranial hemorrhages. Inherited disorders usually present early in life with a positive family history. Previous major surgery without transfusion suggests the absence of an inherited coagulation disorder.

2. How useful are clotting function screening tests?

Prothrombin time (PT) and partial thromboplastin time (PTT), although useful in screening patients with a history of bleeding, have not been shown to have any value as screening tests in asymptomatic patients. Likewise, the routine use of bleeding times to assess platelet function in patients taking aspirin may have little value because of the small correlation between bleeding times and clinical hemorrhage.

3. What are the main components of the hemostatic mechanism?

The four main components of the hemostatic response are vascular reactivity, platelet activity, coagulation, and fibrinolysis. When ruptured, the microvascular system undergoes local reflex vasoconstriction. Simultaneous dilatation of adjacent arterioles diverts local blood flow from the bleeding site. Interaction between the blood vessels and platelets results in the temporary cessation of bleeding by the formation of a platelet plug. Coagulation is the organization of the platelet plug by fibrin formation. Fibrinolysis is the removal of fibrin to reestablish normal blood flow.

4. What is the function of the vascular endothelium?

Normally the vascular endothelium prevents blood from coagulating by secreting coagulation inhibitors such as:
- Glycocalyx, a mucopolysaccharide that prevents the interaction of platelets and coagulation proteins with collagen
- Adenosine diphosphatase (ADPase), which decreases platelet adhesion by inactivating adenosine diphosphate (ADP)
- Prostacyclin (PGI2), a potent vasodilator and platelet aggregation inhibitor
- Protein C, which activates plasminogen and furthers fibrinolysis

If endothelial integrity is broken, the collagen exposed in the subendothelial layers begins the coagulation process by allowing platelet adherence and activation.

5. How do platelets function in the coagulation process?

The platelet membrane enables physical interaction between the vascular endothelium and platelets. It also makes possible platelet interaction with the protein coagulation cascade. The platelet phospholipid, platelet factor 3 (PF3), limits coagulation to the site of platelet aggregation. Activated platelets also release the contents of their granules, including thromboxane A2 and ADP. Thromboxane A2 causes blood vessel constriction and increases ADP release, resulting in additional platelet aggregation and activation.

6. What is an acceptable preoperative platelet count?

A normal platelet count is 150,000–440,000/mm^3. Thrombocytopenia is defined as a count of <150,000/mm^3. Intraoperative bleeding can be severe with counts of 40,000–70,000/mm^3, and spontaneous bleeding usually occurs at counts < 20,000/mm^3. The minimal recommended platelet count before surgery is 75,000/mm^3. Although prophylactic preoperative platelet transfusion is generally advocated to treat preexisting thrombocytopenia, the methods of evaluating clinical need are imprecise.

Qualitative differences in platelet function make it unwise to rely on platelet number as the sole criterion for transfusion. Thrombocytopenic patients with accelerated destruction but active production of platelets have relatively less bleeding than patients with hypoplastic disorders at a given platelet count.

Assessment of preoperative platelet function is further complicated by lack of correlation between bleeding time or any other test of platelet function and a tendency to increased intraoperative bleeding. However, normal bleeding times range from 4–9 minutes, and a bleeding time >1½ times normal (>15 min) is considered significantly abnormal.

7. List the causes of platelet abnormalities.

1. **Quantitative platelet disorders**—thrombocytopenia
   - Dilution after massive blood transfusion
   - Decreased platelet production due to malignant infiltration (aplastic anemia, multiple myeloma), drugs (chemotherapy, cytotoxic drugs, ethanol, hydrochlorothiazide), radiation exposure, or bone marrow depression after viral infection
   - Increased peripheral destruction due to hypersplenism, disseminated intravascular coagulation (DIC), extensive tissue and vascular damage after extensive burns, or immune mechanisms (idiopathic thrombocytopenic purpura, drugs such as heparin, autoimmune diseases)
2. **Qualitative platelet disorders**
   - Inherited (e.g., von Willebrand disease)
   - Acquired (uremia; cirrhosis, particularly after ethanol; drugs, such as aspirin, nonsteroidal anti-inflammatory agents)

8. How does aspirin act as an anticoagulant?

Primary hemostasis is controlled by the balance between the opposing actions of two prostaglandins, thromboxane A2 and prostacyclin. Depending on the dose, salicylates produce a differential effect on prostaglandin synthesis in platelets and vascular endothelial cells. Lower doses preferentially inhibit platelet cyclooxygenase, impeding thromboxane A2 production and inhibiting platelet aggregation. The effect begins within 2 hours of ingestion. Platelets lack a cell nucleus and cannot produce protein. Aspirin effect therefore lasts for the entire life of the platelet (7–10 days). Nonsteroidal anti-inflammatory drugs have a similar but more transient effect than aspirin, lasting for only 1–3 days after cessation of use.

9. Discuss the intrinsic and extrinsic coagulation pathways.

The coagulation cascade requires sequential activation of inactive procoagulant molecules into active cleavage enzymes or serine proteases. Factors V and VIII are the labile factors that serve as cofactors in the cascade. The process of coagulation requires the presence of a phospholipid surface. The intrinsic pathway of coagulation occurs within the blood vessel with platelet phospholipid (PF3) as a catalyst. The extrinsic pathway occurs outside the blood vessel, beginning with the release of tissue thromboplastin (tissue phospholipid) from injured tissues. The phospholipid surface provides a site for the interaction of a complex reaction consisting of the phospholipid surface, calcium, and the activated substrate procoagulant clotting factor. Traditionally, the extrinsic and intrinsic pathways have been considered separate pathways that merge after the formation of activated factor X. In reality they have interrelated steps. The classic two-pathway concept is still useful for the interpretation of in vitro coagulation tests.

10. Discuss factor VIII.

Factor VIII is a large plasma protein complex of two noncovalently bound factors, von Willebrand factor (factor VIII:vWF) and factor VIII antigen, which has anticoagulant activity. The manufacture of each is under separate genetic control. Factor VIII:vWF is necessary both for platelet adhesion and formation of the definitive hemostatic plug through regulation and release of factor VIII antigen. In von Willebrand disease there is a decrease of both factor VIII antigen and factor VIII:vWF.

11. How is coagulation localized?

A number of processes regulate coagulation and confine clotting to sites of vascular damage:
• Rapid blood flow dilutes coagulation factors below coagulation threshold levels.
• Activated coagulation factors are preferentially cleared by the liver and reticuloendothelial system.
• Natural anticoagulants exist in the blood: (1) antithrombin III is a plasma protease inhibitor that serves as a protease scavenger, and (2) protein C and its cofactor protein S inactivate the active cofactor forms of factors VIII and V.
• Activation of the fibrinolytic system digests fibrin both to prevent and to reopen thrombotic occlusion. Fibrinolysis is mediated primarily by plasmin, which is generated from plasminogen. Tissue plasminogen activator (tPA), which is released from endothelial cells, is the most important activator of plasminogen.

12. How does vitamin K deficiency affect coagulation?

Four clotting factors (II, VII, IX, and X) are synthesized by the liver. Each factor undergoes a final vitamin K–dependent enzymatic reaction that adds a carboxyl moiety to each factor. This moiety enables the factors to bind via calcium to the phospholipid surface. Without vitamin K the factors are produced but are not functional. The extrinsic pathway is affected first by vitamin K deficiency or liver dysfunction because the factor with the shortest half-life is factor VII, found only in the extrinsic pathway. With further deficiency both extrinsic and intrinsic pathways are affected.

The warfarin-like drugs compete with vitamin K for binding sites on the hepatocyte. Administration of subcutaneous vitamin K reverses the functional deficiency in 6–24 hours. With active bleeding or in emergency surgery, fresh frozen plasma (FFP) can be administered for immediate hemostasis.

13. How does heparin act as an anticoagulant?

Heparin is a polyanionic mucopolysaccharide that accelerates the interaction between antithrombin III and the activated forms of factors II, X, XI, XII and XIII, effectively neutralizing each. The half-life of heparin's anticoagulant effect is about 90 minutes in a normothermic patient. Patients with reduced levels of antithrombin III are resistant to the effect of heparin. Heparin also may affect platelet function and number through an immunologically mediated mechanism, either acutely or after 5–10 days of exposure.

14. Describe the different coagulation tests.

The basic difference between the intrinsic and extrinsic pathways is the phospholipid surface on which the clotting factors interact before union at the common pathway. Either platelet phospholipid (for the intrinsic pathway) or tissue thromboplastin (for the extrinsic pathway) can be added to the patient's plasma, and the time taken for clot formation is measured. Less than 30% of normal factor activity is required for the tests to be sensitive to decreased levels. The tests are also prolonged in cases of decreased fibrinogen concentration (< 100 mg/dl^{-1}) and dysfibrinogenemias.

Measurement of the intrinsic and common pathways

1. Partial thromboplastin time (PTT)
   • Partial thromboplastin is substituted for platelet phospholipid and eliminates platelet variability.

- PTT measures the clotting ability of all factors in the intrinsic and common pathways except factor XIII.
- Normal PTT is about 40–100 seconds; > 120 seconds is abnormal.
2. Activated PTT (aPTT)
   - An activator is added to the test tube before addition of partial thromboplastin.
   - Maximal activation of the contact factors (XII and XI) eliminates the lengthy natural contact activation phase and results in more consistent and reproducible results.
   - Normal aPTT is 25–35 seconds.
3. Activated clotting time (ACT)
   - Fresh whole blood (providing platelet phospholipid) is added to a test tube already containing an activator.
   - The automated ACT is widely used to monitor heparin therapy in the operating room.
   - Normal range is 90–120 seconds.

Measurement of the extrinsic and common pathways
1. Prothrombin time (PT)
   - Tissue thromboplastin is added to the patient's plasma.
   - Test varies in sensitivity and response to oral anticoagulant therapy whether measured as PT in seconds or simple PT ratio ($PT_{patient}/PT_{normal}$) (normal = the mean normal PT value of the laboratory test system).
   - Normal PT is 10 –12 seconds.
2. International normalized ratio (INR)
   - Developed to improve the consistency of oral anticoagulant therapy.
   - Converts the PT ratio to a value that would have been obtained using a standard PT method.
   - INR is calculated as $(PT_{patient}/PT_{normal})^{ISI}$ (ISI is the international sensitivity index assigned to the test system).
   - The recommended therapeutic ranges for standard oral anticoagulant therapy and high-dose therapy, respectively, are INR values of 2.0–3.0 and 2.5–3.5.

15. How is fresh frozen plasma prepared?

Fresh frozen plasma (FFP) is the fluid portion of human blood that has been centrifuged, separated, and frozen within 6 hours of donation. It contains the labile and stable components of the coagulation, fibrinolytic, and complement systems. With appropriate storage and handling, the loss of labile factors V and VIII is less than 30%. FFP should be used within 24 hours of thawing. Only ABO-compatible plasma should be used, employing a standard 170-µm filter.

16. What are the current indications for transfusion of FFP?

A task force of the American Society of Anesthesiologists (ASA) recommends the use of FFP in the following circumstances:
1. Urgent reversal of warfarin therapy
2. Correction of known anticoagulation deficiencies for which specific concentrates are unavailable
3. Correction of microvascular bleeding in the presence of elevated (> 1.5 times normal) PT or PTT
4. Correction of microvascular bleeding secondary to coagulation factor deficiencies in patients transfused with more than one blood volume, when a PT or PTT cannot be obtained in a timely fashion

The dose given should be calculated to achieve a minimum of 30% of plasma factor concentration (usually about 10–15 ml/kg of FFP).

17. How is platelet concentrate prepared?

Platelet concentrate (PC) is obtained by centrifugation of fresh whole blood to produce supernatant plasma, which is centrifuged again to remove all but about 30–50 ml of plasma.

Storage at room temperature preserves function but is limited to 5 days. Platelet concentrate contains 60–80% of the platelets in a unit of fresh whole blood. Single-donor units, obtained by apheresis from a single donor, contain the equivalent of 5–8 units of PC and are reserved for use in patients with platelet antibodies or to avoid the risk of human leukocyte (HLA) antibody formation. To achieve an increase in platelet count, transfusion should consist of 1 unit of PC for each 10 kg of body weight. The administration of 1 unit of PC should increase the platelet count by 5,000–8,000/mm^3. Administration of ABO-incompatible platelets is accepted practice. The use of a standard 170-µm filter is recommended.

18. What are the current indications for the use of platelets?

The ASA recommends the following:
- Prophylactic platelet transfusion is ineffective and rarely indicated when thrombocytopenia is due to increased platelet destruction
- For surgical patients with thrombocytopenia due to decreased platelet production and surgical and obstetric patients with microvascular bleeding, platelet transfusion is rarely indicated when the count is greater than 100×10^9/L and usually indicated if the count is less than 50×10^9/L. With intermediate values platelet therapy should be based on the risk of bleeding.

19. How is cryoprecipitate obtained?

Cryoprecipitate is obtained from FFP that is thawed in a controlled way. It contains large quantities of factor VIII, von Willebrand factor, fibrinogen, fibronectin, and factor XIII. Cryoprecipitate can be heat-treated to inactivate human immunodeficiency virus (HIV). A single donor unit contains about 100 antihemophiliac units and 250 mg of fibrinogen. Units usually are pooled and should be given through a 170-µm filter.

20. What are the indications for use of cryoprecipitate?

This should be used in the following conditions:
- In bleeding patients with von Willebrand disease
- For prophylaxis in nonbleeding patients with congenital fibrinogen deficiencies or von Willebrand disease (unresponsive to desmopressin)
- In massively transfused patients with fibrinogen concentrations less than 80–100 mg/dl

21. What is DIC?

DIC is not a disease entity but rather a manifestation of disease associated with various well-defined clinical entities:
- Obstetric conditions (amniotic fluid embolism, placental abruption, retained fetus syndrome, eclampsia, saline-induced abortion)
- Intravascular hemolysis (hemolytic transfusion syndromes, minor hemolysis, massive transfusion)
- Septicemia (gram-negative: endotoxin; gram-positive: mucopolysaccharides)
- Viremias (cytomegalovirus, hepatitis, varicella, HIV)
- Disseminated malignancy
- Leukemia
- Burns
- Crush injury and tissue necrosis
- Liver disease (obstructive jaundice, acute hepatic failure)
- Prosthetic devices (LeVeen shunt, aortic balloon)

DIC usually is seen in clinical circumstances in which the extrinsic or intrinsic coagulation pathway or both are activated by circulating phospholipid, leading to generation of thrombin, but the usual mechanisms preventing unbalanced thrombus formation are impaired. After systemic deposition of intravascular fibrin thrombi, consumption of factors V and VIII, and loss of platelets, the resulting circulating level of clotting factors and platelets represents a balance between depletion and production. The fibrinolytic system is activated, and plasmin begins to cleave fibrinogen and fibrin into fibrinogen and fibrin degradation products (FDPs). Recognizing and understanding the syndrome are made difficult by the occurrence of both acute and chronic forms and by a clinical spectrum varying from diffuse thrombosis to diffuse bleeding or both.

22. What tests are used for the diagnosis of DIC?

There is no one pathognomonic test for diagnosis of DIC. In acute DIC, the PT is elevated in about 75% of patients, whereas PTT is prolonged in 50–60%. Platelet count is typically greatly reduced. Hypofibrinogenemia is common. The D-dimer test is a newer diagnostic test. The D-dimer is a neoantigen formed by the action of thrombin in converting fibrinogen to cross-linked fibrin. It is specific for fibrin degradation products formed from the digestion of cross-linked fibrin by plasmin. In 85–100% of patients, FDPs are elevated. Elevated levels are not diagnostic of DIC but indicate the presence of plasmin and plasmin degradation of fibrinogen or fibrin.

23. Describe the treatment of DIC.

The treatment of DIC is confusing and controversial. The triggering process should be identified and treated accordingly. If bleeding continues, heparin is used to stop the consumption process before administration of specific coagulation products. If these measures fail, specific blood components may be depleted and should be replaced after identification. If bleeding still continues, antifibrinolytic therapy with epsilon aminocaproic acid should be considered, but only if the intravascular coagulation process is shown to have stopped and residual fibrinolysis to continue.

BIBLIOGRAPHY

1. Bick RL, Scates SM: Disseminated intravascular coagulation. Lab Med 23:161–165, 1992.
2. Consensus Conference: Fresh frozen plasma: Indications and risks. JAMA 253:551–553, 1985.
3. Consensus Conference: Platelet transfusion therapy. JAMA 257:1777–1780, 1985.
4. Cosby HT: Perioperative haemotherapy: I. Indications for blood component transfusion. Can J Anaesth 39:695–707, 1992.
5. Hardy J, Belisle S, Robitaille D: Blood products: When to use them and how to avoid them. Can J Anaesth 41:R52–R61, 1994.
6. Irving GA: Perioperative blood and blood component therapy. Can J Anaesth 39:1105–1115, 1992.
7. McLaren ID, Crider BA: Monitoring the coagulation system. Anesthesiol Clin North Am 12:211–236, 1994.
8. Miller RD: Update on blood transfusions and blood substitutes. In Review Course Lectures. Cleveland, International Anesthesia Research Society, 1999, pp 71–78.
9. Petrovitch C: Perioperative evaluation of coagulation. In Refresher Courses in Anesthesiology. Philadelphia, J.B. Lippincott, 1992, pp 169–190.
10. Petrovitch CT: Hemostasis and hemotherapy. In Barash PG, Cullen BF, Stoelting RK (eds): Clinical Anesthesia, 3rd ed. Philadelphia, Lippincott Williams & Wilkins, 1997.
11. Practice guidelines for blood component therapy. A report by the American Society of Anesthesiologists Task Force on Blood Component Therapy. Anesthesiology 84:732–747, 1996.
12. Spiess BD: Coagulation function in the operating room. Anesthesiol Clin North Am 8:481–499, 1990.
13. Stehling L: Indications for perioperative blood transfusion in 1990. Can J Anaesth 38:601–604, 1991.

7. AIRWAY MANAGEMENT

James Duke, M.D.

1. List several indications for endotracheal intubation.

Indications in the operating room include (1) the need to deliver positive pressure ventilation; (2) protection of the respiratory tract from aspiration of gastric contents; (3) surgical procedures about the head and neck in which the anesthesiologist is unable to support the airway manually; (4) general anesthesia in nonsupine positions in which it is impossible to support the airway; (5) most situations in which neuromuscular paralysis has been instituted; (6) surgical procedures within the chest, abdomen, or cranium; (7) procedures in which intracranial hypertension must be treated; and (8) protection of a healthy lung from a diseased lung to ensure its continued performance (e.g., hemoptysis, empyema, pulmonary abscess). Nonoperative indications include (1) profound disturbances in consciousness with the inability to protect the airway, (2) tracheobronchial toilet, and (3) severe pulmonary and multisystem injury associated with respiratory failure (e.g., severe sepsis, airway obstruction, hypoxemia, and hypercarbia of various etiologies).

Objective measures that suggest the need to intubate include a respiratory rate > 35 breaths per minute, vital capacity < 15 ml/kg in adults and 10 ml/kg in children, inability to generate a negative inspiratory force of 20 mmHg, arterial partial pressure of oxygen (PaO_2) < 70 mmHg on 40% oxygen, alveolar-arterial (A-a) gradient > 350 mmHg on 100% O_2, arterial partial pressure of carbon dioxide ($PaCO_2$) > 55 mmHg (except in chronic retainers), and dead space (Vd/Vt) > 0.6.

2. How is the airway assessed?

A patient's airway is assessed by historical interview and physical examination and occasionally through inspection of radiographs, pulmonary function tests, and direct fiber-optic examination. Patients should be questioned about adverse events related to previous episodes that required airway management. For instance, have they ever been informed by an anesthesiologist that they had an unexpectedly difficult airway management problem (i.e., "difficult to ventilate, difficult to intubate")? Have they had a tracheostomy or other surgery about the face and neck? Have they sustained significant burns to these areas? Do they have obstructive sleep apnea or temporomandibular joint (TMJ) dysfunction? Unfortunately, patients and family often gloss over the difficulties that other health care providers have experienced in airway management, because such difficulties rarely if ever manifest in activities of daily living. Close review of the patient chart, particularly anesthetic records, is often helpful.

Physical examination is the single most reliable method of detecting and anticipating difficulties in airway management. First, a general assessment of the patient is indicated. Is the patient able to sit and talk without becoming breathless? Is the patient pale or cyanotic, cachectic or acutely ill? Is the patient receiving chronic oxygen therapy? Is the patient markedly obese or scarred, particularly about the chest and neck? Review the vital signs, particularly pulse oximetry (SpO_2) values.

A **focused exam of the airway** follows. Examine the mouth and oral cavity, noting the extent and symmetry of opening (three fingerbreadths is optimal), the health of the teeth (loose, missing, or cracked teeth should be documented), and the presence of dental appliances. Prominent buck teeth may interfere with the use of a laryngoscope. The size of the tongue is noted (large tongues rarely make airway management impossible, only more difficult), as is the arch of the palate (high arched palates have been associated with difficulty in visualizing the larynx).

The appearance of the **posterior pharynx** may predict difficulty in laryngoscopy and visualization of the larynx. Mallampati has classified patients in classes I–IV based on the visualized structures (a diagram of the visualized structures may be found in Chapter 15, The Preoperative Evaluation). Visualization of fewer structures (particularly class III and IV) was associated with difficult laryngeal exposure. With the patient sitting erect, mouth fully open, and tongue protruding, grading is based on visualization of the following structures:

Class I: Pharyngeal pillars, entire palate, and uvula visible

Class II: Pharyngeal pillars and soft palate visible, visualization of uvula obstructed by tongue

Class III: Soft palate visible but pharyngeal pillars and uvula not visualized

Class IV: Only hard palate visible with soft palate, pillars, and uvula not visualized

After examination of the oral cavity is completed, attention is directed at the **size of the mandible and quality of TMJ function**. A short mandibular body (three fingerbreadths) as measured from the mental process to the prominence of the thyroid cartilage (thyromental distance) suggests difficulty in visualizing the larynx. Patients with TMJ dysfunction may have asymmetry or limitations in opening the mouth as well as popping or clicking. Manipulation of the jaw in preparation for laryngoscopy may worsen symptoms postoperatively. Curiously, some patients with TMJ dysfunction have greater difficulty with opening the mouth after general anesthesia and neuromuscular paralysis than when they are awake and cooperative.

Finally, the **anatomy of the neck** is inspected. Again, evidence of prior surgeries (especially tracheostomy) or significant burns is noted. Does the patient have abnormal masses (e.g., hematoma, abscess or cellulitis, lymphadenopathy, goiter, tumor, soft tissue swelling) or tracheal deviation? A short or thick neck may prove problematic. Is the patient especially obese, or does the patient have large breasts (as often in late pregnancy), which may make use of a laryngoscope difficult?

It is also important to have the patient demonstrate the **range of motion of the head and neck**. Preparation for laryngoscopy requires extension of the neck to facilitate visualization. Elderly patients and patients with cervical fusions may have marked limitation of motion. Furthermore, patients with cervical spine disease (disk disease or cervical instability, as in rheumatoid arthritis) may develop neurologic symptoms with motion of the neck. Such problems should be noted and incorporated into the airway management plan. Radiologic views of the neck in flexion and extension also may reveal worrisome cervical instability.

Particularly in patients with **pathology of the head and neck** (such as laryngeal cancer), it is valuable to know the results of indirect laryngoscopy or direct fiber-optic nasolaryngoscopy, which is often performed by otolaryngologists in the course of evaluating such patients. Finally, if history suggests dynamic airway obstruction (as in intrathoracic or extrathoracic masses), **pulmonary function tests**, including flow-volume loops (as discussed in the chapter on pulmonary function testing), may alert the clinician to the potential for loss of airway once paralytic agents are administered. Anatomic differences between adult and pediatric airways are discussed in the chapter on pediatric anesthesia.

3. Discuss the anatomy of the larynx.

The larynx, located in adults at cervical levels 4–6, protects the entrance of the respiratory tract as well as allows phonation. It is composed of **three unpaired cartilages** (thyroid, cricoid, and epiglottis) and **three paired cartilages** (arytenoid, corniculate, and cuneiform). The thyroid cartilage is the largest and most prominent, forming the anterior and lateral walls. The cricoid cartilage is shaped like a signet ring, faces posteriorly, and is the only complete cartilaginous ring of the laryngotracheal tree. The cricothyroid membrane connects these structures anteriorly. The epiglottis extends superiorly into the hypopharynx and covers the entrance of the larynx during swallowing. The corniculate and cuneiform pairs of cartilages are relatively small and do not figure prominently in the laryngoscopic appearance of the larynx or in its function. The arytenoid cartilages articulate upon the posterior aspect of the larynx and are the posterior attachments of the vocal ligaments (or cords). Identification of the arytenoid cartilages may be important during laryngoscopy. In a patient with an "anterior" airway, the arytenoids may be the only visible structures. Finally, the vocal cords attach anteriorly to the thyroid cartilage.

The **innervation of the larynx** consists of the superior laryngeal and recurrent laryngeal nerves, both of which are branches of the vagus nerve. The superior laryngeal nerves decussate into internal and external branches. The internal branches provide sensory innervation of the larynx above the vocal cords, whereas the external branches provide motor innervation to the cricothyroid muscle, a tensor of the vocal cords. The recurrent laryngeal nerves provide sensory innervation below the level of the cords and motor innervation of the posterior cricoarytenoid muscles, the only abductors of the vocal cords. The glossopharyngeal or ninth cranial nerve provides sensory innervation to the vallecula (the space anterior to the epiglottis, a point of contact for curved, Macintosh laryngoscope blades) and the base of the tongue.

Arteries that supply the larynx include the superior laryngeal (a branch of the superior thyroid artery) and inferior laryngeal (a branch of the inferior thyroid) arteries. Venous drainage follows the same pattern as the arteries; there is also ample lymphatic drainage.

4. Discuss the various instruments available to facilitate airway management, especially endotracheal intubation.

The devices, adjuncts, and tubes developed to facilitate airway management and intubation are a tribute to the ingenuity of many individuals; they are also a testament to the anticipated and unexpected difficulties that arise, if not frequently, at least with regularity. The devices described below are divided roughly into those that enhance oxygenation, those that maintain the airway without endotracheal intubation, those that are associated with direct laryngoscopy and intubation, and those that are used for a difficult or awake intubation.

Oxygen supplementation is always a priority when patients are sedated or anesthetized, when the airway is compromised, or when disease processes make tissue oxygenation problematic. Devices range from nasal cannulas, face tents, and simple masks to masks with reservoirs and masks that can be used to deliver positive pressure ventilation. Their limitation is the concentration of oxygen that can be delivered effectively. The limitations and advantages of many such devices are discussed in detail in Chapter 83, Respiratory Therapy.

Devices that help to maintain a patent airway short of endotracheal intubation include oral airways, nasal airways, and laryngeal mask airways. **Oral airways** are usually constructed of hard plastic; they are available in numerous sizes and shaped to curve behind the tongue, lifting it off the posterior pharynx. The importance of these simple devices cannot be overstated, because the tongue is the most frequent cause of airway obstruction, particularly in obtunded patients. Oral airways, which tend to be poorly tolerated in awake, semiconscious, and lightly anesthetized patients, are best inserted under direct visualization, using depressors to manipulate the tongue. Blindly inserting the airway upside down and turning it 180° once it is in the mouth may push the tongue against the posterior pharynx or traumatize oral structures. **Nasal airways** ("trumpets") can be gently inserted down the nasal passages into the nasopharynx and are better tolerated than oral airways in awake or lightly anesthetized patients.

Laryngeal mask airways (LMAs) are useful in maintaining an airway during anesthesia when endotracheal intubation may not be desired (e.g., asthmatic patients, Luciano Pavarotti). In appropriately chosen patients (with difficult airways but no high risk for aspiration), LMAs may prove a successful management strategy. Fiber-optic endotracheal intubation through an LMA also may be performed; all the while the patient is oxygenated and ventilated. LMAs come in various adult and pediatric sizes. They are poorly tolerated in unanesthetized patients.

Laryngoscopes are left-handed tools designed to facilitate visualization of the larynx. The handles are designed for a number of different battery sizes. Some handles are short and work best for patients with obese, thick chests or large breasts.

Laryngoscope blades also come in various styles and sizes. The most commonly used blades include the curved Macintosh (no. 3 or 4) and the straight Miller blades (no. 2 or 3). The curved blades are inserted into the vallecula, immediately anterior to the epiglottis, which is literally flipped out of the visual axis to expose the laryngeal opening. The Miller blade is inserted past the epiglottis, which is simply lifted out of the way of laryngeal viewing. Clinicians usually have a favorite blade, but facility in the use of both is needed. Many agree that in difficult airways, when the larynx is situated anterior to the visual axis or the epiglottis is particularly long or floppy, the straight blade frequently affords improved visualization. An incandescent bulb at the end of the laryngoscope may be the source of illumination, or fiber-optic cables may transmit very bright, high-quality illumination from a light source in the handle.

Endotracheal tubes come in a multitude of sizes and shapes. They are commonly manufactured from polyvinyl chloride, with a radiopaque line from top to bottom, standard size connectors for anesthesia circuits or self-inflating resuscitation bags, a high-volume, low-pressure cuff and pilot balloon, and a hole in the beveled, distal end (the Murphy eye). Internal diameter ranges from 2.0 to 10.0 mm in half-millimeter increments. Endotracheal tubes may be reinforced with wire, designed with laser applications in mind, or unusually shaped so that they are directed away from the surgical site (oral or nasal Rae tubes). A recently developed product, the Lita tube, has an injection port and orifices about the endotracheal cuff for instillation of local anesthetic to the airway, providing local anesthesia, which improves tolerance of the endotracheal tube. The Lita tube may be advantageous when testing of surgical repairs (ventral hernias) or increases in intra-cranial or intraocular pressure secondary to coughing or bucking are undesirable. Double-lumen endotracheal tubes are designed so that one lung may be isolated from the other to facilitate surgery within a hemithorax or to provide differential ventilation to the lungs.

5. What devices and maneuvers are available for patients who are difficult to intubate?

A few available devices that are not often used by clinicians skilled in intubation and fiber-optic endoscopy include the esophageal obturator and combitube. Although they usually can be found in "difficult airway" carts, they find little if any use within most hospital settings.

When inserted into an endotracheal tube, **light wands** may be useful for blind intubation of the trachea. The technique is termed "blind" because the laryngeal opening is not seen directly. When light is well transilluminated through the neck (the jack-o'-lantern effect), the end of the endotracheal tube is at the entrance of the larynx, and the tube can be threaded off the wand and into the trachea in a blind fashion. **Gum elastic bougies** are flexible, somewhat malleable stylets with an anteriorly directed, bent tip that may be useful for intubating a tracheal opening anterior to the visual axis.

Fiber-optic endoscopy is commonly used to facilitate difficult intubations (when visualization with regular laryngoscopes proves impossible). The endoscope is introduced into the nose or mouth of a sedated patient with a topically anesthetized airway or an unconscious, anesthetized patient. Anatomic structures are identified, and the larynx and trachea are entered under direct visualization.

Finally, the trachea may be intubated using a **retrograde technique**. In simplistic terms, a long Seldinger-type wire is introduced through a catheter that punctures the cricothyroid membrane. The wire is directed superiorly and brought out through the nose or mouth, and an endotracheal tube is threaded over the wire and lowered into the trachea.

6. Describe rapid-sequence induction (RSI). Which patients are best managed in this fashion?

It is easiest to appreciate the distinctions of RSI if an induction under non–rapid-sequence conditions is understood. Ordinarily the patient has fasted for at least 6–8 hours and is not at risk for a full stomach and gastric aspiration. The patient is preoxygenated, and an agent is administered to render the patient unconscious. Once it is established that the patient can be satisfactorily mask-ventilated, a muscle relaxant is administered. The patient is then mask-ventilated until complete paralysis is ensured by electrical nerve stimulation. Laryngoscopy and endotracheal intubation are undertaken, and the case proceeds.

In contrast, RSI is undertaken in patients who are thought to have an airway that can be quickly intubated and controlled with direct laryngoscopy but who are at risk for pulmonary aspiration of gastric contents. Aspiration is a serious anesthetic complication with significant potential morbidity (see Chapter 43, Aspiration). Patients with full stomachs are thought to be at risk; other risk factors include pregnancy, diabetes, pain, opioid analgesics, recent traumatic injury, intoxication, and pathologic involvement of the gastrointestinal tract, such as small bowel obstruction. Patients at risk for full stomach should be premedicated with agents that reduce the acidity and volume of gastric contents, such as histamine$_2$ receptor blockers (ranitidine, cimetidine), nonparticulate antacids (Bicitra or Alka-Seltzer), and gastrokinetics, when appropriate (metoclopramide).

The goal of RSI is to secure and control the airway rapidly. The patient is preoxygenated. An induction agent is administered, followed quickly by a rapid-acting relaxant, either succinyl-choline or rocuronium in high doses. Simultaneously an assistant applies pressure to the cricoid cartilage (the only complete cartilaginous ring of the respiratory tract), which closes off the esophagus and prevents entry of regurgitated gastric contents into the trachea and lungs. Known as the Sellick maneuver, such pressure is maintained until the airway is protected by tracheal intubation.

7. Describe the indications for an awake intubation.

If the physical exam leaves in question the ability to ventilate and intubate adequately once the patient is anesthetized and paralyzed, serious consideration should be given to awake intubation.

Patients with a previous history of difficult intubation, acute processes that compromise the airway (e.g., soft-tissue infections of the head and neck, hematomas), mandibular fractures or other significant facial deformities, morbid obesity, or cancer involving the larynx are prudent candidates for awake intubation.

8. How is awake intubation performed?

A frank discussion with the patient is necessary. The anticipated difficulty of airway management and the risks of proceeding with anesthesia without previously securing a competent airway are conveyed in clear terms. Compassion and concern for patient safety are priorities.

Preparation of the operative suite is also important. Topical local anesthetics, intravenous sedatives, a selection of oral and nasal airways and endotracheal tubes, suction, a fiber-optic endoscope, and other airway adjuncts should be readily available. The anesthesiologist should formulate a plan for achieving awake intubation and consider a back-up plan as well. A surgeon capable of creating a surgical airway should be at bedside when loss of airway is a real possibility.

In preparing the patient, intramuscular administration of glycopyrrolate, 0.2–0.4 mg 30 minutes before the procedure, is useful to reduce secretions. Many clinicians also administer nebulized lidocaine to provide topical anesthesia of the entire airway.

Once the patient arrives in the operating suite, standard anesthetic monitors (electrocardiogram [ECG], noninvasive blood pressure, pulse oximetry) are applied and supplemental oxygen is administered. The patient is sedated with appropriate agents (e.g., opioid, benzodiazepine, droperidol, propofol). The choice depends on the clinician's experience and preference as well as patient considerations. Of highest importance, the level of sedation is titrated so that the patient is not rendered obtunded, apneic, or unable to protect the airway.

As sedation is titrated, the route of intubation may be oral or nasal, depending on surgical needs and patient factors. Many anesthesiologists prefer the nasal route, because fiber-optic visualization of the larynx is thought to be easier; again, this is a matter of preference. If nasal intubation is planned, nasal and nasopharyngeal mucosa must be anesthetized; vasoconstrictor substances are applied to prevent epistaxis. Often nasal trumpets with lidocaine ointment are inserted gently; large trumpets are used in sequence to dilate the nasal passages. Simultaneously the tongue, posterior pharynx, and hypopharynx are topically anesthetized with anesthetic sprays. Once the tongue is anesthetized, it is often possible to perform gentle laryngoscopy, spraying tissues deeper and deeper into the hypopharynx until the larynx is visualized. It is inappropriate to introduce an endotracheal tube until the trachea is also anesthetized. Often a transtracheal injection of lidocaine is performed via needle puncture of the cricothyroid membrane; it is also possible to introduce lidocaine into the trachea via a channel of the fiber-optic laryngoscope. Nerve blocks are also useful to provide topical anesthesia (see question 9).

Once an adequate level of sedation and topical anesthesia is achieved, the endotracheal tube is loaded on the fiber-optic endoscope. The endoscope is gently lowered into the chosen passage; with practiced skill, the endoscope is directed past the epiglottis, through the larynx, and down the trachea, visualizing tracheal rings and carina. The endotracheal tube is passed into the trachea, and the endoscope is removed; the endotracheal tube is connected to the anesthesia circuit, and breath sounds and end-tidal carbon dioxide are confirmed. The patient may then be fully anesthetized by intravenous agents or administration of volatile anesthetic.

Useful Medications for Awake Intubations

PURPOSE	MEDICATION	DOSE	ROUTE	COMMENTS
Antisialagogue	Glycopyrrolate	0.2–0.4 mg	IV or IM	Give 30 minutes before intubation
Sedation*	Midazolam	1–2 mg	IV	Amnestic
	Fentanyl	50–250 µg	IV	Analgesic
	Droperidol	1.25–2.5 mg	IV	Neuroleptic

Table continued on next page.

Useful Medications for Awake Intubations

PURPOSE	MEDICATION	DOSE	ROUTE	COMMENTS
Topical anesthesia	Cocaine	40–160 mg	Intranasal	Good anesthetic and vaso-constrictor; may produce coronary vasospasm
	1% Phenylephrine with 4% Lidocaine	1–2 ml 2–4 ml	Intranasal	Vasoconstrictor and local anesthetic
	2% Viscous lidocaine	5–20 ml	Oral	"Swish and swallow"
	Cetacaine spray	2–4 sprays	Oral	Contains benzocaine: excessive use may produce methemoglobinemia
	1% Lidocaine	2–3 ml	Airway blocks	Aspirate before injection
	4% Lidocaine	2–3 ml	Transtracheal	Aspirate before injection

* All sedatives should be slowly titrated to effect. Excessive doses may produce respiratory depression, hypoxemia, and carbon dioxide retention. Suggested doses are for otherwise healthy, approximately 70-kg patients.

9. Are nerve blocks useful when awake intubation is planned?

The glossopharyngeal nerve, which provides sensory innervation to the base of the tongue and the vallecula, may be blocked by transmucosal local anesthetic injection of the tonsillar pillars. The superior laryngeal nerve provides sensory innervation of the larynx above the vocal cords and may be blocked by injection just below the greater cornu of the hyoid. Care must be taken to aspirate before injection, because this is carotid territory. An intravascular injection of local anesthetic into the carotid is likely to produce seizures at a minimum, if not respiratory arrest and vascular collapse. Many clinicians are reluctant to block the superior laryngeal nerves *and* to perform a transtracheal block in patients with a full stomach, because all protective airway reflexes are lost. Such patients are unable to protect themselves from aspiration if gastric contents are regurgitated.

10. The patient has been anesthetized and paralyzed, but the airway is difficult to intubate. Is there an organized approach to handling this problem?

The patient who is difficult to ventilate and difficult to intubate is quite possibly the most serious problem faced by anesthesiologists. Organs that consume practically all of the oxygen delivered to them (the heart and particularly the brain) are at risk for profound and irreversible ischemic injury with relatively brief (5 minutes or so) interruptions in oxygen supply.

It is always wise to consider the merits of regional anesthesia (local anesthetic infiltration of the operative area, nerve blocks, and spinal or epidural anesthesia) to avoid a known or suspected difficult airway. Although a thorough history and physical exam are likely to identify the majority of patients with difficult airways, unanticipated problems occasionally present. Only through preplanning and practiced algorithms are such situations managed optimally. The American Society of Anesthesiologists has prepared a difficult airway algorithm (see following page) to assist the clinician. Key features include anticipating the likelihood of difficult intubation or ventilation. The relative merits of different management options (surgical vs. nonsurgical airway, awake vs. postinduction intubation, spontaneous ventilation vs. assisted ventilation) are weighed. Once these decisions have been made, primary and alternative strategies are laid out to assist in stepwise management, especially if the patient continues to be difficult to ventilate or intubate. This algorithm deserves close and repeated inspection before the anesthesiologist attempts to manage such problems. This is no time for heroism; if intubation or ventilation is difficult, call for help!

11. Transtracheal ventilation is mentioned in the difficult airway algorithm. Describe the technique and its limitations.

Transtracheal ventilation is a nonsurgical technique perhaps best described as a temporizing measure if mask ventilation and oxygenation become inadequate. A catheter (12- or 14-gauge) is connected to a jet-type (Sanders) ventilator, which in turn is connected to an oxygen source capable of delivering gas at a pressure around 50 psi, and inserted into the trachea through the cricothyroid membrane. The gas is delivered intermittently by a hand-held actuator. The duration of ventilation is best assessed by watching the rise and fall of the chest; an inspiratory to expiratory ratio of 1:4 seconds is recommended. Usually oxygenation improves rapidly; however, patients frequently cannot expire fully, perhaps because of airway obstruction, and carbon dioxide retention may limit the duration of the technique's usefulness. An additional risk is barotrauma secondary to high pressures. However, transtracheal ventilation is an effective temporizing measure, allowing team members time to catch *their* breath and to develop and implement further strategies (usually a surgical airway at this point).

12. Define criteria for extubation.

The patient should be awake and responsive with stable vital signs, good grip, and sustained head lift. Adequate reversal of neuromuscular blockade must be established. In equivocal situations, negative inspiratory force should exceed 20 mmHg and vital capacity should exceed 15 ml/kg.

13. The patient has been delivered to the postanesthetic care unit (PACU). The pulse oximeter is attached, and oxygen saturations are noted to be in the upper 80s. Chest wall movement does not appear to be adequate. How should the patient be managed?

As in cardiopulmonary resuscitation (CPR) the ABCs (airway, breathing, and circulation) are fundamental in managing such situations. When the ABCs are so familiar that they are second nature, the clinician may think more deeply about the problem at hand while stabilizing the patient. Assessment, treatment, and reassessment are continuous.

Successful management requires an increase in inspired oxygen concentration. Assess the patient in general (mental status, color, other vital signs) while establishing a patent airway, if needed. A chin lift or jaw thrust may be necessary. Suction the patient's airway, and inspect for foreign bodies. Is the trachea in midline? Are neck masses or swelling problematic? Once the airway appears patent, assess adequacy of ventilation by inspecting and auscultating the chest, observing for normal, symmetric rise and fall. Is respiration paradoxical? Does the abdomen distend and the chest retract with inspiration, suggesting airway obstruction or inadequate reversal of neuromuscular blockade? Auscultate breath sounds, checking for symmetry, wheezing, and other adventitious sounds. Palpate pulses and listen to the heart, because circulatory depression may be associated with oxygen desaturation. Assess the patient's strength by hand grip and sustained head lift. Insufficient strength suggests the need to assess neuromuscular blockade through electrical stimulation. Abnormal findings at any point in the physical exam should be addressed.

14. The patient develops stridorous breath sounds. Describe the likely cause and the appropriate management.

A likely cause of stridorous breath sounds in the early postextubation period is laryngospasm, although other causes of upper airway obstruction (e.g., postextubation croup, expanding hematomas, soft tissue swelling) should be excluded. Laryngospasm may be precipitated by extubation during light planes of anesthesia; secretions falling on the vocal cords or insertion of an oral airway also may produce laryngospasm. If laryngospasm is incomplete, the patient will have stridorous breath sounds. However, if laryngospasm is complete, little if any air movement is possible and breath sounds will be totally absent.

The treatment for laryngospasm is to support ventilation. Call for an assistant, provide a jaw thrust, and assist the patient's inspiratory efforts with positive pressure ventilation, using 100% oxygen. If this approach proves unsatisfactory, administer succinylcholine, 0.15–0.30 mg/kg (about 10–20 mg in adults), to relax the vocal cords. If the patient continues to experience difficulty with ventilation, reintubation with approximately 100 mg of succinylcholine may be necessary. Once intubation is completed and breath sounds have been verified (as well as end-tidal CO_2, if available), the patient should receive assisted ventilation. It may be wise to sedate the patient. When reextubation is attempted in the near future, laryngospasm may recur.

DIFFICULT AIRWAY ALGORITHM†

1. Assess the likelihood and clinical impact of basic management problems:
   A. Difficult intubation
   B. Difficult ventilation
   C. Difficulty with patient cooperation or consent
2. Consider the relative merits and feasibility of basic management choices:
   A. Nonsurgical vs. surgical technique for initial approach to intubation
   B. Awake intubation vs. intubation attempts after induction of general anesthesia
   C. Preservation of spontaneous ventilation vs. ablation of spontaneous ventilation
3. Develop primary and alternative strategies:

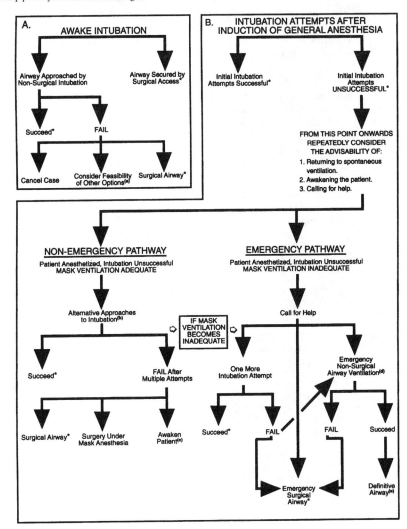

* CONFIRM INTUBATION WITH EXHALED CO_2

(a) Other options include (but are not limited to): surgery under mask anesthesia, surgery under local anesthesia infiltration or regional nerve blockade, or intubation attempts after induction of general anesthesia.

(b) Alternative approaches to difficult intubation include (but are not limited to): use of different laryngoscope blades, awake intubation, blind oral or nasal intubation, fiber-optic intubation, intubating stylet or tube changer, light wand, retrograde intubation, and surgical airway access.

(c) See awake intubation.

(d) Options for emergency nonsurgical airway ventilation include (but are not limited to): transtracheal jet ventilation, laryngeal mask ventilation, or esophageal-tracheal combitube ventilation.

(e) Options for establishing a definitive airway include (but are not limited to): returning to awake state with spontaneous ventilation, tracheotomy, or endotracheal intubation.

† Reproduced with permission of the American Society of Anesthesiologists.

If stridorous breath sounds are due to laryngeal edema, administration of nebulized racemic epinephrine and intravenous steroids may be indicated; reintubation may be necessary if oxygenation continues to deteriorate.

15. The patient is diagnosed and treated for laryngospasm, which resolves. Oxygenation is still not optimal, and chest auscultation reveals bilateral rales. What is the most likely cause?

Although congestive heart failure, fluid overload, adult respiratory distress syndrome, and aspiration of gastric contents need to be considered, negative pressure pulmonary edema (NPPE) is the likely cause. NPPE results from generation of markedly negative intrapleural pressures when the patient inspires against a closed or obstructed glottis. Whereas intrapleural pressures vary between -5 and -10 cm H_2O during a normal respiratory cycle, inspiration against a closed glottis may generate between -50 and -100 cm H_2O pressure. Such increased pressures increase venous return into the thorax and pulmonary vasculature, thereby increasing transcapillary hydrostatic pressure gradients and producing pulmonary edema. Cardiac effects include right ventricular distention, leftward shift of the interventricular septum, and decreased left ventricular compliance, which increases left ventricular end-diastolic pressure and thus pulmonary microvascular resistance.

In addition to its association with laryngospasm, NPPE has been noted with supraglottitis, aspiration, upper airway tumors and foreign bodies, bronchospasm, croup, airway trauma, and strangulation as well as after difficult airway management. Patients who are intubated with small endotracheal tubes and spontaneously breathing also may be at risk. The onset of edema has been noted from 3–150 minutes after the inciting event.

Once the airway obstruction is relieved, treatment is supportive. The pulmonary edema usually resolves between 12 and 24 hours. Continue oxygen therapy; continuous positive airway pressure (CPAP) and mechanical ventilation with positive end-expiratory pressure (PEEP) may occasionally be needed, depending on the severity of gas exchange impairment.

BIBLIOGRAPHY

1. American Society of Anesthesiologists' Task Force on Management of the Difficult Airway: Practice Guidelines for Management of the Difficult Airway. Anesthesiology 78:597–602, 1993.
2. Benumof JL: Management of the difficult adult airway. Anesthesiology 75:1087–1110, 1991.
3. Birmingham PK, Cheney FW, Ward RJ: Esophageal intubation: A review of detection techniques. Anesth Analg 65:886–891, 1986.
4. Bogdomoff DL, Stone DJ: Emergency management of the airway outside of the operating room. Can J Anaesth 39:1069–1089, 1992.
5. Geffin B: Anesthesia and the "problem upper airway." Int Anesth Clin 28:106-114, 1990.
6. Mallampati RS, Gatt SP, Gugino LD, et al: A clinical sign to predict difficult tracheal intubation: A prospective study. Can Anesth Soc J 32:429–435, 1985.
7. McCullough TM, Bishop MJ: Complications of translaryngeal intubation. Clin Chest Med 12:507–521, 1991.
8. Miller KA, Harkin CD, Bailey PL: Postoperative tracheal extubation. Anesth Analg 80:149–172, 1995.
9. Salem MR, Mathrebhotham M, Dennett EJ: Difficult intubation. N Engl J Med 295:879–881, 1976.
10. Salem MR, Wong AY, Mani M, Sellick BA: Efficiency of cricoid pressure in preventing gastric inflation during bag-mask ventilation in pediatric patients. Anesthesiology 40:96–98, 1974.

II. *Pharmacology*

8. VOLATILE ANESTHETICS

Stephan O. Fiedler, M.D.

1. What are the properties of an ideal anesthetic gas?

An ideal anesthetic gas would be predictable in onset and emergence; provide muscle relaxation, cardiostability, and bronchodilation; not trigger malignant hyperthermia or other significant side effects (such as nausea and vomiting); be inflammable; undergo no transformation within the body; and allow easy estimation of concentration at the site of action.

2. What are the chemical compositions of the more common anesthetic gases? Why do we no longer use the older ones?

Molecular structure of contemporary gaseous anesthetics.

Many older anesthetic agents had unfortunate properties and side effects such as flammability (cyclopropane and fluroxene), slow induction (methoxyflurane), hepatotoxicity (chloroform and fluroxene), and nephrotoxicity (methoxyflurane).

3. How are the potencies of anesthetic gases compared?

The potency of anesthetic gases is compared using minimal alveolar concentration (MAC), which is the concentration at one atmosphere that abolishes motor response to a painful stimulus (namely, surgical incision) in 50% of patients. MAC appears to be consistent across species lines. The measurement of MAC assumes that alveolar concentration directly reflects the partial pressure of the anesthetic at its site of action as well as equilibration between the sites.

4. What other uses does MAC have?

MAC allows us not only to predict the required anesthetic dose for a patient but to compare the effects of other factors on MAC itself. The highest MACs are found in infants at term to 6 months of age and decrease with both increasing age and prematurity. For every Celsius degree drop in body temperature, MAC decreases approximately 2–5%. Effect is dependent on partial pressure; hence, higher concentrations are required at elevation.

vioids, barbiturates, calcium channel blockers, and pregnancy are known to
's that do not affect MAC include hypocarbia, hypercarbia, gender, thyroid
'mia.
'ditive. For example, nitrous oxide potentiates the effects of volatile

. Define partition coefficient. Which partition coefficients are important?
A partition coefficient describes the distribution of a given agent at equilibrium between two substances at the same temperature, pressure, and volume. Thus the blood to gas coefficient describes the distribution of anesthetic between blood and gas at the same partial pressure. A higher blood to gas coefficient correlates with a greater concentration of anesthetic in blood (i.e., a higher solubility). Therefore, a greater amount of anesthetic is taken into the blood, which acts as a reservoir for the agent, rendering it unavailable at the site of action and thus slowing the rate of induction.

Other important partition coefficients include brain to blood, fat to blood, liver to blood, and muscle to blood. Except for fat to blood, these coefficients are close to 1 (equally distributed). Fat has partition coefficients for different volatile agents of 30–60; that is, anesthetics continue to be taken into fat for quite some time after equilibration with other tissues.

Compared with equilibration between inspired and alveolar gas partial pressures, equilibration is relatively quick between alveolar and arterial gas tension as well as between arterial and brain anesthetic partial pressure. Thus alveolar concentration ultimately is the principal factor in determining onset of action.

Physical Properties of Contemporary Anesthetic Gases

	ISOFLURANE	DESFLURANE	ENFLURANE	HALOTHANE	NITROUS OXIDE	SEVOFLURANE
Molecular weight	184.5	168	184.5	197.5	44	200
Boiling point (C)	48.5	23.5	56.5	50.2	−88	58.5
Vapor pressure (mmHg)	238	664	175	241	39,000	160
Partition coefficients (at 37°C)						
Blood:gas	1.4	0.42	1.91	2.3	0.47	0.69
Brain:blood	2.6	1.2	1.4	2.9	1.7	1.7
Fat:blood	45	27	36	60	2.3	48
Oil:gas	90.8	18.7	98.5	224	1.4	47.2
MAC (% of 1 atm)	1.15	6.0	1.7	0.77	104	1.7

6. What physical properties of the anesthetic are related to potency?
No one physical property of a volatile anesthetic best predicts potency of the gas. However, at the turn of the century, Meyer and Overton independently observed that an increasing oil to gas partition coefficient correlated with anesthetic potency. Thus they believed that anesthesia was somehow created through incorporation of lipophilic anesthetics into the lipid membrane.

7. What other theories address the mechanism of anesthesia?
Two other theories of anesthetic action include a specific receptor theory for anesthetics and modification of neurotransmission at receptors for gamma-aminobutyric acid (GABA), a naturally occurring neuroinhibitor. The Meyer-Overton lipid solubility theory dominated for nearly half a century before it was modified. Franks and Lieb found that an amphiphilic solvent (octanol) correlated better with potency than lipophilicity and concluded that the anesthetic site must contain both polar and nonpolar sites. Modifications of Meyer and Overton's membrane expansion theories include the **excessive volume theory**, in which anesthesia is created when apolar cell membrane components and amphiphilic anesthetics synergistically create a larger

cell volume than the sum of the two volumes together. In the **critical volume hypothesis**, anesthesia results when the cell volume at the anesthetic site reaches a critical size. Both theories rely on the effects of membrane expansion on and at ion channels.

8. Increasing alveolar concentration is obviously important for rapid induction of anesthesia. What other factors influence speed of induction?

Factors that increase alveolar anesthetic concentration speed onset, whereas factors that decrease alveolar concentration slow onset. Increasing concentrations of anesthetic increases alveolar concentration of anesthetic, and a high-flow breathing circuit enhances delivery. Increasing minute ventilation drives up alveolar concentration. An increase in cardiac output slows induction by decreasing anesthetic partial pressure at the alveolus. Finally, if the partial pressure of anesthesia in the pulmonary artery and veins is nearly equal, alveolar partial pressure rises more rapidly.

9. What is the second gas effect?

In theory, this phenomenon should speed the onset of anesthetic induction. Because nitrous oxide is insoluble in blood, its rapid absorption from alveoli causes an abrupt rise in the alveolar concentration of accompanying volatile anesthetic. However, even at high concentrations (70%) of nitrous oxide, this effect accounts for only a small increase in concentration of volatile anesthetic.

10. Why can nitrous oxide be dangerous if administered to patients with pneumothorax? Are there other conditions in which nitrous oxide should be avoided?

Although nitrous oxide has a low blood to gas partition coefficient, it is 20 times more soluble than nitrogen (which comprises 79% of atmospheric gases). Thus, nitrous oxide can diffuse 20 times faster into closed spaces than it can be removed, resulting in expansion of pneumothorax, bowel gas, or air embolism or in an increase in pressure within noncompliant cavities such as the cranium or middle ear.

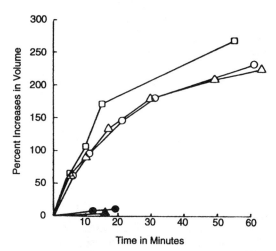

Expansion of a pneumothorax when breathing oxygen (*filled figures*) vs. 75% nitrous oxide (*open figures*). (From Eger EI II, Saidman LJ: Hazards of nitrous oxide anesthesia in bowel obstruction and pneumothorax. Anesthesiology 26:61–68, 1965, with permission.)

11. Describe the ventilatory effects of the volatile anesthetics.

Delivery of anesthetic gases results in a dose-dependent depression of ventilation mediated directly through medullary centers and indirectly through effects on intercostal muscle function. Minute volume decreases secondary to reductions in tidal volume, although rate appears generally to increase in a dose-dependent fashion. Ventilatory drive in response to hypoxia can be easily abolished at one MAC and attenuated at lower concentrations. The ventilatory response to hypercarbia also is attenuated by increasing MAC in a dose-dependent fashion.

12. What effects do volatile anesthetics have on hypoxic pulmonary vasoconstriction? On airway caliber? On mucociliary function?

Hypoxic pulmonary vasoconstriction (HPV) is a locally mediated response of the pulmonary vasculature to decreased alveolar oxygen tension and serves to match ventilation to perfusion. Inhalational agents decrease this response.

All volatile anesthetics appear to decrease **airway resistance** by a direct relaxing effect on bronchial smooth muscle and by decreasing the bronchoconstricting effect of hypocapnia. The bronchoconstricting effects of histamine release also appear to be decreased when an inhalational anesthetic is administered.

Mucociliary clearance appears to be diminished by volatile anesthetics, principally through interference with ciliary beat frequency. The effects of dry inhaled gases, positive pressure ventilation, and high inspired oxygen content also contribute to ciliary impairment.

13. What effects do volatile anesthetics have on the circulation?

In contrast to the pulmonary effects, circulatory effects are best measured with controlled ventilation.

Circulatory Effects of Contemporary Anesthetic Gases

	ISOFLURANE/ DESFLURANE	SEVOFLURANE	HALOTHANE	NITROUS OXIDE
Cardiac output	0	0	–*	+
Heart rate	++/0	0	0	+
Blood pressure	– –*	– –**	–*	0
Stroke volume	–*	–**	–*	–
Contractility	– –*	– –**	– – –*	–*
Systemic vascular resistance	– –	– –	0	0
Pulmonary vascular resistance	0	0	0	+
Coronary blood flow	+	+	0	0
Cerebral blood flow	+	+	+++	0
Muscle blood flow	+	+	–	0
Catecholamine levels	0	0	0	0

* = dose-dependent, ++ = large increase, + = increase, 0 = no change, – = decrease, – – = large decrease.

14. Which anesthetic agent is associated with the greatest frequency of cardiac dysrhythmias?

Halothane has been shown to increase the sensitivity of the myocardium to epinephrine, resulting in more frequent premature ventricular contractions and tachydysrhythmias. The mechanism may be related to the prolongation of conduction through the His-Purkinje system, which facilitates reentrant phenomenon, and α_1 adrenergic receptor stimulation within the heart. Compared with adults, children undergoing halothane anesthesia appear to be relatively resistant to this sensitizing effect, although halothane has been shown to have a cholinergic, vagally induced bradycardic effect in children.

15. Discuss the biotransformation of volatile anesthetics and its significance.

It was initially believed that inhalational anesthetics were inert and underwent no transformation. For the most part, oxidative metabolism occurs within the liver via the cytochrome P-450 system, but metabolism also occurs to a lesser extent in the kidneys, lungs, and gastrointestinal tract. Desflurane and isoflurane are metabolized less than 1%, whereas halothane is more than 20% metabolized by the liver. Under hypoxic conditions, halothane may undergo reductive metabolism, producing metabolites that may cause hepatic necrosis.

Fluoride is another potentially toxic product of anesthetic metabolism. Fluoride-associated renal dysfunction has been linked with the use of methoxyflurane and greatly contributed to the withdrawal of methoxyflurane from the market. The small amount of fluoride produced by other agents, such as sevoflurane, has not been implicated in renal dysfunction. Another rare entity, halothane hepatitis, may be related to the above hypoxic model, but it is more likely secondary to an autoimmune hypersensitivity reaction.

16. Which anesthetic agent has been shown to be teratogenic in animals?

Nitrous oxide, administered to pregnant rats in concentrations greater than 50% for over 24 hours, has been shown to increase skeletal abnormalities. The mechanism is believed to be related to the inhibition of methionine synthesis, which is necessary for DNA synthesis; the mechanism also may be secondary to the physiologic effects of impaired uterine blood flow by nitrous oxide. Although direct effects have not been seen in humans, it may be prudent to limit the use of nitrous oxide in pregnant women.

Several surveys have attempted to quantify the relative risk of operating room personal exposure to nonscavenged anesthetic gases. Pregnant women were found to have a 30% increased risk of spontaneous abortion and a 20% increased risk for congenital abnormalities. However, responder bias and failure to control for other exposure hazards may account for some of these findings.

BIBLIOGRAPHY

1. Albrecht RF, Miletich DJ: Speculations on the molecular nature of anesthesia. Gen Pharmacol 19:339–346, 1988.
2. Atlee JL, Bosnjak ZJ: Mechanisms for cardiac dysrhythmias during anesthesia. Anesthesiology 72: 347–374, 1990.
3. Eger EI II (ed): MAC, Anesthetic Uptake, and Action. Baltimore, Williams & Wilkins, 1974.
4. Eger EI II, Saidman LJ: Hazards of nitrous oxide anesthesia in bowel obstruction and pneumothorax. Anesthesiology 26:61–68, 1965.
5. Quasha AL, Eger EI II, Tinker JH: Determination and applications of MAC. Anesthesiology 53: 315–334, 1980.

9. INTRAVENOUS INDUCTION AGENTS

Gladstone C. McDowell II, M.D.

1. What is an intravenous (IV) induction agent?

An IV induction agent is an intravenously injected drug used to induce unconsciousness at the onset of general anesthesia but allows rapid recovery after termination of its effect.

2. How do IV induction agents work?

Of the multiple theories proposed, perhaps the most widely accepted is that they modulate GABAergic neuronal transmission, thereby interfering with transmembrane electrical activity. GABA (gamma-aminobutyric acid) is the most common inhibitory neurotransmitter in humans.

3. Describe the properties of an ideal induction agent.

1. The drug should be water soluble and stable in aqueous solution with chemical stability and IV fluid compatibility.

2. The onset of anesthesia should be rapid (within 1 arm-brain circulation time) without unwanted movement or unpredictable cardiovascular or neurologic side effects.

3. The drug should possess anticonvulsant, antiemetic, analgesic, and amnestic properties.

4. Recovery from anesthesia should be rapid and predictable (dose-related).

5. There should be no impairment of renal or hepatic function, steroid synthesis, or teratogenicity.

No ideal intravenous induction drug exists, but many agents possess most of the desired physical and pharmacologic properties. With increasing age, the total volume of distribution increases and elimination clearance decreases, resulting in longer lasting drug effects. Older patients are more sensitive to intravenous anesthetics, and dose reductions may be required. Dosage calculation for induction should be based on estimates of lean body mass.

4. What are the properties and side effects of barbiturates?

Barbiturates are derived from barbituric acid; only the shorter acting drugs have clinical use in anesthesia. They produce a dose-dependent central nervous system (CNS) depression with hypnosis and amnesia. The rapid onset of action (1 arm-brain circulation time with maximal effect within 1 minute) reflects lipid solubility. The actions of the long- and medium-acting drugs are terminated by metabolism; the shorter-acting drugs are redistributed from the central compartment. The most commonly used barbiturates are thiopental (Pentothal) and methohexital (Brevital).

Thiopental sodium (Pentothal), the prototypical barbiturate, is a thiobarbiturate usually prepared as a 2.5% solution; it is stable up to 1 week if refrigerated. It has a pH of 10.5 and can be irritating when injected intravenously. The usual IV induction dose of 3–5 mg/kg produces a loss of consciousness within 15 seconds and recovery within 5–10 minutes. It is 99% metabolized by the liver (10–15% per hour), with less than 1% excreted unchanged by the kidneys. The elimination half-life is long (6–12 hours) and may contribute to slow recovery and "hangover" sensation. Approximately 28–30% may be detectable in the body after 24 hours. Because of known accumulation with repeated doses, thiopental is not used to maintain anesthesia. Studies in healthy volunteers demonstrate impairment of driving skills for up to 8 hours.

Methohexital (Brevital) is usually prepared as a 1% solution and is slightly less lipid soluble and less ionized at physiologic pH than thiopental. With induction doses of 1–2 mg/kg, loss of consciousness and recovery rates are similar to thiopental. However, the clearance rate for methohexital is 3–4 times faster with an elimination half-life of 2–4 hours. Reconstituted solutions of methohexital are stable up to 6 weeks. Full recovery from the CNS effects is significantly more rapid than with thiopental.

Barbiturates may cause myoclonus; hiccoughing may occur during induction but is usually brief and self-limiting. Respiratory depression depends on the rate of administration. Cardiovascular depression occurs often in elderly or volume-depleted patients and appears to be dose-related.

5. What are the properties and side effects of propofol?

Propofol (Diprivan), chemically described as an alkylphenol (2,6 diisopropylphenol), is an IV sedative-hypnotic agent used for induction and maintenance of anesthesia as well as sedation. It is a hydrophobic liquid at room temperature and is formulated in a white soybean oil–egg yolk lecithin emulsion (essentially Intralipid 10%). It is highly lipophilic (volume of distribution [Vd] = 2.8 L/kg), which enhances its ability to cross the blood-brain barrier.

Induction doses of 2–2.5 mg/kg produce loss of consciousness in less than 1 minute and last 4–6 minutes. Propofol is cleared rapidly by both redistribution to fatty tissues and rapid clearance via the liver to inactive metabolites that are eliminated by the kidneys. The rapidity of induction is comparable to methohexital and thiopental, but several studies have demonstrated more rapid awakening and discharge from the postanesthetic care unit with propofol. Patients tend to have less residual cloudiness and psychomotor impairment than with barbiturates. The incidence of postoperative nausea and emesis is significantly less. Pain on injection appears to occur in 38–90% of patients. The pain appears to be due to the drug itself and not to the rate of injection or lipid emulsion. The addition of 40 mg of lidocaine to the solution or pretreatment with a small amount of opioid may ameliorate the discomfort. During induction with propofol, rapid arterial and venous vasodilation and mild negative inotropic effects cause a decrease in blood pressure of 20–30%. The decrease is usually most profound in patients who are hypovolemic and may be reduced by a slow rate of infusion and preinduction volume-loading.

6. What are the properties and side effects of etomidate?

Etomidate (Amidate) is a carboxylated imidazole compound dissolved in 35% propylene glycol; it is structurally unrelated to any of the other IV anesthetic agents. The usual induction dosage of 0.2–0.4 mg/kg IV provides rapid loss of consciousness, which lasts 3–12 minutes. The duration of CNS depression is dose-dependent, and recovery of psychomotor function is equivalent to that of thiopental. The short duration of action appears to result from redistribution and rapid hepatic metabolism to inactive carboxylic acid metabolites that are excreted in the urine. Etomidate is cleared 5 times faster than thiopental, and the elimination half-life is shorter (2–5 hours).

Venoirritation with rapid infusion is possible, because etomidate is a weak base dissolved in propylene glycol. Myoclonus during induction may occur secondary to disinhibition of subcortical neuronal activity. Pretreatment with an opioid may blunt this effect. The incidence of nausea and emesis is fairly high, and prophylaxis with an antiemetic is recommended.

7. What are the properties and side effects of ketamine?

Ketamine (Ketalar, Ketaject) is a phencyclidine (PCP) derivative available as a racemic mixture of two isomers; it was released in 1970 for induction of anesthesia. It is 10 times more lipid-soluble than thiopental and produces rapid CNS depression with hypnosis (within 30 seconds), sedation, amnesia, and analgesia. The anesthetic induction doses are 1–2 mg/kg IV, with effects lasting 5–10 minutes, or 10 mg/kg IM, which acts in 3–5 minutes. A stun dose of 4 mg/kg IM is sometimes administered to uncooperative patients (e.g., mentally retarded children) to facilitate intravenous catheter insertion or other procedures.

Ketamine is rapidly redistributed to muscle and fat and metabolized in the liver to a weakly active metabolite, norketamine. Clearance depends on hepatic blood flow, and the elimination half-life is approximately 3 hours. Ketamine is unique in that it stimulates the cardiovascular system, increasing heart rate, blood pressure, and cardiac output; such effects are not dose-dependent. In addition, ketamine tends to provide bronchial smooth muscle relaxation, which may be beneficial in patients with reactive airway disease or bronchospasm.

Ketamine has a high incidence of disturbing "bad trips" or emergence reactions commonly described as vivid dreaming, out-of-body sensation, and illusions. Salivary gland secretions are increased, and pretreatment with an antisialagogue such as glycopyrrolate is recommended. Ketamine also may interact with tricyclic antidepressants, resulting in hypertension and cardiac dysrhythmias. Ketamine increases intracranial pressure and cerebral metabolism and is contraindicated in patients with elevated intracranial pressure.

8. What are the properties and side effects of benzodiazepines?

The three benzodiazepines most commonly used in clinical anesthesia are **midazolam** (Versed), **diazepam** (Valium), and **lorazepam** (Ativan). Midazolam is the most commonly used as a premedicant-sedative or for induction of anesthesia. Midazolam is a water-soluble imidazobenzodiazepine derivative with sedative-hypnotic and amnestic (antegrade) properties. Upon injection, exposure to blood pH renders midazolam lipid soluble. Because of its lipid solubility, midazolam causes the least venoirritation of all benzodiazepines. Onset of action is rapid; an IV induction dose of 0.15–0.2 mg/kg results in loss of consciousness within 60–90 seconds. Tissue distribution peripherally contributes to termination of action; hepatic metabolism plays a smaller role. The elimination half-life is rapid at 2.5 hours. However, in elderly or obese patients, clearance and elimination half-lives may be prolonged, requiring dosage adjustments. Recovery of cognitive function is slower after use of induction doses compared with propofol, methohexital, or etomidate.

The major side effects of diazepam and lorazepam are venoirritation and thrombophlebitis secondary to the use of organic solvents; both compounds are water-insoluble. Prolonged postoperative amnesia, sedation, and rare cases of significant respiratory depression may occur with all benzodiazepines.

9. Can the adverse effects of benzodiazepines be reversed?

Flumazenil (Romazicon) is the first specific benzodiazepine antagonist available for clinical use. The recommended dose of 0.2 mg IV should produce a rapid, reliable reversal of sedation, unconsciousness, and respiratory depression. If reversal is not achieved within 45 seconds, additional doses of 0.2 mg may be administered at 60-second intervals to a maximum of 1 mg. Higher doses are often required to reverse lorazepam compared with diazepam or midazolam. Because of flumazenil's short half-life of 60 minutes (compared with midazolam [1.7–2.5 hours], diazepam [26–50 hours], and lorazepam [11–22 hours]), resedation from the longer acting benzodiazepines may occur.

10. What are the properties and side effects of the opioid IV induction agents?

Fentanyl (Sublimaze) is 100 times as potent as morphine. When used in anesthetic doses of 30–100 µg/kg, it has an onset of action of 1–2 minutes with peak effect within 4–5 minutes. Fentanyl causes minimal histamine release and results in minimal cardiovascular changes (perhaps bradycardia) when used alone for induction.

Sufentanil (Sufenta), a structural analog of fentanyl, is 5–7 times more potent and has a more rapid onset of effect. The elimination half-life of 2–3 hours is slightly shorter than that of fentanyl and produces more rapid awakening and less residual, postoperative respiratory depression. Induction doses range from 5 to 13 µg/kg.

Alfentanil (Alfenta) is a fentanyl analog that is one-fifth to one-third as potent as fentanyl. Because of its decreased lipid solubility, it tends to have a more rapid onset of action and a shorter duration of effect. Its effects are similar to those of fentanyl. Because of its shorter duration of action, it tends to be used more in outpatient anesthesia, although the incidence of nausea and vomiting limits its efficacy in this setting.

All opioids may produce dose-dependent respiratory and CNS depression (fentanyl < sufentanil < alfentanil). Postoperative nausea and emesis may occur with all opioids through stimulation of the chemoreceptor trigger zone in the medulla. Opioids have been suspected to cause spasm of the sphincter of Oddi, resulting in high common bile duct pressures, and should be used judiciously in patients with gallbladder disease (particularly if intraoperative cholangiograms are necessary). Muscle rigidity often accompanies induction doses of all opiates but appears to be of greater magnitude and duration with alfentanil. Recent clinical studies have found that pretreatment with midazolam before induction may diminish this effect. Alternatively, pretreatment with small doses of a nondepolarizing muscle relaxant may attenuate the rigidity and allow mask ventilation.

11. Which are the best agents for outpatient anesthesia?

Propofol is rapidly becoming the most desirable IV agent in outpatient anesthesia because of rapid induction and recovery. The lower incidence of nausea and emesis and the prompt return of cognitive function facilitate a shorter stay in the postanesthesia care unit and increase patient satisfaction.

12. Which IV anesthetics are recommended for use in major trauma or other hypovolemic cases?

Ketamine is recommended for patients who are acutely hypovolemic because of its sympathomimetic effect of increasing heart rate and peripheral vasoconstriction. However, chronically or critically ill patients who have depleted endogenous catecholamines may be unable to respond to the sympathomimetic action of ketamine. In this scenario, the unchecked direct myocardial depressant effect of ketamine may produce even more profound hypotension. Etomidate also may be used as an induction agent in trauma because of its cardiovascular stability.

13. Which induction agents reduce and which increase intracranial pressure (ICP)?

Etomidate, thiopental, propofol, and fentanyl reduce ICP secondary to a decrease in cerebral blood flow and cerebral metabolic consumption of oxygen. Ketamine increases cerebral blood flow, ICP, and cerebral metabolism.

14. Are there additional considerations for IV induction in children?

Children often are given mask inductions to avoid preanesthetic IV initiation. When an IV is already in place, the recommended dose ranges are often higher:

Thiopental: 5–6 mg/kg (neonates: 7–8 mg/kg)
Propofol: 2.5–3.5 mg/kg

BIBLIOGRAPHY

1. Barley PL, Stanley TH: Intravenous opioid anesthetics. In Miller RD (ed): Anesthesia, 4th ed. New York, Churchill Livingstone, 1994, pp 291–387.
2. Chittleborough MC, Osborne GA, Rudkin GE, et al: Double-blind comparison of patient recovery after induction with propofol or thiopental for day-case relaxant general anesthesia. Anaesth Intensive Care 20:169–173, 1992.
3. Gregory GA: Pediatric Anesthesia, 3rd ed. New York, Churchill Livingstone, 1994, pp 547–549.
4. Reves JG, Glass PSA: Non-barbiturate intravenous anesthesia. In Miller RD (ed): Anesthesia, 4th ed. New York, Churchill Livingstone, 1994, pp 247–289.
5. Smith I, White PF, Nathanson M, Gouldson R: Propofol: An update on its clinical use. Anesthesiology 81:1005–1043, 1994.

10. OPIOIDS

John Alden Hatheway, M.D.

1. What are opioids?

Opioids, a class of drugs derived from the poppy (*Papaver somniferum*), are used primarily for analgesia. Opium, from the Greek word for juice, contains more than 20 different alkaloids, all of which belong to one of two classes: phenanthrenes or benzylisoquinolines. Morphine, codeine, and thebaine are the primary phenanthrenes, whereas papaverine and noscapine are the principal benzylisoquinolines. Opioids are either natural (from the poppy), derived from modifying the natural compound (semisynthetic), or completely manufactured (synthetic). The term *opioid* refers to all drugs, synthetic and natural, that have morphine-like actions, including antagonist actions.

2. Define the term *narcotic*.

Narcotic is derived from the Greek word for stupor. For many years narcotic referred to drugs with morphine-like action. Currently, however, the word refers to any drug that can cause dependence; therefore, the term is no longer specific for opioids.

3. Are there any endogenous opioids?

Yes. The realization of specific receptors for substances derived from the poppy sparked research for possible endogenous opioids or endorphins. Endorphins are derived from one of three precursor molecules: (1) proenkephalin, (2) pro-opiomelanocortin, and (3) prodynorphin

These opioids are believed to function as part of an endogenous pain suppression system.

4. Describe the receptor where opioids demonstrate effects.

1. **Mu:** Morphine is the prototype exogenous ligand
   - **Mu$_1$:** The main action at this receptor is analgesia; the endogenous ligands are enkephalins.
   - **Mu$_2$:** Respiratory depression, bradycardia, physical dependence, euphoria, and ileus are elicited by binding at this receptor. No endogenous ligands have been identified.
2. **Delta:** This receptor modulates the activity at the mu receptor. It is thought that mu and delta receptors exist together as a complex. It has the highest selectivity for the endogenous enkephalins, but opioids still bind.
3. **Kappa:** Ketocyclazocine and dynorphin are the prototype exogenous and endogenous ligands, respectively. Analgesia, sedation, dysphoria, and psychomimetic effects are produced by this receptor. Binding to the kappa receptor inhibits release of vasopressin and thus promotes diuresis. Pure kappa agonists do not produce respiratory depression.
4. **Sigma:** N-allylnormetazocine is the prototype exogenous ligand. This receptor is not a pure opiate binding site; many other types of compounds bind at the sigma receptor. Dysphoria, hypertonia, tachycardia, tachypnea, and mydriasis are the principal effects of the sigma receptor.

5. Name the opioids commonly used in the perioperative setting, their trade names, half-lives, equivalent morphine dose, and class.

Commonly Used Opioids

OPIOID	TRADE NAME	HALF-LIFE (hr)	EQUIVALENT MORPHINE DOSE (mg) IM/IV	EQUIVALENT MORPHINE DOSE (mg) PO	OPIOID CLASS
Morphine	Morphine sulfate	2	10	60	Agonist
Fentanyl	Sublimaze	3–4	0.1	–	Agonist
Sufentanil	Sufenta	2–3	0.01–0.02	–	Agonist
Meperidine	Demerol	3–4	75–100	300	Agonist
Alfentanil	Alfenta	1–1.5	0.5–1	–	Agonist
Codeine	Tylenol 3	2–4	130	200	Agonist
Hydrocodone	Vicodin	4	–	30	Agonist
Oxycodone	Percocet, Tylox	–	–	30	Agonist
Hydromorphone	Dilaudid	2–3	1.2	7.5	Agonist
Methadone	Dolophine	15–40	–	20	Agonist
Remifentanil	Ultiva	< 1	–	–	Agonist
Tramadol	Ultram	3–4	100	120	Partial agonist

IM = intramuscularly, IV = intravenously, PO = orally.

6. Do opioids have a place in regional anesthesia?

Because opioid receptors exist in the spinal cord, opioids can be used intrathecally or epidurally for perioperative analgesia. Neuraxial opioids alone do not provide appropriate conditions for surgical anesthesia, but they decrease the required level for inhalational agents. Neuraxial opioids also may be used for postoperative pain management; unlike neuraxial local anesthetics, they do not affect the sympathetic nervous system, skeletal muscle tone, or proprioreception. For instance, epidural morphine infusion provides similar analgesia to 0.5% bupivacaine but with a longer duration of action and a decreased incidence of hypotension. Compared with parenteral opioids, spinal opioids have the advantage of (1) increased potency, (2) decreased daily dose requirements, (3) decreased central nervous system (CNS) depression, (4) decreased incidence of ileus, and (5) decreased potential for abuse.

7. What are the side effects of neuraxial opioids?

Pruritus   Nausea and vomiting   Urinary retention   Ventilatory depression

8. Explain the mechanism of neuraxial opioids.

Opioids that are injected into the epidural or intrathecal space bind to receptors in the dorsal horn of the spinal cord; more specifically, in the substantia gelatinosa. This area of the spinal cord processes afferent pain information and contains mu, delta, and kappa receptors. Mu_1 and delta receptors, when activated, decrease somatic pain. Both kappa and mu_1 receptors inhibit visceral pain. Kappa receptor activation is thought to inhibit release of substance P through blockade of calcium entrance into neurons.

9. Discuss the effect of lipid solubility on neuraxial opioid action.

Lipophilic opioids readily diffuse through the spinal membranes and spinal cord to produce rapid onset. Hydrophilic opioids traverse these tissues much more slowly and hence have a slower onset. However, the more lipophilic an agent is, the more likely it will be absorbed by vasculature and fat; thus lipophilic agents have a shorter duration of action than hydrophilic agents. Metabolism does not affect the duration of action of spinally injected opioids. The spinal duration of action of lipophilic agents is limited by systemic absorption, whereas hydrophilic agents are limited by absorption in rostral arachnoid granulations. Hydrophilic agents remain in the cerebrospinal fluid longer and slowly migrate to higher levels. Lipophilic agents (fentanyl, sufentanil) are appropriate for procedures at the level of opioid injection. Hydrophilic agents (morphine) are appropriate for procedures where the opioid is injected at a distance from the surgical stimulus. Side effects of spinal opioids are also related to lipid solubility. Lipophilic agents are readily absorbed by the local vasculature, rapidly reach significant intravenous concentrations, and may cause the usual parenteral side effects. Lipophilic agnents, which spread rostrally, may depress the respiratory center several hours after injection.

10. What is the effect of combining low-dose local anesthetics with opioids during postoperative infusion?

Evidence suggests that the combination provides an additive analgesic effect; analgesia is greater than with either agent alone. This method allows lower dosage of both agents, hence the propensity for decreased side effects.

11. Describe the onset, duration, and elimination times for the commonly administered opioids morphine and fentanyl.

The onset of action is much shorter for fentanyl than for morphine. The effects of fentanyl may be seen as early as 30 seconds after IV administration, whereas initial effects of morphine take place within a few minutes; the effect of morphine peaks at 10–15 minutes after IV administration. Duration of action is also significantly shorter for fentanyl than for morphine. Fentanyl has a longer elimination half-life (185–219 min) than morphine (114 min).

12. Explain how fentanyl can have a shorter duration of action but a longer elimination half-life than morphine.

Fentanyl is much more lipid-soluble than morphine. Therefore, fentanyl is rapidly redistributed to other tissues, such as fat and skeletal muscle, after initial distribution to vessel-rich tissues. Secondly, 75% of a fentanyl dose is absorbed by the lung—a phenomenon referred to as the pulmonary first-pass effect. Thus, the duration of action of fentanyl is not dictated by elimination but by redistribution and first-pass effect. After redistribution, fentanyl is slowly released into the plasma and hence made available to the liver for clearance. Molecular size, ionization, lipid solubility, protein binding, and elimination determine the onset and duration of action of a particular opioid.

13. What is remifentanil?

Remifentanil is a very short acting opioid agonist. Unlike other opioids, it is broken down by nonspecific esterases in the blood. The drug's clearance is not affected by pseudocholinesterase or cholinesterase inhibitors. The pharmacokinetics of remifentanil are not affected by renal dysfunction and are not significantly affected by hepatic dysfunction. Remifentanil is 20–40 times more potent than alfentanil. The peak onset is within 1–3 minutes, and the duration of action is 5–10 minutes. Remifentanil can be administered for analgesia (to supplement local anesthetic infiltration) during monitored anesthesia care (dose range 0.025–0.2 µg/kg/min). This may follow a single IV bolus dose of 1 µg/kg administered over 30–60 seconds. Alternatively, during general anesthesia, remifentanil may be administered as an infusion running at 0.5–1.0 µg/kg/minute. With such a potent opioid, the patient should be carefully monitored for respiratory depression. Chest wall rigidity is an associated complication, In the case of any associated postprocedural pain, longer acting opioids should be administered at the appropriate time, lest the patient experience significant and unnecessary discomfort.

14. What is tramadol?
Tramadol is a unique analgesic with opioid-like activity as well as catecholamine reuptake inhibition. These properties allow the analgesic to be used for both acute and chronic pain management. It appears to have much lower risk for tolerance and addiction. Major side effects include sedation and dizziness. One concerning but uncommon adverse side effect is seizures. The drug should therefore be used with caution if at all in patients with a history or risk of seizures.

15. What is a fentanyl patch?
A fentanyl patch is a transdermal preparation of the opioid. The patch is constructed as a high-dose (10 mg) reservoir with a microporous membrane. The large amount of fentanyl in the reservoir provides a gradient for diffusion. It takes approximately 8–12 hours to reach steady state after the placement of the patch on the skin. The patch is usually changed every 72 hours. Because the patches are only available in 25-, 75-, and 100-µg per hour doses, they are not extremely titratable. However, this can be an effective alternative analgesic for chronic pain, when oral dosing is no longer an option. Of interest, fentanyl also comes in a transmucosal preparation, sometimes called a "fentanyl lollipop," which can be useful in pediatric patients.

16. Explain why patients with renal failure may have a prolonged ventilatory depressant effect with morphine.
Morphine is metabolized by the liver to morphine-3-glucuronide (75–85%) and morphine-6-glucuronide (5–10%). Both compounds are excreted by the kidney. Morphine-6-glucuronide is an active metabolite that accumulates with renal failure. Therefore, in patients with tenuous renal function, morphine should be used carefully.

17. Describe the cardiovascular effects of opioid agonists.
Opioids are considered to be cardiac-stable drugs. In fact, opioids are often used as the principal anesthetic agent for cardiac anesthesia because of their hemodynamic stability (they are not amnestic). However, important cardiovascular implications must be kept in mind. Opioids may cause a dose-dependent bradycardia. This effect is most likely secondary to direct, central stimulation of the vagal nucleus. An anticholinergic may be used to block or reverse this effect. The one exception to this rule is tachycardia caused by meperidine. Because the structure of meperidine resembles that of atropine, it may elicit atropine-like effects; meperidine is the only opioid to have negative inotropic effects at clinically used doses. Some opioids produce histamine release, which in turn may cause vasodilation and hypotension.

18. Which opioids are known to stimulate the release of histamine?
Morphine, codeine, and demerol stimulate release of histamine, which causes vasodilatation and hence may lead to hypotension. Fentanyl, sufentanil, and alfentanil do not stimulate histamine release.

19. Describe the typical breathing pattern elicited by opioids.

Opioids initially decrease the rate of breathing without affecting the tidal volume. Higher doses decrease the tidal volume, and even higher doses produce apnea. This pattern contrasts with the rapid, shallow breathing common to inhalational agents. Opioids also cause an irregular pattern of breathing.

20. Explain the effect of opioids on the ventilatory response to carbon dioxide.

Opioids shift the carbon dioxide response curve to the right; that is, it takes a higher serum concentration of carbon dioxide to stimulate ventilation.

21. Is it true that opioids should not be used during procedures involving the biliary tract?

No. Opioids have been reported to cause biliary smooth muscle spasm, but the incidence is low. In contemporary practice, opioids are not withheld out of this theoretical concern. (Theoretically, opioid-induced biliary spasm may mimic a common bile duct stone and confuse intraoperative cholangiography.) Naloxone (an opioid antagonist), glucagon, nitroglycerin, or atropine have been given to reverse the spasm. Naloxone may prove problematic if it is given in sufficient doses to reverse analgesia.

22. Name the opioid antagonist most commonly used in clinical anesthesia. Discuss its effects.

Naloxone is the pure mu-receptor antagonist used to treat opioid overdose and to reverse opioid-induced ventilatory depression. However, reversing the ventilatory depressant effects also reverses analgesia. Abrupt reversal of analgesia may produce a catecholamine surge, resulting in tachycardia, hypertension, pulmonary edema, and cardiac dysrhythmias. To avoid the abrupt reversal of analgesia, naloxone, in the perioperative setting, should be administered in doses of about 40 µg (0.1 ml), repeated in a few minutes, if necessary. Because naloxone has a short duration of action, it is often necessary to repeat the dosage or to give a continuous infusion to avoid further depression of ventilation.

23. What are opioid agonist-antagonists?

This term was originally applied to a class of opioids that appeared to cause antagonism at the mu receptor and agonism at the kappa receptor. However, subsequent research revealed that many of the drugs in fact produce partial agonism at more than one receptor. Therefore, the term agonist-antagonist is not entirely accurate. Partial agonist may be more descriptive because these ligands produce less than a maximal effect when bound to the opioid receptor.

24. What is the advantage of using a partial agonist as an antagonist if naloxone is readily available?

As mentioned earlier, naloxone reverses not only respiratory depression but also analgesia. Partial agonists may not reverse analgesia to the same degree as naloxone. Furthermore, some partial agonists do not cause the unfavorable cardiac and pulmonary side effects of naloxone.

CONTROVERSY

25. Can opioids act peripherally?

Peripheral opioid action seems to be present only in conjunction with inflammation. It is thought that during inflammation the usual protective barrier or perineurium is disrupted, allowing access to opioid-binding sites on peripheral nerves.

BIBLIOGRAPHY

1. Bovill JG: Pharmacokinetics and pharmacodynamics of opioid agonists. Anesth Pharm Rev 2:122–134, 1993.
2. Bowdle TA: Partial agonist and agonist-antagonist opioids: Basic pharmacology and clinical applications. Anesth Pharm Rev 2:135–151, 1993.

3. Coda BA: Opioids. In Barash PG, Cullen BF, Stoelting RK (eds): Clinical Anesthesia, 3rd ed. Philadelphia, Lippincott Williams & Wilkins, 1997.
4. Jaffe JH, Martin WR: Opioid analgesics and antagonists. In Hardman JG, Limbird LE (eds): Goodman and Gilman's The Pharmacological Basis of Therapeutics, 9th ed. New York, McGraw-Hill, 1996.
5. Pleuvry BJ: The endogenous opioid system. Anesth Pharm Rev 2:114–121, 1993.
6. Stein C: Morphine-A "local analgesic." Pain Clin Updates 3:1–4, 1995.
7. Stein C: The control of pain in peripheral tissue by opioids. N Engl J Med 332:1685–1690, 1995.

11. BENZODIAZEPINES

Gene Winkelmann, M.D.

1. What drugs are commonly used as amnestics in the practice of anesthesiology?

Benzodiazepines are commonly used in anesthetic practice and include lorazepam, diazepam, and, most commonly, midazolam. Benzodiazepines contain a benzene ring connected to a seven-membered diazepine ring.

2. Where do benzodiazepines exert their amnestic effect?

Benzodiazepine receptors, which are found on postsynaptic nerve endings in the central nervous system (CNS), are part of the gamma-aminobutyric acid (GABA) receptor complex. GABA is the primary inhibitory neurotransmitter of the CNS. The GABA receptor complex is composed of two alpha subunits and two beta subunits. The alpha subunits are the binding sites for benzodiazepines. The beta subunits are the binding sites for GABA. A chloride ion channel is located in the center of the GABA receptor complex.

3. What is the mechanism of action of benzodiazepines?

Benzodiazepines produce their effects by enhancing the binding of GABA to its receptor. GABA activates the chloride ion channel, allowing chloride ions to enter the neuron. The flow of chloride ions into the neuron hyperpolarizes and inhibits the neuron.

4. What are the clinical effects of benzodiazepines?

Benzodiazepines produce anxiolysis, sedation, amnesia, suppression of seizure activity, and in high enough doses, unconsciousness and respiratory depression. The effects depend on the dose. At low concentrations, benzodiazepines produce only anxiolysis. Higher concentrations produce anxiolysis, sedation, and anterograde amnesia; patients will remain conscious but will not remember events during this type of sedation. At still higher concentrations, benzodiazepines produce unconsciousness.

A complete general anesthetic provides unconsciousness, amnesia, analgesia, control of the autonomic nervous system, and sometimes muscular relaxation. Benzodiazepines in low doses may be administered to supplement inhaled or intravenous anesthetics to ensure amnesia. Benzodiazepines in high doses may be used as part of a general anesthetic technique because of their ability to produce unconsciousness and amnesia. Benzodiazepines are not complete anesthetics because they are not analgesics, and they should not be used alone to produce general anesthesia.

5. What are some of the important differences among midazolam, lorazepam, and diazepam?

All three benzodiazepines have different potency, duration of action, and elimination half-lives. The onset and duration of action of a single bolus of benzodiazepine depend on its lipid solubility. Onset of action is a function of rapid distribution to vessel-rich groups, particularly the brain. Awakening depends on redistribution to other body tissues. Midazolam is the most lipid soluble of the three and, as a result, has a rapid onset and a relatively short duration of action. Awakening following an induction dose of midazolam of 0.15 mg/kg occurs at about 17 minutes. The induction dose of diazepam is 0.5 mg/kg and onset is slightly slower than that of midazolam. Initial recovery times for diazepam are similar to those of midazolam. Lorazepam is the least lipid soluble of the three, resulting in a slow onset of action and a long duration of action. The long elimination half-lives of diazepam and lorazepam may lead to prolonged sedation and delayed awakening. In addition, diazepam has two active metabolites that can produce sedation 6–8 hours after its initial administration.

Comparison of Benzodiazepines

DRUG	RELATIVE POTENCY	EQUIVALENT DOSAGES	ELIMINATION HALF-LIFE	INDUCTION DOSE
Diazepam	1	10 mg	21–37 hours	0.3–0.5 mg/kg
Midazolam	3	3.3 mg	1–4 hours	0.1–0.2 mg/kg
Lorazepam	5	2 mg	10–20 hours	0.1 mg/kg*

* Infrequently used for induction.

6. How do benzodiazapines differ in their amnestic properties?
Lorazepam is a more powerful amnestic agent than is diazepam. Midazolam is also a powerful amnestic agent, but its duration of action is much shorter than that of diazepam. The duration of anterograde amnesia produced by benzodiazepines is dose-related and often parallels the degree of sedation. A 4-mg dose of lorazepam produces about 6 hours of anterograde amnesia. Benzodiazepines are not thought to provide retrograde amnesia.

7. Describe some unique properties of midazolam.
Midazolam is both water and lipid soluble. Commercially prepared, midazolam is highly water soluble. Upon entrance into the bloodstream, the pH of blood modifies the structure of midazolam into a lipid-soluble form. This unique property of midazolam improves patient comfort when administered by the intravenous (IV) or intramuscular (IM) route and eliminates the need for an organic solvent like propylene glycol. Both diazepam and lorazepam are insoluble in water and are dissolved in propylene glycol. Injection of diazepam or lorazepam by the IV or IM route may be painful and can cause venoirritation and phlebitis.

8. How are benzodiazepines metabolized?
Benzodiazepines are metabolized in the liver by hepatic microsomal oxidation or glucuronidation. Metabolism may be impaired in the elderly and in patients with liver disease. Diazepam has two active metabolites that may prolong the sedative effects of this drug. Lorazepam has no active metabolites, and midazolam has a metabolite with minimal activity.

9. What are the clinical uses for benzodiazepines?
Benzodiazepines are used in anesthesia for
1. Preoperative medication
2. Intravenous sedation
3. Induction of anesthesia
4. Maintenance of anesthesia
5. Suppression of seizure activity

Amnesia, anxiolysis, and sedation are properties that make benzodiazepines excellent preoperative medications.

10. What are the respiratory side effects of benzodiazepines?
When given in sufficient doses, all benzodiazepines produce respiratory depression. When benzodiazepines are combined with opioids, their respiratory depressant effects are synergistic.

11. Are there any cardiovascular effects from benzodiazepines?

Induction doses of benzodiazepines produce minimal decreases in blood pressure (BP), cardiac output (CO), and systemic vascular resistance (SVR).

12. What are the dosage recommendations for benzodiazepines?

Sedation (anxiolysis, amnesia, and elevation of the local anesthetic seizure threshold): Titrate to effect with endpoints being adequate sedation or dysarthria. Diazepam (5–10 mg) or midazolam (1–2.5 mg) administered IV is useful for sedation during regional anesthesia. Midazolam has a more rapid onset and greater degree of amnesia than diazepam. Lorazepam is slower in onset and longer lasting than midazolam or diazepam. A dose of 2 mg of lorazepam is frequently used for preoperative sedation in cardiovascular procedures.

Treatment of seizures: The efficacy of benzodiazepines as anticonvulsants, especially diazepam, is consistent with the ability of these drugs to enhance the inhibitory effects of GABA, especially in the limbic system. Indeed, diazepam, 0.1 mg/kg IV, is effective in abolishing seizure activity produced by local anesthetics, alcohol withdrawal, and status epilepticus.

Induction and maintenance of anesthesia: Midazolam is the benzodiazepine of choice for anesthetic induction (fast onset, lack of venous complications). An induction dose of midazolam produces about 2 hours of anterograde amnesia. Delayed awakening is a potential disadvantage of administering a benzodiazepine, especially diazepam and lorazepam, for the induction of anesthesia. The slow onset and prolonged duration of action of lorazepam limit its usefulness for preoperative medication or induction of anesthesia when rapid awakening at the end of surgery is desirable.

13. Is there an antagonist for benzodiazepines?

Flumazenil is a competitive antagonist and will reverse unconsciousness, sedation, respiratory depression, and anxiolysis produced by benzodiazepines. Its effect is dose-dependent and influenced by plasma benzodiazepine levels. The onset of flumazenil is rapid, with the peak effect occurring in about 1–3 minutes. Flumazenil is given in increments of 0.2 mg IV until respiratory depression or sedation is reversed. A maximum total dosage of 3 mg is recommended for the reversal of benzodiazepines.

14. Are there any side effects to the use of flumazenil?

Resedation is a possible side effect. The elimination half-life of flumazenil is 1 hour. In comparison, the shortest elimination half-life for the benzodiazepine agonists is 2–3 hours (midazolam). Thus, the potential for resedation is possible following the administration of flumazenil; however, this is more likely to occur with benzodiazepines that have longer half-lives (diazepam and lorazepam). When resedation is likely, the patient should be closely monitored. Resedation can be treated with repeated doses or a continuous infusion (0.5–1.0 µg/kg/min) of flumazenil.

BIBLIOGRAPHY

1. Corssen G, Reves JG, Stanley TH: Intravenous Anesthesia and Analgesia. Philadelphia, Lea & Febiger, 1988, pp 219–255.
2. Reeves GJ, Glass PSA, Lubarsky DA: Nonbarbiturate intravenous anesthetics. In Miller RD (ed): Anesthesia, 4th ed. New York, Churchill Livingstone, 1994, pp 248–259.
3. Stoelting RK: Pharmacology and Physiology in Anesthetic Practice, 2nd ed. Philadelphia, J.B. Lippincott, 1991, pp 118–133, 242–251.
4. Wood M: Intravenous anesthetic agents. In Wood M, Wood Alastair JJ (eds): Drugs and Anesthesia: Pharmacology for Anesthesiologists, 2nd ed. Baltimore, Willliams & Wilkins, 1990, pp 196–206.

12. NEUROMUSCULAR BLOCKING AGENTS

Douglas E. Warnecke, CRNA, M.S.

1. What are neuromuscular blocking agents (NMBs)?

NMBs, commonly called muscle relaxants, are drugs that interrupt transmission at the neuromuscular junction. These drugs provide skeletal muscle relaxation and, consequently, can be used to facilitate tracheal intubation, assist with mechanical ventilation, and optimize surgical conditions. Occasionally, they may be used to reduce the metabolic demands of breathing; in the management of status epilepticus (though they do not diminish central nervous system [CNS] activity), status asthmaticus, or tetanus; and to facilitate the treatment of raised intracranial pressure.

These drugs are very dangerous and inhibit the function of all skeletal muscle, including the diaphragm, and must be administered only by personnel skilled in airway management. NMBs should never be given without preparation to maintain the airway and ventilation. The concomitant use of sedative-hypnotic or amnestic drugs is indicated, because NMBs alone achieve complete paralysis while allowing the patient complete awareness.

2. How are impulses transmitted at the neuromuscular junction?

The neuromuscular junction consists of a prejunctional motor nerve ending and a postsynaptic receptor area on the skeletal muscle membrane. As the impulse arrives at the nerve ending, an influx of calcium causes the release of acetylcholine. Acetylcholine binds to the nicotinic cholinergic receptors located on the postsynaptic membrane. Receptor pores are opened and extracellular ions move down their concentration gradient, causing the transmembrane potential to decrease, with subsequent action potential propagation along the muscle fiber, leading to muscle contraction. The rapid hydrolysis of acetylcholine by acetylcholinesterase (true cholinesterase) and return of normal ionic gradients return the neuromuscular junction and muscle to a nondepolarized, resting state.

3. How are NMBs classified?

These drugs are classified into two groups according to their actions at the neuromuscular junction:

1. **Depolarizing NMB** (succinylcholine): Succinylcholine mimics the action of acetylcholine by depolarizing the postsynaptic membrane at the neuromuscular junction. Because the postsynaptic receptor is occupied and depolarized, acetylcholine has no effect.

2. **Nondepolarizing NMBs**: These agents act by competitive blockade of the postsynaptic membrane, so that acetylcholine is blocked from the receptors and cannot have a depolarizing effect.

4. Describe the mechanism of action of succinylcholine.

Succinylcholine (SCh) is the only depolarizing agent to be used widely in clinical anesthetic practice. The depolarizing agent mimics the action of acetylcholine. However, because SCh is hydrolyzed by plasma cholinesterase, (pseudocholinesterase), which is present only in the plasma and not at the neuromuscular junction, the length of blockade is directly related to the rate of diffusion of SCh away from the neuromuscular junction. Consequently, the resultant depolarization is prolonged when compared to acetylcholine. Depolarization gradually diminishes, but relaxation persists as long as SCh is present at the postsynaptic receptor.

5. What are the indications for using succinylcholine?

In clinical situations in which the patient has a full stomach and is at risk for regurgitation and aspiration when anesthetized, rapid paralysis and airway control are priorities. Such situations include diabetes mellitus, hiatal hernia, obesity, pregnancy, severe pain, and trauma.

SCh provides the most rapid onset of any NMB currently available. In addition, the duration of blockade induced by SCh is only 5–10 minutes. Respiratory muscle function returns quickly should the patient prove difficult to intubate (see question 11).

6. If succinylcholine works so rapidly and predictably, why not use it all the time?

SCh does indeed work rapidly and predictably and has been in clinical use for decades. This extended clinical use has provided ample time to ascertain its drawbacks and dangers.

1. Its duration of action can be unpredictably prolonged in the presence of pseudo-cholinesterase deficiency (seen in liver disease, pregnancy, malnutrition, and malignancies).

2. SCh stimulates all cholinergic receptors—nicotinic in the autonomic ganglia and, especially important, the muscarinic receptors in the sinus node. All types of arrhythmias can be seen, especially bradycardia.

3. Hyperkalemia may result in situations where there is a proliferation of extrajunctional receptors. Extrajunctional receptors are not normally present and are suppressed by normal neural activity. However, any condition that decreases motor nerve activity causes a proliferation of extrajunctional receptors (e.g., burns, muscular dystrophies, prolonged immobility, spinal cord injuries, upper and lower motor neuron disease, and closed head injuries). Depolarization of such receptors by SCh may lead to massive release of intracellular potassium and resultant hyperkalemia, predisposing to malignant ventricular arrhythmias.

4. SCh can trigger malignant hyperthermia and should be avoided when family or previous anesthetic history suggests the likelihood of this disease.

5. In cases of increased intracranial pressure (ICP) or open eye injury, SCh administration may produce increases in intraocular pressure (IOP) and ICP. (However, the modest increases in IOP and ICP should be weighed against the risk of aspiration in these patients, and its careful use may be warranted.)

6. SCh increases intragastric pressure, although the increase in lower esophageal sphincter (LES) tone is greater and there is no increased risk of aspiration unless the patient has an incompetent LES.

7. After prolonged exposure to SCh (7–10 mg/kg), the neuromuscular blockade changes in character and resembles a nondepolarizing block. This is known as a phase II, or desensitization blockade.

7. What questions should an anesthesiologist ask to ascertain if a patient is at risk from SCh administration?

1. Has the patient or any family member had a fever or unexplained death during a previous anesthetic?

2. Has the patient or any family member ever felt weak after a previous anesthetic or needed a breathing machine after a routine surgical problem?

3. Has the patient or any family member had a "crisis" under anesthesia that was unexplained by any known medical problems?

4. Has the patient or any family member ever had a fever or severe myalgias after exercise?

8. What is plasma cholinesterase (pseudocholinesterase)?

Plasma cholinesterase is produced in the liver and metabolizes SCh as well as ester local anesthetics and mivacurium, a nondepolarizing NMB. A reduced quantity of plasma cholinesterase, such as occurs with liver disease, pregnancy, malignancies, malnutrition, collagen vascular disease, and hypothyroidism, may prolong the duration of blockade with SCh.

9. Explain the importance of a dibucaine number.

Plasma cholinesterase can have qualitative as well as quantitative effects, the most common being dibucaine-resistant cholinesterase deficiency. Dibucaine inhibits normal plasma cholinesterase by 80%, while atypical plasma cholinesterase is inhibited only by 20%. A patient with normal SCh metabolism will have a dibucaine number of 80. If a patient has a dibucaine number of 40–60, then that patient is heterozygous for this atypical plasma cholinesterase and will have a moderately prolonged block with SCh. If a patient has a dibucaine number of 20, the patient is homozygous for atypical plasma cholinesterase and will have a very prolonged block with SCh.

It is important to remember that a dibucaine number is a qualitative, and not quantitative, measurement. Consequently, a patient may have a dibucaine number of 80 but have prolonged blockade with SCh related to decreased levels of normal plasma cholinesterase.

10. My patient woke up beautifully after a "textbook" anesthetic but complained of pain all over. What went wrong?

The only NMB commonly used that causes myalgia is SCh. The incidence of muscle pains following the use of this agent ranges from 10% to 70%. It occurs more frequently in muscular individuals and patients who are ambulatory soon after surgery. Though the incidence of myalgias does not appear related to fasciculations, the frequency of myalgias has been shown to decrease with administration of small doses of nondepolarizing NMBs, such as atracurium, 0.025 mg/kg.

11. How are nondepolarizing NMBs classified?

Neuromuscular Relaxants: Doses, Onset of Action, and Duration

RELAXANT	ED95 (mg/kg)	INTUBATING DOSE (mg/kg)	ONSET AFTER INTUBATING DOSE (min)	DURATION (min)*
Short-acting				
Succinylcholine	0.3	1.0	0.75	5–10
Mivacurium	0.08	0.2	1.0–1.5	15–20
Rocuronium	0.3	0.6	2–3	30
Rocuronium	–	1.2	1.0	60
Intermediate-acting				
Vecuronium	0.05	0.15–0.2	1.5	60
Vecuronium	–	0.3–0.4	1.0	90–120
Atracurium	0.23	0.7–0.8	1.0–1.5	45–60
Cisatracurium	0.05	0.2	2	60–90
Long-acting				
Pancuronium	0.07	0.08–0.12	4–5	90
Pipecuronium	0.05	0.07–0.85	3–5	80–90
Doxacurium	0.025	0.05–0.08	3–5	90–120

* Duration measured as return of twitch to 25% of control, ED95 = dose expected to reduce twitch height by 95%.

All competitive antagonists at the neuromuscular junction, including nondepolarizing relaxants, are usually classified by their duration of action (short-, intermediate-, and long-acting), as noted in the table. The times listed are only approximate, as there is a tremendous variation between patients. The best course of action is to titrate whenever possible.

Trends in the development of new nondepolarizing NMBs focus on (1) the development of longer-acting agents free of side-effects and (2) development of a relaxant with quick onset and short duration like SCh without its side effects. Rocuronium seems to have met the challenge of equaling the rapid onset of SCh, though at doses of 1.2 mg/kg, rocuronium's duration of action equals that of the intermediate-acting nondepolarizing NMBs. Rapacuronium is a new aminosteroid NMB currently underoing clinical trials that has the potential to combine rapid onset and short duration in a nondepolarizing NMB.

12. Describe the breakdown and elimination of nondepolarizing NMBs.

Atracurium is unique in that it undergoes spontaneous breakdown at physiologic temperatures and pH (Hoffmann elimination) as well as ester hydrolysis, and thus it is ideal for use in patients with compromised hepatic or renal function. Mivacurium, like SCh, is metabolized by pseudocholinesterase.

Aminosteroid relaxants (pancuronium, vecuronium, pipecuronium, and rocuronium) are deacetylated in the liver, and their action may be prolonged in the presence of hepatic dysfunction. Vecuronium and rocuronium also have significant biliary excretion, and their action may be prolonged with extrahepatic biliary obstruction.

Relaxants with significant renal excretion include tubocurarine, metocurine, doxacurium, pancuronium, and pipecuronium.

13. Do other drugs affect the actions of neuromuscular blockers?

Medications that Potentiate Nondepolarizing Relaxants

All volatile agents	Hexamethonium
Local anesthetics	Trimethaphan
Beta blockers	Immunosuppressants
Calcium channel blockers	High-dose benzodiazepines
Aminoglycosides	Dantrolene
Polymyxins	Magnesium
Lincosamines	

A variety of drugs interfere with nondepolarizing muscle relaxants. Inhalational anesthetics produce CNS depression and a general decrease in neuronal activity. Other drugs interfere at the level of the neuromuscular junction. Local anesthetics decrease propagation of the action potential. Certain antibiotics, such as neomycin and streptomycin, inhibit the formation of acetylcholine. Drugs such as magnesium and lithium inhibit the release of acetylcholine at the nerve terminal.

The duration of effect of SCh can be prolonged by a multitude of drug interactions, the most common being the inhibition of plasma cholinesterase activity. Echothiophate eye drops and organophosphate pesticides fall into this category.

14. Describe the most common side effects of nondepolarizing NMBs. Which drugs are associated with them?

Histamine release is most significant with d-tubocurarine but is also noted with mivacurium, atracurium, and doxacurium. The amount of histamine released is frequently dose-related. Cisatracurium, although chemically related to these NMBs, does not seem to cause the side effect of significant histamine release. **Tachycardia** is usually a side effect of pancuronium (due to ganglionic stimulation and vagolysis).

15. Is it possible to reverse the effects of the nondepolarizing NMBs?

Just as competition at the receptor sites of the neuromuscular junction allows the relaxant to overcome the effects of acetylcholine, medications that increase the amount of acetylcholine at the neuromuscular junction facilitate reversal of relaxation. Reversal agents are **acetylcholinesterase inhibitors**, and include neostigmine, pyridostigmine, and edrophonium. These drugs inhibit the enzyme that breaks down acetylcholine, making more of this neurotransmitter available at each receptor. Physostigmine, another acetylcholinesterase inhibitor, crosses the blood-brain barrier and is not used for reversal of muscle relaxants. Pyridostigmine is used in the management of patients affected with myasthenia gravis. The acetylcholinesterase inhibitors possess positively charged quaternary ammonium groups, are water-soluble, and are renally excreted.

NMB Reversal Agents

DRUG	DOSE (mg/kg)	ONSET (min)	DURATION (min)
Edrophonium	0.5–1.0	2	45–60
Neostigmine	0.035–0.07	7	60–90
Pyridostigmine	0.15–0.25	11	60–120

16. NMB reversal agents cause an increase in available acetylcholine. Is this a problem?

It is important to remember that the muscarinic effects of these drugs at cholinergic receptors in the heart must be blocked by atropine or glycopyrrolate to prevent bradycardia. The degree of bradycardia may be significant. Even asystole has been noted. The most common doses used for this purpose are 0.01 mg/kg of atropine and 0.005-0.015 mg/kg of glycopyrrolate.

To prevent bradycardias associated with the anticholinesterases it is important to administer an anticholinergic with a similar onset of action. Atropine is administered with edrophonium and glycopyrrolate with neostigmine.

17. The heart is a muscle. Do muscle relaxants decrease contraction of the myocardium?

The NMBs have their primary effect at nicotinic cholinergic receptor sites. The myocardium is a muscle with nerve transmission accomplished via adrenergic receptors using norepinephrine as the transmitter. Consequently, muscle relaxants have no effect on cardiac contractility. NMBs also have no effect on smooth muscle.

18. How do we make muscle relaxants work faster if we need to secure the airway sooner?

By overwhelming the sites of action (receptors in the neuromuscular junction), one can provide a competitive advantage for the blocking drug over acetylcholine. This is exactly what is done with the standard intubating dose of a nondepolarizing relaxant. The usual intubating dose (see question 11) is approximately three times the ED95 (the dose expected to show 95% reduction in twitch height on electrical stimulation). For relaxants with cardiovascular stability, further increases in initial dose can provide some decrease in onset time without producing side effects. However, with the exception of the nondepolarizing NMB rocuronium, and possibly the new drug rapacuronium, it is very difficult to decrease the onset time to that of SCh. For drugs with side effects such as histamine release, increases in dose usually increase side effects as well.

Another method of decreasing onset time is the **priming technique**. By giving one-third of the ED95 at 3 minutes before the intubating dose, one can decrease onset time by as much as 1 minute. However, sensitivity to the paralyzing effects of these agents varies greatly among patients, and some patients may become totally paralyzed with a priming dose. Other patients may experience distressing diplopia, dysphagia, or the sensation of not being able to take a deep breath. For this reason, the practice of administering "priming" doses of relaxants is discouraged by many anesthesiologists. Once relaxants are administered at any dose, the caregiver should be in the position to assist ventilations.

BIBLIOGRAPHY

1. Bevan DR, Bevan JC, Donati F: Muscle Relaxants in Clinical Anesthesia. Chicago, Year Book, 1988.
2. Bevan DR, Donati F: Muscle relaxants. In Barash PG, Cullen BF, Stoelting RK (eds): Clinical Anesthesia, 3rd ed. Philadelphia, Lippincott Williams & Wilkins, 1997, pp 385–412.
3. Hunter JM: New neuromuscular blocking drugs. N Engl J Med 332:1691–1699, 1995.
4. Miller RD, Savarese JA: Muscle relaxants. In Miller RD (ed): Anesthesia, 4th ed. New York, Churchill Livingstone, 1994.

13. LOCAL ANESTHETICS

Kevin Fitzpatrick, M.D.

1. What role do local anesthetics play in the practice of anesthesiology?

Local anesthetics enable anesthetists to eliminate pain perception without inducing unconsciousness. For example, a catheter placed in the lumbar epidural space of a pregnant woman can alleviate the pain of labor and delivery. Even if she must be brought to the operating room for a cesarean section, she can be comfortable, awake, and alert, and thus share in the birth of her baby.

Alternatively, local anesthetics may be administered directly into the sheath containing the brachial plexus (nerve roots C5, C6, C7, C8, T1), providing complete anesthesia to the upper extremities and shoulders from 1 to 12 hours or more.

Local anesthetics are also used for selective blocks of the lower extremities, cervical and celiac plexuses, and for areas of the body innervated by the lumbar, thoracic, and cervical spinal cord.

Finally, local anesthetics are useful as adjuncts to general anesthesia (in the unconscious patient) and in the management of acute and chronic pain.

2. How are local anesthetics classified (see Figure)?

1. **Esters:** Esters are local anesthetics whose intermediate chain forms an *ester* link between the aromatic and amine groups. Commonly used esters include procaine, chloroprocaine, cocaine, and tetracaine.

2. **Amides:** Amides are local anesthetics with an *amide* link between the aromatic and amine groups. Commonly used amide anesthetics include lidocaine, bupivacaine, mepivacaine, and etidocaine.

3. How can the name of the local anesthetic identify it as an amide?

Am*i*de local anesthetics contain an *i* in the drug name followed by the *caine*, as in lido-caine or etido-caine.

4. How are local anesthetics metabolized?

Esters undergo hydrolysis by pseudocholinesterases found principally in plasma.

Amides undergo biotransformation in the liver through aromatic hydroxylation, N-dealkylation, and amide hydrolysis.

5. How are impulses conducted in nerve cells?

Transmission of impulses depends on the electrical gradient across the nerve membrane, which, in turn, depends upon the movement of sodium (Na^+) and potassium (K^+) ions. Application of a stimulus of sufficient intensity leads to a change in membrane potential (from $-90mV$ to $-60mV$), subsequent depolarization of the nerve, and propagation of the impulse.

Depolarization is due to inflow of Na^+ ions from the extracellular to the intracellular space.

Repolarization is due to outflow of K^+ ions from the intracellular to the extracellular space.

The Na^+-K^+ pump then restores equilibrium in the nerve membrane after completion of the action potential.

6. What is the mechanism of action of local anesthetics?

The cascade of events (see Figure) is as follows:

1. Diffusion of the unionized (base) form across the nerve sheath and membrane.

2. Re-equilibration between the base and cationic forms in the axoplasm.

3. Binding of the cation to a receptor site inside of the Na^+ channel, resulting in its blockade and consequent inhibition of Na^+ conductance.

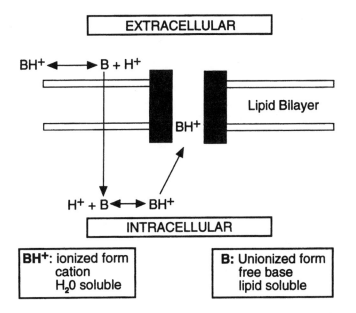

EXTRACELLULAR

$BH^+ \longleftrightarrow B + H^+$

Lipid Bilayer

BH^+

$H^+ + B \longleftrightarrow BH^+$

INTRACELLULAR

| BH^+: ionized form cation H_2O soluble | B: Unionized form free base lipid soluble |

7. Your patient states he was told he is "allergic" to Novocain, which he received for a tooth extraction. Should you avoid using local anesthetics in this patient?

Probably not. Novocain is the trade name for procaine, an ester local anesthetic. Esters are derivatives of *para*-aminobenzoic acid (PABA), reactions to which, although rare, do occur. A thorough history will reveal whether or not the patient experienced the symptoms of a true allergic reaction—hives, wheezing, tachycardia, shock. Symptoms of palpitations and nervousness may represent a response to a local anesthetic additive, like epinephrine, **not** an allergic reaction.

Additionally, the patient may be describing the sequelae of an accidental intravascular injection or overdose of local anesthetic (see question 17). If a true allergy is suspected, another class of local anesthetic may be used, because cross-reactivity between local anesthetics is rare indeed. If the offending allergen remains unidentified, skin testing followed by a subcutaneous challenge injection may be warranted, but is not without hazard.

8. What determines local anesthetic potency?

Lipid solubility: the higher the solubility, the greater the potency. Because bupivacaine and tetracaine are very lipid soluble, they are potent local anesthetics (see Table).

AGENT	LIPID SOLUBILITY	RELATIVE POTENCY	PROTEIN BINDING (%)	DURATION	pKa	ONSET TIME
Procaine	< 1	1	5	Short	8.9	Slow
2-Chloroprocaine	> 1	2	–	Short	9.1	Very quick
Mepivacaine	1	2	75	Medium	7.6	Quick
Lidocaine	4	4	65	Medium	7.7	Quick
Bupivacaine	28	16	95	Long	8.1	Moderate
Tetracaine	80	16	85	Long	8.6	Slow
Etidocaine	140	16	95	Long	7.7	Quick
Ropivacaine	*	?16	94	Long	8.1	Moderate

* Not established.

9. What determines local anesthetic duration of action?

Protein binding: the greater the protein binding, the longer the duration of action. Because bupivacaine, tetracaine, and etidocaine are all highly protein bound, they are long-acting local anesthetics (see table above).

10. What determines local anesthetic onset time?

Degree of ionization: the closer the pKa of the local anesthetic is to tissue pH, the more rapid the onset time. pK_a is defined as the pH at which the ionized and unionized forms exist in equal concentrations (see Figure). Because all local anesthetics are weak bases, those whose pKa lies near physiologic pH (7.4) will have more molecules in the unionized, lipid-soluble form. Recall from the previous figure that it is the unionized form that must cross the axonal membrane in order to initiate neural blockade (see Table above).

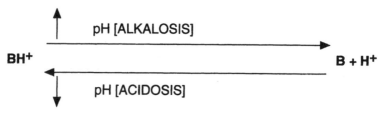

11. How does the onset of anesthesia proceed in a peripheral nerve block?

Conduction blockade proceeds from the outermost (mantle) to the innermost (core) nerve bundles. Generally speaking, mantle fibers innervate **proximal** nerves and core fibers innervate **distal** nerves.

12. You performed an ankle block on your patient who required amputation of his great toe for a nonhealing foot ulcer. You know your technique was impeccable, yet, the moment the incision was made, the patient screamed in agony. What happened?

First, never let the surgeon cut into the patient before confirming the adequacy of the block! A gentle pinch with a small clamp should suffice. Second, since the local tissue pH surrounding the infected toe is likely to be less than 7.4, much of the anesthetic injected near this area will remain in its ionized form and be unable to cross the neuronal membrane. Local infiltration anesthesia near infected tissue suffers from the same limitations. However, a more proximal peripheral nerve block or spinal anesthetic is likely to be effective.

13. What is ion trapping? What is its significance with regard to obstetric anesthesia?

Ion trapping refers to the accumulation of the ionized form of a local anesthetic in acidic environments due to a pH gradient between the ionized and unionized forms. This type of gradient can certainly exist between a mother and an asphyxiated (acidotic, hypercarbic) fetus and may lead to the accumulation of local anesthetic in fetal blood. This accumulation may adversely affect the fetal circulatory system response to asphyxia.

14. Your surgical colleague informs you of her intention to infiltrate a patient's surgical incision at the conclusion of the operative procedure. She is going to use 0.25% bupivacaine (Marcaine), and asks you how many milliliters she may safely inject into the wound site. What is your response?

DRUG	MAXIMUM DOSE (mg/kg)	DRUG	MAXIMUM DOSE (mg/kg)
Procaine	7	Mepivacaine	5
Chloroprocaine	8–9	Bupivacaine	2.5
Tetracaine	1.5 (topical)	Etidocaine	5
Lidocaine	5 or 7 (w/epinephrine)		

The maximum dosages listed in the table above are based on subcutaneous administration and apply only to single-shot injections. Continuous infusions of local anesthetic, as might occur over several hours during epidural anesthesia for labor and delivery, allow for a greater total dose of anesthetic before toxic plasma levels are reached.

Maximum dose of bupivacaine: 2 mg/kg

Patient weight: 70 kg

0.25% bupivacaine = 2.5 mg bupivacaine per milliliter of solution

Maximum total dose of bupivacaine for this patient: 2 mg/kg × 70 kg = 140 mg

Maximum total milliliters 0.25% bupivacaine allowable: 140 mg/(2.5 mg/ml) = 56 ml

15. Why are epinephrine and phenylephrine often added to local anesthetics?

These drugs cause local tissue vasoconstriction, limiting uptake of the local anesthetic into the vasculature and thus prolonging its effects and reducing its toxic potential (see question 17).

16. When are vasoconstrictor additives contraindicated?

1. Unstable angina pectoris
2. Cardiac dysrhythmia
3. Peripheral nerve blocks to fingers, toes, and penis (areas without collateral blood flow)

17. How does a patient become toxic from local anesthetics? What are the clinical manifestations of local anesthetic toxicity?

Systemic toxicity is due to elevated plasma levels of local anesthetic. It is usually a manifestation of overdose or inadvertent subarachnoid or intravascular injection. Toxicity involves the cardiovascular and central nervous systems. Because the central nervous system (CNS) is generally more sensitive to the toxic effects of local anesthetics, it is usually affected first. The manifestations are presented below in chronologic order.

CNS

• Lightheadedness, tinnitus, perioral numbness, confusion
• Muscle twitching, auditory and visual hallucinations
• Tonic-clonic seizure, unconsciousness, respiratory arrest

Cardiac

• Hypertension, tachycardia
• Decreased contractility and cardiac output, hypotension
• Sinus bradycardia, ventricular dysrhythmias, circulatory arrest

18. What anatomic approach in the performance of a regional anesthetic is associated with the greatest degree of systemic vascular absorption of local anesthetic?

Intercostal nerve block > caudal > epidural > brachial plexus > sciatic-femoral > subcutaneous. Because the intercostal nerves are surrounded by a rich vascular supply, local anesthetics injected into this area will be more rapidly absorbed, thus increasing the likelihood of achieving toxic levels.

19. Is there an easy way to remember important data about lidocaine?

Yes. Because lidocaine is one of the safest and most commonly used local anesthetics, it is useful to commit to memory certain information about this drug. Its molecular weight is 234, protein binding 56%, and pK_a 7.8, so just remember 2, 3, 4, 5, 6, 7, 8.

20. What is ropivacaine and what are its potential applications?

Ropivacaine is a new amide local anesthetic that is structurally and behaviorally similar to bupivacaine. Like bupivacaine, it is highly protein bound and has a lengthy duration of action. It is, however, less cardiotoxic.

Ropivacaine is capable of providing differential blockade. In other words, it is possible to separate its sensory and motor anesthetic properties. With ropivacaine, one may provide sensory anesthesia without a significant degree of motor blockade. These characteristics may make ropivacaine an ideal anesthetic for use in obstetric anesthesia.

BIBLIOGRAPHY

 1. Covino BG: Pharmacology of local anesthetics. Rational Drug Therapy 21(8):1–9, 1987.
 2. Covino BG: Toxicity of local anesthetics. Adv Anesth 3:37–65, 1986.
 3. Datta S: Pharmacology of local anesthetics. ASA Refresher Course 21:241–254, 1993.
 4. deJong RH: Local Anesthetics. St. Louis, Mosby, 1994.
 5. Ellis JS: Local anesthetics. In Kirby RR, Gravenstein N (eds): Clinical Anesthesia Practice. Philadelphia, W.B. Saunders, 1994, pp 621–639.
 6. Feldman HS, Arthur GR, Covino BG: Comparative systemic toxicity of convulsant and superconvulsant doses of intravenous ropivacaine, bupivacaine, and lidocaine in conscious dogs. Anesth Analg 69:794–801, 1989.
 7. Finster M, Halston DH, Pedersen H: Perinatal pharmacology. In Schnider SM, Levinson G (eds): Anesthesia for Obstetrics, 3rd ed. Baltimore, Williams & Wilkins, 1993, pp 71–79.
 8. Rowlongson JC: Toxicity of local anesthetic additives. Reg Anesth 18:453–460, 1993.
 9. Schneider M, Ettlin T, Kaufmann M, et al: Transient neurologic toxicity after hyperbaric subarachnoid anesthesia with 5% lidocaine. Anesth Analg 76:1154–1157, 1993.
10. Stoelting RK, Miller RD: Local anesthetics. In Basics of Anesthesia, 3rd ed. New York, Churchill Livingstone, 1994, pp 73–82.
11. Tucker GT: Pharmacokinetics of local anesthetics. Br J Anaesth 58:717, 1986.

14. INOTROPES AND VASOACTIVE DRUGS

Robert F. Bossard, M.D., and Charles W. Whitten, M.D.

1. Why are cardiovascular drugs used clinically?

All of the components of cardiac output and organ perfusion, including preload (end-diastolic volume), afterload (vascular tone), inotropy, heart rate, and even myocardial oxygen supply and demand can be impacted with available cardiovascular drugs. An underlying concept is the Frank-Starling principle, which states that increased myocardial fiber length, or "preload," improves contractility up to a point of ultimate decompensation (see Figure, top of next page).

2. Discuss the use and limitations of drugs that alter vascular tone.

Preload can be altered with drugs that dilate or constrict vascular beds, most importantly the venous or capacitance vessels. In addition, arterial dilators effectively shift failing myocardium to an improved contractility curve, due to afterload reduction and decreased impedance to ventricular ejection. However, the intrinsic inotropic state is not specifically improved by vasodilators, in contrast to the effect of positive inotropic agents. The salutary effects of arterial vasodilators are in most cases somewhat limited by their lesser but parallel impact on venous capacitance, which decreases ventricular preload. Maintenance of preload with volume infusion is an important consideration in the presence of concurrent venodilation. A unique exception to this rule is use of the vasodilating agent nicardipine, the effects of which are largely restricted to the systemic circulation (see question 24).

3. Describe the actions of cardiovascular drugs as agonists and antagonists.

A cardiovascular drug is either an agonist or antagonist. An **agonist** interacts with a receptor, most commonly on the cell surface and causes a change in the receptor, thus initiating a cascade of intercellular events that culminates in a specific clinical effect. An **antagonist**, on the other hand, blocks the cell surface receptor, thereby preventing the unwanted action of an agonist.

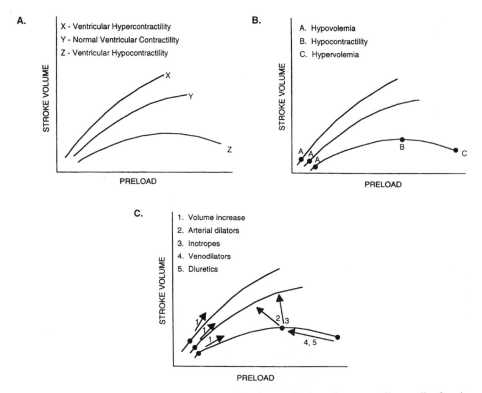

Hemodynamic parameters, intravascular volume, and cardiovascular drugs interact to affect cardiac function and stroke volume. *A*, Classic Frank-Starling relation shows how stroke volume varies with varying preload. *B*, Causes of low stroke volume include hypovolemia, hypocontractility, and hypervolemia. *C*, Various therapeutic maneuvers can be applied to increase stroke volume, depending on the existent ventricular contractility and the volume status of the patient. (Adapted from Bossard RF, Goshi GP, Whitten CW: Perioperative fluid therapy in geriatric patients. In Smith RB, Gurkowski MA, Bracken CA (eds): Anesthesia and Pain Control in the Geriatric Patient. New York, McGraw-Hill, 1995.)

4. What are some commonly used sympathomimetic amines? What is their site of action?

Sympathomimetic Amines Useful in Heart Failure

Catecholamines	Noncatecholamines
Epinephrine	Ephedrine
Norepinephrine	Metaraminol
Isoproterenol	Phenylephrine
Dopamine	Methoxamine
Dobutamine	
Dopexamine	

Adapted from Kaplan JA, Griffin AV: The treatment of perioperative left ventricular failure. In Kaplan JA (ed): Cardiac Anesthesia. Philadelphia, W.B. Saunders.

Most cardiovascular drugs currently used for increasing inotropy or vascular tone, particularly in the acute setting, are sympathomimetic amines, all of which have β-phenylethylamine as a parent compound. Sympathomimetic amines can be classified as either catecholamines or noncatecholamines based on the presence or absence in their structure of a catecholamine moiety, which simply means that the benzene ring has hydroxyl groups substituted at the 3 and 4 positions. Sympathomimetics exert their actions through adrenergic receptors.

5. How are adrenergic receptors classified? What physiologic functions do they subserve?

Adrenergic receptors (ARs) are divided into alpha (α) and beta (β) types, which are further divided into subtypes. Classically, those pertinent to the cardiovascular system include α_1, α_2, β_1, and β_2 subtypes, although modern genetic techniques have led to the identification and cloning of new subtypes. A classification of the AR subtypes from a historical perspective, as well as their cardiovascular and bronchial effects, is delineated in the following figure.

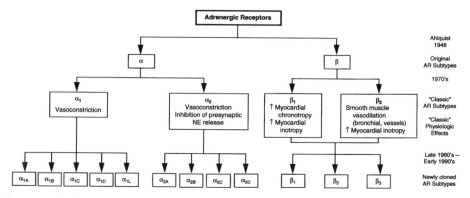

History of adrenergic receptor (AR) subtypes. NE = norepinephrine. (Adapted from Schwinn DA: Cardiac pharmacology. In Estafanous FG, Barash PG, Reves JG (eds): Cardiac Anesthesia: Principles and Practice. Philadelphia, J.B. Lippincott, 1994, p 26.)

6. How selective are the cardiovascular drugs that act on adrenergic receptors?

Most AR agonists and antagonists currently in clinical use are not very subtype-selective. An example is dopamine, which activates dopamine receptors as well as all AR subtypes, depending on the dose used (see question 28).

7. Describe the determinants of myocardial oxygen demand (MVO_2) and supply.

Myocardial oxygen supply is dependent on both the oxygen content of arterial blood and coronary perfusion, the latter of which is influenced by heart rate (slower heart rate increases diastolic time, during which left ventricular subendocardial coronary perfusion occurs), diastolic blood pressure (which determines coronary perfusion pressure), and coronary blood flow (regulated by local metabolic effects, autoregulation, and coronary vascular tone). MVO_2 depends on preload, afterload, inotropy, and heart rate. An increase in preload (increased ventricular diameter) or inotropy increases MVO_2. A decrease in afterload decreases impedence to ventricular ejection and therefore decreases MVO_2. In general, a decrease in heart rate decreases MVO_2 while improving myocardial oxygen supply (unless supply becomes compromised by decreased cardiac output), whereas increased heart rate has the opposite effect.

8. Name the common types of chronic preoperative medications encountered in patients with cardiovascular disease.

1. Digitalis
2. Diuretics
3. Coronary vasodilators (nitrates)
4. β-Adrenergic receptor antagonists
5. Calcium channel blockers
6. Angiotensin-converting enzyme inhibitors

9. Which of these are used to treat angina?

The three major groups of anti-ischemic agents, which form the backbone of therapy for angina, are nitrates, β-adrenergic antagonists, and calcium channel blockers.

10. What are the general goals of inotropic support and the characteristics of the ideal inotrope?
1. Increase cardiac output by improving myocardial contractility.
2. Decrease ventricular diameter, wall tension, and therefore MVO_2.
3. Optimize tissue perfusion and blood pressure.
4. Decrease pulmonary vascular resistance and cor pulmonale.

A perfect inotrope would achieve these goals without tachycardia, arrhythmias, hypertension, or increased myocardial oxygen consumption.

11. What is the mechanism of action of digitalis?
Abnormal intracellular calcium kinetics is a major factor in ventricular failure of various etiologies. Digitalis binds to the alpha-subunit of sarcolemmal sodium-potassium adenosine triphosphatase (Na-K ATPase), completely inhibiting transport processes and thereby increasing intracellular Na and Ca. Increased intracellular Na makes available intracellular Ca more accessible to contractile proteins and also indirectly elevates intracellular Ca levels by decreasing Ca efflux through Na-Ca exchange. Ca interacts with troponin C, the regulatory protein closely associated with myosin, to increase cross-bridging between actin and myosin myofilaments, thus inducing excitation-contraction coupling. Strength of contraction is proportional to the number of Ca binding sites on tropomyosin that are occupied.

12. What are the advantageous effects of digitalis in patients with congestive heart failure?
As inotropy is increased by digitalis, end-systolic volume and pressure are decreased. The decrease in heart size decreases myocardial wall tension, MVO_2, and angina. In addition, digitalis decreases systemic vascular resistance and venomotor tone in patients with congestive heart failure (CHF), again with a salutary impact on MVO_2. In fact, doses of digitalis that show positive results in the treatment of chronic CHF may not produce significant inotropism, suggesting that the benefit comes from modification of reflex responses to heart failure.

13. Discuss factors that predispose to digitalis toxicity.
- Advanced age
- Hypothyroidism
- Hypoxia
- Hypomagnesemia
- Hypokalemia
- Hypocalcemia
- Drugs (such as propranolol, amiodarone, verapamil, or quinidine)

14. What are the manifestations of digitalis toxicity?
Cardiac manifestations result from two mechanisms: enhanced automaticity, almost always junctional or ventricular in origin, and atrioventricular block. Extracardiac symptoms are primarily neurally related and protean in their manifestations, ranging from nausea, vomiting, and diarrhea to confusion, delirium, and convulsions.

15. How is digitalis toxicity managed?
Management of digitalis toxicity includes discontinuation of the drug and normalization of electrolyte derangements. In serious cases, digoxin-immune antibodies can be given. Treatment of serious digitalis-induced arrhythmias may necessitate administration of lidocaine, procainamide, phenytoin, propranolol, or even direct-current countershock. Although countershock itself may result in fatal arrhythmias in this setting, this problem is minimized by use of the lowest amount of energy that is efficacious and administration of lidocaine to suppress ventricular arrhythmias.

16. Is digitalis useful as an inotrope intraoperatively?
Because of its narrow therapeutic ratio and adverse interactions with fluid and electrolyte shifts, digitalis is rarely used intraoperatively as an inotrope.

17. What are the role and physiologic effect(s) of diuretics in the treatment of congestive heart failure?

CHF results in renal hypoperfusion, stimulating the kidney to retain salt and water and thus increasing cardiac preload. Diuretics inhibit solute reabsorption, decreasing congestion. Because cardiac output is often also decreased secondary to decreased preload, diuretic therapy must be carefully monitored. Furosemide can decrease ventricular filling pressures by the additional mechanism of direct vasodilation and increased venous capacitance. Ethacrynic acid, furosemide, and bumetanide increase renal blood flow via decreased renal vascular resistance. On the other hand, thiazide diuretics, although otherwise generally efficacious in CHF, slightly increase renal vascular resistance.

18. What are the mechanism and site(s) of action of nitrovasodilators?

Nitrates such as nitroglycerin and sodium nitroprusside penetrate the vascular endothelium and act as substrates for the formation of nitric oxide. Nitric oxide binds to the enzyme guanyl cyclase, stimulating the formation of cyclic guanosine monophosphate (cGMP), which acts as a second messenger producing relaxation of vascular smooth muscle. Whereas sodium nitroprusside acts primarily on the arterial vasculature, nitroglycerin has its most prominent effect on venous capacitance vessels, although this distinction blurs at higher doses. Nitric oxide can also be delivered to the pulmonary circulation by inhalation, thereby reaching the pulmonary vascular smooth muscle by diffusion across the alveolar-capillary membrane. Direct delivery to the pulmonary circulation reduces potentially undesirable systemic effects (hypotension).

19. Describe the antianginal effect(s) of nitrates.

Beneficial effects of nitroglycerin and other nitrates in anginal therapy result from platelet effects, a reduction in MVO_2, and improved coronary perfusion. Platelet aggregation is inhibited by release of nitric oxide and increased formation of cGMP. Venodilation reduces venous return, ventricular filling pressures, wall tension, and MVO_2 and improves subendocardial and collateral blood flow. Also, coronary artery spasm is ameliorated, and dilation of epicardial coronary arteries, coronary collaterals, and atherosclerotic stenotic coronary segments occurs.

20. What are the beneficial effects of β-AR antagonists in patients with congestive heart failure? Are β-AR blockers useful perioperatively in the management of patients at risk for coronary artery disease?

β-AR antagonists (such as metoprolol) reduce MVO_2 by lowering heart rate, systemic blood pressure, and myocardial contractility. Slower heart rates also augment diastolic function and improve myocardial oxygen delivery. β-ARs, down-regulated by CHF, are normalized by β-AR antagonists. Withholding these antagonists preoperatively exposes an up-regulated pool of receptors to the predictable perioperative surge in endogenous catecholamines, resulting in tachycardia, positive inotropy, worsened myocardial oxygen balance, and increased incidence of myocardial ischemia and infarction. In general, β-AR antagonists are underutilized perioperatively. For example, recent prospective, randomized, controlled trials in patients at risk for coronary artery disease showed that atenolol decreased the incidence of perioperative myocardial ischemia.

21. What are the important interactions of calcium channel blockers with anesthetic agents and other drugs?

Calcium channel blockers (CCBs) can exaggerate the cardiovascular-depressant effects of volatile and narcotic anesthetics. Nevertheless, as with β-AR antagonists, these drugs should not be withheld preoperatively. Muscle relaxants are potentiated by CCBs. Caution should be used when administering β-AR antagonists, particularly intravenously, in the presence of CCBs because of additive effects.

22. How can the hemodynamic and electrophysiologic effects of CCBs be antagonized?

Increasing extracellular Ca ion concentration augments ion flux across unblocked slow Ca channels, thereby antagonizing the effects of CCBs. Hemodynamic effects (negative inotropic and vasodilatory) are impacted more in this way than electrophysiologic effects (negative chronotropic and dromotropic). Both hemodynamic and electrophysiologic effects can be antagonized with catecholamines, which increase the number of Ca channels that can be activated. Atropine may reverse sinoatrial and atrioventricular rhythm disturbances. In addition, both amrinone and glucagon, separately or in combination, have been used successfully in the treatment of hypotension and myocardial depression secondary to CCB overdose. Glucagon is known to stimulate adenyl cyclase through nonadrenergic mechanisms.

23. What are the hemodynamic effects of volatile inhaled agents?

In general, these agents produce dose-dependent decreases in blood pressure secondary to myocardial depression and vasodilation, but the profile of each agent is somewhat different. Halothane and enflurane act principally to decrease myocardial contractility and cardiac output, whereas isoflurane, desflurane, and sevoflurane primarily decrease systemic vascular resistance and therefore tend to support cardiac output. Nevertheless, in a patient with cardiomyopathy, isoflurane, desflurane, or sevoflurane can result in significant myocardial depression. During cardiopulmonary bypass, for example, the perfusionist will usually discontinue administration of any volatile agent for 10 minutes or so before termination of bypass to avoid the myocardial depressive effects of the agent during subsequent emergence from bypass.

24. What cardiovascular drugs are used acutely for hemodynamic control in the perioperative setting?

Efficacious inotropic agents include the sympathomimetic amines, both catecholamines and noncatecholamines. Other inotropes used include phosphodiesterase III (PDE III) inhibitors (sometimes referred to as *inodilators* because of their dual impact on both myocardial contractility ["ino-"] and vascular tone ["-dilator"]), calcium chloride, and thyroid hormone. The traditional vasodilating agents nitroglycerin and nitroprusside are widely used. The newly available CCB nicardipine is a selective arterial vasodilator with minimal venous, inotropic, or dromotropic effects. Vasodilators with efficacy in the treatment of pulmonary hypertension include inhaled nitric oxide and the prostaglandins PGE_1 and prostacyclin (PGI_2). Fenoldopam is a new potent, short-acting peripheral vasodilator with selective dopaminergic agonist properties, thereby maintaining renal and splanchnic blood flow. β-AR antagonists, especially the cardioselective β_1-antagonist esmolol, are important therapeutic options. Labetalol is a useful and unique drug that conveys nonselective β-AR and selective α_1-AR antagonist properties in a 7:1 (β:α) potency ratio with intravenous administration.

25. What intracellular intermediary, or second messenger, is involved in the actions of sympathomimetic amines and PDE III inhibitors?

Cyclic adenosine monophosphate (cAMP). Both classes of drugs increase intracellular cAMP concentrations, albeit through different mechanisms. β-AR stimulation by sympathomimetics activates sarcolemmal adenyl cyclase, resulting in the generation of increased cAMP from adenosine triphosphate, whereas PDE III inhibitors decrease the breakdown of cAMP.

26. How does increased intracellular cAMP affect the myocyte? What are the corresponding effects on myocardial function?

Increased intracellular cAMP activates protein kinases, which phosphorylate proteins in the sarcolemma, sarcoplasmic reticulum (SR), and tropomyosin complex, increasing Ca influx via Ca channels and also amplifying the effect of Ca on contractile elements. In addition, increased protein phosphorylation in the SR and tropomyosin complex, respectively, improves diastolic relaxation (or so-called lusitropy) by stimulating reuptake of Ca into the SR and dissociation of contractile elements. Therefore, β-AR agonists and PDE III inhibitors improve both systolic (increased inotropy and chronotropy) and diastolic (enhanced lusitropy) function.

27. What is the result of combining a β-adrenergic agonist with a PDE III inhibitor?

An additive or synergistic effect results due to the influence of PDE III inhibitors distal to the β-receptor.

28. Describe the hemodynamic profiles of the naturally occurring endogenous catecholamines.

The effects of a low-dose infusion of epinephrine (1–2 μg/min) are primarily limited to stimulation of β_1- and β_2-ARs in the heart and peripheral vasculature, resulting in positive chronotropy, dromotropy, and inotropy, increased automaticity, and vasodilation. Moderate-dose infusion (2–10 μg/min) generates greater α-AR effects and vasoconstriction, and high-dose infusion results in such prominent vasoconstriction that many of the β-AR effects are blocked.

Hemodynamic Dose-Response Relationship of Epinephrine

1–2 μg/min	Primarily β-stimulation
2–10 μg/min	Mixed α- and β-stimulation
10–20 μg/min	Primarily α-stimulation

The potency of **norepinephrine** in stimulating β-ARs is similar to that of epinephrine, but it results in significant α-AR stimulation at much lower doses. **Dopamine** stimulates specific postjunctional dopaminergic receptors in renal, mesenteric, and coronary arterial beds to produce vasodilation. These dopaminergic effects occur at lower doses (0.5–1.0 μg/kg/min), becoming maximal at 2–3 μg/kg/min. At intermediate doses (2–6 μg/kg/min), β_1-AR stimulation is evident. Beginning at doses of about 10 μg/kg/min (but as low as 5 μg/kg/min), α-AR stimulation is seen, which at higher doses overcomes dopaminergic effects, producing vasoconstriction.

29. What are the hemodynamic profiles of the available synthetic catecholamines?

Isoproterenol is the most potent β_1- and β_2-AR agonist, but possesses no α-AR stimulating properties. Therefore, isoproterenol increases heart rate, automaticity, and contractility and also produces marked dilation of both venous capacitance vessels and arterial vessels. **Dobutamine** acts principally on β-ARs, impacting β_1-ARs in a relatively selective fashion. In addition, it has a mild indirect α_1-AR stimulating effect that is secondary to prevention of norepinephrine uptake at adrenergic nerve terminals and is offset by slightly more potent β_2-AR stimulation. Generally, at clinical doses, minimal increases in heart rate, positive inotropy, increased cardiac output, and minimal or modest decreases in systemic and pulmonary vascular resistance occur. Because of the indirect α_1-AR stimulating effect, patients concurrently receiving β-AR antagonists can exhibit marked increases in systemic vascular resistance without improvement in cardiac output. In addition, an occasional patient will display a significant increase in heart rate in a dose-related manner.

30. Which characteristics of β-adrenergic agonists limit their effectiveness?

- Positive chronotropic and arrhythmogenic effects (primarily with epinephrine and isoproterenol and less commonly with dobutamine)
- Vasoconstriction secondary to α_1-AR activation (with norepinephrine and higher dose epinephrine and dopamine)
- Vasodilation due to stimulation of vascular β_2-AR receptors (with isoproterenol and, less commonly, dobutamine)

31. How may the side effects and limitations of β-adrenergic agonists be minimized?

Side effects can be minimized by appropriate dosage adjustments or use of combinations of agents. In modern practice, PDE III inhibitors have assumed a prominent role in this regard (see questions 32 and 34). Often, dopamine is added to infusions of one of the other catecholamines to improve renal perfusion and to minimize the dosage requirement of the first agent. A traditional example of combination therapy is the use of phentolamine (Regitine) with norepinephrine

(Levophed) to minimize the vasoconstrictive effects of the latter. Other agents to consider include lidocaine (for antiarrhythmogenic effects), nitroglycerin, and sodium nitroprusside.

32. Discuss the hemodynamic profile of the PDE inhibitors amrinone and milrinone.

Amrinone and milrinone are approximately as potent in increasing cardiac output as the milder β-AR agonists dopamine and dobutamine. Inotropy is increased, and lusitropy is improved. In addition to direct myocardial effects, prominent vasodilation is produced, and in fact it is difficult to separate out the relative contributions of vasodilation and inotropic effects in increasing cardiac output. Overall hemodynamic effects are intermediate between those of dobutamine and sodium nitroprusside. Both venous and arterial vasodilation occur, which decreases right and left ventricular filling pressures, pulmonary and systemic vascular resistance, pulmonary artery pressure, and mean arterial pressure. Right ventricular dynamics are particularly favorably impacted. Coronary vessels are dilated. In patients with severe CHF, MVO_2 is actually decreased, presumably because of the prominent vasodilatory effects. Compared to the effects seen with the β-AR agonists, heart rate is unchanged or modestly increased, and significant proarrhythmia is less problematic.

33. What untoward effects can result from use of a PDE III inhibitor? How are these minimized?

Because the vasodilatory effects of PDE III inhibitors are profound, concurrent use of a vasoconstrictor (such as epinephrine, norepinephrine, or even phenylephrine) may be needed. This is particularly true after cardiopulmonary bypass, when systemic vascular resistance is typically very low in response to anesthesia, hemodilution, and rewarming. In addition, prolonged infusion of amrinone, but not milrinone, sometimes causes significant thrombocytopenia, which is thought to result from nonimmune-mediated peripheral platelet destruction. Furthermore, milrinone has a significantly shorter half-life, making it more titratable, and therefore milrinone has supplanted amrinone as the PDE III inhibitor of choice.

34. Discuss advantageous characteristics of the PDE inhibitors.

In addition to positive inotropy and lusitropy, vasodilation, and a relative lack of significant tachyarrhythmias, PDE III inhibitors have other advantages. In patients in CHF with down-regulation of β-ARs, PDE III inhibitors can transiently restore $β_1$-AR function by decreasing cAMP breakdown. PDE III inhibitors potentiate the action of β-AR agonists, permitting a decrease in the dose and undesirable side effects (especially vasoconstriction) of these agents. PDE III inhibitors may help reduce myocardial ischemia by several mechanisms, including:

1. Dilation of coronary arteries and arterial conduits, including the internal mammary artery and especially the gastroepiploic artery
2. Improved coronary collateral circulation
3. Attenuation of platelet aggregation and thromboxane activity
4. Decreased MVO_2

35. What are the hemodynamic effects of intravenously administered calcium chloride?

In patients with normal or increased serum Ca levels, an intravenous $CaCl_2$ bolus produces a transient increase in systemic vascular resistance. In patients who are profoundly hypocalcemic, exogenous $CaCl_2$ may generate a significant inotropic response.

36. Can β-adrenergic abnormalities occur secondary to myocardial dysfunction?

Desensitization of the myocardial β-AR–guanine nucleotide protein–adenylyl cyclase (β-AGA) system occurs secondary to cardiomyopathies of multiple etiologies, including coronary artery disease, pulmonary hypertension, and idiopathic causes. Even aging results in a significant decrease in β-AGA responsiveness. Potential abnormalities of the β-AGA system include (1) reduced number of ARs (down-regulation); (2) uncoupling of the AR from the guanine nucleotide protein (G protein); (3) increased activity of the inhibitory G protein; (4) decreased catalytic activity of the adenyl cyclase subunit; and (5) sequestration or internalization of ARs (i.e., redistribution of ARs from the cell surface into the intracellular milieu).

37. What mechanisms of action account for the inotropic effect of thyroid hormone?

Thyroid hormone has chronic actions requiring time for protein synthesis, such as alterations of nuclear synthetic machinery, structural changes in the myosin isozyme, and increased expression of β-adrenergic receptors. In addition, more immediate augmentation of contractility occurs secondary to an increase in mitochondrial respiratory rate and ATP production, enhanced function of sarcolemmal Ca-ATPase, and augmented Na entry into myocytes. Elevated intracellular Na levels increase intracellular Ca concentration and activity (see question 11).

38. In which patient population(s) undergoing heart surgery is use of thyroid hormone indicated?

Although the use of thyroid hormone is certainly indicated in patients with preexisting hypothyroidism, there are at present minimal data confirming its efficacy in euthyroid patients. The use of thyroid hormone after cardiac transplantation has been advocated. These patients are severely ill and more likely to exhibit the euthyroid sick syndrome. Generally speaking, however, the routine use of thyroid hormone in cardiac surgery cannot be recommended at this time. Further study is required to determine its value in this area.

BIBLIOGRAPHY

1. Butterworth JF, Legault C, Royster RL, Hammon JW: Factors that predict the use of positive inotropic drug support after cardiac valve surgery. Anesth Analg 86:461–467, 1998.
2. Kikura M, Levy J: New cardiac drugs. Int Anesth Clin 33:21–37, 1995.
3. Merin RG: Positive inotropic drugs and ventricular function. In Warltier DC (ed): Ventricular Function. Baltimore, Williams & Wilkins, 1995, pp 181–212.
4. Novitsky D: Heart transplantation, euthyroid sick syndrome, and triiodothyronine replacement. J Heart Lung Transplant 11(4 Pt 2):S196–S198, 1992.
5. Post JB, Frishman WH: Fenoldopam: A new dopamine agonist for the treatment of hypertensive urgencies and emergencies. J Clin Pharmacol 38:2–13, 1998.
6. Rathmell JP, Prielipp RC, Butterworth JF, et al: A multicenter, randomized, blind comparison of amrinone with milrinone after elective cardiac surgery. Anesth Analg 86:683–690, 1998.
7. Tobias JD: Nicardipine: Applications in anesthesia practice. J Clin Anesth 7:525–533, 1995.
8. Troncy E, Francoeur M, Blaise G: Inhaled nitric oxide: Clinical applications, indications, and toxicology. Can J Anesth 44:973–988, 1997.
9. Warltier DC: β-adrenergic-blocking drugs. Anesthesiology 88:2–5, 1998.
10. Whitten CW, Latson TW, Klein KW, et al: Anesthetic management of a hypothyroid cardiac surgical patient. J Cardiothorac Anesth 5:156–159, 1991.
11. Zaloga GP, Prielipp RC, Butterworth JF, Royster RL: Pharmacologic cardiovascular support. Crit Care Clin 9:335–362, 1993.

III. *Preparing for Anesthesia*

15. THE PREOPERATIVE EVALUATION

Philip A. Role, M.D., and Frederick M. Galloway, M.D.

1. What are the goals of the preoperative evaluation?

The preoperative evaluation consists of gathering information on the patient and formulating an anesthetic plan. The overall objective is reduction of perioperative morbidity and mortality.

Ideally, the preoperative evaluation is done by the person who will administer the anesthesia. The anesthesiologist should review the surgical diagnosis, organ systems involved, and planned procedure. Through interview, physical exam, and review of pertinent current and past medical records, the patient's physical and mental status are determined. All recent medications are recorded and a thorough drug allergy history is taken. The patient should be questioned about use of cigarettes, alcohol, and illicit drugs. The patient's prior anesthetic experience is of particular interest—specifically, if there has been a history of any anesthetic complications, problems with intubation, delayed emergence, malignant hyperthermia, prolonged neuromuscular blockade, or postoperative nausea and vomiting. From this evaluation, the anesthesiologist decides if any preoperative tests or consultations are indicated and then formulates an anesthetic care plan.

Informed consent is the communication of this anesthetic plan, in terms the patient understands, and covers everything from premedication, preoperative procedures, and intraoperative management, through the recovery room and postoperative pain control. The alternatives, potential complications, and risks versus benefits are discussed, and the patient's questions are answered. If the interview is done by someone other than the person who will administer the anesthesia, the patient should be informed of this and told that the anesthesiologist will have all this information.

Done well, the preoperative evaluation establishes a trusting doctor–patient relationship that significantly diminishes patient anxiety and measurably influences postoperative recovery and outcome.

2. What is the American Society of Anesthesiologists' (ASA) physical status classification?

The ASA classification was created in 1940 for the purposes of statistical studies and hospital records. It is useful both for outcome comparisons and as a convenient means of communicating the physical status of a patient among anesthesiologists. Unfortunately, it is imprecise, and a patient often may be placed in different classes by different anesthesiologists. Also, the higher ASA class only roughly predicts anesthetic risk. The five classes, as last modified in 1961, are:

Class 1—Healthy patient, no medical problems
Class 2—Mild systemic disease
Class 3—Severe systemic disease, but not incapacitating
Class 4—Severe systemic disease that is a constant threat to life
Class 5—Moribund, not expected to live 24 hours irrespective of operation

An *e* is added to the status number to designate an emergency operation. An organ donor is usually designated as a class 6.

3. Describe the two key features of the airway examination.

Current practice includes evaluation of both the oropharynx and mental space. The oropharynx is examined with the patient in the sitting position, with the neck extended, tongue out, and phonating. The four classes of oropharynx, originally described by Mallampati, are grouped according to visualized structures:

Class I—Soft palate, fauces, uvula, anterior and posterior tonsillar pillars
Class II—Soft palate fauces, uvula
Class III—Soft palate, base of uvula
Class IV—Soft palate only

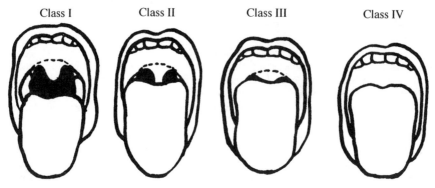

Class I   Class II   Class III   Class IV

Mallampati classification of the oropharynx. (From Benumof JL: Management of the difficult airway. Anesthesiology 75:1087–1110, 1991; adapted from Mallampati SR, et al: A clinical sign to predict difficult tracheal intubation: A prospective study. Can Anaesth Soc J 32:429–434, 1985.)

The **mental space** is the distance from the thyroid cartilage to the inside of the mentum, measured while the patient sits with the neck in the sniff position.

Mallampati found a correlation between higher oropharyngeal class and decreased glottic exposure at laryngoscopy. Benumof more recently demonstrated that higher oropharyngeal class *combined with* a mental space < 2 fingerbreadths better predicted increased difficulty with intubation. Other features on exam that increase the likelihood of difficult intubation include diminished neck extension, decreased tissue compliance, large tongue, overbite large teeth, narrow high-arched palate, decreased temporomandibular joint mobility, and short thick neck.

4. How long should a patient fast before surgery?

Current guidelines for adults with no risk factors for aspiration (see question 4) include no solid food for 6–8 hours; oral preoperative medications may be taken up to 1–2 hours before anesthesia with sips of water.

Current fasting guidelines for pediatric patients are:
1. Clear liquids up to 2 hours preoperatively in newborns ≤ 6 months
2. Solid foods, including milk, up to 4 hours preoperatively in newborns ≤ 6 months; up to 6 hours in children 6 months to 3 years; and up to 8 hours in children > 3 years.

5. Which patients are at higher risk for aspiration?

Higher risk patients are those with any degree of gastrointestinal obstruction, a history of gastroesophageal reflux, diabetes (gastroparesis), recent solid-food intake, abdominal distention (obesity, ascites), pregnancy, depressed consciousness, or recent opioid administration (decreased gastric emptying). In addition, naso-oropharyngeal or upper gastrointestinal bleeding, airway trauma, and emergency surgery are high-risk settings.

6. What particular medical and anesthetic problems are associated with obesity?

Obesity is defined as excess body weight > 20% over the predicted ideal body weight. Obese patients have a higher incidence of diabetes, hypertension, and cardiovascular disease. There is a higher incidence of difficulty with both mask ventilation and intubation. They have a decreased functional residual capacity, increased O_2 consumption and CO_2 production, and often, diminished ventilation ranging from mild ventilation-perfusion mismatch to actual obesity-hypoventilation and obstructive sleep apnea (pickwickian syndrome). These changes result in more rapid apneic desaturation. If the patients are pickwickian, they may have pulmonary hypertension with or without right ventricular failure. Increased intra-abdominal pressure is associated with hiatal hernia and reflux. Because of their higher gastric volume and lower pH, obese patients are at greater risk for aspiration. Pharmacokinetics for many anesthetic agents are altered in them. Finally, regional anesthesia is more difficult and more often unsuccessful.

7. Which conditions identified at preoperative evaluation most commonly result in changes in the anesthetic care plan?

In a study at the University of Florida, care plans were altered in 20% of all patients (including 15% of ASA class 1 and 2 patients) due to conditions identified at the preoperative evaluation. The most common conditions resulting in changes were gastric reflux, insulin-dependent diabetes mellitus, asthma, and suspected difficult airway. These findings indicate that it is preferable in all patients, whenever possible, to do the preoperative evaluation before the day of surgery.

8. What are the appropriate preoperative laboratory tests? Which patients should have an electrocardiogram? Chest radiography?

The trend is to order fewer and fewer laboratory tests, most of which should be based on patient history (see Table).

*Simplified Strategy for Preoperative Testing**

PREOPERATIVE CONDITION	HGB M	HGB F	WBC	PT/PTT	PLT/BT	ELECT	CREAT/BUN	BLOOD GLUCOSE	SGOT/ALK/PTase	X-RAY	ECG	PREGN TEST
Neonates	X	X										
Physiologic age ≥ 75 yr	X	X					X	X		X	X	
Cardiovascular disease							X			X	X	
Pulmonary disease										X	X	
Malignancy	X	X	†	†						X		
Radiation therapy			X							X	X	
Hepatic disease				X					X			
Exposure to hepatitis									X			
Renal disease	X	X				X	X					
Bleeding disorder				X	X							
Diabetes						X	X	X			X	
Smoking ≥ 20 pack-yr	X	X								X		
Possible pregnancy												X
Use of												
Diuretics						X	X					
Digoxin						X	X				X	
Steroids						X		X				
Anticoagulants	X	X		X								
CNS disease			X			X	X	X			X	

* For minimally invasive surgery (cataracts, diagnostic arthroscopy) no tests are indicated. For moderately invasive surgery (procedures in which blood loss or hemodynamic changes are rare), use clinical judgment in test selection.

X = obtain; † = obtain for leukemias only; HGB = hemoglobin; WBC = white blood cell count; PT = prothrombin time; PTT = partial thromboplastin time; PLT = platelets; BT = bleeding time; ELECT = electrolytes; CREAT/BUN = creatine or blood urea nitrogen; SGOT = serum aspartate aminotransferase; ALK PTase = alkaline phosphatase; ECG = electrocardiogram; CNS = central nervous system.

Reproduced with permission from Roizen M: Preoperative lab testing: "What do we need?" In 49th Annual Refresher Course Lectures and Clinical Update Program. San Francisco, ASA, 1998.

9. What is the generally accepted minimum hematocrit for elective surgery?

There *is no* specific minimum; it depends on the clinical setting. The hemoglobin or hematocrit is just one component of oxygen delivery. O_2 delivery is a function of the hematocrit, cardiac output, and arterial O_2 saturation, and blood viscosity (inversely related to the hematocrit). One also must consider medical conditions that place certain organs at increased risk for inadequate oxygenation, such as coronary atherosclerosis, cerebral insufficiency, or renovascular disease. Finally, the potential blood loss and O_2 demands associated with the proposed surgical procedure must be considered.

If there is cardiovascular stability in a volume-resuscitated ASA class 1–2 patient with minimal anticipated blood loss, a hematocrit down to 18% is acceptable before transfusion. A patient with well-compensated systemic disease (ASA class 3) in the same setting should tolerate a hematocrit as low as 24%. In a patient with coronary disease or other significant vascular insufficiency, the hematocrit should be kept > 30%. In the setting of trauma and potential multiorgan failure, keep the hematocrit > 35%.

10. Which patients should have pulmonary function tests (PFTs)?

Because PFTs are relatively insensitive and expensive, they are not recommended routinely for smokers or other patients with underlying lung disease. In most cases, the history, auscultation, and chest radiograph are adequate to formulate the anesthetic plan. In patients undergoing lung resection, PFTs in combination with a ventilation-perfusion lung scan help determine perioperative management and predict outcome. A predicted *postoperative* forced expiratory volume in 1 second (FEV_1) of < 800 ml is a contraindication to pulmonary resection.

PFTs may be useful sometimes in patients with symptomatic lung disease who are having upper abdominal procedures or otherwise prolonged or extensive surgery, in whom they may serve as a predictive device or to monitor the response of the patient's pulmonary condition to preoperative treatment. Flow volume loops can characterize both intra- and extrathoracic airway obstruction.

11. When are preoperative consultations with other specialists indicated?

Preoperative consultations fall into two general categories:

1. Those cases that need more information or expertise to establish or quantify a diagnosis that has implications for the anesthetic management

2. Patients in whom the diagnosis is known, but further evaluation and treatment are needed to optimize their medical condition prior to surgery

An example of the first type of referral would be asking a cardiologist to evaluate a 50-year-old man with recent onset of exertional chest pain.

Referring patients with poorly controlled diabetes, hypertension, or asthma to an internist is a good example of the second type of consultation.

12. What benefits can be derived from preoperative cigarette cessation? How long prior to surgery must the patient quit to realize these benefits?

Carbon monoxide (CO) from cigarette smoking diminishes oxygen delivery to tissues. Nicotine increases heart rate and can cause peripheral vasoconstriction. Within 12–24 hours of discontinuing cigarettes, CO and nicotine levels return to normal. Bronchotracheal ciliary function improves within 2–3 days of cessation, and sputum volume decreases to normal levels within about 2 weeks. However, studies have not demonstrated a significant decrease in postoperative respiratory morbidity until after 6–8 weeks of abstinence.

13. Are there any risks associated with quitting cigarettes?

Following cessation, some smokers will have an initial *increase* in sputum production, and others may have new onset or exacerbation of existing reactive airways disease. Although the risk of *arterial* thrombosis decreases with cessation, there may be an increase in risk of deep venous thrombosis. There are also possible short-term negative effects of the irritability and anxiety associated with nicotine withdrawal.

14. What are current guidelines for perioperative cardiac evaluation for the patient scheduled for noncardiac surgery?

Recognition of potentially serious cardiac disorders (coronary artery disease, congestive heart failure, and arrhythmias) is based on history, physical exam, and ECG interpretation. Besides identifying the *presence* of disease, it is necessary to typify its *severity, stability, and prior treatment.* Other factors important in determining cardiac risk include functional capacity, age, comorbid conditions (e.g., diabetes mellitus, hypertension, chronic renal disease, peripheral vascular disease, etc.), and the invasiveness of the planned surgical procedure.

A recent algorithm has been developed by a group of specialists involved in perioperative cardiac assessment. Clinical markers (or "predictors") of increased perioperative cardiac risk, an assessment of the patient's functional capacity, and the surgery-specific risk are factored together to determine whether a patient is a suitable candidate for the planned surgical procedure or requires further cardiac evaluation and treatment. (Patients who cannot meet the demand of four metabolic equivalents [4 METs] are considered at high risk. Climbing a flight of stairs is considered a 4-MET activity.) The algorithm is reproduced here but all readers are encouraged to review the bibliography reference to better understand these complicated yet important concepts.

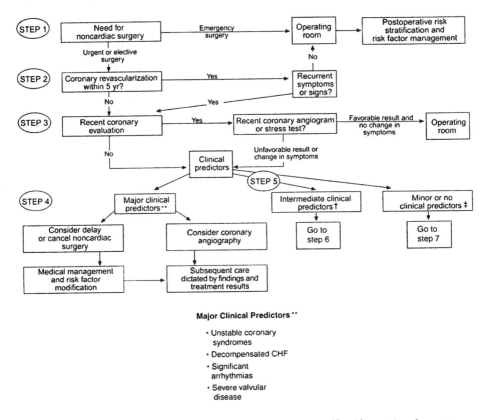

**Major Clinical Predictors **

- Unstable coronary syndromes
- Decompensated CHF
- Significant arrhythmias
- Severe valvular disease

Algorithm continued on next page.

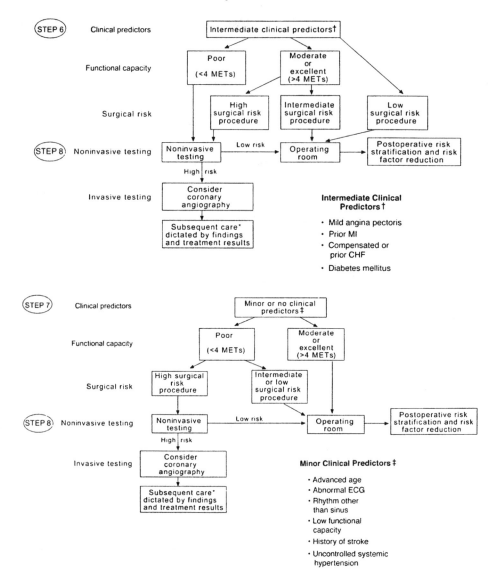

A stepwise approach to preoperative cardiac assessment. *Subsequent care may include cancellation or delay of surgery, coronary revascularization followed by noncardiac surgery, or intensified care. (From American College of Cardiology/American Heart Association Task Force on Practice Guidelines: Executive summary of the ACC/AHA Task Force report: Guidelines for the perioperative cardiovascular evaluation for noncardiac surgery. Anesth Analg 82:854–860, 1996, with permission.)

15. In the evaluation of a patient's coagulation status, what are the key features in the history? What constitutes the basic laboratory evaluation?

The anesthesiologist should *always* ask about **abnormal bleeding** or **bruising**, medical conditions or medications associated with increased bleeding, family history of excessive bleeding, or unusual bleeding with prior surgery. If there is a positive response to any of these, further questioning is indicated: Is there epistaxis, hematuria, or menorrhagia? Hematuria may also occur with a coagulopathy.

Gingival bleeding could be due to primary gum disease, uremia, or thrombocytopenia. Petechiae suggest quantitative or qualitative platelet abnormalities or impaired vascular integrity. Gastrointestinal bleeding may be due to abnormal primary hemostasis, coagulopathy, or fibrinolysis. A history of severe, life-threatening bleeding, bleeding into deep tissue planes, muscles, or the retroperitoneal space, and, especially, spontaneous ecchymoses or hemarthrosis usually are due to a defect in the coagulation pathway. Initial bleeding that stops and then spontaneously recurs also suggests a coagulopathy.

The **basic laboratory** evaluation includes platelet count, bleeding time, prothrombin time (PT), partial thromboplastin time (PTT), and thrombin time. The minimal number of normally functioning platelets to prevent surgical bleeding is 50,000/mm^3. It is important to note that both the PT and PTT require about a 60–80% *loss* of coagulation activity before becoming abnormal, but patients with smaller decreases in function can still have significant surgical bleeding. Therefore the history is still very important.

16. Can a patient with a prosthetic heart valve who is taking anticoagulants undergo a spinal or epidural anesthetic? What about a patient with osteoarthritis on aspirin?

Regional anesthesia in a patient on anticoagulation should be done only when the benefits and risks outweigh those associated with alternative techniques. In a patient with a prosthetic valve, discontinuation of anticoagulants carries a real risk of valvular thrombosis or embolic phenomena. Therefore, the timing is critical to achieve a coagulation "window" short enough to avoid pathologic thrombosis and long enough to avoid neuraxial bleeding. Oral anticoagulants should be stopped 3–5 days prior to surgery, and the patient should be simultaneously started on intravenous heparin. The heparin is stopped 4–6 hours before the spinal or epidural and not resumed for at least 1 hour to avoid epidural hematoma. If there is a possibility of surgical bleeding, the delay should be at least 12 hours before resuming heparin.

Unless there is a history of actual bleeding or bruising, patients receiving antiplatelet medications (aspirin or other nonsteroidal anti-inflammatory drugs) can safely have epidural or spinal anesthesia.

17. Discuss the preoperative evaluation of a diabetic patient.

How long has the patient had diabetes mellitus? How good is the glycemic control? Patients with frequent insulin reactions and episodes of ketoacidosis (i.e., "brittle" diabetics) are more likely to be metabolically unstable perioperatively. Diabetics with a long history of poor control are also more likely to have end-organ disease. Specifically, the anesthesiologist should look for evidence of coronary disease (often "silent"), hypertension, autonomic neuropathy (check for orthostatic changes in vital signs), renal insufficiency, cardiomyopathy, and gastroparesis (ask about reflux and early satiety). Find out what medications the patient takes for the diabetes, the most recent dose, and current blood sugar. Some diabetics may have diminished neck extension due to atlanto-occipital involvement with the stiff joint syndrome.

Serious preoperative metabolic derangements are seen more often in insulin-dependent diabetics, especially in the setting of trauma or infection. Look for high or low glucose levels, electrolyte abnormalities, ketoacidosis, hypovolemia, and hyperosmolarity.

Preoperative testing should include, at a minimum, glucose, electrolytes, BUN, creatinine, urinalysis, and ECG. Additional lab work might include arterial blood gas, ketones, osmolarity, calcium, phosphorus, and magnesium.

18. What are the anesthetic implications of chronic alcohol consumption? What should an alcoholic's preoperative evaluation include?

With an estimated 18 million alcoholics in America, an anesthesiologist can expect to encounter this problem frequently during preoperative evaluations. Alcoholism is a multisystem disease. Increased CNS tolerance to volatile anesthetics and induction agents is observed. Perioperative withdrawal seizures or delirium tremens can occur. Some alcoholics exhibit paradoxical excitation when given sedatives and hypnotics. Peripheral neuropathy may be present with implications for the use of regional anesthesia. Cardiovascular features include an increased incidence of hypertension and alcoholic cardiomyopathy (associated with congestive heart failure, arrhythmias, and enhanced sensitivity to the cardiodepressant effects of volatile anesthetics). Gastrointestinal problems include gastritis, bleeding, hepatitis, and pancreatitis.

Chronic alcohol exposure leads to increased hepatic metabolic activity with increased tolerance of local anesthetics, sedatives, analgesics, and some neuromuscular blockers. Conversely, once liver function becomes impaired, one observes *increased* drug effect, as well as coagulopathy and possible esophageal varices. Metabolic and nutritional abnormalities include thiamine deficiency, hypophosphatemia, hypomagnesemia, and hypocalcemia. Finally, alcoholics may have leukopenia and anemia, and in the presence of liver disease in addition to coagulopathy, they may have thrombocytopenia and a predisposition to disseminated intravascular coagulation.

The diagnosis of alcoholism is often missed because denial is a prominent feature. The brief **CAGE** questionnaire may be more informative than simply asking the patient "how much do you drink?"

C   Do you occasionally cut down on your alcohol intake?
A   Are you annoyed when people criticize your drinking?
G   Do you feel guilty at times about your drinking?
E   Do you ever take an "eye opener" in the morning?

Determine the quantity and frequency of consumption and most recent alcohol intake. Ask about withdrawal symptoms and prior abstinence phenomena. Look for signs of early withdrawal (tremor, agitation, confusion, increased heart rate), stigmata of liver disease (spider angiomata, palmar erythema, jaundice, ascites, gynecomastia, enlarged parotids and lacrimals, abnormal coagulation), and check for hypertension and cardiomyopathy. If a regional technique is planned, document any preexisting neuropathy. Laboratory evaluation should include a complete blood count, platelet count, electrolytes, BUN, creatinine, glucose, liver enzymes, albumin, bilirubin, coagulation tests, calcium, magnesium, and phosphorus. A preoperative ECG is indicated.

If alcohol is noted on the patient's breath, or there is other reason to suspect recent ingestion, an alcohol level should be checked. If the surgery is emergent, the patient should be treated as having a "full stomach." If the surgery is elective, delay the procedure.

19. What are the anesthetic implications of acute alcohol intoxication?

Alcohol is involved in more than 50% of automobile accidents, 67% of homicides, and 35% of suicides. It is the leading killer of persons in the 15–45-year age group. Therefore, many patients presenting for emergency surgery will be intoxicated.

All of these patients are considered as having "full stomachs." Many are dehydrated due to inhibition of antidiuretic hormone (ADH) by alcohol. This, in conjunction with their vasodilation, make them prone to hypotension. Some are hypothermic. Because they are already partially "anesthetized," minimal alveolar concentration (MAC) is decreased, and alcohol works synergistically with the cardiorespiratory depressant effects of sedatives and narcotics. One should not automatically attribute an altered level of consciousness to inebriation, but keep a high index of suspicion for associated head injury or metabolic derangements (lactic acidosis, alcoholic ketoacidosis, hypoglycemia). Laboratory work-up includes a blood alcohol level, drug screen (polydrug consumption is common), complete blood count, electrolytes, glucose, liver function tests, coagulation tests, ECG, calcium, phosphorus, and magnesium.

Most acutely intoxicated patients are *chronic* alcoholics, and therefore all the anesthetic implications outlined in question 18 are also applicable.

CONTROVERSY

20. A 3-year-old child comes in for an elective tonsillectomy. His mother reports that for the last 3 days he has had a runny nose and postnasal drip. Should you postpone surgery?

Viral upper respiratory tract infection (URI) alters the quality and quantity of airway secretions and increases airway reflexes to mechanical, chemical, or irritant stimulation. Some clinical studies have shown associated intraoperative and postoperative bronchospasm, laryngospasm, and hypoxia. There is evidence that the risk of pulmonary complications may remain high for at least 2 weeks, and possibly 6–7 weeks, after a URI. Infants have a greater risk than older children, and intubation probably confers additional risk. An editorial in *Anesthesiology* in 1991 recommended avoiding anesthesia whenever possible for at least several weeks after a URI.

However, as a practical matter, young children can average 5–8 URIs per year, mostly from fall through spring. If a 4–7-week symptom-free interval were rigorously followed, an elective surgery might be postponed indefinitely. Therefore, most anesthesiologists distinguish uncomplicated URI with chronic nasal discharge from nasal discharge associated with more severe URI with or without lower respiratory tract infection (LRI). Chronic nasal discharge is usually noninfectious in origin and caused by allergy or vasomotor rhinitis. An uncomplicated URI is characterized by sore or scratchy throat, laryngitis, sneezing, rhinorrhea, congestion, malaise, nonproductive cough, and temperature < 38°C. More severe URI or LRI may include severe nasopharyngitis, purulent sputum, high fever, deep cough, and associated auscultatory findings of wheezes or rales.

It is generally agreed that chronic nasal discharge poses no significant anesthesia risk. In contrast, children with severe URI or LRI almost always have their elective surgery postponed. Probably *most* anesthesiologists will proceed to surgery with a child with a resolving uncomplicated URI, unless the child has a history of asthma or other significant pulmonary disease.

BIBLIOGRAPHY

1. Abrams KJ: Preanesthetic assessment of the multiple trauma victim. Anesthesiol Clin North Am 8:811–827, 1990.
2. American College of Cardiology/American Heart Association Task Force: Executive summary of the ACC/AHA Task Force report: Guidelines for perioperative cardiovascular evaluation for noncardiac surgery. Anesth Analg 82:854–860, 1996.
3. Benumof JL: Management of the difficult airway. Anesthesiology 75:1087–1110, 1991.
4. Betts EK: In the real world. In Wetchler BV (ed): Anesthesia for Ambulatory Surgery, 2nd ed. Philadelphia, J.B. Lippincott, 1991, pp 506–508.
5. Fiamengo SA: Alcoholism. In Yao FF (ed): Yao and Artusio's Anesthesiology: Problem-Oriented Patient Management, 4th ed. Philadelphia, Lippincott, Williams & Wilkins, 1998.
6. Fong J: Preanesthetic assessment of the patient with coagulopathies. Anesthesiol Clin North Am 8:727–739, 1990.
7. Frost EA, Siedel MR: Preanesthetic assessment of the drug abuse patient. Anesthesiol Clin North Am 8:829–833, 1990.
8. Gibby GL, Gravenstein JS, Layon AJ, Jackson KI: How often does the preoperative interview change anesthetic management [abstract]? Anesthesiology 77:A1134,1992.
9. Goldman L: Cardiac risks and complications of noncardiac surgery. Ann Intern Med 98:504–513, 1983.
10. Goldman L: Cardiac risk in noncardiac surgery: An update. Anesth Analg 80:810–820, 1995.
11. Goldman L: Multifactorial index of cardiac risk in noncardiac surgical procedures. N Engl J Med 287:843–850, 1977.
12. Horlocker TT,Wedel D: Anticoagulants, antiplatelet therapy, and neuraxis blockade. Anesthesiol Clin North Am 10:1–11, 1992.
13. Jacoby DB, Hirshman CA: General anesthesia in patients with viral respiratory infections: An unsound sleep [editorial]? Anesthesiology 74:969–972, 1991.
14. Jones GA: Preanesthetic assessment of the patient with endocrine disease. Anesthesiol Clin North Am 8:697–711, 1990.
15. Levine E: Physiologic effects of acute anemia: Implications for a reduced transfusion trigger. Transfusion 30:11–13, 1990.
16. Lewis M, Keramati S, Benumof JL, Berry CB: What is the best way to determine oropharyngeal classification and mandibular space length to predict difficult laryngoscopy? Anesthesiology 81:69–75,1994.
17. Mallampati SR: A clinical sign to predict difficult tracheal intubation: A prospective study. Can Anaesth Soc J 32:429–434, 1985.
18. Pearce AC, Jones RM: Smoking and anesthesia: Preoperative abstinence and perioperative morbidity. Anesthesiology 61: 576–584, 1984.
19. Schwalbe SS: Preanesthetic assessment of the obstetric patient. Anesthesiol Clin North Am 8:741–758, 1990.

20. Stehling L, Zauder HL: How low can we go? Is there a way to know [editorial]? Transfusion 30:1, 1990.
21. Tait AR, Knight PR: Upper respiratory infection. In Bready LL Smith RB (eds): Decision Making in Anesthesiology, 2nd ed. St. Louis, Mosby, 1992, pp 76–77.
22. Yao FF, Savarese JJ: Morbid obesity. In Yao FF (ed): Yao and Artusio's Anesthesiology: Problem-Oriented Patient Management, 4th ed. Philadelphia, Lippincott Williams & Wilkins, 1998.
23. Zibrak JD, O'Donnell CR, Marton K: Indications for pulmonary function testing: Ann Intern Med 112: 763–771, 1990.

16. PREOPERATIVE MEDICATION

Jeff Nabonsal, M.D.

1. List the possible reasons to use premedication.
Patient comfort
- Anxiolysis
- Sedation
- Amnesia
- Analgesia

Decrease in gastric volume and increase in gastric pH
Decrease in airway secretions
Decrease in incidence of nausea and vomiting
Decrease in autonomic responses (both sympathetic and parasympathetic)
Prophylaxis against allergic reactions
Continued therapy for concurrent disease
Prevention of infection

2. List the most commonly used preoperative medications with the appropriate dose.

Common Preoperative Medications: Dosage, Route, and Indications

DRUG	DOSE*	ROUTE	INDICATIONS
Midazolam	0.5–2 mg doses	Intravenous (IV)	Sedation, amnesia
	0.05–0.1 mg/kg	Intramuscular (IM)	Sedation, amnesia
	0.5–1.0 mg/kg	Oral (PO)	Sedation, amnesia
	(maximum: 20 mg)	(for pediatric patients)	
	0.2–0.3 mg/kg	Intranasal	Sedation, amnesia
Diazepam	5–20 mg	PO	Sedation, amnesia
Methohexital	25 mg/kg	Rectal (PR)	Pediatric sedative
Ketamine	1–2 mg/kg	IM, IV, or PO	Sedation, analgesia
Morphine	0.1–0.2 mg/kg	IM or IV	Analgesia, sedation
Droperidol	5–100 μg/kg	IV	Neuroleptic
Atropine	5–20 μg/kg	IM or IV	Vagolytic
Glycopyrrolate	2–5 μg/kg	IM or IV	Antisialagogue
Scopolamine	5–8 μg/kg	IM or IV	Sedation, amnesia
Ranitidine	1–3 mg/kg	PO or IV	H_2 blockade
Cimetidine	2–4 mg/kg	IM, IV, or PO	H_2 blockade
Metoclopramide	0.1–0.25 mg/kg	IM, IV, or PO	Prophylaxis for
Antacids (nonpar-ticulate)	30 ml	PO (for adults)	aspiration

* Assume 70 kg if not in mg/kg.

3. What factors should always be considered in premedicating patients?

Physical status (as defined by the American Society for Anesthesiologists [ASA])

Age and weight

Levels of anxiety and pain

Previous history of drug use or abuse

Previous nausea and vomiting related to anesthesia

Allergies

Inpatient vs. outpatient

Planned surgical procedure

4. What factors limit one's ability to give depressant medications preoperatively?

Patients at the extremes of age

Head injuries or altered mental status

Minimal cardiac or pulmonary reserve

Hypovolemia

Full stomachs

5. What is meant by psychological preparation? Ideally, how should a patient present in the operating suite for an elective procedure?

Psychological preparation begins with a reassuring preoperative interview by an anesthesiologist in which anticipated events are explained and all the patient's questions are answered. Ideally, for elective operations the patient should be anxiety-free, sedated, easily arousable, and cooperative.

6. Why are gastric volumes and pH a concern for the anesthesiologist? How can they be altered by premedication?

Approximately 40–80% of patients scheduled for elective surgery are at risk of developing aspiration pneumonitis secondary to the presence of a gastric volume > 25 ml and a gastric pH < 2.5 (Mendelson's syndrome). Preanesthetic treatment that reduces gastric volume and increases pH is expected to reduce the incidence and severity of aspiration.

Nonparticulate liquid antacids raise gastric pH and are effective immediately; however, the H_2 blockers need to be given approximately 8 hours before induction of anesthesia to obtain full benefit. Metoclopramide increases gastric motility and relaxes the gastroduodenal sphincter, thereby promoting gastric emptying. Metoclopramide also functions centrally as an antiemetic. Metoclopramide acts within 1–4 minutes if given intravenously and within 30–60 minutes if given orally.

7. Name factors that make the drugs described in question 6 an important consideration.

Pregnancy

Obesity

Opiate use

Pain

Alcohol

Trauma

Diabetes mellitus

Difficult airway

Ileus or obstruction

Increased intra-abdominal pressure

8. Name the most common side effects when opiates are used as a premedication.

Pruritus

Nausea and vomiting

Respiratory depression

Orthostatic hypotension

Histamine release

Delayed gastric emptying

Stiff chest syndrome

Sphincter of Oddi spasm

9. Describe the reasons for choosing an anticholinergic agent as a premedication. Name the three most commonly used anticholinergics.

Anticholinergic premedication is not mandatory and should be tailored to the patient's needs. Reasons for use include vagolytic and antisialagogue effects as well as sedation, amnesia, and antiemetic effects. The three most commonly used anticholinergics are atropine, scopolamine, and glycopyrrolate. The antisialagogue effect is of utmost importance in managing fiber-optic intubations. Decreased secretions improve visualization and topicalization with local anesthesia. Vagolytic effects also may decrease airway responsiveness.

10. Show the relative potencies of the three most commonly used anticholinergic agents and their effects.

Effects of Commonly Used Anticholinergic Agents

	ATROPINE	SCOPOLAMINE	GLYCOPYRROLATE
Tachycardia	+++	+	++
Antisialagogue effect	+	+++	++
Sedation, amnesia	+	+++	0
Central nervous system toxicity	+	++	0
Lower esophageal sphincter relaxation	++	++	++

0 = none, + = mild, ++ = moderate, +++ = marked.

11. List some side effects of anticholinergic medications.
Side effects seen with anticholinergics include:
Central nervous system (CNS) toxicity
Decrease in lower esophageal sphincter tone
Mydriasis and cycloplegia
Increase in physiologic dead space
Prevention of sweating
Hyperthermia

12. Explain why glycopyrrolate has no side effects on the central nervous system.
Glycopyrrolate has no CNS side effects because it is a positively charged quaternary amine, and hence does not cross the blood-brain barrier (BBB). Tertiary amines are neutrally charged and cross the BBB, thus affecting the CNS.

13. A patient in the preoperative holding area is delirious after receiving only 0.4 mg of scopolamine as a premedication. What is the cause of the delirium? Describe its management.
The most likely cause of the delirium is central anticholinergic crisis. The reversal agents for anticholinergics include neostigmine, pyridostigmine, and physostigmine. Physostigmine (Antilirium) is the only acetylcholinesterase inhibitor that crosses the BBB and therefore is the only agent that treats central anticholinergic crisis. The dose of physostigmine is 1 mg, given slowly; the dose may be repeated after 15 minutes.

14. When is it mandatory to use a premedication specifically directed at attenuating sympathetic nervous system (SNS) responses? What options are available?
Patients with known hypertension may develop a marked rise in blood pressure after or during laryngoscopy or intubation. Patients with known coronary artery disease may poorly tolerate the tachycardia associated with instrumentation of a lightly anesthetized airway. Such patients may benefit from premedication that attenuates SNS responses.
Drug regimens that may have beneficial effect on the SNS include clonidine, beta blockers, and high-dose opioids, which cannot be given as a premedication because of respiratory depression. Clonidine is a centrally acting α_2 agonist that attenuates blood pressure and heart rate responses to noxious stimuli and reduces inhaled or injected anesthetic requirements by 40% when given as an oral premedication at 5 µg/kg. Clonidine may produce significant bradycardia or hypotension when combined with beta blockers or calcium channel blockers and may cause marked sedation and drowsiness postoperatively.

15. Describe the medications available for prophylaxis against allergic reactions.
H_1 blockers (diphenhydramine) and H_2 blockers (ranitidine and cimetidine), along with corticosteroids, can be used as prophylaxis against allergic reactions; however, the efficacy is unproved.

16. Why is premedication particularly important in pediatric patients?

Premedication in children is particularly important because children may be difficult to prepare psychologically for the operating suite. Separation from parents and fear of needles may cause great anxiety. Consequently, many children are given oral sedation before induction of anesthesia. Children also have a high vagal tone that responds to laryngoscopy paradoxically with bradycardia as opposed to the tachycardia usually seen in adults. For this reason, immediately before laryngoscopy small children often receive an anticholinergic, given IM or IV once the child is anesthetized.

17. At what age and stage of development do children begin to require sedation?

Children begin to require sedation at approximately 6 months of age, because this is the age at which they develop separation anxiety. Before 6 months of age most children do not respond negatively to separation from their parents.

18. Does preoperative medication of a pregnant woman involve special consideration?

Most procedures are not done electively in pregnant women; however, the need to perform anesthetics in this population is not uncommon.

Psychological preparation can make a big difference. Benzodiazepines and nitrous oxide are the only two commonly used anesthetic drugs that have been implicated as teratogenic during the first trimester. Opioids are considered relatively safe, but because most drugs are listed as pregnancy class C (not tested in pregnant women), attempts are usually made to minimize all preoperative and intraoperative medications. Ideally, one administers regional anesthesia, whenever possible, with only a local premedicant. Many pregnant women agree to this plan when the anesthesiologist explains concerns for the unborn fetus.

19. Name the antiemetic that has caused patients to cancel elective surgery when given preoperatively.

Droperidol, a butyrophenone, is a dopamine antagonist that is a potent antiemetic drug. It may make patients extremely dysphoric and frightened to the point that they cancel surgery. This phenomenon is usually seen when the drug is given alone; however, it has also been seen in patients given fentanyl with droperidol (Innovar). The author recommends a good benzodiazepine base before using droperidol whenever possible.

20. Describe the preoperative management of a morbidly obese patient with a difficult airway. Assume that the patient is otherwise healthy.

A morbidly obese patient is considered a full stomach. Therefore, H_2 blockers given the evening before and the morning of surgery, preoperative metoclopramide, and oral nonparticulate antacids are in order. Glycopyrrolate is useful for planned fiber-optic bronchoscopy. It improves visualization by drying secretions, increases the effectiveness of the topical anesthesia, and decreases airway responsiveness. Sedation with narcotics, benzodiazepines, and droperidol should be judiciously titrated, using supplemental oxygen and close observation to ensure an awake, appropriately responding patient who can protect his or her own airway.

BIBLIOGRAPHY

1. Beecher HK: Preanesthetic medication. JAMA 157:242, 1955.
2. Reves JG, Fragen RJ, Vinick HR, et al: Midazolam: Pharmacology and uses. Anesthesiology 62:310–324, 1985.
3. Lee CM, Yeakel AE: Patient refusal of surgery following Innovar premedication. Anesth Analg 54:224–226, 1975.
4. Manchikanti L, Grow JB, Collvier JA, et al: Bicitra (sodium citrate) and metoclopramide in outpatient anesthesia for prophylaxis against aspiration pneumonitis. Anesthesiology 63:378–384, 1985.
5. Manchikanti L, Kraus JW, Edds SP: Cimetidine and related drugs in anesthesia. Anesth Analg 61:595–608, 1982.
6. Mirakhur RK: Anticholinergic drugs. Br J Anaesth 51:671–679, 1979.

17. THE ANESTHESIA MACHINE

Robert W. Phelps, Ph.D., M.D.

1. What is an anesthesia machine?

A more modern and correct name for an anesthesia machine is an **anesthesia delivery system**. The job of the first anesthesia machines was to supply a mixture of anesthetizing and life-sustaining gases to the patient. A modern anesthesia delivery system not only delivers anesthetic gases, vapors, and oxygen, but also it provides a number of basic monitoring functions and the ability to ventilate the patient automatically. It is virtually impossible to purchase a gas machine today without integrated vaporizers, airway pressure, flow and oxygen monitors, and an automatic ventilator.

2. What is the purpose of an anesthesia machine?

The most important purpose is to help the anesthesiologist keep the patient alive, safe, and adequately anesthetized.

3. Are there different kinds of anesthesia machines?

Anesthesia machines used to be available in many different varieties from many different manufacturers. Today, anesthesia machines have become much more standardized, and currently there are two major manufacturers in the United States: **Dräger** and **Datex-Ohmeda**. Although there are many differences between the machines manufactured by each of the two companies, there are also many similarities, some initiated by user demands, others by governmental and industrial standards.

4. One of the primary determinants of gas delivery is plumbing. Simplify the plumbing of an anesthesia machine to create an overview of its essential interconnections.

Leaving out the safety features and monitors, the anesthesia machine is divided into three sections.

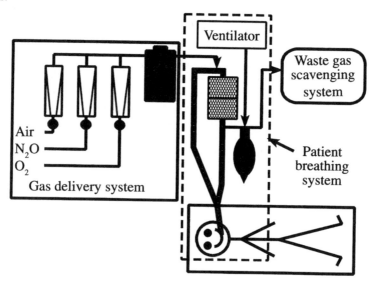

Three main subsystems of an anesthesia machine: gas delivery, patient breathing circuit (which includes the absorber and ventilator), and scavenger.

1. A **gas mixer**, or gas delivery system, supplies at its outlet a defined mixture of gas chosen by the user.

2. The **patient breathing system** includes the patient breathing circuit, absorber head, ventilator, and sometimes gas pressure and flow monitors.

3. A **scavenger system** collects excess gas from the patient and the gas supply section itself and expels the gas outside the hospital to reduce the exposure of operating room personnel to anesthetic gases.

5. Are the three gases—air, oxygen (O_2), and nitrous oxide (N_2O)—standardly available on all anesthesia machines?

This combination of gases is probably the most common, but other combinations are also found. O_2 and N_2O are available on almost every anesthesia machine. The third gas may be absent or may be a number of other gases, including helium (He), heliox (a mixture of He and O_2), carbon dioxide (CO_2), or nitrogen (N_2). If the third gas does not contain O_2 (as do air and heliox), it is possible to deliver a (dangerous) hypoxic mixture to the patient.

6. Where do the gases come from?

Usually the gas source for anesthesia machines in hospitals is from a central supply of gas, called the wall or pipeline supply, that is piped into the operating room. An emergency supply of gases is stored in tanks attached to the anesthesia machine. These tanks should be checked daily to ensure they contain an adequate backup supply in case of a pipeline failure.

7. What is a "regulator" and how does it control the release of gas from the tanks?

The gas in the supply tanks is pressurized to approximately 2200 psig. (The abbreviation "psig" stands for pressure-per-square-inch-gauge. The difference between this and absolute pressure, psi, is the background or atmospheric pressure. Gauges are usually calibrated to read 0 at atmospheric pressure, so their actual reading reflects the pressure above atmospheric pressure.) The "works" of the anesthesia machine require gas at approximately 50 psig, roughly the pressure of the gas from the wall supply. A regulator is used to reduce the pressure. The regulator is designed so that the pressure at its outlet is constant regardless of the starting pressure and the flow rate of gas. There is a separate regulator for each gas supplied by tanks, and the regulators are adjusted so that the resulting pressure is slightly below the usual wall pressure. The wall gas and tank supply are then connected with a check valve. This check valve selects the gas source with the highest pressure for use by the machine. Thus, under normal circumstances, the wall supply is used preferentially and the tank supply only if the wall supply fails.

8. You installed a new tank of N_2O and your pressure gauge reads only about 750 psig. Is the pressure in the N_2O tank different from the pressures of other gases?

At room temperature, N_2O condenses into a liquid at 747 psig. Air and O_2 are compressed gases in their tanks if they are at room temperature, but N_2O is a liquid. The pressure in the tank stays the same until most of the N_2O is released because of the gas-liquid interface. N_2O E-cylinders (those on the back of the machine) hold the equivalent of about 1600 L of gas, whereas E-cylinders of O_2 and air hold only about 600 L.

9. List the uses of O_2 in an anesthesia machine.

- Provides all or part of the fresh gas flow
- Provides gas for the O_2 flush
- Powers the low O_2 alarm (Datex-Ohmeda)
- Is used, along with N_2O, by the Dräger oxygen ratio monitor (ORM) and oxygen ratio monitor controller (ORMC) to prevent delivery of hypoxic mixtures of gas to the patient
- Powers the "fail-safe" valves
- Powers the ventilator

10. How can one be sure that when the O_2 valve is turned on the anesthesia machine really delivers O_2?

1. All wall supply gas connectors are keyed so that only the O_2 supply hose can be plugged into the O_2 connector on the wall, the N_2O hose into the N_2O outlet, and so on. This is known as a Diameter-Index-Safety-System (DISS) and by other similar proprietary names. Several manufacturers make such systems, but they are usually all from one manufacturer (and should be) throughout a particular hospital.

2. The gas cylinders are keyed using a Pin-Index-Safety-System (PISS—no kidding, that's what it's called!) so that only the correct tank can be attached to the corresponding yolk on the anesthesia machine.

3. All anesthesia machines are required to have an O_2 monitoring device attached to it that monitors the O_2 concentration in the gas going to the patient. These devices have alarms that indicate when the delivered O_2 concentration is below a set value.

11. In addition to the distinctions described previously, what other ways are gases distinguished to help prevent human error?

First, the O_2 **flow knob** is distinctively fluted. Knobs for other gases are knurled. Second, a **color code** exists such that each gas knob, flowmeter, tank, and wall attachment bear the corresponding color for its associated gas. In the United States, O_2 is green, air is yellow, and N_2O is blue. International standards differ from the standards in many countries, including the United States. Note that in Germany, the color for O_2 is blue and its flowmeter is always on the left. Thus it is easy for O_2 and N_2O to be confused by someone giving anesthesia in these two countries.

12. How does the hospital piped gas supply compare to the use of tank gas?

The only real differences between the two gas sources are the pressure supplied and the volume of gas available. Wall gases are, for practical purposes, infinite in volume availability (everyone knows this until someone forgets to refill the main hospital tank). Wall gas pressures are typically about 55 psig. Tank pressure is generally regulated by the first-stage regulator to 45 psig. The anesthesia machine preferentially chooses the source with the highest pressure. As long as everything is working correctly, the wall supply is used rather than the tank supply.

13. Is one gas supply preferable to the other? Why?

The wall supply is preferable because it is available in greater volumes and is cheaper. This preserves the tank supply for use only in emergency situations.

14. There are two flowmeters for each gas on an anesthesia machine. Couldn't you safely get away with only one, making the machine less expensive?

Two flowmeters are used on many modern anesthesia machines to increase the range of flows over which an accurate measurement can be obtained. The flow tubes in anesthesia machines are always placed in series (which is not necessarily true on other equipment using flowmeters) so that all the gas flows through both tubes. You can read the flow from either tube, whichever tube is calibrated for the appropriate flow range. To measure flows accurately in the ranges used for low flow or even closed-circuit anesthesia (200–1000 ml/min) to nonrebreathing flows (6 L/min and higher), two flow tubes are essential.

15. Why are the flowmeters for air, O_2, and N_2O arranged in the order they are in?

Part of the reason the flow tubes are arranged in the order they are in is because of a U.S. government standard, part is for safety reasons, and part is determined by the manufacturers' conventions. In the United States, according to government (NIOSH) standards, the O_2 flowmeter must always be on the right. Requiring the O_2 knob to be in the same relative position on all anesthesia machines decreases the risk of the anesthesiologist turning the wrong knob if he or she uses different machines from time to time. There is also an issue of mechanical safety—in this case, the O_2 should enter the common manifold closest to the gas egress side. That way, most leaks will tend to selectively lose gases other than O_2.

16. Can flowmeters be arranged in a different order?
Convention has resulted in some differences. Datex-Ohmeda has the N_2O flowmeter located in the center position, and Dräger has N_2O positioned on the left. Theoretically, you could order your machine with the flowmeters in any order as long as the O_2 was on the right, but the company might not accept your order.

17. All anesthesia machines are required to have "fail-safe" valves to prevent gas administration when no O_2 is present. Have there been any new developments in this area?
Fail-safe valves are a somewhat archaic method of providing a necessary, although not a truly fail-safe, safety feature. The Datex-Ohmeda fail-safe device cuts off the flow of all other gases when the O_2 pressure falls below 25 psig. The figure shows how the flows of O_2 and N_2O change as O_2 pressure is lost. Note that O_2 flow does not start to fall in Datex-Ohmeda machines until the pressure reaches 16 psig because of the second-stage O_2 regulator (part of their Link-25 system). On Dräger machines, the O_2 flow falls proportionately with supplied O_2 pressure because of Dräger's Oxygen Failure Protection Device (OFPD). The proportional decrease begins at full working pressure because Dräger machines have no second-stage regulator.

Output when oxygen pressure is lost

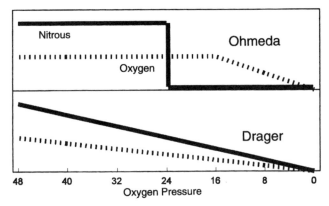

Effect of fail-safe device and OFPD.

18. Is there a distinctive alarm to warn of an O_2 supply failure?
When O_2 pressure fails, Datex-Ohmeda warns of the failure using a reed whistle, which is powered by an internal reserve tank of O_2 that refills every time the machine is turned on. Dräger's O_2 failure alarm is similar to Dräger's other alarms, but the final beep is of a different pitch. Dräger continues to warn the user of the O_2 failure every 30 seconds, but unfortunately it is often mistaken for Dräger's other alarms and frequently ignored. Datex-Ohmeda's distinctive whistle occurs only once.

19. Would it be safer to leave the tank O_2 supply on your machine turned on so that, if the pipeline O_2 failed, the machine would automatically switch immediately to the backup tank supply?
No, for two reasons. **First,** when all equipment is functioning properly, the disadvantage to leaving the tank on is that if a failure in wall O_2 should occur, your machine will use gas from the

tank. You may not know it until the machine (and tank) is totally out of O_2 and the low O_2 pressure alarm begins to sound. At this point, you must really scramble to find O_2 quickly.

The **second reason** allows for equipment failure—there are two parts to the explanation. (1) When no gas is flowing, it is possible for pressure to be maintained in the gauge despite a leak where the tank is connected to the yolk. Thus it is possible to have a full indication on the pressure gauge and an empty tank. The pressure in the tank should be checked *after* the system pressure is bled down, and then the tank should be turned off. (2) As above, if wall O_2 pressure drops too low, the tank could be drained, supplying the anesthesia machine rather than saving tank O_2 for emergencies. A second check valve prevents the tank O_2 from entering the wall supply plumbing should the wall supply fail. If this valve fails, one's tank could, for the short period until the tank empties, backfill the hospital system, helping to supply O_2 to ward patients.

20. How long can you continue to deliver O_2 when the wall supply fails?

The E-cylinders that supply O_2 to most anesthesia machines hold approximately 600 L when full. If the ventilator is not in use (remember that O_2 powers the ventilator), the O_2 flowmeter indicates how much O_2 is being used. With a flow of O_2 of 2 L/min, there is approximately 300 minutes (or 5 hours) of O_2 available. If the ventilator is in use, the additional gas required for this purpose is equal to the minute volume on Datex-Ohmeda ventilators. The amount of O_2 used by Dräger ventilators may be either higher or lower than the minute volume, depending on the settings of the ventilator. In either case, the length of time the tank supply will last will be significantly decreased below the previously estimated 5 hours (for a full tank).

✤ 21. Sometimes your North American Dräger anesthesia machine alarms when you accidentally try to administer a hypoxic mixture of N_2O and O_2 and sometimes it does not. Is there a malfunction in the machine?

The flows of all gases are controlled by the settings of their individual valves. These valves are of a specific type called needle valves. The gas that flows through the valve then enters the corresponding flowmeter so the user can see how much of each gas is flowing. The flow of N_2O is also limited by the ORMC valve if there is an attempt by the user to deliver too much N_2O relative to the flow of O_2. The ORMC limits the flow of N_2O so that the ratio of N_2O to O_2 can never exceed 75%:25%. North American Dräger machines have a switch that controls whether the machine can deliver only N_2O and O_2, or all gases. The table shows the effect of each position of the switch. With regard to this question, you probably had the switch in different positions at different times, and the position of the switch explains the apparent occasional failure of the ORMC alarm.

Dräger Gas Selector Switch Setting

"$O_2 + N_2O$" MODE	"ALL GASES" MODE
ORMC alarms enabled	ORMC alarms disabled
Minimum O_2 flow enabled	Minimum O_2 flow disabled
Third gas disabled at its OFPD	Third gas enabled

✤ 22. Datex-Ohmeda anesthesia machines do not have such a switch. Why is it necessary to have a switch to select "all gases" or "N_2O/O_2"?

It is not necessary. The switch is present for historical reasons. Early anesthesia machines did nothing to prevent delivery of hypoxic mixtures. When Dräger first developed the ORM (not the ORMC), addition of a third gas that did not contain O_2 could easily make the ORM inaccurate

---

✤ This symbolizes victory in the understanding of previous material. The material in this question is considered to be more esoteric and/or difficult and can be skipped on first reading.

and possibly result in delivery of hypoxic mixtures to the patient. Therefore, Dräger chose to allow delivery of either N_2O or a third gas (along with O_2, of course). At that time, the third gas was frequently CO_2 or helium, and the forced choice made some sense. When the third gas is air (which by definition is not hypoxic), such a choice makes little sense. Because of pressure from users, although they insisted on retaining the switch, Dräger changed its function so it selected between all gases and only N_2O and O_2.

✠ 23. How does the ORM and ORMC work?

The **ORM** was originally developed as an alarm to warn the anesthesiologist that he or she was attempting to deliver a hypoxic mixture. It compared the pressure distal to the O_2 needle valve with the corresponding pressure of N_2O. By monitoring the pressure distal to the flow valve, pressure is proportional to flow, and thus a comparison of pressures was equivalent to a comparison of flows. This comparison is accomplished by linking two diaphragms with a rod (see Figure). Mounted on the rod is an electrical contact, which, when the rod moved, could engage an electrical contact, thus powering an alarm. Because the alarm might be incorrect when a third gas is added, the engineers decided simply to disable the alarm when flow of a third gas was allowed. The **ORMC** added an additional "slave" valve to the N_2O gas path, which limited the flow of that gas via a feedback mechanism so that it became impossible to deliver more than 75% N_2O. This limitation occurs whether or not an audible alarm is permitted by the setting of the N_2O/O_2–all gas switch.

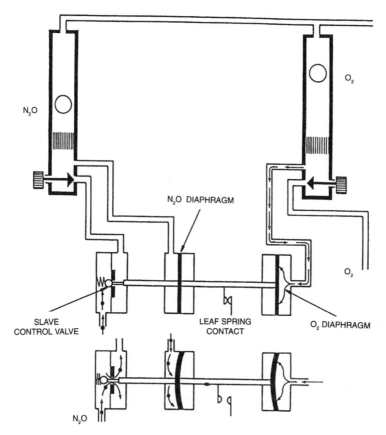

Oxygen ratio monitor controller (ORMC), Dräger's device for preventing delivery of hypoxic mixutres.

24. Datex-Ohmeda machines accomplish the same task with their Link-25 system. How does the Link-25 device work?

Datex-Ohmeda controls the relative flows of O_2 and N_2O mechanically (see Figure). First the pressures of the two gases are carefully regulated with second-stage regulators to 14 and 26 psig. Then two gears with 29 teeth (O_2) and 14 teeth (N_2O) are coupled with a chain. The O_2 gear engages only when an attempt is made to deliver greater than 75% N_2O. At that time, any attempt to deliver more N_2O causes the O_2 knob also to increase at a ratio of 14:29. Similarly an attempt to decrease O_2 delivery also decreases delivery of N_2O. The pressure ratio and gear ratio compensate for various flow rates and the density and viscosity of the two gases.

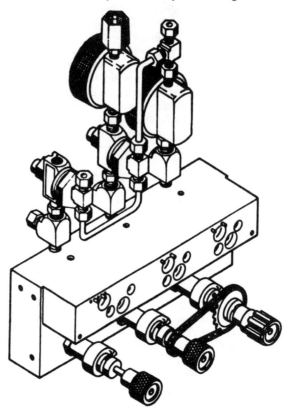

The Datex-Ohmeda Link-25 proportioning system.

25. At an altitude of 7000 ft, you have to administer significantly more desflurane than you would expect given the published minimum alveolar concentration (MAC) of that agent. A similar problem does not occur with other agents. Explain.

Conventional vaporizers (including the Dräger 19.1 and Datex-Ohmeda TEC 3, 4, and 5) are coincidentally "altitude compensated." The altitude compensation occurs because the diverting valve is functionally located at the outlet of the vaporizer, a variation in design that minimizes the pumping and pressurizing effects. The output of these vaporizers is a constant partial pressure of agent with altitude, not a constant volume percent. The desflurane vaporizer (Datex-Ohmeda TEC 6) does not divert a portion of the fresh gas flow through a vaporizing chamber but rather adds vapor to the gas flow to produce a true volume percent output. Because it is the number of molecules of agent (the partial pressure) that anesthetizes the patient, conventional vaporizers provide the same anesthetizing power at altitude. The TEC 6 delivers the set volume percent regardless of altitude, which represents a partial pressure (anesthetizing power) 24% less than the same concentration at sea level. Thus, one must deliver a correspondingly higher percentage of desflurane to achieve MAC at 7000 ft.

26. Can the O_2 flush valve be used to perform jet ventilation instead of purchasing a separate apparatus?

Most anesthesia machines have an internal "pop-off" valve, which limits the maximum pressure that can be delivered via the fresh gas outlet. The actual pressure limit varies with the age and brand of machine, so without testing an individual machine, it is not possible to know for sure exactly what maximum pressure can be delivered. As a rule of thumb, however, most current Datex-Ohmeda machines pop off at about 3–5 psig and Dräger machines at 18 psig. Effective jet ventilation usually requires between 30 and 50 psig.

✠ 27. Compare the performance of "closed circuit" anesthesia using a Dräger ventilator and a Datex-Ohmeda 7000 series ventilator.

On both Datex-Ohmeda and Dräger anesthesia machines, the ventilator exhaust valve opens only when the bellows is completely full and the pressure inside the bellows exceeds the pressure in the clear bellows chamber by approximately 2.5 cm H_2O. If the bellows never reaches the top, the exhaust valve never opens and the circuit is closed. Because the Dräger ventilator's tidal volume is controlled by a mechanical stop, it is difficult to ensure that the circuit stays closed and at the same time ensure continued delivery of the desired tidal volume.

The Datex-Ohmeda bellows always starts its inspiratory excursions from the current position and proceeds down a distance appropriate for the requested tidal volume. It is possible to deliver the same tidal volume from different starting points of the bellows. For example, if the bellows starts at 200 ml from the top, a tidal volume of 1000 ml can be delivered if the bellows descends to 1200 ml. If the fresh gas flow is adjusted to maintain the end expiration position below the top of the bellows enclosure but high enough so the set tidal volume can be delivered, the circuit will remain closed.

28. A patient with malignant hyperthermia needs to be anesthetized. Does the service technician need to remove the vaporizers from the anesthesia machine?

Datex-Ohmeda vaporizers are easily removed simply by releasing a latch and lifting the vaporizer from the machine. On the Dräger anesthesia machines, it is necessary to remove two Allen screws to release the vaporizers. Then unless the vaporizer is being replaced by a second one, it is necessary to install a bypass block to the empty vaporizer slot. These tasks are easily accomplished by anyone capable of manipulating an Allen wrench, but Dräger recommends that their vaporizers be changed only by authorized service personnel. However, flushing the machine with oxygen for several minutes should remove all agent (except from rubber parts in the absorber and circle). The anesthesia provider should ensure that the user of the machine cannot accidentally turn on a vaporizer.

29. One of your O_2 flow tubes broke. Until you can get a replacement, can you put one of the air flowmeters in its place as long as you remember not to turn on the air?

If you remove one of the flow tubes, there will be a leak in the gas collecting manifold unless the hole the tube inserts into is plugged. Remember, the needle valve is located at the inlet of the flow tube, so shutting off the air valve prevents air from entering the (removed) tube fitting. The fitting at which gas exits the tube, however, allows gas from the other flow tubes to flow backward through this opening. You must also remember that flowmeters, also known as Thorp tubes, must be calibrated individually for each gas because the flow characteristics through the tubes vary depending on the density and viscosity of the gas. Finally, each tube must be mated with its own float, and the calibration of each tube and float pair are unique. Using a tube calibrated for air to measure O_2 provides inaccurate flow readings.

✖ 30. Is the airway pressure measured in different places in the Datex-Ohmeda versus the Dräger absorber?

Dräger measures the pressure in the absorber canister both for the reading of the pressure gauge and for the reading from the remote pressure waveform and disconnect sensor. This assumes that the pressure throughout the breathing circuit is the same, which is indeed the case when there is no disconnect or obstruction to gas flow. The **Datex-Ohmeda** senses the pressure on the patient's side of both the inspiratory and expiratory valves. The expiratory pressure is used, among other things, by the ventilator to detect disconnects. The inspiratory pressure may better reflect actual airway pressures, especially in the face of partial tubing kinks, and is the pressure displayed on the pressure gauge on the absorber head.

31. What is the best way to add positive end-expiratory pressure (PEEP) to the patient breathing circuit?

A version of PEEP can be simulated on an anesthesia machine by controlled inhibition of expiration. Several ways of accomplishing this have been devised and are in common use. In anesthesia, two methods predominate, but neither is ideal. The first is by inserting a PEEP valve in the expiratory limb of the anesthesia breathing circuit. These devices use either gravity to hold a marble in the air path or are spring loaded so gravity is immaterial. They prevent expiration until the airway pressure exceeds the set PEEP pressure, usually 5 or 10 cm H_2O. The second way is to place a functionally similar valve in the scavenging limb of the breathing circuit and/or ventilator. This results in the entire breathing circuit being pressurized, not just the expiratory limb, but the result is the same. This is not true PEEP because small perturbations in lung volumes (such as a partial inspiration) eliminate the PEEP temporarily.

32. How can fresh gas flow change the minute volume?

The fresh gas continues to flow into the inspiratory limb of the patient breathing circuit continuously. During inspiration, this gas is added to the gas already going to the patient from the breathing bag or ventilator. The amount of gas added to the patient's tidal volume is simply the amount of fresh gas that enters during the inspiratory portion of the breathing cycle. For example, with a respiratory rate of 10, each ventilatory cycle is 6 seconds long (60 divided by 10). If the inspiratory-to-expiratory (I:E) ratio is 1:2, 2 seconds of each cycle is the inspiratory (I) portion and 4 seconds is the expiratory (E) portion. The fresh gas flowing during these 2 seconds of the inspiratory cycle is what is added to each tidal volume. At a fresh gas flow rate of 6 L/m, 100 ml flows each second, and the tidal volume would be increased by 200 ml because of this fresh gas flow.

33. Why does the patient's breathing bag always become empty on the Dräger anesthesia machine when the ventilator is used?

Both Datex-Ohmeda and Dräger anesthesia machines have a switch that allows the anesthesiologist to choose whether the ventilator or the bag and pop-off (automatic pressure limiting or APL) valve are connected to the breathing circuit. If the switch is in the bag position, the ventilator bellows is disconnected from the breathing circuit. In the ventilator position, the bag and APL valve are disconnected from the circuit, but they are still connected to the scavenger. The bag on the Dräger machine becomes empty because of a difference in the way the APL valve functions on the two machines. The Datex-Ohmeda APL valve is spring loaded. For gas to escape from the circuit, a minimum pressure difference must occur across the valve to force it open. The amount of pressure required is a function of the adjustment of the valve control itself. The Dräger APL valve is a simple variable orifice valve. That is, it always allows gas to flow if any pressure difference at all exists—the flow of gas through the valve is a function of how open the valve is and what the pressure difference is across the valve. Closed scavengers can produce a small negative pressure on the distal side of the APL valve. This negative pressure is too small to open the Datex-Ohmeda APL but can slowly suck gas from the isolated breathing bag of the Dräger machine.

34. What is a scavenger?

Except in a closed circuit situation, gas is always entering and leaving the anesthesia breathing circuit. The exhaust gas is a mixture of expired gas from the patient and excess fresh gas that exceeded the patient's needs but nevertheless contains anesthetic agent. To reduce exposure of operating room personnel to trace amounts of anesthetic agents, it is considered necessary and appropriate to capture and expel this "contaminated" gas from the operating room environment. The device used to transfer this gas safely from the breathing circuit into the hospital vacuum system (or other exhaust system) is called a scavenger. Because of the periodicity of breathing, gas exits the breathing circuit in puffs. The scavenger provides a reservoir for the exhaust gas until the exhaust or vacuum system, which works at a constant flow rate, can dispose of the gas. The scavenger must also prevent excess suction or an occlusion from affecting the patient breathing circuit. It does this by providing both positive and negative relief valves. Thus, if the vacuum system fails or is adjusted to too low a rate, back pressure exits through a positive pressure relief valve. (Granted it contaminates the operating room, but that problem is minimal compared to blowing the patient's lungs up like a balloon.) If the vacuum is adjusted too high, a negative pressure relief valve allows room air to mix with the exhaust gas, preventing buildup of more than a 2.5 mmHg suction at the breathing circuit.

35. Do you need an O_2 monitor on your machine if you have an end tidal anesthesia gas monitor that includes the measurement of end tidal (or inspired) O_2?

No. However, for historical reasons, it has become routine to monitor O_2 with a polarographic or galvanic (fuel cell) sensor located on the absorber head. Some administrators believe that the use of these older sensors is required, but the standards require only that O_2 be monitored. The fact is that monitoring O_2 at the patient's airway is probably safer and more representative of what is actually delivered to the patient.

36. What is more important, your anesthesia machine or your family?

It depends. Excluding time spent asleep (and maybe even counting that time), you will spend more time next to your anesthesia machine than you will spend next to anything or anyone until you retire. It is essential you make the anesthesia machine your friend. Unfortunately, there are certain things your anesthesia machine cannot do for you that your family can. Therefore, understand your anesthesia machine but do not spend any more time with it than you have to. Spend as much time as you can playing with and loving your family.

BIBLIOGRAPHY

1. Bowie E, Huffman LM: The Anesthesia Machine: Essentials for Understanding. Madison, WI, BOC Health Care, 1985.
2. Cicman J, Himmelwright C, Skibo V, Yoder J: Operating Principles of Narkomed Anesthesia Systems. Telford, PA, North American Dräger, 1993.
3. Eisenkraft JB: The anesthesia machine. In Ehrenwerth J, Eisenkraft JB (eds): Anesthesia Equipment: Principles and Applications. St. Louis, Mosby, 1993, pp 27–56.
4. Petty CP: The Anesthesia Machine. New York, Churchill Livingstone, 1987.

18. ANESTHESIA CIRCUITS

Steven J. Luke, M.D.

1. What are the different types of anesthesia circuits?

Breathing circuits are usually classified as open, semiopen, semiclosed, or closed. Features of each type include a source of fresh gas, corrugated tubing, one-way valves, active or passive carbon dioxide scavenging and elimination, rebreathing of exhaled gases, and a pressure relief valve (pop-off).

2. Give an example of an open circuit.

An open circuit is the method by which the first true anesthetics were given 150 years ago. The "circuit" consists simply of a bit of cloth saturated with ether or chloroform and held over the patient's face. The patient breathes the vapors and becomes anesthetized. The depth of anesthesia was controlled by the amount of liquid anesthetic on the cloth; hence, it took a great deal of trial and error to become good at the technique. Later, the cloth was placed over wire-mesh face masks designed to fit the patient's face. Face masks of the same style are still used, albeit without the wire mesh.

3. Give an example of a semiopen circuit.

The various semiopen circuits were fully described by Mapleson and are commonly known as the Mapleson A, B, C, D, E, and F circuits. All have in common a source of fresh gas, corrugated tubing (more resistant to kinking), and a pop-off or adjustable pressure-limiting valve. Differences among the circuits include the location of the pop-off valve and fresh gas input and whether or not a gas reservoir bag is present. Advantages of the Mapleson series are simplicity of design, ability to change the depth of anesthesia rapidly, portability, and lack of rebreathing of exhaled gases (provided fresh gas flow is adequate). Disadvantages include lack of conservation of heat and moisture, limited ability to scavenge waste gases, and high requirements for fresh gas flow.

4. Give an example of a semiclosed circuit.

The prototypical semiclosed circuit is the circle system, which is found in most operating rooms in the United States. Every semiclosed system contains an inspiratory limb, expiratory limb, unidirectional valves, carbon dioxide absorber, gas reservoir bag, and a pop-off valve on the expiratory limb. Advantages of a circle system include conservation of heat and moisture, ability to use low flows of fresh gas (thereby conserving volatile anesthetic and the ozone layer), and the ability to scavenge waste gases. Disadvantages include a complex design with approximately 10 connections, each of which has the potential for failure; a large, bulky design that limits portability; and rebreathing of exhaled gases.

5. Give an example of a closed circuit.

In closed breathing systems the inflow of fresh gas into a circle system is low enough to allow closure of the overflow valve and all carbon dioxide (CO_2) is eliminated by the absorber. Few people use it on a regular basis in the operating room. A full discussion of this complex subject can be found in most standard textbooks.

6. Draw the Mapleson A, B, C, D, E, and F circuits.

(See Figure, top of next page.)

7. What are the fresh gas flow requirements for each Mapleson circuit to prevent rebreathing of CO_2?

A: Spontaneous breathing—equal to patient's minute volume
Controlled ventilation—3× minute ventilation
B: No common clinical use, but requires twice the patient's minute volume
C: No common clinical use, but requires twice the patient's minute volume
D: Spontaneous breathing—2× minute ventilation
Controlled ventilation—70–80 ml $\cdot$ kg^{-1} $\cdot$ min^{-1} or ml/kg/min
E: Spontaneous breathing–3× minute ventilation
Controlled ventilation—unable to use this circuit for controlled ventilation
F: Twice the minute volume is needed for both controlled and spontaneous ventilation

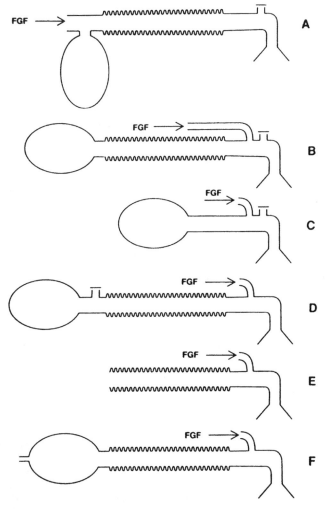

FGF = fresh gas flow. (From Willis BA, Pender JW, Mapleson WW: Rebreathing in a T-piece: Volunteer and theoretical studies of the Jackson-Rees modification of Ayre's T-piece during spontaneous respiration. Br J Anaesth 47:1239–1246, 1975, with permission.)

8. Rank the Mapleson circuits in order of efficiency for controlled and spontaneous ventilation.

Controlled: D > B > C > A (Dead Bodies Can't Argue)

Spontaneous: A > D > C > B (All Dogs Can Bite)

9. What are the other names for the Mapleson circuits?

The Mapleson A circuit is known as the Magill circuit, named for Sir Ivan Whiteside Magill (1888–1986), who introduced endotracheal intubation and Magill's forceps and first described and used circuit A. If the fresh gas flow tubing of a Mapleson D circuit travels within the corrugated tubing, the circuit becomes a Bain circuit. This design was first used by Sir Robert Macintosh (of laryngoscope fame) and E.A. Pask during the second World War to test the buoyant qualities of life jackets with unconscious persons. Pask allowed himself to be anesthetized using the Bain circuit and was then tossed into choppy water on several occasions. Because he did not drown, the life jacket design was deemed a success. The Mapleson E circuit is known as the Ayre's T-piece and was used primarily for pediatric anesthesia years ago; now it is used for weaning patients from mechanical ventilation and is often incorrectly referred to as a "T-bar." The Mapleson F circuit is known as the Jackson-Rees modification of the Ayre's T-piece.

10. Draw a circle system.

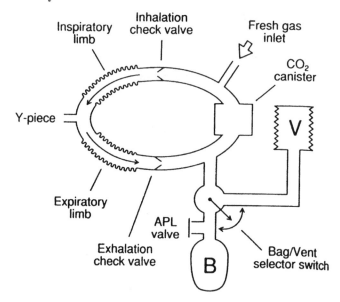

From Andrews JJ: Inhaled anesthetic delivery systems. In Miller RD (ed): Anesthesia, 4th ed. New York, Churchill Livingstone, 1994, pp 185–228, with permission.

11. How can one check for leaks in a circle system?
   One should close the pop-off valve, occlude the Y-piece, and press the oxygen flush valve until the pressure is 30 cm H_2O. The pressure will not decline if there are no leaks. One should then open the pop-off valve to ensure that it is in working order. In addition, one should check the function of the unidirectional valves by breathing down each limb individually, making sure that one cannot inhale from the expiratory limb or exhale down the inspiratory limb. These tests, however, do not substitute for the negative pressure test recommended by Datex-Ohmeda and Dräger for leaks in the machine proximal to the common gas outlet. To perform this test, a no-flow state is first achieved by turning off the machine. The hose connected to the fresh gas outlet is then removed, and the leak detector device (essentially a suction bulb) is attached. After all of the gas is removed from the machine, a flowmeter is opened, and the suction bulb is compressed until it stays flat. If the bulb does not reinflate in 30 seconds, the flowmeter is considered safe. The remaining flowmeters and vaporizers are tested individually in the same way. If all pass, the machine is safe for use. If the machine does not pass, it should be removed for servicing.

12. How does one detect a breathing circuit disconnection during delivery of an anesthetic?
   Breath sounds are no longer detected with an esophageal or precordial stethoscope, and, if the parameters are properly set, the airway pressure monitor and tidal volume-minute volume monitor alarm will sound. The capnograph no longer detects carbon dioxide, and several minutes later the oxygen saturation begins to decline. Exhaled carbon dioxide is probably the best monitor to detect disconnections; a decrease or absence of carbon dioxide is sensitive though not specific for disconnection. To use these monitors most effectively, the alarm limits should be set appropriately for each patient.

13. How is CO_2 eliminated from a circle system?

The exhaled gases pass through a canister containing a CO_2 absorbent such as soda lime or Baralyme. Soda lime consists of calcium hydroxide [$Ca(OH)_2$] with lesser quantities of sodium hydroxide (NaOH) and potassium hydroxide (KOH), along with the amount of water necessary for proper activity. Baralyme consists of barium hydroxide [$Ba(OH)_2$], calcium hydroxide, and water of crystallization. Both soda lime and Baralyme react with CO_2 to form heat, water, and calcium carbonate ($CaCO_3$). For the chemically inclined, the soda lime reactions are as follows:

$$CO_2 + H_2O \rightarrow H_2CO_3$$
$$H_2CO_3 + 2NaOH \rightarrow Na_2CO_3 + 2H_2O + Heat$$
$$Na_2CO_3 + Ca(OH)_2 \rightarrow CaCO_3 + 2NaOH$$

14. How much CO_2 can the absorbent neutralize? What factors affect its efficiency?

Soda lime is the most common absorber and at most can absorb 23 L of CO_2 per 100 g of absorbent. However, the average absorber eliminates 10–15 L of CO_2 per 100 g absorbent in a single-chamber system and 18–20 L of CO_2 in a dual-chamber system. Factors affecting efficiency include the size of the absorber canister (the patient's tidal volume should be accommodated entirely within the void space of the canister), the size of the absorbent granule (optimal size is 2.5 mm or between 4 and 8 mesh), and the presence or absence of channeling (loose packing allowing exhaled gases to bypass absorber granules in the canister).

15. How does one know when the absorbent has been exhausted?

A pH-sensitive dye added to the granule changes color in the presence of carbonic acid. The most common dye in the U.S. is ethyl violet, which is white when fresh and turns violet when the absorbent is exhausted. In the United Kingdom the most common dye indicator is mimosa 2, which is initially pink and turns white when the absorbent is exhausted.

BIBLIOGRAPHY

1. Andrews JJ: Inhaled anesthetic delivery systems. In Miller RD (ed): Anesthesia, 4th ed. New York, Churchill Livingstone, 1994, pp 185–228.
2. Dorsch JA, Dorsch SE: Understanding Anesthesia Equipment, 4th ed. Baltimore, Lippincott Williams & Wilkins, 1998.
3. Morgan GE, Mikhail MS: Clinical Anesthesiology, 2nd ed. Norwalk, CT, Appleton & Lange, 1996, pp 23–46, 696–720.
4. Rushman GB, Davies NJH, Atkinson RS: Lee's Synopsis of Anaesthesia, 11th ed. Oxford, Butterworth-Heinemann, 1993.
5. Willis BA, Pender JW, Mapleson WW: Rebreathing in a T-piece: Volunteer and theoretical studies of the Jackson-Rees modification of Ayre's T-piece during spontaneous respiration. Br J Anaesth 47:1239–1246, 1975.

19. ANESTHESIA VENTILATORS

Robert W. Phelps, Ph.D., M.D.

1. What is the origin of the anesthesia ventilator?

In the early days of anesthesia, patients were rendered unconscious by the anesthesiologist but remained alive only if the patient maintained his or her own spontaneous ventilation and circulation. With the development of breathing circuits and especially with the widespread use of neuromuscular blockers and intubation, anesthesiologists learned, not only could they, but it was essential that they did support the patient's ventilation. Anesthesia ventilators merely automate the "squeezing the bag" function, freeing the anesthesiologist's hands for other tasks.

2. How do anesthesia ventilators "squeeze the bag"?

Any kind of mechanical bag squeezer could be used. On modern anesthesia machines, engaging the ventilator replaces the breathing bag with a second "bag," which is inside an airtight chamber. This second bag is the ventilator bellows, and pumping gas into the chamber surrounding it squeezes it. It is important to remember that the driving gas (the gas in the chamber) and the gas inside the bellows (the gas breathed by the patient) never mix.

3. How do anesthesia ventilators differ from intensive care unit (ICU) ventilators?

First of all, ICU ventilators usually are more powerful (allowing greater inspiratory pressures and tidal volumes) and support more modes of ventilation. Functionally, the gas supplied by ICU ventilators directly ventilates the patient's lungs. The gas supplied by anesthesia ventilators squeezes the bellows but never gets close to the patient. Bellows are an essential component of anesthesia ventilators. Bellows are an optional component of modern ICU ventilators used for monitoring and measuring tidal volumes.

4. What gas is used to drive the bellows in an anesthesia ventilator?

Oxygen is usually used for this purpose because it is cheap and it is always available. It has been argued that oxygen should be used to prevent the patient from breathing a hypoxic mixture if a hole should develop in the bellows. On rising bellows ventilators the pressure inside the bellows is always slightly higher than in the chamber outside the bellows so any net gas flow would decrease tidal volume but not change the composition of the breathing mixture.

5. The pressure inside the bellows is higher than outside?

Yes. This may at first seem counterintuitive, but it's not. Unlike the patient breathing bag, the ventilator bellows floats inside a chamber containing the pressurized ventilator gas. For the bellows to rise, the pressure inside the bellows must exceed the pressure in the bellows chamber by the weight of the bellows itself. This is usually the equivalent of 1–2 cm H_2O. When the bellows reaches the top of its travel, an additional 1–2 cm H_2O cause the exhaust valve to open.

6. What is the status of the scavenger system when the bellows is below the top of its travel?

When the ventilator is engaged and the bellows is below the top of its excursion, the breathing circuit is completely *closed*. Excess gas can escape from the breathing circuit only when a special pneumatic value is activated by the bellows reaching the top of its range. Both Dräger and Datex-Ohmeda anesthesia machines work this way!

7. What is the effect of the extra pressure required to open the exhaust valve on the patient?

A patient being ventilated with an ascending bellows ventilator is usually subjected to 2.5–3.0 cm H_2O of positive end-expiratory pressure (PEEP). Most experts agree this addition of PEEP is actually more physiologic than ventilating the patient with no PEEP.

8. What parameters can be adjusted on an anesthesia ventilator?

Most anesthesia ventilators allow adjustment of tidal volume (or minute volume), respiratory rate, inspiratory-to-expiratory (I:E) ratio, sometimes inspiratory pause (adjusted indirectly using the inspiratory flow rate on Dräger machines), and sometimes PEEP. A few new ventilators including the Datex-Ohmeda 7900 allow adjustment of other parameters and selection of other modes of ventilation.

9. Why have descending bellows been abandoned in favor of ascending bellows?

Bellows are classified according to their movement during expiration—i.e., their position when the ventilator is *not* ventilating the patient. Hanging or descending bellows are considered unsafe for two reasons. First, if a circuit disconnection occurs, the bellows will fill with room air, and although its movement may appear normal, the ventilator will be ventilating the room rather than the patient. Second, since the weight of the bellows creates a slight negative pressure in the circuit, this can cause negative end-expiratory pressure (NEEP) and/or can suck room air backward through the scavenger, interfering with the anesthesiologist's control of gas concentrations breathed by the patient.

10. Is it dangerous to let the patient breathe spontaneously (or to have the ventilator power shut off) when the ventilator/bag switch is in the ventilator position?

The only functional difference between the patient breathing spontaneously when the breathing circuit is connected either to the breathing bag or the ventilator bellows is that the ventilator bellows will generate a small 2.5–3.0 cm H_2O PEEP. In particular, there is no increase in the resistance to breathing. Some anesthesiologists worry about the fact that they cannot monitor the patient's ventilation by feeling the bag.

11. Dräger and Datex-Ohmeda bellows start at different locations in their range. Why is that?

All current Datex-Ohmeda ventilators (7000 series) calculate the inspiratory gas flow rate and duration to produce the set tidal volume and then deliver this to the ventilator bellows chamber. The bellows descends a corresponding amount from the top of its range during inspiration. Typically the bellows never reaches the bottom of the chamber. Dräger uses a stop to set the top of the bellows range so that when the bellows progresses from that stop to the bottom of the bellows chamber, the set tidal volume is delivered. Some of the implications of this difference are discussed later in this chapter.

12. What does it mean if the bellows fails to rise completely between each breath?

The most obvious reason for this is that a leak exists in the breathing circuit, a disconnect has occurred, or the patient has become extubated. When performing low flow or closed circuit anesthesia, the meaning is different for Dräger and Datex-Ohmeda anesthesia machines. On the Dräger anesthesia machine, delivery of a full tidal volume is dependent on full movement of the bellows. On the Datex-Ohmeda anesthesia machine, a full tidal volume can be delivered from any starting position of the bellows as long as the bellows does not reach the bottom of its range. One way to ensure maintenance of a closed circuit is to maintain bellows excursion on a Datex-Ohmeda machine where the bellows touches neither the top nor the bottom of the possible excursion. This technique of maintaining a closed circuit is not possible with Dräger anesthesia machines.

13. What does it mean if the bellows fails to descend completely during each breath?

It is normal on the Datex-Ohmeda anesthesia machine for the bellows to descend only the distance corresponding to the set tidal volume. On the Dräger anesthesia machine, if the bellows does not descend completely, the set tidal volume is not being delivered. This often occurs when the inspiratory flow rate is set too low given the tidal volume and breathing circuit pressure.

14. How does fresh gas flow rate contribute to tidal volume?

Let us assume that the respiratory rate is set at 10 breaths per minute with an I:E ratio of 1:2 and a tidal volume of 1000 ml. Each breath cycle is then 6 seconds long, 2 seconds for inspiration and 4 seconds for expiration. If the fresh gas flow is 6 L/min, $2/60 \times 6000 = 200$ ml of fresh gas is added to each inspiration. If the fresh gas flow is only 600 ml/min, only 20 ml is added to each inspiration.

15. What specifications contribute to the desirability of a ventilator?

In addition to parameters that a user can set, the most important specifications of a ventilator relate to the available airway pressure and peak inspiratory gas flow. In order to supply 1000 ml in 2 seconds (a common requirement for a respiratory rate of 10 and I:E ratio of 1:2), a peak inspiratory flow rate of 30 L/min is required. When ventilating an adult respiratory distress syndrome (ARDS) patient, peak inspiratory flow rates can easily exceed 100 L/min. Peak inspiratory flow rates for the Datex-Ohmeda 7000 ventilator is 60 L/min; for the Dräger ventilator and Datex-Ohmeda 7800 ventilator, it is 80 L/min; and for the Datex-Ohmeda 7900 ventilator, it is 120 L/min. The corresponding limits on a typical ICU ventilator are significantly higher.

16. How and where is tidal volume measured and why are different measures frequently not equal?

Tidal volume is measured using several techniques and at several sites in the breathing circuit. Common measures include the setting on the ventilator control panel (Datex-Ohmeda), setting of the stop limiting bellows excursion (Dräger), actual bellows excursion (Datex-Ohmeda and Dräger), and flow thrugh the inspiratory or expiratory limbs of the circuit. These measures frequently differ because they may or may not include the contribution of the inspiratory flow, are measured at different pressures, and compensate differently for flow rates. None of these measures correspond directly to the volume measurements on ICU ventilators. Since each measure can in theory be an accurate measure of a different parameter, it is more important to record a consistent measure of tidal volume than to debate which measure is correct.

17. When using very low flows of fresh gas, why is there sometimes a discrepancy between inspired oxygen concentration and fresh gas concentration?

At low fresh gas flows, concentrations in the circuit will be slow to change. However, this question refers to the fact that the patient will take up different gases (removing them from the circuit) at rates different than the rates that the gases are added to the circuit. In the case of oxygen, an average adult patient will consume (permanently removing from the circuit) approximately 200–300 ml/min of oxygen. If nitrogen or nitrous oxide is supplied along with the oxygen, the patient will continue to consume oxygen while the nitrogen or nitrous oxide builds up in the circuit. It is possible for a hypoxic mixture to develop in the circuit even though the fresh gas contains 50% or more oxygen.

18. What are the beneficial and adverse effects of PEEP?

Beneficial effects include an increase in functional residual capacity (FRC) by recruitment of partially closed alveoli, improvement in lung compliance, and correction of ventilation-perfusion abnormalities. The overall result is improved oxygenation. Adverse effects include barotrauma and decreased venous return from high pressures, which may lead to pneumothorax, pneumomediastinum, pneumopericardium, subcutaneous emphysema, or decreased cardiac output. In normal patients, PEEP of 5 cm H_2O or less is considered physiologic and advantageous.

BIBLIOGRAPHY

1. Andrews JJ: Inhaled anesthetic delivery systems. In Miller RD (ed): Anesthesia, 4th ed. New York, Churchill Livingstone, 1994, pp 185–228.
2. Atkinson RS, Rushman GB, Davies NJH: Lee's Synopsis of Anaesthesia, 11th ed. Oxford, Butterworth-Heinemann, 1993, pp 97–126, 239–246.
3. Dorch JA, Dorch SE: Understanding Anesthesia Equipment. Baltimore, Williams & Wilkins, 1994, pp 255–280.
4. Morgan GE, Mikhail MS: Clinical Anesthesiology. Norwalk, CT, Appleton & Lange, 1992, pp 23–46, 696–720.

20. VAPORIZERS

Matt Flaherty, M.D.

1. What physical principles are involved in the process of vaporization?

The saturated vapor pressure of the volatile anesthetic, which varies with temperature, determines the concentration of vapor molecules above the liquid anesthetic. The heat of vaporization is the energy required to release molecules of a liquid into the gaseous phase. The liquid phase needs external heat during vaporization, or it will become cooler as molecules leave and enter the gaseous phase. Thermal conductivity is the ability of heat to flow through a substance. Vaporizers are constructed of metals with high thermal conductivity, allowing heat to flow from the vaporizer into anesthetic in the liquid phase, supplying energy for the heat of vaporization.

2. Where is the vaporizer located?

In modern anesthetic systems the vaporizers are located downstream from the flowmeters. Fresh gas passes from the flowmeters to the vaporizer, then on to the common gas outlet. Freestanding vaporizers, added to anesthesia machines after the common gas outlet, are prone to a number of hazards, including tipping, increased resistance to gas flow, and increased output with use of the high-pressure oxygen flush.

3. What does variable bypass mean?

Fresh gas from the flowmeters enters the vaporizer and is divided into two streams. About 80% enters the bypass chamber and is not exposed to the volatile agent. The remaining gas enters the vaporizing chamber and becomes saturated with anesthetic. The concentration dial determines the amount of gas flow that enters each of the two streams. These then reunite near the vaporizer outlet. The fresh gas leaving the vaporizer contains a concentration of vapor as specified by the concentration dial.

4. What does temperature compensation mean?

During vaporization the liquid anesthetic will cool, drawing heat from the metal of the vaporizer, which draws heat from the operating room. As liquid anesthetic cools, the saturated vapor pressure decreases, as does vaporizer output. Temperature compensation means the vaporizer has mechanisms for adjusting the output regardless of cooling. The vaporizer is built of metals that have high thermal conductivity, allowing rapid heat transfer to the liquid anesthetic as it cools. The variable bypass mechanism will direct more gas flow to the vaporizing chamber as the vaporizer cools to compensate for decreased saturated vapor pressure.

5. What is the pumping effect?

Positive pressure can be transmitted back into the vaporizer during ventilation of the patient. The positive pressure can briefly cause gas to reverse flow within the vaporizer, allowing gas in the vaporizing chamber to enter the bypass chamber. The result of the pumping effect is increased vaporizer output beyond that indicated on the concentration dial. Modern vaporizers have mechanisms to compensate for the pumping effect.

6. How does altitude affect modern vaporizers?

The effect of the change in barometric pressure on volumes percent output can be calculated as follows: $x' = x (p/p')$, where x' is the output in volumes percent at the new altitude (p'), and x is the concentration output in volumes percent for the altitude (p), where the vaporizer is calibrated. Example: Consider a vaporizer calibrated at sea level ($p = 760$ mmHg), taken to Denver ($p' = 630$ mmHg), set to deliver 1% halothane vapor (x). The actual output (x') is $1\%(760/630) = 1.2\%$. Remember that partial pressure of the vapor, and not the concentration in volumes percent, is the important factor in depth of anesthesia. Note that 1% at sea level (760 mmHg) is 7.6 mmHg, and that 1.2% at Denver (630 mmHg) is 7.6 mmHg, so regardless of altitude the clinical effect is unchanged.

7. What is the relationship of fresh gas inflow to vaporizer output?

Variable bypass vaporizers have less output than the concentration dial setting specified at very low (250 ml/min) and very high (15 L/min) gas flow rates.

8. What is the relationship of fresh gas composition to vaporizer output?

Most vaporizers are calibrated using 100% oxygen as the fresh gas. Changing to 100% nitrous oxide (which is never actually done) would decrease vaporizer output to about 10% less than the dial setting. This decrease is due to differences in viscosity between the two gases, changing the flow within the vaporizer.

9. What is a copper kettle vaporizer?

This vaporizer is no longer manufactured. A measured amount of fresh gas bubbles up through liquid anesthetic and becomes completely saturated; this vapor then combines with additional fresh gas (calculated by the anesthesiologist) to form the final desired concentration. The copper kettle is not temperature compensated and can use multiple agents. Copper is used because of its high thermal conductivity.

10. What is a multiagent vaporizer?

Most vaporizers in use today are agent specific, meaning they are calibrated and designed for only one anesthetic agent. Multiagent vaporizers, such as the copper kettle, are capable of using any of the common volatile anesthetics. Because the anesthesiologist has to calculate the output, any anesthetic agent can be used if its vapor pressure is known. Some drawover vaporizers have different dial covers, each calibrated for a specific agent, and the dial must match the agent contained in the vaporizer. Multiagent vaporizers never use more than one agent at a time.

11. What happens if you put the wrong agent in a vaporizer calibrated for another agent?

The incorrect agent in an agent-specific vaporizer will deliver either an overdose or underdose. The most important factor in determining the direction of error is the vapor pressure. If an agent with a high vapor pressure is put into a vaporizer meant for a less volatile agent, the output will be excessive. If an agent with a lower vapor pressure than the agent intended for the vaporizer is accidentally used, the anesthetic output will be lower than anticipated. Even if halothane and isoflurane, which have similar vapor pressures, are interchanged, the outputs will still not be accurate. The use of isoflurane in a halothane vaporizer will give 25–50% more anesthetic output than the dial setting. The use of halothane in an isoflurane vaporizer will give less anesthetic output than the dial setting.

12. What is different about the desflurane vaporizer?

The Tec 6 vaporizer is a unique vaporizer designed for desflurane, which has a vapor pressure of 664 mmHg at 20°C. This vaporizer actively heats the liquid agent to 39°C. It was deemed necessary to provide active heating to consistently vaporize desflurane since it boils near room temperature, and small changes in the vaporizer temperature would cause large changes in saturated vapor pressure. Desflurane is less potent than other common agents and up to 18% volumes percent may be delivered. There are electronic alarms for low agent level, no agent output, and low battery. Desflurane boils at room temperature, and the bottles interlock with the vaporizer to prevent loss of agent while filling.

13. What happens if you tip a variable bypass vaporizer on its side?

Liquid anesthetic may spill from the vaporizing chamber to the bypass chamber, effectively creating two vaporizing chambers and increasing vaporizer output.

14. What prevents turning on two vaporizers simultaneously?

Most anesthesia machines have an interlock system or an interlocking manifold that allows only one vaporizer to be turned on at a time. This can be tested by attempting to turn on more than one agent. Improper use of the interlock systems or manifolds can cause gas and anesthetic agent leaks or simultaneous administration of multiple agents. Datex-Ohmeda machines that have three attachment sites for vaporizers must have a vaporizer in the central position to activate the safety interlock mechanism.

15. What prevents filling the vaporizer with the wrong agent?

There are several key-type filling systems. A keyed filler top fits a specific bottle of anesthetic agent, which fits only a specific vaporizer. Funnel-type or open filling port–type vaporizers can easily be misfilled; only vigilance can prevent mistakes.

BIBLIOGRAPHY

1. Andrews JJ: Delivery systems for inhaled anesthetics. In Barash PG, Cullen BF, Stoelting RK (eds): Clinical Anesthesia, 3rd ed. Philadelphia, Lippincott Williams & Wilkins, 1997.
2. Bowie E, Huffman LM: The Anesthesia Machine: Essentials for Understanding. Madison, Ohmeda/BOC Health Care, 1985, pp 91–103.
3. Carter KB, Gray WM, Railton R, Richardson W: Long term performance of Tec vaporizers. Anaesthesia 43:1042–1046, 1988.
4. Coleshill GG: Safe vaporizers. Can J Anaesth 35:667–668, 1988.
5. Dorsch JA, Dorsch SE: Understanding Anesthesia Equipment: Construction, Care and Complications, 3rd ed. Baltimore, Williams & Wilkins, 1994, pp 91–148.
6. James MFM, White JF: Anesthetic considerations at moderate altitude. Anesth Analg 63:1097–1105, 1984.
7. Lewis JJ, Hicks RG: Malfunction of vaporizers. Anesthesiology 27:324–325, 1966.

21. PATIENT POSITIONING

James W. Rosher, M.D.

1. What is the goal of positioning a patient for surgery?

The goal of surgical positioning is to facilitate the surgeon's technical approach while balancing the risk to the patient. The anesthetized patient cannot make the clinician aware of compromised positions; therefore, the positioning of a patient for surgery is critical for a safe outcome. Proper positioning requires that the patient is securely placed on the operating table, all potential pressure areas are padded, intravenous (IV) lines and catheters are free flowing and accessible, endotracheal tube is in proper position, ventilation and circulation are uninterrupted, and general patient comfort and safety are maintained for the duration of the surgery.

2. Describe the most common positions used in the operating room.

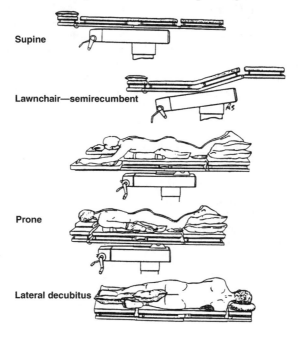

Supine

Lawnchair—semirecumbent

Prone

Lateral decubitus

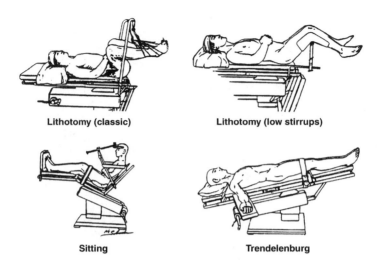

Lithotomy (classic)   Lithotomy (low stirrups)

Sitting   Trendelenburg

Figures on pages 109–110 are reprinted with permission from Martin JT: Positioning in Anesthesia and Surgery, 2nd ed. Philadelphia, W.B. Saunders, 1987.

3. What physiologic effects are related to change in body position?

Most physiologic changes associated with positioning are related to the gravitational effects on the cardiovascular and respiratory systems. The changes in position redistribute blood within the venous, arterial, and pulmonary vasculature, depending on the body position. Pulmonary mechanics also change with varying body positions. Changing from the erect to the supine position increases cardiac output secondary to increases in venous return and stroke volume. There is minimal change in blood pressure, because reflex stimulation of the parasympathetic nervous system produces decreases in heart rate and cardiac contractility. Cardiovascular changes are exaggerated by clinical situations resulting in increased abdominal girth, such as abdominal tumors, ascites, obesity, or pregnancy. The resulting decreased venous return and cardiac output may lead to hypotension in the supine position. The supine position results in decreased functional residual capacity and total lung capacity secondary to the abdominal contents impinging on the diaphragm. Anesthesia and muscular relaxation further diminish these lung volumes. Some improvement is achieved with positive pressure ventilation, but the diaphragm is not restored to the awake position. The Trendelenburg and lithotomy positions may result in further compression of the lung bases, resulting in further decreases in pulmonary compliance. Intracranial pressure increases are seen in these positions as well secondary to increased central venous pressure and decreased cerebral drainage.

4. Name the advantages and disadvantages of the sitting position used for a posterior fossa craniotomy.

Advantages
- Improved surgical exposure owing to decreased pooling of blood in the surgical field
- Optimal positioning for surgical exposure
- Decreased facial swelling
- Easy access to the endotracheal tube
- Ability to monitor the facial nerve easily when indicated by the surgical procedure

Disadvantages
- Possibility of venous air emboli (VAE)
- Hypotension
- Brain-stem manipulations resulting in hemodynamic changes
- Risk of airway obstruction

The risk of VAE requires monitoring with transthoracic Doppler, right atrial catheters, transesophageal echocardiography, capnography, esophageal stethoscope, or mass spectroscopy to help detect or treat the VAE. The sensitivity in decreasing order of detection of VAE are:

Transesophageal echocardiography	End-tidal carbon dioxide
Transthoracic Doppler	Right atrial catheter
End-tidal nitrogen	Esophageal stethoscope

The risk of hypotension may require invasive blood pressure monitoring with an arterial catheter. Care to level the arterial transducer at the external auditory meatus helps correlate the measured arterial pressure with the cerebral perfusion pressure. The sitting or head-up position decreases venous return and subsequently cardiac output. Cerebral blood flow is decreased approximately 20% in these patients and may lead to cerebral ischemia. Often these patients require elastic lower extremity stockings to decrease the venous pooling during surgery, improving blood return to the heart. Prevention of airway obstruction requires vigilance to prevent extreme flexion of the head and neck with resultant kinking of the endotracheal tube.

5. What specific concerns are associated with the prone position?

The anesthesiologist is in charge of controlling the patient's head during positioning. Avoid disconnecting or removing IV lines, Foley catheters, or endotracheal tubes while positioning. The prone position results in a cephalad displacement of the diaphragm. Chest rolls are important to prevent abdominal compression, which impairs diaphragmatic excursion and obstructs the aorta and inferior vena cava. Proper padding of all pressure points, including the face, eyes, ears, nose, arms, knees, hips, ankles, breasts, and genitalia, is necessary in this position. The patient should be free from pressure on the electrocardiogram (ECG) electrodes, wires, and tubing.

6. A patient scheduled for a thoracotomy is being positioned in the lateral decubitus position. What special concerns should the operating room team be aware of in positioning this patient?

1. The dependent lung is underventilated and relatively overperfused. In contrast, the nondependent lung is overventilated because of the increase in compliance. The resulting ventilation-perfusion inequality may result in unexpected hypoxia. Usually, changes in ventilation and perfusion are well tolerated, but in a compromised patient it may prove problematic.

2. All patients in the lateral position should have an axillary roll positioned to prevent compression of the dependent arm's neurovascular bundle. Checking the radial pulse or use of a pulse oximeter on the dependent hand may help to signal impending arterial compression. The arms are usually positioned perpendicular to the torso using a holding device known as an "airplane" or supported and padded with pillows.

3. Proper padding is essential in this position, especially facial structures, breasts, and genitalia. The dependent leg is usually flexed at the hip and knee with padding between the legs. The peroneal nerve at the head of the fibula is also at risk for compression. The head position should remain neutral to prevent stretching of the brachial plexus of the nondependent arm. Often a "bean bag" padding device is used to maintain the patient in a stable lateral position. ECG electrodes, wires, IV tubing, and Foley catheters should all be positioned so they are free and well padded.

7. In the pregnant patient, what is the most desirable position for an abdominal procedure?

The pregnant patient is susceptible to aortocaval compression secondary to the gravid uterus exerting pressure on these vascular structures, potentially decreasing the uteroplacental blood flow and return to the heart. The most favorable position is left uterine displacement by placing a pillow or wedge under the right hip.

8. Which surgical procedures employ the lithotomy position?

- Anal procedures (e.g., hemorrhoidectomy)
- Abdominoperineal procedures (e.g., colorectal procedures)
- Urologic and gynecologic procedures

Depending on the type of surgery, variations of the lithotomy position can be used, such as the classic lithotomy or the low stirrups position.

9. What are the most common complications occurring from the lithotomy position?

The nerves that supply the lower extremity are often damaged because of compression or stretching of the nerves from improper positioning or improper padding. The most common nerves injured are the common peroneal, sciatic, femoral, saphenous, and occasionally the obturator or posterior tibial nerve.

The **common peroneal nerve** may be injured when the head of the fibula (lateral aspect of the knee) is compressed against the leg support device or insufficiently padded. The **sciatic nerve** can be stretched by exaggerated flexion of the hips during positioning. The **femoral nerve** may become kinked under the inguinal ligament from extreme flexion and abduction of the thighs during positioning. The **saphenous nerve** may become injured when the medial tibial condyle is compressed by the leg supports. The **obturator nerve** may be stretched as it exits the obturator foramen during thigh flexion.

Other injuries that occur in the lithotomy position are dislocations of the hips, lower extremity tendon and ligament injuries, and low back discomfort. Occasionally at the end of a procedure, the fingers can be crushed or amputated when the leg section of the table is elevated.

10. Why is it important to move both legs at the same time when positioning patients in the lithotomy position?

The proper way to position a patient in the lithotomy position is to flex both legs at the hips and knees simultaneously, then position the legs in the stirrups. Special care should be taken to prevent extreme flexion of the knees or hips during movement, and a good rule is to avoid flexing the hips greater than 90°. This technique helps prevent nerve injuries and hip dislocations. Proper padding of the ankles, knees, and stirrup braces helps reduce nerve compression injuries.

11. When is it advantageous to use the "lawnchair position"?

The "lawnchair position," a variant of the supine position, is often used for patient comfort, especially in prolonged procedures in which regional anesthesia is used. It is often the preferred position for head and neck procedures. Flexion of the knees and hips places the joints in a more anatomically neutral position. This position also facilitates breathing.

12. How long is it safe to keep an extremity tourniquet inflated and why?

The time limit for inflation of an extremity tourniquet is approximately 2 hours to prevent neurovascular complications. The tourniquet may be deflated to allow recirculation and then re-inflated to ensure adequate perfusion to the limb.

13. What peripheral nerves are most commonly injured during surgery and why?

The **ulnar nerve** is the most frequently injured peripheral never because of its superficial location at the elbow. During surgical procedures, the ulnar nerve may be compressed between the patient and the surgical table. This can be prevented by proper padding of the medial aspect of the elbow.

The **brachial plexus** becomes stretched owing to abduction greater than 90° or with improper head positioning. In all surgical positions, the arms should be properly secured and padded to prevent them from falling off the arm supports.

The **radial nerve** can become injured as a result of improper positioning of the noninvasive blood pressure cuff at the brachial aspect of the arm. It can also be injured by direct external compression of the radial nerve in the spiral groove on the lateral aspect of the humerus.

14. What areas of the body are prone to injury secondary to prolonged or improper positioning?

The eyes are vulnerable to injury by abrading the cornea or direct compression of the globe. The retinal artery can become compressed by external pressure, resulting in retinal ischemia and blindness. This can be prevented by padding around the orbits in the lateral decubitus and prone positions. Taping the eyes shut and using eye lubricants decrease the incidence of corneal abrasion and prevent drying of the cornea.

Skin breakdown can occur owing to improper or prolonged positioning. Pressure on the scalp can result in alopecia. Bony prominences need to be well padded, especially the iliac crest, sacrum, and heels. Nasogastric and endotracheal tubes can produce pressure necrosis of the lips or nares. The face mask may decrease the skin perfusion over the bridge of the nose and should be repositioned frequently during general mask cases. The breast, nipples, scrotum, and penis are susceptible to skin breakdown and require special positioning and padding.

15. Describe the features of the orthopedic fracture table.

The fracture table is designed to facilitate the manipulation of the extremity and to provide access to fluoroscopy of the fractured extremity. The table has a body section to support the head and thorax. A sacral plate is available for support of the pelvis with a well-padded perineal post to allow traction to be applied to the fractured extremity. Adjustable footplates allow for surgical manipulations while maintaining traction and stability.

16. How does the head position affect the position of the endotracheal tube with respect to the carina?

During laryngoscopy and intubation, the endotracheal tube should be placed to the proper depth and verified by auscultation. With patient movement, the head may be flexed or extended in relationship to its original position. A general rule is that the tip of the endotracheal tube follows the direction of the tip of the patient's nose. For example, if the patient's head is flexed, the tip of the endotracheal tube moves toward the carina. The endotracheal tube may enter a main stem bronchus. If the head is extended, the tip of the endotracheal tube moves cephalad, possibly resulting in extubation. Always verify bilateral breath sounds after repositioning a patient.

BIBLIOGRAPHY

1. Anderton JM, Keen RI, Neave R: Positioning the Surgical Patient. London, Butterworth Heinemann, 1988.
2. Cucchiara RF, Faust RJ: Patient positioning. In Miller R (ed): Anesthesia, 4th ed. New York, Churchill Livingstone, 1994, pp 1057–1073.
3. Martin JT: The physiology of the patient's posture. In Collins V (ed): Principles of Anesthesiology. Philadelphia, Lea & Febiger, 1993, pp 163–173.
4. Martin JT: Complications of patient positioning. In Collins V (ed): Principles of Anesthesiology. Philadelphia, Lea & Febiger, 1993, pp 192–206.
5. Martin JT, Warner MA: Patient positioning. In Barash PG, Cullen BF, Stoelting RK (eds): Clinical Anesthesia, 3rd ed. Philadelphia, Lippincott Williams & Wilkins, 1997.
6. Martin JT: Positioning in Anesthesia and Surgery. Philadelphia, W.B. Saunders, 1987.
7. Martin JT, Collins VJ: Technical aspects of patient positioning. In Collins V (ed): Principles of Anesthesiology. Philadelphia, Lea & Febiger, 1993, pp 174–191.

IV. Patient Monitoring and Procedures

22. ELECTROCARDIOGRAPHY

James W. Rosher, M.D.

1. Describe the anatomy and physiology of the cardiac conduction system.

The cardiac impulse originates in the sinoatrial (SA) node, which rapidly conducts across the atria to the atrioventricular (AV) node. There is a normal delay across the AV node of approximately 0.04–0.11 seconds. The impulse is then directed to the common bundle of His and the Purkinje fibers, resulting in ventricular depolarization. The normal cardiac impulse originating in the SA node requires less than 0.2 seconds to depolarize the entire myocardium.

Action potentials from different areas of the heart have characteristic shapes. The particular phases of the various action potentials correlate to the activation and inactivation of ion specific channels, especially sodium and calcium.

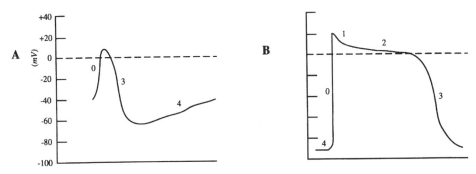

Action potentials demonstrating the action of the ion specific channels. *A,* SA node. *B,* Ventricular muscle.

- **Phase 0** correlates with the activation of the "fast" sodium channels with net movement of sodium into the myocardial cell producing depolarization.
- **Phase 1** represents the early repolarization phase and is the result of inactivation of the sodium channels and transient increases in potassium permeability.
- **Phase 2** represents the plateau phase resulting from activation of the "slow" calcium channels and influx of calcium ions into the cells.
- **Phase 3** represents the final repolarization phase resulting in inactivation of the calcium channels and efflux of potassium ions out of the cell.
- **Phase 4** is the resting potential phase during which normal ion permeability is restored.

Phase 4 of the SA node demonstrates an increase in voltage secondary to the spontaneous influx of sodium and calcium into the SA node, which results in spontaneous diastolic depolarization. This repetitive diastolic depolarization enables the pacing function of the SA node. Note that normal ventricular muscle does not have this capability.

2. What are the components of an electrocardiogram (ECG) complex?

The ECG tracing is a recording of the summed electrical vectors produced during depolarization and repolarization of the heart. Electrical forces directed toward an electrode are represented as positive forces (upward deflections), whereas forces directed away from an electrode are represented as negative forces (downward deflections).

The standard representation of the cardiac cycle is seen in the ECG as the P wave, the QRS complex, and the T wave. These waves and complexes are separated by regularly occurring intervals.

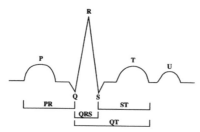

A single normal ECG cycle.

The **P wave** represents the atrial depolarization. The QRS complex represents the ventricular depolarization. The atrial repolarization is usually not seen because it occurs during the QRS complex. The **T wave** represents the repolarization of the ventricles. The **PR interval** represents the time required for an impulse to depolarize the atria, traverse the AV node, and enter the ventricular conduction system. The **QT interval** represents the duration of electrical systole and varies with heart rate. The **ST segment** represents the segment following ventricular depolarization and the preceding ventricular repolarization.

3. Who should have a preoperative 12-lead ECG?
   • Any patient older than 50 years or any patient older than 40 years when risk factors are present.
   • Any other patient who has signs or symptoms of cardiac disease
   • Patients with prior history of cardiac ischemia, dysrhythmias, or pacemaker placement

4. What disorders can be diagnosed perioperatively by the ECG?
   • Dysrhythmias
   • Conduction abnormalities (AV blocks, premature atrial contractions [PACs], premature ventricular contractions [PVCs])
   • Myocardial ischemia
   • Myocardial infarctions
   • Ventricular and atrial hypertrophy
   • Pacemaker function
   • Preexcitation (e.g., Wolff-Parkinson-White syndrome)
   • Drug toxicity (digitalis, antiarrhythmics, tricyclic antidepressants)
   • Electrolyte abnormalities (e.g., disturbances in calcium, potassium)
   • Various medical conditions (e.g., pericarditis, hypothermia, pulmonary emboli, cor pulmonale, cerebrovascular accidents, or increased intracranial pressure)

5. What potential risks may be associated with intraoperative ECG monitoring?
   If the patient is improperly grounded, shocks or burns could occur if the electrodes complete a short circuit. New ECG monitors have minimal risk secondary to patient isolation devices. Older ECG monitors lack these safety devices and may be hazardous.

6. What artifacts can alter the ECG monitor intraoperatively?
   Artifacts on the ECG monitor may lead to inaccurate diagnosis. The following conditions may produce artifacts on the ECG:
   1. Loose or misplaced ECG wires or electrodes

2. Improper electrode placement or adhesion (e.g., electrodes placed on hair or burned tissue, inadequate skin preparation, surgical scrub, loose electrodes, or use of dry electrode gel)

3. Motion (e.g., shivering, tremor, hiccuping, surgical preparation, or diaphragmatic movement)

4. Operating room (OR) equipment (e.g., electrocautery, cardiopulmonary bypass pump, OR lasers, irrigation/suction devices, evoked potential monitoring, and surgical drills and saws)

5. Patient contact by surgeons, nurses, or anesthesia personnel

7. How do you adequately prepare the skin for ECG electrode placement?

Proper skin preparation helps decrease ECG artifact and improve the signal quality for monitoring and diagnostic electrocardiography.

1. Gentle abrasion of the superficial epithelial layer with alcohol and cotton swabs over the intended area of electrode placement helps to decrease the skin resistance and improve adhesion of the electrodes.

2. Hairy skin should be shaved before placement of the skin electrodes to allow optimal adhesion and to decrease discomfort with electrode removal.

3. Wet and oily skin should be cleansed and allowed to dry before electrode placement.

4. Skin electrodes should be completely covered with water-resistant drapes if they are likely to be loosened by preparation solutions.

8. Where do you place the skin electrodes for a unipolar system (5-lead configuration)?

One electrode is placed on the **right shoulder**, one on the **left shoulder**, one on the **left hip area**, one on the **right hip area**, and the V_5 electrode in the **5th intercostal space in the left anterior axillary line**.

This 5-lead configuration allows the clinician to monitor seven different ECG leads (I, II, III, aVR, aVL, aVF, and V_5). Although many OR ECG monitors have only 3-lead systems, the 5-lead system is preferred because it enhances the extent of ECG monitoring possible. If only three leads are available, one can create modified bipolar limb leads to help diagnose specific abnormalities in question.

9. What two leads would you select as primary ECG monitors?

The usefulness of ECG leads in the operative setting was studied by London et al. More than 100 patients with known coronary artery disease were monitored for ischemia during anesthesia and surgery. They found that 75% of the ischemic events occurred in lead V_5. Combining leads V_4 and V_5 resulted in detection of approximately 85% of all the detected events. Lead II is usually best for monitoring P waves, enhancing diagnosis of dysrhythmias, and detecting inferior wall ischemia. Lead V_5 is most sensitive for detection of anterior and lateral ischemia. By monitoring leads II and V_5 simultaneously, the most information can be obtained.

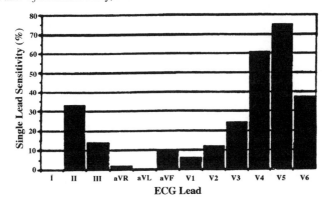

Sensitivity of ECG leads for detection of ischemic events. (From London MJ, Hollenberg M, Wong MG, et al: Intraoperative myocardial ischemia: Localization by continuous 12-lead electrocardiography. Anesthesiology 69:232–241, 1988, with permission.)

10. Which ECG leads monitor specific areas of myocardium?

Ischemia is usually detected as ST segment elevation or depression, T wave inversion, or development of Q waves in leads corresponding to the specific areas of myocardium.

Leads	Ischemia/Infarction
II, III, aVF	Inferior wall
I, aVL, V_4–V_6	Lateral wall
V_1–V_3	Anteroseptal
V_1–V_6	Anterolateral wall

11. What is the difference between diagnostic and monitoring modes for intraoperative electrocardiography?

The diagnostic mode uses ST segment and T wave analysis to diagnose ischemia accurately. The diagnostic mode filters out frequencies below 0.14 Hz but often results in excessive baseline drift and artifact.

The monitoring mode is used to filter out the baseline drift and artifact introduced in ECG signals. This mode filters out all frequencies below 4.0 Hz, which helps remove most of the OR interference. The monitoring mode can introduce artificial elevation and depression of the ST and T wave segments.

12. After orthotopic heart transplantation, what changes can be seen on the ECG tracing?

During orthotopic heart transplantation, the patient's original heart is removed except for the posterior walls of the atria for anastomosis to the donor heart. The patient's original SA node often remains with the original atria, and two P waves can be seen on ECG tracing.

BIBLIOGRAPHY

1. Dubin D: Rapid Interpretation of the EKGs, 4th ed. Tampa, FL, Cover, 1989.
2. Kaplan JA (ed): Cardiac Anesthesia, 4th ed. Philadelphia, W.B. Saunders, 1998.
3. Kotrly KJ, Kotter GS, Montana D, et al: Intraoperative detection of myocardial ischemia with an ST segment trend monitoring system. Anesth Analg 63:343–345, 1984.
4. London MJ, Hollenberg M, Wong MG, et al: Intraoperative myocardial ischemia: Localization by continuous 12-lead electrocardiography. Anesthesiology 69:232–241, 1988.
5. Marriott HJL: Practical Electrocardiography, 7th ed. Baltimore, Williams & Wilkins, 1983.
6. Rao TLK, Jacobs KH, El-Etr AA: Reinfarction following anesthesia in patients with myocardial infarction. Anesthesiology 59:499–505, 1983.
7. Slogoff S, Keats AS: Does perioperative myocardial ischemia lead to postoperative myocardial infarction? Anesthesiology 62:107–114, 1985.
8. Steen PA, Timber JH, Tarhan S: Myocardial reinfarction after anesthesia and surgery. JAMA 239:2566–2570, 1978.
9. Thys D, Hillel Z: Electrocardiography. In Miller RD (ed): Anesthesia, 4th ed. New York, Churchill Livingstone, 1994, pp 1229–1252.

23. PULSE OXIMETRY

Julian M. Goldman, M.D.

1. How does pulse oximetry work?

Pulse oximetry is a noninvasive method by which arterial oxygenation can be approximated. Pulse oximetry is based on the Beer-Lambert law and spectrophotometric analysis. The Beer-Lambert equation is as follows:

$$I_{trans} = I_{in}\, e^{-DCa}$$

where I_{trans} is the intensity of transmitted light, I_{in} is the intensity of the incident light, D is the distance that the light is transmitted through the medium, C is the concentration of the solute (hemoglobin), and the extinction coefficient "a" is a constant for a given solute at a specified wavelength.

Using two wavelengths of light, red at 660 nanometers (nm) and infrared at 940 nm, the changes in absorption of light shone through a pulsatile vascular bed are measured. Given a constant hemoglobin concentraton and light intensity, the oxygen saturation of hemoglobin becomes a logarithmic function of the absorption of light through the blood at the sight of the pulse oximeter probe (see Figure).

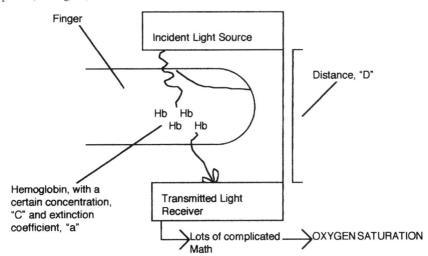

Schematic showing pulse oximetry in action: To understand the complicated math, please read Goldman JM, Souders J: Respiratory monitoring. In Kirby R, Gravenstein N (eds): Clinical Anesthesia Practice. Philadelphia, W.B. Saunders, 1994.[1]

2. How does one know that the color measured by the two lights is due to the color of the blood and not to the color of skin or other tissue?

Simple. With each systolic ejection of blood from the heart, the capillaries and adjacent vessels increase in volume so that less light from the light-emitting diodes (LEDs) passes through the finger tip. Therefore, the pulsatile component of the light transmission signal is detected by the pulse oximeter; the nonpulsatile components (including venous blood) are ignored. It is an elegant concept.

3. What is the normal SpO_2?

Saturation measured by pulse oximetry is denoted by SpO_2 ("p" is for pulse oximetry). Partial pressure of oxygen in arterial blood (PaO_2) and hence SpO_2 vary with age, altitude, and health. Identifying abnormal values is helpful for screening people for cardiopulmonary disease, but perioperative assessment of SpO_2 has a different motive. In general, the SpO_2 should be above the "cliff" of the oxyhemoglobin dissociation curve (see Figure, next page). At and below the cliff, which appears at a saturation of approximately 90%, a small decrease of PaO_2 results in swift desaturation. For example, on the steep part of curve, as PO_2 changes by 1 mmHg, SaO_2 changes by 3%. In the effort to keep the SpO_2 in the safe zone, supplemental oxygen is usually administered to patients who are receiving or recovering from general anesthesia.

4. Why is SpO_2 such a big deal?

One reason, of course, is that SpO_2 can be measured inexpensively and noninvasively. The second reason requires an understanding of oxygen carriage in the blood. The amount of oxygen

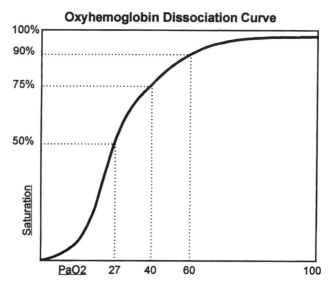

The oxyhemoglobin dissociation curve describes the nonlinear relationship between PaO_2 and percentage saturation of hemoglobin with oxygen (SaO_2). Note that in the steep part of the curve (50% region), small changes in PaO_2 result in large changes in SaO_2. The converse is true when PaO_2 rises above 60 mmHg. Three regions of the curve have been marked (see question 6).

carried by a sample of blood depends on the SaO_2 and hemoglobin concentration. If hemoglobin concentration remains constant, blood that is 50% saturated with oxygen binds one-half as much oxygen as a sample that is 100% saturated. Examination of the oxyhemoglobin dissociation curve tells the rest of the story, because it illustrates the nonlinear relationship between SaO_2 and PaO_2. For example, as PaO_2 increases from 60 mmHg to 100 mmHg, SaO_2 increases only about 6%. In contrast, as PaO_2 increases 33 mmHg, from 27 mmHg to 60 mmHg, SaO_2 increases by 25%.

5. Memorizing the entire oxyhemoglobin dissociation curve is difficult. Are there any tricks to remembering it?

Remember the following key values:

- The PaO_2 at which hemoglobin is 50% saturated, called the P50, is approximately 27 mmHg.
- The saturation of mixed venous blood (in the pulmonary artery) is about 75%, which occurs at a PO_2 of 40 mmHg.
- A PaO_2 of 30 mmHg produces 60% SaO_2, and a PaO_2 of 60 mmHg produces 90% SaO_2.
- A PaO_2 of 75 mmHg produces an SpO_2 of 95%.

6. Many anesthesiologists use the SpO_2 as an indicator of adequate preoxygenation. If the SpO_2 reaches 100% during preoxygenation, does this indicate complete denitrogenation?

No. Hemoglobin may be completely saturated with oxygen before complete pulmonary washout of nitrogen. Replacing all alveolar nitrogen with oxygen provides a depot of oxygen that might be necessary should mask ventilation or intubation prove difficult.

7. The SpO_2 has not risen to 100% despite preoxygenation. What does this mean?

If the SpO_2 has not reached 100% after 2–5 minutes of breathing pure O_2, the patient probably has serious ventilation-perfusion abnormalities (venous admixture or pulmonary shunt). Even complete preoxygenation may not increase SpO_2 to 100% in the presence of pulmonary shunt, because blood that bypasses the alveoli cannot be oxygenated. Before invoking such esoteric explanations, make sure that the probe is well situated on the finger and the patient has a good mask fit and sufficient fresh gas flow to prevent a reduction of inspired O_2 concentration by entrainment of room air.

8. Do carboxyhemoglobin and methemoglobin interfere with obtaining accurate pulse oximetry measurements?

Yes. Just as the patient with carboxyhemoglobin toxicity exhibits the classic cherry red appearance, the pulse oximeter sees carboxyhemoglobin as oxyhemoglobin. Thus oxygenation is overestimated. Therefore, in a victim of smoke inhalation oxygenation should be assessed by arterial blood gas analysis—not pulse oximetry.

The influence of methemoglobinemia on SpO_2 readings is a bit more complicated. At the two wavelengths of light measured, methemoglobin absorbs light about equally. The ratio of absorbances would then approximate 1. The algorithms for estimating SpO_2 would interpret a ratio of 1 as a saturation of about 85%.

9. The saturation plummets after injection of methylene blue. Is the monitor or the patient desaturating?

Methylene blue fools the pulse oximeter into thinking that more reduced hemoglobin is present. The apparent SpO_2 returns to normal within a few minutes.

10. After a struggle to secure the patient's airway, the lungs are ventilated, but the saturation still decreases! What should be done next?

It takes time for O_2 delivered to the lung to influence oxygenation at the fingertip. If the lungs are in fact ventilated (a capnograph can be used for verification), the SpO_2 should rise within approximately 20 seconds. Pulse oximeter signals are also averaged over different periods of time. The benefit is a reduction in spurious pulse oximeter readings, such as those caused by patient movement. The trade-off is that true reductions in pulse oximeter readings are delayed (a patient desaturating faster than the pulse oximeter indicates). Similarly, once adequate delivery of oxygen is restored, there will be a delay in recovery of the pulse oximeter readings. The period of signal averaging can often be changed in commonly used pulse oximeters.

11. What is the appropriate technique to obtain pulse oximetry readings in a cold, shivering patient?

Cold implies vasoconstriction. It is difficult to get an acceptable SpO_2 reading with a small plethysmographic pulsation (i.e., small signal) and lots of movement (i.e., noise). Try warming the patient or applying the probe to a site with better perfusion (earlobe). A digital nerve block improves finger perfusion and facilitates obtaining a reading, but it is a bit extreme. The next generation of pulse oximeters will perform much better under such conditions. Of course, if one cannot get a reliable reading, one cannot chart SpO_2 values.

12. How could pulse oximter technology be improved?

The effects of patient movement and extraneous noise could be lessened. The effects on pulse oximetry by abnormal hemoglobin species could also be taken into account. This might be accomplished by measuring light absorption at more than two wavelengths of light (the current technology). In fact, future pulse oximeters will have technology to decrease technology and estimate carboxyhemoglobin and methemoglobin fractions. Regular preoperative determination of carboxyhemoglobin in smokers may well prove illuminating to caregivers.

BIBLIOGRAPHY

1. Goldman JM, Souders J: Respiratory monitoring. In Kirby R, Gravenstein N (eds): Clinical Anesthesia Practice. Philadelphia, W. B. Saunders, 1994.
2. Nunn JF: Nunn's Applied Respiratory Physiology, 4th ed. Oxford, Butterworth-Heinemann, 1993.

24. CAPNOGRAPHY

Julian M. Goldman, M.D.

1. What is capnography?

The term *capnography* derives from *kapnos*, which means "smoke" in Greek. Capnography is the commonly used, catchall term for measuring and displaying the carbon dioxide concentration of expired and inspired gases. The gas is usually sampled at the connector-end of the tracheal tube, the Y-piece, or the mask or from nasal cannulas. The tracheal tube or Y-piece provides a more reliable sample than the mask or nasal cannula for measuring exhaled CO_2 concentration and evaluating the waveform.

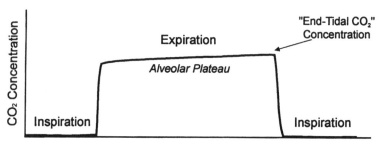

A normal capnogram has the following characteristics: the CO_2 concentration is zero during inspiration, it rises abruptly during expiration, and the alveolar plateau is flat or slightly upsloping. The highest CO_2 concentration is achieved at the end of exhalation and is called the end-tidal CO_2.

2. Why all the fuss about CO_2? What exactly can it tell us?

To get the most out of capnography, we must think about the chain of events required to generate a normal capnogram:

1. The body tissues must generate CO_2.
2. Blood must carry the CO_2 to the lungs.
3. CO_2-containing gas must be exhaled from the lungs and sampled at the mouth or tracheal tube.
4. The capnograph and its sampling line or detector must be in working order.
5. Another CO_2-free inhalation must come along to clear the previously exhaled CO_2 from the sample site.

When CO_2 is exhaled for several breaths in a row (about 5–7), we can be fairly certain that the heart is pumping blood, that ventilating gas is reaching the alveoli and being exhaled, and that the capnograph is functional. An abnormal capnogram may indicate a problem at any point in the chain.

3. Is it possible to see exhaled CO_2 after accidental intubation of the esophagus?

Carbonated beverages or medications (e.g., Alka-Seltzer) would return CO_2 after esophageal intubation. However, usual CO_2 values and waveform would not be expected, and the CO_2 would likely exhaust quickly. Some CO_2 can also reach the stomach if mask ventilation is suboptimal.

4. Can interpreting the shape of the capnogram be as informative as interpreting the electrocardiogram (ECG)?

For some people, the capnograph is much more informative. In general, ECG reading is like bird watching—pure pattern recognition. In contrast, the phenomena that contribute to generating the capnogram are easy to understand, and their effects can be identified as changes in the capnogram.

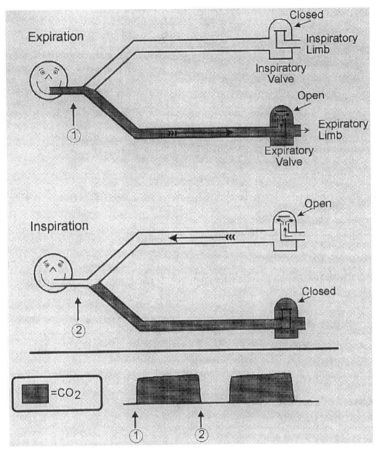

Generation of the capnogram. The capnogram represents the CO_2 concentration at the Y-piece. 1. **Expiration**. CO_2 is present at the Y-piece. Although expiratory gas flow stops at the end of expiration once the lungs have emptied, the capnogram remains elevated because CO_2-containing gas sits in the Y-piece until the next inspiration. 2. **Inspiration**. No CO_2 is present at the Y-piece.

5. Immediately after intubation of the trachea, the capnograph displays a CO_2 concentration of zero. What is the next step?

1. Consider the possibilities:
   - There is no pulmonary blood flow (e.g., cardiac arrest or huge pulmonary embolus)
   - There is no tidal ventilation (e.g., faulty circuit, severe asthma)
   - There is a problem with the capnograph or sampling line.
   - The tracheal tube is not actually in the trachea.
2. Tips for developing the diagnostic and therapeutic plan:
   - Did the tracheal tube pass through the vocal cords? An experienced laryngoscopist usually knows from observation of the initial insertion. Another quick look may be wise.
   - Rule out cardiac arrest by placing a finger on the carotid artery to check for a pulse or by glancing at the pulse oximeter waveform.
   - Assessing the performance of the capnograph is simple: disconnect the sampling line and exhale on it. If it does not register CO_2, the problem is in the instrument. If

CO$_2$ was detected during mask ventilation, this would also suggest the monitor was functioning.

- If (1) the patient has a pulse, (2) the capnograph works, (3) the clinical likelihood of severe acute pulmonary embolism is remote, (4) physical exam rules out airway obstruction, (5) the patient is cyanotic, and (6) the saturation continues to plummet, the tracheal tube probably did not go through the vocal cords. Consider performing another direct laryngoscopy or removing the tracheal tube and ventilating the patient's lungs with a mask.

6. The baseline of the capnogram is elevated. What are the possible causes?

The baseline of the capnogram may not return to zero at high respiratory rates with some capnographs. However, if the baseline is significantly elevated (above approximately 2 mmHg CO$_2$), the patient is receiving CO$_2$ during inspiration. Possible sources for the inspired CO$_2$ include:

1. An exhausted CO$_2$ absorber
2. An incompetent unidirectional inspiratory or expiratory valve
3. Deliberate or inadvertent administration of CO$_2$ from a CO$_2$-equipped anesthesia machine

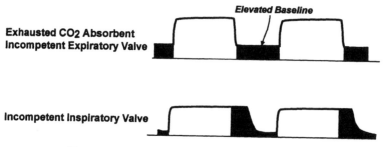

The above capnograms illustrate rebreathing of previously exhaled CO$_2$, which results in elevation of arterial CO$_2$ and exhaled CO$_2$ concentrations. Shaded areas represent CO$_2$ present during inspiration. Note that the CO$_2$ contributed by the exhausted CO$_2$ absorbent or incompetent expiratory valve mixes with CO$_2$-free inspiratory gas at the Y-piece and elevates the inspiratory CO$_2$ concentration by a relatively constant amount. In contrast, when the inspiratory valve is incompetent, exhaled CO$_2$-containing gas flows (backward) into the inspiratory limb. During inspiration this previously exhaled CO$_2$ must flow back into the patient. As the CO$_2$-laden gas passes the Y-piece during inspiration, it registers on the capnograph. The capnogram finally drops to zero after all previously exhaled gas is rebreathed, and fresh gas appears at the Y-piece.

7. What other equipment problems can be detected by examining the capnogram?

A gas leak around a partially deflated tracheal tube cuff produces an abnormal capnogram. A kinked or partially obstructed tracheal tube delays expiration and produces a delayed rise of the capnogram.

8. What other patient problems can be identified by the capnogram?

Many respiratory diseases affect ventilation-perfusion matching and expiratory gas flow. Consequently, such diseases may produce abnormal capnograms. For example, asthma and chronic obstructive pulmonary diseases cause a delayed upslope and steep alveolar plateau (see Figure, next page). Pulmonary hypoperfusion, as in systemic hypotension or pulmonary embolism, decreases CO$_2$ excretion and reduces the end-tidal CO$_2$. However, the capnogram should still have a normal shape.

A commonly seen abnormal capnogram results when the patient makes spontaneous respiratory efforts and inhales before the next mechanical inspiration. This characteristic "cleft" in the alveolar plateau is a useful clinical sign that the patient has started to breathe.

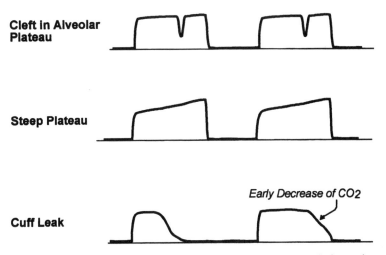

Cleft in Alveolar Plateau

Steep Plateau

Early Decrease of CO2

Cuff Leak

Several abnormal capnograms. The early decrease of CO_2 concentration due to a leak past the tracheal tube cuff is variable. In general, the larger the leak, the earlier the capnogram begins to taper off. This pattern is also evident during mask ventilation with a loose-fitting mask.

BIBLIOGRAPHY

1. Goldman JM, Souders J: Respiratory monitoring. In Kirby R, Gravenstein N (eds): Clinical Anesthesia Practice. Philadelphia, W.B. Saunders, 1994.
2. Gravenstein JS, Paulus DA, Hayes TJ: Capnography in Clinical Practice. Stoneham, MA, Butterworth-Heinemann, 1989.
3. Nunn JF: Nunn's Applied Respiratory Physiology, 4th ed. Oxford, Butterworth-Heinemann, 1993.

25. MONITORING NEUROMUSCULAR FUNCTION

Theresa L. Kinnard, M.D.

1. Describe the anatomy of the neuromuscular junction (NMJ).

The NMJ is composed of a motor nerve ending separated from a highly folded membrane of skeletal muscle (populated with acetylcholine [ACh] receptors) by a synaptic cleft. The synaptic cleft is filled with extracellular fluid and the enzyme acetylcholinesterase. The NMJ transmits the action potential from the nerve to depolarize the muscle and produce muscle contraction. (See Figure, next page.)

2. Name the steps involved in normal neuromuscular transmission.

1. A nerve action potential is transmitted, and the nerve terminal is depolarized.
2. ACh is released from storage vesicles at the terminal.
3. Two ACh molecules bind to the ACh receptor, generating a conformational change.
4. Sodium, potassium, and calcium ions flow down their concentration gradients and through the receptor channel generating an end-plate potential.
5. When between 5% and 20% of the receptor channels are open and a threshold potential is reached, a muscle action potential (MAP) is generated.
6. Propagation of the MAP along the muscle membrane leads to muscle contraction.

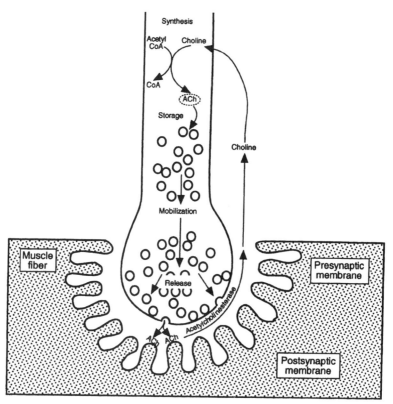

The neuromuscular junction. (From Lebowitz PW, Ramsey FM: Muscle relaxants. In Barash PG, Cullen BF, Stoelting RK (eds): Clinical Anesthesia. Philadelphia, J.B. Lippincott, 1989, pp 339–370, with permission.)

3. What is the structure of the ACh receptor?

The ACh receptor consists of five glycoprotein subunits: two alpha and one each of beta, delta, and epsilon. The receptor is contained within the membrane.

4. Where are the ACh receptors located?

The ACh receptors, also referred to as nicotinic cholinergic receptors, can be found in several areas:

1. Postjunctional receptors are located on the postjunctional muscle membrane in large numbers, approximately 5 million ACh receptors per NMJ.

2. Prejunctional receptors are present on the motor nerve endings and influence the release of ACh. The prejunctional and postjunctional receptors have different binding characteristics (affinity for ACh).

3. Extrajunctional receptors are located throughout the skeletal muscle in relatively low numbers owing to suppression of their synthesis by normal neural activity. In cases of traumatized skeletal muscle or denervation injuries, these receptors proliferate.

5. What is the mode of action of muscle relaxants?

Muscle relaxants block transmission of nerve impulses at the NMJ. **Nondepolarizing muscle relaxants** (NDMR) bind competitively to the ACh receptor, preventing released ACh from binding to the receptor. They may also work by binding to the prejunctional receptors, modulating ACh release.

Depolarizing muscle relaxants (DMR) behave similarly to ACH in that they bind to the ACh receptor and depolarize the postsynaptic membrane at the NMJ. This action produces the characteristic muscle fasciculations of a depolarizing block. The DMR are not hydrolyzed by the acetylcholinesterase present at the junction; thus, they hold the channel open for an extended period of time, rendering the muscle flaccid.

6. Why monitor neuromuscular function?

Monitoring neuromuscular function can aid in the delivery of a correct dose of muscle relaxant, help detect patients who are sensitive to muscle relaxants, and help assess adequate neuromuscular recovery. Relying on standard pharmacokinetic data in dosing muscle relaxants is unreliable because of great patient-to-patient variability.

7. How is neuromuscular function monitored?

Assessments of strength, including hand grip, head lift, tidal volume, vital capacity, and inspiratory pressure have all been used in predicting adequate neuromuscular function. In patients under general anesthesia, the measurement of these variables is often not possible, or their values may be affected by other centrally acting anesthetic agents. The most reliable method of monitoring neuromuscular function uses a portable nerve stimulator to stimulate a peripheral motor nerve and measures the response of the skeletal muscle innervated by that nerve. The stimulus is usually delivered to the nerve via surface electrodes, although needle electrodes have been used in obese patients or experimental situations.

8. What are the common methods of measuring the response of the muscle to stimulation?

The two most common methods of measuring response are mechanomyography and electromyography. **Mechanomyography** measures the contractile responses of the whole muscle to stimulation. Force transducers have been used to make quantitative measurements. In clinical practice, visual or tactile assessment of motor activity is the most commonly used method. **Electromyography** measures the electrical activity associated with the propagation of an action potential in muscle cells. Measurement of the amplified electromyographic signal is related to the number of contracting muscle fibers. This method is not widely used clinically.

9. Which nerves can be chosen for stimulation?

The most common nerve stimulated is the ulnar nerve. The ulnar nerve supplies several hand muscles, including the adductor pollicis muscle. This muscle adducts the thumb at the metacarpophalangeal joint. The contraction of this muscle is most commonly monitored when evaluating the effects of muscle relaxants. It is crucial to monitor the response of the thumb because response of the other fingers may be due to direct stimulation of muscle groups of the hand. The ophthalmic branch of the facial nerve may also be stimulated, monitoring the contraction of the orbicularis oculi muscle. When access to the head and arms is difficult, the peroneal nerve or posterior tibial nerve of the leg can be stimulated. The degree of dorsiflexion of the foot and plantar flexion of the big toe are monitored.

10. Where should the stimulating electrodes be placed on the skin?

There is both a positive and a negative electrode to the nerve stimulator. A negative (black) electrode generates its action potential by depolarizing the membrane. Depolarization, versus hyperpolarization (produced by the positive electrode), makes it easier to stimulate the nerve. Therefore, maximal twitch height occurs when the negative electrode is placed in closest proximity to the nerve. Stimulation is also possible, however, if the positive electrode is placed close to the nerve.

11. Does it make a difference which nerve-muscle is monitored?

Different muscles have different sensitivities to muscle relaxants.

MUSCLE	SENSITIVITY
Vocal cord	Most resistant
Diaphragm	
Orbicularis oculi	
Abdominal rectus	
Adductor pollicis	
Masseter	
Pharyngeal	
Extraocular	Most sensitive

From Rupp SM: Monitoring neuromuscular blockade—twitch monitoring. Anesthesiol Clin North Am 11:361, 1993, with permission.

The fact that a patient is no longer breathing does not mean that he or she is ready to intubate (control of breathing is a complex process). If we attempt intubation based on when a patient becomes apneic, the patient may cough or move because of the relative resistance of the vocal cords and diaphragm to muscle relaxants.

12. Discuss important characteristics of a nerve stimulator.

The stimulator chosen should be able to deliver impulses of 0.1–0.3 milliseconds' (ms) duration to prevent repetitive firing of the nerve. A supramaximal current output of 50–60 mA at all frequencies should be able to be delivered; this would guarantee that all nerve fibers depolarize with stimulation. The pulse waveform generated should be a monophasic square wave, delivering constant current for a specified interval. It should be capable of delivering single-twitch stimulation at 0.1 Hz (1 stimulus every 10 seconds), train of four (TOF) at 2 Hz (2 per second), and tetanic stimulation at 50 Hz (50 per second).

13. What are the different patterns of stimulation and their clinical applicability?

Single stimulus. The simplest mode of stimulation consists of the delivery of single impulses separated by at least 10 seconds (0.1 Hz). Clinically the use of this stimulus is limited owing to the necessity of establishing a baseline response. The single-stimulus response is used when comparing effective doses of muscle relaxants, for instance, the ED 95 of a muscle relaxant is the effective dose for 95% single-twitch suppression of thumb adduction.

Train of four. A stimulus delivered at a frequency fo 2 Hz (2 per second) for a total of four stimuli is known as TOF. Each train is repeated every 10 seconds. The ratio of the amplitude of the fourth to the first response in a train permits the estimation of the degree of block without the need for a control stimulus (T4:T1 ratio). TOF stimulation is the most common modality used to assess degree of blockade. It causes significantly less discomfort in the awake patient than tetanic stimulation and does not affect the subsequent responses to a stimulus. During the onset of neuromuscular blockade, the fourth twitch in the TOF is eliminated at approximately 75% depression of the first twitch. The third twitch is abolished at 80% suppression of the first twitch, and the second twitch is abolished at about 90% block of the first twitch.

Tetanus. Tetanic stimulation consists of repetitive, high-frequency stimulation at frequencies of 50 Hz or greater. Higher frequency stimulation (100 Hz) has been shown to produce fade in the absence of neuromuscular blocking agents owing to depletion of ACh at the NMJ. The response to tetanus is a more sensitive indicator of residual neuromuscular blockade than single twitch. An important consideration in applying a tetanic stimulus is that it changes the response of the NMJ to further stimulation for upward of 30 minutes, thus leading to overestimation of neuromuscular function on further testing. Clinically, a tetanic stimulus is painful to apply in an awake patient, and it is best used in the context of post-tetanic count.

Post-tetanic facilitation and post-tetanic count. This mode of stimulation is useful during periods of intense neuromuscular blockade (when there is no response to TOF stimulation) and extends our range of monitoring. It provides an indication as to when recovery of a single twitch is anticipated and, hence, when reversal of neuromuscular blockade is possible. An application of a 50-Hz stimulus for 5 seconds is followed in 3 seconds by single twitches at 1 Hz. The number of twitches observed is inversely related to the degree of blockade. The number of twitches also may be related to the time until the return of the first response in the TOF.

Double burst. The most recently introduced mode of stimulation that appears to be more sensitive than TOF stimulation for detecting small degrees of residual neuromuscular blockade is double burst. This type of stimulation involves the application of an initial burst of three 0.2-ms impulses at 50 Hz followed by an identical stimulation in 750 ms.[7] The magnitude of the responses to double burst is approximately 3 times greater than that of TOF stimulation, thus making it easier to assess degree of fade present. This method has not gained wide usage.

14. What are the characteristic responses to the various patterns of stimulation produced by nondepolarizing agents and depolarizing agents?

In the presence of an NDMR, repetitive stimulation (TOF or tetanus) is associated with fade of the muscle response. The other distinguishing feature of an NDMR blockade is the presence of posttetanic faciliation. Following a tetanic stimulus, the response to subsequent stimulations is increased. This is thought to be due to increased ACh release or increased sensitivity at the end plate.

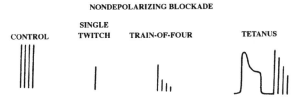

Response to NDMR blockade. (From Bevan DR, Bevan JC, Donati F: Muscle Relaxants in Clinical Anesthesia. Chicago, Year Book Medical Publishers, 1988, pp 49–70, with permission.)

DMR blockade does not exhibit fade in response to repetitive stimuli (TOF and tetanus). It also does not exhibit post-tetanic facilitation. The single-twitch, TOF, and tetanus amplitudes are uniformly decreased in relation to the degree of blockade present. A phase II depolarizing or desensitization block (present with large doses of succinylcholine, over 2 mg/kg) exhibits the same characteristics as an NDMR blockade.

DEPOLARIZING BLOCKADE

Response to DMR blockade. (From Bevan DR, Bevan JC, Donati F: Muscle Relaxants in Clinical Anesthesia. Chicago, Year Book Medical Publishers, 1988, pp 49–70, with permission.)

15. Which responses to stimulation indicate adequate relaxation (blockade)?

The degree of neuromuscular blockade required for a surgical procedure varies greatly, depending on the type of surgery, amount of inhalational agent administered, coexisting disease, medications, and musculature of the patient. Adequate relaxation is generally present when one to two twitches of the TOF response are present, correlating with 80% depression of single-twitch height. To ensure paralysis of the more resistant muscle groups, there should be no response to post-tetanic stimulation.

16. How does the response obtained to various patterns of stimulation correlate with the actual percentage of receptors occupied?

The response to single twitch is not reduced until approximately 75% of receptors are occupied, and the response disappears at 90–95% occupancy. The fourth twitch of the TOF disappears when there are 75–80% of the receptors occupied, the third twitch disappears at 85% occupancy, the second twitch disappears at 85–90% occupancy, and the first twitch disappears at 90–95% occupancy.[13] Sustained tetanus at 50 Hz can be present when up to 75% of receptors are occupied.

17. What results of neuromuscular stimulation indicate adequate muscle relaxant reversal?

Neuromuscular blockade can be reversed when the response to TOF stimulation is at least one twitch and preferably more. No tetanic stimulus should have been applied in the previous 10 minutes. TOF ratio of greater than 0.7 and sustained tetanus at 50 Hz correlate with restoration of neuromuscular function (ability to protect the airway and maintain respiratory function). Unfortunately, the tactile evaluation of fade in TOF and tetanus can be unreliable even in experienced hands. This has led to the development of double-burst stimulation. With the strength of the contractions greater than in TOF, tactile evaluation of the response to double burst appears to be more reliable.

18. What clinical and respiratory parameters correlate with the restoration of neuromuscular function?

An adequate tidal volume is the most insensitive indicator of adequate strength (80% of receptors may still be occupied). The most sensitive respiratory parameter is inspiratory force (50% receptor occupancy) and of intermediate sensitivity is the vital capacity. A negative inspiratory force of –50 cm H_2O is thought to correlate with airway protection and adequate reversal of neuromuscular blockade.[2] The ability to sustain a head lift for 5 seconds and hand grasp are the most sensitive tests of adequate strength (33% receptor occupancy).

19. Which drugs or clinical conditions can prolong neuromuscular blockade?
- Respiratory acidosis
- Metabolic alkalosis
- Hypothermia
- Hypokalemia
- Hypercalcemia
- Hypermagnesemia
- Administration of certain antibiotics such as streptomycin, polymyxin, or neomycin

Cocaine, procaine, lidocaine, and etidocaine have also been shown to have neuromuscular blocking properties. Prolonged blockade has also been shown following lithium therapy owing to its hypokalemic effect. Corticosteroids have been found to have a potentiating effect on neuromuscular blockade. Patients with impaired hepatic or renal function may exhibit increased sensitivity to muscle relaxants depending on their mode of elimination. An important interaction to remember is the potentiation of neuromuscular blockade in the presence of inhaled anesthetics.

20. Which drugs or clinical conditions are associated with resistance to neuromuscular blockade?

1. Antiepileptic drugs tend to shorten the duration of action of neuromuscular blockade drugs.

2. Long-term phenytoin therapy has been shown to shorten the duration of long-acting muscle relaxant blockade by 50%.

3. Patients with burns exhibit resistance to NDMR and sensitivity to succinylcholine with a hyperkalemic response.

21. What is the response to neuromuscular blockade drugs in patients with neuromuscular disease?

Patients with myotonic syndromes exhibit delayed muscle relaxation following contraction. Succinylcholine can induce severe contractions and should be avoided. The response to NDMR blockade in these patients is normal. The patient with myasthenia gravis tends to be extremely sensitive to NDMR blockade and resistant to DMR blockade. Patients with lower motor neuron disorders are sensitive to NDMR blockade and may show marked hyperkalemia in response to succinylcholine. Hemiplegia has been associated with resistance to NDMR, when neuromuscular transmission is monitored on the affected side, and with hyperkalemia in response to succinyl-choline. According to a theory by Brown and Charlton, the level of neurologic lesion determines the response of the NMJ to stimulation.[6] Intracranial lesions cause resistance to muscle relaxants, and spinal cord lesions tend to cause increased sensitivity.

BIBLIOGRAPHY

1. Ali HH: Monitoring of neuromuscular function. In Katz L (ed): Muscle Relaxants: Basic and Clinical Aspects. Orlando, Grune & Stratton, 1985, pp 53–68.
2. Ali HH, Wilson RS, Savarese JJ, et al: The effect of tubocurarine on indirectly elicited train-of-four muscle response and respiratory measurements in humans. Br J Anaesth 47:570–573, 1975.
3. Azar I: Complications of neuromuscular blockers. Anesthesiol Clin North Am 11:379–389, 1993.
4. Berger JJ, Gravenstein JS, Munson ES: Electrode polarity and peripheral nerve stimulation. Anesthesiology 56:402–404, 1982.
5. Bevan DR, Bevan JC, Donati F: Muscle Relaxants in Clinical Anesthesia. Chicago, Year Book, 1988, pp 49–70.
6. Bevan DR, Donati F: Muscle relaxants. In Barash PG, Cullen BF, Stoelting RK (eds): Clinical Anesthesia, 3rd ed. Philadelphia, Lippincott Williams & Wilkins, 1997.
7. Brown JC, Charlton JE: A sensitivity to curare in certain neurological disorders using a regional technique. J Neurol Neurosurg Psychiatry 38:34–39, 1975.
8. Engbaek J, Ostergaard D, Viby-Mogensen J: Double burst stimulation (DBS). A new pattern of nerve stimulation to identify residual neuromuscular block. Br J Anaesth 62:274–278, 1989.
9. Patane PS, Condon BF: Neuromuscular blocking agents and trauma patients. Am J Anesthiol 22:13–22, 1995.
10. Pavlin EG: Clinical tests of recovery from neuromuscular blocking agents. Anesthesiol Clin North Am 11:379–389, 1993.
11. Rupp SM: Monitoring neuromuscular blockade—twitch monitoring. Anesthesiol Clin North Am 11:361–378, 1993.
12. Siverman DG, Brull SJ: Monitoring neuromuscular block. Anesthesiol Clin North Am 12:237–260, 1994.
13. Waud BE, Waud DR: The relation between the response to "train-of-four" stimulation and receptor occlusion during competitive neuromuscular block. Anesthesiology 37:413–416, 1972.

26. CENTRAL VENOUS CATHETERIZATION AND PRESSURE MONITORING

Lyle E. Kirson, D.D.S.

1. What is central venous catheterization?

Central venous catheterization involves inserting a catheter into the venous circulation and advancing it so that its distal orifice is positioned immediately adjacent to, or within, the right atrium of the heart (see Figure, next page). The catheter is introduced into the venous circulation from one of several venous access points.

2. What is central venous pressure?

Central venous pressure refers to the hydrostatic pressure generated by the blood within either the right atrium of the heart or the great veins of the thorax at a point immediately adjacent to the right atrium of the heart.

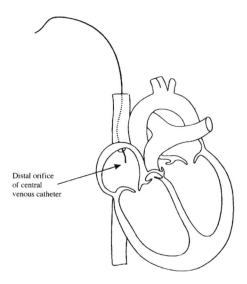

Distal orifice
of central
venous catheter

3. How is central venous pressure measured?

The proximal orifice of the central venous catheter is attached to a fluid-filled manometer. The pressure at the distal orifice is transmitted through the fluid path within the catheter and supports the fluid column within the manometer. If the base of the fluid column is placed at the level of the heart, then the height of the fluid column represents the pressure at the distal orifice of the catheter, the central venous pressure.

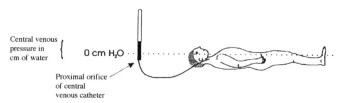

Central venous
pressure in
cm of water

0 cm H_2O

Proximal orifice
of central
venous catheter

In the past, central venous pressure was measured by connecting the catheter to a water manometer and reading the pressure in centimeters (cm) of water. Today, it is more common to attach the catheter to a pressure transducer. The transducer converts the pressure generated at the distal orifice of the catheter into an electrical signal that is then displayed in torr or millimeters of mercury (mmHg) on a real-time display screen. The use of a transducer is more convenient than the manometer and has the added capability of displaying the central venous pressure waveform on the display screen. The waveform provides additional information to the clinician regarding the patient's cardiac function (see question 19). As with a water manometer, the pressure transducer must be positioned at the level of the heart in order to obtain consistently accurate pressure measurements.

4. How is central venous pressure regulated?

Central venous pressure is regulated by a balance between two factors: the volume of blood returning to the heart from the systemic circulation and the ability of the right ventricle to pump the returning blood through the pulmonary circulation.[7] Any physiologic process or event that affects either of these two factors will alter the balance between the two factors and may vary the central venous pressure.[8] Vasodilatation, hemorrhage, fluid infusion, alterations in local tissue metabolism, myocardial ischemia, or changes in sympathetic stimulation of the heart can all alter this balance.

5. At what point on the body should central venous pressure be measured?

The ideal point at which to measure central venous pressure is at the level of the tricuspid valve. It is at this point that, in the healthy heart, hydrostatic pressures caused by changes in body position are almost zero. This phenomenon exists because as the pressure at the tricuspid valve increases from the position change, the right ventricle will fill to a greater degree, right ventricular cardiac output will transiently increase, and the change in pressure at the tricuspid valve will be brought back toward zero. The opposite will occur if pressure at the tricuspid valve decreases.[7]

It is of course difficult to consistently find the precise level of the tricuspid valve in a clinical setting. Therefore, ongoing adjustment is necessary to ensure that the transducer or manometer is at a constant reference point whenever the patient's position or bed height is altered.

6. How does central venous pressure relate to right ventricular preload?

Central venous pressure reflects the preload for the right ventricle. While preload is more accurately defined as the right ventricular end-diastolic volume (RVEDV), RVEDV cannot be easily monitored clinically. Therefore, central venous pressure is the best indicator of right atrial preload currently available to the clinician. Preload is often used to guide the clinician in intravenous fluid replacement. A low or decreasing preload may indicate a need for intravenous fluid administration. An increasing or elevated preload (above 15 mmHg) may indicate over-resuscitation or impaired cardiac performance.

7. Does central venous pressure relate to left ventricular preload?

Central venous pressure is representative of **right** ventricular preload only. It is possible that, in patients whose left and right ventricles are functioning identically, central venous pressure equals or parallels the preload for the **left** ventricle. However, in patients with pulmonary hypertension, pulmonary disease, or right or left ventricular damage, a pulmonary artery catheter provides better information with regard to left ventricular preload than does a central venous catheter.

8. Is there a single normal central venous pressure reading?

There is no single central venous pressure that is normal for all patients, or for that matter, for any individual patient. Measurements may range from 1 to 15 mmHg and depend on the patient's stage of hydration, presence or absence of positive pressure ventilation, position, cardiac function, and chamber compliance. Use several clinical signs (signs of hydration, urine output, blood pressure, etc.) to determine the appropriate range of central venous pressure for any one individual patient.

9. What are the indications for placement of a central venous catheter?

There are perioperative and nonoperative indications for central venous catheterization.
Perioperative indications include:
1. Guiding fluid replacement
2. Evaluating cardiac function
3. Providing access for:
    a. aspiration of air emboli that can occur during neurosurgical procedures
    b. drug infusion
    c. blood and fluid infusion
    d. introduction of a pulmonary artery catheter or transvenous pacer
    e. blood sampling
Nonoperative indications include providing access for:
1. Hyperalimentation
2. Temporary hemodialysis
3. Long-term chemotherapy
4. Frequent therapeutic plasmapheresis[1]

10. Describe several approaches to introduction of the central venous catheter into the venous circulation.

Numerous access points are available for introduction of a catheter into the venous circulation. All approaches carry risks, and none will work successfully for every single patient. Therefore, it is recommended that the clinician become familiar with several different approaches.

The following approaches require that the patient be placed in Trendelenburg position prior to venous puncture. Placing the access point below the level of the heart distends the target vessel and promotes positive venous pressure within the vessel.

As the needle is advanced toward a vessel, slight and constant aspiration is required. However, it is possible that during needle penetration, the vessel walls will collapse upon themselves, allowing the needle to pass through the vessel without demonstrating blood aspiration. Therefore, if blood is not aspirated as the needle is advanced, aspiration should be maintained as the needle is slowly withdrawn.

Finally, be familiar with the anatomy surrounding the vessel and needle puncture site. Advancing the introducer needle too far or in the wrong direction can injure adjacent structures.

The most common approaches to the central venous circulation are:

1. **Subclavian vein.** The subclavian approach is commonly used in the operating room and for quick access in emergency room settings because of the ease of access to the vessel. The subclavian vein is best cannulated from the subclavicular approach. The skin puncture is made just lateral to the costoclavicular ligament, one fingerwidth below the clavicle. The needle is directed along the posterior border of the clavicle in the direction of the sternal notch until the subclavian vein is entered and blood is aspirated.

2. **Internal jugular vein.** There are several approaches to the internal jugular vein, three of which are briefly described here.

• *Low anterior.* Locate the point at which the sternal and clavicular heads of the sternocleidomastoid muscle join. Introduce the needle at this point and direct it at an angle of 30° to the skin. Advance the needle toward the ipsilateral nipple until the internal jugular vein is entered and blood is aspirated.

• *High anterior.* Palpate the carotid artery at the level of the cricothyroid membrane. Introduce the needle just lateral to the carotid pulsation and advance it toward the ipsilateral nipple at a 30° angle to the skin until the internal jugular vein is entered and blood is aspirated. This approach frequently requires penetration of the body of the sternocleidomastoid muscle by the introducer needle.

• *Posterior.* Locate the junction of the posterior border of the sternocleidomastoid muscle and the external jugular vein. Introduce the needle just posterior to this point, and advance it along the deep surface of the muscle toward the ipsilateral corner of the sternal notch until the internal jugular vein is entered and blood is aspirated.

3. **External jugular vein.** When the patient is in Trendelenburg position, the external jugular vein frequently can be visualized where it crosses the sternocleidomastoid muscle. The needle is advanced in a direction paralleling the vessel and introduced into the vein approximately two fingerwidths below the inferior border of the mandible. **Warning:** Difficulty may arise in advancing the catheter or guide wire into the central circulation from the external jugular vein approach because the patient's anatomy frequently directs the catheter into the subclavian vein.

11. Describe the different techniques for introducing the central venous catheter into the venous circulation.

The two most common techniques for introducing a central venous catheter into the venous circulation are passing the catheter through a needle or passing the catheter over a guide wire. In the former, a 14-gauge needle is introduced into the vessel, and the catheter is then threaded through the needle and into the vein. The needle is then removed. In the latter, commonly referred to as the Seldinger technique (named after the individual who first described this technique for arterial catheterization in 1953),[15] an 18- or 20-gauge needle is introduced into the vessel. A guide wire is threaded through the needle and into the vein. The needle is removed, leaving the guide wire in place. The catheter is then passed over the guide wire and into the vessel. Finally, the guide wire is removed. The obvious benefit of the Seldinger technique rests in the use of a smaller gauge introducer needle.

12. Are there different types of central venous catheters?

Several different styles of catheters are available for central venous catheterization. Single-lumen catheters are most commonly used and are available with single port and multiport tips. Triple-lumen catheters are basically three single-lumen, single-port catheters joined together. Each of the three lumens is of slightly different length. The purpose of the triple-lumen catheter is to provide ports for simultaneous drug infusion, blood drawing, and central venous pressure monitoring.

A percutaneous introducer sheath is designed to introduce a pulmonary artery catheter into the central circulation. The introducer sheath is a large-bore catheter (8.5 Fr) with a side-port extension attached at its superior aspect. The side port of the introducer sheath can be used as a central venous catheter, whether or not the pulmonary artery catheter is in place.

13. Where should the distal orifice of the catheter be positioned?

The indication for catheter insertion dictates where the catheter tip should be located. When pressure measurements are to be followed for guidance in fluid management, the tip of the catheter can be positioned within either the atrium or the vena cava near the cava–atrial junction. When monitoring pressures, do not change the position of the catheter tip by advancing or withdrawing the catheter or change the external landmark (approximate level of the tricuspid valve) to which you are referencing your measurements.

For monitoring the waveform of the central venous pressure tracing, position the catheter within the atrium. By so positioning, the waveform will not be damped and will accurately reflect the pressure changes within the right atrium.

Placement of the catheter for aspiration of air emboli during neurosurgical cases requires positioning of the catheter tip (preferably multiport) in the right atrium near the superior vena cava–atrial junction. Embolized air flows past this point and accumulates in the superior aspect of the atrium. Positioning the catheter tip at the superior vena cava–atrial junction allows for optimal aspiration. Locating the tip of the catheter further toward the tricuspid valve reduces its effectiveness for aspirating air emboli.[3]

14. How can you judge the correct positioning of the distal orifice of the catheter?

Judging the appropriate distance for catheter advancement can be accomplished in several ways. Prior to insertion, measurement of the distance from the point of insertion to the right atrium (external projection—immediately right of the third costal cartilage) helps initially define the correct distance for intravascular advancement of the catheter.

When position of the catheter tip is critical, techniques for judging exact catheter location should be employed. Advancement of the catheter under fluoroscopy represents the most accurate method for positioning the catheter tip, but it may be time-consuming and cumbersome in the crowded confines of an operating room or intensive care suite.

An alternative method is to use an electrocardiogram (ECG) to guide placement of the catheter. This technique was first described in 1959[9] and relies on transforming the catheter into an extension of an ECG lead. After insertion of the central venous catheter at the site of choice, the catheter is filled with electrolyte solution—normal saline or 8.4% $NaHCO_3$—and the V lead of the ECG attached to the proximal port.[4] The catheter is then advanced toward the right atrium. The axis and voltage of the P wave on the V lead tracing are indicative of the catheter tip position. As the catheter tip passes the area of the sinoatrial node, the P wave becomes equal in height to the R wave of the ECG. The catheter tip passing the mid-atrial position is demonstrated by a decreasing or biphasic P wave. Low atrial positioning is indicated by an inverted P wave or absence of the P wave.

15. Are any complications associated with placement of the central venous catheter?

Yes. Considering the proximity of the carotid artery to the internal jugular vein, it is not surprising that carotid artery puncture is one of the more common complications associated with all the internal jugular vein approaches. Pneumothorax may occur[5] and is more commonly associated with a subclavian, low anterior (internal jugular), or junctional approach (junction of the internal jugular vein and subclavian vein). Hemothorax is associated primarily with the subclavian vein approach and occurs secondary to subclavian artery laceration.

The thoracic duct, as it wraps around the internal jugular vein, can reach as high as 3 or 4 cm above the sternal end of the clavicle. This places the duct in a vulnerable position for puncture or laceration when a left internal jugular vena puncture is attempted.[10]

A serious complication can occur when a catheter cannot be advanced through an introducer needle and the catheter is then withdrawn from that needle. This maneuver can result in shearing and embolization of the catheter tip. Therefore, if a catheter cannot be advanced through an introducer needle, remove the needle and catheter in unison. A similar event can occur with the Seldinger technique when the tip of the guide wire is sheared and embolized. If a wire cannot be advanced through an introducer needle, remove the needle and wire in unison.

An uncommon but potentially devastating complication is air embolism during central venous catheterization. In order to avoid this problem, the patient should be positioned head down (if entry is at a point superior to the heart) until the catheter is inserted and the hub of the catheter is occluded.

16. What are the _late_ complications associated with central venous catheterization?

Late complications include infection, vascular damage, hematoma formation, dysrhythmia, and extravascular catheter migration.[2,6,12,13]

17. Can you use the central venous catheter for blood transfusions?

Certain clinical implications should be understood before using the central venous catheter for blood transfusions. Most central venous catheters have narrow lumens and long lengths. This configuration creates high resistance, which restricts the flow of blood and creates increased shear force on blood cells. An alternative to the long, narrow catheter is the percutaneous introduce sheath (8.5 Fr) used for pulmonary artery catheter introduction. Caution must be exercised when using this sheath for transfusion. Because the sheath has a large lumen, a great volume of blood can be transfused into the central circulation in a short period of time. The high infusion rate can result in transient right heart volume overload.

18. Are any special precautions needed when removing a central venous catheter?

Before a central venous catheter is removed, the insertion site should be positioned lower than the level of the right atrium. This puts the patient in the head-down position for removal of an internal jugular vein or subclavian vein catheter. The purpose of this positioning is to increase venous pressure at the point of removal and thereby prevent air aspiration into the vein through the evacuated catheter tract. Following removal of the catheter, external pressure should be maintained on the area from which the catheter is withdrawn until clot formation has sealed the vessel.

19. Describe the normal central venous pressure waveform, and relate its pattern to the cardiac cycle.

The normal central venous pressure waveform shows a pattern of three upstrokes and two descents that correspond to certain events in the cardiac cycle (see Figure, next page).

1. The a wave represents the increase in atrial pressure which occurs during atrial contraction.
2. The x' descent is the decrease in atrial pressure as the atrium begins to relax.
3. Before total relaxation is completed, the c wave occurs, which is caused by the bulging of the tricuspid valve into the atrium during the early phases of right ventricular contraction.

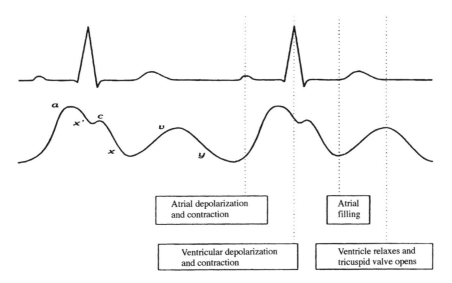

Atrial depolarization and contraction		Atrial filling

Ventricular depolarization and contraction	Ventricle relaxes and tricuspid valve opens

4. The x descent follows the c wave and is a continuation of the x′ descent. The x descent is caused by a drop in pressure brought about by a downward movement of the ventricle and tricuspid valve during the later stages of ventricular contraction.

5. The v wave represents the increase in atrial pressure that occurs while the atrium fills against a closed tricuspid valve.

6. Finally, the y descent represents a drop in pressure as the ventricle relaxes, the tricuspid valve opens (because atrial pressure is higher than ventricular pressure), and blood passively enters the ventricle.

20. What is the significance of the central venous pressure waveform?

The central venous pressure waveform may be used to assist in diagnosis of pathophysiologic events affecting right heart function that may not be detected easily by other monitors. For example, atrial fibrillation is characterized by absence of the normal a wave component. Tricuspid regurgitation results in a "giant V wave" that replaces the normal c, x, and v waves. Other events that can change the normal shape of the central venous pressure waveform include, but are not limited to, atrioventricular dissociation, asynchronous atrial contraction during ventricular pacing, tricuspid stenosis, tamponade, pericardial effusion, increased ventricular afterload, pulmonary hypertension, and right ventricular ischemia and failure.[11,14] Any occurrence, or variation in rhythm, that alters the normal relationship between the events described in question 19 above will alter the normal central venous pressure wave morphology.

BIBLIOGRAPHY

1. Blitt CD, Hines RL (eds): Monitoring in Anesthesia and Critical Care Medicine, 3rd ed. Philadelphia, W.B. Saunders, 1994.
2. Brown CS, Wallace CT: Chronic hematoma—a complication of percutaneous catheterization of the internal jugular vein. Anesthesiology 45:368–369, 1976.
3. Bunegin L, Albin MS, Helsel PE, Hoffman A, Hung T: Positioning the right atrial catheter: A model for reappraisal. Anesthesiology 55:343–348, 1981.
4. Colley PS, Artru AA: ECG-guided placement of Sorenson CVP catheters via arm veins. Anesth Analg 63:953–956, 1984.
5. Cook TL, Dueker CW: Tension pneumothorax following internal jugular cannulation and general anesthesia. Anesthesiology 45:554–555, 1976.
6. Dodson T, Quindlen E, Crowell R, McEnany MT: Vertebral arteriovenous fistulas following insertion of central monitoring catheters. Surgery 87:343–346, 1980.

7. Guyton AC, Hall JE (eds): Textbook of Medical Physiology, 9th ed. Philadelphia, W.B. Saunders, 1995.
8. Hughes RE, McGovern GJ: The relationship between right atrial pressure and blood volume. Arch Surg 79:238–243, 1959.
9. Kaplan JA, Reich DL, Konstadt SN (eds): Cardiac Anesthesia, 4th ed. Philadelphia, W.B. Saunders, 1998.
10. Khalil KG, Parker FB Jr, Mukherjee N, Webb WR: Thoracic duct injury—a complication of jugular vein catheterization. JAMA 221:908–909, 1972.
11. Mark JB: Central venous pressure monitoring: Clinical insights beyond the numbers. J Cardiothorac Vasc Anesth 5:163–173, 1991.
12. Nakayama M, Fujita S, Kawamata M, et al: Traumatic aneurysm of the internal jugular vein causing vagal nerve palsy: A rare complication of percutaneous catheterization. Anesth Analg 78:598–600, 1994.
13. Seldinger SI: Catheter replacement of the needle in percutaneous arteriography. Acta Radiol 39:369–376, 1953.
14. Vender JS, Gilbert HC: Monitoring the anesthetized patient. In Barash PG, Cullen BF, Stoelting RK (eds): Clinical Anesthesia, 3rd ed. Philadelphia, Lippincott Williams & Wilkins, 1997.

27. PULMONARY ARTERY CATHETERIZATION

Michael B. Ochs, D.O.

1. What are the different types of pulmonary artery (PA) catheters?

The basic PA catheter in current use is a balloon-tipped, flow-directed, multilumen catheter inserted percutaneously into the central venous system. These catheters are capable of measuring central venous pressure (CVP), pulmonary artery pressure (PAP), and pulmonary capillary wedge pressure (PCWP). They are also capable of measuring cardiac output using the thermodilution method. A fiber-optic channel capable of continuously measuring mixed venous oxygen saturation is incorporated into some catheters. Other catheters allow pacing of the heart, and some can measure right ventricular ejection fraction. Many catheters contain a lumen known as the VIP lumen, which is usually used for the infusion of vasoactive drugs. New technology allows development of catheters that measure cardiac output continuously instead of intermittently.

2. During which surgical procedures are PA catheters most likely to be placed?

PA catheters are useful in patients undergoing cardiac surgery, cardiac transplantation, lung transplantation, and liver transplantation. PA catheters also may be used to guide the resuscitation of trauma victims who have sustained major blood loss or multiple organ system injury. PA catheters also may be of benefit in patients with poor left ventricular function, left ventricular ejection fraction < 40%, cardiac index < 2 L/min/m^2, recent complicated myocardial infarction, severe ischemic heart disease, pulmonary hypertension, shock states, sepsis, or toxemia of pregnancy, as well as any patient undergoing surgery with anticipated large volume shifts. Many centers also place PA catheters in patients undergoing vascular surgery that involves cross-clamping of the abdominal or thoracic aorta.

3. Are PA catheters useful outside the operating room?

Yes. Swan and Forester stratified patients by data obtained from PA catheters after acute myocardial infarction into one of four groups based on PCWP and cardiac index (CI). Group 1 patients have a CI > 2.2 L/min/m^2 and PCWP < 18 mmHg with an estimated mortality of 3%; group 2 patients have a CI > 2.2 L/min/m^2 and PCWP > 18 mmHg with an estimated mortality of 9%;

group 3 patients have a CI < 2.2 L/min/m^2 and PCWP < 18 mmHg with an estimated mortality of 23%; and group 4 patients have a CI < 2.2 L/min/m^2 and PCWP >18 mmHg with an estimated mortality of 51%. Shoemaker has shown that the use of a PA catheter to guide oxygen delivery in high-risk surgical patients and shock victims may improve survival. PA catheters also are useful for diagnoses and treatment of intracardiac shunts, sepsis, pulmonary hypertension, adult respiratory distress syndrome, and cardiac tamponade.

4. What are the contraindications to placement of a PA catheter?

There are no absolute contraindications for PA catheterization. Suggested relative contraindications include severe coagulopathies, significant thrombocytopenia, prosthetic right-heart valve, endocardial pacemaker leads, and infection or tissue breakdown at the proposed cannulation site. Some clinicians believe that complete left bundle-branch block is a contraindication to PA catheterization because of the risk that the catheter may cause a right bundle-branch block as it passes through the right ventricle and thus lead to complete heart block.

5. What common complications are seen with PA catheters?

Complications may occur during venous access or catheter insertion, while the PA catheter is in place, and during removal of the PA catheter and/or introducer sheath. Shah et al. prospectively studied 6,245 patients who were to have PA catheters inserted in the perioperative period. The majority of catheters were placed in the right internal jugular vein. In 1.9% of patients the carotid artery was inadvertently cannulated, and in 4 patients a 7.5 French introducer sheath was actually placed in the carotid artery. In 31 patients (0.5%), pneumothorax resulted from attempts at central vein cannulation. Cardiac rhythm disturbances occurred in over 70% of the patients, whereas only 3.1% required a bolus of lidocaine to suppress ventricular dysrhythmias. One patient with preexisting left bundle-branch block developed complete heart block and required pacemaker insertion. Four patients (0.064%) suffered an intrapulmonary hemorrhage secondary to pulmonary artery rupture; three occurred during cardiopulmonary bypass. Pulmonary infarction occurred in 4 patients, perforation of the right ventricle in 1 patient, and pulmonary embolus was suspected in 4 patients. The incidence of a positive PA catheter tip culture varies from 5% to 45% depending on the method used. The risk of developing catheter-related sepsis ranges from 0.3% to 0.5% per day.

6. Are any of the complications life-threatening?

Although rare, rupture of the pulmonary artery is the most serious complication associated with PA catheterization. Major risk factors for pulmonary artery rupture include cardiopulmonary bypass, hypothermia, and excessively prolonged balloon inflation and catheter manipulation. Pulmonary artery rupture usually manifests as rapid hypotension with hemoptysis. Management includes reversal of anticoagulation, leaving the PA catheter in place, placement of a double-lumen endotracheal tube to isolate the lung with the bleeding problem, and preparation of the patient for a possible emergent lobectomy or pneumonectomy. Positive end-expiratory pressure (PEEP) also may be useful in cases of hemorrhage.

7. How does one know where the tip of the catheter is?

During placement or flotation of the PA catheter, a pressure transducer is connected through extension tubing to the distal or pulmonary artery port of the catheter. This lumen of the catheter is filled with fluid, the pressure is monitored, and the pressure waveform is continuously displayed on the monitor screen. As the catheter enters the central vein, a central venous pressure waveform is apparent. As the catheter passes the tricuspid valve, a right ventricular waveform is present. When the catheter goes through the pulmonic valve into the main pulmonary artery, the pulmonary arterial waveform is seen; with continued catheter advancement the balloon wedges into a small branch of a pulmonary artery and the waveform reflects PCWP.

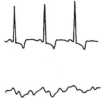

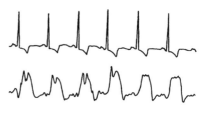

This shows the tip of the catheter in the central venous system.

Now in the right ventricle.

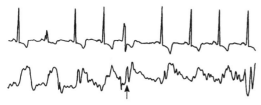

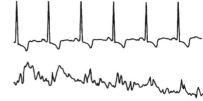

Moving from the right ventricle to the pulmonary artery (at the arrow). Note the presence of a premature ventricular contraction as the catheter passes through the pulmomary outflow tract. This is very common.

Continued advancement of the catheter causes it to wedge in a branch of the pulmonary artery.

8. What hemodynamic parameters are measured by the pulmonary artery catheter?

The most frequently measured hemodynamic parameters are right atrial or central venous pressure, pulmonary arterial pressure, and intermittent measurement of PCWP. All other hemodynamic data are calculated rather than measured.

Calculation of Hemodynamic Variables

VARIABLES	FORMULA	NORMAL VALUES
CI	$\dfrac{\text{CO (L/minute)}}{\text{body surface area (m}^2)}$	2.8–4.2 L/minute/m^2
SV	$\dfrac{\text{CO (L/minute)} \times 1000}{\text{heart rate (beats/minute)}}$	60–90 ml/beat
SI	$\dfrac{\text{SV (ml/beat)}}{\text{body surface area (m}^2)}$	30–65 ml/beat/m^2
RVSWI	$0.0136 \, (\text{MPAP} - \text{CVP}) \times \text{SI}$	5–10 g-m/beat/m^2
LVSWI	$0.0136 \, (\text{MAP} - \text{PCWP}) \times \text{SI}$	45–60 g-m/beat/m^2
SVR	$\dfrac{\text{MAP} - \text{CVP}}{\text{CO (L/minute)}} \times 80$	1200–1500 dyne-second/cm^{-5}
PVR	$\dfrac{\text{MPAP} - \text{PCWP}}{\text{CO (L/minute)}} \times 80$	100–300 dyne-second/cm^{-5}

CI = cardiac index, SV = stroke volume, SI = stroke index, RVSWI = right ventricular stroke work index, LVSWI = left ventricular stroke work index, SVR = systemic vascular resistance, PVR = pulmonary vascular resistance, CO = cardiac output, MPAP = mean pulmonary artery pressure, MAP = mean arterial pressure, PCWP = pulmonary capillary wedge pressure.

9. What is the thermodilution method of measuring cardiac output?

The thermodilution method involves injecting a known volume of fluid with a known temperature (colder than blood) into the proximal or right atrial port of the PA catheter and monitoring the temperature change produced by the cold fluid at the distal end of the PA catheter. The change in temperature of the blood over time is inversely proportional to blood flow. Usually a computer is used to assist with the determination of cardiac output. Typically 10 ml of iced or room-temperature crystalloid solution is injected, and the change in temperature over time is measured by the thermistor at the distal end of the PA catheter. A computation constant based on the type of PA catheter and the volume and temperature of the injected solution should be entered into the cardiac output computer to ensure accurate results. Usually at least three consecutive measurements are obtained a little more than 1 minute apart and then averaged. If the results vary significantly, more determinations should be made to increase the accuracy of the result. The injection for cardiac output should be made at the same point in the respiratory cycle for each determination. Meticulous attention to sterile technique and to absence of air in the injectate is absolutely necessary. If room-temperature injectate is used, there must be at least a 10°C difference between the patient's blood temperature and the injectate temperature to ensure accurate results.

10. Are there any ways to verify that the cardiac output obtained by thermodilution is accurate?

If thermodilution cardiac outputs are performed correctly, the data are generally accurate and reproducible. If one wants to verify the validity of the results, the Fick equation can be used:

$$CO = \frac{\dot{V}O_2}{CaO_2 - C\bar{v}O_2}$$

where CO = cardiac output, $\dot{V}O_2$ = oxygen consumption, CaO_2 = oxygen content of arterial blood, and $C\bar{v}O_2$ = oxygen content of mixed venous blood.

To obtain accurate calculations using the Fick principle, oxygen consumption must be known. Oxygen consumption is relatively easy to calculate in ventilated patients if one knows the alveolar minute ventilation as well as inspired and expired oxygen concentrations. In spontaneously breathing patients it is much more difficult to obtain accurate numbers for oxygen consumption. The cardiac output determined either by thermodilution or the Fick method should always be viewed in light of the patient's clinical condition. If discrepancies exist between the numerical data and the patient's clinical condition, a reason for the discrepancy must be sought.

11. What is the wedge pressure? How do we measure it?

If the balloon at the tip of the catheter is inflated and the catheter is advanced, eventually the catheter will wedge itself into a small branch of the pulmonary artery. If the balloon is left inflated, the pressure monitored distal to the balloon reflects the pulmonary capillary pressure, pulmonary venous pressure, and left atrial pressure. The characteristic venous pressure waveform should be observed on the monitor with its usual A wave, C waves, and V waves.

The A wave represents an increase in left atrial pressure during atrial contraction and usually correlates with the PR interval on the electrocardiogram (ECG). The C wave, which may not always be readily apparent, represents closure of the mitral valve and a small increase in atrial pressure at closure. The next large pressure increase, the V wave,

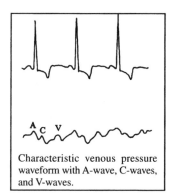

Characteristic venous pressure waveform with A-wave, C-waves, and V-waves.

represents filling of the left atrial chamber concomitantly with left ventricular contraction. An adequate wedge position of the PA catheter may be confirmed using three criteria: (1) the contour of the waveform changes from an arterial to a venous pressure waveform; (2) mean pulmonary artery pressure should drop as the catheter is wedged; and (3) the partial pressure of oxygen of a blood sample taken from the tip of wedge catheter should be at least 19 mmHg higher than a sample taken from a systemic artery, and/or oxyhemoglobin saturation should be approximately 20% higher than that recorded from a freely floating catheter in the pulmonary artery. Just as CVP is proportional to the preload of the right heart, PCWP is proportional to the preload of the left side of the heart. In many patients with cardiac disease, CVP may or may not correlate with PCWP.

12. At what point during the cardiac cycle should wedge pressure be determined?

Wedge pressure is often measured to evaluate the preloading conditions of the left ventricle and correlates with left ventricular end-diastolic pressure (LVEDP). Therefore, to make this correlation accurate, the wedge pressure tracing should be analyzed for the point that correlates with the end of the left ventricular diastolic period. This point correlates with the point on the pressure tracing after the A wave but before the C wave. The C wave represents mitral valve closure, which occurs at the beginning of left ventricular systole. A strip chart recorder that simultaneously records the ECG as well as the wedge pressure tracing is useful for determining pulmonary capillary wedge pressure. Wedge pressure measurements also should be taken at the end of exhalation to eliminate any variation caused by the respiratory cycle.

13. What is the importance of a wedge pressure measurement?

Usually it is desirable to optimize the cardiac output of critically ill patients. Increasing left ventricular end-diastolic volume usually results in an increased cardiac output, but only to a certain point. Further increases in left ventricular end-diastolic volume provide too much stretch of myocardial muscle fibers, and left ventricular performance declines. If wedge pressure can be measured at the end of left ventricular diastole, the result is thought to correlate with left ventricular end-diastolic pressure. Because increases in volume should result in an increase in pressure, there should be some correlation between left ventricular end-diastolic pressure and left ventricular end-diastolic volume. In the normal heart, increases in left ventricular end-diastolic volume result in increases in left ventricular end-diastolic pressure. This correlation is not necessarily found in the failing heart. Obviously any factor that decreases left ventricular compliance (e.g., myocardial ischemia, myocardial contusions, constrictive pericarditis) will result in much larger changes in left ventricular pressures with small changes in left ventricular volumes.

CONTROVERSY

14. Do PA catheters improve outcome in critically ill patients?

This controversy centers on the complications that may occur with catheterization and the ability of clinicians to understand and use the data obtained in a cardiovascular profile. Tuman et al. failed to demonstrate any difference in outcome of patients undergoing coronary artery surgery with or without the use of a PA catheter. Rao et al. showed a decrease in perioperative myocardial infarction in high-risk surgical patients undergoing noncardiac surgery. The investigators used invasive hemodynamic monitoring, including PA catheters in the perioperative period. Shoemaker argues that use of PA catheters to guide therapy that increases cardiac output and oxygen delivery to supranormal values in high-risk surgical patients increases survival rates.

The controversy surrounding the use of PA catheters is likely to continue. Large-scale outcome studies are difficult to control. With appropriate training and vigilance, however, the complication rate associated with PA catheterization is acceptable. Some patients clearly benefit from the data obtained from PA catheters, but only if the clinician interpreting the data has a thorough understanding of the patient's pathophysiology and makes appropriate therapeutic decisions. The following are just three examples of how data from a PA catheter may affect patient care:

Example 1: A 65-year-old man with coronary artery disease undergoing a bowel resection begins to have a progressive decrease in cardiac output, with a concomitant increase in PCWP.

Interpretation. This finding may well represent acute left ventricular dysfunction secondary to myocardial ischemia. If such is the case, the patient probably will benefit from therapy with nitroglycerin.

Example 2: Four hours after surgical repair of fractures of both lower extremities and a ruptured spleen, the urine output of a 35-year-old victim of a motorcycle accident has decreased to 10 ml (over the last hour); cardiac output is low normal, as are CVP and PCWP.

Interpretation. The clinical situation and the data suggest inadequate intravascular volume. Other causes of low urine output (renal dysfunction, urinary obstruction) also should be considered.

Example 3: A 40-year-old woman who underwent laparoscopic cholecystectomy 7 days ago is discovered to be lethargic with low blood pressure at home. She is brought to the hospital and a PA catheter is placed. Blood pressure = 80/40, cardiac index = 6 L/min/m², CVP = 3 mmHg, PCWP = 6 mmHg.

Interpretation. Such data are consistent with septic shock.

BIBLIOGRAPHY

1. Ermakov S, Hoyt JW: Pulmonary artery catheterization. Crit Care Clin 8:773–806, 1992.
2. Fiddian-Green RG, Haglund U, Gutierrez G, Shoemaker WC: Goals for the resuscitation of shock. Crit Care Med 21:S25–S31, 1993.
3. Finegan BA: The pulmonary artery catheter: When and why it should be used. Can J Anaesth 39: R71–R75, 1992.
4. Shah KB, Rao TLK, Laughlin S, El-Etr AA: A review of pulmonary artery catheterization in 6,245 patients. Anesthesiology 61:271–275, 1984.
5. Shoemaker WC: Use and abuse of the balloon-tip pulmonary artery (Swan-Ganz) catheter: Are patients getting their money's worth? Crit Care Med 18:1294–1296, 1990.
6. Shoemaker WC, Appel PL, Kram HB: Hemodynamic and oxygen transport responses in survivors and nonsurvivors of high-risk surgery. Crit Care Med 21:977–990, 1993.

28. ARTERIAL CATHETERIZATION AND PRESSURE MONITORING

Paige Latham, M.D., and Charles W. Whitten, M.D.

1. Why is arterial blood pressure monitored?

Blood pressure monitoring is fundamental in determining the effects of anesthesia on the cardiovascular system. Because decisions about patient care may be based on blood pressure data, it is important to understand how the data are obtained. Arterial pressure is monitored either noninvasively with a blood pressure cuff or invasively with arterial cannulation and a pressure transducer.

2. How do noninvasive blood pressure devices work?

Blood pressure is usually measured either manually (ausculatory method) or with an automated device (oscillometric method).

With the **ausculatory method**, a pneumatic cuff is inflated to occlude arterial blood flow. As the cuff is deflated, audible frequencies called Korotkoff sounds are created by turbulent blood flow in the artery. The pressure at which the sounds are first audible is taken as the systolic pressure, and the pressure at which the sounds become muffled or disappear is taken as the diastolic pressure. Errors in measurement may be due to (1) long stethoscope tubing, (2) poor hearing in the observer, (3) calibration errors in the sphygnomanometer, (4) decreased blood flow in the extremities due either to hypovolemia or to the use of vasopressors, (5) severe atherosclerosis that prevents occlusion of the artery at suprasystolic pressures, (6) inappropriate cuff size, or (7) too rapid of a deflation rate.

With the **oscillometric method**, a pneumatic cuff is also inflated to occlude the arterial blood flow. As the cuff is deflated, the arterial pulsations cause pressure changes in the cuff that are analyzed by a computer. The systolic pressure is taken as the point of rapidly increasing oscillations, the mean arterial pressure as the point of maximal oscillation, and the diastolic pressure as the point of rapidly decreasing oscillations. Errors in measurement may occur from inappropriate cuff size or factors that prevent detection of cuff pressure variations, such as patient shivering. Prolonged use of the stat mode, in which the cuff reinflates immediately after each measurement is obtained, may lead to complications such as ulnar nerve paresthesia, thrombophlebitis, or compartment syndrome.

3. What are the indications for intra-arterial blood pressure monitoring?

Intra-arterial blood pressure monitoring is indicated when (1) blood pressure changes may be rapid, (2) moderate blood pressure changes may cause end-organ damage, (3) frequent arterial blood gases may be needed, or (4) noninvasive blood pressure monitoring is inaccurate. Clinical examples include anticipated cardiovascular instability (e.g., massive fluid shifts, intracranial surgery, significant cardiovascular disease, valvular heart disease, diabetes), direct manipulation of the cardiovascular system (cardiac surgery, major vascular surgery, deliberate hypotension), frequent sampling of blood gases for pulmonary disease or single lung ventilation, or morbid obesity, which prevents accurate noninvasive measurements.

4. What are the complications of invasive arterial monitoring?

Complications include distal ischemia, arterial thrombosis, hematoma formation, catheter site infection, systemic infection, necrosis of the overlying skin, and potential blood loss due to disconnection. The incidence of infection increases with duration of catheterization. The incidence of arterial thrombosis increases with (1) duration of catheterization, (2) increased catheter size, (3) catheter type (Teflon catheters cause more thrombosis than catheters made of polypropylene), (4) proximal emboli, (5) prolonged shock, and (6) preexisting peripheral vascular disease.

5. How is radial artery catheterization performed?

The wrist is dorsiflexed and immobilized, the skin is cleaned with an antiseptic solution, the course of the radial artery is determined by palpation, and local anesthetic is infiltrated into the skin overlying the artery. A 20-gauge over-the-needle catheter apparatus is inserted at a 30–45° angle to the skin along the course of the radial artery. After arterial blood return, the angle is decreased, and the catheter is advanced slightly to ensure that both the catheter tip and the needle have advanced into the arterial lumen. The catheter is then threaded into the artery. Alternatively, the radial artery may be transfixed. After arterial blood return, the apparatus is advanced until both the catheter and the needle pass completely through the front and back walls of the artery. The needle is withdrawn into the catheter, and the catheter is pulled back slowly. When pulsatile blood flow is seen in the catheter, the catheter is advanced into the lumen. If the catheter will not advance into the arterial lumen and blood return is good, a sterile guide wire may be placed into the lumen through the catheter and the catheter advanced over the wire. Some arterial cannulation kits have a combined needle-guide wire-cannula system, where the guide wire is advanced into the lumen after good blood flow is obtained, and the catheter is then advanced over the guide wire. After cannulation, low-compliance pressure tubing is fastened to the catheter, a sterile dressing is applied, and the catheter is securely fastened in place. Care must be taken to ensure that the pressure tubing is free from bubbles before connection.

6. Describe the normal blood supply to the hand.

The hand is supplied by the ulnar and radial arteries. These arteries anastomose via four arches in the hand and wrist (the superficial and deep palmar arches, the anterior and posterior carpal arches) and between their metacarpal and digital branches. Because of the dual arterial blood supply, the hand usually has collateral flow, and the digits can be supplied by either artery if the other is occluded. Both ulnar and radial arteries have been removed and used successfully as coronary artery bypass grafts without ischemic sequelae to the hand. Preoperative evaluation is performed with an Allen's test and an ultrasonic Doppler flowmeter to determine if the collateral circulation is adequate prior to removal of the artery.

7. Describe Allen's test. Explain its purpose.

Allen's test is performed before radial artery cannulation to determine whether ulnar collateral circulation to the hand is adequate in case of radial artery thrombosis. The hand is exsanguinated by having the patient make a tight fist. The radial and ulnar arteries are occluded by manual compression, the patient relaxes the hand, and the pressure over the ulnar artery is released. Collateral flow is assessed by measuring the time required for return of normal coloration. Return of color in less than 5 seconds indicates adequate collateral flow; whereas return in 5–10 seconds suggests an equivocal test and more than 10 seconds indicates inadequate collateral circulation.

8. Is Allen's test an adequate predictor of ischemic sequelae?

Although some clinicians advocate use of Allen's test, others have demonstrated that Allen's test of radial artery patency has no relationship to distal blood flow as assessed by fluoroscein dye injection. There are many reports of ischemic sequelae in patients with normal Allen's tests; conversely patients with abnormal Allen's tests may have no ischemic sequelae. Apparently Allen's test alone does not reliably predict adverse outcome.

9. What alternative cannulation sites are available?

The ulnar, brachial, axillary, femoral, dorsalis pedis, and posterior tibial arteries are all acceptable cannulation sites. The ulnar artery may be cannulated if the radial artery provides adequate collateral flow. The brachial artery does not have the benefit of collateral flow, but many studies have demonstrated the relative safety of its cannulation. Cannulation of the axillary artery is also relatively safe, but the left side is preferred because of a lower incidence of embolization to the carotid artery. The femoral artery is an excellent site for cannulation because of the large size, the technical ease of cannulation, and the low risk of ischemic sequelae. While some studies have indicated a slightly higher incidence of infection with a femoral catheter, other studies have not demonstrated this increase. The small size of the dorsalis pedis and posterior tibial arteries make cannulation difficult and pose an increased risk for ischemic complications; cannulation of these arteries is relatively contraindicated for patients with peripheral vascular disease and diabetes mellitus.

10. How does a central waveform differ from a peripheral waveform?

As the arterial pressure is transmitted from the central aorta to the peripheral arteries, the waveform is distorted. Transmission is delayed, high frequency components such as the dicrotic notch are lost, the systolic peak increases, and the diastolic trough is decreased. The changes in systolic and diastolic pressures result from a decrease in the arterial wall compliance and from resonance (the addition of reflected waves to the arterial waveform as it travels distally in the arterial tree). The systolic blood pressure in the radial artery may be as much as 20–50 mmHg higher than the pressure in the central aorta. (See Figure, next page.)

11. What information can be obtained from an arterial waveform?

The arterial waveform provides valuable information about the patient's hemodynamic status: (1) the waveform determines the heart rate during ECG electrocautery interference and whether the electrical spikes from a pacemaker result in ventricular contractions; (2) the slope of the upstroke may be used to evaluate myocardial contractility; (3) large respiratory variations suggest hypovolemia; and (4) the waveform provides a visual estimate of the hemodynamic consequences of various arrhythmias.

12. How is the arterial waveform reproduced?

Reproduction of the arterial waveform requires the following equipment: (1) an intravascular catheter, (2) fluid-filled pressure tubing and a stopcock, (3) electromechanical transducer, and (4) electronic analyzer and display system. The mechanical energy at the catheter tip is transmitted to the transducer by the fluid-filled tubing and then converted to an electrical signal. The electrical signal is then converted to a waveform by the analyzer and displayed.

13. Describe the conversion of the mechanical energy of a pressure wave to an electrical signal.

Transducers convert the mechanical energy of a pressure wave into electrical current or voltage. The design of most transducers is based on the strain-gauge principle, which states that

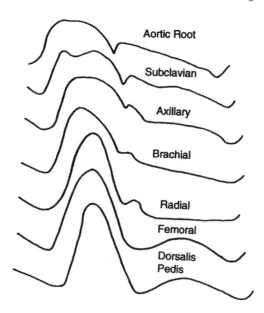

Aortic Root

Subclavian

Axillary

Brachial

Radial

Femoral

Dorsalis
Pedis

Configuration of the arterial waveform at various sites in the arterial tree. (From Blitt CD, Hines RL: Monitoring in Anesthesia and Critical Care Medicine, 3rd ed. New York, Churchill Livingstone, 1995, with permission.

stretching a wire or silicone crystal changes its electrical resistance. Consequently, distortion in the shape of the diaphragm in the transducer (due to changes in mechanical pressure) results in a small electrical current. The sensing elements are arranged as a Wheatstone-Bridge circuit so that the voltage output is proportionate to the mechanical pressure applied to the diaphragm.

14. How is the waveform reproduced from an electrical signal?

The waveform is reproduced by the summation of a series of sinusoidal waves. Waveforms consist of the fundamental waveform and ten harmonics. The frequency of the fundamental waveform depends on the patient's heart rate. If the heart rate is 60 bpm, the fundamental frequency is 1 Hz (cycles/second), and frequencies up to 10 Hz contribute to the waveform.

15. Define damping coefficient and natural frequency.

Natural frequency, a property of the catheter-stopcock-transducer apparatus, is the frequency at which the monitoring system resonates and amplifies the signals it receives. The natural frequency is directly proportional to the diameter of the catheter lumen and inversely proportional to (1) the square root of the length of the tubing connection, (2) the square root of the system compliance, and (3) the density of the fluid contained in the system. Because the natural frequency of most monitoring systems is in the same range as the frequencies used to recreate the arterial waveform, significant amplification and distortion of the waveform may occur.

The **damping coefficient** reflects the rate of dissipation of the energy of a pressure wave. This property may be adjusted to counterbalance the erroneous amplification that results when the natural frequency of the monitoring system overlaps with the frequencies used to recreate the waveform.

16. What are the characteristics of overdamped and underdamped monitoring systems?

The damping coefficient is estimated by evaluating the time for the system to settle to zero after a high-pressure flush. An underdamped system continues to oscillate for 3–4 cycles; it overestimates the systolic and underestimates the diastolic blood pressure. An overdamped system settles to baseline slowly without oscillating; it underestimates the systolic and overestimates the diastolic blood pressure. In both cases, however, the mean blood pressure is relatively accurate.

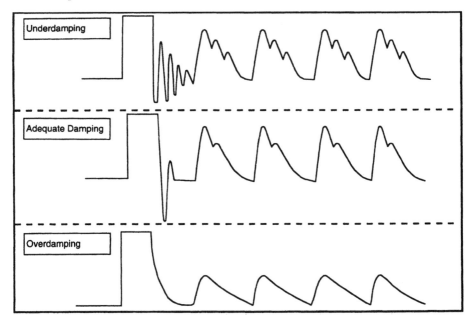

Underdamped, adequately damped, and overdamped arterial pressure tracings after a high pressured flush.

17. How can the incidence of artifacts in arterial monitoring systems by reduced?

The incidence of artifacts can be reduced by meticulous care of the monitoring system:

1. The connecting tubing should be rigid with an internal diameter of 1.5–3 mm and a maximal length of 120 cm.

2. The lines should be kept free of kinks, clots, and bubbles, which cause overdamping of the system.

3. Only one stopcock per line should be used to minimize possible air introduction.

4. The mechanical coupling system should be flushed with heparinized saline to maintain patency of the arterial line and to minimize the risk of distal embolization and nosocomial infection.

5. The transducer should be placed at the level of the right atrium, the midaxillary line in the supine position.

6. The transducer should be electrically balanced or rezeroed periodically because the zero point may drift if the room temperature changes.

BIBLIOGRAPHY

1. Bedford RF, Shah NK: Blood pressure monitoring: Invasive and non-invasive. In Blitt CD, Hines RL (eds): Monitoring in Anesthesia and Critical Care Medicine, 3rd ed. New York, Churchill Livingstone, 1995, p 100.
2. Buxton BF, Chan AT, Dixit AS, et al: Ulnar artery as a coronary bypass graft. Ann Thorac Surg 65:1020–1024, 1998.
3. Frezza EE, Mezghebe H: Indications and complications of arterial catheter use in surgical or medical intensive care units: Analysis of 4932 patients. Am Surg 64:127–131, 1998.
4. McGregor AD: The Allen test—An investigation of its accuracy by fluorescein angiography. J Hand Surg 12:82–85, 1987.
5. Meyer RM, Katele GV: The case for a complete Allen's test. Anesth Analg 62:947, 1983.
6. Reich DL, Moskowitz DM, Kaplan JA: Hemodynamic monitoring. In Kaplan JA, Reich DL, Konstadt SN (eds): Cardiac Anesthesia, 4th ed. Philadelphia, W.B. Saunders, 1999, pp 321–329.

7. Skeehan TM, Thys DM: Monitoring the cardiac surgical patient. In Hensley FA, Martin DE (eds): A Practical Approach to Cardiac Anesthesia, 2nd ed. Boston, Little, Brown, 1995, pp 101–111.
8. Slogoff S, Keats AS, Arlund C: On the safety of radial artery cannulation. Anesthesiology 59:42, 1983.
9. Stanley TE, Reves JG: Cardiovascular monitoring. In Miller RD (ed): Anesthesia, 4th ed. Philadelphia, Churchill Livingstone, 1994, pp 1163–1171.
10. Vender JS, Gilbert HC: Monitoring the anesthetized patient. In Barash PG, Cullen BF, Stoelting RK (eds): Clinical Anesthesia, 3rd ed. Philadelphia, Lippincott Williams & Wilkins, 1997, pp 626–629.

V. Perioperative Problems

29. HYPOXEMIA AND PULMONARY PHYSIOLOGY

Jeff Nabonsal, M.D.

1. In the operating room the patient's oxygen saturation begins to decrease. What is the appropriate response?

When a true hypoxic event is identified, apply 100% oxygen immediately; then adequacy of ventilation must be assessed. The problem usually represents an intrapulmonary process, but one must rule out mechanical causes first. If the patient is not intubated, attempt mask ventilation; if the patient is intubated, hand ventilation by bag is appropriate. At this point check the inspired oxygen concentration, capnograph, and peak pressures required to move the chest. A calibrated oxygen analyzer, in the inspired limb of the circuit, is the only way to ensure that a hypoxic mixture is not delivered to the patient. In the intubated patient a ruptured endotracheal tube cuff is recognized by an audible leak with bagging, whereas poor compliance should make one consider obstruction, bronchospasm, or tension pneumothorax. Listen to the chest for bilateral breath sounds, decreased breath sounds, wheezing, or rales. Inspect the endotracheal tube for kinks, plugging (if one can pass a suction catheter, the tube is most likely patent), and position. If necessary, perform laryngoscopy to check for endotracheal tube placement. Check the circuit for mechanical problems and for possible failure of the oxygen supply. If there is any question about the machine, do not hesitate to switch to an Ambu bag and an alternate oxygen tank. As a last resort, reintubate; do not allow the patient to deteriorate before intervening. If pneumothorax is high on the differential diagnosis, consider decompressing the chest, first with a needle, then with a chest tube if appropriate. Obtain arterial blood gases, chest radiograph, and electrocardiogram (ECG) and review recent events.

Other causes to consider after ruling out mechanical problems and endotracheal tube problems include surgical causes (uncontrolled bleeding, hypotension, compression of vital structures) and other patient-related causes (ventilation-perfusion mismatch, pulmonary embolism, pulmonary edema, fat embolism, anemia, decreased cardiac output). Lastly, consider adding positive end-expiratory pressure (PEEP) and inserting a pulmonary artery catheter to aid in diagnosing and treating a hypoxic event.

2. Discuss the determinants of pulmonary blood flow and include the effects of hypotension and PEEP.

The major determinants of pulmonary blood flow are gravity and hypoxic pulmonary vasoconstriction (HPV). The actual perfusion to an alveolus depends on multiple factors. West describes four zones of perfusion in an upright lung, starting at the apices and moving downward to the bases:

In **zone 1**, alveolar pressure (P_{Alv}) exceeds pulmonary artery pressure (P_{pa}), leading to ventilation without perfusion (alveolar dead space). Zone 1 is essentially nonexistent in healthy patients.

In **zone 2**, arterial pressure exceeds alveolar pressure, but alveolar pressure still exceeds venous pressure (P_{pv}). Blood flow in zone 2 is determined by arterial-alveolar pressure differences, which steadily increase down the zone.

In **zone 3**, pulmonary venous pressure now exceeds alveolar pressure, and flow is determined by the arterial-venous pressure difference.

In **zone 4**, interstitial pressure ($P_{interstitium}$) is greater than venous and alveolar pressures; thus flow is determined by the arterial-interstitial pressure difference.

To simplify: Zone 1 $P_{Alv} > P_{pa} > P_{pv}$
Zone 2 $P_{pa} > P_{Alv} > P_{pv}$
Zone 3 $P_{pa} > P_{pv} > P_{Alv}$
Zone 4 $P_{pa} > P_{interstitium} > P_{pv} > P_{Alv}$

Decreased pulmonary artery pressure increases the size of zones 1 and 2 at the expense of zones 2 and 3; this may occur with hypotension or extreme blood loss. Increased pulmonary artery pressure has the opposite effect. PEEP increases P_{Alv} and the size of zones 1 and 2 at the expense of zones 2 and 3.

3. What is meant by the term ventilation-perfusion (V/Q) mismatch? Describe how HPV aids in avoiding this problem.

Both ventilation and perfusion increase toward the gravity-dependent portion of the lungs but at different rates. Thus, V/Q is >1 at the top of the lungs, 1 at the third rib in the upright lung, and <1 below the third rib. HPV is a local response of pulmonary artery smooth muscle that decreases blood flow when a low alveolar oxygen pressure is sensed. This response aids in keeping normal V/Q relationships by diversion of blood from underventilated areas but is effective only when normoxic areas of the lungs are available to receive the diverted blood flow. HPV is inhibited to a degree by the volatile anesthetics and some vasodialators but is not affected by intravenous anesthesia.

V/Q = infinity = dead space
V/Q = 0 = absolute shunt

4. Why does general anesthesia worsen V/Q mismatch?

Under general anesthesia functional residual capacity (FRC) is reduced by approximately 400 ml in an adult. The supine position decreases FRC another 800 ml. Obesity, pregnancy, ascites, abdominal surgery, and multiple other causes may further decrease FRC. A large enough decrease in FRC may bring end-expiratory volumes or even the entire tidal volume to levels below the closing volumes. Closing volumes are the volumes at which small airways begin to close. When small airways begin to close, low V/Q areas develop. Closing capacity is equal to the sum of the closing volume and the residual volume. Surgical compression or clamping of the pulmonary vasculature creates high V/Q areas or increased pulmonary dead space, which is also a source of V/Q mismatch.

5. Define the terms *anatomic, alveolar,* and *physiologic dead space.*

Dead space (V_D) is the portion of the tidal volume that does not participate in gas exchange. **Anatomic dead space** is the volume of gas that ventilates the conducting airways. **Alveolar dead space** is the volume of gas that reaches the alveoli but does not take part in gas exchange because the alveoli are not perfused (West zone 1). In awake, healthy, supine patients alveolar dead space is negligible. **Physiologic dead space** is the sum of anatomic and alveolar dead space.

V_D/V_T is the ratio of the physiologic dead space to the tidal volume and is usually approximately 33%. Clinically, V_D/V_T is determined by the Bohr method, which assumes that all expired CO_2 comes from perfused alveoli and not dead space.

$$V_D/V_T = \frac{\text{(alveolar } P_{CO_2} - \text{expired } P_{CO_2})}{\text{alveolar } P_{CO_2}}$$

where we assume alveolar P_{CO_2} = arterial P_{CO_2}, and expired P_{CO_2} = the average P_{CO_2} in an expired gas sample (not the same as end-tidal P_{CO_2}).

6. What is the significance of the alveolar-arterial oxygen gradient? What is the most common reason for an increase in this value?

The alveolar-arterial oxygen gradient (A-a gradient or A-aDO_2) is a gradient that normally exists in humans and occurs for three reasons:

1. Absolute shunting
2. V/Q mismatch
3. Diffusion impairment

$$A\text{-}aDO_2 = \text{alveolar oxygen pressure} - \text{arterial oxygen pressure.}$$

$$\text{Alveolar oxygen pressure} = P_AO_2 = FiO_2\,(P_B - P_{H_2O}) - P_aCO_2/RQ,$$

where P_B = barometric pressure, P_{H_2O} = vapor pressure of water = 47 mmHg, RQ = respiratory quotient (approximately 0.8; this value changes with diet), FiO_2 = fraction of inspired oxygen, and P_aCO_2 = arterial partial pressure of carbon dioxide. Arterial oxygen pressure (P_aO_2) is determined by blood gas analysis.

The most common cause of a widened A-aDO_2 is shunt.

7. Define absolute shunt. How does one calculate the shunt fraction (Q_S/Q_T)?

Absolute shunt is defined as blood that reaches the arterial system without passing through ventilated regions of the lung. The fraction of cardiac output that passes through a shunt is determined by the following equation:

$$Q_S/Q_T = C_c - C_a/C_c - C_v$$

where C_c = oxygen content of end pulmonary capillary blood, C_v = mixed venous oxygen content, and C_a = arterial oxygen content.

The formula for calculating blood oxygen content is discussed in question 10.

8. What are the five causes of hypoxemia and how can they be differentiated?

Differential Diagnosis of Hypoxemia

CAUSES	PaCO$_2$	A-aDO$_2$	RESPONSE TO 100% OXYGEN*
Hypoventilation	↑	Normal	Often improves
Absolute shunt (V/Q = 0)	Normal	↑	None
V/Q mismatch	Normal	↑	Improves
Diffusion abnormality	Normal	↑	Improves
Decreased FiO$_2$	Normal	Normal	Improves

* All causes are improved by 100% oxygen therapy except absolute shunt.

9. What is responsible for normal physiologic shunt?

It is estimated that 2–5% of cardiac output is normally shunted through postpulmonary shunts, thus accounting for the normal A-aDO_2. Postpulmonary shunts include thebesian, bronchial, mediastinal, and pleural veins.

10. Calculate normal arterial C_aO_2 and venous C_vO_2 oxygen content.

Oxygen content is calculated by summing the oxygen bound to hemoglobin (Hgb) and the dissolved oxygen of blood:

$$\underset{\text{Bound}}{\text{Oxygen content (ml } O_2/dl) = 1.34 \text{ ml } O_2/g \text{ Hgb} \times [\text{Hgb}] \times S_aO_2} + \underset{\text{Dissolved}}{(P_aO_2 \times 0.003)}$$

where S_aO_2 is the percent of saturated hemoglobin. If [Hgb] = 15 g/dl, arterial saturation = 96%, and P_aO_2 = 90 mmHg, mixed venous saturation = 75%, and P_vO_2 = 40 mmHg, then

$$C_aO_2 = (1.34 \text{ ml } O_2/g \text{ Hgb} \times 15 \text{ g Hgb/dl} \times .96) + (90 \times 0.003) = 19.6 \text{ ml } O_2/dl$$

$$C_vO_2 = (1.34 \text{ ml } O_2/g \text{ Hgb} \times 15 \text{ g Hgb/dl} \times .75) + (40 \times 0.003) = 15.2 \text{ ml } O_2/dl$$

Note the difference between arterial and venous oxygen (VO$_2$) content is 4.4 ml O$_2$/dl.

11. How is oxygen consumption determined?

According to the Fick equation, oxygen consumption is determined when the difference between the C_aO_2 and the C_vO_2 is multiplied by cardiac output. Using values from question 10:

$$VO_2 = \text{Cardiac output (L/min)} \times (C_aO_2 - C_vO_2) \text{ in ml } O_2/dl$$

Thus, if cardiac output is 5 L/min or 50 dl/min:

$$50 \text{ dl/min} \times 4.4 \text{ ml } O_2/dl = 220 \text{ ml } O_2/min.$$

12. What are the normal P_AO_2, P_aO_2, and A-a gradient at sea level on room air?

The P_AO_2 can be calculated using the alveolar gas equation (see question 6):

$$P_AO_2 = FiO_2 (P_B - PH_2O) - P_aCO_2/RQ$$
$$P_AO_2 = 0.21 (760 - 47) - 40/0.8 = 99.7$$

The P_aO_2 of normal room air is about 90–100 at sea level ($P_B = 760$) and can be estimated by the equation:

$$P_aO_2 = 102 - (\text{age in years})/3$$

A normal A-a gradient on room air is about 10–15 mmHg and increases with age. If the A-a gradient is negative, consider the possibility of a bubble in the sample.

13. Define compliance. Give the normal value as well as the value considered to be abnormal.

Compliance is defined as the change in volume per unit change in pressure. Normal compliance is 100 ml/cm H_2O; compliance is considered abnormal when it decreases to less than 50 ml/cm H_2O.

14. Describe the nature of the elastic forces taking place between the chest wall and the lungs.

The lungs have elastic recoil forces that attempt to collapse the lung. The chest wall has elastic recoil forces that try to expand the chest. Under normal circumstances the chest wall and lung pleura are opposed, and the elastic chest wall forces create a small negative interpleural pressure. However, when two entities separate, as in pneumothorax, the lung collapses due to a loss of this negative pressure.

15. A fetus is born at 32 weeks' gestation, appears dusky after delivery, and is difficult to ventilate. What is the likely cause?

Infant respiratory distress syndrome (IRDS), which is found in premature infants with an immature surfactant system, is characterized by respiratory failure secondary to poor lung compliance. Surfactant is a substance that decreases the alveolar surface tension and thus the pressure required to distend the alveolus. The alveoli are made up of two different types of cells. Type II cells manufacture surfactant, otherwise known as dipalmityl phosphatidylcholine (DPPC). DPPC, a phospholipid, is synthesized from fatty acids. Surfactant molecules appear hydrophobic on one end and hydrophilic on the other. The hydrophobic portion projects into the alveolar cavity, whereas the hydrophilic end lies within the alveolar fluid. The molecule is confined to the alveolar surface, where, during expiration, the area of the alveolus diminishes, leaving the surfactant molecules more densely packed. Just as soap reduces the surface tension of water, surfactant reduces the normal forces between surface molecules, thus lowering surface tension and increasing lung compliance.

16. Discuss Laplace's law with respect to the alveolus.

The Laplace equation states:

$$P = 2 \times T/R$$

where P = distending pressures within the alveolus (dyne/cm^2), T = surface tension of the alveolar fluid (dyne/cm), and R = radius of the alveolus (cm). The relationship shows that the pressure necessary to expand the alveolus is (1) directly proportional to the surface tension and (2) inversely proportional to the radius. Thus, the combination of lowering surface tension and increasing alveolar radius lowers the pressure required to expand alveoli.

17. Internists are having difficulty weaning a 100-kg man from mechanical ventilation. The patient has a 7.0-mm endotracheal tube that is 29 cm long. The internists want to know whether cutting off 4 cm of endotracheal tube length will be as helpful as changing to a tube of larger diameter. What is the correct answer?

Because pressure = flow × resistance (Ohm's law), resistance = pressure/flow. For laminar gas flow, according to Poiseuille's law,

$$resistance = 8NL/\pi R^4$$

where R = radius, N = viscosity (poises), and L = length.

The single most important factor in determining airway resistance is the radius of the tube. If the radius is halved, the resistance within the tube increases to 16-fold; if the length of the tube is doubled, however, the resistance is only doubled. The clinical significance is that cutting the length of the tube minimally affects resistance; however, increasing the tube diameter makes a dramatic difference in resistance. Therefore, to reduce the work of breathing and the driving pressure necessary for the patient, the endotracheal tube should be changed to a larger size.

18. A 5-year-old child with multiple large laryngeal papillomas is stridorous before arrival at the OR for laser removal of the lesions. The surgeon requests helium to help ventilate the child. Discuss the physical explanation behind the use of helium. Is it acceptable to use helium with a laser?

Helium's utility as a therapeutic gas is based on its low density. When flow is turbulent, driving pressure is mostly related to gas density. Because flow in large airways is mainly turbulent, use of low-density gas mixtures in place of air or oxygen lowers the driving pressure needed to move gas in and out of the area. With less pressure required to move the gas through the large airways, the patient or ventilator's work of breathing decreases. Helium also can be used in the treatment of bronchospastic disease, but this effect is limited strictly to large airway obstruction.

Because helium is inert (one of the noble gases), it can be used safely with laser without the worry of combustion. But some oxygen must be delivered with the helium; therefore, all patients are at risk of airway fires with laser.

19. What is Reynolds' number?

In 1883 Osborne Reynolds showed that the transition from laminar to turbulent flow in a tube is determined by the value of a dimensionless parameter known as the Reynolds' number.

$$Reynolds'\ number = \frac{2rvd}{N}$$

where d = density, v = average velocity, r = radius, and N = viscosity. Reynolds showed that for any size tube, transition from laminar to turbulent flow occurs when the Reynolds' number reaches a value of approximately 2100.

BIBLIOGRAPHY

1. Harrison RA: Physiologic basis for evaluation and treatment of hypoxemia. In ASA Regional Refresher Course Lectures. Park Ridge, IL, American Society of Anesthesiologists, 1985.
2. Scanlan CL, Spearman CB, Sheldon RL (eds): Egan's Fundamentals of Respiratory Care. St. Louis, Mosby, 1995.
3. West JB: Respiratory Physiology: The Essentials, 5th ed. Philadelphia, Lippincott Williams & Wilkins, 1994.

30. HYPERCARBIA

Teresa J. Youtz, M.D.

1. What is the normal range for arterial partial pressure of carbon dioxide ($PaCO_2$)?
At sea level, the normal range of $PaCO_2$ is 36–44 mmHg.

2. How is CO_2 transported in the blood?
CO_2 is transported to the lungs as dissolved CO_2, bicarbonate ions (HCO_3^-), and carbamino-hemoglobin, which transport an average of 4 ml CO_2 per 100 dl of blood. Of the 4 ml of CO_2, 7% is dissolved CO_2, 23% carbaminohemoglobin, and 70% HCO_3^-.

3. What are the clinical signs of hypercarbia?
Signs of hypercarbia are sympathetic in origin and include hyperventilation, hypertension, tachycardia, and elevated pulse pressure. Symptoms of hypercarbia may include dyspnea, headache, restlessness, excitement, and hallucinations.

4. Discuss the mechanisms of hypercarbia.
1. **Hypoventilation**
   - Increased difficulty in breathing may be due to surgical position, increased airway resistance, or decreased compliance.
   - Decreased respiratory drive secondary to anesthetic drugs' effect on central respiratory drive.
2. **Increased dead space ventilation** (the portion of minute ventilation or tidal volume that does not participate in gas exchange)
   - Decreased pulmonary artery pressure (e.g., during deliberate hypotension) may increase zone I and alveolar dead space ventilation (the volume of gas that enters nonperfused lung).
   - Increased airway pressure (i.e., positive end-expiratory pressure) may increase zone I and dead space ventilation.
   - Pulmonary embolus, thrombosis, etc.
   - Short, rapid inspirations may be distributed preferentially to noncompliant and poorly perfused alveoli. Slow inspiratory time allows more compliant distribution and better perfused alveoli.
   - Anesthetic apparatus increases total dead space. Normal apparatus increases total dead space by 33–46% in intubated patients and by 64% in patients breathing by mask. Anesthetic circuits may cause rebreathing of expired gases if fresh gas flow is insufficient or if valves are defective.
3. **Increase in CO_2 production**. All causes of increased oxygen (O_2) consumption increase CO_2 production:
   - Hyperthermia (temperature of 40° C may increase CO_2 production by 25%)
   - Shivering
   - Catecholamine release
   - Hyperthyroidism
   - Malignant hyperthermia
   - Hyperalimentation
4. **Inspired CO_2**
   - CO_2 absorber channeling or exhaustion
   - CO_2 directly into circuit
   - Laparoscopic procedures (CO_2 insufflation)

5. What should be done when a patient has an elevated PaCO$_2$?
- Determine cause (see question 4).
- Tailor treatment to cause.
- Increase minute ventilation.
- Decrease anesthetic level.
- Check integrity of circuit.
- Determine if CO$_2$ absorbent is exhausted.
- Determine if monitors have been zeroed.

6. What is normal CO$_2$ production? How does it change during general anesthesia?
A 70-kg man at rest produces approximately 200 ml/min of CO$_2$. General anesthesia produces a 10–40% decrease in CO$_2$ production secondary to hypothermia, decreased work of breathing with controlled ventilation, and pharmacologic paralysis.

7. What is the rate of increase of PaCO$_2$ during apnea?
During steady-state where CO$_2$ production equals CO$_2$ elimination, there is about a 6 mmHg gradient between alveolar partial pressure of CO$_2$ (P$_A$CO$_2$) and mixed venous CO$_2$ (PvCO$_2$). If CO$_2$ elimination is stopped, P$_A$CO$_2$ and PvCO$_2$ equilibrate rapidly during the first minute of apnea, as is reflected by a 5–10 mmHg increase in the PaCO$_2$. Subsequently, there is a 2–4 mmHg increase in PaCO$_2$ per minute.

8. Define apneic threshold. At what level of PaCO$_2$ does it occur?
Apneic threshold is the maximal PaCO$_2$ that does not initiate spontaneous ventilation, which is about 5 mmHg below resting PaCO$_2$ regardless of its baseline level.

9. What is the ventilatory response to an increase in inspired CO$_2$?
In awake patients, in the range of 20–80 mmHg, for each mmHg increase in PaCO$_2$ minute ventilation increases by 2 L/min.

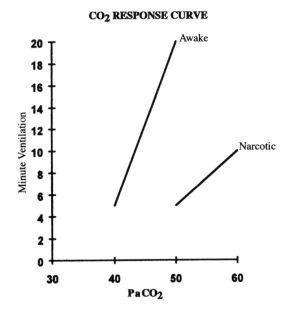

Ventilating response to increase in inspired CO$_2$.

10. What can change the slope of the CO_2 response curve?

Volatile anesthetics, opioids, barbiturates, and other IV sedatives will decrease the slope and shift it rightward. In other words, the patient will tolerate a high level of CO_2 for a given minute ventilation. It is not unusual to observe end-tidal CO_2 levels above 50 mmHg in anesthetized, spontaneously breathing patients demonstrating this effect.

11. What are the effects of hypercarbia on the circulatory system? How are these effects modified by inhaled anesthetics?

Moderate hypercarbia directly stimulates the sympathoadrenal system with an increase in catecholamines, which compensates for the direct cardiac and vascular depression. Increases in $PaCO_2$ between 20 and 80 mmHg are associated with a linear increase in heart rate and cardiac output. CO_2 acts as a direct vasodilator except in pulmonary vasculature, in which it is a direct vasoconstrictor. The overall effects in awake patients are increases in systolic blood pressure, pulse pressure, stroke volume, myocardial contractility, and heart rate and a decrease in systemic vascular resistance.

12. Discuss mechanisms by which oxygenation can be affected by CO_2.

1. An increase in P_ACO_2 must displace oxygen from the alveoli. At sea level, a P_ACO_2 of 80 mmHg decreases the alveolar partial pressure of oxygen (P_AO_2) from 100 to 60 mmHg, with a resulting decrease in arterial partial pressure of oxygen (PaO_2).

2. Increased $PaCO_2$ produces a decrease in pH, with a resulting shift to the right of the oxyhemoglobin dissociation curve. The result is a decreased affinity of hemoglobin for oxygen.

13. What are the advantages and disadvantages of using an opioid antagonist to treat hypercarbia due to an opioid-induced decrease in ventilatory drive?

The advantage is rapid reversal of narcosis. The disadvantages are nausea, vomiting, pulmonary edema, hypertension, tachycardia, and reversal of analgesia.

14. When is mechanical ventilation needed for ventilatory failure?

Many signs and symptoms need to be considered: whether the patient shows changes in mental status; whether the $PaCO_2 > 80$; whether the rate of $PaCO_2$ increase is progressive or stable; whether the patient is in distress, tachypneic, or dyspneic; whether the work of breathing increases with intercostal retractions and tracheal tug; and whether the patient is hypoxic.

15. What is the effect of $PaCO_2$ on cerebral blood flow?

Cerebral blood flow increases or decreases 1 ml/100 g/min for every mmHg increase or decrease in $PaCO_2$ from baseline. The cerebral vasculature maximally dilates at a $PaCO_2$ of 80 mmHg.

16. How does end-tidal CO_2 ($ETCO_2$) monitoring correlate with $PaCO_2$?

$ETCO_2$ monitors gas from end exhalation of the lungs, which is measured by spectrophotometry or mass spectrometry. The exhaled CO_2 from the alveoli mixes with the gas from the conducting airways and the breathing circuit that was not involved in gas exchange. The exhaled CO_2 is diluted so that the $ETCO_2$ is usually lower than the $PaCO_2$. In healthy lungs the $ETCO_2$ is usually 5 cm less than the $PaCO_2$. With increasing dead space ventilation, the difference between the $ETCO_2$ and $PaCO_2$ becomes greater.

17. What is the preterm infant's response to hypercarbia?

The preterm infant has smaller increases in minute ventilation than full-term infants and adults.

18. How does hypercarbia affect uteroplacental blood flow?

Moderate hypercarbia has no effect on uteroplacental blood flow. Uterine blood flow increases with $PaCO_2 > 60$, secondary to an increase in mean arterial pressure (MAP). Uterine vascular resistance is unchanged.

19. Discuss some electrolyte changes associated with hypercarbia.

Increased $PaCO_2$ creates respiratory acidosis. The CO_2 combines with water to form carbonic acid, and the carbonic acid then breaks down to a hydrogen ion and a bicarbonate ion. Chronic hypercarbia (e.g., chronic lung disease) increases the reabsorption of bicarbonate by the kidneys, causing a compensatory metabolic alkalosis.

Hypercarbia also produces a leakage of potassium ions from cells into the plasma. This increase is associated with hyperclycemia, which is a response to the increased catecholamines that mobilize glucose from cells, especially in the liver. Because it takes time for potassium ions to reenter the cells, repeated episodes of hypercarbia at brief intervals may result in an increase of plasma potassium.

BIBLIOGRAPHY

1. Benumof JL: Respiratory physiology and respiratory function during anesthesia. In Miller RD (ed): Anesthesia, 4th ed. New York, Churchill Livingstone, 1994, pp 611–615.
2. Gal TJ: Causes and consequences of impaired gas exchange. In Benumof JL, Saidman LJ (eds): Anesthesia and Perioperative Complications. St. Louis, Mosby, 1992, pp 205–208.
3. Gravenstein N, Kirby RR (eds): Complications in Anesthesiology, 2nd ed. Philadelphia, Lippincott Williams & Wilkins, 1996.
4. Kopman AF: Differential diagnosis of hypercarbia. In Ravin MB (ed): Problems in Anesthesia: A Case Study Approach. Boston, Little, Brown, 1981, pp 29–36.
5. Nunn JF: The effects of changes in the carbon dioxide tension. In Nunn's Applied Respiratory Physiology, 4th ed. Oxford, Butterworth-Heinemann, 1993, pp 526–527.
6. Stoelting RK, Miller RD: Effects of inhaled anesthesia on ventilation and circulation. In Basics of Anesthesia, 3rd ed. New York, Churchill Livingstone, 1994, pp 47–51.

31. HYPOTENSION

Cindy Griffiths, M.D., and Rita Agarwal, M.D.

1. Broadly categorize the causes of hypotension.

The mnemonic "DDD VITAMINS" is useful for differential diagnoses.

		EXAMPLE
D	Developmental	Valvular heart lesions
D	Drugs	Anesthetics and other drugs
D	Degenerative	Neurologic
V	Vascular	Cardiovascular instability
I	Infectious/Iatrogenic	Adverse reactions, surgical
T	Toxic/Traumatic	Hemorrhage, sepsis
A	Autoimmune/Anoxic	Anoxic brain injury
M	Metabolic/Medical	Medical causes
I	Endocrine	Pregnancy
N	Neoplastic	(Self-explanatory)
S	Special	Postoperative, deliberate

2. What is orthostatic hypotension?

Orthostatic hypotension is commonly defined as a decrease in systolic blood pressure of greater than 20% accompanied by an increase in heart rate of 20 beats per minute or more when the patient goes from the supine to upright position. Young people may maintain normal blood pressure despite a 20% reduction in circulating volume, whereas elderly patients may become orthostatic with a normal blood volume.

3. How do valvular heart lesions produce hypotension?

1. **Mitral stenosis.** Tachycardia can decrease blood pressure by limiting diastolic time, impairing left ventricular filling. Also, left atrial pressures increase, predisposing to pulmonary hypertension and right ventricular dysfunction, all contributing to decreased cardiac output. Hypotension can be treated by augmenting preload and reduction in heart rate.

2. **Aortic stenosis.** The heart relies on volume to overcome increased afterload and a noncompliant ventricle. Decreased perfusion to a greatly distended ventricle produces ischemia, decreasing cardiac output and producing hypotension. Extremes of heart rate may likewise decrease cardiac output. Peripheral resistance must be maintained to facilitate diastolic perfusion of the coronary arteries.

3. **Mitral regurgitation.** Forward left ventricular ejection fraction is reduced (though total LV ejection fraction may actually be increased) from regurgitation of some of each stroke volume into the left atrium through an incompetent mitral valve. Hypotension occurs if the heart rate decreases or systemic vascular resistance (SVR) increases. Maintain intravascular volume to ensure adequate filling and ejection fraction. Use agents that mildly increase heart rate and decrease SVR. Keep the heart "full and fast."

4. **Aortic regurgitation.** "Forward" stroke volume is decreased by regurgitation through an incompetent aortic valve. Decreased diastolic blood pressure produces coronary hypoperfusion. Treatment is directed toward avoiding extremes of heart rate or increased afterload, while maintaining contractility and intravascular volume.

4. Which drugs and materials common to the operating room have hypotension as a side effect?

1. **Antihypertensive agents** may inadvertently cause hypotension, especially in hypovolemic patients.

2. **Intravenous contrast agents** may cause hypotension in 5–8% of patients by anaphylaxis, release of vasoactive substances, or activating the complement system.

3. **Methylmethacrylate,** a cement used in joint replacement, undergoes an exothermic reaction that causes it to adhere to imperfections in the bony surface. Hypotension usually occurs 30–60 seconds after placement of the cement but can occur up to 10 minutes later. Postulated mechanisms include tissue damage from the reaction, release of vasoactive substances when it is hydrolyzed to methacrylate acid, embolization as the bone is reamed, and vasodilation caused by absorption of the volatile monomer.

4. **Allergens.** Latex and other histamine-releasing agents (e.g., morphine, atracurium, mivacurium) should be considered.

5. **Opioids** may cause hypotension by decreasing sympathetic tone. More commonly, they cause bradycardia.

6. **Antibiotics** are the most common drug class to cause allergic reactions. Vancomycin, if rapidly infused, can cause "red man syndrome," an anaphylactoid reaction due to histamine release and characterized by flushing and hypotension.

5. By what mechanism(s) do commonly used anesthetic agents cause hypotension?

1. **Inhalational agents:** Halothane lowers cardiac output by directly depressing myocardial contractility. Isoflurane, by contrast, reduces preload and afterload through vasodilation.

2. **Hypnotics:** Both propofol and sodium pentothal cause hypotension through vasodilation.

3. **Neuromuscular blocking agents:** A side effect of rapidly injected atracurium and mivacurium is histamine release with resultant hypotension.

6. In what ways can regional anesthetics lead to hypotension?

1. **Epidural anesthesia.** Conduction blockade of sympathetic fibers causes vasodilation below the level of the block. There is less chance of hypotension with blocks lower than the fifth thoracic level (T5) because of compensatory vasoconstriction of the upper extremities. Blocks higher than T2 may affect cardioaccelerator nerves, reducing cardiac output and heart rate. The

vagus nerve may remain unaffected, causing further vasovagal reductions in heart rate and blood pressure. Rapid-acting agents such as chloroprocaine and etidocaine produce a faster sympathectomy and more abrupt hypotension.

2. **Spinal (subarachnoid) anesthesia.** Because the local anesthetic is injected directly into the cerebrospinal fluid, spinal blockade generally has a faster onset than epidural blockade and may decrease blood pressure faster and more dramatically. Hypovolemic patients are especially susceptible to hypotension after regional blockade. They have compensated by vasoconstriction, and when sympathetic tone is abolished, they vasodilate and become profoundly hypotensive.

7. Which neurologic conditions cause hypotension?

1. **Head injury.** A transient decrease in blood pressure is common. Suspect occult bleeding, because prolonged hypotension is likely due to hemorrhage. The injured brain is more vulnerable to the ischemic effects of hypotension. Scalp and facial lesions are deceptive and may be a source of significant blood loss.

2. **Brain death.** There is loss of descending vascular control, exacerbated by hypovolemia from hemorrhage or the diuresis used to reduce cerebral edema.

3. **Spinal shock.** Loss of sympathetic tone leads to bradycardia, vasodilation, and hypotension. Pressors may be required if hypotension persists despite normovolemia. Bradycardia can be treated with atropine.

8. Describe the hemodynamic changes associated with aortic cross-clamping.

The most common **iatrogenic** causes of hypotension are side effects from drugs and regional anesthetic techniques.

Aortic cross-clamping and unclamping can lead to hypotension. Clamping the abdominal aorta, to repair an aneurysm for example, leads to hypertension in the segment proximal to the clamp with hypoperfusion distally. **Infrarenal clamping** leads to a mild increase in afterload and usually preserves myocardial contractility. **Suprarenal clamping** elevates mean arterial pressure (MAP), central venous pressure, pulmonary artery pressure, and pulmonary capillary wedge pressure and decreases cardiac index. The increase in afterload may lead to overdistention of an impaired left ventricle, impairing performance and producing hypotension.

"Unclamping shock" is a short-lived, moderately hypotensive episode (approximately 40% reduction in MAP) associated with increased oxygen requirements and metabolic acidosis, usually for approximately 30 minutes after unclamping. Two theories as to the cause of unclamping shock have been developed. The first theory proposes that hypotension is due to washout of vasoactive mediators and acids from ischemic limbs. The second theory is that there is a reactive hyperemia at the newly revascularized area, causing a relative hypovolemia when fluid is redistributed after unclamping. Vascular resistance diminishes, producing hypotension.

9. What causes of hypotension are associated with pregnancy and childbirth?

1. **Supine hypotension syndrome.** Beyond the first trimester, weight of the gravid uterus produces aortocaval compression, decreasing venous return and compromising uteroplacental perfusion. Only 10% of women at term are symptomatic (dizziness, nausea, hypotension), although 90% have complete caval obstruction when supine. All pregnant patients should have a wedge under the right hip when supine, displacing the uterus to the left.

2. Hypotension after **regional block.** Prehydration is important. If the patient remains hypotensive, ensure that the uterus is displaced, increase fluids, place the patient in slight head-down position, and administer ephedrine, which is conventionally thought to preserve uterine blood flow better than phenylephrine.

3. **Postpartum hemorrhage.** Normal blood loss is approximately 500 ml from a vaginal delivery and 1000 ml from a cesarean section. Further losses, from uterine atony, an unidentified bleeding source, or severe lacerations, may significantly diminish the parturient's blood volume.

4. Rapid infusion of **intravenous oxytocin (Pitocin).** Bolus administration of intravenous oxytocin produces systemic vasodilation, tachycardia, hypotension, and antidiuresis.

5. **Amniotic fluid embolism.** Absorption of amniotic fluid and particulate fetal matter through large uterine blood vessels occurs in approximately 3 in 100,000 births. The biphasic response consists initially of pulmonary vasospasm in response to vasoactive substances, followed by right-sided heart failure, decreased cardiac output, pulmonary edema, hypoxia, hypotension, and death.

10. How is hypotension treated intraoperatively?

First, determine the cause. Estimate blood loss and prior fluid resuscitation, check hematocrit, urine output, and electrocardiogram (ECG). Invasive monitoring may be indicated.

CAUSES	TREATMENT
Decreased preload	Fluids then pressors
Decreased cardiac output	
ST segment depression	Treat ischemia with nitroglycerin
Decreased contractility	Inotropes
Increased afterload	Decrease afterload (sodium nitroprusside [Nipride])
Decreased afterload	Volume, pressors

11. Describe the major causes of postoperative hypotension.

- **Spurious** or incorrect readings may be obtained using a blood pressure cuff that is too large or an arterial line that is improperly zeroed, malpositioned, or damped.
- **Decreased SVR** caused by a sympathectomy from regional anesthesia.
- **Hypovolemia** caused by unreplaced fluid deficit, unrecognized blood loss, third spacing, or ongoing fluid loss. The patient may require reoperation to investigate persistent occult bleeding.
- **Ventricular dysfunction** can be produced by ischemia, impaired contractility, fluid overload, or mobilization of fluid after regional anesthesia.
- **Mechanical problems** such as a tension pneumothorax or tamponade may impair venous return.
- **Arrhythmias** are more common in patients with preexisting heart disease. They can be triggered by ischemia, decreasing cardiac output, or medications including alpha blockers, venodilators, and histamine-releasing drugs.

12. How is postoperative hypotension treated?

Review all vital signs for clues. Review input and output during surgery as well as the procedure. Perform a physical exam and assess urine output. A fluid trial is usually indicated and often curative. Consider myocardial ischemia and mechanical reasons preventing return of blood to the heart. Hematocrit, electrolytes, blood gas, ECG, and chest x-ray may be required to establish a diagnosis or corroborate a clinical suspicion. Pressors or inotropes occasionally may be necessary.

13. Discuss concerns about hypotension in pediatrics.

Mask induction with halothane causes hypotension by directly depressing the myocardium. Children have an increased incidence of bradycardia, hypotension, and cardiac arrest compared with adults because they have rapid anesthetic uptake, immature baroreflexes that are blunted by anesthesia, and less vasoconstrictive responses to hemorrhage than adults.

14. What techniques are used to cause deliberate hypotension?

Sodium nitroprusside, an afterload reducer, is commonly used because it has a rapid onset and short half-life and is easy to titrate. Perfusion is preserved at pressures greater than 50 mmHg in normal patients. Disadvantages of sodium nitroprusside include rebound hypertension, tachyphylaxis, increased intracranial pressure, and cyanide toxicity.

Nitroglycerin has a short half-life and no toxic metabolites. It causes increased cerebral blood flow by venodilation.

Esmolol is a cardioselective β_1-adrenergic blocking agent with a half-life of 9 minutes and is easily titratable. Advantages in neurosurgery include a lack of cerebral vasodilation, tachycardia, rebound hypertension, or toxic metabolites.

Less commonly used agents include ganglionic blockers (trimethaphan), alpha antagonists (phentolomine), and inhalational agents. Modest hypotension can also be a benefit of a regional technique that causes a sympathectomy because blood loss may be diminished.

BIBLIOGRAPHY

1. Bernards CM: Epidural and spinal anesthesia. In Barash PG, Cullen BF, Stoelting RK (eds): Clinical Anesthesia, 3rd ed. Philadelphia, Lippincott Williams & Wilkins, 1997.
2. Chestnut DH: Obstetrical Anesthesia: Principles and Practice. St. Louis, Mosby, 1994.
3. Cottrell JE, Hartung J: Induced hypotension. In Cottrell JE, Smith DS (eds): Anesthesiology and Neurosurgery. St. Louis, Mosby, 1994, pp 425–434.
4. Ellis JE, Roizen MF, Mantha S, Wilke H-J: Anesthesia for vascular surgery. In Barash PG, Cullen BF, Stoelting RK (eds): Clinical Anesthesia, 3rd ed. Philadelphia, Lippincott Williams & Wilkins, 1997.

32. HYPERTENSION

Tanya Argo, M.D., and Theresa L. Kinnard, M.D.

1. What is hypertension?

Hypertension (HTN) is a disease process in which the patient has higher than normal blood pressure (BP) on more than one occasion. As a rule, the upper limit of normal BP is considered around 140/90. Over time, elevated BP leads to end-organ damage.

2. Contrast systolic and diastolic hypertension.

Systolic HTN is associated with advancing age and is related to a decreased compliance of the aorta and arterioles. In adults with a diastolic BP (DBP) < 90 mmHg, a systolic BP (SBP) of 140–159 mmHg is borderline isolated systolic HTN, whereas SBP > 160 mmHg is isolated systolic HTN.

Diastolic HTN is associated with an increase in systemic vascular resistance and believed to be the major contributor to hypertensive morbidity. In adults, a DBP of 90–104 mmHg is mild HTN; 105–114 mmHg is moderate HTN; and > 115 mmHg is severe HTN.

3. What are the causes of HTN?

1. Essential HTN—unknown cause; > 90% of all cases fall into this category.

2. Endocrine—adrenocortical dysfunction, pheochromocytoma, myxedema, acromegaly, birth control pills, thyrotoxicosis.

3. Renal—chronic pyelonephritis, renovascular stenosis, acute and chronic glomerulonephritis, polycystic kidney disease.

4. Neurogenic—psychogenic, familial dysautonomia, increased intracranial pressure, spinal cord transection, polyneuritis.

5. Systolic hypertension with wide pulse pressure—arteriosclerosis, aortic valvular insufficiency, patent ductus arteriosus, arteriovenous fistula.

6. Miscellaneous—increased intravascular volume, polyarteritis nodosa, hypercalcemia, toxemia of pregnancy, coarctation of the aorta, acute intermittent porphyria.

4. Why should HTN be treated?

Many HTN patients develop smooth muscle hypertrophy in the precapillary resistance arterioles. Hypertrophied arterioles develop increased resting resistance and an exaggerated response to vasomotor stimuli. Uncontrolled HTN is also associated with early arteriosclerosis, which leads to coronary artery disease; intracerebral occlusions or hemorrhage; and renal failure. Men with isolated systolic HTN have a two- to threefold increase in cardiovascular disease. Recently, however, the results of the Systolic Hypertension in the Elderly Program (SHEP) suggested that treatment with a thiazide diuretic decreases the risk of cerebrovascular accident by 36%. Decreasing DBP to a normal range also has been associated with a decrease in morbidity and mortality of HTN-related diseases.

5. Identify current drug therapies for hypertensive patients.

Five classes of drugs are used in the medical treatment of hypertension:

1. Diuretics
2. Antiadrenergics—alpha and beta blockers
3. Calcium channel blockers
4. Vasodilators
5. Angiotensin-converting enzyme (ACE) inhibitors

6. Describe common preanesthetic considerations in hypertensive patients.

1. What is the cause of the hypertension? Surgical mortality is fairly high in patients with renovascular hypertension. Undiagnosed pheochromocytoma may have devastating operative consequences, such as catecholamine-induced coronary artery spasm or sustained malignant hypertension.

2. When did the patient become hypertensive? If HTN was of sudden onset, it probably has an identifiable cause.

3. How long has the patient had hypertension? A longer duration of disease may mean more severe end-organ damage.

4. What medications is the patient taking now?

5. What medications has the patient taken in the past?

6. Has the patient been compliant with medication?

7. Have medications adequately controlled the HTN? Poorly controlled HTN leads to an increased incidence of end-organ damage.

8. Is there any evidence of end-organ damage? More than 50% of untreated hypertensives develop end-organ disease, including left ventricular hypertrophy, congestive heart failure, cardiomyopathy, renal insufficiency, strokes, and retinopathy.

9. Are the electrolytes within normal limits, especially in patients taking diuretics?

7. What findings from physical and laboratory exams may indicate end-organ damage from HTN?

1. Left ventricular lift with cardiac palpation
2. Loud aortic closure and S_4 upon cardiac auscultation
3. Left ventricular hypertrophy on an electrocardiogram (ECG) suggests long-term HTN
4. Arteriovenous nicking on retinal exam
5. Orthostatic hypotension
6. Elevated serum creatinine
7. Abdominal bruits
8. Congestive heart failure

8. What antihypertensive medications should be taken until the time of surgery?

A well-controlled hypertensive patient has less intraoperative lability in blood pressure. Acute withdrawal of antihypertensives may precipitate rebound HTN or myocardial ischemia. In general, antihypertensive therapy should be maintained until the time of surgery and restarted as soon as possible after surgery. However, Coriate et al. found that discontinuation of ACE inhibitors 24 hours before the scheduled surgery decreased the incidence of severe hypotension on induction. Diuretics may be withheld when depletion of intravascular volume is a concern.

9. What preoperative premedication is appropriate for hypertensive patients?

Hypertensive patients, like all patients, have increased anxiety before surgery and may benefit from anxiolytics such as the benzodiazepines. Clonidine, an α_2-adrenergic agonist, also has been shown to decrease preoperative anxiety and to reduce lability of intraoperative blood pressure and anesthetic requirements. If an anticholinergic is required, glycopyrrolate is a better choice than atropine, because it is associated with a lower incidence of tachycardia.

10. Discuss alternative induction agents for general anesthesia in hypertensive patients.

Any induction agent can be successfully used with careful titration and monitoring.

- Barbiturates, benzodiazepines, and propofol are likely to lead to an exaggerated decrease in BP if not titrated slowly to effect. Untreated or poorly controlled hypertensive patients are often volume-depleted and especially prone to significant falls in BP.
- Propofol, a diisopropylphenol, exhibits dose-dependent cardiovascular depression.
- Ketamine is rarely recommended, because its sympathomimetic effects may exaggerate HTN.
- Etomidate is a nonbarbiturate hypnotic with a lower incidence of cardiovascular effects. It is probably the most cardiovascularly stable drug available for induction of hypertensive patients.
- Opioids also may be used with minimal cardiovascular effects but may require doses not conducive to immediate extubation at the end of surgery.
- Intravenous or topical laryngotracheal lidocaine (1.5 mg/kg) before intubation may help to minimize the sympathetic response to the stimulation of intubation.
- Sodium nitroprusside (1–2 µg/kg), nitroglycerin (1–2 µg/kg), or esmolol also helps to blunt rise in BP and heart rate with laryngoscopy and intubation.
- The most important factor for limiting the exaggerated BP response to intubation is to limit the duration of laryngoscopy to 15 seconds or less.

11. Is regional anesthesia a viable option for hypertensive patients?

Yes, but a high level of sympathetic blockade in hypertensive patients may produce excessive reductions in BP, because decreased intravascular fluid volume exacerbates vasodilatation. Regional blocks should be administered to an adequately medicated and sedated patient to prevent stress-related release of catecholamines. Epinephrine should not be added to local anesthetics because of its association with tachycardia and exacerbation of HTN.

12. Discuss common intraoperative considerations for hypertensive patients.

Long-term hypertension often leads to **left ventricular functional abnormalities**. Left ventricular hypertrophy (LVH) results from the increased pressure against which the left ventricle is required to eject. The hypertrophied left ventricle requires a greater filling pressure to produce adequate end-diastolic stretching of heart muscle to maintain stroke volume, as illustrated by the Frank-Starling curve (see Chapter 38, Congestive Heart Failure). The left ventricle also may exhibit diastolic dysfunction, in which the ventricle does not relax enough to allow adequate filling for maintenance of stroke volume (unless end-diastolic pressures increase). Subsequently, hypertensive patients with LVH depend on preload to maintain cardiac output and arterial blood pressure.

The autoregulation curve of cerebral blood flow (CBF) also shifts to the right. Autoregulation is the ability of the brain to maintain a constant cerebral blood flow over a range of BPs. In hypertensive patients the higher pressure required for normal blood flow is reflected in the shifting of the curve. Symptoms of cerebral ischemia are more likely to occur at higher pressures in hypertensive patients than in normotensive controls.

Other considerations include constant monitoring of the ECG for evidence of myocardial ischemia, keeping in mind that an increase in heart rate and BP may lead to increased myocardial oxygen consumption. Intraoperative hypertension also promotes increased bleeding in the operative site. Renal dysfunction may influence choice of agents or dosage requirement. Centrally acting antihypertensives (e.g., clonidine, methyldopa) promote sedation and therefore may decrease anesthetic needs.

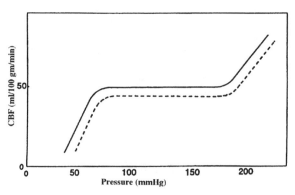

Autoregulation of cerebral blood flow.

13. Provide a differential diagnosis for intraoperative HTN.
Related to preexisting disease

Preexisting HTN	Elevated intracranial pressure
Early acute myocardial infarction	Autonomic hyperreflexia
Aortic dissection	

Related to surgery

Prolonged tourniquet time	Postmyocardial revascularization
Aortic cross-clamping	Postcarotid endarterectomy

Related to anesthetic

Pain/catecholamine release	Malignant hyperthermia
Inadequate depth of anesthesia	Shivering
Hypoxia	Improperly sized (too small) BP cuff
Hypervolemia	Transducer artifact-increased resonance
Hypercarbia	(improperly low position of transducer)

Related to medication
Rebound hypertension (from discontinuation of clonidine, beta blockers, or methyldopa)
Systemic absorption of vasoconstrictors
Intravenous indigo carmine dye

Others
Bladder distention, hypothermia and vasoconstriction, hypoglycemia

14. Is acute postoperative HTN significant?
It is fairly common for postoperative patients to exhibit hypertension. Prompt diagnosis of cause and appropriate treatment are needed to prevent associated complications. Acute hypertension increases afterload and therefore myocardial work and thus may precipitate myocardial ischemia. Increased systemic vascular resistance also may impair left ventricular ejection of blood, decreasing cardiac output and leading to pulmonary edema. Other complications include wound hematomas, intracerebral hemorrhage, arrhythmias, acute renal failure, headache, and changes in mental status.

15. How is postoperative HTN managed?
Pain is the most common cause of postoperative hypertension, but the first step is thorough assessment for other causes. The best approach is to diagnose the problem and to individualize treatment. Normally careful titration of labetalol or esmolol is sufficient to gain quick control of postoperative HTN. Occasionally, one may need to consider a nitroprusside drip, especially if tight control is required (i.e., postoperative craniotomy patients, patients prone to myocardial ischemia).

CONTROVERSIES

16. Are hypertensive patients undergoing general anesthesia at increased risk for perioperative cardiac morbidity?

The hypertensive patient's risk for perioperative cardiac complications is difficult to assess because of differences in study design and patient selection. A study by Prys-Roberts noted that poorly controlled hypertensive patients with an average mean blood pressure of 129.5 mmHg demonstrated an increased incidence of hypotension and ECG changes, suggesting myocardial ischemia during maintenance of general anesthesia. Other studies also suggest that a DBP > 110 mmHg is a risk factor for cardiac morbidity.

17. Is there a BP above which elective surgery should be cancelled?

The answer to this question is highly individualized and depends on the anesthesiologist, surgeon, surgical procedure, and patient. Elevated BP in a patient who is normally well controlled but very nervous preoperatively should be treated with an anxiolytic and reevaluated. The available data suggest that the patient with a DBP ≥ 110 mmHg should not undergo elective anesthesia because of an increased incidence of cardiac complications (myocardial ischemia, congestive heart failure, or cardiac death).

BIBLIOGRAPHY

1. Coriate P, Richer C, Douraki T, et al: Influence of chronic angiotensin converting enzyme inhibition on anesthetic induction. Anesthesiology 81:299–307, 1994.
2. Goldman L, Caldera DL: Risks of general anesthesia and elective operation in the hypertensive patient. Anesthesiology 50:285–292, 1979.
3. Prys-Roberts C: Anesthesia and hypertension. Br J Anaesth 56:711–724, 1984.
4. SHEP Cooperative Research Group: Prevention of stroke by antihypertensive drug treatment in older persons with isolated systolic hypertension. JAMA 265:3255–3264, 1991.
5. Steen PA, Tinker JH, Tarhan S: Myocardial reinfarction after anesthesia and surgery. JAMA 239:2566–2570, 1978.

33. AWARENESS DURING ANESTHESIA

James A. Ottevaere, M.D.

1. What is awareness under anesthesia?

Patient perception under general anesthesia takes the form of either explicit or implicit memory. Anesthetic awareness refers to explicit memory of intraoperative events, which involves spontaneous or conscious recall. In contrast, implicit memory is subconscious processing of information by the brain. Explicit recall of intraoperative events may occur with or without the sensation of pain, and recollections may be vivid, such as operating room conversation, or vague, such as dreams or unpleasant sensations associated with the operation. Implicit memory during anesthesia has been tested by hypnosis and behavioral suggestion. A commonly used behavioral suggestion is intraoperative instructions to touch a designated body part during the postoperative interview. The results of such investigations are variable but indicate that implicit memory during anesthesia exists in some form.

2. What is the significance of implicit memory during general anesthesia?

Implicit memory in anesthetized patients has prompted investigation into improving postoperative outcomes by using intraoperative suggestion. Patients listen to audiotapes containing positive messages while undergoing general anesthesia. Studies using this technique have demonstrated a decrease in both hospital stay and use of postoperative analgesia. Patients also report an improved sense of well-being. The subject, however, remains controversial because some studies found no difference in outcomes after positive suggestion.

3. Discuss the incidence of awareness during anesthesia.

The incidence of awareness during anesthesia varies greatly, depending on clinical situation and anesthetic technique. Awareness under anesthesia is divided into two categories, consciousness with pain and consciousness without pain. Awareness with painful sensation has the greatest effect on postoperative sequelae. The incidence of awareness with pain is approximately 1 in 3000 general anesthetics. Consciousness without pain has a higher incidence—approximately 3 in 1000 general anesthetics. Absence of pain may result from the concomitant use of local anesthetics or opioids or the analgesic properties of volatile anesthetics at low doses. Evidence suggests that the incidence of awareness under anesthesia has decreased over the last 2 decades as nitrous narcotic techniques decrease. However, medicolegal claims for awareness are increasing.

4. Describe common clinical situations associated with awareness.

Anesthesiologists often intentionally use light general anesthesia when it is indicated by the clinical situation. Common surgeries associated with an increased incidence of awareness are cesarean section, major trauma, and cardiac procedures. General anesthesia in obstetric patients may produce neonatal suppression; therefore, doses and concentrations of anesthetics have traditionally been minimized. As a result, the incidence of awareness in obstetric patients is approximately 1%. The hemodynamic instability associated with major trauma often requires reduced dosages of anesthetics. The incidence of postoperative awareness in trauma patients may be as high as 48%, depending on the severity of trauma. Patients undergoing cardiac surgery with cardiopulmonary bypass also have a higher incidence of postoperative recall because of the reliance on narcotic-based anesthesia, which minimizes myocardial depression but produces unreliable amnesia. Recent data suggest an incidence of 1%.

5. Describe the clinical signs and symptoms of light anesthesia.

Motor signs in response to light anesthesia frequently precede hemodynamic changes or sympathetic activation. Specific motor signs include eyelid or eye motion, swallowing, coughing, grimacing, and movement of the extremities or head. Increased respiratory effort is due to activity of intercostal and abdominal muscles, which are suppressed at deeper levels of anesthesia. With the use of neuromuscular blockade, motor signs do not provide information about anesthetic depth. Consequently, sympathetic activation represents an additional method for assessing light anesthesia. Sympathetic effects associated with light anesthesia include hypertension, tachycardia, mydriasis, tearing, sweating, and salivation. Such findings are nonspecific and modified by anesthetic agents; thus their presence or absence is an unreliable indicator of awareness. In fact, a recent review of closed claims for awareness reported that signs of "light" anesthesia (tachycardia, hypertension) were found in only a minority of patients claiming awareness.

6. What is the last sensory modality suppressed by anesthesia?

The auditory pathway is the most metabolically active part of the conscious brain. Thus, hearing is the last sense suppressed by anesthesia. This fact has significant implications. Because hearing plays an important role in implicit memory, intraoperative events or conversation may affect postoperative well-being both positively and negatively. In addition, monitoring of auditory-evoked potentials (AEPs) provides a window into anesthetic depth and may be used to evaluate the effects of anesthetic drugs.

7. What monitor can be used to tell how deeply anesthetized a patient is?

No single monitor can give a complete answer to how deeply anesthetized a patient is. Depth of anesthesia involves several parameters, including the degree of analgesia, areflexia, and hypnosis. Traditionally, analgesia has been judged by vital signs, and areflexia can be monitored by patient movement or nerve stimulation. BIS monitoring is a newer technology that uses processed parameters of the electroencephalogram (EEG) waveform to give the anesthesiologist an objective measure of the degree of hypnosis that the patient is under.

8. Describe the BIS monitor further.

The monitor collects raw EEG data from a small electrode placed over the forehead and temporal area. The raw data undergo bispectral analysis (a proprietary process involving lots of math) and other processed EEG parameters. Once the processing is complete, a number between 1 and 100 is displayed on the screen, which should correspond to the degree of sedation or hypnosis of the patient. Lower numbers indicate deeper hypnosis while higher numbers indicate a lightly sedated or awake patient.

9. Which anesthetic techniques are associated with increased risk of intraoperative awareness?

Several anesthetic techniques increase the risk of awareness. Use of muscle relaxants, particularly in combination with nitrous oxide and opioids alone, may mask signs of light anesthesia and contribute to increased incidence of intraoperative awareness. Incidence of recall is also increased in opioid-based anesthetics used in cardiac and other selected surgeries. Total intravenous anesthesia (TIVA) may predispose patients to awareness under anesthesia because of the variability in dosage requirements and elimination rates, which is not seen with volatile agents.

10. What are the common preventable causes of intraoperative awareness?

Mislabeling or misuse of succinylcholine drips have a high association with awake paralysis, as do syringe swaps. These are clearly due to lack of vigilance. Difficult intubations are associated with awareness when the caregiver neglects to redose with hypnotics or maintains volatile anesthesia. Vaporizers should be checked for adequate content. Use of muscle relaxants (eliminating patient movement as a sign) may also contribute to awareness.

11. What dose of volatile agent is sufficient to prevent awareness?

Volatile agents have amnestic properties. However, the concentration of volatile anesthetics necessary to eliminate intraoperative awareness is not clearly established. Variability among patients and clinical situations contributes to altered alveolar concentrations necessary to suppress recall. Evidence indicates that 0.4–0.6 minimum alveolar concentration (MAC) of isoflurane prevents response to commands and eliminates awareness in volunteers. The fact that these volunteers did not receive surgical stimulation has led to recommendations of at least 0.8 MAC to guarantee unconsciousness during surgery when volatile agents are used as the primary anesthetic. Addition of amnestic agents such as benzodiazepines, scopolamine, and intravenous anesthetics lowers the concentration of volatile agent necessary to prevent recall.

12. Identify common clinical situations that increase anesthetic requirements.

Unrecognized increases in anesthetic requirements may contribute to intraoperative awareness. Certain clinical situations are associated with increased minimum alveolar concentration (MAC) of volatile anesthetics. Multiple general anesthetics may produce long-term tolerance to subsequent anesthetics. Chronic alcoholism, hypernatremia, and hyperthermia increase MAC. Drugs that increase central nervous system catecholamines, such as monoamine oxidase inhibitors, tricyclic antidepressants, cocaine, and amphetamines, also increase the MAC of inhaled anesthetics.

13. What are some sequelae of intraoperative awareness?

The postoperative interview allows the anesthesiologist to elicit information about anesthetic recall. Because few patients spontaneously complain of intraoperative awareness, underreporting is common. Direct inquiry about the patient's subjective feelings about the anesthetic may elicit complaints of fear, anger, sadness, or simply a feeling that something is "not quite right."

Complaints involving recall of intraoperative conversation, pain, weakness or paralysis, or intubation should be pursued to determine their validity. Some cases of awareness may manifest months to years postoperatively as post-traumatic stress disorder (PTSD). PTSD results from distressing events outside normal human experience; in anesthesia, it is usually associated with intraoperative awareness involving pain. PTSD symptoms include flashbacks or nightmares, avoidance behaviors, emotional numbing, preoccupation with death, and hyperarousal.

14. How should patients who have experienced intraoperative awareness be managed?

When a case of awareness is identified either by staff or during the postoperative interview, several steps should be taken immediately. The anesthesiologist should determine the validity of the claim by eliciting details from the patient and comparing them with intraoperative events. The timing of any recollection of pain should be assessed, because patients may confuse postoperative and intraoperative pain. The anesthesiologist should question patients compassionately and acknowledge belief in their accounts. Detailed documentation of the interview and findings should be recorded in the hospital chart. Prompt referral to a psychologist or psychiatrist trained in treatment of PTSD is warranted, particularly in patients who exhibit psychological symptoms or experience pain as part of their intraoperative recall.

15. How can the anesthesiologist help to prevent intraoperative awareness?

Prevention of awareness is an important consideration in the proper administration of anesthesia. Research and experience have led to the development of specific recommendations for prevention. Preoperatively the anesthesiologist should perform a thorough machine check. Amnestic agents such as benzodiazepines or scopolamine are helpful when used as premedicants or adjuvants to anesthesia. Additional doses of induction agents during prolonged or difficult intubations helps to ensure adequate levels of anesthesia. Intraoperatively, muscle relaxants should be avoided unless necessary for surgical conditions. Nitrous oxide and opioids alone or in combination are unreliable in the prevention of awareness and should be supplemented with volatile or intravenous agents. Volatile agents should be administered in at least 0.8 MAC when used as the sole anesthetic. Finally, given the potential effect of auditory input on postoperative outcomes, discouraging negative comments or using headphones or earplugs during anesthesia may have some value in the prevention of explicit and implicit recall.

BIBLIOGRAPHY

1. Aitkenhead AR: Awareness during anaesthesia: What should the patient be told? [editorial]. Anaesthesia 45:351–352, 1990.
2. Domino KB, Posner KL, Caplan RA, Cheney FW: Awareness under anesthesia: A closed claims analysis. Anesthesiology 90:1053–1061, 1999.
3. Eldor J, Frankel DZN: Intra-anesthetic awareness. Resuscitation 21:113–119, 1991.
4. Ghoneim MM, Block RI: Learning and consciousness during general anesthesia. Anesthesiology 76:279–305, 1992.
5. Heneghan C: Clinical and medicolegal aspects of conscious awareness during anesthesia. Int Anesthesiol Clin 31:1–11, 1993.
6. Jones JG: Perception and memory during general anesthesia. Br J Anaesth 73:31–37, 1994.
7. Liu WHD, Thorp TAS, Graham SG, Aitkenhead AR: Incidence of awareness with recall during general anesthesia. Anaesthesia 46:435–437, 1991.
8. Lyons G, Macdonald R: Awareness during caesarean section. Anaesthesia 46:62–64, 1991.
9. Newton DEF, Thornton C, Konieczko K, et al: Levels of consciousness in volunteers breathing sub-MAC concentrations of isoflurane. Br J Anaesth 65:609–615, 1990.
10. Phillips AA, McLean RF, Devitt JH, Harrington EM: Recall of intraoperative events after general anaesthesia and cardiopulmonary bypass. Can J Anaesth 40:922–926, 1993.

34. CARDIAC DYSRHYTHMIAS

Kelli Lambert Weiner, M.D.

1. Describe the relationship between the electrocardiogram (ECG) tracing and the intracellular action potential.

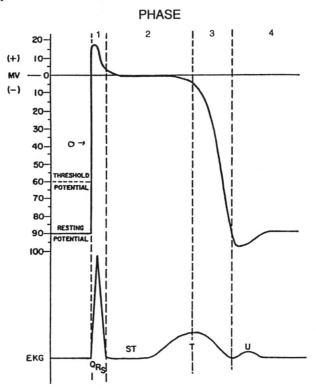

Action potential and surface ECG.

There are five phases to the action potential. The **resting membrane potential** is predominantly determined by the concentration gradient between intracellular and extracellular potassium and, to a lesser extent, the sodium gradient. As demonstrated in the figure above, phase 0 is the rapid depolarization of the action potential and corresponds to the initiation of the QRS complex of the ECG. This occurs when an electrical stimulus causes an increase in sodium permeability and allows an influx of sodium into the cell.

There are four phases to repolarization. The earliest phase of recovery—**phase 1**—proceeds quickly to the plateau portion of the action potential—**phase 2**—corresponding to the QT interval. **Phase 3** is related to the T wave of the ECG. Repolarization is due to the efflux of potassium from the cell and the inactivation of the sodium and calcium channels. **Phase 4** is the time when the cell is at its resting membrane potential, between the end of the T wave and the beginning of the QRS complex.

Each portion of the conduction system has a specific type of action potential, designated either as fast or slow action potentials. The primary current for the fast action potentials is sodium movement, and for the slow channels, calcium. The sinus node and the arterioventricular node have slow action potentials. The atrium, His-Purkinje network, and the ventricle have fast action potentials.

2. Interpret the following 12-lead ECG.

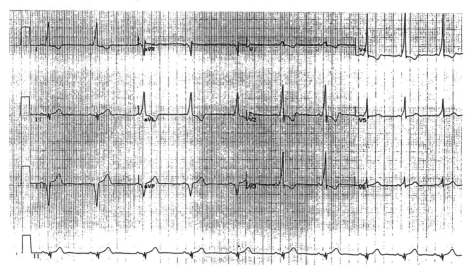

This tracing is a classic example of the **Wolff-Parkinson-White** (WPW) phenomenon. The ECG findings are a short P-R interval of ≤ 0.12 seconds, initial slurring of the QRS, and prolongation of the QRS. The slurring of the QRS—the delta wave—is caused by early depolarization of the portion of the ventricle due to an accessory pathway.

In the past, two patterns of WPW have been described: type A and type B. When aberrant conduction occurs down a left-sided accessory pathway, a pattern resembling right bundle branch block exists, and this is known as type A. With a right-sided accessory pathway, a pattern resembling left bundle branch block is seen and is known as type B. In patients with WPW, the atrial stimulus may conduct only through the normal pathway, down both pathways, or down the accessory pathway. Accessory atrioventricular (AV) connections may be capable of conduction in the retrograde direction only, and these are termed "concealed pathways," as there are no delta waves present on the ECG.

3. What are the mechanisms of reentry and of AV reentrant tachycardia?

Reentrant tachycardia can occur when two conduction pathways are available that form a potentially circular path. If an unidirectional block is present in one pathway, and conduction time is slow enough over the nonblocked pathway to allow recovery time in the blocked pathway, this allows retrograde conduction over the previously blocked pathway.

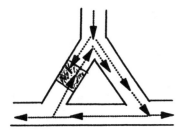

Requirements for a reentry circuit.
1. A potentially circular pathway
2. A zone of depressed conduction
3. An area of unidirectional block

Orthodromic AV reentrant tachycardia is the most frequent form of tachycardia that utilizes an accessory pathway (see Figure below).

Orthodromic AV reentry.

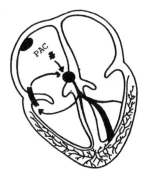

This term refers to the propagation of an impulse down the normal AV conduction system and retrograde conduction over the accessory pathway back to the atrium. The QRS morphology is narrow, unless an underlying bundle branch block is present. This type of tachycardia can be initiated by either a premature atrial contraction (PAC) or premature ventricular contraction (PVC). **Antidromic tachycardia** uses the accessory pathway for anterograde conduction, with retrograde conduction through the normal ventricular to atrial (VA) conduction system. This pattern also can be started by either a PAC or PVC, and during the tachycardia, the QRS will be broad and often bizarre.

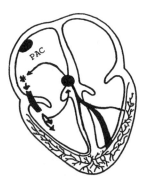
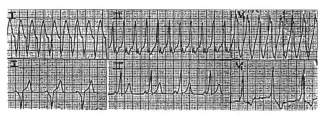

Antidromic AV reentry. Note the rhythm strip with the broad QRS, and after conversion, delta waves are present in the second strip.

4. What is the treatment of AV reentry tachycardia?

The first step in treatment is to determine if the patient is hemodynamically stable. If the patient is not stable, the first choice is synchronized cardioversion. If the patient is stable, the first choice is to increase vagal tone by carotid massage or Valsalva maneuver. The next step is to administer verapamil, 5–10 mg intravenously, or adenosine, 6 mg intravenously followed by 12 mg if necessary. These measures can be repeated, if necessary, and followed by synchronized cardioversion if the rhythm persists or the patient becomes unstable.

5. Identify this patient's rhythm.

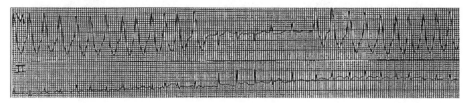

In this ECG, the rhythm is **atrial fibrillation** in a patient with an **AV accessory pathway**. The normal and abnormal QRS complexes indicate two possible pathways for conduction. This combination of an irregular rhythm with narrow and wide QRS complexes is virtually diagnostic of atrial fibrillation with preexcitation. It is important to recognize this pattern, because the treatment differs from that for a patient with atrial fibrillation without preexcitation. Lead II is uninformative in this ECG and demonstrates the importance of multiple ECG lead analysis.

6. What is the treatment of atrial fibrillation with preexcitation?

In the usual patient with atrial fibrillation, digitalis is often used to decrease the number of stimuli that are conducted through the AV node. However, in WPW, digitalis may increase the conductivity of the accessory pathway and lead to ventricular fibrillation. β-adrenergic blockers prolong conduction time and increase the refractoriness in the AV node; however, they do not terminate AV reentry tachycardia and can cause profound hypotension. Although calcium channel blockers can terminate orthodromic AV reentry, they are dangerous during atrial fibrillation because they can increase the ventricular rate by increasing the number of preexcited ventricular complexes. The use of adenosine in these patients is controversial, because adenosine can terminate reentrant supraventricular arrhythmias involving the AV node. However, the drug can also cause increased conduction through the accessory pathway, possibly leading to ventricular fibrillation. The recommended treatment for atrial fibrillation with an accessory pathway in a hemodynamically stable patient is **procainamide**, 50 mg/min intravenously to a total dose of 10 mg/kg. If the patient is hemodynamically unstable, the treatment is **synchronized cardioversion**.

7. Discuss the anesthetic considerations for patients with preexcitation syndromes.

Adequate suppression of the sympathetic response is the key to avoiding these potentially serious arrhythmias. **Halothane** is a poor choice for a volatile anesthetic because it sensitizes the myocardium to catecholamines. It also has the least effect on refractoriness. **Droperidol** depresses accessory pathway conduction and may prevent the rapid ventricular response during AV reentrant tachycardia. **Opiates** and **barbiturates** have no proven electrophysiologic effect on accessory pathways. **Pancuronium** enhances AV conduction and is contraindicated.

8. What is the differential diagnosis for the following 12-lead ECG?

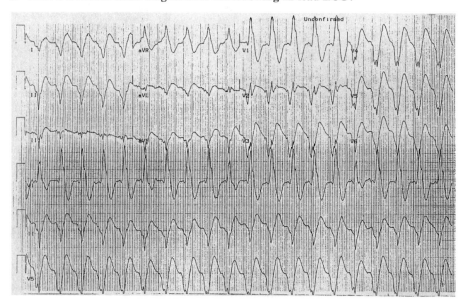

The differential diagnosis of a **wide complex tachycardia** includes ventricular tachycardia, supraventricular tachycardia with aberrant conduction, supraventricular tachycardia with a preexisting bundle branch block, or antidromic AV reentrant tachycardia.

9. What is the interpretation of the preceding ECG?

Determining the etiology of a wide complex tachycardia is often difficult. The following criteria can be seen in the ECG in question 8, supporting the diagnosis of **ventricular tachycardia**:

1. QRS duration > 0.14 seconds
2. Axis: quadrant III (negative in lead I, negative in lead aVF)
3. AV dissociation
4. VA association (ventricular to atrial conduction)
5. Morphology is unlike the pattern of right or left bundle branch block
6. Concordance: QRS complexes in all precordial leads are positive or negative

10. What is Brugada's rule?

Brugada et al. addressed the difficulty of interpreting wide complex tachycardias. They measured the interval from the onset of the R wave to the deepest part of the S wave in all tachycardias showing an RS complex in at least one precordial lead. An RS interval of > 100 msec was consistent with ventricular tachycardia. **The absence of an RS complex in all precordial leads or an RS interval > 100 msec was 100% specific for ventricular tachycardia** in their study. The ECG in question 8 illustrates the absence of RS complexes in all precordial leads.

11. What is a fusion beat?

A fusion beat occurs when there is activation of the ventricle from an atrial stimulus and from a ventricular focus simultaneously. This beat has a morphology intermediate between the normal beat and ventricular complex and identifies **AV dissociation**.

12. What is a Dressler beat?

A Dressler beat also indicates AV dissociation—a "capture beat." It occurs when there is a normal QRS due to ventricular activation from an atrial stimulus. If these beats are present during a wide complex tachycardia, the diagnosis is ventricular tachycardia. Fusion (F) and capture (C) beats are demonstrated in this ECG strip.

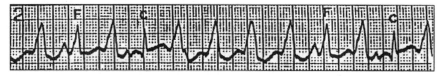

ECG courtesy of Dr. Henry J.L. Marriott.

13. Interpret the following ECG.

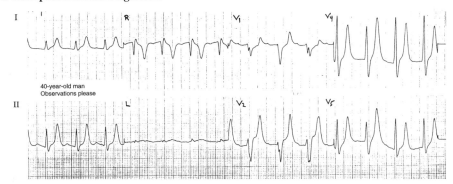

40-year-old man
Observations please

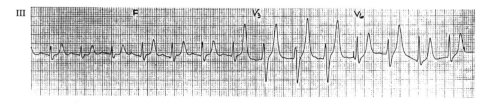

This ECG reveals the characteristic findings of **hyperkalemia**. Hyperkalemia causes a decrease in the resting membrane potential, therefore making the potential less negative. There is a decrease in the velocity of phase 0, leading to slowing of intraventricular conduction and a variable widening of the QRS on ECG. Hyperkalemia also causes acceleration of repolarization by increasing the steepness of the slope of phase 3. This is caused by increased membrane permeability to potassium and accounts for the tall and peaked T waves that are characteristic of hyperkalemia. This ECG was obtained in a 40-year-old man with diabetic ketoacidosis with a potassium concentration of 7.8 mmol/L. Note the prolonged PR interval, moderate increase in QRS duration, and marked increase in T-wave amplitude.

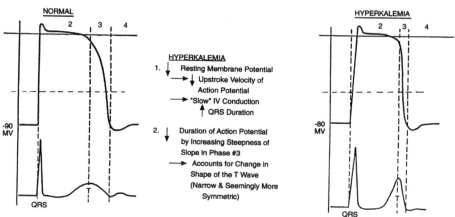

Effects of hyperkalemia on the action potential.

14. Describe the electrophysiologic changes that occur with hypokalemia.

Hypokalemia causes an increase in the resting membrane potential and an increase in the duration of the action potential (see Figure on following page). Phase 3 increases in duration, prolonging repolarization. A decrease in phase 2 and the increase in phase 3 cause shortening of the ST segment, flattened T waves, and the appearance of a U wave. The QRS may widen if hypokalemia is severe. The height of the P wave may be increased and the PR segment prolonged. The ECG below reveals a U wave in a patient with an aldosterone-secreting tumor and a potassium level of 1.8 mmol/L.

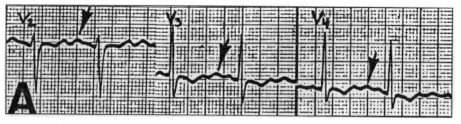

HYPOKALEMIA

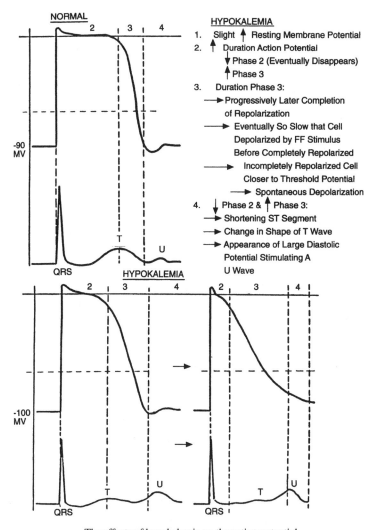

The effects of hypokalemia on the action potential.

15. What electrolyte abnormality is detected on this ECG strip?

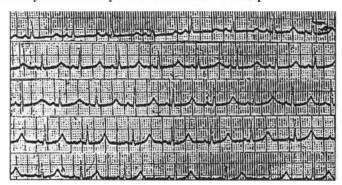

This ECG reveals a prolonged QT interval, primarily affecting the interval between the beginning of the QRS and the onset of the T wave. **Hypocalcemia** results in such prolongation. During the preceding rhythm strip, the QT normalizes as calcium is being administered.

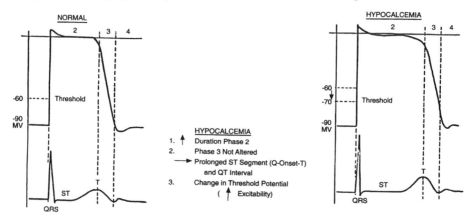

16. Describe the causes of QT prolongation.

The causes of a prolonged QT can be grouped as either congenital or acquired. The acquired causes can be due to **antiarrhythmic drugs** that prolong repolarization, such as quinidine, procainamide, sotalol, and amiodarone. Other offending drugs include phenothiazines, tricyclic antidepressants, and lithium. **Electrolyte imbalances** can result in QT prolongation, particularly hypokalemia, hypomagnesemia, and hypocalcemia. **Central nervous system disturbances**, such as subarachnoid or intracerebral hemorrhage, head trauma, and cerebral tumors, may cause marked repolarization abnormalities. **Myocarditis** and **myocardial ischemia** are additional causes.

17. What arrhythmia can occur with prolonged QT syndrome?

The arrhythmia associated with this syndrome is torsades de pointes. It is initiated by a ventricular beat in the setting of prolonged ventricular repolarization. This arrhythmia frequently resolves spontaneously, but it can lead to ventricular fibrillation.

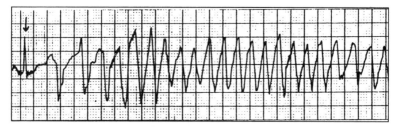

An example of torsades de pointes. A single sinus beat (*arrow*) is followed by ventricular tachycardia with an oscillating or swinging pattern of the QRS complexes.

ACKNOWLEDGMENT

The author thanks Dr. William P. Nelson, Saint Joseph's Hospital, Denver, Colorado, for his assistance with this chapter and the use of his illustrations.

BIBLIOGRAPHY

1. Brugada P, Brugada J, Mont L, et al: A new approach to the differential diagnosis of a regular tachycardia with a wide QRS complex. Circulation 83:1649–1659, 1991.

2. Durakovie Z, Durakovie A, Kastelan A: The preexcitation syndrome: Epidemiological and genetic study. Int J Cardiol 35:181–186, 1992.
3. Exner DV, Muzyka T, Gillis AM: Proarrhythmia in patients with the Wolff-Parkinson-White syndrome after standard doses of intravenous adenosine. Ann Intern Med 122:351–352, 1995.
4. Gursoy S, Brugada R, Brugada J: Which ventricular tachycardia is dangerous? Clin Cardiol 15:43–44, 1992.
5. Kaplan JA: Cardiac Anesthesia, 3rd ed. Philadelphia, W.B. Saunders, 1993, pp 781–818.
6. Lowenstein SR, Harken AH: A wide, complex look at cardiac dysrhythmias. J Emerg Med 5:519–531, 1987.
7. Lubarsky D, Kaufman B, Turndorf H: Anesthesia unmasking benign Wolff-Parkinson-White syndrome. Anesth Analg 68:172–174, 1989.
8. Podrid PJ, Kowey PR: Cardiac Arrhythmia: Mechanisms, Diagnosis, and Management. Baltimore, Williams & Wilkins, 1995.
9. Prystowky EN: Diagnosis and management of the preexcitation syndromes. Curr Probl Cardiol 13:225–310, 1988.
10. Sager PT, Khandari AK: Wide complex tachycardias: Differential diagnosis and management. Cardiol Clin 9:595–640, 1991.
11. Sharpe MD, Dobkowski WB, Murken JM, et al: The electrophysiologic effects of volatile anesthetics and sufentanil on the normal atrioventricular conduction system and accessory pathways in Wolff-Parkinson-White syndrome. Anesthesiology 80:63–70, 1994.
12. Steurer G, Gursoy S, Frey B, et al: The differential diagnosis of the electrocardiogram between ventricular tachycardia and preexcited tachycardia. Clin Cardiol 17:306–308, 1994.
13. Surawicz B: Electrophysiologic Basis of ECG and Cardiac Arrhythmias. Baltimore, Williams & Wilkins, 1995.
14. Wolff L, Parkinson J, White PD: Bundle-branch block with short P-R interval in healthy young people prone to paroxysmal tachycardia. Am Heart J 5:685–704, 1930.
15. Wrenn K: Management strategies in wide QRS complex tachycardia. Am J Emerg Med 9:592–597, 1991.

35. TEMPERATURE MONITORING AND DISTURBANCES

John H. Yang, M.D.

1. What are acceptable sites for temperature monitoring?

Monitoring temperature is a standard of care in anesthesia. The site for monitoring temperature during anesthesia depends on the surgical procedure, type of anesthesia, and reason for temperature monitoring:

1. **Skin**—may not reflect core temperature (skin is as much as 3–4°C lower).

2. **Axilla**—temperature monitored over the brachial artery with the arm adducted to the side is approximately 1°C below core.

3. **Rectum**—does not reflect rapid changes; rectal perforation is a rare complication.

4. **Esophagus**—a probe in the lower one-third of the esophagus accurately reflects core and blood temperature; combined with an esophageal stethoscope, the temperature probe is also useful for auscultation.

5. **Nasopharynx**—reflects brain temperature because of its proximity to the internal carotid artery; complications include nosebleed, especially if the patient is pregnant or has a coagulopathy; contraindicated in head trauma or with evidence of cerebrospinal fluid rhinorrhea.

6. **External auditory meatus**—because the tympanic membrane is in close proximity to the internal carotid artery, it reflects core temperature well; eardrum perforation is a possible complication.

7. **Bladder catheter**—approximates core temperature when urine flow is high.

8. **Pulmonary artery catheter**—an accurate measure of core temperature but expensive and invasive.

2. Define hypothermia.

Hypothermia is a clinical state of subnormal body temperature in which the body is unable to generate enough heat for bodily functions. A core temperature of 35°C (95°F) is the upper limit of hypothermia. Cold signals travel to the hypothalamus primarily via delta fibers traversing the spinothalamic tracts in the anterior spinal cord. Below this temperature shivering and autonomic and endocrinologic responses are unable to compensate completely without assisted warming.

3. How does anesthesia predispose to hypothermia?

Heat loss is common in all patients during general anesthesia, because anesthetics alter thermoregulation, prevent shivering, and produce peripheral vasodilation. Volatile anesthetics impair the thermoregulatory center in the hypothalamus and also have direct vasodilatory properties. Opioids reduce the vasoconstrictive mechanisms of heat conservation by their sympatholytic properties. Barbiturates cause peripheral vasodilation. Muscle relaxants reduce muscle tone and prevent shivering thermogenesis. Regional anesthesia also may produce sympathetic blockade, muscle relaxation, and sensory blockade of thermal receptors, thus inhibiting compensatory responses.

4. What are the clinical signs of hypothermia?

Shivering, decreased sweating, and vasoconstriction are early signs of hypothermia. If hypothermia is prolonged, patients may present with altered mental status and muscle weakness. Anesthetized patients behave as poikilotherms, reflecting the temperature of the external environment. Decreased motor activity is also an early manifestation of hypothermia.

The physiologic effects of hypothermia depend on the degree of temperature depression. With mild hypothermia (32–35°C, 90–95°F), one sees central nervous system (CNS) depression, decreased basal metabolic rate, tachycardia, and shivering. The patient also may have dysarthria, amnesia, ataxia, and apathy. Moderate hypothermia (27–32°C, 80–90°F) involves further depression in level of consciousness, mild depression of vital signs, arrhythmias, and cold diuresis. In severe hypothermia (< 27°C, 80°F), the patient may be comatose and areflexic and have significantly depressed vital signs.

5. Which patients are at risk for hypothermia?

Patients at risk include the elderly, who have reduced autonomic vascular control, and infants, who have a large surface area–to-mass ratio. Patients with burns, spinal cord injuries that involve autonomic dysfunction, and endocrine abnormalities are also at risk.

6. What is the function of shivering?

Shivering is the spontaneous, asynchronous, random contraction of skeletal muscles in an effort to increase the basal metabolic rate. Shivering is modulated through the hypothalamus and can increase the body's heat production by up to 300% in young, muscular individuals. Shivering increases oxygen consumption and carbon dioxide production. This effect may be undesirable in the patient with coronary artery disease or pulmonary insufficiency.

Nonshivering thermogenesis increases metabolic heat production without producing mechanical work. Infants younger than 3 months of age cannot shiver and mount a caloric response by nonshivering thermogenesis. Skeletal muscle and brown fat tissue are the major energy sources for this process, which does not occur in anesthetized adults.

7. What are the pathophysiologic effects of hypothermia?

1. **Vascular**—vasoconstriction leads to hypoperfusion of peripheral tissues and promotes tissue hypoxia. Systemic vascular resistance and central venous pressure are increased; the reliability of pulse oximetry and intrarterial pressure monitoring is decreased

2. **Cardiac**—shivering increases oxygen consumption by up to 300% and thus increases myocardial oxygen demand. As hypothermia worsens, heart rate, cardiac output, and oxygen consumption decrease. Later symptoms include ventricular arrhythmias and further myocardial depression.

3. **Pulmonary**—pulmonary vascular resistance increases and hypoxic pulmonary vasoconstriction decreases, resulting in increased ventilation-perfusion mismatch and hypoxemia. Ventilatory drive is depressed. Bronchomotor tone is diminished, thus increasing anatomic dead space. The carbon dioxide content of blood (PCO_2) drops 50% per 8°C-decrease in temperature; thus there is little respiratory stimulus to breathe. In blood the carbon dioxide and oxygen solubility increase with cooling. The pH of arterial blood gases rises 0.015 units per centigrade decrease in temperature. The rule of thumb is that the body temperature in centigrade should approximate arterial carbon dioxide partial pressures ($PaCO_2$).

4. **Renal**—renal blood flow is decreased, glomerular filtration is reduced, and protein catabolism and diuresis are increased, with spilling of urinary nitrogen. Cold diuresis due to impaired sodium reabsorption may lead to hypovolemia. The ability to concentrate or dilute urine is decreased.

5. **Hepatic**—hepatic blood flow is decreased and the metabolic and excretory functions of the liver are diminished.

6. **Central nervous system**—cerebral blood flow is decreased, and cerebral vascular resistance is increased. Cerebral metabolic oxygen consumption decreases by 7% per centigrade decrease in temperature. Both motor and somatosensory evoked potential latencies are increased by hypothermia. At about 33°C sedation occurs, and at 30°C cold narcosis results. The minimal alveolar concentration (MAC) of volatile agents is decreased, resulting in delayed emergence, drowsiness, and confusion.

7. **Hematologic**—decreased platelet function, visceral sequestration, and platelet aggregation result in thrombocytopenia. Activity of clotting factors is reduced, resulting in impaired coagulation, whereas fibrinolysis is increased. Leukocytes are also sequestered. Blood viscosity increases about 3% with each centigrade decrease in temperature. Increases in hematocrit (2–3% per centigrade decrease in temperature) are associated with rouleaux formation. The oxygen-hemoglobin dissociation curve shifts to the left, and hemoglobin affinity for oxygen increases 6% per centigrade decrease in temperature. Plasma volume decreases 25% for each 11°C decrease because of cold diuresis and impaired sodium resorption.

8. **Metabolic**—the basal metabolic rate and tissue perfusion decrease, leading to metabolic acidosis. Acute hyperkalemia is a risk with rewarming. Moderate hyperglycemia may result from the catecholamine response, decreased insulin levels, and decreased insulin responsiveness. Oxygen consumption and carbon dioxide production decrease by 8% per centigrade decrease in temperature.

9. **Intraocular pressure**—decreases because of a decrease in aqueous humor production and vasoconstriction.

10. **Healing**—hypothermia may contribute to wound infection by directly impairing the immune system and by triggering thermoregulatory vasoconstriction that reduces oxygen delivery to the wound.

8. Describe the electrocardiographic (ECG) manifestations of hypothermia.

Mild hypothermia may be associated only with sinus bradycardia. Moderate hypothermia may result in prolonged PR intervals, widened QRS complexes, and a prolonged QT interval. Below 32°C an elevation of the junction of the QRS and ST segments known as the hypothermic hump or Osborne or J wave may be seen. Its size increases with decreasing body temperature; it usually is seen in leads II and V_6 and may spread to leads V_3 and V_4. The J wave is not specific for hypothermia; it also may be seen in hypothalamic lesions and cardiac ischemia. Nodal rhythms are common below 30°C. Below 28°C, premature ventricular contractions, atrioventricular blocks, and spontaneous atrial or ventricular fibrillation also occur. Ventricular fibrillation or asystole below 28°C is relatively unresponsive to atropine, countershock, or pacing. Resuscitative efforts should persist until the patient is rewarmed.

9. What are the pharmacologic effects of hypothermia?

Drug effects are prolonged by decreased hepatic blood flow and metabolism and decreased renal blood flow and clearance. Protein binding increases as body temperature decreases. The

MAC of inhalational agents is decreased about 5–7% per centigrade decrease in core temperature, but decreased cardiac output and increased blood solubility result in no change in speed of inhalational induction. Hypothermia may prolong the duration of neuromuscular blocking agents because of decreased metabolism. Monitoring of neuromuscular function may also be impaired. Hypothermia delays discharge from the postanesthetic care unit and may prolong the need for mechanical ventilation.

10. Describe the major mechanisms of heat loss.

1. **Radiation** (i.e., dissipation of heat to cooler surroundings) accounts for about 60% of heat loss, depending on cutaneous blood flow and exposed body surface area.

2. **Evaporation** accounts for 20% of heat loss due to the latent heat of vaporization, which is the energy required to vaporize liquid from serosal and mucosal surfaces. Evaporation depends on exposed surface area and the relative humidity of ambient air.

3. **Convection** is responsible for about 15% of heat loss and depends on the air flow over exposed surfaces.

4. **Conduction** depends on the transfer of heat between adjacent surfaces and accounts for about 5% of the total heat loss. The degree of loss is a function of the temperature gradient and thermal conductivity.

11. What are the major causes of heat loss in the operating room?

Cool rooms, cold intravenous and prepping solutions, and exposure of the patient contribute significantly to hypothermia. One unit of refrigerated blood or 1 liter of room-temperature crystalloid decreases the body temperature about 0.25°C. Cutaneous heat loss is proportional to exposed surface area and accounts for 90% of heat loss. General anesthetics cause vasodilation and decrease heat production. In addition, loss of hypothalamic responsiveness due to volatile anesthetics results in the inability to mount a caloric response to decreasing body temperature. Neuromuscular blocking agents prevent muscle heat production by shivering. Less than 10% of heat loss is through the respiratory tract.

12. What disease processes are associated with hypothermia?

Hypothyroidism and hypothalamic lesions may predispose a patient to intraoperative hypothermia. Difficulty in maintaining normothermia during general anesthesia is age-related. The elderly and the very young are at increased risk of hypothermia because of poor temperature regulation. The basal metabolic rate declines by approximately 1% per year after age 30 years. Infants also may become hypothermic more easily because of their decreased ability to shiver.

13. Discuss methods of rewarming.

Passive rewarming uses the body's ability to provide necessary heat if continued heat loss is minimized by covering exposed areas. Because passive rewarming relies on shivering thermogenesis, hypothalamic mechanisms must be intact and sufficient glycogen stores must be available.

Active rewarming involves methods readily available in the operating room, including the administration of warmed intravenous fluids and use of radiant heat lamps and warming blankets, especially those that blow warm air over body surfaces. Airway rewarming is less effective, because the heat content of gases is poor. Heated irrigation fluids administered by peritoneal lavage or bladder instillation and extracorporeal rewarming with cardiopulmonary bypass may be required. A core temperature afterdrop (a secondary decline in core temperature with rewarming) may result from the return of cold blood from the periphery.

14. Describe ways to prevent hypothermia in the surgical patient.

Operating rooms are commonly cool. Use of a passive heat and moisture exchanger (artificial nose) is beneficial. Humidification of respiratory gases is important to prevent airway drying and to maintain normal ciliary function, but it is not a major method of rewarming. Other steps include the following:

1. Raise the ambient temperature in the operating room; all patients become hypothermic at common operating room temperatures.

2. Cover exposed areas to minimize conductive and convective losses.

3. Use intravenous fluid warmers when administering intravenous fluids and transfusing blood. Depending on the rate of infusion, fluids may be warmed up to 40–42°C.

4. Use heated humidifiers to the anesthetic circuit to minimize evaporative losses and to warm compressed gases.

5. Maintain closed or low-flow semiclosed circuits to decrease evaporative losses and conserve anesthetic vapors.

6. Use warming blankets for conductive transfer of heat.

7. Use radiant warmers and heat lamps, especially in pediatric patients, who have a high surface area–to-weight ratio and cannot mount a caloric response.

8. Irrigate with warm solutions if possible.

15. Define hyperthermia.

Hyperthermia is a rise in body temperature of 2°C per hour. Because it is uncommon in the operating room, its cause must be investigated. The usual cause is sepsis or fever. Hypothalamic lesions and hyperthyroidism are less common. Malignant hyperthermia, catecholamine surges, and production of bacteremia in the course of surgery may elevate body temperature. Occasionally overly vigorous warming techniques, usually in peripheral surgical procedures, may be responsible.

16. Describe the manifestations of hyperthermia.

The awake patient may manifest general malaise, nausea, light-headedness, and tachycardia, accompanied by sweating, vasodilation, and increased basal metabolic rate. With prolonged hyperthermia the patient may exhibit symptoms of heat exhaustion or even heat stroke. In the anesthetized patient signs and symptoms include tachycardia, hypertension, increased end-tidal carbon dioxide, increased drug metabolism, and possibly dehydration, as suggested by a decline in urine output and decreased skin turgor. Hyperthermia is a hypermetabolic state with increased oxygen consumption, increased minute ventilation, sweating, and vasodilation. Intravascular volume and venous return are decreased. Heart rate increases by 10 bpm per centigrade increase in temperature.

17. What conditions are associated with hyperthermia?

1. Malignant hyperthermia is a possible cause in patients with a genetic predisposition. However, it may manifest initially as tachycardia, hypercapnia, muscle rigidity, tachyarrhythmias, ventilatory difficulties, and metabolic acidosis. Treatment consists of discontinuing triggering agents, administering dantrolene, cooling the patient, and ensuring adequate renal output. Blood gases should be checked and metabolic acidosis corrected.

2. Hypermetabolic states, including sepsis, infection (endogenous pyrogens), thyrotoxicosis (thyroid storm), and pheochromocytoma

3. Hypothalamic lesions secondary to trauma, anoxia, or tumor

4. Neuroleptic malignant syndrome

5. Transfusion reaction

6. Medications

18. Do any drugs increase the risk of hyperthermia?

Sympathomimetic drugs, monoamine oxidase inhibitors, cocaine, amphetamines, and tricyclic antidepressants increase the basal metabolic rate and heat production. Anticholinergics and antihistamines may elevate temperature by suppression of sweating.

19. What are the pharmacologic effects of hyperthermia?

Increases in basal metabolic rate and hepatic metabolism decrease the half-life of anesthetic drugs. Anesthetic requirements may be increased.

20. What is the treatment for the hyperthermic patient in the operating room?

Exposure of skin surfaces is helpful, as are cooling blankets and cool intravenous fluids. Administration of antipyretics is prudent. Correctable causes of hyperpyrexia should be ruled out.

BIBLIOGRAPHY

1. Sessler DI: Physiologic responses to mild perianesthetic hypothermia in humans. Anesthesiology 75:594–610, 1991.
2. Sessler DI: Skin surface warming: Heat flux and central temperature. Anesthesiology 73:218–224, 1990.
3. Sessler DI: Temperature monitoring. In Miller RD (ed): Anesthesia, 4th ed. New York, Churchill Livingstone, 1994, pp 1363–1382.
4. Slotman GJ: Adverse effects of hypothermia in postoperative patients. Am J Surg 149:495–501, 1985.
5. Solomon A: The electrocardiographic features of hypothermia. J Emerg Med 7:169–173, 1989.
6. Zoll RH: Temperature monitoring. In Ehrenwerth J, Eisenkraft JB (eds): Anesthesia Equipment: Principles and Applications. St. Louis, Mosby, 1993, pp 264–273.

36. POSTANESTHETIC CARE AND COMPLICATIONS

Roger A. Mattison, M.D.

1. Which patients should be cared for in the postanesthetic care unit (PACU)?

Perioperative care should be continued in the PACU for all patients who are likely to require a period of physiologic stabilization. A mandatory period of high-intensity care for every postoperative patient is an obsolete requirement. PACU care is generally divided into phase 1, during which monitoring and staffing ratios are equivalent to an intensive care unit (ICU), and phase 2, during which a transition is made from intensive observation to stabilization for care on a surgical ward or at home. After general anesthesia, many patients exhibit stable hemodynamics and cognitive functioning and can be discharged to phase 2 care. Most patients who have had monitoring plus sedation or extremity regional anesthesia should be appropriate for phase 2 care. After neuroaxis regional anesthesia, a period of phase 1 care will be required. Preexisting disease, surgical procedure, and pharmacologic implications of the perioperative anesthetic agents ultimately determine the most appropriate sequence of postoperative care for each patient. Alterations in preoperative status during postoperative recovery caused by anesthetic agents and procedures are often more intense but usually shorter in duration than alterations caused by systemic illness.

2. How long should a patient stay in the PACU?

No specific period is required for PACU care. On admission, a report is given by the anesthesiologist or anesthetist to the PACU nurse about the patient's prior health status, surgical procedure, intraoperative events, and anesthetic course. This report guides the intensity and duration of observations in the PACU. Anesthetic technique, administered agents, and type and reversal of neuromuscular blockade should be included in the report. Initial assessment of the patient by the PACU nurse includes baseline responsiveness, ventilation, pain, and vital signs. Initial PACU vital signs become the final entry on the intraoperative anesthetic record. Subsequent PACU nursing observations are recorded on a flow sheet. Various scoring systems have been used to allow numeric scoring of subjective observations as an indicator of progress toward discharge. The Aldrete scoring system tracks five observations: activity, respiratory effort, circulation, consciousness, and oxygenation. Scales for each are 0–2, and a total score of 8–10 indicates readiness to move to the next phase of care. Regression of motor block in the case of regional anesthesia is also an important assessment.

The Aldrete Score

Activity	• Able to move four extremities	2
	• Able to move two extremities	1
	• Not able to move extremities voluntarily or on command	0
Respiration	• Able to breathe and cough	2
	• Dyspnea or limited breathing	1
	• Apneic	0
Circulation	• BP ± 20% of preanesthetic level	2
	• BP ± 21–49% or preanesthetic level	1
	• BP ± 50% of preanesthetic level	0
Consciousness	• Fully awake	2
	• Arousable on calling	1
	• Not responding	0
O_2 Saturation	• Maintain O_2 sat > 92% in room air	2
	• Needs O_2 to maintain O_2 sat > 90%	1
	• O_2 saturation < 90% with O_2 supplement	0

Modified from Aldrete AJ, Krovlik D: The postanesthetic recovery score. Anesth Analg 49:924–933, 1970, with permission.

3. What problems should be resolved during postanesthetic care?

1. **Poor respiratory effort:** the patient should be breathing easily and able to cough on command and oxygenate to preanesthesia levels.

2. **Hemodynamic instability:** blood pressure should be within 20% of preanesthetic measurements with stable heart rate and rhythm.

3. **Attenuated sensorium:** the patient should be fully awake and able to move all extremities voluntarily.

4. **Postoperative pain:** pain management should no longer require continuous nursing intervention.

4. Describe the appearance of residual neuromuscular blockade.

The patient appears "floppy" with poorly coordinated and ineffective abdominal and intercostal muscle activity. A patient who can verbalize complains that breathing is restricted and that efforts to deliver supplemental oxygen are suffocating. Although apparently willing to respond to commands, the patient is unable to sustain a head lift or hand grasp. In the worst case, weakness of the pharyngeal muscles results in upper airway collapse and respiratory obstruction after extubation. Neither a good response to train-of-four testing in the operating room nor spontaneous rhythmic ventilation before extubation rules out residual neuromuscular blockade.

5. How do opioids and residual volatile anesthetics affect breathing?

Slow rhythmic breathing or apneic pauses in a patient who is hard to arouse suggest residual narcosis. In contrast to the patient with residual muscle relaxation, the narcotized patient often is unconcerned about ventilation despite obvious hypoxia. Because analgesia and narcotic depression of ventilation are both dose-dependent, the patient may appear quite comfortable. As narcosis slows ventilation, the route of elimination of inhalation agents is suppressed. Residual volatile anesthetic reduces tidal volume and depresses respiratory effort. This synergism may cause significant postoperative hypoventilation. Surprising degrees of hypercapnia may be found, even with relatively normal pulse oximetry values.

6. How should these causes of hypoventilation be treated?

Hypoventilation due to residual neuromuscular blockade should be treated urgently and aggressively. Additional reversal agents may be given in divided doses up to the usual dose limitations. Cholinergic effects of reversal agents at the sinoatrial node may result in significant bradycardia.

Treatment decisions for residual narcosis may prove more problematic. Opioid antagonism for the sake of ventilatory support reverses adequate analgesia. The agonist/antagonist class of analgesic drugs seldom yields a net improvement in ventilation when used for reversal and may excessively obtund the patient. Usually, the best alternatives are ventilatory support with nasal or oral airway and continuous tactile and verbal stimulation until the clinical effects of the opioid on ventilation and responsiveness have resolved. Other supportive measures include increasing inspired oxygen concentrations (FiO_2) by switching from nasal cannula to mask.

Volatile anesthetic agents are eliminated by exhalation. All of the agents in current use have low blood-gas partition coefficients and thus should be eliminated effectively in the PACU if minute ventilation is sufficient. In severe respiratory depression of any cause, reintubation and mechanical ventilation are possible interventions.

Ventilation Problems in the PACU

PROBLEM	SIGNS/SYMPTOMS	TREATMENT
Inadequate reversal of neuro-muscular block	Uncoordinated, ineffectual respiration effort	Neostigmine, 0.05 mg/kg intravenously
Narcosis	Slow ventilation, sedated or asleep	Respiratory support, Naloxone, 0.04–0.40 mg intravenously
Residual inhalation anesthesia	Sleepy, shallow breathing	Encourage deep breathing, tactile stimulation

7. What other problems with ventilation should be considered in the PACU?

Whereas residual effects of the anesthetic drugs reduce respiratory effort, other intraoperative events may interfere with gas exchange. Aspiration of gastric contents or reactive airway disease leads to segmental bronchiolar obstruction resulting in wheezing, prolonged expiratory phase, and hypoxia. Bronchial foreign body and pneumothorax may present with signs such as asymmetric breath sounds and hypoxia but can be differentiated readily by postoperative chest radiography. Supraglottic obstruction may result in stridor and hypercarbia rather than hypoxia. Rarely, in susceptible patients (poor cardiac output, compromised renal function, hypoproteinemia), fluid overload results in pulmonary edema with hypoxia. The common physiologic pathway for any of these difficulties is ventilation-perfusion mismatch. The secondary physiologic effect is a hypertensive response to hypercarbia or hypoxia. Review of the operative procedure and the intraoperative anesthetic record will suggest possible etiologies. Past medical history of smoking, asthma, or chronic obstructive pulmonary disease is also important for the recognition of patients at higher risk for reactive small airway obstruction.

8. What is negative pressure pulmonary edema?

A phenomenon unique to the postextubation period and thus pertinent to the PACU is negative pressure pulmonary edema. Findings include coarse breath sounds and production of pink frothy sputum, as with other causes of pulmonary edema, but often hypoxia and hypertension precede the telltale physical signs. The cause of the edema is the patient's vigorous ventilatory effort against a partially closed glottis or occasionally a small endotracheal tube. The clinical presentation follows a rapid emergence, often when the patient has been intoxicated at the time of induction. This phenomenon should be anticipated in young muscular individuals but may occur in any patient with some degree of laryngospasm after extubation. Often, preceding the obstructive event, reversal of opioids has been required to achieve sufficient responsiveness for extubation. Chest radiographs confirm the presence of a normal-sized heart and rarely show any lung parenchymal changes except alveolar infiltrates. The edema usually responds to supportive measures and minimal diuretic treatment. Extended PACU observation or hospitalization of these patients is recommended.

9. Describe an orderly approach to treatment of respiratory emergencies in the PACU.

1. Supplemental oxygen plus measures to support airway patency:
   - Chin lift, neck extension, steady positive pressure ventilation by mask to overcome supraglottic obstruction.
   - Occasionally inhalation of nebulized epinephrine or intravenous steroid to reduce mucosal swelling.

2. Subcutaneous or inhaled β-adrenergic agonists (e.g., albuterol) are appropriate if respiratory difficulties are related to distal bronchoconstriction:
   - Inhaled route is less likely to exacerbate hypertension from other causes.
   - If bronchoconstriction is part of a full-blown anaphylactic episode, a more aggressive approach (beyond the scope of this chapter) is required.

3. Mechanical causes of lower airway obstruction, if suspected, should be vigorously investigated by radiography and bronchoscopy and treated. However, most hypoxia in the PACU is cauded by simple atelectasis, which is treated with supplemental oxygen and instructions to breathe deeply and cough. Incentive spirometry is not used in the PACU.

4. Maximize treatment of postoperative pain.

5. Avoid treatment of hypertension and tachycardia with drugs until hypercarbia and hypoventilation are ruled out.

Predicted FiO_2 with Supplemental Oxygen Delivery

SYSTEM	DELIVERY FLOW	FiO_2 PREDICTED
Nasal cannula	2 L/min	0.28
Nasal cannula	4 L/min	0.36
Face mask	6 L/min	0.50
Partial rebreathing mask	6 L/min	0.6
Partial rebreathing mask	8 L/min	0.8

10. Describe an approach to the evaluation of postoperative hypertension and tachycardia.

A hyperdynamic postoperative phase is not an uncommon event. While etiologies recur with regularity, it is always wise to keep a broad differential diagnosis in mind. Frequently observed and readily treatable causes include pain, hypothermia with shivering, bladder distention, and essential hypertension. Also consider hypoxemia, hypercarbia, fever and its causes, anemia, hypoglycemia, tachydysrhythmias, withdrawal (ethyl alcohol, etc.), myocardial ischemia, medications taken, past medical history, surgical procedures, and intraoperative events. Rarely, the hyperdynamic state may reflect hyperthyroidism, pheochromocytoma, and malignant hyperthermia.

Despite appropriate treatment based on etiology, the patient may require antihypertensive therapy. The accompanying table lists medication options, dosages, and concerns. Often blood pressure elevations of 20% above baseline will resolve spontaneously as the patient recovers.

Treatment of Hypertension (Intravenous Preparations)

	BENEFIT	HAZARD	PREPARATION
β-adrenergic antagonist (cardioselective)	Short-acting preparation available; slows heart rate	Bradycardia, decreased contractility	Esmolol,* 0.3 mg/kg intravenous
			Labetalol, 5–50 mg/kg intravenous
Calcium channel blocker	Less effect on contractility	Not given as bolus	Nicardipine infusion, 0.1 mg/ml; up to 5 mg over 1 hour
Angiotensin-converting enzyme inhibitors	Least effect on contractility	Long-acting effects	Enalapril, 1.25–2.5 mg intravenous
Direct vasodilator	Infusion administration	Potent; requires continuous monitor	Sodium nitroprusside, 0.2–8 μg/kg/min

* Bolus may be followed by infusion.

11. What might cause hypotension in the postoperative phase?

Emergence from inhalation anesthesia is characterized by resolving vasodilation, increasing muscle tone, and increasing sympathetic tone, which usually results in an expansion of central blood volume and at least a temporary increase in blood pressure at the end of the operative procedure. As the patient is warmed and pain control is begun in the PACU, sympathetic tone is reduced and blood volume is redistributed to the periphery. The effects of surgical blood loss, third-space sequestration of fluid, ongoing hemorrhage and inadequate volume replacement manifest as hypotension. Less commonly, heart failure may present as hypotension. Dysrhythmias and preexisting ischemic heart disease may be causative. Sepsis or anaphylaxis may result in expansion of peripheral capillary beds.

12. When should hypotension be treated?

Treatment must be swift and aggressive. Volume expansion with crystalloid is the first-line therapy. Elevate the legs and place the patient in the Trendelenburg position. Circumstances may require administration of colloid (not albumin, that's expensive!) or packed red blood cells. Review available data as the differential diagnosis widens. Consider the surgical procedure, intraoperative events, medications, and past medical history. Evaluate blood loss and urine output. Review the rhythm strip and consider a 12-lead electrocardiogram (ECG). Should volume expansion prove unsatisfactory, vasopressors or inotropes may be necessary, including ephedrine, neosynephrine, dopamine, epinephrine, and dobutamine.

13. Under what circumstances is a patient slow to awaken?

Most patients do not achieve a state of complete conscious awareness during the PACU stay because short-term memory function remains unreliable. However, they are said to be "awake" if they are oriented to time, place, and person and respond meaningfully in conversation. Patients are considered slow to awaken when they fail to progress beyond protective airway reflexes and minimal conscious awareness. Some patients may make transient progress only to lapse to a lower level of consciousness.

A reasonable initial assumption is that such patients are displaying residual drug effects. Should decreased awareness persist beyond a reasonable period of observation, ventilatory, metabolic, and central nervous system (CNS) etiologies must be considered. Blood gas analysis will reveal hypoxemia or hypercarbia. Hyponatremia and the extremes in serum glucose may be causative. CNS ischemia caused by decreased perfusion air embolic phenomena should be considered. Has the patient had documented CNS ischemic events or strokes? Does the patient have a seizure history? Again, review the surgical procedure and intraoperative events. Difficult neurosurgical procedures and cardiopulmonary bypass are well associated with delayed awakening.

14. When is aggressive evaluation of slow awakening necessary?

Patients who have had carotid endarterectomy or craniotomy require prompt radiographic (computed tomography or angiography) evaluation if slow to awaken. Surgically correctable causes such as increased intracranial pressure, intracranial hemorrhage, or major cerebral vascular occlusion cannot be distinguished by clinical examination in the PACU. Patients who awaken over hours to days but have no surgically correctable lesion usually have sustained insult to the microcirculation of the brain stem and may require substantial time for recovery.

15. How should analgesic drugs be selected for PACU use?

1. Consider previous allergies and adverse reactions.
   - Nausea with one opioid may predict similar reaction to others.
   - Documented allergic reaction may be avoided by choosing a structurally different drug.
2. Avoid dose-dependent adverse reactions to opioids by adding nonsteroidal anti-inflammatory drugs (NSAIDs) for nonnarcotic analgesia; ketorolac (Toradol) may be administered parenterally if contraindications (renal insufficiency, peptic ulcer disease, and platelet disturbances) are absent.

3. Coordinate initial analgesic therapy with longer range pain management modalities, such as patient controlled analgesia (PCA) or epidural infusion.

4. Consider whether the patient will be discharged to home postoperatively or remain an inpatient who can be given supplemental oxygen and more intense observation.

5. Review the patient's history for preoperative opioid use, which might predict greater tolerance and higher dosage limits for postoperative opioid analgesia.

16. Discuss the issues surrounding postoperative nausea and vomiting (PONV).

PONV remains a significant, troublesome postanesthetic problem. It results in delayed PACU discharge and occasional unplanned hospital admissions, and is a recurring cause of patient dissatisfaction. Both the surgical procedure and anesthetic agents administered may be factorial. Females, patients with a prior PONV history, and children are at risk. Laparoscopic surgery and surgery on internal female genitalia or middle ear are problematic. Anesthetic agents with a high association with PONV include the opioids and nitrous oxide. Propofol has the lowest incidence of any of the induction agents. Prophylactic antiemetics appear a more effective therapy when administered near care conclusion; likewise, prophylaxis is superior to rescue (treatment once PONV has ensued). Suggested medications are discussed in Chapter 65, Outpatient Anesthesia.

17. Should ambulatory patients be treated differently in the PACU?

The goal of postanesthetic care of the ambulatory patient is to render the patient "street ready." Nausea and vomiting are treated aggressively, avoiding butyrophenones (e.g., droperidol), which may be excessively sedating. When possible, pain should be treated with short-acting agents such as fentanyl. Nonnarcotic agents should be used whenever possible. Oral analgesics should be used in phase 2 recovery as prescribed for postoperative care. After regional anesthesia, extremities should be protected while the patient is mobilized, and ambulation should be assisted if transient segmental paresthesia makes movement unsteady. No ambulatory surgery patient should be discharged after receiving any sedating medication without a companion to ensure safe transportation to a place of residence.

18. What are safe guidelines for discharging a patient to home after ambulatory surgery?

By the time the patient arrives in phase 2, issues of cardiovascular stability, orientation and conscious awareness, and ventilation should be resolved. Resolution of postoperative nausea or pain may extend into phase 2, but the continued use of intravenous agents should rarely be required. Patients should be able to stand and to take a few steps (or to sit upright if the surgical procedure will not permit standing). They should sip fluids and urinate. They should be able to repeat postoperative management and follow-up instructions and to identify their escort home (allowing for baseline cognitive function). Prescriptions for postoperative care at home should be provided to patients in phase 2 recovery so that a separate pharmacy stop is not required. All conditions that require further intervention after discharge should be manageable with oral therapy. Finally, the patient and any companions should be provided with telephone number(s) for contacting health care providers at the facility if any untoward postoperative events occur. It is good practice to plan on a follow-up telephone call from the ambulatory PACU to the patient 24 hours after discharge to review postoperative progress and satisfaction.

BIBLIOGRAPHY

1. Aldrete AJ, Krovlik D: The postanesthetic recovery score. Anesth Analg 49:924–933, 1970.
2. Bellati RG Jr: Common post anesthesia problems. In Vendor JS, Speiss BD (eds): Post Anesthesia Care. Philadelphia, W.B. Saunders, 1992, pp 9–20.
3. Don H: Hypoxemia and hypercapnia during and after anesthesia. In Orkin EK, Cooperman LH (eds): Complications in Anesthesiology. Philadelphia, J.B. Lippincott, 1983, pp 191–194, 200–202.
4. Malley RA: Delayed return to consciousness. In Frust EAM, Galdiner PL (eds): Postanesthetic Care. Norwalk, CT, Appleton & Lange, 1990, pp 9–16.

5. Marymount JH, O'Connor BS: Postoperative cardiovascular complications. In Vendor JS, Spiess BD (eds): Post Anesthesia Care. Philadelphia, W.B. Saunders, 1992, pp 25–33.
6. Rosenberg H: Postoperative emotional responses. In Orkin EK, Cooperman LH (eds): Complications in Anesthesiology. Philadelphia, J.B. Lippincott, 1983, pp 355–361.
7. Wetchler BV: Problem solving in the postanesthesia care unit. In Wetchler BV (ed): Anesthesia for Ambulatory Surgery, 2nd ed. Philadelphia, J.B. Lippincott, 1990, pp 400–410.

VI. Anesthesia and Systemic Disease

37. ISCHEMIC HEART DISEASE AND MYOCARDIAL INFARCTION

Richard B. Allen, M.D.

1. Name the known risk factors for the development of ischemic heart disease (IHD).

Age, male gender, positive family history, hypertension, smoking, hypercholesterolemia, and diabetes mellitus. Sedentary lifestyle and obesity are often associated factors.

2. Explain the determinants of myocardial oxygen supply and demand.

Oxygen (O_2) supply to the myocardium is determined by oxygen content and coronary blood flow. Oxygen content can be calculated by the following equation:

$$O_2 \text{ content} = [1.39 \text{ ml } O_2/g \text{ of hemoglobin} \times \text{hemoglobin (g/dl)} \times \% \text{ saturation}] + [0.003 \times PaO_2]$$

Coronary blood flow occurs mainly during diastole, especially to the ventricular endocardium. Coronary perfusion pressure is determined by the difference between diastolic blood pressure and left ventricular end-diastolic pressure (LVEDP). Anemia, hypoxemia, tachycardia, diastolic hypotension, hypocapnia (coronary vasoconstriction), coronary occlusion (IHD), vasospasm, increased LVEDP, and hypertrophied myocardium all may adversely affect myocardial O_2 supply.

Myocardial O_2 demand is determined by heart rate, contractility, and wall tension. Increases in heart rate increase myocardial work and decrease the relative time spent in diastole (decreased supply). Contractility increases in response to sympathetic stimulation, which increases O_2 demand. Wall tension is the product of intraventricular pressure and radius. Increased ventricular volume (preload) and increased blood pressure (afterload) both increase wall tension and O_2 demand.

3. What is the pathophysiology of ischemia?

Ischemia occurs when coronary blood flow is inadequate to meet the needs of the myocardium. Atherosclerotic lesions that occlude 50–75% of the vessel lumen are considered hemodynamically significant. Nonstenotic causes of ischemia include aortic valve disease, left ventricular hypertrophy, ostial occlusion, coronary embolism, coronary arteritis, and vasospasm.

The right coronary artery system is dominant in 80–90% of people and supplies the sinoatrial node, atrioventricular node, and right ventricle. Right-sided coronary artery disease often manifests as heart block and dysrhythmias. The left main coronary artery gives rise to the circumflex artery and left anterior descending artery, which supply the majority of the interventricular septum and left ventricular wall. Significant stenosis of the left main coronary artery (left main disease) or the proximal circumflex and left anterior descending arteries (left main equivalent) may cause severely depressed myocardial function during ischemia.

4. Describe the pathogenesis of a perioperative myocardial infarction.

A myocardial infarction (MI) is usually caused by platelet aggregation, vasoconstriction, and thrombus formation at the site of an atheromatous plaque in a coronary artery. Sudden increases in myocardial O_2 demand (tachycardia, hypertension) or decreases in O_2 supply (hypotension, hypoxemia, anemia), can precipitate MI in patients with IHD. Complications of MI include

189

dysrhythmias, hypotension, congestive heart failure, acute mitral regurgitation, pericarditis, ventricular thrombus formation, ventricular rupture, and death.

5. What clinical factors increase the risk of a perioperative MI following noncardiac surgery?

IHD (prior MI or angina) and congestive heart failure are historically the strongest predictors of an increased risk for perioperative MI. Other risk factors include valvular heart disease (particularly aortic stenosis), arrhythmias due to underlying heart disease, advanced age, type of surgical procedure, and poor general medical status. Hypertension alone does not place a patient at increased risk for perioperative MI, but these patients are at increased risk for IHD, congestive heart failure, and stroke.

6. How can cardiac function be evaluated on history and physical examination?

If a patient's exercise capacity is excellent, even in the presence of IHD, then chances are good that the patient will be able to tolerate the stresses of surgery. Poor exercise tolerance in the absence of pulmonary or other systemic disease indicates an inadequate cardiac reserve. All patients should be questioned about their ability to perform daily activities, such as cleaning, yard work, shopping, and golfing, for example. The ability to climb two to three flights of stairs without significant symptoms (angina, dyspnea, syncope) is usually an indication of adequate cardiac reserve. Signs and symptoms of congestive heart failure including dyspnea, orthopnea, paroxysmal nocturnal dyspnea, peripheral edema, jugular venous distension, a third heart sound, rales, and hepatomegaly must be recognized preoperatively.

7. What is the significance of a history of angina pectoris?

Angina is the symptom of myocardial ischemia, and nearly all patients with angina have coronary artery disease. Stable angina is defined as no change in the onset, severity, and duration of chest pain for at least 60 days. Syncope, shortness of breath, or dizziness that accompanies angina may indicate severe myocardial dysfunction due to ischemia. Patients with unstable angina are at high risk for developing an MI and should be referred for medical evaluation immediately. Patients with diabetes mellitus and hypertension have a much higher incidence of silent ischemia. Perioperatively, most ischemic episodes are silent (as determined by ambulatory and postoperative electrocardiogram [ECG]) but probably significant in the final outcome of surgery.

8. Should all cardiac medications be continued throughout the perioperative period?

Patients with a history of IHD are usually taking medications intended to decrease myocardial oxygen demand by decreasing the heart rate, preload, or contractile state (beta-blockers, calcium channel antagonists, nitrates) and to increase the oxygen supply by causing coronary vasodilation (nitrates). These drugs are generally continued throughout the perioperative period. Abrupt withdrawal of beta-blockers can cause rebound increases in heart rate and blood pressure. Calcium channel blockers can exaggerate the myocardial depressant effects of inhaled anesthetics but should be continued perioperatively.

9. What ECG findings support the diagnosis of IHD?

The resting 12-lead ECG remains a low cost, effective screening tool in the detection of IHD. It should be evaluated for the presence of ST-segment depression or elevation, T-wave inversion, old MI as demonstrated by Q waves, disturbances in conduction and rhythm, and left ventricular hypertrophy. Ischemic changes in leads II, III, and aVF suggest right coronary artery disease, leads I and aVL monitor the circumflex artery distribution, and leads V_3–V_5 look at the distribution of the left anterior desending artery. Poor progression of anterior forces suggests significant left ventricular dysfunction, possibly related to IHD.

10. What tests performed by medical consultants can help further evaluate patients with known or suspected IHD?

Exercise ECG is a noninvasive test, that attempts to produce ischemic changes on ECG (ST depression ≥ 1 mm from baseline) or symptoms by having the patient exercise to maximum capacity.

Information obtained relates to the thresholds of heart rate and blood pressure that can be tolerated. Maximal heart rates and blood pressure response, as well as symptoms, guide interpretation of results.

Exercise thallium scintigraphy increases the sensitivity and specificity of the exercise ECG. The isotope thallium is almost completely taken up from the coronary circulation by the myocardium and can then be visualized radiographically. Poorly perfused areas that later refill with contrast delineate areas of myocardium at risk for ischemia. Fixed perfusion defects indicate infarcted myocardium.

Dipyridamole thallium imaging is useful in patients who are unable to exercise. This testing is frequently required in patients with peripheral vascular disease who are at high risk for IHD and limited by claudication. Dipyridamole is a potent coronary vasodilator that causes differential flow between normal and diseased coronary arteries detectable by thallium imaging.

Echocardiography can be used to evaluate left ventricular and valvular function and to measure ejection fraction. Stress echocardiography (dobutamine echo) can be used to evaluate new or worsened regional wall motion abnormalities in the pharmacologically stressed heart. Areas of wall motion abnormality are considered at risk for ischemia.

Coronary angiography is the gold standard for defining the coronary anatomy. Valvular and ventricular function can be evaluated and measurements of hemodynamic indices taken. Because angiography is invasive, it is reserved for patients who require further evaluation based on previous tests or who have a high probability of severe coronary disease.

11. Based on the initial evaluation, which patients should be referred for further testing?

Patients at risk for IHD but with good exercise tolerance may not require further work-up, especially if they are undergoing procedures with a low to moderate risk of perioperative MI. Patients with decreased exercise tolerance for unclear reasons or with unreliable histories should be evaluated with dipyridamole thallium testing.

Patients with documented IHD (prior MI or chronic stable angina) with good exercise tolerance can sometimes proceed with low-risk surgery without further evaluation. Patients with known IHD and poor exercise tolerance should be referred for dipyridamole thallium testing or coronary angiography prior to all but the most minor surgical procedures.

12. Which surgical procedures carry the highest risk of perioperative MI?

In general, major abdominal, thoracic, and emergency surgery carry the highest risk of perioperative MI. The highest risk noncardiac procedure is aortic aneurysm repair. These patients have a high incidence of IHD, and cross-clamping of the aorta during surgery and postoperative complications can place great stress on the heart.

13. How long should a patient with a recent MI wait before undergoing elective noncardiac surgery?

The risk of reinfarction during surgery after a prior MI has traditionally depended on the time interval between the MI and the procedure. The highest risk of reinfarction is between 0 and 3 months post-MI, lower risk is from 3 to 6 months, and a baseline risk level is reached after 6 months (approximately 5% in most studies).

14. What if surgery cannot safely be delayed for 6 months?

The patient's functional status following rehabilitation from an MI is probably more important than the absolute time interval. Patients with ongoing symptoms may be candidates for coronary revascularization prior to their noncardiac procedure. Patients who quickly return to good functional status following an MI can be considered for necessary noncardiac surgery between 6 weeks and 3 months without undue added risk.

15. How is premedication useful in the setting of IHD and surgery?

Patient anxiety can lead to catecholamine secretion and increased oxygen demand. In this regard, the goal of premedication is to produce sedation and amnesia without causing deleterious myocardial depression, hypotension, or hypoxemia. Morphine, scopolamine, and benzodi-azepines, alone or in combination, are popular choices to achieve these goals. All premedicated patients should receive supplemental oxygen. Patients who use sublingual nitroglycerin should have access to their medication. Transdermal nitroglycerin can be applied in the perioperative period as well.

16. Outline the hemodynamic goals of induction and maintenance of general anesthesia in patients with IHD.

The anesthesiologist's goal must be to maintain the balance between myocardial O_2 supply and demand throughout the perioperative period. During induction, wide swings in heart rate and blood pressure should be avoided. Ketamine should be avoided because of the resultant tachycardia and hypertension. Prolonged laryngoscopy should be avoided, and the anesthesiologist may wish to blunt the stimulation of laryngoscopy and intubation by the addition of opiates, beta-blockers, or laryngotracheal or intravenous lidocaine.

Maintenance drugs are chosen with knowledge of the patient's ventricular function. In patients with good left ventricular function, the cardiac depressant and vasodilatory effects of inhaled anesthetics may reduce myocardial O_2 demand. A narcotic-based technique may be chosen to avoid undue myocardial depression in patients with poor left ventricular function. Muscle relaxants with minimal cardiovascular effects are usually preferred.

Blood pressure and heart rate should be maintained near baseline values. This can be accomplished by blunting sympathetic stimulation with adequate analgesia and aggressively treating hypertension (anesthetics, nitroglycerin, nitroprusside, beta-blockers), hypotension (fluids, sympathomimetics, inotropic drugs), and tachycardia (fluids, anesthetics, beta-blockers).

17. What monitors are useful for detecting ischemia intraoperatively?

The V_5 precordial lead is the most sensitive single ECG lead for detecting ischemia and should be monitored routinely in patients at risk for IHD. Lead II can detect ischemia of the right coronary artery distribution and is the most useful lead for monitoring P waves and cardiac rhythm.

Transesophageal echocardiography can provide continuous intraoperative monitoring of left ventricular function. Detection of regional wall motion abnormalities with this technique is the most sensitive monitor for myocardial ischemia.

The pulmonary artery occlusion (wedge) pressure gives an indirect measurement of left ventricular volume and is a useful guide to optimizing intravascular fluid therapy. Sudden increases in the wedge pressure may indicate acute left ventricular dysfunction due to ischemia. The routine use of pulmonary artery catheters in patients with IHD has not been shown to improve outcome. However, close hemodynamic monitoring (including pulmonary artery catheter data) may be beneficial depending on the patient's condition and the nature of the surgical procedure.

BIBLIOGRAPHY

1. Eagle KA, Coley CM, Newell JB, et al: Combining clinical and thallium data optimizes preoperative assessment of cardiac risk before major vascular surgery. Ann Intern Med 110:859–866, 1989.
2. Fleisher LA, Barash PG: Preoperative cardiac evaluation for noncardiac surgery: A functional approach. Anesth Analg 74:586–598, 1992.
3. Goldman L: Cardiac risk in noncardiac surgery: An update. Anesth Analg 80:810–820, 1995.

38. CONGESTIVE HEART FAILURE

Richard D. Abbott, M.D.

1. Name the classifications and causes of heart failure.

Heart failure may be classified as left-sided versus right-sided, high output versus low output, backward versus forward, acute versus chronic, and compensated versus decompensated. One needs to be cautious in recognizing the difference between underlying causes and precipitating factors. The causes may be classified as cardiac or noncardiac. The cardiac causes may be divided further into conditions that directly alter myocardial or ventricular function and conditions that do not.

Causes of Heart Failure Conditions

CARDIAC	NONCARDIAC
Ischemia	Hypertension
Cardiomyopathy	Pulmonary embolus
Toxic	High output states
Metabolic	Thyrotoxicosis
Infectious, inflammatory	
Infiltrative	
Genetic	
Idiopathic	
Valvular heart diseases	
Aortic stenosis, regurgitation	
Mitral stenosis, regurgitation	
Restrictive disease	
Pericardial	
Myocardial	
Congenital disease	
Electrical abnormalities	
Tachydysrhythmias	
Ventricular dyssynergy	

2. What major alterations in physiology occur in patients with heart failure?

Myocardial hypertrophy allows the heart to overcome pressure overload, whereas dilation occurs with volume overload. Ventricular dilation allows the chamber to eject an adequate stroke volume with less muscle shortening, but wall stress is increased, as described by the Laplace relationship.

There is a loss of arterial compliance and arteriolar narrowing, associated with vascular smooth muscle hypertrophy. There is enhanced vasoconstrictor activity secondary to elevated sympathetic nervous system (SNS) activity, renin-angiotensin activation (resulting in sodium and water retention), increased levels of arginine vasopressin and endothelin, and possibly decreased local release of endothelium-derived relaxing factor (nitric oxide).

3. What are the presenting symptoms of heart failure?

Exertional dyspnea and fatigue are most often the primary complaint. However, ankle swelling may be the first symptom recognized by the patient. Dyspnea that is more prominent in the supine position is strongly suggestive of heart failure. Nocturia, coughing, wheezing, right upper quadrant pain, anorexia, nausea and vomiting, and palpitations also may be complaints.

4. What physical signs suggest heart failure?

Cardiac palpation may reveal an expanded impulse area (ventricular dilatation) or a forceful sustained impulse with left ventricular hypertrophy (LVH). Auscultation reveals a gallop rhythm (S_3) or an S_4 secondary to forceful atrial contraction. Murmurs of valvular diseases should be looked for. Severe failure may result in cyanosis.

Pulmonary examination often reveals rales located most prominently over the lung bases. Decreased breath sounds secondary to pleural effusions occur more often in patients with chronic heart failure.

Jugular venous distention (JVD) > 10 cm H_2O above the right atrium is considered abnormal. Close examination may reveal a large A wave due to a noncompliant right ventricle, a large v wave associated with tricuspid regurgitation, or a rapid y descent secondary to restrictive disease.

5. What laboratory studies are useful in evaluating the patient with heart failure?

The posteroanterior and lateral chest radiograph may detect cardiomegaly or evidence of pulmonary vascular congestion, including perihilar engorgement of the pulmonary veins, cephalization of the pulmonary vascular markings, or pleural effusions. The electrocardiogram (ECG) is often nonspecific, although 70–90% of patients may demonstrate ventricular or supraventricular dysrhythmias. Echocardiography characterizes chamber size, wall motion, valvular function, and left ventricular wall thickness. Radionuclide angiography provides a fairly reproducible and accurate assessment of left ventricular ejection fraction.

Blood work, including serum electrolytes, arterial blood gases (ABG), liver function tests (LFTs), and blood counts (CBC), is frequently evaluated. Many patients with heart failure are hyponatremic from activation of the vasopressin system. Treatment with diuretics and aldosterone activation may lead to hypokalemia and hypomagnesemia. Some degree of prerenal azotemia is often present. Hypocalcemia and hypophosphatemia also are often present. Hepatic congestion may result in elevated bilirubin levels and elevated LFTs.

6. Differentiate between systolic and diastolic dysfunction.

Systolic dysfunction occurs when myocardial sarcomere shortening is reduced and may result from global or regional reduction in contractility or high impedance to ventricular ejection. Elevated preload, as evidenced by elevated left ventricular end-diastolic volume, provides at least short-term compensation. Myocardial hypertrophy and new sarcomere generation provide longer term compensation. With diastolic dysfunction the principal abnormality involves impaired relaxation of the ventricle. Ventricular relaxation is energy-dependent and relies on reuptake of calcium into the sarcoplasmic reticulum of the myocyte. It is also related to myocardial mass, collagen content, and extrinsic forces such as pericardial disease.

7. What is the Frank-Starling law?

The Frank-Starling law basically states that the force or tension developed in a muscle fiber depends on the extent to which the fiber is stretched. There is an optimal sarcomere length and thus an optimal fiber length from which the most forceful contraction occurs. The left ventricle normally operates at a left ventricular end-diastolic volume (LVEDV) that results in less than optimal fiber lengths. Stroke volume increases to an extent with increasing preload (see Figure, next page).

8. How is the severity of heart failure classified?

Typically, the status of patients with congestive heart failure (CHF) can be classified on the basis of either symptoms and impairment of lifestyle or severity of cardiac dysfunction. The New York Heart Association classification is used to assess symptomatic limitations of heart failure and response to therapy:

Class I—ordinary physical activity does not cause symptoms.
Class II—ordinary physical activity will result in symptoms.
Class III—less than ordinary activity results in symptoms.
Class IV—symptoms occur at rest.

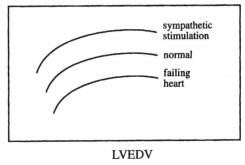

Effects of changes in preload on normal, failing, and sympathetically stimulated hearts.

Stroke Volume

sympathetic stimulation

normal

failing heart

LVEDV

Prognosis of the patient with CHF does not necessarily relate to symptomatic classifications. Left ventricular ejection fraction (LVEF) has been linked to mortality rates in some studies. An EF < 25% has been associated with an annual mortality rate as high as 40%, whereas an EF > 35–40% has been associated with mortality rates below 10%.

9. What treatment strategies are used in heart failure?

Diuretics are used when patients with heart failure exhibit signs or symptoms of circulatory congestion. Thiazide diuretics are often used for mild fluid retention. Loop diuretics such as furosemide may be substituted when thiazides fail to result in an adequate response. Addition of a second diuretic, such as metolazone, may induce an effective diuresis in patients resistant to loop diuretics alone.

Angiotensin-converting enzyme (ACE) inhibitors are effective therapy for patients who can tolerate them. Therapy with ACE inhibitors improves LV function and exercise tolerance and may prolong life. Hypotension and azotemia are the major side effects. A dry cough is fairly common but rarely necessitates discontinuation of therapy. A combination of the vasodilators hydralazine and isosorbide dinitrate also has been shown to be effective in improving exercise tolerance and life span.

The currently used **calcium channel blockers** may produce favorable hemodynamic responses but negative inotropic effects. These agents are used in patients with concurrent myocardial ischemia.

Digitalis is effective in patients with underlying atrial fibrillation or a dilated LV with poor systolic function. **Beta blockers** may produce favorable long-term effects in patients with ischemic heart disease.

10. What clinical findings would you expect in a patient with digitalis toxicity?

Patients may present with complaints of anorexia, nausea, and vomiting. Other symptoms include abdominal pain, confusion, paresthesias, amblyopia, and scotomata.

ECG manifestations are nonspecific. Increased automaticity, as evidenced by atrial or ventricular dysrhythmias such as premature ventricular contractions, bigeminy, trigeminy, or ventricular tachycardia, may be present. Delayed atrioventricular node conduction is common, with complete heart block sometimes occurring. Advanced age, hypothyroidism, decreased renal function, hypokalemia, hypercalcemia, and hypomagnesemia predispose to digitalis toxicity.

11. What should be considered in preparing to conduct an anesthetic on the patient with heart failure?

Patients in a decompensated state are not candidates for elective procedures. Often, waiting a few days to optimize cardiac performance is indicated. In emergent circumstances, invasive monitoring is indicated to guide fluid therapy and assess response to anesthetic agents and inotropic or vasodilator therapy.

12. What are the goals of intraoperative fluid management in patients with heart failure?

Principles of fluid management include optimizing preload, correcting electrolyte disturbances (slowly), and avoiding sodium overload. Again, these goals might be best achieved through invasive monitoring and frequent blood analysis. Replacement of blood losses with blood products might be preferable to replacement with crystalloid.

13. When conducting a general anesthetic in patients with a history of or active CHF, is there a perfect choice of anesthetic agents?

No. Patients with decreased myocardial reserve are more sensitive to the cardiovascular depressant effects caused by anesthetic agents, but careful administration with close monitoring of hemodynamic responses can be accomplished with most agents.

The barbiturates and propofol generally produce the most profound depression of cardiac function and blood pressure when used for induction of general anesthesia. Etomidate produces few aberrations in cardiovascular status, although hypotension may occur in the setting of hypovolemia. Ketamine administration may result in elevated cardiac output and blood pressure secondary to increased sympathetic activity, although this effect may be blunted in patients with CHF and when ketamine is coadministered with benzodiazepines, inhalational anesthetics, or thiopental. Cardiovascular side effects are mild when the benzodiazepines are given in sedative doses but become more pronounced when induction doses are given or when administered in combination with opioids. Induction doses of opioids are usually well tolerated by patients with decreased cardiac reserve but may not be well suited to short surgical procedures (remember, opioids are *not* complete anesthetics). Slower administration, smaller induction doses, and infusions of the IV anesthetics generally result in less dramatic alterations of blood pressure and myocardial function. Each of the inhaled anesthetics produces some degree of myocardial depression.

14. Is regional anesthesia contraindicated in patients with heart failure?

Regional anesthesia, when prudently administered, is an acceptable anesthetic technique. In fact, modest afterload reduction may enhance cardiac output. Continuous regional techniques (spinal or epidural) are preferable because they are associated with gradual loss of sympathetic tone, which may be treated with titration of fluids and vasoactive drugs. Isobaric local anesthetics may be associated with slightly less hypotension compared to hyperbaric local anesthetics.

BIBLIOGRAPHY

1. Clark NH, Stanley TH: Anesthesia for vascular surgery. In Miller RD (ed): Anesthesia, 4th ed. New York, Churchill Livingstone, 1994, pp 1857–1858.
2. Cohn JN: Heart failure. In Willerson JT, Cohn JN (eds): Cardiovascular Medicine. New York, Churchill Livingstone, 1995, pp 947–979.
3. Lake CL: Chronic treatment of congestive heart failure. In Kaplan JA (ed): Cardiac Anesthesia, 3rd ed. Philadelphia, W.B. Saunders, 1993, pp 125–149.
4. Stoelting RK: Pharmacology and Physiology in Anesthetic Practice, 2nd ed. Philadelphia, J.B. Lippincott, 1991, pp 289–291.

39. VALVULAR HEART DISEASE

Richard B. Allen, M.D.

1. Discuss the basic pathophysiology of cardiac valvular disease.

Mitral and aortic stenosis cause pressure overload of the left ventricle, which produces hypertrophy with a cardiac chamber of normal size. Mitral and aortic regurgitation cause volume overload, which leads to hypertrophy with a dilated chamber. The net effect of left-sided valvular lesions is an impedance to forward flow of blood into the systemic circulation. Although right-sided valvular lesions occur, left-sided lesions are more common and usually more hemodynamically significant. This chapter deals only with left-sided lesions.

2. Describe common findings of the history and physical exam in patients with valvular disease.

A history of rheumatic fever, intravenous drug abuse, or heart murmur should alert the examiner to the possibility of valvular disease. Exercise tolerance is frequently decreased. Patients may exhibit signs and symptoms of congestive heart failure, including dyspnea, orthopnea, fatigue, pulmonary rales, jugular venous congestion, hepatic congestion, and dependent edema. Compensatory increases in sympathetic nervous system tone manifest as resting tachycardia, anxiety, and diaphoresis. Angina may occur in patients with a hypertrophied left ventricle even in the absence of coronary artery disease. Atrial fibrillation frequently accompanies diseases of the mitral valve.

3. Which tests are useful in the evaluation of valvular disease?

The **electrocardiogram** (EGC) should be examined for evidence of ischemia, arrhythmias, atrial enlargement, and ventricular hypertrophy. The **chest radiograph** may show enlargement of cardiac chambers, suggest pulmonary hypertension, or reveal pulmonary edema and pleural effusions. **Cardiac catheterization** is the gold standard in the evaluation of such patients and determines pressures in various heart chambers as well as pressure gradients across valves. **Cardiac angiography** allows visualization of the coronary arteries and heart chambers.

4. How is echocardiography helpful?

Doppler echocardiography characterizes ventricular function and valve function. It can be used to measure the valve orifice area and transvalvular pressure gradients, which are measures of the severity of valvular dysfunction. The function of prosthetic valves is also measured echocardiographically.

5. Which invasive monitors aid the anesthesiologist in the perioperative period?

An arterial catheter provides beat-to-beat blood pressure measurement and continuous access to the bloodstream for sampling. Pulmonary artery catheters enable the anesthetist to measure cardiac output and provide central access for the infusion of vasoactive drugs. The pulmonary capillary wedge pressure is an index of left ventricular filling and is useful for guiding intravenous fluid therapy. Transesophageal echocardiography can be used intraoperatively to evaluate left ventricular volume and function, to detect ischemia (segmental wall motion abnormalities) and intracardiac air, and to examine valve function before and after repair.

6. What is a pressure-volume loop?

A pressure-volume loop plots left ventricular pressure against volume through one complete cardiac cycle. Each valvular lesion has a unique profile that suggests compensatory physiologic changes by the left ventricle.

7. How does a normal pressure-volume loop appear?

A = mitral opening, B = mitral closure, C = aortic opening, and D = aortic closure.

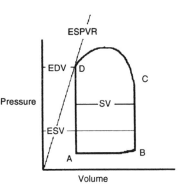

Basic Flow-Volume Loop

The segment DA is isovolumetric relaxation, AB is ventricular filling, BC is isovolumetric contraction, and CD is ejection. Stroke volume (SV), end-systolic volume (ESV), and end-diastolic volume (EDV) are labelled. The end-systolic pressure–volume relationship (ESPVR) slope is a measure of contractility. A horizontal-clockwise shift of the slope represents a decrease in contractility.

8. Discuss the pathophysiology of aortic stenosis.

Aortic stenosis is a fixed outlet obstruction to left ventricular ejection. Concentric hypertrophy (thickened ventricular wall with normal chamber size) develops in response to the increased intraventricular systolic pressure and increased wall tension necessary to maintain forward flow. Ventricular compliance decreases, and end-diastolic pressures increase. Contractility and ejection fraction are usually maintained until late in the disease process. Atrial contraction may account for up to 40% of ventricular filling (normally 20%). Aortic stenosis is usually secondary to calcification of a congenital bicuspid valve or rheumatic heart disease. Patients often present with angina, dyspnea, syncope, or sudden death. Angina occurs in the absence of coronary artery disease because the thickened myocardium is susceptible to ischemia (increased oxygen demand) and elevated end-diastolic pressure reduces coronary perfusion pressure (decreased oxygen supply).

9. How are the compensatory changes in the left ventricle represented by a pressure-volume loop?

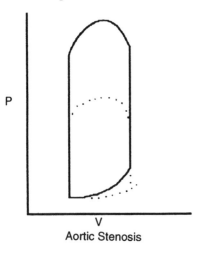

The dotted line represents a normal pressure-volume loop. Note the significant increase in left ventricular end-disatolic pressure and end-systolic pressure.

P

V

Aortic Stenosis

10. What are the hemodynamic goals in the anesthetic management of patients with aortic stenosis?

Patients must have adequate intravascular volume to fill the noncompliant ventricle. Reductions in afterload lead to reduced blood pressure and coronary perfusion because cardiac output is relatively fixed by the stenotic valve. Extremes of heart rate should be avoided. Bradycardias lead to a decrease in cardiac output, whereas tachycardias may produce ischemia as well as limit ejection time. A sinus rhythm is imperative, and emergent cardioversion is indicated if the patient suffers severe hemodynamic compromise due to supraventricular arrhythmia (remember the importance of the atrial "kick").

11. Discuss the pathophysiology of aortic insufficiency.

Chronic aortic insufficiency is usually rheumatic in origin. Acute aortic insufficiency may be secondary to trauma, endocarditis, or dissection of a thoracic aortic aneurysm. The left ventricle experiences volume overload, because part of the stroke volume regurgitates across the incompetent aortic valve in diastole. Eccentric hypertrophy (dilated and thickened chamber) develops. A dilated orifice, slower heart rate (relatively more time spent in diastole), and increased systemic vascular resistance increase the amount of regurgitant flow. Compliance and stroke volume may be markedly increased in chronic aortic insufficiency, whereas contractility gradually diminishes. Ideally, such patients should have valve replacement surgery before the onset of irreversible myocardial damage. In acute aortic insufficiency, the left ventricle is subjected to rapid, massive volume overload with elevated end-diastolic pressures and displays poor contractility. Hypotension and pulmonary edema may necessitate emergent valvular replacement.

12. What does the pressure-volume loop look like in acute and chronic aortic insufficiency?

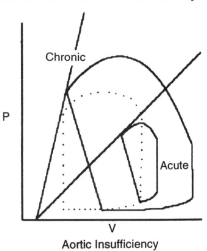

The dotted line represents a normal flow-volume loop. Note the markedly increased ventricular volumes. In chronic aortic insufficiency the ventricle has time to dilate massively without a large increase in end-diastolic pressure. In acute aortic insufficiency the end-diastolic pressures increase significantly, and the compliance is diminished. Also note the increase in ventricular volume in diastole due to regurgitant flow.

Aortic Insufficiency

13. What are the hemodynamic goals in the anesthetic management of patients with aortic insufficiency?

"Fast, full, and forward" is a phrase to remember in managing such patients. Afterload reduction augments forward flow, and additional intravascular volume may be necessary to maintain preload. Modest tachycardia reduces ventricular volumes and limits the time available for regurgitation. The natural heart rate should be maintained if the heart has had time to compensate for the disease state.

14. What is the pathophysiology of mitral stenosis?

Mitral stenosis is usually secondary to rheumatic disease. Critical stenosis of the valve occurs 10–20 years after the initial infection. As the orifice of the valve narrows, the left atrium experiences pressure overload. In contrast to other valvular lesions, the left ventricle shows relative volume underload due to the obstruction of forward blood flow from the atrium. The elevated atrial pressure may be transmitted to the pulmonary circuit and thus lead to pulmonary hypertension and right-heart failure. The overdistended atrium is susceptible to fibrillation with resultant loss of atrial systole, leading to reduced ventricular filling and cardiac output. Symptoms (fatigue, dyspnea on exertion, hemoptysis) may be worsened when increased cardiac output is needed, as with pregnancy, illness, anemia, and exercise. Blood stasis in the left atrium is a risk for thrombus formation and systemic embolization.

15. How is the pressure-volume loop changed from normal in mitral stenosis? (See Figure, next page.)

16. What are the anesthetic considerations in mitral stenosis?

The intravascular volume must be adequate to maintain flow across the stenotic valve. Increases in pulmonary vascular resistance may exacerbate right ventricular failure, and treatment

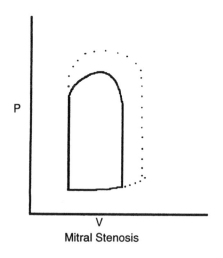

P

V

Mitral Stenosis

The dotted curve represents a normal flow-volume loop. Note that the peak systolic pressure and stroke volume are reduced in the volume-underloaded left ventricle.

of hypotension with systemic vasoconstrictor drugs must be undertaken cautiously. Hypoxemia, hypercarbia, and acidosis increase pulmonary vascular resistance. For this reason, the respiratory depressant effects of preoperative medications may prove particularly deleterious. A slower heart rate is beneficial to allow more time for blood to flow across the valve and to increase ventricular filling.

17. Describe the pathophysiology of mitral regurgitation.

Chronic mitral regurgitation is usually due to rheumatic heart disease, ischemia, or mitral valve prolapse. Acute mitral regurgitation may occur in the setting of myocardial ischemia and infarction with papillary muscle dysfunction or chordae tendineae rupture. In chronic mitral regurgitation, the left ventricle and atrium show volume overload, which leads to eccentric hypertrophy. Left ventricular systolic pressures decrease as part of the stroke volume escapes through the incompetent valve into the left atrium, leading to elevated left atrial pressure, pulmonary hypertension, and eventually right-heart failure. As in aortic insufficiency, regurgitant flow depends on valve orifice size, time available for regurgitant flow, and transvalvular pressure gradient. The valve orifice increases in size as the left ventricle increases in size. In acute mitral regurgitation, the pulmonary circuit and right heart are subjected to sudden increases in pressure and volume in the absence of compensatory ventricular dilatation, which may precipitate acute pulmonary hypertension, pulmonary edema, and right-heart failure.

18. How is the pressure-volume loop in mitral regurgitation changed from normal?

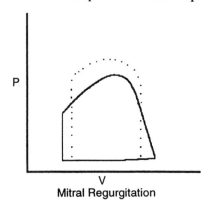

P

V

Mitral Regurgitation

The dotted curve represents a normal pressure-volume loop. The left ventricle shows volume overload but does not develop increased end-diastolic pressures. Systolic pressures are low. Note that intraventricular volume begins decreasing at the onset of systole rather than after a period of isovolumetric contraction as the blood flows across the incompetent valve into the left atrium.

19. What are the hemodynamic goals in anesthetic management of mitral regurgitation?

The intravascular volume should remain full, although slight decreases in volume may decrease the regurgitant fraction by shrinking the size of the ventricle. A slightly elevated heart rate also helps to decrease ventricular volume. Decreasing systemic vascular resistance augments forward flow. As in mitral stenosis, drugs and maneuvers that increase pulmonary vascular resistance must be avoided.

BIBLIOGRAPHY

1. Barash PG, Mathew JP: Mitral stenosis. In Bready LL, Smith RB (eds): Decision Making in Anesthesiology, 2nd ed. St. Louis, Mosby, 1992, pp 188–189.
2. Barash PG, Mathew JP: Mitral regurgitation. In Bready LL, Smith RB (eds): Decision Making in Anesthesiology, 2nd ed. St. Louis, Mosby, 1992, pp 190–191.
3. Deutsch N, Hantler CB: Aortic stenosis. In Bready LL, Smith RB (eds): Decision Making in Anesthesiology, 2nd ed. St. Louis, Mosby, 1992, pp 192–193.
4. Deutsch N, Hantler CB: Aortic regurgitation. In Bready LL, Smith RB (eds): Decision Making in Anesthesiology, 2nd ed. St. Louis, Mosby, 1992, pp 194–195.
5. Reich DL, Brooks JL III, Kaplan JA: Uncommon cardiac diseases. In Katz J, Benumof J, Kadis L (eds): Anesthesia and Uncommon Diseases, 3rd ed. Philadelphia, W.B. Saunders, 1990, pp 333–377.
6. Wray DL, Rothstein P, Thomas SJ: Anesthesia for cardiac surgery. In Barash PG, Cullen BF, Stoelting RK (eds): Clinical Anesthesia, 3rd ed. Philadelphia, Lippincott Williams & Wilkins, 1997.

40. AORTO-OCCLUSIVE DISEASE

Michael Leonard, M.D.

1. Define aorto-occlusive disease.

Aorto-occlusive disease is characterized by pathophysiologic, atherosclerotic changes within the aorta (almost always abdominal) that extend into the iliac or even femoral arteries and result in inadequate perfusion of vital organs and the lower extremities. Aneurysmal changes are common.

2. List pathophysiologic changes commonly present during anesthesia for vascular surgery on the aorta and its major branches.

- Acute hemodynamic changes
- Hypoperfusion of vital organs from underlying disease or vascular cross-clamping
- Potential for massive transfusion and attendant complications
- Severe increases in left ventricular afterload from aortic cross-clamping
- Acid-base disturbances

3. How significant is the incidence of coexisting disease in patients undergoing major vascular surgery?

Because peripheral vascular disease is clinically evident between the fifth and eighth decades of life, the majority of these patients have multiple medical problems.

Coronary artery disease—65%   Angina pectoris—15%
History of myocardial infarction—25%   Hypertension—35%
Congestive heart failure (CHF)—10%–15%   Renal insufficiency—10%
Pulmonary disease—25%   Diabetes mellitus—8%
Cerebrovascular disease—13%

4. What is the risk associated with major vascular surgery in patients with coexisting disease?

A mortality rate of roughly 5% is associated with elective abdominal aortic aneurysm (AAA) repair. The major cause of postoperative death is cardiac, primarily myocardial infarction. Some 30% of these patients have their postsurgical course complicated by CHF. Patients presenting for surgery with poorly controlled CHF, as evidenced by S_3 gallop or distended neck veins, have a 20% mortality with AAA repair.

5. What are the perioperative concerns arising from concurrent disease?

Cardiac. Because cardiac problems are so prevalent in this population, careful evaluation and perioperative management are paramount. Optimal control of CHF, angina, and hypertension is critically important. Patients with a clinical history of ischemic heart disease may require extensive testing. Holter monitoring, exercise treadmill testing, dipyridamole-thallium scanning, and coronary arteriography are appropriate to assess these patients. Current practice is to continue all cardiac medications up to surgery with the possible exception of angiotensin-converting enzyme (ACE) inhibitors in hypertensives because these patients may experience marked intraoperative hypotension.

Pulmonary. Many vascular patients are heavy smokers. Chronic obstructive pulmonary disease (COPD), chronic bronchitis, and bronchospasm are common problems. Preoperative intervention with antibiotics in chronic bronchitics, cessation of smoking, incentive spirometry, and appropriate use of bronchodilators minimizes the incidence of atelectasis, pneumonia, and respiratory failure after surgery.

Renal. The presence of renal insufficiency necessitates careful evaluation of renal function. These patients are more sensitive to the toxicity associated with arteriographic contrast agents and must be watched closely to ensure renal function is not diminished during the diagnostic evaluation. Postoperative renal failure in this population carries a 50% mortality.

Cerebrovascular disease. A decreased ability to autoregulate cerebral blood flow may be present in these individuals, and they require tighter control of blood pressure intraoperatively. The presence of ongoing symptoms of the cerebral circulation dictates further work-up.

Diabetes. These patients have a high incidence of cardiac, vascular, and renal disease. They are also prone to silent myocardial ischemia. Autonomic neuropathy in diabetics frequently results in hemodynamic instability intraoperatively.

6. Describe the primary aspects of management when a patient presents with an acute abdominal aortic rupture.

If the rupture is retroperitoneal, enough blood may be contained for the patient to maintain hemodynamic stability. With free intraperitoneal rupture, survival is unusual. Patients should be stabilized in the operating room (not the emergency room) to a systolic blood pressure of 80–100 mmHg. At least 10 units of blood should be set up, multiple large-bore intravenous (IV) lines placed, and anesthesia induced gently. Invasive monitoring may be obtained either preinduction or postinduction, depending on the clinical situation. In cases of acute rupture, poor outcome is associated with advanced age, cardiac disease, free rupture, preoperative shock, acute coronary ischemia, and cardiac arrest.

7. List the appropriate intraoperative monitors for aortic surgery.
- Electrocardiogram (ECG) monitoring (preferably both lead II for rhythm assessment and V_5 for detecting intraoperative ischemia)
- Arterial line for continuous pressure monitoring and blood gas analysis
- Pulmonary artery catheter
- Esophageal stethoscope and temperature probe

Critically important in patient management:
- Indwelling urinary catheter
- Estimation of intravascular volume

• Ability to detect myocardial ischemia
• Assessment of hematologic, acid-base, and electrolyte values

In high-risk patients, transesophageal echocardiography to assess the effect of aortic cross-clamping on left ventricular function can be helpful.

8. What are the factors to consider in choosing alternative anesthetic agents?

Hemodynamic stability and **cardiac function** are major determinants in the choice of anesthetic agents. Unstable patients are best induced with ketamine, etomidate, or small amounts of opioids and benzodiazepines. In stable patients, gradual and gentle inductions are preferred with the goals being avoidance of tachycardia and hypertension. Intratracheal lidocaine is useful in blunting the response to intubation. Patients with poor ventricular function are candidates for high-dose opioid anesthetics, which depress cardiac contractility to a lesser extent than inhalation agents do. Combinations of regional epidural anesthetics and light general anesthetics offer the benefit of less intraoperative myocardial depression and airway control; local anesthetic and opioid infusions for postoperative pain control are an additional benefit. In the past, concerns have been raised about the risk of epidural hematomas resulting from regional anesthesia in patients receiving surgical anticoagulation, but studies have shown this to be a safe practice.

9. What percentage of AAAs involve the renal arteries?

Approximately 70% are infrarenal, whereas 30% include renal arteries.

10. Discuss the physiologic implications of cross-clamping the abdominal aorta.

Aortic cross-clamping produces an acute, tremendous increase in left ventricular afterload. Cardiac ischemia, acute left ventricular failure, and severe hypertension can all accompany cross-clamping. This abrupt increase in afterload can be treated through use of vasodilators such as nitroprusside and nitroglycerin and α-adrenergic blockers such as phentolamine. Renal ischemia and interruption of spinal cord perfusion are possible. Lack of perfusion below the cross-clamp produces metabolic acidosis in the lower extremities.

11. Does infrarenal clamping adversely affect renal function?

Infrarenal clamping causes increases in plasma renin activity, alterations in intrarenal blood flow, and decreases in glomerular filtration rate and renal perfusion. In addition, the surgery itself may result in arterial emboli to the kidney and hypoperfusion. These emboli are usually composed of atheromatous debris or thrombus from within the diseased vessel.

12. What physiologic changes can be expected with removal of the cross-clamp?

The decrease in peripheral vascular resistance from the maximally dilated vascular beds below the clamp results in an acute decrease in arterial blood pressure. Additionally, washout of the lactate and accumulated metabolites in the ischemic extremities produces an acute metabolic acidosis. Maneuvers to ameliorate the effects of cross-clamp removal include increasing arterial and central venous pressure by fluid loading the patient before the clamp comes off. Also, infusion of bicarbonate before clamp removal can buffer the acid load and minimize the acute acidosis.

13. What considerations for intraoperative fluid and blood replacement are warranted?

1. Adequate hydration must be maintained intraoperatively to maximize perfusion and urine output.
2. Volume loading should be performed before clamp removal.
3. The ability to replace blood loss quickly is important because rapid, severe hemorrhage is common.
4. Use of a cell saver may minimize or prevent use of products from the blood bank.
5. Massive transfusion may necessitate administration of clotting factors and platelets.
6. Using IV fluid warmers helps maintain the patient's body temperature.

14. Discuss important elements of postoperative care.

All patients should be admitted to the intensive care unit. The patient's cardiac status requires careful observation. The peak incidence of postoperative myocardial infarction is at about 72 hours postoperatively. This is probably related to the reabsorption of fluid that was "third spaced" during the operation, which can lead to CHF and myocardial ischemia. Pulmonary function can be enhanced with incentive spirometry, pulmonary toilet, and bronchodilators when appropriate. Close attention should be given to renal function and urine output, because postoperative renal failure has ominous implications. Pain must be well controlled to minimize physiologic stress. Other miscellaneous postoperative complications include gastrointestinal ischemia, bleeding, stroke, graft infection, distal arterial thrombosis, and pulmonary embolism.

BIBLIOGRAPHY

1. Clark NJ, Stanley TH: Anesthesia for vascular surgery. In Miller RD (ed): Anesthesia, 4th ed. New York, Churchill Livingstone, 1994.
2. Eagle KA, Coley CM, Nussbaum SR, et al: Combining clinical and thallium data optimizes preoperative assessment of cardiac risk before major vascular surgery. Ann Intern Med 110:859–866, 1989.
3. Goldman L, Caldera DL, Nussbaum SR, et al: Multifactorial index of cardiac risk in patients in noncardiac surgical procedures. N Engl J Med 297:845–850, 1977.
4. Lunn JK, Dannemiller FJ, Stanley TH: Cardiovascular responses to clamping of the aorta during epidural and general anesthesia. Anesth Analg 58:372–376, 1979.
5. Rao TL, El-Etr AA: Anticoagulation following placement of epidural and subarachnoid catheters: An evaluation of neurologic sequelae. Anesthesiology 55:618–620, 1981.

41. CEREBROVASCULAR INSUFFICIENCY

Cynthia K. Hampson, M.D.

1. What is cerebrovascular disease?

Cerebrovascular disease refers to abnormalities in both extracranial and intracranial blood vessels that may lead to an inadequate supply of blood and therefore oxygen to the brain. When the supply of oxygen is inadequate to meet the needs of the brain, cerebral ischemia results; this is termed cerebrovascular insufficiency.

2. What are the neurologic manifestations of cerbrovascular insufficiency?

The two major groups of symptoms include transient ischemia attack (TIA) and stroke. A TIA develops suddenly, involves neurologic dysfunction for minutes to hours (by definition, never lasting more than 24 hours), clears spontaneously, and is associated with a normal computed tomography (CT) scan. Strokes may develop rapidly or in a stepwise fashion over a period of hours, days, or weeks. Their major differentiating feature from TIAs is that the resultant neurologic dysfunction either requires a period of months to years to resolve or, more commonly, never resolves completely. Strokes can be classified as minor, with eventual full or nearly full recovery, or major, with severe and permanent disability or death. In addition to cerebrovascular abnormalities, strokes are associated with many other disease states, including but not limited to hypertension, diabetes, coagulopathies, atrial fibrillation, mitral valve disease, substance abuse, and endocarditis. A third group of patients experiences neurologic dysfunction for longer than 24 hours with spontaneous and complete recovery within 1–2 weeks. This phenomenon is termed reversible ischemic neurologic deficit (RIND) and should be pathophysiologically grouped with TIAs.

3. What is the major cause of TIAs?

TIAs have two presumed causes, depending on the area of brain affected. Ischemia of the frontal and parietal lobes or the retina of the eye are believed to be caused by embolism of platelet aggregates and debris from atheroscerotic plaques in the extracranial carotid arteries and verte-brobasilar arteries. The quick resolution of TIAs (within 24 hours) is the result of the body's inherent mechanisms for dissolving and breaking down such emboli. In contrast, ischemia of the brain stem or the temporal and occipital lobes is believed to be caused by a transient decrease in blood flow or blood pressure in the vertebrobasilar system.

4. Contrast the symptoms of vertebrobasilar and carotid TIAs.

Carotid artery emboli usually present as transient ipsilateral visual loss, contralateral motor or sensory disturbance, or both. The visual loss results from the passage of emboli into the first branch of the internal carotid, the ophthalmic artery. The visual loss is often described as a shade pulled down over one eye, a syndrome called amaurosis fugax. Motor or sensory loss, including tingling, numbness, clumsiness, altered mentation, and difficulty with speaking, is caused by the passage of emboli into a cerebral hemisphere; consciousness is rarely affected. In contrast, symptoms of vertebrobasilar artery disease result from ischemia to the occipital lobes and the brain stem. Visual disturbance is common, but it is bilateral and frequently described as dim or blurry. Diplopia, nausea, vomiting, vertigo, and unsteadiness are also common. A characteristic of vertebrobasilar disease is the "drop-attack," a sudden loss of postural tone in the legs. Transient episodes of global amnesia, probably resulting from ischemia to the temporal lobes of the thalamus, are most likely due to basilar insufficiency. Vertebrobasilar symptoms, in contrast to carotid symptoms, are often linked to patient position or movement. Abrupt changes in position resulting in orthostatic hypotension may precipitate symptoms, and turning the head or reaching above the head may cause compression of the involved arteries.

5. What is the incidence of stroke in the United States?

Stroke affects approximately 500,000 persons annually; it is the third most common cause of death in the United States.

6. List the risk factors for stroke.

Hypertension is the strongest risk factor. Both systolic and diastolic elevations in blood pressure are associated with increased risk, and the degree of elevation is directly proportional to the risk of stroke. Two other major risk factors are cardiac disease (left ventricular hypertrophy, atrial fibrillation, cardiovascular disease) and smoking. Other less significant factors include age, diabetes, and hyperlipidemia.

7. What is the significance of an asymptomatic carotid bruit?

Asymptomatic bruits are heard in 5–10% of the adult population. A 1989 prospective study of 566 patients with asymptomatic carotid bruits revealed a 1-year stroke or TIA rate of 2.5% compared with a rate of 0.7% in patients without carotid bruits. The recent European Carotid Surgery Trial (ECST) demonstrated that carotid endarterectomy (CEA) is not indicated for most patients with moderate (30–69%) stenoses, even if they are symptomatic. However, the rate of stroke or TIA increases dramatically with increasing stenosis, reaching a 1-year stroke or TIA rate of 46% for stenoses greater than 80%. It is well accepted that symptomatic patients and asymptomatic patients with a stenosis > 70% are candidates for CEA.

8. What are the two most common means of evaluating carotid disease?

The most common noninvasive means of evaluating carotid stenosis is the duplex scan. A duplex scan involves B-mode ultrasonography of the carotid bifurcation, which provides a two-dimensional assessment of plaques, ulcerations, and patency; Doppler ultrasonography measures red blood cell velocity and further defines the degree of stenosis. Angiography, an invasive test that carries a low risk of stroke, is the most accurate means of assessing carotid stenosis and of measuring the size of plaques. The accuracy of the duplex scan in estimating the degree of stenosis is 95% compared with angiography.

9. List the most common coexisting medical problems of symptomatic patients presenting for CEA.

Analysis of patients enrolled in the North American Symptomatic Carotid Endarterectomy Trial (NASCET) made it possible to determine the prevalence of specific coexisting medical conditions.

Coexisting Medical Conditions

MEDICAL CONDITION	PREVALENCE (%)
Angina	24
Previous myocardial infarction	20
Hypertension	60
Claudication	15
Smoking, current	37
Smoking, previous	40
Diabetes	19

10. What is the major cause of morbidity and mortality in patients undergoing CEA?

Cardiac complications, mainly myocardial infarction, are the primary source of mortality associated with CEA. A study of 1,546 endarterectomies noted that patients with a preoperative history of angina had a mortality of 18% compared with less than 5% in patients free of cardiac symptoms. The overall incidence of fatal infarction in patients undergoing CEA is 0.5–4%, which represents approximately 40% of the total 30-day perioperative mortality. Other factors predictive of increased cardiac mortality with CEA are congestive heart failure, myocardial infarction within the previous 6 months, and severe hypertension.

11. Describe a risk stratification scheme that considers medical status, neurologic status, and extent of carotid disease.

Carotid Endarterectomy and Risk Stratification

RISK GROUP	CHARACTERISTICS	TOTAL MORBIDITY AND MORTALITY (%)
1	Neurologically stable; no major medical or angiographic risk	1
2	Neurologically stable, significant angiographic risk, no major medical risk	2
3	Neurologically stable, major medical risk, ± major angiographic risk	7
4	Neurologically unstable, ± major medical or angiographic risk	10

TYPE OF RISK	RISK FACTORS	
Medical	Angina	
	Myocardial infarction (< 6 months ago)	
	Congestive heart failure	
	Severe hypertension (> 180/110 mmHg)	
	Chronic obstructive pulmonary disease	
	Age > 70 years	
	Severe obesity	
Neurologic	Progressing deficit	
	New deficit (< 24 hours)	
	Frequent daily TIAs	
	Multiple cerebral infarcts	

Table continued on next page.

Carotid Endarterectomy and Risk Stratification (Continued)

TYPE OF RISK	RISK FACTORS
Angiographic	Contralateral internal carotid artery occlusion
	Internal carotid artery siphon stenosis
	Proximal or distal plaque extension
	High carotid bifurcation
	Presence of soft thrombus

From Herrick IA, Gelb AW: Occlusive cerebrovascular disease: Anesthetic considerations. In Cottrell JE, Smith DS (eds): Anesthesia and Neurosurgery. St. Louis, Mosby, 1994, p 484, with permission.

12. Define cerebral autoregulation. How is it affected in cerebrovascular disease? What are the anesthetic implications?

Cerebral autoregulation is the ability of the brain to maintain cerebral blood flow relatively constant (40–60 ml/100 g/min) over a wide range (50–150 mmHg) of mean arterial pressure. Stenosis or obstruction in the internal carotid artery causes a pressure drop beyond the obstruction. In an effort to maintain cerebral blood flow and avoid ischemia, the cerebral vasculature dilates. As the degree of carotid obstruction progresses, the cerebral vasculature distal to the obstruction maximally dilates. At this point, the cerebral vasculature loses its autoregulatory ability. Cerebral blood flow becomes passive and depends on systemic blood pressure. It thus becomes critically important to maintain the blood pressure of the CEA patient within very narrow limits, because they have minimal or no autoregulatory reserve to counter anesthetic-induced reductions in blood pressure. The anesthesiologist must have multiple preoperative blood pressures and heart rates to define the range over which the patient's cerebral blood flow is currently maintained.

13. How are the cerebral responses to hyper- and hypocapnia altered in cerebrovascular disease? What are the anesthetic implications?

Normal cerebral vessels are highly sensitive to arterial carbon dioxide partial pressure ($PaCO_2$), dilating in response to hypercapnia and constricting in response to hypocapnia. Cerebral blood flow normally increases approximately 4% (1–2 ml/100 g/min) for each 1 mmHg increase in $PaCO_2$ between 20 and 100 mmHg. However, in ischemic, already maximally vasodilated areas of the brain, this relationship breaks down, and responses to hyper- and hypocapnia may be paradoxical. Because cerebral vessels in an area of ischemia are already maximally dilated, hypercapnia may result in dilation of only normally responsive vessels outside the area of ischemia. This phenomenon, termed "steal," may divert blood flow away from the ischemic area, further compromising perfusion. On the other hand, hypocapnia may cause vessels in normal areas to undergo constriction, diverting blood to marginally perfused areas. This phenomenon is termed the "Robin Hood" or "inverse steal" effect. It is therefore generally recommended that normocapnia be maintained in patients undergoing endarterectomy.

14. What is normal cerebral blood flow? At what level is cerebral blood flow considered ischemic?

Normal cerebral blood flow in humans is 40–60 ml/100 g/min (15% of cardiac output). The cerebral metabolic rate for oxygen in adults is 3–4 ml/100 g/min (20% of whole-body oxygen consumption). The cerebral blood flow at which ischemia becomes apparent on electroencephalogram (EEG), termed the critical regional cerebral blood flow (rCBF), is 18–20 ml/100 g/min. Metabolic failure occurs at approximately 10–12 ml/100 g/min.

15. How do inhalational anesthetics affect cerebral perfusion and cerebral metabolic rate?

In the normal, unanesthetized brain, cerebral blood flow varies directly with the cerebral metabolic rate for oxygen. Inhalational agents are said to "uncouple" this relationship. They decrease the cerebral metabolic rate for oxygen but concurrently cause dilation of cerebral blood vessels, thus increasing cerebral blood flow. Isoflurane reduces rCBF to less than 10 ml/100 g/min, thus providing relative brain protection. In comparison, enflurane reduces rCBF to about 15 and halothane to about 20 ml/100 g/min. Although it has not been proved or disproved by formal studies, isoflurane is theoretically the inhaled anesthetic of choice for CEA.

16. How should patients scheduled for CEA be monitored?

All patients undergoing CEA should be monitored with leads II and V of the ECG, noninvasive arterial blood pressure, end-tidal capnometry, temperature, and pulse oximetry. Because of the need to maintain the patient's blood pressure within a specified range and to perform repetitive blood gas and coagulation studies, intra-arterial blood pressure monitoring is also indicated. As always, additional monitors should be guided by individual patient characteristics. Carotid surgery does not involve large fluid shifts and does not require a pulmonary artery catheter in the patient with normal ventricular function. A 16-gauge or larger intravenous line is the recommended peripheral venous access for the typical CEA. Additional intravenous lines are started to administer vasoactive or anesthetic infusions.

17. Is regional or general anesthesia preferred for the endarterectomy patient?

No controlled, randomized, prospective study exists that demonstrates a long-term benefit of one technique over the other. A simple aggregation of results from 23 mostly retrospective studies of CEA outcomes involving 9160 cases revealed little difference in the overall rate of postoperative myocardial infarction (MI) between general anesthesia (2.8%) and regional anesthesia (2.1%). Ultimately, the choice between regional and general anesthesia is based on patient suitability and preference, on surgeon and anesthesiologist experience and expertise, and on the availability of cerebral perfusion monitoring.

18. Describe a regional anesthetic technique suitable for CEA.

Suitable anesthesia requires sensory blockade of cervical nerves C2–C4, which is provided by blockade of the deep cervical plexus. This block is performed with the patient in the supine position, with the head and neck slightly extended and turned away from the side that is to be blocked. The anesthesiologist should stand at the shoulder of the side to be blocked. A line is drawn from the tip of the mastoid process to Chassaignac's tubercle (the transverse process of the sixth cervical vertebra, the most easily palpable transverse process of the cervical vertebrae). A second line 1 cm posterior and parallel to this line overlies the the tips of the transverse processes of C2–C4. Each of these three processes should be located and marked before injection. The C2 process is located 1–2 cm below the mastoid process and is the most difficult to palpate. The C3 process is approximately 1.5 cm below the C2 process (along the second line), and the C4 process is approximately 1.5 cm more cauded than C3. A 2" 22-gauge needle is then inserted just superior and posterior to the marks and is angled slightly anterior and caudad. This angle decreases the chance of inadvertently advancing the needle between the transverse processes and into the vertebral artery. The needle should contact C2 process at a depth of 2.5–3 cm; the C3 and C4 processes are slightly more superficial. After aspiration, 6 ml of local anesthesia is injected at each of the three locations. An alternate technique (attributed to Winnie) involves location of all three processes but injection only at the C4 process of 10–12 ml of local anesthesia. A paresthesia should be obtained with this technique, which relies on spread within the neurovascular space to achieve adequate anesthesia. If a paresthesia is not obtained with initial needle placement, the needle should be walked in an anteroposterior plane in a stepwise manner. Sensory blockade is provided by lower concentrations of local anesthetics, such as 0.5–1% lidocaine or 0.25% bupivacaine. Contraindications to this block are relative, including coagulopathy, previous surgery in the area of blockade, and poor patient cooperation. Patients with significant chronic obstructive pulmonary disease or otherwise borderline respiratory status may not be good candidates, because phrenic nerve palsy is a frequent complicaton of deep cervical plexus blockade. Care should be taken not to palpate the neck excessively, because the carotid plaque may fragment and embolize.

19. What are the advantages and disadvantages of regional anesthesia for CEA?

The main advantage of regional anesthesia is the ability to perform continuous neurologic assessment of the awake, cooperative patient and thus to evaluate the adequacy of cerebral perfusion. This, however, can quickly become a disadvantage if the patient develops cerebral ischemia. Cerebral ischemia in this setting may lead to disorientation, inadequate ventilation and oxygenation, and a disrupted surgical field. Providing maximal cerebral protection often requires conversion to a general anesthetic, but endotracheal intubation in this setting may prove difficult. In addition, sedation may impair the value of the awake neurologic assessment and therefore must be titrated carefully. Proponents of regional anesthesia believe that greater inherent control of blood pressure is maintained, thus reducing the need for vasopressors and perioperative myocardial ischemia. However, studies supporting this claim are limited.

A recognized complication of deep cervical block is phrenic nerve block, which may cause ventilatory compromise in some patients and is the major contraindication for bilateral deep cervical blocks. Other disadvantages of the deep cervical block include seizures from intra-arterial injection of local anesthetic, total spinal or epidural anesthesia, and recurrent laryngeal nerve block.

20. Describe a general anesthetic technique for a typical CEA patient.

Many general anesthetic techniques are acceptable for CEA. Any technique that provides prompt awakening of the patient at the end of surgery and affords myocardial and cerebral protection is acceptable. The following guidelines are designed to attain these goals.

Because of the desire to have the patient awake and responsive soon after the completion of CEA, heavy premedication with long-acting agents is to be avoided. Anxiety generally is alleviated by an effective preoperative interview. The intra-arterial catheter is placed before induction, as induction often involves unacceptable hemodynamic changes. The patient is preoxygenated, and induction is begun with a short-acting opioid until the patient is comfortably sedated but able to maintain relative normocapnea. The patient is then induced with 2–3 mg/kg of thiopental; controlled ventilation is begun with 100% oxygen by mask with isoflurane added as tolerated. Paralysis is generally instituted with a muscle relaxant possessing hemodynamic stability, such as vecuronium or rocuronium. Succinylcholine may be used, but it is contraindicated in hemiparetic patients because of the risk of hyperkalemia. Additional opioid is also given to blunt the sympathetic response to intubation (i.e., 3–5 µg/kg of fentanyl). In addition, 1–1.5 minutes before intubation, 100 mg of lidocaine is given intravenously to help blunt the response to intubation. With complete paralysis verified by train-of-four monitoring, intubation is then performed. Reduction of hypertension, coughing, and straining can be achieved at the end of surgery with the use of an endotracheal tube, which permits intratracheal instillation of lidocaine prior to awakening.

A light general anesthetic is maintained with oxygen—up to 50% nitrous oxide and isoflurane. Additional opioids are administered judiciously as needed, with the goal of a smooth but prompt awakening. Remifentanil offers significant benefit in this regard, since it can be infused at doses beneficial in controlling hypertensive episodes and reducing myocardial ischemia without delaying awakening. Light general anesthesia is associated with a decreased incidence of transesophageal echocardiography (TEE)–diagnosed myocardial ischemia compared with deep anesthesia with phenylephrine to maintain blood pressure. However, a recent Canadian study comparing propofol and isoflurane revealed no evidence of Holter-monitored ischemia during phenylephrine infusion. This suggests that the combination of a pure α-agonist with a negative inotrope produces wall-motion abnormalities that are over-diagnosed as ischemic in origin. Holter monitoring has been shown to be more sensitive than TEE in the detection of intraoperative ischemia.

Blood pressure is usually maintained within a narrow predefined range based on multiple observations of the patient's baseline vital signs. This range is defined by the highest preoperative value that is not associated with myocardial ischemia and the lowest preoperative value that is not associated with cerebral ischemia. Vasoactive agents, such as phenylephrine, dopamine, nitroglycerin, and nitroprusside, are commonly used as necessary to maintain blood pressure within this range.

Before carotid occlusion, anesthetic depth is minimized and blood pressure is allowed to rise to the upper limit previously defined as acceptable. This goal may require the addition of vasopressors. To insure that the patient does not move during carotid clamping, muscle relaxants may be added. Stretching of the carotid baroreceptor and significant bradycardia and hypotension can be avoided by having the surgeon infiltrate the carotid bifurcation with 1% lidocaine.

Maintenance of normothermia, through supplemental warming if necessary, has recently been demonstrated to reduce the risk of serious postoperative cardiac events (unstable angina, ischemia, MI) by 55% in patients with coronary artery disease undergoing noncardiac surgery when compared to permitting relative hypothermia.

21. Discuss the conflicting goals of myocardial protection and cerebral protection during CEA.

The main goals of CEA anesthesia are to protect the heart and the brain from ischemia. However, the means of achieving these goals are often in direct conflict. Decreasing myocardial oxygen requirements involves decreasing heart rate, blood pressure, and contractility, whereas increasing cerebral perfusion involves increasing blood pressure and contractility and avoiding bradycardia. Suggested compromises, which have been incorporated into the general guidelines described in question 20, include decreasing both cerebral and myocardial metabolic rate with anesthetics such as thiopental and isoflurane, and maximizing afterload reduction while monitoring the EEG for ischemia. While injection of the carotid sinus with local anesthetics to avoid sudden bradycardia and hypotension has been suggested in the past, a recent study suggests that this procedure is in fact associated with an increased incidence of postoperative hypertension.

Conflicts in Myocardial and Cerebral Protection

HEMODYNAMIC VARIABLE	TO PROTECT THE HEART FROM ISCHEMIA	TO PROTECT THE BRAIN FROM ISCHEMIA
Heart rate	Slow	Do not slow
Blood pressure	Decrease	Increase cerebral perfusion pressure
Contractility	Decrease	Increase

Compromise solutions:
1. Inject area of carotid bifurcations with 1% lidocaine for 10–15 minutes.
2. Decrease cerebral and myocardial metabolic rate and contractility.
3. Use normal findings of EEG or processed EEG to guide afterload reduction.

From Roizen MF, Ellis JE: Anesthesia for vascular surgery. In Barash PG, Cullen BF, Stoelting RK (eds): Clinical Anesthesia. Philadelphia, J.B. Lippincott, 1992, pp 1059–1072, with permission.

22. What are the advantages and disadvantages of general anesthesia for patients undergoing CEA?

Advantages of general anesthesia include control of the airway, a quiet operative field, and the ability to maximize cerebral perfusion if ischemia develops. The main disadvantage of general anesthesia is loss of the continuous neurologic evaluation of the awake patient.

23. What methods of monitoring cerebral perfusion during general anesthesia are available?

Available techniques include stump pressure monitoring, intraoperative EEG, monitoring of somatosensory-evoked potentials, monitoring of jugular venous or transconjunctival oxygen saturation, transcranial Doppler, and tracer wash-out techniques. None is as reliable as an awake cooperative patient. None of the methods has been demonstrated to improve outcome, and none has gained widespread acceptance as the monitor of choice. In addition, the availablity of proper equipment and personnel to perform the monitoring varies by institution.

24. Do stump pressures provide reliable cerebral perfusion information?

No. The stump pressure is the pressure in the portion of the internal carotid artery immediately cephalad to the carotid cross-clamp. This pressure is presumed to represent pressure transmitted from the contralateral carotid artery and vertebrals via the circle of Willis. In the past, it was believed that a stump pressure of 50 mmHg was indicative of adequte cerebral blood flow and perfusion. However, studies have shown that stump pressures have **no** correlation with flow. Some patients with stump pressures less than 50 mmHg are adequately perfused, whereas some patients with "adequate" stump pressures have suffered ischemic injury. Studies have also shown a lack of correlation between stump pressures and EEG and between stump pressures and neurologic exam in awake patients.

25. Does intraoperative EEG provide clinically useful information during CEA?

No data show that EEG during CEA results in improved patient outcomes. Although the EEG is a highly sensitive and early indicator of global cortical ischemia, it is not highly specific and results in many false-positive (though few false-negative) warnings. It is also affected by multiple variables, including temperature, blood pressure, $PaCO_2$, PaO_2, serum glucose and sodium levels, anesthetic depth, and preexisting neurologic deficits. The value of the EEG may lie in myocardial protection. Monitoring of the EEG with the goal of maximally reducing blood pressure without producing EEG evidence of cerebral ischemia reduces myocardial afterload and the incidence of perioperative myocardial ischemia. Recent trends toward processed EEG data, such as density spectral array, have made this monitor more "user friendly" but less sensitive.

26. What are the common postoperative complications of CEA?

Hypotension associated with decreased systemic vascular resistance is common and is believed to be caused by an intact carotid sinus responding to higher arterial pressures after removal of the atheromatous plaque. Such hypotension responds well to fluid administration and vasopressors. Hypotension also may result from myocardial ischemia. The incidence of postoperative myocardial ischemia and infarction has already been discussed and obviously indicates a need for continued careful control of postoperative blood pressure, heart rate, and oxygenation. Therefore, a 12-lead ECG should be obtained soon after the patient arrives in the recovery room, and leads II and V of the ECG should be continuously monitored.

Hypertension is also common but less understood. Obviously, the high incidence of preoperative hypertension, particularly when it is poorly controlled, may result in labile postoperative hypertension. It may also be the result of denervation of the carotid sinus or trauma to the sinus intraoperatively. Other causes of postoperative hypertension must also be sought, such as bladder distention, hypoxia, hyercarbia, and pain. Given the high association of postoperative hypertension with onset of new neurologic deficit, postoperative hypertension must be aggressively monitored and treated.

Cerebral hyperperfusion caused by increased cerebral blood flow is also a recognized postoperative complication. It typically results from an increase in flow of not less than 35%, but the increase may approach 200%. Poorly controlled hypertension contributes to this complication. Symptoms and side effects of hyperperfusion are headache, face and eye pain, cerebral edema, nausea and vomiting, seizure, and intracerebral hemorrhage. The blood pressure of such patients should be very carefully controlled, preferably without the use of cerebral vasodilators.

Respiratory difficulties may result from several different mechanisms. Hematomas and tissue edema may form postoperatively and lead to airway compromise and cranial nerve palsies. Treatment involves drainage of the hematoma followed by intubation of the patient as needed. Respiratory problems also may result from vocal cord paralysis due to intraoperative damage to laryngeal nerves and from phrenic nerve paresis after cervical plexus block. Depending on the severity of the respiratory compromise, intubation may be indicated. The chemoreceptor function of the carotid bodies is predictably lost in most patients after CEA, as evidenced by a complete loss of the respiratory response to hypoxia and an average increase in the resting pCO_2 of 6 mmHg. Thus, patients should receive supplemental oxygen postoperatively for at least 24 hours; adequate attention to pulmonary toilet is mandatory.

Most **strokes** associated with CEA occur postoperatively as a result of surgical factors involving carotid thrombosis and emboli from the surgical site.

BIBLIOGRAPHY

1. Chambers BR, Norris JW: Outcome in patients with asymptomatic neck bruits. N Engl J Med 315:860–865, 1986.
2. Eisenberg MJ, London MJ, Leung JM, et al: Monitoring for myocardial ischemia during non-cardiac surgery: A technology assessment of transesophageal echocardiography and 12-lead electroencephalography. JAMA 268:210–216, 1992.
3. European Carotid Surgery Trialist's Collaborative Group: Endarterectomy for moderate symptomatic carotid stenosis: Interim results from the MRC European Carotid Surgery Trial. Lancet 347: 1591–1593, 1996.
4. Frank SM, Fleisher L, Breslow MJ, et al: Perioperative maintenance of normothermia reduces the incidence of morbid cardiac events. JAMA 277:1127–1134, 1997.
5. Frost EAM: The patient for carotid endarterectomy. Anesthesiol News, Dec 18–25, 1994.
6. Lien CA, Poxnak AV: Carotid endarterectomy. In Yao FF (ed): Yao and Artusio's Anesthesiology: Problem-Oriented Patient Management, 4th ed. Philadelphia, Lippincott Williams & Wilkins, 1998.
7. Multch WAC, White IWC, Donen N, et al: Hemodynamic instability and myocardial ischemia during carotid endarterectomy: A comparison of propofol and isoflurane. Can J Anesth 42:577–587, 1995.
8. North American Symptomatic Carotid Endarterectomy Trial Steering Committee: North American Symptomatic Carotid Endarterectomy Trial. Methods, patient characteristics, and progress. Stroke 22:711–720, 1991.
9. O'Donnell TF, Callow AD, Willet C, et al: The impact of coronary artery disease on carotid endarterectomy. Ann Surg 198:705–712, 1983.
10. Roederer GO, Langlois YE, Joger KA, et al: The natural history of carotid arterial disease in asymptomatic patients with cervical bruits. Stroke 15:605–613, 1984.
11. Smith JS, Roizen MF, Cahalan MK, et al: Does anesthetic technique make a difference? Augmentation of systolic blood pressure during carotid endarterectomy: Effects of phenylephrine versus light anesthesia and of isoflurane versus halothane on the incidence of myocardial ischemia. Anesthesiology 69:846–853, 1988.
12. Sundt TM Jr, Whinant JP, Houser OW, et al: Prospective study of the effectiveness and durability of carotid endarterectomy. Mayo Clin Proc 65:625–635, 1990.
13. Tuman KJ: Anesthesia for surgery of the carotid artery. In 49th Annual Refresher Course Lectures Presented at the 1998 Annual Meeting of the American Society of Anesthesiologists. Park Ridge, IL, ASA, 1998, pp 261–267.
14. Wade JG, Larson CP, Hickey RF, et al: Effect of carotid endarterectomy on carotid chemoreceptor and baroreceptor function in man. N Engl J Med 282:823–829,1970.

42. REACTIVE AIRWAY DISEASE

Malcolm Packer, M.D.

1. Define reactive airway disease.

This term is used to describe a family of diseases that share an airway sensitivity to physical, chemical, or pharmacologic stimuli. This sensitivity results in a bronchoconstrictor response and is seen in patients with asthma, chronic obstructive pulmonary disease (COPD), emphysema, viral upper respiratory illness, and other disorders.

Asthma is defined by the American Thoracic Society as "a disease characterized by an increased responsiveness of the trachea and bronchi to various stimuli manifested by a widespread narrowing of the airways that changes in severity either spontaneously or as a result of therapy. Asthma is manifested by episodes of dyspnea, cough and wheezing." These symptoms are related to the increased resistance to airflow in the patient's airways.

2. What are the different types of asthma?

Although the common denominator lies in hyperreactivity of the airways, patients may fit into two subgroups: allergic (extrinsic) and idiosyncratic (intrinsic). Many believe that the terms extrinsic and intrinsic should be discarded. Underlying all types of asthma are airway hyperreactivity and inflammation, and the cause includes the interaction of allergic and nonallergic stimuli.

The allergic type of asthma is thought to result from an immunoglobulin E (IgE)–mediated response to certain antigens such as dust and pollen. Among the mediators released are histamine, leukotrienes, prostaglandins, bradykinin, thromboxane, and eosinophilic chemotactic factor. Their release leads to capillary leakage in the airways, along with mucous secretions and smooth muscle contraction surrounding the airway. Inflammation is a prominent feature.

The idiosyncratic type of asthma is not mediated by IgE but by nonantigenic stimuli, such as exercise, cold, pollution, and infection. Bronchospasm is caused by increased parasympathetic (vagal) tone. Patients in the idiosyncratic group also have release of the same mediators as the allergic group. Conversely, certain patients with allergic asthma have increased vagal tone.

3. What diseases mimic asthma?

Upper and lower airway obstruction from tumor, aspirated foreign bodies, or stenosis may mimic asthma. Left ventricular failure (cardiac asthma) and pulmonary embolism both simulate airway hyperreactivity. Gastroesophageal reflux and aspiration also may produce airway hyperreactivity. Viral respiratory illnesses (e.g., respiratory syncytial virus) also produce bronchospasm. A careful history and physical exam help to define the cause.

4. What are the important historical features of an asthmatic patient?

A careful history allows a close estimate of the severity of disease. Questions should include:

1. How and when the patient was first diagnosed.
2. How often the patient has "attacks," what typically initiates them, and how long the illness has lasted.
3. Whether the patient has been treated as an outpatient or inpatient.
4. If the patient was an inpatient, ask for details of hospital stay, including length of admission, requirement of intensive care, and intubation.
5. What medications the patient takes, including as-needed usage and over-the-counter medications. Has the patient ever taken steroids?

5. What physical findings are associated with asthma?

The most common physical finding is expiratory wheezing. Wheezing is a sign of obstructed airflow and is often associated with a prolonged expiratory phase. As asthma progressively worsens, patients use accessory respiratory muscles. A significantly symptomatic patient with quiet auscultatory findings may signal impending respiratory failure because not enough air is moving to elicit a wheeze. Patients also may be tachypneic and probably are dehydrated; they prefer an upright posture and demonstrate pursed-lip breathing. Cyanosis is a late and ominous sign.

6. What preoperative tests should be ordered?

The patient's history guides the judicious ordering of preoperative tests. A mild asthmatic on as-needed medication who is currently healthy will not benefit from preoperative testing. Symptomatic patients with no recent evaluation deserve closer attention.

The most common test is a pulmonary function test, which allows simple and quick evaluation of the degree of obstruction and its reversibility. The important measures are FEV_1 (the amount of air forcefully expired in 1 second), FVC (the total amount of air expired or forced vital capacity), MMEFR (the flow rate noted while expiring 25–75% of the forced vital capacity), and PEFR (peak expiratory flow rate). A comparison of values obtained from the patient with predicted values helps to assess the degree of obstruction. Severe exacerbation correlates with a PEFR or FEV_1 less than 30–50% of predicted, which for most adults is a PEFR of less than 120

L/min and a FEV_1 of less than 1 L. Tests should be repeated after a trial of bronchodilator therapy to assess reversibility and response to treatment.

Arterial blood gases are usually not helpful. Hypoxia may be evaluated with a pulse oximeter, and hypercapnia is not noted until the FEV_1 is less than 25%. Electrocardiograms, chest radiographs, and blood counts are rarely indicated for evaluation of asthma unless particular features of the patient's presentation suggest alternative diagnoses (e.g., fever and rales suggesting pneumonia).

7. What specific medications and routes of delivery are used in asthma?

The mainstay of therapy remains inhaled beta agonists. Specific $beta_2$ agonists, such as albuterol, terbutaline and fenoterol, have become available over the last 10 years. They offer greater specificity for $beta_2$-mediated bronchodilation and fewer side effects (e.g., $beta_1$-associated tachydysrythmias and tremors). Albuterol can be administered orally or by metered dose inhaler (MDI). Terbutaline is effective via nebulizer, subcutaneously, or as a continuous intravenous infusion (beware of hypokalemia, lactic acidosis, and cardiac tachydysrhythmias with intravenous use). Epinephrine is available for subcutaneous use in severely asthmatic patients. Patients with coronary artery disease have difficulty with tachycardia and need the more $beta_2$-specific agents. The data on delivery of beta agonists support the inhaled route over parenteral administration for routine treatment. Adult dosages of commonly used drugs are as follows:

Albuterol: 2.5 mg in 3 ml of normal saline for nebulization or 2 puffs by MDI. Patients with active asthma may need repeat treatments.

Terbutaline: 0.3–0.4 mg subcutaneously; may repeat as required every 20 minutes for 3 doses.

Epinephrine: 0.3 mg subcutaneously; may repeat as required every 20 minutes for 3 doses.

The use of theophylline in asthma is controversial. Theophylline has some bronchodilatory effects and improves diaphragmatic action. Such benefits must be weighed against a long list of side effects: tremor, nausea and vomiting, palpitations, tachydysrhythmias, and seizures. Careful monitoring of serum levels is mandatory. Theophylline is the oral form, whereas aminophylline (its water-soluble form) is for intravenous use. Dosage for adults is as follows:

Theophylline: 5 mg/kg intravenously over 30 minutes (loading dose in patients not previously taking theophylline). After loading dose, start continuous infusion of 0.4 mg/kg/hr. Check level in 6 hours. Beware of drug interactions and certain diseases that alter theophylline clearance.

The use of anticholinergic compounds has increased over the years. Atropine, glycopyrrolate, and ipratropium are useful in bronchospasm associated with COPD and beta blockade. Anticholinergics also may be helpful in severe airway obstruction ($FEV_1 < 25\%$ predicted). Ipratropium, glycopyrrolate, and atropine may be given via nebulizer; ipratroprium is available in an MDI. The following dosages are for adults:

Anticholinergics: ipratroprium, 0.5 mg by nebulization or 4–6 puffs by MDI; atropine, 1–2 mg per nebulization.

Corticosteroid medications reverse airway inflammation, decrease mucus production, and potentiate beta agonist–induced smooth muscle relaxation. Steroids should be considered seriously in patients with moderate to severe asthma or patients who have required steroids in the last 6 months. Onset of action is 1–2 hours after administration. Methylprednisolone is popular because of its strong anti-inflammatory powers but weak mineralocorticoid effect. Side effects include hyperglycemia, hypertension, hypokalemia, and mood alterations, including psychosis. Long-term steroid use or prolonged use with muscle relaxants is associated with myopathy. Steroids may be given orally, via MDI, or intravenously. The following dosages are for adults:

Corticosteroids: methylprednisolone, 60–125 mg IV as required every 6 hours, or prednisone, 30–50 mg orally every day.

Cromolyn sodium is a mast cell stabilizer that is useful for long-term maintenance therapy in certain patients. Patients younger than 17 years of age and with moderate to severe exercise-induced asthma appear to benefit the most. Side effects include some minimal local irritation on delivery. Cromolyn sodium may be administered via multidose inhaler or as a powder in a turboinhaler. Cromolyn sodium is not effective and in fact is contraindicated in acute asthmatic attacks.

Patients with severe asthma may require **methotrexate** or **gold salts**. Both medications have undesirable side effect profiles and are reserved for patients who have major difficulties with corticosteroids.

8. What is the best approach to preoperative medical management?

First the anesthesiologist should classify each patient in one of several groups. Asymptomatic patients with no recent bouts of asthma, no current medications, and no history of serious illness usually require only careful observation. Currently, asymptomatic patients who have a history of recurrent asthma and use bronchodilators require optimization of pulmonary function. The dosing of beta agonists should be guided by symptoms and pulmonary function tests. Theophylline dosing may be adjusted if levels are inadequate or toxic. The decision to start corticosteroids is difficult, but in general they should be used to pretreat (1) patients with a history of moderate to severe asthma, especially with intensive care admissions and mechanical ventilation; (2) patients who required steroids in the last 6 months; and (3) patients at risk for adrenal insufficiency.

The final group is the symptomatic patient with ongoing bronchospasm. If at all possible, surgery should be delayed. If emergent surgery is required, treatment with beta agonists, up to and including continuous nebulizations, is useful. For patients who do not improve on this regimen, a trial of intravenous terbutaline or subcutaneous epinephrine should be made. Corticosteroids should be started early and continued. For patients taking theophylline, therapy should be optimized on the basis of serum levels. Consider whether regional anesthesia is possible.

9. Should theophylline be initiated in symptomatic patients?

Available data allow no definite recommendation. In some studies, patients taking theophylline show ventilatory improvement in the first 24 hours of use, whereas other studies show no benefit in patients with acute asthma. The use of theophylline increases the incidence of tremor, nausea, palpitations, and tachycardia. Until definite proof is available, many investigators suggest that theophylline therapy should be initiated only in patients with acute asthma who do not improve with maximal beta agonist and corticosteroid therapy.

10. What are the safe methods of inducing general anesthesia in asthmatic patients?

Intravenous induction agents used in asthmatic patients include oxybarbiturates, thiobarbiturates, ketamine, and propofol. Thiobarbiturates constrict airways in laboratory investigations and may have a loose association with clinical bronchospasm. The most common cause of bronchospasm is the stimulus of intubation, and large doses of barbiturates are required to block this effect successfully. Ketamine has well-known bronchodilatory effects secondary to the release of endogenous catecholamines with beta$_2$ agonism. Ketamine also has a small, direct relaxant effect on smooth muscles. In a recent study, propofol demonstrated no significant effect on peripheral airway tone. Intravenous lidocaine is a useful adjunct to the above induction agents in blunting the response to laryngoscopy and intubation.

Mask induction with halothane or sevoflurane is an excellent method to block airway reflexes and to relax airway smooth muscles directly. These agents are much more palatable to the airway than isoflurane or enflurane.

11. What agents may be used for maintenance anesthesia?

Inhaled anesthetics are excellent for maintenance anesthesia in asthmatic patients. Halothane, isoflurane, and enflurane appear equally effective in blocking airway reflexes and bronchoconstriction. Inhaled anesthetics have been used in the intensive care unit to provide bronchodilation in intubated patients with severe asthma, improving indices of respiratory resistance (inspiratory and expiratory flows), decreasing hyperinflation, and lowering intrinsic positive end-expiratory pressure (PEEP).

Opioids at higher doses block airway reflexes but do not provide direct bronchodilation. Morphine remains controversial because of its histamine-releasing activity. Anesthetics relying primarily on opioids may cause problems with respiratory depression at emergence (particularly in patients with COPD that has an asthmatic component).

Neuromuscular blocking agents, such as d-tubocurarine, atracurium, and mivacurium, release histamine from mast cells upon injection. They also may bind directly to muscarinic receptors on ganglia, nerve endings, and airway smooth muscle. Both mechanisms theoretically may increase airway resistance. Pancuronium and vecuronium continue to be used safely in asthmatic patients. In patients with bronchospasm neuromuscular blocking agents improve chest wall compliance, but smooth muscle airway tone and lung compliance remain the same. Prolonged use of muscle relaxants in ventilated asthmatic patients is associated with increases in creatine kinase and clinically significant myopathy.

12. What are the complications of intubation and mechanical ventilation in asthmatic patients?

The stimulus of intubation causes significant increases in airway resistance. Lung hyperinflation occurs when diminished expiratory flow prevents complete emptying of the alveolar and small airway gas. Significant gas trapping may cause hypotension by increasing intrathoracic pressure and reducing venous return. Pneumomediastinum and pneumothorax are also potential causes of acute respiratory decompensation.

Several measurements of ventilator function may give some insight into a patient's improving or worsening status. Plateau pressures (the pressure measured at end inspiration and before expiration starts, averaged over a 0.4-second pause) correlate loosely with complications at pressures greater than 30 cm H_2O. Auto-PEEP is the measurement of end-expiratory pressure (taken at end expiration while the expiratory port is momentarily occluded) and may correlate with alveolar pressures in the bronchospastic patient. Auto-PEEP, however, does not specifically correlate with complication. Plateau pressure and auto-PEEP measurements require a relaxed patient.

Several strategies for mechanically ventilating bronchospastic patients have been developed:

1. Increase expiratory time by decreasing ventilator rate, increasing inspiratory flow rates to decrease inspiratory time, and directly increasing the inspiratory to expiratory ratio.

2. Avoid ventilator-applied PEEP.

3. Decrease minute volume, allowing controlled hypoventilation and permissive hypercapnea.

13. What are the causes of intraoperative wheezing and the correct responses to asthmatic patients with acute bronchospasm?

Airway secretions, foreign body, pulmonary edema (cardiac asthma), obstructed endotracheal tube, endotracheal tube at the carina or down a mainstem bronchus, allergic or anaphylactic response to drugs, and asthma cause wheezing in intubated patients. A number of medications cause wheezing in asthmatic patients, including beta blockers, muscle relaxants, and aspirin.

After carefully checking the endotracheal tube and listening for bilateral breath sounds, one should increase the inspired oxygen to 100% and deepen the anesthetic if hemodynamically tolerated by the patient. Provoking factors such as medication infusions, misplaced endotracheal tubes, or other causes of airway stimulation should be corrected. Manipulating the ventilator (see question 15) may help. Reversal of bronchospasm may be attempted with such medications as beta$_2$ agonists and corticosteroids. Aminophylline and anticholinergics may be added for patients with poor response to beta$_2$ agonists and corticosteroids.

14. Describe the emergence techniques for asthmatic patients under general endotracheal anesthesia (GETA).

Awake and deep extubations are alternatives in patients under GETA. The endotracheal tube is a common cause of significant bronchospasm, and its removal under deep-inhaled anesthetic in a spontaneously ventilating patient often leads to a smooth emergence. Deep extubations should be avoided in patients with difficult airways, morbidly obese patients, and patients with full stomachs.

15. What new therapies are available to anesthesiologists treating asthmatic patients in bronchospasm?

Recently, intensivists have administered magnesium sulfate to patients in status asthmaticus. Hypothetically magnesium interferes with calcium-mediated smooth muscle contraction and decreases acetylcholine release at the neuromuscular junction. Magnesium reduces histamine- and methacholine-induced bronchospasm in controlled studies, but so far clinical studies have failed to show a significant response.

Heliox, a blend of helium and oxygen, has been successful in reducing airway resistance, peak airway pressures, and $PaCO_2$ levels when administered to spontaneously and mechanically ventilated patients. The mixture contains 60–80% helium and 20–40% oxygen and is less dense than air. The decrease in density allows less turbulent flow and significant declines in resistance to flow. The device for heliox administration in intubated patients is cumbersome unless the anesthesia machine is already equipped.

The Lita-Tube endotracheal tube allows intraoperative instillation of lidocaine at and below the cords of the intubated patient. This technique decreases airway stimulation from the endotracheal tube and may prevent reflex bronchospasm.

BIBLIOGRAPHY

1. Corbridge TC, Hall JB: The assessment and management of adults with status asthmatics. Am J Respir Crit Care Med 151:1296–1316, 1995.
2. Fung D, Smith NT: Anesthetic considerations in asthmatic patients. In Gershwin ME (ed): Bronchial Asthma. London, Grune & Stratton, 1986, pp 525–540.
3. Hudgel DW: Bronchial asthma. In Baum GL, Wolinsky E (eds): Textbook of Pulmonary Diseases, 5th ed. Boston, Little, Brown, 1994, pp 647–685.
4. Kiu HK, Rook GA, Ryan-Dykes MA, Bishop MJ: Effect of prophylactic bronchodilator treatment on lung resistance after tracheal intubation. Anesthesiology 81:43–48, 1994.
5. Pizov R, Brown RH, Weiss YS, et al: Wheezing during induction of general anesthesia in patients with and without asthma. Anesthesiology 82:1111–1116, 1995.
6. Stoller JK, Wiedemann HP: Chronic obstructive lung diseases: Asthma, emphysema, chronic bronchitis, bronchiectasis and related conditions. In George RB (ed): Chest Medicine Essentials of Pulmonary and Critical Care Medicine, 2nd ed. New York, Churchill Livingstone, 1990, pp 161–203.

43. ASPIRATION

Malcolm Packer, M.D.

1. What is aspiration?

Aspiration is the passage of material from the pharynx into the trachea. Aspirated material can originate from the stomach, esophagus, mouth, or nose. The materials involved can be particulate, such as food or a foreign body, or fluid, such as blood, saliva, or gastrointestinal contents. Aspiration of gastric contents may occur by vomiting, which is an active propulsion from the stomach up the esophagus, or by regurgitation, which is the passive flow of material along the same path.

2. Who first described aspiration associated with anesthesia?

Sir James Simpson described the death of a 15-year-old girl given chloroform for toenail removal in the mid 19th century. Simpson reasoned that she died from choking on her own secretions. In 1946 Curtis Mendelson reported 60 cases of aspiration associated with patients receiving general anesthesia for vaginal delivery. Mendelson performed an animal study describing the physiologic response to the different types of aspirates: liquid versus particulate and acidic versus neutral pH. This compilation of clinical and animal study data opened physicians' eyes to the serious sequence of events following the aspiration of gastric contents. This sequence is known as Mendelson's syndrome.

3. How often does aspiration occur?

The results of several different retrospective and prospective surveys place the incidence at 1–7 cases of significant aspiration per 10,000 anesthetics.

4. Name the risk factors for aspiration.

Extremes of age

Emergency cases

Type of surgery (most common in cases of esophageal, upper abdominal, or
    emergency laparotomy surgery)

Recent meal

Delayed gastric emptying and/or decreased lower esophageal sphincter tone (diabetes,
    gastric outlet obstruction, hiatal hernia, medications [e.g., narcotics, anticholinergics])

Trauma

Pregnancy

Pain and stress

Depressed level of consciousness

Morbid obesity

Difficult airway

Poor motor control (neuromuscular disease)

Esophageal disease (e.g., scleroderma, achalasia, diverticulum, Zenker's diverticulum)

5. Describe the different clinical pictures caused by the three broad types of aspirate: acidic fluid, nonacidic fluid, and particulate matter.

Acidic aspirates with a pH less than 2.5 and volumes of more than 0.4 ml/kg immediately cause alveolar-capillary breakdown, resulting in interstitial edema, intra-alveolar hemorrhage, atelectasis, and increased airway resistance. Hypoxia is common. Although such changes usually start within minutes of the initiating event, they may worsen over a period of hours. The first phase of the response is direct reaction of the lung to acid; hence the name chemical pneumonitis. The second phase, which occurs hours later, is due to leukocyte or inflammatory response to the original damage and may lead to respiratory failure.

Aspiration of **nonacidic fluid** destroys surfactant, causing alveolar collapse and atelectasis. Hypoxia is common. The destruction of lung architecture and the late inflammatory response are not as great as in acid aspiration.

Aspiration of **particulate food matter** causes both physical obstruction of the airway and a later inflammatory response related to the presence of a foreign body. Alternating areas of atelectasis and hyperexpansion may occur. Patients show hypoxia and hypercapnia due to physical obstruction of airflow. If acid is mixed with the particulate matter, damage is often greater and the clinical picture worse.

6. What is the incidence of clinical signs and symptoms after aspiration of gastric contents?

Fever occurs in over 90% of aspiration cases, with tachypnea and rales in at least 70%. Cough, cyanosis, and wheezing occur in 30–40% of cases. Aspiration may occur "silently"—without the anesthesiologist's knowledge—during anesthesia. Any of the above clinical deviations from the expected course may signal an aspiration event. Patients undergoing anesthesia should be monitored according to the recommendations of the American Society of Anesthesiologists. Included are temperature, breath sound, and oxygenation monitoring, which ensure early detection of aspiration.

7. When is a patient suspected of aspiration believed to be out of danger?

The patient who shows none of the above signs or symptoms and has no increased oxygen requirement at the end of 2 hours should recover completely.

8. Describe the treatment of aspiration.

Supportive care remains the mainstay. Immediate suctioning should be instituted. Supplemental oxygen and ventilatory support should be initiated if respiratory failure is a problem. Patients with respiratory failure often demonstrate atelectasis with alveolar collapse and may respond to positive end-expiratory pressure (PEEP). Patients with particulate aspirate may need bronchoscopy to remove large obstructing pieces.

9. What are the major controversies in the treatment of aspiration?

Discussions about treating patients with prophylactic antibiotics and corticosteroids continue. Presently no evidence suggests that antibiotics are helpful unless intestinal obstruction causes the aspirated fluid to be fecally contaminated. Corticosteroids have not been shown to be helpful in human studies. Lastly, some practitioners advocate lavaging the trachea with normal saline or sodium bicarbonate in the case of acid aspiration. This procedure, however, has not been shown to be helpful and may actually worsen the patient's status.

10. What precautions prior to anesthetic induction are required to prevent aspiration or mollify its sequelae?

The main precaution is to recognize which patients are at risk. Patients should have an adequate fasting period to improve the chances of an empty stomach. Gastrokinetic medications such as metaclopramide immediately improve gastric emptying and increase esophageal sphincter tone. It is also helpful to increase gastric pH by either nonparticulate antacids such as sodium citrate or H_2 receptor antagonists, which decrease acid production.

The market now includes several H_2 antagonists, giving anesthesiologists a choice (e.g., cimetidine, ranitidine, and famotidine). Cimetidine was first on the market and is still widely used. Although cimetidine increases gastric pH, it also has a significant side-effect profile, including hypotension, heart block, central nervous dysfunction, decreased hepatic blood flow, and significant retardation of the metabolism of many drugs. Ranitidine, a newer H_2 antagonist, is much less likely to cause side effects; only a few cases of central nervous dysfunction and heart block have been reported. Famotidine is equally as potent as cimetidine and ranitidine and has no significant side effects.

11. What are considered adequate fasting times?

In general, adults should have no solid food for 6–8 hours prior to surgery. Over the years anesthesiologists have shortened the time during which no oral ingestion (NPO) is permitted and currently allow clear liquid intake 3–4 hours before surgery. Infant NPO times are usually 4–6 hours for formula and 2–3 hours for clear liquids or breast milk.

12. Define rapid-sequence induction.

Patients with an airway that is by exam easy to intubate may receive a rapid-sequence induction, which consists of preoxygenating the patient and placing pressure over the cricoid cartilage (Sellick maneuver). This pressure prevents gastric contents from leaking into the pharynx by extrinsic obstruction of the esophagus. The cricoid cartilage is the only complete cartilaginous ring of the tracheal tree. After preoxygenation and cricoid pressure, general anesthesia is induced and a paralyzing dose of relaxant is administered. The patient's trachea is intubated, and the endotracheal balloon cuff is inflated. To ensure proper placement, breath sounds should be symmetrical and end-tidal carbon dioxide detected. Cricoid pressure should be released only after endotracheal tube placement is assured.

13. Which procedures are safer for patients at risk for aspiration?

Patients with airways thought to be difficult to intubate may require placement of an endotracheal tube while awake to allow spontaneous breathing and to protect the airway from aspiration.

Awake intubations are facilitated by such devices as light wands, fiber-optic bronchoscopes, and retrograde intubation kits. Patient comfort is aided by the judicious use of sedation and topical local anesthetic. Oversedation as well as a topicalized airway may make the patient unable to protect the airway. Therefore, keeping the patient conscious and applying topical local anesthetic only to the airway above the glottis lead to safe intubation.

Endotracheal intubation does not guarantee that no aspiration will occur. Material may still slip past a deflated or partly deflated cuff. In pediatric patients younger than 8 years old, an endotracheal cuff is not recommended; thus leakage of material into the lungs is common.

14. Describe the morbidity and mortality associated with pulmonary aspiration of stomach contents.

The average hospital stay is 21 days, much of which is in intensive care. Complications range from bronchospasm and pneumonia to acute respiratory distress syndrome, lung abscess, and empyema. The average mortality rate is 5%.

BIBLIOGRAPHY

1. Gibbs C, Modell J: Management of aspiration pneumonitis. In Miller R (ed): Anesthesia, 4th ed. New York, Churchill Livingstone, 1994, pp 1437–1464.
2. Kallar SK, Everett LL: Potential risks and preventive measures for pulmonary aspiration: New concepts in preoperative fasting guidelines. Anesth Analg 77:171–182, 1993.
3. Mecca RS: Postoperative recovery. In Barash PG, Cullen BF, Stoelting RK (eds): Clinical Anesthesia, 3rd ed. Philadelphia, Lippincott Williams & Wilkins, 1997.
4. Mendelson CL: The aspiration of stomach contents into the lungs during obstetric anesthesia. Am J Obstet Gynecol 52:191–205, 1946.
5. Rout CC, Rocke A, Gouws E: Intravenous ranitidine reduces the risk of acid aspiration of gastric contents at emergency cesarean section. Anesth Analg 76:156–161, 1993.
6. Vaughan GG, Gryeko RJ, Montgomery MT: The prevention and treatment of aspiration of vomiting during pharmacosedation and general anesthesia. J Oral Maxillofac Surg 50:874–879, 1992.
7. Warner MA, Warner ME, Weber JG: Clinical significance of pulmonary aspiration during the perioperative period. Anesthesiology 78:56–62, 1993.

44. CHRONIC OBSTRUCTIVE PULMONARY DISEASE

Howard J. Miller, M.D.

1. Define chronic obstructive pulmonary disease (COPD).

COPD is a clinical spectrum of diseases including emphysema, chronic bronchitis, and asthmatic bronchitis. It is a common disorder characterized by progressive increased resistance to flow of gases in the airways. Airflow limitation (obstruction) may be due to loss of elastic recoil or obstruction of small or large (or both) conducting airways. The increased resistance may have some degree of reversibility. Cardinal symptoms are cough, dyspnea, and wheezing.

2. What are the features of asthma and asthmatic bronchitis?
Asthma
- A heterogeneous disorder characterized by reversible airway obstruction
- Asthma "attacks" may be gradual or sudden in onset and are associated with a variety of precipitating factors (i.e., exercise, dander, pollen, intubation)
- After treatment, complete or near-complete resolution of symptoms

Asthmatic bronchitis
- Consists of airway obstruction, chronic productive cough, and episodic bronchospasm
- It can result from progression of asthma or chronic bronchitis
- Major reversibility cannot be achieved in asthmatic bronchitis and some degree of airway obstruction exists at all times

Asthma, with the strict definition of reversibility, should not be included in the COPD spectrum, whereas asthmatic bronchitis should.

3. Describe chronic bronchitis and emphysema.

Chronic bronchitis is characterized by cough, sputum production, recurrent infection, and airway obstruction for many months to several years. Historically, chronic bronchitis has been defined as a chronic cough with sputum production for at least 3 months per year for 2 consecutive years. Chronic bronchitis consists of mucous gland hyperplasia, mucous plugging, inflammation and edema, peribronchiolar fibrosis, narrowing of airways, and bronchoconstriction. Decreased airway lumina owing to mucus and inflammation increase resistance to flow of gases.

Emphysema is characterized by progressive dyspnea and variable cough. Destruction of the elastic and collagen network of alveolar walls without resultant fibrosis leads to abnormal enlargement of air spaces. Additionally the loss of airway support leads to airway narrowing and collapse during expiration (air trapping).

4. List contributory factors associated with the development of COPD.

1. **Smoking:** Smoking impairs ciliary function, depresses alveolar macrophages, leads to increased mucous gland proliferation and mucus production, increases the inflammatory response in the lung leading to increased proteolytic enzyme release, reduces surfactant integrity, and causes increased airway reactivity.

2. **Occupational exposure:** Animal dander, toluene and other chemicals, various grains, cotton.

3. **Environmental exposure:** Air pollution in industrialized areas (e.g., sulfur dioxide and nitrogen dioxide).

4. **Recurrent infection:** Viral or bacterial (or both), including human immunodeficiency virus (HIV), which can produce an emphysema-like picture.

5. **Familial and genetic factors:** A predisposition to COPD exists among family members and is more common in men than women. Also, alpha$_1$-antitrypsin deficiency exists in heterozygous and homozygous forms. This disorder results in autodigestion of pulmonary tissue by proteases and should be suspected in younger patients with basilar bullae on chest x-ray. Smoking accelerates its presentation and progression.

5. What historical information should be obtained preoperatively?

1. Smoking history: number of packs per day (PPD) and duration
2. Presence and severity of dyspnea, especially exercise tolerance (for example, one would be reassured if the patient could climb two to three flights of stairs comfortably)
3. Productive cough and the patient's ability to produce a forceful cough
4. History of wheezing
5. Prior and most recent hospitalizations for COPD and length of stay
6. Prior intubations secondary to COPD or respiratory failure
7. Medications, including home oxygen therapy and steroids, either systemic or inhaled
8. Allergies
9. Recent pulmonary infections, exacerbations, or change in character of sputum
10. Weight loss in the absence of other factors suggests end-stage disease
11. Symptoms of right-sided heart failure, including peripheral edema, right upper quadrant pain from an enlarged liver, jaundice, and anorexia secondary to liver and splanchnic congestion
12. Problems with previous surgeries or anesthetics, including postoperative intubation and mechanical ventilation

6. What are "pink puffers" and "blue bloaters"?

Pink puffers	Blue bloaters
Usually older (> 60 years)	Relatively young
Pink in color	Cyanotic
Thin	Heavier in weight
Have minimal cough	Frequently wheeze
Have predominantly emphysema	Have chronic productive cough
	Have predominantly chronic bronchitis or asthmatic bronchitis

7. List pertinent physical findings in patients with COPD.

- Breathing pattern, including respiratory rate, depth, use of accessory muscles
- Chest auscultation for presence of focally or unilaterally decreased breath sounds, wheezing, or rhonchi
- Presence of jugular venous distention (JVD), a hepatojugular reflux, and peripheral edema indicating right-sided heart failure
- Palpation of peripheral pulses, assessing stroke volume and ease of obtaining arterial blood samples if needed

8. What laboratory examinations are useful?

1. **White count and hematocrit:** Elevation suggests infection and chronic hypoxemia, respectively.

2. **Electrolytes:** Bicarbonate levels are elevated to buffer a chronic respiratory acidosis if the patient retains carbon dioxide. Hypokalemia can occur with repeated use of β-adrenergic agonists.

3. **Chest x-ray:** Look for lung hyperinflation, bullae or blebs, flattened diaphragm, increased retrosternal air space, atelectasis, cardiac enlargement, infiltrate, effusion, cancer, or pneumothorax.

4. **Electrocardiogram:** Look for decreased voltage amplitude, signs of right atrial (peaked P waves in leads II and V_1) or ventricular enlargement (right axis deviation, R/S ratio in $V_6 \leq 1$, increased R wave in V_1 and V_2, right bundle-branch block), and arrhythmias. Atrial arrhythmias are common, especially multifocal atrial tachycardia and atrial fibrillation.

5. **Arterial blood gas:** Hypoxemia, hypercarbia, and acid-base status, including compensation, can be evaluated.

6. **Pulmonary function tests (PFTs):** Determine the degree of obstruction and bronchodilator response.

9. What are normal PFT values? How are these changed in COPD?

PFT	NORMAL	EMPHYSEMA	BRONCHITIS	ASTHMA
FVC	≥ 3–4 L	Decreased	Normal to slightly decreased	Decreased
FEV_1	> 2–3 L	Decreased	Normal to slightly decreased	Decreased
TLC	5–7 L	Increased	Normal to slightly increased	Decreased
RV	1–2 L	Increased	Increased	Increased
$FEF_{25-75\%}$	60–70% predicted	Decreased	Normal to slightly decreased	Decreased
Hypoxemia/ hypercarbia		Late in disease	Early in disease	Acute attack only
Air trapping		Moderate to marked	Moderate, partly reversible	Mild, intermittent
Diffusion capacity		Decreased	Normal to slightly decreased	Normal

Key: FVC = forced vital capacity; FEV_1 = forced expiratory volume in 1 second; TLC = total lung capacity; RV = residual volume; $FEF_{25-75\%}$ = forced expiratory flow, midexpiratory phase at 25–75%. PFT values are based on sex, age, and height of the patient, not on weight.

10. How does a chronically elevated arterial carbon dioxide partial pressure ($PaCO_2$) affect the respiratory drive in a person with COPD?

Persons with COPD have a reduced ventilatory drive in response to carbon dioxide (CO_2). Chronically elevated $PaCO_2$ produces increased cerebrospinal fluid bicarbonate concentrations. The respiratory chemoreceptors at the medulla become "reset" to a higher concentration of CO_2. Thus, diminished ventilatory drive secondary to CO_2 exists. In these patients, ventilatory drive may be more dependent on oxygen. If given high concentrations of oxygen, these persons may hypoventilate because of the loss of the hypoxic stimulus and the relative insensitivity to hypercarbia.

Additionally, inhalation of 100% oxygen may increase ventilation-perfusion (V-Q) mismatch by inhibiting hypoxic pulmonary vasoconstriction (HPV). HPV is an autoregulatory mechanism in the pulmonary vasculature that decreases blood flow to poorly ventilated areas of the lung. Therefore, more blood flow is available for gas exchange in better ventilated areas of the lung. Inhibition of HPV results in increased perfusion of poorly ventilated areas of lung contributing to hypoxemia and/or hypercarbia.

11. How do general anesthesia and surgery affect pulmonary mechanics?

Vital capacity (VC) is reduced by 25–50% and residual volume (RV) increases by 13% following many general anesthetics and surgical procedures. Expiratory reserve volume (ERV) decreases by 25% after lower abdominal surgery and 60% after upper abdominal and thoracic surgery. Tidal volume (V_T) decreases 20%, and pulmonary compliance (PC) and functional residual capacity (FRC) decrease 33%. Atelectasis, hypoventilation, hypoxemia, and pulmonary infection may result. Many of these changes require a minimum of 1–2 weeks to resolve.

PULMONARY FUNCTION	CHANGE WITH SURGERY
VC, ERV, V_T, PC, FRC	Decrease
RV	Increase

12. Does one site of surgery affect pulmonary mechanics more than another?

Upper abdominal incisions and thoracotomy affect pulmonary mechanics the greatest, followed by lower abdominal incisions and sternotomy. These changes are secondary to supine position, decreased diaphragmatic excursion, and decreased effective cough secondary to pain.

13. What factors are associated with an increased perioperative morbidity or mortality?

FACTOR	ABDOMINAL SURGERY	THORACOTOMY	LOBECTOMY/PNEUMONECTOMY
FVC	< 70% predicted	< 70%	< 50% or < 2 L
FEV_1	< 70%	< 1 L	< 1 L
FEV_1/FVC	< 50%	< 50%	< 50%
$FEF_{25-75\%}$	< 50%	< 50%	
RV/TLC			> 40%
$PaCO_2$	> 45–50 mmHg	> 45–50 mmHg	

Increased morbidity includes hypoxemia, hypoventilation with elevated PCO_2, pulmonary infection, and the need for reintubation and mechanical ventilation. All of these can prolong intensive care unit and overall hospital stay as well as increase mortality. Additionally, an FEV_1 less than 800 ml in a 70-kg person is probably incompatible with life and is an absolute contraindication to lung resection because of the high incidence for prolonged or even lifetime mechanical ventilation.

Patients presenting for lung resection (lobectomy and pneumonectomy) must have pulmonary function and arterial blood gas values that are superior to the values in the table. If any of the aforementioned criteria are not satisfied, further preoperative testing is indicated to determine the risk-benefit ratio for lung resection. Further tests include split-lung function, regional perfusion, regional ventilation, regional bronchial balloon occlusion, and pulmonary artery balloon occlusion studies. Additionally, spirometry should yield a predicted postresection FEV_1 greater than 800 ml.

14. List the common pharmacologic agents used to treat COPD and their mechanism of action.

Agents Used to Treat COPD

AGENT	MECHANISM OF ACTION

β-adrenergic agonists
  Albuterol
  Metaproterenol
  Isoetharine
  Terbutaline
  Epinephrine
	Stimulation of beta$_2$ receptors leads to an increase in adenylate cyclase, increasing intracellular cAMP, resulting in decreased smooth mucle tone (bronchodilation). Excessive use may lead to hypokalemia owing to β$_2$-adrenergic stimulation that causes redistribution of potassium into cells. Typically inhaled in nebulized or metered dose inhaler forms.

Methylxanthines
  Aminophylline
  Theophylline
	Inhibition of phosphodiesterase produces increased cyclic adenosine monophosphate (cAMP). Facilitates endogenous catecholamines. Improved contraction of respiratory muscles, e.g., the diaphragm. Respiratory system stimulant. Administered orally or intravenously.

Corticosteroids
  Cortisol
  Methylprednisolone
  Dexamethasone
  Prednisone
	Anti-inflammatory. Membrane stabilization of mast cell reduces/prevents release of histamine and other vasoactive agents. Potentiate β-adrenergic agonists. These agents are either inhaled or given systemically.

Anticholinergics
  Atropine
  Glycopyrrolate
  Ipratropium
	Inhibition of acetylcholine on postganglionic cholinergic receptors of airway smooth muscle, decreasing intracellular cyclic guanosine monophosphate (cGMP), producing smooth muscle relaxation. Ipratropium, administered as an aerosol, has the advantage of being poorly absorbed by the gastrointestinal tract. Therefore, if swallowed, systemic side effects (e.g., tachycardia and increased secretion viscosity) are reduced.

Membrane stabilizers
  Cromolyn sodium
  Corticosteroids
	Stabilizes mast cell membrane to prevent degranulization. Cromolyn is for prevention of bronchoconstriction only and must be given prophylactically.

15. What therapies are available to reduce perioperative pulmonary risk?
1. **Stop smoking**
   a. Cessation for 48 hours prior to surgery decreases carboxyhemoglobin levels. The oxyhemoglobin dissociation curve shifts to the right, allowing increased tissue oxygen availability.
   b. Cessation for 4–6 weeks before surgery has been shown to decrease the incidence of postoperative pulmonary complications.
   c. Cessation for 2–3 months before surgery results in all the above benefits plus improved ciliary function, improved pulmonary mechanics, and reduced sputum production.
2. Optimize pharmacologic therapy. Continue medications even on the day of surgery.
3. Recognize and treat underlying pulmonary infection.
4. Maximize nutritional support, hydration, and chest physiotherapy.
5. Institute effective postoperative analgesia allowing the patient to cough effectively, take large tidal volumes, and ambulate early after surgery.

16. Do advantages exist with regional anesthesia techniques in patients with COPD?
Regional anesthesia, such as extremity and neuraxial blockade, offers several advantages in certain surgical procedures and is an excellent choice for surgery involving the extremities,

perineum, and lower abdomen. Under regional anesthesia, the patient breathes spontaneously and does not require intubation. Neuraxial techniques that produce surgical anesthesia at levels higher than a T10 dermatome may reduce effective coughing secondary to abdominal muscle dysfunction, leading to decreased sputum clearance and atelectasis. Additionally, one must be careful with certain brachial plexus techniques, which may anesthetize the phrenic nerve or cause a pneumothorax. Sedatives may depress respiratory drive and should be titrated to effect.

Continuous regional anesthetic techniques can be used during the postoperative period as well. For example, continuous lumbar and thoracic epidurals, continuous brachial plexus catheters, and intrathecal narcotics can all be used for optimizing postoperative pain control, resulting in improved pulmonary mechanics. These techniques accomplish this goal with lower doses of narcotics than intramuscular or intravenous methods and with less sedation.

17. What agents can be used for induction of general anesthesia? Should certain drugs be avoided? Do certain agents offer any advantages?

Induction of general anesthesia can be accomplished with any of the common induction agents, including barbiturates, benzodiazepines, opioids, propofol, etomidate, or ketamine. One should be cautious with agents that are known to release histamine (i.e., morphine sulfate), which may cause bronchospasm. Ketamine has the advantage of producing bronchodilation secondary to its sympathomimetic effects and by direct antagonism of bronchoconstricting mediators. Ketamine may be the induction drug of choice if the patient does not have underlying cardiac disease or pulmonary hypertension.

Once induction of anesthesia has been accomplished, complete suppression of airway reflexes must be ensured before tracheal intubation. Muscle relaxants facilitate intubation. The patient is commonly mask-ventilated with a volatile anesthetic to deepen the plane of anesthesia, thereby decreasing airway reflexes. Volatile anesthetics have the advantage of producing bronchodilation. Intravenous lidocaine given before intubation can help blunt airway reflexes.

18. What are the advantages and disadvantages of different agents for general anesthesia?

Volatile agents (halothane, isoflurane, enflurane, sevoflurane, and desflurane). All produce bronchodilation and are useful in patients with COPD. Most, especially desflurane, are quickly eliminated and produce little, if any, respiratory depression postoperatively. Halothane has the highest cardiac arrhythmogenic potential and should be used with extreme caution in the presence of sympathomimetics.

Muscle relaxants and their reversal agents. Depolarizing and nondepolarizing muscle relaxants are commonly used and include succinylcholine, vecuronium, rocuronium, and pancuronium. They facilitate endotracheal intubation and mechanical ventilation. They are skeletal muscle, not smooth muscle, relaxants. Agents that may cause histamine release (atracurium and d-tubocurarine) should be avoided or used with extreme caution.

Neuromuscular reversal agents (neostigmine and edrophonium). These agents reverse the effects of nondepolarizing relaxants. They may theoretically precipitate bronchospasm and bronchorrhea secondary to stimulation of postganglionic cholinergic and muscarinic receptors. Clinically, however, bronchospasm is rarely seen after administration of these agents, possibly because anticholinergic agents (atropine or glycopyrrolate) are concurrently administered with the reversal agents.

Opioids. Opioids blunt airway reflexes and deepen anesthesia. Morphine produces histamine release and should be used with caution. Fentanyl, sufentanil, and alfentanil do not cause histamine release. One must always consider the residual respiratory depressant affects of opioids at the end of surgery.

Nitrous oxide. Nitrous oxide increases the volume and pressure of blebs or bullae, thereby increasing the risk of barotrauma and pneumothorax. Additionally, nitrous oxide may increase pulmonary vascular resistance and pulmonary artery pressures. This would be especially deleterious in patients with coexisting pulmonary hypertension or cor pulmonale (or both). Therefore, nitrous oxide should be avoided or used with extreme caution in patients with COPD.

19. Discuss the use of mechanical ventilation during general anesthesia.

As discussed in question 11, pulmonary mechanics are greatly affected by general anesthesia. Mechanical ventilation of the lungs is employed to optimize oxygenation and ventilation. Extended expiratory time is needed in patients with COPD. Too short of an expiratory phase leads to air trapping and increased peak airway pressures.

20. Define auto-PEEP.

Air trapping is known as auto-PEEP (positive end-expiratory pressure) and results from "stacking" of breaths when full exhalation is not allowed to occur. Auto-PEEP results in impairment of oxygenation and ventilation as well as hemodynamic compromise by decreasing preload and increasing pulmonary vascular resistance. Increasing expiratory time, by increasing inspiratory flow and increasing tidal volume with decreasing respiratory rate, reduces the likelihood of auto-PEEP. All people have some degree of intrinsic PEEP (PEEPi); however, PEEPi may be higher in patients with COPD. One may use PEEP to improve oxygenation in patients with COPD; however, studies have shown that PEEP levels should not exceed 85% of PEEPi to avoid further hyperinflation, compromised hemodynamics, and impairment of gas exchange.

21. Form a differential diagnosis for intraoperative wheezing.

Bronchoconstriction can cause wheezing; however, it is not the only cause. Other causes may be considered before appropriate treatment can begin:
* Mechanical obstruction of the endotracheal tube by secretions or kinking
* Aspiration of gastric contents or of a foreign body (i.e., a dislodged tooth)
* Endobronchial intubation (most commonly right mainstem intubation)
* Inadequate anesthesia
* Pulmonary edema (cardiogenic and noncardiogenic)
* Pneumothorax

22. How would you treat intraoperative bronchospasm?

1. Administer 100% oxygen and manually ventilate with sufficient expiratory time.
2. Identify and correct the underlying condition.
   a. Relieve mechanical obstruction by suctioning or unkinking the endotracheal tube.
   b. Remove foreign bodies if present.
   c. Ensure that the endotracheal tube is not endobronchial or resting on the carina.
   d. Treat pulmonary edema.
   e. Relieve a pneumothorax.

Once bronchoconstriction is established as the diagnosis, pharmacologic therapy can be instituted. Options include:
* Deepening the anesthetic with volatile agents
* Beta-adrenergic agonists aerosolized via the endotracheal tube (e.g., albuterol), subcutaneously (e.g., terbutaline), or intravenously (e.g., epinephrine or terbutaline)
* Ketamine intravenously or intramuscularly
* Intravenous aminophylline
* Intravenous lidocaine
* Intravenous corticosteroids

Although controversial, extubation may be beneficial because the endotracheal tube may contribute to or be the stimulus causing bronchoconstriction.

23. Do patients with COPD need to have postoperative mechanical ventilation?

Every patient must be considered individually. Those patients that exhibit a resting $PaCO_2$ > 45–50, FEV_1 < 1 L, FVC < 50–70% of predicted, or FEV_1/FVC < 50% may require postoperative intubation and ventilation, especially for upper abdominal and thoracic surgeries. In addition, consider how well the patient was prepared preoperatively, the respiratory rate and observed work of breathing, the patient's spontaneous tidal volume, the negative inspiratory force generated by the patient, arterial blood gas parameters, and body temperature. Is the patient fully reversed from muscle relaxation or are residual anesthetic drugs affecting the patient? Does the patient have adequate pain control?

CONTROVERSIES

24. Should H_2-receptor antagonists be avoided in patients with COPD?

Two types of histamine receptors have been identified: H_1-receptor stimulation results in bronchoconstriction, and H_2-receptor stimulation results in bronchodilation. Theoretically, H_2-receptor antagonist administration would result in unopposed H_1-receptor stimulation causing bronchoconstriction. H_2-receptor antagonists have been safely used in patients with COPD; however, their administration should be determined individually based on a risk-benefit ratio. Because many patients with COPD take corticosteroids, which can cause gastritis or peptic ulcers, concomitant H_2-antagonists are prescribed as well.

25. At the conclusion of surgery, should a patient with COPD be extubated "deep" or awake?

"Deep" extubation involves removing the endotracheal tube while the patient remains in a deep plane of anesthesia, while airway reflexes are suppressed. Typically, deep extubation is accomplished with the patient breathing spontaneously, deeply anesthetized with a volatile agent. Deep extubation, however, does not guarantee against bronchospasm while the patient awakens. Furthermore, many patients are not suitable for deep extubation. Patients at risk for aspiration and those with difficult airways usually require awake extubation. If awake extubation is required, attempts should be made to blunt airway reflexes. Appropriate interventions include intravenous or intratracheal lidocaine and aerosolized β-adrenergic agonists for smooth muscle relaxation.

Preoperatively, alternatives to general endotracheal anesthesia should be considered, including regional anesthesia or general anesthesia by mask or laryngeal mask airway (LMA). Use of an LMA and mask anesthesia does not require placement of an endotracheal tube in the trachea, which may act as a bronchoconstriction stimulus. LMA use allows the anesthesiologist to have free hands to perform other tasks and can provide a conduit for positive pressure ventilation. Positive pressure ventilation via an LMA, however, is often limited secondary to an inadequate seal surrounding the glottic opening.

BIBLIOGRAPHY

1. Aubier M, Murciano D, Milic-Emili J, et al: Effects of the administration of O2 on ventilation and blood gases in patients with chronic obstructive pulmonary disease during acute respiratory failure. Am Rev Respir Dis 122:747–754, 1980.
2. Beckers S, Camu F: The anesthetic risk of tobacco smoking. Acta Anaesthesiol Belg 42:45–56, 1991.
3. Egan TD, Wong KC: Perioperative smoking cessation and anesthesia: A review. J Clin Anesth 4:63–72, 1992.
4. Eisenkraft JB, Cohen E, Neustein SM: Anesthesia for thoracic surgery. In Barash PG, Cullen BF, Stoelting RK (eds): Clinical Anesthesia, 3rd ed. Philadelphia, Lippincott Williams & Wilkins, 1997.
5. Gateau O, Bourgain J, Gaudy J, Benveniste J: Effects of ketamine on isolated human bronchial preparations. Br J Anaesth 63:692–695, 1989.
6. Ingram RH: Chronic bronchitis, emphysema, and airways obstruction. In Isselbacher KJ, Braunwald E, Wilson JD, et al (eds): Harrison's Principles of Internal Medicine, 13th ed. New York, McGraw-Hill, 1993, pp 1197–1206.
7. Konrad FX, Schreiber T, Brecht-Kraus D, Georgieff M: Bronchial mucus transport in chronic smokers and nonsmokers during general anesthesia. J Clin Anesth 5:375–380, 1993.
8 Kroenke K, Lawrence VA, Theroux JF, Tuley MR: Operative risk in patients with severe obstructive pulmonary disease. Arch Intern Med 152:967–971, 1992.
9. Martin RJ: Reexamining theophylline for asthma. Contemp Intern Med 5:8–14, 1993.
10. Moorthy SS, Dierdorf SF: Anesthesia for patients with chronic obstructive pulmonary disease. In Kirby RR, Gravenstein N (eds): Clinical Anesthesia Practice. Philadelphia, W.B. Saunders, 1994, pp 963–968.

11. Pearce AC, Jones RM: Smoking and anesthesia: Preoperative abstinence and perioperative morbidity. Anesthesiology 61:576–584, 1984.
12. Pepe PE, Marini JJ: Occult positive end-expiratory pressure in mechanically ventilated patients with air-flow obstruction. Am Rev Respir Dis 126:166–170, 1982.
13. Petty TL: Chronic obstructive pulmonary disease—can we do better? Chest 97:2s–5s, 1990.
14. Petty TL: Definitions in chronic obstructive pulmonary disease. Clin Chest Med 11:363–373, 1990.
15. Ranieri VM, Giuliani R, Cinnella G, et al: Physiologic effects of positive end-expiratory pressure in patients with chronic obstructive pulmonary disease during acute ventilatory failure and controlled mechanical ventilation. Am Rev Respir Dis 147:5–13, 1993.
16. Sassoon CSH, Hassell KT, Mahutte CK: Hyperoxic-induced hypercarbia in stable chronic obstructive pulmonary disease. Am Rev Respir Dis 135:907–911, 1987.
17. Stock MC: Respiratory function in anesthesia. In Barash PG, Cullen BF, Stoelting RK (eds): Clinical Anesthesia, 3rd ed. Philadelphia, Lippincott Williams & Wilkins, 1997.
18. Stoelting RK, Deirdorf SF, McCammon RL: Obstructive airways disease. In Stoelting RK, Deirdorf SF, McCammon RL (eds): Anesthesia and Coexisting Disease, 2nd ed. New York, Churchill Livingstone, 1988, pp 195–225.
19. Warner MA, Divertie MB, Tinker JH: Preoperative cessation of smoking and pulmonary complications in coronary artery bypass patients. Anesthesiology 60:380–383, 1984.

45. PULMONARY HYPERTENSION AND VASODILATOR THERAPY

James Duke, M.D.

1. Define pulmonary hypertension.

Pulmonary hypertension (PH) exists when the pulmonary systolic pressure exceeds 25–30 mmHg and diastolic pressures exceed 12 mmHg.

2. List conditions that produce pulmonary hypertension.

PH may be primary or secondary. Pulmonary hypertension is said to be primary in the absence of secondary causes, such as pulmonary disease (congenital or parenchymal), cardiac disease (shunts, mitral stenosis, left ventricular failure), thromboembolic or obliterative pulmonary vascular disease, collagen vascular disease, exogenous vasoconstrictive substances, or portal hypertension.

3. Discuss the natural history of pulmonary hypertension.

The pulmonary circulation has high flow and low resistance. The right ventricle (RV) is thin-walled and accommodates changes in volume better than changes in pressure. To accommodate increases in flow, such as during exercise, unopened vessels are recruited, and patent vessels distended, and pulmonary vascular resistance (PVR) may decrease. Such normal adaptive mechanisms can accommodate threefold to fivefold increases in flow without significant increases in pulmonary artery (PA) pressures. Early in the evolution of PH, the pressure overload results in hypertrophy of the RV without significant changes in cardiac output (CO) or RV filling pressures either at rest or during exercise. As the disease progresses, the vessels become less distensible, and the actual cross-sectional area of the pulmonary circulation decreases. Initially with exercise, CO eventually declines despite modest increases in right ventricular end-diastolic pressures (RVEDP). In time, RV failure ensues, and the patient is symptomatic even at rest. RV myocardial blood flow becomes compromised, and tricuspid regurgitation develops secondary to RV distention, further increasing RVEDP and worsening failure. In addition, left ventricular (LV) diastolic function may deteriorate, and LV filling may be compromised by excessive septal incursion into the left ventricle, with a resultant decrease in cardiac output.

4. What are some electrocardiographic and radiologic features of the disease?

The **electrocardiogram** (ECG) commonly shows right axis deviation, right ventricular hypertrophy (tall R waves in V_1–V_3), RV strain (T-wave inversion in V_1–V_3), S wave in V_6, and enlarged P waves in II, III, and aVF. Although atrial fibrillation is rare, its presence should be viewed with concern because the contribution of "atrial kick" to ventricular filling is unavailable. In the presence of stiff pulmonary vasculature and a noncompliant right ventricle, cardiac output may become significantly diminished. **Radiologic abnormalities** have been observed in over 90% of cases. Abnormalities on chest radiographs suggestive of PH include prominence of the right ventricle as well as the hilar pulmonary artery trunk, rapid tapering of vascular markings, and a hyperlucent lung periphery.

5. What signs and symptoms suggest pulmonary hypertension?

Early findings
Increase in pulmonic component of S_2
Narrowly split S_2
Right-sided fourth heart sound (gallop)
Early diastolic murmur of tricuspid regurgitation
RV heave

Late findings
Jugular venous distention
Peripheral edema
Cyanosis
RV third heart sound

Symptoms
Dyspnea, initially on exertion*
Angina (50% of patients)
Fatigue (20% of patients)
Syncope

* Eventually, virtually all patients with PH become dyspneic.

6. Discuss the observed abnormalities on pulmonary function testing.

Pulmonary function tests demonstrate mild restrictive defects secondary to the effects of the noncompliant pulmonary vasculature. Arterial blood gases reveal varying degrees of hypoxemia.

7. What additional diagnostic tests are available for evaluating pulmonary hypertension? What results may be expected?

An **echocardiogram** is an excellent noninvasive method for following progression of the disease. Echocardiographic features of PH include enlarged RV dimension, small LV dimension, thickened interventricular septum, systolic mitral valve prolapse, and abnormal septal motion. Determination of pulmonary artery pressures and PVR by pulsed Doppler echocardiography correlates well with values determined at cardiac catheterization.

Perfusion lung scans are particularly important in patients in whom thromboembolic disease is suspected. Thromboembolic disease is remediable with thromboendarterectomy and anticoagulation, whereas primary (PPH) is not. Lung scan demonstrates segmental defects in patients with thromboemboli but not in patients with PPH. **Pulmonary angiography** is indicated in patients demonstrating segmental perfusion scan defects, but pulmonary angiography should be undertaken cautiously in patients with PH. Although they are not contraindications, the associated risks of this procedure, including hypotension, worsening oxygenation, and cardiac arrest, should be weighed carefully against the potential benefit. In particular, patients with RV failure and increased RVEDP tolerate this procedure poorly.

Finally, **cardiac catheterization** is mandatory for confirming the diagnosis of PH and ruling out intracardiac shunts as a cause. In PH, catheterization may prove to be technically demanding and require guide wire assistance. Detection of an elevated wedge pressure is an indication for left-sided heart catheterization to rule out mitral stenosis, congenital heart disease, and left-sided heart failure as causes of PH.

8. Discuss standard therapies for patients suffering from pulmonary hypertension.

Supplemental oxygen therapy is common, the goal being to maintain saturations above at least 90%. **Diuretics** may be prescribed to patients with RV failure, hepatic congestion, and peripheral edema, although excessive diuresis may decrease RV preload and CO. Anti-coagulation is often instituted (usually oral warfarin), because patients are at great risk for throm-boembolic events (which may prove to be terminal). The use of cardiac glycosides is controversial; no studies clearly suggest a beneficial or detrimental effect. **Vasodilator therapy** is discussed in question 9. Finally, **lung or heart-lung transplantation** must be considered a con-temporary yet expensive option in selected patients with PH.

9. What medications are available to treat increased pulmonary artery pressures?

Virtually all classes of vasodilators have been investigated, including direct smooth muscle vasodilators, α-adrenergic antagonists, β-adrenergic agonists, calcium channel blockers, prosta-glandins, and angiotensin-converting enzyme (ACE) inhibitors. Intravenous medications avail-able for intraoperative use and intensive care management include nitroglycerin, nitroprusside, prostaglandin E_1, prostacyclin (PGI_2), phentolamine, and isoproterenol. Calcium channel block-ers are the current outpatient therapy of choice. Rich et al. found that 20% reductions in PVR in patients taking nifedipine or hydralazine were associated with increased long-term survival.[6] High doses of nifedipine or diltiazem have produced reductions in PA pressures and PVR as well as regression of RV hypertrophy.

10. A patient with a history of pulmonary hypertension presents for a surgical procedure. How should this patient be monitored intraoperatively?

In addition to the routine monitors for every general anesthetic (pulse oximetry, ECG, tem-perature, precordial or esophageal stethoscope, and noninvasive blood pressure), invasive moni-toring is standard management for patients with PH. **Invasive arterial pressure** monitoring allows beat-to-beat assessment of blood pressure and frequent blood analysis. A **PA catheter** should be introduced preoperatively to allow direct monitoring of PA pressure and right atrial pressure, and indirect assessment of LV volume and performance through determination of pul-monary occlusion pressures. Other standard monitors of particular use include **end-tidal carbon dioxide** and **inspired oxygen concentrations. Transesophageal echocardiography** is particu-larly useful in assessing volume status, left and right ventricular performance and valvular regur-gitation, and early detection of segmental wall motion abnormalities secondary to myocardial ischemia.

11. What intraoperative measures may lessen pulmonary hypertension?

1. As hypoxemia and hypercarbia increase PA pressures, optimize the patient's oxygenation and ventilation.

2. Assess myocardial performance; increasing PA pressures may be secondary to a failing left ventricle.

3. If ischemia is associated with a decreasing CO, consider infusing nitroglycerin to im-prove coronary perfusion. Inotropic drugs such as dobutamine or dopamine may enhance con-tractility and improve CO.

4. Assess volume status. Patients may be highly volume-dependent to maintain CO, yet hy-pervolemia may increase PA pressures.

5. Correct acid-base status, and ensure the patient is not becoming hypothermic. Both acid-base abnormalities and hypothermia may cause increased PA pressure.

6. Deepen the anesthetic.

7. Consider the use of direct-acting vasodilators.

12. What is nitric oxide?

Nitric oxide (NO) is a small molecule produced by vascular endothelium. Formed from the action of NO synthetase on arginine, NO crosses into vascular smooth muscle and stimulates guanylate cyclase, resulting in formation of 3',5'-cyclic guanosine monophosphate (cGMP). Subsequently, cGMP produces smooth muscle relaxation and vasodilation. Donation of NO groups is the mechanism of action of the nitrovasodilators.

13. Discuss therapeutic usefulness and limitations of NO in pulmonary hypertension.

A frequently associated complication of intravenous vasodilator therapy for PH is systemic hypotension. NO is administered by inhalation and crosses the alveolar membrane to the vascular endothelium, producing smooth muscle relaxation. But when it crosses into the circulation, it is rapidly bound to hemoglobin (with an affinity 1,500 times greater than carbon monoxide) and deactivated; thus it has no vasodilator effect on the systemic circulation. Deactivation on entering the circulation also limits the effectiveness of NO to the period in which it is administered by inhalation. Because storage in oxygen produces toxic higher oxides of nitrogen, especially nitrogen dioxide (NO_2), NO is stored in nitrogen and blended with ventilator gases immediately before administration. The potential for increased methemoglobin levels during NO administration should also be recognized.

14. Is NO useful in other conditions besides PPH?

Numerous reports document the efficacy of NO in improving oxygenation and PH in adult respiratory distress syndrome (ARDS). NO has been shown to reverse hypoxic pulmonary vasoconstriction. PH associated with congenital diaphragmatic hernias, congenital heart disease and persistent PH of the neonate, PH associated with adult mitral valve disease, and PH after cardiopulmonary bypass have been successfully managed through inhalation of NO. Doses have ranged from as high as 80 parts per million (ppm) to as low as 2 ppm. Individual dose-response relationships should be determined for each patient, and the lowest dose that produces a satisfactory pulmonary vasodilator response should be used to ensure the smallest possible production of methemoglobin. Methemoglobin levels should be assessed regularly. What constitutes a satisfactory dose of NO may depend on the desired endpoint; for instance, improvement in oxygenation in ARDS or reduction in PA pressures in PH.

CONTROVERSIES

15. Discuss the advantages and disadvantages of the intravenous nitrovasodilators.

Because of their ready availability, titratability, and common use, intravenous nitrovasodilators are popular in the acute management of increased PA pressures. Commonly used nitrovasodilators include nitroglycerin and sodium nitroprusside. **Nitroglycerin** has the advantage of providing coronary vasodilation. Principally a venodilator, nitroglycerin may excessively decrease preload. Nitroglycerin infusion is started at about 1 μg/kg/min and ordinarily produces a smooth reduction in vascular pressures. Above 3 μg/kg/min, venodilation may become excessive, decreasing preload and requiring intravenous fluid augmentation. **Sodium nitroprusside** (SNP) is an extremely potent, principally arterial vasodilator. Infusions begin about 0.5–1.0 μg/kg/min and are carefully adjusted upward to effect. SNP is extremely effective at afterload reduction. Despite its potency and potential for creating excessive hypotension, SNP is safe for short-term use. Long-term use is associated with tachyphylaxis and the potential for cyanide toxicity.

16. Are any anesthetic agents effective in lowering pulmonary artery pressures?

When used as part of a maintenance anesthetic, isoflurane, a volatile anesthetic agent, has been demonstrated to lower PA pressure and PVR and to improve CO in this setting. Its presumed mechanism is direct action on pulmonary vascular smooth muscle. Of the volatile anesthetics, isoflurane has probably the greatest effect on vascular smooth muscle.

Few data suggest a beneficial effect of other agents commonly used during general anesthesia. Muscle relaxants have no pulmonary vasodilator effect. Opioids do not have a direct vasodilator effect but may attenuate the vasoconstrictor effect of noxious pain stimuli. Studies suggest that nitrous oxide should be used cautiously if at all; it is best avoided in the presence of significant RV dysfunction. In children with intracardiac shunts, ketamine may prevent reversal of left-to-right shunts, because it increases systemic vascular resistance to a greater extent than PVR.

BIBLIOGRAPHY

1. Cheng DCH, Edelist G: Isoflurane and primary pulmonary hypertension. Anaesthesia 43:22–24, 1988.
2. D'Alonzo GE, Barst RJ, Ayres SM, et al: Survival in patients with primary pulmonary hypertension: Results from a national prospective registry. Ann Intern Med 115:343–349, 1991.
3. McLaughlin VV, Rich S: Pulmonary hypertension: Advances in medical and surgical interventions. J Heart Lung Transplant 17:739–743, 1998.
4. Moser KM, Page GT, Ashburn WL, Fedullo PF: Perfusion lung scans provide a guide to which patients with apparent primary pulmonary hypertension merit angiography. West J Med 148:167–170, 1988.
5. Reeves JT, Groves BM, Turkevich D: The case for treatment of selected patients with primary pulmonary hypertension. Am Rev Respir Dis 134:342–346, 1986.
6. Rich S, Brundage BH, Levy PS: The effect of vasodilator therapy on the clinical outcome of patients with primary pulmonary hypertension. Circulation 71:1191–1196, 1985.
7. Roissant R, Falke KJ, López F, et al: Inhaled nitric oxide for the adult respiratory distress syndrome. N Engl J Med 328:399–405, 1993.
8. Rubin LJ: Primary pulmonary hypertension (ACCP consensus statement). Chest 104:236–250, 1993.
9. Zapol WM, Rimar S, Gillis N, et al: Nitric oxide and the lung. Am J Respir Crit Care Med 49:1375–1380, 1994.

46. ANESTHESIA AND PERIOPERATIVE HEPATIC DYSFUNCTION

M. Susan Mandell, M.D., Ph.D.

1. What is the rate of transmission for hepatitis B and hepatitis C following an accidental needlestick?

Anesthesiologists are at increased risk for acquiring hepatitis as shown by a prevalence of 19–49% for hepatitis B serum markers compared to 3–5% for healthy blood donors. Based on information from the Centers for Disease Control, 30% of hepatitis B and 3% of hepatitis C exposed individuals will become infected following a needlestick from an infected patient.

2. What is recommended following a needlestick injury in a health care worker from a patient with hepatitis?

Hepatitis A. Immune globulin when given intramuscularly within 4 weeks of exposure provides passive immunity for 6 months. No vaccine is available.

Hepatitis B. High anti–hepatitis B surface antigen titer immune globulin (HBIG) is recommended following percutaneous exposure in health care workers who have no antibodies to hepatitis B surface antigen. This is followed by hepatitis B vaccine.

Hepatitis C. The effectiveness of immune globulin following exposure to hepatitis C virus is uncertain but offered in some institutions. No vaccine is available. Laboratory testing for virus and elevations of liver enzymes is performed at the time of injury and repeated at 3 and 6 months to detect infection. Treatment with alpha interferon may be recommended if viral infection is detected although the efficacy of treatment is unknown.

3. What is cirrhosis of the liver?

Cirrhosis of the liver is characterized by diffuse death of liver cells causing formation of fibrous tissue and nodular regeneration of hepatic tissue. The consequent distortion of the hepatic circulation further propagates cellular damage and results in a progressive reduction of liver cells, which eventually manifests as impairment of liver function. Hepatic synthetic failure, indicated by a prolonged prothrombin time (PT) and fall in albumin or impairment of detoxification mechanisms resulting in encephalopathy, is often termed end-stage liver disease.

4. Describe the changes in the cardiovascular system of patients with cirrhosis.

As liver disease progresses, most patients develop a hyperdynamic circulatory state, characterized by a fall in total peripheral resistance and a compensatory rise in cardiac output. The circulating plasma volume increases in response to vasodilation, and peripheral blood flow is enhanced. The arteriovenous oxygen gradient narrows due to increased peripheral shunting. Consequently, the mixed venous oxygen saturation of blood is higher than normal.

5. What pulmonary changes occur in a patient with cirrhosis?

Arterial hypoxemia with compensatory hyperventilation occurs in liver disease and is multifactorial in origin. Intrinsic and extrinsic pulmonary venous shunts form in response to portal hypertension and neovascularization. Deoxygenated blood that does not participate in pulmonary exchange is returned to the arterial circulation and reduces oxygen content.

Circulating vasoactive substances normally metabolized by the liver inhibit hypoxic pulmonary vasoconstriction, the mechanism responsible for optimal matching of ventilation and perfusion. Inhibition may be so profound that the patient becomes short of breath in the upright position (platypnea) due to gravity-induced pooling within the lung. Encephalopathy, pleural effusion, and reduced functional capacity from ascites also worsen arterial hypoxemia.

Anesthesia in cirrhotic patients is complicated by an increased risk of hypoxemia. Oxygen supplementation and positive pressure ventilation may improve ventilation-perfusion mismatch intraoperatively. However, pulmonary shunt and alveolar hypoventilation are generally worsened by anesthesia and postoperative narcotic analgesics.

6. What is hepatorenal syndrome? How does it differ from acute tubular necrosis?

Both types of acute renal failure occur in patients with cirrhosis and are characterized by increases in serum creatinine and oliguria. Differentiation is important, because treatment and prognosis vary.

Hepatorenal syndrome occurs in cirrhotic patients with portal hypertension and ascites. Intense vasoconstriction of the afferent arteriole reduces renal blood flow and impairs glomerular filtration. Abnormalities in the renin-angiotensin system, prostaglandins, catecholamines, and other endogenous factors probably contribute to vasoconstriction.

Acute tubular necrosis (ATN) is caused by renal tubular injury from ischemic or toxic injury. Tubular debris produces high intraluminal pressures and glomerular vasoconstriction. ATN may respond to diuretics, dopamine, calcium channel blockers, or angiotensin-converting enzyme inhibitors and is often reversible. In contrast, hepatorenal failure is minimally responsive to the above drug therapy and only reversible by normalization of hepatic function. The onset of hepatorenal syndrome is indicative of a poor prognosis.

7. How can hepatorenal syndrome be differentiated from acute tubular necrosis by urinanalysis?

The two conditions can be differentiated by the clinical pattern of onset and the laboratory values listed in the table.

Differential Diagnosis of Renal Failure in Liver Disease

MEASUREMENT	HEPATORENAL	ATN
Onset	Slow	Acute
Urine sodium concentration	< 10 mmol/L	50–70 mmol/L
Urine/plasma creatinine	> 10	< 10
Urine specific gravity	>1.010	1.010–1.015
Casts in urine	Seldom	Frequent

8. Describe volume assessment and fluid management in patients with hepatorenal syndrome.

Optimization of renal blood flow by correction of hypovolemia may prevent further renal injury during anesthesia and surgery in patients with liver disease. Volume assessment, however, can be misleading as central venous pressures are often elevated despite relative hypovolemia due to increased back pressure in the inferior vena cava from hepatic enlargement or scarring. The pressure profiles of a pulmonary artery catheter are often required for accurate volume assessment.

A trial of volume expansion should be undertaken as the initial treatment of low urine output. Although immediate improvement occurs in more than one-third of patients treated, hepatorenal syndrome leads to progressive renal failure unless hepatic function improves.

9. Which liver function tests are used to detect hepatic cell damage?

The cytosolic enzymes alanine aminotransferase (ALT) and aspartate aminotransferase (AST) are released into the blood as a result of increased membrane permeability or cell necrosis. They tend to rise and fall in parallel, although AST is cleared more rapidly from the circulation by the reticuloendothelial system. Their levels are not affected by changes in renal or biliary function. In contrast to ALT, which is mainly confined to hepatocytes, AST is found in heart and skeletal muscle, pancreas, kidney, and red blood cells. Therefore AST lacks specificity as a single diagnostic test. ALT is more specific but less sensitive for hepatic disease detection.

10. Briefly describe the laboratory tests used to assess hepatic synthetic function and their limitations.

All clotting factors except factor VIII are synthesized by the liver. PT indirectly determines the amount of clotting factors available and therefore is used to assess hepatic synthetic function. Elevation in PT is not specific for liver disease, and is altered, for instance, by the hemophilias and disseminated intravascular coagulation. Vitamin K deficiency due to gastrointestinal diseases and anticoagulant therapy can also prolong PT. Once other disease processes have been excluded, PT becomes a sensitive prognostic indicator for acute hepatocellular injury.

Albumin is made only by the liver and reflects hepatic synthetic ability. However, renal and gastrointestinal losses can affect plasma levels as can vascular permeability changes in critically ill patients. A reduction in synthesis due to liver disease may require 20 days to detect changes in serum levels because of the long plasma half-life. Low serum albumin levels are therefore indicators of chronic liver disease.

11. What laboratory enzyme assays are used in the diagnosis of cholestatic liver disease?

Alkaline phosphatase (ALP), gamma-glutamyl transferase (GGT) and 5'-nucleotidase are commonly used to assess biliary tract function. These enzymes are located in the biliary epithelial cell membranes. ALP occurs in a wide variety of tissues and is elevated in a number of conditions, notably bone disease and pregnancy. Hepatic origin of an elevated ALP can often be suggested by clinical context and simultaneous elevations of GGT and 5'-nucleotidase.

12. How can laboratory results be used to predict outcome in liver disease?

In acute liver disease such as viral hepatitis, plasma transaminase concentrations often reach levels 10–100 times normal. The higher plasma concentrations are associated with greater hepatocyte death and therefore an increased mortality rate. Relatively normal plasma levels can also be found in patients with acute liver disease, signifying massive cellular necrosis and associated with a very high mortality. PT is usually grossly prolonged and correlates with hepatic synthetic ability. Albumin levels are often normal. The mortality for intra-abdominal surgery in patients with severe acute hepatic disease approaches 100%.

Liver function tests have also been used to predict outcome following surgery in patients with chronic hepatic impairment. Child's scoring system (see Table, next page) was originally used to stratify risk in patients undergoing portosystemic shunting procedures. Using this method, mortality rates of 10%, 31%, and 76% were identified in Child's class A, B, and C, respectively. This scoring system has been tested and found to have predictive value for operative outcome of hepatobiliary procedures. This classification is generally associated with outcome for nonoperative patients, but specific survival and mortality rates for each category are unknown.

Child's Classification of Liver Failure*

GROUP	A	B	C
Serum bilirubin (mg/dl)	Below 2.0	2.0–3.0	Over 3.0
Serum albumin (g/dl)	Over 3.5	3.0–3.5	Under 3.0
Ascites	None	Easily controlled	Poorly controlled
Encephalopathy	None	Minimal	Advanced
Nutrition	Excellent	Good	Poor

* The Pugh modification replaces nutrition with prothrombin time prolongation (A: 1–4 seconds; B: 5–6 seconds; C: > 6 seconds).

13. What risk factors for liver disease can be identified by medical history?

The following table lists risk factors for liver disease easily obtained in a brief medical history. Patients with these problems, previous jaundice, or a history of liver disease should have liver function tests evaluated before anesthesia and surgery.

Risk Factors for Liver Disease

RISK FACTOR	EXAMPLE
Viral hepatitis	Intravenous drug abuse, transfusion, tattoos, contact with infected person
Drugs	Alcohol, prescription medications (e.g., acetaminophen, haloperidol, tetracycline, isoniazid, hydralazine, captopril, and amiodarone)
Autoimmune disease	Systemic lupus erythematosus, sarcoidosis, mixed connective tissue disorder
Metabolic disease	Hemochromatosis, Wilson's disease, cystic fibrosis, alpha$_1$ antitrypsin deficiency, and glycogen storage disease
Inflammatory bowel disease	Crohn's disease and ulcerative colitis

14. What is jaundice?

Jaundice is a visible yellow or green discoloration, usually first observed in the sclera, caused by elevation of the total serum bilirubin. Levels of 2.0–2.5 mg/dl (normal 0.5–1.0 mg/dl) result in jaundice. The oxidation of bilirubin to biliverdin gives the green hue often observed on physical exam.

15. What are the common causes of jaundice?

The distinction between unconjugated and conjugated hyperbilirubinemia is essential to the differential diagnosis of jaundice. Elevations in the serum unconjugated bilirubin fraction are usually related to changes in the turnover of red blood cells and their precursors. Conjugated hyperbilirubinemia always signifies dysfunction of the liver or biliary tract.

16. List the common causes of increases in unconjugated bilirubin.

Unconjugated hyperbilirubinemia is defined as an elevation of the total serum bilirubin of which the conjugated fraction does not exceed 15%. The causes are listed in the table below.

Causes of Unconjugated Bilirubin

CAUSE	EXAMPLE
Hemolysis	Incompatible blood transfusion, arterial/venous bypass circuit, congenital or acquired defects (autoimmune and drug-induced hemolytic anemia, glucose-6-phosphatase deficiency)
Hematoma resorption	Retroperitoneal or pelvic hematoma
Enzymatic deficiencies	Congenital deficiency (Gilbert's syndrome) to complete absence (Crigler-Najjar syndrome) of hepatic uridine diphosphate glucuronyl transferase

17. List the common causes of biliary obstruction.

Elevations of conjugated bilirubin are due to hepatocyte dysfunction and intrahepatic or extrahepatic stasis. A differential diagnosis of biliary stasis is listed below.

Causes of Biliary Obstruction

EXTRAHEPATIC OBSTRUCTION	INTRAHEPATIC OBSTRUCTION
Tumor (bile duct, pancreas and duodenum)	Primary biliary cirrhosis
Cholecystitis	Drugs (estrogens, anabolic steroids, tetracycline, and valproic acid)
Biliary stricture	Total parenteral nutrition
Ascending cholangitis	Pregnancy
Sclerosing cholangitis	Sclerosing cholangitis

18. What are the main causes of hepatocyte injury?

Causes of Hepatocyte Injury

CAUSE	EXAMPLE
Infection	Hepatitis A, B, C, D, and E, cytomegalovirus, Epstein-Barr
Drugs	Acetaminophen, isoniazid, phenytoin, hydralazine, alpha methyldopa, sulfasalazine
Sepsis	
Total parenteral nutrition	Abnormal liver function tests in 68–93% of patients given TPN for longer than 2 weeks
Hypoxemia	Lower arterial oxygen or interference with peripheral use as in cyanide and carbon monoxide poisoning
Ischemia	Increased venous pressure (congestive heart failure, pulmonary embolus, and positive pressure ventilation)
	Decreased arterial pressure (hypovolemia, vasopressors, and aortic cross-clamp)

19. How do inhalational anesthetic gases produce liver dysfunction?

Though rare, all inhalational agents can cause inflammation or death of hepatocytes by direct toxicity. Adverse reactions are caused by metabolic products of inhalational agents. Halothane, the most extensively metabolized agent, is associated with mild liver dysfunction in up to 30% of individuals exposed, reflected as an asymptomatic transient elevation of hepatic AST and ALT.

20. What is halothane hepatitis?

Anesthetic exposure to halothane results in severe hepatic impairment in approximately 1 in 30,000 individuals. This is termed an idiosyncratic reaction and is immunologically mediated. Halothane is metabolized by the liver and produces acyl chloride, which acts as a hapten. This results in trifluoroacetylation of hepatocyte membranes. The membrane–hapten complex induces an immune response resulting in hepatic necrosis. Risk factors associated with halothane hepatitis include obesity, female gender, familial factors, and prior exposure.

21. How is halothane hepatitis diagnosed?

Unfortunately, because there is no specific test for halothane-induced hepatitis, it has been considered a diagnosis of exclusion once other etiologies for perioperative hepatic dysfunction have been excluded. Careful screening of the history and laboratory results, however, will help diagnose halothane hepatitis. Most patients will have at least one of the risk factors cited in question 20. In addition, since this is an immunologically mediated reaction, there is usually a delay of 7–28 days in the development of hepatic dysfunction. Associated findings include pyrexia, arthralgia, rash, eosinophilia, autoantibodies, and circulating immune complexes.

If halothane hepatitis is strongly suspected, there are several centers in the United States and Europe that test for immune-modified hepatocyte complexes that are diagnostic for this condition.

22. Do any other inhalational anesthetic agents cause immune-mediated hepatitis?

Enflurane has rarely been associated with immune-based hepatitis with a documented incidence of 1 in 800,000. There have also been only a few case reports of isoflurane hepatitis. In general, the potential of an inhalational anesthetic agent to induce immune complexes is related to the extent of metabolism. Generally the degree of metabolism of agents is: halothane > enflurane > isoflurane > desflurane.

23. How do inhalational anesthetic agents alter hepatic blood flow?

All these agents vasodilate the hepatic artery and preportal blood vessels. This decreases mean hepatic artery pressure and increases venous pooling in the splanchnic vessels. Portal flow decreases. Overall the result is suboptimal perfusion of the liver. In addition, autoregulation of the hepatic artery is abolished and blood flow becomes pressure dependent. This is usually tolerated well in patients with normal hepatic function, as metabolic demand is also decreased by these drugs. Patients with hepatic disease are more susceptible to injury secondary to preexisting impaired perfusion.

24. Why is drug metabolism altered in cirrhosis of the liver?

Cirrhosis generally leads to a decrease in blood flow through the liver due to fibrotic changes, leading to ischemia in regions most distant from branches of the hepatic artery. The cytochrome P450 system is concentrated in these regions and is responsible for the metabolism of a wide variety of drugs. Damage to this area causes a decrease in the rate of drug metabolism and leads to a prolonged plasma half-life.

BIBLIOGRAPHY

1. Berry AJ, Issacson IJ, Kane MA, et al: A multicenter study of the prevalence of hepatitis B viral serological markers in anesthesia personnel. Anesth Analg 63:738–742, 1984.
2. Epstein M, Berk DP, Hollenber NK, et al: Renal failure in patients with cirrhosis. Am J Med 49:175–185, 1970.
3. Hawker F: Liver function tests. In Hawker F (ed): The Liver. Philadelphia, W.B. Saunders, 1993, pp 43–70.
4. Kenna J, Van Pelt F: The metabolism and toxicity of inhaled anaesthetic agents. Anaesth Pharmacol Rev 2:29–42, 1994.
5. Maze M: Anesthesia and the liver. In Miller RD (ed): Anesthesia, 4th ed. New York, Churchill Livingstone, 1994, pp 1969–1980.
6. Stoelting RK, Blitt CD, Cohen PJ, et al: Hepatic dysfunction after isoflurane anesthesia. Anesth Analg 66:147–151, 1987.

47. RENAL FUNCTION AND ANESTHESIA

James Duke, M.D.

1. Describe the anatomy of the kidney.

The kidneys are paired organs lying retroperitoneally against the posterior abdominal wall. Although their combined weight is only 300 g (about 0.5% of total body weight), they receive 20–25% of total cardiac output. The renal arteries are branches of the aorta, originating below the superior mesenteric artery. There are numerous arterial anastomoses with the mesenteric and suprarenal vessels. The renal veins drain into the inferior vena cava. Nerve supply is abundant; sympathetic constrictor fibers originate from the fourth thoracic to first lumbar spinal segments

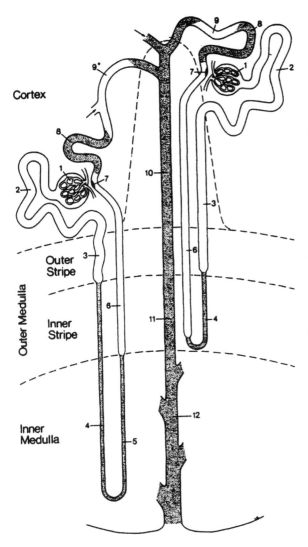

Cortex

Outer Medulla

Outer
Stripe

Inner
Stripe

Inner
Medulla

This scheme depicts a short-looped and a long-looped nephron together with the collecting system (not drawn to scale). Within the cortex a medullary ray is delineated by a dashed line. *1*, Renal corpuscle including Bowman's capsule and the glomerulus (glomerular tuft); *2*, proximal convoluted tubule; *3*, proximal straight tubule; *4*, descending thin limb; *5*, ascending thin limb; *6*, distal straight tubule (thick ascending limb); *7*, macula densa located within the final portion of the thick ascending limb; *8*, distal convoluted tubule; *9*, connecting tubule; *9**, connecting tubule of the juxtamedullary nephron that forms an arcade; *10*, cortical collecting duct; *11*, outer medullary collecting duct; *12*, inner medullary collecting duct. (From Kriz W, Bankir I: A standard nomenclature for structures of the kidneys. Am J Physiol 254:F1, 1988, with permission.)

and are distributed via celiac and renal plexuses. There is no sympathetic dilator or parasympathetic innervation. Pain fibers, mainly from the renal pelvis and upper ureter, enter the spinal cord via splanchnic nerves.

On cross-section of the kidney, three zones are apparent: cortex, outer medulla, and inner medulla. Eighty percent of renal blood flow is distributed to cortical structures. Each kidney contains about 1 million nephrons. Nephrons are classified as superficial (about 85%) or juxtamedullary, depending on location and length of tubules. The origin of all nephrons is within the cortex, where abundant glomerular capillary networks (continuations of interlobular arteries) surround the Bowman's capsule of each nephron.

The glomerulus and capsule are known collectively as the renal corpuscle. Each Bowman's capsule is connected to a proximal tubule that is convoluted within its cortical extent but becomes straight-limbed within the outer cortex; at this point the tubule is known as the loop of Henle. The loop of Henle of superficial nephrons descends only to the intermedullary junction, where it makes a hairpin turn, becomes thick-limbed, and ascends back into the cortex, where it approaches and touches the glomerulus with a group of cells known as the juxtaglomerular apparatus (JGA). The superficial nephrons form distal convoluted tubules that merge to form collecting tubules within the cortex. About 5 thousand tubules join to form collecting ducts. Ducts merge at minor calyces, which in turn merge to form major calyces. The major calyces join and form the renal pelvis, the most cephalic aspect of the ureter. The renal corpuscles of juxtamedullary nephrons are located at juxtamedullary cortical tissue. They have long loops of Henle that descend deep into medullary tissue; the loops also reascend into cortical tissue, where they form distal convoluted tubules and collecting tubules. These nephrons (15% of the total) are responsible for conservation of water.

2. List the major functions of the kidney.
1. Regulation of body fluid volume and composition
2. Acid-base balance
3. Detoxification and excretion of nonessential materials, including drugs
4. Elaboration of renin, which is involved in extrarenal regulatory mechanisms
5. Endocrine and metabolic functions, such as erythropoietin secretion, vitamin D conversion, and calcium and phosphate homeostasis

3. Discuss glomerular and tubular function.
Glomerular filtration results in production of about 180 L of glomerular fluid each day. Filtration does not require the expenditure of metabolic energy; rather it is due to a balance of hydrostatic and oncotic forces. The glomerular membrane possesses negatively charged pores that allow passage of water, ions, and negatively charged ions of less than approximately 40 Å (molecular weight < 15,000). Substances between 40 and 80 Å (molecular weight ~40,000) ordinarily pass if they are neutrally charged; substances > 80 Å are unfiltered. Normal glomerular filtration rate (GFR) is 125 ml/min.

Tubular function reduces the 180 L/day of filtered fluid to about 1 L/day of excreted fluid, altering its composition through active and passive transport. Transport is passive when it is the result of physical forces, such as electrical or concentration gradients. When transport is undertaken against electrochemical or concentration gradients, metabolic energy is required and the process is termed active.

Substances may be either reabsorbed or secreted from tubules; both processes may be active or passive. Substances may move bidirectionally, taking advantage of both active and passive transport. The direction of transit for reabsorbed substances is from tubule to interstitium to blood, whereas the direction for secreted substances is from blood to interstitium to tubule. Secretion is the major route of elimination for drugs and toxins, especially when they are plasma protein-bound.

4. How is urine concentrated or diluted?
Loops of Henle allow formation of urine that is hypertonic relative to plasma. The greater the length of the loops, the more concentrated the urine can become. Throughout the animal kingdom, production of hypertonic urine requires the presence of loops of Henle.

The most energetically efficient manner for concentrating tubular fluid involves active transport of ions and osmotic equilibration of water. The passive transport of water is known as countercurrent multiplication of concentration.

Beginning at the glomerulus, the balance of hydrostatic and oncotic forces favors filtration of plasma at the rate of about 180 L/day. At the proximal convoluted tubule (PCT), sodium passively moves down a concentration gradient into the sodium-poor milieu of the cells lining the PCT. Chloride passively follows to maintain electrical neutrality, and water moves into the cells passively as well in response to osmotic gradients. Sodium is then transported *against* a concentration gradient into the renal interstitium. This energy-dependent process (active transport) uses the intracellular Na-K-ATPase–driven sodium pump, exchanging intracellular sodium for extracellular potassium. Again, chloride and water passively follow. About 75% of the filtered tubular fluid is then taken back up into the circulation via peritubular capillaries with no net change in osmotic activity.

At the level of the thin descending loop of Henle the nephron reaches medullary tissue with its hypertonic interstitium. Water moves along its osmotic gradient, but the cells are poorly permeable to sodium and incapable of active transport; sodium remains intratubular. By the time of reversal of flow at the ascending loop of Henle, the volume of tubular fluid has decreased and its osmolality has increased substantially. The thin ascending loop is impermeable to water, but some diffusion and active transport of sodium and chloride take place. The thick ascending loop is also impermeable to water but allows active transport of chloride and passive movement of sodium. This active transport of chloride is the driving force for urinary concentration and dilution.

By the time tubular fluid reaches the distal convoluted tubule (DCT), its volume is only about 15% of the originally filtered fluid, and it is hypotonic relative to the interstitium. The cells of the DCT and collecting ducts are hormonally responsive; when antidiuretic hormone (ADH) levels are high, water moves out of the tubules and back into the circulation. What remains is a fluid rich in urea. By the time tubular fluid has reached the midpoint of the PCT, the tubule is once again cortical; the osmotic difference between tubule and cortical interstitium is small. Active transport of sodium and passive movement of water continue, leaving only 5–8% of the original filtered fluid within the tubules.

Entering the ADH-responsive collecting tubules and again descending into medullary tissue, water moves into the hypertonic interstitium. The tubular fluid that finally enters the renal pelvis is only about 0.5% of the originally filtered fluid.

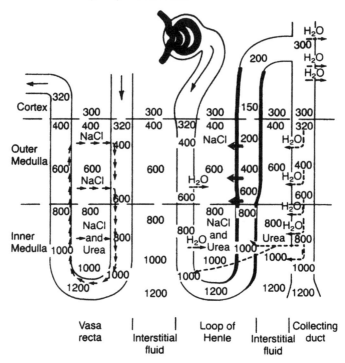

The countercurrent mechanism for concentrating the urine. Numerical values are in mOsm/L. (From Guyton AC: Textbook of Medical Physiology, 8th ed. Philadelphia, W.B. Saunders, 1991, with permission.)

5. Discuss diuresis and the site of action of commonly used diuretics.

An appreciation of the site and mode of diuretic action reinforces understanding of nephronal function. For instance, diuretics such as acetazolamide, which act on the PCT, do not significantly affect urine volume or concentration because the majority of sodium and water reabsorption occurs in the loop of Henle. On the other hand, diuretics that interfere with the active transport of chloride within the loop of Henle affect urine formation greatly. With the exception of osmotic diuretics, all diuretics interfere with sodium conservation.

Diuretics

DRUG	SITE OF ACTION	ACTION/SIDE EFFECTS
Carbonic anhydrase inhibitors (acetazolamide)	Proximal convoluted tubule	Inihibits sodium reabsortpion Interferes with H^+ excretion Hyperchloremic, hypokalemic acidosis
Thiazides (hydrochlorothiazide)	Cortical diluting segment (between ascending limb and aldosterone-responsive DCT)	Inhibits sodium reabsorption Accelerates sodium-potassium exchange—hypokalemia Decreases GFR in volume-contracted states
Potassium-sparing diuretics (spironolactone, triamterene)	Competitive inhibition of aldosterone in DCT	Inhibiting aldosterone prevents sodium reabsorption and sodium-potassium exchange Modest diuretic that often supplements thiazides
Loop diuretics (furosemide, bumetanide, ethacrynic acid)	Inhibit Cl^- reabsorption at thick ascending loop of Henle	Potent diuretic; acts on critical urine concentrating process Renal vasodilation, significant hypokalemia Can produce significant volume contraction
Osmotic diuretics (mannitol, urea)	Filtered at glomerulus but not reabsorbed; creates osmotic gradient into tubules; excretion of water and some sodium	Hyperosmolality reduces cellular water Limited ability to excrete sodium Renal vasodilator

6. Describe the unique aspects of renal blood flow (RBF) and control. How does RBF affect urine concentration?

RBF of about 1200 ml/min is well maintained (autoregulated) at blood pressures of 80–180 mmHg. Blood flow to cortex, outer medulla, and inner medulla has a distinct relationship to function. The cortex requires about 80% of blood flow to achieve its excretory and regulatory functions, and the outer medulla receives 15%. The inner medulla receives a small percent of blood flow; a higher flow would wash out solutes responsible for the high tonicity (1200 mOsm/kg) of the inner medulla. Without this hypertonicity, urinary concentration would not be possible.

Control of RBF is through extrinsic and intrinsic neural and hormonal influences; a principal goal of blood flow regulation is to maintain GFR. As mentioned, the potential sympathetic vasoconstrictor capacity is extensive, but the euvolemic, nonstressed state has little baseline sympathetic tone. Under mild-to-moderate stress, RBF decreases slightly, but efferent arterioles constrict, maintaining GFR. During periods of severe stress (hemorrhage, hypoxia, major surgical procedures) both RBF and GFR decrease secondary to sympathetic stimulation. This phenomenon is also observed when high concentrations of epinephrine or norepinephrine are infused.

The renin-angiotensin-aldosterone axis also has an effect on RBF. A proteolytic enzyme formed at the macula densa of the juxtaglomerular apparatus, renin acts on angiotensinogen within the circulation to produce angiotensin I. Enzymes within lung and plasma convert angiotensin I to angiotensin II, a potent pressor and renal vasoconstricting agent (especially of the efferent arteriole) as well as a factor in the release of aldosterone. Stimuli for renin release include tubular sodium content, catecholamine levels, sympathetic stimulation, and afferent arteriolar tone. During periods of stress, levels of angiotensin are elevated and contribute (along with sympathetic stimulation and catecholamines) to decrease RBF.

Prostaglandins (PG) are also found within the kidney. PGE_2 and PGE_3 are intrinsic mediators of blood flow, producing vasodilation.

Blood flows to the medulla through the vasa recta, which are continuations of juxtamedullary glomerular efferent arterioles. Bundles of vasa recta do not descend deeply into the medulla, and the inner medulla receives only 1–3% of RBF. The hairpin arrangement of the vasa recta functions as a countercurrent exchanger. Water leaves the descending limb and enters the more hypertonic ascending limb, thus bypassing the inner medulla. Medullary solute travels in the opposing direction, leaving the hypertonic ascending limb and entering the less tonic descending limb. An osmotic gradient is thus maintained; the tip of the renal papilla has an osmolality of 1200 mOsm/kg.

7. Describe the sequence of events associated with decreased RBF.

The initial response to decreased RBF is to preserve ultrafiltration through redistribution of blood flow to the kidneys, selective afferent arteriolar vasodilation, and efferent arteriolar vasoconstriction. Renal hypoperfusion also results in active absorption of sodium and passive absorption of water in the ascending loop of Henle; paradoxically, oxygen demand is increased in an area particularly vulnerable to decreased oxygen delivery (75–80% of the energy expended in the kidney is for active sodium transport). Compensatory sympathoadrenal mechanisms redistribute blood flow from outer cortex to inner cortex and medulla. If renal hypoperfusion persists or worsens despite early compensatory mechanisms, and as sodium is resorbed in the ascending loop, increased sodium is delivered to the macula densa, producing afferent arteriolar vasoconstriction and decreasing glomerular filtration. Because GFR is decreased, less solute is delivered to the ascending loop. Because less solute is delivered, less is resorbed (an energy-requiring process); thus less oxygen is needed, and the net effect is that afferent arteriolar vasoconstriction decreases oxygen-consuming processes. The result, however, is oliguria. **Oliguria is a symptom of decreased RBF and oxygen delivery and a result of compensatory mechanisms designed to prevent ischemic renal injury.**

8. What preoperative risk factors are associated with postoperative renal failure?

Variability in the definition of renal failure (impaired glomerular function as measured by blood urea nitrogen [BUN], creatinine, or GFR or impaired tubular function as measured by urine specific gravity, osmolality, or fractional excretion of sodium), nonuniformity of statistical methods, and inconsistent criteria for establishing risk factors have made meta-analysis of published studies impossible. Nonetheless, a few patterns emerge. Preoperative renal risk factors (increased BUN and creatinine and a history of renal dysfunction), left ventricular dysfunction, advanced age, jaundice, and diabetes mellitus are predictive of postoperative renal dysfunction. Patients undergoing cardiac or aortic surgery are particularly at risk for developing postoperative renal insufficiency.

9. Discuss the relationship between aortic surgery and renal dysfunction.

The incidence of acute renal failure (ARF) associated with aortic surgery is about 8%; the mortality rate in such cases is about 60%. The most common cause of ARF is ischemic injury leading to acute tubular necrosis. An association with preexisting renal insufficiency (creatinine > 2.3 mg/dl) is particularly worrisome. Complicated aneurysms (e.g., expanding, ruptured, suprarenal, thoracic, and pararenal aneurysms) have a higher incidence of ARF (10–30%) than uncomplicated infrarenal aneurysms (5%). When ARF accompanies repair of an expanding or ruptured aneurysm, the mortality rate ranges between 75% and 95%. Suprarenal cross-clamping carries a higher incidence of ARF compared with infrarenal cross-clamping. The higher incidence may be associated with enhanced atheromatous embolization to renal vessels; curiously, *supraceliac* cross-clamping and infrarenal cross-clamping have a nearly equal incidence of ARF.

10. What is the effect of cardiopulmonary bypass on renal blood flow?

Cardiopulmonary bypass decreases RBF and GFR by 30%. Nonpulsatile cardiopulmonary bypass appears more detrimental to renal blood flow. The correlation between length of cardiopulmonary bypass and ARF is linear. Hemolysis associated with cardiopulmonary bypass and pigment nephrotoxicity may be a cause of ARF, although renal ischemia associated with cardiopulmonary bypass is by far the leading cause. Valvular surgical procedures have twice the incidence of ARF compared with coronary artery bypass grafting.

11. Discuss the major causes of perioperative ARF.

ARF is defined as a significant decrease in GFR over a period of 2 weeks or less. Renal failure, or azotemia, can be categorized broadly into prerenal, renal, and postrenal etiologies. Prerenal azotemia is due to decreased blood flow to the kidney and accounts for about 60% of all cases of ARF. Causes include renal vascular disease and renal ischemia. In the perioperative setting, ischemia is most likely due to inadequate perfusion from blood and volume losses. Other mechanisms of prerenal azotemia include hypoperfusion secondary to myocardial dysfunction and congestive heart failure or shunting of blood away from the kidneys, as in sepsis.

Renal causes account for 30% of all cases of ARF. Acute tubular necrosis is the leading cause and may be due to either ischemia or toxins. Nephrotoxins include radiocontrast media, aminoglycosides, and fluoride associated with volatile anesthetic metabolism. Hemolysis or muscular injury (producing hemoglobinuria and myoglobinuria) are also causes of intrinsic ARF.

Postrenal causes (10% of cases) are due to obstructive nephropathy and may be observed in men with prostatism, women with pelvic malignancies, diabetes-associated neuropathy that affects bladder function, ureteral obstruction, and anticholinergic-associated bladder dysfunction from anesthetic agents or antihistamines.

12. Discuss the utility of urine output in assessing renal function.

Urine output is easily measured through insertion of an indwelling Foley catheter and connection to a urimeter. A daily output of 400–500 ml of urine is required to excrete obligatory nitrogenous wastes. In adults, an inadequate urine output (oliguria) is often quoted as < 0.5 ml/kg/hour. In the absence of preexisting renal disease and urinary obstruction, oliguria is usually a manifestation of diminished renal perfusion and glomerular filtration, either from hypovolemia or renal vasoconstriction. As discussed in question 7, oliguria is both a symptom and a compensatory mechanism in the setting of renal perfusion. GFR also may be decreased by the effects of anesthesia, sympathetic activity, hormonal influences, and surgical procedure via redistribution of blood away from outer cortical nephrons.

Despite reliance on urine output to gauge adequacy of volume resuscitation and renal function, numerous studies show no correlation between urine volume and histologic evidence of acute tubular necrosis, GFR, creatinine clearance, or perioperative changes in the levels of BUN or creatinine. This lack of correlation has been noted in patients with burns, trauma, shock states, or cardiovascular surgery.

Finally, a normal urine output does not rule out renal failure. Nonoliguric renal failure is not uncommon perioperatively. Levels of renin, aldosterone, and ADH may affect tubular secretion of water and solute independent of GFR. At best, urinary flow rate and volume are indirect measures of the adequacy of renal function.

13. How useful are urine specific gravity and osmolality in assessing perioperative renal function?

Specific gravity (SpGr), a measure of the kidney's concentrating ability, is determined by comparing the mass of 1 ml of urine to 1 ml of distilled water. Normal values range between 1.010 and 1.030. In prerenal azotemia, the kidney's attempts to conserve sodium and water are reflected in a concentrated urine with SpGr > 1.030; loss of concentrating ability, as in acute tubular necrosis, is reflected by SpGr < 1.010. However, many factors can change SpGr, including protein, glucose, mannitol, dextran, diuretics, radiographic contrast, extremes of age, and thyroid, parathyroid, adrenal, or pituitary disease. Hence, measurement of specific gravity is a nonspecific measure of renal function.

The same factors that render SpGr nonspecific also affect the reliability of urine osmolality as an assessment of renal function. Traditionally, an osmolality > 500 mOsm/kg H_2O has been used as a guideline to identify prerenal azotemia and an osmolality < 350 mOsm/kg H_2O to identify acute tubular necrosis, but these values are not particularly predictive.

14. What are the limitations in using serum creatinine and BUN to assess renal function?

Many nonrenal variables may be responsible for elevation of BUN and creatinine, including increased nitrogen absorption, hypercatabolism, hepatic disease, diabetic ketoacidosis, hematoma resorption, gastrointestinal bleeding, hyperalimentation, and many drugs (e.g., steroids). In addition, elevation of serum creatinine is a late sign of renal dysfunction. GFR may be reduced as much as 75% before abnormal elevation is observed. Because creatinine production is proportionate to muscle mass, settings in which substantial wasting has already occurred (e.g., chronic illness, advanced age) may have "normal" creatinine levels despite markedly reduced GFR. Postoperative creatinine measurements are not particularly predictive of renal dysfunction.

15. Are estimates of urine-to-plasma ratios of creatinine or urea predictive of renal dysfunction?

Urine-to-plasma creatinine ratios are neither sensitive nor specific for renal dysfunction. Only at extremes do they indicate renal dysfunction (may indicate acute tubular necrosis if < 10 or prerenal azotemia if > 40). Because so many nonrenal variables may influence BUN levels, the urine-to-plasma urea ratio is also neither sensitive nor specific for renal dysfunction.

16. Is measurement of urinary sodium useful in assessing renal function? What factors influence urinary sodium excretion?

Urinary sodium levels appear to correlate more with the amount and type of resuscitation fluid than with renal function. Factors that influence urinary sodium levels include secretion of aldosterone and ADH, diuretic therapy, saline content of IV fluids, sympathetic tone, and coexisting sodium avid states, such as cirrhosis and congestive heart failure.

17. How is the fractional excretion of sodium (FENa) determined? Is it of value in assessing renal function?

FENa represents the fraction of all filtered sodium that is excreted:

$$\text{FENa} = \text{excreted Na/filtered Na} \times 100 = (U_{Na} \times P_{Cr}/U_{Cr} \times P_{Na}) \times 100$$

where U_{Na} is urinary sodium, U_{Cr} is urinary creatinine, P_{Cr} is plasma creatinine, and P_{Na} is plasma sodium.

Numerous retrospective and prospective investigations demonstrated a high sensitivity and specificity in differentiating prerenal azotemia (FENa < 1%) from acute tubular necrosis (FENa > 1%), but more recent reports dispute the earlier studies, noting that the determination is not particularly accurate early in the course of renal impairment, when it would be most useful. Conditions other than acute tubular necrosis that may have an FENa > 1% include normal renal function with high salt intake and volume depletion with preexisting chronic renal disease. Other conditions that may have an FENa < 1% include congestive heart failure, acute glomerulonephritis, myoglobinuric and hemoglobinuric renal failure, acute urinary tract obstruction, renal transplant rejection, and contrast nephrotoxicity.

18. What is free water clearance (C_{H_2O})? Is it predictive of renal dysfunction?

$$C_{H_2O} = UV - \{(U_{osm}/P_{osm}) \times UV\}$$

where UV is urine volume, U_{osm} is urinary osmolality and P_{osm} is plasma osmolality. Free water clearance is a measure of the kidney's ability to dilute or concentrate urine. Because numerous nonrenal factors may affect urine osmolality, this determination is often not likely to have value. Free water clearance is not as useful as determination of creatinine clearance.

19. How is creatinine clearance (CrCl) determined? What does it measure? What is its usefulness in assessing acute renal dysfunction?

CrCl approximates glomerular filtration and measures the ability of the glomerulus to filter creatinine from plasma:

$$CrCl = (Urine\ Cr \times UV)/Plasma\ Cr$$

where Urine Cr is urinary creatinine, UV is urine volume, and Plasma Cr is plasma creatinine.

CrCl is the most efficient test available for assessing glomerular filtration. A significant limitation is the necessity for 24-hour urine collection, clearly an obstacle if an immediate assessment of renal function is needed. CrCl estimated from 2-hour urine collections has been shown to be reasonably valid if urine is collected conscientiously, although longer collection periods always provide more accurate assessments.

20. Given the preceding discussions about methods that may be useful in assessing perioperative renal dysfunction, can any generalizations be made?

The majority of renal function tests are neither sensitive nor specific in predicting perioperative renal dysfunction. Currently, we rely on a number of indirect variables that do not reliably correlate with glomerular filtration. Creatinine clearance is the most sensitive test available but is limited by the need for prolonged urine collection; in the operative setting it is clearly not practical.

In daily anesthetic practice, considerable attention continues to be given to urine output. In most patients, an output of 0.5–1.0 ml/kg/hr reassures the anesthesiologist that renal function is probably intact. However, an "adequate" urine output should be considered only in the context of preexisting renal disease or other conditions associated with increased renal morbidity, recent or ongoing renal insults (e.g., surgical procedure, renal toxins, volume losses, resuscitation), and medications (e.g., osmotic diuretics, volatile anesthetics, anticholinergics, nonsteroidal anti-inflammatory drugs [NSAIDs]).

21. Discuss dopamine and its effect on renal blood flow.

Dopamine is a precursor in the synthetic pathway of norepinephrine and epinephrine. When infused in low concentrations, norepinephrine and epinephrine produce an increase in systemic blood pressure accompanied by a decrease in total RBF with maintenance of GFR; when they are infused in higher concentrations, GFR also decreases.

In contrast, low-dose dopamine increases RBF, GFR, and urinary sodium excretion secondary to intracortical redistribution of blood flow. This effect is observed when dopamine receptors are differentially activated. Infusion rates of 0.5–2.0 µg/kg/min (some say 1–3 µg/kg/min) stimulate primarily dopaminergic receptors (DA_1 and DA_2). Infusion of 2–5 µg/kg/min stimulate β-adrenergic receptors, whereas rates above 5 µg/kg/min stimulate α-adrenergic receptors. Some clinicians fail to appreciate the significant variability within patients due to receptor activation and binding affinities as well as up- and downregulation of receptors. Thus, it is at best difficult to characterize an observed effect as purely dopaminergic. It is also likely that dopamine is not a usual modulator of renal hemodynamics and function.

In euvolemic adults with normal renal function, dopamine is natriuretic, because it inhibits reabsorption at the proximal convoluted tubule. But in most critically ill patients, natriuresis is not often seen because of multiple influences; the goal of the kidney is sodium conservation. In fact, when baseline GFR is < 70 ml/min, low-dose dopamine is not likely to increase GFR, perhaps because blood flow in chronic renal dysfunction has already been redistributed toward inner cortex and medulla. Marik observed that in a group of critically ill, oliguric patients only those with low plasma renin responded with an improved urine output.

Dopamine, in combination with loop diuretics, increases urine output in patients with acute oliguric renal failure who were previously unresponsive to volume expansion or furosemide; however, this effect may not be due to dopamine's effect on GFR but rather to its effect on RBF, which enhances delivery of furosemide to its site of action. In conclusion, dopamine increases urine output in healthy, hydrated patients and in some oliguric patients.

22. Describe the effects of anesthetics on renal function.

It is difficult to separate the effects of anesthetic agents on renal function from the effects of surgical stress. Likewise, the indirect effects of general anesthesia on renal hemodynamics, sympathetic activity, and humoral regulation confound interpretation of direct anesthetic effects, although it appears that the indirect effects of anesthetic agents have a greater influence on RBF and GFR.

General anesthesia temporarily depresses renal function as measured by urine output, GFR, RBF, and electrolyte excretion. Renal impairment is usually short-lived and completely reversible. Maintenance of systemic blood pressure and especially preoperative hydration lessen the effect on renal function. Spinal and epidural anesthesia also appear to depress renal function, but not to the same extent as general anesthesia. In this setting decrements in renal function parallel the magnitude of sympathetic blockade.

Agents that produce myocardial depression (such as volatile anesthetics) are associated with an increase in renal vascular resistance to maintain blood pressure; RBF and GFR decrease. The effects of volatile anesthetics on renal autoregulation are conflicting, but their indirect effects of renal hemodynamics are probably of greater significance.

Methoxyflurane is no longer used because its significant degree of biotransformation (50%) produced toxic amounts of fluoride (peak concentrations > 50 μmol). **Enflurane**, also through production of fluoride, is potentially nephrotoxic, but the duration of exposure necessary to produce toxic levels is far beyond normal limits (although transient impairment in renal concentrating ability has been noted). In any case, with the introduction of newer volatile anesthetics, clinical use of enflurane appears to be declining. A recently introduced volatile anesthetic, **sevoflurane**, is metabolized to fluoride ions; about 3.5% of a dose appears in the urine as inorganic fluoride. Peak concentrations of about 25 μmol appear within 2 hours of discontinuing the agent. Despite peaks in fluoride concentration consistent with renal dysfunction (with methoxyflurane), extensive experience with sevoflurane (especially in Japan) confirms its safety. Its remarkable insolubility when compared to methoxyflurane may be explanatory; there is simply less sevoflurane deposited in lipid stores to be later metabolized to fluoride, and the overall fluoride "burden" is less.

Opioids, barbiturates, and **benzodiazepines** also reduce GFR and urine output. When **droperidol** is administered in combination with opioids to produce general anesthesia (neurolepanesthesia), its α-adrenergic blocking properties maintain the normal distribution of blood flow within the kidney and may result in somewhat smaller changes in renal hemodynamics. **Anticholinergic agents** may predispose patients with obstructive uropathies to postrenal azotemia.

Ketorolac is an NSAID and anesthetic adjuvant that may be administered intramuscularly or intravenously. As a prostaglandin inhibitor, ketorolac interferes with prostaglandin-associated intrinsic renal vasodilation and is a well known cause of drug-induced acute renal failure. In patients at risk and in patients with preexisting renal dysfunction, its use must be avoided.

In conclusion, preexisting cardiovascular and renal function, extent of surgery, and intravascular volume status appear to be the major determinants of the duration and extent of renal impairment associated with anesthetic agents.

23. What muscle relaxants have substantial renal excretion?

Because virtually all relaxants have some degree of renal excretion, their duration of action is prolonged in patients with renal insufficiency. Atracurium undergoes spontaneous degradation under physiologic conditions (Hofmann degradation and ester hydrolysis) and may be preferred in patients with significant renal impairment. Because atracurium is water-soluble, patients with altered body water composition may require larger initial doses to produce rapid paralysis but smaller and less frequent doses to maintain paralysis.

Muscle Relaxants and Renal Excretion

Gallamine > 90%	Doxacurium 30%
Tubocurarine 45%	Vecuronium 15%
Metocurine 43%	Atracurium 10%
Pancuronium 40%	Rocuronium 10%
Pipecuronium 38%	Mivacurium < 10%

24. Does mechanical ventilation affect renal function?

Increases in intrathoracic pressure may decrease urine volume and sodium excretion. Because the magnitude of increased pressure is influential in depressing renal function, ventilatory techniques that use only partial ventilatory support (intermittent mandatory ventilation, pressure support ventilation, continuous positive airway pressure with spontaneous ventilation) are less deleterious. Increases in ADH secretion are noted during controlled ventilation but may be attenuated by volume loading. Decreases in intrathoracic blood volume and changes in transmural pressures do not appear to have a major direct influence on renal function. However, reduced systemic pressures may produce reflex increases in renal sympathetic neural tone. Activation of the renin-angiotensin-aldosterone system by mechanical ventilation also probably acts to reduce renal function.

25. Describe management strategies to prevent renal failure in high-risk patients.

In patients with elevated creatinine or suspected renal insufficiency with "normal" creatinine, determining the CrCl is useful in adjusting the doses of renally excreted and renally toxic drugs, such as aminoglycosides. When radiocontrast must be given, the dose should be limited to the minimum needed, and the patient should be hydrated. Laboratory studies should be appropriate to the patient group. Before surgery, the patient must be euvolemic; pulmonary artery catheterization may be indicated to guide fluid management and to optimize hemodynamics and therefore RBF. Medications that may be nephrotoxic (e.g., amphotericin, NSAIDs, aminoglycosides) or produce an obstructive uropathy (anticholinergics, antihistamines) should be avoided if possible.

26. Do diuretics have a role in preventing renal failure in high-risk patients?

Mannitol may be of use because (1) it is a renal vasodilator, increasing cortical blood flow; (2) it increases tubular flow, clearing tubules of necrotic cellular debris that may contribute to acute tubular necrosis; and (3) as an oxygen scavenger, it may be of benefit in preventing ischemia-reperfusion injuries. However, with the exception of contrast nephrotoxicity, no controlled prospective studies clearly demonstrate the benefit of mannitol in preventing acute renal failure in high-risk patients. Diuretics may convert oliguric renal failure to nonoliguric renal failure; management may be easier but prognosis is not improved. Mannitol may also potentiate acute renal failure if it precipitates congestive heart failure and produces renal hypoperfusion. Finally, like mannitol, furosemide has been shown to be of benefit in high-risk groups only anecdotally.

27. How are patients with chronic renal failure best managed perioperatively?

The surgical mortality rate for patients with end-stage renal disease (ESRD) is about 4%, but when such patients require emergency procedures, the rate increases to 20%. Clearly preoperative preparation is of benefit. Primary causes of death include sepsis, dysrhythmias, and cardiac dysfunction.

The morbidity rate is substantial, approaching 50%. Hyperkalemia is the most common cause of morbidity, although infections, hemodynamic instability, bleeding, and arrhythmias are extremely common and problematic. Renal causes for increased morbidity include decreased ability to concentrate and dilute urine, decreased ability to regulate extracellular fluid and sodium, impaired handling of acid loads, hyperkalemia, and impaired excretion of medications. Renal impairment is confounded by anemia, uremic platelet dysfunction, arrhythmias, pericardial effusions, myocardial dysfunction, chronic hypertension, neuropathies, malnutrition, and susceptibility to infection. Of note, patients with chronic renal failure who are not yet on dialysis are at greater risk for developing acute renal failure.

Preoperatively patients must be euvolemic, normotensive, normonatremic, and normokalemic, not acidotic or severely anemic, and without significant platelet dysfunction. Suggested laboratory values include complete blood count, electrolytes, arterial blood gases, and template bleeding time. Bleeding time measured at the thigh rather than the arm is a better predictor of bleeding in the perioperative period. Dialysis usually corrects uremic platelet dysfunction and is best performed within the 24 hours before surgery. Administration of 1-deamino-8-D-arginine vasopressin (DDAVP) or cryoprecipitate is also of benefit.

Other indications for acute dialysis include uremic symptoms, pericardial tamponade, bleeding, hypervolemia, congestive heart failure, hyperkalemia, and severe acidosis.

Patients with ESRD who have left ventricular dysfunction or undergo major procedures with significant fluid shifts require pulmonary artery monitoring to guide fluid therapy. Sterile technique should be strictly followed when inserting any catheters. In minor procedures, fluids should be limited to replacement of urine and insensible losses. Hypotension and drugs with substantial renal excretion must be avoided. Succinylcholine increases extracellular potassium. Meperidine has a renally excreted, active toxic metabolite (normeperidine). As in the operative phase, postoperative potassium restriction and close monitoring of potassium levels is a must. Hyperkalemia should be considered in patients with ESRD who develop ventricular arrhythmias and experience a cardiac arrest. Rapid administration of calcium chloride temporizes the cardiac effects of hyperkalemia until further measures (administration of glucose and insulin, hyperventilation, administration of sodium bicarbonate and potassium-binding resins, and dialysis) can be taken to shift potassium intracellularly and to decrease total body potassium.

BIBLIOGRAPHY

1. Amoroso P, Lanigan C: Renal dysfunction and anesthesia. Curr Opin Anesth 8:267–270, 1995.
2. Aronson S: Monitoring renal function. In Miller RD (ed): Anesthesia, 4th ed. New York, Churchill Livingstone, 1994, pp 1293–1317.
3. Aronson S: Controversies: Should anesthesiologists worry about the kidney? Review Course Lectures. Anesth Analg 80(Suppl):68–73, 1995.
4. Aronson S, Thisthelwaite R, Walke R, et al: Safety and feasibility of renal blood flow determination during kidney transplant surgery with perfusion ultrasonography. Anesth Analg 80:353–359, 1995.
5. Burchardi H, Kaczmarczyk: The effect of anaesthesia on renal function. Eur J Anaesth 11:163–168, 1994.
6. Charlson ME, MacKenzie CR, Gold JP, et al: Postoperative changes in serum creatinine: When do they occur and how much is important? Ann Surg 209:328–333, 1989.
7. Guyton AC: Textbook of Medical Physiology, 8th ed. Philadelphia, W.B. Saunders, 1991.
8. Hock R, Anderson RJ: Prevention of drug-induced nephrotoxicity in the intensive care unit. J Crit Care 10:33–43, 1995.
9. Kellen M, Aronson S, Roizen MF, et al: Predictive and diagnostic tests of renal failure: A review. Anesth Analg 78:134–142, 1994.
10. Kellerman PS: Perioperative care of the renal patient. Arch Intern Med 154:1674–1688, 1994.
11. Kriz W, Bankir I: A standard nomenclature for structures of the kidney. Am J Physiol 254:F1, 1988.
12. Marik PE: Low-dose dopamine in critically ill oliguric patients: The influence of the renin angiotensin system. Heart Lung 22:171–175, 1993.
13. Sladen RN: Renal physiology. In Miller RD (ed): Anesthesia, 4th ed. New York, Churchill Livingstone, 1994, pp 663–688.
14. ter Wee PM, Smit AJ: Effects of intravenous infusion of low-dose dopamine on renal function in normal individuals and in patients with renal disease. Am J Nephrol 6:42–46, 1986.

48. INCREASED INTRACRANIAL PRESSURE

William D. Sefton, M.D.

1. Define elevated intracranial pressure.

Elevated intracranial pressure (ICP) is usually defined as a sustained pressure of 20 mmHg or greater within the subarachnoid space. The normal ICP is 10–20 mmHg.

2. What are the determinants of ICP?

The space-occupying contents of the skull—i.e., brain, cerebrospinal fluid (CSF), extracellular fluid, and blood perfusing the brain—are contained in the virtually fixed volume of the cranium. If any of these contents increases in volume, the ICP will increase.

3. How is ICP measured?

Various techniques are available. The standard method is a ventriculostomy, in which a burr hole is made in the cranium and a soft plastic catheter is introduced into the lateral ventricle. Saline-filled tubing is attached, and an external transducer measures the pressure in the fluid column of the tubing. Another common method is the subarachnoid bolt, which is also placed through a burr hole but does not require insertion through brain tissue or identification of the position of the ventricle. Pressure is transduced via saline-filled tubing. A third technique involves the insertion of a fiber-optic bundle through a small burr hole. The fiber-optic bundle senses changes in the amount of light reflected off a pressure-sensitive diaphragm at its tip. This system, commonly called a Camino (it is manufactured by Camino Laboratories), has recently gained popularity because of ease of placement and avoidance of difficulties associated with the fluid-filled transducing systems.

4. Summarize the conditions that commonly cause elevated ICP.

Common Causes of Elevated ICP

CSF DISORDERS	MASSES	HEAD TRAUMA	MIXED CAUSES
Communicating hydrocephalus	Neoplasm	Contusion	Bleeding from cerebral aneurysm or arteriovenous malformation
Obstructing hydrocephalus (e.g., from a posterior fossa lesion)	Hematoma (epidural or subarachnoid)	Cerebral edema	Hepatic encephalopathy
	Cysts	Cerebral lacerations	Malignant hypertension
			Cerebrovascular accident with edema

5. Describe the symptoms of increased ICP.

Symptoms associated with increased ICP alone include headache, vomiting, papilledema, drowsiness, loss of consciousness, and behavioral changes. Several other symptoms, such as pathologic (decerebrate) posturing, oculomotor nerve palsy, abnormalities of brain stem reflexes, and abnormal respiratory patterns (including apnea), are probably caused by brain stem distortion or ischemia secondary to elevated ICP. The classic Cushing reflex, consisting of hypertension and bradycardia, is probably due to medullary ischemia and generally occurs when ICP approaches systemic arterial pressure.

6. Discuss the possible consequences of increased ICP.

In addition to producing the above symptoms, the ultimate danger of increased ICP is a decrease in cerebral perfusion pressure, which may result in regional or global cerebral ischemia and possible irreversible neurologic damage. In addition, sufficient elevation of ICP may result in herniation of brain contents (across the falx cerebri or tentorium or inferiorly from the foramen magnum).

7. What are the determinants of cerebral perfusion pressure?

Cerebral perfusion pressure is defined as the difference between mean arterial pressure (MAP) and either ICP or central venous pressure (CVP), whichever is higher.

8. What is intracranial elastance? Why is it clinically significant?

Intracranial elastance, commonly misnamed intracranial compliance, refers to the variation in ICP in accordance with intracranial volume. Because intracranial components can shift their volumes to an extent (for example, CSF movement from the intracranial compartment to the spinal compartment), ICP remains somewhat constant over a certain range of volume. However, when compensatory mechanisms are exhausted, ICP rises rapidly with further increases in volume.

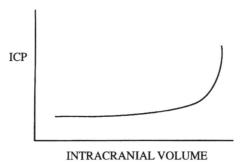

Intracranial elastance.

9. How is cerebral blood flow regulated?

Cerebral blood flow (CBF) is coupled to cerebral metabolic rate by an as yet uncharacterized mechanism. In general, increases in the cerebral metabolic rate for oxygen ($CMRO_2$) lead to increases in CBF, although the increase in flow is delayed by 1–2 minutes. Several other parameters influence flow. Specifically, an increase in the partial pressure of carbon dioxide in arterial blood ($PaCO_2$) is a powerful vasodilator that increases flow. Similarly, a decrease in the partial pressure of oxygen (PaO_2) in arterial blood below 50 mmHg greatly increases flow. Variations in MAP also may result in large increases or decreases in flow, but over a broad range flow is nearly constant. When the brain has been injured, as in stroke, tumor accompanied by edema, or trauma, autoregulation may not be intact. Systemic hypertension may result in precipitous increases in flow, with secondary increases in ICP leading to regional ischemia elsewhere.

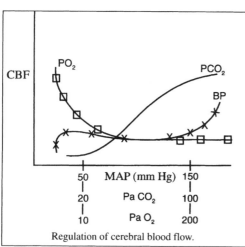

Regulation of cerebral blood flow.

10. What is the goal of anesthetic care for patients with elevated ICP?

Because patients with elevated ICP may be located on the elbow of the elastance curve, wherein a small change in volume leads to a large increase in ICP and probable decrease in cerebral perfusion, the goal of anesthetic care is to use all possible measures to reduce intracranial volume.

11. Can this goal be aided by preoperative interventions?

Traditionally, several techniques have been used to decrease intracranial volume before surgery, particularly when the volume is already increased by local edema surrounding brain tumors. Mild fluid restriction (intake of one-third to one-half of daily maintenance requirements) may decrease ICP over a period of several days. Corticosteroids are particularly effective in decreasing edema associated with tumors.

12. How is the goal of reduced intracranial volume achieved at induction of anesthesia?

Generally, the measures used at induction of anesthesia are geared specifically to reduce cerebral blood volume. If conscious and cooperative, the patient is encouraged to hyperventilate during preoxygenation to reduce $PaCO_2$. Most commonly used intravenous anesthetics, such as the barbiturates (usually thiopental), propofol, benzodiazepines, and etomidate lower CBF either by reducing cerebral metabolic rate or by direct cerebral vasoconstriction. Narcotics have a variable effect on CBF but are commonly used to blunt the sympathetic response to laryngoscopy and tracheal intubation. Common adjuncts include intravenous lidocaine, which is also a cerebral vasoconstrictor and may blunt the response to intubation, and short-acting beta blockers such as esmolol, which blunt systemic hypertension due to laryngoscopy. Ketamine is to be avoided, because it increases CBF and ICP.

13. How is ICP moderated during maintenance of anesthesia?

Most intraoperative maneuvers for controlling ICP rely on reduction of cerebral blood volume or total brain water content. Blood volume is minimized by hyperventilation to lower $PaCO_2$ (25–30 mmHg), which results in cerebral vasoconstriction, and by using anesthetic agents that decrease CBF. Maintaining the patient in a slightly head-up position promotes venous drainage. To shrink brain water content acutely, furosemide and mannitol are commonly used to promote diuresis. In addition, intravenous fluids are limited to the minimal amount necessary to maintain cardiac performance. The surgeon may drain CSF directly from the surgical field or use spinal drainage to decrease total intracranial volume. If oxygenation is not problematic, positive end-expiratory pressure should be avoided, because it can be transmitted to the intracranial compartment. Lastly, moderate hypothermia (approximately 35°C) decreases $CMRO_2$ and thus CBF.

14. Which intravenous fluids are used during surgery to minimize ICP?

In general, hypotonic crystalloid infusions should be avoided, because they may increase brain water content. Glucose-containing solutions are avoided because of evidence of worsened neurologic outcome if ischemia occurs in the setting of hyperglycemia. Therefore, hyperglycemia (serum glucose > 180 mg/dl) should be treated with insulin. Colloidal solutions are not superior to crystalloid. Glucose-free isotonic crystalloid appears to be the standard infusion in neurosurgical cases. Hetastarch has been associated with an elevation of prothrombin and partial thromboplastin times when given in volumes > 1 L.

15. What are the effects of volatile anesthetics on CBF?

All of the commonly used inhaled anesthetics have been noted to increase CBF and to uncouple $CMRO_2$ and CBF. The response of CBF to $PaCO_2$ is preserved.

16. How do neuromuscular blocking agents affect ICP?

Succinylcholine has been reported to increase ICP, but the clinical significance of this transient increase remains doubtful. The increase also appears to be attenuated by pretreatment with a defasciculating dose of a nondepolarizing relaxant. Therefore, in cases of emergent surgery in patients with a full stomach, rapid-sequence induction with succinylcholine is acceptable. Commonly used nondepolarizing agents have no effect on ICP and can be used safely.

17. Discuss strategies for controlling ICP at emergence from anesthesia.
Usually beta blockers such as esmolol and labetalol are given in divided doses to attenuate the increased sympathetic tone present at emergence. Nitroprusside, a direct-acting vasodilator, is also useful in controlling blood pressure when administered by infusion. In addition, as at induction, normo- or hypocarbia is preferred.

18. If the above measures fail to control ICP, what other measures are available?
Barbiturate coma has been used in patients refractory to other methods of ICP control. Typical doses of pentobarbital are 10 mg/kg given over 30 minutes to load, followed by three hourly doses of 5 mg/kg. This regimen usually provides a therapeutic serum level of 30–50 µg/ml. Maintenance is usually achieved by dosing of 1–2 mg/kg/hr.

19. In a patient with traumatic head injury, how should fluid resuscitation be prioritized?
As a general rule, hemodynamic stability takes precedence because cerebral hypoperfusion is clearly detrimental. Isotonic crystalloid and packed red blood cells are fluids of choice. Hetastarch is probably best avoided because of its ability to produce coagulopathy when given in larger volumes.

BIBLIOGRAPHY

1. Bendo A, Kass I, Hartung J, Cottrell JE: Anesthesia for neurosurgery. In Barash PG, Cullen BF, Stoelting RK (eds): Clinical Anesthesia, 3rd ed. Philadelphia, Lippincott Williams & Wilkins, 1997.
2. Cucchiara RF, Mahla ME: Anesthesia in patients with elevated intracranial pressure. In Barash PG, Deutsch S, Tinker J (eds): Refresher Courses in Anesthesiology, vol 21. Philadelphia, J.B. Lippincott, 1993, pp 177–188.
3. Gopinath SP, Robertson CS: In Cottrell JE, Smith DS (eds): Anesthesia and Neurosurgery, 3rd ed. St. Louis, Mosby, 1994, pp 676–677.
4. Michenfelder JD: Intracranial pressure. In Cucchiara RF, Michenfelder JD (eds): Clinical Neuroanesthesia. New York, Churchill Livingstone, 1990, pp 81–82.
5. Zornow MH, Scheller MS: Intraoperative fluid management during craniotomy. In Cottrell JE, Smith DS (eds): Anesthesia and Neurosurgery, 3rd ed. St. Louis, Mosby, 1994, pp 254–257.

49. MUSCULAR DISORDERS AND NEUROPATHIES

Timothy Fry, D.O.

1. What are major clinical features of muscular dystrophy?
The most severe form of muscular dystrophy, Duchenne's muscular dystrophy, is associated with painless degeneration and atrophy of skeletal muscle. Muscular dystrophy is a sex-linked recessive disease with signs and symptoms presenting between 2 and 5 years of age. Death is typically due to congestive heart failure or pneumonia.

2. Name the important systems involved with muscular dystrophy.
Degeneration of cardiac muscle, as demonstrated by progressive decrease in R-wave amplitude on electrocardiogram (ECG), may lead to a decrease in contractility and mitral regurgitation secondary

to papillary muscle dysfunction. The respiratory system also may be affected with degeneration of ventilatory muscles. A restrictive pattern is observed on pulmonary function testing. Patients are more prone to aspiration.

3. What are the anesthetic considerations in patients with muscular dystrophy?

Patients with muscular dystrophy may be more sensitive to the myocardial depressant effects of inhaled anesthetics. Succinylcholine should not be used because of the possibility of massive rhabdomyolysis, hyperkalemia, and subsequent cardiac arrest. In fact, cardiac arrest has been reported in patients with unrecognized muscular dystrophy. One should be aware of this possibility and have calcium readily available as an antidote. Nondepolarizing relaxants are acceptable but may be associated with longer than normal recovery times. Because smooth muscle may be affected, patients may have gastrointestinal tract hypomotility, delayed gastric emptying, and impaired swallowing, which may lead to increased risk of aspiration.

4. What is myotonic dystrophy?

Myotonic dystrophy, an autosomal dominant disease that usually presents in the second or third decade, is characterized by persistent contraction of skeletal muscle after stimulation. The contractions are not relieved by regional anesthetics, nondepolarizing muscle relaxants, or deep anesthesia. Deterioration of skeletal, cardiac, and smooth muscle function is progressive.

5. How does myotonic dystrophy affect the cardiopulmonary system?

Heart failure is rare, but dysrhythmias and atrioventricular block are common. Mitral valve prolapse occurs in 20% of patients. Restrictive lung disease, with mild hypoxia on room air and a weak cough, may lead to pneumonia.

6. What are the important relaxant considerations with myotonic dystrophy?

Succinylcholine produces exaggerated contraction of skeletal muscles, possibly making ventilation of the lungs and tracheal intubation difficult or impossible. The response to nondepolarizing muscle relaxants is normal.

7. What are the clinical manifestations of Guillain-Barré syndrome?

Guillain-Barré syndrome usually presents as a postinfectious state with sudden onset of weakness or paralysis, typically in the legs, that spreads cephalad over several days. The symptoms may involve the skeletal muscles of the arms, trunk, and head. Patients may have dysphagia due to pharyngeal muscle weakness and impaired ventilation due to intercostal muscle paralysis. Complete spontaneous recovery may occur within weeks. Mortality (3–8%) is typically due to sepsis, adult respiratory distress syndrome, pulmonary embolism, or cardiac arrest.

8. How is the autonomic nervous system affected?

Autonomic dysfunction is a common finding. Patients may experience wide fluctuations in blood pressure, profuse diaphoresis, peripheral vasoconstriction, tachycardia, cardiac conduction abnormalities, and orthostatic hypotension.

9. What are the major anesthetic considerations for patients with Guillain-Barré syndrome?

Because compensatory cardiovascular responses may be absent, patients may become hypotensive with changes in posture, mild blood loss, or positive pressure ventilation. On the other hand, laryngoscopy may produce exaggerated increases in blood pressure. Succinylcholine should not be used because of the potential for exaggerated potassium release in the presence of lower motor neuron lesions. Postoperative ventilation may be necessary and should be explained to the patient preoperatively.

10. What are the pathophysiologic features of Parkinson's disease?

Parkinson's disease, an adult-onset degenerative disease of the extrapyramidal system, is characterized by the loss of dopaminergic fibers and dopamine depletion in the basal ganglia.

The results are diminished inhibition of the extrapyramidal motor system and unopposed action of acetylcholine.

11. What are the clinical manifestations of Parkinson's disease?

Patients with Parkinson's disease display increased rigidity of the extremities, facial immobility, shuffling gait, rhythmic resting tremor, dementia, depression, diaphragmatic spasms, and oculogyric crisis. Oculogyric crisis is a form of dystonia in which the eyes are deviated in a fixed position for minutes to hours.

12. Why is orthostatic hypotension a common side effect in patients treated with levodopa?

Levodopa crosses the blood-brain barrier, where it is converted to dopamine. Increased levels of dopamine may increase myocardial contractility and heart rate. Renal blood flow is likely to increase, causing an increase in glomerular filtration rate and excretion of sodium. Intravascular fluid volume is therefore decreased, and the renin-angiotensin-aldosterone system is depressed. Orthostatic hypotension is a common finding. High concentrations of dopamine may cause negative feedback for norepinephrine production, which also causes orthostatic hypotension.

13. Describe the complications that may occur when patients with Parkinson's disease need anesthesia.

1. Abrupt withdrawal of levodopa may lead to skeletal muscle rigidity that interferes with adequate ventilation. Levodopa should be administered on the morning of surgery throughout the perioperative period.

2. Orthostatic hypotension, cardiac dysrhythmias, and even hypertension may occur.

3. Phenothiazines (e.g., chlorpromazine, promethazine, fluphenazine, prochlorperazine) and butyrophenones (e.g., droperidol) may antagonize the effects of dopamine in the basal ganglia. Metoclopramide inhibits dopamine receptors in the brain. These medications should be avoided.

4. Patients may be intravascularly volume-depleted; therefore, aggressive administration of crystalloid or colloid solutions may be required before induction of anesthesia.

14. What are the clinical signs and symptoms of Alzheimer's disease?

Alzheimer's disease accounts for 60% of the severe cases of dementia in the United States. The disease follows an insidious onset with progressive worsening of memory despite a normal level of consciousness. Computed tomography (CT) scan shows ventricular dilation and marked cortical atrophy.

15. What is the most significant anesthetic problem associated with Alzheimer's disease?

The inability of some patients to understand their environment or to cooperate with providers of medical care becomes an important anesthetic consideration. Sedative drugs may exacerbate confusion and probably should be avoided in the perioperative period. Regional techniques may be used with the understanding that the patient may be frightened or confused by the operating room environment. However, they avoid administration of volatile anesthetics and reduce opioid administration, which may be of benefit.

16. What are the hallmark features of multiple sclerosis?

The corticospinal tract neurons of the brain and spinal cord show random and multiple sites of demyelination, which result in visual and gait disturbances, limb paresthesias and weaknesses, and urinary incontinence. The onset of disease is typically between the ages of 15 and 40 years. The cause appears to be multifactorial, including viral and genetic factors. The course of multiple sclerosis is characterized by periods of exacerbations and remissions of symptoms. Residual symptoms eventually persist.

17. Do steroids have a role in the treatment of multiple sclerosis?

Steroids may shorten the duration of an attack but probably do not influence progression of the disease.

18. How do patient temperature and stress play a role in exacerbation?

It is thought that elevated temperature causes complete blocking of conduction in demyelinated neurons. Emotional stress and excessive fatigue should be avoided, because they may exacerbate symptoms.

19. What perioperative problems must be anticipated in patients with multiple sclerosis?

Surgical stress most likely will exacerbate the symptoms of multiple sclerosis. Even modest increases in body temperature ($> 1°C$) must be avoided. Spinal anesthesia has been implicated in postoperative exacerbation of symptoms. The mechanism is unknown, but epidural or peripheral nerve blocks may be a better choice for regional techniques. There are no known unique interactions between multiple sclerosis and drugs selected for general anesthesia, although succinylcholine may cause an exaggerated release of potassium.

20. Describe the neuropathies associated with diabetes.

1. Autonomic neuropathy. The diabetic patient with an autonomic neuropathy may manifest with one or all of the entities in the table below. A patient with autonomic neuropathy may not have angina pectoris in the presence of ischemic heart disease. Once an autonomic neuropathy develops, the mortality rate exceeds 50% over a 5-year period. Gastroparesis may place such patients at an increased risk of aspiration due to delayed gastric emptying.

2. Peripheral neuropathies. Diabetic patients may complain of sensory discomfort of the lower extremities or carpal tunnel syndrome. They also may develop segmental demyelination of the cranial, median, and ulnar nerves; numbness and tingling or burning and itching of the lower extremities; and skeletal muscle weakness of the upper and lower extremities.

Manifestations of Diabetic Autonomic Neuropathy

Orthostatic hypotension	Gastroparesis
Resting tachycardia	Bladder atony
Cardiac dysrhythmias	Impotence
Sudden death syndrome	Hypoglycemia

21. Describe postpoliomyelitis syndrome.

Postpoliomyelitis syndrome (postpolio syndrome) is characterized by progressive weakness that begins years after a severe attack of poliomyelitis. The syndrome typically presents many years after the acute disease as a progression of weakness in the originally affected muscles. Normal muscles are less often affected. Common signs and symptoms include fatigue, cold intolerance, joint deteriorations, muscle pain, atrophy, respiratory insufficiency, dysphagia, and sleep apnea. Patients with postpolio syndrome who complain of dysphagia may have some degree of vocal cord paralysis. Some patients have decreased lung function; considerable cardiorespiratory deconditioning also may be present.

22. What are the anesthetic considerations for patients with postpolio syndrome?

Patients should be informed about the possibility of postoperative mechanical ventilation after general anesthesia. If sleep apnea is present, the patient may have coexisting pulmonary hypertension. Dysphagia and vocal cord paralysis may place patients at increased risk for aspiration. If progressive skeletal muscle weakness is present, succinylcholine should be avoided because of the possibility of exaggerated potassium release.

BIBLIOGRAPHY

1. Ackerman MS: The patient with Parkinson's disease. In Frost EAM (ed): Preanesthetic Assessment 2. Boston, Birkhauser, 1989, pp 289–302.
2. Dierdorf SF: Anesthesia for patients with rare and coexisting disease. In Barash PG, Cullen BF, Stoelting RK (eds): Clinical Anesthesia. Philadelphia, 3rd ed. Philadelphia, Lippincott Williams & Wilkins, 1997.

3. Driscoll BP, Gracco C, Coelho C, et al: Laryngeal function in postpolio patients. Laryngoscope 105:35–41, 1995.
4. Eriksson LI: Neuromuscular disorders and anaesthesia. Curr Opin Anesthesiol 8:275–281, 1995.
5. Jubelt B, Drucker J: Post-polio syndrome: An update. Semin Neurol 13:283–290, 1993.
6. Katzman R: Alzheimer's disease. N Engl J Med 314:964–973, 1983.
7. Mitchell MM, Ali HH, Savarese JJ: Myotonia and neuromuscular blocking agents. Anesthesiology 49:44–48, 1978.
8. Stoelting RK, Dierdorf SF: Diseases of the nervous system. In Anesthesia and Co-existing Disease, 3rd ed. New York, Churchill Livingstone, 1993, pp 181–250.
9. Stoelting RK, Dierdorf SF: Skin and musculoskeletal diseases. In Anesthesia and Co-existing Disease, 3rd ed. New York, Churchill Livingstone, 1993, pp 427–457.

50. ANESTHETIC CONCERNS IN PATIENTS WITH SPINAL CORD INJURY

Andrew A. Shultz, M.D., and Kenneth Niejadlik, M.D.

1. What are the more common causes of spinal cord injuries (SCIs)?

Motor vehicle accidents are the most common cause of acute SCIs, followed by falls and sports injuries (especially diving accidents). It is estimated that cervical SCIs occur in approximately 1.5–3% of all major traumatic accidents. The most common nontraumatic cause of spinal cord transection is multiple sclerosis. Rheumatoid arthritis of the spine may cause subluxation of the C1 on the C2 vertebra, leading to progressive quadriparesis. In major urban regions, gunshot wounds are a major cause of SCIs. Lastly, vascular, infectious, and developmental abnormalities may cause damage to the spinal cord with neurologic sequelae.

2. Describe the blood supply to the spinal cord.

The superior cervical spinal cord derives the majority of its blood supply from the anterior spinal artery (ASA) and posterior spinal artery (PSA). The ASA originates from a medial branch of the vertebral arteries at the level of the foramen magnum and courses inferiorly along the anterior median fissure of the spinal cord, supplying approximately two-thirds of the anterior spinal cord. The paired PSAs originate from the intracranial portions of either the vertebral arteries or the posterior inferior cerebellar arteries and run down the posterior region of the spinal cord, supplying the posterior one-third of the spinal cord.

From the inferior cervical spinal cord caudally, the ASA and paired PSAs are joined by the radicular arteries, which form a plexus surrounding the cord. In the cervical regions, the radicular arteries originate from the vertebral, cervical, and inferior thyroid arteries. In the thoracic and lumbar regions, the radicular arteries originate from the intercostal, lumbar, or lateral sacral arteries.

3. What is the artery of Adamkiewicz?

The artery of Adamkiewicz is any one of a number of anterior radicular arteries from either an intercostal or lumbar branch of the aorta that supply the lumbar region of the spinal cord.

4. Which region of the spinal cord seems most predisposed to ischemia? Why?

The lower cervical spinal cord, specifically C5–C8, seems most predisposed to ischemic injury. This region is supplied almost exclusively by the small anterior and posterior spinal arteries and is deficient of the radicular artery plexus that supplies the more caudal regions of the spinal cord. Of note, manipulation of the head and neck during surgical positioning may further compromise blood flow to this already vulnerable area of the spinal cord.

5. What is the approximate range of autoregulation of blood supply to the spinal cord?

At least in animals, autoregulation of spinal cord perfusion is similar to autoregulation of cerebral blood flow; that is, blood flow between mean arterial pressures (MAPs) of 60–120 mmHg is held relatively constant. In contrast, blood flow above or below these values becomes flow dependent.

6. Describe the innervation of the diaphragm and accessory muscles of respiration.

Each hemidiaphragm is supplied by the ipsilateral phrenic nerve, which originates principally from the fourth cervical nerve (C4) with lesser contributions from the C3 and C5 segments.

Accessory Muscles of Respiration

MUSCLE	FUNCTION	INNERVATION
Sternocleidomastoid	Lifts sternum during inspiration	Accessory (cranial nerve XI)
Anterior serrati	Lift ribs during inspiration	Long thoracic
Scaleni	Lift the first two ribs during inspiration	Ventral rami of the cervical nerves
External intercostal	Lifts the ribs during inspiration	Intercostal or thoracoabdominal
Rectus abdominis	Used during forced expiration and coughing	Thoracoabdominal or subcostal
Internal intercostal	Pulls the ribs downward during expiration	Intercostal or thoracoabdominal

7. Describe the respiratory sequelae of acute SCI.

The major cause of death in patients with acute SCI is respiratory failure secondary to paralysis of the respiratory muscles. The level of SCI dictates the degree of ventilatory compromise.

Pentaplegia describes a state of SCI at the junction of the brain stem and spinal cord. Voluntary diaphragmatic contraction is not possible because of phrenic nerve paralysis. In addition, accessory muscles of respiration, including those controlled by cranial nerves (sternocleidomastoid, trapezius, pharyngeal), are no longer under voluntary control. As a result, the patient is chronically ventilator dependent.

Respiratory quadriplegia results from cervical lesions at approximately C2–C3, sparing the cranial and uppermost cervical nerves. Because of paralysis of the phrenic nerves and the nerves that innervate the accessory muscles of respiration, this condition also results in chronic ventilator dependence.

Cervical lesions below C4 permit partial functioning of the phrenic nerve, resulting in at least some degree of voluntary control of respiration. Vital capacities, however, are approximately 20–25% of normal.

Cervical lesions at or below C6 allow full diaphragmatic control. However, accessory muscles of respiration are affected, depending on the level of the spinal cord lesion. Expansion of the rib cage via the accessory muscles contributes to approximately 60% of tidal volume in healthy people.

Of note, acute reactions to injury may extend several segments superiorly and inferiorly from the level of the original lesion. This phenomenon may resolve, leading to eventual improvement of respiratory function.

8. Are other pulmonary complications seen in the quadriplegic patient?

Accessory muscle weakness or paralysis may result in absent or weak cough, predisposing to retained secretions, atelectasis, and hypoxia. Hypoxia, superimposed on acute gastric dilatation, may result in conditions ideal for regurgitation and aspiration, especially in pentaplegics with ineffective upper airway reflexes.

9. Which position facilitates ventilation in the quadriplegic patient—supine or upright? Why?

In the person without spinal injury, the upright position facilitates respiration, because the caudal migration of abdominal contents results in greater excursion of the diaphragm and lower end-expiratory volumes. In contrast, the supine position greatly improves ventilation in the quadriplegic patient. During inspiration, diaphragmatic contraction leads to compression of abdominal contents, which results in anterior displacement of the abdominal wall. Conversely, return of the diaphragm during expiration is facilitated by the elastic recoil of the abdominal wall as well as the cephalad movement of the abdominal contents. The net result of the supine position is decreased end-expiratory volume and greater excursion of the diaphragm.

The beneficial effects of gravity and abdominal wall recoil are lost when the quadriplegic patient assumes the upright position, in which the abdominal wall protrudes and the abdominal contents move toward the pelvis. In addition, the resting position of the diaphragm is lower. These factors result in decreased excursion and greater end-expiratory volumes. The anatomic advantages of the supine position should be exploited whenever the patient is breathing spontaneously in the intensive care unit (ICU) or operating room (OR).

10. What derangements in pulmonary function tests are seen in quadriplegics?

Vital capacity (VC) is reduced by 36–91% and is affected by the patient's posture (VC is greater in the supine and Trendelenburg positions than in the upright position).

Forced vital capacity (FVC) and forced expiratory volume at 1 second (FEV_1) are surprisingly not found to be lower in quadriplegics than in patients with lumbar lesions.

Total lung capacity (TLC) and **expiratory reserve volume** (ERV) are lower. **Reserve volumes** are higher, and **functional residual capacity** (FRC) is normal.

FEV_1/FVC ratio is normal, indicating no significant degree of airway obstruction.

Pulmonary function in quadriplegics generally tends to deteriorate from the time of acute injury to approximately day 4, at which time a gradual improvement through the second and third weeks is seen. Early deterioration in pulmonary function tests (PFTs) is thought to be secondary to the acute and transient upward spread of the spinal cord lesion due to edema and hemorrhage. Resolution of these acute processes and return of motor function result in improvement of PFTs.

11. What is Ondine's curse? Why is it seen in patients with acute SCI?

Ondine's curse, also called idiopathic or primary alveolar hypoventilation syndrome, is a condition in which spontaneous ventilation occurs only with voluntary effort and ceases during periods of inattention to breathing or sleep. This condition was named by Severinghaus and Mitchell after the 1939 play entitled *Ondine,* in which a knight, Hans, is unfaithful to a sea nymph, Ondine. In a jealous rage, Ondine places a curse on Hans whereby he must pay constant attention to his breathing.

Although mostly idiopathic, Ondine's curse also may occur after surgical or traumatic injury to the brain stem and high cervical regions of the spinal cord (especially the anterolateral region of C2–C4). Studies have demonstrated that the greatest danger of sleep apnea occurs during the first 5 nights after an acute SCI. Therefore, close observation of patients with high cervical lesions is warranted during this period.

12. Describe the nature and cause of neurogenic pulmonary edema.

A condition seen immediately after SCI, neurogenic pulmonary edema (NPE) is secondary to central nervous system insult, such as trauma to the spinal cord, stroke, increased intracranial pressure, seizures, tumors, or intracerebral hemorrhage. As the name implies, there must be a complete absence of concurrent cardiac or pulmonary disease.

The cause of NPE is controversial, but two mechanisms have been postulated. Animal studies have shown an acute increase in sympathetic activity after mechanically induced SCI, resulting in increased MAP, systemic vascular resistance (SVR), and pulmonary vascular resistance (PVR). The mediators of this response act at the pulmonary vascular bed to increase vascular permeability to proteins, leading to a pulmonary alveolar exudate and fluid accumulation. An alternative proposal suggests that increased hydrostatic forces in the pulmonary capillary secondary to transient afterload-induced left ventricular failure lead to NPE.

13. What hemodynamic changes can be seen in patients with acute SCI?

The initial hemodynamic findings, described as "spinal shock," may persist for 1–3 weeks after acute injury. Profound systemic hypotension may result from loss of vascular tone and consequent diminished preload. The extent of hypotension is directly related to the level of the spinal cord lesion and is more pronounced in cervical than lumbar lesions.

A broad spectrum of cardiac dysrhythmias is observed in the patient with acute SCI, including sinus bradycardia, P-wave changes, increased P-R interval, ectopic beats, and complete heart block. Supraventricular arrhythmias such as atrial fibrillation and multifocal atrial tachycardia may occur. Ventricular arrhythmias such as premature ventricular contractions (PVCs) and ventricular tachycardia (VT) are also observed. Bradycardia is also noted in cervical lesions because of a predominance of vagal tone at the sinoatrial (SA) node of the heart. This predominance results from a lack of sympathetic input (so-called cardioaccelerator fibers, T1–T4) to the heart.

The significance of such circulatory derangements is that the patient with acute SCI compensates poorly for sudden changes in posture, blood loss, or anesthetics with cardiodepressant or vasodilating properties.

14. Define autonomic hyperreflexia. What are its clinical manifestations?

Autonomic hyperreflexia (AH) is a syndrome of massive, disinhibited reflex sympathetic discharge in response to cutaneous or visceral stimulation below the level of a spinal cord lesion in paraplegic and quadriplegic patients. AH is seen only after the resolution of spinal shock and the return of spinal cord reflexes (approximately 1–3 weeks after injury). In AH, the sympathetic nervous system below the level of spinal cord transection is functionally isolated from all inhibiting influences of the brain stem and hypothalamus. Therefore, any afferent cutaneous or visceral stimulus that enters the spinal cord below the level of the lesion has the potential to trigger a widespread reaction called a "mass reflex" below the level of the lesion.

In general, the clinical manifestations of AH are a result of sympathetic nervous system (SNS) stimulation below the spinal cord lesion and compensatory parasympathetic nervous system (PNS) stimulation above the spinal cord lesion. The classic syndrome includes paroxysmal hypertension and compensatory bradycardia. Below the transection, sympathetically mediated pallor, pilomotor erection, somatic and visceral muscle contraction, and increased spasticity may be seen. Above the lesion, the PNS mediates internal vasodilation, resulting in flushing of the face and mucous membranes. Sweating and mydriasis are also common. If left untreated, severe hypertension may lead to confusion, seizures, encephalopathy, retinal and cerebral bleeds, subarachnoid hemorrhage, strokes, or death. Cardiac manifestations include left ventricular failure secondary to acute increased SVR, pulmonary edema, and myocardial ischemia. Electrocardiogram (ECG) findings may include atrioventricular dissociation, premature atrial contractions, PVCs, and acute atrial fibrillation.

15. What factors provoke AH?

In short, almost anything. Bladder distention seems to be the most common eliciting factor. However, almost any genitourinary stimulus may elicit AH, e.g., bladder catheterization, urinary tract infections, testicular torsion, or cystoscopy. The second most common cause of AH is gastrointestinal insults, including sigmoidoscopy, enemas, acute appendicitis, or perforated duodenal ulcers. Almost any stimulus below the level of the spinal cord lesion may cause AH, including temperature extremes, decubitus ulcers, sunburn, and tight clothing.

16. Which factors affect the severity and incidence of AH?

For any given spinal cord lesion, the more caudad the peripheral stimulus, the greater the sympathetic response. In other words, the severity of the response is proportional to the number of spinal cord segments interposed between the spinal cord lesion and the stimulus level. Therefore, the maximal SNS response results from stimulation of the anorectal area (S2–S4).

The critical level of spinal cord lesion for development of AH seems to be midthoracic, approximately T7. In fact, AH in some form is observed in 85% of patients with spinal cord lesions at or above T7. Lesions between T6 and T10 seem to produce minimal hemodynamic changes. Lesions at or below T10 produce no consistent hemodynamic changes consistent with AH. Such data indicate that the lower the spinal cord lesion, the greater the potential for compensatory vasodilation above the lesion; therefore, the lesser the hemodynamic response.

17. Discuss the prevention and treatment of AH.

Prevention of AH incorporates good comprehensive medical care of patients with spinal cord injury. In the operating room one must provide appropriate anesthesia even for operative procedures on insensate parts of the body; AH is an autonomic phenomenon independent of the patient's perception of pain.

Topical anesthetics are unreliable in preventing AH. Their inability to effectively block afferent transmissions from the deeper underlying muscle layers is the proposed explanation.

Subarachnoid blocks are highly effective in preventing AH in procedures involving the lower abdomen, pelvis, and lower extremities. Epidural anesthesia also may be effective; however, the most intense stimuli provoking AH originate from the S2–S4 segments, an area sometimes missed with epidural blocks. All regional techniques are plagued by technical difficulties secondary to vertebral column distortion, positioning, determining the level of blockade, and ruling out subarachnoid injection with epidural anesthesia. General anesthetics are effective if a deep plane of anesthesia is achieved before the surgical stimulus is begun.

AH, once suspected, should be treated immediately and aggressively. The stimulus should immediately be discontinued. Deepening the plane of anesthetic during a general anesthesia or raising the level of epidural anesthesia may prove to be effective.

Pharmacologic intervention includes several options. Sodium nitroprusside seems to be the drug of choice because of its titratability with sudden blood pressure changes; an arterial line is recommended. Calcium channel blockers are increasing in popularity, and nifedipine and nicardipine have been successfully used. Calcium channel blockers may be used both for prophylaxis (given 30 minutes before the procedure) and for an acute crisis. Alpha-adrenergic blocking agents have been used with limited efficacy, because they are most effective on receptors susceptible to circulating levels of norepinephrine (i.e., adrenal release) rather than to norepinephrine released at nerve terminals, which is thought to be the mechanism of AH.

18. How should the airway be managed in patients with potential or diagnosed SCI?

Patients with high cervical lesions have probably been intubated early in the course of treatment, either in the field or in the emergency department. Patients who present to the OR in acute respiratory distress, unconscious, or uncooperative should be managed with oral intubation; direct laryngoscopy should follow general anesthesia with a rapid-sequence technique. Manual in-line stabilization is used to counter extension or flexion during laryngoscopy and tracheal intubation. **Elective intubation** in the OR should be performed in an awake patient to allow neurologic evaluation both before and after intubation. After adequate topical anesthesia of the pharynx, transtracheal and superior laryngeal nerve blocks (contraindicated in patients with a full stomach) may be performed in preparation for fiber-optic oral or nasal tracheal intubation.

19. What about the use of succinylcholine in patients with SCI?

Within 48–72 hours after acute SCI, the denervated muscles respond with proliferation of extrajunctional acetylcholine receptors along the muscle cell membrane. Depolarization in response to administration of succinylcholine (SCh) involves both the neuromuscular junction and extrajunctional receptors. A large release of potassium into the circulation may result in ventricular fibrillation and cardiac arrest. Prior administration of a nondepolarizing muscle relaxant does not reliably decrease the potassium release associated with SCh administration in patients with SCI. Peak release of potassium in response to SCh occurs when the injury is approximately 2 weeks old. The duration of exaggerated potassium release is unknown, but it is thought to be reduced in 3–6 months. However, some authors advocate waiting at least 8 months after SCI to use SCh.

BIBLIOGRAPHY

1. Albin MS: Spinal cord injury. In Cottrell JE, Smith DS (eds): Anesthesia and Neurosurgery. St. Louis, Mosby, 1994, pp 713–743.
2. Amzallag M: Autonomic hyperreflexia. Int Anesthesiol Clin 31:87–102, 1993.
3. Ditunno JF, Formal CS: Chronic spinal cord injury. N Engl J Med 330:550–556, 1994.
4. Erickson RP: Autonomic hyperreflexia: Pathophysiology and medical management. Arch Phys Med Rehabil 61:431–440, 1980.
5. Lam AM: Acute spinal cord injury: Monitoring and anaesthetic implications. Can J Anaesth 38:R60–73, 1991.
6. Stoelting RK, Dierdorf SF: Anesthesia and Co-existing Disease, 3rd ed. New York, Churchill Livingstone, 1993, pp 226–230.

51. ANESTHETIC MANAGEMENT OF MYASTHENIA GRAVIS

James Duke, M.D.

1. Describe the clinical presentation of myasthenia gravis (MG).

Myasthenic patients present with generalized fatigue and weakness of striated muscles that worsen with repetitive muscular use and improve with rest. Very commonly, extraocular muscles are the first affected, and the patient complains of diplopia or ptosis. Of particular concern are myasthenic patients who develop weakness of their respiratory muscles or the muscles controlling swallowing and the ability to protect the airway from aspiration. Depending on whether extraocular, airway, or respiratory muscles are affected, MG may be described as ocular, bulbar, or skeletal, respectively.

2. What is the pathophysiologic process that leads to MG?

Myasthenia gravis is an autoimmune disease of the neuromuscular junction (NMJ). Antibodies to the acetylcholine (ACh) receptor (see question 3) may reduce the absolute number of functional receptors by direct destruction of the receptor, by blockade of the receptor, or by complement-mediated destruction. Antibodies are found in about 90% of all myasthenics. Additionally, when all myasthenics are compared, the absolute level of antibody correlates poorly with disease severity, though changes in antibody levels within individual patients may correlate with disease progression.

3. Discuss the anatomy and physiology of the NMJ.

The NMJ is a nicotinic cholinergic receptor at the synaptic juncture of a motor neuron and striated muscle. The small area of skeletal membrane known as the junction is chemically sensitive to ACh. Vesicles containing about 10,000 molecules of ACh congregate along thickened patches of axonal membrane known as "active zones." Across from the active zones on the postjunctional membrane are invaginations known as "junctional folds," which are the location of the ACh receptors. An action potential reaches the terminal neuron and stimulates binding of the vesicles with the membrane with the release of ACh. Diffusing across the synapse, ACh binds to and depolarizes the receptors, eventually producing an action potential that propagates along the muscular membrane, leading to the excitation-contraction mechanisms that result in muscular contraction. The action of ACh is terminated either through hydrolysis by the enzyme acetylcholinesterase (AChE) or by diffusion away from the NMJ.

4. Besides the abnormalities at the NMJ, can MG be pathologically associated with any other tissue?

Abnormalities of the thymus gland are associated with MG. The thymus is derived primarily from the third and fourth branchial arches and tends to be four-lobed, residing posterior to the sternum, although thymic tissue may be found throughout the mediastinum. Thymic hyperplasia, defined as a greater abundance of germinal centers, is more often seen in younger patients with MG. The typical patient is a female in the third decade of life. Thymomas are also associated with MG. These neoplasias of thymic epithelial cells are found in older myasthenics, often males in their fifth or sixth decade. Myasthenia gravis is also associated with other autoimmune diseases, including hyperthyroidism, diabetes mellitus, rheumatoid arthritis, and collagen vascular diseases. Malignancies are also noted with greater incidence in myasthenics.

5. How is MG diagnosed?
The very characteristic pattern of progressive fatigue that improves with rest suggests the diagnosis. Once suspected, careful electromyographic evaluation or provocative testing substantiates the clinical impression. Repetitive stimulation of muscle groups of myasthenic or normal individuals results in progressive diminution of motor action potentials. Nonmyasthenic individuals, with their normal complement of motor end plates, do not clinically manifest any signs that the motor action potentials are declining with repetitive stimulation. Myasthenics, with their markedly reduced population of receptors, manifest the diminution in action potentials electromyographically. The diminution is known as "fade." If at least three muscle groups are tested in myasthenics, 95% of these individuals demonstrate fade electromyographically. Provocative testing is undertaken by intravenously administering dilute solutions of the neuromuscular relaxant curare into an extremity isolated with a blood pressure cuff. A positive response is considered a 10% decrement in electromyographic testing from baseline values. Edrophonium chloride, a short-acting AChE inhibitor, is also useful in diagnosing MG. An intravenous dose of 2–10 mg produces a transient improvement in strength in most myasthenics tested.

6. Describe immunosuppressant therapy for MG.
Because MG is an autoimmune process, corticosteroids and other immunosuppressants (azathioprine and cyclophosphamide) have long been used in medical management. Rarely are they first-line therapy, because patients develop the sequelae of long-term steroid use, such as hypertension, hyperglycemia, poor wound healing, fluid and electrolyte disturbances, gastric erosions, and impaired immunity, as well as the potential for steroid-induced myopathy and enhanced weakness. Plasmapheresis may be of transient benefit in profoundly weakened myasthenics who have failed medical management and are awaiting thymectomy.

7. Discuss the pros and cons of anticholinesterase therapy. Where else in the practice of anesthesia are anticholinesterases used?
Anticholinesterase agents have been employed in the therapy of MG for more than 50 years. Their mechanism of action is through reversible inhibition of AChE, the enzyme that metabolizes ACh. Because of its prolonged duration of effect, pyridostigmine is most commonly prescribed. A sustained-release preparation is available for myasthenics so profoundly affected that they may experience difficulty swallowing their morning doses. Anticholinesterases are used daily by anesthesiologists to reverse the residual effects of nondepolarizing muscle relaxants. By inhibiting ACh breakdown, anticholinesterases essentially overcome the competitive antagonism of the nondepolarizing relaxants at the NMJ. Doses to reverse motor blockade are much greater than are needed to treat myasthenic symptoms.

8. What is the role of surgery in the treatment of MG?
Numerous studies document that thymectomy arrests progress of the disease, decreases mortality, and accelerates remission. The exact indications, timing of surgery, and surgical approach are matters of controversy. Thymomas, generalized MG, and the necessity to administer steroids to control symptoms are considered indications for surgery. Formerly, surgery was undertaken only if the patient failed medical management, but it is now recognized that thymectomy early in the clinical course of the disease favors greater postoperative symptomatic improvement and possibly even remission. The alternative surgical approaches are transcervical and transsternal

thymectomy. Surgeons who favor the former approach believe there is less postoperative embarrassment in respiration, whereas those who favor the latter approach believe that mediastinal exenteration is necessary to obliterate all remains of thymic tissue.

9. What are some of the principal anesthetic concerns in the management of a myasthenic patient for any operative procedure?

Principal concerns include the degree of pulmonary impairment produced by the disease, the magnitude of bulbar involvement with attendant impairment in handling oral secretions (risk of pulmonary aspiration), and adrenal suppression from long-term steroid use. It is best to continue oral anticholinesterases the morning of surgery, though some practitioners believe that skipping the morning dose may later avoid the need for neuromuscular blockade. Although uncommon, cardiac disease that is MG-related should be considered in the preoperative evaluation. Because symptoms are primarily related to arrhythmias, an electrocardiogram (ECG) should be evaluated. Symptoms of congestive heart failure should be sought as well.

10. Can the likelihood of postoperative ventilation be predicted?

Postoperative mechanical ventilation has been required in up to 30% of all myasthenic patients studied. Because the potential need for ventilatory assistance is significant, attempts have been made to identify predictors of postoperative ventilation. Leventhal et al. identified four risk factors that correctly identified the need for ventilatory support in 91% of those studied:

1. Duration of disease longer than 6 years
2. History of chronic respiratory disease
3. Pyridostigmine dose 48 hours preoperatively of greater than 750 mg/day
4. Preoperative vital capacity of less than 2.9 L.

Eisenkraft et al. found this scoring system greatly overestimated the number of myasthenic patients requiring postoperative ventilation. His group found advanced, generalized disease, a previous history of MG-related respiratory failure, and associated steroid therapy more predictive. Perhaps the utility of any scoring system is to draw attention to the significant clinical features that may portend ventilatory failure.

11. Describe the altered responsiveness of myasthenic patients to muscle relaxants.

Because of the decreased number of functional NMJs, understanding the altered responsiveness of myasthenic patients to relaxants is absolutely fundamental. Depolarizing and nondepolarizing relaxants have been administered safely, although at altered doses, to myasthenic patients. But consideration should always be given to alternatives to muscle relaxants. Because these patients are clinically weak, pharmacologic relaxation is often unnecessary. The inhalational anesthetics are well known to facilitate muscular relaxation and intubation and often prove suitable. Perhaps the surgical procedure contemplated could be performed under a regional anesthetic or nerve block, eliminating the need for relaxation altogether. Muscle relaxants sometimes may be indicated, however, and understanding the pharmacodynamic principles is essential.

Like ACh, succinylcholine (SCh), a **depolarizing** muscle relaxant, is dependent on binding to the NMJ, where under normal situations it depolarizes the NMJ for a prolonged period, relative to ACh. Numerous case reports have demonstrated that in MG, where there are fewer functional receptors, patients actually have been resistant to SCh. However, the degree of resistance does not appear to be of great clinical significance. Myasthenic patients, when given 2 mg/kg (still considered a normal acceptable dose) instead of 1 mg/kg of SCh, experienced satisfactory intubating conditions only seconds after nonmyasthenic persons.

Myasthenic patients are more sensitive than nonmyasthenic persons to the **nondepolarizing** relaxants. Numerous case reports have demonstrated that nondepolarizing relaxants of short or intermediate duration may be safely used in MG. Dosing should start at about one-tenth of usual recommended doses. Recovery time for these reduced doses is quite variable but may be quite prolonged. Close electromyographic monitoring is essential. Relaxation should be reversed at case conclusion and the patient carefully evaluated for return of strength.

Patients in remission should be presumed to persist in their sensitivity to the nondepolarizing relaxants. A case report describes a physically vigorous myasthenic patient, 9 years postthymectomy, on no medications, who experienced prolonged paralysis after receiving a normal intubating dose of 0.1 mg/kg of vecuronium. One might say, "once a myasthenic, always a myasthenic."

12. Are there any medications (besides the relaxants) that might potentiate the weakness found in MG?

Aminoglycosides, magnesium, lithium, calcium channel blockers, and antiarrhythmics all have been reported to exacerbate myasthenic symptoms. The effects may be prejunctional (decreasing ACh release), postjunctional (decreasing sensitivity of the receptor), or secondary to intrinsic weak relaxant properties.

13. Do intravenous anesthetic agents have altered effects in persons with MG?

Intravenous agents do not appear to offer significant disadvantages in myasthenic individuals. Opioids and sedatives do have the potential to depress respiratory drive, could become problematic in a myasthenic patient with respiratory impairment, and are best titrated to effect. The action of ester anesthetics may be prolonged, as they are metabolized by plasma cholinesterases, enzymes that may be impaired by anticholinesterase medications.

14. How might a myasthenic patient respond to volatile anesthetic agents?

Potent inhaled agents have muscle relaxant properties in general and may be used to advantage in myasthenic patients. Often they are the sole agent used to facilitate muscular relaxation. Neuromuscular transmission may by impaired by volatile agents through inhibition of ACh release and by desensitization of the postjunctional receptor.

15. What are the postanesthetic concerns in a patient with MG?

Assessing whether the patient has adequate respiratory capabilities is a primary concern prior to extubation. Neuromuscular function should be assessed electromyographically. If relaxants were given, they should be reversed with an appropriate anticholinesterase. Strength should be assessed. The patient should be able to demonstrate a sustained head-lift for 5 seconds. Vital capacity should be at least 15 ml/kg, and the patient should generate a negative inspiratory force of 25 cm H_2O. Because these patients can have weakness of upper airway musculature, be wary of the patient who may generate apparently adequate respiratory activity while still intubated but suffer upper airway collapse and obstruction after extubation. At least 3 hours of clinical stability should be observed in a postoperative care unit (PACU) if consideration is being given to discharging a recovering myasthenic patient to a routine surgical floor. Otherwise, in a patient who was significantly compromised prior to surgery or whose immediate recovery period has proved somewhat problematic, postoperative disposition should be made to an intermediate care or intensive care unit. Anticholinesterase agents are usually introduced orally once the patient is awake and strong enough to swallow.

16. What are myasthenic and cholinergic crises, and how might they be differentiated?

Receptors responsive to ACh are described as cholinergic and further subclassified as nicotinic or muscarinic. The NMJ is a nicotinic receptor. Ganglionic receptors are muscarinic. Efforts to increase nicotinic (NMJ) receptor stimulation, a goal in myasthenic therapy, run the risk of overstimulation of the muscarinic, cholinergic receptors, producing a cholinergic crisis. Cholinergic crises result from relative overdosing of anticholinesterases. Should a patient's myasthenic symptoms improve, either spontaneously, after thymectomy, or from corticosteroid administration, a "usual" dose of anticholinesterase may prove excessive, precipitating a cholinergic crisis. Patients with ocular myasthenia may be particularly at risk, as extraocular muscles tend to be resistant to the effects of anticholinesterases. Adequate doses to improve ptosis and diplopia may produce generalized muscarinic symptoms and weakness of other muscle groups.

Signs and symptoms of muscarinic overstimulation include excessive salivation, lacrimation, urinary incontinence, diarrhea, bronchorrhea, pulmonary edema, miosis and paralysis of accommodation (blurred vision), as well as weakness. Collectively, this is known as the **SLUDGE syndrome**.

The hallmark of a myasthenic crisis is acute respiratory insufficiency and may be precipitated by infections, exertion, menstruation, emotional stress or acute illness, or underdosing of anticholinesterase medication. Pupils tend to be mydriatic. Because both crises involve weakness and acute respiratory failure, recognition and differentiation depend on review of historical information, searching for SLUDGE symptoms, and examination of the pupils. Edrophonium chloride, given cautiously in 1-mg doses, should improve a myasthenic crisis. Anticholinesterases are withheld if a cholinergic crisis is likely. In either case, the airway should be protected and the patient ventilated.

BIBLIOGRAPHY

1. Adams SL, Matthews J, Grammer LC: Drugs that may exacerbate myasthenia gravis. Ann Emerg Med 13:532–538, 1984.
2. Baraka A: Anaesthesia and myasthenia gravis. Can J Anaesth 39:476–486, 1992.
3. Drachman DB: Myasthenia gravis. N Engl J Med 330:1797–1810, 1994.
4. Eisenkraft JB, Book WJ, Mann SM, et al: Resistance to succinylcholine in myasthenia gravis: A dose-response study. Anesthesiology 69:760-763, 1988.
5. Eisenkraft JB, Papatestas AE, Kahn CH, et al: Predicting the need for postoperative mechanical ventilation in myasthenia gravis. Anesthesiology 65:79–82, 1986.
6. Leventhal SR, Orkin FK, Hirsh RA: Prediction of the need for postoperative mechanical ventilation in myasthenia gravis. Anesthesiology 53:26–30, 1980.
7. Lumb AB, Calder I: "Cured" myasthenia gravis and neuromuscular blockade. Anaesthesia 44:828–830, 1989.
8. Wilkins KB, Bulkley GB: Thymectomy in the integrated management of myasthenia gravis. Adv Surg 32:105–133, 1999.

52. MALIGNANT HYPERTHERMIA

Lee Weiss, M.D.

1. Define malignant hyperthermia.

Malignant hyperthermia (MH) is an inherited myopathy characterized by a hypermetabolic state after exposure to an appropriate triggering agent. A defect at the sarcoplasmic reticulum leads to decreased calcium reuptake. Specifically, the ryanodyne receptor (a calcium release channel) fails, and intracellular calcium increases 500-fold, leading to sustained muscle contractions, glycolysis, and heat production. The incidence is 1 out of 15,000 pediatric and 1 out of 50,000 adult anesthetics.

2. Name the MH triggers.

MH is an anesthetic-related disease. Medications definitely identified as triggers include:
- Depolarizing muscle relaxants (e.g., succinylcholine)
- Potent inhalational agents (e.g., halothane, isoflurane, enflurane, desflurane, sevoflurane)

3. Which anesthetic agents are safe?

The following agents have been found safe in patients susceptible to MH:
- Benzodiazepines • Barbiturates

• Local anesthetics   • Nondepolarizing muscle relaxants
• Propofol   • Ketamine

Ketamine and pancuronium should be used with caution in MH-susceptible patients, because the resulting tachycardia may mask the onset of MH.

4. Describe the clinical syndrome and intraoperative diagnosis.

The initial signs are an increase in end-tidal carbon dioxide and decrease in arterial oxygen saturation, tachycardia and dysrhythmias, rigidity (despite the use of a muscle relaxant), and tachypnea (in spontaneously breathing patients). An unexplained tachycardia, however, is usually the first sign. Other findings are hyperthermia and cyanosis. When clinical signs are suggestive of MH, several laboratory tests may lead to a presumptive diagnosis. Blood gas analysis reveals metabolic acidosis. Other metabolic abnormalities include hyperkalemia, hypercalcemia, hyperphosphatemia, creatinine kinase levels > 1000 IU, and myoglobinuria. All of these tests are suggestive of the diagnosis, but a caffeine and halothane contracture test performed postoperatively is more definitive.

5. Define masseter muscle rigidity (MMR). What is its relationship to malignant hyperthermia?

After administering succinylcholine and documenting loss of twitches on neuromuscular stimulation, difficulty in opening the mouth represents MMR. Such patients may be susceptible to MH; a full-blown episode typically occurs 20–30 minutes after the onset of MMR. The incidence of MMR is 1% in children induced with halothane and succinylcholine and 2.8% in children having strabismus surgery. Such patients are prone to an increase in creatinine kinase, myoglobinuria, tachycardia, and dysrhythmias independent of MH. It is controversial whether to proceed with an anesthetic if the patient develops MMR. Some anesthesiologists elect to cancel the scheduled procedure, whereas others continue the case using an anesthetic that does not involve triggering agents.

6. How is MH diagnosed?

The diagnosis of MH is immensely more difficult than its treatment. A suspicion that testing is needed is based on patient history, positive family history, or previous anesthetic remarkable for clinical features of MH. Key features in the patient's history include strabismus, myalgias on exercise, tendency to fever, myoglobinuria, muscular disease, and intolerance of caffeine. Patients requiring a more definitive diagnosis are referred for muscle biopsy. A caffeine and halothane contraction test (the gold standard) is performed on muscle obtained by biopsy. Caffeine and halothane decrease the threshold for muscle contraction and therefore facilitate diagnosis. This test is 85% specific and 100% sensitive. Creatine phosphokinase is elevated in 70% of susceptible patients. A genetic test of the ryanodyne receptor may eventually be developed.

7. How is MH treated?

1. Call for help; management is involved and difficult for one person.
2. Discontinue triggering agents.
3. Hyperventilate the patient with 100% oxygen.
4. Expedite or abort procedure.
5. Administer dantrolene (2.5 mg/kg bolus; may repeat 2 mg/kg every 5 minutes, then 1–2 mg/kg/hr).
6. Cool patient (cold intravenous normal saline, cold body cavity lavage, ice bags to body, cold nasogastric lavage, cooling blanket).
7. Change to a clean circuit not exposed to volatile agents.
8. Monitor and treat acidosis (follow serial arterial blood gases and administer sodium bicarbonate).
9. Promote urine output (maintain > 2 ml/kg/hr urine output with conscientious fluid management; furosemide, 0.5–1.0 mg/kg IV; and 20% mannitol, 1 g/kg IV).

10. Treat hyperkalemia (0.1–0.2 U/kg regular insulin + 500 mg/kg dextrose IV).

11. Treat dysrhythmias with procainamide and calcium chloride, 2–5 mg/kg IV (calcium chloride is used to treat the hyperkalemia-associated dysrhythmias).

12. Monitor creatinine kinase, urine myoglobin, and coagulation for 24–48 hours.

8. Why is procainamide the drug of choice for dysrhythmias?

Most antiarrhythmic agents can be used without difficulty. However, in addition to controlling multiple arrhythmias, procainamide inhibits abnormal drug-induced contraction in MH-susceptible muscle in vitro. On the other hand, calcium channel blockers should not be used; in combination with dantrolene, they may cause hyperkalemia and cardiovascular collapse.

9. Describe the mechanism of action of dantrolene.

Dantrolene impairs calcium-dependent muscle contraction. Side effects are muscle weakness, hyperkalemia, gastrointestinal upset, and thrombophlebitis. The solution is prepared by mixing 20 mg of dantrolene with 3 g of mannitol in 60 ml of water. Preparation is tedious and time-consuming, requiring several people to mix the dantrolene into solution; this is one reason to call for help.

10. Describe the preparation of an anesthetic for MH-susceptible patients.

1. Clean machine; remove vaporizers; and replace CO_2 canisters, bellows, and gas hose.

2. Flush the machine for 20 minutes with 10 L/min.

3. Have the MH cart in the operating room (this cart contains all the supplies needed to resuscitate a patient with MH).

4. Schedule the patient as the first case of the day, and notify the postanesthesia care unit to be prepared to provide the necessary manpower.

5. Consider dantrolene and sedation for premedication.

6. Check creatinine kinase and complete blood count preoperatively.

7. Consider anesthetic alternatives; monitor anesthetic care with sedation and local anesthesia, regional anesthesia, or a general anesthetic using nontriggering agents (e.g., oxygen, propofol, and vecuronium).

8. After surgery check laboratory values and monitor patient in an appropriate setting (intensive care unit vs. step-down unit, depending on the need for invasive monitoring).

11. What syndromes are associated with MH?

There is a strong correlation between central core disease (a sarcoplasmic myopathy characterized by proximal muscle weakness) and MH. Other syndromes with decreasing risk include Duchenne's dystrophy (an X-linked myopathy), King-Denborough syndrome (characterized by short stature, musculoskeletal abnormalities, and mental retardation), myoadenylate deaminase deficiency, Fukuyama's muscular dystrophy, and Becker's muscular dystrophy.

12. Compare neuroleptic malignant syndrome with MH.

Neuroleptic malignant syndrome (NMS), which may be confused with MH, may appear 24–72 hours after administration of a psychotropic drug (e.g., haloperidol, fluphenazine, clozapine, perphenazine, thioridazine). The cause of NMS is related to dopamine receptor blockade in the hypothalamus and basal ganglia. NMS is characterized by akinesia, muscle rigidity, hyperthermia, tachycardia, cyanosis, autonomic dysfunction, sensorium change, diaphoresis, and elevated levels of creatinine kinase. NMS has a mortality rate of 10%. Treatment is with dantrolene or bromocriptine (a dopamine receptor agonist). Patients with NMS are not prone to MH.

CONTROVERSY

13. Should patients with MH be pretreated with dantrolene?

MH can be prevented by giving dantrolene preoperatively. However, many problems are associated with its use. Dantrolene may mask or delay the diagnosis of MH. Pretreatment depletes the supply of this expensive medication and may induce or worsen muscle weakness; dantrolene is synergistic with muscle relaxants. The anesthesiologist still needs to prepare a nontriggering anesthetic.

BIBLIOGRAPHY

1. Gronert GA, Antognini JF: Malignant hyperthermia. In Miller RD (ed): Anesthesia, 4th ed. New York, Churchill Livingstone, 1994, pp 1075–1094.
2. Levitt RC: Prospects for the diagnosis of malignant hyperthermia susceptibility using molecular approaches. Anesthesiology 76:1039–1048, 1992.
3. Maclennan DH, Phillips MS: Malignant hyperthermia. Science 256:789–794, 1992.
4. Miller JD, Lee C: Muscle diseases. In Katz J, Benumof JL, Kadis LB (eds): Anesthesia and Uncommon Diseases, 3rd ed. Philadelphia, W.B. Saunders, 1990, pp 590–644.
5. Rosenberg H: Understanding Malignant Hyperthermia. Westport, CT, Malignant Hyperthermia Association of the United States, 1992.

53. ALCOHOLISM

Andrew M. Veit, M.D.

Ninety percent of Americans consume alcohol at some point in their lives. Alcoholism affects 15% of the American population: 200,000 deaths per year are attributed to alcohol, and one-third of all adults have medical problems related to alcohol use. Because of the high prevalence of alcoholism and alcohol use in the U.S., it is important to understand the pharmacologic and physiologic effects of alcohol and how they affect the delivery of an anesthetic.

1. How is alcohol absorbed and metabolized?

Alcohol is absorbed across the gastrointestinal mucosa by simple diffusion. Absorption is greater in the small intestine than in the stomach. The volume of distribution (Vd) of alcohol is that of body water, which is equal to approximately 80% of total body weight. The distribution of alcohol to the tissues is related directly to tissue blood flow, and alcohol easily crosses the blood-brain barrier. Five to ten percent of consumed alcohol is excreted unchanged in the breath and urine. Alcohol **excretion** follows first-order kinetics: the rate of excretion is directly proportional to the concentration of alcohol in the blood. Arterial blood levels of alcohol correlate well with concentrations in lung alveoli, hence the basis of the breathalyzer test used by law enforcement officers.

Alcohol is **metabolized** primarily in the liver. The majority of consumed alcohol is metabolized to acetaldehyde by the enzyme alcohol dehydrogenase. Alcohol metabolism follows Michaelis-Menten zero-order kinetics. When alcohol dehydrogenase is saturated with ethanol, the rate of metabolism is constant, although alcohol concentration may increase. Nicotinamide adenine dinucleotide (NAD) acts as a cofactor in the oxidation of alcohol to acetaldehyde by accepting a hydrogen molecule. The hepatic conversion of reduced NAD to NAD is the rate-limiting step in alcohol metabolism. When the liver can no longer keep up with the demand for production of NAD, normal liver function is impaired. In addition, an insignificant amount of alcohol is also metabolized during first-pass through the gastric mucosa and in the microsomes of endothelial cells.

An average adult is able to metabolize approximately 10 ml of alcohol per hour. Four ounces of whiskey or 1.2 L of beer require approximately 5–6 hours for metabolism. At this slow rate it is not difficult to envision how blood alcohol levels rise to intoxicating levels quite quickly. The maximal amount of alcohol that an average adult can metabolize in a 24-hour period is 450 ml.

Oxidation of alcohol to acetaldehyde.

2. What is the mechanism of action of alcohol?

The exact mechanism of action of alcohol is unknown. Alcohol is thought to have a widespread disordering effect on cell membranes, which, in turn, alters the action of membrane-bound proteins. Centrally, the inhibitory action of alcohol, thought to be mediated by gamma-aminobutyric acid [GABA] receptors, results in disinhibition.

3. What are the acute and chronic effects of alcohol on the nervous system?

In **acute** terms, alcohol depresses the central nervous system by inhibiting polysynaptic function. Disorder of polysynaptic pathways is manifested by generalized blunting and loss of higher motor, sensory, and cognitive function. Although the behavioral effects of alcohol consumption may seem excitatory or stimulating to observers and users, this impression is probably due to a depressive effect on inhibitory pathways (disinhibition).

Chronic alcohol use is associated with peripheral nerve and neuropsychiatric disorders, many of which—such as Wernicke's encephalopathy, Korsakoff's psychosis, and nicotinic acid deficiency encephalopathy—may be linked to nutritional deficiencies. Alcohol-related neuropathy usually involves pain and numbness in the lower extremities, often with concomitant weakness of the intrinsic muscles of the feet. Patients may exhibit hypalgesia in a stocking-foot distribution, and the Achilles tendon reflex may be absent. Finally, generalized weakness in the proximal limb musculature also may be seen with chronic alcohol use.

4. What are the effects of alcohol on the cardiovascular system?

Moderate **acute** ingestion of alcohol produces no significant changes in blood pressure (BP) or myocardial contractility. Cutaneous vasodilatation occurs and heart rate increases via sympathetic reflex. At toxic levels of acute alcohol ingestion, a decrease in central vasomotor activity causes respiratory and cardiac depression.

The leading cause of death in **chronic** users of alcohol is cardiac dysfunction. Consumption of 60 ounces of ethanol per month (8 pints of whiskey or 55 cans of beer) may lead to the development of alcohol-induced hypertension. An intake > 90 ounces per month over a 10-year period may lead to the development of congestive cardiomyopathy. The cardiomyopathy of alcoholism is associated with pulmonary hypertension, right-heart failure, and dysrhythmias. The most common dysrhythmias are atrial fibrillation and premature ventricular contractions. Patients with left ventricular disease, however, are subject to ventricular tachydysrythmias, ventricular fibrillation, and sudden death.

5. How does alcohol affect the respiratory system?

Acute alcohol intake may cause hyperventilation via disinhibition of central respiratory regulation centers. Hyperventilation increases dead-space ventilation (ventilation of the bronchial air space as opposed to the alveolar air spaces). Despite hyperventilation, alcohol depresses the ventilatory response to carbon dioxide. The most significant danger to the respiratory tract associated with acute alcohol intoxication is chemical pneumonitis caused by the aspiration of gastric contents.

Chronic alcohol use may lead to dysfunction of the cilia lining the respiratory tract, inhibition of macrophage mobility, and reduction in surfactant production. Chronic alcohol users are more susceptible to pulmonary infection, often by staphylococci or gram-negative organisms. Chronic alcohol users with concurrent liver and heart disease may have pulmonary hypertension and pulmonary congestion as well as a generalized decrease in all lung capacities: vital capacity, functional residual capacity, and inspiratory capacity.

6. How does alcohol affect the gastrointestinal and hepatobiliary systems?

Phrenohepatology is a historical technique defined as the study of determining a patient's alcohol history by palpating the bumps on his liver. Acute alcohol use may cause esophagitis, gastritis, and pancreatitis. Chronic alcohol use leads to delayed gastric emptying and relaxation of the lower esophageal sphincter. This, in turn, increases the risk of gastric acid aspiration.

The liver undergoes transient and reversible fatty infiltration during acute alcohol use. Although such changes resolve with abstinence and the cycle can repeat itself many times, prolonged alcohol exposure leads to chronic infiltration of fat, which over time progresses to necrosis and fibrosis of liver tissue. The initial presentation of fatty liver changes is hepatomegaly. When necrosis, fibrosis, and cirrhosis become apparent, the liver regresses in size. Consumption of 90 ounces of ethanol per day over a 10-year period leads to irreversible cirrhosis, and 10–15% of such patients later suffer from alcohol-induced hepatitis. Alcohol-induced hepatitis is a serious complication of cirrhosis and carries a 30% mortality rate.

In addition to structural changes, the synthetic function of the liver is also impaired. Production of albumin and coagulation factors II, V, VII, X, and XIII is decreased. Reduction of albumin results in lower intravascular oncotic pressure and may lead to tissue edema. A reduction in circulating coagulation factors may predispose to bleeding, which is evidenced by a prolonged prothrombin time (PT).

7. How is the blood supply to the liver altered by cirrhosis?

The blood supply to the liver is derived from the portal vein and hepatic artery. The portal vein provides 75% of hepatic blood flow and 55% of hepatic oxygen supply. The structural changes that occur with cirrhosis reduce portal blood flow, making the liver more dependent on the hepatic artery for blood supply. Blood from the splanchnic beds, no longer able to pass through the liver, is diverted through portosystemic collateral channels: the esophageal venous plexus, splenic vein, epigastric venous plexus, perineal venous plexus, and mediastinal veins. Over time the collateral vessels dilate and undergo varicose changes.

8. Which nutritional deficiencies are seen in chronic alcohol users?

Chronic alcohol use leads to deficiencies of thiamine and folic acid. Beriberi (thiamine deficiency), which is commonly seen in third-world countries where milled rice is a dietary staple, presents as Wernicke's encephalopathy, polyneuropathy, and cardiac failure. The cardiac failure in thiamine deficiency is characterized by high cardiac output, low systemic vascular resistance, and loss of vasomotor tone. Folic acid deficiency causes bone marrow depression and leads to thrombocytopenia, leukopenia, and anemia.

9. What are the effects of alcohol on inhalational anesthetics?

In acutely intoxicated, nonhabituated patients the requirement for inhalational anesthetics is decreased. In other words, the minimal alveolar concentration (MAC) of inhalational agents is reduced. By definition, MAC describes the alveolar concentration of inhalational anesthetic that prevents 50% of patients from moving away from surgical stimulation. The alveolar concentration of an inhalational anesthetic necessary to provide adequate analgesia in healthy patients is close to the lethal level in intoxicated patients. Studies demonstrate that the concentration of halothane required to produce respiratory arrest in nonhabituated, intoxicated patients is not significantly different from the concentration that causes cardiac arrest. For chronic users of alcohol, the MAC for inhalational agents is increased. This is evidenced by the fact that chronic alcohol exposure leads to the development of tolerance to the pharmacodynamic and central nervous system depressant effects of inhalational agents.

10. What are the effects of alcohol ingestion on intravenous narcotics such as barbiturates, benzodiazepines, and opioids?

Acutely intoxicated patients are more sensitive to the effects of barbiturates, benzodiazepines, and opioids. Cross-tolerance develops to intravenous agents with chronic alcohol exposure.

11. How does alcohol affect muscle relaxants?

The choice of muscle relaxant in **nonhabituated** acutely intoxicated patients should be based more on the requirements of the surgical procedure than the physiologic state of the patient. Most acutely intoxicated patients require rapid-sequence induction for intubation and a rapid-acting muscle relaxant (succinylcholine, rocuronium). Choice of a particular muscle relaxant should be based on the duration of the procedure and medical history of the patient. The pharmacokinetics of muscle relaxants is not affected by acute alcohol intoxication in nonhabituated patients.

The pharmacodynamic profile of muscle relaxants is altered in **alcohol-habituated** patients. In healthy patients, succinylcholine is rapidly hydrolyzed and thus inactivated by plasma cholinesterases produced in the liver. Patients with liver disease may have decreased levels of circulating plasma cholinesterase; therefore, the effects of succinylcholine may be prolonged in alcoholic patients. Cirrhotic patients with poor liver function have a greater Vd for injected drugs and thus require a larger dose of nondepolarizing relaxants. Relaxants that rely on hepatic clearance may have a prolonged duration of action. Muscle relaxants that are metabolized independently of organ function (e.g., cisatracurium) are good choices in patients with liver disease.

12. Describe special considerations in the preoperative assessment of alcohol-abusing patients.

A complete history and physical exam should be performed for all patients before they receive an anesthetic. Special consideration must be given to the cardiovascular system of chronic alcohol users. Tachycardia, dysrythmias, or cardiomegaly may indicate alcohol-related cardiac dysfunction. A 12-lead electrocardiagram (ECG) should be evaluated for dysrhythmias and signs of cardiomegaly and ischemia. Useful laboratory studies include measurement of serum electrolytes to check for hypokalemia and hypoglycemia, complete blood count to evaluate the anemia associated with chronic alcohol use, and coagulation studies (PT, partial prothrombin time, platelet count) to evaluate propensity toward a bleeding diathesis secondary to hepatic disease. Ten percent of intoxicated trauma patients have a cervical spine injury; a lateral cervical spine radiograph should be evaluated before manipulation of the neck and intubation.

13. What are the special monitoring considerations in alcohol-abusing patients?

All patients brought to the operating theater should be monitored in accordance with standards of practice outlined by the American Society of Anesthesiology: noninvasive blood pressure measurement, continuous ECG, pulse oximetry, and temperature monitoring. Invasive monitoring should be considered on an individual basis. Chronic alcohol abusers with hepatic dysfunction and well-developed portosystemic collateral circulation rely on hepatic arterial blood flow for hepatic perfusion. Inhalational agents may cause vasodilatation of preexisting hepatic shunts and increase the liver's dependence on arterial flow. Placement of an arterial catheter in such patients maintains beat-to-beat control of systemic blood pressure and reduces the risk of hypotensive hepatic ischemia. In addition, an arterial catheter provides access for blood gas sampling. Because acutely intoxicated patients are subject to hypoglycemia, serum glucose levels should be followed closely.

Volume status may be assessed by placement of an indwelling bladder catheter and central venous catheter. Patients with alcohol-induced cardiac disease are less sensitive to endogenous or parenteral catecholamines and may benefit from pulmonary artery catheterization and close monitoring of cardiac filling pressures and cardiac output.

Instrumentation of the esophagus should be avoided in patients with known liver disease because of the possibility of rupturing esophageal varices. Patients have been known to exsanguinate and die as a result of bleeding from esophageal varices. A precordial stethoscope and cutaneous temperature probe are safe alternatives to the esophageal stethescope.

14. Is premedication necessary in alcohol-abusing patients?

Special premedication is not necessary for sober chronic alcohol abusers scheduled for routine elective surgery. Acutely intoxicated patients, to a certain degree, have provided their own premedication. Alcohol is, after all, a sedative. Acutely intoxicated patients should also be premedicated with oral sodium citrate (Bicitra or Alka-Seltzer Gold) to neutralize gastric acid and with metoclopramide to enhance gastric motility and facilitate gastric emptying. Pretreatment with an H_2-receptor blocker also may assist in reducing the acidic output from the gastric mucosa.

15. How does one anesthetize sober chronic alcohol abusers?

No one anesthetic technique is safer than another. As previously mentioned, sober chronic alcohol users may demonstrate tolerance to many intravenous and inhalational anesthetic agents. Isoflurane is thought by many to be the best inhalational agent for maintaining hepatic blood flow and should be considered in patients with hepatic disease. An opioid-based anesthetic may be more appropriate in patients with cardiac disease because of its minimal effects on myocardial contractility and heart rate. Anesthetic techniques for patients with severe organ dysfunction are discussed elsewhere in this text. In general, a balanced anesthetic technique using amnestics, opioids, nitrous oxide, and an inhalational agent will suffice.

16. How does one anesthetize intoxicated patients?

One must first determine whether the operation is elective or emergent. An elective procedure should be postponed until the patient is sober and meets the fasting (NPO) guidelines for elective surgery. In an emergent situation, rapid-sequence induction and general endotracheal anesthesia are usually indicated. Rapid-sequence induction involves adequate preoxygenation with 100% oxygen via face mask at high flow rates for 3–5 minutes of normal breathing, or 4 full vital-capacity breaths. This regimen adequately denitrogenates the lungs. The next step is to administer an induction dose of an intravenous anesthetic, followed by a rapid-acting muscle relaxant. During this step, an assistant applies firm downward pressure over the cricoid cartilage to compress and occlude the esophagus (Sellick maneuver). This maneuver prevents passive regurgitation of gastric contents. The trachea is then intubated with a cuffed endotracheal tube. Position of the tube in the trachea is confirmed by auscultating breath sounds bilaterally, visualizing bilateral chest wall movement with respiration, and noting the presence of end-tidal carbon dioxide on the capnograph. Once correct placement of the tube is confirmed, cricoid pressure may be released.

17. What are the signs and symptoms of alcohol withdrawal?

Alcohol withdrawal syndrome presents as anorexia, insomnia, weakness, combativeness, tremors, disorientation, auditory and visual hallucinations, and convulsions. The peak onset is 10–30 hours after abstinence from alcohol. The symptoms may last for 40–50 hours. Prolonged abstinence may lead to delirium tremens or hyperactivity of the autonomic nervous system that manifests as tachycardia, diaphoresis, fever, anxiety, and confusion. Delirium tremens carries a 10% mortality rate. Alcohol withdrawal syndrome may occur in anesthetized patients in the operating theater. Under anesthesia it can present as uncontrolled tachycardia, diaphoresis, and hyperthermia. The treatment for alcohol withdrawal syndrome is the administration of benzodiazepines or intravenous infusion of ethanol. Often chronic alcohol abusers receive benzodiazepines as prophylaxis against withdrawal. This treatment should be continued during anesthesia or may be initiated during induction.

BIBLIOGRAPHY

1. Fiamengo SA: Alcoholism. In Yao FS (ed): Yao and Artusio's Anesthesiology: Problem-Oriented Patient Management, 4th ed. Philadelphia, Lippincott Williams & Wilkins, 1998, pp 693–707.
2. Hardman JG, Limbird LE (eds): Goodman and Gilman's The Pharmacological Basis of Therapeutics, 9th ed. New York, McGraw-Hill, 1996, pp 372–381.
3. Schuckit MA: Alcohol and alcoholism. In Braunwald E, Isselbacher KJ, Petersdorf RG, et al (eds): Harrison's Principles of Internal Medicine, 14th ed. [international]. New York, McGraw-Hill, 1998, pp 2503–2508.

5. Stoelting RK: Pharmacology and Physiology in Anesthetic Practice, 2nd ed. Philadelphia, J.B. Lippincott, 1991, pp 783–785.
6. Stoelting RK, Dierdorf SF: Anesthesia and Co-existing Disease, 3rd ed. New York, Churchill Livingstone, 1993, pp 223, 262–268, 445, 526–528.

54. DIABETES MELLITUS

Robert H. Slover, M.D., and Robin B. Slover, M.D.

1. Describe the two principal types of diabetes mellitus.

Type I diabetes mellitus is an autoimmune disorder in which destruction of the pancreatic islet cells results in the inability to produce insulin. Type I diabetes, also called insulin-dependent diabetes mellitus (IDDM), is common in children, adolescents, and young adults. Type II diabetes mellitus is a disorder in the body's ability to use insulin. Early in the course of the disease the patient is able to make sufficient insulin, but cell receptor impairment results in high blood glucose levels despite normal or high insulin levels. Type II diabetes is usually a disease of older adults; onset in the sixth decade and beyond is common. Type II diabetes is also called non–insulin-dependent diabetes mellitus because, at least early in the disease, most adults can be managed with diet and oral hypoglycemic agents alone.

2. Why should glucose be controlled during surgery?

Sustained hyperglycemia results in increased risk for infection, impaired wound healing, and increased length of postsurgical hospitalization. The underlying insulin deficiency associated with hyperglycemia may lead to ketogenesis, acidosis, and protein catabolism. Specific complications include:

1. Hyperglycemia producing osmotic diuresis
2. Hyperosmolar states with hyperviscosity, thrombogenesis, and cerebral edema
3. Ketogenesis and the risk of diabetic ketoacidosis
4. Proteolysis and decreased amino acid transport, resulting in retarded wound healing
5. Loss of polymorphonuclear cell phagocytic function

3. What factors affect metabolic decompensation?

The following factors favor metabolic decompensation—a shift from glucose homeostasis toward catabolism—in patients with poorly controlled diabetes:

1. Insulin deficiency
2. Increased counterregulatory hormones (epinephrine, cortisol, glucagon growth hormone)
3. Fasting states (glycogen depletion)
4. Dehydration

4. Describe glucose metabolism in the setting of surgery.

Insulin enhances glucose uptake, glycogen storage, protein synthesis, amino acid transport, and fat formation. The counterregulatory hormones promote glycogenolysis, gluconeogenesis, proteolysis, and lipolysis. Basal insulin secretion is essential even in the fasting state to maintain glucose homeostasis.

Surgery leads to increased stress and high counterregulatory hormone activity with a decrease in insulin secretion. In diabetic patients this leads to lipolysis, gluconeogenesis, and glycogenolysis—and thus to increased glucose production and decreased utilization. Therefore, in diabetics without adequate insulin replacement, the combination of insulin deficiency and excessive counterregulatory hormones may lead to severe hyperglycemia and diabetic ketoacidosis, which are associated with hyperosmolarity, and increases in protein catabolism, fluid loss, lipolysis, and protein breakdown.

5. What other complications are associated with diabetes mellitus?

1. Hypertension is seen in 40% of poorly controlled diabetics who undergo surgery. The effect of potassium-wasting diuretic agents must be closely monitored, because even mild acidosis results in total body potassium loss.

2. Diabetic autonomic neuropathy may compromise neuroreflexic control of cardiovascular and pulmonary function, manifesting as orthostatic hypotension and loss of variations in cardiac rhythm with deep breathing and the Valsalva maneuver as well as urinary retention, ileus, and gastric retention.

3. Disturbances in renal function are common, including increased blood urea nitrogen and creatinine, protein loss and hypoalbuminemia, and electrolyte disturbances.

4. Occult infections are present in 17% of diabetics.

6. Describe the goals of diabetic therapy in the perioperative state.

Given the potential and demonstrable complications in patients with diabetes, certain reasonable goals should be kept in mind:

1. Avoid hypoglycemia, severe hyperglycemia, protein catabolism, electrolyte imbalance, and ketoacidosis.

2. Anticipate, prevent, and treat imbalances of potassium, magnesium, and phosphate.

3. Avoid significant glycosuria and osmotic diuresis.

7. What preoperative considerations influence the management of diabetes?

First, the type of diabetes and previous therapy must be considered. For example, a patient with type I diabetes certainly requires insulin, usually as an intravenous infusion during surgery. On the other hand, a patient with type II diabetes who does not normally require insulin should be well managed with dietary control only. A patient with type II diabetes who requires daily insulin will require insulin on the day of surgery. If the procedure is short or minimally invasive, the patient is not likely to require an insulin infusion. The second consideration is obviously the nature of the surgery. Control of postoperative infection should be considered. If the procedure involves a significant risk of postoperative infection, insulin infusion may be considered to establish tighter glucose control. Underlying fluid and electrolyte imbalances should be corrected and severe hyperglycemia or ketosis should be controlled. Insulin requirements are increased by infection, hepatic disease, obesity, steroids, stress (including pain), and cardiovascular surgery. Consider the following questionnaire for a surgical patient with diabetes:

1. Type of diabetes and duration of disease
2. Daily therapy at home: amount of insulin dose, diet, oral hypoglycemics
3. Underlying diabetic complications
   - Renal disease
   - Neuropathy (early satiety and reflux suggest gastroparesis)
   - Retinopathy
   - Hypertension and medications
   - Hepatic disease
   - Infections, skin disease, foot disease, vaginitis
   - Cardiac disease, silent ischemia
4. Evidence of overt infectious disease
5. Status of electrolytes, phosphate, and magnesium
6. Blood glucose, ketones, acidosis
7. Does the procedure involve high risk of postoperative infection or pain?

8. Describe effective preoperative management for the diabetic patient.

Patients undergoing more serious and invasive procedures have higher levels of counter-regulatory hormones and require closer attention to good glucose control. Blood glucose levels under 200 mg/dl in the days preceding surgery are ideal and ensure adequate glycogen stores and insulin sufficiency. Insulin requirements may be lower during prolonged preoperative hospitalization than at home because of inactivity. If the patient is hospitalized, it is possible to control the diet (with cooperation, of course, the same control is possible at home) to help in achieving glucose control. On the day before surgery glucose should be monitored at bedside before each meal, at bedtime, and in the early morning. The goal is to have most glucose levels under 200 mg/dl. Underlying complications should be managed, and electrolytes, phosphate, magnesium, and hydration should be normal. A baseline electrocardiogram (ECG) is important in adult patients.

9. A patient has been admitted for a lengthy procedure with the anticipation of significant postoperative recovery time and risk of infection. How should this patient's diabetes be managed during surgery?

It is ideal, especially in children with type I diabetes, to schedule the surgery early in the day. This allows a subcutaneous insulin injection on the night before the procedure and initiation of insulin infusion on the morning of surgery.

At least 1 hour before surgery, a combined insulin-dextrose infusion should be initiated. The infusion is made by adding 0.32 units of insulin per gram of glucose (16 units of insulin to 1000 ml of 5% dextrose [D5] in water). Ensure that electrolytes and phosphate are normal. Glucose should be under 200 mg/dl. No parenteral insulin is given on the morning of surgery.

Glucose and potassium should be checked hourly during surgery and in the postanesthetic care unit, using rapid bedside monitoring of glucose levels. The recommended infusion of insulin is 32 units with 20 mEq/L of potassium in 1000 ml of D10 at 100 ml/hr. The infusion may be increased or decreased by 4-unit increments. Potassium should be omitted if the blood level is > 5.5 mEq/L or increased to 40 mEq/L if the blood level is < 4 mEq/L.

10. Describe the postoperative management of the same patient.

In significant procedures with prolonged recovery time and a period of decreased intake, it is easier to manage the patient by continuing the insulin and glucose infusion for up to 48 hours, matching increased or decreased insulin needs with changes in rate of concentration of the infusate. The following guidelines are recommended:

1. Continue bedside monitoring of glucose, electrolytes, and fluids.
2. Using the insulin-glucose infusion, alter the rate or concentration as needed.
3. A glucose goal of 100–250 mg/dl is reasonable.
4. With the resumption of oral feeding, insulin is given subcutaneously according to the patient's preoperative schedule. If pain or stress is still significant, it will be necessary to increase the dose by as much as 20%. Monitor glucose at bedside before meals, at bedtime, and early in the morning, adjusting doses as necessary.
5. Monitor nutrition! If total parenteral nutrition is used, the insulin rate may need to increase and should be adjusted based on glucose monitoring.

11. Describe the management of diabetic patients who require emergency surgery.

If at all possible, electrolyte and glucose imbalance should be corrected before surgery. Sufficient rehydration, electrolyte replacement, and insulin treatment can be achieved in 4–6 hours to improve hyperglycemia and to suppress ketogenesis and acidosis. Rehydration is initiated with 10–20 ml/kg of normal saline (NS). Insulin infusion should be 0.1U kg/hr, using 0.45 NS (or D10 in 0.45 NS if glucose is < 150 mg/dl). If the patient is in ketoacidosis and immediate surgery is imperative, the following guidelines may be useful.

Insulin Infusion Rate for Emergency Surgery

BLOOD GLUCOSE (mg/dl)	RATE (ml/hr)	INSULIN RATE (U/HR)*	
		A	B
0–50	5	0.25	0.50
50–100	10	0.50	1.00
100–150	15	0.75	1.50
150–200	20	1.00	2.00
200–250	25	1.25	2.50
250–300	30	1.50	3.00
300–350	35	1.75	3.50
350–400	40	2.00	4.00
> 400	50	3.00	6.00

* Solution A is used for patients with an insulin requirement of < 50 units/day and is made with 50 units of insulin in 1000 ml NS with potassium, 20 mEq/L. Solution B is used for patients with an insulin requirement > 50 units/day and is made with 100 units insulin in 1000 ml NS with potassium 20 mEq/L. Pediatric patients require 0.1 units/kg/hr of insulin for ketoacidosis and 0.05 unit/kg/hr for maintenance.

12. What type of insulin should be used during surgery?

During the preoperative period and after the patient has returned to subcutaneous insulin postoperatively, both long-acting insulin (neutral protamine Hagedorn [NPH], lente) and short-acting insulin (regular) are used. However, during the operative period only regular insulin is used. All of the infusion suggestions in this chapter refer to human regular insulin. Given subcutaneously, regular insulin has an onset of action within 20–30 minutes and a duration of up to 2–3 hours. Given intravenously, regular insulin acts within 3–5 minutes and has a duration of 20–30 minutes.

13. What specific assessments should be performed during the anesthetic evaluation of an insulin-dependent diabetic?

Cardiovascular, renal, and autonomic and peripheral nervous systems may be affected. A diligent search should be made for signs and symptoms of congestive heart failure or myocardial ischemia. Frequently, myocardial ischemia is silent in diabetics, even without signs of associated neuropathy. A preoperative ECG should be performed on all diabetics. Because myocardial infarction carries a higher risk of morbidity and mortality in diabetic patients, myocardial ischemia should be minimized in the perioperative period. Congestive heart failure and valvular heart disease are significant risk factors for perioperative cardiac complications in diabetic patients. Decisions about intraoperative monitoring should be individualized, recognizing the increased risk in such patients for silent perioperative myocardial ischemia. Because diabetics have an increase in small-vessel disease throughout the body, cerebrovascular or peripheral vascular disease also may be present. Proteinuria is an early manifestation of diabetic nephropathy. Preoperative evaluation should include measurement of electrolytes, serum blood urea nitrogen and creatinine, and urinalysis. In patients with end-stage renal disease on dialysis, the type of dialysis and schedule of dialysis in relationship to the date of surgery should be determined. Optimally, surgery should occur the day after dialysis. Peripheral neuropathies are common in diabetics; they should be documented carefully preoperatively. Diabetic patients may be more susceptible to iatrogenic peripheral nerve injuries. Autonomic neuropathy may affect cardiovascular (silent ischemia), gastrointestinal (gastroparesis with increased risk of aspiration), thermoregulatory (decreased ability to alter blood vessel flow to conserve temperature), and neuroendocrine systems (decreased catecholamine production in response to stimulation). Patients with autonomic neuropathy should receive aspiration prophylaxis: an H_2-blocking agent, a gastric stimulant to decrease gastroparesis, and a nonparticulate antacid. Autonomic neuropathy can be assessed by four simple exams. The first two tests examine the sympathetic nervous system; the last two tests examine the parasympathetic nervous system.

1. A normal response in diastolic pressure (from lying to standing) is a change of at least 16 mmHg; an affected patient has a response of < 10 mmHg.

2. A larger change in postural systolic blood pressure (from lying to standing). A normal decrease is < 10 mmHg; an affected patient has a decrease of at least 30 mmHg.

3. Decreased heart rate response to deep breathing. Normal patients increase heart rate by at least 15 beats per minute. Affected patients have an increase of 10 or fewer beats per minute.

4. If the ECG is recorded, the R-R ratio can be determined with a Valsalva maneuver. A normal ratio is > 1.20; an abnormal response is < 1.10.

Oral intubation may be difficult in some diabetic patients because of stiff joint syndrome, with decreased mobility at the atlantooccipital joint. The remainder of the airway exam may be normal. Stiff joint syndrome is suggested by the inability to approximate the palmar aspect of the pharyngeal joints (touch the palmar aspects of the fingers together when the palms are together—the prayer sign) and correlates with duration of insulin-dependent diabetes and microvascular complications. Atlanto-occipital joint mobility can be evaluated radiographically. If decreased mobility is documented or stiff joint syndrome is suspected clinically, an awake intubation may be required.

14. Are regional anesthetics helpful in insulin-dependent diabetics?

Regional anesthetic techniques (epidural anesthetics, spinal anesthetics, and peripheral nerve blocks) decrease the stress response of the patient. In insulin-dependent diabetics, this can help to maintain a more stable blood glucose as well as decrease stress on the cardiovascular system. Epinephrine should not be used in peripheral nerve blocks (e.g., ankle blocks) because of the risk of decreasing blood flow to the area; insulin-dependent diabetics often already have diseased microcirculation. In blocks with high systemic absorption, such as brachial plexus or intercostal blocks, low-dose epinephrine may be used.

BIBLIOGRAPHY

1. Gavin LA: Management of diabetes mellitus during surgery. West J Med 151:525–529, 1989.
2. George K, Alberti MM, Gill GV, Elliott MJ: Insulin delivery during surgery in the diabetic patient. Diabetes Care 5(S1):65–75, 1982.
3. Hirsh IB, McGill JB: The role of insulin in management of surgical patients with diabetes mellitus. Diabetes Care 13:980–991, 1990.
4. MacKenzie CR, Charlson ME: Assessment of perioperative risk in the patient with diabetes mellitus. Surg Obstet Gynecol 167:293–299, 1988.
5. Rosenstock J, Raskin P: Surgery! Practical guidelines for diabetes management. Clin Diabetes 5:49–61, 1987.
6. Schade DS: Surgery and diabetes. Med Clin North Am 72:1531–1543, 1988.
7. Schuman CR, Podolsky S: Surgery in the diabetic patient. In Podolsky S (ed): Clinical Diabetes: Modern Management. New York, Appleton-Century-Crofts, 1980, pp 509–535.
8. Wissler RN: The patient with endocrine disease. Probl Anesth 6:61–89, 1992.

55. THYROID AND ADRENAL DISEASE

Kenneth M. Swank, M.D.

1. Describe four steps involved in thyroid hormone synthesis.

1. **Uptake of iodide**. Iodide from the bloodstream is concentrated in thyroid cells by an active transport mechanism.

2. **Iodination of thyroglobulin**. Thyroglobulin, a large glycoprotein rich in tyrosine, is enzymatically iodinated and stored in the thyroid follicles.

3. **Coupling reactions**. The monoiodotyrosine and diiodotyrosine moieties within the thyroglobulin molecule are coupled to one another to form triiodothyronine (T_3) and thyroxine (T_4).

4. **Release of hormones**. T_3 and T_4 are enzymatically cleaved from thyroglobulin within the follicular cell and released into the bloodstream.

2. How much T_3 and T_4 is produced? What regulates their production?

Approximately 8 µg of T_3 and 90 µg of T_4 are produced daily. Additional T_3 is formed from the peripheral conversion of T_4 to T_3. T_3 is approximately four times more potent than T_4 but has a much shorter half-life; therefore the contribution of each to total thyroid activity is approximately equal. Thyroid-stimulating hormone (TSH) (produced by the anterior pituitary gland) acts on thyroid tissue to increase the rates of all steps involved in thyroid hormone synthesis and release. Thyrotropin-releasing hormone (TRH) (produced by the hypothalamus), in turn, regulates the amount of TSH produced by the pituitary. T_3 and T_4 inhibit release of TSH and to a much smaller degree the release of TRH, thus establishing a negative feedback control mechanism.

3. List the common thyroid function tests and their use in assessment of thyroid disorders.

Total T_4 level, total T_3 level, TSH level, and resin T_3 uptake (T_3RU). The T_3RU is useful in conditions that alter levels of thyroid binding globulin, which would alter total T_4 results.

Unity of Thyroid Function Tests in the Diagnosis of Hypothyroid or Hyperthyroid States

DISEASE	T_4	T_3	TSH	T_3RU
Primary hypothyroidism	−	−	+	−
Secondary hypothyroidism	−	−	−	−
Hyperthyroidism	+	+	0	+
Pregnancy	+	0	0	+

+, Increased; −, decreased; 0, no change.

4. Discuss some common signs, symptoms, and causes of hypothyroidism.

Symptoms	Signs
Fatigue	Bradycardia
Cold intolerance	Hypothermia
Constipation	Deep tendon reflex relaxation
Dry skin	phase prolongation
Hair loss	Hoarseness
Weight gain	Periorbital edema

The signs and symptoms observed in patients with mild hypothyroidism are nonspecific, and clinical detection is extremely difficult. Patients with severe long-term untreated hypothyroidism may progress to myxedema coma, which is frequently fatal. Myxedema coma is characterized by hypoventilation, hypothermia, hypotension, hyponatremia, hypoglycemia, obtundation, and adrenal insufficiency.

Factors that may lead to myxedema coma in hypothyroid patients include cold exposure, infection, trauma, and administration of central nervous system depressants.

The most common cause of hypothyroidism is surgical or radioiodine ablation of thyroid tissue in the treatment of hyperthyroidism, most commonly Graves' disease. Other causes of hypothyroidism include chronic thyroiditis (Hashimoto's thyroiditis), drug effects, iodine deficiency, and pituitary or hypothalamic dysfunction.

5. Of the numerous manifestations of hypothyroidism, which are most important in relation to anesthesia?

With regard to the **cardiovascular system**, hypothyroidism causes depression of myocardial function owing to protein and mucopolysaccharide deposition within the myocardium and depression of intracellular myocardial metabolism. Cardiac output declines as a result of decreased heart rate and stroke volume. Decreased blood volume, baroreceptor reflex dysfunction, and pericardial effusion may accompany hypothyroidism as well. All of these effects make the hypothyroid patient sensitive to the hypotensive effects of anesthetics. The **respiratory system** can be affected, causing hypoventilation; in severe hypothyroidism, respiratory failure can be present. The ventilatory responses to both hypoxia and hypercarbia are significantly impaired, making the hypothyroid patient sensitive to drugs that cause respiratory depression. Hypothyroidism also decreases the hepatic and renal clearance of drugs. These patients are also prone to hypothermia because of lowered metabolic rate and consequent lowered heat production.

6. How does hypothyroidism affect minimum alveolar concentration (MAC) of anesthetic agents?

Animal studies show that MAC is not affected by hypothyroidism. Clinically, it has been noted that hypothyroid patients have increased sensitivity to anesthetic agents. This is due not to a decrease in MAC per se but to the patient's metabolically depressed condition.

7. How is hypothyroidism treated?

Treatment consists of supplementation with exogenous thyroid hormones, most frequently levothyroxine because its long half-life results in a more constant serum level. The principal risk with treatment is in patients with coronary artery disease (CAD). An increase in the basal metabolic rate may result in myocardial ischemia.

Suggested thyroid supplementation protocol for hypothyroid patients:
- Patients without CAD: T_4 50 μg/day increasing monthly by 50-μg/day increments until a euthyroid state is reached.
- Patients with CAD: T_4 25 μg/day increasing monthly by 25-μg/day increments until a euthyroid state is achieved.
- In urgent situations, thyroid supplementation may be cautiously given intravenously. Recommended dose is T_4 300 μg/m^2 by slow infusion.

Hypothyroid patients receiving intravenous supplementation must be monitored closely for signs and symptoms of cardiac ischemia as well as adrenal insufficiency.

8. Under what circumstances should elective surgery be delayed for a hypothyroid patient?

Patients with **mild to moderate hypothyroidism** are not at increased risk undergoing elective surgical procedures. Some authors suggest that elective surgery in patients who are symptomatic should be delayed until the patient is rendered euthyroid. Other authorities recommend against delaying surgery if thyroid replacement can begin before surgery (in patients without CAD). In patients with **severe hypothyroidism**, elective surgery should be delayed until they have been rendered euthyroid. This may require 2–4 months of replacement therapy for complete reversal of cardiopulmonary effects. Normalization of the patient's TSH level reflects reversal of hypothyroid-induced changes.

9. List common signs, symptoms, and causes of hyperthyroidism.

Signs	Symptoms	Causes
Goiter	Anxiety	Graves' disease
Tachycardia	Tremor	Toxic multinodular goiter
Proptosis	Heat intolerance	
Atrial fibrillation	Fatigue	
	Weight loss	
	Muscle weakness	

10. How is hyperthyroidism treated?

There are three approaches to treatment.

1. **Antithyroid drugs** such as propylthiouracil (PTU) inhibit iodination and coupling reactions in the thyroid gland, thus reducing production of T_3 and T_4. PTU also inhibits peripheral

conversion of T_4 to T_3. **Iodine** in large doses not only blocks hormone production, but also decreases the vascularity and size of the thyroid gland, making iodine useful in preparing hyperthyroid patients for thyroid surgery.

2. **Radioactive iodine**, I^{131}, is actively concentrated by the thyroid gland, resulting in destruction of thyroid cells and thus a decrease in the production of hormone.

3. **Surgical subtotal thyroidectomy**

All of these approaches may render the patient hypothyroid. In the short term, β-adrenergic blockers control symptoms of hyperthyroidism.

11. Which effects of hyperthyroidism are the most important with regard to anesthesia?

In hyperthyroidism, the metabolic rate of the body is increased, causing significant changes in the **cardiovascular system**, the magnitude of which are proportional to the severity of the thyroid dysfunction. Because of the elevated oxygen consumption, the cardiovascular system is hyperdynamic. Tachycardia and elevated cardiac output are present, and tachyarrhythmias, atrial fibrillation, left ventricular hypertrophy, and congestive heart failure may develop. Hyperthyroid patients with **proptosis** are more susceptible to ocular damage during surgery because of difficulty with taping their eyelids closed.

12. How is MAC affected by hyperthyroidism?

As in hypothyroidism, MAC is not affected by hyperthyroidism, although clinically hyperthyroid patients appear to be resistant to the effects of anesthetic agents. Induction with volatile agents is slowed by the increased cardiac output. The rate of drug metabolism is increased, giving the appearance of resistance. Hyperthyroidism-induced hyperthermia may indirectly elevate MAC.

13. Define thyrotoxicosis.

Also known as **"thyroid storm,"** this is an acute exacerbation of hyperthyroidism usually caused by a stress such as surgery or infection. It is characterized by extreme tachycardia, hyperthermia, and possibly severe hypotension. Perioperatively, it usually occurs 6–18 hours after surgery but can occur intraoperatively and be confused with malignant hyperthermia.

14. How is thyrotoxicosis treated?

Intraoperative treatment must be immediate, consisting of careful β-adrenergic blockade, infusion of intravenous fluids, and temperature control if hyperthermia is present. Corticosteroids should be considered for refractory hypotension because hyperthyroid patients may have a relative cortisol deficiency. Antithyroid drugs should be added postoperatively.

15. What complications may occur after a surgical procedure involving the thyroid gland?

Because of the close proximity of the thyroid gland to the trachea and larynx, many of the complications that occur (such as laryngeal edema or cervical hematoma) can cause airway obstruction. Chronic pressure on the trachea from a goiter, for example, can lead to tracheomalacia, rendering the patient prone to tracheal collapse and airway obstruction following extubation. Inadvertent resection of the parathyroid glands, in turn, can lead to hypocalcemia, which may produce laryngospasm. Innervation to the vocal cord musculature may be compromised by surgical damage to the recurrent laryngeal nerves (RLN). Bilateral RLN injury can result in the vocal cords being passively drawn together during inspiration, leading to severe obstruction that necessitates emergent tracheostomy. Unilateral injury results in dysfunction of the ipsilateral vocal cord. Damage to the nerve fibers innervating the vocal cord adductors results in unopposed abduction of the ipsilateral vocal cord, increasing the risk of aspiration. Damage to the innervation of the abductor muscles results in an abnormally adducted vocal cord, which can cause hoarseness. Vocal cord function may be assessed following surgery with direct or fiberoptic laryngoscopy.

16. Why is levothyroxine given to organ donors?

Hypotension in the donor before organ donation decreases organ perfusion, which adversely affects the viability and function of the donor organs after transplantation. This hypotension may be due to cardiac dysfunction from a hypothyroid state induced by failure of the hypothalamic-pituitary axis. Infusion of levothyroxine appears to improve donor hemodynamics, thus improving the quality of the donated organs.

17. Describe the functions and regulation of the adrenal gland.

The adrenal gland can be functionally divided into the adrenal cortex and the adrenal medulla. The **adrenal cortex** principally produces the steroid hormones cortisol and aldosterone. Production of cortisol is regulated by adrenocorticotropic hormone (ACTH) produced by the anterior pituitary. The release of ACTH is promoted by corticotropin-releasing hormone (CRH) derived from the hypothalamus. Cortisol inhibits release of both CRH and ACTH, establishing negative feedback control. Ectopic ACTH can be produced by various neoplasms, such as small cell lung carcinomas. Aldosterone secretion is regulated by the renin-angiotensin system. The **adrenal medulla** secretes epinephrine and norepinephrine. Their release is governed by the sympathetic nervous system.

18. Define pheochromocytoma.

A pheochromocytoma is a neoplasm arising from the adrenal medulla or paravertebral chromaffin tissue. Ninety percent of these tumors arise from the adrenal medulla, and 10% are bilateral. Pheochromocytomas may secrete norepinephrine, epinephrine, or other catecholamines. The ratio of secreted norepinephrine to epinephrine is higher than that found in normal adrenal medullary tissue. Most extra-adrenal pheochromocytomas secrete only norepinephrine.

19. How much cortisol is produced by the adrenal cortex?

Normally, approximately 20–30 mg of cortisol per day is produced. This amount increases dramatically as a response to a stress, such as infection or surgery. Under stressful conditions, 75–150 mg per day may be produced, with the increase in production being generally proportional to the severity of the stress.

20. What is the most common cause of hypothalamic-pituitary-adrenal (HPA) axis disruption?

Exogenous steroids (glucocorticoids) result in HPA axis suppression. Short-term steroid administration—no longer than 7–10 days—results in suppression of CRH and ACTH release, which usually returns to normal about 5 days after discontinuation of steroid therapy. Long-term administration of exogenous steroids results in adrenocortical atrophy secondary to a lack of ACTH. This results in prolonged adrenocortical insufficiency, which can last a year or more following steroid discontinuation. Therefore, long-term steroid administration should not be abruptly terminated; rather it should be gradually tapered off over a period of 1–4 weeks.

21. What is addisonian crisis?

Also referred to as acute adrenocortical insufficiency, an addisonian crisis is caused by a relative lack of cortisol or other glucocorticoid in relation to a stress such as surgery. It is a shock-like state characterized by refractory hypotension, hypovolemia, and electrolyte disturbances. Causes of adrenocortical insufficiency include
- HPA axis suppression by exogenous corticosteroid administration
- Autoimmune adrenalitis
- Adrenal hemorrhage
- Adrenal tuberculosis
- Septic shock

22. How is addisonian crisis treated?

Treatment must be immediate and consists of intravenous cortisol, fluid replacement, physiologic monitoring, and correction of electrolyte abnormalities.

CONTROVERSY

23. Is perioperative stress steroid supplementation for patients on steroid therapy necessary?

Few documented cases of acute perioperative adrenal insufficiency, addisonian crisis, exist. Studies have shown that patients who have been on long-term steroid therapy undergoing even major surgery rarely become hypotensive because of glucocorticoid deficiency. If observed, hypotension is usually due to hypovolemia or cardiac dysfunction. The possible side effects of perioperative steroid supplementation include:

- Hyperglycemia
- Aggravation of hypertension
- Impaired wound healing
- Fluid retention
- Gastric ulceration
- Immunosuppression

One answer to this question might be that no supplementation is required unless hypotension refractory to standard treatment occurs. However, although considerable data exist regarding the problems associated with long-term steroid therapy, few data indicate any significant problems related to short-term perioperative steroid supplementation. Despite its rarity, acute adrenal insufficiency is associated with significant morbidity and mortality. Therefore, alternatively, because perioperative steroid supplementation is associated with few risks in itself and because acute adrenal insufficiency can potentially lead to death, supplemental steroids should be given. Currently, this seems to be the view of most authors.

24. If supplemental corticosteroids are to be administered perioperatively, how much should one give?

The dosage is highly dependent on the amount of stress that the surgery is likely to cause. **For minor surgery**, no supplementation or minimal supplementation, such as hydrocortisone, 25 mg, may suffice. **For major surgery**, a variety of dosages have been suggested, with none being shown to be superior to the rest. One regimen consists of hydrocortisone, 25 mg, intraoperatively followed by an infusion of hydrocortisone, 100 mg, over the immediate 24 hours postoperatively. Another is to give 200–300 mg/70 kg in divided doses each day. The goal of these regimens is to give the lowest dose that provides sufficient supplementation while avoiding potential side effects.

BIBLIOGRAPHY

1. Knudsen L, Christiansen A, Lorentzen JE: Hypotension during and after operation in glucocorticoid-treated patients. Br J Anaesth 53:295–300, 1981.
2. Lampe GH, Roizen MF: Anesthesia for patients with abnormal function at the adrenal cortex. Anesthesiol Clin North Am 5:245–267, 1987.
3. Murkin JM: Anesthesia and hypothyroidism: A review of thyroxine physiology, pharmacology, and anesthetic implications. Anesth Analg 61:371–383, 1982.
4. Napolitano LM, Chernow B: Guidelines for corticosteroid use in anesthetic and surgical stress. Int Anesthesiol Clin 26:226–232, 1988.
5. Orlowski JP: Evidence that thyroxine (T4) is effective as a hemodynamic rescue agent in management of organ donors. Transplantation 55:959–960, 1993.
6. Stoelting RK, Dierdorf SF: Endocrine diseases. In Anesthesia and Co-existing Disease, 3rd ed. New York, Churchill Livingstone, 1993, pp 347–367.
7. Streck WF, Lockwood DH: Pituitary adrenal recovery following short-term suppression with corticosteroids. Am J Med 66:910–914, 1979.
8. Weatherill D, Spence AA: Anaesthesia and disorders of the adrenal cortex. Br J Anaesth 56:741–749, 1984.
9. Wenning GK, Wietholter H, Schnauder G, et al: Recovery of the hypothalamic-pituitary-adrenal axis from suppression by short-term, high-dose intravenous prednisolone therapy in patients with MS. Acta Neurol Scand 89:270–273, 1994.

56. OBESITY

Lisa Leonard, CRNA, M.H.S., and Elizabeth Ward, CRNA

1. Define obesity and morbid obesity.

Obesity is defined as body weight 20% greater than ideal weight. Approximately 20% of males and 30% of females are obese. Morbid obesity is defined as body weight more than two times ideal weight or greater than 100 lbs over ideal weight. In morbidly obese men, aged 23–34 years, the death rate is increased 12 times, primarily because of cardiovascular impairments.

2. How is ideal body weight calculated?

The Broca index is a practical way to determine ideal body weight:

Height (cm) – 100 = ideal weight (kg) for males
Height (cm) – 105 = ideal weight (kg) for females
For example, a male 6' tall (72") 180 cm – 100 = 80 kg ideal body.

Body mass index (BMI) is another method of determining ideal body weight:

$BMI = weight (kg) / height (m^2)$
Ideal body weight = BMI of 22–28
Obesity = BMI of 28–35
Morbid obesity = BMI > 35

3. Do obese patients have an altered response to CO_2?

Obesity per se has not been found to decrease the respiratory center's sensitivity to CO_2. Yet approximately 5–10% of obese patients experience an apparent decreased ventilatory response to CO_2, resulting in one or more of the following syndromes.

    1. Obstructive sleep apnea syndrome (OSAS)—defined as 30 apneic periods of > 20 seconds over 7 hours.

    2. Obesity hypoventilation syndrome (OHS)—decreased ventilatory response to CO_2 and O_2, resulting in sleep apnea, hypoventilation, hypercapnea, pulmonary hypertension, and hypersomnolence.

    3. Pickwickian syndrome—symptoms include OHS, hypoxemia, hypercarbia, pulmonary hypertension, polycythemia, and biventricular failure.

4. Discuss the respiratory changes that occur in morbidly obese patients.

Obesity is typically accompanied by hypoxemia, the mechanisms of which include:

    1. An increased work of breathing 2–4 times greater than normal. An increased chest wall mass decreases chest wall compliance and diaphragmatic excursion.

    2. The large tissue mass increases total oxygen (O_2) consumption and increases carbon dioxide (CO_2) production.

    3. Changes in lung volumes result in closure of small airways during tidal respiration and ventilation-perfusion (V-Q) mismatch. An altered response to CO_2 is seen in some obesity syndromes. The pulmonary function tests of obese patients show a restrictive pattern of lung disease.

Changes in Pulmonary Volumes and Function Tests Associated with Obesity

LUNG VOLUMES	CHANGES WITH OBESITY
Tidal volume (V_T)	Normal or increased
Inspiratory reserve volume (IRV)	Decreased

Table continued on next page.

Changes in Pulmonary Volumes and Function Tests Associated with Obesity (Cont.)

LUNG VOLUMES	CHANGES WITH OBESITY
Expiratory reserve volume (ERV)	Greatly decreased
Residual volume (RV)	Normal
Functional residual capacity (FRC = RV + ERV)	Greatly decreased
Vital capacity (VC) (VC = IRV + V_T + ERV)	Decreased
Total lung capacity	Decreased
Forced expiratory volume at 1 second (FEV_1)	Normal or slightly decreased
Maximal midexpiratory flow rate (MMEF)	Normal or slightly decreased

5. What arterial blood gas changes are common in obese patients?

The most common alteration is hypoxemia due to V-Q mismatching. Pulmonary perfusion is increased because of increased cardiac output, circulating blood volume, and pulmonary hypertension. Progressive obesity results in tidal volumes resting below closing volume, resulting in collapsed airways during tidal respiration and the tendency to undergo oxygen desaturation.

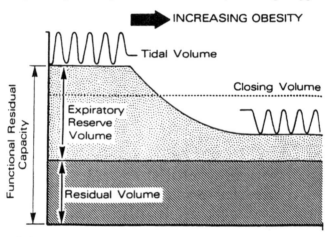

Changes in ventilation associated with weight gain. (From Fox GS: Anaesthesia for intestinal short circuiting in the morbidly obese with reference to the pathophysiology of gross obesity. Can Anaesth Soc J 22:307, 1975, with permission.)

6. Describe the changes in the cardiovascular system of obese patients.

Cardiac output (CO) and stroke volume (SV) increase in proportion to oxygen consumption and weight gain. An increase in CO of 100 ml/min accompanies each kilogram increase in adipose tissue. Circulating blood volume is also increased proportionately with increasing weight. Systemic hypertension is 10 times more prevalent in obese patients because of the increases in CO and blood volume. Pulmonary hypertension is present in pickwickian patients as a result of increased CO and hypoxic pulmonary vasoconstriction (the reflex constriction of pulmonary arterioles in areas of atelectasis). Right and left end-diastolic pressures may be elevated. Ventricular hypertrophy and biventricular failure are common; as many as 10% of obese patients develop congestive heart failure.

7. What changes in gastrointestinal and hepatic function can be expected in obese patients?

The large tissue mass in obese patients increases intra-abdominal and intragastric pressures. Hiatal hernias and gastric reflux are common. Several studies have shown that, despite an 8-hour fast, 85–90% of morbidly obese patients have gastric volumes > 25 ml and gastric pH < 2.5, greatly increasing their risk for pulmonary aspiration. Obese patients typically have fatty infiltration of the liver and may have hepatic inflammation, focal necrosis, and cirrhosis. At present no causal relationship between fatty infiltration and cirrhotic changes is known. Hepatic enzymes are generally elevated, especially after jejunoileal bypass operations.

8. Do obese patients metabolize anesthetic drugs differently from nonobese patients?

Alterations in drug metabolism in obese patients may be unpredictable. Obesity increases the biotransformation rate of methoxyflurane, enflurane, and halothane, resulting in increased serum levels of fluoride ions. Prolonged exposure to increased concentrations of fluoride ions is associated with renal toxicity. Isoflurane and desflurane have not been associated with significant increases in the rate of biotransformation in obese patients and are therefore the volatile agents of choice. Lipophilic or fat-soluble drugs such as opioids, benzodiazepines, and barbiturates have an increased volume of distribution and decreased elimination half-life, resulting in lower serum drug concentrations and decreased clearance. Exceptions include fentanyl, a lipophilic opioid that shows similar pharmacokinetics in obese and nonobese patients. In obese patients, hydrophilic, water-soluble drugs generally have similar volumes of distribution, elimination half-lives, and rates of clearance in obese and nonobese patients. Pseudocholinesterase activity is increased with obesity, and larger doses of succinylcholine are required (1.2–1.5 mg/kg). Nondepolarizing muscle relaxants show variability in dosing, duration, and recovery and should be followed closely with a peripheral nerve stimulator for return of neuromuscular function.

9. Discuss the relationship between obesity and diabetes mellitus.

Adult-onset diabetes mellitus occurs 7 times more frequently in obese than in nonobese patients. Insulin resistance is a prominent feature of both obesity and non–insulin-dependent diabetes mellitus (NIDDM). Several studies have shown a relationship between obesity and impairment of insulin action in NIDDM. Insulin action in obese patients is impaired by decreasing insulin suppression of hepatic glucose production and decreasing glucose utilization at the muscle. Obese patients, therefore, are at increased risk for hyperglycemia and hyperinsulinemia.

10. What factors should be considered in preparing an obese patient for surgery?

1. **History.** A thorough medical history should include incidence of sleep apnea, snoring, somnolence, and periodic breathing as well as assessment of hypertension, congestive heart failure, and coronary artery disease. Obese patients are frequently inactive, and determination of impaired cardiac performance may be difficult. Questions involving symptoms of gastroesophageal reflux, hiatal hernia, diabetes mellitus, and deep vein thrombosis should also be asked.

2. **Physical examination.** Airway evaluation is extremely important and should include cervical and mandibular range of motion, thyromental distance, and oral airway assessment. Subjective evaluation of chest and neck fat may suggest difficulties with intubation. If the airway examination suggests a potentially difficult intubation, the patient should be counseled on the procedure and benefits of an awake, sedated fiber-optic intubation. Adequacy of arterial and venous access also should be evaluated.

3. **Preoperative tests.** An electrocardiogram should be obtained for all obese patients to look for increased voltage, signs of atrial or ventricular enlargement, and arrhythmias. Ventricular arrhythmias are common. Chest radiographs are necessary and may reveal atelectasis, cardiac enlargement, infiltrates, effusion, or pneumothorax. A complete blood count and electrolytes should be obtained. Elevations in the white cell count and hematocrit may suggest infection and chronic hypoxemia, respectively. Bicarbonate levels are elevated to buffer a chronic respiratory acidosis if the patient retains carbon dioxide. Hypokalemia may occur with repeated use of diuretics. A room-air arterial blood gas analysis helps to identify baseline hypoxemic and hypercarbic patients and to determine acid-base status. Pulmonary function tests characterize pulmonary impairment. Liver function tests may prove valuable if hepatic dysfunction is suspected.

11. Is preoperative medication of an obese patient desirable?

An obese patient's increased risk of pulmonary aspiration should be prophylactically treated with H_2-receptor antagonists, such as cimetidine or ranitidine, combined with metoclopramide and nonparticulate antacids. Current recommendations suggest that ranitidine, 150 mg orally on the night before surgery and 1–2 hours before surgery, may be preferable to cimetidine. The side effects of cimetidine include inhibition of hepatic microsomal enzymes and decreased liver blood flow, which may decrease the metabolism of certain drugs.

12. What are the primary operative concerns in morbidly obese patients?

1. **Airway and ventilatory management.** Before induction of anesthesia, preparation for a difficult airway should be completed. A fiber-optic bronchoscope, cricothyrotomy equipment, a variety of laryngoscope blades, endotracheal tubes, and oral and nasal airways should be available. Preoxygenation and denitrogenation of the patient are critical, using 3 minutes of spontaneous breathing with 100% oxygen. If the airway exam suggests that laryngoscopy and intubation are not problematic, rapid-sequence induction and intubation with cricoid pressure may be used. Otherwise, awake, sedated fiber-optic intubation is the technique of choice. Rarely can the awake obese patient tolerate a supine position, and a head-elevated position of at least 30° may be necessary for induction of anesthesia. Careful attention to airway positioning before induction greatly facilitates intubation. A wedge under the patient's shoulder blades, combined with good head extension, is frequently helpful. Capnography is necessary to help verify endotracheal tube placement, because auscultation through the thick chest wall can be difficult. Pulse oximetry is mandatory for detection of hypoxemia in obese patients, and an inspired oxygen of greater than 50% is strongly recommended once intubation is obtained. Positive-pressure ventilation is necessary, because spontaneous ventilation may predispose the patient to atelectasis and hypoxemia. Adequate ventilation may require the addition of positive end-expiratory pressure (PEEP) to maintain arterial oxygenation; increases in tidal volume may worsen oxygenation if high peak pressures impair return of blood to the chest, decreasing cardiac output and producing V-Q mismatch.

2. **Cardiovascular management.** Cardiovascular monitoring in obese patients can be difficult. Large blood pressure (BP) cuffs (the bladder of the cuff encloses 70% of the arm) are used to avoid false readings. A small cuff falsely elevates BP readings, whereas an excessively large cuff gives falsely low readings. Despite an appropriate cuff size, an invasive arterial line may be necessary to follow blood pressure closely and offers the option of serial arterial blood gas analysis for monitoring of ventilatory status. Monitoring of central venous pressure (CVP) and pulmonary artery pressure (PAP) may be advantageous to follow volume status and cardiac function, but catheters are difficult to place because landmarks and pulses may be obscured. Generally PAP catheter placement is unnecessary unless the patient is undergoing extensive surgery or shows evidence of cardiac or pulmonary disease, especially pulmonary hypertension or cor pulmonale.

3. **Positioning.** The operating table may be of inadequate width to accommodate an obese patient. Care must be taken to protect and pad all pressure points. It may become necessary to secure two operating tables together for extremely obese patients.

13. What criteria should be used for extubation of an obese patient?

Before extubation the obese patient should be awake, alert, and able to sustain a head-lift for 5 seconds. Muscle relaxants should be adequately reversed, as indicated by peripheral nerve stimulator findings (sustained tetanus with no post-tetanic facilitation of twitches). The patient should have a respiratory rate of less than 30 breaths per minute. Arterial blood gases on 40–50% oxygen should be equal to or better than preoperative values; the PaO_2 should be greater than 80 mmHg and the $PaCO_2$ less than 45–50 mmHg if no preoperative values are available. A maximal inspiratory force of at least 25–30 cm H_2O, a vital capacity of 10–15 ml/kg, and a tidal volume greater than 5 ml/kg lean body weight are acceptable for extubation. The patient must be stable hemodynamically.

14. Discuss the postoperative course of morbidly obese patients.

Morbidly obese patients are at increased risk for hypoxemia for 4–7 days postoperatively. Therefore, supplemental oxygen is mandatory with the patient in a sitting or semirecumbent position. Aggressive pulmonary care with incentive spirometry, cough, deep breathing, and early ambulation is advised. Admission to an intensive care unit postoperatively may be necessary for close monitoring. An increased incidence of deep vein thrombosis in obese surgical patients necessitates early ambulation, which may be difficult because of relative postoperative immobility. Low-dose heparin and leg compression stockings are suggested. Postoperative pain control is important for both improved pulmonary function and early ambulation. Opioids may be used cautiously with adequate monitoring for respiratory depression. Intramuscular injections are likely to be subcutaneous and demonstrate unpredictable blood levels; therefore, intravenous narcotics are preferable. Patient-controlled analgesia (PCA) is a desirable option. Studies have shown that epidural opioids and local anesthetics facilitate earlier ambulation and decrease pulmonary complications as well as hospital stay compared with intramuscular narcotics. Epidural local anesthetic and opioid doses are similar to those for nonobese patients. In all patients, opioid epidural analgesia has the potential for unpredictable delayed respiratory depression and requires adequate monitoring at all times.

BIBLIOGRAPHY

1. Cork RC: General anesthesia for the morbidly obese patient—An examination of postoperative outcomes. Anesthesiology 54:310–313, 1981.
2. Fox DJ: Obesity. In Bready LL, Smith RB (eds): Decision Making in Anesthesiology, 2nd ed. St. Louis, B.C. Decker, 1992, pp 116–117.
3. Fox G: Anesthesia for the morbidly obese, experience with 110 patients. Br J Anaesth 53:811–815, 1981.
4. Lee J: Airway maintenance in the morbidly obese. Anesthesiol Rev 7:33–36, 1980.
5. Polk SL: Anesthesia for the morbidly obese patient. Trends Anesthesiol 6:3–9, 1987.
6. Snyder DS, Humphrey LS: Evaluation of the obese patient. In Rogers MC, Covino BG, Tinker JH, Longnecker DE (eds): Principles and Practice of Anesthesiology. St. Louis, Mosby, 1993, pp 514–532.

57. ANESTHESIA FOR TRAUMA

Laurel Mahonee, M.D., and Matt Flaherty, M.D.

1. Name the more common conditions that predispose trauma patients to increased anesthetic risk.

Depressed level of consciousness may lead to hypoventilation, loss of protective airway reflexes, inappropriate behavior, and decreased ability to examine and interview the patient. **Full stomachs** increase the risk of pulmonary aspiration of gastric contents. **Hypothermia** and **major blood loss**, either obvious or concealed internally, are common. **Alcohol and drug ingestion** is often associated with major trauma, particularly with death from trauma. Because of blood loss, intoxication, and organ injury, these patients are prone to altered responsiveness to anesthetic agents.

2. Paramedics relate that an incoming patient has a Glasgow Coma Scale (GCS) score of 3. What is the significance of this score?

The GCS is a system for assessment of patients with brain injury. The actual score is composed of scores for best eye opening, and best motor and verbal responses. Scores range from 3 to 15, with higher scores indicating higher levels of consciousness. Generally, the GCS for severe head injury is 9 or less; for moderate injury, 9–12; and for minor injury, 12 and higher. The described patient has the lowest possible score, which indicates no eye opening and no motor or verbal responses. The Advanced Trauma Life Support (ATLS) protocol mandates immediate tracheal intubation of all patients with a GCS ≤ 8.

3. Describe the progressive deterioration as a patient loses blood.

Healthy patients who acutely lose 10–15% of blood volume may experience anxiety secondary to pain, their accident, and blood loss. Changes in blood pressure, heart rate, pulse pressure, urine output, and respiratory rate are usually minimal. As the loss increases to 20–25% of blood volume, the vital signs become deranged. A patient with an acute loss of 30% of blood volume typically has a systolic blood pressure of 70–90 mmHg and a diastolic blood pressure > 50–60 mmHg; in addition, the heart rate usually increases to 120–130 beats per minute, the pulse pressure narrows to 20–30 mmHg, urine output falls to 5–15 ml/hr, and the respiratory rate increases to 30–40 breaths per minute.

4. What is the initial therapy for hypovolemic shock?

Initial therapy for hypovolemia is replacement of the lost volume with crystalloid infusion. The volume administered is 3 times the estimated blood loss. Failure to improve hemodynamically with this initial crystalloid infusion indicates a need for blood transfusion (consider tension pneumothorax, etc.). Patients who have lost more than 25–30% of blood volume are likely to require transfusion with packed red blood cells (PRBCs).

5. Outline the initial management of an unconscious 70-kg patient who has lost 2000 ml of blood.

As in all types of resuscitation, the airway and breathing must be addressed first. All trauma patients are assumed to have full stomachs. For protection of the airway against pulmonary aspiration of gastric contents and for maintenance of oxygenation and ventilation, the patient must undergo immediate tracheal intubation and ventilation with 100% oxygen. The rapid-sequence intubation technique is frequently used (see question 11). Establishing numerous large-gauge IV access points is paramount. The patient has lost approximately 40% of blood volume, so volume resuscitation is an ongoing priority. If cross-matched blood is not available, the transfusion of O-negative PRBCs is accepted practice until type-specific or cross-matched PRBCs are available. If more than 2 units of O-negative PRBCs are given, transfusions should continue with O-negative PRBCs. Intra-arterial catheterization allows for continuous monitoring and repetitive serologic analysis (ABGs, hematocrit, platelet count, coagulation profiles, and blood chemistries).

6. What is the significance of lactic acidosis in a trauma patient?

Lactate is a product of anaerobic metabolism at the cellular level. Any tissue experiencing inadequate oxygen delivery will produce lactate. Lactate levels above 2 mEq/L suggest the need for further resuscitation. Persistent lactic acidosis has been identified as an independent risk factor for multiple organ failure. There is some time delay for an adequately resuscitated patient to clear lactate. Patients with preexisting liver disease have notorious difficulty accomplishing this.

7. Why is the rapid-sequence induction frequently used for airway management in trauma patients?

The rapid-sequence induction is used because it minimizes the time between loss of consciousness and paralysis and protection of the airway with a cuffed endotracheal tube. All trauma patients are considered to have a full stomach, which places them at increased risk for aspiration. The usual rapid-sequence induction begins with preoxygenation with 100% oxygen. Often used induction agents in the hemodynamically unstable patient include ketamine and etomidate. The moribund patient may require only paralysis. Reduced doses are used in trauma patients because of contracted blood volume. The muscle relaxant of choice is succinylcholine, which has the fastest onset of paralysis sufficient for intubation. Prior to administration of the anesthetic and succinylcholine, pressure is applied firmly over the cricoid ring (Sellick maneuver) to prevent regurgitation of gastric contents. The patient is intubated as soon as adequate muscle relaxation is achieved (usually around 45–60 seconds). The endotracheal tube cuff is immediately inflated. The presence of end-tidal CO_2 is confirmed, and breath sounds are auscultated over the chest before the cricoid pressure is released. Positive pressure ventilation is usually avoided during the rapid-sequence induction to minimize the risk of aspiration.

8. How does trauma to the cervical spine modify the approach to the airway?

There is no airway management technique that results in no cervical motion. However, there is no documentation of iatrogenic neurologic injury in patients with cervical fractures when cervical spine precautions were used. These precautions include an appropriately sized Philadelphia collar, sand bags placed on each side of the head and neck, and the patient resting on a hard board with the forehead taped and secured to the board.

Alternative airway management techniques in the traumatized patient include rapid-sequence induction with in-line stabilization, use of the Bullard laryngoscope, blind nasal intubation, and fiber-optic bronchoscopic-assisted ventilation. When a cervical fracture or cervical spinal cord injury is documented, most anesthesiologists would choose fiber-optic intubation, facilitated by some form of topical anesthesia to the airway and sedation, titrated to effect, keeping in mind the patient's other injuries and hemodynamic status. This allows postintubation assessment of neurologic status prior to induction of unconsciousness. It would not be advisable to ablate all protective airway reflexes in a patient with a full stomach.

The Bullard laryngoscope is a rigid oral laryngoscope, the physical characteristics of which result in decreased cervical motion at the atlanto-occipital, atlantoaxial, and other high cervical articulations.

9. What are the signs of a tension pneumothorax?

Pneumothoraces may develop quickly with positive pressure ventilation. The chest may rise unevenly with inspiration. The breath sounds become unequal. Percussion of the chest over the pneumothorax is tympanitic. The trachea may shift away from the affected side. Neck veins may become distended (in the normovolemic patient). The patient becomes progressively more hypotensive, and peak airway pressures progressively rise. Immediate treatment for tension pneumothorax is the placement of a large-bore needle through the chest wall in the second intercostal space in the midclavicular line. A rush of air confirms the diagnosis. The needle should be left in place until a tube thoracostomy is performed. Tension pneumothorax is a clinical diagnosis; **do not delay treatment for radiologic confirmation** of this life-threatening condition.

10. How may a pulmonary contusion manifest during general anesthesia?

Blunt chest trauma may result in pulmonary contusion, a major cause of post-traumatic morbidity and mortality. Often associated with pulmonary contusion are multiple rib fractures. Parenchymal hematoma and edema are pathologic findings; lungs become poorly compliant, airway pressures increase, and gas exchange is impaired. Therapeutic measures include increased inspired oxygen concentration, positive end-expiratory pressure, and optimization of volume status, best achieved with the guidance of invasive pressure monitoring. Air entrainment into the pulmonary circulation is a risk and may result in air emboli to the central nervous system (CNS) and coronary circulation.

11. The patient becomes hypoxemic and peak airway pressures have doubled over 1 hour. How is tension pneumothorax differentiated from pulmonary contusion?

Both conditions may be caused by blunt chest trauma; penetrating trauma is more likely to cause tension pneumothorax.

Pulmonary Contusion vs. Tension Pneumothorax

SIGN	PULMONARY CONTUSION	TENSION PNEUMOTHORAX
Hypoxemia	+	+
Increased airway pressure	+	+

Table continued on next page.

Pulmonary Contusion vs. Tension Pneumothorax (Continued)

SIGN	PULMONARY CONTUSION	TENSION PNEUMOTHORAX
Tympany on percussion	−	+
Differential chest rise on inspiration	−	+
Tracheal shift	−	+
Bilateral breath sounds	+	−
Pulmonary edema, rales	+	−

12. Describe the presentation of a cardiac contusion.

Blunt chest trauma may cause cardiac contusion. Associated injuries include sternal fractures, multiple rib fractures, and pulmonary contusion. The right ventricle lies posterior to the sternum and is often affected. Dysrhythmias are common, and a patient without dysrhythmias for 24 hours is likely not contused. Pump failure is an ominous finding. Cardiac enzyme elevation is a nonspecific finding. Echocardiography is useful and reveals segmental wall motion defects.

13. What is Beck's triad?

Beck's triad consists of hypotension, distant heart sounds, and distended neck veins, the classic signs associated with cardiac tamponade. Neck vein distention may not be found because of hypovolemia. Central venous pressure is increased in tamponade, because right atrial filling is impaired. Stroke volume decreases, and tachycardia may compensate for decreased cardiac output. Some patients have electrical alternans, a rhythmic variation in electrocardiogram (ECG) voltage that originates as the heart begins to float more freely in the expanded pericardium, causing axis shifts.

14. A patient with undetected cardiac tamponade undergoes general anesthesia for laparotomy. What happens to cardiac filling as positive pressure ventilation begins?

Cardiac tamponade may arise from either blunt or penetrating trauma. When bleeding into the pericardial space causes pericardial pressures to equal or exceed right atrial pressures, cardiac filling is impaired. Positive pressure ventilation further decreases venous return and may greatly exacerbate the reduction in cardiac output.

15. A patient with blunt chest trauma develops hypotension and increased central venous pressure (CVP) during emergency left thoracotomy. Differentiate cardiac tamponade from cardiac contusion.

Either condition may arise after blunt chest trauma, or the two may coexist.

Cardiac Contusion vs. Cardiac Tamponade

SIGN	CARDIAC CONTUSION	CARDIAC TAMPONADE
Elevated central venous pressure	+	+
Hypotension	+	+
Distant heart sounds	−	+
Dysrhythmias	Common	Uncommon
Hypotension exacerbated by positive pressure ventilation	Minimal	+
Pulsus paradoxus (spontaneous ventilation)	−	+

16. What risks are incurred when trauma patients are given analgesia and/or sedation?

It was thought that analgesia might mask undiagnosed conditions. However, it is inhumane to deny analgesia to a patient who has sustained painful traumatic injury. Analgesia may in fact be beneficial if it promotes patient cooperation. A brief yet thorough examination is reasonable prior to sedation and analgesia administration. The intoxicated, hemodynamically unstable, or elderly patient may have an exaggerated response to these medications, so they should be titrated to effect while monitoring the patient's vital signs. That analgesia masks undiagnosed injuries is an unsupported allegation.

17. Which induction agents are best for trauma patients?

Far more important than the particular drug is the dose given. Thiopental and propofol are appropriate for some trauma patients if given in reduced dosages. The intravascular volume is reduced in hypovolemic patients; thus usual doses may result in higher-than-expected plasma concentrations. Ketamine may be used in the hypovolemic patient as its sympathetic stimulation supports the blood pressure; it should be recognized that, on occasion, its direct myocardial depressant effects may result in hypotension. Etomidate is often used in hemodynamically unstable patients because of its minimal effect on hemodynamic variables. Fentanyl has minimal cardiac depressive action but may cause a drop in endogenous catecholamine output.

18. When are trauma patients prone to coagulopathy?

Coagulopathies often begin after transfusion of approximately 1 blood volume (consider after transfusion of 5 units PRBCs). Dilutional thrombocytopenia is most common. Plasma coagulation factors are also decreased (~ 40% of normal). This level of coagulation factors may or may not be adequate; fresh frozen plasma transfusion should be guided by laboratory analysis. Diffuse intravascular coagulopathy and fibrinolysis may occur after massive transfusion. Patients with increasing shock and tissue ischemia are particularly at risk. Hypothermia induces coagulopathy through alterations in platelet number and function, inhibition of coagulation enzymes, and possibly increased fibrinolytic activity.

19. What are the best intravenous lines for fluid resuscitation?

Increasing the gauge of the catheter is the most important intervention because flow rate is a function of the 4th power of the radius (Poiseuille's law). There is a direct inverse relationship between flow and catheter length (i.e., use the shortest catheter possible). The most desirable catheter would be the 14-gauge or 9-French catheter introducer.

20. Describe management of the pregnant trauma patient.

The patient should be positioned with left uterine displacement. Immediate consultation with an obstetrician to ascertain the viability of the fetus is advised. If fetal distress occurs, an emergency cesarean section may be required. If ultrasound or fetal heart tones indicate fetal demise and cesarean section is not indicated, all efforts are directed toward resuscitation of the mother. After surgery the patient may experience premature labor. Monitoring for uterine contractions may detect premature labor and allow intervention, if necessary.

The usual concerns for pregnant women apply. Airway management may be difficult, and the patients are at risk for pulmonary aspiration. The gravid uterus may render the patient hypotensive, especially if there has been blood loss. Pregnant women may be sensitive to sedatives and local anesthetics. They have a dilutional anemia, and the uterus may interfere with abdominal exam. Seat belts may produce uterine rupture.

Always consider the fetus and assess fetal heart tones. Premature labor may ensue during the postoperative phase yet may go unrecognized due to the administration of opioids; vigilance and fetal monitoring are therefore indicated. Occasionally, emergent cesarean section is necessary, but the life of the mother takes precedence.

21. Describe strategies to maintain a trauma patient's body temperature.

Patients often arrive hypothermic because of environmental exposure and are immediately stripped, exacerbating this condition. Hence, it is not unusual to begin anesthetic care with the patient's temperature between 35° and 36°C. The following strategies are recommended:

• Warm the room prior to arrival.
• Warm all fluids and blood products.
• Keep the patient covered whenever possible and use convective air warming blankets over nonoperative sites.

Warming of gases is not particularly useful because the heat content of gas is negligible.

22. What is the abdominal compartment syndrome (ACS)?

A victim of polytrauma experiencing hypotension, oliguria, and respiratory failure manifesting as increasing airway pressures (on mechanical ventilation) and decreasing oxygenation may have ACS. The most common scenario is coagulopathy after massive resuscitation. Diagnosis is by clinical suspicion and confirmed by measuring bladder pressure (> 25 cm H_2O is suspicious). Treatment involves fluid resuscitation and abdominal decompression.

23. What is polyheme?

The search is ongoing for a blood substitute. Polyheme is manufactured from outdated PRBCs. The cellular stroma is removed, and the hemoglobin is polymerized to limit renal filtration (and failure!). It binds to oxygen similar to the hemoglobin in normal red blood cells. Its life in the circulation is on the order of days. Its concentration is about 8 g/dl, so one would not likely be able to exceed this hemoglobin level during its use. Methemoglobin concentrations are significant and interfere with pulse oximetry.

BIBLIOGRAPHY

1. Abrams K: Preanesthetic evaluation. In Grande CM (ed): Textbook of Trauma Anesthesia and Critical Care. St. Louis, Mosby, 1993, pp 421–431.
2. Capan LM, Miller SM: Trauma and burns. In Barash PG, Cullen BF, Stoelting RK (eds): Clinical Anesthesia, 3rd ed. Philadelphia, Lippincott Williams & Wilkins, 1997.
3. Hastings RH, Vigil AC, Hanna R, et al: Cervical spine movement during laryngoscopy with Bullard, Macintosh, and Miller laryngoscopes. Anesthesiology 82:859–869, 1995.
4. Landow L, Shahnarian A: Efficacy of large bore intravenous fluid administration sets designed for rapid volume resuscitation. Crit Care Med 18:540, 1990.
5. Mizock BA, Falk JL: Lactic acidosis in critical illness. Crit Care Med 20:80–91, 1992.
6. Pavlin EG: Hypothermia in traumatized patients.In Grande CM (ed): Textbook of Trauma Anesthesia and Critical Care. St Louis, Mosby, 1993, pp 1131–1139.
7. Ryder IG, Brown D: Anesthetic risks for trauma patients. In Grande CM (ed): Textbook of Trauma Anesthesia and Critical Care. St. Louis, Mosby,1993, pp 445–452.
8. Schumaker PT, Cain SM: The concept of critical oxygen delivery. Intens Care Med 13:223–229, 1987.

58. ANESTHESIA AND BURNS

Alma N. Juels, M.D., and Philip R. Levin, M.D.

1. Who gets burned?

Approximately 50,000 people are hospitalized in the United States for thermal injury; one-half are children. Over 1.25 million persons are treated annually for burns. Of thermal-related deaths, one-third are children younger than 15 years of age. The highest incidence occurs in children younger than 5 years of age. The majority of burns are thermal injuries. Electrical burns usually cause tissue destruction by thermal injury and associated injuries. In chemical burns, the degree of injury depends on the particular chemical, its concentration, and duration of exposure.

2. What are the consequences of skin damage?

The skin is the largest organ of the human body. It has three principal functions, all of which are disrupted by burn injury: (1) it is an important sensory organ; (2) it performs a major role in thermoregulation for the dissipation of metabolic heat; and (3) it acts as a barrier to protect the body against the entrance of microorganisms in the environment. A burn patient may have extensive evaporative heat and water loss, and loss of thermoregulation may lead to hypothermia. Burn patients have a profound risk of infection and sepsis.

3. How are burns classified?

The severity of the burn is graded by its depth, which depends on the extent of tissue destruction. **First-degree burns** involve the upper layers of the epidermis; the skin is painful and appears red and slightly edematous, much like a sunburn. **Second-degree burns** occur when tissue damage extends into the dermis, which is still lined with intact epithelium that proliferates and regenerates new skin. Second-degree burns develop blisters and have red or whitish areas that are very painful. **Third-degree burns** are due to the destruction of all layers of skin, including the nerve endings; therefore, there is no sensation. The skin appears charred. Skin will not regenerate. **Fourth-degree burns** involve destruction of all layers of skin and extend into the subcutaneous tissue, muscle, and fascia—even as far as the bone.

4. What systems are affected by burns?

All physiologic functions can be affected by burns, including the cardiovascular and respiratory systems, hepatic, renal, and endocrine function, the gastrointestinal tract, hematopoiesis, coagulation, and immunologic response.

5. How is the cardiovascular system affected?

A transient decrease in cardiac output, as much as 50% from baseline, is followed by a hyperdynamic response. In the acute phase, organ and tissue perfusion decrease because of hypovolemia, depressed myocardial function, increased blood viscosity, and release of vasoactive substances. The acute phase starts immediately after injury; the second phase of burn injury, termed the metabolic phase, begins about 48 hours after injury and involves increased blood flow to organs and tissues. Geriatric patients may have a delayed or nonexisting second phase. Hypertension of unknown cause develops and may be quite extensive.

6. How is the respiratory system affected?

Pulmonary complications can be divided into three distinct syndromes based on clinical features and temporal relationship to the injury. Early complications, occurring 0–24 hours postburn, include carbon monoxide poisoning and direct inhalation injury and can lead to airway obstruction and pulmonary edema. Delayed injury, occurring 2–5 days after injury, includes adult respiratory distress syndrome. Late complications, occurring days to weeks after the injury, include pneumonia, atelectasis, and pulmonary emboli.

7. What is inhalation injury?

Inhalation injury occurs when hot gases, toxic substances, and reactive smoke particles reach the tracheobronchial tree. These substances result in wheezing, bronchospasm, corrosion, and airway edema and should be suspected if the burn was sustained in a closed space. The presence of carbonaceous sputum, perioral soot, burns to the face and neck, stridor, dyspnea, or wheezing are indications for complete respiratory tract evaluation. There should be a low threshold for elective intubation of a suspicious airway.

8. What are the features of carbon monoxide (CO) poisoning?

CO is produced by incomplete combustion associated with fires, exhaust from internal combustion engines, cooking stoves, and charcoal stoves. Its affinity for hemoglobin is 200 times that of oxygen. When CO combines with hemoglobin, forming carboxyhemoglobin (COHb), the pulse oximeter may overestimate hemoglobin saturation. Symptoms are caused by tissue hypoxia, shift in the oxygen-hemoglobin dissociation curve, direct cardiovascular depression, and cytochrome inhibition. Treatment is initiated with 100% oxygen, which decreases the serum half-life of COHb. Indications for hyperbaric oxygen include coma, myocardial ischemia, persistent symptoms after 4 hours of 100% oxygen at atmospheric pressure, or acidosis; hyperbaric oxygen is also indicated in neonates.

9. How do burns affect the gastrointestinal tract?

Adynamic ileus may occur at any time after a burn injury. Acute ulceration of the stomach or duodenum, referred to as Curling's ulcer, may lead to gastrointestinal bleeding. The small and large intestine may develop acute necrotizing enterocolitis with abdominal distention, hypotension, and bloody diarrhea. During the second and third week after injury acalculous cholecystitis is common.

10. How is renal function affected?

Renal blood flow and glomerular filtration diminish immediately, activating the renin-angiotensin-aldosterone system. Antidiuretic hormone (ADH) is released, resulting in retention of sodium and water and loss of potassium, calcium, and magnesium. The incidence of acute renal failure in burned patients varies from 0.5% to 38%, depending primarily on the severity of the burn. The associated mortality rate is very high (77–100%). Hemoglobinuria, secondary to hemolysis, and myoglobinuria, secondary to muscle necrosis, can lead to acute tubular necrosis and acute renal failure.

11. How is myoglobinuria treated?

Vigorous fluid resuscitation, maintenance of urine output with osmotic diuretics (mannitol), and administration of bicarbonate to alkalinize the urine may reduce the incidence of pigment-associated renal failure.

12. How is hepatic function affected?

Acute reduction of cardiac output, increased viscosity of blood, and splanchnic vasoconstriction can cause hepatic hypoperfusion, which can result in decreased hepatic function.

13. Are drug responses altered?

Drugs administered acutely by any route other than intravenously have delayed absorption. After 48 hours the plasma albumin concentration is decreased, and albumin-bound drugs, such as benzodiazepines and anticonvulsants, have an increased free fraction and therefore a prolonged effect. The effect of drugs metabolized in the liver by oxidative metabolism (phase-I reaction) is prolonged (e.g., diazepam). However, drugs metabolized in the liver by conjugation (phase II) are not affected (e.g., lorazepam). Opioid requirements are increased, most likely because of habituation and hypercatabolism. Ketamine may cause hypotension secondary to hypovolemia and depleted catecholamine stores, exerting its direct cardiodepressant effect. Thiopental, propofol, and etomidate may cause hypotension secondary to hypovolemia in the acute phase. Inhalational agents are likewise poorly tolerated in hypovolemic patients.

14. What is the endocrine response to a burn?

The endocrine response to a thermal burn involves massive release of catecholamines, glucagon, adrenocorticotropic hormone, antidiuretic hormone, renin, angiotensin, and aldosterone. Glucose levels are elevated, and patients are susceptible to nonketotic hyperosmolar coma. Adrenal necrosis has been noted in burn patients and should be suspected in the hypotensive patient who is unresponsive to volume infusion.

15. What are the hematologic complications that occur with burns?

Anemia is a common finding in severely burned patients. In the immediate postburn period, erythrocytes are damaged or destroyed by heat and are removed by the spleen in the first 72 hours. This decrease in red cell mass is not immediately apparent because of the loss of plasma fluid and hemoconcentration. With fluid resuscitation, the deficit becomes more apparent. In the early postburn period, more red cell loss occurs secondary to decreased erythropoiesis. Also, ongoing infection can result in subacute activation of the coagulation cascade. Consumption of circulating procoagulants results in various degrees of coagulopathy. Platelet function is both qualitatively and quantitatively depressed.

16. How are patients with burns resuscitated?

The initial goal of resuscitation is to correct hypovolemia. Burns cause a generalized increase in capillary permeability with loss of fluid and protein into interstitial tissue; this loss is greatest in the first 12 hours. Two formulas are recommended for treating burn shock in the first 24 hours. The **Parkland formula** involves giving 4 ml of lactated Ringer's solution (LR) per kilogram of body weight per percent of total body surface area (BSA) burned. One half of the calculated amount is given during the first 8 hours, and the remainder is given over the next 16 hours, in addition to daily maintenance fluid. The **Brooke formula** requires 3 ml of LR per kilogram of body weight per percent of BSA burned. One half of the calculated amount is given in the first 8 hours, and one half in the next 16 hours. Most burn centers use crystalloid as the primary fluid for burn resuscitation. In the United States, most authors believe colloid solutions should not be used in the first 24 hours. There is abundant evidence that outcome is not influenced by early colloid resuscitation. On the second day after injury, capillary integrity is restored, and the amount of required fluid is decreased. Infusion of crystalloid is decreased after the first day, and colloids are administered. The endpoint of fluid therapy is hemodynamic stability and urine output at a rate of 1 ml/kg/hr.

17. How do you calculate the percent of total body surface burned?

The severity of a burn injury is based on the amount of surface area covered in second- and third-degree burns. In the "rule of nines" method of estimation, the major body parts are portioned as follows:

Head and neck	9%
Upper extremities	9% each
Chest (anterior and posterior)	9% each
Abdomen	9%
Lower back	9%
Lower extremities	18% each
Perineum	1%

The rule of nines is modified in children because the head and neck are proportionately larger than in adults.

Rule of Nines Modified for Children

	PERCENT OF BODY SURFACE ACCORDING TO AGE		
	NEWBORN	3 YEARS	6 YEARS
Head	18%	15%	12%
Trunk	40%	40%	40%
Arms	16%	16%	16%
Legs	26%	29%	32%

18. What is important in the preoperative history?

It is important to know at what time the burn occurred for fluid replacement. The type of burn is also important to assess airway damage, associated injuries, and the possibility of more extensive tissue damage than initially appreciated (electrical burns). A standard preoperative anesthetic history also must be taken, including past coexisting medical conditions, medications, allergies, and anesthetic history.

19. What should the anesthesiologist look for on the preoperative physical exam?

In addition to the conventional concerns of any patient about to undergo surgery, most important to the anesthesiologist is the status of the patient's airway. Excessive sputum, wheezing, and diminished breath sounds may suggest inhalation injury to the lungs. The cardiovascular system should be evaluated, noting pulse rate and rhythm, blood pressure, cardiac filling pressures (if available), and urine output. Neurologic evaluation should include an assessment of the level of consciousness and orientation. A complete airway examination is always a must.

20. What preoperative tests are required before induction?

Special emphasis should be placed on correcting the acid-base and electrolyte imbalance during the acute phase. Therefore, an arterial blood gas analysis and a chemistry panel are required. A chest radiograph also should be obtained in patients suspected of smoke inhalation, although a normal chest radiograph does not preclude significant injury. In the presence of CO poisoning, the pulse oximeter may overestimate the saturation of hemoglobin; therefore, a COHb level, determined by cooximetry, may be helpful to assess the degree of CO poisoning and to guide treatment. Coagulation tests are also helpful, because such patients often have bleeding diathesis.

21. What monitors are needed to give a safe anesthetic?

Access for monitoring may be difficult. Needle electrodes or electrocardiogram (ECG) pads sewn on the patient may be required for the ECG monitor and nerve stimulator. A blood pressure cuff may be placed on a burned area, but an arterial catheter may be better and allows frequent blood analysis. Temperature measurement is a must because of exaggerated decreases in body temperature. Invasive monitors are placed as deemed necessary, taking into account the patient's previous baseline medical condition. If the procedure involves a large amount of blood loss, central venous pressure (right atrial pressure) should be monitored through an introducer sheath. If myocardial dysfunction is likely, a pulmonary artery catheter may be necessary, though authorities disagree on this point.

22. How are muscle relaxants affected?

From about 24 hours after injury until the burn has healed, succinylcholine may cause hyperkalemia, because of proliferation of extrajunctional neuromuscular receptors. On the other hand, burned patients tend to be resistant to the effects of nondepolarizing muscle relaxants and may need 2–5 times the normal dose.

23. What induction drugs are good for burn patients?

Various medications have been given successfully to burn patients. Ketamine offers the advantage of stable hemodynamics and analgesia and has been used extensively as the primary agent for both general anesthesia and analgesia for burn dressing changes. Unfortunately, it tends to produce dysphoric reactions. If the patient is hemodynamically unstable, etomidate is a reasonable induction alternative to ketamine. In patients who are adequately volume resuscitated and not septic, thiopental and propofol are acceptable induction agents.

24. Describe specific features of electric burns.

Care of electrical burns is similar to care of thermal burns, except that the extent of injury may be misleading. Areas of devitalized tissue may be present under normal-appearing skin. The extent of superficial tissue injury may result in underestimation of initial fluid requirements. Myoglobinuria is common, and urine output must be kept high to avoid renal damage. The development of neurologic complications after electrical burns is common, including peripheral neuropathies or spinal cord deficits. Many believe that regional anesthesia is contraindicated. Cataract formation may be another late sequela of burn injury. Cardiac dysrhythmias and ventricular fibrillation or asystole may occur up to 48 hours after injury. Apnea may result from tetanic contraction of respiratory muscles or cerebral medullary injury.

BIBLIOGRAPHY

1. Capan LM, Miller SM: Trauma and burns. In Barash PG, Cullen BF, Stoelting RK (eds): Clinical Anesthesia, 3rd ed. Philadelphia, Lippincott Williams & Wilkins, 1997.
2. Davies MP, Evans J, McGonigle RJ: The dialysis debate: Acute renal failure in burn patients. Burns 20:71–73, 1994.
3. MacLennan N, Heimback D, Cullen B: Anesthesia for major thermal injury. Anesthesiology 89:749–770, 1998.
4. Monafo WW: Initial management of burns. N Engl J Med 335:1581–1586, 1996.
5. Nguyen TT, Gilpin DA, Meyer NA, Herndon DN: Current treatment of severely burned patients. Ann Surg 223:14–25, 1996.
6. Sheridan RL, Prelack KM, Petras LM, et al: Intraoperative reflectance oximetry in burn patients. J Clin Monit 11:32–34, 1995.

VII. Special Anesthetic Considerations

59. NEONATAL ANESTHESIA

Rita Agarwal, M.D.

1. Why are neonates and preterm infants at increased anesthetic risk?

1. **Pulmonary factors.** Differences in the neonatal airway, including large tongue and occiput, floppy epiglottis, small mouth, and short neck, predispose infants to upper airway obstruction. The more premature the infant is, the higher the incidence of airway obstruction. The carbon dioxide response curve is shifted further to the right in neonates than in adults; that is, infants have a decreased ventilatory response to hypercarbia. Newborn vital capacity is about one-half of an adult's vital capacity, respiratory rate is twice that of an adult, and oxygen consumption is 2–3 times greater. Consequently, opioids, barbiturates, and volatile agents have a more profound effect on ventilation in neonates than in adults.

2. **Cardiac factors.** Newborn infants have relatively stiff ventricles that function at close to maximal contraction. Cardiac output is heart rate dependent, and neonates are highly sensitive to the myocardial depressant effects of many anesthetic agents, especially those that may produce bradycardia. Inhalational agents and barbiturates should be used cautiously.

3. **Temperature.** Infants have poor central thermoregulation, thin insulating fat, increased body surface area to mass ratio, and high minute ventilation. These factors make them highly susceptible to hypothermia in the operating room. Shivering is an ineffective mechanism for heat production because infants have limited muscle mass. Nonshivering thermogenesis uses brown fat to produce heat, but it is not an efficient method to restore body temperature and increases oxygen consumption significantly. Cold-stressed infants may develop cardiovascular depression and hypoperfusion acidosis.

4. **Pharmacologic factors.** Neonates have a larger volume of distribution and less tissue and protein binding of drugs than older children and adults. They also have immature livers and kidneys and a larger distribution of their cardiac output to the vessel-rich tissues. Neonates often require a larger initial dose of medication but are less able to eliminate the medication. Uptake of inhalation agents is more rapid and minimum alveolar concentration (MAC) is lower.

2. Do neonates have normal renal function?

Glomerular function of the kidneys is immature, and the concentrating ability is impaired. Renal clearance of drugs may be delayed. Extra salt and water are not handled well.

3. Why is it important to provide infants with exogenous glucose?

Neonates have low stores of hepatic glucose, and mechanisms for gluconeogenesis are immature. Infants who have fasted may develop hypoglycemia. Symptoms of hypoglycemia include apnea, cyanosis, respiratory difficulties, seizures, high-pitched cry, lethargy, limpness, temperature instability, and sweating.

4. What are the differences in the gastrointestinal or hepatic function of neonates?

Gastric emptying is prolonged, and the lower esophageal sphincter is incompetent; thus the incidence of reflux may be increased. Elevated levels of bilirubin are common in neonates. Kernicterus, a complication of elevated levels of bilirubin, may lead to neurologic dysfunction and even death in extreme cases. Commonly used medications such as furosemide and sulfon-amide may displace bilirubin from albumin and increase the risk of kernicterus. Diazepam contains the preservative benzyl alcohol, which also may displace bilirubin. Hepatic metabolism is immature, and hepatic blood flow is less than in older children or adults. Drug metabolism and effect may be prolonged.

5. What is retinopathy of prematurity?

Retinopathy of prematurity is a disorder that occurs in premature and occasionally full-term infants who have been exposed to high inspired concentrations of oxygen. Proliferation of the retinal vessels, retinal hemorrhage, fibroproliferation, scarring, and retinal detachment may occur, with decreased visual acuity and blindness. Premature and full-term infants should have limited exposure to high concentrations of inspired oxygen. Oxygen saturation should be maintained between 92% and 95%, except during times of greater risk for desaturation.

6. How is volume status assessed in neonates?

Blood pressure is not a reliable measure of volume in neonates. If the anterior fontanelle is sunken, skin turgor is decreased, and the infant cries without visible tears, the diagnosis is dehydration. Capillary refill after blanching of the big toe should be less than 5 seconds. The extremities should not be significantly cooler than the rest of the body. Finally, the skin should look pink and well perfused—not pale, mottled, or cyanotic.

7. What problems are common in premature infants?

Common Problems in Premature Infants

PROBLEM	SIGNIFICANCE
Respiratory distress syndrome (RDS)	Surfactant, which is produced by alveolar epithelial cells, coats the inside of the alveolus and reduces surface tension. Surfactant deficiency causes alveolar collapse. BPD occurs in about 20% of cases.
Bronchopulmonary dysplasia (BPD)	Interstitial fibrosis, cysts, and collapsed lung impair ventilatory mechanics and gas exchange.
Apnea and bradycardia (A and B)	Most common cause of morbidity in postoperative period. Sensitivity of chemoreceptors to hypercarbia and hypoxia is decreased. Immaturity and poor coordination of upper airway musculature also contribute. If apnea persists > 15 sec, bradycardia may result and worsen hypoxia.
Patent ductus arteriosus (PDA)	Incidence of hemodynamically significant PDA varies with degree of prematurity but is high. Left-to-right shunting through the PDA may lead to fluid overload, heart failure, and respiratory distress.
Intraventricular hemorrhage (IVH)	Hydrocephalus usually results from IVH. Avoiding fluctuations in blood pressure and intracranial pressure may reduce the risk of IVH.
Retinopathy of prematurity (ROP)	See question 5.
Necrotizing enterocolitis (NEC)	Infants develop distended abdomen, bloody stools, and vomiting. They may go into shock and require surgery.

8. What special preparations are needed before anesthetizing a neonate?

1. Routine monitors in a variety of appropriately small sizes should be available.

2. The room should be warmed at least 1 hour before the start of the procedure to minimize radiant heat loss. A warming blanket and warming lights also help to decrease heat loss. Covering the infant with plastic decreases evaporative losses. Forced-air warming blankets have been shown to be very efficient at keeping infants warm. They work equally well if the infant is placed on them or if the blanket is placed on the infant. Temperature should be monitored carefully, because it is easy to overheat a small infant.

3. At least 2 pulse oximeter probes are helpful in measuring preductal and postductal saturation. Listening to heart and breath sounds with a precordial or esophageal stethoscope is invaluable.

4. Placing 25–50 ml of balanced salt solution in a buretrol prevents inadvertent administration of large amounts of fluid.

5. Five percent albumin and blood should be readily available.

6. Calculate estimated blood volume and maximal acceptable blood loss.

9. What intraoperative problems are common in small infants?

Common Intraoperative Problems in Infants

PROBLEM	POSSIBLE CAUSES	SOLUTION
Hypoxia	1. Short distance from cords to carina; ETT easily dislodged or displaced into bronchus.	1. After intubation, place ETT into right mainstem and, carefully listening to breath sounds, pull tube back. Tape ETT 1–2 cm above level of carina.
	2. Pressure on abdomen or chest by surgeons may decrease FRC and vital capacity.	2. Inform surgeons when they are interfering with ventilation. Hand ventilation helps to compensate for changes in peak pressure.
Bradycardia	1. Hypoxia	1. Preoxygenate before intubation or extubation; all airway manipulations should be performed expeditiously.
	2. Volatile agents	2. Minimize amount of volatile agent administered, especially halothane.
	3. Succinylcholine	3. Give atropine before administering succinylcholine.
Hypothermia	See question 1.	Warm operating room, warming blanket, warming lights, humidifier; keep infant covered whenever possible. Warming fluids may be helpful.
Hypotension	1. Bradycardia	1. Treat bradycardia with anticholinergics and ensure oxygenation.
	2. Volume depletion	2. Many neonatal emergencies are associated with major fluid loss. Volume status should be carefully assessed, with replacement as needed.

ETT = endotracheal tube, FRC = forced residual capacity.

10. What are the most common neonatal emergencies?

Tracheoesophageal fistula (TEF) Gastroschisis
Congenital diaphragmatic hernia (CDH) Patent ductus arteriosus (PDA)
Omphalocele Intestinal obstruction
Pyloric stenosis

11. Discuss the incidence and anesthetic implications of congenital diaphragmatic hernia.

1. The incidence is 1–2:5000 live births.

2. The diaphragm fails to close completely, allowing the peritoneal contents to herniate into the thoracic cavity. Abnormal lung development and hypoplasia usually occur on the side of the hernia but may be bilateral.

3. The majority of hernias occur through the left-sided foramen of Bochdalek.

4. Cardiovascular abnormalities present in 23% of patients.

5. Patients present with symptoms of pulmonary hypoplasia. The severity of symptoms and prognosis depend on the severity of the underlying hypoplasia.

6. Mask ventilation may cause visceral distention and worsen oxygenation. The infant should be intubated while awake. Low pressures must be used for ventilation to prevent barotrauma. Pneumothorax of the contralateral (healthier) lung may occur when high pressures are needed. Some patients may require high-frequency ventilation or extracorporeal membrane oxygenation (ECMO).

7. A nasogastric tube should be used to decompress the stomach.

8. A transabdominal approach is used for the repair.

9. Good intravenous access is mandatory. An arterial line may be necessary if the infant has significant lung or cardiac abnormalities.

10. Pulmonary hypertension may complicate management by impairing oxygenation and decreasing cardiac output. Most patients need to remain intubated in the postoperative period.

11. Opioids and muscle relaxants should be the primary agents used. Inhalational agents may be used to supplement the anesthetic if tolerated by the infant.

12. Which congenital anomalies are associated with tracheoesophageal fistula (TEF)?

TEFs may occur alone or as part of a syndrome. The two most common syndromes are the VATER and the VACTERL syndromes. Patients with VATER have vertebral anomalies, imperforate anus, tracheoesophageal fistula, and renal or radial abnormalities. Patients with VACTERL have all of the above in addition to cardiac and limb abnormalities.

13. How should patients with TEF be managed?

1. Patients usually present with excessive secretions, inability to pass a nasogastric tube, and regurgitation of feedings. Respiratory symptoms are uncommon.

2. Positive pressure ventilation may cause distention of the stomach. In a spontaneously breathing patient, either an awake intubation or inhalational induction may be carried out.

3. The endotracheal tube (ETT) should be placed into the right mainstem and gradually withdrawn until bilateral breath sounds are heard. The stomach should be auscultated to ensure that it is not overinflated. If the infant has significant respiratory distress because of overinflation of the stomach, it may be necessary to perform a gastrostomy before anesthetizing the patient.

4. An arterial line is frequently not necessary in an otherwise healthy infant with no other congenital anomalies. In selected patients, it may be helpful to monitor blood gas values.

5. Pulse oximetry is invaluable. Probes should be placed at a preductal (right hand or finger) and postductal site (left hand or feet).

6. Once the airway has been secured, the infant is placed in the left lateral decubitus position. Placing a precordial stethoscope on the left chest helps to detect displacement of the ETT.

7. A right-sided thoracotomy is made, and the fistula is divided. If possible, the esophagus is reanastomosed; if not, a gastrostomy tube is placed.

8. It is desirable to extubate the infant as soon as possible to prevent pressure on the suture line.

14. What are the differences between omphalocele and gastroschisis?

1. An omphalocele is a hernia within the umbilical cord caused by failure of the gut to migrate into the abdomen from the yolk sac. The bowel is completely covered with chorioamnionic membranes but otherwise usually normal. Patients with omphalocele frequently have associated cardiac, urologic, and metabolic anomalies.

2. The exact cause of gastroschisis is unknown; it may be due to vascular occlusion of blood supply to the abdominal wall or fetal rupture of an omphalocele. The bowel is often covered with an inflammatory exudate and may be abnormal. There are usually no associated anomalies.

15. How are patients with omphalocele or gastroschisis managed in the perioperative period?

1. It is important to prevent evaporative and heat loss from exposed viscera. The exposed bowel should be covered with warm, moist saline packs and Saran wrap until the time of surgery. The operating room should be warmed before the arrival of the infant. Warming lights and a warming blanket help to decrease conductive and radiation loss. Covering the head and extremities with plastic prevents evaporative loss.

2. Respiratory distress is uncommon; therefore, infants usually arrive in the operating room breathing spontaneously. Awake intubation or rapid-sequence induction quickly establishes airway control.

3. Ventilation is controlled with muscle relaxants to facilitate return of the bowel into the abdomen.

4. After intubation a nasogastric tube should be placed if not already present.

5. Patients need good IV access to replace third-space and evaporative losses. An arterial line is frequently unnecessary.

6. Once the surgeons begin to put the viscera into the abdomen, the ventilatory requirements change. Hand ventilation during this phase allows the anesthesiologist to feel peak airway pressures and changes in airway pressures. If peak airway pressures are greater than 40 cm H_2O, the surgeons must be notified.

7. The abdominal cavity may be too small for the viscera. Venous return from or blood flow to the lower extremity may be compromised. A pulse oximeter on the foot helps to detect such changes. Renal perfusion may decrease and manifest as oliguria.

8. If primary closure is not possible, the surgeons choose either to do a fascial (skin) closure or to place a synthetic mesh silo over the defect. Both approaches necessitate return trips to the operating room for the final corrective procedure.

9. Patients usually remain intubated after surgery.

16. How does pyloric stenosis present?

Pyloric stenosis is a common surgical problem, occurring in 1 out of 300 live births. First-born males are more commonly affected, and it usually presents between 2 and 6 weeks of age. Patients present with persistent vomiting. Dehydration, hypochloremia, and alkalosis can develop. Continued vomiting and dehydration can lead to metabolic acidosis. An olive-like mass can be felt in the epigastrium. Confirmation of the diagnosis by barium swallow roentgenogram has largely been replaced by abdominal ultrasound.

17. Discuss the perioperative management of patients with pyloric stenosis.

1. Electrolyte and volume imbalances need to be corrected prior to taking the patient to the operating room.

2. A gastric tube should be placed and continuous suction applied. Watch out for barium!

3. Patients are at risk for aspiration; therefore, rapid-sequence intubation or awake intubation should be performed.

4. Choice of anesthetic agents and muscle relaxants will be guided by the speed of the surgeon (duration of surgery can be 10–60 minutes).

5. Opioids are usually unnecessary and should be avoided intraoperatively.

CONTROVERSIES

18. At what age should the former premature infant be allowed to go home afer surgery?

Premature infants are at increased risk for the development of postoperative apnea even after relatively minor surgery. Postoperative apnea has been reported in ex-premature infants up to 60 weeks postconceptual age (PCA). Côté et al. showed that, in ex-premature infants born at a gestional age of 32 weeks undergoing inguinal herniorrhaphy, the risk of postoperative apnea was not less than 1% until 56 weeks PCA.[3] Anemia appropriate for gestational age or high for gestational age infants and a history of continuing apnea at home increased the risk of postoperative apnea.

19. Does regional anesthesia protect the patient from developing postoperative anesthesia?

Spinal anesthesia without supplemental sedation has been associated with less apnea than general anesthesia. Caudal epidural blockade may also be used. The addition of sedation may increase the incidence of postoperative apnea.

BIBLIOGRAPHY

1. Badgewell JM (ed): Clinical Pediatric Anesthesia. Philadelphia, Lippincott-Raven, 1997.
2. Côté CJ, Ryan JF, Todres ID, Goudsouzian NG (eds): A Practice of Anesthesia in Infants and Children, 2nd ed. Philadelphia, W.B. Saunders, 1993.
3. Côté CJ, Zaslavsky A, Downes JJ, et al: Postoperative apnea in former preterm infants after inguinal herniorrhaphy. A combined analysis. Anesthesia 82:809–822, 1995.
4. Diaz JH (ed): Perinatal Anesthesia and Critical Care. Philadelphia, W.B. Saunders, 1991.
5. Gregory GA (ed): Pediatric Anesthesia, 3rd ed. New York, Churchill Livingstone, 1994.
6. Klaus MH, Fanaroff AA (eds): Care of the High Risk Neonate, 4th ed. Philadelphia, W.B. Saunders, 1993.

60. PEDIATRIC ANESTHESIA

Rita Agarwal, M.D.

1. What are the differences between the adult and pediatric airway?

Differences between the Adult and Pediatric Airway

INFANT AIRWAY	SIGNIFICANCE
Obligate nose breathers, narrow nares	Infants can breathe only through their nose, which can become easily obstructed by secretions
Large tongue	May obstruct airway and make laryngoscopy and intubation more difficult
Large occiput	Sniffing position achieved with roll under shoulder
Glottis located at C3 in premature babies, C3–C4 in newborns, and C5 in adults	Larynx appears more anterior; cricoid pressure frequently helps with visualization
Larynx and trachea are funnel-shaped	Narrowest part of the trachea is at the cricoid; the patient should have an ETT leak of < 30 cm H_2O to prevent excessive pressure on the tracheal mucosa, barotrauma
Vocal cords slant anteriorly	Insertion of ETT may be more difficult

ETT = endotracheal tube.

2. Are there any differences in the adult and pediatric pulmonary system?

Differences in the Pediatric and Adult Pulmonary System

PEDIATRIC PULMONARY SYSTEM	SIGNIFICANCE
Decreased, smaller alveoli	13-fold growth in number of alveoli between birth and 6 yr; threefold growth in size of alveoli between 6 yr and adulthood
Decreased compliance Decreased elastin	Increased likelihood of airway collapse
Increased airway resistance Smaller airways	Increased work of breathing and vulnerability to disease affecting small airways
Horizontal ribs, more pliable ribs and cartilage	Inefficient chest wall mechanics
Less type-1, high-oxidative muscle	Babies tire more easily
Decreased total lung capacity (TLC), faster respiratory and metabolic rate	Faster desaturation
Higher closing volumes	Increased dead-space ventilation

3. How does the cardiovascular system differ in a child?

1. Newborns are unable to increase cardiac output (CO) by increasing contractility; they can increase CO only by increasing heart rate.

2. Babies have an immature baroreceptor reflex and limited ability to compensate for hypotension by increasing heart rate. They are more susceptible, therefore, to the cardiac depressant effects of volatile anesthetics.

3. Babies and infants have increased vagal tone and are prone to bradycardia. The three major causes of bradycardia are hypoxia, vagal stimulation (laryngoscopy), and volatile anesthetics. **Bradycardia is bad!**

4. What are normal vital signs in children?

Normal Vital Signs in Children

AGE (YR)	HR	RR	SBP	DPB
<1	120–160	30–60	60–95	35–69
1–3	90–140	24–40	95–105	50–65
3–5	75–110	18–30	95–110	50–65
8–12	75–100	18–30	90–110	57–71
12–16	60–90	12–16	112–130	60–80

HR = heart rate, RR = respiratory rate, SBP = systolic blood pressure, DBP = diastolic blood pressure. A good rule of thumb is: normal BP = 80 mmHg + 2 × age.

5. When should a child be premedicated? Which drugs are commonly used?

Children may have a great deal of fear and anxiety when they are separated from their parents and during induction of anesthesia. Vetter recommends premedicating children who are 2–6 years old and have had previous surgery or no preoperative tour and education or who fail to interact positively with health care providers in the preoperative area. There is increasing evidence that children who are anxious during induction will suffer from negative postoperative behavioral changes.

Commonly Used Preoperative Medications and Routes of Administration

DRUG	ROUTE OF ADMINISTRATION	ADVANTAGES	DISADVANTAGES
Midazolam	po, pr, in, iv, sl	Quick onset, minimal side effects	Tastes bad when given orally, burns intranasally
Ketamine	po, pr, in, iv, sl	Quick onset, good analgesia	May slow emergence, tastes bad, burns intranasally
Fentanyl	otfc	Tastes good, good analgesic, onset at 45 min.	Possible hypoxemia, nausea
Diazepam	po, pr, im	Cheap, minimal side effects	Long onset time, may prolong emergence

po = by mouth, pr = per rectum, iv = intravenous, sl = sublingual, im = intramuscular, in = intranasal, otfc = oral transmucosal fentanyl citrate.

6. Describe the commonly used induction techniques in children.

1. **Inhalational induction** is the most commonly used induction technique in children younger than 10 years. The child is asked to breathe 70% nitrous oxide (N_2O) and 30% oxygen for approximately 1 minute; halothane is then turned on slowly. The halothane concentration is increased 0.5% every 3–5 breaths. If the child coughs or holds the breath, the concentration of halothane is not increased until the coughing or breath-holding resolves. Sevoflurane can also be used with or without N_2O.

   2. **Rapid inhalational or "brutane" induction** is used in an uncooperative child. The child is held down, and a mask containing 70% N_2O, 30% oxygen, and 3–5% halothane or 8% sevoflurane is placed on the child's face. This unpleasant technique should be avoided if possible. Once anesthesia has been induced, the concentration of halothane or sevoflurane should be decreased.

   3. **Steal induction** may be used if the child is already sleeping. Inhalational induction is accomplished by holding the mask away from the child's face and gradually increasing the concentration of halothane or sevoflurane. The goal is to induce anesthesia without awakening the child.

   4. **Intravenous induction** is used in a child who already has an IV line in place and in children > 10 years. Typical medications used in children are thiopental, 5–7 mg/kg; propofol, 2–3 mg/kg; and ketamine, 2–5 mg/kg. EMLA cream (eutectic mixture of local anesthesia) applied at least 90 minutes before starting the IV infusion makes this an atraumatic procedure.

7. How does the presence of a left-to-right shunt affect inhalational induction? Intravenous induction?

   A left-to-right intracardiac shunt leads to volume overload of the right side of the heart and the pulmonary circulation. Patients develop congestive heart failure and decreased lung compliance. Uptake and distribution of inhaled agents are minimally affected; onset time for intravenous agents is slightly prolonged.

8. How about a right-to-left shunt?

   Right-to-left shunting causes hypoxemia and left ventricular overload. Patients compensate by increasing blood volume and hematocrit. It is important to maintain a high systemic vascular resistance to prevent increased shunting from right to left. Such shunts may slightly delay inhalation induction and shorten the onset time of intravenous induction agents.

9. What other special precautions need to be taken in a child with heart disease?

   1. The **anatomy** of the lesion(s) and **direction of blood flow** should be determined. Pulmonary vascular resistance (PVR) needs to be maintained. If the PVR increases, right-to-left shunting may increase and worsen oxygenation, whereas a patient with a left-to-right shunt may develop a reversal in the direction of blood flow (Eisenmenger's syndrome). If a patient has a left-to-right shunt, decreasing the PVR may increase blood flow to the lungs and lead to pulmonary edema. Decreasing the PVR in patients with a right-to-left shunt may improve hemodynamics.

Conditions that Can Increase Shunting

LEFT-TO-RIGHT SHUNT	RIGHT-TO-LEFT SHUNT
Low hematocrit	Decreased SVR
Increased SVR	Increased PVR
Decreased PVR	Hypoxia
Hyperventilation	Hypercarbia
Hypothermia	Acidosis
Anesthetic agent:	Anesthetic agents:
Isoflurane	?Nitrous oxide; ?Ketamine

SVR = systemic vascular resistance; PVR = pulmonary vascular resistance.

   2. **Air bubbles** should be meticulously avoided. If there is a communication between the right and left sides of the heart (ventricular septal defect, atrial septal defect), air injected intravenously may travel across the communication and enter the arterial system. This may lead to central nervous system symptoms if the air obstructs the blood supply to the brain or spinal cord (paradoxical air embolus).

   3. **Prophylactic antibiotics** should be given to prevent infective endocarditis. Recommendations for medications and doses can be found in the American Heart Association guidelines.

   4. **Avoid bradycardia**.

   5. **Recognize and be able to treat a "tet spell."** Children with tetralogy of Fallot have right outflow tract (RVOT) obstruction, an overriding aorta, ventricular septal defect, and pulmonary stenosis or atresia. They may or may not have cyanosis at rest. However, many are

prone to hypercyanotic spells ("tet spells") with stimulation as they get older. Such episodes are characterized by worsening RVOT obstruction, possibly as a result of hypovolemia, increased contractility, or tachycardia during times of stimulation or stress. Patients are frequently treated with beta blockers, which should be continued perioperatively. Hypovolemia, acidosis, excessive crying or anxiety, and increased airway pressures should be avoided. The systemic vascular resistance (SVR) should be maintained. If a hypercyanotic spell occurs in the perioperative period, treatment includes maintaining the airway, volume infusion, increasing the depth of anesthesia, or decreasing the surgical stimulation. Phenylephrine is extremely useful in increasing SVR. Additional doses of beta blockers also may be tried. Metabolic acidosis should be corrected.

10. How does one choose an endotracheal tube of appropriate size?

Guidelines for Endotracheal Tube (ETT) Size

AGE	SIZE (mm INTERNAL DIAMETER)
Newborns	3.0–3.5
Newborn–12 months	3.5–4.0
12–18 months	4.0
2 years	4.5
> 2 years	ETT size = $\frac{16 + age}{4}$

1. An ETT a half size above and a half size below the estimated size should be available.
2. The leak around the tube should be < 30 cm H_2O.
3. The ETT should be placed to a depth of approximately 3 times its internal diameter.

11. Can cuffed ETTs be used in children?
Cuffed ETTs can be used in children. Of course, the cuff takes up space, thus limiting the size of the ETT. However, Khine et al. have shown that cuffed tubes can be successfully used even in neonates without increasing complications.[7]

12. Can a laryngeal mask airway (LMA) be used in children?
LMAs can be very useful in pediatrics. They can help secure a difficult airway, either as the sole technique or as a conduit to endotracheal intubation.

13. How does one choose an appropriate size LMA?

Laryngeal Mask Airways for Children

SIZE OF CHILD	LMA SIZE
Neonates up to 5kg	1
Infants 5–10 kg	1½
Children 10–20 kg	2
Children 20–30 mg	2½
Children/small adults > 30 kg	3

14. How does the pharmacology of commonly used anesthetic drugs differ in children?
1. The minimal alveolar concentration (MAC) of the volatile agents is higher in children than adults. The highest MAC is in infants aged 1–6 months. Premature babies and neonates have a lower MAC.
2. Children have a higher tolerance to the dysrhythmic effects of epinephrine during general anesthesia with volatile agents.

3. In general children have higher drug requirements (mg/kg) because they have a greater volume of distribution (more fat, more body water).

4. *Opioids* should be used carefully in children less than 1 year old, who are more sensitive to the respiratory depressant effects.

15. How is perioperative fluid managed in children?

1. Maintenance is calculated as follows:

Infant < 10 kg	4 ml/kg/hr
10–20 kg	40 + 2 ml/kg/hr for every kg < 10
Child > 20 kg	60 + 1 ml/kg/hr for every kg > 20

2. Estimated fluid deficit (EFD) should be calculated and replaced as follows:

EFD = maintenance × hours since last oral intake
½ EFD + maintenance given over the 1st hour
¼ EFD + maintenance given over the 2nd hour
¼ EFD + maintenance given over the 3rd hour

3. All EFD should be replaced for major cases. For minor cases, 10–20 ml/kg of a balanced salt solution with or without glucose is usually adequate.

4. Estimated blood volume (EBV) and acceptable blood loss (ABL) should be calculated for every case.

16. What is the most common replacement fluid used in children? Why?

A balanced salt solution (BSS) such as lactated Ringer's with glucose (D5LR) or without glucose (LR) is recommended. Welborn showed that hypoglycemia may occur in healthy children undergoing minimally invasive procedures if glucose-containing fluids are not used. However, she also found that administration of 5% glucose-containing solutions resulted in hyperglycemia in the majority of children. Some authors recommend using fluid containing 1% or 2.5% glucose. Others still use 5% glucose solutions for maintenance but recommend non–glucose-containing BSS for third space or blood loss. In major operations it is prudent to check serial glucose levels and to avoid hyper- or hypoglycemia.

17. What is the EBV in children?

Guidelines for Estimated Blood Volume in Children

AGE	EBV (ml/kg)
Neonate	90
Infant up to 1 year old	80
Older than 1 year	70

18. How is acceptable blood loss calculated?

$$ABL = \frac{EBV \times (pt\ hct - lowest\ acceptable\ hct)}{average\ hct}$$

where ABL = acceptable blood loss, EBV = estimated blood volume, pt = patient, and hct = hematocrit. The lowest acceptable hematocrit varies with individual circumstances. Blood transfusion is usually considered when the hematocrit is less than 21–25%. If problems with vital signs develop, blood transfusion may need to be started earlier. For example, a 4-month-old infant is scheduled for craniofacial reconstruction. He is otherwise healthy, and his last oral intake was 6 hours before arriving in the operating room. Weight = 6 kg, preoperative hct = 33%, lowest acceptable hct = 25%.

Maintenance	=	weight × 4 ml/hr = 24 ml/hr
EFD	=	maintenance × 6 kg = 144 ml
EBV	=	weight × 80 ml/kg = 480 ml

$$\text{ABL} \quad = \quad \frac{\text{EBV} \times (\text{pt hct} - \text{lowest acceptable hct})}{\text{average hct}}$$

$$= \quad \frac{480 \times (33 - 25)}{29} = 132 \text{ ml}$$

19. How do the manifestations of hypovolemia differ in children?

Healthy children compensate for acute volume loss of 30–40% before blood pressure changes. The most reliable early indicators of compensated hypovolemic shock in a child are persistent tachycardia, cutaneous vasoconstriction, and diminution of pulse pressure.

20. What are the systemic responses to blood loss?

Sysemic Response to Blood Loss in Children

ORGAN SYSTEM	< 25% BLOOD LOSS	25–40% BLOOD LOSS	> 45% BLOOD LOSS
Cardiac	Weak, thready pulse; ↑HR	↑HR	↓BP, ↑HR, bradycardia indicates severe blood loss and impending circulatory collapse
Central nervous system	Lethargic, confused, irritable	Change in LOC, dulled response to pain	Comatose
Skin	Cool, clammy	Cyanotic, ↓capillary refill, cold extremities	Pale, cold
Kidneys	↓UOP; ↑specific gravity	Minimal UOP	Minimal UOP

HR = heart rate, BP = blood pressure, LOC = level of consciousness, UOP = urine output.

21. What is the most common type of regional anesthesia performed in children?

Caudal epidural block is the most common regional technique performed in children. It is usually performed in an anesthetized child and provides good adjunct intraoperative and postoperative analgesia. It is used most commonly for surgery of the lower extremities, perineum, and lower abdomen. Lumbar and thoracic epidural blocks can also be used for postoperative pain relief. These should only be placed by experienced operators, however.

22. Which local anesthetic is usually used?

Bupivacaine in a concentration of 0.125–0.25% is the most commonly used local anesthesia. Bupivacaine 0.25% produces good adjunct intraoperative analgesia and decreases the required MAC of volatile anesthetic. However, it may produce postoperative motor blockade that interferes with hospital discharge of outpatients. Bupivacaine 0.125% causes minimal postoperative motor block but may not provide intraoperative analgesia or decrease the MAC requirements. Gunter showed that 0.175% bupivacaine produces good intraoperative analgesia and minimal motor block and decreases the required MAC of volatile anesthetics.

23. What is the dose?

Commonly Used Doses of Local Anesthetic for Caudal Block

DOSE (CC/KG)	LEVEL OF BLOCK	TYPE OF OPERATION
0.5	Sacral/lumbar	Penile, lower extremity
1	Lumbar/thoracic	Lower abdominal
1.2	Upper thoracic	Upper abdominal

Toxic dose of bupivacaine in the child is 2.5 mg/kg; in the neonate, 1.5 mg/kg.

24. What is a fascia iliaca block and what are its indications?

The fascia iliaca block is a technique to anesthetize the femoral, obturator, and lateral cutaneous nerves. The block provides analgesia to the upper thigh and is good for patients with femur fractures or patients undergoing procedures such as femoral osteotomy, muscle biopsy, or skin grafting.

25. Describe the common postoperative complications.

1. **Nausea and vomiting** continue to be the most common cause of delayed discharge or unplanned admission in children. The best treatment for postoperative nausea and vomiting is prevention. Prophylactic administration of an antiemetic should be considered for patients at high risk for emesis. Avoiding opioids will decrease the incidence of postoperative nausea and vomiting as long as pain relief is adequate (e.g., patient has a functioning caudal block). Management includes administering intravenous fluid and stopping oral intake. If vomiting persists, metoclopramide, droperidol, or ondansetron can be tried. If the vomiting does not resolve, the patient should be admitted for observation.

Factors Associated with Increased Incidence of Postoperative Nausea and Vomiting

PATIENT FACTORS	SURGICAL/ANESTHETIC FACTORS
Patient age > 6 yr	Length of surgery > 20 min
Previous history of postoperative nausea and vomiting	Eye surgery
History of motion sickness	Tonsillectomy/adenoidectomy
Preoperative nausea	Use of narcotics
Extreme preoperative anxiety	? Nitrous oxide

2. **Respiratory problems,** particularly laryngospasm and stridor, are more common in children than in adults. Management for laryngospasm includes oxygen, positive pressure, the Fink maneuver (painful jaw thrust), succinylcholine, and reintubation if necessary. Stridor is usually treated with humidified oxygen, steroids, and racemic epinephrine.

CONTROVERSIES

26. What is the significance of masseter muscle rigidity?

1. Rigidity of the masseter muscles occurs in 1% of children receiving halothane and succinylcholine. Addition of sodium thiopental may decrease the incidence, although its mechanism of action is unknown.

2. Masseter muscle rigidity may be the first symptom of malignant hyperthermia (MH), but it also may occur in patients who are not susceptible to MH.

27. How is the patient who develops masseter muscle rigidity managed?

1. The incidence of MH after masseter muscle rigidity is a source of controversy. Most authors believe that the incidence is 1% or less; however, one recent study showed that it may be as high as 59% in patients referred for muscle biopsy.

2. When masseter muscle rigidity develops, the major issue is whether to substitute a nontriggering technique or to stop the procedure. The author usually switches to a nontriggering technique and continues with the operation unless other signs of possible MH develop or such severe masseter muscle spasm occurs that intubation is impossible.

3. Patients should be admitted and followed postoperatively for increased levels of creatine phosphokinase (CPK) and other signs of MH (heart rate, blood pressure, temperature, urine myoglobin). If the postoperative CPK levels are > 20,000, the patient should be managed and diagnosed with MH. If the CPK is < 20,000 but still significantly elevated, an MH work-up should be considered, including a muscle biopsy. If CPK is normal or minimally elevated, the patient is probably not at increased risk for MH.

28. Describe the management of a patient with an upper respiratory infection.

1. The risk of adverse respiratory events is 9–11 times greater up to 2 weeks after an upper respiratory infection (URI). Underlying pulmonary derangements include:
   - Decreased diffusion capacity for oxygen
   - Decreased compliance and increased resistance
   - Decreased closing volumes
   - Increased shunting (ventilation-perfusion mismatch), lung oxygen uptake
   - Increased incidence of hypoxemia
   - Increased airway reactivity

2. Endotracheal intubation increases the risks of such respiratory events.

3. General recommendations for a child with mild URI:
   - Discuss increased risk with parents.
   - Try to avoid intubation.
   - Use anticholinergics to help decrease secretions and airway reactivity

4. The child who has a fever, rhonchi that do not clear with coughing, an abnormal chest x-ray, elevated white count, or decreased activity levels should be rescheduled.

29. What are the advantages and disadvantages of the pediatric circle system and the Bain circuit?

Advantages and Disadvantages of the Pediatric Circle System and Bain Circuit

CIRCUIT	ADVANTAGES	DISADVANTAGES
Circle system	Relatively constant inspired concentration of gases Conservation of moisture and heat Minimal pollution in operating room	Complex design, with unidirectional valves Small babies (< 10 kg) may have an increased work of breathing to overcome resistance to valves
Bain circuit	Lightweight Good for spontaneous or controlled ventilation Minimal resistance Exhaled gases in outer tubing add warmth and humidity to inspired gases (in theory)	Most anesthesia machines require special attachment for this circuit Inner tubing may kink or become disconnected

30. Should parents be allowed to accompany children for induction of anesthesia?

Young children may become extremely anxious and frightened when they are separated from their parents before surgery. Allowing parents to accompany children to the operating room may facilitate induction of anesthesia in some cases. Parents and children should be educated and prepared for what to expect. Parents should be prepared to leave when the anesthesiologists believe that it is appropriate. Highly anxious, reluctant, or hysterical parents are a hindrance. An anesthesiologist who is not comfortable with allowing parents to be present during induction probably should not allow them to be so. An uncooperative or frightened child may or may not benefit from parental presence.

BIBLIOGRAPHY

1. Badgewell JM (ed): Clinical Pediatric Anesthesia. Philadelphia, Lippincott-Raven, 1997
2. Berry FA (ed): Anesthetic Management of Difficult and Routine Pediatric Patients, 2nd ed. New York, Churchill Livingstone, 1990.
3. Cohen MM, Cameron CB: Should you cancel the operation when a child has an upper respiratory tract infection? Anesth Analg 72:282–286, 1991.
4. Gregory GA (ed): Pediatric Anesthesia, 3rd ed. New York, Churchill Livingstone, 1994.
5. Gunter JB, Dunn CM, Bennie JB, et al: Optimum concentration of bupivacaine for combined caudal-general anesthesia in pediatric patients. Anesth Analg 66:995–998, 1982.

6. Kain ZN, Mayes LC, Wang SM, Hofstadler MD: Postoperative behavioral outcomes in children: Effects of sedative premedication. Anesthesiology 90:758–765, 1999.
7. Khine HH, Corddry DH, Kettrick RG, et al: Comparison of cuffed and uncuffed endotracheal tubes in young children during general anesthesia. Anesthesiology 86:627–631, 1997.
8. Motoyama EK, Davis PJ (eds): Smith's Anesthesia for Infants and Children, 5th ed. St. Louis, Mosby, 1990.
9. O'Flynn RP, Shutack JG, Rosenberg H, Fletcher JE: Masseter muscle rigidity and malignant hyperthermia susceptibility in pediatric patients: An update on management and diagnosis. Anesthesiology 80:1228–1233, 1994.
10. Vetter TR: The epidemiology and selective identification of children at risk for preoperative anxiety reactions. Anesth Analg 77:96–99, 1993.
11. Welborn LG, McGill WA, Hannallah RS, et al: Perioperative blood glucose concentrations in pediatric operations. Anesthesiology 65:543–547, 1986.

61. FUNDAMENTALS OF OBSTETRIC ANESTHESIA

Ana M. Lobo, M.D., M.P.H.

1. What are the cardiovascular changes associated with pregnancy?

Cardiovascular Changes Associated with Pregnancy

Heart rate	↑ (15–20 bpm)
Cardiac output	↑ (40–50%)
Stroke volume	↑ (50% by term)
Systemic vascular resistance	↓ (21%)
Pulmonary vascular resistance	↓ (34%)
Uterine blood flow	↑ (40%)
Mean arterial blood pressure	↓ 15 mmHg (normal by 2nd trimester)
Arterial blood pressure	↓ (normal by 2nd trimester)
Vascular tone	↓
Central venous pressure	No change

In pregnancy, the heart may appear enlarged on chest x-rays, as the diaphragmatic rise shifts the heart position to the left. There is a high incidence of asymptomatic pericardial effusion during pregnancy. Because of increased blood flow and vasodilation, a low grade (I to II) systolic murmur may be heard. The electrocardiogram (ECG) may show benign dysrhythmias and left axis deviation.

2. Discuss the respiratory changes associated with pregnancy.

Changes in the Respiratory System at Term in Pregnant Women

Minute ventilation	↑ (50%)
Alveolar ventilation	↑ (70%)
Tidal volume	↑ (50%)
Oxygen consumption	↑ (20%)

Table continued on next page.

Changes in the Respiratory System at Term in Pregnant Women (Continued)

Respiratory rate	↑ (15%)
Dead space	No change
Lung compliance	No change
Total compliance	↓ (30%)
Airway resistance	↓ (36%)
Expiratory reserve volume	↓ (20%)
Residual volume	↓ (20%)
Closing volume	No change or ↓
Vital capacity	No change
Total lung capacity	↓ (0–5%)
Functional residual capacity	↓ (20%)

Respiratory tract mucosa is friable and edematous. Functional residual capacity is reduced and oxygen consumption increased. Laryngoscopy may be difficult as the pregnant patient's enlarged breasts interfere with use of a laryngoscope. For these reasons pregnant patients experience precipitous declines in oxygen saturation at the time of anesthetic induction and neuromuscular blockade, complicated by the difficulties of airway management.

3. What blood gas changes are associated with pregnancy?

Changes in Blood Gases at Term Pregnancy

Arterial PO_2	↓ (10 mmHg)
Arterial PCO_2	↓ (10 mmHg)
Arterial pH	No change
Serum bicarbonate	↓ (4 mEq/L)

4. What gastrointestinal changes occur with pregnancy?

Decreases in gastric motility and incompetence of the gastroesophageal junction render the patient prone to regurgitation of gastric contents. All parturients are at risk for aspiration. A gastric volume > 25 ml and gastric pH < 2.5 increase the risk of aspiration pneumonitis. Aspiration prophylaxis prior to surgery includes an H_2 blocker, nonparticulate antacid, and metoclopramide to enhance gastric motility. Appendectomy and cholecystectomy are common nonobstetrical surgeries during pregnancy.

5. List the central nervous system changes that occur during pregnancy.

Pregnancy causes a decrease in anesthetic requirements. The minimum alveolar concentration (MAC) for inhalational agents is decreased by as much as 40%. The mechanism for this decrease is uncertain, but may be secondary to increased progesterone levels. Dosage requirements for regional anesthesia are reduced. This decrease in local anesthetic requirement may be due to a decrease in epidural space volume (due to epidural vein engorgement) and/or an increase in nerve sensitivity to local anesthetics. The lumbar lordosis of pregnancy may increase cephalad spread of subarachnoid local anesthetics. Also, an increase in cerebrospinal fluid pressure caused by labor may contribute to reduced local anesthetic requirements during spinal anesthesia. This increased sensitivity should be taken into account when administering both general and regional anesthetics.

6. How are the hematologic and coagulation systems changed by pregnancy?

Hematologic Changes in Pregnancy

Total erythrocyte volume	↑ (20%)
Plasma volume	↑ (45%)
Blood volume	↑ (35%)
Hemoglobin	↓
Hematocrit	↓ (31.9–36.5%)
Platelets	No change or ↓
Factors I, VII, VIII, IX, X, XII	↑
Fibrinogen	↑
Fibrinolysis	↓

Plasma volume increases from 40 to 70 ml/kg, near term blood volume increases by 1000 ml to 1500 ml. The relative anemia of pregnancy is caused by a relatively slower rise in red blood cell mass compared to plasma volume. Maternal anemia, usually due to iron deficiency, occurs if the hemoglobin falls below 10 g or the hematocrit is less than 30%.

Parturients are hypercoagulable and at risk for thrombotic events (such as deep venous thrombosis). Platelet activation and consumption are increased during pregnancy. Increased platelet consumption is compensated for by increased platelet production, and the platelet count usually remains unchanged or slightly reduced. Thrombocytopenia (platelet count < 100,000/mm^3) occurs in approximately 0.9% of normal parturients. Bleeding time is shortened during pregnancy.

The concentration of most coagulation factors increases during gestation. Fibrinolysis increases, and fibrin degradation products and plasminogen levels are increased. Prothrombin and partial thromboplastin times are shortened.

7. Do plasma proteins change during pregnancy?

Plasma albumin concentrations decrease during pregnancy. Free fractions of protein-bound drugs increase with falling albumin levels. Total protein levels also decrease during pregnancy, as does maternal colloid osmotic pressure (by approximately 5 mmHg). Plasma cholinesterase concentrations decrease by about 25% before delivery and 33% by 3 days postpartum. These reductions rarely result in clinically significant increases in the duration of depolarizing (succinylcholine) neuromuscular blockade. Monitoring neuromuscular blockade is important in *any* patient receiving muscle relaxants.

8. Discuss the hepatic changes of pregnancy.

Liver size, blood flow, and liver morphology do not change during pregnancy. Lactate dehydrogenase (LDH), serum bilirubin, alanine aminotransferase (ALT, SGPT), aspartate aminotransferase (AST, SGOT), and alkaline phosphatase increase during pregnancy. Alkaline phosphatase activity increases mostly due to production of this compound by the placenta. Gallbladder emptying slows, and the bile tends to be concentrated. These changes predispose the parturient to gallstone formation.

9. How is the renal system altered in pregnancy?

Renal calices, pelvices, and ureters dilate after the third trimester due to progesterone production. Late in pregnancy, the enlarged uterus compresses the ureter at the pelvic brim, leading to urinary stasis and contributing to the frequency of urinary tract infections during pregnancy.

Renal blood flow and glomerular filtration rate increase with pregnancy. Aldosterone levels also increase, causing increased total body sodium and water. Creatinine clearance is increased as a result of increased renal blood flow and glomerular filtration rate; therefore, serum creatinine and blood urea nitrogen (BUN) levels are decreased. Glucosuria (1–10 g/day) and proteinuria (<300 mg/day) are not pathologic in the pregnant patient. Bicarbonate excretion is increased in compensation for the respiratory metabolic alkalosis.

10. What causes labor pain?

During the first stage of labor, pain is caused by cervical dilation and effacement and dilation of the lower uterine segment. This pain is transmitted by autonomic C fibers that enter the dorsal horn of the spinal cord at T11–T12. It is usually described as a dull, aching pain. Throughout the second stage of labor, the pain is mediated by A-delta fiber stimulation, secondary to lower vagina, vulva, and perineum distention. These impulses enter the spinal cord through posterior roots of S2–S4.

11. Describe the most important intrapartum physiologic changes and their significance.

Cardiac output doubles during active labor, with the maximal increase occurring immediately after delivery. This rise in cardiac output is due to increasing catecholamine levels and autotransfusion during uterine contractions. Hyperventilation is common during active labor and may magnify the preexistent respiratory alkalosis, producing uterine vasoconstriction and compromised placental perfusion, hypoxemia, and fetal distress. Regional anesthesia during the intrapartum period may attenuate the hemodynamic changes, hyperventilation, and stress response associated with active labor.

12. How quickly do the organ systems recover after delivery?

Cardiac output rises immediately after birth because of autotransfusion of 500–750 ml of blood from the uterus (patients with pulmonary hypertension and stenotic valvular lesions are at risk during this time). Cardiac output returns to normal about 4 weeks postpartum. Functional residual capacity and residual volume rapidly return to normal. Many of the pulmonary changes due to mechanical compression by the gravid uterus resolve quickly. Alveolar ventilation returns to normal by 4 weeks postpartum, and there is a rise in maternal arterial pCO_2 as the progesterone level decreases. The "dilutional" anemia of pregnancy resolves and the hematocrit returns to normal within 4 weeks, due to a postpartum diuresis. Serum creatinine, glomerular filtration rate, and BUN return to normal levels in less than 3 weeks. Mechanical effects of the gravid uterus on the gastrointestinal system resolve within 2–3 days postpartum, although gastric emptying may be delayed for several weeks as serum progesterone levels are maintained. Therefore, precautions against pulmonary aspiration of gastric contents should be continued for several weeks postpartum.

13. How is the aortocaval compression syndrome treated?

Aortocaval compression becomes a significant concern by the second trimester and occurs when a pregnant woman assumes the supine position. Signs and symptoms of aortocaval compression are similar to those of shock—hypotension, tachycardia, pallor, sweating, nausea, vomiting, and changes in cerebration. These are caused by impaired venous return to the heart. The gravid uterus compresses the inferior vena cava, decreasing venous return and resulting in these symptoms. If the gravid uterus compresses the aorta, there may be a decrease in uterine and placental blood flow resulting in fetal distress. Aortocaval compression is prevented by uterine displacement (lateral position) to increase venous return. If symptomatic, patients should receive intravenous fluid administration, supplemental oxygen, and ephedrine (to increase cardiac output without producing uterine artery constriction).

14. What are the three stages of labor?

The first stage begins with the onset of regular contractions and ends with full cervical dilation (10 cm at term). The second stage of labor begins with full cervical dilation and is complete with delivery of the infant. The period of time from delivery of the infant to delivery of the placenta is referred to as the third stage of labor.

15. Describe the phases of cervical dilation in first-stage labor.

Cervical dilation in the first stage of labor occurs over time in an S-shaped curve. This stage is separated into latent and active phases. During the latent phase, many hours of painful uterine contractions may occur with little change in cervical dilation. The cervix effaces and becomes softer during this preparatory phase. The transition between the latent and active phases of the first stage of labor does not occur at a specific cervical dilation but is distinguished by an increase in the rate of cervical dilation. The active phase is often entered abruptly, and progression in cervical dilation should occur. About 60% of women reach the transition phase to active labor by 4 cm of cervical dilation and about 90% reach it by 5 cm.

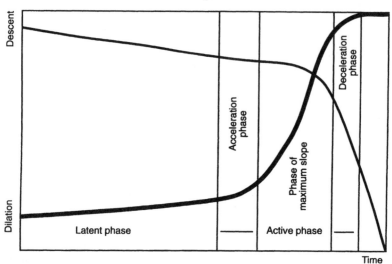

The first stage of labor—The Friedman curve. (From Friedman EA: Patterns of labor as indicators of risk. Clin Obstet Gynecol 16:172–183, 1973, with permission.)

16. Describe the vessels of the umbilical cord.

Two umbilical arteries carry blood away from the fetus; a single umbilical vein carries oxygenated blood to the fetus.

17. Which five factors influence uteroplacental perfusion?

1. **Aortocaval compression:** When lying supine, gravid patients compress their abdominal aorta, decreasing uteroplacental perfusion.

2. **Hypotension:** A fall in maternal arterial pressure (MAP) of 25% is associated with a decrease in uterine blood flow. Uteroplacental perfusion is compromised at MAP of 100 mmHg systolic.

3. **Increases in uterine vascular resistance:** Increases in uterine vascular resistance occur during contractions and parturition, with use of intravenous ketamine (> 1.5 mg/kg) and oxytocin, and with abruptio placentae.

4. **Maternal hypoxia, hypercarbia, and hypocarbia:** These changes are associated with decreased uteroplacental perfusion.

5. **Catecholamines:** Ephedrine acts indirectly and increases mean MAP by stimulating a release of catecholamines, not by adrenergic receptor agonism. Phenylephrine is a direct-acting α-adrenergic agonist but may be contraindicated because it decreases uterine blood flow in pregnant sheep and decreases placental and myometrial blood flow. Ephedrine affects uterine blood flow less than the other vasopressor agents, and for this reason it is usually used to increase blood pressure in pregnant patients.

18. What factors affect placental transfer of drugs and other substances?

Placental transfer is accomplished by simple diffusion, active transport, bulk flow, facilitated diffusion, and "breaks" in the chorionic membrane. Anesthetic compounds cross the placenta mostly by simple diffusion, as described by the equation:

$$Q/t = [k \times A \times (C_m - C_f)]/D$$

This equation states that the quantity of free drug (nonionized and nonprotein bound, Q) that crosses the placenta per unit of time (t) is directly proportional to the diffusion coefficient of the drug (k), the total area of the chorionic membrane available for transfer (A), and the difference between the maternal (C_m) and fetal concentrations (C_f) of free drug and is indirectly proportional to the distance across the membrane (D).

A drug's molecular weight, spatial configuration, degree of ionization, and lipid solubility determine its diffusion coefficient (k). The greater the diffusion coefficient, the greater the quantity of drug transferred. Compounds that are low in molecular weight, small in spatial configuration, poorly ionized, and lipid soluble have high rates of placental transfer. Most anesthetic drugs are highly lipid soluble and have molecular weights < 600, and for this reason their rates of placental transfer are high.

19. Describe the management of the pregnant patient undergoing nonobstetric surgery.

In the pregnant patient, nonemergent surgery should be avoided to protect the developing fetus. If a procedure must be done, the second trimester is the safest time, avoiding organogenesis. Surgery during pregnancy increases perinatal mortality, and manipulation of the uterus should be minimal to decrease the risk of premature labor. The most common surgical condition during pregnancy is appendicitis, followed by torsion, rupture, or hemorrhage of ovarian cysts. Cholecystectomies and trauma-related surgery are not uncommon.

Drugs with a long history of safe use are best employed, including thiopental, morphine, fentanyl, succinylcholine, pancuronium, and isoflurane. Nitrous oxide has been associated with DNA-synthesis inhibition and should be avoided. Diazepam use has been associated with fetal abnormalities (cleft lip and palate), so all benzodiazepines are best avoided.

If general anesthesia is chosen, the patient should receive an antacid regimen prior to careful preoxygenation and rapid-sequence intubation with cricoid pressure. Employ uterine displacement, avoiding aortocaval compression. Treat hypotension with fluids and IV ephedrine; high concentrations of oxygen are advisable. When considering regional anesthesia, consider the patient's altered responsiveness to local anesthetics.

20. How is fetal heart rate (FHR) monitoring used to evaluate fetal well-being?

The most important index is the relationship of FHR patterns to maternal uterine contractions. The **baseline FHR** is evaluated between contractions and is normally 120–160 bpm. Fetal tachycardia (> 160 bpm) may be caused by fever, hypoxia, beta-sympathomimetic agents, maternal hyperthyroidism, or fetal hypovolemia. Fetal bradycardia (< 120 bpm) may result from hypoxia, complete heart block, beta blockers, local anesthetics, or hypothermia. The moment-to-moment change in FHR is the **beat-to-beat variability**. Increased variability is seen with uterine contractions and maternal activity. Decreased variability may be due to central nervous system depression, hypoxia, acidosis, sleep, narcotic use, vagal blockade, and magnesium therapy for preeclampsia.

21. Describe the different types of fetal heart rate decelerations.

Early decelerations in FHR are caused by head compressions (vagal stimulation), are uniform in shape, begin near the onset of a uterine contraction, and are benign.

Variable decelerations are caused by umbilical cord compression and are nonuniform in shape, abrupt in onset and cessation, and severe if the FHR is < 70 bpm and of > 60 seconds duration. They usually do not reflect fetal acidosis.

Late decelerations are caused by uteroplacental insufficiency, are uniform in shape, and are severe when the FHR decreases by > 45 beats below baseline. When severe, they are associated with fetal acidosis. These decelerations are associated with maternal hypotension, hypertension, diabetes, preeclampsia, or intrauterine growth retardation. These are ominous patterns and indicate that the fetus has inadequate reserves (it is not able to maintain normal oxygenation and pH in the face of decreased blood flow). If fetal distress is present, the anesthesiologist should administer oxygen to the mother, maintain maternal blood pressure, and place the parturient in the left uterine displacement position.

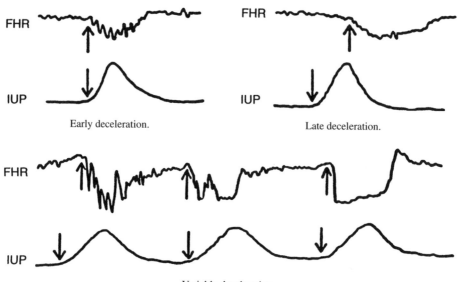

Early, late, and variable FHR deceleration during labor. (IUP = intrauterine pressure). (From Ackerman WE, Juneja MM: Obstetric Anesthesia Pearls. East Norwalk, CT, Appleton & Lange, 1992, pp 98–100, with permission.)

22. What are normal fetal capillary pH and arterial blood gas values at birth and at 30 minutes of life?

Normal fetal capillary pH is ≥ 7.25. Fetal acidosis is diagnosed when the pH is < 7.20. At birth, normal values for arterial blood gases are pH 7.25, PCO_2 of 40 mmHg, and PO_2 of 60 mmHg. At 30 minutes of life, the normal values are 7.33, 35, and 68, respectively.

23. How does one evaluate the neonate?

The Apgar score, originally introduced in 1952, is the most frequently used index for evaluating neonatal well-being and success of resuscitation. The Apgar score is measured at 1 and 5 minutes of life and assigns a value to five physiologic variables, with a possible total score of 10. Heart rate and respiratory effort are the most important evaluations. An Apgar score of 0–3 indicates a severely depressed neonate, whereas a score of 7–10 is considered normal.

The Apgar Score

	0	1	2
Heart rate	Absent	< 100 bpm	> 100 bpm
Respirations	Absent	Irregular, shallow	Good, crying
Reflex irritability	No response	Grimace	Cough, sneeze
Muscle tone	Flaccid	Good tone	Spontaneous flexed arms/legs
Color	Blue, pale	Body pink, extremities blue	Entirely pink

From Chantigan RC: Neonatal evaluation. In Ostheimer GE (ed): Manual of Obstetric Anesthesia. New York, Churchill Livingstone, 1992, p 49, with permission.

24. What drugs are useful in neonatal resuscitation?

A mnemonic for remembering which drugs may be administered via endotracheal tube is **LANE** (lidocaine, atropine, naloxone, epinephrine).

Drugs Used in Neonatal Resuscitation

DRUG	DOSE	ROUTE	INDICATION
Atropine	0.02 mg/kg	IV/ETT/IM	Bradycardia
Epinephrine	0.01 mg/kg	IV/ETT	Asystole
$CaCl_2$	5–20 mg/kg	IV	Low cardiac output, hypermagnesemia
Isoproterenol	Titrate to 16 μg/kg/min	IV	Persistent bradycardia
Lidocaine	1 mg/kg	IV/ETT	Ventricular arrhythmia
$NaHCO_3$	1–2 mg/kg	IV	Acidosis (pH < 7.1)
Naloxone	0.1 mg/kg 0.2 mg/kg	IV IM	Reverse narcotic-related depression

IV = intravenous, IM = intramuscular, ETT = endotracheal tube.
A mnemonic for remembering which drugs may be administered via endotracheal tube is **LANE** (lidocaine, atropine, naloxone, epinephrine).

25. What are the major concerns of anesthesiologists during neonatal resuscitation?

1. **Airway/breathing:** Laryngoscope blade size 0; endotracheal tube 2.5–3.5 mm; suction trachea to prevent aspiration; administer 100% oxygen.

2. **Circulation:** Cardiac compressions 100/min; defibrillation dose 2 J/kg once, then 4 J/kg.

3. **Hypovolemia:** Poor capillary refill; usually blood pressure is 50–70 mmHG systolic, 35–50 mmHG diastolic; treat with volume expansion (10 ml/kg), repeat if necessary.

4. **Hypothermia:** Neonates lose heat quickly because of their large body surface area to mass ratio; blankets, humidified oxygen, and heating lamp should be available.

5. **Hypoglycemia:** Dextrose, 2 mg/kg intravenously, then 5–8 mg/kg/min; may be due to asphyxiation or maternal hyperglycemia; document hypoglycemia prior to dextrose use.

6. **Hypocalcemia:** Calcium chloride given to patients suspected of having low ionized calcium levels contributing to poor cardiac function, for prolonged persistent asystole, and for the urgent treatment of hyperkalemia.

BIBLIOGRAPHY

1. Ackerman WE, Juneja MM: Obstetric Anesthesia Pearls. Norwalk, CT, Appleton & Lange, 1992.
2. Cheek TG, Gutsche BB: Maternal physiologic adaptations during pregnancy. In Shnider SM, Levinson G (eds): Anesthesia for Obstetrics, 3rd ed. Baltimore, Williams & Wilkins, 1993, pp 3–17.
3. Conklin KA: Physiologic changes of pregnancy. In Chestnut DH (ed): Obstetric Anesthesia Principles and Practice. St. Louis, Mosby-YearBook, 1994, pp 24–28.
4. Ostheimer GW (ed): Manual of Obstetric Anesthesia. New York, Churchill Livingstone, 1992.
5. Palahniuk RJ, Shnider SM, Eger EI: Pregnancy decreases requirements for inhaled anesthetic agents. Anesthesiology 41:82–83, 1974.
6. Peisner DB, Rosen MG: Transition from latent to active labor. Obstet Gynecol 68:448–451, 1986.
7. Santos AC, Pedersen H, Finster M: Obstetric anesthesia. In Barash PG, Cullen BF, Stoelting RK (eds): Clinical Anesthesia, 3rd ed. Philadelphia, Lippincott Williams & Wilkins, 1997.

62. OBSTETRIC ANALGESIA AND ANESTHESIA

Ana M. Lobo, M.D., M.P.H.

1. What are the most commonly used parenteral opioids for labor analgesia? Which side effects are of special concern to the parturient?

Intravenous and Intramuscular Analgesics for Labor

DRUG	USUAL DOSE	ONSET	DURATION	COMMENTS
Meperidine	25 mg IV 50 mg IM	5–10 min IV 40–45 min IM	2–3 hr	Active metabolite is normeperi- dine; neonatal effects most likely if delivery occurs between 1 and 4 hr after administration
Morphine	2–5 mg IV 10 mg IM	5 min IV 20–40 min IM	3–4 hr	Infrequent use during labor; greater respiratory depression in neonate than with meperidine
Fentanyl	25–50 µg IV 100 µg IM	2–3 min IV 10 min IM	30–60 min	Short-acting, potent respiratory de- pressant, used as continuous in- fusion and/or PCA; cumulative effect with large doses over time

IV = intravenous, IM = intramuscular, PCA = patient-controlled analgesia.
(Adapted from Wakefield ML: Systemic analgesia. Opioids, ketamine and inhalational agents. In Chestnut DH (ed): Obstetric Anesthesia: Principles and Practice. St. Louis, Mosby, 1994, p 341.)

In general, the above intravenous (IV) drugs help the parturient to tolerate labor pain but rarely provide complete analgesia. The incidence of side effects and efficacy of analgesia are dose-dependent. Opioids easily cross the placenta and may cause a decrease in fetal heart rate with beat-to-beat variability. In addition, IV opioids may cause neonatal respiratory depression and neurobehavioral changes.

2. What advantages does patient-controlled analgesia (PCA) offer over conventional intermittent bolus dosing?

PCA has been associated with greater patient satisfaction, less risk of maternal respiratory depression, less need for antiemetic use, and better pain relief with lower drug doses. PCA is especially useful if epidural anesthesia is contraindicated or not available.

3. Discuss the benefits of epidural anesthesia for labor and delivery.

In most laboring women, epidural analgesia is effective and reduces maternal catecholamine levels, potentially improving uteroplacental perfusion. Catecholamine secretion as a result of painful contractions may prolong labor by adversely affecting uterine contractility. Painful contractions may also lead to maternal hyperventilation and respiratory alkalosis, which in turn shifts the oxyhemoglobin dissociation curve to the left, decreasing delivery of oxygen to the fetus. Most importantly, the benefits of enhanced maternal well-being should not be underestimated.

4. What are the indications and contraindications for epidural analgesia in labor and delivery?

Relief of labor-induced pain is sufficient reason for placing an epidural catheter. Analgesia can be readily deepened to anesthesia by increasing the local anesthetic concentration, facilitating instrumental or cesarean delivery. Labor analgesia benefits preeclamptic patients and may be useful in patients with cardiac disease (e.g., mitral stenosis) because it blunts the hemodynamic effects that accompany uterine contractions (increased preload, tachycardia, increased systemic vascular resistance [SVR], hypertension, and hyperventilation). The contraindications to epidural anesthesia include patient refusal, coagulopathy, uncontrolled hemorrhage, increased intracranial pressure, and infection at the site of needle introduction. Relative contraindications include systemic maternal infection and certain neurologic diseases.

5. Discuss the importance of a test dose and suggest an epidural test-dose regimen. When and why is this regimen used?

The importance of a local anesthetic test dose is to recognize subarachnoid or intravenous placement of the epidural catheter, thereby preventing total spinal anesthesia or systemic toxicity. A common test dose is 3 ml of 1.5% lidocaine with 1:200,000 epinephrine. If the dose of local anesthetic is given in the subarachnoid space, a spinal block will appear within 3–5 minutes. If the local anesthetic is injected intravenously, tachycardia may result within 45 seconds (increase in heart rate of 30 bpm) because of the epinephrine additive. Every time an epidural catheter is injected, it is a test dose of sorts; one should always monitor for signs of IV or subarachnoid local anesthetic injection. Aspiration of the catheter is not adequate to identify all intrathecal or intravascular catheters. If there is any doubt in the anesthesiologist's mind about the exact site at which the epidural catheter is placed, the catheter should be removed and replaced.

6. What are the characteristics of the ideal local anesthetic for use in labor? Discuss the three most common local anesthetics used in obstetric analgesia. How does epinephrine affect the action of local anesthetics?

The ideal local anesthetic in labor would have rapid onset of action, minimal risk of toxicity, minimal motor blockade with effective sensory blockade, and a minor effect on uterine activity and placental perfusion. Bupivacaine, lidocaine, and chloroprocaine are most commonly used in obstetric analgesia.

Bupivacaine, an amide, is the most commonly used local anesthetic for obstetric analgesia. Pain relief after epidural injection is first noted by the patient after 10 minutes; 20 minutes are required to achieve peak effect. Analgesia usually lasts approximately 2 hours. Dilute solutions provide excellent sensory analgesia with minimal motor blockade. During early labor, a 0.125% solution is often adequate, whereas a 0.25% solution is usually required during the active phase. Because bupivacaine is highly protein-bound, its transplacental transfer is limited. Addition of epinephrine (1:200,000) to bupivacaine speeds its onset and lengthens its duration of action. Epinephrine also increases the intensity of motor blockade (which is not desirable in laboring patients).

Lidocaine is also an amide local anesthetic used in concentrations of 0.75–1.5% for sensory analgesia. It crosses the placenta more readily than bupivacaine and may not provide analgesia comparable to that of bupivacaine. Analgesia lasts approximately 45–90 minutes and is usually apparent within 10 minutes.

2-Chloroprocaine is an ester local anesthetic. Onset of analgesia is rapid. Effective analgesia is provided for approximately 40 minutes; this short duration limits its usefulness in labor. The efficacy of bupivacaine or opioids is diminished by prior use of chloroprocaine. Chloroprocaine 3% is frequently used to increase the anesthetic level quickly for cesarean section or instrumental vaginal delivery. Chloroprocaine has a very short half-life in maternal and fetal blood.

7. Ropivacaine is a recently introduced local anesthetic. Describe its properties and benefit in obstetric anesthesia.

Ropivacaine is slightly less potent than bupivacaine. Sensory block is similar to or slightly slower in onset and less intense and shorter in duration than equipotent doses of bupivacaine. Motor blockade is also slightly less than bupivacaine and may be an advantage. It is reported to have less cardiotoxicity (if inadvertently injected intravenously) because it binds less avidly to sodium channels of cardiac conduction tissue. It is currently approved for epidural use and is available in 2-, 5-, 7.5-, and 10-mg/ml preparations. On an equipotent cost basis, it is roughly twice as much as bupivacaine.

8. Name three methods for administering epidural analgesia. State the concerns and appropriate doses associated with each.

The three methods of maintaining an epidural block include intermittent bolus injection, continuous infusion, and patient-controlled epidural anesthesia (PCEA).

Intermittent injection requires that the catheter be checked for migration into the subarachnoid space or a blood vessel via aspiration and a repeat test dose. After multiple injections, the patient may develop intense motor blockade.

Epidural analgesia may also be accomplished by continuous infusion of dilute local anesthetic (with or without added opioid). The possible benefits of this method include (1) maintenance of a stable level of analgesia, (2) stable maternal hemodynamics, and (3) improved patient satisfaction. The patient should be assessed hourly for adequacy of analgesia, motor blockade, and progress of labor. The infusion pump should be different from that of intravenous infusion lines and infusion tubing free of side-ports to minimize the chance of accidental injection of other substances into the epidural space.

With PCEA, each patient may adjust the dose received to control her level of analgesia. PCEA may result in greater patient satisfaction and less total dose of drug than other techniques. As with a continuous infusion, the patient should be checked frequently for degree of analgesia and motor blockade.

Maintaining an Epidural Block: Intermittent Injection and Continuous Infusion Techniques

DRUGS	INTERMITTENT INJECTION	CONTINUOUS INFUSION
Bupivacaine	5–10 ml of a 0.125–0.375% solution every 90–120 minutes	0.0625–0.25% solution at 8–15 ml/hr
Lidocaine	5–10 ml of a 0.75–1.5% solution every 60–90 minutes	0.5–1.0% solution at 8–15 ml/hr
2-Chloroprocaine	5–10 ml of a 1–2% solution every 45–60 minutes	0.75% solution at 27 ml/hr

From Glosten B: Epidural and spinal anesthesia/analgesia—local anesthetic techniques. In Chestnut DH: Obstetric Anesthesia Principles and Practice. St. Louis, Mosby, 1994, p 363, with permission.

9. Discuss the complications of epidural anesthesia and their treatments.

Hypotension (a decrease in systolic pressure of 20–30% from baseline) may accompany epidural local anesthetic administration and result in decreased uteroplacental perfusion and fetal distress. Hypotension results from sympathetic blockade, peripheral venodilation, and decreased venous return to the heart. Treatment includes volume expansion, supplemental oxygen, and placement of the mother in the full lateral and Trendelenburg positions. Ephedrine (5–10 mg IV) should be administered if blood pressure does not promptly return to normal.

Septa within the epidural space may limit spread. The catheter may also thread into a spinal nerve foramina, similarly limiting spread.

Intravenous local anesthetic injection may produce dizziness, restlessness, tinnitus, seizures, and loss of consciousness. Cardiovascular (CV) collapse may follow central nervous system (CNS) symptoms. Bupivacaine CV toxicity secondary to large IV doses is especially severe and may be fatal. Treatment of IV toxicity includes:

1. Give the patient 100% O_2 and intubate if necessary (to oxygenate, ventilate, and protect the airway).
2. Stop convulsions with a barbiturate or a benzodiazepine.
3. Support blood pressure (IV fluids and pressors).
4. Use cardiopulmonary resuscitation if necessary.
5. Treat bradycardia with atropine.

6. Treat ventricular tachycardia with bretylium.
7. Treat ventricular fibrillation with bretylium, epinephrine and defibrillation.
8. Consider delivery of the fetus.

The incidence of **unintentional dural puncture** is about 1–8%. If cerebrospinal fluid (CSF) is noted, the needle should be removed and the epidural catheter placed at an alternate interspace. Whether a postdural puncture headache may be prevented by injecting saline or blood via the epidural catheter is controversial. Local anesthetic subsequently injected epidurally may pass into the subarachnoid space and result in a block that is unexpectedly high.

The incidence of an **unexpected high block** or total spinal block is approximately 1 in 4,500 lumbar epidurals during labor. Risk is minimized by aspirating the catheter and giving a test dose each time the catheter is bolused. The signs and symptoms of a total spinal include hypotension, dyspnea, inability to speak, and loss of consciousness. Treatment includes intubation, oxygen administration, ventilation, and support of maternal circulation.

10. Explain the mechanism of action of intrathecal and epidural opioids. What effect do they have on pain perception, sympathetic tone, sensation, and movement?

Opioids administered intrathecally or epidurally provide excellent analgesia without appreciably affecting sympathetic tone, sensation, and voluntary motor function. Opioids given via these routes bind to presynaptic and postsynaptic receptor sites in the dorsal horn of the spinal cord (Rexed's laminae I, II, V), altering nociceptive transmission. Some of the effects of lipid-soluble opioids may be due to the systemic absorption.

11. What opioids are used to provide spinal and epidural analgesia during labor? Name their most common side effects. Do they provide adequate analgesia for labor and delivery when used alone?

The most commonly used epidural opioids include fentanyl and sufentanil. Pruritus, nausea, and vomiting are the most common side effects; delayed respiratory depression is the most serious complication though distinctly uncommon in this population. Intrathecal or epidural opioids alone may provide adequate relief for the early stages of labor, but they are unreliable in producing adequate analgesia for the second stage of labor. Concurrent administration of local anesthetic is necessary for late cervical dilation and delivery of the infant. However, opioids alone are useful in patients who cannot tolerate sympathetic blockade.

Opioids Used to Provide Intrathecal Analgesia During Labor

DRUG	DOSE
Fentanyl	10–20 μg
Sufentanil	5–10 μg
Morphine	0.25–0.3 mg
Meperidine	10 mg

Adapted from Ross BK: Epidural and spinal anesthesia/analgesia—opioid techniques. In Chestnut DH (ed): Obstetric Anesthesia Principles and Practice. St. Louis, Mosby, 1994, p 382.

12. Is there a cause-and-effect relationship between epidural anesthesia and prolonged labor or operative delivery?

This issue is highly controversial. Though it has been reported that epidural analgesia prolongs labor and leads to increased operative delivery, there are numerous studies that do not support this assertion. Though labor analgesia may prolong the second stage, there appears to be no harm to mother or fetus.

13. Relate the advantages and disadvantages of spinal anesthesia for cesarean section. Which drugs are frequently used in the technique?

Spinal anesthesia produces a dense neural blockade, is relatively easy to perform, has a rapid onset, and is most likely to be associated with local anesthetic toxicity. The development of small-gauge, noncutting needles has significantly reduced the incidence of postdural-puncture headache (PDPH). Hypotension is a disadvantage and can be prevented by prehydration (1–2 L crystalloid), positioning to avoid aortocaval compression, and use of ephedrine (5–10 mg IV) if blood pressure does not improve with these measures.

Drugs Used for Spinal Anesthesia for Cesarean Section

DRUG	DOSAGE RANGE (mg)	DURATION (min)
Lidocaine	60–75	45–75
Bupivacaine	7.5–15.0	60–120
Tetracaine	7.0–10.0	60–120
Procaine	100–150	30–60
Adjuvant drugs		
Epinephrine	0.2	
Morphine	0.25–0.4	—
Fentanyl	0.015–0.025	—

Adapted from Reisner LS: Anesthesia for cesarean section. In Chestnut DH (ed): Obstetric Anesthesia: Principles and Practice. St. Louis, Mosby, 1994, p 468.

14. What are the advantages and disadvantages of cesarean section with epidural anesthesia? What are the most commonly used local anesthetics?

Epidural analgesia provides pain relief during labor and delivery, and should circumstances require operative delivery, greater doses of increased concentration can create surgical anesthesia. Epidural catheters allow the local anesthetic to be given in increments, titrating to the desired sensory level. Titration of local anesthetic dose results in more controlled sympathetic blockade. Thus, the risk of hypotension is decreased, as is the risk of reduced uteroplacental blood flow. Typically, epidural blocks produce less intense motor blockade than spinal anesthesia.

Disadvantages include slower onset of analgesia, large local anesthetic dose requirement, occasional patchy block unsuitable for surgery, and risk of total spinal anesthesia or systemic toxicity if the epidural catheter migrates. Unintentional dural puncture may occur, and 50–85% of such patients experience headache.

Drugs commonly used for cesarean section with epidural include 0.5% bupivacaine, 2% lidocaine, and 3% chloroprocaine. Epinephrine (1:200,000) may be added to prolong the duration of the block, to decrease vascular absorption of the local anesthetic, and to improve the quality of the block. The addition of epinephrine to a local anesthetic does not appear to affect uterine blood flow adversely. Opioids enhance intraoperative analgesia and provide postoperative pain relief. It is frequently necessary to add epinephrine to lidocaine for cesarean section, because lidocaine alone is unreliable in providing consistently satisfactory anesthesia.

15. How is combined spinal and epidural anesthesia performed? What are its advantages?

The anesthesiologist first finds the epidural space by loss-of-resistance technique with a Touhy needle. Subsequently, a long (4.5"), small-gauge (24-G), noncutting (Sprotte) spinal needle is advanced through the epidural needle and clear CSF is noted. A spinal dose of local anesthetic (plus narcotic, if desired) is injected into the subarachnoid space, and the spinal needle is removed. The epidural catheter is subsequently threaded into the epidural space. Small doses of local anesthetics and opioids provide rapid and reliable analgesia for much of stage I labor. Later, as labor progresses and pain becomes more intense, dilute local anesthetic and opioid epidural infusions can satisfy analgesic requirements. This technique also results in a low incidence of PDPH.

16. List the indications for general anesthesia for cesarean section.
• Extreme fetal distress (in the absence of a functioning epidural catheter)
• Significant coagulopathy

• Inadequate regional anesthesia
• Acute maternal hypovolemia/hemorrhage
• Patient refusal of regional anesthesia

17. What concerns the anesthesiologist when he or she administers general anesthesia for cesarean section? How is it performed?

This population is at high risk for difficulty in intubation, rapid oxygen desaturation, and aspiration of gastric contents. The goal is to minimize maternal risk of aspiration and neonatal depression. This goal is accomplished by following certain guidelines. After monitors are placed, while the patient is being carefully preoxygenated, the abdomen is prepared and draped, and the obstetricians are ready to begin. Rapid-sequence induction with cricoid pressure is always used, and incision occurs when correct endotracheal tube placement is verified. Frequently used induction agents include thiopental, propofol, ketamine, and etomidate. Succinylcholine is the muscle relaxant of choice for most patients (1–1.5 mg/kg), and only small amounts cross the placenta. To prevent maternal awareness until the neonate is delivered, frequently a combination of 30–50% nitrous oxide in oxygen is used with a low concentration of a halogenated agent (0.5 minimum alveolar concentration [MAC]). Larger concentrations of a volatile agent may cause vasodilation of the uterus and excessive uterine bleeding. However, this population is identified as being at increased risk for intraoperative awareness.

After delivery of the child, the concentration of nitrous oxide is increased, opioids, benzodiazepines, and a nondepolarizing muscle relaxant (lower doses, remember!) are administered. Concentrations of volatile agents are decreased if uterine atony appears to be a problem. Oxytocin (Pitocin) is also administered to facilitate generalized uterine contracture. At the conclusion of the procedure, the neuromuscular blockade is reversed, and the patient is extubated after thorough orogastric and airway suctioning and after the patient has demonstrated return of strength and mentation.

BIBLIOGRAPHY

1. Bromage PR: Choice of local anesthetics in obstetrics. In Shnider SM, Levinson G (eds): Anesthesia for Obstetrics, 3rd ed. Baltimore, Williams & Wilkins, 1993, p 84.
2. Chestnut DH (ed): Obstetric Anesthesia: Principles and Practice. St. Louis, Mosby, 1994.
3. Hawkins JL, Hess KR, Kubicek MA, et al: A re-evaluation of the association between instrumental delivery and epidural analgesia. Reg Anesth 20:50–56, 1995.
4. McClure JH: Ropivacaine. Br J Anaesth 76:300–307, 1996.
5. Ostheimer GW (ed): Manual of Obstetric Anesthesia. New York, Churchill Livingstone, 1992.
6. Santos AC, Pedersen H, Finster M: Obstetric anesthesia. In Barash PG, Cullen BF, Stoelting RK (eds): Clinical Anesthesia, 3rd ed. Philadelphia, Lippincott Williams & Wilkins, 1997.

63. HIGH-RISK OBSTETRICS AND COEXISTING DISEASE

Ana M. Lobo, M.D., M.P.H.

1. Define high-risk pregnancy.

A pregnant patient is placed into the high-risk category when she has a condition(s) that significantly increases the likelihood of maternal or fetal morbidity or mortality.

High-risk Conditions in Pregnancy

Hypertension	7% of all pregnancies
Preeclampsia	5–7% of all pregnancies
Preterm birth	7–10% of all births
Abruptio placentae	0.2–2.4% of all pregnancies
Placenta previa	0.5% of term deliveries
Uterine atony	2–5% of all vaginal deliveries
Gestational diabetes mellitus	1–5% of all pregnancies
Hyperthryoidism	0.2% of all pregnancies
Obesity	6% of all pregnancies
Morbid obesity	1–2% of all pregnancies
Renal disease	1–2% of all pregnancies
Cardiac disease	1–2% of all pregnancies

2. Describe the four categories of hypertension associated with pregnancy.

Hypertension occurs in 7% of pregnancies and may result in perinatal death and prematurity. **Gestational hypertension** is characterized by an increase in mean arterial pressure after 20 weeks' gestation, without proteinuria. **Preeclampsia**, also known as pregnancy-induced hypertension, is characterized by hypertension and proteinuria with or without edema. **Chronic hypertension** may also be present during pregnancy, as can **chronic hypertension with superimposed preeclampsia**.

3. What is the etiology of preeclampsia?

Preeclampsia is characterized by vasoconstriction, hypovolemia, coagulation abnormalities, and poor organ perfusion. Although the etiology is unknown, many theories have been proposed. Circulating vasoconstrictive toxins have been isolated from the blood, placenta, and amniotic fluid of women with preeclampsia. The immunologic theory states that circulating immune complexes, which result in vascular damage, are formed in response to an inadequate maternal antibody response to the fetal allograft. Others propose that primary endothelial damage causes an increase in thromboxane A_2 (vasoconstrictor) and a decrease in prostacyclin production (vasodilator). Some theorize that primary disseminated intravascular coagulation (DIC), causing the formation and deposition of microvascular thrombin, is responsible. Endogenous vasoconstrictors have also been implicated, as these patients are particularly sensitive to norepinephrine, epinephrine, and vasopressin and have an increased hypertensive response to angiotensin II. Uteroplacental insufficiency is thought to occur in these patients, although the precise etiology is unclear.

4. What clinical findings are present in preeclampsia?

Preeclampsia consists of the triad of hypertension, proteinuria, and edema developing after 20 weeks' gestation. It usually occurs after the 24th week of gestation. It is seen more frequently in nulliparous black women and in women at the extremes of child-bearing age, of lower socioeconomic status, and with underlying chronic hypertension, multiple gestations, diabetes mellitus, and hydatidiform moles. Clotting factors may be decreased in up to 20% of patients. Pulmonary edema and left ventricular failure are common if the patient is fluid-overloaded.

Symptoms and Signs of Preeclampsia

SYMPTOM/SIGN	MILD	SEVERE
Headache	—	+
Visual disturbance	—	+

Table continued on next page.

Symptoms and Signs of Preeclampsia (Continued)

SYMPTOM/SIGN	MILD	SEVERE
Cerebral disturbances	—	+
Seizures (eclampsia)	—	+
Serum creatinine	N	↑
Thrombocytopenia	—	+
Hyperbilirubinemia	—	+
AST (SGOT) elevation	N	_
Fetal growth retardation	—	+
Epigastric pain	—	+

N = normal; AST = aspartate aminotransferase
Adapted from Horowitz IR, Gomella LG: Obstetrics and Gynecology on Call. Norwalk, CT, Appleton & Lange, 1993, p 78.

5. List the criteria for diagnosing preeclampsia.

Criteria for Diagnosing Preeclampsia

	MILD	SEVERE
Systolic blood pressure*	> 140 mmHg or increase of 30 mmHg	> 160 mmHg
Diastolic blood pressure*	> 90 mmHg or increase of 15 mmHg	> 110 mmHg
Proteinuria*	> 300 mg in 24-hr urine Trace, 1+, or 2+ semiquantitative	> 5 gm in 24-hr urine 3+ or 4+ semiquantitative
Oliguria	—	≤ 400 ml/24 hr
Pitting edema	1+	> 2+

* Values must be duplicated at least 6 hr after the initial reading.
Adapted from Horowitz IR, Gomella LG: Obstetrics and Gynecology on Call. Norwalk, CT, Appleton & Lange, 1993, p 77.

6. What conditions contribute to maternal and perinatal mortality in preeclampsia?

Preeclampsia is the leading cause of maternal mortality in pregnancy and results in death in 0.4–11.9% of patients who develop it. Maternal mortality may be the result of cerebral hemorrhage, hepatic rupture, myocardial infarction with cardiac arrest, or pulmonary edema. Perinatal mortality occurs in 20–30% of affected mothers and may be due to placental infarction or placental growth retardation.

7. What is the HELLP syndrome?

The HELLP syndrome is characterized by **h**emolytic anemia, **e**levated **l**iver enzymes, and **l**ow **p**latelets occurring in the setting of preeclampsia and is associated with high maternal and fetal mortality. The HELLP syndrome usually occurs before 36 weeks' gestation and is considered a severe form of preeclampsia. The most common complaints of patients with this disorder are epigastric pain (90%), malaise (90%), and nausea and vomiting (50%). Hepatic rupture can occur and is a dramatic, life-threatening event requiring massive blood transfusion, correction of multiple coagulation disturbances, and heroic surgical intervention. Some patients present with a nonspecific viral flu-like syndrome. Hypertension and proteinuria may be very mild at first, but a rapidly accelerating downhill course is usually noted, leading to DIC and renal and liver failure.

To prevent maternal and fetal mortality, immediate delivery is indicated on diagnosis, regardless of the gestational age of the fetus. Platelet counts usually reach their lowest level 24–48 hours after delivery (frequently < 50,000/ml). Platelet counts recover within 11 days postpartum, depending on the severity of the thrombocytopenia.

8. How is preeclampsia managed?

Aspirin may be used in small doses prior to delivery to alter the prostacyclin to thromboxane ratio. Initial results have been positive in women who are at risk for this disorder.

Magnesium sulfate is used as prophylaxis against the development of seizures by increasing the patient's seizure threshold. Magnesium therapy is started with an IV loading dose of 4–6 g over 15 minutes, followed by an intravenous infusion of 1–3 g/hr. Magnesium blood levels must be monitored to prevent toxicity.

A rapid-acting **antihypertensive agent** is initiated when diastolic blood pressures are consistently high (> 110 mmHg). Hydralazine is the most commonly used drug of this class. Its vasodilating properties can increase uterine blood flow and maternal renal blood flow. The diastolic blood pressure should be maintained around 90 mmHg, as uterine perfusion may be compromised with rapid lowering of blood pressure.

Invasive monitoring should be considered in patients who require vigorous hydration or remain oliguric after a fluid challenge. An arterial line should be placed in patients with severe preeclampsia and with symptoms of pulmonary edema.

Definitive treatment of preeclampsia involves **delivery** of the placenta and neonate.

Diuretics are usually avoided because patients are vasoconstricted and volume-depleted.

9. What potential problems may occur in the patient receiving magnesium sulfate?

The therapeutic range of magnesium sulfate is 4–8 mEq/L. As plasma milligram levels increase, the patient develops electrocardiogram (ECG) changes with widening of the QRS complex and a prolonged P-Q interval. Deep tendon reflexes are lost at 10 mEq/L; sinoatrial and atrioventricular block as well as respiratory paralysis occur at 15 mEq/L; and cardiac arrest occurs at 25 mEq/L. In therapeutic doses, magnesium sulfate increases the sensitivity of the mother and fetus to muscle relaxants. Magnesium rapidly crosses the placenta, so the newborn may have decreased muscle tone, respiratory depression, and apnea. Intravenous calcium slowly administered to the newborn may decrease the neuromuscular-blocking properties of magnesium. Magnesium also decreases catecholamine release and systemic vascular resistance.

10. What are the anesthetic considerations in the patient with preeclampsia?

The standard preoperative considerations for a pregnant woman at term apply (discussed in Chapter 62, Obstetric Analgesia and Anesthesia). Labor epidurals are standard for management of labor pain (or cesarean section) once coagulation disturbances have been ruled out. Platelet counts less than 100,000/ml are considered a contraindication by many, though the *trend* of the count may be considered as well. Once placed, catheters should be dosed with local anesthetics judiciously because these patients may be relatively hypovolemic.

Should general anesthesia be required, the standard concerns for rapid oxygenation desaturation, difficult, edematous airways, and full stomach apply. Additionally, a severe hypertensive response to intubation may be observed. Rapid-acting vasodilators or beta-antagonists may be necessary.

11. How is eclampsia diagnosed? How does it affect different organ systems?

Eclampsia is diagnosed in the preeclamptic patient when seizures or coma develop. Cerebral edema and focal hemorrhages may occur. Liver necrosis, hemorrhage, and thrombosis may develop. DIC and hyaline degeneration of the kidneys may also occur.

12. How are eclamptic seizures treated?

Maternal mortality increases (in part) with the number of convulsions the patient has experienced. The airway should be supported and oxygen administered. A rapid-acting anticonvulsant, such as thiopental (50–100 mg), diazepam (2.5–5 mg), midazolam (1–2 mg), or magnesium (2–4 g), should be administered intravenously to stop the seizure. The patient should then receive seizure prophylaxis with magnesium sulfate. Consider the benefits of intubation as well as delivery of the fetus.

13. Discuss preterm labor.

Preterm labor is associated with placental abruption, uterine abnormalities, breech presentation, and multiple gestations. It is common following premature rupture of the membranes. This condition is seen in 5–10% of all pregnancies and is more common in women who are younger than 20 years of age, who are of low socioeconomic status, and who smoke. Urinary tract infection, systemic infections, dehydration, vaginitis, or cervicitis may contribute to the development of preterm labor. The major consequence of preterm labor is neonatal prematurity (< 37 weeks or weight < 2500 g), leading to an increased risk of neonatal mortality (due mostly to pulmonary immaturity) and morbidity.

14. How is preterm labor treated?

Uterine relaxants are used routinely to abolish labor prior to 34 weeks' gestation. The most widely used drugs are β_2 adrenergic agonists and magnesium sulfate. B_2 adrenergic agonists, such as ritodrine and terbutaline, may be administered intravenously or orally. They cause bronchodilation, vasodilation, and uterine relaxation. Common side effects include hypotension, tachycardia, arrhythmias, hypokalemia, hyperglycemia, and pulmonary edema. Magnesium sulfate is also used for tocolysis, but serum levels must be monitored. Infusions of both agents are continued for 24 hours after tocolysis is accomplished. Prostaglandin synthetase inhibitors (indomethacin and ibuprofen) and calcium channel blockers (verapamil and nifedipine) are used as second-line tocolytics because of their respective fetal and neonatal side effects. Steroids may also be administered to improve fetal lung maturity and decrease the risk of neonatal hyaline membrane disease. If tocolysis fails, delivery of a premature neonate is certain.

15. Discuss third-trimester vaginal bleeding.

The most common causes are abruptio placentae and placenta previa. Abruptio placentae is the separation of the placenta after 20 weeks' gestation and may be internal (painful and occult) or external (perhaps painless vaginal bleeding). The cause of this disorder is not completely understood, but factors associated with it include pregnancy-related and chronic hypertension, previous abruption, uterine abnormalities, advanced parity, smoking, and cocaine use. Abruptions are classified in terms of severity:

Grade 0	No signs or symptoms (recognized after delivery)
Grade 1 (mild)	Vaginal bleeding, abdominal pain, contractions, uterine tenderness
Grade 2 (moderate)	Same symptoms as grade 1 plus uterine tetany and fetal distress
Grade 3 (severe)	Maternal shock, uterine tetany, coagulopathy, fetal demise, distal organ necrosis, and DIC

16. What is placenta previa?

In placenta previa, the placenta obstructs the descent of the neonatal presenting part. Its etiology is not known, but this condition is more common in multiparous patients and those with a previous cesarean section. A partial placenta previa occurs when only part of the internal os is covered. A marginal placenta previa occurs when the placental edge is at the os but does not cover it. The main symptom is painless vaginal bleeding. The diagnosis of placenta previa may be made with ultrasonography or by direct examination of the cervical os (usually done in an operating room with all preparations for hemorrhage and emergency cesarean section, a "double set-up").

17. Describe the anesthetic management of abruptio placentae and placenta previa.

Cesarean section is frequently indicated. In grade 0 or 1 abruptions, regional anesthesia is appropriate. In grade 2 or 3 abruptions, general anesthesia is often indicated, due to urgency, maternal hypotension, and coagulopathy. Hemoglobin, hematocrit, platelet count, prothrombin time (PT), partial thromboplastin time (PTT), fibrinogen level, and fibrin degradation products should be measured, although the emergent nature of this situation precludes delaying surgery for lab results. It is crucial to have two large-bore intravenous lines for access and resuscitation, and blood products for transfusion should be readily available. Rapid-sequence induction of anesthesia may be accomplished safely with ketamine (0.5–1 mg/kg) or etomidate (0.2–0.3 mg/kg). Uterine atony is a postdelivery concern.

18. What is postpartum uterine atony? How is it treated?

Uterine atony occurs when the uterus will not contract after delivery and may result in a severe hemorrhage, with a blood loss measured in liters. Conditions associated with it include multiple gestation, macrosomia, polyhydramnios, high parity, prolonged labor, chorioamnionitis, precipitous labor, augmented labor, uterine distension, and tocolytic agents.

Obstetric management of this condition includes bimanual compression, uterine massage, and administration of drugs that stimulate uterine contractions. **Oxytocin** (Pitocin), the first-line drug for treating this condition, is a synthetic hormone that is administered intravenously in a solution of 20 U/1000 ml of crystalloid, and its onset of action is immediate. If atony is severe, 1–2 U of oxytocin may be given as an intravenous bolus. Oxytocin may not be rapidly administered intravenously, because it causes hypotension, coronary artery spasm, and intracranial hemorrhage. **Methylergonovine maleate** (Methergine) is given in a dose of 0.2 mg intramuscularly, and its onset of effect is rapid. It may also be administered in doses of 0.02 mg intravenously but may cause hypertension. **Prostaglandin $F_{2\alpha}$** (Hemabate) is used to treat refractory uterine atony. The dose is 250 µg intramuscularly or intramyometrially and may be repeated every 15–30 minutes (total dose < 2 mg). This drug may cause nausea, vomiting, and fever. If these agents are not successful, either internal iliac artery ligation or hysterectomy is indicated. Always consider decreasing the level of volatile anesthetic because these are uterine relaxants as well.

19. Discuss gestational diabetes and its anesthetic concerns.

Pregnant patients may have preexisting diabetes or develop glucose intolerance during pregnancy. Hyperglycemia may be controlled by diet though oral hypoglycemics or insulin may be necessary. The incidence of abortion, polyhydramnios, preeclampsia, dystocia, and cesarean section are increased. Infants can be large and suffer postpartum hypoglycemia. Anesthetic concerns include obesity, full stomach, aortocaval compression due to polyhydramnios, and placental insufficiency.

20. What is the significance of hyperthyroidism in pregnancy?

Hyperthyroidism complicating pregnancy is most likely caused by Graves' disease, trophoblastic disease, or excessive thyroid supplementation. Maternal hyperthyroidism secondary to Graves' disease is due to stimulation of thyroxine synthesis by autoantibodies. Maternal symptoms include heat intolerance, poor weight gain, diarrhea, nervousness, and tachycardia. These autoantibodies cross the placenta, resulting in fetal thyroid stimulation with possible fetal prematurity, in utero death, intrauterine growth retardation, goiter, and exophthalmos. A low thyroid-stimulating hormone and increased thyroxine, triiodothyronine, and free thyroid index are noted.

Thyroid storm, or thyrotoxicosis, is a life-threatening disorder that is precipitated by stress, such as that experienced during infection, labor, or cesarean section. Clinically it is manifested by tachycardia, atrial fibrillation, hyperpyrexia, dehydration, altered consciousness, and hemodynamic instability.

21. Describe the anesthetic management of the patient with hyperthyroidism.

Nonemergent surgery should be delayed until the patient is euthyroid. Propylthiouracil (PTU) is administered, though this crosses the placenta and may render the fetus hypothyroid. Beta blockers are administered for their sympatholytic effect and glucocorticoids supplemented. Avoid medications that produce tachycardia; thiopental is said to have an antithyroid effect. Airway management may be difficult due to an enlarged thyroid.

The anesthesiologist should be prepared to treat thyroid storm, should this occur. Treatment includes oxygen supplementation, intravenous hydration with chilled crystalloid solution containing glucose, cooling blankets as needed, electrolyte replacement, glucocorticoid administration (dexamethasone, 2–4 mg intravenously), antithyroid medication (PTU, 600–1000 mg/day), sodium iodide (1 gm intravenously), and beta-adrenergic blocking agents (propranolol, esmolol). Invasive monitoring may be needed, as these patients may develop high-output cardiac failure.

22. What causes DIC in the obstetric patient?

DIC is the result of abnormal activation of the coagulation system. In pregnant women the most frequent causes of DIC include shock, infection, abruptio placentae, amniotic fluid embolism, intrauterine fetal death, and preeclampsia or eclampsia. Increased PT, PTT, and thrombin time (TT) and a decreased platelet count and fibrinogen level are laboratory findings. Treatment involves removing the precipitating cause, providing multisystem organ support, and replacing depleted coagulation factors.

23. What types of renal disease are most frequently seen in the obstetric patient?

Glomerular disease and acute renal failure are the most common renal disorders observed during pregnancy. **Glomerular disease** may be secondary to infection, inflammatory processes, or systemic diseases such as diabetes mellitus or systemic lupus erythematosus. Hypertension and proteinuria occur in up to 50% of patients with glomerular disease.

Acute renal failure may occur in patients with preexisting renal disease who experience the superimposed stress of pregnancy. It is usually due to complications that occur late in pregnancy (such as abruption, hemorrhage, amniotic fluid embolism, or preeclampsia/eclampsia). Renal failure is treated in a supportive fashion.

24. How is anesthetic management affected in patients with renal disorders?

Regional anesthesia maintains renal blood flow and glomerular filtration rate (GFR) if the patient is maintained euvolemic. However, the uremic patient may have functional platelet defects. A coagulation profile should be reviewed prior to administering a regional anesthetic. The benefits of a bleeding time are hotly debated, though a grossly abnormal bleeding time would preclude regional anesthesia.

Other concerns in the renal patient are hyperkalemia (avoid potassium-containing solutions), hypoalbuminemia (altered drug binding), hypertension, anemia, and metabolic acidosis, hypocalcemia, and hyperphosphatemia.

25. Which cardiac disease most commonly complicates pregnancy?

Valvular heart disease is the most common cardiac disease in obstetric patients. Most valvular lesions are due to rheumatic heart disease, with mitral stenosis being the predominant lesion (in up to 90% of cases) and a most clinically important one. Half of all deaths in patients with valvular heart disease occur within 24 hours after delivery, and 30% occur within the following 4 days, usually from pulmonary edema and congestive heart failure (75%). Mortality approaches 1–3%.

26. How is mitral stenosis managed?

Mitral stenosis prevents filling of the left ventricle, resulting in decreased stroke volume and cardiac output, and prevents emptying of the left atrium, resulting in increased left atrial and pulmonary artery pressures (PAP). Signs and symptoms include a diastolic murmur, dyspnea, hemoptysis, chest pain, right heart failure, and thromboembolism. Normal pregnant patients have increased cardiac output, heart rate, and blood volume. Pregnancy aggravates mitral stenosis because an increased heart rate limits ventricular filling, further increases left atrial pressure, and increases PAP. Mitral stenosis limits the patient's ability to increase her cardiac output despite an increase in blood volume. Atrial fibrillation may occur, decreasing cardiac output and increasing the risk of atrial thrombus and systemic emboli. These patients are prone to pulmonary edema.

Anesthetic goals include the following: maintain a slow heart rate (to increase ventricular filling time), maintain sinus rhythm (to improve cardiac output), avoid aortocaval compression, maintain normal PAP, maintain normal systemic vascular resistance (SVR) (a decreased SVR will lower coronary perfusion and a high SVR will decrease cardiac output), and prevent increases in pulmonary vascular resistance (PVR) (due to pain, hypoxemia, hypercarbia, or acidosis). **Epidural analgesia** reduces preload and prevents postpartum pulmonary edema. A combined **spinal-epidural technique** is excellent for labor analgesia. Intravenous administration of crystalloid should be judiciously given (hemodynamic monitoring helps here). If **general anesthesia** is indicated, drugs that produce tachycardia (atropine, ketamine, pancuronium) should be avoided. A beta blocker, such as esmolol, is useful in slowing the heart rate. Acute tachydysrhythmias may require cardioversion.

BIBLIOGRAPHY

1. Biehl DR: Antepartum and postpartum hemorrhage. In Shnider SM, Levinson G (eds): Anesthesia for Obstetrics, 3rd ed. Baltimore, Williams & Wilkins, 1993, pp 389–391.
2. Busch RL: Valvular disease. In Ostheimer GW (ed): Manual of Obstetric Anesthesia. New York, Churchill Livingstone, 1992, pp 276–280.
3. Datta S: Diabetes mellitus. In Ostheimer GW (ed): Manual of Obstetric Anesthesia. New York, Churchill Livingstone, 1992, pp 298–299.
4. Gutsche BB, Cheek TG: Anesthetic considerations in preeclampsia-eclampsia. In Shnider SM, Levinson G (eds): Anesthesia for Obstetrics, 3rd ed. Baltimore, Williams & Wilkins, 1993, pp 305–329.
5. Gutsche BB, Samuels P: Anesthetic considerations in premature birth. Int Anesthesiol Clin 28:33–43, 1990.
6. Lechner RB: Hematologic and coagulation disorders. In Chestnut DH (ed): Obstetric Anesthesia: Principles and Practice. St. Louis, Mosby, 1994, pp 826–828.
7. Mayer DC, Spielman FJ: Antepartum and postpartum hemorrhage. In Chestnut DH (ed): Obstetric Anesthesia: Principles and Practice. St. Louis, Mosby, 1994, pp 708–709.
8. Santos AC, Pedersen H, Finster M: Obstetric anesthesia. In Barash PG, Cullen BF, Stoelting RK (eds): Clinical Anesthesia, 3rd ed. Philadelphia, Lippincott Williams & Wilkins, 1997.
9. Thornhill ML, Camann WR: Cardiovascular disease. In Chestnut DH (ed): Obstetric Anesthesia: Principles and Practice. St. Louis, Mosby, 1994, pp 747–760.

64. THE GERIATRIC PATIENT

David E. Strick, M.D.

1. In what ways does body composition change with aging?
- Increase in the proportion of body fat
- Diminished skeletal muscle mass (approximately 10%)
- Reduction in intracellular water

Although intracellular volume contracts with age, in otherwise healthy individuals, intravascular volume is preserved. In chronically ill, hypertensive, or otherwise debilitated patients, in addition to those on diuretics, the plasma volume may be contracted.

2. What are the anesthetic implications of the changes in body composition?

Changes in body composition can affect the distribution and elimination of anesthetic drugs. The **increase in the percentage of body fat** leads to a larger proportion of total body mass that can serve as a reservoir for lipid-soluble drugs. Thus, elderly patients may have an extended elimination time and prolongation of effect. The effect of the **loss of skeletal muscle** is a decrease in maximal and resting oxygen consumption, a slightly lowered resting cardiac output, and diminished production of body heat. Despite a smaller muscle mass, elderly patients are not more sensitive to muscle relaxants, probably because of fewer receptors at the neuromuscular junction. Patients who do have a **diminished plasma volume** may develop higher than expected plasma concentrations of drugs if dosing is based on body weight alone. Therefore, these patients may have a greater than anticipated response to drugs and thus appear to be more sensitive.

3. What changes in pulmonary function are seen with advancing age?

Total lung capacity	Decreased	Residual volume	Increased
Vital capacity	Decreased	Functional residual capacity	Increased
Forced expiratory volume	Decreased	Dead space	Increased
in 1 second (FEV$_1$)		Closing capacity	Increased

Aging affects chest wall mechanics, lung function, gas exchange, and ventilatory regulation resulting in decreased lung volumes and reduced gas exchange. The bellows function of the lung is reduced by fibrosis and calcification of the thoracic cage, loss of height of intervertebral disks, and declining respiratory muscle strength. The lung itself undergoes a loss of elastic recoil secondary to diminished elastin and increasing connective tissue. The break-up of alveolar septa leads to enlarged alveoli with diminished surface area. The lungs become more compliant but lose their ability to keep small airways open. Airway collapse leads to air trapping and uneven inhaled gas distribution, whereas parenchymal changes cause abnormal blood flow patterns. This produces ventilation-perfusion ($\dot{V}/\dot{Q}$) mismatching and less efficient alveolar gas exchange, resulting in a decrease in resting arterial oxygen (Pao$_2$). Older patients also have a reduced ventilatory response to hypercarbia and hypoxia in the awake state.

4. Describe the effects of a reduced vascular elasticity on associated organ systems.

Inelastic vasculature creates increased afterload for the heart and leads to elevated systolic blood pressures. As a result of the increased work, the left ventricle becomes hypertrophied and the aorta dilates. Inadequate control of chronic hypertension can lead to a contracted intravascular volume, which contributes to intraoperative blood pressure lability.

5. What changes occur in the autonomic function of the elderly?

The changes in autonomic function have been referred to as a **physiologic beta blockade**. Elderly patients, despite having higher levels of endogenous catecholamines, develop lower maximal heart rates in response to stress. Elderly patients also have a reduced chronotropic and inotropic response to exogenous β-adrenergic agonists. Possible explanations include a reduced number of receptors, abnormal receptor affinity, or reduced cyclic adenosine monophosphate (cAMP) production. A reduced affinity of β-adrenergic receptors to both agonists and antagonists has definitely been documented. In addition, the elderly have fewer responsive vascular adrenergic receptors, requiring higher doses of phenylephrine to attain a given blood pressure rise when compared with younger patients.

6. What are the consequences of physiologic beta blockade?

The decline in autonomic function impairs the cardiovascular reflexes that normally maintain hemodynamic stability. Inadequate autonomic responses can lead to cardiovascular decompensation. Elderly patients have a diminished heart rate response to hypotension produced by postural changes or alpha-antagonists as well as to acute hemodilution. Drugs or anesthetic techniques (e.g., spinal or epidural anesthesia) that reduce or block autonomic function tend to cause more hypotension in older patients.

7. Is there a change in cardiac output with aging?

Studies on active, otherwise healthy older subjects have shown that cardiac output at rest and during moderate exercise does not significantly decline with age. Maximal cardiac output does decline with age owing to the progressive decrease in maximum heart rate.

8. Is coronary artery disease easy to detect in the aging population?

Because coronary artery disease does not become clinically apparent until a critical stenosis develops, many older, inactive patients may have occult disease and be asymptomatic. Consequently the incidence of coronary artery disease in the elderly is underestimated if based on history and resting electrocardiogram (ECG) criteria. The incidence of silent myocardial infarction also increases with age. Thus ECG findings during the preoperative evaluation may reveal a prior unrecognized myocardial infarction. Peripheral vascular disease is also an important prognostic factor for the presence of coronary artery disease.

9. Discuss the disturbances in cardiac rhythm associated with aging.

Signs of aging:	Common disturbances in rhythm:
• Fibrosis of the sinoatrial node	• Sick sinus syndrome
• Atrophy of conduction pathways	• Hemiblocks
• Loss of normal pacemaker cells	• Bundle-branch blocks
	• Supraventricular and ventricular ectopic beats

Left anterior hemiblock, atrioventricular conduction delays, and atrial flutter or fibrillation suggest underlying cardiac disease and should prompt additional evaluation. Right bundle-branch block does not appear to be associated with an increased incidence of cardiac disease. Premature ventricular and supraventricular beats are common in the elderly and are not necessarily pathologic in healthy elderly individuals. These ectopic beats, however, may indicate underlying coronary artery disease or left ventricular hypertrophy in some individuals.

10. Why is the hepatic clearance of drugs diminished in the elderly?

Decreased clearance is most likely due to the marked reduction in the size of the liver that accompanies aging. By age 80, liver mass may be reduced by as much as 40%. Hepatic blood flow declines proportionally to the loss of liver mass. This decline in hepatic blood flow results in elevated blood levels of drugs that undergo extensive first-pass metabolism. Qualitatively the microsomal and nonmicrosomal enzymatic function of elderly patients is preserved.

11. What changes occur in the kidneys of geriatric patients?

The kidneys become smaller with age. As much as 30% of an adult's renal mass can be lost by the age of 70. By age 80, the number of functioning glomeruli may be one half that of a young adult. Renal blood flow also decreases with age and is associated with a glomerular filtration rate (GFR) that declines by 1.0–1.5% per year. Creatinine clearance decreases by approximately 1% per year after age 40 and can be estimated by the following formula:

$$\text{creatinine clearance} = \frac{(140 - \text{age}) \times \text{wt (kg)}}{72 \times \text{serum creatinine}}$$

Serum creatinine levels usually remain within normal limits despite the lower GFR because of reduced creatinine production from a declining muscle mass. Thus, unless the serum creatinine is elevated, it is not a sensitive test of renal function in the elderly. The kidneys of geriatric patients are also less responsive to antidiuretic hormone and have an impaired ability to concentrate urine.

12. How do the changes in renal function affect anesthetic management?

Deterioration of renal function leaves geriatric patients with minimal renal reserve and places them at risk for intraoperative fluid and electrolyte disturbances. Renal blood flow, which diminishes with age, may be compromised by dehydration or congestive heart failure. These factors contribute to an increased risk for acute renal failure, which is responsible for 20% or more of perioperative deaths in geriatric surgical patients. Thus, the anesthetic plan must include careful management of fluids and electrolytes as well as maintenance of urine output of at least 0.5 ml/kg/hour. Finally, anesthetic drugs and their metabolites that depend on renal clearance have prolonged elimination half-lives and longer durations of action.

13. Why is intraoperative body temperature difficult to control in older patients?

During general anesthesia, older patients have a greater decrease in body temperature when compared with younger patients and are less likely to reestablish normal body temperature in the recovery phase. Elderly patients have a reduced basal metabolic rate and produce less body heat. Elderly patients tend to have smaller amounts of subcutaneous tissue, which provides insulation, as well as diminished reflex cutaneous vasoconstriction to prevent heat loss.

14. Do anesthetic requirements increase or decrease with advancing age?

The minimum alveolar concentration (MAC) for volatile anesthetics decreases 4–5% per decade after age 40 years. The median effective dose (ED_{50}) for IV agents decreases as well. The basis for these changes is unclear, but because this decrease in anesthetic requirement occurs with a wide variety of agents, a physiologic as opposed to a pharmacologic cause is suggested.

15. Are geriatric patients more at risk for pulmonary aspiration?

Older patients have been shown to have attenuated airway reflexes, and this places them at increased risk for pulmonary aspiration. This risk is compounded by sedatives commonly used for premedication. Routine use of antacids is warranted as is waiting to extubate until airway reflexes are fully recovered.

16. How are the pharmacokinetics and quality of spinal anesthesia affected by age?

Elderly patients have decreased blood flow to the subarachnoid space, resulting in slower absorption of anesthetic solutions. Older patients also have a smaller volume of cerebrospinal fluid, the specific gravity of which tends to be higher than that of younger patients. This leads to a higher final concentration for a given dose and may alter the spread of the anesthetic. Elderly patients may have accentuated degrees of lumbar lordosis and thoracic kyphosis, increasing cephalad spread and pooling in the thoracic segments. Thus, one might see higher levels of spinal anesthesia, accompanied by faster onset of action and prolonged duration. Finally, older patients have a lower incidence of postdural puncture headaches when compared with younger patients.

17. Do the dynamics of epidural anesthesia change with age?

Older patients require a smaller local anesthetic dose to achieve the same level of block when compared with younger patients. This change in dose requirement is magnified when larger volumes of anesthetic solution are used and may be the result of narrowing of the intervertebral spaces.

BIBLIOGRAPHY

1. Brommage PR: Aging and epidural dose requirements. Br J Anaesth 41:1016–1022, 1969.
2. Lakatta EG: Heart and circulation. In Schneider EL, Rowe JW (eds): Handbook of the Biology of Aging, 3rd ed. San Diego, Academic Press, 1990, pp 181–216.
3. Muravchick S: Anesthesia for the elderly. In Miller RD (ed): Anesthesia, 4th ed. New York, Churchill Livingstone, 1994, pp 2143–2156.
4. Stiff J: Evaluation of the geriatric patient. In Rogers MC (ed): Principles and Practice of Anesthesiology. St. Louis, Mosby-Year Book, 1993, pp 480–492.
5. Stoelting RK, Dierdorf SF: Physiologic changes and disorders unique to aging. In Stoelting RK, Dierdorf SF (eds): Anesthesia and Co-existing Disease, 3rd ed. New York, Churchill Livingstone, 1993, pp 631–637.
6. Vaughn MS, Vaughn RW, Cork RC: Postoperative hypothermia in adults: Relationship of age, anesthesia, and shivering to rewarming. Anesth Analg 60:746–751, 1981.
7. Wahba WM: Influence of aging on lung function—clinical significance of changes from age twenty. Anesth Analg 62:764–776, 1983.

65. OUTPATIENT ANESTHESIA

Lora Manning, B.S.N., MSNA

1. What types of operative procedures can be performed on an outpatient basis?

Many types of operations are successfully completed in ambulatory surgery, including pediatric, ophthalmic, gynecologic, orthopedic, ear, nose, and throat (ENT), diagnostic, and reconstructive procedures. Both general and regional anesthetics are routinely performed in ambulatory settings.

2. What physical status, as defined by the American Society of Anesthesiologists (ASA), is appropriate in candidates for outpatient surgery?

It is common practice for relatively healthy ASA I and II patients to return home the day of surgery, provided complications from surgery or anesthesia do not arise. More controversial are geriatric and ASA III patients scheduled for outpatient surgery. Well-controlled ASA III patients are accepted on an outpatient basis, but three important points must be kept in mind: (1) the degree to which the systemic disease is under control, (2) the complexity of the surgery, and (3) the level of postoperative care and availability of assistance at home. The clinician's responsibility to the patient is to ensure that a safe and stable postoperative course extends to the home. Patients who do not have the resources to care for themselves should not be discharged home, even if they meet discharge criteria. It is imperative that provisions for home care are made well in advance.

3. List the criteria for discharge from ambulatory settings.

In addition to an Aldrete score of 8 (see Chapter 36, Postanesthetic Care and Complications) and stable vital signs, before discharge from the postanesthetic care unit, patients must demonstrate:

- Ability to ambulate
- Ability to ingest fluids without nausea and vomiting
- Pain controlled with oral analgesics
- Recovery of sensorimotor function after conduction block with ability to void
- Lack of respiratory distress
- Regression of upper extremity blocks and adequate protection of the arm (the patient should receive specific instructions on care)

4. What types of anesthesia are appropriate for outpatients?

Approximately 50% of all anesthetics administered are regional, and many are given to outpatients. Certainly general anesthetics, using either the laryngeal mask airway, mask, or endotracheal tube, are appropriate choices. Appropriate short-acting opioids include fentanyl (2–5 µg/kg) and sufentanil (up to 0 .4 µg/kg). Morphine is a less popular opioid because of its sedating properties. Propofol, either as an induction agent or in total intravenous anesthesia (TIVA), is a popular alternative. Drugs with prolonged sedative effects, such as phenothiazines or butyrophenones (droperidol) should be avoided. Because of its minimal side effects, ondansetron is becoming more popular as an antiemetic. Premedication with midazolam (0.025 mg/kg IV; 0.5–0.75 mg/kg orally) is common. The effects of benzodiazepines may be reversed with flumazenil (0.2-mg increments), realizing resedation may occur due to disparity in half-lives when compared to diazepines.

5. What are the most common postoperative problems in surgical outpatients? How can they be managed?

Pain, nausea, and vomiting. Local infiltration of the wound either before or after surgical incision has proved effective in relieving postoperative pain. Ejlersen et al. found that preincisional infiltration with lidocaine afforded longer lasting analgesia than postincisional infiltration. Bupivacaine (0.25% with or without epinephrine) is also an effective local anesthetic. Ketorolac (30 mg IV; 30–60 mg IM) is a nonsteroidal anti-inflammatory drug (NSAID) and useful analgesic adjuvant. Advantages include intact ventilatory function and decreased nausea and vomiting. As with all NSAIDs, platelet function is depressed, and patients with impaired renal function are at increased risk for renal failure. Pediatric caudal blocks are also effective in providing postoperative pain relief. Bupivacaine, 0.25%, provides analgesia to the T10–L2 sensory level.

Postoperative nausea and vomiting (PONV) are among the most common postoperative complaints, with an incidence of 10–30%. The many causes include pain, dehydration, opioid use, type of surgery, and gender. Women undergoing gynecologic surgery are at increased risk for PONV. Women menstruating at the time of surgery demonstrate an even higher incidence, peaking at the fourth and fifth day of their cycle. Although routine prophylactic treatment may not be warranted, certain surgeries (laparoscopy, middle ear surgery, gynecologic) are more prone to induce nausea and vomiting and may best be managed prophylactically. Initial treatment should include ensuring adequate hydration and pain relief, followed by any of the following:

1. Ondansetron, a serotonin antagonist, has received favorable results in studies compared with placebo and more traditional antiemetics. Doses of 4–8 mg have decreased the incidence of postoperative nausea by 57–75%; antiemetic effects may last up to 24 hours. It is free of many of the side effects of older drugs; however, elevated transaminase levels have been infrequently reported.

2. Droperidol, a butyrophenone, is also commonly used in doses of 0.0625–0.125 mg/kg. However, it produces drowsiness and occasional extrapyramidal effects.

3. Metoclopramide, in a dose of 10 mg given close to or at the end of surgery, is also effective in reducing PONV. It may cause extrapyramidal symptoms and is contraindicated in patients with bowel obstruction, concomitant use of tricyclic antidepressants or monoamine oxidase inhibitors, and Parkinson's disease.

4. Scopolamine and scopolamine patches have been successfully used in ambulatory surgery. The patches provide long-term (3–7 days) relief of nausea and vomiting, but undesirable side effects (dry mouth, somnolence, blurred vision, fever) may necessitate discontinuation. Patches should be applied behind the ear 4 hours before they are needed.

6. What are the common causes of an unplanned admission?

The most common causes are surgically related, but anesthetic complications may occur, with nausea and vomiting topping the list. Other common causes are (1) persistent hypoxemia, (2) unresolving conduction block, (3) postdural puncture headache, (4) pain, and (5) persistent hypertension.

7. What laboratory tests are necessary preoperatively?

A thorough history and physical exam should be the guide for deciding which, if any, lab tests are necessary. The trend is to order fewer and fewer tests, basing such evaluations on strong anticipation of abnormal findings from the history and physical exam. Chronic medical conditions require a baseline evaluation. For example, diabetics require assessment of glucose level, and renal patients require an electrolyte profile, blood urea nitrogen, creatinine, and hematocrit. If a consultation is necessary, the condition requiring evaluation should be clearly described and reasons for the consultation clearly conveyed. See Chapter 15, The Preoperative Evaluation, for a useful guide to appropriate preoperative testing.

8. What preoperative medications are necessary?

Medications that patients must take for chronic conditions should be continued the morning of surgery and include β-adrenergic blockers, angiotensin-converting enzyme inhibitors, central acting antihypertensives, beta agonists, anticonvulsants, H_2 blockers, corticosteroids, aminophylline, and other cardiac drugs, such as antianginal or antidysrhythmic agents. Patients taking Coumadin are evaluated on a case-by-case basis but rarely are candidates for outpatient surgery. (Cataracts may be an exception.)

Non–insulin-dependent diabetics should be counseled not to take oral hypoglycemic agents in the hope of preventing perioperative hypoglycemia. Diabetics can be managed several different ways: (1) Hold morning insulin dose, and check blood sugar on arrival at ambulatory anesthesia. (2) Have the patient take one half of the usual morning insulin dose, and check blood sugar on arrival at ambulatory anesthesia.

Routine aspiration prophylaxis is recommended for high-risk patients and obstetrics and may include a nonparticulate antacid, an H_2 blocker, and metoclopramide.

9. Are patients with a history of malignant hyperthermia suitable for outpatient surgery?

This issue is controversial. If patients are permitted to go home on the day of surgery, strict guidelines must be followed: (1) avoid all triggering agents perioperatively; (2) use a clean machine (inactivate or remove vaporizors; change bellows, CO_2 absorber and breathing tubes; and flush the machine with high-flow oxygen for at least 10 minutes); (3) schedule the patient as the first case of the day, allowing for prolonged postoperative evaluation; (4) ensure that dantrolene is readily available; and (5) observe the patient for a minimum of 6 hours postoperatively. Some centers admit susceptible patients for overnight observation.

10. What are the current fasting guidelines for pediatric patients?

Studies indicate that clear liquid intake accelerates gastric emptying. Parents are encouraged to give clear liquid feedings up to 2–3 hour before surgery. Breast milk is considered a clear liquid. Formula or solids are withheld 6–8 hours before surgery. To prevent hypovolemia and hypoglycemia, clear liquids should continue to be given up to the prescribed times. Small children should be scheduled at the beginning of the day.

11. Is the patient selection different for pediatric patients?

ASA I or II patients continue to be appropriate candidates for ambulatory surgery. Pediatric patients classified as ASA III or IV may be appropriate for ambulatory surgery if their medical condition is well controlled. Immunocompromised pediatric patients are often well suited as outpatients because their risk of hospital-acquired illness will be minimized. Premature infants require careful consideration because of an increased risk of apnea, poor temperature control, and immature gag reflex. Generally, term infants less than 44 weeks and ex-premature infants less than 55–60 weeks postconceptual age are at risk for developing apnea and are best admitted for apnea monitoring.

12. What types of surgery can be performed on pediatric patients on an outpatient basis?

(1) Ophthalmic procedures, (2) lower abdominal and genitourinary surgery, (3) ENT surgeries, (4) extremity surgery, (5) plastic surgery, and (6) peripheral orthopedic procedures. Exceptions include major procedures performed within body cavities, unless performed laparoscopically.

13. What different anesthetic techniques are common in pediatrics?

Sedatives, if used preoperatively, may be given orally, nasally, or rectally. Pediatric patients < 14 months tend not to experience separation anxiety, and sedation may not be necessary. In young children, general anesthesia is accomplished with mask induction. Halothane and sevoflurane are less irritating to the airways and are commonly chosen induction agents. In healthy patients, minimal monitoring (pulse oximetry) is acceptable until the child is sufficiently anesthetized to permit complete monitoring. Alternatively, some centers allow the parents to be in the operating room, holding the child during induction. This approach may provide a more cooperative patient. Intravenous access, if necessary, is established after the child is asleep. Most older children are allowed to choose between an IV line or mask induction so that they can maintain some sense of control. Caudal blocks with 0.25% bupivacaine are also becoming more common as an adjuvant to general anesthesia for inguinal or perineal surgery in pediatric patients. They can be administered before the start of surgery or immediately before awakening and provide postoperative analgesia. Doses are based on the site of surgery: inguinal region, 0.5 ml/kg; umbilical region, 0.75 ml/kg.

14. What other special considerations should be kept in mind for pediatric patients?

Patients with a current upper respiratory infection require further consideration, because infection increases the incidence of respiratory complications (bronchospasm, laryngospasm, hypoxemia) when intubation is required. However, many children have frequent clear nasal discharge. It is important to question the parent further about cough, fever, purulent discharge, or any other change in symptoms. If nasal discharge is due to allergic rhinitis, surgery may continue. It is common practice to delay surgery for 2–3 weeks after a significant upper respiratory infection.

BIBLIOGRAPHY

1. Ejlersen E, Andersen HB, Eliasen K, Mogensen T: A comparison between preincisional and postincisional lidocaine infiltration and postoperative pain. Anesth Analg 74:495-498, 1992.
2. Henderson JA: Ambulatory surgery: Past, present, and future. In Wetchler BV (ed): Anesthesia for Ambulatory Surgery. Philadelphia, J.B. Lippincott, 1991, pp 1–27.
3. Holzman RS: Morbidity and mortality in pediatric anesthesia. Pediatr Clin North Am 41:239–256, 1994.
4. Kurth CS, Spitzer AR, Broennle AM, et al: Postoperative apnea in preterm infants. Anesthesiology 66:483–486, 1987.
5. Mulroy MF: Regional anesthetic techniques. In White PF (ed): Anesthesia for Ambulatory Surgery. Boston, Little, Brown, 1994, pp 81–98.
6. Patel R, Hannallah R: Pediatric anesthetic techniques. In White PF (ed): Anesthesia for Ambulatory Surgery. Boston, Little, Brown, 1994, pp 37–53.
7. Scuderi P, Wetchler B, Sung YF, et al: Treatment of postoperative nausea and vomiting after outpatient surgery with the 5-HT3 antagonist ondansetron. Anesthesiology 78:15–20, 1993.
8. Splinter WM, Stewart JA, Muir JG: The effect of preoperative apple juice on gastric contents, thirst, and hunger in children. Can J Anaesth 36:55–60, 1989.
9. Stoelting RK: Pharmacology and Physiology in Anesthetic Practice, 3rd ed. Philadelphia, Lippincott Williams & Wilkins, 1999.
10. Watcha MF, White PF: Postoperative nausea and vomiting. Anesthesiology 77:162–184, 1992.

66. ANESTHESIA OUTSIDE THE OPERATING ROOM

Michael Duey, M.D., and Kevin Fitzpatrick, M.D.

1. For what procedures and in what locales outside the operating room (OR) or obstetric suite is anesthesia conducted?

- Diagnostic radiology, which includes angiographic procedures or sedation for computed tomography (CT) and magnetic resonance imaging (MRI)
- Cardiac catheterizations, insertion of implantable cardiac defibrillators (ICD), and coronary arteriography
- Cardioversions, which may be conducted in various locations, including the intensive care unit (ICU)
- Therapeutic radiation
- Electroconvulsive therapy
- Sedation for bone marrow biopsies and other minor procedures on the pediatric ward
- Emergency airway management anywhere in the hospital
- Transport of the anesthetized or critically ill patient

2. To what safety standards must one adhere when conducting an anesthetic outside the OR?

Standards developed by the Department of Anesthesia at Harvard are the same as those used in the OR.

Requirements for the Safe Conduct of Anesthesia

Piped oxygen in addition to oxygen cylinders	Adequate illumination
Suction	Immediate access to the patient
Anesthesia machine and supplies equivalent to those in the OR	Emergency resuscitation cart with defibrillator
	Attending anesthesiologist
Sufficient electrical outlets	Two-way communication to summon help

3. What situations may interfere with maintenance of the above standards?

Most facilities for nonsurgical procedures are not designed to meet the needs of anesthesiologists. Physical space is often cramped. Limited access to the patient may pose a safety risk. During certain procedures, as in MRI, the anesthesiologist may not be present in the same room as the patient. Suboptimal lighting, especially in the radiology suite, may lead to unrecognized airway obstruction or cyanosis, circuit disconnections, and exhaustion of gas (oxygen) cylinders.

4. What monitoring is necessary for administration of an anesthetic outside the OR?

Required monitoring includes (1) continuous display of electrocardiogram (ECG) throughout the anesthetic; (2) determination of blood pressure and heart rate at least every 5 minutes; (3) pulse oximetry; and (4) capnography. When mechanical ventilation is required, a breathing system disconnect alarm must be in continuous use. In addition, an oxygen analyzer with a low oxygen concentration alarm must be used.

5. How may the equipment necessary for the conduction of an anesthetic in a remote location be different from that in the OR?

Often, as new anesthesia machines and monitors are purchased by an anesthesia department, the older equipment is relegated to remote locations. The anesthesiologist must be familiar with the operation of such equipment before using it to provide an anesthetic.

6. What other equipment is required?

1. Tools for airway management
   - Bag/mask ventilation system
   - Oral airways of various sizes
   - Laryngoscopes
   - Endotracheal tubes
2. Medications for induction of anesthesia
3. Muscle relaxants
4. Drugs for cardiac resuscitation. These items may be easily stored and carried in an emergency airway box to any location.

7. What are the dangers of dyes (contrast agents) used in radiologic imaging?

Approximately 5–8% of patients receiving an intravenous injection of contrast medium experience an allergic reaction to the dye. The method of injection (slow or bolus), type of dye used, and dose influence the risk of systemic reaction. Patients with a prior history of allergy to shellfish or seafood are more prone to reactions.

8. What are the manifestations of an allergic reaction?

Contrast Dye Allergic Reactions

MILD	MODERATE	SEVERE (ANAPHYLAXIS)
Nausea	Bronchospasm	Prolonged hypotension
Vomiting	Hypotension	Cyanosis
Facial flushing	Tissue edema	Anoxia
Fever	Seizures	Pulmonary edema
Chills		Angina
Urticaria		Dysrhythmias

9. How can anesthesiologists protect themselves from radiation exposure?

Protective garments, including radiation-shielding aprons, thyroid shields, and protective eyewear, are recommended. Radiation exposure badges that measure cumulative exposure also should be considered.

10. What specific side effects are most common during cerebral angiography?

Contrast dyes may cross the blood-brain barrier, causing seizures and increased intracranial pressure. During cerebral angiography it is advantageous to keep patients awake and talking for continuous neurologic assessment.

11. Discuss specific challenges involved in the administration of an anesthetic in the CT suite.

Movement of the patient on the CT gantry may cause kinking of oxygen tubing or disconnection of the breathing circuit. Patients receiving oral contrast or undergoing emergency procedures must be considered at risk for aspiration of gastric contents. Temperature monitoring of pediatric patients is essential because of the cold temperatures required for CT equipment to function properly.

12. Define the unique problems associated with providing an anesthetic in the MRI suite.

Difficulties in providing a safe anesthetic in the MRI suite arise from the necessity of using a powerful magnetic field. The MRI suite is often located in a remote, isolated area of the hospital. The cylindrical large-bore magnet surrounding the body limits access to the patient. Ferromagnetic objects may be hurled toward the scanner, creating lethal projectiles. Large metal objects may interfere with the quality of the image. Many electronic instruments may not function normally when placed in close proximity to the magnet. Implantable ferrous magnetic devices, such as older cerebrovascular clips, surgical clips, and pacemakers, are hazardous.

13. What modifications in the anesthesia machine, ventilator, and monitoring equipment must be made to provide an anesthetic in the MRI suite?

All monitoring equipment is affected by the magnetic fields generated by the MRI machine. Monitors with ferromagnetic components must be located outside the magnetic field. The distance depends on the strength of the field and shielding in the suite. If the anesthesia machine, monitoring equipment, and ventilator are located several meters from the patient, long monitoring leads and ventilation tubing, with a large compressible volume in the circuit, are required, and risk of disconnection is increased. Anesthetic and monitoring equipment with nonferromagnetic components is available and allows much closer proximity to the patient and MRI machine. Many newer institutions have anesthesia machines built into the structure of the MRI suite, which allows easier and safer conduction of anesthesia. The lack of availability of a piped oxygen source into the MRI suite in older institutions may be a significant problem, because standard gas cylinders are ferromagnetic and may become dangerous projectiles when introduced into the magnetic environment. Aluminum cylinders are a safe alternative, but they cannot be recharged because metal fatigue from repeated pressurizations predisposes these tanks to explosion. Nonferromagnetic ventilators are available.

Electrocardiography. Many MRI manufacturers now produce ECG and respiratory monitors compatible with their equipment. Unfortunately, these monitors do not allow reliable qualitative assessment of the ECG, but they may be used to provide an index of heart rate and to serve as a gating signal for other monitoring equipment (e.g., pulse oximeters). If such equipment is not available, modification of existing equipment is necessary. When unshielded ferromagnetic wiring is used, the ECG demonstrates significant changes in the strong magnetic field produced by the MRI scanner. Changes in ECG potentials are greatest in the early T waves and late ST segments, mimicking the changes seen in conditions such as hyperkalemia and pericarditis. The rapidly changing magnetic fields may cause spikes in the ECG trace, leading to an artificially elevated heart rate on the monitor. Positioning the electrodes as close as possible to the center of the magnetic field, keeping the limb leads close together and in the same plane, and braiding or twisting the leads help to minimize the changes produced by the magnetic field.

Pulse oximetry. Problems similar to those encountered with the ECG may be experienced. The use of nonferromagnetic probes and shielded wiring minimizes distortion of the signal.

Capnography. To function properly, the capnograph should be placed outside the magnetic field. The long connecting tubing causes significant lag and alarm times. The waveform may show a prolonged upslope, even in patients with healthy lungs. Trends and respiratory rate, however, may be observed.

Blood pressure. Noninvasive blood pressure readings may be obtained if all ferrous connections are removed from the cuff and tubing. Invasive pressure readings may be obtained if the lead from the pressure transducer is passed through a radiofrequency filter. Dampening of the waveform is minimized by resting the transducer within 1.5 m of the patient.

Auscultation. Use of precordial or esophageal stethoscopes may be difficult because of the length of tubing required and the noise produced by the MRI machine.

BIBLIOGRAPHY

1. Gillies BS, Lecky JH: Anesthesia for nonoperative locations. In Barash PG, Cullen BF, Stoelting RK (eds): Clinical Anesthesia, 3rd ed. Philadelphia, Lippincott Williams & Wilkins, 1997.
2. Manninen PH: Anaesthesia outside the operating room. Can J Anaesth 38:R126–R129, 1991.
3. Messick JM, MacKenzie RA, Southorn P: Anesthesia at remote locations. In Miller RD (ed): Anesthesia, 4th ed. New York, Churchill Livingstone, 1994, pp 2247–2276.
4. Patteson SK, Chesney JT: Anesthetic management for magnetic resonance imaging: Problems and solutions. Anesth Analg 74:121–128, 1992.
5. Peden CJ, Menon DK, Hall AS, et al: Magnetic resonance for the anaesthetist. Part II: Anesthesia and monitoring in MR units. Anaesthesia 47:508–517, 1992.
6. Rasch DK, Bready LL: Anesthesia for magnetic resonance imaging. Prog Anesthesiol 5:158–165, 1991.

67. ARTIFICIAL CARDIAC PACEMAKERS

Kevin Fitzpatrick, M.D.

GENERAL CONSIDERATIONS

1. What are some indications for the placement of a cardiac pacemaker?

1. Acquired atrioventricular (AV) block in adults
2. AV block associated with myocardial infarction
3. Chronic bifascicular or trifascicular block
4. Sinus node dysfunction
5. AV block and dysrhythmias in children
6. Tachydysrhythmias

THE LANGUAGE OF PACEMAKERS

2. What is a lead? An electrode?

The lead is the insulating wire that connects the pacemaker to the electrode. The electrode is the metal end of the lead that makes contact with the myocardium.

3. What is unipolar pacing? Bipolar pacing?

In a **unipolar pacemaker**, the stimulating electrode (negative) is located in the atrium or ventricle and the ground electrode (positive) is placed in a location distant from the heart. With **bipolar pacemakers**, both the positive and the negative electrodes are placed within the paced cardiac chamber.

4. What is a triggered pacemaker? An inhibited pacemaker?

A **triggered pacemaker** senses atrial and/or ventricular depolarization and paces immediately. An **inhibited pacemaker** senses an intrinsic atrial and/or ventricular depolarization and promptly shuts off.

5. Define R-wave sensitivity.

R-wave sensitivity describes the minimum voltage of intrinsic R wave necessary to activate the sensing circuit of the pacemaker and inhibit it from pacing. In other words, when the intrinsic R-wave is greater in magnitude than the R wave sensitivity programmed into the pacemaker, the pacemaker will not interfere with cardiac conduction.

TYPES OF PACEMAKERS

6. What is the 5-letter coding system used to describe cardiac pacemakers?

Most pacemakers are referred to by the first three letters of the code. The first letter indicates the location of the pacing electrode. The second letter signifies the location of the pacemaker's sensor. The third letter is indicative of the mode of activity. The fourth letter describes programmability. The fifth letter describes implantable cardioverter-defibrillators (ICD) (see tables).

Coding System Describing Cardiac Pacemakers

I	II	III	IV	V
CHAMBER PACED	CHAMBER SENSED	MODE OF RESPONSE	PROGRAMMABILITY	ANTITACHYCARDIC FUNCTIONS
O = none	O = none	O = none	O = none	O = none
A = atrium	A = atrium	T = triggered	P = simple programmable	P = pacing
V = ventricle	V = ventricle	I = inhibited	M = multiprogrammable	S = shock
			C = communicating	
D = dual (A + V)	D = dual (A + V)	D = dual (T + I)	R = rate responsive	D = dual (P + S)

Types of Pacemakers

LETTER CODE	PACEMAKER FUNCTION
AOO	Atrial fixed-rate (asynchronous) pacemaker: it paces the atrium regardless of intrinsic cardiac activity.
VOO	Ventricular fixed-rate pacemaker: it stimulates the ventricle regardless of intrinsic cardiac activity.
AAI	Atrial demand pacemaker: it senses and paces only in the atrium; it is inhibited from pacing by intrinsic P waves.
VVI	Ventricular demand pacemaker: it senses and paces only in the ventricle; intrinsic R waves inhibit it from pacing.
AAT	Atrial triggered pacemaker: it senses and paces in the atrium; it is triggered to pace by sensing intrinsic (nonconducted) P waves.
VVT	Ventricular triggered pacemaker: it senses and paces in the ventricle; it is triggered to stimulate by sensing intrinsic (nonconducted) R waves.
DVI	Sequential pacemaker: it senses only in the ventricle; it paces the atrium and then the ventricle and is inhibited by intrinsic ventricular depolarization.
VDD	The pacemaker senses in both the atrium and ventricle and paces in the ventricle; it is able to pace the ventricle after atrial contraction, even if AV conduction is impaired; likewise, it may pace only the atrium and permit intrinsic AV conduction and ventricular contraction.

7. What is a fixed-rate pacemaker? Give an example.

These are known as asynchronous pacemakers. Electrical impulses are delivered at regular, pre-set intervals, *independent* of the patient's intrinsic heart rate. These pacemakers are good for pacing during bradycardia secondary to new-onset third degree AV block. Ventricular tachycardia may result when competition with a patient's intrinsic rate leads to a pacing spike that occurs on a T wave.

8. What is a single-chamber demand pacemaker?

Demand pacemakers are also known as noncompetitive pacemakers. They stimulate the heart "on demand" only when spontaneous impulses do not occur during a preselected time interval. This type of pacemaker is inhibited by intrinsic R waves when the patient's own heart rate is greater than the preset rate. When this occurs, the electrocardiogram (ECG) will not demonstrate any pacemaker "spikes" (impulses). In order to assess whether the pacemaker is functioning properly, vagal maneuvers (Valsalva or carotid massage) may slow the intrinsic rate sufficiently so that the pacemaker begins transmitting impulses to the myocardium.

9. Why is it occasionally necessary to convert a demand pacemaker to an asynchronous pacemaker? How is this accomplished?

A demand pacemaker may malfunction because of faulty circuitry, incorrect programming, or extrinsic radio frequency interference (see question 20). Under these circumstances, it may be useful to convert the pacemaker to asynchronous mode so that the myocardium is depolarized at regular intervals and cardiac output is maintained.

Mode conversion may be achieved by reprogramming the pacemaker through an external remote control radio device or by bringing a specially designed magnet in close to the pacemaker. A pacemaker magnet should always be nearby when patients with pacemakers undergo surgical procedures.

10. What is the most common type of pacemaker?

The VVI demand pacemaker is the most commonly placed pacemaker today.

11. What are sequential pacemakers?

Sequential pacemakers are designed to preserve the AV conduction sequence. They may be useful in young, exercising patients because these pacemakers are able to increase the ventricular rate in response to increases in the intrinsic rate of atrial depolarization. The ventricle, then, may be paced independently of the atrium.

12. What type of pacemaker is known as the "universal" pacemaker?

The DDD pacemaker is the universal pacemaker. It can behave as a VDD pacemaker during normal atrial rates with abnormal AV conduction. It is an AAI pacemaker during atrial bradycardia and normal AV conduction. It becomes a DVI pacemaker during sinus bradycardia with abnormal AV conduction.

13. What is an implantable cardioverter-defibrillator (ICD)?

An ICD continuously monitors the patient's cardiac rhythm. ICDs are placed in patients prone to ventricular dysrhythmias and in whom medical management has failed. When ventricular tachycardia or fibrillation is detected, this device will deliver countershocks in an attempt to convert the heart to its baseline rhythm.

PREOPERATIVE EVALUATION IN THE PATIENT WITH A PACEMAKER

14. What kinds of diagnostic information and data from the history and physical exam are particularly relevant in these patients?

Many of these patients have multiple medical problems, including cardiovascular disease. Cardiac medications should probably be continued throughout the perioperative period. It is important for the anesthetist to know the original indications for placement of the pacemaker and whether the patient is experiencing a return of pre-pacemaker symptoms, e.g., light-headedness, dizziness, or fainting.

A chest radiograph may be helpful to verify pacemaker lead continuity and to look for signs of congestive heart failure, e.g., cardiomegaly or prominent vascularity and pulmonary edema. These patients must have a recent ECG available. Sample ECG tracings demonstrating pacemaker activity may be found at the end of this chapter. Do not forget to palpate the patient's pulse while watching a continuous ECG monitor. In this way, one may verify that paced cardiac beats are conducted. A recent hematocrit will serve to assess oxygen-carrying capacity in patients with cardiac disease. A serum potassium is also useful in order to identify acute changes in extracellular potassium concentration which may affect myocardial sensitivity to pacing (see question 23).

15. What kind of data should be gathered regarding the pacemaker itself?

The type of pacemaker (letter code) and date of placement should be determined. If the patient cannot remember, he or she may be able to produce the pacemaker identification card. Otherwise, a chest x-ray will reveal not only the type of pacemaker (since the letter code is radiopaque), but also the location of the pacemaker.

16. Do these patients require any type of special monitoring?

Indicated monitoring is predicated on the patient's overall medical condition and the operation to be performed. The presence of a pacemaker is not necessarily an indication for invasive monitoring (pulmonary artery catheter, arterial line).

INTRAOPERATIVE MANAGEMENT OF THE PATIENT WITH A PACEMAKER

17. What type of anesthetic is best for procedures involving the pacemaker?

In general, no one technique is better than another. Usually, intravenous sedation (minimum alveolar concentration–monitored anesthesia care) with local anesthetic infiltration is performed for pacemaker placement and battery changes. General endotracheal anesthesia (GETA) is performed for ICD placement.

18. Is succinylcholine contraindicated for general anesthetics in patients with pacemakers?

Random muscular contractions, or fasciculations, often occur after the administration of depolarizing muscle relaxants and may be perceived by the pacemaker sensor as an intrinsic cardiac impulse. Depending on the type of pacemaker, it may be inhibited from firing an impulse resulting in deleterious reductions in heart rate and cardiac output, even cardiac standstill. A "defasciculating" dose of a nondepolarizing muscle relaxant should be given 5–10 minutes before succinylcholine is administered. Additionally, the pacemaker may be reprogrammed to asynchronous (VOO) mode, so that it stimulates the ventricle regardless of intrinsic cardiac activity.

19. Can etomidate be used as an induction agent?

The myoclonus typically occurring after induction doses of etomidate and, to a lesser extent, methohexital and thiopental can also fool a pacemaker's sensor and lead to cardiac standstill. This is, however, a rare occurrence.

20. How does electrocautery affect pacemaker function?

Electromagnetic interference (EMI) from electrocautery ("Bovie") is probably the most common cause of intraoperative pacemaker failure. Its use may cause the pacemaker to stop firing because EMI is interpreted as normal intrinsic cardiac activity. The sensing function of the pacemaker may be circumvented by the application of an external magnet or by reprogramming the pacemaker to asynchronous mode. Electrocautery will not affect a VOO pacemaker.

Most demand pacemakers are programmed to institute a default rhythm in the presence of continuous EMI. **Multiprogrammable** pacemakers, however, could be reprogrammed to any of a number of modes during the application of electrocautery, and a magnet applied to these pacemakers can actually worsen its response to electrocautery.

21. What can be done to protect the pacemaker from the untoward effects of EMI?

An attempt should be made to use bipolar cautery. The electrocautery energy level should be kept as low as possible; short bursts are safer than continuous activation. Finally, the current dispersal unit (CDU, or "Bovie pad") should be placed remote from the pacemaker.

22. Your patient with a pacemaker is found pulseless; ECG demonstrates ventricular tachycardia. The defibrillator is charged and ready to go. Do you proceed with external defibrillation?

Yes. Most pacemakers are constructed with protective circuits designed to withstand external defibrillation. The paddles, however, should not be placed directly over the pacemaker. Pulselessness or any dysrhythmia must be confirmed by palpation of a major artery. The carotid and femoral arteries are usually the easiest to identify.

CONTROVERSY

23. Your patient with a pacemaker has a serum potassium of 2.9 mEq/L. His only medication is furosemide, which he has been taking for 2 years. Should he receive supplemental potassium before receiving an anesthetic?

Probably not. The normal intracellular-to-extracellular ratio of potassium is 30:1, which is equivalent to a –90 mV resting membrane potential (RMP). Acutely increasing extracellular potassium, e.g., rapid intravenous administration of potassium, or acidosis, will create a less negative RMP. Action potential threshold is thus lowered and, consequently, the myocardium is more sensitive to electrical depolarization. This may precipitate ventricular tachycardia or fibrillation.

Acutely decreasing extracellular potassium through, for example, hyperventilation (respiratory alkalosis), creates a more negative RMP, rendering the myocardium less excitable. Clinically, hypokalemia could increase the pacing threshold and lead to loss of pacing.

Acute changes in extracellular potassium are of concern in patients with pacemakers. Chronic imbalances invoke compensatory mechanisms that restore RMP to normal levels. With regard to this patient, he is probably chronically hypokalemic and not at increased risk. If chronic hypokalemia cannot be established, i.e., there is no previous serum potassium level available or the potassium level is less than 2.9 mEg/L, anesthetic administration should be postponed.

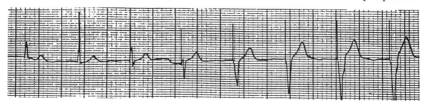

Normal VVI pacing. (From Zaidan JR: Pacemakers. In Barash PG (ed): Refresher Courses in Anesthesiology, Vol 21. Philadelphia, J.B. Lippincott, 1993, with permission.)

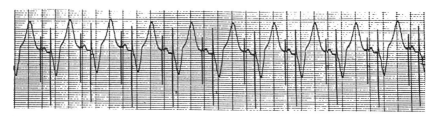

Normal atrioventricular (sequential) pacing. (From Zaidan JR: Pacemakers. In Barash PG (ed): Refresher Courses in Anesthesiology, Vol 21. Philadelphia, J.B. Lippincott, 1993, with permission.)

BIBLIOGRAPHY

1. Eckenbrecht PD: Pacemakers and implantable cardioverter defibrillators. 45th Annual Refresher Course Lectures and Clinical Update Program 234:1–7, 1994.
2. Domino KB, Smith TC: Electrocautery-induced reprogramming of a pacemaker using a precordial magnet. Anesth Analg 62:609–612, 1983.

3. Mangar D, Atlas GM, Kane PB: Electrocautery-induced pacemaker malfunction during surgery. Can J Anesth 38:616–618, 1991.
4. Stoelting RK, Dierdorf SF: Abnormalities of cardiac conduction and cardiac rhythm. In Anesthesia and Coexisting Disease, 3rd ed. New York, Churchill Livingstone, 1993, pp 63–77.
5. Zaidan JR: Pacemakers. In Barash PG (ed): Refresher Courses in Anesthesiology, Vol 21. Philadelphia, J.B. Lippincott, 1993, pp 1–12.
6. Zaidan JR: Pacemakers. Anesthesiology 60:319–334, 1984.

68. CONGENITAL HEART DISEASE

Robert H. Friesen, M.D.

1. What is the incidence of congenital heart disease?

Although a range can be found in the literature, a reasonable estimate of the incidence is 1 in 250 live births.

2. What causes pulmonary hypertension in association with congenital heart disease?

Pulmonary hypertension is the result of high blood flow and pressure in the pulmonary vasculature caused by left-to-right intracardiac shunting at the ventricular level. This situation is typically present with ventricular septal defects or atrioventricular septal (endocardial cushion) defects, in which blood flows along a pressure gradient from the high pressure left ventricle to the lower pressure right ventricle.

3. Describe the pulmonary vascular effects of left-to-right shunts.

Chronic high flow and pressure in the pulmonary vasculature leads to medial hypertrophy of the pulmonary arteries, resulting in a progressive increase in pulmonary vascular resistance (PVR). This pulmonary vascular obstructive disease eventually becomes irreversible. This is rare in patients younger than 1 year of age, except in special situations (Down syndrome, high altitude, or concurrent existence of cyanotic heart disease, for example).

Several years of progression of pulmonary vascular obstructive disease can result in PVR being greater than systemic vascular resistance (SVR). When this happens, the intracardiac shunt is reversed and flows right-to-left. This life-threatening situation is called Eisenmenger's syndrome.

4. How do left-to-right shunts affect the heart?

Over time, both ventricles suffer from such shunting. The right ventricle must pump a higher than normal volume of blood through a progressively resistant pulmonary vasculature. The left ventricle is overworked because it receives a higher volume load from pulmonary venous return and because maintenance of cardiac output is less efficient when some blood exits the left ventricle through a septal defect rather than the aorta. Biventricular dilatation, hypertrophy, and, eventually, ischemia, fibrosis, and dysfunction are the result.

5. What is a pulmonary hypertensive crisis and how is it treated?

In patients with pulmonary hypertension, the pulmonary vasculature is hyperreactive to various stimuli that cause pulmonary vasoconstriction. These stimuli include hypoxia, acidosis, hypercarbia, and stress associated with such noxious stimuli as pain or tracheal suctioning. When PVR suddenly increases as a result of such hyperreactivity to a point at which right ventricular pressure equals or exceeds left ventricular pressure, a pulmonary hypertensive crisis is said to occur. This is a dangerous situation in which death can occur as a result of rapidly progressive right ventricular failure, diminishing pulmonary blood flow and cardiac output, and hypoxia.

Treatment of Pulmonary Hypertension

GOAL	METHOD
Increase P_{O_2}	Increase FiO_2
	Treat atelectasis
	Control ventilation
Alkalosis	Hyperventilation
	Treat metabolic acidosis
Control stress response	Adequate analgesia
Pulmonary vasodilatation	Inhaled nitric oxide
	Intravenous prostacyclin (PGI_2)

P_{O_2} = partial pressure of oxygen; FiO_2 = fractional concentration of oxygen in inspired gas

6. How are shunts calculated?

Using cardiac catheterization data, relative flows in the pulmonary and systemic circulations can be calculated using the Fick principle (flow is inversely related to oxygen extraction):

$$Qp/Qs = \frac{Sao_2 - Svo_2}{Spvo_2 - Spao_2}$$

Qp = pulmonary blood flow; Qs = systemic blood flow; Sao_2 = systemic arterial oxygen saturation; Svo_2 = systemic mixed venous oxygen saturation; $Spvo_2$ = pulmonary venous oxygen saturation; $Spao_2$ = pulmonary arterial oxygen saturation.

7. How is PVR calculated?

Resistance is related to pressure and flow:

$$PVR = \frac{PAP - LAP}{Qp} \qquad SVR = \frac{MAP - CVP}{Qs}$$

(Expressed in Wood units. Multiply by 80 to express in dyne $\cdot$ sec $\cdot$ cm^{-5}).
PAP = pulmonary artery pressure; LAP = left atrial pressure; Qp = pulmonary blood flow; MAP = mean arterial pressure; CVP = central venous pressure; Qs = systemic blood flow.

8. Do anesthetic drugs affect PVR?

Most anesthetics do not have undesired effects on the pulmonary vasculature. Inhalational anesthetics are vasodilators and probably have similar effects on both SVR and PVR. Fentanyl does not have direct effects on the pulmonary vasculature, but can prevent the stress response to noxious stimuli. Ketamine can increase PVR significantly in some patients who have pulmonary hypertension, especially if accompanied by hypoventilation. Almost any sedative drug can depress ventilation and cause changes in oxygen saturation or carbon dioxide tension that could increase PVR.

9. What causes cyanosis in congenital heart disease?

When at least 5 g/dl of desaturated hemoglobin is present in arterial blood, the lips, nailbeds, and mucous membranes appear blue, or cyanotic. Cyanosis occurs in patients with congenital heart lesions involving a right-to-left shunt and decreased pulmonary blood flow (including tetralogy of Fallot, pulmonary stenosis or atresia with septal defect, and tricuspid atresia), in lesions involving mixing of right- and left-sided blood without decreased pulmonary blood flow (including truncus arteriosus, anomalous pulmonary venous return, single ventricle, and double-outlet right ventricle), and in parallel right and left circulations (transposition of the great arteries).

10. Describe the clinical problems associated with cyanotic congenital heart disease.

In response to chronic hypoxemia, these patients develop polycythemia. When hematocrit exceeds about 65%, increased blood viscosity is associated with a greater risk of intravascular thrombosis, stroke, and poor flow in the microcirculation. The combination of hypoxemia and impaired blood flow can lead to tissue ischemia and organ dysfunction. In the heart, ventricular dysfunction occurs as the myocardium is subjected to chronic ischemia and is exacerbated by the hypertrophy associated with ventricular outflow obstruction, as in pulmonary stenosis.

In the presence of right-to-left shunting, air bubbles inadvertently injected into a vein can cross to the left side of the heart and enter the systemic arterial circulation, where they may cause stroke or myocardial ischemia.

11. What is the tetralogy of Fallot, and what are "tet spells?"

The tetrad of anatomic findings described by Fallot for this congenital heart lesion are pulmonary stenosis, overriding aorta, ventricular septal defect, and right ventricular hypertrophy. The pulmonary stenosis has a dynamic component: the subvalvular right ventricular outflow tract is muscular and contracts in response to inotropic stimuli (catecholamines). When such contraction occurs—or if SVR decreases significantly—less blood can flow into the pulmonary artery, so more desaturated blood is shunted right-to-left across the ventricular septal defect into the left ventricle. An acute hypercyanotic episode, or "tet spell," is the result.

Hypercyanotic spells and their treatment illustrate the importance of the balance between SVR and PVR. In the presence of a shunt, such as a ventricular septal defect, blood flow will follow the path of least resistance. If SVR is lower than PVR or right ventricular outflow tract resistance, as is the case in a "tet spell," blood will shunt right to left. Treatment is aimed toward alteration of the resistance relationships.

Treatment of Hypercyanotic Spells

GOAL	METHOD
Relax the right ventricle outflow tract	β-blockade with propranolol 0.1 mg/kg or esmolol 0.5–1.0 mg/kg
Increase SVR	Phenylephrine 5 µg/kg Compress femoral arteries or abdominal aorta
Increase stroke volume	Intravenous fluid bolus
Improve oxygenation	Increase FiO_2

12. What effects do anesthetic agents have on shunting in patients with cyanotic congenital heart disease?

Anesthetics can affect myocardial contractility, SVR, and PVR, and shunting can be influenced by any of these. Although it has been postulated that halothane or isoflurane may cause hypercyanotic spells because of their effect on SVR, studies have demonstrated that right-to-left shunting usually does not change significantly as long as ventilation and oxygenation are maintained. Nevertheless, as with any patient with cardiovascular disease, it is wise to avoid great changes in hemodynamic parameters by careful dosing, combining anesthetic drugs to achieve a balanced technique, and using muscle relaxants.

13. What is the main problem associated with ventricular obstructive lesions?

Obstruction to ventricular outflow, such as is observed in aortic stenosis, interrupted aortic arch, coarctation of the aorta, or pulmonary stenosis, is associated with progressive deterioration of ventricular performance because of ventricular hypertrophy and myocardial ischemia. The hypertrophy develops because the ventricle must work extra hard to overcome the obstruction and maintain stroke volume. Eventually, oxygen demand exceeds supply, and tissue ischemia occurs. Fibrosis and deterioration of function follow. Neonates with left-sided obstructive lesions commonly present with ventricular failure and acidosis and have a high mortality rate.

14. What is a "ductal dependent lesion"?

In some congenital heart defects, a patent ductus arteriosus is the only route by which blood can flow into either the pulmonary artery or the systemic aorta. For example, neither tricuspid atresia nor pulmonary atresia allows direct blood flow from the right ventricle into the pulmonary artery. Instead, blood must be shunted into the left side of the heart across an atrial or ventricular septal defect, flow into the aorta, and then flow through the ductus arteriosus into the pulmonary artery for gas exchange in the lungs. Similarly, the hypoplastic left heart has no direct blood flow from the heart to the aorta for systemic circulation; blood must flow from the pulmonary artery across the ductus arteriosus into the descending aorta. In these cases, maintenance of ductal patency by infusion of prostaglandin E_1 is essential to support life until a palliative or corrective procedure can be performed.

15. What is the best anesthetic technique for patients with congenital heart disease?

This depends on assessment of the patient's condition and the type of surgical procedure to be performed. Assessment of the patient should include a history (symptoms of cardiac limitation, recent changes, medications), physical examination (cyanosis, tachypnea, signs of heart failure), and laboratory tests (hematocrit for polycythemia, electrolytes when diuretics are used, chest x-ray for cardiomegaly or pulmonary infiltrates, electrocardiogram [ECG] for cardiac rhythm and ischemic changes). Review of cardiac catheterization or echocardiographic data will provide information concerning shunts, valve function or obstruction, pulmonary hypertension, and ventricular function.

There is no simple recipe for anesthetic management of the patient with congenital heart disease, and many rational approaches can be used. In some ways, the choice of anesthetic technique is easier for long and complicated major surgery (high-dose fentanyl, invasive monitoring, and postoperative mechanical ventilation) than it is for shorter or less complicated operations when rapid return to consciousness and spontaneous ventilation are goals. The availability of shorter duration nondepolarizing muscle relaxants and newer inhalational anesthetics with minimal cardiovascular depressant effects makes this job easier. Most anesthetics depress cardiovascular function and ventilation to some extent. Uptake of inhalational anesthetics (anesthetic induction) is slower in patients with cyanotic lesions.

Anesthetic Management

Avoid cardiovascular depressants

Maintain good oxygenation and ventilation

Understand the anatomy and pathophysiology of congenital heart disease

Know the cardiovascular effects of anesthetic drugs and techniques

Maintain shunt balance

Avoid hemodynamic stress triggers

Provide prophylaxis for bacterial endocarditis

---

16. How soon does cardiac function return to normal after surgical repair?

Although restoration of improved cardiac function is a very rewarding aspect of pediatric cardiac surgery, some experts believe that normal function is rarely achieved. Long-term cardiac function following repair of congenital heart disease depends on the duration and severity of cardiac impairment prior to correction and on the surgical result. Myocardial ischemia and fibrosis associated with obstructive or cyanotic lesions are irreversible changes that can have permanent effects on cardiac function. Residual postoperative valvular stenosis or regurgitation may be associated with progression of cardiac disease. Inadequate myocardial preservation during cardiopulmonary bypass can injure the heart. Even years after straightforward repair of ventricular septal defects, cardiac function has been observed to be abnormal. Therefore, one should not assume that cardiac function is normal in a child or adult who has undergone successful surgical repair of congenital heart disease in the past.

17. Why are cardiac surgical operations always named after surgeons?

Cardiac surgeons seem to enjoy naming innovative operations after themselves or their colleagues. Thus, we have operations called Blalock-Taussig shunt, Damus-Kaye-Stansel, Ross,

Rastelli, Norwood, and many others. Unfortunately, the rest of us are left to scratch our heads and wish that more descriptive names were used, even if they are longer. A few reference books will help here.

18. What is subacute bacterial endocarditis (SBE) and how can it be prevented?

Turbulent or high-velocity blood flow in the heart associated with congenital heart defects can cause damage to the endocardium of the heart or valves or to the endothelium of the great vessels. Damaged endocardium is rough and can be a nidus for infection in the presence of bacteremia or septicemia. Bacteremia can occur during dental or surgical procedures in the oral cavity, the alimentary tract, or the genitourinary system. Prophylactic administration of antibiotics during these procedures can prevent the development of an endocardial infection. Current recommendations involve the use of ampicillin and gentamicin or, in case of penicillin allergy, clindamycin or vancomycin. The precise recommendations, which are generated by the American Heart Association, depend on the type of operation and change from time to time; they are published periodically in the *Journal of the American Medical Association*.

BIBLIOGRAPHY

1. Arnon RG, Steinfeld L: Medical management of the cyanotic patient with congenital heart disease. Cardiovasc Rev Rep 6:145–156, 1985.
2. Dajani AS, Bisno AL, Chung KJ, et al: Prevention of bacterial endocarditis: Recommendations by the American Heart Association. JAMA 264:2919–2922, 1990.
3. Garson A Jr, Bricker JT, Fisher DJ, Neish SR (eds): The Science and Practice of Pediatric Cardiology, 2nd ed. Baltimore, Williams & Wilkins, 1998.
4. Graham TP Jr: Ventricular performance in congenital heart disease. Circulation 84:2259–2274, 1991.
5. Huntington JH, Malviya S, Voepel-Lewis T, et al: The effect of a right-to-left intracardiac shunt on the rate of rise of arterial and end-tidal halothane in children. Anesth Analg 88:759–762, 1999.
6. Hickey PR, Hansen DD, Cramolini GM, et al: Pulmonary and systemic hemodynamic responses to ketamine in infants with normal and elevated pulmonary vascular resistance. Anesthesiology 62:287–293, 1985.
7. Hickey PR, Hansen DD, Wessel DL, et al: Blunting of stress responses in the pulmonary circulation of infants by fentanyl. Anesth Analg 64:1137–1142, 1985.
8. Laishley RS, Burrows FA, Lerman J, Roy WL: Effect of anesthetic induction regimens on oxygen saturation in cyanotic congenital heart disease. Anesthesiology 65:673–677, 1986.
9. Lake CL: Pediatric Cardiac Anesthesia, 3rd ed. Stamford, CT, Appleton & Lange, 1997.
10. Morray JP, Lynn AM, Mansfield PB: Effect of pH and PCO_2 on pulmonary and systemic hemodynamics after surgery in children with congenital heart disease and pulmonary hypertension. J Pediatr 113:474–479, 1988.
11. Nudel D, Berman N, Talner N: Effects of acutely increasing systemic vascular resistance on oxygen tension in tetralogy of Fallot. Pediatrics 58:248–251, 1976.
12. Nussbaum J, Zane EA, Thys DM: Esmolol for the treatment of hypercyanotic spells in infants with tetralogy of Fallot. J Cardiovasc Anesth 3:200–202, 1989.
13. Rabinovitch M, Haworth SG, Castaneda AR, et al: Lung biopsy in congenital heart disease: A morphometric approach to pulmonary vascular disease. Circulation 58:1107–1122, 1978.
14. Rudolph AM, Yuan S: Response of the pulmonary vasculature to hypoxia and H^+ ion concentration changes. J Clin Invest 45:399–411, 1966.
15. Wessel DL, Hickey PR: Anesthesia for congenital heart disease. In Gregory GA (ed): Pediatric Anesthesia, 3rd ed. New York, Churchill Livingstone, 1994.
16. Wood P: The Eisenmenger syndrome or pulmonary hypertension with reversed central shunt. Br Med J 2:701–709, 1958.

VIII. Regional Anesthesia

69. SPINAL ANESTHESIA

Stephanie E. May, M.S.A., CRNA

1. Define spinal anesthesia.

A local anesthetic is injected into the subarachnoid space, mixing with cerebrospinal fluid (CSF), creating conduction blockade of the spinal nerves; this is also known as subarachnoid block (SAB). The resultant nerve block provides surgical anesthesia as far cephalad as the upper abdomen. Distribution of the local anesthetic determines the extent of the sympathetic, sensory, and motor effects, and elimination of the local anesthetic determines their duration. SAB is frequently administered as a single injection, although an indwelling catheter may be used for intermittent or continuous injections.

2. Does spinal anesthesia have advantages over general anesthesia?

Regional anesthesia such as SAB has been shown to be of benefit in several areas:

1. The metabolic stress response to surgery and anesthesia is much more effectively reduced by SAB than general anesthesia.

2. Many studies (especially in elective hip surgery) have shown a reduction in blood loss of 20–30% in patients receiving regional anesthesia versus general anesthesia.

3. Several studies demonstrated that regional techniques decrease the incidence of venous thromboembolic complications by as much as 50%, especially in lower extremity procedures.

4. Data regarding pulmonary complications are mixed; however, pulmonary compromise appears to be less in peripheral procedures performed under regional anesthesia. Other areas of potential benefit include avoidance of endotracheal intubation in patients with a difficult airway or reactive airway disease and decreased risk of gastric aspiration.

5. There may be a slight trend toward reduced cardiac complications in patients receiving regional versus general anesthetics.

6. SAB is widely used in obstetric anesthesia, especially for abdominal delivery. Less medication is administered to the mother and fetus. The mother is able to remain awake and participate in the delivery.

3. What is the duration of SAB?

Duration of Spinal Anesthetic Agents

AGENT	DURATION*
Lidocaine 5%	Short-to-intermediate acting, up to 60–75 minutes; possible 90+ minutes with a vasoconstrictor.
Tetracaine 1%	90–120 minutes; up to twice as long with a vasoconstrictor.
Bupivacaine 0.75%	Approximately 120–150 minutes; little increase with a vasoconstrictor.

* Times are based on the more commonly used hyperbaric preparations of local anesthetics (see question 4). Isobaric solutions tend to produce a more prolonged block.

Termination of action is due to reabsorption of the agent from the CSF into the systemic circulation, where metabolism and elimination occur. Duration of neural blockade may be prolonged by addition of a vasoconstrictor, such as phenylephrine or epinephrine, to the local anesthetic solution. Vasoconstrictor efficacy varies with the type of local anesthetic.

4. Describe the factors involved in distribution (and therefore level) of spinal anesthetics.

1. Patient characteristics: height, position, gender (a woman in the lateral position is slightly head down because of the width of pelvis relative to the shoulders), intra-abdominal pressure, and anatomic configuration of the spinal canal.

2. Type of needle, site of injection, and direction of needle.

3. Amount or dosage of local anesthetic (the most influential factor).

4. Physical characteristics of the local anesthetic solution. The baricity of the local anesthetic solution is defined as the ratio of the density of the local anesthetic solution to the density of CSF. A solution with a ratio > 1 is defined as hyperbaric and tends to sink with gravity in the CSF. The level of block is greatly affected by patient position. An isobaric solution has a baricity of 1 and tends to remain in the immediate area of injection. It is not significantly affected by patient position. A ratio < 1 defines a hypobaric solution, which tends to rise against gravity in the CSF. A hypobaric solution is useful when administered in unusual positions, such as the jack-knife position.

5. Volume of CSF in the spinal canal. Volume may be decreased by engorgement of the epidural veins due to increased intra-abdominal pressure from ascites or pregnancy.

The table below illustrates the anesthetic dermatomal levels necessary for different surgical procedures.

Dosing Guidelines for Spinal Anesthesia*

	T10	T6	T4
Dermatomal level	Umbilicus	Xiphoid	Nipple
Surgical area	Vaginal	Small bowel	Stomach
	Anal/rectal	Colon	Liver
	Bladder	Appendix	Pancreas
	Lower extremities	Pelvis	Gallbladder
Drug (mg)			
Tetracaine	6–10,10–12, 14	12, 14, 16	12–14, 16, 18
Bupivacaine	10, 7.5–12, 14	12, 10.5–14, 16	14, 16, 20
Lidocaine	50, 50–60, 70	60, 70, 80	70, 80, 90

* Dosage given for respective patient heights of 60, 66, and 72 inches (hyperbaric solutions).

5. How and where is a spinal anesthetic administered?

A typical SAB is performed in the lumbar region below the level of the spinal cord (L3–L4 in young children, L2 in adults) to avoid direct injury to the cord. The interspace between L3–L4 is the first interspace just above an imaginary line connecting the iliac crests. The patient is positioned in the sitting or lateral decubitus position, and the lumbar spine is flexed as much as possible to open the vertebral interspaces. The spinal needle is placed midline through the skin, subcutaneous structures, interspinous ligament, ligamentum flavum, dura, and arachnoid membrane. If the patient cannot adequately flex the lumbar spine or the ligaments are heavily calcified, one may use a lateral or paramedian approach. A slight "pop" may be felt as the dura and arachnoid membranes are punctured. When flow of CSF occurs, the local anesthetic agent is injected. The patient is then properly positioned and carefully observed for adverse affects, such as high spinal or hemodynamic instability.

6. Discuss the mechanism of action of spinal anesthesia.

Neural transmission of impulses in the nerve roots or possibly the spinal cord itself is interrupted by the local anesthetic; progression of the blockade may require 10–15 minutes. The nerve fibers vary in function, diameter, and thickness of the myelin sheath, which affects susceptibility to local anesthetics. Preganglionic autonomic fibers (B fibers) are small and more permeable to local anesthetics than the larger sensory C fibers. Sympathetic blockade is found 1–2 segments above the sensory block and motor blockade 1–2 segments below the sensory block.

7. List the most common complications of spinal anesthesia.

1. **Hypotension** occurs frequently with SAB. It is due to a combination of decreased vascular resistance and diminished cardiac output. Factors that increase the incidence and severity of hypotension include hypovolemia, sensory level greater than T4, baseline systolic blood pressure below 120, performance of the block at or above L2–L3, addition of phenylephrine to the local anesthetic solution, and SAB combined with general anesthesia. Hypotension may be ameliorated with prehydration of the patient. Hypotension may be treated with volume expansion or sympathomimetics. Trendelenburg position, used to treat other forms of hypotension, may raise the level of blockade and should be used with caution. Volume loading should also be used with caution in patients with limited cardiac reserve. As the block recedes, vascular tone increases, raising the central blood volume (preload), which may precipitate heart failure.

2. **Bradycardia** also may be seen. The mechanism is usually multifactorial and may include unopposed vagal tone from a high sympathectomy, blockade of the cardioaccelerator fibers (T1–T4), and the Bezold-Jarisch reflex (slowing of the heart rate secondary to a drop in venous return). Bradycardia may be treated with anticholinergic agents, such as atropine, or β-adrenergic agonists, such as ephedrine.

3. **Cardiac arrest** is occasionally reported during SAB. Studies have shown two major causes: oversedation and poor understanding of the physiology of sympathectomy. Oversedation is not unique to spinal anesthesia but in combination with a sympathectomy may be life-threatening. Oversedation during placement of the block (especially if one is distracted by events surrounding injection, positioning, and assessment of the level of block) may lead to respiratory compromise and hypoxemia. The patient with SAB has lost hemodynamic reserve, and this combination has led to cardiac arrest. Treatment consists of immediate assurance of adequate ventilation with reversal of hypoxia and early use of vasopressors.

4. **Nausea and vomiting** are common, perhaps because of unopposed vagal tone or hypotension that decreases cerebral blood flow. Anticholinergic medication or blood pressure elevation may be used to treat this side effect.

Total spinal, postdural puncture headache (PDPH), and other **uncommon neurologic sequelae** are discussed below.

8. What is a total spinal?

A total spinal is local anesthetic depression of the cervical spinal cord and brain stem. Signs and symptoms include dysphonia, dyspnea, upper extremity weakness, loss of consciousness, pupillary dilation, hypotension, bradycardia, and cardiopulmonary arrest. Early recognition is the key to management. Treatment includes securing the airway, positive pressure ventilation, volume infusion, and pressor support. The patient should receive sedation once ventilation is instituted and hemodynamics stabilize.

9. Describe a postdural puncture headache.

A potentially severe headache may develop after dural puncture, presumably secondary to the rent in the dura and resultant CSF leak, which may cause traction on the meninges and cranial nerves. The headache typically occurs 24–48 hours after the puncture, although it may occur immediately. The headache is characteristically intense in the occipital region and neck when the patient assumes the upright position and improves when the patient is recumbent. Diplopia or blurring of vision may occur. Tinnitus and hearing loss have been reported. Cranial nerve deficits also may be seen. Patients at higher risk for PDPH include those who have been instrumented with large-bore spinal needles with sharp bevel tips. Newer pencil-point needles, ranging from 24–27 gauge, have a low incidence of PDPH. Women, younger patients, parturients, and obese patients tend to have a higher incidence of PDPH. Treatment usually begins with hydration, analgesia, and caffeine. It is important to rule out central nervous system infection as a cause of the symptoms. Refractory or severe headaches may be treated effectively with an epidural blood patch. Epidural administration of dextran, hetastarch, and even saline has been shown to be of some benefit.

10. What is the risk of neurologic injury after spinal anesthesia?

Neurologic problems after SAB may be due to nerve compression secondary to improper patient positioning, direct surgical trauma, or unrecognized preexisting neurologic disease. Direct trauma to nerve fibers may occur from the spinal needle and may be heralded by a paraesthesia, for which the spinal needle should be redirected. Space-occupying lesions may occur after a SAB because of epidural venous bleeding (from direct trauma or coagulopathy) or abscess formation (from direct inoculation due to poor sterile technique or bacteremic seeding). Early recognition and management are imperative to avoid permanent neurologic sequelae. In patients who have received any medication with anticoagulant potential, it is important not to attribute persistent neurologic deficits to residual effects of local anesthesia. Adhesive arachnoiditis has been reported, presumably due to injection of an irritant into the subarachnoid space, and may be prevented by using preservative-free local anesthetics and opioids and avoiding contamination of the spinal needle with betadine and talc.

Nerve injury also has been reported from the direct effect of local anesthetics or their additives. Neurotoxicity may be due to prolonged exposure to high concentrations of local anesthetics. Evidence indicates that local anesthetics may inhibit fast axonal transport, disrupt the axonal cytoskeleton, cause axonal degeneration, and possibly contribute to ischemic nerve injury via inhibition of local vasodilating compounds. Microbore continuous spinal catheters have been associated with cauda equina syndrome, most likely due to direct high concentrations of local anesthetic at the nerve roots. Metabisulfite, a local anesthetic additive used as an antioxidant for epinephrine, has been shown to be neurotoxic in combination with the low pH of chloroprocaine. Epinephrine may increase and prolong the intraneural concentration of anesthetic, resulting in neurotoxicity. Vasoconstrictors may theoretically render ischemic injury to patients with already compromised circulation. Despite half a century of use, lidocaine has recently been recognized to produce transient (usually on the order of days) painful dysesthesias and radicular symptoms in some individuals.

11. What are the contraindications to spinal anesthesia?

Absolute contraindications include local infection at the puncture site, bacteremia, and intracranial hypertension. **Relative contraindications** include hypovolemia, aortic stenosis, progressive degenerative neurologic disease, low back pain, and coagulopathy.

12. What risk is associated with coagulation abnormalities?

The risk of spinal hematoma and neurologic dysfunction in patients with coagulopathy is small but real. A detailed history of abnormal bleeding and medication that affects coagulation should be obtained. In patients fully anticoagulated with intravenous heparin, the infusion should be discontinued 4–6 hours before SAB. The time of administration of recently introduced low–molecular-weight heparin compounds should be noted and the SAB performed in the window of time immediately prior to a scheduled dose (and the dose held for at least 2 hours). Oral warfarin therapy should be discontinued for several days, and prothrombin time should be measured before SAB. Patients who receive heparin after receiving nonsteroidal anti-inflammatory drugs (NSAIDs), including aspirin, may be at higher risk for spinal hematoma. Use of NSAIDs alone probably does not pose undue risk. Bleeding times are frequently measured in such patients before the block. No data support this practice. SAB probably should be avoided in patients who have recently received thrombolytic therapy. Avoidance of SAB in patients with underlying pathologic coagulopathies, such as disseminated intravascular coagulation or thrombocytopenia, seems wise.

13. Describe the various spinal needles.

A wide range of needles of varying type and size is available for spinal anesthesia. Standard length is 3.5"; longer needles are available for larger patients. Needle diameter ranges from 20 to 27 gauge. In general, the smaller the diameter, the less the incidence of PDPH. The larger bore needles (22-gauge and below) are useful in elderly patients, whose spinal ligaments may be calcified and who are at lower risk of PDPH, or in any patient in whom placement of SAB is difficult. Tip designs may also influence the incidence of PDPH as well as CSF flow characteristics through the needle. Small (24–27 gauge), pencil-point needles, such as the Whitacre or Sprotte brands, are thought to have the lowest incidence of PDPH and the best flow characteristics.

14. Discuss briefly the use of intrathecal opioids.
Opioids may be administered into the subarachnoid space with or without local anesthetics. They produce intense visceral analgesia without affecting motor or sympathetic function. The major site of action is at the opiate receptors within the second and third laminae of the substantia gelatinosa in the dorsal horn of the spinal cord. Lipophilic agents such as fentanyl and sufentanil have a much more localized effect than the hydrophilic agents such as morphine; the spread of hydrophilic agents is greater. Fentanyl and sufentanil have a rapid onset of action and a duration of 2–8 hours. Morphine lasts 6–24 hours. The long durations of action make these drugs desirable for postoperative analgesia. Addition of these agents to local anesthetic SABs may prolong the sensory block without increasing the postoperative duration of motor blockade or time to voiding. Toxicity includes respiratory depression (which may occur late with hydrophilic agents), nausea, vomiting, pruritus, and urinary retention. Opioid antagonists or agonist/antagonists are useful in treating such complications.

BIBLIOGRAPHY

1. Bevacqua BK: Spinal catheter size and hyperbaric lidocaine dosing. Reg Anesth 19:136–141, 1994.
2. Brown DL: Atlas of Regional Anesthesia. Philadelphia, W.B. Saunders, 1992, pp 267–282.
3. Caldwell LE: Subarachnoid morphine and fentanyl for labor analgesia: Efficacy and adverse effects. Reg Anesth 19:2–8, 1994.
4. Caplan RA: Unexpected cardiac arrest during spinal anesthesia: A closed claims analysis of predisposing factors. Anesthesiology 68:5–11, 1988.
5. Carpenter RL: Incidence and risk factors for side effects of spinal anesthesia. Anesthesiology 76:906–916, 1992.
6. de Jong RH: Local Anesthetics. St. Louis, Mosby, 1994.
7. Grass JA: Surgical outcome: Regional anesthesia and analgesia versus general anesthesia. Anesth Rev 20:117–125, 1993.
8. Greene NM: Distribution of local anesthetic solutions within the subarachnoid space. Anesth Analg 64:713–730, 1985.
9. Jaradeh S: Cauda equina syndrome: A neurologist's perspective. Reg Anesth 18:473–480, 1993.
10. Rowlingson JC: Toxicity of local anesthetic additives. Reg Anesth 18:453–460, 1993.

70. EPIDURAL ANALGESIA AND ANESTHESIA

Joy L. Hawkins, M.D.

1. Where is the epidural space? Describe the relevant anatomy.
The epidural space lies just outside the dural sac containing the spinal cord and cerebrospinal fluid (CSF). As the epidural needle enters the midline of the back over the bony spinous processes, it passes through (1) skin, (2) subcutaneous fat, (3) supraspinous ligament, (4) interspinous ligament, (5) ligamentum flavum, and (6) epidural space. Beyond the epidural space lie the spinal meninges and CSF. The epidural space has its widest point (5 mm) at L2. In addition to the traversing nerve roots, it contains fat, lymphatics, and an extensive venous plexus. Superiorly the space extends to the foramen magnum, where dura is fused to the base of the skull. Caudally it ends at the sacral hiatus. The epidural space can be entered in the cervical, thoracic, or lumbar regions to provide anesthesia. In pediatric patients the caudal epidural approach is commonly used (see question 3).

2. Differentiate between a spinal and an epidural anesthetic.

For a **spinal anesthetic**, a small amount of local anesthetic drug is placed directly in the CSF, producing rapid, dense, predictable neural blockade. An **epidural anesthetic** requires a tenfold increase in dose of local anesthetic to fill the potential epidural space and penetrate the nerve coverings; hence onset is slower. The anesthesia produced tends to be segmental; that is, a band of anesthesia is produced, extending upward and downward from the injection site. The degree of segmental spread depends largely on the volume of local anesthetic. For example, a 5-ml volume may produce only a narrow band of anesthetic covering 3–5 dermatomes, whereas a 20-ml volume may produce anesthesia from the upper thoracic to sacral dermatomes. An epidural anesthetic requires a larger needle, often uses a continuous catheter technique, and has a subtle endpoint for locating the space. The epidural space is located by the "feel" of the ligaments as they are passed through, whereas the subarachnoid space is definitively identified by CSF at the needle hub.

3. How is caudal anesthesia related to epidural anesthesia? When is it used?

Caudal anesthesia is a form of epidural anesthesia in which the injection is made at the sacral hiatus (S5). Because the dural sac normally ends at S2, accidental spinal injection is rare. Although the caudal approach to the epidural space provides dense sacral and lower lumbar levels of block, its use is limited by major problems: (1) the highly variable anatomy in adults, (2) the risk of injection into a venous plexus, and (3) the difficulty in maintaining sterility if a catheter is used. Caudal anesthesia is primarily used in children (whose anatomy is predictable) to provide postoperative analgesia after herniorrhaphy or perineal procedures. A catheter can be inserted if desired for long-term use.

4. What are the advantages of using epidural anesthesia over general anesthesia?

- Avoidance of airway manipulation; useful for asthmatics, known difficult intubations, and patients with a full stomach.
- Decreased stress response; less hypertension and tachycardia.
- Less thrombogenesis and subsequent pulmonary embolism; a proven benefit in orthopedic hip surgery.
- Improved bowel motility with less distention; sympathetic blockade provides more parasympathetic tone.
- The patient can be awake during the procedure if desired; useful for cesarean section and certain arthroscopic and laparoscopic procedures.
- Less postoperative nausea and sedation.
- Better postoperative pain control, especially for thoracic, upper abdominal, and orthopedic procedures.
- Less pulmonary dysfunction, both from better pain control and absence of airway manipulation.
- Faster turnover at the end of the case because there is no emergence time.

5. What are the disadvantages of epidural compared with general anesthesia?

- Initiation is slow at the beginning of the case.
- Less reliability, with higher failure rate.
- Occasional contraindications, including coagulopathy, hemodynamic instability, or spinal anomalies.

6. What are the advantages of epidural anesthesia over spinal anesthesia?

- Epidural anesthesia can produce a segmental block focused only on the area of surgery or pain; for example, during labor or for thoracic procedures.
- The gradual onset of sympathetic block allows time to manage associated hypotension.
- Duration of anesthesia can be prolonged by redosing through indwelling epidural catheters.
- There is more flexibility in the density of block; if less motor block is desired (for labor analgesia or postoperative pain management), a lower concentration of local anesthetic can be used.

• Decreased incidence of headache. Theoretically with no hole in the dura there is no spinal headache; however a wet tap occurs 0.5–4% of the time with the large-bore epidural needle, and about 50% of such patients require treatment for headache. Because newer technology in spinal needles has decreased the incidence of headache requiring treatment to less than 1%, this advantage probably no longer holds true.

7. What are the disadvantages of epidural compared with spinal anesthesia?

• The induction of epidural anesthesia is slower because of more complex placement, the necessity of incremental dosing of the local anesthetic, and the slow onset of anesthesia in the epidural space.
• Because of the greater amounts of local anesthetic used, there is a risk of local anesthetic toxicity if a vein is accidentally entered with the needle or catheter.
• Epidural anesthesia is less reliable; it is not as dense, the block can be patchy or one-sided, and there is no definite endpoint during placement.

8. What factors should the anesthesiologist look for in the preoperative assessment before performing an epidural anesthetic? Should special laboratory tests be performed?

In addition to the general preoperative assessment of every patient before surgery, the following specific items should be assessed before performing epidural anesthesia:

1. **History**
   • Previous back injury or surgery
   • Neurologic symptoms or history of neurologic disease (e.g., diabetic neuropathy, multiple sclerosis)
   • Bleeding tendencies or disease associated with coagulopathy (e.g., preeclampsia)
   • Prior regional anesthesia and associated problems
2. **Physical exam**
   • Neurologic exam for strength and sensation
   • Back exam for landmarks and potential anatomic abnormalities (scoliosis) or pathology (infection at the site of placement)
3. **Surgery**
   • Expected duration and blood loss
   • Positioning required
   • Amount of muscle relaxation necessary
4. **General**
   • The patient should be given a detailed explanation of the procedure, risks, benefits, and options (including general anesthesia if the block fails).
   • Discuss the patient's desire for sedation.
5. **Lab tests**
   • None are specifically necessary except as based on the history and physical exam.

9. Describe the technique for performing a lumbar epidural anesthetic.

• Have immediately available: oxygen, equipment for positive pressure ventilation and intubation, and pressors to treat hypotension.
• Place a well-running intravenous (IV) line and give an appropriate preload of fluid to protect against hypotension after sympathetic blockade.
• The patient may be sitting or in lateral position with the spinous processes aligned in the same vertical or horizontal plane and maximally flexed. Administer sedation as deemed appropriate.
• Mark a line between the iliac crests to locate the L4 spinous process. Palpate the L2–L3, L3–L4, and L4–L5 interspaces, and choose the widest or the closest to the desired anesthetic level.
• Make a skin wheal after sterile preparation and draping of the field. The anesthesiologist must wear a hat, mask, and sterile gloves.

- The epidural needle is inserted in the midline through the skin wheal until increased resistance of ligaments is felt. Remove the needle stylet and attach a syringe with 3–4 ml of air or saline. When the barrel of the syringe is tapped, it should feel firm and bounce back while the tip of the needle is in ligament.
- Advance several millimeters at a time, tapping the syringe intermittently. The ability to recognize the feel of various layers of ligament comes with experience. Ligamentum flavum is often described as leathery, gritty, or simply as having a marked increase in resistance. This is the last layer before the epidural space.
- As the needle passes through ligamentum flavum and enters the epidural space, there is often a "pop" or "give," and the air or fluid in the syringe injects easily because of loss of resistance.
- The syringe is removed, and while the nondominant hand grasps the hub of the needle to brace it, the dominant hand threads the catheter 3–5 cm into the space.
- The epidural needle is withdrawn carefully so as not to remove the catheter. After attaching the injector port to the catheter, it is aspirated for blood or CSF; if negative, a test dose is given. The catheter is then taped in place.

10. Are there any contraindications to epidural anesthesia?
Absolute contraindications
- Patient refusal. Sometimes a more thorough explanation will allay the patient's fears and make the technique acceptable. Some common concerns include (1) having to watch surgery or remain wide awake; (2) fear of a needle in the spinal cord; and (3) pain. Reassure patients that a curtain will block their view and that the desired degree of sedation can be provided. Explain that the spinal cord ends at about L1 in adults and that the needle is placed below that level. Compare the procedure to the placement of the IV line, which also uses a 16- or 18-gauge needle, and explain that a local anesthetic will be used in the skin.
- Sepsis with hemodynamic instability. The induction of sympathetic blockade decreases systemic vascular resistance (SVR) even further. There is also a remote risk of epidural abscess if bacteremic blood is introduced into the epidural space without prior antibiotic coverage.
- Uncorrected hypovolemia. With ongoing hemorrhage, the fall in SVR can produce severe refractory hypotension.
- Coagulopathy. If a vessel is injured within the epidural space, an epidural hematoma could form, causing neurologic damage.

Relative contraindications (often more medicolegal than medical)
- Elevated intracranial pressure.
- Prior back injury with neurologic deficit.
- Progressive neurologic disease, such as multiple sclerosis.
- Chronic back pain.
- Localized infection at the injection site.

11. What are the potential complications of epidural anesthesia? Can they be anticipated or prevented?
- Hypotension due to sympathetic blockade, which sometimes may be prevented by fluid preload and patient positioning.
- Intravascular injection of local anesthetic, which can be prevented by aspirating the catheter for blood, using a marker, such as epinephrine, that will cause tachycardia if injected into a vessel, and using incremental dosing (no more than 5 ml at a time). If an intravascular injection occurs, one must (1) stop convulsions with an induction agent or rapid-acting anticonvulsant; (2) intubate the trachea, if necessary for ventilation or airway protection; and (3) treat cardiovascular collapse with pressors, inotropes, and advanced cardiac life support (ACLS) protocols.

- Subarachnoid injection of a large volume of local anesthetic ("total spinal"). This can be prevented by aspirating the catheter for CSF and giving a small initial dose of local anesthetic to look for rapid onset of sensory block if the drug enters the CSF (remember: the onset of an epidural anesthetic is slow). If a total spinal occurs, one must treat hypotension with pressors and support ventilation with mask ventilation or intubation.
- Postdural puncture headache due to accidental dural puncture with the large-bore epidural needle. This can be treated in various ways, depending on the preference of the patient and anesthesiologist. Common therapies include analgesics, caffeine, or an epidural "blood patch." Determining factors include severity of the headache and how aggressively the patient wishes to be treated. To provide a blood patch, up to 20 ml of the patient's blood is placed in the epidural space to seal the dural hole and to elevate low CSF pressure.
- Epidural hematomas, which are extremely rare and usually occur spontaneously in clinical settings outside the operating room. When they are associated with regional anesthesia, there is usually a preexisting coagulopathy. Epidural hematomas present as back pain and leg weakness and must be diagnosed by computed tomography (CT) or magnetic resonance imaging (MRI). If the hematoma is not surgically decompressed in 6–8 hours, neurologic recovery is rare.

12. What physiologic changes should be expected after successful initiation of an epidural anesthetic?

- Decrease in blood pressure. However, afterload reduction can be useful for patients with hypertension or congestive heart failure if preload is maintained.
- Changes in heart rate. Tachycardia may occur as cardiac output increases to compensate for a drop in SVR. Bradycardia may occur if blockade above T4 disrupts the cardiac sympathetic accelerator fibers.
- Ventilatory changes. In normal patients, ventilation is maintained as long as the diaphragm is not impaired (phrenic nerve: C3–C5), but patients may become subjectively dyspneic as they become unable to feel their intercostal muscles. Patients dependent on accessory muscles of respiration may be impaired at lower levels of anesthesia. The ability to cough and protect the airway may be lost even if ventilation is adequate.
- Bladder distention. Sympathetic blockade and loss of sensation may require catheterization for urinary retention.
- Intestinal contraction. Sympathetic blockade with parasympathetic predominance contracts the bowel.
- Change in thermoregulation. Peripheral vasodilation lowers core body temperature if the patient is not covered. Shivering is common during epidural anesthesia.
- Neuroendocrine changes. Neural blockade above T5 blocks sympathetic afferents to the adrenal medulla, inhibiting the neural component of the stress response. Sympathetic and somatic pathways for pain also are blocked. Glucose control is better maintained.

13. How does one choose which local anesthetic to use?

The choice of local anesthetics usually is based on their onset, duration, and safety profile as well as on the special clinical characteristics of the patient and surgical procedure.

Local Anesthetics Commonly Used in Epidural Techniques

ANESTHETIC	SURGICAL CONCENTRATION	ONSET	DURATION	COMMENTS: MAXIMAL DOSE (WITH EPINEPHRINE)
Chloroprocaine	3%	Rapid	45 min	Ester, rapid metabolism → least toxic, intense sensory and motor block; 15 mg/kg
Lidocaine	2%	Intermediate	60–90 min	Amide, intense sensory and motor block; 7 mg/kg

Table continued on next page.

Local Anesthetics Commonly Used in Epidural Techniques (Continued)

ANESTHETIC	SURGICAL CONCENTRATION	ONSET	DURATION	COMMENTS: MAXIMAL DOSE (WITH EPINEPHRINE)
Bupivacaine	0.75%[a] 0.5%[b]	Slow	2–3 hr	Amide, most cardiotoxic; motor < sensory block; 3 mg/kg
Ropivacaine	0.75%	Slow	2–3 hr	Amide, less cardiotoxic than bupivacaine; motor < sensory; expensive; 3 mg/kg

[a] Not available for obstetric use.
[b] May not always produce surgical anesthesia.

14. Why is epinephrine used? Should it be included in all cases?

Epinephrine (and phenylephrine, another adjuvant vasoconstrictor) is often added to local anesthetic solutions in a concentration of 5 µg/ml (1:200,000) or less. There are several benefits to this practice:

- Prolongs blockade, especially of lidocaine, by reducing uptake into the bloodstream and thereby metabolism.
- Improves quality and reliability of blockade, either by increasing the available local anesthetic through decreased uptake or by an intrinsic anesthetic mechanism on central α-adrenergic receptors.
- Reduces peak blood levels by slowing vascular absorption.
- Helps to identify an intravascular injection as a "test dose." If the epinephrine-containing solution is unintentionally injected into a blood vessel, tachycardia usually results.

Epinephrine may be added to the local anesthetic solution for all blocks except those involving end arteries (digits, penis) or for patients in whom the tachycardia and hypertension may be detrimental (coronary artery disease, preeclampsia).

15. When should opioids be included in the epidural anesthetic?

Opioids may be mixed with the local anesthetic solution to intensify the block or to manage postoperative pain, either alone or with a dilute local anesthetic solution. Examples of epidural bolus doses: fentanyl, 50–100 µg; sufentanil, 20–30 µg; and morphine, 2–5 mg. The opioids act at the mu receptors in the substantia gelatinosa of the spinal cord. The more lipophilic opioids such as fentanyl and sufentanil have fast onset (5 min), short duration (2–4 hrs), and lower incidence of side effects. Morphine is hydrophilic and does not attach to the receptor as easily. It has a long onset (1 hr), long duration (up to 24 hr), and a high incidence of side effects, such as itching and nausea. Respiratory depression, although rare, is the most serious concern and requires special monitoring for the duration of the drug.

16. Why can some patients with epidural blocks move around and even walk, whereas others have a dense motor block?

Preserving motor function is especially important in postoperative patients and laboring women. The degree of motor block can be decreased by lowering the concentration of local anesthetic and by choosing a local anesthetic with favorable sensory-motor dissociation. As local anesthetic concentration decreases, the intensity of the block decreases and fewer motor nerves are affected. Sensory block can be augmented by the addition of epidural opioids if desired. Bupivacaine provides relatively more sensory block for a given amount of motor block (so-called sensory-motor dissociation). This property accounts for much of its popularity in obstetric anesthesia. For example, a common epidural infusion for postoperative pain and labor is 0.1% bupivacaine with 2–5 µg/ml fentanyl.

17. When is analgesia preferable to anesthesia?

Anesthesia implies an intense sensory and motor blockade, which is necessary to perform a surgical procedure. It usually is obtained by using the highest available concentration of local anesthetic (for example, 2% lidocaine or 3% chloroprocaine). **Analgesia** implies sensory blockade only, usually for pain or labor, and may be achieved with dilute local anesthetic or epidural opioids.

18. How does one know what level of anesthesia is needed for different types of surgery? What is a segmental block? When is it used?

To provide adequate surgical blockade with an epidural anesthetic, one must know the innervation of the structures stimulated during the procedure. For example, a transurethral resection of the prostate requires a T8 level because the bladder is innervated by T8 through its embryologic origins. A laparotomy such as a cesarean section requires a T4 level to cover the innervation of the peritoneum.

Epidural anesthesia is segmental; that is, it has an upper and lower level. The block is most intense near the site of catheter insertion and diminishes with distance. The needle and catheter should be placed as close to the site of surgery as possible; for example, a thoracic injection is used for chest surgery, whereas a midlumbar injection is used for hip surgery. In labor, the lower limit of block can be kept above the sacral nerve roots until the second stage of labor to preserve pelvic floor tone and the perineal reflex.

19. How does one know how much local anesthetic solution to use for different procedures? What factors affect spread in the epidural space?

The extent of epidural blockade is determined primarily by the volume of local anesthetic; more dermatomes are blocked by more milliliters of local anesthetic. To achieve a T4 level from a lumbar epidural catheter, 20–30 ml of solution is required. Other factors affecting spread in the epidural space include (1) age (older patients require less local anesthetic); (2) pregnancy—requires less; (3) obesity—probably requires less; and (4) height—taller patients may require more.

20. What is a combined spinal-epidural anesthetic? Why use both?

For a combined spinal-epidural anesthetic, a long spinal needle is passed through an epidural needle once it has been placed in the epidural space. When CSF is obtained from the spinal needle, a dose of local anesthetic is placed in the subarachnoid space, and the spinal needle is removed. The epidural catheter is then threaded into the epidural space and the epidural needle is removed. This technique combines the advantages of both spinal and epidural anesthesia: fast onset of an intense spinal block so that the surgery can proceed quickly and an epidural catheter to extend the length of the block if necessary for a long surgical procedure or for postoperative pain management.

21. What is a combined epidural-general anesthetic? Why give the patient two anesthetics?

In some surgical procedures, controlled ventilation may be safer for the patient or necessary for the surgical procedure. Examples may be intrathoracic or upper abdominal operations. Because these procedures often result in moderate-to-severe postoperative pain, an epidural anesthetic can be an ideal way to provide pain relief and to aid in mobilization to prevent pulmonary and thromboembolic complications. The epidural anesthetic is usually placed prior to induction of general anesthesia. By using the epidural catheter intraoperatively, smaller amounts of the general anesthetic agents are required, which may result in fewer hemodynamic consequences and faster awakening. At the same time, the patient's airway can be protected, ventilation controlled, and hypnosis and amnesia provided.

22. What should the anesthesiologist ask the patient after use of an epidural anesthetic?

- Satisfaction with the anesthetic. Was there anything that the patient would like to have been done differently? Assess patient satisfaction and try to correct any misunderstandings.

- Regression of sensory and motor block. Is there any residual blockade? Can the patient ambulate? Does the patient have any problem with bowel or bladder function? Any of these complaints requires a thorough neurologic exam to localize the deficit. Although the complaint may be due to residual local anesthetic or nerve compression during the surgical procedure (which usually resolves with time), further evaluation may be needed. Depending on the pattern and severity of the neurologic dysfunction, further evaluation by a formal neurology consultation, electromyogram, or CT may be needed to rule out pathology in the epidural space (such as hematoma).
- Complaints of back pain. Examine the site for bruising, redness, or swelling.
- Complaints of headache. If an accidental dural puncture occurred, the patient should be followed for several days; such headaches can appear up to 1 week later.
- Adequacy of postoperative pain relief. Did any side effects of epidural narcotics (itching, nausea) require treatment?

BIBLIOGRAPHY

1. Badner NH: Epidural agents for postoperative analgesia. Anesthesiol Clin North Am 10:321–337, 1992.
2. Batra MS: Epidural and spinal analgesia and anesthesia: Contemporary issues. Anesthesiol Clin North Am, Vol. 10, 1992.
3. Cousins MJ, Veering BT: Epidural neural blockade. In Cousins MJ, Bridenbaugh PO (eds): Neural Blockade, 3rd ed. Philadelphia, Lippincott Williams & Wilkins, 1998, pp 243–321.
4. Mulroy MF, Norris MC, Liu SS: Safety steps for epidural injection of local anesthetics: Review of the literature and recommendations. Anesth Analg 85:1346–1356, 1997.

71. PERIPHERAL NERVE BLOCKS

David M. Glenn, M.D., and Jose M. Angel, M.D.

1. How are peripheral nerve fibers classified? How do they differ anatomically and functionally?

Nerve roots of the spinal cord, which become the peripheral nerves, are a mix of motor, sensory, and autonomic fibers. Because these fibers have individual sensitivities to local anesthetics (LAs), the totality of block is not always uniform. The table below describes these classifications and how their anatomic features affect ease and speed of blockade. Generally speaking, small myelinated fibers are more easily blocked than large unmyelinated fibers. Each fiber has a specific minimal concentration (Cm) of LA for blockade. The Cm is higher for motor fibers than for sensory fibers and lowest for sympathetic fibers. Hence, as the LA diffuses away from the site of injection and the concentration decreases by dilution, sympathetic nerves are more completely blocked, sensation is moderately blocked, and motor function is only partially blocked.

Anatomic and Functional Classification of Peripheral Nerve Fibers

GROUP	SUBGROUP	ACTION/FUNCTION	MYELIN	SIZE	RELATIVE EASE OF BLOCKADE
A	Alpha	Motor, proprioception	Present	Large	4
	Beta	Motor, proprioception light touch, pressure	Present	Medium	3
	Gamma	Muscle tone (spindle)	Present	Medium	3
	Delta	Pain, temperature, touch	Present	Small	2
B		Preganglionic, sympathetics	Present	Small	1

Table continued on next page.

Anatomic and Functional Classification of Peripheral Nerve Fibers (Continued)

GROUP	SUBGROUP	ACTION/FUNCTION	MYELIN	SIZE	RELATIVE EASE OF BLOCKADE
C		Deep pain, temperature, pressure, postganglionic sympathetics	Absent	Extra small	2

1 = most easily blocked, 4 = least easily blocked.

2. What are the basic principles and techniques underlying successful peripheral nerve block (PNB)?

1. One must have knowledge of the anatomy and landmarks (specific bones, vessels, and muscles) involved in locating the nerve to be blocked.

2. The appropriate LA, concentration, and volume must be chosen.

3. The appropriateness of additives (e.g., epinephrine, bicarbonate) must be decided.

4. The tactile sensation of loss of resistance as the needle passes through the nerve sheath or a paresthesia when the needle touches the nerve may be helpful in localizing the nerve.

5. A nerve stimulator connected to the advancing needle may provide additional sensitivity in locating the desired nerve (twitching of the specific muscle group supplied by the nerve).

3. What are the risks in performing PNB?

Two categories of risks are involved in a PNB: anatomic and physiologic. The anatomic structures and organs surrounding the nerve to be blocked may be damaged by the needle. Examples include pneumothorax and hemothorax in a supraclavicular block, total spinal blockade in an interscalene block, and, in any nerve block, direct nerve laceration or major vessel damage resulting in pseudoaneurysm or hematoma. Physiologic risks may be systemic or local. Systemic side effects affect the central nervous system (CNS) and the cardiovascular (CV) systems. Systemic effects occur from overdosage and circulatory absorption or inadvertent intravascular injection. Symptoms usually occur in the following sequence: tongue or lip numbness, tinnitus, light-headedness, visual disturbances, muscular spasms or twitching, seizures, coma, and cardiorespiratory arrest. More potent LAs are usually more toxic. Bupivacaine is the most cardiotoxic, not only because of its potency but also because its slow dissociation from myocardial sodium channels results in refractory cardiac depression.

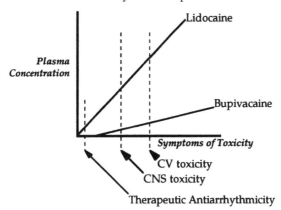

Comparison of plasma concentration to systemic toxic symptoms for lidocaine versus bupivacaine.

Finally, there are the possible allergic side effects of aminoester LAs (tetracaine, chloroprocaine, procaine, cocaine). These LAs are derivatives of para-aminobenzoic acid (PABA), a known allergen. Hypersensitivy reactions to various preservatives used in some LAs have been noted in the past.

4. How can the risks from PNB be minimized?

It is essential to ensure that the needle is placed correctly before injecting the LA. Effective methods are simple but important:

1. Continuous aspiration is mandatory while advancing the needle; a flow of blood or cerebrospinal fluid (CSF) is an obvious sign of improper needle position and indicates that the needle needs to be redirected.

2. Reports of symptoms experienced by the patient, such as paresthesia, hiccups, or cough, help to determine whether the needle is touching a nerve.

3. Dilute epinephrine may be added to the LA to test needle placement; it causes a transient increase in heart rate and blood pressure if injected intravascularly. (Exception: do not use epinephrine in digital or facial blocks.)

4. Using no more than the recommended dosage (mg/kg body weight) of LA affords a good margin of safety; however, plasma levels resulting from absorption vary with the type and location of the block. This recognition is of vital importance to avoid toxic systemic levels from the "recommended dose."

UPPER EXTREMITIES

5. Describe the indications and landmarks for PNBs at the elbow and wrist.

PNBs at the elbow are primarily useful to supplement incomplete brachial plexus blocks. PNBs at the wrist are useful for surgery distal to the metacarpophalangeal (MCP) joints. The following table describes the useful landmarks for identifying the nerve. In practice, a large volume of LA is more likely to produce an adequate block. Blocks at the wrist and elbow are also useful for diagnosis in some chronic pain syndromes.

Landmarks for PNB Injection at the Wrist and Elbow

NERVE		LANDMARK		LANDMARK	DOSAGE OF LA
Landmark at the wrist					
Ulnar		Flexor carpi ulnaris tendon, styloid process of ulna		Ulnar artery pulsation	3–5 ml 1% lidocaine or 0.5% bupivacaine
Radial	is medial	Anatomic snuff box	and lateral	Radial artery pulsation	3–5 ml 1% lidocaine or 0.5% bupivacaine
Median	to	Flexor carpi radialis tendon	to	Palmaris longus tendon (identified best in the flexed wrist)	3–5 ml 1% lidocaine or 0.5% bupivacaine
Landmark at the elbow					
Ulnar		Olecranon process		Medial epicondyle of humerus	5–10 ml 1% lidocaine or 0.5% bupivacaine
Radial	is medial to	Brachioradialis muscle (antecubital space)	and lateral to	Biceps tendon (antecubital space)	5–10 ml 1% lidocaine or 0.5% bupivacaine
Median		Medial epicondyle of humerus		Brachial artery pulse	3–5 ml 1% lidocaine or 0.5% bupivacaine

6. Describe the anatomy of the brachial pleus. What nerve or nerves are missed in performing brachial plexus blocks of the interscalene, supraclavicular, and axillary nerves?

The nerves of the brachial plexus originate from the spinal roots of C4–T2. They crisscross in an array of trunks, divisions, and cords; pass over the first rib and under the clavicle with the subclavian artery and vein; branch in the axilla as the ulnar, median, radial, and musculocutaneous nerves; and continue to supply the arm. Certain important anatomic factors must be considered in deciding which block is most appropriate:

- The C8–T2 roots join the plexus inferior to and distant from the site of injection of an **interscalene block**. As a result, C8–T2 roots are often missed; nerves potentially missed include the ulnar, medial brachial, and antebrachial cutaneous nerves, certain radial and thoracodorsal nerves, and the medial aspect of the upper and lower arm, hand, and fingers. This block is therefore appropriate for surgery to the lateral aspect of the shoulder, upper arm, and hand.
- The musculocutaneous and axillary nerves exit from the plexus before entering the axilla and are therefore unaffected by an **axillary block**, leaving the shoulder and upper arm without anesthesia. The musculocutaneous nerve can be blocked by infiltration of the coracobrachialis muscle. If a tourniquet is expected to be used, further LA infiltration along the axillary fold is necessary for blockade of the medial brachial cutaneous and intercostobrachial nerves. This block is best for surgery below the elbow.
- **Supraclavicular block** is most likely to anesthetize all of these nerves in a single shot and therefore is the most effective block for the entire arm (with the occasional exception of the skin overlying the shoulder, which can be blocked by a supplemental injection of the superficial cervical plexus nerves). The risk of pneumothorax, however, is greater with the supraclavicular than infraclavicular block.

7. How is a digital block performed? What is the most important thing to remember about your choice of local anesthetic?

The digital nerves of the fingers originate from the web spaces and run along both sides of each finger. They branch into dorsal and ventral arrays and are quite superficial. The best way to achieve a good block is to inject LA in a ring-like fashion around the base of the finger. Well-performed basic techniques and general principles are important:

- Continuous aspiration while advancing the needle and LA injection while withdrawing.
- Too large a volume may cause traumatic pressure injury to the nerves.
- **Do not** use vasoconstrictors, such as epinephrine, in the LA. Vasoconstriction may cause severe ischemia, necrosis, and loss of the finger. This caveat also applies to local infiltration blocks of the toes, tip of the nose, and ears.

8. Describe the Bier block. How is it performed?

Otherwise known as intravenous regional anesthesia, the Bier block is most commonly performed on the upper extremity for forearm and hand surgery of short duration. It is reliable and safe and has a high degree of patient satisfaction. The Bier block involves the following steps:

1. A small-gauge intravenous cannula is placed as distally as possible, usually in a vein of the hand.

2. A double tourniquet is placed around the upper arm.

3. The arm is exsanguinated by elevating and wrapping it tightly with a wide elastic band, called an esmarch.

4. With the proximal tourniquet inflated, 40–50 ml of 0.5% lidocaine is injected through the intravenous catheter. Within minutes anesthesia sets in and the operation may proceed.

5. When the patient begins to experience discomfort from the proximal tourniquet, the distal cuff, under which anesthetic has been infused, is inflated; only then is the proximal cuff deflated.

6. Eventually the distal cuff becomes uncomfortable as the total allowable ischemic time limit is approached and must be deflated as well. This method enables complete anesthesia up to approximately 90 minutes.

The main side effect to watch for is LA toxicity as the tourniquet is deflated. This complication is rare unless the tourniquet time is < 30 minutes. In such cases the tourniquet may be repeatedly and briefly deflated and reinflated, monitoring for LA toxicity. Repeating this procedure several times allows slower release of the LA and minimizes the risk of toxic effects. As always, constant communication with the patient is essential to detect early symptoms of toxicity. Hence oversedation is to be avoided.

A Bier block also may be performed on the lower extremities, although for surgery it is somewhat less efficacious. It is useful mostly in the diagnosis and treatment of some chronic pain syndromes in the lower extremities.

HEAD AND NECK

9. Describe the PNBs that are useful for surgery on the lateral and anterior neck.

The nerve roots arising from the plexus of cervical segments C2–C4 supply motor and sensory function to the anterior and lateral neck and some sensory function to the shoulder. Patients scheduled for carotid endarterectomy or thyroidectomy are good candidates for cervical plexus blocks (deep and/or superficial). Bilateral blockade is necessary for midline surgery such as thyroidectomy. In nearly all cases, however, some local infiltration should be performed by the surgeons because of the innervation by cranial nerves (i.e., blockade of the glossopharyngeal innervation of the carotid bodies alleviates reflex cardiovascular changes). Interscalene or supraclavicular blocks are the preferred regional anesthesia for shoulder surgery. If the patient still experiences pain, cervical plexus blockade as a supplement usually remedies the problem.

LOWER EXTREMITIES

10. What PNBs can be performed for surgery of the lower extremity?

As with PNBs of the upper extremity, knowledge of anatomy, especially the nerve routes and innervations, is essential. The most commonly performed and useful blocks are listed in the table below.

Lower Extremity PNBs: Examples, Innervation, and Injection Sites

NERVE	EXAMPLES	INNERVATION	INJECTION SITE	LA AND DOSE
Femoral	Acute femur fracture pain for placement in traction or transport; knee surgery	Motor to quadriceps, pectineus, and sartorius muscles, sensory to medial and anterior thigh	Inferior to inguinal ligament and lateral to femoral pulse	20 ml 1% lidocaine or 0.5% bupivacaine (40 ml for 3-in-1 block)
Lateral cutaneous femoral	Muscle biopsy, tourniquet pain	Sensory to proximal two-thirds of lateral hip and thigh	Medial and inferior to anterior superior iliac spine through inguinal ligament	10–15 ml 1% lidocaine or 0.5% bupivacaine
Obturator	Muscle biopsy, tourniquet pain, adductor relaxation for surgery	Sensory to medial thigh and hip, knee joint, motor to thigh adductors	"Walking" off the inferior ramus into the obturator foramen	20 ml 1% lidocaine or 0.5% bupivacaine
Sciatic	All surgery of the lower extremity that does not require a tourniquet	All of the lower extremity below the knee	Anterior approach: 2 cm medial from the femoral artery at the level of and "walking" off the lesser trochanter Posterior approach: midway between sacral hiatus and greater trochanter	20 ml 1% lidocaine or 0.5% bupivacaine

Table continued on next page.

Lower Extremity PNBs: Examples, Innervation, and Injection Sites (Continued)

NERVE	EXAMPLES	INNERVATION	INJECTION SITE	LA AND DOSE
Popliteal	Surgery of ankle and foot, usually in conjunction with sural nerve block	Muscles and skin of the posterior and lateral leg and foot	Lateral to the popliteal artery and vein in popliteal fossa	20–30 ml 1% lidocaine or 0.5% bupivacaine
Ankle block	See below			

11. Which nerves are affected by an ankle block? Where are they accessible to a needle? What region of the foot does each supply?

The table and figure below describe the three injection points for the five nerves of the ankle block.

Ankle Block Injection Site and Innervation

NERVE	LOCATION OF INJECTION	REGION OF INNERVATION
Sural	Lateral to Achilles tendon, posterior to lateral malleolus	Lateral heel, ankle, and foot
Posterior tibial	Medial to Achilles tendon, posterior to medial malleolus	Posterior and medial heel and plantar foot and toes
Superficial peroneal and saphenous	Subcutaneous across anterior one-third aspect of foot from lateral to medial malleoli	Top of foot and toes and medial ankle
Deep peroneal	Medial to tendon of hallucis longus	Web space of big toe

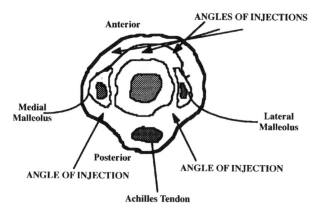

Sites of injection in an ankle block: cross section at the level of the malleoli.

CONTROVERSY

12. Should paresthesias be used as an indicator of nerve localizations in PNBs?

Pros: Increased certainty of nerve localization and therefore increased success rate of adequate block.

Cons: Increased risk of nerve damage or laceration, discomfort to the patient, requires greater patient cooperation than other techniques; therefore must be done with minimal sedation and reliable mental status.

Note: Use of a peripheral nerve stimulator technique has not been definitively shown to be less likely to cause nerve damage than use of a paresthesia technique.

BIBLIOGRAPHY

1. Brown DL: Atlas of Regional Anesthesia. W.B. Saunders, Philadelphia, 1992.
2. Ellis H, Feldman S: Anatomy for Anesthetists. London, Saunders/Blackwell, 1977.
3. Goldberg ME, Gregg C, Larijani GE, et al: A comparison of three methods of axillary approach to brachial plexus blockade for upper extremity surgery, Anesthesiology 66:814–816, 1987.
4. Moore DC: Regional Block, 4th ed. Springfield, IL, Charles C Thomas, 1965.
5. Mulroy MF: Regional Anesthesia: An Illustrated Procedural Guide. Boston, Little, Brown, 1989.
6. Tetzlaff JE: Peripheral nerve blocks. In Morgan GE, Mikhail MS (eds): Clinical Anesthesia. Norwalk, CT, Appleton & Lange, 1992, pp 230–268.
7. Tetzlaff JE, Yoon HJ, Brems J: Interscalene brachial plexus block for shoulder. Reg Anesth 19:339–343, 1994.
8. Urban MK, Urquhart B: Evaluation of brachial plexus anesthesia for upper extremity surgery. Reg Anesth 19:175–182, 1994.

IX. Anesthetic Considerations in Selected Surgical Procedures

72. CARDIOPULMONARY BYPASS

Michael Leonard, M.D.

1. What is the function of a cardiopulmonary bypass (CPB) pump?

A CPB pump functions as the temporary equivalent of an intact cardiopulmonary system. The machine perfuses the patient's vital organs, while oxygenating the blood and removing carbon dioxide (CO_2). Isolation of the cardiopulmonary system allows for surgical exposure of the heart and great vessels.

2. What are the basic components of the CPB pump?

A CPB circuit has a venous line, which siphons central venous blood from the patient into a reservoir. This blood then becomes oxygenated and has CO_2 removed before being returned to the patient's arterial circulation. Pressure to perfuse the arterial circulation is supplied by either a roller head or a centrifugal pump. The machine also has roller head pumps for cardioplegia administration, a ventricular vent to drain the heart during surgery, and a pump sucker to remove blood from the surgical field. Additionally the circuit contains filters for air and blood microemboli, because both can cause devastating central nervous system injury if delivered to the arterial circulation. A heat exchanger is present to produce hypothermia on bypass and warm the patient before separating from CPB.

3. Define the levels of hypothermia.

Mild: 32–35°C
Moderate: 26–31°C
Deep: 20–25°C
Profound: 14–19°C

4. Why is hypothermia used on CPB?

Systemic oxygen demand decreases 9% for every degree of temperature drop. The main concern on CPB is the prevention of myocardial and central nervous system injury.

5. Discuss the common cannulation sites for bypass.

Venous blood is obtained through cannulation of the superior and inferior vena cavae at the level of the right atrium. Arterial blood is returned to the ascending aorta proximal to the innominate artery. Occasionally the femoral artery and vein are used as cannulation sites. Drawbacks to femoral bypass include ischemia of the leg distal to the arterial cannula, inadequate venous drainage, possible inadequate systemic perfusion secondary to a small inflow cannula, and difficulty in cannula placement owing to atherosclerotic plaques.

6. What are the basic anesthetic techniques used in CPB cases?

Patients with poor ventricular function receive high-dose opioid anesthetics, usually with fentanyl or sufentanil. Healthier patients with reasonably good ventricular function can be given less opioid and supplemented with propofol or inhalation agents. The potential advantage of this latter approach is earlier postoperative extubation and transfer from the intensive care unit. Amnestic agents, such as midazolam, are a must to prevent intraoperative awareness. Neuromuscular blocking agents prevent shivering on bypass, which increases systemic oxygen demand, as well as contraction of the diaphragm during the surgical procedure.

7. List the two basic types of oxygenators.

1. **Bubble oxygenators** work by bubbling oxygen (O_2) through the patient's blood and then defoaming the blood to minimize air microemboli.

2. In **membrane oxygenators**, O_2 and CO_2 diffuse across a semipermeable membrane. Membrane units are generally preferable owing to a decreased risk of gas microemboli and less damage to blood elements.

8. What is meant by "pump prime," and what is the usual hemodynamic response to initiating bypass?

Priming solutions of either crystalloid or crystalloid-colloid are used to fill the CPB circuit. When bypass is initiated, the circuit must contain fluid to perfuse the arterial circulation until the patient's blood can circulate through the pump. The usual prime volume is 1.5–2.5 L. The acute hemodilution from the patient's circulating blood volume mixing with the prime causes an acute reduction in mean arterial pressure.

9. Why is systemic anticoagulation necessary?

Contact of the synthetic surfaces of the CPB circuit with nonheparinized blood leads to diffuse thrombosis, oxygenator failure, and frequently death. Even in a dire emergency, a minimum standard dose of 3–4 mg/kg of heparin must be given through a central line before the initiation of bypass. Postbypass, protamine is used to complex heparin and reverse the anticoagulant effect.

10. How is the adequacy of anticoagulation measured before and during bypass?

Activated clotting time (ACT) is measured about 3–4 minutes after heparin administration and every 30 minutes on CPB. An ACT of 400 seconds or longer is considered acceptable. Heparin levels are frequently measured, but only the ACT is a measure of anticoagulant activity. This is particularly important in patients with heparin resistance (seen with preoperative heparin infusions) and antithrombin III deficiency.

11. What must be ascertained before placing the patient on CPB?
- Adequate arterial inflow of oxygenated blood
- Sufficient venous return to the bypass pump
- ACT of at least 400 seconds
- Core temperature monitoring site
- Baseline assessment of the patient's pupils relative to size and symmetry
- Adequate depth of anesthesia

12. Why is a left ventricular vent used?

Left ventricular distention on bypass can be caused by aortic regurgitation or blood flow through the bronchial and thebesian veins. The resultant increase in myocardial wall tension can lead to serious myocardial ischemia by precluding adequate subendocardial cardioplegia distribution. A left ventricular vent, placed through the right superior pulmonary vein, decompresses the left side of the heart and returns this blood to the CPB pump.

13. Define cardioplegia.

Cardioplegia is a hypothermic, hyperkalemic solution containing some metabolic energy substrate. Perfused through the coronary arteries, cardioplegia induces diastolic electromechanical dissociation. Myocardial oxygen and energy requirements are dramatically reduced to those of cellular maintenance. Cardioplegia is perfused either anterograde via the aortic root coronary ostia or retrograde through the right atrial coronary sinus.

14. Myocardial protection refers to steps taken during bypass to minimize myocardial ischemia. What elements constitute myocardial protection?
- Cardioplegia
- Hypothermia
- Topical cooling of the heart with icy saline slush
- Left ventricular venting
- Insulating pad on the posterior cardiac surface to prevent warming from mediastinal blood flow
- Minimizing bronchial vessel collateral flow (which also rewarms the arrested heart)

15. What is the function of an aortic cross-clamp?
Clamping across the proximal aorta isolates the heart and coronary circulation. The arterial bypass perfusate enters the aorta distal to the clamp. Cardioplegia is infused between the clamp and aortic valve, thus entering the coronary circulation. This isolation of the heart from the systemic circulation allows for prolonged cardioplegia activity and profound cooling of the heart.

16. What are the pH-stat and alpha-stat methods of blood gas measurement?
In **pH-stat** measurements during hypothermic bypass, blood gases are temperature corrected to 37°C. In **alpha-stat**, blood gases are all measured as if drawn at 37°C and not temperature corrected. Some evidence suggests cerebral autoregulation of blood flow is better preserved on bypass with alpha-stat measurement of pH 7.4 and PCO_2 of 40 mmHg.

17. Develop an appropriate checklist for discontinuing bypass.
1. Check acid-base balance, hematocrit, electrolytes, and platelet count.
2. Ascertain adequate systemic rewarming.
3. Recalibrate all pressure transducers.
4. Ensure adequate cardiac rate and rhythm (may require pacing).
5. Reexamine the electrocardiogram (ECG) for rhythm and ischemia.
6. Remove intracardiac or intra-aortic air if aorta or cardiac chambers were opened.
7. Initiate ventilation of lungs.

18. Why is cardiac pacing frequently useful postbypass?
Between the ischemic insult of bypass and residual effect of cardioplegia, cardiac conduction may be impaired and myocardial wall motion is suboptimal. Cardiac pacing, with an atrial kick, at a rate of 80–100 beats per minute can significantly improve cardiac output.

BIBLIOGRAPHY

1. Bull BS, Korpman HA, Huse WM, Briggs BD: Heparin therapy during during extracorporeal circulation: I. Problems inherent in existing heparin protocols. J Thorac Cardiovasc Surg 69:674–684, 1975.
2. DiNardo JA: Management of cardiopulmonary bypass. In DiNardo JA, Schwartz MJ (eds):Anesthesia for Cardiac Surgery. Norwalk, CT, Appleton & Lange, 1990.
3. Hindman BJ, Lillehaug SL, Tinker JH: Cardiopulmonary bypass and the anesthesiologist. In Kaplan JA (ed): Cardiac Anesthesia, 3rd ed. Philadelphia, W. B. Saunders, 1993.
4. Murkin JM, Farrar JK, Tweed WA, et al: Cerebral autoregulation and flow/metabolism coupling during cardiopulmonary bypass: The influence of PaCO2. Anesth Analg 64:576–581, 1987.
5. Robinson RJS, Boright WA, Ligier B, et al: The incidence of awareness, and amnesia for perioperative events, after cardiac surgery with lorazepam and fentanyl anesthesia. J Cardiothorac Anesth 1:524–530, 1987.

73. DOUBLE-LUMEN ENDOTRACHEAL TUBES AND ONE-LUNG VENTILATION

Matt Flaherty, M.D.

1. What is one-lung ventilation?

One lung-ventilation involves preparation of the airway so that each lung can function independently. Double-lumen endotracheal tubes have a separate lumen to each lung and thus allow ventilation of one lung while the other is collapsed or independently ventilated. Typically, one-lung ventilation is used for respiratory support when thoracic surgical procedures necessitate either partial or complete collapse, retraction, or removal of the contralateral lung. Occasionally disease states require the isolation of one lung from the other.

2. What are the absolute indications for double-lumen tubes or one-lung ventilation?

Absolute indications for isolation of one lung or one-lung ventilation include protection of a healthy lung from a contaminated lung, such as gross infection in one lung or massive hemoptysis from one side. Lavage of one lung for pulmonary alveolar proteinosis requires isolation of the affected side. Other absolute indications include bronchopleural or bronchopleural cutaneous fistulas, surgical opening of major airways, disruption of the trachea or bronchial system, and giant unilateral cyst or bulla. Such disease states generally require diversion of ventilation to avoid loss of volume at leak sites or damage to the airway or lung at fragile sites.

3. What are the relative indications for double-lumen tubes or one-lung ventilation?

Relative indications for isolation of the lungs and one-lung ventilation arise from the need to collapse one lung for surgical exposure. Procedures involving the thoracic aorta, upper lobes, or complete pneumonectomy have the highest priority among the relative indications for one-lung ventilation. Moderate need for surgical exposure arises with middle and lower lobectomies, subsegmental lung resections, esophageal surgery, thoracoscopy, and thoracic spine procedures. Lower priority still is the occasional need to separate the lungs when a chronic, unilateral, totally occluding pulmonary embolus is removed.

4. Describe common equipment used to separate the two lungs.

Separating the lungs requires either a double-lumen tube or a single-lumen tube with a blocking device (bronchial blocker) to occlude one of the mainstem bronchi. The use of a single-lumen endotracheal tube is possible if it is placed distal to the carina and the cuff isolates one side. The advantage of the double-lumen tube is the presence of a lumen to each side. The lungs can be ventilated independently and suctioned as needed, and either side may be visualized directly with a fiber-optic bronchoscope. A vent port distal to the clamp site of each lumen allows deflation of the contralateral lung.

5. What are the different types of double-lumen tubes?

There are both right- and left-sided double-lumen tubes. Robertshaw types, by far the most common, are designed with a bronchial lumen that has its own cuff and extends distal to the carina. The tracheal lumen, with its cuff, opens proximal to the carina. Carlens tubes are similar to the Robertshaw design but have a hook that catches at the carina. Carlens tubes are rarely used today, because the hook may cause airway trauma during placement. Both designs have sizes 41, 39, 37, and 35 French (F); the Robertshaw tubes also come in 28 F. The inflatable bronchial cuffs are a bright blue color to help visualization during positioning with the fiber-optic bronchoscope.

6. What size are the individual lumens inside the double-lumen tube?

Both lumens are the same size in double-lumen tubes. The inner diameters are 6.5, 6.0, 5.5, and 5.0 mm for the 41, 39, 37, and 35 F, respectively.

7. What is the difference between a right- and left-sided double-lumen tube?

The difference between right- and left-sided double-lumen tubes is based on the difference between the length of the right and left mainstem bronchi. The right upper lobe bronchus branches from the right mainstem bronchus at about 2.1–2.3 cm. The bronchial lumen of right-sided double-lumen tubes must pass the carina far enough to let the cuff isolate the bronchial from the tracheal lumen, yet not so far that it blocks the right upper lobe take-off. The fact that the right upper lobe take-off is sometimes less than 2.1 cm or even tracheal in origin makes placement of the right-sided double-lumen tube difficult without obstructing the right upper lobe bronchus. The bronchial cuff is shaped asymmetrically, and the lumen has an additional slotted opening to help prevent this complication. The left mainstem bronchus is about 5.0–5.4 cm long and thus allows more room to place the bronchial lumen and cuff. The bronchial lumen of a left-sided double-lumen tube has a simple round opening and symmetric cuff.

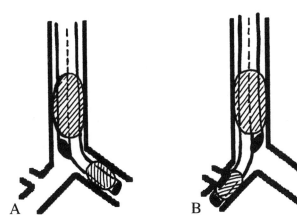

A, Left Robertshaw endotracheal tube, properly placed at the carina. *B*, Right Robertshaw endotracheal tube, properly placed at the carina.

8. When is a right-sided double-lumen tube used?

Right-sided double-lumen tubes are hard to place because of the short right mainstem bronchus. The cuff has the potential to move 1 cm or less and block the right upper lobe take-off. Because of this risk, left-sided double-lumen tubes are usually preferred. Because both right- and left-sided double-lumen tubes have a lumen to each lung, the left-sided double-lumen tube works well for procedures on either side, unless the bronchus itself is involved in the pathology or surgical procedure. When left-sided double-lumen tubes cannot be used or left bronchial surgery is planned, the right-sided double-lumen tube may be the best option.

9. What are the contraindications for use of a right- or left-sided double-lumen tube?

The left-sided double-lumen tubes cannot be used when the left mainstem bronchus is stenotic or obstructed or has an acute take-off. For left pneumonectomy, left-sided double-lumen tubes work well and can be pulled back out of the bronchus before it is stapled. The tube can be replaced with or used as a single-lumen tube. The same anatomic problems may prevent right-sided double-lumen tube placement, in addition to the technical difficulty involved in ventilation of the right upper lobe.

10. How is the double-lumen tube placed?

The double-lumen tube is supplied with a specialized stylet that, like conventional stylets, helps to stiffen the tube as it is passed through the upper airway past the vocal cords. Because it is a relatively large endotracheal tube, it should be lubricated before placement. Selecting a double-lumen tube that is too small may require excessive inflation of the cuffs to create a seal for positive pressure ventilation and increase the risk of airway injury. Tracheal cuff inflation usually requires 6–8 ml, whereas the bronchial cuff usually needs only 2–3 ml. Rupture of the mainstem bronchus due to excessive cuff inflation has been reported. The stylet also can be used to ensure the initial orientation of the longer endobronchial lumen as it is advanced toward the carina. Many anesthesiologists then remove the stylet and advance the tube blindly until it is seated in the mainstem bronchus. A possible complication is disruption of the mainstem bronchus; thus a double-lumen tube should not be forced. An alternative technique is to remove the stylet, pass a flexible fiber-optic bronchoscope through the bronchial lumen, and advance the tube with the bronchoscope as a guide. The bronchoscope also may be passed via the tracheal lumen and used to observe the endobronchial lumen as it passes into the appropriate mainstem bronchus. The placement of the right-sided double-lumen tube usually requires a fiber-optic bronchoscope; the margin for error is less because of the shorter right mainstem bronchus.

11. How does one confirm the position of a double-lumen tube?

The properly placed double-lumen tube, with both cuffs inflated, allows separation of the two lungs during ventilation; proper placement can be confirmed by auscultation and visualization of chest movement. When the bronchial lumen is clamped and the vent opened, breath sounds and chest rise should be minimal on the involved side and normal on the other. There should be no leak at the vent port. The reverse is true when the tracheal lumen is clamped and the vent opened: breath sounds and chest rise should be minimal over the tracheal side and normal over the side with the bronchial lumen. Again, there should be no leak at the vent port. Auscultation is the least sensitive method to confirm proper placement. In one study, when double-lumen tube placement was thought to be correct by auscultation, fiber-optic examination detected malpositioning in 48% of cases. Fiber-optic examination is made by passing the bronchoscope through the tracheal lumen and ensuring that the bronchial cuff (always colored bright blue) is located just distal to the carina on the desired bronchial side. The anterior trachea has complete cartilage rings, and the posterior aspect has the membranous band, which may continue down the posterior portions of the mainstem bronchi. Once the anterior tracheal wall is identified, the right and left mainstem bronchi can be positively identified. Right-sided double-lumen tubes are further examined by passing the bronchoscope through the bronchial lumen and ensuring that the slot for right upper lobe ventilation is facing and open to the right upper lobe bronchus. The final and most sensitive test of proper placement is observation of the lung when the chest is surgically opened. The double-lumen tube may move when the patient is turned to a lateral position and should be checked after the patient is in the surgical position.

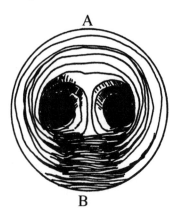

Fiber-optic bronchoscopic view of the trachea showing anterior and posterior anatomical landmarks. *A,* Cartilaginous rings, anterior. *B,* Membranous trachea, posterior.

12. Does one need a fiber-optic bronchoscope for placement and confirmation of placement?

Although double-lumen tubes can be placed blindly, if there appears to be a problem with placement, the fiber-optic bronchoscope should be used. Placement confirmation is much more sensitive with the fiber-optic bronchoscope, especially with right-sided double-lumen tubes. As mentioned above, when double-lumen tube placement was thought to be correct by auscultation, fiber-optic examination detected malpositioning in 48% of cases. Standard adult fiber-optic bronchoscopes usually have an outer diameter of 4.9 mm and barely fit through the lumens of the 37-F double-lumen tubes. If one uses a 35-F double-lumen tube or smaller, a pediatric or "slim" style bronchoscope is required.

13. How is a bronchial blocker used?

Bronchial blockers involve the placement of a Fogarty embolectomy catheter through a conventional endotracheal tube. The balloon is positioned in one of the mainstem bronchi, using the fiber-optic bronchoscope for guidance. When one-lung ventilation is desired, the balloon is inflated, blocking ventilation to that side. Venting and ventilation of the blocked lung is not possible.

14. What is a Univent tube?

The Univent tube is a endotracheal tube containing a bronchial blocker. The bronchial blocker is located in a small channel built into the wall of the endotracheal tube. The bronchial blocking balloon is connected to a venting port. Once the balloon is inflated, the blocked lung can be vented to the atmosphere and allowed to collapse. The balloon can be advanced when needed and retracted when not in use.

15. What are the common problems encountered in placing double-lumen tubes or bronchial blockers?

The most common problems involve malpositioning of the bronchial end of the double-lumen tube. If the bronchial lumen and cuff do not reach distally to either mainstem bronchus, either side may ventilate both lungs. If the bronchial lumen is in the trachea and the cuff is over-inflated, it may be possible to ventilate both lungs via the bronchial lumen, whereas the tracheal lumen displays very high airway pressures and ventilates neither lung. If the bronchial lumen is placed on the wrong side, it will isolate the wrong side when one-lung ventilation is attempted. When the bronchial lumen is too far down one of the mainstem bronchi, it may block the upper lobe bronchi on the involved side, and the tracheal lumen may also ventilate the same side. Double-lumen tube cuffs may herniate like any other cuff, possibly obstructing part or all of the airway. The bronchial cuff may be overinflated and rupture the mainstem bronchus.

Bronchial blockers involve the risk of misplacement or migration into the trachea, with major airway obstruction. The balloon also can be overinflated and injure the bronchus. Univent tubes should be used only by personnel familiar with the purpose of the bronchial blocker that they contain. Usually this blocker is deflated and retracted into its channel at the end of a case. If the patient remains intubated with the Univent tube postoperatively, it may accidentally be inflated in a tracheal site and obstruct the airway.

When double-lumen tubes are placed, their shape and size lead to a higher incidence of laryngeal trauma. The incidence of trauma with the Carlens tube (with the carinal hook) may be around 1.5%. An airway device in the mainstem bronchus runs a risk of being sutured into the surgical closure at that site. Endobronchial lumens of double-lumen tubes, bronchial blockers, and suction catheters have been sutured into bronchial stumps during pneumonectomy and lobectomy. When such devices are sutured into the bronchial stump, their removal may cause significant damage to the airway.

16. What are standard ventilator settings for one-lung ventilation?

Most anesthesiologists use approximately the same tidal volume for one-lung ventilation as for two-lung ventilation—typically around 10 ml/kg. Higher tidal volumes increase airway pressures and vascular resistance, which may cause more blood flow to the nonventilated lung and more shunting. Lower tidal volumes may allow more atelectasis in the ventilated lung. The FiO_2 (fractional concentration of oxygen in inspired gas) will usually be 0.8–1.0, giving the greatest margin of safety against hypoxia. The respiratory rate is usually adjusted to maintain a $PaCO_2$ around 40 mmHg.

17. Describe pulmonary changes that occur with one-lung ventilation.

Most thoracic surgery is performed in the lateral decubitus position with the surgical site up and nonventilated. The nonventilated lung is also referred to as the nondependent lung. When ventilation is interrupted, the remaining blood flow to the nondependent lung becomes shunted (ventilation-perfusion ratio of zero), contributing to hypoxia. Several factors help to decrease nondependent lung blood flow: gravity, which favors blood flow to the ventilated (dependent) lung; surgical compression and retraction; surgical ligation of nondependent lung blood vessels; and hypoxic pulmonary vasoconstriction. The total benefit of the above factors is a reduction of ~50% shunt to ~30%. The dependent lung physiology also changes because of loss of lung volume due to compression from the abdomen and mediastinum. Absorption atelectasis may occur in marginally ventilated areas. Hypoxic pulmonary vasoconstriction in the dependent lung may favor blood flow to the nondependent lung. Secretions in the dependent lung may be difficult to remove through the double-lumen tube.

18. Which changes more during one lung ventilation—PaO_2 or $PaCO_2$?

During one-lung ventilation change is much greater in PaO_2 than in $PaCO_2$ because of the greater diffusibility of CO_2.

19. Describe an approach to management of hypoxia during one-lung ventilation.

PaO_2 usually decreases significantly when ventilation changes to one lung. The first step is to check the FiO_2 to ensure that it is 0.8–1.0; the second is to check tidal volumes (optimal value—around 10 ml/kg). The fiber-optic bronchoscope should be used to ensure that the double-lumen tube or bronchial blocker is in proper position. The respiratory rate should be adjusted to keep the $PaCO_2$ around 40 mmHg, because hypocapnia may decrease hypoxic pulmonary vaso-constriction. The next step is to add ~5 cm H_2O pressure of continuous positive airway pressure (CPAP) to the nondependent lung. This step may expand the retracted lung and the surgeon should be informed before CPAP is initiated. CPAP supplies oxygen to some of the alveoli that are perfused in the nondependent lung by decreasing shunt. The next step is to add ~5cm H_2O pressure of positive end-expiratory pressure (PEEP) to the dependent lung; this may increase volume in the dependent lung, which is highly prone to atelectasis. The PEEP may have a negative effect, however, by increasing vascular resistance in the dependent lung and causing more blood to flow to the nondependent lung, thereby increasing shunt. For this reason CPAP should be initiated in the nondependent lung; only small increments of PEEP should be added each time. If hypoxia continues, CPAP and PEEP can be incrementally increased in the nondependent and dependent lungs, respectively. If severe hypoxia continues, the surgeon may be able to ligate or clamp the pulmonary artery to the nondependent lung (for pneumonectomy), eliminating shunt from this source. Finally, return to two-lung ventilation may be necessary.

20. Describe the extubation of patients with a double-lumen tube.

If the patient is to be ventilated postoperatively, it may be desirable to remove the double-lumen tube and replace it with a conventional endotracheal tube. Some patients are extubated in the operating room when they demonstrate usual extubation criteria. Both lumens of the double-lumen tube are suctioned. Removal of a double-lumen tube is a potent laryngeal stimulus; this stimulus may be attenuated somewhat by intravenous lidocaine, 1 mg/kg 3–5 minutes before extubation. After lobectomy and pneumonectomy, positive pressure should be limited to less than 30 cm H_2O if possible, because the bronchial stump may be damaged by high airway pressures. The stump is usually tested for a leak at 35–40 cm H_2O, under saline, before closure of the chest.

21. When should one consider leaving a double-lumen tube or bronchial blocker in place for postoperative management?

Changing to a single-lumen endotracheal tube may be undesirable for a number of reasons. Changing the double-lumen tube may entail risk of airway loss in patients with airway edema or prior difficult intubation. The lungs may benefit from continued differential ventilation modes postoperatively, as in the case of lung transplant. There may be continued risk of contamination of one lung from the other or continued bronchopleural fistula. The double-lumen tube may be used for an extended period postoperatively. Case reports describe up to 10 days' duration without tracheal or bronchial trauma. The primary difficulty is increased airway resistance and difficulty in suctioning secretions because of the relatively small lumens. Leaving a bronchial blocker in place postoperatively is not advised because of the risk of severe airway obstruction if the inflated blocker migrates into the trachea.

22. What should be done if the patient is too small for the double-lumen tube?

The smallest double-lumen tube is the 28 F. Pediatric patients requiring one-lung ventilation may be managed with a single-lumen tube and a small Fogarty embolectomy catheter, which is passed outside the lumen of the endotracheal tube. The pediatric fiber-optic laryngoscope via the endotracheal tube is used to guide placement of the bronchial blocker.

BIBLIOGRAPHY

1. Benumof JL: Anesthesia for Thoracic Surgery. Philadelphia, W.B. Saunders, 1987, pp 223–287.
2. Benumof JL, Partridge NL, Salvaiterra C, et al: Margin of safety in positioning modern double-lumen endotracheal tubes. Anesthesiology 67:729–738, 1987.
3. Brodsky JB, Shulman MS, Mark JB: Malposition of left-sided double-lumen endotracheal tubes. Anesthesiology 62:667–669, 1985.
4. Brodsky JB, Mihm FG: Split-lung ventilation. In Hall JB, Schmidt GA, Wood LDH (eds): Principles of Critical Care. New York, McGraw-Hill, 1992, pp 160–164.
5. Eisenkraft JB, Cohen E, Neustein SM: Anesthesia for thoracic surgery. In Barash PG, Cullen BF, Stoelting RK (eds): Clinical Anesthesia, 3rd ed. Philadelphia, Lippincott Williams & Wilkins, 1997.
6. Eisenkraft JB, Neustein SM: Anesthetic management of therapeutic procedures of the lungs and airway. In Kaplan JA (ed): Thoracic Anesthesia, 2nd ed. New York, Churchill Livingstone, 1991, pp 371–388.
7. Lee BS, Sarnquist FH, Sarner VA: Anesthesia for bilateral single-lung transplantation. J Cardiothorac Vasc Anesth 6:201–203, 1992.
8. Smith GB, Hirsch NP, Ehrenwerth J: Sight and sound: Can double-lumen endotracheal tubes be placed accurately without fiberoptic bronchoscopy? Br J Anaesth 58:1317–1320, 1986.
9. Veil R: Selective bronchial blocking in a small child. Br J Anaesth 41:453–454, 1969.
10. Wilson RS: Endobronchial intubation. In Kaplan JA (ed): Thoracic Anesthesia, 2nd ed. New York, Churchill Livingstone, 1991, pp 371–388.

74. SOMATOSENSORY-EVOKED POTENTIALS AND SPINAL SURGERY

Patricia A. Gottlob, M.D.

1. What are somatosensory-evoked potentials (SSEPs)?

SSEPs are the electrophysiologic responses of the nervous system to the application of a discrete stimulus at a peripheral nerve anywhere in the body. They reflect the ability of a specific neural pathway to conduct an electrical signal from the periphery to the cerebral cortex.

2. How are SSEPs generated?

Using a skin surface disc electrode or subcutaneous fine-needle electrode placed near a major peripheral sensory nerve, a square wave electrical stimulus of 0.2–2 milliseconds is applied to the nerve at a rate of 1–2 Hz. The stimulus intensity is adjusted to produce minimal muscle contraction (usually 10–15 mA). The resulting electrical potential is recorded at various points along the neural pathway from the peripheral nerve to the cerebral cortex.

3. What major peripheral nerves are most commonly stimulated?

In the upper extremity, the common sites of stimulation are the median and ulnar nerves at the wrist. In the lower extremity, the common peroneal nerve at the popliteal fossa and the posterior tibial nerve at the ankle are used. Less commonly, the tongue, trigeminal nerve, and pudendal nerve have been studied.

4. Trace the neurosensory pathway from the peripheral nerves to the cerebral cortex.

The axons of the peripheral sensory nerves enter the spinal cord via the dorsal spinal roots. These first-order neurons continue rostrally in the ipsilateral posterior column of the spinal cord until they synapse with nuclei at the cervicomedullary junction. Second-order neurons from these nuclei immediately cross to the opposite side of the brain stem, where they continue their ascent via the medial lemniscus through the midbrain, synapsing in the thalamus. Third-order neurons then travel via the internal capsule to synapse in the postcentral gyrus, the primary somatosensory cortex.

5. At what points along the neurosensory pathway are SSEPs most commonly recorded?

After upper limb stimulation, potentials are recorded at the brachial plexus (Erb's point, 2 cm superior to the clavicular head of the sternocleidomastoid muscle); the cervicomedullary junction (posterior midline of the neck at the second cervical vertebra); and the scalp overlying the somatosensory cortex on the contralateral side.

After stimulation of the lower extremity, potentials are recorded at the popliteal fossa, lumbar spinal cord, and somatosensory cortex.

6. Describe the characteristics of the SSEP waveform.

The SSEP is plotted as a waveform of voltage versus time. It is characterized by

1. **Amplitude** (A), which is measured in microvolts from baseline to peak or peak to peak.

2. **Latency** (L), which is the time, measured in milliseconds, from onset of stimulus to occurrence of a peak or the time from one peak to another.

3. **Morphology**, which is the overall shape of the waveform, described as positive (P, below the baseline) or negative (N, above the baseline).

A waveform is identified by the letter describing its deflection above or below the baseline followed by a number indicating its latency (e.g., N20).

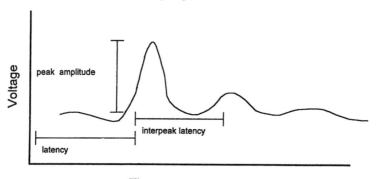

Characteristics of the SSEP waveform.

7. Name several characteristic peaks important for the evaluation of SSEPs.

Characteristic Peaks for Evaluation of Median Nerve Stimulation

PEAK	GENERATOR
N9	Brachial plexus (Erb's point)
N11	Dorsal root entry zone (cervical spine)
N13, 14	Posterior column (nucleus cuneatus)
P14	Medial lemniscus
N20	Somatosensory cortex

Characteristic Peaks for Evaluation of Posterior Tibial Nerve Stimulation

PEAK	GENERATOR
N20	Dorsal root entry zone (lumbar spine)
N40	Somatosensory cortex

8. What is the central somatosensory conduction time (CCT)?

CCT is the latency between the dorsal column nuclei (N14) and the primary sensory cortex (N20) peaks and reflects nerve conduction time through the brain stem and cortex.

9. What are the indications for intraoperative use of SSEP monitoring?

SSEP monitoring is indicated in any setting with the potential for mechanical or vascular compromise of the sensory pathways along the peripheral nerve, within the spinal canal, or within the brain stem or cerebral cortex. SSEP monitoring has been used in the following:

1. **Orthopedic procedures**
   - Correction of scoliosis with Harrington rod instrumentation
   - Spinal cord decompression and stabilization after acute spinal cord injury
   - Spinal fusion
2. **Brachial plexus exploration**
3. **Neurosurgical procedures**
   - Resection of a spinal cord tumor or vascular lesion
   - Tethered cord release
   - Resection of a sensory cortex lesion (e.g., aneurysm or thalamic tumor)
   - Repair of a thoracic or abdominal aortic aneurysm
   - Carotid endarterectomy

10. What constitutes a significant change in the SSEP?

Any decrease in amplitude greater than 50% or increase in latency greater than 10% may indicate a disruption of the sensory nerve pathways. The spinal cord can tolerate ischemia for about 20 minutes before SSEPs are lost.

11. Summarize the effects of anesthetic agents on the amplitude and latency of SSEPs.

Effects of Anesthetic Agents on Amplitude and Latency of SSEPs

DRUG	AMPLITUDE	LATENCY
Premedication		
Midazolam (0.3 mg/kg)	↓	0
Diazepam (0.1 mg/kg)	↓	↑
Induction agents		
Thiopental (5 mg/kg)	↑/0	↑
Etomidate (0.4 mg/kg)	↑↑↑	↑
Propofol (0.5 mg/kg)	0	↑
Ketamine (1 mg/kg)	↑	*

(Table continued on next page.)

Effects of Anesthetic Agents on Amplitude and Latency of SSEPs (Cont.)

DRUG	AMPLITUDE	LATENCY
Opioids		
Fentanyl		↑
Sufentanil		↑
Morphine		↑
Meperidine	↑/↓	↑
Inhaled anesthetics		
Nitrous oxide	↓	↑
Isoflurane	↓	↑
Halothane	↓	↑
Enflurane	↓	↑
Desflurane	↓	↑
Others		
Droperidol	↓	↑
Muscle relaxants	0	0

↑ = increase, ↓ = decrease, 0 = no change, * = not known.

12. What is the take-home message of the effects of anesthetic agents on SSEPs?

1. All of the halogenated inhaled anesthetics probably cause roughly equivalent dose-dependent decreases in amplitude and increases in latency that are further worsened by the addition of 60% nitrous oxide.

2. If possible, bolus injections of drugs should be avoided, especially during critical stages of the surgery. Continuous infusions are preferable.

13. What other physiologic variables can alter SSEPs?

1. **Temperature:** Hypothermia increases latency, whereas amplitude is either decreased or unchanged. For each decrease of 1°C, latency is increased by 1 millisecond. Hyperthermia (4°C) decreases amplitude to 15% of the normothermic value.

2. **Hypotension:** With a decrease of the mean arterial blood pressure (MAP < 40 mmHg), progressive decreases in amplitude are seen. The same change also is seen with a rapid decline in MAP to levels within the limits of cerebral autoregulation.

3. **Hypoxia:** Decreased amplitude due to hypoxia has been reported.

4. **Hypocarbia:** Increased latency has been described at an end-tidal $CO_2 < 25$ mmHg.

5. **Isovolemic hemodilution:** Latency is not increased until the hematocrit is < 15%, and amplitude is not decreased until the hematocrit is < 7%. This effect is likely due to tissue hypoxia.

14. If SSEPs change significantly, what can the anesthesiologist and surgeon do to lessen the insult to the monitored nerves?

The **anesthesiologist** can:

1. Increase mean arterial blood pressure, especially if induced hypotension is used.
2. Correct anemia, if present.
3. Correct hypovolemia, if present.
4. Improve oxygen tension.

The **surgeon** can:

1. Reduce excessive retractor pressure.
2. Reduce surgical dissection in the affected area.
3. Decrease Harrington rod distraction, if indicated.

If changes in the SSEPs persist despite corrective measures, a wake-up test may be performed to confirm or refute the SSEP findings. The patient's anesthetic level is lightened, and a clinical assessment of neurologic function is performed.

15. Despite "normal" SSEPs, can patients awaken with neurologic deficits?

Although SSEP monitoring is a useful tool in preventing neurologic damage during spinal surgery, it is by no means foolproof. Because motor tracts are not monitored, the patient may awaken with preserved sensation but lost motor function. The monitoring of motor-evoked potentials (MEPs) along with SSEPs provides a more complete assessment of neural pathway integrity.

BIBLIOGRAPHY

1. Black S, Cucchiara R: Neurologic monitoring. In Miller R (ed): Anesthesia, 4th ed. New York, Churchill Livingstone, 1994.
2. Deletic V: Evoked potentials. In Lake C (ed): Clinical Monitoring for Anesthesia and Critical Care. Philadelphia, W.B. Saunders, 1994, pp 288–314.
3. Goodrich JT: Electrophysiologic measurements: Intraoperative evoked potential monitoring. Anesthesiol Clin North Am 5:477–488, 1987.
4. Kalkman CJ: Monitoring the central nervous system. Anesthesiol Clin North Am 12:173–191, 1994.
5. McPherson R: Intraoperative neurologic monitoring. In Rogers M, Tinker J, Covino B, Longnecker D (eds): Principles and Practice of Anesthesiology. St. Louis, Mosby, 1992, pp 803–826.
6. Moller A: Evoked Potentials in Intraoperative Monitoring. Baltimore, Williams & Wilkins, 1988.
7. Schramm J, Kerthen M: Recent developments in neurosurgical spinal cord monitoring. Paraplegia 30:609–616, 1993.
8. Thiagarajah S: Anesthetic management of spinal surgery. Anesthesiol Clin North Am 5:587–600, 1987.

75. DELIBERATE HYPOTENSION

Jefferson P. Mostellar, M.D.

1. Define deliberate hypotension.

Deliberate hypotension is defined as the intentional reduction of systemic perfusion pressure.

2. Describe the indications for deliberate hypotension.

The major indication for using a deliberate hypotensive technique is to reduce intraoperative blood loss and to produce a relatively bloodless surgical site. This technique has been used in neurosurgical, orthopedic, vascular, and major craniofacial and other plastic procedures. Deliberate hypotension also may be used to help manage patients who refuse blood transfusions (e.g., for religious reasons).

3. What are the benefits of deliberate hypotension?

Deliberate hypotension decreases blood loss and thereby reduces the need for blood transfusion. In addition, reducing blood loss may enhance surgical visualization, lessening operating time. However, it is important to consider the risk-benefit ratio with each individual patient.

4. What are the contraindications to deliberate hypotension?

The contraindications to deliberate hypotension include inexperience or lack of understanding of the technique; inability to monitor the patient appropriately; any systemic disease that compromises organ function, oxygenation, or perfusion (e.g., diabetes mellitus, coronary or carotid artery disease, renal insufficiency, cirrhosis); polycythemia; and allergy to hypotensive agents. The use of deliberate hypotension in a patient with increased intracranial pressure (ICP) is controversial, because all hypotensive drugs and inhalational agents have been shown to increase ICP.

5. What are the possible complications of deliberate hypotension?

Hypoperfusion and ischemic injury, particularly to the brain and heart, are the most serious concerns. Blood pressure (BP) must be measured at the level of the brain, not heart, to accurately monitor cerebral perfusion pressure. Most complications, however, are due to lack of vigilance in monitoring. With a healthy patient and attention to detail, the benefits of deliberate hypotension outweigh the potential risks.

6. What is autoregulation? How is it affected by chronic hypertension?

Autoregulation is the maintenance of a constant blood flow over a wide range of pressures. Autoregulation maintains constant cerebral blood flow (CBF) over a range of cerebral perfusion pressures (CPP) from 50–150 mmHg. Chronic hypertension causes a shift to the right in the autoregulation curve.

7. How is the central nervous system affected by deliberate hypotension?

Cerebral perfusion pressure (CPP = mean arterial pressure – ICP) should be maintained above 50 mmHg in the normotensive patient and higher in the chronically hypertensive. Inhalational anesthetics and vasodilators alter the ratio of CBF to cerebral metabolic rate of oxygen consumption ($CMRO_2$). Vasodilators (e.g., sodium nitroprusside or nitroglycerin) dilate cerebral vessels directly with no effect on the $CMRO_2$. These drugs, as well as inhalational agents, attenuate the autoregulation of CBF in a dose-dependent fashion and decrease blood flow from baseline levels. If the decrease in CBF is greater than the decrease in $CMRO_2$, cerebral ischemia may occur. Spinal cord blood flow (SCBF) is also affected by deliberate hypotension. Because SCBF is regulated like CBF, factors that affect CBF have similar affects on SCBF.

8. How should ventilation be maintained when deliberate hypotension is planned?

Ventilation during deliberate hypotension should be aimed at maintaining normocarbia. Hypocapnia decreases CBF by 2%/mm of mercury decline in arterial partial pressure of carbon dioxide ($PaCO_2$). Therefore, it is important to keep the $PaCO_2$ at normal levels to ensure adequate CBF and to prevent cerebral ischemia.

9. How is the cardiovascular system affected?

Most vasodilators improve left ventricular function by reducing afterload, decreasing cardiac work and myocardial oxygen requirements. Coronary blood flow depends on diastolic filling pressure. Large reductions in diastolic filling pressures may lead to myocardial ischemia, especially in patients with coronary artery disease. Vasodilation causes a relative decrease in circulating blood volume by increasing the capacitance of blood vessels, potentially requiring volume infusions to maintain preload (and CVP). Increased capitance results in decreased venous return, which may cause baroreceptor reflex–mediated tachycardia. Drugs that cause tachycardia (atropine and pancuronium) should not be used. In addition hypercarbia causes catecholamine secretion, which increases BP and heart rate.

10. How is the pulmonary system affected?

Pulmonary blood flow is reduced by all vasodilating drugs due to redistribution of blood to the peripheral circulation. During controlled hypotension, both alveolar dead space and intrapulmonary shunting are increased. These changes are thought to be due to decreases in pulmonary artery pressures, increased blood flow through dependent areas of the lung, and inhibition of the hypoxic pulmonary vasoconstriction. Such changes, however, are usually not clinically significant, but pulse oximetry should be followed closely and arterial blood gases should be measured regularly to detect changes in oxygenation and ventilation.

11. How is the hepatic system affected?

The splanchnic circulation is poorly autoregulated in the hepatic arterial bed and probably nonexistent in the portal bed. Because clinical monitoring of this system is not commonplace, it would be best to use a hypotensive technique that maintains cardiac output. The use of deliberate hypotension in patients with cirrhosis is relatively contraindicated.

12. How is the renal system affected?

The renal circulation is well autoregulated. Glomerular filtration rate is maintained above an MAP of 75 mmHg. As long as normovolemia is maintained, modest oliguria is acceptable during deliberate hypotension. Many clinical studies have demonstrated return of normal urine volumes after return of normotension and no subsequent renal impairment. A balanced hypotensive technique may be best.

13. Describe the different techniques and agents used for deliberate hypotension.

1. **Inhalational technique.** All volatile anesthetics have been used as the sole agent in producing deliberate hypotension because of their ability to depress directly the myocardium and cardiac output and to promote vasodilation. Such effects are dose-dependent. This technique is not recommended, however, because of the inability to quickly reverse the cardiovascular depression that may accompany an inhalational overdose. The most common method of inducing deliberate hypotension uses a combination of inhalational agent and direct vasodilator.

2. **Vasodilator agents.** Because of their potency, vasodilators are best administered by continuous infusion, which allows easy titration through a dedicated intravenous line, avoiding inadvertent bolusing and a precipitous drop in BP. Direct, continuous arterial BP monitoring is imperative. The three commonly used vasodilators are sodium nitroprusside, nitroglycerin, and trimethaphan.

3. **β-adrenergic blockers.** These drugs decrease MAP by their negative inotropic properties. Labetalol and esmolol are the most commonly used β-adrenergic blockers. Labetalol combines both alpha$_1$ and beta blockade and may attenuate the compensatory tachycardia associated with hypotension. Because their hypotensive potency is considerably less than that of inhalational agents and vasodilators, they usually are used as a supplement to attain the desired level of hypotension. Among their advantages are lack of rebound hypertension and absence of toxic metabolites. It must be remembered that beta blockade removes the clinical signs of hypovolemia and light anesthesia.

14. Discuss the actions of sodium nitroprusside.

The most commonly used drug to induce deliberate hypotension, sodium nitroprusside (SNP), is a direct vascular smooth-muscle relaxant that causes arteriolar dilation, some venodilation, and a decrease in BP. This response is due to a nitrose (-NO) group on the molecule that diffuses into the vascular smooth muscle and increases cyclic guanosine monophosphate (cGMP), thus producing relaxation. It has a rapid onset of action (seconds), brief duration of action (minutes), and minimal side effects when used appropriately. SNP tends to maintain adequate blood flow to vital organs with MAP above 50 mmHg and provides a more homogeneous distribution of cerebral blood flow by its direct cerebral vasodilating properties. It has no direct effect on CMRO$_2$ but shifts the autoregulation curve to the left in a dose-dependent fashion. Depression of myocardial contractility is minimal, and cardiac output is usually improved with decreased afterload. Coronary blood flow is maintained, and myocardial oxygen demand is reduced. Tachycardia may result from the reduced BP. SNP also decreases right ventricular afterload by directly relaxing pulmonary vasculature. Hypoxic pulmonary vasoconstriction is attenuated, causing an increase in intrapulmonary shunting. Rebound systemic and pulmonary hypertension may occur with sudden discontinuation of SNP. Tachyphylaxis is common and may be a sign of toxicity. It is recommended to begin infusion of SNP at 0.2–0.5 μg/kg/min and to increase the dose slowly until the desired level of hypotension is achieved. The maximal infusion rate is 10 μg/kg/min. The contraindications to SNP include liver and renal failure, anemia, unstable cardiovascular system, and Leber's optic atrophy. High doses or prolonged administration may cause toxic side effects.

15. Discuss the actions of nitroglycerin.

Nitroglycerin (NTG) is a direct-acting, smooth-muscle relaxant that primarily affects venous capacitance vessels, causing a decrease in preload. It also has some effect on arterial smooth-muscle at higher doses, decreasing BP. NTG has a relatively rapid onset of action (minutes), has a brief duration of action (minutes), and lacks significant tachyphylaxis and toxicity. It produces a smooth reduction in BP with minimal risk of sudden hypotension. CBF is maintained in a homogeneous fashion by direct cerebral vasodilation, and $CMRO_2$ is unaffected. Coronary blood flow is increased by coronary artery vasodilation, which increases myocardial oxygen supply. Cardiac output and pulmonary artery pressure may be decreased secondary to an increase in the capacitance bed. Rebound hypertension due to abrupt discontinuation of NTG is usually not seen. Renal and hepatic blood flow is also well maintained. The usual starting infusion rate is 0.2–0.5 µg/kg/min, increasing slowly until the desired level of hypotension is reached.

16. Discuss the pharmacodynamics of trimethaphan.

Trimethaphan (TMP) is a ganglionic blocking drug with direct vasodilating properties. It decreases BP by blockade of sympathetic output, direct vasodilation, and histamine release. It has the advantages of rapid onset (minutes), brief duration (minutes), and easy titration. Because its effects are related to ganglionic blockade and sympathetic tone, the response is somewhat variable from patient to patient. CBF is reduced with a redistribution of flow away from cortical areas. Higher doses produce mydriasis, which compromises neurologic examination. Renal vascular resistance is increased with a reduction in renal blood flow. The disadvantages of TMP include impaired cerebral and spinal cord blood flow; decreases in coronary, hepatic, and renal blood flow; tachycardia; histamine release; inhibition of pseudocholinesterase enzymes; potentiation of nondepolarizing muscle relaxants; and tachyphylaxis. TMP is contraindicated in patients with asthma because of histamine release and risk of bronchospasm. Infusions are usually started at 25 µg/kg/min and titrated to effect.

17. What are the toxic side effects of agents used to induce hypotension?

Fortunately, the majority of such drugs are without toxic side effects. However, prolonged use of SNP may be associated with cyanide toxicity. Three signs should alert one to the possibility of cyanide toxicity from SNP infusion: (1) the need for doses > 10 µg/kg/min, (2) tachyphylaxis occurring within 60 minutes, or (3) resistance to SNP. If any of these occur, the infusion of SNP should be stopped. Cyanide toxicity should be suspected if unexplained metabolic acidosis occurs, if lactate levels increase, or if mixed venous oxygen content rises.

SNP is rapidly metabolized by interaction with sulfhydryl groups of red blood cells, with the resultant release of cyanide. The cyanide is converted to thiocyanate by the rhodanase enzyme system in the liver and then excreted by the kidneys. High doses of SNP may exceed the ability of the enzyme system to metabolize cyanide to thiocyanate, thereby allowing free cyanide to bind irreversibly to the cytochrome electron transport system, resulting in cytotoxic hypoxia. This binding causes a change from aerobic to anaerobic metabolism with metabolic acidosis and death.

18. How is cyanide toxicity treated?

Because cyanide binds irreversibly to the cytochrome enzymes, treatment is directed at introducing an alternative source of binding with greater affinity for cyanide. Administration of amyl nitrate produces methemoglobin, which has a higher affinity for cyanide than the cytochrome enzymes. Methemoglobin reacts with cyanide to form cyanmethemoglobin. Thiosulfate is then administered and reacts with cyanide to form thiocyanate, which is excreted by the kidneys. (In the setting of renal insufficiency, thiocyanate can accumulate and result in central nervous system excitation.) Therefore, the initial steps in the treatment of cyanide toxicity are to stop the infusion of SNP, to deliver 100% oxygen, and to administer amyl nitrite by inhalation for 30 seconds every 2 minutes. The next step is to give sodium nitrite in an intravenous dose of 10 mg/kg bolus, followed by an infusion of 5 mg/kg over 30 minutes. Immediately after this infusion, sodium thiosulfate, 150 mg/kg (not to exceed 12.5 g), is given.

19. What monitoring should be used? What laboratory studies should be followed?

Continuous invasive arterial pressure monitoring is indicated. Monitoring of central venous pressure (CVP) or pulmonary artery pressure (PAP) is also indicated if urine output does not accurately reflect volume status. Once anesthesia has been induced, baseline blood gases, oxygen saturation, hematocrit, blood glucose, and CVP or PAP should be measured before the planned level of hypotension is reached. These values should be repeated every 30–60 minutes or sooner if necessary. Once baseline CVP or PAP has been assessed, it should be maintained throughout the procedure. Normovolemia must be maintained at all times. A change of even 1–2 mmHg in CVP or PAP may represent a significant reduction in blood volume during induced hypotension. Normocarbia and hyperoxia should be maintained to ensure adequate cerebral perfusion pressure and to prevent hypoxia due to intrapulmonary shunting. As mentioned earlier, oliguria may occur. In this setting, central pressures should be monitored closely, maintaining normovolemia. If beta blockers are used as supplements, glucose levels need to be followed, because beta blockers inhibit glycogenolysis and hypoglycemia may develop. Temperature also must be monitored, because vasodilation results in substantial heat loss and hypothermia.

20. Can vision be affected by deliberate hypotension?

There are reports of patients having spinal surgery in the prone position developing vision deficits postoperatively, despite the usual manipulations to safeguard the eyes. Factors may be obesity and impaired return of blood to the central circulation secondary to the increased intra-abdominal pressure in the prone position.

BIBLIOGRAPHY

1. Bendo AA, Kass IS, Hartung J, Cottrell JE: Anesthesia for neurosurgery. In Barash PG, Cullen BF, Stoelting RK (eds): Clinical Anesthesia, 3rd ed. Philadelphia, Lippincott Williams & Wilkins, 1997.
2. Brown TCK, Fisk GF: Induced hypotension. In Brown TCK, Fisk GC (eds): Anaesthesia in Children. Oxford, Blackwell, 1992, pp 324–329.
3. Collins VJ: Controlled hypotension. In Collins VJ (ed): Principles of Anesthesiology. Philadelphia, Lea & Febiger, 1993, pp 1056–1095.
4. Cote CJ: Strategies to reduce blood transfusions: Controlled hypotension and hemodilution. In Cote CJ, Ryan JF, Todres ID, Goudsouzian NG (eds): A Practice of Anesthesia for Infants and Children. Philadelphia, W.B. Saunders, 1993, pp 201–210.
5. Lerman J: Special techniques: Acute normovolemic hemodilution, controlled hypotension, and hypothermia, ECMO. In Gregory GA (ed): Pediatric Anesthesia. New York, Churchill Livingstone, 1994, pp 319–347.
6. Roth S, Nunez R, Schreider BD: Unexplained visual loss after lumbar spinal fusion. J Neurosurg Anesthesiol 9:346–348, 1992.
7. Salem MR, Bikhazi GB: Hypotensive anesthesia. In Motoyama EK, Davis PJ, Cohn EL (eds): Anesthesia for Infants and Children. St. Louis, Mosby, 1990, pp 345–370.
8. Van Aiken H, Miller ED: Deliberate hypotension. In Miller RD (ed): Anesthesia, 4th ed. New York, Churchill Livingstone, 1994, pp 1481–1504.

76. ANESTHESIA FOR CRANIOTOMY

Roger A. Mattison, M.D.

1. Are there particular anesthetic problems associated with intracranial surgery?

Space-occupying intracranial lesions are associated with disturbed autoregulation in adjacent tissue, vascular malformations and aneurysms are accompanied by altered vasoreactivity (particularly if preceded by subarachnoid hemorrhage), and traumatic injuries require sometimes contradictory efforts to minimize brain swelling while maximizing systemic resuscitation.

In addition, there are specific neurophysiologic concerns: control of cerebral blood flow and volume, anticipation of the effects of surgery and anesthetic management on intracranial pressure dynamics, and maintenance of perfusion. Additionally, as for any operative procedure, the patient should be unconscious and remain unaware of intraoperative stimuli; adrenergic responses of the patient to intraoperative events should be attenuated; and the surgeon's approach to the operative site should be facilitated.

2. How is the anesthetic requirement different in the brain and related structures?

During anesthesia for craniotomy, the level of nociceptive stimulus varies greatly. Laryngoscopy and intubation regulate deep levels of anesthesia to block potentially harmful increases in heart rate, blood pressure, and brain metabolic activity, which may increase cerebral perfusion and brain swelling. Except for placement of pins in the skull for head positioning, considerable time may pass during positioning and operative preparation with no noxious stimulus. Then, incision of scalp, opening of the skull, and reflection of the dura provide increased surgical stimulus, only to be followed by dissection of the brain or pathologic tissue which is almost completely free of nociceptive nerve fibers. Occasionally, vascular structures of the brain may respond with adrenergic surge during surgery, particularly if a subarachnoid hemorrhage has occurred in the region of the procedure.

3. Should monitoring be different during a craniotomy?

The usual noninvasive monitors are used for every patient, including pulse oximetry, stethoscope, noninvasive blood pressure cuff, electrocardiogram, end-tidal and inspired gas monitors, and peripheral nerve stimulator. End-tidal anesthetic agent monitoring has some theoretical value, particularly in managing emergence. Continuous arterial pressure monitoring is often used to assess hemodynamic changes, which may develop acutely with cranial nerve root stimulation or slowly because of minimal intravascular volume repletion. Some forgo the radial artery catheter for very superficial craniotomies, such as mapping of the seizure focus directly with cortical electrodes; few anesthesiologists would use a central venous catheter unless there was a high risk of air entrainment in the venous system or a likelihood of using vasoactive infusions perioperatively. Occasionally, continuous electroencephalography is used, not so much as an intraoperative monitor but rather as a means for the surgeon to localize diseased tissue. Comparison of ipsilateral and contralateral evoked potentials has been reported during aneurysm surgery. Jugular bulb venous oxygen saturation and transcranial oximetry have been described as monitors of oxygen delivery and metabolic integrity of the brain globally but are not used regularly in intraoperative settings. Some patients, especially after trauma, have subdural, intraventricular, or cerebrospinal fluid pressure monitors in use intraoperatively.

4. Discuss the considerations for fluid administration during craniotomy.

Volume depletion from overnight fasting and volume redistribution from vasodilating anesthetic agents result in relative hypovolemia. Each patient should be evaluated individually to ensure adequate myocardial, central nervous system, and renal perfusion. Special attention must be directed toward stability of intracranial volume. Prior to opening of the dura, sudden increases in intravascular volume may cause deleterious increases in intracranial pressure, especially in situations involving intracranial masses or contusions or intraparenchymal, subdural, or epidural hematomas. Therefore, although fluids must be given to avoid hypovolemia and hypotension, exuberant bolus administration is to be avoided.

The content of the fluids used during a craniotomy is also important. An isosmolar intravenous fluid should be chosen. Unless hypoglycemia is documented, glucose-containing solutions should be avoided. In both clinical and experimental settings where glucose is used in the resuscitation fluids after head injury, outcome is worse. Saline is the appropriate fluid for use during craniotomy. Balanced salt solutions may be used if their osmolarity approximates or exceeds that of the serum. Ringer's lactate has a slight theoretical disadvantage because lactate is metabolized and the solution becomes hypotonic. Colloid solutions or 3% NaCl are equivalent solutions for acute volume replacement prior to packed red cell administration. Often, 25% albumin is used for pressure support when blood replacement is not needed. Hetastarch solutions are generally not used during craniotomies because of concerns that they are associated with impaired coagulation in vitro.

5. When are measures for brain protection required?

"Brain protection" refers to the maneuvers by the anesthesiologist to maintain a balance between brain metabolism and substrate delivery and to prevent secondary injury to regions of the brain after an episode of ischemia. The need for brain protection should be anticipated after head trauma and brain contusion as well as during procedures for the correction of intracranial aneurysms or arteriovenous malformations.

6. How can the brain be protected?

Historically, long-acting barbiturates have been used for metabolic suppression for refractory intracranial hypertension. The goal is suppression of brain activity with resultant reduction of metabolism which is reflected by a flat electroencephalogram (EEG).

In the intraoperative setting, metabolic suppression is needed when a major artery is temporarily clipped to facilitate access to an aneurysm. The EEG correlate is "burst suppression" wherein the typical anesthetic slow-wave activity slows to random bursts of electrical activity. Burst suppression can be achieved by rapid infusion of thiopental, propofol, or etomidate. Hypothermia has long been known to reduce brain metabolism (and to slow the EEG). Mild to moderate hypothermia (32.5–34°C) has been found to be useful for intraoperative brain protection. The global metabolic suppression secondary to hypothermia decreases not only neuronal electrical activity but also "housekeeping" functions, including cellular homeostasis and membrane integrity. Production of excitatory neurotransmitters during reperfusion of ischemic tissue also may be suppressed by modest hypothermia.

Much attention has been directed to suppression of the neuroexcitation that occurs with reperfusion after regional or global brain ischemia. Calcium influx into glial cells and vascular smooth muscle may be suppressed by calcium channel blockade, free radicals that are generated may be "scavenged" by mannitol, and increased intracellular hyperglycemia may be prevented by avoiding systemic hyperglycemia. Cerebral protection remains a fruitful area of investigation.

7. How is the choice of anesthetic agent made?

Choice of anesthesia for craniotomy is based on an understanding of the pharmacologic properties of hypnotic agents, inhalation agents, opioids, and muscle relaxants and on a balancing of beneficial and potentially adverse effects. Whichever agents are chosen, the goals are postoperative hemodynamic stability associated with an awake, neurologically assessable patient.

Hypnotic agents: Thiopental effectively blocks conscious awareness and reduces the functional activity of the brain and brain metabolism. Propofol has similar effects and is eliminated more rapidly. Etomidate and midazolam are only slightly less effective in metabolic suppression. An agent is selected on the basis of associated hemodynamic effects, anticipated difficulty of regaining consciousness, and cost.

Inhalation agents: The differences between halothane, isoflurane, desflurane, and sevoflurane concerning metabolic suppression and cerebral blood flow are slight. All cause suppression of brain activity while preserving or enhancing cerebral blood flow. Cost and speed of elimination are concerns in selection.

Opioids: All opioids have negligible effects on cerebral blood flow and small effects on cerebral metabolism. Chiefly, they block adrenergic stimulation, which increases brain activity. They are useful as part of a balanced anesthesia. More fat-soluble opioids, such as morphine and hydromorphone, may be eliminated so slowly that they cause respiratory depression after the procedure is completed. Respiratory depression that causes hypercarbia results in undesirable increases in cerebral blood flow and potentially increased intracranial pressure (ICP), which is to be avoided after a craniotomy. Newer short-acting synthetic opioids may also cause residual respiratory depression after prolonged infusion.

Muscle relaxants: Depolarizing muscle relaxants are generally not used in the setting of intracranial pathology. Although theoretical hemodynamic differences exist among the nondepolarizing muscular relaxants, these are of little importance during a craniotomy. The main criteria for choosing a nondepolarizing muscular relaxant is the duration of neuromuscular blockade desired, route of elimination, and cost.

8. What are the concerns for patient positioning during a craniotomy?

Because craniotomies tend to be lengthy procedures, protecting vulnerable peripheral nerves and pressure-prone areas from injury is essential. Provisions must be made to prevent prep solutions from entering the eyes. Generally, the head is fixed in position with pins clamped against the outer table of the skull. Because the head is held in a fixed position, any patient movement will stress the cervical spine. Muscle paralysis must be maintained all the time the head is secured in the holding device.

In every craniotomy, the risk of air entrainment into the venous system must be estimated. Whenever the head is positioned 10 cm above the mid-thorax (> 20° elevation), a potential negative pressure exists between the venous sinuses of the head and the central venous system. Air entrained in the central venous system may collect in the right side of the heart and interfere with preload and pulmonary flow. Air can potentially cross the intra-atrial septum and, if a patent foramen ovale is present (20% of patients), become a paradoxical air embolus to the systemic circulation. This risk is very significant in sitting-position craniotomies. End-tidal CO_2, end-tidal nitrogen, and precordial Doppler are sensitive indicators of venous air. In high-risk situations, a multiorificed right atrial catheter should be placed for removal of air bubbles.

9. Why do some patients awaken slowly after a craniotomy?

Continuous infusion of opioid as part of balanced anesthesia leads to prolonged redistribution and persistent sedation. Residual volatile anesthetic or barbiturate may contribute to slow awakening. However, all these residual anesthetic effects are overcome simply by waiting and providing respiratory support. Use of agents of short duration may prove beneficial. Slow awakening that persists for more than 2 hours is virtually never an effect of residual anesthesia. The patient who is unresponsive for several hours after a craniotomy should be evaluated for increased ICP, embolic phenomenon, brain stem ischemia, or intracranial masses. Evaluation should be a joint effort of the neurosurgeon and anesthesiologist.

10. What anesthesia problems are unique to surgery on the intracranial blood vessels?

1. **Subarachnoid hemorrhage (SAH):** Aneurysms of the intracerebral arteries may be diagnosed after SAH. Neurologic impairment after SAH ranges from headache and stiff neck (stage I) to deep coma (stage V). Initial resuscitation includes observation, tight control of blood pressure, and support of intravascular volume (hypervolemic, hyperosmolar, normotensive). The optimal time for surgical clipping of the aneurysm is within the first few days of hemorrhage. After 5–7 days following SAH, the risk of rebleeding remains high, but the risk of vasospasm of the vessel feeding the aneurysm markedly increases due to irritation from the breakdown of old blood. Invasive monitoring of arterial pressure and central venous pressure is required to facilitate maintenance of hemodynamic stability and guide volume replacement. The minimal approach to brain protection is to maintain mild hypothermia. Metabolic suppression by electroencephalographic burst suppression may be done at the time of temporary vessel clipping but may result in poor outcome when accompanied by hypotension.

2. **Rebleeding:** Approximately 30% of intracranial aneurysms that have bled will rebleed at some time if untreated. In the initial few days, the hydrodynamic forces on the aneurysm wall are caused by the systolic blood pressure resisted by the tension of the aneurysmal wall. Larger aneurysms have less wall tension for any part of the aneurysmal surface. Rebleeding of the aneurysm prior to the opening of the dura is catastrophic, requiring the surgeon to approach the

bleeding vessel blindly, perhaps temporarily clipping major feeding vessels. Although it might seem reasonable to induce hypotension during the opening of the dura, hypotension, should a rebleed occur, adversely affects regional perfusion and may promote vasospasm.

3. **Vasospasm:** Vasospasm can occur after any SAH, regardless of clinical stage. The end result of persistent vasospasm is ischemic stroke in the region of distribution of the aneurysmal artery, resulting in permanent neurologic damage after SAH. Diagnosis is by angiography, and many times an angiogram is requested on the first postoperative day to guide therapy. Maintaining hypervolemic normotensive hemodynamic status is the first line of prevention of vasospasm and should be maintained intraoperatively. Physiologically, vasospasm is caused by mediator release in the vascular smooth muscle in response to hemoglobin in the interstitium, ending in calcium influx into the cellular walls of the artery and causing persistent vasoconstriction. Calcium channel blockade has been advocated but has shown mixed results. Thromboplastin activators have been used experimentally by irrigation in the region of the aneurysmal bleed with some success. The main line of prevention is intraoperative irrigation of the hematoma early in SAH course and maintenance of favorable hemodynamics postoperatively.

11. Are there special anesthetic problems associated with brain tumors?

Mass lesions of the brain cause problems for the anesthesiologist because of their size and location. Frontal tumors grow to large size without producing neurologic symptoms or increased ICP. Supratentorial tumors of the motor and sensory cortical regions present with seizures, localizing neurologic signs, and increased ICP. Posterior fossa masses in adults cause disturbances in gait, balance, proprioception, or cranial nerve impingement. There is a "penumbra" around all intracranial tumors where the adjacent brain loses autoregulatory function. Thus, on induction, regional blood flow in these areas may increase in response to aggressive fluid replacement or increased systolic blood pressure. After the resection is completed, this penumbra may respond to reperfusion with swelling. The end result may be either preincisional or postoperative increases in ICP. Infratentorial posterior fossa tumors cause particular problems for the anesthesiologist. Tumors are generally small but may surround complex vascular channels of the basilar, posterior communicating, and cerebellar arteries. Tumors may arise from the glia surrounding the cranial nerve roots or impinge on them. Simple dissection of a brain stem tumor can cause disturbance of heart rate and rhythm or blood pressure when nerve roots are retracted. The surgical approach to the posterior fossa involves awkward positioning, from sitting to lateral to prone to "park bench." At the least, any of these positions requires careful attention to the position of the endotracheal tube to avoid migration to an endobronchial position or out of the glottis. Venous air embolism must be anticipated. The plan for anesthesia must also allow for intraoperative monitoring of auditory-evoked potentials, somatosensory-evoked potentials, or motor-evoked potentials if indicated. Any of these evoked potentials can be suppressed by hypnotic and inhaled anesthetic agents.

12. Are there other anesthetic concerns during craniotomies?

Transsphenoidal surgery, although not strictly a craniotomy, involves manipulation of ventilation to raise the $PaCO_2$ and ICP, which forces the pituitary into a more easily visualized position.

Rapidly deteriorating neurologic status after closed head injury often leads to emergency intubation, neuroradiologic studies, and emergent craniotomy. The increase in ICP that causes the clinical deterioration sometimes progresses to involve brain stem compression. The physiologic response to increased ICP is systemic hypertension and, in the late stages, bradycardia known as the Cushing reflex. This reflex should be anticipated and treated by measures to reduce ICP rather than pharmacologic treatment of the hypertension per se. Typically, when the cranium is opened and brain stem pressure is reduced, the blood pressure decreases, but if aggressive treatment of elevated blood pressure has been undertaken, the drop in blood pressure may have disastrous consequences.

Craniotomies in pediatric patients are, in principle, the same as in adults but fortunately more rare. The intracranial pathology that is most common in the pediatric group is the posterior fossa tumor, particularly cerebellar astrocytoma. Positioning, cranial nerve root stimulation, and venous air embolus are concerns during posterior fossa resections in children.

BIBLIOGRAPHY

1. Drummond JC: Brain protection during anesthesia. Anesthesiology 79:877–880, 1993.
2. From RP, Warner DS, Todd MM, Sokoll MD: Anesthesia for craniotomy: A double-blind comparison of alfentanil, fentanyl and sufentanil. Anesth Analg 73:896–904, 1990.
3. Hartung J, Cottrell JE: Mild hypothermia and cerebral metabolism. J Neurosurg Anesth 6:1–3, 1994.
4. Illievich UM, Petricek W, Schramm W, et al: Electroencephalographic burst suppression by propofol in humans: Hemodynamic consequences. Anesth Analg 77:155–160, 1993.
5. Lam AM, Mayberg TS: Anesthetic management of head trauma. In Lake CL, Rice LJ, Sperry RJ (eds): Advances in Anesthesia, vol. 12, St. Louis, Mosby, 1995, pp 333–339.
6. Marx W, Shaw N, Long C, et al: Sufentanil, alfentanil and fentanyl: Impact on cerebrospinal fluid pressure in patients with brain tumors. J Neurosurg Anesth 1:3–7, 1989.
7. Prough DS, Johnson JC, Stump DA: Effects of hypertonic saline versus lactated Ringer's on cerebral oxygen transport during resuscitation from hemorrhagic shock. J Neurosurg 64:627–632, 1986.
8. Smith M-L: Cerebral ischemia and brain protection. Curr Opin Anaesth 5:626–631, 1992.
9. Todd MM, Warner DS, Sokoll MD, et al: A prospective, comparative trial of three anesthetics for elective supratentorial craniotomy. Anesthesiology 78:1005–1020, 1993.
10. Young ML: Posterior fossa: Anesthetic considerations. In Cottrell JE, Smith DS (eds): Anesthesia and Neurosurgery. St. Louis, Mosby, 1994, pp 346–356.

77. LAPAROSCOPY

Donald G. Crino, M.D.

1. What are the origins of modern laparoscopic surgery?

Endoscopic procedures were first introduced in the early 20th century. In 1901, George Kelling used a cystoscope to examine the abdomen of a dog. In 1910, Jacobeus performed the first clinical laparoscopic exam. It wasn't until the 1960s, with improvements in equipment safety and technology, that a number of gynecologists pioneered the way for the therapeutic application of laparoscopy. In 1987, with advances in optics, video imaging, and light transmission, Phillipe Mouret described the first successful laparoscopic cholecystectomy. One year later, Reddick and Olsen introduced the technique into the United States. Since that time a revolution in laparoscopic procedures has occurred. It is now estimated that by the year 2000, 50–60% of all intra-abdominal procedures will be performed laparoscopically.

2. List some currently practiced laparoscopic or thoracoscopic procedures.

The following is a list of the more common procedures being performed today.

- **Gynecologic procedures:** Diagnostic laparoscopy for chronic pelvic pain, laparoscopic-assisted vaginal hysterectomy, tubal ligation, and pelvic lymph node dissection.
- **Gastrointestinal procedures:** Appendectomy, peritoneal adhesolysis, inguinal hernia repair, cholecystectomy, fundoplication for hiatal hernia, tumor staging, evaluation of abdominal trauma, vagotomy, diaphragmatic hernia repair, colectomy and other bowel resections, nephrectomy, splenectomy, adrenalectomy, common bile duct exploration, and feeding tube placement.
- **Thoracoscopic procedures:** Drainage of pleural effusions and pleurodesis, evaluation of blunt or pulmonary trauma, resection of solitary pulmonary nodules, tumor staging, repair of esophageal perforations, and pleural biopsy.
- **Video-assisted thoracic surgery:** Lobectomy, pneumonectomy, wedge resection, implantation of implantable cardioverter, excision of mediastinal masses, transthoracic sympathectomy,

splanchnicectomy, pericardiocentesis, pericardiectomy, esophagectomy, and thoracic spine surgeries.

3. **What are the contraindications for laparoscopic procedures?**
   Relative or absolute contraindications for laparoscopy include:
   • Increased intracranial pressure
   • Patients with ventriculoperitoneal or peritoneojugular shunts
   • Hypovolemia
   • Congestive heart failure or severe cardiopulmonary disease
   • Previous abdominal surgery with significant adhesions
   • Morbid obesity
   • Pregnancy
   • Coagulopathy

4. **What are the benefits of laparoscopic procedures?**
   The benefits of any laparoscopic procedure must be viewed in comparison to its open counterpart. Many of the reported benefits have been based on clinical study outcomes; however, a number are theoretical in nature and have not yet been shown to actually exist. Benefits may be conferred either intra- or postoperatively.

   Intraoperative benefits include a reduction in acute phase reactants (C-reactive protein and interleukin-6), though this has not been universally observed. Compared to its open counterparts, laparoscopy produces similar plasma concentrations of cortisol and catecholamines. Another benefit is the avoidance of prolonged exposure and manipulation of abdominal contents and reduction in large abdominal incisions, which would have a significant effect on postoperative outcome.

   One of the most noticeable postoperative benefits is improved pulmonary function, thought to be secondary to preserved diaphragmatic function, earlier ambulation, and smaller abdominal incisions. Postoperative ileus is also decreased. Although postoperative pain is not always reported as less, the overall analgesic requirement is reduced. Finally, these patients typically have a shorter hospitalization and a quicker resumption of normal daily activities.

5. **Why has carbon dioxide (CO_2) become the insufflation gas of choice during laparoscopy?**
   The choice of an insufflating gas for the creation of a pneumoperitoneum is influenced by the gas's blood solubility, tissue permeability, combustibility, expense, and its potential to cause side effects. An ideal gas would also be physiologically inert, colorless, and capable of pulmonary excretion. Although a number of gases have been used, CO_2 has become the gas of choice. Other gases that have been considered include air, nitrous oxide, helium, and oxygen.

   CO_2 is colorless, odorless, inexpensive, and does not support combustion. Its blood solubility enhances tissue diffusion, thus decreasing the risk of gas emboli. CO_2 does possess a number of disadvantages, however, including hypercarbia, respiratory acidosis, and sudden death secondary to cardiac dysrhythmias. It is also associated with more postoperative neck and shoulder pain due to diaphragmatic irritation.

   Compared to CO_2, the other gases have significant drawbacks. Nitrous oxide causes less peritoneal irritation and cardiac dysrhythmias than CO_2; however, it supports combustion and may lead to intra-abdominal explosions when hydrogen or methane are present. It also is associated with a greater decline in blood pressure and cardiac index. Air supports combustion and has a higher risk of gas emboli. The lethal embolic dose of CO_2 is 5 times that of air and is not associated with the bronchoconstriction and pulmonary compliance changes seen with air. Helium, which is inert and not absorbed from the abdomen, has the greatest risk of gas emboli. Finally, oxygen's main drawback is its high combustibility.

6. **How does CO_2 insufflation affect $PaCO_2$?**
   The change in $PaCO_2$ is dependent on the duration of the pneumoperitoneum, the intra-abdominal pressure, the patient's age and underlying medical conditions, patient positioning, and

the mode of ventilation. The maximum rate of CO_2 diffusion has been calculated at approximately 14 ml/minute, but this would account for only 10% of the observed increase in $PaCO_2$, so ventilatory impairment secondary to ventilation-perfusion mismatch must also be factorial. In fact, increases in intra-abdominal pressures result in diaphragmatic dysfunction and increased alveolar dead space.

The mode of ventilation and type of anesthetic chosen can also significantly affect $PaCO_2$ levels. When laparoscopy is performed under local anesthesia with spontaneous ventilation, $PaCO_2$ remains unchanged because of the patient's increased respiratory efforts. During general anesthesia with spontaneous ventilation, $PaCO_2$ increases despite hyperventilation, due in part to the respiratory depressant effects of the anesthetic. Finally, during laparoscopy performed under general anesthesia with controlled ventilation, $PaCO_2$ will increase if minute ventilation is maintained at preinsufflation levels.

Usually observed is an initial rise in $PaCO_2$ approximately 5–10 minutes after CO_2 insufflation, leveling off after 20–25 minutes. The final $PaCO_2$ levels tend to be significantly higher in patients with cardiopulmonary disease than in healthy patients undergoing similar procedures. There also appears to be a direct correlation between increases in intra-abdominal pressures and $PaCO_2$ levels obtained. During pelviscopy, which has been associated with the highest intra-abdominal pressures, $PaCO_2$ tends to increase beyond the plateau stage.

7. How does patient positioning affect hemodynamics and pulmonary function during laparoscopy?

During laparoscopic surgery, the patient is positioned to utilize gravitational displacement of the abdominal contents away from the surgical site. Depending on the surgery, the Trendelenburg, reverse Trendelenburg, or lithotomy positioning is regularly used. When possible, head up or head down tilting should not exceed 15° and should be instituted gradually, in order to prevent significant hemodynamic or respiratory impact.

The cardiovascular changes associated with the Trendelenburg position are influenced by the degree of head down tilt, intravascular status, ventilation techniques, anesthetic drugs administered, and patient's associated cardiovascular disease. In euvolemic patients, increases in central venous pressure (CVP) and cardiac output are noted. Patients with intact baroreceptor reflexes will typically experience vasodilatation and bradycardia. In patients with cardiac disease, especially depressed left ventricular function, the hemodynamic changes can be significantly greater and could lead to further myocardial dysfunction. The Trendelenburg position does decrease the transmural pressure in the pelvic organs, possibly decreasing blood loss but increasing the risk of gas emboli. The reverse Trendelenburg is associated with decreased preload. This in turn causes decreased cardiac output and mean arterial pressure (MAP), worsening the hemodynamic changes associated with CO_2 insufflation. There is also an increase in blood pooling in the lower extremities, possibly increasing the risk of venous thrombosis and pulmonary emboli.

As with the cardiovascular changes associated with the Trendelenburg position, the pulmonary changes are dependent on the patient's age, pulmonary function, weight, extent of tilt, ventilation technique, and anesthetic agents used. The Trendelenburg position causes impaired diaphragmatic function secondary to the cephalad displacement of abdominal viscera. This results in a decreased functional residual capacity, total lung capacity, and pulmonary compliance with the development of atelectasis. These changes are greater in the obese, elderly, and debilitated patients. In healthy patients, the changes are of minimal consequence. Also of concern is the potential for mainstem intubation as the lungs and carina are displaced cephalad by the diaphragm. The reverse Trendelenburg position is not associated with any deleterious pulmonary consequences and may improve pulmonary function.

8. What is considered a safe increase in intra-abdominal pressure?

The associated increase in intra-abdominal pressure secondary to CO_2 insufflation may have deleterious effects on preload, afterload, and myocardial performance. The hemodynamic impact is proportional to the intra-abdominal pressures obtained and patient characteristics. Healthy gynecologic patients undergoing short procedures have only minor hemodynamic changes as long as intra-abdominal pressures are maintained below 18 mmHg.

Animal and human studies have found a biphasic response to increasing intra-abdominal pressures. At intra-abdominal pressures less than 10 mmHg, vascular return to the heart appears to increase secondary to decreased sequestration of blood in the splanchnic vasculature, resulting in increased cardiac output and MAP. The response appears to be absent in hypovolemic patients. At intra-abdominal pressures of up to 16 mmHg, no significant changes in systemic vascular resistance (SVR) and cardiac index (CI) are seen. As the intra-abdominal pressure is increased to greater than 20 mmHg, preload and cardiac output decrease, and SVR increases. Renal blood flow, glomerular filtration rate, and urine output also decline. At intra-abdominal pressures of greater than 30 mmHg, CVP falls significantly, and the CI decreases up to 50% of preinsufflation values. At intra-abdominal pressures greater than 40 mmHg, marked decreases in CVP and cardiac output are noted and are associated with tachycardia and hypotension. Lactic acidosis is also noted secondary to the marked decrease in cardiac output and impairment of hepatic blood lactate clearance. Based on animal and human studies, the current recommendation for intra-abdominal pressure during laparoscopy is less than 15 mmHg.

9. Summarize the hemodynamic effects of laparoscopy.

The changes in CI are biphasic during abdominal laparoscopy. After anesthetic induction and patient positioning, CI can decrease up to 35–40% of preduction values. After CO_2 insufflation, reductions in CI up to 50% of preinduction values can occur. Five to ten minutes after the insufflation, the CI begins to increase, approaching preinsufflation values.

Pulmonary artery occlusion pressure (PAOP) and CVP also decline during anesthetic induction and patient positioning but begin to increase after CO_2 insufflation. However, this effect may be due to rise of intrathoracic pressure secondary to increased intra-abdominal pressure, rather than an increase in intrathoracic blood volume. SVR also significantly increases during the initial stages of insufflation. Though these changes partially resolve approximately 10–15 minutes after insufflation, the changes in cardiac filling pressures and SVR increase left ventricular wall stress. In healthy patients, left ventricular function appears to be preserved; however, in patients with underlying cardiovascular disease, the changes could be deleterious. In a study evaluating patients with ASA 3–4 classification who were exposed to up to 15 mmHg, the decrease in cardiac output and increase in SVR significantly decreased mixed venous oxygenation and oxygen delivery in 50% of the subjects.

Hemodynamic Changes During Laparoscopy

Cardiac output/cardiac index	Decreased
Mean arterial pressure	Increased
Systemic vascular resistance	Increased
Central venous pressure	Decreased initially then increased
PAOP	Decreased initially then decreased
Left ventricular wall stress	Increased
Heart rate	No change

10. What are the pulmonary changes associated with laparoscopy?

Upon anesthetic induction and patient positioning, cephalad displacement of the diaphragm and respiratory muscle relaxation result in reductions in functional residual capacity (FRC) and compliance; CO_2 insufflation exacerbates these deleterious changes. When the FRC is reduced relative to the patient's closing capacity, hypoxemia may result from atelectasis and intrapulmonary shunting. Hypoxemia is uncommon in healthy patients but becomes a concern in obese patients or those with underlying cardiopulmonary disease. There are reductions in both pulmonary and chest wall compliance, and resistance may increase as well.

Pulmonary Changes Associated with Laparoscopy

Peak inspiratory pressure	Increased
Intra-thoracic pressure	Increased
Vital capacity	Decreased
Functional residual capacity	Decreased
Respiratory compliance	Decreased
Respiratory resistance	Increased
$PaCO_2$	Increased
pH	Decreased
PaO_2	No significant change (may have reductions in patients with cardiopulmonary disease)

11. What are the neurohumoral responses associated with laparoscopy?

Plasma concentrations of dopamine, vasopressin, epinephrine, norepinephrine, renin, angiotensin, and cortisol all significantly increase. The increases correspond to the onset of abdominal insufflation. Of interest, serum levels of vasopressin and norepinephrine parallel the changes noted in CI, MAP, and SVR. Hypercarbia, the mechanical effects of the pneumoperitoneum, and stimulation of the autonomic nervous system have all been implicated as potential causes of these observed changes.

12. Should nitrous oxide (N_2O) be used as an anesthetic during laparoscopy?

Studies have shown during laparoscopic procedures there are no clinically significant differences in bowel distension and postoperative nausea and vomiting when N_2O-oxygen was compared to air-oxygen. Currently, there is no conclusive evidence suggesting N_2O cannot be used during laparoscopy.

13. What anesthetic techniques can be used for laparoscopy?

Local anesthesia with IV sedation, regional techniques, and general anesthesia have all been used with good results. The unexpected conversion from a laparoscopic to any open procedure must be considered when choosing anesthetic technique.

The advantages of local anesthesia with IV sedation include reduced anesthetic time, quicker recovery time, decreased postoperative nausea and vomiting, earlier recognition of complications, and fewer hemodynamic changes. The success of this technique is dependent on patient motivation, precise surgical technique, and short procedure time. Occasionally, extremes in administration of sedatives and analgesics during manipulation of pelvic organs may result in hypoventilation. This technique should be avoided in any procedure of long duration that requires multiple trocar sites, steep Trendelenburg or reverse Trendelenburg, and a large increase in intra-abdominal pressure.

Regional techniques, such as epidural anesthesia, share similar benefits and disadvantages with local anesthesia with IV sedation. In addition, there may be a decreased need for sedation and analgesia and improved muscle relaxation. However, the high level of sympathetic denervation in concert with abdominal insufflation and positioning extremes could be associated with adverse ventilatory and circulatory changes.

Out of concern for patient discomfort and the ventilation issues associated with CO_2 insufflation and positioning extremes, the most frequently used anesthetic technique is balanced general anesthesia with endotracheal intubation and controlled ventilation. The advantages of general anesthesia include optimal muscle relaxation, complete analgesia, ability to control ventilation, protection from gastric aspiration, and a quiet surgical field. The laryngeal mask airway (LMA) has been substituted for endotracheal intubation but does not protect against pulmonary aspiration of gastric contents. Controlled ventilation is also difficult when a LMA is used. Urinary bladder and gastric decompression should be performed to decrease the risk of visceral puncture and improve the surgical field.

14. What complications are associated with laparoscopic procedures?

Laparoscopic surgery is considered a safe alternative to open procedures. Most of the larger studies on mortality were conducted in the early 1970s during gynecologic procedures. The rate of mortality has decreased from 1–2/1000 to 1/100,000. Most deaths resulted from cardiac complications (25%). Currently, mortality associated with laparoscopy is 0–0.13%.

The rate of major intraoperative events is usually below 1–2% with vascular injury accounting for about a third of these. Complications are most likely to occur during placement of the trocar through the abdominal wall and during CO_2 insufflation. Although major vessels can be injured, the more common vessels injured include the superficial and inferior epigastric vessels and the superficial and deep circumflex iliac vessels. Gastrointestinal perforations, hepatic and splenic tears, avulsions of adhesions, omental disruptions, bile duct injury, and herniation at the torcar site have also been reported. Extraperitoneal insufflation of CO_2 is also common, with an incidence of 0.4–2.0%. This complication can lead to subcutaneous emphysema, pneumomediastinum, unilateral and bilateral pneumothorax, pneumopericardium, pneumoscrotum, and ocular emphysema. Gas embolization is a rare but catastrophic event, likely caused by the inadvertent injection of insufflating gases into a vessel or abdominal organ. This complication usually occurs during the induction of the pneumoperitoneum. Cardiac dysrhythmias such as atrioventricular dissociation, nodal rhythms, sinus bradycardia, tachycardia, and asystole have also been reported. These dysrhythmias are probably vagally mediated or secondary to the hypercarbia typically seen.

Postoperative complications are usually benign compared to intraoperative misadventures but can lead to delayed hospital discharge and patient discomfort. The most frequent complications reported include pain, headache, sore throat, and postoperative nausea and vomiting. The postoperative pain is described as vague abdominal, neck, or shoulder discomfort. Pain at the trocar insertion site is usually very minimal. Most troublesome, 40–70% of patients recovering from laparoscopy suffer from nausea or vomiting, with 50% requiring antiemetic therapy; 7% experience delayed hospital discharge.

BIBLIOGRAPHY

1. Bernard HR, Hartman TW: Complications after laparoscopic cholecystectomy. Am J Surg 165:533–535, 1993.
2. Chui PT, Gin T, Oh TE: Anaesthesia for laparoscopic general surgery. Anaesth Intens Care 21:163–174, 1993.
3. Cunningham AJ, Brull SJ: Laparoscopic cholecystectomy: Anesthetic implications. Anesth Analg 76:1120–1133, 1993.
4. Deziel DJ, Millikan KW, Economou SG, et al: Complications of laparoscopic cholecystectomy: A national survey of 4,292 hospitals and an analysis of 77,604 cases. Am J Surg 165:9–14, 1993.
5. Goodale RL, Beebe DS, McNevin MP, et al: Hemodynamic, respiratory, and metabolic effects of laparoscopic cholecystectomy. Am J Surg 166:533–537, 1993.
6. Hasel R, Arora SK, Hickey DR: Intraoperative complications of laparoscopic cholecystectomy. Can J Anaesth 40:459–464, 1993.
7. Ishizaki Y, Bandai Y, Shimomura K, et al: Safe intraabdominal pressure of carbon dioxide pneumoperitoneum during laparoscopic surgery. Surgery 114:549–554, 1993.
8. Joris JL, Noirot DP, Legrand MJ, et al: Hemdynamic changes during laparoscopic cholecystectomy. Anesth Analg 76:1067–1071, 1993.
9. Kendall AP, Bhatt S, Oh TE: Pulmonary consequences of carbon dioxide insufflation for laparoscopic cholecystectomy. Anaesthesia 50:286–289, 1995.
10. Lee VS, Chari RS, Cucchiaro G, Meyers WC: Complications of laparoscopic cholecystectomy. Am J Surg 165:527–532, 1993.
11. Pelosi P, Foti G, Cereda M, et al: Effects of carbon dioxide insufflation for laparoscopic cholecystectomy on the respiratory system. Anaesthesia 51:744–749, 1996.

12. Puri GD, Singh H: Ventilatory effects of laparoscopy under general anaesthesia. Br J Anaesth 68:211–213, 1992.
13. Sharma KC, Brandstetter RD, Brensilver JM, Jung LD: Cardiopulmonary physiology and pathophysiology as a consequence of laparoscopic surgery. Chest 110:810–815, 1996.
14. Soper NJ, Brunt LM, Kerbl K: Laparoscopic general surgery. N Engl J Med 330:409–419, 1994.
15. Taylor E, Feinstein R, White PF, Soper N: Anesthesia for laparoscopic cholecystectomy: Is nitrous oxide contraindicated? Anesthesiology 76:541–543, 1992.
16. Wahba RW, Beique F, Kleiman SJ: Cardiopulmonary function and laparoscopic cholecystectomy. Can J Anaesth 42:51–63, 1995.
17. Wittgen CM, Andrus CH, Fitzgerald SD, et al: Analysis of the hemodynamic and ventilatory effects of laparoscopic cholecystectomy. Arch Surg 126:997–1001, 1991.

78. TRANSURETHRAL RESECTION OF THE PROSTATE

Lyle E. Kirson, D.D.S.

1. What is transurethral resection of the prostate?

Transurethral resection of the prostate (TURP) involves the resection of benign hypertrophic prostatic tissue by means of a movable electrocautery–cutting wire loop located at the end of a resectoscope. The resectoscope is passed through a sheath that has been positioned within the patient's urethra. As the surgical field is visualized through the resectoscope, the cutting wire loop is moved back and forth, carving away a small piece of prostatic tissue each time the loop is withdrawn toward the surgeon. Simultaneously, an irrigating solution flows into the surgical site via a channel in the resectoscope to distend the bladder and to bathe the surgical site, washing away blood and tissue debris removed by the wire loop. Thus a clear operative field is maintained for the surgeon.

2. Describe the anatomy of the prostate gland.

The prostate gland underlies the apex of the male bladder and surrounds the prostatic portion of the urethra. The prostate is formed by enlargement of urethral glands. A fibrous sheath surrounds the prostate, and the body of the gland consists of a fibromuscular stroma that envelops the glandular tissue. Venous drainage is via the thin-walled veins, or sinuses, of the prostatic plexus.

Although developmentally divisible into two lobes, the prostate gland is anatomically divisible into five lobes. The median and lateral two lobes of the prostate gland most frequently undergo benign prostatic hypertrophy. The nerve supply to the prostate derives from the prostatic plexus, which originates from the inferior hypogastric (pelvic) plexus. Afferent pain fibers of the prostate, urethra, and mucosa of the bladder originate primarily from sacral nerves 2, 3, and 4 (S2, S3, and S4). Pain impulses from an overstretched bladder travel with sympathetic fibers that have their origin in the twelfth thoracic and first and second lumbar nerves (T12, L1, and L2). Proprioceptive impulses from the muscular wall of the bladder, which are activated by stretching of the muscular wall as the bladder fills, are carried by the parasympathetic fibers of S2, S3, and S4.

3. What pathologic process is treated by TURP?

Benign prostatic hypertrophy is the most common tumor of the prostate and affects a high proportion of elderly men. The hyperplasia involves growth of both smooth muscle of the prostatic urethra and glandular tissue. Some patients appear to have a preponderance of muscle tissue growth, whereas others may tend toward glandular development. As the hyperplasia develops, primarily in the lateral and middle lobes, (1) the urethral orifice narrows, and (2) the normal prostatic tissue becomes compressed against the outer fibrous capsule. The compressed normal prostatic tissue and sinuses may be referred to as the surgical capsule.

The goal of TURP is to remove the hyperplastic tissue while sparing the surgical capsule. The hyperplastic tissue does not produce a smooth junction with the compressed normal prostatic tissue but instead involves areas of the surgical capsule. It is therefore difficult to avoid some exposure of venous sinuses of the normal prostatic tissue during transurethral resection of the hyperplastic tissue.

4. What is the primary concern and complication associated with TURP?

The primary concern associated specifically with TURP is intravascular absorption of large volumes of irrigating fluid during the procedure. The absorption occurs predominantly through exposed venous sinuses of the surgical capsule. A spectrum of clinical and physiologic conditions results. The clinical manifestations brought about by intravascular fluid absorption are referred to as the TURP syndrome, and the degree of symptoms depends on the type, magnitude, and extent of absorbed fluid.

Several irrigants are currently in clinical use. All irrigants are nonelectrolyte solutions, and all but one are either isosmolar or slightly hyposmolar in make-up. Some symptoms of TURP syndrome (see question 5) may result from the specific make-up of the irrigating solution; however, the majority of symptoms are common to all irrigants and result from the acute intravascular fluid overload or hyponatremia.

As the fluid is absorbed, intravascular pressure increases, and proteins, as well as electrolytes, become diluted. The cumulative effect of increased intravascular pressure, decreased protein oncotic pressure, and decreased electrolyte concentration favors the movement of fluid from the vascular compartment into the interstitial spaces. Fluid moving out of the intravascular space produces edema in various tissue beds, including the pulmonary and cerebral beds. Decline in sodium and chloride levels results in electrolyte disturbances. Myocardial contractility may diminish, and conduction disturbances may arise in the face of vascular overload, electrolyte abnormalities, and cell edema. In addition, cerebrospinal fluid (CSF) pressure increases and electrolyte disturbances occur in the CSF.

5. What are the first signs and symptoms of TURP syndrome?

The anesthesiologist must recognize signs and symptoms of developing TURP syndrome. For the patient undergoing TURP with major conduction anesthesia (subarachnoid block or epidural block), the first sign has been described classically as restlessness and mental confusion. However, presentation of symptoms is variable, and the syndrome may manifest initially in other ways, such as nausea, vomiting, dizziness, headache, unresponsiveness, or transient visual changes. Other symptoms associated with hemodynamic instability may be the first indication of a developing problem, especially in patients under general anesthesia. Signs and symptoms may include hypertension, hypotension, heart rate changes, cardiac arrhythmias, pulmonary edema, or cyanosis.

Whereas it is the responsibility of the anesthesiologist to recognize symptoms, it is the responsibility of the surgeon to notify the anesthesiologist of problems that may be evident from a surgical perspective. Excessive bleeding, deep cuts, and visualization of sinuses are signs of an increased potential for development of TURP syndrome. The anesthesiologist should take note when a surgeon states, "Let's give him a little Lasix." The surgeon has recognized that conditions may be appropriate for excessive fluid absorption.

6. Why is isosmolar solution used for irrigation?

The irrigating solution originally used for TURP was distilled water. It was quickly recognized, however, that patients who absorbed a significant amount of distilled water developed intravascular hemolysis due to a decrease in serum osmolarity. In addition to hemolysis were signs and symptoms of (1) water intoxication and (2) renal failure, resulting from hemoglobin precipitation in the renal tubules. For these reasons, distilled water was all but abandoned as an irrigant;

isosmolar or slightly hyposmolar irrigating solutions were developed (normal serum osmolality = 280–300 mOsml/kg).

7. Normal saline, an isoelectric solution, seems to be the safest irrigant. Why is normal saline irrigation not used for TURP?

Only nonelectrolyte solutions can be used for irrigation during TURP. Electrolyte solutions are avoided to minimize the dispersion of current throughout the bladder when electrocautery is used. Dissemination of electrocautery current would be uncomfortable for the patient and dangerous to both patient and surgeon. After completion of surgery and before the patient is moved to the postanesthesia care unit, however, bladder irrigation should be changed to normal saline. Because fluid absorption from continuous bladder irrigation may continue in the postoperative period, eliminating nonelectrolyte solutions reduces the risk of postoperative hyponatremia.

8. Is more than one type of irrigation available for TURP?

Yes. Below is a list of available irrigants for TURP.

Distilled water. The danger of using distilled water as an irrigating solution is discussed above (see question 6). A few centers, however, still use it because it provides excellent optical qualities during resection (pH: 5.0–7.0).

Sorbitol (3% or 3.3%). Sorbitol, a nontoxic isomer of mannitol, is rapidly metabolized to 70% carbon dioxide and 30% dextrose. A small portion is excreted by the kidneys. Sorbitol at this concentration is nonhemolytic. It has a calculated osmolarity of 165 mOsml/L (pH: 5.0–7.0).

Resectisol (mannitol 5%). Resectisol, a 5% solution of mannitol, is the only isosmolar irrigating solution (275 mOsml/L). Mannitol is not metabolized and relies on elimination solely through renal excretion. Because Resectisol is not metabolized, large intravascular volume expansion may result in cardiac decompensation if large amounts of the irrigant are absorbed (pH: 4.5–7.0).

Cytal. Cytal, a 3% solution of sorbitol and mannitol, is an attempt to combine the best qualities of both agents. The calculated osmolarity is 178 mOsml/L. Metabolism of the absorbed sorbitol portion reduces the potential for vascular overload (pH: 4.9).

Glycine. Glycine is an amino acid constituted in a 1.5% solution. The osmolarity of the solution is 200 mOsml/L. Although glycine is excreted to some extent by the kidneys, it is also metabolized to ammonia by the liver. Among the more disturbing features of glycine are the temporary visual changes (including blindness) associated with its absorption. Whether such visual changes result from the glycine itself, cortical edema, or ammonia intoxication remains unknown (pH: 4.5–6.5).

9. When is TURP syndrome likely to occur?

The time to onset of TURP syndrome depends on numerous factors, including the experience of the surgeon, the surgeon's aggressiveness with the electrocutting loop, the pathology of the gland, and the amount of tissue removed. The incidence of morbidity increases as resection time exceeds 60 minutes, and for many years it was believed that TURP syndrome was unlikely during the first hour of resection. We now recognize that TURP syndrome can develop more rapidly.

The patient is not free of risk once the resection is completed. If the integrity of the prostatic capsule or wall of the bladder is violated during surgery, irrigating fluid may be sequestered in the intraperitoneal and extraperitoneal space during resection. The fluid may be absorbed into the intravascular space during the postoperative period and result in intravascular fluid overload and symptoms of TURP syndrome.

10. What is the treatment for TURP syndrome?

Treatment of TURP syndrome should begin the moment the problem is recognized.

1. Terminate surgery as quickly as possible and switch to normal saline for continuous bladder irrigation. Be sure that the irrigation is warm, as all bladder irrigation should be, to prevent the development of hypothermia.

2. Support ventilation as needed and obtain the following baseline laboratory tests: complete blood count, platelet count, electrolytes, and clotting studies if a bleeding problem is suspected. Prothrombin time, partial thromboplastin time, and fibrinogen level should be included in the coagulopathy work-up.

3. Administration of intravenous normal saline and diuretics may be all that is needed to correct the problem. Administer furosemide, 20 mg, intravenously. If the patient is on chronic diuretics, a dose of 40 mg or more may be required, but dosing should be based on the diuresis obtained initially from 20 mg. Maintain intravascular volume with normal saline as diuresis progresses.

4. If the patient demonstrates significant effects from hyponatremia, intravenous administration of hypertonic saline may be appropriate (see question 11). Our protocol restricts the use of hypertonic saline to patients who have developed central seizures or cardiac dysfunction.

5. Consider placement of a central venous catheter to guide fluid replacement during the immediate postoperative period.

6. If hemodynamic instability develops, consider placement of an arterial catheter and pulmonary artery catheter to aid in resuscitation.

7. Monitor the serum potassium level. Patients frequently become hypokalemic as diuresis occurs.

8. Reassure patients that any symptoms, especially visual changes, are only temporary and that their symptoms will dissipate as their condition improves.

11. Why not replace sodium deficit with hypertonic saline in patients suffering from TURP syndrome?

The use of hypertonic saline for correction of hyponatremia associated with TURP syndrome should be restricted to patients demonstrating significant symptoms, namely, central seizures or cardiac dysfunction due to electrolyte imbalance. If hypertonic saline is chosen for fluid replacement, close attention must be paid to the patient's electrolyte and intravascular fluid status. The patient has not lost sodium; he has gained water. Excessive administration of hypertonic saline results in additional fluid overload and complicates an already difficult management problem. Hypertonic saline should be administered through a central line at a rate no greater than 100 ml/hr.

12. Is it possible to calculate how much irrigating fluid has been absorbed?

The amount of irrigating solution absorbed can be estimated by comparing sodium levels at any time during the procedure with levels at the start of the procedure.

Volume absorbed = (preoperative serum sodium/postoperative serum sodium $\times$ ECF) – ECF

where ECF = extracellular fluid.

Example: A 70-kg man undergoes TURP under subarachnoid block (spinal anesthetic). After 50 minutes of resection, he complains of headache and appears somewhat disoriented. The procedure is immediately terminated, and a blood sample is sent to the laboratory for electrolyte analysis. The patient's preoperative serum sodium concentration was 142 mEq/L compared with the immediate postoperative value of 106 mEq/L. If the patient has an ECF compartment of approximately 20% of body weight, his ECF volume at the start of the procedure was about 14 L $(0.20 \times 70 = 14$ L$)$. Using the above formula, $(142/106) \times 14$ L $= 18.75$ L. Subtracting his initial extracellular volume of 14 L from the postoperative extracellular volume of 18.75 L yields an absorption of 4.75 L. This figure represents a minimal volume of absorption, because any fluid that has shifted into the intracellular space is lost in the calculation.

A more accurate technique for calculating fluid absorption is to add a trace amount of ethanol to the irrigating solution and then to monitor and quantify the amount of ethanol that the patient expires. This technique is complex and requires special instrumentation.

13. What can be done to minimize the risk of developing TURP syndrome?

1. The patient must be prepared properly for surgery. Preparation should include adequate hydration, electrolyte analysis, and coagulation profile. Patients who are debilitated and demonstrate

poor reserve benefit from the placement of hemodynamic monitors for preoperative assessment and treatment as well as for intraoperative monitoring.

2. The most important step in minimizing the risk of TURP syndrome is to limit the duration of surgery. Because fluid can be absorbed at a rate greater than 50 ml/min, it is possible to place nearly 3 L of fluid into the intravascular and interstitial spaces within 1 hour of resection time. Limit resection time to 1 hour or less.

3. The hydrostatic pressure created by the fluid irrigating the surgical site must be minimized. Because the irrigating fluid flows by gravity, the bag of irrigation should not hang higher than 60 cm above the operative field.

4. The surgeon should limit the extent of bladder distention created by the irrigant. Frequent drainage of the bladder by the surgeon reduces the amount of irrigant absorbed.

5. Careful surgical resection minimizes exposure of the venous sinuses and preserves the capsule of the prostate.

6. Blood pressure must be stable. A decrease in pressure lowers the periprostatic venous pressure and allows increased absorption of fluid.

14. How difficult is it to estimate blood loss during TURP?

It is very difficult to estimate true blood loss during TURP because of the mixing of irrigating solution with shed blood and the manner in which the irrigant–blood mixture is discarded (frequently directly into a drain). One way to calculate true blood loss is to collect all of the irrigant–blood mixture and to measure its hematocrit:

(Hematocrit of irrigant × volume of irrigant)/starting hematocrit = blood loss

Example: A 70-kg man undergoes TURP under general anesthesia. His starting hematocrit is 40%. Two liters of irrigant are used and collected during resection. A sample of the irrigant–blood mixture spun in a centrifuge reveals a hematocrit of 5%. Using the above formula: $(0.05 \times 2000 \text{ ml})/0.40 = 250 \text{ ml}$ blood loss.

15. Is there a preferred anesthetic technique for TURP?

Because early recognition of the TURP syndrome is paramount in preventing significant sequelae, the anesthetic technique that lends itself to early recognition is the optimal choice. Spinal or epidural anesthesia in a patient who has received minimal sedation allows early detection of various signs and symptoms of the syndrome, especially changes in mental status (see question 5). For this reason, most clinicians agree that regional anesthesia, if not contraindicated for a particular patient, is the technique of choice for TURP.

16. What level of spinal anesthetic is required for TURP?

A spinal anesthetic with a T12 sensory level is sufficient to eliminate pain associated with resection of hypertrophied prostatic tissue as well as discomfort due to bladder distention (see question 2). It is possible, however, to perform TURP with an anesthetic level involving only the sacral nerves. In such a situation, the surgeon needs to evacuate irrigant from the bladder frequently to avoid bladder distention and the resulting discomfort.

17. What other complications are associated with TURP?

Perforation of the bladder during TURP may occur because of the proximity of the surgical site to the bladder wall (see question 9). Diagnosing bladder perforation is difficult. Symptoms may include abdominal pain, respiratory compromise, and a tense abdominal wall. If the patient has received a spinal anesthetic, abdominal pain may not become evident until the anesthetic level begins to recede. In such patients and in patients receiving a general anesthetic, difficulty in breathing or an unexplained change in airway pressure may be the first indication of bladder perforation. As fluid accumulates in the intraperitoneal cavity, abdominal compliance decreases and movement of the diaphragm becomes limited. The result is respiratory compromise. Diagnosis of bladder perforation can be confirmed by obtaining a cystogram. The sequestration of irrigating fluid into the intraperitoneal and extraperitoneal space through bladder perforation is frequently self-limiting and normally requires no treatment.

Intraoperative and postoperative hemorrhage has been associated with TURP. Bleeding may occur by several mechanisms, and it is the clinician's responsibility to identify the cause.

Thrombocytopenia may develop and produce a coagulopathy. Thrombocytopenia may be secondary to a dilutional effect from irrigant absorption or to excessive blood loss. The diagnosis of dilutional thrombocytopenia is based on platelet count, serum sodium, and hematocrit. If these indices are low in the presence of normal or elevated central venous pressure or pulmonary capillary wedge pressure, the diagnosis is dilutional thrombocytopenia secondary to irrigant absorption. Diuresis alone may correct the problem. A low platelet count and hematocrit, with a normal serum sodium level and a normal or low central venous pressure or pulmonary capillary wedge pressure, indicate thrombocytopenia secondary to blood loss. Platelet transfusion may be appropriate in this setting.

Coagulopathy may develop secondary to fibrinolysis. Tissue thromboplastin and urokinase are released from the prostate during resection and may initiate either primary or secondary fibrinolysis. The treatment for primary fibrinolysis is administration of epsilon-aminocaproic acid (EACA). EACA, however, is contraindicated in patients with secondary fibrinolysis (disseminated intravascular coagulation). Therefore, a coagulation pathologist can be very helpful in distinguishing and treating these conditions.

Late complications associated with TURP include secondary bladder neck contracture, secondary urethral stricture, and incontinence.

18. How uncomfortable are patients after TURP? What can be done to minimize their discomfort?

Postoperative pain is thought to be due primarily to the development of a surgically induced reflex arc that results in uninhibited detrusor contraction and pain, often termed bladder spasm. Current analgesic methods directed toward minimizing spasm include suppositories containing belladonna and opium.

19. What other modalities are available for postoperative pain control?

Oral and parenteral administration of narcotics is, of course, useful in controlling postoperative pain. Intrathecal narcotics also may be used. A small dose of intrathecal morphine administered concomitantly with a spinal anesthetic results in significant postoperative analgesia, even in low doses (0.1 mg) that may be inadequate for blocking pain associated with other surgical procedures. The manner in which intrathecal morphine eliminates pain associated with TURP probably involves elimination at the spinal level, via spinal opioid receptor mechanisms, of the surgically induced reflex arc and bladder spasm.

BIBLIOGRAPHY

1. Azar I: The transurethral prostatectomy syndrome. In Moya F (ed): Current Reviews in Clinical Anesthesia. Miami Lakes, Current Reviews, 1987, pp 167–171.
2. Defalque RJ, Miller DW: Visual disturbances during transurethral resection of the prostate. Can Anaesth Soc J 22:620–621, 1975.
3. Hahn RG, Ekengren JC: Patterns of irrigating fluid absorption during transurethral resection of the prostate as indicated by ethanol. J Urol 149:502–506, 1993.
4. Hoekstra PT, Kahnoski R, McCamish MA, et al: Transurethral prostatic resection syndrome—a new perspective: Encephalopathy with associated hyperammonemia. J Urol 130:704–707, 1983.
5. Kirson LE, Goldman JM: Low-dose intrathecal morphine for postoperative pain control in patients undergoing transurethral resection of the prostate. Anesthesiology 71:192–195, 1989.
6. Maluf NSR, Boren JS, Brandes GE: Absorption of irrigating solution and associated changes upon transurethral electroresection of prostate. J Urol 75:824–836, 1956.
7. Ovassapian A, Joshi CW, Brunner EA: Visual disturbances: An unusual symptom of transurethral prostatic resection reaction. Anesthesiology 57:332–334, 1982.

79. ANESTHETIC CONSIDERATIONS FOR LASER SURGERY

J. Todd Nilson, M.D.

1. What is a laser?

Laser = light amplification by stimulated emission of radiation. Lasers produce coherent light, a source of light that does not occur naturally. To produce coherent light, atoms, ions, or molecules are stimulated by an energy source. The stimulated medium spontaneously radiates energy in the form of light. The radiated light is then amplified and emitted as the laser beam. Laser light has three defining characteristics:

- **Coherence**—all waves are in phase, both in time and in space.
- **Collimation**—the waves travel in parallel directions.
- **Monochromaticity**—all waves have the same wavelength.

2. Why do surgeons use lasers?

Lasers are very precise, with minimal dissipation of damaging heat and energy to surrounding tissues. Depending on the type of laser, it is preferentially absorbed by different types of tissues. In addition, controversial issues of faster healing and fewer infections are associated with their use.

3. What makes lasers behave differently from one another?

Wavelength depends on the lasing medium (the atoms stimulated). The longer the wavelength, the more strongly it is absorbed. Thus, the power of the light is converted to heat in shallower tissues. Conversely, the shorter the wavelength, the more scattered the light; therefore the light is converted to heat in deeper tissues. For example, a carbon dioxide (CO_2) laser has a longer wavelength and is absorbed almost entirely at the tissue surface. As a result, precise excision of superficial lesions is possible. Conversely, an Nd:YAG laser (neodymium:yttrium-aluminum-garnet) has a shorter wavelength and therefore deeper penetration. It is good for heating large tissue masses and debulking tumor.

Characteristics of Lasers Commonly Used in the Operating Room

LASER TYPE	WAVELENGTH	ABSORBER	TYPICAL APPLICATIONS
CO_2	10,600 Invisible (far infrared)	All tissues, water	General, precise surgical cutting
Nd:YAG	1,064 Invisible (near infrared)	Darkly pigmented tissues	General coagulation (via fiber optics), tumor debulking
Nd:YAG-KTP (neodymium:yttrium-aluminum-garnet:potassium-titanyl-phosphate)	532 Visible (emerald green)	Blood	General, pigmented lesions
Argon	488-514 Visible (blue-green)	Melanin, hemoglobin	Vascular, pigmented lesions
Krypton	400–700 Visible (blue-red)	Melanin	General, pigmented lesions

Power density (irradiance) is the energy delivered per unit area of cross section. Power density is usually measured as W/cm^2. Coherent light is focused into small spots of very high power density that can cut or vaporize tissue. Lower power density is used for coagulation.

4. What are the hazards of lasers?

Atmospheric contamination (particularly common in surgery for laryngeal papillomas). The vaporization of tissue and dispersion of diseased particulate matter is a hazard for all operating room personnel. The smoke produced by vaporization of tissues with lasers may be mutagenic, transmit infectious diseases, and cause acute bronchial inflammation.

Fire and explosion. Laser beam contact with flammable materials such as anesthetic gas tubing, surgical drapes, and sponges may cause fires or explosion. Endotracheal tube fires have an estimated incidence of 0.5–1.5%. Fires result in minimal or no harm to the patient if the situation is handled swiftly but may be catastrophic if not (see question 8).

Embolism. Although rare, a venous gas embolism may occur during laparoscopic surgery or hysteroscopy. Reported cases have been associated primarily with Nd:YAG lasers, in which coolant gases circulate at the probe tips. The gas from the probe tips caused embolism in the reported cases.

Inappropriate energy transfer. Laser light vaporizes whatever tissue lies in its path. Precise aim by the surgeon and a cooperative (well-anesthetized, paralyzed) patient are mandatory. In addition, laser light is easily reflected by surgical instruments and may be hazardous to all operating room personnel. Laser contact with the eyes is of particular concern, because it may impair vision or cause blindness. The nature of ocular damage depends on the wavelength of the laser light. For example, CO_2 lasers cause corneal opacification, whereas Nd:YAG lasers cause damage to the retina.

Perforation. Misdirected laser energy may perforate a viscus or large blood vessel. Laser-induced pneumothorax after laryngeal surgery also has been reported. Sometimes the perforations do not occur until several days after surgery when edema and tissue necrosis are at a maximum.

5. What is the best technique for anesthetic induction in a patient undergoing airway surgery?

In patients in whom the airway is likely to collapse after induction, an awake intubation should be strongly considered. In conscious patients with obstructive airway lesions, tracheal intubation is best performed over a fiber-optic endoscope; blind intubation may cause tissue edema or trauma and further obstruction of the airway. Sometimes awake tracheotomy is needed to secure an adequate airway before induction. When airway obstruction is mild and laryngoscopy and intubation appear feasible, preoxygenation and intravenous administration of a rapid-induction agent and succinylcholine are performed to secure intubation as quickly as possible. Regardless of whether awake or postinduction intubation is planned, a surgeon capable of emergent tracheotomy should be present during induction. Equipment for emergent cricothyrotomy also should be readily available.

6. What are the intraoperative considerations for laser surgery of the airway?

Upper airway lesions. In laser resection of upper airway lesions, tracheal intubation is optional. Techniques that do not involve an endotracheal tube allow better visualization of the operative field by the surgeon and also remove potentially flammable materials from the airway.

Lower airway lesions. Lower airway lesions are accessed through rigid bronchoscope or fiber optically. The CO_2 laser beam is directed at the lesion through a rigid metal bronchoscope, coated with a matte finish to reduce reflected laser light. Ventilation is accomplished through the side arm of the bronchoscope, using saline-soaked gauze to form a seal around the bronchoscope. Jet ventilation (see question 7) is another option. If the lesion is to be accessed fiber optically (e.g., lower tracheal and bronchial lesions), the Nd:YAG laser is required, because it can travel through fiber-optic cables, whereas the CO_2 laser cannot.

7. What ventilation techniques are commonly used in laser surgery of the airway?

Jet ventilation. In this technique the surgeon aims a high-velocity jet of O_2 at the airway opening. The high flow of O_2 entrains room air as a result of the Venturi effect, thus ventilating the lungs with a high volume of O_2-air mixture. Ventilation is accomplished by attaching a metal Fraser-tipped suction catheter to wall O_2 and a Sanderson-type jet injector. This apparatus is mounted to the operating laryngoscope. Sometimes the mass of the airway lesion makes this method impossible. If the jet stream is not aimed in the trachea, gastric dilatation may occur. Barotrauma to the airway and subsequent pneumothorax are also risks and may in turn lead to mediastinal or subcutaneous air.

Spontaneous ventilation. Allowing the patient to inhale volatile agents via the operating laryngoscope is also an option, although it is not feasible for some procedures. It is difficult to control the depth of anesthesia during spontaneous ventilation, and it is often necessary to paralyze the patient during many airway procedures. Of note, however, hypoventilation, hypercarbia, and aspiration (surgical debris, secretions, vomitus, and smoke) are additional complications related to both jet and spontaneous ventilation.

Endotracheal intubation. This method allows excellent ventilation and airway protection of the anesthetized patient but often obscures the operative field and puts flammable materials in the path of the laser beam.
- Flammability studies have shown that of the available pliable tubes (polyvinyl chloride [PVC], red rubber, silicone), PVC tubes are the least flammable.
- Some authors advocate wrapping the endotracheal tube with metal tape; however, this method limits the tube's pliability and increases the risk of a reflected laser beam and loss of metal tape fragments in the trachea.
- Others advocate using a PVC endotracheal tube with an O_2-helium mixture to deliver the anesthetic agent, thus reducing flammability. Helium has a high thermal diffusivity and decreases the heat of materials in laser contact. Nitrous oxide is not used in the same fashion, because it has a much lower thermal diffusivity and supports combustion.

8. Describe the correct management of airway fires.
Two strategies minimize the potential hazard of an airway fire: (1) reduce the flammability of the airway by decreasing the O_2 concentration and covering potentially flammable tissue with wet lap sponges, and (2) remove flammable materials (such as endotracheal tubes) from the airway by using metallic Venturi jet ventilation cannulas or by ventilating with intermittent extubation.

Airway fire protocol
1. Stop ventilation.
2. Disconnect the O_2 source, remove the endotracheal tube, and flood the surgical field with saline.
3. Mask-ventilate the patient with 100% O_2, then reintubate.
4. Perform rigid laryngoscopy and bronchoscopy (using Venturi jet ventilation) to assess the damage and remove debris.
5. Monitor the patient for 24 hours.
6. Use short-term steroids.
7. Continue ventilatory support and antibiotics as needed.

BIBLIOGRAPHY
1. Pashayan AG, Gavenstein JS: Helium retards endotracheal tube fires from carbon dioxide lasers. Anesthesiology 62:274–277, 1985.
2. Rampil IJ: Anesthetic considerations for laser surgery. Anesth Analg 74:424–435, 1992.
3. Rampil IJ: Anesthesia for laser surgery. In Miller RD (ed): Anesthesia, 4th ed. New York, Churchill Livingstone, 1994, pp 2197–2211.
4. Van der spek AFL, Spargo PM, Norton ML: The physics of lasers and implications for their use during airway surgery. Br J Anaesth 60:709–729, 1988.
5. Wolf GL, Simpson JI: Flammability of endotracheal tubes in oxygen and nitrous oxide enriched atmosphere. Anesthesiology 67:236–239, 1987.

80. ANESTHESIA FOR ELECTROCONVULSIVE THERAPY

Steven J. Stein, M.D., and Kevin Fitzpatrick, M.D.

1. What is the historical background of electroconvulsive therapy?

Ladislas von Meduna, a Hungarian neuropsychiatrist and pathologist, erroneously believed that schizophrenia and epilepsy were mutually antagonistic and that the symptoms of schizophrenia were ameliorated by generalized seizures. In 1934 he successfully treated a catatonic man through chemically induced epileptic fits. Electrically induced seizures, first performed in 1937, are the only form of electroconvulsive therapy (ECT) used currently. Early ECTs did not involve the use of sedatives, analgesics, muscle relaxants, supplemental oxygen, or ventilation. Indeed, awareness and cyanosis were believed to be therapeutic and thus were encouraged.

2. What are the main indications for ECT?

The primary role of ECT is treatment of major depressive disorders associated with psychotic features. As many as 90% of psychotically depressed patients respond to ECT. Occasionally, ECT is used to treat nonchronic schizophrenia, mania, and catatonia unresponsive to drug therapy.

3. Describe the preanesthetic management of patients scheduled for ECT.

A preanesthetic visit with the patient and chart review are essential for administering anesthesia for ECT. Compassionate reassurance and prudent explanation of risks, benefits, and reasonable expectations of events before and after the procedure allay fears and misconceptions. The preoperative history and physical examination should concentrate on the cardiopulmonary and central nervous systems in addition to careful evaluation of the airway. In particular, the presence of hypertension, coronary artery disease, and elevated intracranial pressure must be assessed (see questions 12, 13, and 14).

4. How is anesthesia for ECT performed?

ECT is not usually performed in the operating room. However, it is often done in close proximity, for example, in the postoperative anesthesia care unit (PACU). The patient is placed on a gurney, and an intravenous infusion is started. Monitors are placed, and 100% oxygen is given by face mask. The induction agent is administered, followed by a muscle relaxant. At this point the anesthesiologist must assume control of the patient's airway through mask ventilation. The psychiatrist applies the electroshock after the muscle relaxant has taken effect, and the seizure is monitored, both centrally and peripherally (see question 6). The anesthetist continues ventilatory support until the patient is able to take control. Parameters such as vital signs and adequacy of oxygenation and ventilation must be carefully observed until the patient has safely emerged from the general anesthetic and seizure.

5. What are the requirements for monitoring the anesthetized patient during ECT?

Standard monitors include continuous electrocardiography, noninvasive blood pressure, pulse oximetry, and precordial stethoscope. Equipment and medications appropriate for full cardiopulmonary resuscitation must be readily available, including oral airways, styletted endotracheal tubes, laryngoscopes, suction, and emergency drugs (e.g., atropine, phenylephrine, ephedrine, beta blockers). The vast majority of patients do not require endotracheal intubation.

6. How is seizure activity monitored?

Centrally, an electroencephalogram (EEG) monitors the duration of the seizure. **Peripherally**, an arm or foot is isolated from the circulation with a tourniquet before injection of the muscle relaxant. Once the electroshock has been delivered, the ensuing hand or foot movement is used as an indicator of seizure duration.

7. Describe the characteristics of the seizure evoked by ECT.

The electrical stimulus is applied through electrodes that are usually fixed to the scalp by a headband. Bilateral ECT requires electrode placement over each cerebral hemisphere, whereas with unilateral ECT both electrodes are placed over a single hemisphere. The electroshock produces a grand mal seizure by acting on the cerebral cortex. A **latent period** of 2–3 seconds is followed first by a **tonic phase** of 10–12 seconds, then by a **clonic phase** lasting 30–50 seconds.

8. What are the typical electroencephalographic findings during ECT?

The EEG shows a build-up of alpha and beta rhythmic activity during the tonic phase, which is followed by repetitive polyphasic spikes and wave complexes in the clonic phase, synchronous with the clonic movements. The electrical seizure (central) always lasts longer than the clonic manifestation (peripheral).

9. Does the duration of seizure affect the therapeutic efficacy?

Most definitely. In current practice, a series of 8–12 treatments is administered at a rate of 2–3 treatments per week. It has been reported that seizures < 30 seconds in duration are not clinically effective. The cumulative seizure time over several treatments must also be noted. Cumulative seizure duration of < 210 seconds is without benefit; cumulative seizure duration of > 1000 seconds demonstrates no additional improvement in symptoms. However, many patients have had a full remission with 100 seconds of total seizure time. A 500-mg dose of intravenous caffeine is often given just before the induction of anesthesia to prolong the seizure. It is important to recognize that over the course of several treatments seizure threshold tends to increase.

10. Discuss the various induction agents used for ECT.

Methohexital (Brevital), a barbiturate, is the most commonly used induction agent. As with all barbiturates, methohexital decreases seizure duration and raises seizure threshold. Paradoxically, methohexital has been noted to induce seizures in adults and children with temporal lobe epilepsy.

Thiopental, another barbiturate, seems to offer no unique advantage over methohexital. Compared with methohexital, thiopental has a slower onset and longer duration of action. However, the incidence of hiccups, muscle twitching, and excessive salivation is lower with thiopental.

Diazepam (Valium), like thiopental, increases the seizure threshold and shortens seizure duration. Its slow onset and delayed recovery make it a poor choice.

Ketamine is the only intravenous induction agent that has been shown to increase seizure duration in both humans and animals. Unfortunately, its slow onset of action, prolonged recovery time, and association with a greater incidence of nausea and ataxia after ECT preclude its general use.

Etomidate has been used to induce general anesthesia for ECT, but it is associated with involuntary muscle movement, increased muscular tone, and longer recovery time.

Propofol has recently been shown to attenuate the hypertensive response to ECT compared with methohexital (see question 12). However, it is also associated with a shorter seizure duration. Finally, propofol in fact may behave as an anticonvulsant.

Alfentanil, a potent synthetic opioid, does not affect seizure threshold. It may substitute for a barbiturate in patients who have decreasing seizure duration over a series of ECT treatments.

11. What is the rationale for adding a muscle relaxant to the anesthetic regimen?

The violent muscular contractions accompanying the seizure may lead to skeletal injury, including vertebral fractures. Addition of succinylcholine essentially negates this risk. A bite block is placed to protect the teeth and tongue from masseter muscle contraction (which occurs even with the use of muscle relaxants) due to direct muscle stimulation.

12. How does ECT affect the autonomic nervous system?

A **parasympathetic discharge** immediately after application of the current (coincident with the tonic phase of seizure activity) is followed seconds later by a **sympathetic surge** (coincident with the clonic phase). This parasympathetic–sympathetic sequence may cause an initial brady-cardia or even asystole, followed by tachycardia, dysrhythmias, and hypertension. Less than 1 minute after the seizure, plasma epinephrine concentrations increase about fifteenfold and plasma norepinephrine threefold. The generalized increase in oxygen demand and pronounced sympathetic activity may result in myocardial ischemia or even infarction in patients with coro-nary artery disease.

13. How does ECT affect the cerebrovascular system?

An initial brief period of cerebral vasoconstriction after the electrical stimulus is followed by a sustained increase in cerebral blood flow (up to 7 times baseline) and a 400% increase in cere-bral metabolism. The resulting increase in intracranial pressure (ICP) may be of concern in pa-tients with intracranial mass lesions, vascular anomalies, or elevated ICP of any origin.

14. What can be done to treat the sympathetic response to ECT?

Labetalol (a mixed alpha and beta receptor antagonist), esmolol (a beta$_1$ selective receptor antagonist), and fentanyl (a potent opioid) are commonly used to attenuate the sympathetic re-sponse to ECT. Clonidine (a centrally active alpha$_2$ agonist), phenoxybenzamine (an alpha recep-tor blocker), and trimethaphan (a ganglionic blocking agent) also have been used successfully. Nitroglycerin (a nitrate compound like nitroprusside) is an effective venodilating agent with anti-hypertensive properties.

15. How do oxygenation and ventilation affect the duration of the seizure?

Aggressive ventilation by mask after anesthetic induction and before application of the elec-troshock may lower seizure threshold and increase seizure duration. This beneficial effect is as-sociated with both oxygenation and hypocapnia. Conversely, hypoxemia and hypercapnia shorten seizure duration.

16. List the strong and moderate contraindications to ECT.

As with any decision-making process in medicine, the risks and benefits must be carefully considered for each patient. In the case of ECT, the risks of a general anesthetic and seizure must be weighed against the benefits of potential freedom from disabling severe depression.

Strong contraindications
- Recent myocardial infarction (< 3 months)
- Recent cerebrovascular accident (< 3 months)
- Intracranial mass lesion (with or without changes in ICP)
- High risk for aspiration

Moderate contraindications
- Angina pectoris
- Congestive heart failure
- Cardiac pacemakers
- Pheochromocytoma (risk of malignant pressor crisis)
- Glaucoma (ECT elevates intraocular pressure)
- Retinal detachment
- Severe osteoporosis
- Major bone fractures
- Thrombophlebitis
- Severe acute and chronic pulmonary disease
- Pregnancy (theoretical risk of fetal hypoxemia)—
  fetal monitoring is essential

17. What are the anesthetic considerations for tricyclic antidepressants (TCAs), monoamine oxidase inhibitors (MAOIs), and lithium?

TCAs. Patients scheduled for ECT are frequently taking psychotropic agents. TCAs (e.g., imipramine, noripramine) are structurally related to phenothiazines and block the reuptake of norepinephrine and serotonin into presynaptic nerve terminals. The pressor response to direct-acting sympathomimetics is increased many-fold in patients taking TCAs; therefore, drugs such as phenylephrine must be administered with caution.

MAOIs. Monoamine oxidase selectively deaminates amine neurotransmitters (norepinephrine, epinephrine, dopamine, and serotonin) by oxidation. Blocking this enzyme causes accumulation of amine neurotransmitters in nerve terminals. Like TCAs, MAOIs may precipitate hypertensive crises when given in conjunction with direct or indirect sympathomimetics. Therefore, it is recommended that MAOIs be discontinued 2 weeks brefore starting ECT. Examples of MAOIs include deprenyl, isocarboxazid, phenelzine, and tranylcypromine. Both TCAs and MAOIs augment the effects of barbiturates, increasing sleep time and duration of anesthesia. Hence, lower doses of barbiturates should be used if patients are taking either of these medications.

Lithium. Lithium carbonate is occasionally used in the treatment of recurrent depression. It is associated with prolonged recovery when used in conjunction with barbiturates. In addition, it may prolong the duration of action of succinylcholine.

18. What are frequent side effects of ECT?

Muscle aches, headaches, and memory disturbances tend to be the most common side effects. Headaches may be treated with opioids. Both retrograde and anterograde amnesia may occur. The most common long-term side effect of ECT is memory disturbance, which usually improves with time and is insignificant after 6 months. In addition, many patients emerge from the anesthetic highly agitated. Agitation is treated first by reassurance and periodic reorientation of the patient. Judicious administration of midazolam or lorazepam may be indicated. Status epilepticus is a rare complication of ECT and may be treated with barbiturates, benzodiazepines, or phenytoin (Dilantin). Vertebral and long-bone fractures have not been reported since 1976. The overall mortality associated with ECT is very low—on the order of 1 in 28,000 treatments. Dysrhythmias, myocardial infarction, congestive heart failure, and cardiac arrest are the most frequent causes of death.

BIBLIOGRAPHY

1. Consensus Conference: Electroconvulsive therapy. JAMA 254:2103–2108, 1985.
2. Gaines GY, Rees DI: Electroconvulsive therapy and anesthetic considerations. Anesth Analg 65:1345–1346, 1986.
3. Jones RM, Knight PR: Cardiovascular and hormonal responses to electroconvulsive therapy. Modification of an exaggerated response in an hypertensive patient by beta blockade. Anaesthesia 36:795–799, 1981.
4. Maletsky BM: Seizure duration and clinical effect in electroconvulsive therapy. Compr Psychiatry 19:541–550, 1978.
5. McPherson R, Lipsey J. Electroconvulsive therapy. In Rodgers M (ed): Current Practices in Anesthesiology. Philadelphia, B.C. Decker, 1990, pp 180–185.
6. Pitts FN, Woodruff RA, Craig AG, Rich CL: The drug modification of ECT. Part 2: Succinylcholine dosage. Arch Gen Psychiatry 19:595–598, 1968.
7. Selvin BL: Electroconvulsive therapy—1987. Anesthesiology 67:367–385, 1987.

X. Pain Management

81. ACUTE PAIN MANAGEMENT

Robin B. Slover, M.D., and Rose A. Gates, R.N., M.S.N.

1. Define acute pain.

Pain is defined as "an unpleasant sensory and emotional experience associated with actual or potential tissue damage, or described in terms of such damage." Acute pain refers to pain of short duration (< 6 weeks), usually associated with surgery, trauma, or an acute illness. Acute pain differs from chronic pain because (1) its cause is usually known; (2) it is usually temporary and located in the area of trauma or damage; and (3) it resolves spontaneously with healing.

2. Why has acute pain been undertreated?

Acute pain has been undertreated for various reasons. Training in appropriate pain assessment and the appropriate medication choices has been minimal for most health care providers. In addition, the risks associated with the use of opioids, such as respiratory depression and addiction, are perceived as much higher than in fact they are. The fact that poorly treated pain may result in higher morbidity and mortality rates has become appreciated only recently.

3. How is pain assessed?

Pain is a subjective experience; no machine can measure pain. Changes in vital signs such as blood pressure or pulse rate correlate poorly with the degree of pain control. The only person who can determine the presence and degree of pain is the patient. However, the magnitude of pain and the response to treatment can be monitored in several ways. A scale of 10 faces, ranging from very happy to very sad, can be used in young children.

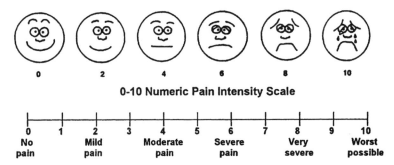

0-10 Numeric Pain Intensity Scale

Pain scales for children and adults. (From Wong D, Whaley L: Clinical Manual of Pediatric Nursing. St. Louis, Mosby, 1990, with permission.)

The child points to the face matching the way he or she feels. Similar scales using color (from blue for minimal pain through violet hues to bright red for maximal pain) or numbers (from zero for no pain through ten for maximal pain) have been devised for adults. A visual analog scale uses a 10-cm line on which the patient marks a point corresponding to the amount of pain. Verbal descriptive scales, such as the McGill Pain Questionnaire, are useful both for clinical and research purposes. Functional ability is also a useful measure of pain. In some patients, especially

411

those who also have chronic pain, function may be more useful than pain scores. For example, in assessing a patient with chronic pancreatitis who always gives a 10/10 pain score, one can monitor the number of times the patient spontaneously leaves the room to smoke. On days with very bad pain, spontaneous activity is likely to be curtailed. In addition to documenting the current pain scale at rest, pain should also be measured during activity. The activity score may be a more sensitive measure of efficacy of pain control, because it is easier to control pain at rest. The pain scale can be used to ensure that an intervention, such as an increased dose of analgesia, is effective in decreasing the patient's pain.

4. What medications are useful in treating acute pain?

The medications useful in treating acute pain are similar to those used in treating other types of pain. The World Health Organization (WHO) analgesic ladder developed for treating patients with cancer pain also provides a useful approach to treating acute pain. At the lowest level (mild pain), nonopioid analgesics such as nonsteroidal anti-inflammatory drugs (NSAIDs) (e.g., ibuprofen or acetaminophen) are useful. Such drugs have an analgesic ceiling; above a certain dose, no further analgesia is expected. For moderate pain, compounds combining acetaminophen or aspirin with an opioid are useful. The inclusion of acetaminophen limits the amount of such agents that should be used within a 24-hour period, because toxic accumulations can occur. For severe levels of pain, an opioid such as morphine or hydromorphone is a better choice; such opioids have no analgesic ceiling. Most postoperative or trauma patients initially respond better to a morphine-equivalent opioid. By the time the patient is eating and ready for discharge, opioid-acetaminophen agents or NSAIDs are often adequate.

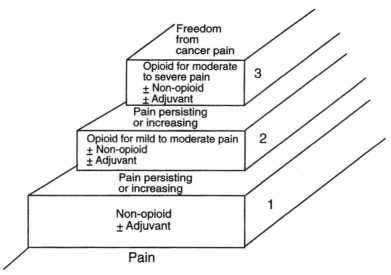

Analgesic ladder. (From Cancer Pain Relief and Palliative Care: Report of a WHO Expert Committee. Geneva, World Health Organization, 1990. Technical Report Series, No. 804, Fig. 1, with permission.)

Not all types of pain respond equally to the same medication. Opioid analgesics are helpful in controlling somatic or visceral pain. Bone pain may be helped partially by opioids. However, NSAIDs and steroids are highly effective in treating bone pain. The combination of NSAIDs and opioids is synergistic in controlling pain. Neuropathic pain, often described as pain with a burning, hyperesthetic quality, responds to a diverse group of drugs, including antidepressants (amitriptyline), anticonvulsants (carbamazepine or clonazepam), antiarrhythmics (mexiletine), baclofen, and α-adrenergic agonists (clonidine). Recommended regimens are listed below. Opioids may also be helpful. Frequently, pain control is improved after 1–2 days of using adjuvant drugs.

Alternate medications may also help to control somatic or visceral pain. Drugs that control pain by different mechanisms may be synergistic when used together (such as NSAIDs and opioids). By using lower doses of two different agents, the patient may have good pain control with fewer side effects.

Adjuvant Drug Doses

DRUG	INITIAL DOSE	MAXIMUM DOSE
Baclofen	10 mg	40–80 mg
Clonazepam	0.5 mg	2–3 mg
Carbamazepine	100 mg twice daily	Blood level Therapeutic range
Amitriptyline	10–25 mg	100–200 mg
Clonidine patch	0.1 mg	0.1–0.3 mg
Mexiletine	150 mg twice daily	600–750 mg

5. What is the risk of addiction with opioids?

Addiction (or psychological dependence) needs to be differentiated from physical dependence. Physical dependence, a physiologic adaptation of the body to the presence of an opioid, develops in all patients maintained on opioids for a period of several weeks. If the opioid is stopped abruptly without tapering, the patient may show signs of withdrawal. The patient can stop opioids at any time and by tapering down avoids withdrawal symptoms. Tolerance is the need for a higher dose of opioid to produce the same pharmacologic effect. Neither physical dependence nor tolerance indicates addiction. The psychological dependence seen with addiction is characterized by a compulsive behavior pattern involved in acquiring opioids for non-medical psychic effects as opposed to pain relief. The risk of iatrogenic addiction is very low; several studies have shown it to be less than 0.1%. Patients who are inadequately treated may seem to be drug-seeking, because they repeatedly request opioids and are concerned with the timing of their next dose. Such "pseudoaddiction" may mimic addictive behavior but is due to inadequate pain treatment. This iatrogenic condition can be avoided by listening to the patient and carefully assessing his or her pain. With proper doses of pain medication, pseudoaddiction disappears.

6. How should opioids be given? Are some opioids better than others?

Opioids can be given in various ways. Oral administration is usually the easiest and least expensive. Tablets should be provided on a schedule (e.g., oxycodone-acetaminophen tablets every 4 hours) rather than on an "as needed" (prn) or "as requested" basis. Many studies have shown that prn schedules usually provide only 25% of the maximal possible daily dose of opioids, despite the patient's repeated requests. If a patient cannot take medication orally, opioids can be administered intramuscularly, intravenously (including patient-controlled analgesia [PCA] pumps), subcutaneously, rectally, transdermally, epidurally, intrathecally, and through buccal mucosa. Because PCA pumps are safe and effective, they are often used when the patient cannot take oral medication.

The opioids usually given parenterally include morphine, meperidine, and hydromorphone. Meperidine has the highest incidence of allergic reactions; in addition, its first metabolite, normeperidine, can accumulate and cause central nervous system excitation, including seizures. Normeperidine accumulation is dose-dependant and more common in patients with renal impairment. Normeperidine seizures are rare with intramuscular meperidine, because the amount of medication is small and given as needed. However, with the larger doses available through a PCA pump, more cases of normeperidine seizures have been reported. Morphine has an active metabolite—morphine-6-glucuronide—that is analgesic and has a longer half-life than morphine. This metabolite can be useful in many cases, because it allows a slow, sustained increase in analgesia.

However, in patients with decreased renal function, the accumulation of an active metabolite may lead to increased side effects, including increased risk of respiratory depression. Fentanyl acts more rapidly than morphine or meperidine and has no active metabolites. It is a safer choice for patients with impaired renal or liver function. Hydromorphone also has no active metabolites. It is 5 times as potent as morphine and less dysphoric; however, its onset of action and duration are more similar to morphine than fentanyl.

7. How should a PCA pump be set?

Several decisions must be made in setting up a PCA pump. The first is what drug to use. As discussed above, the most commonly used agents are morphine and hydromorphone. The use of meperidine has decreased significantly over the last 5 years because of the risk of seizures from normeperidine. Fentanyl also can be used, particularly in patients with end-organ failure. Morphine comes prepackaged in a 1-mg/ml concentration; because hydromorphone is 5 times as potent, a 0.2-mg/ml concentration is equivalent. After choosing the drug, a decision should be made about the type of infusion: increment dosing only, basal (continuous) and incremental dosing, or incremental dosing with a basal dose only at night (between 10 p.m. and 6 a.m.) to help the patient sleep. Studies have shown no significant benefit to a basal rate, although anecdotally patients prefer a basal rate at night to help them sleep. Finally, the length of the lock-out period needs to be determined. Lock-out refers to the time between actual delivery of opioid doses; for example, if a 6-minute lock-out period is selected, the patient cannot receive opioid doses closer than 6 minutes apart, regardless of how often he or she activates the PCA pump. The lock-out period should be short enough to allow the patient to titrate the opioid level but long enough to allow the patient to feel the effect of one dose before delivering another. The usual lock-out ranges are 6–10 minutes.

PCA Opioid Guidelines for Acute Pain (Adults)

OPIOID	BASAL DOSE (AFTER LOADING)	INCREMENT DOSE	USUAL LOCK-OUT (min)
Morphine 1.0 mg/ml	1.0 mg	1.0–2.0 mg	6–10
Hydromorphone 0.2 mg/ml	0.2 mg	0.2–0.4 mg	6–10
Fentanyl 10–25 mcg/ml	10–25 µg	10–50 µg	6–10

8. What are common side effects of opioids? How are they treated?

The common side effects of opioids are sedation, pruritus, nausea and vomiting, urinary retention, and respiratory depression. In patients who have taken opioids previously, the risk of respiratory depression and sedation is less. Pruritus is treated by applying lotion to the affected area, by intravenous or oral delivery of diphenhydramine (25–50 mg) and, in severe cases, by using an opioid antagonist or agonist-antagonist (e.g., nalbuphine, 5 mg every 6 hours). Propofol, 10 mg every 6 hours, is also effective. Urinary retention is treated by urinary catheter drainage or nalbuphine. Nausea and vomiting respond to a decrease in opioid dose (elimination of a basal rate), nalbuphine, and antiemetics. Ondansetron, 4 mg intravenously, has proved to be a much more effective antiemetic than droperidol. Respiratory depression is treated by using an antagonist (naloxone) or agonist-antagonist (nalbuphine).

9. How do peridural opioids work?

Opioid receptors are present in levels I and II of the substantia gelatinosa of the dorsal horn. Opioids given either intrathecally or epidurally bind to these receptors. The dose of morphine can be decreased to 10% of the usual intravenous dose when given epidurally and to 1% when given intrathecally.

Approximate Equinalgesic Conversions of Morphine among Routes of Administration

PARENTERAL	EPIDURAL	SUBARACHNOID
100	10	1

The clinical behavior of the opioid can be predicted by its lipid solubility. Highly lipid-soluble opioids, such as fentanyl, pass through membranes and bind quickly. Fentanyl has a rapid onset, short duration, and limited spread. Morphine, which is highly hydrophilic, moves through membranes more slowly and has a slower onset but longer duration, because it stays suspended in solution and is released slowly to bind to the opioid receptors. Because of its poor lipid solubility, it spreads throughout the entire length of the spinal fluid and can help to control pain from several different anatomic sites. The termination of clinical activity of peridural opioids is due to vascular absorption and breakdown. Local anesthetics, such as lidocaine and bupivacaine, can be used alone or in combination with opioids (0.05–0.1% bupivacaine is used to minimize motor block).

Epidural Opioids

DRUG	ONSET (MIN)	DURATION (HR)	NUMBER DERMATOMES COVERED	SINGLE DOSE	INFUSION RATE
Morphine	60	12–24	All	2–5 mg	0.05–0.01 mg/ml 0.5–1.0 mg/hr
Hydromorphone	45	6–10	10–12	200–300 μg	10–30 μg/ml 100–300 μg/hr
Fentanyl	5–10	3–5	5–6	50–100 μg	1–5 μg/ml 10–50 μg/hr

10. How do agonist-antagonists differ from opioids such as morphine?

Mu, delta, and kappa opioid receptors have been identified in the central nervous system. Most morphine equivalent opioids are primarily mu agonists, with some delta and kappa effect. Agonist-antagonists are mu antagonists and kappa agonists. Because kappa receptors provide weaker analgesia, agonist-antagonists are adequate for mild-to-moderate pain, whereas mu agonists are adequate for moderate-to-severe pain.

11. How should patients with epidural analgesia or PCA pumps be monitored?

Patients receiving analgesia do not need elaborate monitoring equipment. Pulse oximetry can be used if there is any question of oxygen saturation, but usually nurses are able to monitor patients safely by checking respiratory rate every hour and level of sedation every hour the patient is awake. Vital signs are taken as scheduled.

Monitoring Guidelines for Acute Pain Patients

Any additional narcotics or sedatives must be authorized by the pain service before they are administered to a patient with an epidural catheter.

Respiratory rate every 1 h × 4 h, then every 2 h × 16 h after the initial dose of epidural narcotic; then every 4 hr as long as epidural medications are administered

If respiratory rate is 6–7 breaths per minute, call anesthesia pain resident.

If respiratory rate is less than 5 breaths per minute, administer naloxone, 0.2 mg (½ ampule) by intravenous push, and oxygen by mask at 6 L/min. Call anesthesia resident immediately. Arouse patient and encourage patient to breathe.

Sedation scale every 1 h × 4 h, then every 2 hr × 8 h, then every 4 h as long as epidural medications are administered.

Sedation scale: 1 = wide awake; 2 = drowsy; 3 = sleeping, arousable; 4 = difficult to arouse; 5 = not able to awaken

12. How is an oral agent chosen for a patient who preveiously received intravenous opioids?
Choice of an oral agent should be based on how much pain the patient still has and how much opioid was needed to control the pain. Opioid-acetaminophen compounds are adequate for patients whose pain required 0–2 mg/h of morphine. Hydrocodone-acetaminophen is a milder analgesic than oxycodone-acetaminophen and is useful for patients who require minimal opioids. An equal analgesic dosing chart can be used to select equivalent levels of analgesics.

Equianalgesic Doses

ANALGESIC	EQUIANALGESIC DOSES		DOSE INTERVAL (hr)
	PARENTERAL (mg)	ORAL (mg)	
Opioid agonist			
Morphine	10	30–60	3–6
Slow-release morphine	—	30–60	8–12
Hydromorphone (Dilaudid)	1.5	7.5	3–5
Fentanyl (Sublimaze, Innovar)	0.1	—	0.5–1
Transdermal fentanyl (Duragesic)	—	—	72
Levorphanol (Levo-Dromoran)	2	4	3–6
Meperidine (Demerol)	75	300	3–4
Methadone (Dolophine)	10	20	4–6
Oxycodone	—	30	3–6
Codeine	130	200	3–6
Hydrocodone	—	30	3–4
Agonist-Antagonist			
Nalbuphine (Nubain)	10	—	3–6
Butorphanol (Stadol)	2	—	3–4

Oral Drugs Approximately Equianalgesic to Aspirin (650 mg)

Codeine	50 mg	Propoxyphene	65 mg
Hydrocodone	5 mg	Acetaminophen	650 mg
Meperidine	50 mg	Ibuprofen	200 mg
Oxycodone	5 mg	Naproxen	275 mg

13. Which NSAID should be used?
If the patient can take oral medication, an oral agent should be used. Most oral agents have the same degree of analgesia as anti-inflammatory activity. The degree of potency of analgesia parallels the risk of gastric upset with oral agents. Agents such as etodolac and nabumetone reportedly have a decreased risk of gastric upset. The number of doses needed per day also varies. Epironicam and oxaprozin are once-a-day agents. One or two specific agents may work better for a given patient, but their identification is usually a matter of trial and error. Price also may be a factor. Older NSAIDs that are off patent may be significantly cheaper and just as effective (e.g., naproxen, indomethacin, and ibuprofen).

For patients who cannot take oral medication, parenteral ketorolac is the available option. Ketorolac has a more potent analgesic than anti-inflammatory effect. It may be given intravenously (IV) or intramuscularly (IM). The dose for most patients is 30 mg IV or IM every 6 hours. For a single dose for outpatients, 30 mg IV or 60 mg IM should be used. In patients who are over 65 years old, who weigh under 100 pounds, or who are frail, 15 mg every 6 hours should be used. In patients with a creatinine ≥ 1.3 or renal failure, the use of ketorolac should be carefully considered.

The side effects of NSAIDs may be observed with either oral or parenteral use. Patients who have active gastric disease, who are anticoagulated or hypovolemic, or who have a history of triad asthma, congestive heart failure, or renal disease may have complications from NSAID use.

14. What other techniques can be used for acute pain management?

In addition to PCA pumps and epidurals, intrathecal narcotics can be used, especially if spinal anesthesia is used for the procedure. Preservative-free morphine can be used for inpatients and fentanyl for outpatients. Morphine doses of 0.1–0.3 mg are adequate for many lower extremity, urologic, and gynecologic procedures and have a minimal risk of respiratory depression. For thoracic procedures, higher doses are needed (0.3–0.75 mg) and involve a risk of respiratory depression. Fentanyl also can be used intrathecally; 10–15 µg of intrathecal fentanyl is equal to 0.1–0.3 µg of intrathecal morphine. Because fentanyl is more lipid-soluble than morphine, it does not spread as far but still may be given through lumbar spinal injection.

Other types of blocks can be useful. Intercostal blocks decrease pain and improve ventilation in patients with rib fractures or flail chests. Continuous brachial plexus blocks increase blood flow in patients with collagen vascular diseases or arterial spasm (Beuzer's disease) and patients who have digital reattachment, improving healing as well as providing good pain control.

15. How does good management of acute pain make a difference?

Pain is a form of stress and produces elevation in stress hormones and catecholamines. Good pain management has been shown to result in shorter hospital stays, improved mortality rates (especially in patients with less physiologic reserve, such as those in the intensive care unit), better immune function, less catabolism and endocrine derangements, and fewer complications. In addition, specific benefits have been shown for patients undergoing specific procedures. Patients who undergo amputation under a regional block with local anesthetic have a decreased incidence of phantom pain. Patients in whom a vascular graft is placed have a lower rate of thrombosis. A decreased mortality rate has been shown in patients with flail chests who have epidural analgesia.

Recent studies have shown the value of preemptive analgesia in some surgical situations. The blockade of the pathways involved in pain transmission before surgical stimulation may decrease the patient's postoperative pain. Local infiltration along the site of skin incision in patients having inguinal hernia repairs with general anesthesia is beneficial if the infiltration is done before the skin incision. Several studies using intravenous or epidural opiates in patients having thoracotomies and hysterectomies have also shown a preemptive effect. The use of local anesthetic with spinal and epidural anesthetics has not been shown to be preemptive. NSAIDs have not shown a preemptive effect. Further studies with larger patient groups are needed to provide definitive answers regarding preemptive analgesia.

Proper pain management not only keeps patients more comfortable, but also may decrease the risk of morbidity and mortality, thus improving utilization of health resources.

BIBLIOGRAPHY

1. Agency for Health Care Policy and Research: Acute Pain Management: Operative or Medical Procedures and Trauma. Clinical Practice Guideline. Washington, DC, U.S. Department of Health and Human Services, 1992, AHCPR publication 92-0032.
2. American Pain Society: Principles of Analgesic Use in the Treatment of Acute Pain and Cancer Pain, 3rd ed. Skokie, IL, American Pain Society, 1992.
3. American Society of Regional Anesthesia: Comprehensive Review of Pain Management. Richmond, VA, American Society of Regional Anesthesia, 1994.
4. Batra MS (ed): Adjuvants in epidural and spinal anesthesia. Anesthesiol Clin North Am 10:13–30, 1992.
5. Goresky GV, Klassen K, Waters JH: Postoperative pain management for children. Anesthesiol Clin North Am 9:801–820, 1991.
6. Hannallah RS: Regional anesthesia. Anesthesiol Clin North Am 9:837–848, 1991.
7. Lubenow TR, McCarthy RJ, Ivankovich AD: Management of acute postoperative pain. Clin Anesth Updates 3:801–820, 1992.
8. McQuay HJ: Do preemptive treatments provide better pain control? In Gebhard GF, Hammond DC, Jensen TS (eds): Proceedings of the 7th World Congress on Pain. Seattle, IASP Press, 1993, pp 709–723.
9. Sinatra RS, Hord AH, Ginsberg B, Preble LM: Acute Pain Mechanisms and Management. St. Louis, Mosby, 1992.
10. Yaster M, Nicholas E, Maxwell LG: Opioids in pediatric anesthesia and in the management of childhood pain. Anesthesiol Clin North Am 9:745–762, 1991.

82. CHRONIC PAIN

Jose M. Angel, M.D.

1. How does normal pain perception occur?

1. A noxious stimulus causes stimulation of nociceptors (pain receptors) in the receptor organ (e.g., skin).

2. This stimulation leads to activation of cells in the dorsal horn of the spinal cord and transmission of the nerve impulse to the midbrain and cortex.

3. Transmission of sensory information is modulated (inhibited or potentiated) throughout the nervous system by neurons from the midbrain and spinal cord that release endogenous opioids, catecholamines, and other neurotransmitters.

4. Peripheral nociceptor sensitization (i.e., transmission of impulses at subnormal thresholds) occurs following release of chemical mediators (e.g., prostaglandins, leukotrienes) at the site of injury.

5. Continued stimulation by peripheral nociceptors then leads to sensitization of neurons in the spinal cord. This is known as central sensitization.

2. Define chronic pain.

Chronic pain is that which persists beyond the normal duration of recovery from an acute injury or disease. Chronic pain may also be due to an ongoing or intermittent disease. Although a thorough work-up may reveal the presence of obvious pathology, sometimes no identifiable cause is found. Whether or not such a cause is determined, a chronic painful condition commonly also affects the patient's self-image and sense of well-being.

3. Discuss the causes of chronic pain.

Different chronic pain syndromes may involve different mechanisms. When there is clear pathophysiology, the source of pain is thought to be the constant stimulation of pain receptors, i.e., **chronic nociception**. This happens in chronic diseases such as rheumatoid arthritis or migraine headaches. The disease process may also cause a malfunction of the nervous system itself, i.e., **neuropathic pain**. A persistent pain state may follow peripheral nerve damage if there is neuroma formation (following nerve transection) or increased afferent activity (following nerve compression). Chronic neuropathic pain may also result from ongoing peripheral nociceptor input causing changes in spinal cord sensory neurons. These changes may involve increased spontaneous activity of spinal neurons or loss of inhibitory spinal neurons. When chronic pain does not have an obvious cause, other etiologies such as psychological causes must be considered.

4. What are the treatment goals in the management of chronic pain?

According to the American Society of Anesthesiologists practice guidelines (1997), the goals in the management of chronic pain are:

1. to optimize pain control, recognizing that a pain-free state may not be achievable
2. to minimize adverse outcomes and costs
3. to enhance functional abilities and physical and psychological well-being
4. to enhance quality of life for patients with chronic pain

5. Are psychological factors important in the diagnosis and therapy of chronic pain?

Because of the chronic nature of their symptoms, many aspects of patients' lives may have been profoundly affected. Often, there is associated depression, sleep disturbances, anger, and other psychological effects of chronic illness. There may also be general physical deterioration and weight gain or loss. In addition, secondary gain issues, such as a pending litigation or the need for social attention, may reinforce pain behavior and adversely affect recovery. Furthermore, some evidence suggests a higher incidence of prior physical or sexual abuse among chronic pain patients than in the general population. All these factors must be investigated and addressed by the staff and patient to maximize the patient's chances for improvement.

6. How are nerve blocks helpful in the treatment of chronic pain?

1. **Diagnosis:** Pain relief following a series of nerve blocks can help to identify the nerve site causing the symptoms.

2. **Therapy:** Nerve blocks eliminate or reduce pain symptoms temporarily. In certain situations (e.g., sympathetically maintained pain), nerve blocks may be used in conjunction with other therapies such as physical therapy to treat the overall pain problem.

3. **Prognosis:** Nerve blocks can help determine whether more invasive and potentially irreversible therapies, such as radiofrequency ablation, cryotherapy, neurolysis, or surgical neurectomy, are appropriate and amenable to the patient.

7. What is the prognosis for someone who develops back pain?

Most people experience back pain at some point in their lives; however, approximately 85% of patients recover within 2 weeks to 3 months with conservative therapy (e.g., nonsteroidal anti-inflammatory drugs [NSAIDs], physical therapy). No known effective therapy exists for back pain that persists for more than 3 months. The prognosis is worse with increased duration of symptoms, with lower socioeconomic status, and with pending litigation.

8. Name the possible causes of chronic back pain.

Back pain (confined to the spinal and paraspinal areas) may be due to pathologic changes in any of the midline structures, including discs, vertebrae, ligaments, paraspinal muscles, and nerves. These changes may result from congenital or degenerative disease, surgery, or trauma. For example, degenerative disease may lead to spinal stenosis, in which narrowing of the spinal canal or the spinal foramina causes impingement on the nerve roots. Intervertebral facet joint degeneration may also cause low back pain. Chronic pain may also result from muscle spasms owing to repetitive strain or poor posture.

9. How can pain of muscular origin be a factor in chronic pain in general and chronic back pain in particular?

Muscle fibers may become a source of localized chronic pain due to initial sprain or strain injuries or underlying bone or joint disease. It has been hypothesized that a muscle area with initial spasm may develop vasoconstriction and tissue hypoxia, which would then result in pain and tenderness. This leads to further spasm and continued vasoconstriction and hypoxia. Digital pressure over specific muscle areas, known as trigger points, causes worsening and spreading of the pain to other parts of the muscle. Therapy for this syndrome, known as **myofascial pain**, comprises a combination of trigger point injections and physical therapy. In chronic back pain, the lumbar paraspinal muscles and quadratus lumborum are common sites where trigger points are found.

10. Are there other causes of chronic pain of muscular origin?

Fibromyalgia presents as a diffuse bilateral muscular tenderness involving the upper and lower body and without clear trigger points. Proposed causes include intrinsic muscle cell abnormalities, changes in neurotransmitter levels, chronic sleep disruption, and changes in immune system function. Therapy with tricyclic antidepressants, muscle relaxants, physical therapy, and biofeedback and behavioral therapy may improve symptoms significantly.

11. A patient presents with unilateral leg pain associated with a corresponding bulging or protruding herniated disc and without evidence of a neurologic deficit. Discuss treatment.

These symptoms are consistent with a radicular syndrome. The patient, however, does not present with symptoms that warrant surgical intervention. In addition to NSAIDs, the patient may benefit from a trial of lumbar epidural steroids. A series of three injections is given as close as possible to the affected root, usually 2–3 weeks apart. The patient may also benefit from a trial of physical therapy in conjunction with the above.

12. Discuss the rationale behind the use of epidural steroids for the treatment of a radiculopathy (pain associated with a herniated disc).

Radiculopathy may be due to mechanical nerve root compression by a herniated disc; this is usually associated with a clear neurologic deficit and can be confirmed with neuroradiologic studies. Such a presentation may require surgical decompression. In some patients with radicular symptoms, however, no nerve root compression can be shown. Animal studies suggest that a ruptured disc can release substances (prostaglandin derivatives) that, in minute concentrations, cause nerve root irritation and pain. Steroids are known to be effective anti-inflammatory agents, and they have been shown in experimental animals to decrease transmission along C-fibers, which are involved in pain transmission. In addition, numerous clinical reports and some double-blind, randomized studies suggest that patients may benefit from epidural steroid therapy. Further studies are needed to determine fully the value of epidural steroids in the treatment of radicular pain. Nevertheless, this therapy remains a useful, low-risk alternative in the treatment of this syndrome.

13. Define sympathetically maintained pain (SMP).

SMP is a chronic pain associated with localized dysfunction of the sympathetic nervous system. SMP may, therefore, be considered a subset of neuropathic pain. The pain usually involves an extremity and is described as a burning sensation. SMP may be present in association with many other neuropathic syndromes including complex regional pain syndrome (see question 18).

14. What is the mechanism of SMP?

Several hypotheses, not mutually exclusive, have been proposed:

1. Damaged afferent fibers in peripheral nerves become hypersensitive to norepinephrine released from sympathetic fibers.

2. Damage to a peripheral nerve leads to abnormal healing with formation of synapses between sensory and sympathetic fibers (ephaptic transmission).

3. A hyperactive sympathetic system eventually leads to sensitization of spinal cord neurons.

The common pathway may be increased sensory fiber sensitivity to, or hyperactivity of, the sympathetic nervous system leading to pain perception in the absence of noxious stimuli. The α_1-receptor may, therefore, be important in this type of pain. Finally, it has also been proposed that over time changes induced in the central nervous system may become irreversible, leading to a sympathetically independent pain state.

15. Why are nerve blocks useful in the treatment of SMP?

Isolated blockade of sympathetic nerves can help diagnose whether the pain symptoms are due solely or partially to a dysfunction of the sympathetic nervous system. Moreover, if the patient's pain improves after a series of diagnostic blocks, further sympathetic blockade is indicated in combination with physical therapy. This type of nerve blockade can be achieved by injection of local anesthesia in the cervical and lumbar paravertebral areas, where the sympathetic ganglia are located. Because of the deep location of the sympathetic ganglia, performance of these blocks often requires fluoroscopic guidance to maximize success and decrease risk. The specific nerve block is chosen based on the location of the patient's pain.

Appropriate Nerve Blocks for Sympathetically Maintained Pain

PAINFUL AREA	SYMPATHETIC INNERVATION	APPROXIMATE NERVE BLOCK LOCATION
Head, neck, upper extremity	Cervicothoracic ganglia (including stellate ganglia)	Transverse process of C6 vertebra

Table continued on next page.

Appropriate Nerve Blocks for Sympathetically Maintained Pain (Continued)

PAINFUL AREA	SYMPATHETIC INNERVATION	APPROXIMATE NERVE BLOCK LOCATION
Chest	Thoracic ganglia	Thoracic paravertebral area
Upper abdomen	Splanchnic nerves, celiac plexus	T12 or L1 paravertebral area
Lower abdomen, pelvis	Hypogastric plexus	Anterolateral edge of L5–S1
Leg, lower abdomen	Lumbar plexus	Anterolateral edge of L2–L4

16. Are there other techniques available for sympathetic nerve blockade?

When pain is circumscribed to the upper or lower extremity, bretylium, which affects norepinephrine release, can be used to achieve a functional sympathetic blockade. This technique, termed **intravenous regional block**, involves the use of a tourniquet to isolate functionally the affected extremity from the rest of the body; as a result, the medication is delivered only to the affected site, which allows the concomitant use of local anesthetics and may decrease the risks and incidence of side effects. When pain involves anatomically distant areas (e.g., the upper and lower body), systemic intravenous phentolamine, an α-adrenergic blocker, can be used as a diagnostic test. A decrease in pain with either one of these drugs suggests a sympathetically maintained mechanism.

17. List other medications that are helpful in the therapy of SMP.

Drugs that produce a pharmacologic blockade of the sympathetic system, such as:
- Alpha-blocking agents, including prazosin, terazosin, and phenoxybenzamine
- Clonidine (an alpha$_2$ agonist)
- Beta-blocking agents such as propranolol

18. Define complex regional pain syndrome (CRPS).

This term has been recently introduced to describe pain involving a distal part of an extremity and that is associated with edema, skin blood flow changes, or abnormal sudomotor activity. CRPS may be considered a subset of neuropathic pain, and it is divided into type I and type II. CRPS type I refers to the syndrome previously known as reflex sympathetic dystrophy (RSD), whereas CRPS type II refers to the syndrome previously known as causalgia. This new nomenclature attempts to standardize the diagnosis of these poorly understood disorders by emphasizing the presenting signs and symptoms rather than any presumed etiology.

Complex Regional Pain Syndrome (CRPS)

CRPS describes a variety of painful conditions following injury that appear regionally and has a distal predominance of abnormal findings, exceeds in both magnitude and duration the expected clinical course of the inciting event often resulting in significant impairment of motor function, and shows variable progression over time.

CRPS type I (RSD)
- Type I is a syndrome that develops after an initiating noxious event.
- Spontaneous pain or allodynia/hyperalgesia occurs, is not limited to the territory of a single peripheral nerve, and is disproportionate to the inciting event.
- There is or has been evidence of edema, skin blood flow abnormality, or abnormal sudomotor activty in the region of the pain since the inciting event.
- This diagnosis is excluded by the existence of conditions that would otherwise account for the degree of pain and dysfunction.

CRPS type II (Causalgia)
- Type II is a syndrome that develops after a nerve injury.
- Spontaneous pain or allodynia/hyperalgesia occurs and is not necessarily limited to the territory of the injured nerve.

Table continued on next page.

Complex Regional Pain Syndrome (CRPS) (Continued)

- There is or has been evidence of edema, skin blood flow abnormality, or abnormal sudomotor activity in the region of the pain since the inciting event.
- This diagnosis is excluded by the existence of conditions that would otherwise account for the degree of pain and dysfunction.

Adapted from Stanton-Hicks M, Janig W, Hassenbusch S, et al: Reflex sympathetic dystrophy: Changing concepts and taxonomy. Pain 63:127–133, 1995.

19. How does damage to the nervous system result in chronic pain?

Nerve damage with or without significant involvement of the sympathetic nervous system may lead to chronic pain. Such neuropathic pain may stem from a number of entities, including:

Systemic diseases (diabetes mellitus, AIDS, Friedreich's ataxia)

Trauma

Chemotherapy

Surgery

Stroke

Herpes zoster

Consequently, demyelination, axonal damage, alterations in nerve transport, and neuroma formation may all be factors in chronic pain. Neuropathy may manifest as isolated loss of sensory or motor function, but occasionally it is associated with pain described as an electric shock or pins and needles, and sometimes as burning pain as seen in patients with SMP. In contrast to SMP, however, sympathetic nerve blocks are ineffective in relieving this type of neuropathic pain. Therefore, this pain has also been termed **sympathetically independent pain**.

20. How is neuropathic pain treated?

If the pain results from a single damaged nerve, therapy includes nerve blockade with local anesthetics. Steroids are also used when neuroma formation is observed. When only short-term pain relief is obtained after several of these blocks, cryotherapy or surgical neurectomy may be used to achieve more long-lasting pain relief. Concomitant therapy with anticonvulsants such as gabapentin (Neurontin) and with certain antidysrhythmics such as mexiletine may also be effective. These medications have been shown to decrease spontaneous ectopic impulse transmission while having a lesser effect on normal nerve function.

21. Are there other medications that can be used in the therapy of chronic pain?

Tricyclic antidepressants (amitriptyline, doxepin) produce analgesia at doses much lower than those required for therapy of depression. They have been shown to be superior to placebo for the treatment of several chronic pain conditions, including diabetic neuropathy, postherpetic neuralgia, migraine headaches, and possibly central pain syndrome. Anxiolytic agents (benzodiazepines) and neuroleptics (fluphenazine [Prolixin]) have also been used, but their efficacy remains unproven.

22. Can spinally administered drugs be useful in the therapy of chronic nonmalignant pain?

Spinal drug administration has the potential advantage of improved analgesia with much lower dose requirements and decreased side effects. Opioids and local anesthetics delivered into the epidural or intrathecal space have proved to be an effective therapy for patients with cancer pain who have failed to respond to more conservative therapies. In addition, epidural clonidine has also been shown to be an effective analgesic when symptoms do not improve with opioid therapy alone. Long-term use of epidural drugs, however, may be ineffective owing to the development of fibrosis. Intrathecal opioids have been used for chronic nonmalignant pain, but their use, as is the use of opioids in general for this type of pain, is controversial.

BIBLIOGRAPHY

1. Benzon HT: Epidural steroid injections. Pain Digest 1:271–280, 1992.
2. Kozin F: Reflex sympathetic dystrophy syndrome: A review. Clin Exp Rheumatol 10:401–409, 1992.
3. Magni G: The use of antidepressants in the treatment of chronic pain. Drugs 42:730–748, 1991.
4. McQuay HJ: Pharmacological treatment of neuralgic and neuropathic pain. Cancer Surv 7:141–159, 1988.
5. Nachemson AL: Newest knowledge of low back pain. Clin Orthop 279:8–20, 1992.
6. Portenoy RK: Chronic opioid therapy for nonmalignant pain: From models to practice. APS Journal 1:171–186, 1992.
7. Practice Guidelines for chronic pain management. A report by the American Society of Anesthesiologists Task Force on Pain Management, Chronic Pain Section. Anesthesiology 86:995–1004, 1997.
8. Wall PD, Melzack R (eds): Textbook of Pain, 3rd ed. New York, Churchill Livingstone, 1994.

XI. Critical Care

83. RESPIRATORY THERAPY

Mark Wilson, R.R.T.

1. Discuss the various oxygen (O_2) delivery devices.

There are three basic classifications for O_2 delivery devices.

1. **Low-flow systems** provide supplemental O_2 at flows ranging from 0 to 8 L/min. The nasal cannula is the most commonly employed low-flow device. The delivered O_2 concentration (FiO_2) can be estimated by adding 4% per liter of O_2 delivered. The nasopharynx acts as an anatomic reservoir that collects O_2 from the nasal cannula, enabling a maximum of 40% O_2 to be delivered.

2. **Reservoir systems** use a volume reservoir to accumulate oxygen during exhalation, thereby increasing the amount of oxygen for the next breath. The **simple mask** covers the patient's nose and mouth and provides an additional reservoir of O_2 beyond the nasal cannula. It is fed by small-bore O_2 tubing at a rate of no less than 6 L/min to ensure that exhaled CO_2 is flushed through the exhalation ports on each side of the mask and not rebreathed. An FiO_2 of 0.55 can be achieved at O_2 flow rates of about 10 L/min. The **nonrebreather mask** adds a reservoir bag and a series of one-way valves that direct gas flow from the bag on inhalation and allow egress of expired gases on exhalation. O_2 flows of 10–15 L/min are commonly needed to maintain reservoir bag inflation and should deliver an FiO_2 greater than 0.8. The performance of these masks greatly depends on obtaining a tight seal between the mask and the patient's face. A poorly fitting mask allows the entrainment of room air, diluting the delivered O_2 concentration.

3. **High-flow systems** must generate a minimum of 50–60 L/min to be classified as such and should be sufficient to meet or exceed a patient's inspiratory flow requirement. **Air entrainment devices**, such as the large volume nebulizer, deliver high gas flows only at low to moderate FiO_2s (0.21–0.40). Air entrainment devices are considered high flow only at O_2 concentrations at or below 40%. The higher the FiO_2 that the device is set to deliver, the less air is entrained, and the total flow to the patient is diminished. Venturi masks are also examples of high-flow entrainment devices.

Large-volume nebulizers produce a cool mist aerosol, which can help minimize inflammation, humidify the airway, and sooth the recently extubated pharynx. **Air-oxygen blending devices** provide complete inspiratory flow, over a full range of O_2 concentrations, and are considered the only true high-flow system.

2. Are pulmonary complications important in the postoperative patient?

Pulmonary complications are a major cause of morbidity following surgical procedures. In elderly patients, they are the second most important cause of postoperative death. Atelectasis, aspiration, and postoperative pneumonia are the three most common pulmonary complications following surgery.

1. **Atelectasis** results from areas of collapsed alveoli and leads to approximately 90% of postoperative febrile episodes. Atelectasis can develop in response to hypoventilation, a transient decrease in surfactant production, or airway obstruction due to secretions.

2. **Aspiration** of gastric materials with a pH level below 2.5 causes an immediate chemical pneumonitis leading to inflammation, local edema, and bronchospasm. In addition to the pH of the aspirate, the extent of injury depends on the amount aspirated. Atelectasis may also develop in response to reflex bronchospasm and aspiration of large particles.

3. Gross aspiration progressing to **pneumonia** has a 30% mortality rate owing to ensuing sepsis, adult respiratory distress syndrome (ARDS), and multiorgan failure.

3. How should pulmonary complications be treated?

Prevention is the best treatment for perioperative pulmonary complications.

The risk of pulmonary **aspiration** can be minimized by avoiding general anesthesia if the patient has recently eaten. When surgery cannot be delayed, use of cricoid pressure (the Sellick maneuver) during rapid-sequence induction is indicated and should be maintained until a cuffed endotracheal tube is inserted and proper position verified. Antacids, histamine$_2$ blockers, antiemetics, and gastrokinetic drugs are used to elevate stomach acid pH and reduce gastric fluid volume.

Atelectasis can be minimized with good pulmonary toilet. Deep breathing and coughing, and early ambulation are probably the easiest, most effective maneuvers. Incentive spirometry, postural drainage and chest physiotherapy, proper fluid and electrolyte management, and adequate pain control are helpful. Endotracheal and nasotracheal suction may also be needed.

4. What is proper tracheal suctioning technique?

Always preoxygenate with 100% O_2 for 3–5 minutes before suctioning. This should reduce the risk of the most common complications, hypoxemia, and cardiac arrhythmias; however, vagal stimulation may also produce bradycardia.

Atelectasis may develop during airway suctioning and can be minimized by four methods:

1. The outer diameter of the suction catheter should not exceed one half to two thirds of the inner diameter of the airway. A helpful formula for determining catheter size is:

$$\text{Catheter size (French)} = \frac{\text{Inner diameter (mm)} \times 3}{2}$$

2. Limit duration of suctioning to 10–15 seconds.

3. Avoid excessive negative pressure. The recommended negative pressure is –100 to –120 cm H_2O for adults, –80 to –100 cm H_2O for children, and –60 to –80 cm H_2O for infants.

4. Hyperinflation before and after suctioning may also help prevent atelectasis.

If elevated intracranial pressures are a concern, temporary hyperventilation before and after suctioning may be indicated. Sterile technique should always be used.

5. What role does positive end-expiratory pressure (PEEP) play in ventilation?

Low to moderate levels of PEEP (5–8 cm H_2O) may help resolve atelectasis and maintain alveolar patency in conditions associated with decreased pulmonary compliance or increased capillary-alveolar wall permeability. PEEP should be used as is hemodynamically tolerated.

6. How much PEEP should be used?

This often depends on the patient's hemodynamic status. If the patient has a low intravascular volume, even low levels of PEEP can impede venous return and occlude pulmonary capillary beds, resulting in a decreased cardiac output and ventilation-perfusion mismatch. Generally the best PEEP is that level which allows the lowest safe level of FiO_2 without hemodynamic compromise. In the presence of alveolar hemorrhage or fulminant pulmonary edema, temporary PEEP levels of 20 cm H_2O are commonly employed until the alveolar capillary abnormality is corrected. Rarely, situations require levels of PEEP above 20 cm H_2O. During high PEEP therapy (> 12 cm H_2O), delivered tidal volume should be adjusted to avoid injury from overdistention of normal lung units. PEEP also increases intravascular pressures, and this data should be evaluated accordingly.

7. What is a good tidal volume?

A tidal volume of 10–12 mL/kg, based on ideal body weight, is usually sufficient. Tidal volumes as low as 5 mL/kg have been used with PEEP levels of 10–15 cm H_2O in patients with ARDS. The lung with ARDS has three types of alveoli:

- **Consolidated alveoli**, which do not reexpand regardless of the amount of PEEP applied
- **Recruitable alveoli**, which respond to PEEP therapy
- **Normal functional alveoli**

Ventilating the volume-compromised lung with an otherwise acceptable tidal volume may lead to overdistention and barotrauma of normal alveoli.

8. Define postextubation stridor. How should postextubation stridor be treated?

Stridor is a high-pitched, coarse, musical sound associated with laryngeal inflammation and edema, occurring during inspiration. Stridor is associated with increased airway resistance and work of breathing.

Aerosolized 2.25% racemic epinephrine reduces laryngeal edema via mucosal vasoconstriction. A cool mist aerosol may also aid in reducing laryngeal inflammation. Owing to its low density, a helium and O_2 gas mixture (heliox) may enhance spontaneous ventilation but may not be tolerated if the patient has a high O_2 requirement. The most common heliox mixture is 70% helium and 30% O_2. Should a stridulous patient require intubation, reextubation becomes problematic. The risk for stridor exists for up to 24 hours postextubation. Steroid therapy for acute stridor is of questionable efficacy secondary to the delayed onset of action.

9. What is the most effective modality for delivering aerosolized bronchodilators to the mechanically ventilated patient?

The alternatives are the small volume nebulizer and the metered-dose inhaler (MDI). An MDI with an in-line spacer/reservoir has been shown to produce better particle deposition at the alveolar level and deliver a more accurate dose in half the time, with one-third the cost of the jet nebulizer system.

10. Define an in-line spacer/reservoir.

An in-line spacer is a device that adapts to the ventilator tubing and is inserted into the inspiratory limb. This spacer prevents "rain out" of the aerosolized bronchodilator, enhancing delivery of the active agent into the tracheobronchial tree. The MDI should be actuated just before the inspiratory phase of ventilation, preferably with a slow deep breath and inspiratory pause.

11. How much bronchodilator therapy should be given with an MDI?

Manufacturers recommend 2–4 puffs every 3–4 hours. Clinically the dose should be titrated to effect. For example: Administer 5 puffs (1 puff per breath), wait 5 minutes, and repeat as needed.

It is important to shake the MDI between puffs to remix the medication and ensure proper dosing for each actuation.

12. Can principles of nebulizer therapy be useful in providing anesthesia of the airway?

Lidocaine (4%), administered via small volume nebulizer and aerosol mask, can adequately anesthetize the upper airway, facilitating awake intubation or bronchoscopy. Systemic uptake of aerosolized lidocaine is relatively small, less than 1.5 µg/ml, with a therapeutic level of 1.0–6.0 µg/ml.

13. What is the oxyhemoglobin dissociation curve?

It is a sigmoidal curve that describes the nonlinear binding reaction or affinity of O_2 for hemoglobin. The upper, relatively flat part of the curve demonstrates that under normal conditions, minor fluctuations in PO_2 have little effect on hemoglobin saturation. When the PO_2 decreases to below 60 mmHg (as in the systemic capillary bed), the slope of the curve steepens, and hemoglobin's affinity for O_2 is decreased, allowing greater amounts of O_2 to be unloaded at the tissue level.

14. What is the P-50?

The P-50 is that O_2 tension associated with 50% hemoglobin saturation. Its utility is in describing the position of the curve and for comparing the O_2-binding characteristics of differing hemoglobin species. A normal P-50 is about 26.6 (at a pH of 7.40, $PaCO_2$ 40 mmHg, and 37°C). The lower the P-50, the greater the affinity of hemoglobin for O_2.

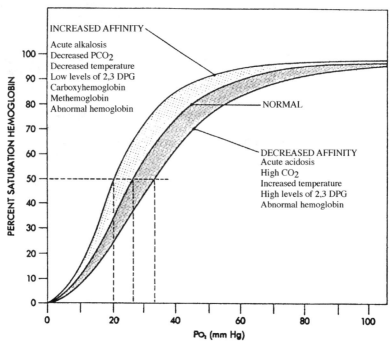

Oxyhemoglobin dissociation curve. The normal P-50 at 26.6, how its position changes with left or right shifts of the O_2 dissociation curve, and factors that affect the position of the curve. (From Egan DF: Fundamentals of Respiratory Care, 6th ed. St. Louis, Mosby, 1995, with permission.)

15. Discuss static (plateau) and dynamic (peak inspiratory) pressures and their significance.

Dynamic pressure is a reflection of the amount of pressure necessary to deliver a given volume and is affected by frictional resistance. The two major components of frictional resistance are tissue and airway resistance. The tissue component represents the amount of energy required to displace the muscle and organs of the thorax and abdomen, to allow for lung expansion. Tissue resistance accounts for about 20% of total frictional resistance. The remaining 80% is created by the resistance of air moving through the anatomic airways and the artificial ventilator circuit. The effect that frictional resistance has on dynamic pressure is greatly influenced by the flow characteristics of the cycling ventilator. The higher the inspiratory flow, the more turbulent the air becomes, and the more resistance it encounters.

Static pressure is a measurement taken at a point of no airflow. It is the pressure recorded during an inspiratory breath hold, or "plateau" maneuver, and represents the impedance to lung inflation caused by elastic forces. Lung compliance must be measured under static conditions to eliminate the factor of dynamic tissue and airway resistance.

Significance

Although dynamic pressure measurements are important in the detection of acute airway changes such as mucus accumulation, pneumothorax, bronchospasm, and inadvertent disconnection, they should not be the sole determinant of the patient's compliance and risk for lung injury. Situations may arise that demand high peak inspiratory flow rates, so higher dynamic pressures are to be expected from increased tubing and conducting airways resistance. Static pressures of 30–35 cm H_2O and dynamic pressures of 35–40 cm H_2O suggest a high risk for lung injury.

BIBLIOGRAPHY

1. Burton GG, Hodgkin JE, Ward JJ, et al: Respiratory Care: A Guide to Clinical Practice, 4th ed. Philadelphia, Lippincott Williams & Wilkins, 1997.
2. Darmon JY, Rauss A, Dreyfuss D, et al: Evaluation of risk factors for laryngeal edema after tracheal extubation in adults and its prevention by dexamethasone. Anesthesiology 77:245–251, 1992.
3. Fuller HD, Dolovich MB, Turpie FH, et al: Efficiency of bronchodilator aerosol delivery to the lungs from the metered dose inhaler in mechanically ventilated patients. Chest 105:214–218, 1994.
4. Kiiski R, Takala J, Kari A, et al: Effect of tidal volume on gas exchange and oxygen transport in the adult respiratory distress syndrome. Am Rev Respir Dis 146:1131–1135, 1992.
5. Macdonnell SPJ, Timmins AC, Watson JD: Adrenaline administered via a nebulizer in adult patients with upper airway obstruction. Anesthesia 50:35–36, 1995.
6. Rau JL, Harwood RJ, Groff JL: Evaluation of a reservoir device for metered dose bronchodilator delivery to intubated adults. Chest 102:924–930, 1992.
7. Scanlon CL, Wilkins RL, Stoller JK: Egan's Fundamentals of Respiratory Care, 7th ed. St. Louis, Mosby, 1998.

84. PULMONARY FUNCTION TESTING AND INTERPRETATION

Theresa L. Kinnard, M.D., and William V. Kinnard, M.D.

1. What are pulmonary function tests?

The term pulmonary function test (PFT) refers to a standardized measurement of a patient's airflow (spirometry), lung volumes, and diffusing capacity for inspired carbon monoxide (DLCO). These values are always reported as a percentage of a predicted normal value, which is calculated based on the age and height of the patient. Used in combination with the history, physical exam, blood gas analysis, and chest radiograph, PFTs facilitate the classification of respiratory disease into obstructive, restrictive, or mixed disorders.

2. When are PFTs indicated as part of the preoperative evaluation?

The primary goal of preoperative pulmonary function testing is to identify a group of patients at either high or prohibitive risk of postoperative pulmonary complications in whom institution of aggressive therapy before and/or after surgery may decrease complications, or in whom surgery should be avoided entirely. Risk factors for pulmonary complications include (1) age > 70 years; (2) obesity; (3) upper abdominal or thoracic surgery; (4) history of lung disease; (5) greater than 20-pack/year history of smoking; and (6) resection of an anterior mediastinal mass.

3. What factors need to be taken into consideration before interpreting PFT results?

PFTs are standardized according to predicted values based on tests of healthy individuals. The predicted values vary according to age, height, gender, and ethnicity. For example, several studies have demonstrated that vital capacity and total lung capacity are 13–15% lower in blacks than in whites. Reliable testing requires patient cooperation and understanding as well as a skilled technician.

4. What are the subdivisions of lung volumes and capacities?

The tidal volume (V_T) is the volume of air inhaled and exhaled with each breath during normal breathing. Inspiratory reserve volume (IRV) is the volume of air that can be maximally inhaled beyond a normal V_T, expiratory reserve volume (ERV) is the maximal volume of air that can be exhaled beyond a normal V_T, and residual volume (RV) is the volume of air that remains in the lung after maximal expiration. By definition, lung capacity is composed of two or more lung volumes, including total lung capacity (TLC), vital capacity (VC), inspiratory capacity (IC), and functional residual capacity (FRC).

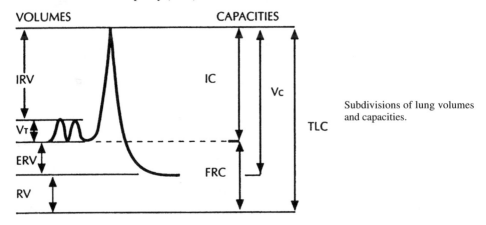

Subdivisions of lung volumes and capacities.

5. What techniques are used in the determination of lung volumes?

The determination of FRC is the cornerstone for the measurement of the remainder of the lung volumes. The FRC is the volume of air in the lung at the end of a normal expiration and is composed of RV and ERV. The FRC can be measured by three different techniques: (1) helium dilution, (2) nitrogen washout, and (3) body plethysmography. Plethysmography is more accurate for determining FRC in patients with obstructive airway disease and is considered the approach of choice. It involves a direct application of Boyle's law, which states that the volume of gas in a closed space varies inversely with the pressure to which it is subjected. All measurements of FRC, if performed correctly, are independent of patient effort.

6. What information is obtained from spirometry?

Spirometry provides timed measurements of expired volumes from the lung and forms the foundation of pulmonary function testing. With automated equipment it is possible to interpret more than 15 different measurements from spiromety alone. Forced vital capacity (FVC), forced expiratory volume in one second (FEV_1), FEV_1/FVC ratio, and flow between 25% and 75% of the FVC (MMF_{25-75}) are the most clinically helpful indices obtained from spirometry.

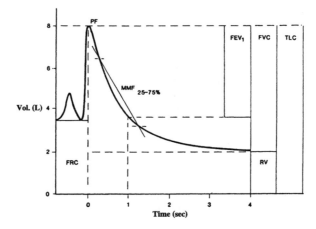

Spirogram. (Adapted from Harrison RA: Respiratory function and anesthesia. In Barash PG, Cullen BF, Stoelting RK (eds): Clinical Anesthesia. Philadelphia, J.B. Lippincott, 1989, pp 877–904.)

7. What information is not obtained from spirometry?

Spirometry may demonstrate airflow limitation but does not determine its cause (e.g., airway obstruction vs. decreased elastic recoil of the alveolus vs. decreased expiratory muscle activity). Nor does it provide information about lung volumes and capacities, which require the application of different techniques of measurement.

8. What is maximum voluntary ventilation?

Maximal voluntary ventilation (MVV) or maximal breathing capacity (MBC) is an extremely effort-dependent spirometric test that measures the maximal volume of air that a patient can expire in 1 minute by voluntary effort. This is a nonspecific test that evaluates a variety of factors important to lung function (e.g., patient motivation, strength, and endurance as well as pulmonary mechanics). A decrease in MMV has been shown to predict increased morbidity and mortality in patients undergoing thoracic surgery.

9. What is the diffusing capacity for DLCO?

The DLCO is the rate of uptake of carbon monoxide (CO) per driving pressure of alveolar CO. It is a function of both membrane diffusing capacity and pulmonary vascular components and thus is a reflection of functioning alveolar capillary units. CO is used as a nonphysiologic gas because of its affinity for hemoglobin and because it reflects the diffusing capacity of the physiologic gases (oxygen and carbon dioxide). This test has been used as an indicator of suitability for pulmonary resection and as a predictor of postoperative pulmonary morbidity.

10. What disease states cause a decrease in DLCO?

As implied above, any disease process that compromises the alveolar capillary unit may cause a decrease in DLCO. Three major types of pulmonary disorders cause a decrease in DLCO: (1) obstructive airway disease, (2) interstitial lung disease, and (3) pulmonary vascular disease. Differential diagnosis must take into account other clinical, physiologic, and radiographic findings.

11. What disease states cause an increase in DLCO?

In general, conditions that cause a relative increase in the amount of hemoglobin in the lung may result in an increased DLCO. Congestive heart failure, asthma, and diffuse pulmonary hemorrhage are the most common causes of an increased DLCO. A perforated tympanic membrane may cause an artifactually high DLCO by permitting an escape of CO by a nonpulmonary route.

12. What PFT abnormalities are present in patients with obstructive airway disease?

Obstructive airway diseases, which include asthma, chronic bronchitis, emphysema, cystic fibrosis, and bronchiolitis, exhibit diminished expiratory airflow. These conditions involve airways anatomically distal to the carina. The FEV_1, FEV_1/FVC ratio, and the forced expiratory flow at 25–75% of FVC (FEF_{25-75}) are decreased below normal predicted values. A decreased FEF_{25-75} reflects collapse of the small airways and is a sensitive indicator of early airway obstruction. The FVC may be normal or decreased due to respiratory muscle weakness, or dynamic airway collapse with subsequent air trapping. The table below grades the severity of obstruction based on the FEV_1/FVC ratio.

Severity of Obstructive and Restrictive Airway Diseases as Measured by FEV_1/FVC and TLC

	NORMAL	MILD	MODERATE	SEVERE
FEV_1/FVC	> 73%	61–73%	51–60%	< 50%
TLC	> 81%	66–80%	51–65%	< 50%

13. What PFT abnormalities are present in patients with restrictive lung disease?

The characteristic pattern in patients with restrictive pulmonary disease is a reduction in lung volumes, particularly TLC and VC, whereas air flow rates can be normal or increased. Disorders that result in decreased lung volumes include abnormal chest cage configuration, respiratory muscle weakness, loss of alveolar air space (pulmonary fibrosis, pneumonia), and encroachment of the lung space by disorders of the pleural cavity (effusion, tumor).

14. What is a flow-volume loop and what information does it provide?

The flow-volume loop can be constructed from routine clinical spirometric data and aids in the anatomic localization of airway obstruction. Forced expiratory and inspiratory flow at 50% of FVC (FEF_{50} and FIF_{50}) are shown in the following figure. Note that expiratory flow is represented above the x axis, whereas inspiratory flow is represented below the axis. In a normal flow-volume loop the FEF_{50}/FIF_{50} ratio is 1.0.

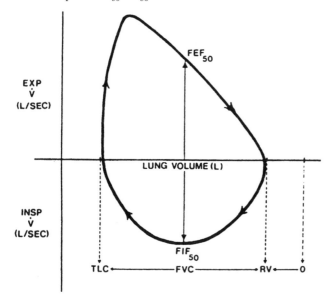

Idealized flow-volume loop. (Flow in l/sec is abbreviated v̇.) (From Harrison RA: Respiratory function and anesthesia. In Barash PG, Cullen BF, Stoelting RK (eds): Clinical Anesthesia. Philadelphia, J.B. Lippincott, 1989, pp 877–904, with permission.)

15. What are the characteristic patterns of the flow-volume loop in a fixed airway obstruction, variable extrathoracic obstruction, and intrathoracic obstruction?

Upper airway lesions are categorized as fixed when there is a plateau during both inspiration and expiration of the flow-volume loop (tracheal stenosis). The FEF_{50}/FIF_{50} ratio remains unchanged. An extrathoracic obstruction occurs when the lesion (tumor) is located above the sternal notch and is characterized by a flattening of the flow-volume loop during inspiration. The flattening of the loop represents no further increase in airflow because the mass causes airway collapse. The FEF_{50}/FIF_{50} ratio is > 1. An intrathoracic obstruction is characterized by a flattening of the expiratory loop of a flow-volume loop, and the FEF_{50}/FIF_{50} ratio is < 1. The lesion causes airway collapse during expiration. (See Figure, next page.)

16. How can flow-volume loops be utilized in the preoperative assessment of patients with an anterior mediastinal mass scheduled for surgical resection?

General anesthesia in patients with an anterior mediastinal mass (lymphoma, thymoma, thyroid mass) may lead to a potentially catastrophic situation. After induction of anesthesia (conversion from negative-pressure to positive-pressure ventilation), the mass may compress the vena cava, pulmonary vessels, heart, or tracheobronchial tree, producing acute cardiovascular collapse. The preoperative evaluation of a flow-volume loop in different positions (sitting and supine) helps to assess potentially obstructive lesions of the airway and to identify patients in whom alternative management may be indicated.

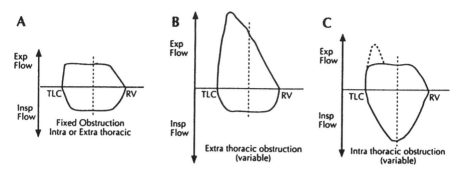

Flow-volume loops in a fixed, extrathoracic, and intrathoracic airway obstruction. (The hash marks represent flow at 50% of vital capacity.) (From Kryger M, Bode F, Antic R, et al: Diagnosis of obstruction of the upper and central airways. Am J Med 61:85–93, 1976, with permission.)

17. What are the effects of surgery and anesthesia on pulmonary function?

All patients undergoing surgery and general anesthesia exhibit changes in pulmonary function that promote the development of postoperative pulmonary complications. Such changes, which are more significant in patients undergoing upper abdominal and thoracic procedures, include a decrease in lung volumes, particularly VC and FRC. The VC is reduced to approximately 40% of preoperative values and remains depressed for at least 10–14 days after open cholecystectomy. The FRC has been shown to decrease approximately 10–16 hours after upper abdominal surgery and gradually returns to normal by 7–10 days. The normal pattern of ventilation is also altered, with decreased sigh breaths and decreased clearance of secretions.

18. Why is the postoperative decrease in FRC important?

The decrease in FRC is important in terms of its relationship to closing volume (CV)—the volume of the lung at which small airways close. When the CV is greater than FRC, small airway collapse during normal tidal volume breathing leads to atelectasis and hypoxemia.

19. What PFT values predict increased perioperative pulmonary complications?

Pulmonary Function Criteria Suggesting Increased Risk for Abdominal and Thoracic Surgery

	ABDOMINAL	THORACIC
FVC	< 70% predicted	< 70% predicted or < 1.7 L
FEV_1	< 70% predicted	< 2 L*, < I L†, < 0.6 L‡
FEV_1/FVC	< 65%	< 35%
MVV	< 50% predicted	< 50% predicted or < 28 L/min
RV		< 47% predicted
DLCO		< 50%
VO_2		< 15 ml/kg/min

* Pneumonectomy.   † Lobectomy.   ‡ Segmentectomy.
Adapted from Gass GD, Olsen GN: Preoperative pulmonary function testing to predict postoperative morbidity and mortality. Chest 89:127–135, 1986, with permission.

20. What is VO_{2max}? How is it used to predict postoperative pulmonary complications?

The VO_{2max} is the maximal oxygen consumption that a patient attains during exercise. It reflects the patient's pulmonary, cardiac, and peripheral vascular function as well as motivation and endurance. It has been used to predict postoperative pulmonary complications after lung resection. In a study by Bechard and Wetstein, 50 patients scheduled for lung resection who had an $FEV_1 > 1.7$ L underwent exercise testing. There was no morbidity or mortality in patients who could consume more than 20 ml/kg/min of oxygen. The group that could not exercise to 10 ml/kg/min had a 29% mortality rate and a 43% morbidity rate. The authors concluded that oxygen consumption should be used preoperatively in patients scheduled for lung resection.

21. Are there absolute values of specific pulmonary function tests below which the risk of surgery is prohibitive?

Multiple factors are highly predictive of postoperative pulmonary complications, but there is no preoperative pulmonary function test result that absolutely contraindicates surgery. It is ultimately the decision of the surgeon, anesthesiologist, and patient whether the risk of pulmonary complications outweighs the benefits of a surgical procedure.

BIBLIOGRAPHY

1. Bechard D, Wetstein L: Assessment of exercise oxygen consumption as preoperative criterion for lung resection. Ann Thorac Surg 44:344–349, 1987.
2. Boysen PG, Block AJ, Moulder PV: Relationship between preoperative pulmonary function tests and complications after thoracotomy. Surg Gynecol Obstet 152:813–815, 1981.
3. Craig DB: Postoperative recovery of pulmonary function. Anesth Analg 60:46–52, 1981.
4. Eisenkraft JB, Cohen E, Neustein SM: Anesthesia for thoracic surgery. In Barash PG, Cullen BF, Stoelting RK (eds): Clinical Anesthesia, 3rd ed. Philadelphia, Lippincott Williams & Wilkins, 1997.
5. Gass GD, Olsen GN: Preoperative pulmonary function testing to predict postoperative morbidity and mortality. Chest 89:127–135, 1986.
6. Kryger M, Bode F, Antic R, et al: Diagnosis of obstruction of the upper and central airways. Am J Med 61:85–93, 1976.
7. Mahler DA, Horowitz MB: Pulmonary function testing. In Bone RC (ed): Pulmonary and Critical Care Medicine. St. Louis, Mosby, 1994, pp 1–19.
8. Schoenberg JB, Beck GJ, Bouhuys A: Growth and decay of pulmonary function in healthy blacks and whites. Respir Physiol 33:367–393, 1978.
9. Stock MC: Respiratory function in anesthesia. In Barash PG, Cullen BF, Stoelting RK (eds): Clinical Anesthesia, 3rd ed. Philadelphia, Lippincott Williams & Wilkins, 1997.
10. Stoller JK, Holden DH, Matthay MA: Preoperative evaluation. In Bone RC (ed): Pulmonary and Critical Care Medicine. St. Louis, Mosby, 1994, pp 1–17.
11. Tisi GM: Preoperative evaluation of pulmonary function. Am Rev Respir Dis 119:293–310,1979.

85. MODES OF MECHANICAL VENTILATION

Stuart G. Rosenberg, M.D.

1. What is mechanical ventilation?

Mechanical ventilation (MV) is a form of artificial ventilation that performs the task normally done by the respiratory muscles. It allows oxygenation and ventilation (carbon dioxide removal) of the patient. The two major types of MV are positive-pressure ventilation and negative-pressure ventilation. Positive-pressure ventilation (PPV) may be invasive (via an endotracheal tube) or noninvasive (via face mask). It also may be volume- or pressure-cycled (see question 4). The many different modes of PPV include controlled mechanical ventilation (CMV), assist-control ventilation (ACV), intermittent mandatory ventilation (IMV), synchronized IMV (SIMV), pressure-controlled ventilation (PCV), pressure-support ventilation (PSV), inverse ratio ventilation (IRV), pressure-release ventilation (PRV), and high-frequency modes.

It is important to distinguish endotracheal intubation from MV as one does not necessarily imply the other. For example, a patient may require endotracheal intubation for airway protection and still be able to breathe spontaneously through the endotracheal tube without the need for MV.

2. Why might a patient require MV?

MV may be indicated in many disorders. In many cases
clear-cut. The main reasons for instituting MV are the patient's
and the loss of adequate alveolar ventilation, which may be seco
of the pulmonary parenchyma, such as pneumonia or pulmonary ea
indirectly compromises pulmonary function, such as sepsis or centra
tion. In addition, administration of a general anesthetic frequently req
agents are respiratory depressants, and neuromuscular blocking drugs cau
piratory muscles. The principal goal of MV in the setting of respiratory fai
exchange while the underlying disease process is reversed.

3. Describe noninvasive ventilation and when it may be appropriate.

Noninvasive ventilation may be either a negative- or positive-pressure mode. Negative-pressure ventilation (usually via an iron lung or cuirass ventilator) is occasionally used in patients with neuromuscular disorders or chronic fatigue of the diaphragm due to chronic obstructive lung disease (COLD). The ventilator shell encompasses the body below the neck, and a negative pressure is generated, creating a gradient for flow of gas from the upper airway into the lungs. Exhalation is passive. This mode of ventilation avoids the need for endotracheal intubation and its attendant problems. The upper airway must be clear, and it is left unprotected from aspiration. Hypotension may occur from splanchnic pooling of blood.

Noninvasive ventilation using positive pressure (NIPPV) can be delivered in various ways, including mask continuous positive airway pressure (CPAP), mask bilevel positive airway pressure (bi-PAP), mask PSV, or combinations of these. This mode of ventilation may be used to avoid endotracheal intubation in certain subgroups of patients, such as those who are terminally ill or have certain types of respiratory failure (e.g., hypercapnic COLD exacerbation). In terminally ill patients with respiratory compromise, NIPPV has been shown to be a safe, effective, and more comfortable means of ventilatory support. It allows the patient to maintain autonomy and verbal communication and is simpler and less stressful to terminate if indicated.

4. Describe CMV, ACV, and IMV, the most commonly used modes of PPV.

These three modes of conventional volume-cycled ventilation are in essence three different ways of triggering the ventilator. With CMV, the patient is entirely under the control of the preset tidal volume (V_T) and respiratory frequency (f). CMV is used in patients making no respiratory effort at all, e.g., those with respiratory depression or pharmacologically induced paralysis, as seen under general anesthesia. The ACV mode allows the patient to trigger a breath (hence, the element of assist) so that a preset tidal volume is delivered. If the patient becomes bradypneic or apneic for any reason, the ventilator provides a back-up control mode. IMV, which originally was developed as a weaning tool, allows the patient to breathe spontaneously through the ventilator circuit. The ventilator intermittently delivers positive-pressure breaths based on a preset V_T and f. SIMV prevents the ventilator from delivering a mechanical breath during a spontaneous breath.

The debate over the advantages and disadvantages of ACV and IMV continues to rage. Theoretically, IMV may allow a decreased mean airway pressure (Paw) and possibly less barotrauma, because not every breath is a positive-pressure breath. It also may be easier to synchronize the patient with the ventilator in the IMV mode. ACV probably causes respiratory alkalosis more often, because the patient receives a full V_T with every breath, even when tachypneic. Either mode requires some work of breathing on the patient's part (usually more with IMV). It may be advantageous initially to relieve as much of the work as possible in patients with acute respiratory failure (ARF) while allowing the underlying disease process to reverse itself. This usually requires sedation, occasionally muscle paralysis, and CMV.

5. What are the initial ventilator settings in ARF? What are the goals of these settings?

Most patients with ARF require full ventilatory support. The basic goals are to preserve arterial oxygen saturation and to prevent ventilator-induced complications. Complications may arise

...y pressures or persistently high inspired concentrations of oxygen (FiO_2) (see

...t commonly one begins with the **ACV mode**, which ensures delivery of a preset volume. ...sure-cycled modes are, however, becoming more popular.

An FiO_2 needs to be chosen. One usually starts at 1.0 and titrates downward as tolerated. Prolonged exposure to high FiO_2 values (> 60–70%) may lead to oxygen toxicity.

Tidal volume is based on body weight and the pathophysiology of lung injury. Currently, volumes in the range of 10–12 ml/kg body weight are acceptable. Conditions such as acute respiratory distress syndrome (ARDS), however, decrease the volume of the lung available for ventilation. Because large pressures or volumes may exacerbate the underlying lung injury, smaller volumes are chosen, in the range of 6–10 ml/kg body weight.

A **respiratory rate** (f) is chosen, usually in the range of 10–20 breaths per minute (bpm). Patients with high minute volume requirements may need a rate in the 20s. Carbon dioxide (CO_2) elimination does not improve significantly with rates > 25, and rates > 30 predispose to gas trapping secondary to abbreviated expiratory times.

Positive end-expiratory pressure (PEEP; see question 6) is typically chosen in small amounts initially (e.g., 5 cm H_2O) and may be titrated upward if necessary to improve oxygenation. A small amount of PEEP in most cases of acute lung injury helps to maintain the patency of recruitable alveoli. Recent data show that a small amount of PEEP avoids the alveolar shear forces that result from the repetitive opening and closing of alveoli. Such shear forces may aggravate lung injury.

Flow rate, pattern, and inspiratory-to-expiratory (I:E) ratio are frequently set by the respiratory therapist, but they should be understood also by the intensivist. The peak flow rate determines the maximal inspiratory flow rate delivered by the ventilator during the inspiratory cycle. An initial flow rate of 50–80 L/min is usually satisfactory. The I:E ratio is determined by the minute ventilation and flow rate; that is, inspiratory time is determined by flow and V_T, whereas expiratory time is determined by flow and frequency. An I:E of 1:2 to 1:3 is reasonable in most situations; however, patients with COLD may require even longer expiratory times to allow adequate exhalation of gases. This can be accomplished by increasing flow, thus decreasing the I:E ratio. High flow rates, however, may increase airway pressures and worsen gas distribution in some cases. Slower flow rates may reduce airway pressures and improve gas distribution by increasing the I:E ratio. An increased (or "reversed," as discussed below) I:E ratio increases mean Paw but also may increase cardiovascular side effects. The shortened expiratory time is not well tolerated in obstructive airways disease. The flow pattern or waveform also has a small effect on ventilation. A constant flow pattern (square wave) provides flow at the value selected. The descending or ramp waveform may increase airway pressures yet improve gas distribution. Inspiratory hold, expiratory retard, and periodic sigh also may be chosen.

6. Explain PEEP. How is optimal PEEP determined?

PEEP is a supplement to many of the modes of ventilation whereby the airway pressure at end expiration remains above ambient pressure. PEEP tends to prevent alveolar collapse and to recruit a portion of atelectatic alveoli in acute lung injury states. Functional residual capacity (FRC) and oxygenation are increased. PEEP is applied initially at approximately 5 cm H_2O and increased in small increments to a total of 15–20 cm H_2O. High levels of PEEP may have a deleterious effect on cardiac output (see question 8). Optimal PEEP strives for the best arterial oxygenation, with the least decrement in cardiac output, and maintenance of acceptable airway pressures. Optimal PEEP is actually the point of maximal alveolar recruitment, which can be assessed quickly at the bedside by increasing PEEP to the point of lung inflation at which compliance (see question 14) begins to decrease. One simply watches the airway pressure after each incremental increase in PEEP. The airway pressure should rise only by the amount of PEEP dialed in. When the pressure begins to rise more than the amount of PEEP dialed in, the alveoli are overdistended and the point of maximal alveolar recruitment has been exceeded. Continuous positive airway pressure (CPAP) is a form of PEEP delivered throughout the respiratory cycle during spontaneous breathing.

7. What is intrinsic or auto-PEEP?

As first described by Pepe and Marini in 1982, intrinsic PEEP (PEEPi) is the development of positive pressure and continued flow within the alveoli at end expiration without application of extrinsic PEEP (PEEPe). Normally the lung volume at end expiration (FRC) is determined by the opposing forces of elastic recoil and the chest wall. These forces are normally balanced so that there is no flow or pressure gradient at end expiration. PEEPi occurs by two major mechanisms. In healthy lungs during MV, if the respiratory f is too rapid or the E time too short, there is not enough time for full exhalation before the next breath is delivered. This results in stacking of breaths and generation of positive airway pressure at end exhalation. Therefore, patients with high minute volume requirements (e.g., sepsis, trauma) or patients receiving high I:E ratios are at risk for PEEPi. Small-diameter endotracheal tubes also may limit exhalation and contribute to PEEPi. The other major mechanism for development of PEEPi is related to the underlying pulmonary pathology. Patients with increased airway resistance and pulmonary compliance (e.g., asthma, COLD) are at high risk for PEEPi. Such patients have difficulty in exhaling gas because of airway obstruction and are prone to development of PEEPi during spontaneous ventilation as well as MV. PEEPi has the same side effects as PEEPe, but it requires more vigilance. As ventilators are normally vented to ambient pressure, the only way to detect and measure PEEPi is to occlude the expiratory port at end expiration while monitoring airway pressure. This should be done routinely in all patients receiving MV, especially those at high risk. Treatment is based on etiology. Manipulating ventilator parameters (such as decreasing f or increasing inspiratory flow to decrease I:E) may allow time for full exhalation. Treatment of the underlying disease process (e.g., bronchodilators) also helps. PEEPe has been used with some benefit to relieve air trapping in patients with expiratory flow limitation from obstructive airways disease. This may work by theoretically stenting open airways to allow full exhalation. As PEEPe approaches PEEPi, however, severe hemodynamic and gas exchange compromise may occur.

8. What are the side effects of PEEPe and PEEPi?

1. Barotrauma may occur from overdistention of alveoli.

2. Cardiac output may be decreased by several mechanisms. PEEP increases intrathoracic pressure, leading to an increase in transmural right atrial pressure and a decrease in venous return. PEEP also tends to increase pulmonary artery pressure, which impedes right ventricular output. Dilation of the right ventricle may cause bowing of the interventricular septum into the left ventricle, thus impairing filling of the left ventricle and contributing to decreased cardiac output. Hypotension ensues, especially if the patient is hypovolemic. In a common scenario, an emergency endotracheal intubation is performed in a patient with COLD and respiratory failure. Such patients usually have been in distress for several days with decreased oral intake and increased insensible fluid losses. On intubation the patient is vigorously bagged to improve oxygenation and ventilation. Auto-PEEP rapidly worsens, and in the face of hypovolemia severe hypotension ensues. Treatment (if prevention fails) consists of rapid volume infusion, allowing a longer expiratory phase, and resolution of bronchospasm.

3. Incorrect interpretation of cardiac filling pressures (e.g., central venous pressure or pulmonary artery occlusion pressure) also may occur with PEEP. Pressure transmitted from the alveolus to the pulmonary vasculature may falsely elevate the readings. The more compliant the lung, the greater the pressure that is transmitted. A rule of thumb is to subtract one-half of the PEEP applied over five from the pulmonary artery occlusion pressure (PAOP).

4. Overdistention of alveoli from excessive PEEP decreases blood flow to these areas, increasing dead space (Vd/V_T).

5. Work of breathing may be increased with PEEP (with positive-pressure breathing that requires the patient to trigger the ventilator or with spontaneous breathing on the ventilator), because the patient is required to generate a larger negative pressure to trigger flow from the ventilator.

6. Other potential side effects of PEEP include an increase in intracranial pressure (ICP) and fluid retention.

9. Describe pressure-limited types of ventilation.

The ability to deliver pressure-limited breaths—either triggered by the patient (pressure support ventilation) or the ventilator (pressure-controlled ventilation)—has been added to most adult ventilators in recent years. Pressure-limited modes are used routinely in neonatal ventilation. With pressure support ventilation (PSV) the patient initiates the breath, causing the ventilator to deliver a preset pressure, augmenting the V_T. The positive-pressure portion of the breath is cycled off after the inspiratory flow drops to a predetermined level, typically 25% of its peak value. Note that the pressure is sustained until the flow tapers. This flow characteristic readily meets the patient's demands and results in greater comfort. This spontaneous mode of ventilation can be used to decrease work of breathing by overcoming resistance in the breathing circuit and augmenting V_T in marginal patients. It may be combined with IMV or used alone. PEEP or CPAP may be added. PSV also has been shown to expedite weaning from MV.

In pressure-controlled ventilation (PCV) the patient receives a positive-pressure breath that ceases when a preset maximal pressure is reached. Volume varies, depending on airway resistance and pulmonary compliance. PCV may be used alone or combined with other techniques such as IRV (see question 10). The inherent flow characteristics of PCV (high initial flow followed by a decelerating wave pattern) seem to improve compliance and gas distribution. It has been suggested that PCV may be used safely and is well tolerated as an initial mode of ventilation in patients with acute hypoxic respiratory failure. Pressure-control modes with volume-guarantee ventilators are beginning to appear on the market.

10. Does inverse ratio ventilation have a role in patient ventilation?

IRV may have some benefit in severe ARDS. It is a controversial mode of ventilation in which the I time is extended beyond the usual maximum of 50% of the respiratory cycle in a pressure- or volume-cycled mode. As the I time is prolonged, the I:E ratio inverts (e.g., 1:1, 1.5:1, 2:1, 3:1). Most intensivists do not recommend going beyond 2:1 because of the increasing risks of hemodynamic compromise and barotrauma. Oxygenation has been shown to improve by lengthening I time, although no prospective randomized trials have been done. The mechanism for improvement in oxygenation may be related to several factors: increase in mean Paw (without an increase in peak Paw), recruitment of additional alveoli with longer opening time constants due to slower inspiratory flow, and development of PEEPi. The slower inspiratory flow also may decrease the development of volutrauma or barotrauma. This technique, however, may be counterproductive in patients with airflow obstruction (e.g., COLD or asthma) by worsening PEEPi. Because IRV may be an uncomfortable mode of ventilation for patients, deep sedation or muscle paralysis may be required. In summary, although of unproven benefit, IRV may have a role in advanced ARDS.

11. Does MV cause problems in organ systems other than the cardiopulmonary system?

Yes. Increased intrathoracic pressure may cause or contribute to increased ICP. Sinusitis may result from prolonged nasotracheal intubation. Nosocomial pneumonia is always a concern in ventilated patients. Gastrointestinal bleeding is common from stress ulceration, and prophylaxis should be initiated. Water and salt retention may result from increased vasopressin secretion and decreased levels of atrial natriuretic compound. Bedridden, critically ill patients are always at risk for thromboembolic phenomena; prophylaxis is thus appropriate. Many patients receiving MV require sedation and occasionally muscle paralysis (see question 17).

12. What is controlled hypoventilation with permissive hypercapnia?

Controlled hypoventilation is a method used in patients requiring MV to prevent overinflation of alveoli and possible damage to the alveolar-capillary membrane. Recent data indicate that high levels of volume and pressure may induce or potentiate lung injury by alveolar overdistention. Controlled hypoventilation (or permissive hypercapnia) is a pressure-limiting, lung-protective strategy whereby less significance is given to the pCO_2 value than to the inflation pressure of the lung. Several studies in ARDS and status asthmaticus have shown a decrease in barotrauma, intensive care days, and mortality. One lowers the set V_T to a range of approximately 6–10 ml/kg in an attempt to keep the peak Paw below 35–40 cm H_2O and the static Paw below 30 cm H_2O. A small V_T is appropriate in ARDS, which is a heterogeneous lung disease with small lung volumes available for ventilation. Gattinoni et al. described three zones in this disease process: a zone of consolidated diseased alveoli that cannot be recruited, a zone of collapsed yet recruitable alveoli, and a small zone (25–30% of normal) of alveoli available for ventilation. Traditional V_Ts much in excess of volume available for ventilation may cause overdistention of available alveoli, potentially exacerbating acute lung injury. Because only a small area of lung is available for ventilation, the term "baby lung" has been coined. The pCO_2 is allowed to rise slowly to a level of up to 80–100 mmHg. The pH falls and may be treated with buffer below 7.20–7.25. Alternatively one may wait for the normal kidney to retain bicarbonate in response to the hypercapnia. Permissive hypercapnia is usually well tolerated. Potential adverse effects include cerebral vasodilatation leading to increased ICP. In fact, intracranial hypertension is the only absolute contraindication to permissive hypercapnia. Increased sympathetic activity, pulmonary vasoconstriction, and cardiac arrhythmias may occur, although they are rarely of significance. Depression of cardiac contractility may be a problem in patients with underlying ventricular dysfunction.

13. Are there other methods to control pCO_2?

There are several other approaches to the control of pCO_2. Decreased production of CO_2 can be achieved by deep sedation, muscle paralysis, cooling (certainly avoiding hyperthermia), and a decrease in the amount of ingested carbohydrate. Tracheal gas insufflation (TGI) is a simple method of increasing CO_2 clearance. A small (suction-type) catheter is placed through the endotracheal tube to the level of the carina. Oxygen and blended nitrogen are insufflated at approximately 4–6 L/min. This in effect creates a wash-out of dead space (Vd/V_T) without a change in minute ventilation or airway pressure. The average reduction in pCO_2 is 15%. This technique is helpful in head-injured patients who may benefit from controlled hypoventilation. Extracorporeal techniques for CO_2 removal are also occasionally used.

14. What is lung compliance? How is it calculated?

Compliance is a measure of distensibility and is expressed as the change in volume for a given change in pressure. Pulmonary compliance is calculated as $V_T/(Paw - PEEP)$. Normal static compliance is 70–100 ml/cm H_2O. In ARDS the compliance is less than 40–50 ml/cm H_2O. Compliance is a global value and does not describe what is happening regionally in the lung with ARDS, in which diseased regions are interspersed with relatively healthy regions. Trending of compliance is a useful parameter in determining the course of a patient with ARF.

15. Is ventilation in the prone position an option in patients who are difficult to oxygenate?

Studies have shown that pO_2 improves significantly in most patients with ARDS when they are prone, probably because of improvement in ventilation-perfusion matching in the lung. Ventilation in the prone position is not routine, however, because it makes nursing care much more difficult.

16. How does one approach the patient who is "fighting the ventilator"?

Agitation, respiratory distress, or "fighting the ventilator" must be taken seriously, because several of the causes may be life-threatening. A diagnosis must be arrived at swiftly to prevent irreversible harm to the patient. Initially, one separates the potential causes into ventilator (machine, circuit, and airway) problems and patient-related problems. The many patient-related causes include hypoxemia, secretions or mucous plugging, pneumothorax, bronchospasm, infection such as pneumonia or sepsis, pulmonary embolus, myocardial ischemia, gastrointestinal bleed, worsening PEEPi, and anxiety. The ventilator-related issues include system leak or disconnection; inadequate ventilator support or delivered FiO_2; airway-related problems, such as extubation, obstructed endotracheal tube, cuff herniation or rupture; and improper triggering sensitivity or flows. Until the problem is sorted out, one should ventilate the patient manually with 100% O_2. Breath sounds and vital signs (including pulse oximetry and end tidal CO_2) should be immediately checked. If time permits, an arterial blood gas analysis and portable chest radiograph should be obtained. A suction catheter may be placed rapidly through the endotracheal tube to ensure patency and to suction secretions or plugs. Suspicion of a pneumothorax with hemodynamic compromise should prompt immediate decompression before obtaining a chest radiograph. Once it is determined that the patient is well oxygenated and ventilated as well as hemodynamically stable, sedation may be administered, if required, and a more detailed assessment can be undertaken.

17. Should neuromuscular blockade be used to facilitate MV?

Neuromuscular blockade (NMB) is commonly used to facilitate MV. It modestly improves oxygenation, decreases peak Paw, and improves the patient-ventilator interface. Muscle paralysis may be of greater benefit in specific situations, such as intracranial hypertension or unconventional modes of ventilation (e.g., IRV or extracorporeal techniques). Drawbacks to the use of NMB include loss of neurologic exam; abolished cough; potential for an awake, paralyzed patient; numerous medication and electrolyte interactions; and potential for prolonged paralysis. Furthermore, improvement in patient outcome has not been scientifically proved. Use of NMB must not be taken lightly. Adequate sedation should be attempted first to avoid NMB. If deemed absolutely necessary after a careful risk-benefit analysis, NMB may be instituted. Use should be limited to 24–48 hours, if possible, to prevent prolonged paralysis.

18. Is split-lung ventilation ever useful?

Split-lung ventilation (SLV) refers to differential ventilation of each lung independently usually via a double-lumen endotracheal tube and two ventilators. Originally developed in the operating suite to facilitate thoracic surgery, its use has been extended to occasional patients in the intensive care unit. Patients with severe unilateral lung disease may be candidates for split-lung ventilation. Split-lung ventilation has been shown to improve oxygenation in patients with unilateral pneumonia, pulmonary edema, and contusion. Isolation of the lungs can save the life of patients with massive hemoptysis or lung abscess by protecting the good lung from spillage. Patients with a bronchopleural fistula also may benefit from SLV. Different modes of ventilation may be applied to each lung individually, including V_T, flows, PEEP, and CPAP. The two ventilators need not be synchronized, and in fact hemodynamic stability is better maintained by using the two ventilators asynchronously.

BIBLIOGRAPHY

1. Brodsky JB, Mihm FG: Split-lung ventilation. In Hall JB, Schmid GA, Wood LDH (eds): Principles of Critical Care. New York, McGraw-Hill, 1992, pp 160–164.
2. Gattinoni L, Pesenti A, Avalli L, et al: Pressure-volume curve of total respiratory system in acute respiratory failure. Computed tomographic scan study. Am Rev Respir Dis 136:730–736, 1987.
3. Hyzy RC, Popovich J: Mechanical ventilation and weaning. In Carlson RW, Geheb MA (eds): Principles and Practice of Medical Intensive Care. Philadelphia, W.B. Saunders, 1993, pp 924–943.
4. Marini JJ: New options for the ventilatory management of acute lung injury. New Horizons 1:489–503, 1993.
5. Pappert D, Rossaint R, Slama K, et al: Influence of positioning on ventilation-perfusion relationships in severe adult respiratory distress syndrome. Chest 106:1511–1516, 1994.
6. Pepe PE, Marini JJ: Occult positive end-expiratory pressure in mechanically ventilated patients with airflow obstruction. Am Rev Respir Dis 126:166–170, 1982.
7. Pilbeam SP: Mechanical Ventilation: Physiologic and Clinical Applications. St. Louis, Mosby, 1992.
8. Rappaport SH, Shpiner R, Yoshihara G, et al: Randomized, prospective trial of pressure-limited versus volume-controlled ventilation in severe respiratory failure. Crit Care Med 22:22–32, 1994.
9. Ravenscraft SA, Burke WC, et al: Tracheal gas insufflation augments CO_2 clearance during mechanical ventilation. Am Rev Respir Dis 148:345–351, 1993.
10. Shanholtz C, Brower R: Should inverse ratio ventilation be used in adult respiratory distress syndrome? Am J Respir Crit Care Med 149:1354–1358, 1994.
11. Tobin MJ: What should the clinician do when a patient "fights the ventilator"? Respir Care 36:395–406, 1991.
12. Tuxen DV: Permissive hypercapnic ventilation. Am J Respir Crit Care Med 150:870–874, 1994.
13. Williams JE, Bartolome RC: How to mechanically ventilate the critically ill patient. Intern Med 13:10–18, 1992.

86. NEUROMUSCULAR BLOCKING AGENTS IN THE INTENSIVE CARE UNIT

Stuart G. Rosenberg, M.D.

1. What are the indications for neuromuscular blocking drugs in the intensive care unit?

The main indication is facilitation of endotracheal intubation and mechanical ventilation. Ease of laryngoscopy, a flaccid patient, and prevention of laryngospasm greatly improve intubating conditions. Use of neuromuscular blocking (NMB) drugs in mechanically ventilated patients improves the patient–ventilator interface, decreases peak airway pressure, and may improve gas exchange. A flaccid, paralyzed patient is a prerequisite for newer modes such as inverse-ratio ventilation. Other indications include increased intracranial pressure (ICP), optimal oxygen transport, tetanus, hypermetabolic states, and assurance of an immobile patient for radiographic and invasive procedures. NMB drugs also control muscle activity and lactate production in status epilepticus. Electroencephalographic monitoring is required in the paralyzed patient, because the seizure activity is masked. Because of complications associated with the use of NMBs (see question 9), a trial of adequate sedation before instituting paralysis for any indication should be made.

2. What is the effect of NMB agents on pulmonary gas exchange?

Scant data indicate slight improvement in the partial pressure of oxygen (pO_2) and carbon dioxide (pCO_2) in some patients. This effect is thought to be due primarily to a decrease in oxygen consumption and carbon dioxide production in skeletal muscle. Lung volumes also may improve if the patient has been coughing or fighting the ventilator. On the other hand, ventilation-perfusion (V/Q) matching may worsen because of changes in diaphragmatic position secondary to paralysis. The overall net effect is variable and difficult to predict. Because some patients show improvement in gas exchange, a trial of NMBs may be worthwhile to decrease toxic oxygen concentration and other ventilatory requirements.

3. Does the use of NMB agents in mechanically ventilated patients improve morbidity or mortality?

No. Currently no evidence supports this claim.

4. Do NMBs have active metabolites?

Yes. The 3-hydroxy metabolites of vecuronium and pancuronium are active at the neuromuscular junction and may accumulate in renal failure, producing a prolonged block. Laudanosine, one of the metabolites of atracurium, causes central nervous system excitation and seizures at high plasma levels in dogs. These levels have not been reached in humans, even with renal or hepatic failure. Succinylcholine, which in fact is diacetylcholine (two molecules of acetylcholine linked together), is metabolized to monoacetylcholine, which may cause bradycardia.

5. How does one determine if the patient is adequately paralyzed?

Clinical observation and direct monitoring of neuromuscular function are important to ensure that the goals of paralysis are met and to avoid overdose. Observation of a relaxed patient synchronous with the ventilator is desirable. Monitoring of depth of neuromuscular blockade is accomplished most readily with a peripheral nerve stimulator. A series of impulses (most commonly a train-of-four [TOF]) is delivered to a peripheral nerve, such as the facial, ulnar, or posterior tibial, and the muscle response in the form of contraction or twitches is measured. Typically a fading pattern develops as the block deepens, with progressive loss of twitches until complete blockade is established. The number of twitches remaining corresponds to the percentage of receptor blockade at the neuromuscular junction. In the intensive care unit (ICU), the presence of

1–2 twitches is desirable, corresponding to an 85–90% neuromuscular junction receptor blockade. This level ensures adequate paralysis and avoids overdose and prolonged recovery.

6. How does one know that the pharmacologically paralyzed patient is adequately sedated?

In patients who are unable to respond with movement or eye opening, assessment of the autonomic nervous system is necessary, just as one gauges the depth of a general anesthetic from autonomic signs. One should look for large reactive pupils, tearing, diaphoresis, piloerection, tachycardia, and hypertension as possible signs of inadequate sedation. Discontinuation of the NMB (if tolerated) allows return of skeletal muscle function and further assessment of the adequacy of sedation. Sedation may not be necessary in the unresponsive, comatose patient. Sedation also may not be tolerated if the patient is hemodynamically unstable. In this situation a cardiostable, amnestic drug such as scopolamine should be considered.

7. Do other medications used in the ICU interact with NMBs?

Yes. Many classes of drugs used in the ICU affect neuromuscular transmission and thereby interact with NMB drugs, including aminoglycosides, magnesium, class I antiarrhythmics, and calcium channel blockers. NMBs may predispose the patient receiving exogenous steroids to steroid myopathy (see question 9). Close monitoring of neuromuscular function is essential.

8. Which blood chemistry abnormalities affect NMBs?

Hypophosphatemia, hypermagnesemia, hypokalemia, respiratory acidosis, and metabolic alkalosis cause muscle weakness and potentiate NMBs. Increased creatinine or liver function tests may lead to accumulation of NMBs and their metabolites.

9. Describe the complication of prolonged muscle weakness.

Prolonged muscle weakness is a known and dreaded complication of NMBs. It may occur in patients who have received NMBs for several days to weeks. The incidence is not clear but may be as high as 10% in patients deemed at risk. More than 100 cases are documented in the literature. Prolonged muscle weakness is a proximal and distal tetraparesis that may last up to several months. It is not to be confused with the shorter term prolonged effect of an overdose of NMBs, which usually resolves in hours to days and is due to the lingering effect of the drugs or active metabolites at the neuromuscular junction. Monitoring the TOF should prevent this shorter term effect. Prolonged muscle weakness appears to be related to a myopathic process with normal neuromuscular transmission. The actual pathology is not well characterized but resembles a steroid-like myopathy. Patients at risk include those receiving exogenous steroids and NMBs for longer than 5 days. Asthmatics seem particularly susceptible. Concurrent aminoglycoside administration also may be a risk factor. Profound weakness may last for months, requiring ventilatory support. Many authors have recommended close monitoring of the TOF, intermittent withholding of the NMB, and physical therapy to prevent muscle atrophy with the hope of preventing prolonged muscle weakness. Unfortunately, none of these precautions has been proved to be of benefit. The use of atracurium was previously recommended to prevent prolonged muscle weakness; early reports implicated only the steroid-based NMBs, pancuronium and vecuronium, which have a steroid-ring nucleus in their structure. It was suspected that some interaction or synergistic effect between the steroidal NMBs and exogenous steroids was directly toxic to muscle tissue. More recently, however, atracurium (a nonsteroidal NMB) also has been implicated in prolonged paralysis. There is no specific treatment other than supportive measures. Prolonged ventilation may be required. Physical therapy is essential. Tapering steroids as soon as possible may be of some benefit. Survival is the rule. As the condition is so morbid, one must carefully weigh the benefits and risks of long-term neuromuscular blockade in the ICU.

10. What is the differential diagnosis of muscle weakness in the critically ill patient?

In addition to NMB-induced prolonged muscle weakness (see question 9), numerous other entities seen in the ICU lead to muscle weakness. Cervical spinal cord pathology, such as trauma, infection, or vascular accident, may lead to quadriparesis. Poliomyelitis affects the upper motor neurons and causes weakness. Peripheral neuropathies from diabetes mellitus, alcohol, human immunodeficiency virus (HIV), or porphyria cause weakness. In severely ill patients with sepsis or multiple organ failure, involvement of the peripheral nerves may lead to critical illness polyneuropathy (CIP), an axonal degeneration of motor and sensory nerves that resembles a toxic or nutritional neuropathy. Many of the above states have sensory involvement in addition to motor weakness. Prolonged muscle weakness affects motor function only. Unrecognized myasthenia gravis may cause prolonged muscle weakness after NMBs. Eaton-Lambert syndrome is a paraneoplastic syndrome that causes a decrement in neuromuscular transmission. Other myopathies, such as polymyositis, HIV-related myopathy, or alcohol-induced myopathy, should be considered. Guillain-Barré syndrome is a postinfectious ascending paralysis occasionally seen in the ICU. Of course, electrolyte abnormalities and drugs affecting neuromuscular transmission also should be considered. Prolonged muscle weakness from NMBs is a diagnosis of exclusion. Patients with weakness require a thorough neurologic exam, full chemistry panels, cranial and/or spinal cord imaging, cerebrospinal fluid examination, nerve conduction studies, electromyography, and possibly muscle or nerve biopsies. Treatment obviously depends on the specific diagnosis.

11. What other concerns are related to the patient receiving NMBs?

A major concern is the inability to perform a neurologic exam in critically ill patients. A central event such as a cerebrovascular accident may go unrecognized for some time. Patients cannot blink or protect their eyes. Drying and corneal abrasions may occur. Artificial tears and taping the eyes closed help. Inability to cough reduces the ability to mobilize pulmonary secretions. Suctioning and meticulous respiratory care are warranted. Immobile patients are prone to decubitus ulcers. An airbed may be of help in preventing ulcers. Immobile patients are also prone to thromboembolic complications. Prophylaxis of deep vein thrombosis should be instituted. Peripheral nerve injuries may occur if the patient is not positioned properly. Passive range-of-motion exercises may help to prevent muscle atrophy. Sedation may be crucial to avoid an awake, paralyzed patient. If possible, it is good practice occasionally to stop the NMB and to re-examine the patient fully.

BIBLIOGRAPHY

1. Apte-Kakade S: Rehabilitation of patients with quadriparesis after treatment of status asthmaticus with neuromuscular blocking agents and high-dose corticosteroids. Arch Phys Med Rehabil 72:1024–1028, 1991.
2. Argov Z, Mastaglia F: Disorders of neuromuscular transmission caused by drugs. N Engl J Med 301:409–413, 1979.
3. Bishop M: Hemodynamic and gas exchange effects of pancuronium bromide in sedated patients with respiratory failure. Anesthesiology 60:369–371, 1984.
4. Durbin C: Neuromuscular blocking agents and sedative drugs: Clinical uses and toxic effects in the critical care unit. Crit Care Clin 7:489–506, 1991.
5. Hansen-Flaschen J, Cowen J, Raps E: Neuromuscular blockade in the intensive care unit: More than we bargained for. Am Rev Respir Dis 147:234–236, 1993.
6. Loper KA, Butler S, Nessly M, Wild L: Paralyzed with pain: The need for education. Pain 37:315–316, 1989.
7. Segredo V, Matthay M: Prolonged neuromuscular blockade after long term administration of vecuronium in two critically ill patients. Anesthesiology 72:566–570, 1990.
8. Topulos G: Neuromuscular blockade in adult intensive care. New Horizons 1:447–462, 1993.

87. SEDATION IN THE INTENSIVE CARE UNIT

John D. Lockrem, M.D., and James Rosher, M.D.

1. Why is sedation a special problem in the intensive care unit (ICU)?

Patients in the ICU often experience pain, fear, anxiety, and discomfort, all of which make sedation an important part of their medical care. The goals of sedation in the ICU are analgesia, amnesia, anxiolysis, and hypnosis. The objective is to produce a calm, comfortable, but communicative patient. Each patient presents with various medical conditions that require various levels of sedation. The needs of the patient must guide the appropriate selection of drug therapy. A patient's requirements may vary throughout the ICU stay, and the patient's condition needs to be addressed frequently. Sedation is needed for postoperative pain control; injuries received during trauma; placement and presence of endotracheal tubes, thoracostomy, and drainage catheters; endotracheal suctioning; bladder catheterization; invasive monitoring; physical therapy; and routine nursing care. Fear and anxiety are heightened by the inability to communicate during artificial ventilation, awareness of the critical situation, physical restraints, and loss of orientation to time and place. Sedation is often required for procedures such as elective cardioversion. Critically ill patients often require proper sedation for severe respiratory failure, tolerance of mechanical ventilation, neuromuscular blockade, septic shock, and combative or severely agitated states.

2. Is there an ideal sedative regimen for all ICU patients?

Unfortunately, no. Many factors play a role in selection of the sedative regimen, including age, personality, drug therapy, smoking and alcohol usage, prior experiences, surgical incision site, and current medical condition. Clinical objectives that should be considered in every ICU patient include maintenance of a relaxed state, adequate pain control, allowance of sufficient cooperation for neurologic examination and therapeutic interventions, tolerance of mechanical ventilation, reduction in barotrauma, and conservation of energy. Although general recommendations can be made, the individual needs of each patient must be considered.

3. Isn't the best method of sedation obvious to ICU staff?

Because a wide variety of drugs are used for ICU sedation, an adequate understanding is essential for proper usage. A 1989 survey in the journal *Pain* revealed that many health care workers misunderstand the sedative and analgesic properties of several commonly used medications. For example, 10% of ICU nurses and 5% of house staff physicians believed that pancuronium (a neuromuscular blocker) relieved anxiety. In the same study, 80% of physicians and 43% of ICU nurses believed that diazepam (a sedative) relieves pain. This chapter is meant to familiarize health care providers with several medications used in mechanically ventilated patients for sedation, analgesia, anxiolysis, amnesia, and hypnosis. Among the available sedatives are the **benzodiazepines, opioids, antipsychotics**, and the **nonbarbiturate anesthetic, propofol**. Various aspects of each class of drugs are discussed, including the mechanism of action, metabolism and excretion, indications, contraindications, pharmacodynamics and kinetics, cost analysis, and advantages versus disadvantages. The use of neuromuscular blocking agents or pain management protocols is not discussed.

4. Which common characteristics of benzodiazepines affect ICU sedative choice?

The most frequently used agents in the ICU are **midazolam, lorazepam**, and **diazepam**, all of which have anxiolytic, amnestic, mild muscle relaxant, and hypnotic effects. They are unique in that they produce deep amnesia while the patient remains conscious. Although they do not have analgesic properties, they reduce opioid requirements. They also possess anticonvulsant properties and are used in the prevention of alcohol withdrawal syndrome.

The administration of benzodiazepines results in minimal respiratory effects except for a decreased ventilatory response to hypoxia and hypercarbia and a decrease in minute ventilation with carbon dioxide (CO_2) retention. Cardiac effects in normovolemic patients include a mild decrease in systemic vascular resistance (SVR) secondary to venodilation, a 10% decrease in mean arterial pressure (MAP), and a slight increase in heart rate (HR). In cases of hypovolemia, benzodiazepines should be used with caution, because decreases in sympathetic tone and venodilation may precipitate hypotension. A synergistic response with a further decrease in MAP is observed when opioids are used concomitantly. Central nervous system (CNS) effects include a decrease in cerebral blood flow (CBF) and cerebral metabolic rate for oxygen ($CMRO_2$). Seizure activity is promptly terminated by many benzodiazepines. Caution should be used in patients with renal or hepatic disease, because metabolism and excretion of most benzodiazepines occur in the kidney and liver. A dose reduction is necessary in such patients. Tolerance to benzodiazepines in general develops quickly, within 1–2 days. The most effective means of avoiding tolerance is a combination of opioids and benzodiazepines, which decreases the dosage requirement of each medication and delays the onset of tolerance. Because of withdrawal reactions after long-term therapeutic use, dosages should be tapered before discontinuation.

Potential risks include oversedation or coma, hypotension, and respiratory depression. Another adverse reaction, especially in the elderly, is paradoxical agitation, which is thought to result from the amnestic effects; patients may become disoriented, confused, and even combative. When reassured, they often settle down but may become restless again as they forget what they have been told. An important consideration with the use of benzodiazepines is the lack of analgesic effects. By combining benzodiazepines and opioids, the dose of each can be decreased because of synergistic effects. Benzodiazepines bind to inhibitory gamma-aminobutyric acid (GABA) receptors, thereby increasing the membrane conductance of chloride ions in the CNS. The resultant change in membrane polarization inhibits normal neuronal function.

5. Describe the properties of midazolam.

Midazolam is a short-acting, water-soluble benzodiazepine with a beta elimination half-life of 1–12 hours (average: 1–4 hr). Although midazolam is water-soluble in its prepared state, its imidazole ring closes at physiologic pH, causing an increase in lipid solubility. Hepatic metabolism produces active metabolites that are excreted by the kidneys. Hepatic biotransformation results in the active metabolites alpha-1-hydroxy-midazolam and 4-hydroxy-midazolam. Midazolam and its metabolites are excreted principally by the kidneys.

With continuous infusion, patients with normal liver and renal function usually awaken within 12 hours. However, in septic patients or patients with hepatic dysfunction, active metabolites may result in prolonged coma. Neither midazolam nor its metabolites are removed effectively by hemodialysis. In critically ill patients, the unpredictability and variability in duration of effect may be due to the altered volume of distribution and protein-binding. Midazolam can be administered by intermittent intravenous (IV) dosing for short-term sedation in doses of 1–2 mg every 1–4 hours. The usual sedative dose of midazolam begins by loading with 0.05–0.1 mg/kg followed by 2–3 mg/hr IV infusion with an opioid supplement. When used alone for sedation, the dose range may be as high as 10–40 mg/hr. One study reported the use of doses of 0.25–0.3 mg/kg/hr for ICU sedation of ventilated patients. The mean time to return to baseline mental status after discontinuation of the infusion was 30 hours. A drug that is usually short-acting may become long-acting under clinical conditions often encountered in the ICU.

6. Does lorazepam have unique properties that make it useful for ICU sedation?

Yes. Lorazepam (Ativan) is an intermediate-acting, lipid-soluble benzodiazepine with a beta elimination half-life of 10–20 hours. Lorazepam is less lipid-soluble than midazolam or diazepam; hence maximal effects may not occur for 15–30 minutes after IV injection because of equilibration within the CNS. The CNS effects are attributed directly to the parent compound; no active metabolites are formed. Hepatic biotransformation by glucuronide conjugation yields lorazepam glucuronide, which is inactive. Excretion occurs primarily through the kidneys.

Lorazepam is frequently administered in the ICU by intermittent injection and continuous infusions. The duration of sedation achieved by continuous infusion is much shorter than the duration of other benzodiazepines because no active metabolites are produced. Infusions of lorazepam, 1–5 mg/hr (0.01–0.1 mg/kg/hr), for ICU sedation are common. Intermittent IV boluses of 1–2 mg every 2–6 hours also provide adequate sedation. The cardiopulmonary effects of lorazepam are consistent with the features of midazolam except for the previously discussed pharmacokinetics. Care also must be taken in patients with hepatic and renal dysfunction, and dosage must be adjusted accordingly.

7. Why isn't diazepam used more frequently in the ICU?

Diazepam (Valium) is a long-acting, rapid-onset, highly lipid-soluble benzodiazepine with a beta elimination half-life of 20–70 hr. Diazepam is poorly dissolved in aqueous media (propylene glycol/alcohol/diazepam) and produces venous irritation and pain on IV injection. Hepatic biotransformation results in pharmacologically active metabolites, including desmethyldiazepam. These metabolites are excreted through bile into the gastrointestinal tract, where they are reabsorbed with further sedative action (half-life: 36–90 hr). Clinical activity results from a combination of the parent compound and active metabolites, which makes diazepam undesirable for repetitive IV injections. In addition, because diazepam is not soluble in aqueous solution, it cannot be given by continuous infusion. Bolus dosage of IV diazepam is 2–10 mg (average: 2.5–5 mg).

After repeated injections, diazepam may accumulate because of its long elimination half-life and active metabolites. In the ICU, diazepam typically is used for treatment of muscle spasms and alcohol withdrawal syndrome, anticonvulsant therapy, and mild sedation for therapeutic interventions. Diazepam has similar characteristics to the other benzodiazepines in respect to cardiopulmonary and hepatorenal physiologic effects. The metabolism of diazepam is reduced when it is used concurrently with cimetidine; thus the amount of free diazepam is increased.

8. Can the effects of benzodiazepines be reversed?

Yes. Flumazenil is an imidazobenzodiazepine that acts as a specific benzodiazepine receptor antagonist. It competitively antagonizes most of the CNS effects of the benzodiazepines through a neutral receptor principle. That is, flumazenil has no direct receptor activity except to displace the active benzodiazepine from the receptor; therefore, it is not a true antagonist. The drug may be used for rapid reversal of oversedation from benzodiazepines and is helpful in differentiating the cause of coma. The dose of flumazenil is 0.2 mg IV every 1–2 minutes (maximum: 3 mg/hr). It is rapidly metabolized via the liver and has a beta elimination half-life of approximately 1–1.5 hours. Occasional side effects include anxiety, headache, dizziness, nausea and vomiting, blurred vision, pain on injection, and resedation.

9. What role should opioids play in ICU sedation?

Because pain and discomfort are so commonly experienced by ICU patients, particularly in the postoperative period, opioids for analgesia and sedation are often primary agents in the effort to make patients more comfortable. Opioids are easy to administer and relatively inexpensive and often provide a pleasant euphoria. Most opioids have similar side effects; however, each has its own advantages and disadvantages.

10. What are the major disadvantages of opioids?

Side effects of opioids include dose-dependent respiratory depression, bradycardia, drowsiness, euphoria, dysphoria, hallucinations, cough suppression (which may be beneficial; for example, in helping a patient accommodate to a recently placed endotracheal tube), nausea and vomiting, pruritus, decreased gastrointestinal motility, constipation, urinary retention, biliary sphincter spasm, allergic reactions, and potentiation of cardiopulmonary effects of other sedatives, hypnotics, or analgesics. Opioids do not produce amnesia at commonly used doses. In large doses they significantly depress respiration and inhibit central respiratory drive. Respiratory depression may be a desirable effect in mechanically ventilated patients but may pose a problem when patients are weaned from the ventilator.

11. How are opioids administered? How do they work?

Opioids can be administered to ventilated patients by intermittent injections or continuous infusions. The mechanism of action involves opioid receptors (mu, kappa, sigma, delta) located in the brain, spinal cord, and peripheral tissues. Mu receptors mediate supraspinal analgesia, euphoria, respiratory depression, and physical dependence. Kappa receptors are involved in spinal analgesia, sedation, and miosis. Delta receptors mediate analgesia and potentiate the effects of other receptors, whereas sigma receptors play a role in hallucinations, dysphoria, and stimulation of vasomotor and respiratory centers. Opioid receptor activation inhibits the presynaptic release of and the postsynaptic response to excitatory neurotransmitters (acetylcholine and substance P). This inhibition alters the potassium and calcium ion conductance at the cellular level, resulting in central effects. Opioids also interfere with pontine and medullary respiratory control.

12. Which properties affect the use of morphine as a sedative?

Morphine is an inexpensive, reliable, commonly used opioid—the prototype to which all other opioids are compared. Its low lipid solubility results in slower onset of action and prolonged duration of effect compared with the synthetic narcotics (e.g., fentanyl). Morphine is commonly given in bolus injections of 1–5 mg every 1–2 hours.

Dosage requirements vary greatly, depending on the patient's needs. Because morphine has a peak onset time of 15–20 minutes and a duration of 4–5 hours, it is easily dosed to effect. Continuous infusion is usually at rates of 2–4 mg/hr but should be titrated to effect. The pulmonary effects consist of dose-dependent respiratory depression. Minimal cardiac depression is seen in normal doses. If rapid, large doses are given intravenously, histamine release may result in hypotension and bronchospasm. The effect may be prolonged in patients with hepatic and renal disease. Metabolism occurs in the liver by conjugation with glucuronic acid to form morphine-3-glucuronide and morphine-6-glucuronide, which are minimally active metabolites. Approximately 5–10% of morphine is excreted in the urine unchanged; therefore, renal failure prolongs the effect. Less than 10% of morphine metabolites undergo biliary excretion.

13. Does fentanyl have specific advantages and disadvantages in the ICU?

Fentanyl is a rapid-acting, potent synthetic piperidine opioid agonist that is 100 times more potent than morphine. Rapid onset and short duration of action reflect its greater lipid solubility compared with morphine and make fentanyl the preferred narcotic in the postoperative or post-traumatic period for many clinicians. Intravenous injections of fentanyl (25–50 µg every 10–20 minutes) is common for initial postoperative analgesic management. Intermittent boluses of fentanyl (50–200 µg IV every 1–4 hours) can be given once pain control is achieved. Because fentanyl has a peak onset of 5–10 minutes, it is easily titrated to effect. The beta elimination half-life is 1–3 hours; however, the analgesic duration is approximately 1 hour because of redistribution into fat and muscle. Continuous infusions are administered at rates of 0.025–0.25 µg/kg/min or 1.5–15 µg/kg/hr. Cardiovascular effects result in minimal changes in MAP, SVR, and cardiac output. Decreases in HR are caused by withdrawal of sympathetic tone and activation of vagal efferents. Pulmonary effects include depression of ventilation by decreases in respiratory rate (RR) and increases in CO_2 retention. Maximal respiratory depression occurs in 3–5 minutes and persists for 3–4 hours. Rigidity of the abdominal and chest wall musculature may occur with large doses and may make ventilation difficult. CNS effects result in decreases in cerebral blood flow and $CMRO_2$.

Renal function is not affected by normal doses of fentanyl. Metabolism of fentanyl occurs via hepatic oxidation to norfentanyl and hydrolysis to 4-N-anilino piperidine and propionic acid (all active metabolites). Renal excretion of unchanged fentanyl accounts for 10–25% of an administered dose and of inactive metabolites for 75%. In the ICU fentanyl helps to maintain hemodynamic stability, to control tachycardia, and to suppress catecholamine release. Tachyphylaxis has been known to occur with continuous infusions of fentanyl.

14. Which drug is useful for managing the severely agitated or psychotic patient?

Haloperidol, a butyrophenone derivative, is an antipsychotic drug used in ICU patients for treatment of extreme agitation, delirium, or disorientation. Severely agitated patients require considerable nursing time to ensure that they do not pull out catheters, endotracheal tubes, or arterial or venous lines or cause physical harm to themselves or others. Haloperidol is used for elderly confused patients in whom excessive sedation or respiratory depression should be avoided. Most patients who receive haloperidol have minimal amnesia, hypnosis, or analgesia; they usually are awake and calm in appearance. The diagnosis of acute ICU psychosis is made by ruling out hypoxia, hypercarbia, electrolyte abnormalities, concurrent medication reactions, gastric or urinary distention, exacerbation of previous psychiatric conditions, septicemia, renal or hepatic dysfunction, and withdrawal symptoms. It is essential to provide adequate analgesia to patients sedated with haloperidol. It should be used with caution if at all in patients with allergic reactions to droperidol, prior history of seizures, possibility of pregnancy, or parkinsonian symptoms.

15. How is haloperidol dosed in severely agitated or psychotic patients?

Dosing regimens vary greatly among patients, and florid psychotic patients may require large amounts for adequate sedation. One rational approach is to calculate the expected dose required to achieve the effective plasma concentration of 20 ng/ml. The amount of drug is the product of weight of the patient (kg), volume of distribution (Vd), and effective plasma concentration (C_{plasma}):

$$\text{Haloperidol dose} = (kg) \cdot (V_d) \cdot (C_{plasma})$$

For a 70-kg person, the maximal loading dose is (70 kg) • (18 L/kg) • (20 ng/ml) or 25.2 mg. Haloperidol would be given at doses of 5 mg every 30 minutes, titrating to appropriate sedation up to the maximal dose calculated. The maintenance dose is one-fourth of the loading dose, given every 6 hours.

16. What complications are associated with haloperidol?

Complications of haloperidol include cardiac dysrhythmias, extrapyramidal symptoms (reversed with diphenhydramine), acute dystonic reactions, parkinsonian symptoms, tardive dyskinesias, and neuroleptic malignant syndrome. The extrapyramidal symptoms are occasionally quite troubling and hard to manage and in rare patients even permanent. Neuroleptic malignant syndrome is a rare disorder characterized by muscle tremors, catatonia, hyperthermia, autonomic dysfunction, and muscle destruction. The mortality rate is > 10%. Several incidents of cardiac dysrhythmias, including torsades de pointes, have been reported. Haloperidol has alpha-blocking properties that are associated with hypotension. Minimal respiratory effects are seen with haloperidol infusions.

17. Describe the mechanism of action and pharmacokinetics of haloperidol.

The mechanism of action of haloperidol is thought to be through central inhibition of the postsynaptic dopaminergic receptor and inhibition of catecholamine reuptake at the nerve terminals. The pharmacokinetics of haloperidol are best described by a three-compartment model. The beta elimination half-life is 6–8 hours, and the drug may accumulate with infusions. Ninety percent is protein-bound; the large volume distribution (18 L/kg) suggests extensive tissue redistribution. Metabolism of haloperidol is through hepatic biotransformation with oxidation to inactive metabolites and reduction to hydroxyhaloperidol (minimal activity). Haloperidol and its metabolites are excreted in urine and feces.

18. What is propofol? Does it have a place in ICU sedation?

Propofol is a nonbarbiturate agent used for general anesthesia, for sedation for local procedures, and for ICU sedation of ventilated patients. Propofol is a milky white, lipid-soluble diisopropyl phenol. Rapid onset, rapid awakening, and minimal residual accumulation have made propofol nearly ideal for ICU sedation. Onset occurs in less than 30 seconds after IV injection, and awakening occurs in 4–8 minutes without continued infusion. Propofol can be dosed intermittently to a given effect or, more commonly, given as a continuous infusion. It is formulated in a lipid, preservative-free emulsion and must be given intravenously. The unique pharmacokinetic profile of propofol includes not only a rapid distribution phase (alpha half-life of approximately 1.8–8.3 minutes) but also a rapid metabolic elimination phase (beta half-life of approximately 34–64 minutes). Metabolism is via hepatic enzyme degradation to inactive metabolites, which are rapidly excreted by the kidney without significant accumulation, even when infused for days.

19. What are the physiologic effects of propofol? What special precautions must be observed?

Cardiovascular effects are related to dose and speed of injection. Rapid injection decreases MAP by approximately 30% in normovolemic patients. Exaggerated responses are seen with hypovolemia, depressed myocardial function, and debilitated patients; therefore, careful titration and reduced dosage are essential in these settings. Slow rates of infusion have been used in patients with poor left ventricular function and in critically ill patients; the mild negative hemodynamic effects are not statistically different from those of other sedatives.

Approximately 10–15% of patients note pain on initial injection; hence, large veins are preferred when available. No significant phlebitis occurs despite initial discomfort. Often pretreatment with opioid or lidocaine (25 mg IV) decreases the incidence of pain. Patients with renal or hepatic disease exhibit no adverse response or accumulation. CNS effects include reduction in CBF and $CMRO_2$ corresponding to the decrease in MAP. Respiratory depression occurs acutely with intravenous doses and is directly proportional to the dose. Therefore, propofol should be used with caution in ICU patients who are not mechanically ventilated. There is no evidence of adrenal axis suppression with infusions, and propofol has no analgesic or muscle-relaxing properties. Propofol reduces the proliferative responses of lymphocytes and may interfere with immune function. Strict aseptic techniques must be followed in administering propofol, because no preservatives are used in the formulation. Unused propofol must be discarded every 12 hours for sterility. Caution must be exercised in patients with egg allergy; lecithin is a component of egg whites and the fat emulsion in propofol. Minimal nausea, vomiting, and pruritus have been observed with the use of propofol. Some studies demonstrate antiemetic properties.

20. What are the advantages and dosing recommendations of propofol?

Specific advantages of propofol include minimal long-term effects, rapid awakening that ensures cooperation for exams and facilitates extubation, and easy titration to the desired level of sedation. Propofol is comparable to or even less expensive than several benzodiazepine infusions. The combination of propofol and an opioid infusion allows significantly reduced doses of each. Propofol is prepared in 10% Intralipid, which provides 1 kcal/ml and may account for 10–25% of daily caloric requirements. In critically ill patients, it is best to start a slow infusion of propofol at doses of 20–40 µg/kg/min (1–2 mg/kg/hr). Most patients tolerate a maintenance infusion rate of 20–100 µg/kg/min (1.2–6.0 mg/kg/hr). The rate of infusion depends on the desired level of sedation, the patient's age and overall health, and concurrent medications. If rapid unconsciousness is desired (e.g., rapid-sequence induction), propofol should be administered at 0.5–2.0 mg/kg (mean: 1.5 mg/kg).

21. How is the level of sedation monitored in the ICU?

Sedation scales are available to facilitate communication among the ICU staff and to standardize the assessment of sedation. The Ramsay sedation scale is easily adapted to the ICU. Most patients can be maintained at Ramsay scale level 3 (sedated, responsive to commands). At times deeper levels of sedation (levels 5 and 6) are required, such as postoperatively, after major trauma, or during use of muscle relaxants. Conversely, stable patients may benefit from level 2 (cooperative, calm) sedation. The goal of ICU sedation of mechanically ventilated patients is to achieve Ramsay scale scores of 2–3 for maximal patient comfort and cooperation.

The Ramsay Sedation Score

SCORE	CHARACTERISTICS
1	Anxious, agitated, restless
2	Cooperative, tranquil, accepting ventilator support
3	Sedated, but responsive to commands
4	Asleep, brisk response to sound or glabellar tap
5	Asleep, sluggish response to sound or glabellar tap
6	Asleep, no response to sound or glabellar tap

BIBLIOGRAPHY

1. Aitkenhead AR, Pepperman ML, Willatts SM, et al: Comparison of propofol and midazolam for sedation in critically ill patients. Lancet 2(8665):704–708, 1989.
2. Bailie GR, Cockshott ID, Douglas EJ, Bowles BJ: Pharmacokinetics of propofol during and after long-term continuous infusion for maintenance of sedation in ICU patients. Br J Anaesth 68:486–491, 1992.
3. Barvais L, Dejonckheere M, Dernovoi B, et al: Continuous infusion of midazolam or bolus of diazepam for postoperative sedation in cardiac surgical patients. Acta Anaesthesiol Belg 39:239–245, 1988.
4. Bell J, Sartain J, Wilkinson GA, Sherry KM: Propofol and fentanyl anaesthesia for patients with low cardiac output state undergoing cardiac surgery: Comparison with high-dose fentanyl anaesthesia. Br J Anaesth 73:162–166, 1994.
5. Bodenham A, Park GR: Reversal of prolonged sedation using flumazenil in critically ill patients. Anaesthesia 44:603–605, 1989.
6. Cammarano WB, Pittet JF, Weitz S, et al: Acute withdrawal syndrome related to the administration of analgesic and sedative medications in adult intensive care unit patients. Crit Care Med 26:676–684, 1998.
7. Carrasco G, Molina R, Costa J, et al: Propofol vs midazolam in short-, medium-, and long-term sedation of critically ill patients. Chest 103:557–564, 1993.
8. Degauque C, Dupuis A: A study to compare the use of propofol and midazolam for the sedation of patients with acute respiratory failure. J Drug Dev 4(Suppl 3):95–97, 1991.
9. Deppe SA, Sipperly ME, Sargent AI, et al: Intravenous lorazepam as an amnestic and anxiolytic agent in the intensive care unit: A prospective study. Crit Care Med 22:1248–1252, 1994.
10. Durbin CG Jr: Sedation in the critically ill patient. New Horizons 2:64–74, 1994.
11. Loper KA, Butler S, Nessly M, Wild L: Paralyzed with pain: The need for education. Pain 37:315–316, 1989.
12. Malacrida R, Fritz ME, Suter PM, Crevoisier C: Pharmacokinetics of midazolam administered by continuous intravenous infusion to intensive care patients. Crit Care Med 20:1123–1126, 1991.
13. McMurray TJ, Collier PS, Carson IW, et al: Propofol sedation after open heart surgery: A clinical and pharmacokinetic study. Anaesthesia 45:322–326, 1990.
14. Nimmo GR, Mackenzie SJ, Grant IS: Haemodynamic and oxygen transport effects of propofol infusion in critically ill adults. Anaesthesia 4:485–489, 1994.
15. Pholman AS, Simpson KP, Hall JB: Continuous intravenous infusion of lorazepam versus midazolam for sedation during mechanical ventilatory support: A prospective, randomized study. Crit Care Med 22:1241–1247, 1994.
16. Shelly MP, Mendel L, Park GR: Failure of critically ill patients to metabolize midazolam. Anaesthesia 42:619–626, 1987.
17. Simpson PJ, Eltringham RJ: Lorazepam in intensive care. Clin Ther 4:150–163, 1981.
18. Smith I, White PF, Nathanson M, Gouldson R: Propofol: An update on its clinical use. Anesthesiology 81:1005–1043, 1994.
19. Valente JF, Anderson GL, Branson RD, et al: Disadvantages of prolonged propofol sedation in the critical care unit. Crit Care Med 22:710–712, 1994.

88. SEPSIS AND THE SYSTEMIC INFLAMMATORY RESPONSE SYNDROME

John D. Lockrem, M.D.

1. What makes sepsis and multiple organ dysfunction an important critical care problem?

Multiple organ dysfunction has been identified as the most common cause of mortality in the surgical intensive care unit (ICU). The mortality rate for septic shock is generally reported at 50–70%. In addition to high mortality, prolonged ICU care and enormous health care costs make improvements in the treatment of sepsis a high priority.

2. Define the following terms: *infection, bacteremia, systemic inflammatory response syndrome, sepsis, septic shock,* and *multiple organ dysfunction syndrome.*

The use of varying definitions of basic terms has made the results of many studies of innovative therapies hard to interpret. The American College of Chest Physicians and the American Society for Critical Care Medicine have made a plea for consistent use of terms based on a consensus conference.

Infection: an inflammatory response to the presence of microorganisms or the invasion of normally sterile host tissue by such organisms.

Bacteremia: the presence of viable bacteria in the blood.

Systemic inflammatory response syndrome (SIRS): the systemic inflammatory response to a variety of severe clinical insults. The response is manifested by two or more of the following conditions: (1) temperature > 38°C or < 36°C; (2) heart rate > 90 beats per minute; (3) respiratory rate > 20 breaths per minute or $PaCO_2$ < 32 mmHg; and (4) white blood cell count (WBC) > 12,000/mm^3, < 4,000/mm^3, or > 10% immature forms.

Sepsis: the same definitions as SIRS, but limited to infection as a cause.

Septic shock: sepsis associated with hypotension, despite adequate fluid resuscitation, and perfusion abnormalities that may include, but are not limited to, lactic acidosis, oliguria, or acute alteration in mental status. Patients who are receiving inotropic or vasopressor agents may not be hypotensive at the time that perfusion abnormalities are measured.

Multiple organ dysfunction syndrome (MODS): altered organ function in an acutely ill patient such that homeostasis cannot be maintained without intervention.

3. Why is SIRS important?

The signs that for so long have been associated with infection—fever, elevated WBC count, and organ dysfunction—are actually signs of the body's inflammatory response to infection rather than a direct result of the infecting organism. Disease processes that trigger the inflammatory cascade may be clinically indistinguishable from sepsis and have the same outcome. The inflammatory cascade accounts for the clinical picture associated with trauma, pancreatitis, burns, or other noninfectious insults. Recognition that the common factor in many life-threatening illnesses is uncontrolled inflammation has led to the design of treatment strategies aimed at modulation of the inflammatory response.

4. The inflammatory response is a normal reaction to infection. Should it not be encouraged?

Yes and no. Teleologically, the classic *tumor, calor, rubor,* and *dolor* response to infection can be viewed as the organism's attempt to keep an infection localized. However, when the response is no longer under local control (e.g., as in a swollen finger), the systemic response may be more harmful than the inciting infection. The cascading inflammatory response leads to increased capillary permeability throughout the body, and diffuse endothelial injury leads to multiple organ dysfunction.

5. What treatments for SIRS have proven utility?

At this point, the commonly accepted treatments are aimed mainly at the underlying condition and supporting the organism through the stressful period. Treatment of the underlying condition involves finding and treating the source of infection or inflammation, drainage of abscess, debridement of necrotic tissue, and early fixation of fractures. Essential support of vital functions includes hemodynamic support with the goal of maintaining oxygen delivery, nutritional support, and support of failing organs with appropriate therapy, including ventilation, dialysis, and replacement of platelets and clotting factors.

6. Is the exact endpoint of hemodynamic support controversial?

Yes. Several studies have shown improved survival among patients with a hyperdynamic cardiovascular performance as demonstrated by an approximately 30% increase in cardiac index (CI), oxygen delivery index (DO_2I), oxygen consumption index (VO_2I), and left ventricular stroke work index (LVSWI). Some patients with adequate cardiac reserve achieve such performance values on their own, whereas others require augmentation with inotropes or vasodilators. There is no uniform agreement that adding hemodynamic support to "supranormal" values improves outcome from sepsis, but it appears likely that the ability to respond to metabolic stress, such as sepsis, with improved hemodynamic performance is beneficial. It is possible that, in an effort to achieve a hyperdynamic state, some patients may be harmed when their cardiovascular limit is exceeded. Clearly SIRS imposes metabolic stress, but we have no way of knowing for any individual exactly what the ideal level of oxygen consumption should be; therefore, we do not know how much support is required to meet the demand.

7. What is the significance of lactic acidosis in patients with septic shock?

Experts debate how far the clinician should go to support the circulation and the specific endpoints of therapy, but in the setting of septic shock they generally agree that lactic acidosis indicates inadequate perfusion until proved otherwise. CI, DO_2I, and VO_2I should be followed and therapy directed at restoring cellular oxygen metabolism.

8. How should patients with septic shock be resuscitated?

Adequate perfusion must be restored promptly. The initial response should be fluid resuscitation, because sepsis results in increased capillary leak and increased fluid requirements. In the most severe cases or in patients at highest risk for organ damage, a pulmonary artery (PA) catheter is useful to guide therapy. The pressure recorded at the distal port of the catheter with the PA occluded (PAOP), sometimes referred to as the wedge pressure, is used as an approximation of left ventricular preload. Fluid is given until signs of shock are reversed, up to a PAOP of approximately 18–20 cm H_2O. If at that point the patient is still hypotensive or oliguric or still has altered mental status, hemodynamic parameters are measured and treatment with vasoactive infusions is begun.

9. How does one decide which vasoactive drug to use?

The choice is tempered by the situation. If the mean arterial pressure (MAP) is greater than 60 mmHg with a PAOP greater than 18 cm H_2O, but the CI, DO_2I, or VO_2I are low, an inotrope such as dobutamine is warranted. If the MAP is low, dopamine is useful because of its greater pressor effect. When shock is most severe, pressor and inotropic support with a norepinephrine (Levophed) infusion is indicated. When MAP and PAOP indicate adequate filling but systemic vascular resistance (SVR) is increased, the cautious use of a vasodilator may be appropriate. Most commonly, patients in septic shock have low SVR; thus the use of vasodilators is unusual.

10. Does the use of norepinephrine presage progressive deterioration?

When the rate of infusion of norepinephrine is titrated to a desired pressure, the usual result is administration of increasing amounts of drug while perfusion diminishes and vasoconstriction predominates. When, however, the goal is to maximize perfusion rather than pressure, CI and

DO_2I are monitored and maintained; with this approach, norepinephrine is a valuable aid to resuscitation.

11. What are the specific recommendations for anesthetic management in patients in septic shock?

Obviously, no elective operations are performed with a patient in septic shock, and surgery most often is related to the shock itself. Drainage of abscess, debridement of necrotic tissue, and diagnostic biopsies are often performed in hemodynamically unstable patients. In general, the anesthetic period amounts to a continuation of the resuscitation, with maintenance of perfusion a priority. The use of circulatory depressants and vasodilators should be minimized, and the use of vasoactive infusions may well be necessary intraoperatively.

12. Are steroids useful in septic shock?

Septic shock has been described as "autodigestive inflammation"; thus it is easy to understand why treatment with corticosteroids, as general anti-inflammatory agents, was attempted. Although animal studies showed improved survival with steroid treatment in sepsis, several large, multicenter randomized human trials have shown no overall benefit; moreover, the mortality rate in the subset of patients with renal insufficiency was increased.

13. What is the role of monoclonal antibodies directed against proinflammatory mediators?

Many different innovative treatments have been developed in an effort to interrupt the inflammatory cycle. Monoclonal murine and human antibodies to bacterial endotoxin have been studied extensively, and although animal and early human trials generated tremendous excitement, randomized outcome trials have failed to justify clinical use. Unfortunately, the same experience has been reported for other agents, such as monoclonal antibodies to tumor necrosis factor (TNF), a soluble TNF receptor that in essence inactivates TNF, and a bioengineered receptor antagonist for interleukin-1.

14. What are the prospects for future pharmacotherapy in SIRS?

Recent research into new medical treatments for SIRS has been discouraging. Nonetheless, amazing new technologies have been developed, and much has been learned about the control of the inflammatory system. Activation of the many cytokines, the complement system, the cyclooxygenase pathway (which results in the generation of thromboxanes), and the many other pathways involved in the inflammatory response is a complicated and interdigitating system. Interference with one pathway is unlikely to control accelerated inflammation, and multiple treatments to block each step of the cascade, although theoretically possible, are likely to be prohibitively expensive and perhaps even harmful. Rather than trying to block each proinflammatory agent, future research may focus on attempts to stimulate the natural anti-inflammatory mediators, such as interleukins 4, 8, 10, and 13, prostaglandin E_2, macrophage deactivation factor, and platelet-derived growth factor. As we learn more about the regulation and balance of the system, the likelihood of being able to modulate and control the inflammatory response should increase.

Despite intense investigative interest over the last 3 decades relating to the proinflammatory response of severe infection, the treatment of sepsis remains targeted toward medical and surgical treatment of the infection nidus and support of organ dysfunction. Therapy can be divided into immediate steps taken to stabilize the patient followed by more definitive therapeutic intervention. Other diseases and states may mimic sepsis and need to be considered during the initial evaluation. A wide variety of organisms may be associated with sepsis. Hypotension and hypoperfusion accompany severe sepsis and septic shock and warrant intense efforts to optimize organ perfusion. Other supportive care issues, such as stress ulcer prophylaxis and nutritional support, are important adjuncts to therapy.

Therapies that block the actions of interleukin-1 (IL-1) or TNF-alpha have been proposed to be potentially beneficial in critically ill patients with sepsis. Clinical trials demonstrated no survival benefit when the actions of IL-1 were blocked. In contrast, inhibition of TNF-alpha with either monoclonal antibodies or TNF receptor fusion proteins appeared to improve survival in prospectively defined groups of patients with severe sepsis, including those with dysfunction of two or more organ systems or with septic shock associated with the dysfunction of at least one organ system. Although none of the clinical trials has demonstrated statistically significant improvement in mortality for patients who received anticytokine therapy 28 days before, few of the completed studies were initially powered to achieve statistical significance at the day 28 endpoint. While that available data suggest that anti-TNF therapies improve survival in groups of patients with sepsis that can be identified by clinical criteria, confirmation of the potentially beneficial effects of anti-TNF agents awaits completion of the large multicenter clinical trials that are currently examining the utility of these therapies.

BIBLIOGRAPHY

1. Abraham E: Cytokine modifiers: Pipe dream or reality? Chest 113(3 Suppl):224S–227S, 1998.
2. Bone RC, Balk RA, Cerra FB, et al: Definitions for sepsis and organ failure and guidelines for the use of innovative therapies in sepsis. Chest 101:1644–1655, 1992.
3. Cronin L, Cook DJ, Carlet J, et al: Corticosteroid treatment for sepsis: A critical appraisal and meta-analysis of the literature. Crit Care Med 23:1430–1439, 1995.
4. Dellinger RP: Current therapy for sepsis. Infect Dis Clin North Am 13:495–509, 1999.
5. Eidelman LA, Sprung CL: Why have new effective therapies for sepsis not been developed? Crit Care Med 22:1330–1334, 1994.
6. Fisher CJ, Dhainau JFA, Opal SM, et al: Recombinant human interleukin 1 receptor antagonist in the treatment of patients with sepsis syndrome. JAMA 271:1836–1842, 1994.
7. Knaus WA, Sun X, Nystrum PE, et al: Evaluation of definitions for sepsis. Chest 101:1656–1662, 1992.
8. Suffredini AF: Current prospects for the treatment of clinical sepsis. Crit Care Med 22:S12–S18, 1994.
9. Veterans Administration Systemic Sepsis Cooperative Study Group: Effect of high-dose glucocorticoid therapy on mortality in patients with clinical signs of systemic sepsis. N Engl J Med 317:653–665, 1987.
10. Ziegler, EJ, Fisher CJ, Sprung CL, et al: Treatment of Gram-negative bacteremia and septic shock with JA-1A human monoclonal antibody against endotoxin. N Engl J Med 324:429–436, 1991.

89. ARDS

Paul K. Miller, M.D.

1. What is ARDS?

ARDS stands for acute respiratory distress syndrome. Formerly this disease entity was called adult respiratory distress syndrome, to distinguish it from infant respiratory distress syndrome, which was thought to be secondary to inadequate surfactant production. The current thinking is that both adult and infant disease entities have pathophysiologic features that are more similar than not.

2. What are other names for ARDS?

Historically, this disease entity has been called adult hyaline membrane disease, adult respiratory insufficiency syndrome, congestive atelectasis, hemorrhagic lung syndrome, Da Nang lung, stiff lung syndrome, shock lung, white lung, postperfusion lung, and wet lung.

3. When was ARDS first described?

In 1967, in a now landmark paper, Drs. Petty and Ashbaugh described the features of acute respiratory distress in adults. They have been credited with coining the term adult respiratory distress syndrome.

4. How can I recognize ARDS?

Petty and Ashbaugh described 12 patients whose respiratory distress syndrome was manifested by the acute onset of tachypnea, hypoxemia, and reduced pulmonary compliance.[1] They noted that the pathophysiology of the illness closely resembled infant respiratory distress syndrome.

5. Are there any known etiologies of ARDS?

Yes. Sepsis syndrome, aspiration of gastric contents, and multitrauma have all been shown to be causative factors in the development of ARDS. Additionally, massive blood transfusions, adverse drug reactions or overdoses, pulmonary inhalation injury, cardiopulmonary bypass, severe pneumonia, pancreatitis, near drowning, and anoxic pulmonary injury (shock) have all been associated with increased risk of ARDS.

6. Are trauma patients more likely to get ARDS?

Not necessarily. However, certain traumatic injuries have a high incidence of associated ARDS. Specifically, severe closed head injuries, multiple major fractures, and pulmonary contusions may lead to the development of ARDS.

7. How do we know for sure when a patient has ARDS?

In 1994, participants in an American and European conference established a consensus definition of ARDS in the hope of furthering research efforts related to the disease mechanism, patient outcomes, and coordination of clinical trials. That definition is as follows:

1. Acute onset.
2. Partial pressure of oxygen in alveolar gas (PAO_2) to fractional concentration of oxygen in inspired gas (FiO_2) ratio ≤ 200 (regardless of level of positive end-expiratory pressure [PEEP]).
3. Bilateral infiltrates seen on frontal chest radiograph.
4. Pulmonary artery wedge pressure ≤ 18 mmHg when measured, or no clinical evidence of left atrial hypertension.

If a patient meets these criteria, he or she may be diagnosed as having ARDS.

8. Describe the pathologic lesion in ARDS.

ARDS is essentially a capillary-leak phenomenon. The hallmark lesion is diffuse alveolar damage. The pathologic insult occurs at the alveolar-capillary membrane, resulting in a loss of integrity of alveolar cellular junctions and resultant leakage of proteinaceous fluid into the alveolar interstitium and alveolar space proper. Inflammatory mediators result in neutrophil recruitment and further alveolar injury, manifested by increased capillary permeability and alveolar edema.

9. What are some of the clinical features of ARDS?

As mentioned above, the defining clinical features of ARDS are the acute onset of respiratory distress, hypoxemia, and bilateral chest infiltrates in the absence of cardiogenic pulmonary edema. Other clinical features include reduced pulmonary compliance, increased atelectasis, reduced functional residual capacity, increased airway resistance, and increased intrapulmonary shunting. Some patients may also develop pulmonary hypertension.

10. How do we manage ARDS?

Effective treatment requires resolution of the underlying disease process (e.g., pancreatitis, sepsis) that resulted in the lung injury. In spite of enormous amounts of research on ARDS, the treatment of this disease remains largely supportive. Typically, these patients require endotracheal intubation and positive pressure ventilation. Controversy rages over which specific ventilation modes and strategies may be most beneficial (or perhaps least harmful). PEEP is typically employed to restore lung volumes, decrease intrapulmonary shunting, and improve ventilation-perfusion (V/Q) mismatching. FiO_2 is titrated to counter hypoxemia, as well as minimize oxygen toxicity.

11. Suppose an ARDS patient remains difficult to oxygenate. What then?

The patient's oxygen demand should be minimized, if possible. Hemoglobin and cardiac output should be optimized. Normothermia should be maintained, because both fever and hypothermia with shivering dramatically increase oxygen demand. Infection should be treated aggressively. Judicious sedation and even neuromuscular blockade should be employed as necessary.

12. Does inverse-ratio ventilation help?

Inverse-ratio ventilation—where the ventilator is set such that the inspiratory time of each breath is longer than the expiratory time—has been used with varying degrees of effectiveness in the treatment of severe ARDS. It has not been shown to be superior to any other mode of mechanical ventilation in ARDS. It may be beneficial if the patient's pulmonary compliance is severely reduced.

13. What about pressure control ventilation?

Pressure control ventilation (PCV) has become popular in the management of ARDS. The ventilator delivers a preset number of breaths, with each breath augmented by a preset amount of inspiratory pressure. Gas flow is delivered in a decelerating pattern, unlike the square or sinusoidal flow-wave patterns commonly used with volume-cycled modes of ventilation. This decelerating flow-wave pattern naturally results in flow-rate decay as the patient's lungs fill with air during inspiration. Tidal volume is variable, depending on set inspiratory pressure, set respiratory rate, set inspiratory time, pulmonary compliance, and resistance in the patient's airway as well as the ventilator circuit. Thus PCV is thought to be a "gentler" mode of mechanical ventilation that may result in less iatrogenic lung injury in the ARDS patient with poor lung compliance. In pure PCV mode, each breath is time-triggered, machine-cycled, and mandatory. The patient is unable to trigger the ventilator him- or herself and cannot take additional breaths above the set rate. Because the patient has no control over the ventilatory pattern, PCV is a very uncomfortable mode of mechanical ventilation and typically requires heavy sedation or neuromuscular blockade. It has not been shown to be superior to any other mode of mechanical ventilation in the management of ARDS.

14. Are there any other modes of mechanical ventilation that have been shown to be beneficial in ARDS?

Enthusiasm exists in some circles for high-frequency jet ventilation (HFJV), airway pressure-release ventilation (APRV), and partial-liquid ventilation (PLV), as well as pressure control ventilation with low tidal volumes (6 ml/kg). Extracorporeal membrane oxygenation (ECMO) and extracorporeal carbon dioxide removal (ECCOR) have been used with mixed results. Small studies of these modes and strategies have been alternately promising and discouraging. Larger clinical trials have been proposed, completed, or are pending.

15. Do steroids work?

Since ARDS is an inflammatory disease process, it seems that steroids ought to be indicated early in its treatment. Some multicenter clinical trials in the 1980s were disappointing in that they failed to demonstrate improved outcomes with high-dose methylprednisolone. Recently there has been renewed interest in using high-dose corticosteroids *late* in the treatment of ARDS, specifically to attenuate the progressive alveolar fibrosis and attendant hypoxemia associated with a thickened alveolar-capillary membrane (diffusion defect).

16. What is the mortality rate associated with ARDS?

Despite advances in supportive care and ventilator technology, the mortality rate from ARDS has remained high and has been believed to be greater than 50%, with no real improvement since this disease was first described in 1967. Recent data suggest, however, that the mortality rate may be improving and indeed may be somewhere around 40%.

17. Where are current research initiatives being directed?

Recent studies involving exogenous surfactant administration (ARDS patients may have dysfunctional surfactant), late steroids (in the fibroproliferative phase), ketoconazole (a potent inhibitor of thromboxane and leukotriene synthesis), nitric oxide (a selective pulmonary vasodilator), eicosanoids (anti-inflammatory agents), pentoxifylline (a phosphodiesterase inhibitor), antiendotoxin and anticytokine agents, and PLV have been proposed, completed, or are in progress. Additionally, some investigators have been experimenting with positioning ARDS patients prone.

BIBLIOGRAPHY

1. Ashbaugh DG, Bigelow DB, Petty TL, et al: Acute respiratory distress in adults. Lancet 2(7511):310–323, 1967.
2. Bass TL, Miller PK, Campbell DB, et al: Traumatic adult respiratory distress syndrome. Chest Surg Clin North Am 7:429–441, 1997.
3. Bernard GR, Artigas A, Brigham KL, et al: The American-European consensus conference on ARDS. J Respir Crit Care Med 149:818–824, 1994.
4. Bernard GR, Luce JM, Sprung CL, et al: High-dose corticosteroids in patients with the adult respiratory distress syndrome. N Engl J Med 317:1565–1570, 1987.
5. Kollef MH, Schuster DP: The acute respiratory distress syndrome. N Engl J Med 332:27–37, 1995.
6. Luce JM, Montgomery AB, Marks JD, et al: Ineffectiveness of high-dose methylprednisolone in preventing parenchymal lung injury and improving mortality in patients with septic shock. Am Rev Respir Dis 138:62–68, 1988.
7. Meduri GU, Belenchia JM, Estes RJ, et al: Fibroproliferative phase of ARDS: Clinical findings and effect of corticosteroids. Chest 100:943–952, 1991.
8. Meduri GU, Headley AS, Golden E, et al: Effect of prolonged methylprednisolone therapy in unresolving acute respiratory distress syndrome. JAMA 280:159–165, 1998.
9. Milberg JA, Davis DR, Steinberg KP, et al: Improved survival of patients with acute respiratory distress syndrome (ARDS): 1983–1993. JAMA 273:306–309, 1995.

INDEX

Entries in **boldface type** indicate complete chapters.